AMERICAN HISTORY

THE MODERN ERA SINCE 1865

AMERICAN HISTORY

THE MODERN ERA SINCE 1865

DONALD A. RITCHIE

Glencoe
McGraw-Hill

New York, New York   Columbus, Ohio   Woodland Hills, California   Peoria, Illinois

Authors

★★

Donald A. Ritchie is Associate Historian of the United States Senate Historical Office. Dr. Ritchie received his doctorate in American history from the University of Maryland after service in the U.S. Marine Corps. He has taught American history at various levels, from high school to the university. He edits the Historical Series of the Senate Foreign Relations Committee and is the author of several books, including *Press Gallery: Congress and the Washington Correspondents*, which received the Organization of American Historians' Richard W. Leopold Prize. Dr. Ritchie has served as president of the Oral History Association and as a council member of the American Historical Association.

Glencoe/McGraw-Hill

A Division of The **McGraw·Hill** *Companies*

Printed in the United States of America.

Send all inquiries to:
Glencoe/McGraw-Hill
8787 Orion Place
Columbus, Ohio 43240

ISBN 0-07-821613-3 (Student Edition)
ISBN 0-07-821614-1 (Teacher's Wraparound Edition)

6 7 8 9 10 11 027/046 04 03 02

Academic Consultants

****

Sarah Witham Bednarz
Visiting Assistant Professor
Texas A&M University
College Station, Texas

Barbara Anne Egypt
Bruce R. Watkins Cultural
  Heritage Center
Kansas City, Missouri

Delbert A. Jurden
Instructor (retired)
Johnson County Community
  College
Overland Park, Kansas

Keith Ian Polakoff
Associate Vice President for
  Academic Affairs and
  Dean of Graduate Studies
California State University, Long
  Beach
Long Beach, California

John F. Waukechon
Assistant Instructor
University of Texas
Austin, Texas

Teacher Reviewers

****

Rose Marie Floyd
Social Studies Teacher
Jefferson Davis High School
Montgomery, Alabama

Janice A. Hardeman
Department Chair, Social Studies
Ephrata High School
Ephrata, Pennsylvania

George W. Henry, Jr.
Teacher, Chair History
  Department
St. Mark's School
Salt Lake City, Utah

Marjorie B. Hollowell
Chairman, Social Studies
  Department
John A. Holmes High School
Edenton, North Carolina

Alan Kaplan
Social Studies Educator
Huntington High School
Huntington, West Virginia

James LaMastus
Social Studies Teacher
North High School
Evansville, Indiana

Michael L. Manson, Ed. D.
Teacher of Social Studies (retired)
Townsend Harris High School
Flushing, New York

Todd Kent Meyer
History Teacher
Watertown Senior High School
Watertown, South Dakota

Susan P. Owens
Social Studies Teacher
K-12 Department Chair
Howard L. Goff Middle School
East Greenbush, New York

Simmie G. Plummer
History Teacher
Valley High School
Aluquerque, New Mexico

Irene Ramnarine
Secondary Social Studies
  Resource Teacher
Brevard County School Board
Melbourne, Florida

James M. Wolfe
History Teacher
Suitland University High School
Forestville, Maryland

Contents

UNIT FOUR
Entering a New Century
1867–1920

★ ★ ★ ★ ★ ★ ★ ★ ★ ★ ★ ★ ★ ★ ★ ★ ★ ★ ★

UNIT FIVE
Crusade and Disillusion
1914–1932

★ ★ ★ ★ ★ ★ ★ ★ ★ ★ ★ ★ ★ ★ ★ ★ ★ ★ ★

UNIT SIX
Times of Crisis 1932–1960

★ ★

UNIT SEVEN
Redefining America
1954–Present

★ ★

APPENDIX

★ ★

Features

Cultural Kaleidoscope

 **THE PRINCETON REVIEW** ## Standardized Test Practice

Features

Linking Past and Present

Let the Children Kodak

For after all the home pictures are what count. We by the personal pictures that tell of our travels and tions—but the intimate home pictures of the chil- by the children—those are the pictures that are ed as the years go by.

a Kodak or a Brownie it's all very simple. even from their kindergarten days, have astering the Brownie or one of the smaller en in picture making has been made by the Kodak system. Brownie lve dollars, and Kodaks from five ety to suit all pockets and

COMPANY,
N. Y., The Kodak City.

Features

★ ★

| THE ARTS | GEOGRAPHY | History AND ECONOMICS | SCIENCE | MATH |

SCIENCE

MATH

Features

BUILDING SKILLS

Social Studies Skills

The Tet Offensive, 1968

Critical Thinking Skills

Europe in 1914

Technology Skills

Study and Writing Skills

Features

American Literary Heritage

Features

★★★★★★★★★ AMERICAN PORTRAITS

Features

Footnotes to History

Features

★ ★

★★★ AMERICA'S FLAGS ★★★

Features

Cause-and-Effect Charts

Rebuilding Europe

CAUSES

- Communist guerrillas control much of Greece
- European countries suffer economic devastation after World War II

• The Marshall Plan

EFFECTS

- Congress responds by voting [mili]tary and economic aid to Gre[ece]
- Western European econom[ies] prosper

The Move Toward Equality

CAUSES

- 1955   Rosa Parks is arrested
- 1955   Montgomery bus boycott
- 1957   Conflict at Little Rock
- 1957   SCLC is organized
- 1960   Students stage sit-ins
- 1963   March on Washington

• Toward Equality

EFFECTS

- 1962   James Meredith enters University of Mississippi
- 1967   Thurgood Marshall appointed to Supreme Court
- 1968   Shirley Chisholm elected to House
- 1972   Barbara Jordan and Andrew Young are first Southern African Americans elected to House since 1901

The Beginning of the Civil War

CAUSES

- 1850   Compromise of 1850
- 1854   Kansas-Nebraska Act
- 1855-1856   Guerrilla warfare in Kansas
- 1857   Dred Scott decision on slavery in the territories
- 1859   John Brown raids Harpers Ferry, Virginia
- 1860   Election of Abraham Lincoln

• The War Begins

EFFECTS

- [18]60   South Carolina secedes
- [18]61   Confederacy formed
- [186]1   Attack on Fort Sumter

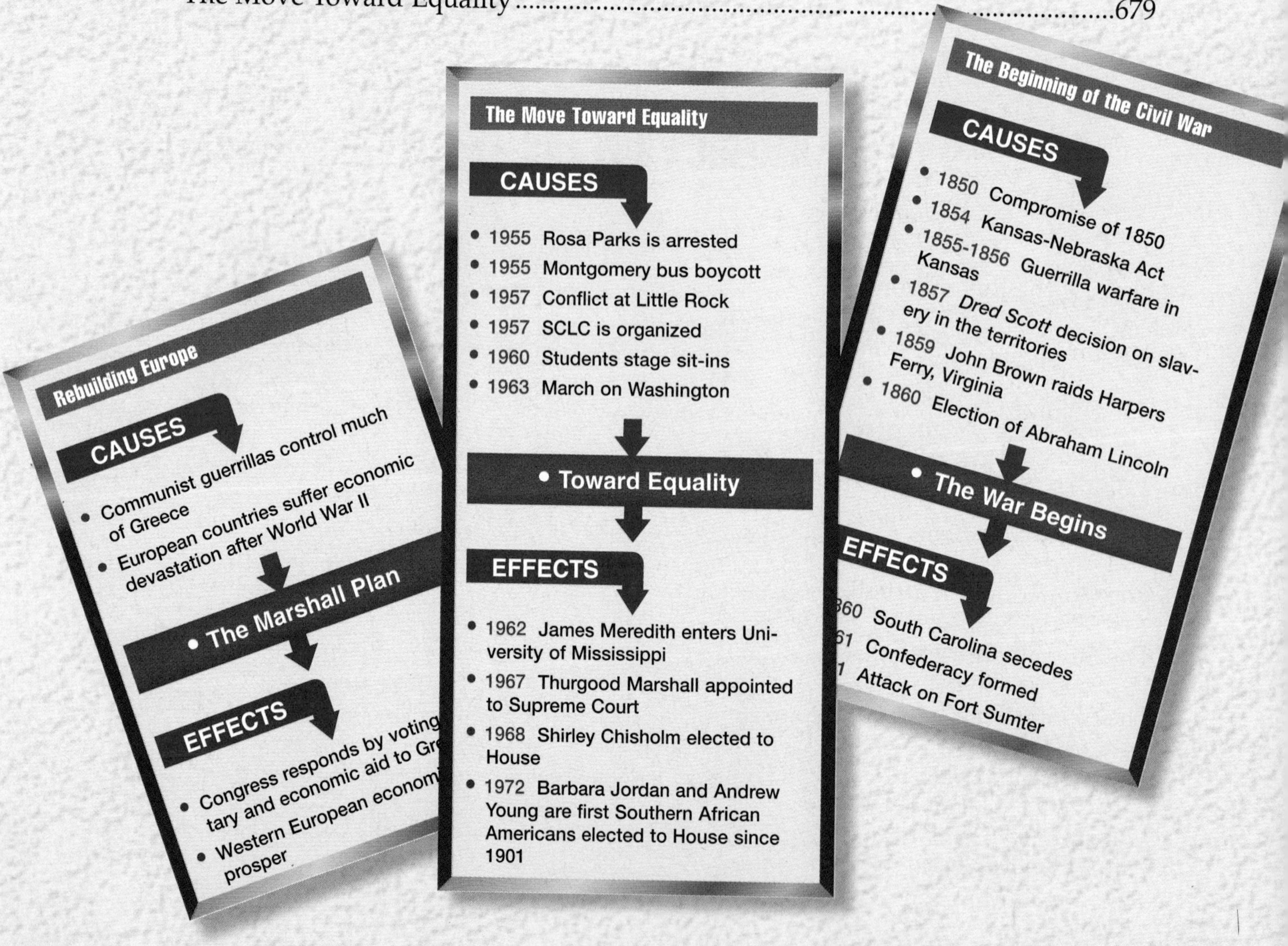

Features

Maps, Charts, Graphs, and Tables

The Mexican War, 1846–1848

← American troops
★ American victory
← Mexican troops
★ Mexican victory
🌐 U.S. naval blockade
▨ Disputed area

0   200   400 miles
0   200   400 kilometers

Map Study

The Mexican War was spread over a vast territory. Unable to defend distant California, Mexico concentrated its efforts south of Texas. **When was the Battle of Buena Vista fought?**

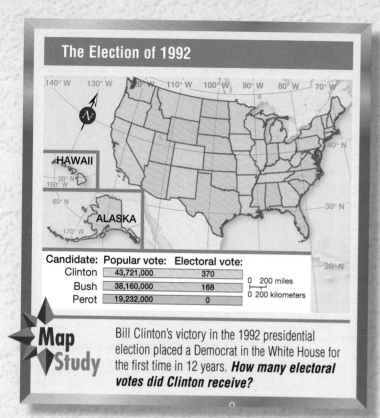

The Election of 1992

Candidate:	Popular vote:	Electoral vote:
Clinton	43,721,000	370
Bush	38,160,000	168
Perot	19,232,000	0

0 — 200 miles
0 — 200 kilometers

Map Study

Bill Clinton's victory in the 1992 presidential election placed a Democrat in the White House for the first time in 12 years. **How many electoral votes did Clinton receive?**

Charts, Graphs, and Tables

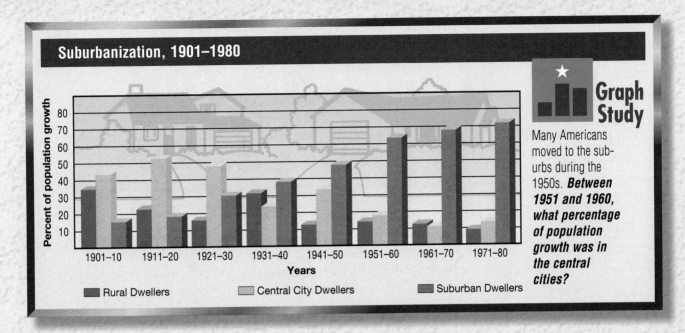

Suburbanization, 1901–1980

Percent of population growth vs **Years** (1901–10, 1911–20, 1921–30, 1931–40, 1941–50, 1951–60, 1961–70, 1971–80)

■ Rural Dwellers　　■ Central City Dwellers　　■ Suburban Dwellers

Graph Study

Many Americans moved to the suburbs during the 1950s. *Between 1951 and 1960, what percentage of population growth was in the central cities?*

GNP, Stock Values, and Unemployment

Year	Gross National Product (in billions)	Stock Values, New York Stock Exchange (in billions)	Unemployment (Percent)
1920	$140.0	$5.5	5.2
1921	127.8	4.7	11.7
1922	148.0	5.7	6.7
1923	165.9	5.9	2.4
1924	165.5	5.9	5.0
1925	179.4	7.6	3.2
1926	190.0	8.6	1.8
1927	189.8	10.5	3.3
1928	190.9	13.7	4.2
1929	203.6	17.9	3.2
1930	183.5	14.4	8.7
1931	169.3	7.5	15.9
1932	144.2	3.8	23.6

Chart Study

Study each column heading, noting the years that show the greatest change. *What was the worst year of the Great Depression for both business and labor?*

Reading for Information

Think about your textbook as a tool that helps you learn more about the world around you. It is an example of non-fiction writing—it describes real-life events, people, ideas, and places. Here is a menu of reading strategies that will help you become a better textbook reader. As you come to passages in your textbook that you don't understand, refer back to these reading strategies for help.

✔ BEFORE YOU READ

Set a Purpose
- Why are you reading the textbook?
- How does the subject relate to your life?
- How might you be able to use what you learn in your own life?

Preview
- Read the chapter title to find what the topic will be.
- Read the subtitles to see what you will learn about the topic.
- Skim the photos, charts, graphs, or maps. How do they support the topic?
- Look for vocabulary words that are boldfaced. How are they defined?

Draw From Your Own Background
- What have you read or heard about concerning new information in the topic?
- How is the new information different from what you already know?
- How will the information that you already know help you understand the new information?

✔ AS YOU READ

Question
- What is the main idea?
- How do the photos, charts, graphs, and maps support the main idea?

Connect
- Think about people, places, and events in your own life. Are there any similarities with those in your textbook?
- Can you relate the textbook information to other areas of your life?

Predict
- Predict events or outcomes by using clues and information that you already know.
- Change your predictions as you read and gather new information.

Visualize
- Pay careful attention to details and descriptions.
- Create graphic organizers to show relationships found in the information.

LOOK FOR CLUES AS YOU READ

- **Comparison-and-Contrast Sentences:**

  Look for clue words and phrases that signal comparison, such as *similarly, just as, both, in common, also,* and *too.*

  Look for clue words and phrases that signal contrast, such as *on the other hand, in contrast to, however, different, instead of, rather than, but,* and *unlike.*

- **Cause-and-Effect Sentences:**

  Look for clue words and phrases such as *because, as a result, therefore, that is why, since, so, for this reason,* and *consequently.*

- **Chronological Sentences:**

  Look for clue words and phrases such as *after, before, first, next, last, during, finally, earlier, later, since,* and *then.*

✔ AFTER YOU READ

Summarize
- Describe the main idea and how the details support it.
- Use your own words to explain what you have read.

Assess
- What was the main idea?
- Did the text clearly support the main idea?
- Did you learn anything new from the material?
- Can you use this new information in other school subjects or at home?
- What other sources could you use to find more information about the topic?

Themes in American History

★ ★

*I*MAGINE a United States without computers, telephones, or automobiles, where women and most minorities cannot vote, a place where 8 of 10 people work on farms, and higher education is a privilege reserved for the fortunate few.

That we live today in a totally different country—yet one that is indeed still the United States—is no accident. What connects past generations and our own is an unbroken chain of events that shapes our lives. Every event in our personal lives has contributed to who we are today. So too have events throughout our nation's history created the American people of the 1990s. Like individual threads in a cloth, events by themselves may lack substance and seem insignificant. Seen together as part of the whole, however, events gain clarity and form.

To help make sense of countless events in history, historians use themes to organize events into meaningful patterns. Themes are recurrent threads, surfacing within an assortment of events, making up the substance of history's fabric—a rich design emblazoned with brilliant colors on the cloth of time.

American Democracy

Abraham Lincoln perhaps explained the meaning of democracy best when he called it "government of the people, by the people, for the people." Democracy at its best, according to many of our nation's leaders, is "among" the people, as exhibited by this "stump-speaking" politician of the mid-1800s, an era of frontier democracy championed by Andrew Jackson.

▲ *STUMP SPEAKING* by George Caleb Bingham, 1853–1854

Civil Rights and Liberties

The foundation of democracy is the right of every person to take part in government and to voice one's views on issues. Not all people in our nation's past have had this basic right. This lithograph illustrates when all African American men were granted suffrage in 1870 with the passage of the Fifteenth Amendment. Preservation of such civil rights and liberties for all citizens is how we guarantee that "we the people" control the government.

◀ MISSOURI'S COMMEMORATION OF THE FIFTEENTH AMENDMENT

Economic Development

The Preamble to the Constitution sets out the purposes of American government, one of which is to "promote the general welfare." Framers of the Constitution recognized that one of government's purposes must be to provide a climate in which citizens can better themselves economically. With few government restrictions, the nation's economy was built on the hard work of farmers and agricultural business.

▶ **CLASSIC LANDSCAPE**
by Charles Sheeler, 1931

Geography and Environment

The United States succeeded in part because of its rich natural resources and its vast open spaces. But in most regions of the nation, the natural landscape was transformed to accommodate ambitions that hard work could make dreams come true. The steel plow and the railroad helped Americans settle the West, but the unblemished environment of the Native American gave way to the demands of expansion.

◀ **MERCED RIVER, YOSEMITE**
by Albert Bierstadt, 1861

Conflict and Cooperation

It has been said that democracy is a poor form of government, but that no better form has been invented. President George Washington established the principle of placing the good of the nation above individual or sectional grievances in 1794, when he led troops against Pennsylvania farmers protesting a tax on whiskey. The conflict over, Washington pardoned the convicted leaders in the spirit of cooperation.

▶ *WASHINGTON RECEIVING THE WESTERN ARMY AT FORT CUMBERLAND, MARYLAND* by Frederick Kemmelmeyer, c. 1795

Influence of Technology

Americans have always been quick to embrace innovations—the country was settled and built by people who gave up old ways and sought new. Americans' lives are profoundly influenced by technology, the use of science and machines. Perhaps no machine has so shaped modern life as the automobile.

◀ FORD AUTOMOBILE, EARLY 1900s

The Individual and Family Life

Americans have a strong tradition of individual freedom sheltered by the protective core of the family unit. Families during the 1950s moved to suburban areas outside the central city to provide themselves with more living space and protection from the perceived dangers of the city. Our earliest experiences of freedom, which were limited by the rights of other individuals, come from interactions within our homes.

◀ Young suburban family of the 1950s

Ideas, Beliefs, and Institutions

An important part of this nation's story is the origin and spread of social, religious, and educational ideas and values. The belief in fundamental rights lies at the heart of United States citizenship and enables people to worship as they wish, speak freely, and read and write what they choose. Along with the enjoyment of these rights, however, comes a responsibility to ensure their strength and endurance.

▶ ANNE HUTCHINSON PREACHING IN HER BOSTON HOME, from a painting by Howard Pyle

Cultural Diversity

American is not a pure nationality but a peculiar mosaic of ideals and ideas. People from around the world for generations have sung of this "land of the Pilgrims' pride, land where our fathers died" even though their ancestors arrived on these shores long after such events transpired. The public schools were the method by which those seeking a new future were transformed into Americans. These immigrant children in New York in the early 1900s pledged allegiance to a flag under which none had been born but which was justly theirs in every way.

◀ Students at a New York City school pledge allegiance, early 1900s.

U.S. Role in World Affairs

A nation composed of peoples from around the world—buying and selling goods around the world, with economic and military might felt across continents, displaying a form of government emulated in all four corners of the globe—cannot but play a leading role in world affairs. The American people have carried on a long tradition as champions of democracy.

▶ President Clinton addressing Jordan's parliament, 1994

Geography in History

★ ★

EOGRAPHY—the study of Earth's surface and the processes that shape it, the relationship between people and their environments, and people and place connections—is an integral part of the web of history.

Indeed, all history happens somewhere. It is the task of geography to supply answers about where a place is, what it is like, how the people live there, how people from different places interact with one another, and how one place on Earth is like others on Earth.

The geography of a region not only includes its physical landscape, natural resources, and climate but also the people who have settled there and their distinctive way of life. The history of the American people—the countless events that make up who we are—is notably influenced by the interplay of our nation's geographic features.

Like historians, geographers use themes to help organize their study of geography into purposeful patterns. Organizing information by themes helps make sense of the vast amount of information we have learned about the myriad of distinctive places that make up the United States.

SPACE PORTRAIT: U.S.A.
The First Color Photomosaic of the Contiguous UNITED STATES
Produced by
GENERAL ELECTRIC COMPANY
Beltsville Photographic Engineering Laboratory
From 569 Landsat Satellite Images
In Cooperation with
The National Geographic Society and
National Aeronautics and Space Administration

Location

A place's position on the earth's surface—its location—constitutes one of the five themes of geography. Location can be either absolute (one particular spot of ground) or relative (position as compared to some other place). *Location* answers the question "Where is that and why is its location significant?"

▶ The Southeast, by virtue of its location on the Atlantic Coast, was one of the first parts of North America settled by Europeans. Colonial Williamsburg recreates daily life as it unfolded in the Southeast three centuries ago.

◀ Los Angeles, California, one of the most densely populated urban areas in the United States, is located atop a network of active fault lines. Its Southwest location is a mixed blessing for Los Angeles—the city enjoys a Mediterranean climate, but it lives with the knowledge that earthquakes can strike at any time.

Place

A place's physical and human characteristics tell what is special about it and what makes it different from all others. Landforms, climate, and culture combine to make up the particular flavor of a particular place. *Place* answers the question "What is that place like?"

▶ Settlement of the Great Plains coincided with the development of machines for plowing, planting, and harvesting on a grand scale; the combination made the Midwest a supplier of meat and grain to the world.

◀ Rivers have had a tremendous impact on American history and life. The confluence of the Mississippi (left) and Ohio (right) rivers south of Cairo, Illinois, in the heart of the Midwest, imparts a special quality to land that is quite different from that found in the desert Southwest. Water is of paramount importance to both places—in the Midwest for its abundance, in the Southwest for its lack.

Human/Environment Interaction

The theme of human/environmental interaction describes how people use, affect, and are affected by their surroundings. Through such interaction, people change the environment in which they live. *Human/environment interaction* answers the question "How does the interaction of people within an environment affect their way of life?"

▶ *WHERE COTTON IS KING* by Konstantin Rodko, 1908
Warm climate, abundant rainfall, and rich soil combined to make large parts of the Southeast ideally suited for the cultivation of cotton. The use of slave labor for this industry set the stage for a confrontation between North and South that became this nation's bloodiest war.

◀ Fishing boats ply the coastal waters of the Northeast in search of such delicacies as lobster. The nutrient-rich waters of the Atlantic drew people to the sea. Yet centuries of fishing have reduced the ocean's bounty.

Movement

People interacting across the globe exemplifies interdependence, the need humans have to utilize skills and resources from around the earth. People travel, communicate, and trade goods, ideas, and information. *Movement* answers the question "How do the people in this place interact with peoples in other places?"

▲ Southwesterners who live along the border between the United States and Mexico can experience dramatic changes in culture and lifestyle by simply walking a few feet from one country to another. The movement of people between countries has political, social, and economic implications.

◀ *DANIEL BOONE ESCORTING SETTLERS THROUGH THE CUMBERLAND GAP* by George Caleb Bingham, 1851–1852

Regions

Regions is the ultimate theme of geography. Regions—how areas form and change—display unity through their characteristics, some physical, some human. The study of regions allows geographers to answer the question "How is this place like other places on the earth?"

◀ The Northeast, like other coastal regions around the world, used its natural advantages to become a center of fishing, shipping, and trade. Yankee clipper ships were the fastest merchant vessels in the world; in 1854 the *Flying Cloud* set a record of 89 days, 8 hours, between Boston and San Francisco.

▶ New England is known not only for its brilliant foliage but also for its charming countryside of small villages inhabited by descendants of early settlers whose motto was, "Use it up, wear it out, make it do."

UNIT ONE
CREATING A NATION
PREHISTORY TO 1815

★★★

CHAPTER
1
Exploration and Settlement
Prehistory–1763

CHAPTER
2
A New Nation
1750–1789

CHAPTER
3
Launching the Republic
1789–1815

▲ ASTROLABE, ITALY, 1500s

History AND ART

Prehistoric Drawing
Baja California, Mexico

Native Americans came to the Western Hemisphere thousands of years ago. Artists have provided a glimpse of their way of life through cave and rock paintings.

Setting the Scene

Why It's Important

The Americas had long been inhabited by a rich variety of Native American cultures. Hundreds of years ago, however, other peoples—Europeans and enslaved Africans—set foot in what was to them a new world. They brought with them their talents and know-how and began to create what is today the United States of America.

To learn more about the colonists' struggles to found a new nation, view the *Historic America: Electronic Field Trips* Side 1, Chapter 6; Side 1, Chapter 7 video lessons:
- *Lexington and Concord*
- *Independence Hall*

Themes

- Geography and the Environment
- The Individual and Family Life
- Beliefs, Ideas, and Institutions
- American Democracy
- Cultural Diversity

Key Events

- First Americans cross the Bering Strait
- Height of Mayan culture
- Voyages of Columbus
- Spanish bring enslaved Africans to America
- Founding of English colonies
- Declaration of Independence
- Ratification of the Constitution
- Louisiana Purchase
- War of 1812

PRIMARY SOURCES Library See pages 856–857 for the primary source readings to accompany Unit 1.

▲ SOUTHWESTERN POTTERY

◀ EARLY AMERICAN FULLER CRADLE

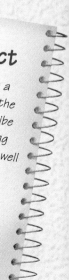

Portfolio Project

Prepare a short report on a Native American culture in the United States today. Describe its peoples' occupations, living standards, and social life as well as traditional crafts, legends, and beliefs.

Global Perspectives

The World

	Prehistory			1600 A.D.
Asia and Oceania	c. 4000 B.C. *Civilizations develop in Asia and Africa*	660 B.C. *Jimmu becomes first emperor of Japan*	1368 *Ming dynasty begins rule of China*	
Europe	509 B.C. *Romans set up a republic*		1400s *Age of Exploration begins*	
Africa	c. 1,750,000 B.C. *First groups of people appear in Africa*			1652 *Cape Town is founded*
South America			◀ 1400s *Inca and Aztec empires flourish*	
North and Central America			1492 *Columbus lands in the Americas*	1650 *Spanish introduce horses to the Plains people*

The United States

Pacific and Northwest	c. 1500 B.C. *People learn metalworking techniques*		1578 *Sir Francis Drake explores the California coast*	
Southeast			1607 *First permanent English settlement is formed at Jamestown*	
Midwest	▶ 200 B.C.–A.D. 400 *Hopewell culture reaches its zenith*			
Southwest		◀ 1050-1200 *Great Pueblo period flourishes*		
Atlantic Northeast			1620 *Pilgrims found Plymouth*	

Prehistory   1600 A.D.

Linking Across TIME

Native Americans have left an indelible mark on American life. Perhaps the most obvious sign of our country's Native American heritage is the hundreds of place names that dot the map. Some of these names offer a vivid physical description of the place. Chattanooga, for example, means "rock rising to a point," while Nantucket means "the far away place." Other names indicate what went on at the place. Milwaukee was the "gathering place by the river" and Kalamazoo was the "boiling pot."

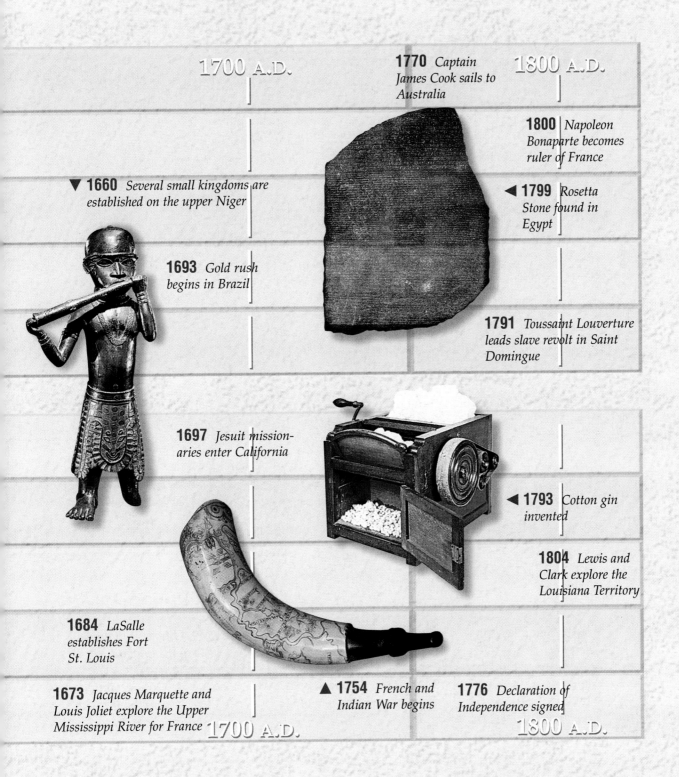

1700 A.D.

1770 *Captain James Cook sails to Australia*

1800 A.D.

1800 *Napoleon Bonaparte becomes ruler of France*

▼ **1660** *Several small kingdoms are established on the upper Niger*

◄ **1799** *Rosetta Stone found in Egypt*

1693 *Gold rush begins in Brazil*

1791 *Toussaint Louverture leads slave revolt in Saint Domingue*

1697 *Jesuit missionaries enter California*

◄ **1793** *Cotton gin invented*

1804 *Lewis and Clark explore the Louisiana Territory*

1684 *LaSalle establishes Fort St. Louis*

1673 *Jacques Marquette and Louis Joliet explore the Upper Mississippi River for France*

▲ **1754** *French and Indian War begins*

1776 *Declaration of Independence signed*

1700 A.D.

1800 A.D.

CHAPTER 1

★★

Exploration and Settlement
Prehistory–1763

▼ ARROWHEAD, HAND-CHIPPED

Setting the Scene

Focus

The first people came to North America long before written history. Their descendants, known as Native Americans, developed unique cultures and civilizations in North America and South America. Then a series of events in Europe, Asia, and Africa opened the way to European exploration and settlement in the Americas. Thereafter, various nations—Spain, Portugal, France, England, and the Netherlands—sought to build a colonial empire.

Concepts to Understand

★ How different ways of life among the Native American societies created **cultural diversity**

★ What political, social, and economic **values and beliefs** the European colonists developed in America

Read to Discover . . .

★ who were the major Native American groups.

★ why European nations wanted to explore and colonize the Americas.

Journal Notes

How do the accomplishments and ideas of a culture reflect values? Note important details about various cultures in your journal as you read the chapter.

HISTORY Online

Chapter Overview
Visit the *American History: The Modern Era Since 1865* Web site at **me.glencoe.com** and click on **Chapter 1—Chapter Overviews** to preview chapter information.

CULTURAL			
	● **c. 4500 B.C.** *Writing develops*	● **900s** *Chinese advance the art of printing*	● **1149** *University founded at Oxford, England*
	Prehistory–A.D. 500	**A.D. 900**	**1100**
POLITICAL	● **1000 B.C.** *People inhabit present-day Peru and Ecuador*	● **900s** *Mayan civilization begins to decline* ● **900s** *Feudalism spreads throughout western Europe*	● **1152** *Frederick I becomes Holy Roman Emperor*

Cabot's Departure, 1497
by Ernest Board, 1906

English merchants persuaded their king to send John Cabot, an Italian navigator, to Asia by a northwest route. This painting, completed more than 400 years after the event, communicates a feeling of solemn pageantry.

◀ JAPANESE MILITARY EQUIPMENT

- **1300** *Cahokia is largest North American community*
- **1337** *Hundred Years' War begins*

1300

- **1505** *Michaelangelo paints Sistine Chapel*
- **1570** *Iroquois form League of Five Nations*

1500

- **1740** *Great Awakening stimulates revivalist spirit*
- **1763** *Peace of Paris ends Seven Years' War*

1700

★★

World in Transition

Guide to Reading

Main Idea

The cultures of the Americas developed without any contact with those of Africa, Asia, or Europe.

Reading Strategy

Classifying Information As you read about the world in transition on the eve of European exploration, summarize the state of the countries and regions discussed in a chart similar to the one shown here.

Region/Country	Summary

Objectives

After studying this section, you should be able to

★ explain the differences among the Native American cultures of the region.

★ describe how European society changed as a result of the Crusades, the Renaissance, and the Reformation.

★ identify the leading empires of Asia and Africa.

Key Terms

confederation, feudalism, shogun, joint-stock company

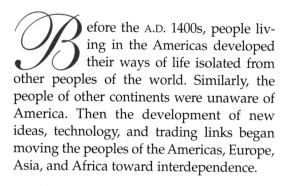

▶ PAINTED CLAY IMAGE

Before the A.D. 1400s, people living in the Americas developed their ways of life isolated from other peoples of the world. Similarly, the people of other continents were unaware of America. Then the development of new ideas, technology, and trading links began moving the peoples of the Americas, Europe, Asia, and Africa toward interdependence.

■ The First Americans

Twenty thousand years ago, much of the water in today's oceans was frozen. Huge ice sheets covered much of present-day Canada and the northern United States. Scientists today believe that people from Asia walked across a "land bridge" that once connected Alaska and Asia. They also may have traveled

in simple boats down the Pacific Coast. In small groups, they gradually spread throughout North and South America, following great herds of game animals. Over time these people adapted to their environments. Their descendants became known as Native Americans.

In time Native Americans formed into many diverse groups based on language and customs. Despite their diversity, Native Americans had many similar ideas. For example, all Native Americans felt a close relationship to the land and their environment.

Native American Empires

Groups of Native Americans in present-day Mexico and South America gradually developed highly organized and sophisticated societies. In western South America, the Inca ruled a large empire that stretched 3,000 miles (4,800 km) from present-day Colombia to the middle of Chile. A complex system of roads linked the various regions of the Inca Empire, and terraced hillside farms with complicated irrigation systems produced abundant food.

To the north, in the area called Mesoamerica—parts of the nations of Mexico, Guatemala, and Honduras—other powerful Native American civilizations arose. One of the earliest, the Olmec, developed large temple complexes and pyramids along the Gulf of Mexico. Farther south, in the Yucatán Peninsula, the Maya established city-states dominated by even larger pyramids. The Maya excelled in trade and mathematics. Mayan mathematicians invented the concept of zero and developed complicated calendars linked to the study of the stars.

Many other equally advanced groups emerged in Mesoamerica. The last was the Aztec. Their city, Tenochtitlán, is the site of modern Mexico City. By the late 1400s, Tenochtitlán had gold-adorned temples, floating gardens, and an enormous market.

Cultures North of Mexico

Native Americans living in the present-day southwestern United States and in the fertile Mississippi Valley traded with Mexico.

In these two areas, the population was only one-tenth that of Mexico and the Inca Empire. The way of life was also much different. Most people lived in small villages or bands.

In the Southwest, the Anasazi built large, multistory apartment-like buildings of adobe. Another southwestern group, the Hohokam, built large villages that had irrigation canals and temple mounds. During the 1300s, severe drought and climate change ended both cultures. The Hohokam did not survive, but the descendants of the Anasazi remain as the Pueblo people of New Mexico.

Around A.D. 900, in the Mississippi Valley, farmers and traders built great temple mounds and towns. Such cities as Cahokia (near present-day St. Louis) grew to great size, with hundreds of temple mounds. Another group of moundbuilders, the Hopewell culture, arose in the Ohio Valley about 200 B.C. and lasted about 700 years.

In other parts of North America, a variety of Native American groups flourished: the buffalo-hunters of the Great Plains, the rich fishing cultures of the Pacific Northwest, and the seed gatherers of California. In the Northeast, the Iroquois set up a **confederation,** or government made up of independent units, about A.D. 1580. The confederation worked to maintain peace between the various Iroquois nations. In the

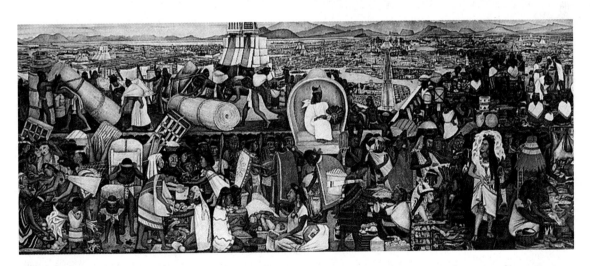

▲ *MARKETPLACE OF TLATEOLCO* by Diego Rivera, 1920s Rivera's murals portray the culture and history of Mexico. Cities grew up around market centers, which drew great crowds of people. *What peoples developed complex road and irrigation systems?*

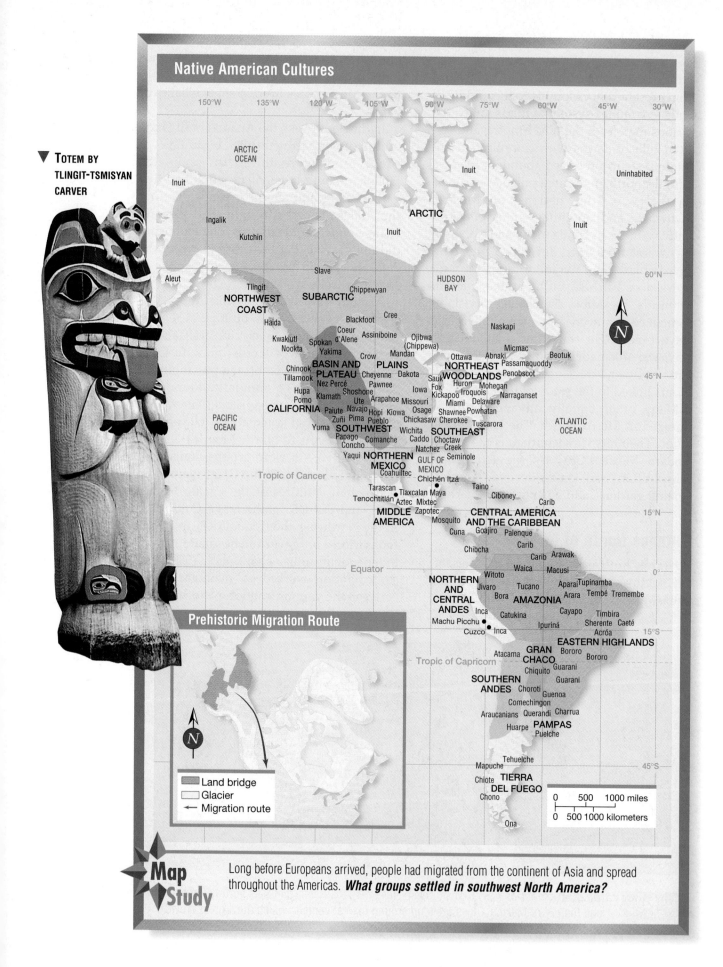

Native American Cultures

▼ **Totem by Tlingit-Tsmisyan Carver**

Prehistoric Migration Route

- ▨ Land bridge
- ☐ Glacier
- ← Migration route

Map Study

Long before Europeans arrived, people had migrated from the continent of Asia and spread throughout the Americas. *What groups settled in southwest North America?*

Southeast, the Creek, Cherokee, Choctaw, Seminole, and Chickasaw formed a confederation called the Five Civilized Tribes. This group later devised a written language and a dictionary, and practiced a loose-knit form of democracy.

■ A New Europe

Across the Atlantic Ocean, Europe entered a period known as the Middle Ages, which lasted from about A.D. 500 until about A.D. 1500. During the Middle Ages, central government in Europe was replaced by **feudalism,** a system in which powerful lords gave land to nobles in return for pledges of loyalty. The majority of Europe's people were peasants who worked on farmlands held by the nobles.

The Crusades

During the Middle Ages, the Roman Catholic Church, the western branch of Christianity, became a powerful force in Europe. From 1095 to about 1300, Church leaders asked Europeans to carry out a series of Crusades, or "holy wars," to recapture the "Holy Land" of Palestine from the Muslims, or people who follow the religion of Islam.

Although the Crusades were a failure, they had a major impact on western Europe. The Crusades helped break down feudalism. Contact with the East spurred a new demand in Europe for Asian luxury goods, such as spices and silk. European cities—especially Venice and Genoa in Italy—became more prosperous due to increased trading in the Mediterranean area.

Renaissance and Reformation

In Europe, a wealthy and educated middle class developed from an increase in commerce and the growth of cities. Prosperity, optimism, and an emphasis on human abilities led to a profound cultural awakening known as the Renaissance. Renaissance ideas and values began about 1350 in the city-states of northern Italy and spread to other parts of Europe. The Renaissance was

Visualizing History

▲ **RELIGIOUS ART** Artists decorated books, crosses, and other items with religious images. Shrines in which sacred relics are kept, called reliquaries (shown above), were frequently made of gilded copper and decorated with precious stones. *What impact did the Crusades have on western Europe?*

a turning point in Europe's history. While the Middle Ages had emphasized faith and spiritual values, the Renaissance exalted human creativity and talent.

Religion was one area of European life in which traditional ways were challenged by these developments. In the early 1500s, the German monk and scholar Martin Luther attacked several church practices. In taking a stand against church authorities, Luther sparked what became known as the Protestant Reformation. A new form of Christianity—Protestantism—developed and grew throughout northern Europe. In other parts of Europe, most people remained loyal to the Roman Catholic Church.

Emerging Nations

During the 1400s, strong monarchs brought unity to the countries of England, France, Portugal, and Spain. All four lands had seaports on the Atlantic Ocean—soon to become a great avenue of trade and exploration.

Europeans, once isolated and bound by a rigid feudal system, were developing a spirit of curiosity and adventure. Unified monarchies and national rivalry led to competition for trade with Asia. The search for an all-water route to East Asia encouraged explorers to cross unknown oceans and seek new lands.

Medieval Asia and Africa

Since ancient times, trade had linked the peoples of Europe, Asia, and Africa. Europe's share in foreign trade declined during much of the Middle Ages, but trade between Asia and Africa flourished.

The Influence of Islam

The most important influence in medieval Africa and Asia was the rise of the religion of Islam in the 600s. Inspired by the teachings of the prophet Muhammad, the prophet's followers spread Islam from the Arabian Peninsula through Southwest Asia to India and North Africa into Spain and the Mediterranean region.

As Islam spread, Muslims and Christians came into direct conflict. Contact between the groups, however, influenced trade and learning and brought new ideas. Muslim Arab scholars had made advances in medicine, astronomy, mathematics, and other sciences. From the Arabs, Europeans learned algebra and the system of Arabic numerals, which had come to Southwest Asia from India.

China

In the early 1200's the ancient empire of China was conquered by invading Mongols from central Asia. China prospered under Mongol rule. East-west trade revived, along with cultural exchanges among China, Europe, and Muslim Asia. European

▲ **ILLUMINATED MANUSCRIPT**, illustrated and hand-written document

traders, such as Marco Polo, returned with silk, spices, and important Chinese inventions, such as the compass, printing, and gunpowder. Polo's description of the luxury of the Chinese ruler's court stirred the imaginations of his European readers:

> ❝ *Inside, the walls and halls and chambers are all covered with gold and silver and decorated with pictures of dragons and birds and horsemen and various breeds of beasts and scenes of battle.... The hall is so vast that a meal might be served there for more than 6,000 men.* ❞

In 1294, the Chinese overthrew their Mongol rulers and set up the Ming Empire. Ming rulers at first encouraged trade, sending expeditions to India and East Africa. By the late 1400s, they ended China's contacts with the world. While the spirit of the Renaissance was transforming Europe, the mood in China was to preserve tradition against foreign influences. China would remain relatively isolated for centuries.

Japan

Like medieval Europe, Japan had a feudal society, based on bonds between landowning nobles and warriors who served them.

• •
Footnotes to History

Illuminated Manuscript Scholars of the Byzantine empire created an art form called the illuminated manuscript. These were books decorated with elaborate designs, beautiful lettering, and miniature paintings. The brilliantly colored paintings portrayed religious themes as well as scenes of Byzantine daily life. Adopted in western Europe, the art of illuminating manuscripts provided a vivid record of daily life between A.D. 300 and 1200.

Since the 1100s, the country had been led by **shoguns**, military dictators who had far more power than the Japanese emperor. By the late 1400s, the shogun's government had weakened, and local lords were almost constantly at war. Nonetheless, towns and trade prospered in medieval Japan.

African Trading Kingdoms

From ancient times, trade linked the continent of Africa with other cultures. The earliest African civilizations developed in northeastern Africa. From their base in the Nile River valley, Egyptians and, later, Kushites ruled extensive empires. A Christian African empire, Axum, arose during the Middle Ages in the area that is present-day Ethiopia.

Between A.D. 500 and 1500, three wealthy kingdoms—Ghana, Mali, and Songhai—developed one after the other in western Africa. The Muslim conquest of North Africa greatly increased trade, and Muslim culture spread throughout the area. East Africa, on the other hand, looked eastward, trading with Arabia, Persia, India, and China. In central and southern Africa, civil wars brought internal disorder to the Bantu-speaking nations. The resulting loss of power left little defense against Europeans who arrived in the 1500s.

■ Expansion of Europe

The Renaissance spirit of curiosity and adventure that swept over Europe helped launch the bold voyages of the Age of Exploration. Europeans wanted luxury goods and food-preserving spices from Asia. Western European merchants hoped to break the monopoly that Arab and Italian traders had on the overland routes to Asia. European monarchs desired to enrich their countries, and church leaders wanted to send missionaries overseas to spread Christianity.

Linking Past and Present

African Art

In Africa, the arts are interwoven with many aspects of daily life. From ancient times to the present, Africans have used visual arts in many different forms and materials.

Then

Medieval Art

In ancient times, African artists and craftspeople created an extraordinary variety of art forms—from sculpted figures and masks to decorated cloth to the multi-rhythmic music of traditional dances. Because of the forced migration of enslaved Africans to other parts of the world, these styles spread throughout the Americas, the Caribbean, and parts of Europe.

Now

A Heritage of Beauty

The influence of African masks, sculptures, and weavings can be seen in museums and in everyday life. Modern European artists such as Pablo Picasso drew inspiration from the abstract masks of the Yoruba of Nigeria. The bronze castings of the Benin are known around the world. So are the many types of textiles designed by Africans. Prized by many are Ghana's brightly colored *kente* cloth, Nigeria's *adire* cloth, and East Africa's *kong* cloth—complete with a Swahili proverb on each piece.

Today there are thousands of artists in the towns and cities of Africa fashioning pots, carving wood masks, designing buildings, sculpting statues, and weaving and dyeing cloth.

▲ YORUBA MASKS

▶ ANTELOPE FIGURINE

Commerce and Technology

The great expense of ocean voyages made new ways of raising finances necessary. In England, France, and the Netherlands, the **joint-stock company** became a useful form for raising money. The company sold shares, called stock, to investors, thus providing money or capital for its venture.

No matter how well financed, long voyages could not have succeeded without better technology. By the 1400s, ship captains were using precise maps of the coasts of Europe and North Africa. From Arab sailors, Europeans learned to use improved navigational instruments, such as the compass, the astrolabe, and the quadrant—that allowed navigators to determine direction and distance. Ships were also built to new designs that made them faster and more seaworthy. The carrack had several masts and a rudder. Smaller but easier to handle was the Portuguese caravel, a double-rigged ship with both square and triangular sails. **$**

The Pioneering Portuguese

Portugal was the first European country to search for a sea route to Asia. This small nation had a long Atlantic coast with good ports and a rich seafaring tradition.

In the early 1400s, Prince Henry, son of King John I of Portugal, brought together mapmakers, astronomers, and shipbuilders to plan voyages of exploration. One of Henry's plans was to have his ships sail around Africa and find a path to India. Expedition after expedition, the Portuguese inched their way down the west coast of Africa. By the time Prince Henry—known as "the Navigator"—died in 1460, his ships had reached just beyond the westernmost tip of Africa.

By this time, the Portuguese had established trading posts and sugar plantations on the West African coast. They acquired gold, ivory, pepper, palm oil, and slaves from African merchants. Using war captives as slaves had long been a practice throughout the world. The Portuguese used enslaved Africans as servants in Portugal or as laborers on their West African plantations.

Meanwhile, Portuguese navigators moved on to find a sea route to India. In 1487 and 1488, a Portuguese expedition led by Bartholomeu Dias rounded the southern tip of Africa. The area was soon named the "Cape of Good Hope" because it seemed to promise the existence of a new sea route to India. Ten years later, another Portuguese expedition led by Vasco da Gama rounded the Cape of Good Hope, sailed up the eastern coast of Africa, and crossed the Indian Ocean to Calicut on the coast of India. Da Gama finally returned home to Portugal in 1499. The sea route that he opened challenged other European nations to make their own explorations. In the following four centuries, western Europe's quest for wealth and empire would affect the lives of people on every continent.

Section 1 ★ Assessment

Checking for Understanding

1. **Define** confederation, feudalism, shogun, joint-stock company.
2. **Summarize** the process by which the Americas were first settled.
3. **Analyze** the way in which the spread of Islam affected Europe, Asia, and Africa.

Critical Thinking

4. **Outlining** Use the outline format shown to list the changes that took place in Europe and to show how they helped usher in the Age of Exploration.

Changes in Europe

I. A.   II. A.   III. A.
    B.   B.   B.

INTERDISCIPLINARY ACTIVITY

5. **The Arts** Select one of the Native American groups from the map on page 10. Research its way of life. Write a one-page paper that describes your findings.

★★★

European Explorations

Guide to Reading

Main Idea

In search of new trade routes, Europeans reached the Americas—where they began to build new and lasting societies.

Reading Strategy

Sequencing Information As you read about European exploration of the Americas, create a time line of significant events. Use the dates provided as a guide.

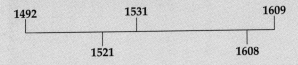

1492   1531   1609
    1521   1608

Objectives

After studying this section, you should be able to
★ describe Spanish exploration, conquests, and settlement in the Americas.
★ discuss English, French, and Dutch ventures in North America.

Key Terms

line of demarcation, conquistador, mestizo, *encomienda*, mercantilism, northwest passage

▶ EXPLORER'S LOG BOOK

The first Europeans to arrive in the Americas were Norse seafarers from Scandinavia. Between A.D. 800 and 1100, the Norse established settlements in Iceland, Greenland, and along the coast of North America, which they called Vinland. Conflicts with Native Americans and lack of support from home, however, made the Norse settlements in Vinland unsuccessful. Not until the voyage of Christopher Columbus in 1492 did European exploration of the Americas begin in earnest.

■ Early Voyages

As a result of his studies and calculations, the Italian-born navigator Christopher Columbus came to believe that it would be easier to reach Asia by traveling west. He eagerly sought to lead such a voyage, and for years sought financial backing. Columbus finally persuaded King Ferdinand and Queen Isabella of Spain that his plan would bring them wealth, empire, and converts to the Catholic religion. The monarchs provided Columbus with three ships, the *Niña*, the *Pinta*, and the *Santa Maria*.

Voyages of Columbus

Columbus left Spain in August 1492 with 90 sailors. Two months later, after a difficult Atlantic voyage, Columbus went ashore onto a small island in the Bahamas (San Salvador) and claimed it for Spain. Believing he had reached the East Indies off the coast of Asia, he called the local people Indians. Columbus made three more voyages across the Atlantic. Despite his achievements, Columbus died in 1506 unaware that he had reached new continents in the Western Hemisphere.

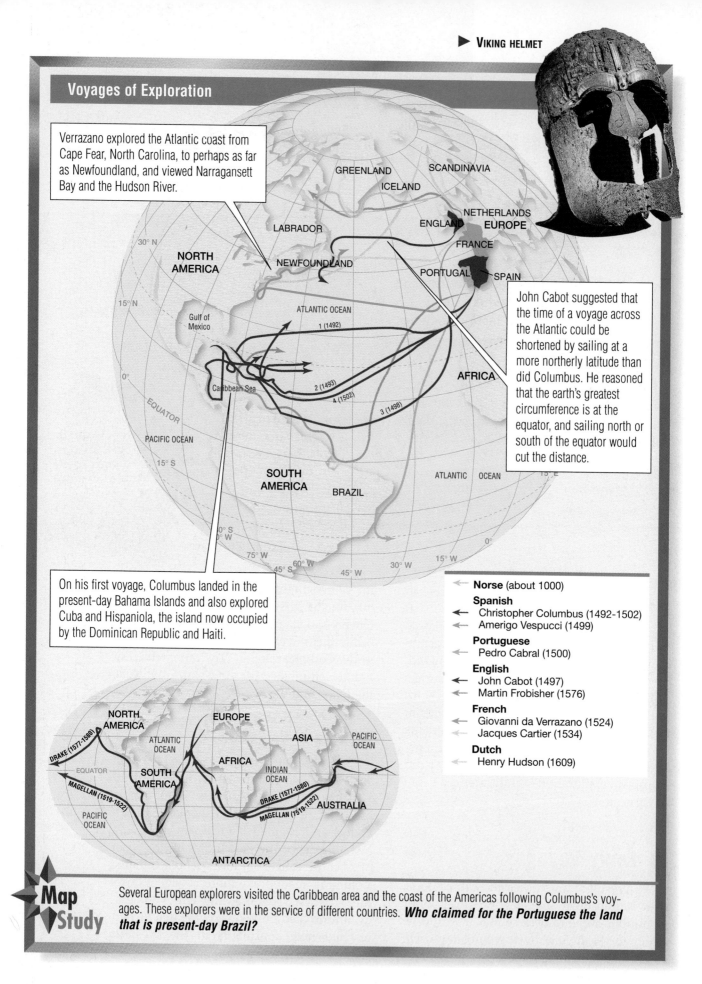

Voyages of Exploration

Verrazano explored the Atlantic coast from Cape Fear, North Carolina, to perhaps as far as Newfoundland, and viewed Narragansett Bay and the Hudson River.

John Cabot suggested that the time of a voyage across the Atlantic could be shortened by sailing at a more northerly latitude than did Columbus. He reasoned that the earth's greatest circumference is at the equator, and sailing north or south of the equator would cut the distance.

On his first voyage, Columbus landed in the present-day Bahama Islands and also explored Cuba and Hispaniola, the island now occupied by the Dominican Republic and Haiti.

GREENLAND
SCANDINAVIA
ICELAND
NETHERLANDS
ENGLAND EUROPE
LABRADOR
FRANCE
NEWFOUNDLAND
PORTUGAL SPAIN
NORTH AMERICA
30° N
15° N
Gulf of Mexico
ATLANTIC OCEAN
1 (1492)
AFRICA
0°
Caribbean Sea
2 (1493)
4 (1502)
3 (1498)
EQUATOR
PACIFIC OCEAN
15° S
SOUTH AMERICA
BRAZIL
ATLANTIC OCEAN
0° S
75° W 60° W 45° S
45° W 30° W 15° W
0°

← Norse (about 1000)

Spanish
← Christopher Columbus (1492-1502)
← Amerigo Vespucci (1499)

Portuguese
← Pedro Cabral (1500)

English
← John Cabot (1497)
← Martin Frobisher (1576)

French
← Giovanni da Verrazano (1524)
← Jacques Cartier (1534)

Dutch
← Henry Hudson (1609)

NORTH AMERICA
EUROPE
ATLANTIC OCEAN
ASIA
PACIFIC OCEAN
DRAKE (1577-1580)
AFRICA
EQUATOR
INDIAN OCEAN
SOUTH AMERICA
MAGELLAN (1519-1522)
DRAKE (1577-1580)
MAGELLAN (1519-1522)
AUSTRALIA
PACIFIC OCEAN
ANTARCTICA

Map Study

Several European explorers visited the Caribbean area and the coast of the Americas following Columbus's voyages. These explorers were in the service of different countries. *Who claimed for the Portuguese the land that is present-day Brazil?*

Division of the World

Columbus's exploration put Spain and Portugal in direct competition for trade and empire. In 1493, Pope Alexander VI convinced the two Catholic nations to divide any new overseas territories between them. He set a **line of demarcation,** an imaginary north-south line, west of the Azores, a group of islands in the North Atlantic about 800 miles off the coast of Portugal. The agreement gave Spain rights to all the non-Christian lands to the west of the line, and Portugal rights to all those to the east.

A New Land

In 1499, a Portuguese expedition led by the Italian-born navigator and explorer Amerigo Vespucci (veh•SPOO•chee) sailed along the coast of South America. Vespucci concluded that this land was a vast new continent. In 1504 Vespucci's sensational account was published, and he erroneously received credit for reaching the mainland of this land before Columbus. German mapmakers named the land "America," and the name stuck.

A Vast New Ocean

On expeditions into present-day Panama, the Spanish explorer Vasco Núñez de Balboa (VAHS•koh NOO•nyayth day bal•BOH•uh) was guided by local Native Americans to a vast body of water. Having climbed a peak alone to see the water first, Balboa in 1513 became the first European to see the eastern coast of the Pacific Ocean. It now appeared that the lands Columbus had reached were separated from Asia by this seemingly endless ocean.

Magellan's Voyage

Balboa's expedition revived hope of sailing west to reach Asia. Since only an isthmus, or strip of land, separated the oceans at Panama, it was thought that perhaps there was a strait, or narrow waterway, connecting the two bodies of water. Portuguese navigator Ferdinand Magellan believed he could find such a passage.

Magellan hoped to sail around the world to the Spice Islands, a center for the valuable spice trade located in present-day Indonesia. Spain's King Charles I agreed to finance Magellan, and in 1519 Magellan set sail with five ships. By October 1520, Magellan had reached the strait that now bears his name at the southern tip of South America.

The strait, with its fierce winds, was difficult to navigate. Because the ocean on the other side seemed so calm, Magellan called it the Pacific, meaning "peaceful." Magellan later died in April 1521 as the result of a local war in the Philippines. Only one of his ships, the *Victoria* carrying 18 survivors, finally reached Spain in 1522. These survivors and their ship were the first to circumnavigate the world.

■ Spain in America

After Columbus's voyages, Spanish **conquistadors** (kahn•KEES•tuh•dawrs), or conquerors, made their way to the Americas in hope of finding gold and silver. In the West Indies, the conquistadors enslaved the local Native Americans, forcing them to search for gold or to raise crops. Most of the Native Americans in the West Indies succumbed to such European diseases as smallpox and measles, from which they had no immunity. The Spaniards then began to abduct West Africans to work as slaves.

Cortés and Moctezuma

In 1519, the conquistador Hernán Cortés (kawr•TEHZ) led an expedition of 600 soldiers from the West Indies island of Cuba to the eastern shore of Mexico. The Spanish force had firearms and horses, both of which the local Native Americans had never seen. Believing that Cortés was a returning god, the Aztec emperor Moctezuma welcomed the Spaniards and lodged them in the Aztec capital of Tenochtitlán. Cortés wrote:

❝ *The city itself is as big as Seville or Córdoba. . . . [it] has many squares where . . . markets are held continuously. . . .*

> *There are . . . many temples. . . . Amongst these temples there is one . . . whose great size and magnificence no human tongue could describe.* **"**

To ensure their safety, the Spaniards took Moctezuma captive. They also looted the city of gold and silver. Eight months later, when Moctezuma was killed by one of his subjects, the Aztec rose up against the Spaniards and forced them to retreat.

In 1521, Cortés returned to the Aztec capital, having amassed huge numbers of allies among local Native Americans dissatisfied with Aztec rule. After a long siege, the Spaniards destroyed Tenochtitlán whose splendor had so impressed them. Mexico City was built on its ruins, and the area's rich silver mines soon produced vast wealth.

Fall of the Inca

Another conquistador, Francisco Pizarro, set out to conquer the mighty and fabulously rich Inca Empire. In 1531 Pizarro sailed from Panama to present-day Peru with an army of only 180 soldiers. Reaching the Incan city of Cajamarca (KAH•

Visualizing History

▲ **COLUMBUS AND ISABELLA**
Columbus believed Asia was accessible by traveling westward. Queen Isabella of Spain agreed to finance Columbus's explorations across the Atlantic. **What did Columbus's explorations mean for Spain?**

huh•MAHR•kuh), the Spaniards seized the Incan ruler, Atahualpa (AH•tah•WAHL•pah) and later executed him. Already weakened by civil war, the Inca Empire easily fell to the Spaniards.

Junípero Serra
1713–1784

★★★★★★★★ AMERICAN PORTRAITS

Most Spanish conquests in the Americas were marked by a terrible slaughter of the local people. In contrast, a gentle priest established Spanish control in California by setting up a string of missions to care for and convert the Native Americans.

Born on an island off the Spanish coast, Junípero Serra became a Franciscan priest and professor of philosophy. Because he wanted to work as a missionary among Native Americans, in 1749 he left Spain to travel to Mexico.

At the age of 55, he was sent to take control of Upper California. He established a mission at San Diego, and later founded several missions stretching up the California coast to San Francisco. Taking as his motto "Always go forward and never turn back," Junípero Serra traveled by foot from mission to mission, making sure that Native Americans were not abused.

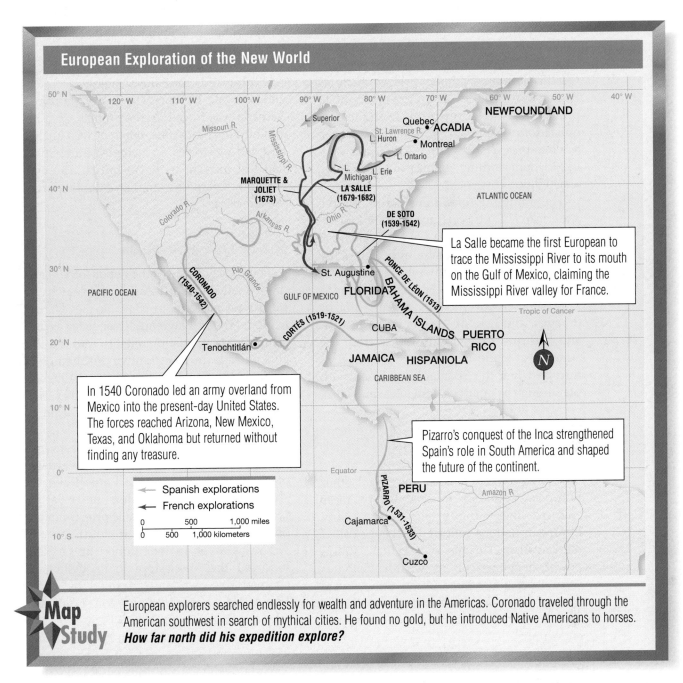

European Exploration of the New World

La Salle became the first European to trace the Mississippi River to its mouth on the Gulf of Mexico, claiming the Mississippi River valley for France.

In 1540 Coronado led an army overland from Mexico into the present-day United States. The forces reached Arizona, New Mexico, Texas, and Oklahoma but returned without finding any treasure.

Pizarro's conquest of the Inca strengthened Spain's role in South America and shaped the future of the continent.

← Spanish explorations
← French explorations

0   500   1,000 miles
0   500   1,000 kilometers

Map Study European explorers searched endlessly for wealth and adventure in the Americas. Coronado traveled through the American southwest in search of mythical cities. He found no gold, but he introduced Native Americans to horses. *How far north did his expedition explore?*

Pizarro's conquest of the Inca Empire brought many Spanish settlers to Peru, where they mined silver and gold.

Colonial Life

Other Spanish conquistadors explored areas to the north, in the present-day southern and western United States. Because these northern lands appeared inhospitable, the Spanish considered them unsuitable for colonization. In other areas of the Americas, the Spaniards worked to strengthen their empire.

The people of Spain's American colonies formed a structured society, where position was determined predominately by birth. Spaniards born in Spain or in the Americas made up the highest social classes. **Mestizos** (meh•STEE•zohs), those born of Native American and Spanish parents, made up the next level of society. At the lowest levels were Native Americans, enslaved Africans, and people of mixed ancestry.

Through the *encomienda* system, the Spanish monarch rewarded conquistadors with land and the right to demand both labor and taxes from the Native Americans. The

Spanish colonists often treated the Native Americans cruelly, overworking them and using their forced labor to gain vast personal wealth. Roman Catholic priests, such as Father Bartolome de Las Casas, sought to protect the Native Americans from the conquistadors. Many clergy established missions to provide the Native Americans with work, food, clothing, a European education, and religious instruction.

The mingling of Spanish and Native American cultures produced a new kind of society in the Spanish colonies. Spanish became the major language, although many Native Americans continued to speak their original languages. The Spanish introduced European crops, such as wheat, alfalfa, oranges, and figs, as well as horses, cattle, and firearms. Likewise, products from the Americas made significant changes in Europe when the Spaniards returned with plants such as potatoes, tomatoes, and corn.

■ New Ventures

Spain's colonial success convinced other European countries to establish overseas empires. Beginning in the 1600s, many European nations followed a theory called **mercantilism.** This theory held that a state's power depended on its wealth. Colonies were especially valued because they were sources of raw materials and provided markets for the manufactured goods of the parent country.

English-Spanish Rivalry

In 1497, John Cabot explored the Atlantic shores of present-day Canada and claimed the land for England. But poor finances, religious conflict, and the threat of war with Spain kept the English from following up on Cabot's claims.

In the late 1500s, daring English sea captains, such as Francis Drake, cruised the shores of Spanish America, capturing treasure ships and looting towns. In 1588, seeking revenge for English attacks on Spanish ships and colonies, King Philip II of Spain sent a huge fleet of ships, known

as the Spanish Armada, to sail against the English fleet.

The outnumbered, but swift, English vessels attacked the slow, heavy Spanish galleons one by one. The badly damaged Armada was forced up the English Channel and into the North Sea, where it was further crippled by storms. In a single battle, Spain had lost most of its naval forces. The way was now cleared for English colonization in the Americas.

The French in America

In the early 1500s, French-sponsored expeditions sailed to North America in search of a **northwest passage.** In 1534, Jacques Cartier explored the St. Lawrence River as far as present-day Montreal, but failed to find the elusive passage. In 1608, Samuel de Champlain founded the first French settlement, Quebec, on the banks of the St. Lawrence River. Few French settlers, however, were attracted to this northern outpost.

French explorers soon ventured from present-day Canada south into the heartland of North America. In 1673 Louis Joliet, an American-born fur trader, and Father Jacques Marquette, a Catholic priest, canoed on the Mississippi as far south as the Arkansas River. In 1682 Robert de La Salle followed the Mississippi to its delta and claimed the vast lands drained by it for France. He named the region Louisiana after the French king Louis XIV.

France's colonies in North America eventually formed a long string of outposts from Canada to the Gulf of Mexico. Rather than encourage settlements and farms, the French directed their interests toward devel-

• •

Footnotes to History

The Spanish Empire   The Spanish empire in the Americas included more than one-half the continental United States. The oldest surviving building in the United States is the Spanish fort at St. Augustine, Florida. The city of Santa Fe was founded by the Spanish at about the same time the English Pilgrims were crossing the Atlantic on the *Mayflower.*

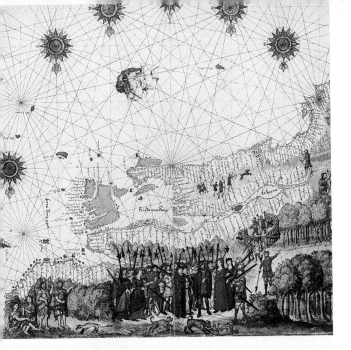

▲ NEW FRANCE The French explored and settled in a vast region that included the St. Lawrence River valley, the Great Lakes, and the Mississippi River valley. *Where did the French make settlements?*

oping the fur trade. Beaver skins sent to France and made into hats were a particularly profitable item.

The French generally had better relations with Native Americans than did the Spanish. French trappers and traders known as *coureurs de bois*—"runners of the woods"—lived among the Native Americans and learned their ways. Without soldiers accompanying them, French missionaries bravely journeyed into the American wilderness to convert Native Americans to Catholicism.

The Dutch in America

The Netherlands, which had won its independence from Spain in the late 1500s, was also interested in exploration. In 1609, the Dutch funded an expedition by an English navigator, Henry Hudson. He reached New York Harbor and sailed up the river, which today bears his name, as far as present-day Albany, New York. The Dutch soon set up trading posts on Manhattan Island, which they named New Amsterdam, and along the Hudson River. A profitable fur trade was established with the Native Americans. The Dutch promised land to settlers in an attempt to populate the colony; however, few were interested. Because of poor leadership and weak government, the Dutch colony easily fell to the English in 1664.

◀ FUR TRADER

Section 2 ★ Assessment

Checking for Understanding

1. **Define** line of demarcation, conquistador, mestizo, *encomienda*, mercantilism, northwest passage.
2. **Contrast** patterns of French settlement with colonization patterns of other European nations.

Critical Thinking

3. **Organizing Information** Use a chart like the one shown here to list what goods were introduced to Europe and the Americas as a result of exploration.

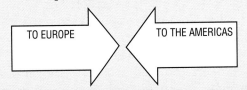

TO EUROPE   TO THE AMERICAS

INTERDISCIPLINARY ACTIVITY

4. **The Arts** Create a time line poster of important explorations during the 1500s.

Stock Exchanges

The age of exploration brought sweeping changes to European society and to culture. Overseas trade and colonial ventures stimulated the European economy and helped it develop and grow. Business practices and banking practices soon became more sophisticated in order to facilitate profit from the flourishing world trade.

Launching an overseas trading venture was a major financial undertaking. Merchants in the sixteenth century reduced the risks of ocean trade by forming trading companies. Governments of western European states controlled the trade of their merchants and provided company charters that included the rights of stock ownership. Shares of stock allow the buyer a certain part of the future profits and assets of the company selling the stock. The person buying stock, therefore, becomes part owner of a company.

The early trading companies eventually led to the establishment of joint-stock companies such as the Dutch United East India Company, formed in the early 1600s. In order to sell large blocks of shares to investors, this company created a stock exchange in Amsterdam. The money raised became a permanent fund the company could draw money from when it initiated trading ventures.

In 1650 the English adopted the Dutch method of creating a permanent fund to finance trading enterprises. Before 1773, however, when English investors wanted to buy or sell shares of stock, they had to locate a broker to carry out their transactions. Then the London brokers founded the first English stock exchange. The first stock exchanges in the United States were organized in Philadelphia in 1791 and in New York City a year later.

▲ THE MONEY CHANGER AND HIS WIFE BY GUENTIN METYS, 1514

Not all the trading companies made money. England's Virginia Company was a costly failure, as were other European companies. By 1700, however, joint-stock companies had proved that free enterprise could raise the capital necessary for costly ventures, regardless of the risk.

Making the Economics Connection

1. Why did merchants form joint-stock companies?

2. What advantage did the Dutch United East India Company have over English companies in 1690?

ACTIVITY

3. Select three stocks that are listed on the New York Stock Exchange. Graph the performance of these stocks over a two-week period.

★★

The English Colonies

Guide to Reading

Main Idea

For various reasons, many English citizens established colonies along the eastern shore of North America.

Reading Strategy

Classifying Information As you read about the English colonies, create a chart similar to the one shown here, and list each colony under the appropriate heading.

Southern Colonies	Middle Colonies	New England

Objectives

After studying this section you should be able to

★ examine the different kind of English colonies that were formed in America.

★ discuss the ways in which American colonists differed from the British by 1750.

Key Terms

indentured servant, proprietor, congregation, commonwealth, constitution

▶ PINE TREE SHILLING, 1652

In 1587, Sir Walter Raleigh, an English nobleman, tried to establish a permanent English colony on Roanoke Island near the coast of present-day North Carolina. He named the land "Virginia" in honor of the "Virgin Queen" Elizabeth I. This effort to build a colony failed because Spanish control of the sea delayed Raleigh's efforts to resupply the settlement until after England defeated the Spanish Armada in 1588. When English ships finally returned to Roanoke, they found none of the settlers. The fate of this "Lost Colony" remains a mystery.

■ The Southern Colonies

In 1606 King James I created the Virginia Company made up of merchants who had petitioned for permission to found colonies. Two parts of the company, the Virginia Company of London and the Virginia Company of Plymouth, were given exclusive settlement rights in North America.

Virginia

The London Company sent settlers to Virginia, where it was believed precious metals abounded. In the spring of 1607, the settlers founded Jamestown, named after King James I, a settlement 60 miles up the James River. Most of them were "gentlemen" who wanted to look for gold—not carpenters to build houses or farmers to raise crops for survival. The tragic result was that most of the 500 colonists who came in the first few years died. George Percy, one of the survivors, wrote of the sufferings at Jamestown:

❝ *Our men were destroyed with cruell diseases as Swellings, Flixes, Burning Fevers, and by*

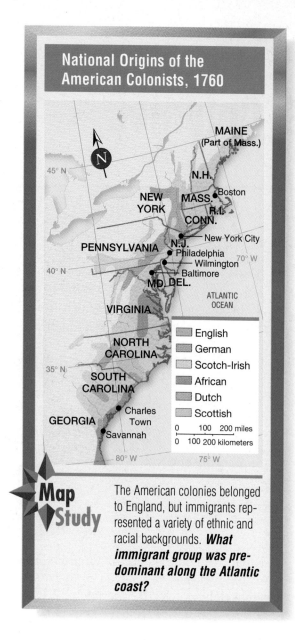

Map Study

National Origins of the American Colonists, 1760

MAINE (Part of Mass.)

N.H.

NEW YORK

MASS. • Boston

R.I.

CONN.

New York City

PENNSYLVANIA

N.J.

Philadelphia

Wilmington

Baltimore

MD. DEL.

VIRGINIA

ATLANTIC OCEAN

NORTH CAROLINA

SOUTH CAROLINA

GEORGIA

Charles Town

Savannah

45° N

40° N

35° N

70° W

80° W

75° W

English
German
Scotch-Irish
African
Dutch
Scottish

0   100   200 miles
0   100 200 kilometers

The American colonies belonged to England, but immigrants represented a variety of ethnic and racial backgrounds. *What immigrant group was predominant along the Atlantic coast?*

warres, and some departed suddenly, but for the most part they died of mere famine. There were never Englishmen left in a forreigne Countrey in such miserie. . . .

"

By 1618, the company had expanded land sales, extended English law and rights to the colonists, and allowed settlers a representative assembly—the House of Burgesses. Soon after, new recruits, including various craftspeople, arrived in Virginia. Settlers, however, continued to die in large numbers from disease. Meanwhile the company

failed to realize any significant profits for its shareholders. In 1624, King James I dissolved the company and took control of the colony.

From nearby Native Americans, the settlers learned to grow corn, beans, squash, and tobacco, which soon became a profitable cash crop. Thousands of settlers streamed into Virginia, lured by the promise of free, abundant farmland. One source of workers for wealthy settlers were **indentured servants,** who worked for a set period of time to pay off their Atlantic passage and then were free to start their own farms.

In 1619 a Dutch warship brought 20 enslaved Africans to Jamestown. Virginians, desiring an additional source of labor for their tobacco fields, purchased the Africans. From 1600 to 1850, Europeans brought 15 million enslaved Africans to the Americas.

Maryland

In 1632 King Charles I gave his friend George Calvert, Lord Baltimore, a grant of land north of Virginia that became the colony of Maryland. The grant made Lord Baltimore **proprietor,** meaning that he had authority over the colony's government. Baltimore's son, Cecil Calvert, established Maryland as a refuge for Catholics. Protestants, however, soon outnumbered Catholics in Maryland. In 1649, the legislative assembly affirmed religious freedom to all Christian settlers by passing the Toleration Act, the first of its kind in America.

Carolina

Profits from tobacco in Virginia and Maryland lured settlers to Carolina, a proprietary colony located farther south along the Atlantic coast. In northern Carolina, subsistence farmers grew only enough to live on, while merchants exported tar, pitch, and turpentine from the area's pine forests. Southern Carolina, however, offered a better harbor and attracted more settlers. Charles Town—present-day Charleston—became a major port city in the South. Settlers in southern Carolina built large plantations to grow rice and indigo, a plant that produced a purple dye. In 1729, King George II made the two parts of Carolina separate royal colonies.

Georgia

Georgia, named after King George II, was the last of the 13 English colonies. Its wealthy proprietor, James Oglethorpe, planned Georgia as a refuge for debtors and a military outpost against the Spaniards in Florida. This plan did not succeed, however; and in 1752, Georgia became a royal colony.

■ New England

Unlike most of the southern colonies, New England was settled by people seeking a religious haven, not investors seeking a fortune. In England, Anglicans known as Puritans wanted to "purify" the Anglican Church of its remaining Catholic practices. Another group, called Separatists, believed that it was better to separate themselves entirely from Anglicanism and to form their own church. Some Separatist "Pilgrims" settled in Holland to escape persecution by English authorities. Hoping to preserve their English language and culture, the Pilgrims finally decided to settle in America.

Plymouth

In 1619, the Pilgrims secured a grant of land in Virginia from the London Company. A year later, they and other passengers set sail from England on the *Mayflower*. The ship, however, accidentally landed far to the north of Virginia on the Massachusetts coast. Because they had no charter that applied to this area, the Pilgrims drew up the Mayflower Compact and established Plymouth Colony. The Compact stated that a government derives its just powers from the people who are governed.

The Pilgrims survived a difficult winter with the help of Native Americans, such as Squanto, who taught them about their new environment. The Pilgrims' deep sense of religious purpose also sustained the colony.

▼ WILLIAM BRADFORD'S BIBLE

History AND ART

▲ *PILGRIMS GOING TO CHURCH* by George H. Boughton, 1867 Religion was important in Pilgrim life. *What evidence shown in this picture suggests that the settlers did not yet feel safe?*

▲ ANNE HUTCHINSON

Although Plymouth grew, it never became very large. It ran its own affairs until it became part of the larger Massachusetts Bay Colony in 1691.

Puritan Massachusetts

In 1629, prominent Puritans in England bought a trading company, changed its name to the Massachusetts Bay Company, and secured a charter directly from the king. Their plan was to built in Massachusetts a Christian society they believed would be a lighthouse for all the world. The first governor of Massachusetts, John Winthrop, made their intentions clear:

“ *We shall be as a city upon a hill. The eyes of all people are upon us.* ”

During the 1620s, thousands of Puritans escaping from religious persecution sailed for Massachusetts. Boston, the leading town, and its surrounding settlements flourished.

In Massachusetts, the Puritans set up churches governed by each **congregation,** or body of church members. They also transformed the Massachusetts Bay Company from a trading company into a **commonwealth,** a self-governing political unit, the first of its kind in America.

Dissent and Division

The Puritans who came to Massachusetts to worship as they pleased had no intention of granting the same freedom to those who were not Puritans. Roger Williams, a minister who disagreed with official Puritan views, preached that church and government should remain separate because involvement in political affairs would corrupt the church. He also asserted that the colonists had no right to settle on the land unless the land was purchased from the Native American people. Because of these views, Williams was banished from Massachusetts.

In 1644, Williams moved south and started the colony of Rhode Island on land purchased from the Native Americans. The new colony welcomed Jews as well as all Christians and guaranteed their religious freedom. In Rhode Island, church and state were completely separate, a principle that was to become an important part of America's political heritage.

Other dissenters fleeing Puritan persecution included Anne Hutchinson, who openly challenged Puritan interpretations of the Bible. She and her followers went to Rhode Island. Dissenters also founded colonies in New Hampshire and Connecticut. In 1639, the colony of Connecticut adopted the Fundamental Orders of Connecticut, the first written **constitution,** or plan of government, in America.

■ Middle Colonies

England's neglect of the American colonies between 1640 and 1660 enabled traditions of self-government to develop firmly in America. Colonial legislatures in New England and the South made their own laws, and local courts enforced them. The Middle Colonies also developed a degree of independence from England.

New York

In 1664 King Charles II granted his brother James, the Duke of York, the land west and south of New England, from the Connecticut River to the Delaware River. He did this even though the territory had already been settled by the Dutch. In 1664, English warships captured the Dutch settlement of New Amsterdam and ended Dutch rule. The Duke of York did not hesitate to change the colony's name to New York.

Political affairs in New York were dominated by continual conflict between the royal governor and the elected representative assembly. Few settlers came at first because powerful landowners held much of the land. New York City provided a magnificent harbor, but the small population of the colony did not supply enough goods for export. Although Dutch customs remained strong, New York eventually had a varied population that included Dutch, Swedes, Native Americans, Africans, English, French, and people of other nationalities.

New Jersey

Shortly after the Duke of York received his grant of land in 1664, he started giving out parts of it to his friends. He gave New Jersey to two nobles who granted religious freedom and large land grants to settlers. By 1682, the colony had been sold to members of a religious group called the Society of Friends, or Quakers, who were seeking escape from persecution. In 1702, New Jersey finally became a royal colony under the authority of New York's governor.

Penn's Colonies

William Penn, the son of an English admiral, wanted to found a colony in America that would serve as a refuge for persecuted Quakers. In England, Quakers were considered religious radicals because they believed that paid clergy were unnecessary and that every person could know God's will through his or her own "inner light." Taking advantage of a debt that King Charles II owed his father, Penn asked the king for land in America. In 1681, Charles gave Penn authority over a vast area west of the Delaware River named "Penn's Woods," or Pennsylvania.

Arriving in Pennsylvania in 1682, Penn worked out a plan for a "city of brotherly love," Philadelphia. His promise of religious freedom and tolerance drew many settlers from Europe. Pennsylvania gave the right to vote to a large number of colonists. Penn also insisted that Native Americans be paid for their land. These measures meant rapid growth for the colony. By 1700 Philadelphia rivaled Boston and New York City as both a commercial and cultural center.

In 1682 William Penn bought the three counties south of Pennsylvania along the Atlantic coast from the Duke of York. These "lower counties," known as Delaware, had first been settled by the Dutch, then the Swedes, before the English captured them in 1664.

Section 3 ★ Assessment

Checking for Understanding

1. **Define** indentured servant, proprietor, congregation, commonwealth, constitution.

2. **Explain** the factors that created hardships and initially limited the success of the Virginia colony.

Critical Thinking

3. **Analyzing Motives** Most New England colonies were settled by people escaping religious persecution. Which of these groups sought true religious freedom? How did they differ from the others?

4. **Comparing and Contrasting** Use a diagram like the one shown here to list the similarities and differences between the establishment of Virginia and New England colonies.

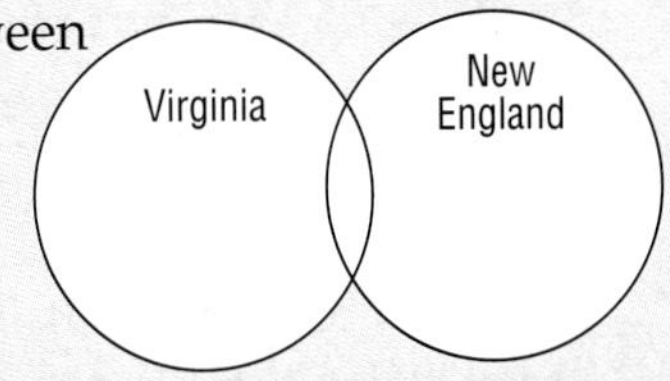

Virginia — New England

INTERDISCIPLINARY ACTIVITY

5. **Geography** Turn to the map on page 24. Which groups had settled in New Hampshire by 1760? What immigrant group had settled the farthest west?

BUILDING SKILLS
Study and Writing Skills

Interpreting Primary Sources

One often learns about the past by studying primary sources, or the original records of events made by people who witnessed them. Primary sources include letters, journals, legal documents, drawings, photographs, and artifacts. Historians have used documents, such as the following from the records of the Suffolk County Court in Massachusetts, to uncover information about life for women in the colonies. Read the excerpts, then answer the questions that follow.

▲ ACCUSED OF WITCHCRAFT BY DOUGLAS VOLK

Learning the Skill

Order abt Hitt (8 July, 1674)

In Answer to the request of Anne Hitt widdow . . . that Shee might have Liberty to dispose of & put to Sale some part of [her husband's] *Estate for the paiment of debts & Legacies & maintenance of herselfe & Children: The Court Orders & Empowres the saide Anne Hitt (with the consent & advice) of those that are Sureties for her true Administracion upon the said Estate to dispose of & put to Sale the house & ground at Charlestown valued in the Inventory at L:170. Shee rendring an Account of Sd Sale unto the Court of this County.*

Walsebee's discharge (28 April, 1674)

The wife of David Walsebee of Brantery being presented for his Idleness and sottish carriage [drunken behavior]. *Upon hearing of the case The Court judge there is noe ground for the presentment and so discharge her.*

Licenses (28 April, 1674)

Anne Puglice upon certificate from the Selectmen of Boston had her license renewed to distill *& retail strong waters by small quantities for ye yeare ensuing; provided shee did not sell any of the inhabitants of the Town to drincke it in her house. . . .* [O]n condicion that Anne Puglice *should observe all the Laws . . .*

Practicing the Skill

1. When were the documents written?

2. What does the charge against the wife of David Walsebee indicate about the manners expected of women?

Glencoe's **Skillbuilder Interactive Workbook, Level 2** provides instruction and practice in key social studies skills.

APPLYING THE SKILL

3. Why are these excerpts primary sources? What is the advantage of studying primary sources?

★★★★★★★★★★★★★★★★★★★★★★

Colonial Life

Guide to Reading

Main Idea
The English colonies gradually developed a uniquely American society.

Reading Strategy

Organizing Information As you read about colonial life, list the different groups living in the colonies, and briefly describe their position in a diagram similar to the one shown here.

People in the English Colonies

Objectives

After studying this section, you should be able to

★ describe social classes and the role of women, indentured servants, and African Americans.

★ discuss the relationship between English colonists and Native Americans.

★ explain why religious toleration and freedom developed during the colonial period.

Key Term

gentry

▶ **SCRIMSHAW, CARVED ARTICLE MADE FROM WHALE IVORY**

By European standards, the society of England during the 1600s and 1700s was remarkably mobile. An apprentice might become rich and marry his daughter to a noble. In turn, a noble's younger son, who inherited no property, might become an apprentice or hire himself out as a soldier. Like England, the colonies' social structure had many classes, but from the start it was more democratic.

■ Colonial Social Classes

In each of the 13 colonies, there was an upper class. In New England, merchants, shipowners, and the clergy composed this class. In the South and along the Hudson River in New York, great landowners imitated the country **gentry,** or upper class, of England. Early colonial laws permitted only upper-class men to wear silver buttons and upper-class women and girls to wear silk dresses. Social rank was indicated on marriage certificates and even on tombstones.

Near the bottom of society were indentured servants, bound by contract to work in the colonies in return for their passage to America. When the contract expired, the servant was free to work for wages. Because labor was scarce, wages in the colonies were two or three times those in England. Indentured servants could move up in society. For example, in the 1660s, 13 of 28 members of the Virginia House of Burgesses had come to the colony as indentured servants.

Quality of Life

For most people, life in colonial America was better than it had been in Europe. Still, many died within the first year because of hardships encountered during the ocean voyage. Frontier settlements faced conflict with Native Americans, starvation due to crop failures, disastrous fires, and epidemics of smallpox, dysentery, malaria, diphtheria, and yellow fever.

By the 1700s, conditions had improved, although epidemics continued to make life uncertain. There was widespread prosperity—a product of cheap land, a ready market for colonial exports, and hard work.

A Varied Population

By 1775 people of English origin accounted for just under half the population. The high birthrate—an average of seven births per woman in New England—and the long period of colonial history—1607 to 1776—meant that most of these children were born in the colonies. From about the time of the founding of Pennsylvania in 1681, people of different nationalities and religions—Scots, Irish Catholics, French Huguenots, Spanish Jews, and German Protestants—arrived in increasing numbers. Together with the Dutch in New York, these accounted for nearly one-third of the colonists.

Beginning in Virginia in 1619, the first enslaved Africans were brought by the Dutch from the West Indies. Africans, both enslaved and free, made up about 20 percent of the total population. The proportion of African Americans was highest in the southern colonies because slave labor proved profitable on plantations.

■ Women in the Colonies

The only respectable option for women in the English colonies was thought to be marriage. Women generally married in their early twenties and had five or six children. Their principal task was rearing children,

▲ *THE MASON CHILDREN: DAVID, JOANNA, AND ABIGAIL* Unknown Artist, c. 1670 Usually a person's place in colonial society was obvious from his or her appearance and dress. ***What can you conclude about the children's family from this painting?***

although most women died during the child-bearing years.

The second occupation for most women was farming. A farm could not carry on without the skills of women in making cloth, garments, candles, soap, and breadstuffs. A visitor to the North Carolina-Virginia border region in 1710 gave this description of a frontierswoman:

> ❝ . . . [S]he is a very civil woman and shows nothing of ruggedness or Immodesty in her carriage, yett she will carry a gunn in the woods and kill deer, turkeys, etc., shoot down wild cattle, catch and tye hoggs, knock down beeves with an axe. . . . ❞

In the South, plantation wives helped direct the workforce. When seafaring New England husbands left their wives, sometimes for years at a time, women were successful as merchants or storekeepers. Widespread home manufacturing allowed women to learn trades. Some women were printers, newspaper publishers, druggists, and doctors.

HISTORY Online

Student Web Activity
Visit the *American History: The Modern Era Since 1865* Web site at **me.glencoe.com** and click on *Chapter 1—Student Web Activities* for an activity on life in the colonies.

■ Slavery in the Colonies

At first it was not clear that enslaved Africans were to be treated differently from white indentured servants. Gradually legal distinctions were adopted. Indentured servants retained the rights of English people and the protection of the law. Africans were protected by no law or tradition. The South gave marriages between enslaved persons no legality, and children could be sold away from their mothers. Enslaved persons owned no property and had little legal protection against irresponsible or cruel slaveholders.

Slavery and Southern Plantations

Slave labor was adopted for the southern plantations, where the work was done in fields and easily overseen. Southern colonial laws declared Africans to be enslaved for life. It was illegal to teach Africans to read for fear that learning would spoil them for physical labor.

There were, in the South, slaveholders who disapproved of slavery but hesitated to act on their beliefs because free blacks faced serious discrimination. In addition, whites feared them as possible leaders of slave insurrections. Most southern colonies passed laws that made it difficult to give enslaved people their freedom.

Slavery in the North

In the North, slavery was less profitable and enslaved people less numerous. New England not only allowed, but required, people who were enslaved to marry; they could acquire property and testify in court. A slaveholder might punish a slave, but an owner who killed a slave could be charged with murder. A growing number of people argued that slavery was a moral wrong.

In Pennsylvania, Quakers and Mennonites, a German Protestant sect, denounced slavery. The number of free African Americans increased. In Jaffrey, New Hampshire, Amos Fortune bought other African Americans out of slavery and left money for the town school. But the northern colonies did not permit equality to free African Ameri-

▲ SLAVE TRADE Trade that furnished Africans to markets was a horrible example of inhumanity. It has been estimated that about 30 percent of the enslaved Africans died crossing the Atlantic. *How were Africans treated in the northern colonies?*

cans. Custom usually kept them in menial positions, and the laws denied them the right to vote or hold office.

■ Native Americans

The first meetings between English settlers and Native Americans gave little evidence of the eventual destruction of the Native Americans' ways of life. A few colonial leaders, notably Roger Williams and William Penn, tried to treat them fairly, and some Protestant ministers regarded the Native Americans principally as souls to be converted to Christianity.

Land Ownership

The expansion of colonial farms became the principal cause of numerous conflicts. The colonists reasoned that since Native Americans did not have settled dwellings, but were on the move like "the foxes and wild beasts . . . so it is lawful now to take a land which none useth; and make use of it."

Some of the conflicts resulted from misunderstandings each culture had of the other's values. Europeans viewed land ownership as essential to progress.

Individual Native Americans did not own land, but jointly shared territory with all the members of the group. Native Americans viewed the land as a resource to be used and left unchanged. Those who sold or by treaty gave up lands did so without any authority, since no chief could dispose of land.

Colonists justified wars against Native Americans in many ways. Some Puritan ministers even claimed that Native Americans were children of the devil, so they could be killed in good conscience.

Weapons of Conquest

Individually, a colonist may not have been a match for a Native American who had learned the art of war in struggles over territory; but because of sheer numbers and weapons, the whites were destined to win. They also had grim allies in diseases such as smallpox. European diseases sometimes wiped out whole Native American communities that had not developed immunities. Of the estimated 120,000 Native Americans who had lived in the area occupied by the 13 colonies, perhaps only 20,000 survived. Most Native American nations, too small to resist,

simply disappeared as social units. The Iroquois were the only group that had the ability to protect its members from destruction.

■ The Colonial Mind

Although many came to America to worship as they pleased, they were not ready to grant others the same freedom. In New England and the Southern Colonies, a single official church was "established"—that is, supported by taxes. Massachusetts Puritans believed that religious toleration was a weakness inspired by the devil. Anyone who advocated it would suffer the consequences. While they expelled many like Roger Williams, they hanged Quakers on Boston Common. Anglican Virginia, on the other hand, expelled Puritan ministers from Massachusetts.

The Great Awakening

In the 1740s, the colonies experienced a religious revival called the Great Awakening. Some Puritan ministers in Massachusetts, concerned over declining religious

Visualizing History

▲ RELIGION IN THE COLONIES In the 1600s and 1700s, most European countries had state religions. Persecution of religious dissenters was common, and many colonists who came to America sought the freedom to worship in their own way. Religion in the colonies was characterized by a growing tolerance. *What was the Great Awakening?*

▲ EDUCATION IN THE COLONIES Education was closely related to religion. The first colleges—William and Mary (above), Harvard, and Yale—were established mainly to train ministers. By the end of the colonial period, nine colleges had been founded, eight of them by churches. *How did formal education in the colonies differ from modern education?*

fervor, began to preach sermons that warned of the impending dangers of hell. They were influenced by Jonathan Edwards, one of America's greatest colonial theologians.

As ministers took sides favoring or opposing the revivalists, new churches sprang up. The diversity of churches helped to make religious toleration even more essential. Other products of the revival were new colleges such as Princeton, Brown, Rutgers, and Dartmouth.

By the late 1700s, open religious persecution in the colonies was largely a thing of the past, although not all religious groups were equal before the law. Visitors from other countries were especially struck by the freedom granted Jews, who still suffered severe persecution in most European countries.

Colonial Education

The Puritans believed that citizens should learn enough English to read the Bible and understand the laws. The Massachusetts General School Act of 1647 stated two principles of education that remain today: local communities have a duty to set up schools, and this duty is enforced by law.

In the Middle Colonies, schooling was not as universal as in New England, but it was widespread. In the Southern Colonies,

formal education was generally limited to children of large landowners and professionals. Even where schools were desired, the widely separated plantations and farms of the South made them impractical.

By modern standards schools in the colonies were primitive. There were few books, and instruction was given only two or three months a year. Most girls received little formal education. Two-thirds of the women whose names appear on Massachusetts legal documents in the early 1700s could not write their signatures. Despite these shortcomings, no other region of equal size in the world had such a high proportion of the population that could read and write.

Religion was the principal force behind most institutions of higher learning in the colonies. The earliest colleges—Harvard, William and Mary, and Yale—were founded to train young men for the ministry.

The Enlightenment

By the mid-1700s, the college curriculum began to change, as interest in science and a demand for practical subjects arose. When King's College—later Columbia—opened in New York City in 1754, it announced that studies would include not only the traditional Latin, Greek, and Hebrew, but also:

> *Surveying and Navigation, Geography, History, Husbandry, Commerce, Government, the Knowledge of ALL Nature in the Heavens above us and in the Air, Water, and Earth Around us. . . .*

This interest in science originated in Europe, where it was known as the Enlightenment. English philosopher John Locke produced works that were widely read in America. In *An Essay Concerning Human Understanding,* Locke maintained that people could best gain knowledge of the universe by observing and by experimenting. This knowledge would guide them in developing a reasonable society. In the second of two *Treatises on Government,* Locke taught that people were born with certain natural rights to life, liberty, and property; that people formed governments to protect these rights; and that a government interfering with these might rightfully be overthrown. Many readily accepted the idea that government was the agent of the people, not their ruler.

■ The Press in America

In addition to schools and colleges, newspapers, almanacs, and books helped raise the level of public information. Because paper and type were expensive and the reading public in America small, most books came from Britain. But by 1750, there were 25 or 30 American newspapers, mostly 4 pages long, printed weekly. Printed on tough rag paper, these newspapers were passed from hand to hand at the local inn until often half the men in a village had read a single copy. European travelers in the colonies were amazed to find that political discussions in public inns were joined intelligently by everybody, from the college educated to stable help.

Colonial editors occasionally criticized British laws or officials. In 1735, John Peter Zenger of the *New York Weekly Journal* accused the royal governor of corruption. As a result, Zenger was brought to trial on a charge of libel. His lawyer, Andrew Hamilton, argued that the editor was not guilty since the charges were true and since free speech was a basic right of English people. As a result, Zenger was acquitted. At the time the case attracted little attention, but today it is regarded as a landmark in the development of the free press in America.

■ New Directions

By 1776 America was well on its way to establishing economic independence. Thirty percent of the ships in the British merchant marine were American, and most of these sailed from New England ports.

The Economy

New Englanders carried on a share of the African slave trade. They were the first to hunt whales in the Antarctic; in 1774, 360 whaling ships sailed from the island of Nantucket alone. While New England was a formidable competitor in trade, no colony offered much competition to the British in manufacturing. The American colonists usually obtained manufactured goods from Britain.

To pay for fine European goods, such as clothing, books, wine, and cutlery, the colonies had to trade staples that Europeans needed or to pay in gold or silver. Trade with the West Indies netted Spanish dollars, the common colonial currency. Later the new nation, the United States, would adopt

. . . .
Footnotes to History

An American Style   Imitating English ways was common in America at first. Slowly the colonists began to develop their own ways of doing things. Building styles were modified to suit local conditions. Cabinetmakers began to turn out excellent furniture of their own design. Silversmiths like Paul Revere put their own designs on their products. Colonists found ways of putting beauty into things they made for practical use, such as quilts and guns.

the dollar instead of the British pound as its monetary unit. Gradually the colonies developed a culture distinctly different from that of Europe.

GOVERNMENT
Stirrings of Independence

The degree of power exercised by British officials varied from colony to colony, but it was limited everywhere. In all colonies the voters elected their own legislature, and in charter colonies, their governor as well. In proprietary colonies the governor was appointed by the proprietor or by his heirs; in royal or crown colonies the governor was chosen by the king. The governor of a proprietary or crown colony had wide powers, such as a veto over the legislature and control of land grants.

Government at the town and county levels was run entirely by the colonists themselves. In New England, the important local unit was the township. Decisions were made at the town meeting, which most heads of families had a right to attend. The town meeting was the most direct form of democracy in the colonies. In the Southern and Middle colonies, local government was usually less democratic but, nevertheless, entirely independent of British control.

None of the colonies was so democratic as to allow full political rights to all men or to any women. Active citizenship and the right to vote and hold office were limited to

Visualizing History

▲ **FREEDOM OF THE PRESS** John Peter Zenger, publisher of the *New York Weekly Journal*, was arrested and imprisoned for criticizing the governor of New York, and copies of the newspaper were burned. Andrew Hamilton, Zenger's lawyer, argued that the publisher had the right to speak and write the truth and to oppose arbitrary power. *What was the outcome of the trial?*

adult white males owning property, who usually had to be members of the established church. In spite of these limitations, a higher proportion of people were involved in government than anywhere in the European world. This wide participation gave Americans training that was valuable when the colonies later became independent.

Section 4 ★ Assessment

Checking for Understanding

1. **Define** gentry.

2. **Give** reasons for the development of religious freedom and toleration in the British colonies.

Critical Thinking

3. **Evaluating Cause and Effect** What factors contributed to social mobility in the colonies? What factors restricted it?

4. **Drawing Conclusions** Create a diagram like this one to show how the Enlightenment helped prompt the colonists to eventually rebel against the British.

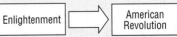

INTERDISCIPLINARY ACTIVITY

5. The Arts Which illustration in this section do you think best represents life in the colonies? Why?

American Literary Heritage

Among the Native American groups with the richest oral literary traditions are the Iroquois and Navajo. During the 1500s a prophet named Dekanawida (dek•uhn•uh•WEE•duh) appeared among the Iroquois and urged them to lay down their weapons and join hands in the spirit of friendship and peace. His influence led to the formation of the Iroquois Confederation of the Five Nations. The Navajo expressed themselves in songlike chants and legends that provide a window on their ideals and beliefs.

Read to Discover

What values does Dekanawida stress in the Constitution of the Five Nations? Find examples of words or parts of lines that are repeated throughout the "Song of the Rain Chant." Why do you think these particular words are repeated?

Reader's Dictionary

confederacy   an alliance for mutual support or common action

lodgement   a place of rest or deposit

The Constitution of the Five Nations (excerpts)

I am Dekanawida and with the Five Nations confederate lords I plant the Tree of the Great Peace. I name the tree the Tree of the Great Long Leaves. Under the shade of this Tree of the Great Peace we spread the soft white feathery down of the globe thistle as seats for you . . . and your cousin lords.

We place . . . at the top of the Tree of the Long Leaves an eagle who is able to see afar. If he sees in the distance any evil approaching or any danger threatening he will at once warn the people of the confederacy. . . .

All lords of the Five Nations Confederacy must be honest in all things. . . . It shall be a serious wrong for anyone to lead a lord into trivial affairs, for the people must ever hold their lords high in estimation out of respect to their honorable positions. . . .

We now do crown you with the sacred emblem of the deer's antlers, the emblem of your lordship. You shall now become a mentor of the people of the Five Nations. The thickness of your skin shall be seven spans—which is to say that you shall be proof against anger, offensive actions and criticism. Your heart shall be filled with peace and good will and your mind filled with a yearning for the welfare of the people of the confederacy. With endless patience you shall carry out your duty and your firmness shall be tempered with tenderness for your people. Neither anger nor fury shall find lodgement in your mind and all your words and actions shall be marked with calm deliberation. . . .

Navajo Song of the Rain Chant

Far as man can see,
Comes the rain,
Comes the rain with me.

From the Rain-Mount,
Rain-Mount far away,
Comes the rain,
Comes the rain with me.

O'er the corn,
O'er the corn, the tall corn,
Comes the rain,
Comes the rain with me.

'Mid the lightnings,
'Mid the lightning zigzag,
'Mid the lightning flashing
Comes the rain,
Comes the rain with me.

'Mid the swallows,
'Mid the swallows blue
Chirping glad together,
Comes the rain,
Comes the rain with me.

Through the pollen,
Through the pollen blest,
All in pollen hidden,
Comes the rain,
Comes the rain with me.

Far as man can see,
Comes the rain,
Comes the rain with me.

▶ IROQUOIS NOTCHED STAFF

▶ NAVAJO RUG

Responding to Literature

1. In the Iroquois Constitution, what is the function of the eagle that sits atop the Tree of the Long Leaves?

2. How does the Rain Chant reflect Navajo beliefs about nature?

3. In what ways are the qualities desired for Iroquois leaders similar to or different from those desired for today's leaders in the United States government?

ACTIVITY

4. Research information about one aspect of Iroquois or Navajo life. Subjects could include lifestyles, occupations, religious practices, or achievements. Present your information in a report to the other students.

Self-Check Quiz

Visit the *American History: The Modern Era Since 1865* Web site at **me.glencoe.com** and click on *Chapter 1—Self-Check Quizzes* to prepare for the chapter test.

Using Vocabulary

Classify each term below into one of the following categories: Political Structures and Systems, Economic Activity and Systems, Religion and Culture

confederation

shogun

joint-stock company

line of demarcation

conquistador

mestizo

mercantilism

feudalism

proprietor

commonwealth

constitution

gentry

encomienda

congregation

Reviewing Facts

1. **Discuss** key changes in the political and social structure of Europe during the late Middle Ages.

2. **Identify** advanced cultures of Africa and Asia and the importance of their trade with Europe.

3. **Summarize** Spanish exploration, exploitation, and colonization in America.

4. **Analyze** why slavery became more prevalent in the South than in New England.

Understanding Concepts

Cultural Diversity

1. Compare the differences and similarities between each of the following sets of cultures: medieval European and medieval Japanese cultures; the West African trading kingdoms and the Aztec Empire.

Values and Beliefs

2. Use a diagram like the one shown here to name the two main reasons English colonists settled in America, and then list which colonies fit under each reason.

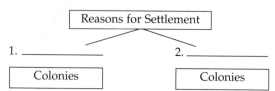

Reasons for Settlement

1. _____   2. _____

Colonies   Colonies

3. What values and beliefs helped establish democratic institutions in the British colonies?

Critical Thinking

1. **Proposing Solutions** Imagine you are appointed to resolve disputes between Native Americans and European colonists who want farmland. Propose a fair plan for expansion.

2. **Analyzing Fine Art** Analyze the two paintings on this page and answer the questions that follow.
   a. What details in the paintings give you clues about the people's occupations?
   b. What can you tell about town life in the British American colonies from these paintings?

COLONIAL WORKERS

History and Geography

African Trading Kingdoms

Study the map of African trading kingdoms on this page. Then answer the questions that follow.

1. **Movement** In which direction would a trading party from Timbuktu travel to reach Ghat?

2. **Location** What city is the easternmost trade partner?

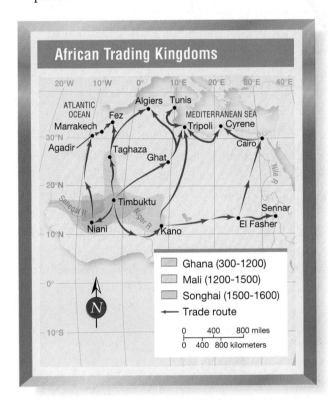

African Trading Kingdoms

Ghana (300–1200)
Mali (1200–1500)
Songhai (1500–1600)
⟵ Trade route

0   400   800 miles
0   400   800 kilometers

Practicing Skills

Interpreting Primary Sources

Read the account below by an English settler who visited Native American towns during the 1580s. Then answer the questions that follow.

Their towns are small and few . . . a village may contain but ten or twelve houses—some perhaps as many as twenty. . . .

The houses are built of small poles . . . covered from top to bottom either with bark or with mats woven of long rushes. . . .

1. How does the writer describe the size of the towns?

2. Would you describe the account as factual and objective or biased? Explain.

Technology Activity

Using a Word Processor

Use the Internet and library sources to find out more about an ocean or land voyage of exploration that interests you. Write a brief report about the journey.

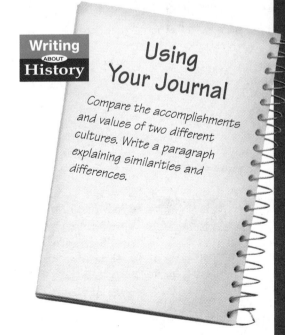

Writing ABOUT History

Using Your Journal

Compare the accomplishments and values of two different cultures. Write a paragraph explaining similarities and differences.

Cooperative Learning Interdisciplinary Activity: Cultural Studies

Working in a group with four members, study slavery around the world and throughout history. Assign each member one or more cultures or geographic areas to study. Report your findings and conduct a discussion comparing and contrasting slavery in other cultures with slavery in the British colonies.

★★

CHAPTER 2

A New Nation
1750–1789

◀ EAGLE AND
CROSSED FLAGS

Setting the Scene

Focus

Once the colonists' need for British protection ended, the road to independence was not far behind. The insurmountable breach between Britain and America led the thirteen colonies to issue a Declaration of Independence on July 4, 1776. Under General George Washington's leadership, the new United States fought a war for independence over six long years. During this period of experiment and uncertainty, American political leaders laid the foundations of a democratic government embodied in a new constitution.

Concepts to Understand

★ What steps the colonists took to secure and protect their **rights and freedom**
★ Why a strong central **authority** was needed to keep the new republic intact

Read to Discover . . .

★ what factors caused the American Revolution.
★ what important compromises made the Constitution possible.

Journal Notes

What contributions did women, African Americans, and Native Americans make to the American Revolution? Note details in your journal as you read the chapter.

HISTORY *Online*

Chapter Overview
Visit the *American History: The Modern Era Since 1865* Web site at **me.glencoe.com** and click on **Chapter 2—Chapter Overviews** to preview chapter information.

CULTURAL			
	• **1751** *Ben Franklin writes* Experiments on Electricity	• **1759** *Michael Hillegas of Philadelphia opens first music store in America*	• **1767** Letters from a Farmer *published by John Dickinson*
	1750	**1758**	**1766**
POLITICAL	• **1754** *French and Indian War begins*	• **1765** *Stamp Act passed*	• **1767** *Townshend Acts passed* • **1773** *Colonists dump tea in Boston Harbor*

History AND ART

The Signing of the Constitution
by Howard Chandler Christy, 1940

The delegates sign the final draft of the Constitution in Independence Hall. Despite mixed feelings regarding some aspects of the Constitution, most of those present were hopeful about the future.

◀ REVOLUTIONARY WAR DRUM

● **1775** *Quakers establish first antislavery society in the United States*

● **1783** *Noah Webster publishes first spelling book*

● **1790** *Samuel Hopkins receives first United States patent*

1774	1782	1790

● **1775** *Revolutionary War begins*
● **1776** *Declaration of Independence is signed*

● **1783** *Treaty of Paris is signed*
● **1787** *Constitutional Convention is held*

● **1790** *Congress hears first formal petition for abolition of slavery*

★★

The Road to Revolution

Guide to Reading

Main Idea
As the increasingly independent-minded English colonists rebelled against Great Britain, the two sides moved closer to war.

Reading Strategy
Sequencing Information As you read about the colonists' struggle against Britain, create a time line of key events along the road to revolution. Use dates provided as a guide.

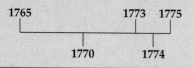

1765 ⎯⎯⎯⎯ 1773 1775

1770 1774

Objectives
After studying this section, you should be able to

★ explain the interests of both the British and the colonists between 1763 and the beginning of the Revolution.

★ discuss the events that led the colonists to armed resistance to British control over the colonies.

Key Terms
salutary neglect, militia, direct tax, boycott, minutemen

◄ **AMERICAN REVOLUTIONARY BANNER**

*D*uring most of the colonial era, the British government followed a policy of **salutary neglect,** or non-interference, which allowed America's colonists to do as they wished. Britain, however, gradually tightened its control of the colonists' foreign trade in order to increase revenue. From the British point of view the colonies existed to supply raw materials and to provide markets for British goods.

■ New Policies

In 1651, the British Parliament passed a Navigation Act requiring all goods shipped between England and the colonies to be carried in ships built either in England or in the colonies. Then in 1660, it declared that specific colonial products—tobacco, cotton, indigo, and sugar—could be shipped only to Britain.

A number of other British laws also had a serious impact on the colonies. The Molasses Act of 1733 placed a heavy tax on the colonists' importation of sugar and molasses from the Spanish and French West Indies. The Woolen Act of 1699, the Hat Act of 1732, and the Iron Act of 1750 placed restrictions on colonial industries to keep them from competing with British industries. Benjamin Franklin's reaction to these laws was typical of the Americans' views:

❝ *A colonist cannot make a button, a horse shoe, nor a hobnail but some sooty iron monger or respectable buttonmaker of Britain shall bawl . . . that his honor's worship is . . . injured, cheated and robbed by the rascally Americans.* ❞

The French and Indian War

While Britain passed trade laws for its colonies, a struggle for empire developed between Britain and France. Anglo-French wars fought between 1689 and 1713 brought areas of present-day Canada—Nova Scotia, Newfoundland, and Hudson's Bay Territory—under Britain. The French and Indian War, fought between 1754 and 1763, gave the British further opportunity to expand their territory in North America.

The Albany Plan

In 1754, at a meeting in Albany, New York between colonial delegates and representatives of the Iroquois, Benjamin Franklin proposed a union of the colonies with the power to levy taxes, raise troops, and regulate trade. The delegates adopted Franklin's plan, but the colonial and British governments feared a loss of power and rejected it. This lack of cooperation seriously handicapped the war effort against the French.

On the Battlefield

The final struggle between Britain and France for control of North America began in the Ohio Valley. There the French drove out English fur traders and in 1754 established Fort Duquesne (doo•KAYN). This move threatened the safety of both Virginia and Pennsylvania. A force of Virginia **militia**—a group of civilians trained as soldiers to fight in emergencies—under the command of a young officer named George Washington failed until 1758 in their attempt to seize the fort. One military disaster after another followed for the British. The British made an advance on Montreal by way of Lake George and Lake Champlain that met with utter failure. The British also failed to take the French fort of Louisbourg on Cape Breton Island, a key to the control of the mouth of the St. Lawrence River. These and other colonial defeats caused many Native Americans to switch their support from the British to the French.

The tide of battle shifted in Britain's favor when William Pitt became British minister of war in 1758. By giving aid to France's enemies in Europe, Pitt forced France to split its forces. Pitt also sent talented young officers to lead the campaigns in North America. After a series of victories, the British finally staged a showdown with the French at Quebec on the St. Lawrence River. British troops under Commander James Wolfe landed at night below Quebec and scaled a wooded cliff located under the guns of Quebec's fortress. On the Plains of Abraham at the top of the cliffs, the British soldiers forced French forces under Commander Louis Montcalm to surrender.

Treaty of Paris, 1763

Great Britain won its war with France—in America, Europe, and Asia. Under the Treaty of Paris of 1763, Great Britain gained the areas of Canada it did not already control and all the land east of the Mississippi River. From Spain, France's ally, Great Britain received Florida. Spain, in turn, obtained the Louisiana Territory from France. North America was now divided between Great Britain and Spain with the Mississippi River forming the boundary.

▲ GEORGE WASHINGTON AT FORT DUQUESNE, 1758

■ Control and Protest

Victory in the French and Indian War brought Britain vast new territories—and new problems. Britain had to cope with a huge war debt and the handling of the recently acquired territory between the Appalachian and Allegheny mountains.

In 1763 Pontiac, chief of the Ottawa people, united several Native American groups into a fighting force against the British. He feared the further loss of Native American lands to the ever-advancing settlers of the British colonies. Pontiac's warriors captured a chain of British forts northwest of the Ohio River but failed to drive colonial settlers back across the Appalachian Mountains.

During Pontiac's Rebellion, the British government issued the Proclamation of 1763, which ended all settlement west of the Appalachian Mountains. Through the Proclamation, the British hoped to win the friendship of the Native Americans. But the colonists protested that the Proclamation deprived them of land for settlement.

Between 1764 and 1767, Parliament passed new taxes that shifted part of the burden of the war debt to the American colonies. The British felt that the colonists benefited from British protection and that it was only fair that they pay some of the cost of running the empire.

In 1764, Parliament enacted the Sugar Act. Although this law cut the rates of the Molasses Act of 1733, the British government had always winked at the colonists evading payment. The troubling thing about the Sugar Act was that the British intended to enforce it. Colonial merchants often evaded poorly enforced British revenue laws and smuggled foreign goods into the colonies. They realized that strict enforcement would wipe out their profits from the illegal trade with the Spanish and French West Indies.

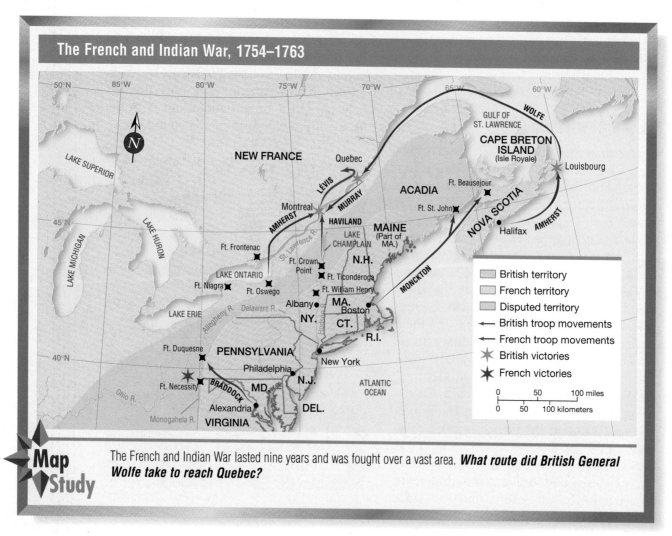

The French and Indian War, 1754–1763

The French and Indian War lasted nine years and was fought over a vast area. *What route did British General Wolfe take to reach Quebec?*

Map Study

Linking Past and Present

Dancing

From rural farms to urban mansions, dance in colonial America was a common recreation. While some clergy members condemned dancing as evil, others recommended it as healthy exercise.

▶ **DANCING THE MINUET**

▶ **MODERN DANCERS**

Then

Colonial Dance

During the colonial period, the minuet, a gliding dance in 3/4 time, dominated European social dancing. Couples performed line dances such as the reel to the accompaniment of a fiddler. The reel soon gave way to a more daring dance called the cotillion, a dance imported from the courts of France. In this forerunner of modern square dancing, four couples formed a group and moved to the directions of a "caller."

Now

Modern Forms

During the twentieth century, American popular music incorporated African American, Cuban, and South American rhythms to create new dances. Just as the minuet characterized its era, such dances as the Charleston, the tango, the samba, and the bossa nova dominated different eras during the twentieth century. These new popular dances mirrored the speedy pace of contemporary life. Eventually, the new forms combined to produce today's highly individualized and free moving dancing.

In 1765, Parliament passed another revenue law called the Stamp Act. It required that stamps be placed on many kinds of articles and documents. Unlike earlier tax measures, the Stamp Act provided for a **direct tax**—a tax paid directly to the government rather than being included in the price of goods. Previous tax laws had affected only merchants, but the Stamp Act affected colonists everywhere. Colonists protested the Act by staging a **boycott**—a refusal to buy British goods—until Parliament repealed the law. Affected by declining revenue, British merchants pressured Parliament to repeal the Stamp Act in 1766.

The next year Parliament passed the Townshend (TOWN•zehnd) Acts, which placed import duties on tea, paper, glass, and paint. Unable to collect these taxes either, the British repealed the Acts in 1770, except the tax on tea. It was retained to assert the principle that Parliament had a right to tax the colonies.

■ American Resistance

American resistance took a variety of forms, including disobedience to British laws, protests, cooperation among the 13 colonies, boycotts, and violence. One of the first public protests took place in Virginia in 1765 when the House of Burgesses met to consider the Stamp Act. Patrick Henry introduced the Virginia Resolutions protesting Parliament's action. Henry claimed that since Americans elected no members to the British Parliament, they could not be taxed by that body. Colonial assemblies alone had the right to levy taxes on colonists. This bold stand encouraged other colonists to support the principle of "no taxation without representation."

Resistance to the Stamp Act brought the first real cooperation among the 13 colonies. At the Stamp Act Congress, held in New York in October 1765, delegates drew up resolutions against the Act and organized the boycott of British-made goods.

▲ THE BOSTON MASSACRE Bitter feelings erupted in bloodshed on March 5, 1770, in Boston, when British soldiers fired into a crowd, killing five. *What happened when news of the Boston Massacre spread?*

Although most colonial leaders who opposed efforts of the British Parliament to tax Americans were from the wealthy classes, they were also supported by shopkeepers, clerks, and laborers. These ordinary colonists were the driving force between two groups that ensured the boycott was carried out—the Sons and Daughters of Liberty. Its members carried on demonstrations throughout the colonies and intimidated English agents who tried to sell stamps.

The Boston Massacre

In March 1770, the first clash between Americans and British troops took place in Boston. When a crowd of Americans threw sticks and snowballs at British soldiers, the soldiers panicked and opened fire, killing five men. News of the event, which became known as the "Boston Massacre," spread throughout the colonies. But instead of heightening the crisis, the incident was followed by a three-year lull. During this time, committees of correspondence kept in contact with each other and helped keep the resistance movement going.

■ The Boston Tea Party

The period of calm finally ended in 1773 when the British Parliament voted to grant a British company sole control of the tea trade with America. Colonists objected to this control because they suspected that it was an attempt to bribe them into acknowledging Parliament's right to tax the colonies.

Opposition groups organized to prevent the sale of the East India tea. In Boston, colonists led by Sam Adams were determined that no tea would come ashore. On a signal from Adams, a group of colonists, disguised as Mohawks, rushed to the wharf. Before a cheering crowd, they boarded the tea ships and heaved 342 chests of tea into Boston's harbor.

To the British government, the Boston Tea Party was an act of lawlessness that deserved swift punishment. In March 1774, Parliament passed the Coercive Acts. One of the acts closed the port of Boston until payment was made for the tea. Another act provided for British officials accused of a crime to be tried in British rather than in American courts. Still another declared that British troops could be quartered in any private home. Finally, Massachusetts saw its right of self-government greatly reduced. Colonists considered the Coercive Acts so harsh that they called them the "Intolerable Acts."

■ The Final Break

The Coercive Acts convinced many Americans that Britain was trying to take away their liberties. In response, 56 delegates came to the First Continental Congress that met in Philadelphia in September 1774. The Congress vowed to stop trade with Britain until the acts were repealed. To enforce its boycott, Congress set up an organization called "The Association." The Association exerted a surprising degree of control over Americans, telling them what they should eat, drink, and wear, as well as how they should behave in public.

Lexington and Concord

Meanwhile, every colony organized military forces. Fighting between the Americans and the British soon broke out near Boston, which had been occupied in 1774 by a British army. Early on April 19, 1775, a detachment of 700 British soldiers was secretly sent to destroy the military supplies colonists had collected at Concord, 21 miles from Boston.

Learning of the soldiers' destination, the Boston Sons of Liberty took action. The organization sent Paul Revere and William Dawes, later joined by Samuel Prescott, to alert the **minutemen,** or militia members so named because they could be ready for battle on a minute's notice, in the towns and villages along the way. When the British reached the town of Lexington, about 70 armed minutemen awaited them. In the skirmish eight colonists were killed. The British force pushed on to the neighboring town of Concord and burned what little gunpowder the colonists had not used for themselves.

By the time the British began their march toward Boston, the countryside was swarming with minutemen, who fired at the redcoats from behind trees, buildings, and stone walls. Only a brigade sent out from Boston saved the British from annihilation. About 270 British and 100 Americans were killed or wounded at Concord.

Battle of Bunker Hill

In June 1775, the British discovered that American troops had occupied Breed's Hill, a peninsula overlooking Boston. The British commander made a frontal attack uphill. Because the range of a musket was scarcely more than 50 yards, the Americans were ordered to hold their fire until they could see the "whites of their enemies' eyes." After turning back two British attacks, the Americans ran out of ammunition. The Battle of Bunker Hill, as it came to be called, was a moral victory for the Americans because their untrained militia had stood up to professional troops.

Second Continental Congress

On May 10, 1775, a Second Continental Congress met in Philadelphia. The Congress assumed the powers of a central government and took steps to conduct the war that had, in fact, begun at Lexington. The Congress voted to ask the colonies for supplies and troops.

For commander in chief, Congress chose George Washington. It valued his experience and ability, but the fact that he was a Virginian was also important because it would keep the Southern and Middle colonies from thinking of the conflict as New England's war. Although it would be more than a year until independence was declared, the American Revolution had begun.

Section 1 ★ Assessment

Checking for Understanding

1. **Define** salutary neglect, militia, direct tax, boycott, minutemen.

2. **State** two ways in which the interests of the British and the colonists differed immediately before the Revolution.

3. **Explain** the purpose and significance of the two Continental Congresses that met in Philadelphia, Pennsylvania.

4. **List** the major provisions of the Treaty of Paris.

Critical Thinking

5. **Analyzing Issues** Use a chart like the one shown here to summarize the colonial reaction to each British action listed.

British Action	Colonial Reaction
Proclamation of 1763	
Stamp Act	
Intolerable Acts	

INTERDISCIPLINARY ACTIVITY

6. **The Arts** Compose American newspaper headlines describing British actions and American reactions between 1763 and 1775.

Identifying Alternatives

In order to make an informed decision, you must identify the alternatives or the possible options in each situation. Almost any decision you make has alternatives, even if the choices are unpleasant.

Learning the Skill

Use the following steps to identify and evaluate alternatives:
- **State** the problem or decision to be made.
- **List** all the possible options you can think of.
- **Gather** information to evaluate the alternatives. Map out both positive and negative consequences of each alternative.

◄ **SAMUEL ADAMS**

Revolutionary leader and public official Samuel Adams early on took a firm position for independence. In 1765 he was elected to the Massachusetts House of Representatives, where he was linked with the colonists arousing public feeling against British measures. As one of the main spokespersons for this position, Adams agitated against the Stamp Act, the Townshend duties, and other measures imposed by Parliament.

Adams wrote many articles alerting Americans of Parliament's actions and helped organize the committees of correspondence in New England. A leading force behind the Boston Tea Party and a delegate to the Continental Congress, Adams was one of the first American leaders to call for immediate independence.

In 1772 Adams wrote *A List of Infringements and Violations of Rights,* detailing what he considered to be the wrongs committed by Great Britain against the colonists. Adams wrote to convince other colonists of his position:

> "We cannot help thinking, that an enumeration [list] of some of the most open infringements of our rights [by Great Britain], will by every candid person be judged sufficient to justify whatever measures have been already taken, or may be thought proper to be taken, in order to obtain a redress of the grievances under which we labour. . . ."

Practicing the Skill

1. What is the topic Adams is discussing?
2. What position does Adams advocate?
3. Identify at least two alternative viewpoints to Adams's position.

 Glencoe's **Skillbuilder Interactive Workbook, Level 2** provides instruction and practice in key social studies skills.

APPLYING THE SKILL

4. Suppose you have to decide whether to work after school, take part in an extracurricular activity, or use the time to study. Create a chart in which you list the alternatives and the pros and cons for each.

★★

War for Independence

Main Idea
The colonists declared their independence from Great Britain and achieved a victory in the American Revolution.

Reading Strategy
Classifying Information As you read about the war for independence, use a chart like the one shown here to explain what actions each group took in the war effort.

Group	Actions
Africans	
Native Americans	
Women	

Objectives
After studying this section, you should be able to
★ state what factors caused the American Revolution.
★ explain why the Americans were able to win the war.

Key Terms
treason, propaganda, republic, Patriot, Loyalist, social contract, mercenary

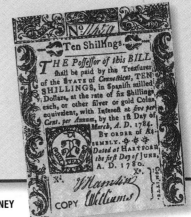

► CONTINENTAL MONEY

After the bloodshed in Massachusetts, colonial leaders such as Patrick Henry of Virginia appealed for separation from Great Britain. Most colonists, however, were not ready for independence. They wanted the colonies to remain part of the British Empire but rule themselves through their legislatures.

Moving Toward Separation

The Second Continental Congress, which convened in Philadelphia in May 1775, sent a petition to the king that blamed all of the recent troubles on the king's ministers. The king, however, refused to accept the petition and charged the American leaders with **treason,** or attempting to overthrow the government.

Influential in swaying the colonists toward the idea of separation was Thomas Paine's *Common Sense,* which first appeared in January 1776. Paine, who had come to America from England in 1774, was a writer of revolutionary **propaganda,** or ideas spread deliberately to help a cause. Paine called upon Americans to proclaim their independence. He felt that they should not only break from Great Britain, but cast off kings altogether and form a **republic,** a government in which the highest power belongs to the citizens, who choose representatives to act for them.

Paine's stirring words divided Americans into **Patriots,** who favored separation, and **Loyalists,** who supported the king. Many Patriots hoped that independence would bring military aid from France and help replace lost British markets with new markets in other countries.

■ Declaration of Independence

The Continental Congress, sensing growing public support for independence, assigned five of its best thinkers to prepare a Declaration of Independence. The purpose of the Declaration was to justify the American cause, to state that the colonies were independent, and to express the new nation's principles.

Writing the Declaration

Thomas Jefferson, a young Virginian, was the principal author of the Declaration. Jefferson, like many other American leaders, knew and valued the works of John Locke and other European political thinkers. He incorporated many of their ideas into the Declaration.

Basic Rights

The Declaration of Independence stated that individuals have certain basic rights that cannot be taken away by any government. Like Locke, Jefferson believed that government is created by a **social contract,** or agreement between the rulers and those ruled. If a government loses the support of the people by taking away basic rights, the people have a right to change the government through rebellion. The beginning of the Declaration reads:

> *We hold these truths to be self-evident, that all men are created equal, that they are endowed by their Creator with certain unalienable Rights, that among these are Life, Liberty, and the pursuit of Happiness. That to secure these rights, Governments are instituted among Men, deriving their just powers from the consent of the governed; that whenever any Form of Government becomes destructive of these ends, it is the right of the People to alter or to abolish it.*

The Declaration continued with a list of the ways Great Britain and George III had abused their power and concludes that "these United Colonies are and of Right ought to be Free and Independent States."

Influence of the Declaration

On July 4, 1776, Congress adopted the Declaration of Independence, which became one of the world's most important political documents. Throughout the years, the American Declaration of Independence has inspired supporters of freedom in many parts of the world.

The Move Toward Independence

CAUSES

- 1763 Treaty of Paris ends French and Indian War
- 1764 Parliament passes Sugar Act
- 1765 Stamp Act is passed
- 1767 Townshend Acts are passed
- 1770 Boston Massacre takes place
- 1774 Parliament passes Intolerable Acts

• Declaring Independence

EFFECTS

- 1765 Stamp Act Congress meets
- 1773 Colonists carry out Boston Tea Party
- 1774 First Continental Congress meets
- 1775 Fighting occurs at Lexington and Concord

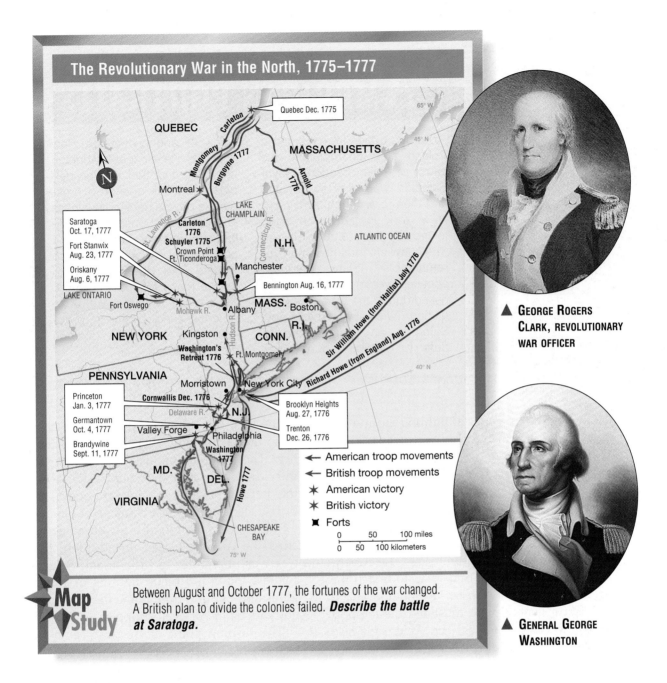

The Revolutionary War in the North, 1775–1777

Quebec Dec. 1775

QUEBEC

MASSACHUSETTS

65° W

45° N

Montreal

Saratoga
Oct. 17, 1777

Fort Stanwix
Aug. 23, 1777

Oriskany
Aug. 6, 1777

LAKE CHAMPLAIN

Carleton
1776

Schuyler 1775

Crown Point
Ft. Ticonderoga

Manchester

N.H.

ATLANTIC OCEAN

Bennington Aug. 16, 1777

LAKE ONTARIO

Fort Oswego

Mohawk R.

Albany

MASS.

Boston

Sir William Howe (from Halifax) July 1776

NEW YORK

Kingston

CONN.

R.I.

Washington's
Retreat 1776

Ft. Montgomery

Richard Howe (from England) Aug. 1776

40° N

PENNSYLVANIA

Morristown

New York City

Princeton
Jan. 3, 1777

Cornwallis Dec. 1776

Delaware R.

N.J.

Brooklyn Heights
Aug. 27, 1776

Germantown
Oct. 4, 1777

Valley Forge

Trenton
Dec. 26, 1776

Brandywine
Sept. 11, 1777

Philadelphia

Washington
1777

MD.

DEL.

Howe 1777

VIRGINIA

CHESAPEAKE
BAY

75° W

← American troop movements
← British troop movements
✳ American victory
✳ British victory
◼ Forts

0   50   100 miles
0 50 100 kilometers

Map Study

Between August and October 1777, the fortunes of the war changed. A British plan to divide the colonies failed. ***Describe the battle at Saratoga.***

▲ GEORGE ROGERS CLARK, REVOLUTIONARY WAR OFFICER

▲ GENERAL GEORGE WASHINGTON

◼ Fighting for Independence

The signing of the Declaration of Independence made war between Britain and the American colonies a certainty. Both the British and Americans had taken steps that made a peaceful reconciliation impossible. The only course that remained for the colonists was revolution. For American leaders, failure would mean disgrace and even death. As Benjamin Franklin said, "We must all hang together now, or assuredly we shall hang separately."

Advantages and Disadvantages

The first battles of the American Revolution were concentrated in the states of New York and New Jersey. The British hoped to gain control of the middle states and separate New England from the southern states. Great Britain devised its plans from a position of military strength. Its troops were well led, well trained, and well equipped. Its navy, the most powerful in the world, controlled the Atlantic seacoast. The British government also had enough money to pay 30,000 German **mercenaries,** or hired soldiers, to fight with

★★★★★AMERICAN PORTRAITS

Haym Salomon
1740(?)–1785

Forced to flee from his native Poland after championing the cause of Polish freedom, Haym Salomon went first to England and then to America. Arriving in New York in 1772, he soon joined the Patriot struggle.

A Jewish businessman of remarkable ability, Salomon acquired wealth, all of which he risked during the American Revolution. Twice arrested as a spy, Salomon was condemned to death for plotting to burn British ships at anchor outside New York City. He escaped by bribing his jailer and fled to Philadelphia. There he opened a prosperous private banking business and donated thousands of dollars for military supplies and government salaries. He also worked with Robert Morris to secure loans for the war effort. As a result of his devotion to America—and business problems after the war—Salomon died penniless.

---

them. After decades of fighting around the world, the British forces were prepared for war.

The American colonists, on the other hand, had no navy, little battle experience, and lacked money, clothing, guns, ammunition, and food. Officers identified themselves with colored ribbon on their hats because they had no uniforms. The Americans, however, did find ways to match the seasoned British forces. Washington was a skillful general who mustered the support of the colonial forces. The Americans also found it easier to fight a war on familiar territory in defense of their homes.

Carrying Out the War

Volleys from British muskets scattered the colonial army in the first battles waged in the war. But the colonists began to surprise the British with their ability and tactics. They would ambush British troops, then disappear into the countryside with the help of neighbors and friends. The British also had the disadvantage of having to wait weeks or months for supplies to cross the Atlantic Ocean. In addition, the war was unpopular in Britain; and British soldiers found it difficult fighting in a war thousands of miles from home that they did not understand or even support.

The turning point of the war came in October 1777, with a decisive American victory against the British at Saratoga in New York. The French—anxious to strike back at the British—decided that the Americans were a good political risk and entered the war on the American side.

Before French military aid reached America, Washington's army had to endure the unusually harsh winter of 1777 and 1778 encamped at Valley Forge, Pennsylvania. The Prussian Baron Friedrich W.A. von Steuben and the French Marquis de Lafayette joined Washington at Valley Forge, bringing discipline and encouragement. By spring, the tattered army began to regain morale as new provisions arrived from France.

Student Web Activity
Visit the *American History: The Modern Era Since 1865* Web site at **me.glencoe.com** and click on *Chapter 2—Student Web Activities* for an activity on the Revolutionary War.

■ Difficult Choices

When the Declaration of Independence called the United States "one people," it expressed a hope rather than a fact. Only about one-third of the American people actively supported the war. Another third were indifferent to the Patriot cause. The rest were Loyalists who supported the British. The struggle between Patriots and the Loyalists was as bitter a struggle as the struggle between the rebels and the British. Patriots thought of the Loyalists as traitors to the American cause.

African Americans

From the beginning of the war, at Lexington, Concord, and Bunker Hill, African American soldiers fought for the American cause. Slaveholders were afraid to give guns to African Americans, however, whether enslaved or free. In November 1775, the Continental Congress ordered the discharge of all African American soldiers in the Continental Army and banned the enlistment of other African Americans.

When the British promised to free any enslaved person who joined their army, the Congress reversed its policy and allowed free African Americans to reenlist. Enslaved African Americans who were recruited into the army either won freedom from the start or at the end of their military service.

Native Americans

Some groups of Native Americans remained neutral, but many joined the

▲ *MOLLY PITCHER AT THE BATTLE OF MONMOUTH* by Dennis Malone Carter, 1854 Several women took an active part in the fighting. At the Battle of Monmouth, New Jersey, in 1778, Molly Pitcher takes her husband's place firing a cannon. ***In what other ways did women aid the American cause?***

British. They knew the Americans opposed the Proclamation Act of 1763, which reserved land west of the Appalachians for Native Americans. British agents encouraged the Native Americans to attack frontier settlements in Virginia, Georgia, the Carolinas, and the Northwest. These actions diverted many state militia from fighting against British troops.

In New York four nations of the Iroquois Confederation supported the British. General Washington sent troops against the Iroquois and broke their confederation. Many Native Americans—including almost all of the Mohawk—moved permanently to Canada.

Women

Many women actively supported the American cause. Women often served as secret agents supplying information about British positions and plans. They raised money to equip troops. They ran farms and businesses while their husbands were away at war. Women also accompanied the troops, serving as cooks, medics, laundresses, and guides. A few even fought in the ranks.

Women who supported the Revolution expected to gain from its ideals of democracy and equality. However, the American Revolution did little to change the political rights of women. Although new state bills

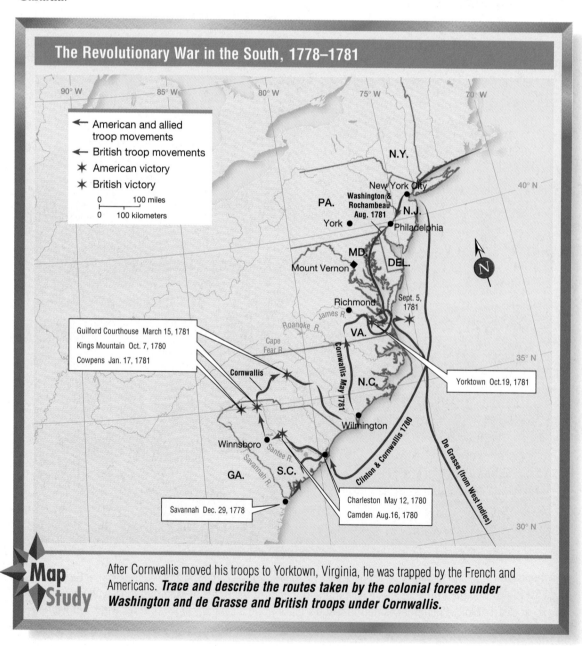

The Revolutionary War in the South, 1778–1781

American and allied troop movements
British troop movements
✳ American victory
✳ British victory

0   100 miles
0   100 kilometers

N.Y.
New York City
Washington & Rochambeau Aug. 1781
PA.
York
Philadelphia
N.J.
MD.
DEL.
Mount Vernon
Richmond
Sept. 5, 1781
James R.
Roanoke R.
VA.
Cape Fear R.
Cornwallis May 1781
Guilford Courthouse March 15, 1781
Kings Mountain Oct. 7, 1780
Cowpens Jan. 17, 1781
N.C.
Yorktown Oct.19, 1781
Cornwallis
Wilmington
Winnsboro
Santee R.
Clinton & Cornwallis 1780
De Grasse (from West Indies)
Savannah R.
GA.
S.C.
Savannah Dec. 29, 1778
Charleston May 12, 1780
Camden Aug.16, 1780

Map Study

After Cornwallis moved his troops to Yorktown, Virginia, he was trapped by the French and Americans. *Trace and describe the routes taken by the colonial forces under Washington and de Grasse and British troops under Cornwallis.*

▲ WOMEN AND RIGHTS Abigail Adams was a crusader for women's rights, demonstrating the careful thought of educated women of this period. *To what group did the new state bills of rights reserve the full privileges and rights of citizenship?*

of rights declared that all people are equal, they reserved full privileges of citizenship for white males. Women would have to wait until the twentieth century before they won full privileges of citizenship.

■ The War's End

Unable to capture Washington's army or to put down the rebellion in the north, the British turned their main military efforts to the south. For three years, beginning in 1778, British forces marched through Georgia, the Carolinas, and Virginia. Although they were successful at first, the British could not keep their conquests in the south because they could not win the loyalty of the inhabitants.

The Southwest

The British were also unsuccessful in the southwest. General Bernardo de Galvez, the governor of Spanish Louisiana, helped Americans ship supplies up the Mississippi River. When Spain officially entered the war in 1779, Galvez's troops defeated the British at Baton Rouge, Natchez, and Pensacola. These battles forced the British to divert troops from their campaigns along the Atlantic coast.

Yorktown

In 1780 and 1781, the British suffered serious naval defeats at the hands of the French, causing them to lose control of the Atlantic. This made possible the capture of the principal British force in the south under Lord Cornwallis. In October 1781, with the aid of the French, the Americans defeated the British army. George Washington accepted the British surrender at Yorktown, Virginia.

★★★ AMERICA'S FLAGS ★★★

Flags of the American Revolution The flag of the British Union flew over the

English colonies in America, beginning with Jamestown, Virginia, in 1607 until the American Revolution. The *Congress Colors* or *Grand Union* flag served as America's first national flag from 1775 to 1777. Its 13 stripes stood for the thirteen

colonies. The crosses represented the British flag and symbolized the colonists' loyalty to Britain at that time. After the Declaration of Independence, the British flag lost its meaning as a part of the United States flag. Thus the Continental Congress on June 14, 1777, designed the first Stars and Stripes. It determined that "the Flag of the United States be 13 stripes, alternate red and

white; that the Union be 13 stars, white in a blue field representing a new constellation."

★★★★★★★★★★★★★★★★★★★★★★

▲ *SURRENDER OF LORD CORNWALLIS AT YORKTOWN* by John Trumbull, 1824 Surrounded by American and French forces, General Charles Cornwallis was forced to surrender. Although other skirmishes followed, the victory at Yorktown assured America's independence. *What were the terms of the treaty ending the war?*

The Treaty of Paris, 1783

The Treaty of Paris in 1783 acknowledged American independence and granted the new nation land from the Atlantic Ocean to the Mississippi River. Although several provisions of the treaty led to later disputes, it was a great diplomatic victory for the Americans. The United States gained an area that was four times the size of France and nearly ten times that of the British Isles.

Section 2 ★ Assessment

Checking for Understanding

1. **Define** treason, propaganda, republic, Patriots, Loyalists, social contract, mercenary.

2. **Explain** the decisions facing African Americans and Native Americans during the Revolution.

Critical Thinking

3. **Analyzing Beliefs** The American Revolution has been described as a civil war as well as a rebellion. Analyze this theory based on the conflict between Loyalists and Patriots during the Revolution.

4. **Analyzing Issues** Use a diagram like the one shown here to highlight the factors that helped the colonists win the war.

Reasons for Colonial Victory

INTERDISCIPLINARY ACTIVITY

5. **Government** Imagine that you are living in the early 1770s. Record your observations and feelings about such events as the writing of the Declaration of Independence.

The Revolutionary Pen

In the years leading up to the American Revolution, few colonists could claim to be professional writers. Yet Americans from every walk of life wrote on the topics of liberty, the nature of government, and law. By 1765 there were more than 20 newspapers in the colonies, publishing locally written poems, songs, and satires on the issues of the day as well as news from abroad and debates of colonial assemblies. Broadside ballads—emotionally charged story poems printed on a single sheet of paper that could be pasted on lampposts, nailed to trees, or slipped under doors for everyone to read— helped fuel colonists' passion for freedom.

▲ TARRED AND FEATHERED TAX COLLECTOR, 1774 CARTOON

As relations between Great Britain and the colonies frayed, Thomas Paine made an impassioned appeal in his pamphlet *Common Sense:*
Everything that is right or natural pleads for separation. The blood of the slain, the weeping voice of nature cries, 'TIS TIME TO PART.

After reading Paine's pamphlet, thousands of colonists converted to the cause of independence and answered his call.

◄ POET PHILLIS WHEATLEY

Such measures as the Sugar Act, the Stamp Act, the Quartering Act, and the Townshend Acts stirred even more colonists to write expressing their views. Poet Phillis Wheatley, who was born in Africa and taken as a slave to Massachusetts, wrote her first poem in 1766. It was to King George III when he repealed the Stamp Act:
And may each clime with equal gladness see
A monarch's smile can set his subjects free!

Making the Art Connection

1. What kinds of stories and features did newspapers of the period include?

2. What events influenced more colonists to express their views?

ACTIVITY

3. Think about something you believe in, some concern or issue you'd like others to view as you do. Write a broadside ballad that makes a convincing argument for believing as you do and build a case that will sway your reader to share your beliefs.

The Declaration of Independence

*D*elegates at the Second Continental Congress faced an enormous task. The war against Great Britain had begun, but to many colonists the purpose for fighting was unclear. As sentiment increased for a complete break with Britain, Congress decided to act. A committee was appointed to prepare a document that declared the thirteen colonies free and independent from Britain. More important, the committee needed to explain why separation was the only fitting solution to long-standing disputes with Parliament and the British Crown. Thomas Jefferson was assigned to prepare a working draft of this document, which was then revised. It was officially adopted on July 4, 1776. More than any other action of the Congress, the Declaration of Independence served to make the American colonists one people.

★★★

The printed text of the document shows the spelling and punctuation of the parchment original. To aid in comprehension, selected words and their definitions appear in the side margin, along with other explanatory notes.

impel *force*

endowed *provided*

People create governments to ensure that their natural rights are protected.

If a government does not serve its purpose, the people have a right to abolish it. Then the people have the right and duty to create a new government that will safeguard their security.

Despotism *unlimited power*

In Congress, July 4, 1776. The unanimous Declaration of the thirteen united States of America,

Preamble

When in the Course of human events, it becomes necessary for one people to dissolve the political bands which have connected them with another, and to assume among the powers of the earth, the separate and equal station to which the Laws of Nature and Nature's God entitle them, a decent respect to the opinions of mankind requires that they should declare the causes which impel them to the separation.—

Declaration of Natural Rights

We hold these truths to be self-evident, that all men are created equal, that they are endowed by their Creator with certain unalienable Rights, that among these are Life, Liberty, and the pursuit of Happiness.—

That to secure these rights, Governments are instituted among Men, deriving their just powers from the consent of the governed,—

That whenever any Form of Government becomes destructive of these ends, it is the Right of the People to alter or to abolish it, and to institute new Government, laying its foundation on such principles and organizing its powers in such form, as to them shall seem most likely to effect their Safety and Happiness. Prudence, indeed, will dictate that Governments long established should not be changed for light and transient causes; and accordingly all experience hath shewn, that mankind are more disposed to suffer, while evils are sufferable, than to right themselves by abolishing the forms to which they are accustomed. But when a long train of abuses and usurpations, pursuing invariably the same Object evinces a design to reduce them under absolute Despotism, it is their right, it is their duty, to throw off such Government, and to provide new Guards for their future security.—

★★★★★★ ▲ *DECLARATION OF INDEPENDENCE IN CONGRESS* by John Trumbull, 1824 ★★★★★★★★★★★★★★★★★★★★★★★★★★★★★★

List of Grievances

Such has been the patient sufferance of these Colonies; and such is now the necessity which constrains them to alter their former Systems of Government. The history of the present King of Great Britain is a history of repeated injuries and usurpations, all having in direct object the establishment of an absolute Tyranny over these States. To prove this, let Facts be submitted to a candid world.—

He has refused his Assent to Laws, the most wholesome and necessary for the public good.—

He has forbidden his Governors to pass Laws of immediate and pressing importance, unless suspended in their operation till his Assent should be obtained; and when so suspended, he has utterly neglected to attend to them.—

He has refused to pass other Laws for the accommodation of large districts of people, unless those people would relinquish the right of Representation in the Legislature, a right inestimable to them and formidable to tyrants only.—

He has called together legislative bodies at places unusual, uncomfortable, and distant from the depository of their public Records, for the sole purpose of fatiguing them into compliance with his measures.—

He has dissolved Representative Houses repeatedly, for opposing with manly firmness his invasions on the rights of the people.—

He has refused for a long time, after such dissolutions, to cause others to be elected; whereby the Legislative powers, incapable of Annihilation, have returned to the People at large for their exercise; the State remaining in the meantime exposed to all the dangers of invasion from without, and convulsions within.—

He has endeavoured to prevent the population of these States; for

usurpations
unjust uses of power

Each paragraph lists alleged injustices of George III.

relinquish *give up*
inestimable *priceless*

Annihilation *destruction*

convulsions
violent disturbances

Naturalization of Foreigners
process by which foreign-born persons become citizens

tenure *term*

Refers to the British troops sent to the colonies after the French and Indian War.

Refers to the 1766 Declaratory Act.

quartering *lodging*

Refers to the 1774 Quebec Act.

render *make*

abdicated *given up*

perfidy *violation of trust*

insurrections *rebellions*

Petitioned for Redress
asked formally for a correction of wrongs

that purpose obstructing the Laws for Naturalization of Foreigners; refusing to pass others to encourage their migrations hither, and raising the conditions of new Appropriations of Lands.—

He has obstructed the Administration of Justice, by refusing his Assent to Laws for establishing Judiciary powers.—

He has made Judges dependent on his Will alone, for the tenure of their offices, and the amount and payment of their salaries.—

He has erected a multitude of New Offices, and sent hither swarms of Officers to harass our people, and eat out their substance.—

He has kept among us, in times of peace, Standing Armies without the Consent of our legislatures.—

He has affected to render the Military independent of and superior to the Civil power.—

He has combined with others to subject us to a jurisdiction foreign to our constitution, and unacknowledged by our laws; giving his Assent to their Acts of pretended Legislation:—

For quartering large bodies of troops among us:—

For protecting them, by a mock Trial, from punishment for any Murders which they should commit on the Inhabitants of these States:—

For cutting off our Trade with all parts of the world:—

For imposing Taxes on us without our Consent:—

For depriving us in many cases, of the benefits of Trial by Jury:—

For transporting us beyond Seas to be tried for pretended offences:—

For abolishing the free System of English Laws in a neighbouring Province, establishing therein an Arbitrary government, and enlarging its Boundaries so as to render it at once an example and fit instrument for introducing the same absolute rule into these Colonies:—

For taking away our Charters, abolishing our most valuable Laws, and altering fundamentally the Forms of our Governments:—

For suspending our own Legislatures, and declaring themselves invested with power to legislate for us in all cases whatsoever.—

He has abdicated Government here, by declaring us out of his Protection and waging War against us.—

He has plundered our seas, ravaged our Coasts, burnt our towns, and destroyed the Lives of our people.—

He is at this time transporting large Armies of foreign Mercenaries to compleat the works of death, desolation and tyranny, already begun with circumstances of Cruelty & perfidy scarcely paralleled in the most barbarous ages, and totally unworthy the Head of a civilized nation.—

He has constrained our fellow Citizens taken Captive on the high Seas to bear Arms against their Country, to become the executioners of their friends and Brethren, or to fall themselves by their Hands.—

He has excited domestic insurrections amongst us, and has endeavoured to bring on the inhabitants of our frontiers, the merciless Indian Savages, whose known rule of warfare, is an undistinguished destruction of all ages, sexes and conditions.

In every stage of these Oppressions We have Petitioned for Redress in the most humble terms: Our repeated Petitions have been answered only by repeated injury. A Prince, whose character is thus marked by every act which may define a Tyrant, is unfit to be the ruler of a free people.

Nor have We been wanting in attentions to our British brethren. We have warned them from time to time of attempts by their legislature to extend an unwarrantable jurisdiction over us. We have reminded them of the circumstances of our emigration and settlement here. We have appealed to their native justice and magnanimity, and we have conjured them by the ties of our common kindred to disavow these usurpations, which would inevitably interrupt our connections and correspondence. They too have been deaf to the voice of justice and of consanguinity. We must, therefore, acquiesce in the necessity, which denounces our Separation, and hold them, as we hold the rest of mankind, Enemies in War, in Peace Friends.—

unwarrantable jurisdiction *unjustified authority*

consanguinity *originating from the same ancestor*

Resolution of Independence by the United States

We, therefore, the Representatives of the united States of America, in General Congress, Assembled, appealing to the Supreme Judge of the world for the rectitude of our intentions, do, in the Name, and by Authority of the good People of these Colonies, solemnly publish and declare, That these United Colonies are, and of Right ought to be Free and Independent States; that they are Absolved from all Allegiance to the British Crown, and that all political connection between them and the State of Great Britain, is and ought to be totally dissolved; and that as Free and Independent States, they have full Power to levy War, conclude Peace, contract Alliances, establish Commerce, and to do all other Acts and Things which Independent States may of right do.—

And for the support of this Declaration, with a firm reliance on the protection of divine Providence, we mutually pledge to each other our Lives, our Fortunes and our sacred Honour.

rectitude *rightness*

The signers, as representatives of the American people, declared the colonies independent from Great Britain. Most members signed the document on August 2, 1776.

John Hancock
    President from
    Massachusetts

Georgia
Button Gwinnett
Lyman Hall
George Walton

North Carolina
William Hooper
Joseph Hewes
John Penn

South Carolina
Edward Rutledge
Thomas Heyward, Jr.
Thomas Lynch, Jr.
Arthur Middleton

Maryland
Samuel Chase
William Paca
Thomas Stone
Charles Carroll
    of Carrollton

Virginia
George Wythe
Richard Henry Lee
Thomas Jefferson
Benjamin Harrison
Thomas Nelson Jr.
Francis Lightfoot Lee
Carter Braxton

Pennsylvania
Robert Morris
Benjamin Rush
Benjamin Franklin
John Morton
George Clymer
James Smith
George Taylor
James Wilson
George Ross

Delaware
Caesar Rodney
George Read
Thomas McKean

New York
William Floyd
Philip Livingston
Francis Lewis
Lewis Morris

New Jersey
Richard Stockton
John Witherspoon
Francis Hopkinson
John Hart
Abraham Clark

New Hampshire
Josiah Bartlett
William Whipple
Matthew Thornton

Massachusetts
Samuel Adams
John Adams
Robert Treat Paine
Elbridge Gerry

Rhode Island
Stephen Hopkins
William Ellery

Connecticut
Samuel Huntington
William Williams
Oliver Wolcott
Roger Sherman

★★★★★★★★★★★★★★★★★★★★★★★★★★★★★★★★★★★★★★★

The Confederation

Guide to Reading

Main Idea
The colonists' first attempt to establish a government, under the Articles of Confederation, failed to bring stability to the new nation.

Reading Strategy
Classifying Information As you read about the colonists' attempt to form a new government, list the provisions of the Articles of Confederation in a chart like the one shown here.

Articles of Confederation

Objectives
After studying this section, you should be able to

★ explain how political control was allocated within the government under the Articles of Confederation.

★ list the strengths and weaknesses of the Articles of Confederation.

Key Terms
bicameral, veto, emancipation, confederation, unicameral, public land, speculator, depression

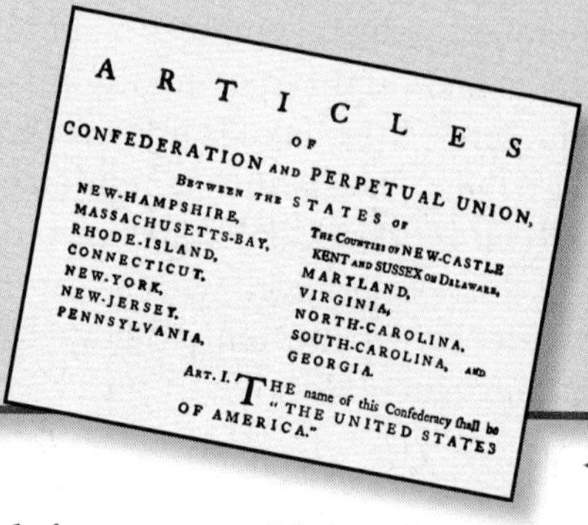

A R T I C L E S
OF
CONFEDERATION AND PERPETUAL UNION,
BETWEEN THE STATES OF
NEW-HAMPSHIRE,
MASSACHUSETTS-BAY,
RHODE-ISLAND,
CONNECTICUT,
NEW-YORK,
NEW-JERSEY,
PENNSYLVANIA,

THE COUNTIES OF NEW-CASTLE
KENT AND SUSSEX ON DELAWARE,
MARYLAND,
VIRGINIA,
NORTH-CAROLINA,
SOUTH-CAROLINA, AND
GEORGIA.

ART. I. **T**HE name of this Confederacy shall be
"THE UNITED STATES
OF AMERICA."

◀ THE ARTICLES OF CONFEDERATION

*A*s the fighting spread from Massachusetts in 1775, royal governors throughout the colonies watched their authority collapse. At first a few tried to organize Loyalist resistance, but eventually all royal governors abandoned their offices and fled. In May 1776, Congress urged the colonies to replace their colonial charters with new constitutions.

■ New State Governments

Most of the new state constitutions set up state governments similar to the colonial governments they replaced. All states except Pennsylvania and Georgia created **bicameral,** or two-house, legislatures. Members of each house represented geographic districts and, in nearly all the states, were directly elected by the voters.

Major changes were made in the executive branch, however. Many Americans had come to distrust strong executive power. So most state governors were elected to one-year terms by their legislatures and had no power to **veto,** or reject, bills passed.

For the most part, citizenship was restricted to white male property owners. However, because of the ideal of equality, many Americans began to question the institution of slavery. By 1804, every state north of Maryland had provided for the **emancipation,** or freeing, of enslaved African Americans.

In addition, many states upheld religious freedom by ending ties with established churches. In Virginia a bill for religious freedom written by Jefferson proclaimed that:

❝ *. . . [N]o man shall be compelled to frequent or support any religious worship, place, or ministry . . . nor shall otherwise*

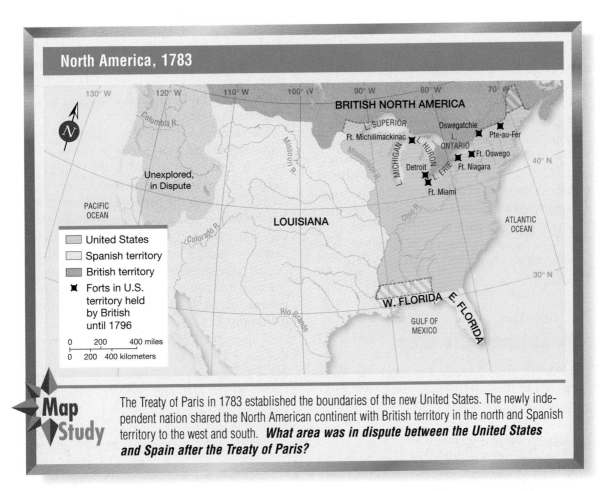

North America, 1783

BRITISH NORTH AMERICA

United States
Spanish territory
British territory
Forts in U.S. territory held by British until 1796

Unexplored, in Dispute

PACIFIC OCEAN

LOUISIANA

ATLANTIC OCEAN

W. FLORIDA E. FLORIDA

GULF OF MEXICO

0   200   400 miles
0 200 400 kilometers

Map Study

The Treaty of Paris in 1783 established the boundaries of the new United States. The newly independent nation shared the North American continent with British territory in the north and Spanish territory to the west and south. *What area was in dispute between the United States and Spain after the Treaty of Paris?*

suffer on account of his religious opinions or belief, but that all men shall be free to profess, and by argument to maintain, their opinion in matters of religion. "

Although states discriminated against their residents on the basis of race, sex, religion, and economic standing, most state constitutions included bills of rights that guaranteed trial by jury, freedom of the press, and other "unalienable rights."

■ The Articles of Confederation

America needed a workable central government that would unite the separate states. Instead, the states, reluctant to give up control, formed a **confederation,** a league of independent states, under an agreement called the Articles of Confederation. Congress completed the document in 1777, but not until 1781 did all the states approve it.

The Articles' Provisions

Governing authority was placed in a **unicameral,** or one-house, Congress in which each state had one vote. Congress could wage war and make treaties. It could raise an army and navy, borrow money, establish a postal system, and manage Native American affairs.

Despite these features, the national government under the Articles was too weak to operate effectively. There was not an executive branch to carry out laws, and no federal courts to interpret them. Executive power was divided among several congressional committees. Two important functions were denied to Congress—the power to tax and the power to regulate commerce. Unable to collect taxes, Congress had to depend on the generosity of the states for its income. Between 1781 and 1789, however, the states gave Congress only about one-sixth of the funds it requested. Without money or real power over the states, the Confederation Congress commanded so little respect that its members often did not bother to attend sessions.

Foreign Affairs

After independence, the United States did not want European alliances. The country's economy, however, depended on trade with Europe. In addition, the United States had ongoing disputes with European nations about North American territory. Therefore, in spite of its wish to remain isolated, the United States had to carry on trade and diplomatic exchanges with Europe. In many cases, foreign relations were complicated because other nations treated the United States with disdain, believing that the new nation was too weak and disunited to last very long.

GEOGRAPHY

Settling the West

During this period, the term *the West* referred to the land that lay just beyond the Appalachian Mountains. Between 1780 and 1790, the population in this area grew from about 2,000 to 100,000. In agreeing to the Articles of Confederation, eastern states with western lands declared their holdings to be **public land,** or land belonging to the central government.

The central government, however, was powerless to meet the needs of western settlers. It could not dislodge the British or persuade Spain to allow westerners free navigation along the Mississippi River in the South. Without money, Congress could neither purchase Native American land nor provide troops to protect settlers. In addition to the central government's weakness, westerners resented eastern land **speculators,** or dealers, buying large tracts of western land from the government.

When settlers in Tennessee and Kentucky threatened to leave the United States, Congress responded with two laws: the Land Ordinance of 1785 and the Northwest Ordinance of 1787.

▲ *DANIEL BOONE ESCORTING SETTLERS THROUGH THE CUMBERLAND GAP* by George Caleb Bingham, 1851–2 In many of his works, George Caleb Bingham depicts life along the Missouri and Mississippi Rivers. ***What problems did western settlers face?***

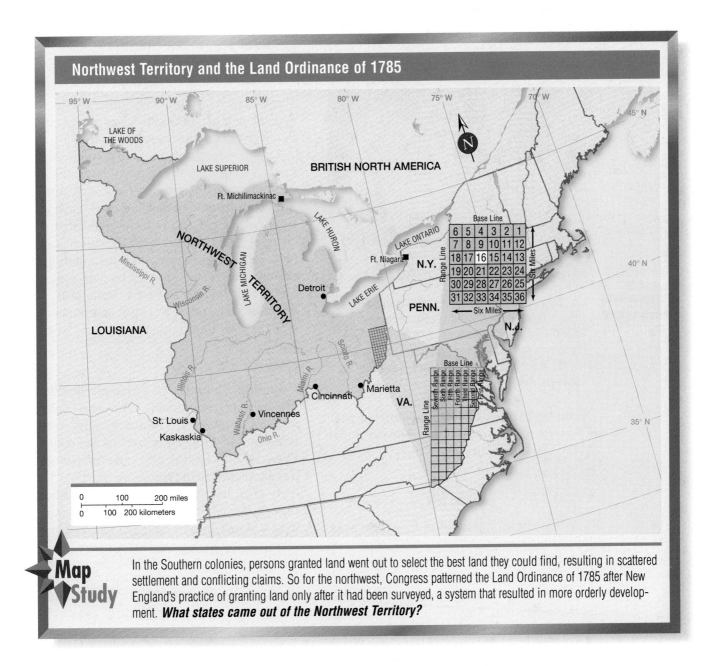

Northwest Territory and the Land Ordinance of 1785

Map Study

In the Southern colonies, persons granted land went out to select the best land they could find, resulting in scattered settlement and conflicting claims. So for the northwest, Congress patterned the Land Ordinance of 1785 after New England's practice of granting land only after it had been surveyed, a system that resulted in more orderly development. **What states came out of the Northwest Territory?**

Land Ordinance of 1785

The Land Ordinance of 1785 provided an orderly method for settling public land north of the Ohio River. The land would be surveyed and divided into townships six miles square. Every township was to contain 36 sections of one square mile, 640 acres each. Proceeds from the sale of Section 16 in each township had to be used to establish public schools. The land would sell for $1 per acre. To attract land speculators, the law required that buyers take at least one whole section. Speculators could divide their sections into smaller rectangular tracts and sell them to settlers at a profit.

Northwest Ordinance of 1787

To provide for a strong government, Congress passed the Northwest Ordinance of 1787. The region bounded by the Ohio River, the Great Lakes, and the Mississippi River was to be divided into three to five territories. Whenever 5,000 adult male citizens settled in a territory, they could set up a territorial government with an elected legislature.

The national government appointed and paid judges and a territorial governor. When the population of a territory reached 60,000, its people could organize as a state and apply for admission to the Union. The

▲ SHAYS'S REBELLION Some states printed so much paper money that it became virtually worthless. Jacobb Shattucks and Daniel Shays led the farmers' rebellion in western Massachusetts. *What grievances did these rebelling farmers have?*

Northwest Ordinance also guaranteed personal freedoms and prohibited slavery north of the Ohio River. ⊕

■ State Disputes

While the Confederation Congress was providing for stability in the West, the eastern states engaged in disputes with one another. These difficulties resulted from the postwar **depression**—or economic slowdown—and from the weak central government.

Boundary and Tax Disputes

Conflicts erupted as states engaged in boundary disputes. Parts of present-day Vermont were claimed by other states. A serious conflict between Connecticut and Pennsylvania almost resulted in war.

Congress was powerless to regulate commerce, so each state passed laws taxing goods from its neighbors. New York taxed firewood from Connecticut and cabbage from New Jersey. New Jersey retaliated by charging New Yorkers high fees for using a New Jersey lighthouse. Without a national currency, each state printed its own money. The notes' values differed from state to state, and they often were not accepted outside the state issuing them.

Shays's Rebellion

In Massachusetts, the economic situation became explosive. Unable to pay their debts, farmers in western Massachusetts were jailed or had property seized by the courts. These farmers felt the new government was just another form of tyranny. In late 1786 and early 1787, led by former Continental Army captain Daniel Shays, they closed the courts in two Massachusetts counties, stopped land seizures, and took over a local arsenal. Only through donations was Massachusetts able to raise a militia force to defeat Shays's ragtag band. Although defeated, the rebellion caused great alarm among people who believed in orderly government.

Section 3 ★ Assessment

Checking for Understanding

1. **Define** bicameral, veto, emancipation, confederation, unicameral, public land, speculator, depression.

2. **Specify** the reasons for the rebellion led by Daniel Shays.

Critical Thinking

3. **Expressing Viewpoints** Imagine that you live in the new United States. Based on your sex, race, and religion, tell to what extent the Revolution has brought about equality for you.

4. **Examining Issues** Use a diagram like the one shown here to list the strengths and weaknesses of the Articles of Confederation.

```
        Articles of Confederation
        /                      \
   Strengths              Weaknesses
```

INTERDISCIPLINARY ACTIVITY

5. **The Arts** Create a political cartoon that illustrates one of the weaknesses of the Articles of Confederation.

★★★★★★★★★★★★★★★★★★★★★★★★★★★★★★

The Constitution

Main Idea

American leaders abandoned the Articles of Confederation and crafted a new document—the Constitution.

Reading Strategy

Classifying Information As you read about the crafting of the Constitution, create a chart like the one shown here, and explain the opposing views of the Federalists and Anti-Federalists.

Federalists	Anti-Federalists

Objectives

After studying this section, you should be able to
★ explain the arguments for and against the new constitution.
★ explain how the Constitution corrected the weaknesses of the Confederation government.

Key Terms

ratification, federalism, amendment

▶ SURVEYOR'S TOOLS, EIGHTEENTH CENTURY

fter the war, George Washington had retired to Mount Vernon, his Virginia estate on the Potomac River. But his concern about the nation's problems moved him to action once again. In 1785 he invited representatives of Virginia and Maryland to Mount Vernon to discuss their differences. The meeting's success inspired Maryland and Virginia to invite all the states to meet at Annapolis, Maryland, to discuss common problems.

When the Annapolis Convention met in September 1786, delegates from only five states were present, so they could do little. Included in this group, however, was Alexander Hamilton of New York, an outspoken supporter of a strong national government. Hamilton persuaded the delegates to propose another convention. Its purpose would be to regulate commerce and to propose measures making the national government more effective.

■ The Philadelphia Convention

Congress responded by calling a meeting of the states in Philadelphia, "for the sole and express purpose of revising the Articles of Confederation." The date set for the Convention was May 14, 1787, but it was May 24 before enough delegates arrived to do business. Eventually 12 of the 13 states were represented. Only Rhode Island was not represented.

Assembling the Delegates

The 55 delegates at the convention included many of the most able political leaders in the United States. More than half had sat in the Continental Congress and so had seen for themselves the unhappy consequences of a weak central government. Benjamin Franklin, the oldest delegate at 81,

Visualizing **History** ▲ THE PHILADELPHIA CONVENTION
Several important leaders of the
Revolution did not attend the
Philadelphia Convention. Thomas
Jefferson (above) was serving as minister to France,
and Massachusetts did not send Samuel Adams or
John Hancock. Despite the absence of such notables,
the gathering at Philadelphia brought together one of
the greatest combinations of intelligence, knowledge,
and ability in American history. *What was the
"Great Compromise"?*

was in poor health and did not attend regularly. Washington was elected to preside over the proceedings, so, like Franklin, his participation in the discussions was limited. They were the best-known Americans of their time and their presence gave the convention great prestige.

The Virginia Plan

James Madison, a 36-year-old Virginian, was the first delegate to arrive at the convention, and he was the most prepared. He came to Philadelphia with a draft of a completely new framework of government. Virginia governor Edmund Randolph immediately presented Madison's proposal, known as the Virginia Plan. This document became the basis for discussion in the convention; it is the foundation for the Constitution of the United States.

■ Conflicting Plans

Almost all delegates at the convention agreed that the Articles were hopelessly weak, but there were two serious conflicts that proved difficult to resolve. Differences developed between large states and small states over representation in Congress and between northern and southern states over economic issues and the institution of slavery.

Representation

The dispute between large and small states nearly broke up the convention. The large states demanded that each state be represented by population in the bicameral Congress Madison had proposed. By what possible right, they asked, should Delaware's 59,000 people have equality with Virginia's 692,000? The small states insisted that they would never give up the equal power they enjoyed under the Articles of Confederation to be swallowed up by the large states. William Paterson of New Jersey presented an alternative proposal, known as the New Jersey Plan, which would have merely strengthened the Articles of Confederation.

Disagreement also arose over the structure of the new government. Large-state delegates generally favored Madison's plan for a national government with separate executive, legislative, and judicial branches and with the states subordinate to the national government. Most small-state delegates supported the New Jersey Plan, which continued the Confederation and left the states supreme.

For two weeks, bitter debate raged over these differences. The deadlock was finally broken when the delegates took a day off to celebrate the Fourth of July. During the recess, a committee worked out what became known as the "Great Compromise." According to this agreement, state representation in the lower house of Congress would be based on population; in the upper house each state would have an equal vote. The delegates' ability to resolve this dispute increased their confidence in compromise as the key to a successful convention.

68 UNIT 1 Creating a Nation: Prehistory to 1815

Economic Interests

A dispute arose between the commercial interests of the North and the plantation interests of the South. Southerners wanted to count slaves to determine representation to Congress but not for direct taxation. The North wanted to count slaves for taxation but not for representation. A "three-fifths compromise" established that five slaves would be equal to three free persons for both representation and taxation.

South Carolina and Georgia, afraid that a strong national government might act against slavery, insisted that the Constitution forbid interference with the slave trade. The delegates agreed that for 20 years the national government would not prevent the importation of slaves nor charge an import duty of more than ten dollars a head.

Compromises Yield a New Government

These compromises allowed the delegates to complete their two essential tasks: to give the national government more power and to provide a framework for a workable government. The delegates granted to the central government the powers it had needed most under the Articles of Confederation. The new government could levy and collect taxes, provided such taxes were "uniform throughout the United States." It could regulate commerce with foreign nations and between the states. Thus it could write and enforce commercial treaties that would increase foreign trade, and it could keep trade among the states free of barriers. It could also coin money and regulate its value, so there could be a national standard of money instead of state currency with different values.

The Executive Branch

Although the greatest disputes at the convention were over the structure and powers of the legislative branch, the delegates also disagreed about the executive branch. Everyone at the convention agreed on the need for an executive branch to operate the government, but some delegates favored a group executive, so that no one individual could become too powerful. The executive committees of the Confederation Congress had not worked out well, and Hamilton's proposal for a single executive chosen by Congress for life was too reminiscent of monarchy. In the final weeks of the convention, two more compromises were achieved. A single executive would serve a four-year term. This person would be chosen not directly by the people but indirectly by special electors named by the legislature of each state.

The Judicial Branch

As the long hot summer drew to a close, the exhausted delegates merely roughed out the framework of the judicial branch. In so doing, they created only a Supreme Court and empowered the new government to create "such inferior Courts as the Congress may from time to time ordain and establish."

Their work concluded, the delegates reviewed their efforts. No one was completely happy with the final plan, but most

Visualizing History

▲ **JAMES MADISON** As one of the delegates from Virginia, James Madison participated in the lengthy, often heated debates that created a foundation of government for the United States. ***What other contributions did Madison make to the Constitution?***

 Visualizing History

▲ **CELEBRATION** Ratification of the Constitution set off a wave of celebration. *How many states had to ratify the Constitution for it to become law?*

agreed it was a vast improvement on the Articles. Madison recorded the reaction of Benjamin Franklin:

" *Doctor Franklin, looking toward the President's chair, at the back of which a rising sun happened to be painted . . . "I have," said he, "often and often in the course of the Session . . . looked at that [sun] behind the President without being able to tell whether it was rising or setting; but now, at length I have the happiness to know it is a rising and not a setting Sun.* "

■ The Ratification Struggle

On September 17, 1787, after four months of work, the delegates to the Constitutional Convention gathered one last time to sign their work. Of the 55 who had come to Philadelphia that spring, 42 were still on hand, and all but 3 agreed to sign the document.

The Framers of the Constitution anticipated that **ratification,** or approval, of the document would be difficult. Rhode Island, which had boycotted the convention, certainly would not approve. So it seemed foolish to insist on the unanimous approval required to amend the Articles. Instead, the Constitution provided that "the ratification of nine States shall be sufficient for the establishment of this Constitution."

The Constitution Opposed

To get even nine states to ratify the Constitution was no small task. Some states objected to surrendering their power and independence to the national government. Nor were supporters of states' rights pleased that the new Constitution bypassed state governments in the ratification process. Ratification was to be decided by special conventions to be called in each state, a process implementing the idea expressed in the Declaration of Independence that governments "derive their just powers from the consent of the governed."

Even among the "governed," however, opposition was strong. Debtors and paper-money advocates were opposed to any plan forcing full payment of debts and restoring sound currency. There was certainly suspicion of a powerful central government. Why revolt from Great Britain, people asked, simply to fall under a new kind of tyranny? Popular leaders such as John Hancock, Samuel Adams, and Patrick Henry opposed it.

Support Organized

Those who favored the new plan of government called themselves "Federalists." They took this name to emphasize that the Constitution was based on the principle of **federalism,** a system in which power is divided between a central government and regional governments, and to remind Americans that the states would retain many of their powers. Of course, those who opposed the Constitution were "Federalists" too, because the league of states created by the Articles also was based on federalism. The real issue was whether the national government or state governments would be supreme. By taking the name "Federalists," however, the supporters of the Constitution caused their opponents to be tagged with the negative label "Anti-Federalists."

Although the two sides were almost equally divided, several factors worked against the Anti-Federalists. Their campaign was a negative one. They attacked almost everything about the Constitution and complained that it failed to protect basic liberties such as freedom of speech and religion. But the Anti-Federalists had nothing to offer in its place.

The Federalists, on the other hand, presented a definite program to meet the difficulties facing the nation. They promised that if the Constitution was ratified, **amendments,** or additions and changes, would be made to provide a Bill of Rights to protect the people.

The Federalists also made better use of communications. They were supported by most of the nation's newspapers. They presented their case more convincingly in sermons, pamphlets, and debates in state conventions.

The Federalists' campaign for ratification produced one of the finest pieces of political writing in the history of the world, *The Federalist*—a collection of 85 essays written by Hamilton, Madison, and John Jay. Originally published in the *New York Journal,* the essays explained in detail the importance of the Constitution to the success of the nation.

The Constitution Is Ratified

The Federalists succeeded in getting the Constitution ratified not merely because they were good speakers and writers, but because they were politically shrewd. In the states where strong opposition existed, the Federalists were able to outmaneuver their opponents.

In Pennsylvania, the Federalists called the election for the state's ratifying convention before the Anti-Federalists had an opportunity to organize. In Massachusetts, the Federalists used influential Anti-Federalist leader John Hancock to gain support for the Constitution. They suggested that if the Constitution were ratified, Hancock could be the first President of the United States.

In New York, two-thirds of the State Convention were Anti-Federalists. But the persuasiveness of John Jay and the news that 10 states had already ratified the Constitution convinced enough Anti-Federalists to change sides so that New York became the "eleventh pillar" of the new federal roof.

The vote in several key states—Massachusetts, Virginia, and New York—was extremely close. By July 1788, however, all the states except Rhode Island and North Carolina had ratified, and preparations were made to launch the new government without them.

Section 4 ★ Assessment

Checking for Understanding

1. **Define** ratification, federalism, amendment.
2. **Distinguish** between the positions of the Federalists and the Anti-Federalists.

Critical Thinking

3. **Summarizing** Use a chart like the one shown here to explain how the Constitution corrected the weaknesses of the Articles of Confederation.

Weakness		Correction
	→	
	→	

4. **Making Inferences** Why would it have been considered significant when people such as John Hancock, Samuel Adams, and Patrick Henry opposed the new Constitution?

INTERDISCIPLINARY ACTIVITY

5. **Government** Find photographs of buildings, people, or actions that illustrate the concept of a living Constitution. Write captions for each image that explain how illustrations represent this concept.

Using Vocabulary

Each of the following terms has a meaning that relates to government. Find the definition of each word and then write a sentence in which you give an example of its meaning.

direct tax	veto
treason	federalism
bicameral	amendment

Reviewing Facts

1. **Identify** the incidents that became turning points in the relationship between the American colonies and Britain.

2. **List** the organizations that came into being in the colonies to protest British tax laws and describe the ways in which the colonists defied those laws.

3. **Compare** the plan the British devised to win the Revolutionary War with that of the American and French, noting similarities and differences.

4. **Explain** the contributions and achievements made by women to the Revolutionary war effort.

5. **Describe** the problems faced by the United States under the Articles of Confederation.

6. **Identify** the disagreements that divided the delegates at the Constitutional Convention.

7. **Detail** why *The Federalist* helped win public support for the new Constitution.

Understanding Concepts

Civil Rights and Liberties

1. Jefferson turned to natural rights and the contract theory of government when he was writing the Declaration of Independence. Explain why he used these particular concepts.

2. When the colonists refused to pay the taxes imposed by Parliament, the crown took measures to force obedience. Use a diagram like the one shown here to list the measures and tell what effect each had on British-American relations.

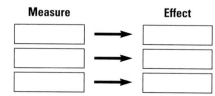

Authority

3. **Propose** possible reasons why a distrust of strong central authority after the Revolutionary War gradually gave way to its acceptance at the Constitutional Convention.

Critical Thinking

1. **Identifying Alternatives** Historians argue whether any war is inevitable. How could war between Britain and the American colonies have been avoided?

2. **Linking Past and Present** Detail the relationship you see between the theory of government as outlined in the Declaration of Independence

▲ **TRANSPORTING TOBACCO**

and political changes that have occurred in eastern Europe in recent years.

3. **Analyzing Illustrations** Study the illustration on page 72 and answer the questions that follow.

   a. What is each of the two groups doing?

   b. What clues in the painting suggest a particular period of time or era? Explain.

History and Geography

Lexington and Concord

Study the information on the map. Then answer the questions that follow.

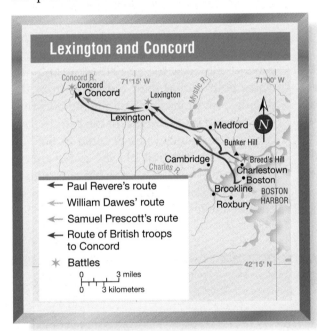

Lexington and Concord

← Paul Revere's route
← William Dawes' route
← Samuel Prescott's route
← Route of British troops to Concord
✶ Battles

1. **Movement** Which of the Patriots reached Concord?

2. **Place** What battle sites are shown on the map?

3. **Location** Why was Boston an important strategic site for the Americans?

Cooperative Learning **Interdisciplinary Activity: Citizenship**

Work in a group of four on the following activity. Imagine that your group is being sent to the moon in order to establish a colony there. Together, write a constitution for your colony. Decide which portions of the United States Constitution will work for your new situation and the changes that will need to be made to serve the best interests of your group.

Practicing Skills

Identifying Alternatives

Suppose you are a colonist who has to decide whether to join the Sons or Daughters of Liberty.

1. What three questions might you ask about the organization?

2. What alternatives do you have besides joining?

3. What are the positive and negative consequences of each alternative?

Technology Activity

Using a Word Processor

Use the Internet and other resources to find out more about one of the signers of the Declaration of Independence (see page 61 for a listing). Write a brief biographical sketch of the person.

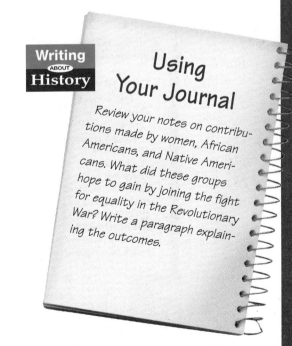

Writing ABOUT History

Using Your Journal

Review your notes on contributions made by women, African Americans, and Native Americans. What did these groups hope to gain by joining the fight for equality in the Revolutionary War? Write a paragraph explaining the outcomes.

Constitution Handbook

The entire system of federal government in the United States rests on a single document: the Constitution. It has served as the "supreme law of the land" for more than 200 years, making it the oldest written constitution in the world. Institutions that we take for granted—the Congress, the President, the Supreme Court—were created by the Constitution. Major governmental decisions that are made every day depend upon constitutional authority.

The authors of the Constitution created a strong central government. Article I, Section 8, which has been called the "heart of the Constitution," gave the new Congress various powers not possessed by the Confederation Congress, including the authority to levy taxes and regulate interstate commerce. The power to levy taxes enabled Congress to finance the federal government.

Through its authority over interstate commerce, Congress has enacted laws ranging from prohibitions against racial discrimination to regulations on consumer credit.

The "elastic clause" that appears in Article I, Section 8, says that Congress shall make all laws "necessary and proper" for putting into effect its enumerated powers. Determining what laws are necessary and proper has provided for ongoing debate and controversy over the years, beginning with the debate over the National Bank in 1790.

The Constitution reinforced the idea that the states were to remain sovereign in some matters. Through their authority in common law and criminal law, the state governments were left in control of local affairs. Their separate identities were protected, and their authority in matters not specifically given to the national government was limited only by the rights of the people within each state. The Tenth Amendment assured this basic protection of each state's sovereignty.

Another assurance of state and popular sovereignty is provided by the amending process. Because the Constitution and the states both derive their authority from the people, provisions for changing the Constitution depend upon the will of the people. This careful arrangement has resulted in only 27 amendments. The first 10 were added almost immediately—in 1791—as a Bill of Rights to protect against national government encroachments on individual freedom.

Division of Powers

EXCLUSIVE POWERS GRANTED TO THE FEDERAL GOVERNMENT	CONCURRENT POWERS SHARED BY THE FEDERAL AND STATE GOVERNMENTS	RESERVED POWERS SET ASIDE FOR THE STATES
• Regulate interstate and foreign commerce • Establish an army and navy • Declare war • Coin money • Establish postal system • Establish federal courts • Set standards for weights and measures • Regulate patents and copyrights • Admit new states • Establish laws of citizenship • Pass laws needed to carry out its powers	• Enforce the laws • Borrow money • Lay and collect taxes • Establish courts • Charter banks • Provide for the general welfare	• Regulate intrastate commerce • Conduct elections • Determine voting requirements • Establish local governments • Provide for public safety • Tenth Amendment reserves to the state governments all powers not granted to the federal government or prohibited by the Constitution

Chart Study

When the Constitution was written, the states reserved certain powers. The Constitution gave certain powers and rights to the national government. ***Who retains all other rights?***

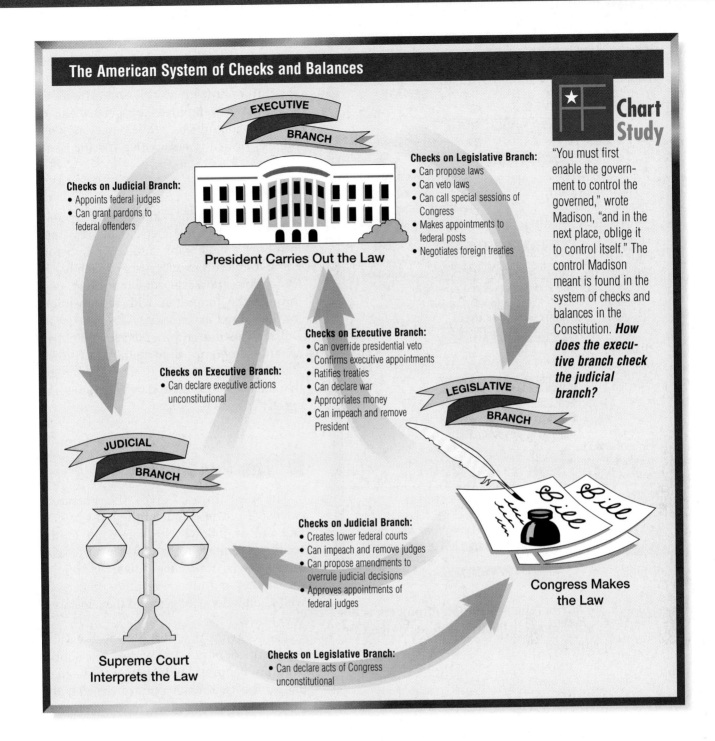

The American System of Checks and Balances

EXECUTIVE BRANCH

Checks on Judicial Branch:
- Appoints federal judges
- Can grant pardons to federal offenders

President Carries Out the Law

Checks on Legislative Branch:
- Can propose laws
- Can veto laws
- Can call special sessions of Congress
- Makes appointments to federal posts
- Negotiates foreign treaties

"You must first enable the government to control the governed," wrote Madison, "and in the next place, oblige it to control itself." The control Madison meant is found in the system of checks and balances in the Constitution. *How does the executive branch check the judicial branch?*

Checks on Executive Branch:
- Can override presidential veto
- Confirms executive appointments
- Ratifies treaties
- Can declare war
- Appropriates money
- Can impeach and remove President

Checks on Executive Branch:
- Can declare executive actions unconstitutional

JUDICIAL BRANCH

LEGISLATIVE BRANCH

Checks on Judicial Branch:
- Creates lower federal courts
- Can impeach and remove judges
- Can propose amendments to overrule judicial decisions
- Approves appointments of federal judges

Congress Makes the Law

Supreme Court Interprets the Law

Checks on Legislative Branch:
- Can declare acts of Congress unconstitutional

■ Congress

The Constitution provided different legislative powers for the Senate and House. The Senate approves treaties and presidential appointments and tries all **impeachment** cases of government officials formally accused of wrongdoing in office; the House originates all revenue bills, and has the power to impeach members of the executive and judicial branches. Legislation must pass both Houses before it can be sent to the President to be signed into law.

Most of the enumerated powers of Congress leave little room for interpretation. When the constitutional authority of Congress seems to conflict with the authority of the President, it is often because of a deliberate effort by the Constitutional Convention to limit the power of government. The framers of the Constitution chose to divide government powers among three separate

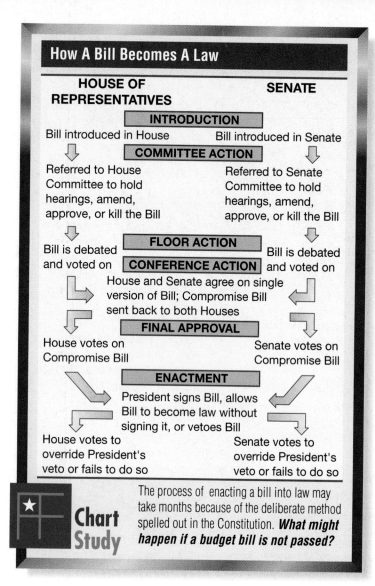

How A Bill Becomes A Law

HOUSE OF REPRESENTATIVES   **SENATE**

INTRODUCTION

Bill introduced in House   Bill introduced in Senate

COMMITTEE ACTION

Referred to House Committee to hold hearings, amend, approve, or kill the Bill

Referred to Senate Committee to hold hearings, amend, approve, or kill the Bill

FLOOR ACTION

Bill is debated and voted on   Bill is debated and voted on

CONFERENCE ACTION

House and Senate agree on single version of Bill; Compromise Bill sent back to both Houses

FINAL APPROVAL

House votes on Compromise Bill   Senate votes on Compromise Bill

ENACTMENT

President signs Bill, allows Bill to become law without signing it, or vetoes Bill

House votes to override President's veto or fails to do so

Senate votes to override President's veto or fails to do so

Chart Study The process of enacting a bill into law may take months because of the deliberate method spelled out in the Constitution. *What might happen if a budget bill is not passed?*

branches. This separation of powers is one of the most distinctive features of the Constitution.

Duties

The federal government is separated into legislative, executive, and judicial branches. These branches, described in the first three articles of the Constitution, are each given separate authority. Under this **separation of powers**, each branch exercises a check on the powers of the other two.

The Constitution describes the duties of the three branches, but it does not detail how those duties are to be carried out. To handle the heavy volume of legislation efficiently, both houses of Congress, from the very beginning, divided into committees.

These smaller units do most of the work of both houses. Each committee deals with particular problems, such as labor, banking, agriculture, foreign affairs, and armed services. Some committees are permanent, or standing committees, while others are temporary, formed to deal with a specific issue.

Legislation

Legislation begins with written proposals called bills. Any member of Congress may introduce a bill on any subject. Long before going to the full membership of each house for a vote, however, the bill must pass through the committee with responsibility for the subject in question.

The Constitution provided for a deliberate and sometimes slow method of passing legislation. One factor is the requirement that the legislation passed by both houses be exactly the same.

■ The Presidency

The Constitution gives the President extensive powers. Four of the most important are as follows: the command of the country's military forces; the power to conduct foreign affairs; the power to appoint the cabinet and other executive officers, as well as all federal judges; and the legislative veto power.

The Constitution did not foresee the development of political parties, one source of additional presidential power. As head of one of the two major political parties, the President can exert pressure for legislation and can give or withhold support for a senator's or representative's reelection.

Presidential power increases during crises involving actual or perceived danger from abroad. It is affected by the tendency of Congress to yield much of its power to the President for the duration of the crisis.

The President, who has access to a vast military and foreign service network, can control information that Congress receives. In addition, Congress, working as a whole or through committees, is inherently less capable of exercising decisive action quickly.

In domestic policy the Constitution clearly gives "the power of the purse" to Congress. Over time, the President has come to dominate many processes of allocating the government's money. The creation of the Bureau of the Budget in 1921 (now the Office of Management and Budget), whose director was appointed by the President, heralded the transfer of major budgetary power out of the hands of Congress.

◼ The Courts

The judiciary is only briefly described in the Constitution. Article III provides that there shall be "one Supreme Court" and such lower courts as Congress may establish.

The Court System

The first Congress passed the Judiciary Act of 1789. This law set up the federal court system, the basics of which are still in place today. The federal judiciary may be envisioned as a three-tiered pyramid, with many district courts at the bottom, a smaller number of circuit courts in the middle, and one Supreme Court at the top.

Cases from a district court may be appealed, or taken for review, to the circuit court for the area in which the district court is located. Cases may be appealed to the Supreme Court, which currently consists of nine members: eight associate justices and one Chief Justice. Because the cases that reach them are so complex, the justices must decline to rule upon all but a small fraction of the cases they are asked to hear.

The main purpose of the federal judiciary is to provide a forum for disputes involving federal laws. The most important power of the federal courts, that of **judicial review**, is not stated in the Constitution. This is the power of the Court to decide whether a given law, federal or state, conflicts with the Constitution. If so, the law can be declared unconstitutional and ceases to have effect. This acts as a form of veto power over laws. If the Supreme Court rules a law unconstitutional, the Congress or the states may initiate an amendment to the Constitution.

The Court cannot rule on just any law, but only on those that come before it. In this sense its role is passive; it cannot take the initiative to correct problems that the justices see or hear about, but must wait for others to file lawsuits. The Court also must rely on the President to enforce its rulings.

Unlike Congress and the President, federal judges do not have to face reelection. The Constitution provides that they shall hold office "during good behavior"—which generally means for life or until they choose to resign—and that their salaries may not be reduced. The Framers wanted to protect federal judges from political pressures so they could rule fairly and wisely, without fear of popular hostility. A federal judge can be removed through the difficult process of impeachment by Congress.

◼ A Living Document

When the Constitution reached its bicentennial year in 1989, it inspired interest in the significance of the document. Two broadly different views emerged. Some people saw the limitations and problems that the federal government faced and suggested a new constitutional convention to restructure the government to meet today's difficult challenges. Others emphasized the remarkable enduring quality of the Constitution and its basic principles that remain important today.

It is likely that if changes are to be made in basic principles of government, they will come by amendment or interpretation. Amendment, however, has historically been approached with caution. The founders wanted the Constitution to be safe from the passions of the public and political schemes.

The Constitution's adaptability to new circumstances has made it a lasting framework of government. It has permitted, perhaps even encouraged, debate over the proper role of each branch of government, or of government itself. Through the first two centuries of federal government, the Constitution has served to moderate change in government. It has also ably guarded those freedoms that we the people have entrusted it to preserve.

The Constitution of the United States

*T*he Constitution of the United States
is truly a remarkable document. It was one of the
first written constitutions in modern history. The Framers
wanted to devise a plan for a strong central government that would
unify the country, as well as preserve the ideals of the Declaration of
Independence. The document they wrote created a representative legislature, the
office of president, a system of courts, and a process for adding amendments. For over
200 years, the flexibility and strength of the Constitution has guided the nation's
political leaders. The document has become a symbol of pride and a force for
national unity. For easier study of the Constitution, those passages that have
been set aside or changed by the adoption of amendments are printed in blue.
Also included are explanatory notes that will help clarify the
meaning of each article and section.

▲ THE CAPITOL, WASHINGTON, D.C.

Preamble

We, the people of the United States, in Order to form a more perfect Union, establish Justice, insure domestic Tranquility, provide for the common defence, promote the general Welfare, and secure the Blessings of Liberty to ourselves and our Posterity, do ordain and establish this Constitution for the United States of America.

Article I

Section 1

All legislative Powers herein granted shall be vested in a Congress of the United States, which shall consist of a Senate and House of Representatives.

Section 2

1. The House of Representatives shall be composed of Members chosen every second Year by the People of the several States, and the Electors in each State shall have the Qualifications requisite for Electors of the most numerous Branch of the State Legislature.

2. No Person shall be a Representative who shall not have attained to the Age of twenty-five Years, and been seven Years a Citizen of the United States, and who shall not, when elected, be an Inhabitant of that State in which he shall be chosen.

3. Representatives and direct Taxes shall be apportioned among the several states which may be included within this Union, according to the respective Numbers, which shall be determined by adding to the whole Number of free Persons, including those bound to Service for a Term of Years, and excluding Indians not taxed, three-fifths of all other Persons. The actual Enumeration shall be made within three Years after the first Meeting of the Congress of the United States, and within every subsequent Term of ten Years, in such Manner as they shall by Law direct. The Number of Representatives shall not exceed one for every thirty Thousand, but each state shall have at Least one Representative; and until such enumeration shall be made, the State of New Hampshire shall be entitled to chuse three; Massachusetts eight, Rhode Island and Providence Plantations one, Connecticut five, New York six, New Jersey four, Pennsylvania eight, Delaware one, Maryland six, Virginia ten; North Carolina five, South Carolina five, and Georgia three.

4. When vacancies happen in the Representation from any State, the Executive Authority thereof shall issue Writs of Election to fill such Vacancies.

5. The House of Representatives shall chuse their Speaker and other Officers; and shall have the sole Power of Impeachment.

The Preamble introduces the Constitution and sets forth the general purposes for which the government was established. The preamble also declares that the power of the government comes from the people.

The printed text of the document shows the spelling and punctuation of the parchment original.

Article I. The Legislative Branch

Section 1. Congress

The power to make laws is given to a Congress made up of two chambers to represent different interests: the Senate to represent the states; the House to be more responsive to the people's will.

Section 2. House of Representatives

1. Election and Term of Office

"Electors" means voters. Every two years the voters choose new Congress members to serve in the House of Representatives. The Constitution states that each state may specify who can vote. But the 15th, 19th, 24th, and 26th Amendments have established guidelines that all states must follow regarding the right to vote.

2. Qualifications

Representatives must be 25 years old, citizens of the United States for 7 years, and residents of the state they represent.

3. Division of Representatives Among the States

The number of representatives from each state is based on the size of the state's population. Each state is divided into congressional districts, with each district required to be equal in population. Each state is entitled to at least one representative. The number of representatives in the House was set at 435 in 1929. Since then, there has been a reapportionment of seats based on population shifts rather than on addition of seats.

Only three-fifths of a state's slave population was to be counted in determining the number of representatives elected by the state. Native Americans were not counted at all.

The "enumeration" referred to is the census, the population count taken every 10 years since 1790.

4. Vacancies

Vacancies in the House are filled through special elections called by the state's governor.

5. Officers

The speaker is the leader of the majority party in the House and is responsible for choosing the heads of various House committees. "Impeachment" means indictment, or bringing charges against an official.

Section 3. The Senate
1. Number of Members, Terms of Office, and Voting Procedure
Originally, senators were chosen by the state legislators of their own states. The 17th Amendment changed this, so that senators are now elected directly by the people. There are 100 senators, 2 from each state.

2. Staggered Elections; Vacancies
One-third of the Senate is elected every two years. The terms of the first Senate's membership was staggered: one group served two years, one four, and one six. All senators now serve a six-year term.

The 17th Amendment changed the method of filling vacancies in the Senate.

3. Qualifications
Qualifications for the Senate are more restrictive than those for the House. Senators must be at least 30 years old and they must have been citizens of the United States for at least 9 years. The Framers of the Constitution made the Senate a more elite body in order to produce a further check on the powers of the House of Representatives.

4. President of the Senate
The Vice President's only duty listed in the Constitution is to preside over the Senate. The only real power the Vice President has is to cast the deciding vote when there is a tie. However, modern Presidents have given their Vice Presidents new responsibilities.

5. Other Officers
The Senate selects its other officers, including a presiding officer (president pro tempore) who serves when the Vice President is absent or has become President of the United States.

6. Trial of Impeachments
When trying a case of impeachment brought by the House, the Senate convenes as a court. The Chief Justice of the Supreme Court acts as the presiding judge, and the Senate acts as the jury. A two-thirds vote of the members present is necessary to convict officials under impeachment charges.

7. Penalty for Conviction
If the Senate convicts an official, it may only remove the official from office and prevent that person from holding another federal position. However, the convicted official may still be tried for the same offense in a regular court of law.

Section 4. Elections and Meetings
1. Holding Elections
In 1842 Congress required members of the House to be elected from districts in states having more than one Representative rather than at large. In 1845 it set the first Tuesday after the first Monday in November as the day for selecting presidential electors.

2. Meetings
The 20th Amendment, ratified in 1933, has changed the date of the opening of the regular session of Congress to January 3.

Section 3
1. The Senate of the United States shall be composed of two Senators from each State, chosen by the Legislature thereof; for six Years; and each Senator shall have one Vote.

2. Immediately after they shall be assembled in Consequence of the first Election, they shall be divided as equally as may be into three Classes. The Seats of the Senators of the first Class shall be vacated at the Expiration of the second Year, of the second Class at the Expiration of the fourth Year, and of the third Class at the Expiration of the sixth Year, so that one-third may be chosen every second Year; and if Vacancies happen by Resignations, or otherwise, during the Recess of the Legislature of any State, the Executive thereof may make temporary Appointments until the next Meeting of the Legislature, which shall then fill such Vacancies.

3. No person shall be a Senator who shall not have attained the Age of thirty Years, and been nine Years a Citizen of the United States, and who shall not, when elected, be an Inhabitant of that State in which he shall be chosen.

4. The Vice President of the United States shall be President of the Senate, but shall have no vote, unless they be equally divided.

5. The Senate shall chuse their Officers, and also a President pro tempore, in the absence of the Vice-President or when he shall exercise the Office of the President of the United States.

6. The Senate shall have the sole Power to try all impeachments. When sitting for that purpose they shall be on Oath or Affirmation. When the President of the United States is tried, the Chief Justice shall preside: And no person shall be convicted without the Concurrence of two-thirds of the Members present.

7. Judgment in Cases of Impeachment shall not extend further than to removal from Office, and disqualification to hold and enjoy any Office of Honor, Trust or Profit under the United States: but the Party convicted shall nevertheless be liable and subject to Indictment, Trial, Judgment and Punishment, according to Law.

Section 4
1. The Times, Places, and Manner of holding Elections for Senators and Representatives, shall be prescribed in each state by the Legislature thereof; but the Congress may at any time by Law make or alter such Regulations, except as to the Places of Chusing Senators.

2. The Congress shall assemble at least once in every Year, and such Meeting shall be on the first Monday in December, unless they shall by Law appoint a different Day.

▲ THE WILL OF THE PEOPLE The idea of representative democracy works well when the legislature is responsive to the citizens. *Which chamber was not originally elected by the people?*

Visualizing History

Section 5

1. Each House shall be the Judge of the Elections, Returns and Qualifications of its own Members, and a Majority of each shall constitute a Quorum to do Business; but a smaller Number may adjourn from day to day, and may be authorized to compel the Attendance of absent Members, in such Manner, and under such Penalties as each House may provide.

2. Each House may determine the Rules of its Proceedings, punish its Members for disorderly Behaviour, and, with the Concurrence of two-thirds, expel a Member.

3. Each House shall keep a Journal of its Proceedings, and from time to time publish the same, excepting such Parts as may in their Judgment require Secrecy; and the Yeas and Nays of the Members of either House on any question shall, at the desire of one-fifth of those Present, be entered on the Journal.

4. Neither House during the Session of Congress, shall, without the Consent of the other, adjourn for more than three days, nor to any other Place than that in which the two Houses shall be sitting.

Section 6

1. The Senators and Representatives shall receive a Compensation for their Services, to be ascertained by Law, and paid out of the Treasury of the United States. They shall in all Cases, except Treason, Felony and Breach of the Peace be privileged from Arrest during their attendance at the Session of their respective Houses, and in

Section 5. Organization and Rules of Procedure

1. Organization

Until 1969 Congress acted as the sole judge of qualifications of its own members. In that year, the Supreme Court ruled that Congress could not legally exclude victorious candidates who met all the requirements listed in Article I, Section 2.

A "quorum" is the minimum number of members that must be present for the House or Senate to conduct sessions. For a regular House session, a quorum consists of the majority of the House, or 218 of the 435 members.

2. Rules

Each house sets its own rules, can punish its members for disorderly behavior, and can expel a member by a two-thirds vote.

3. Journals

In addition to the journals, a complete official record of everything said on the floor, as well as the roll call votes on all bills or issues, is available in the *Congressional Record*, published daily by the Government Printing Office.

4. Adjournment

Neither house may adjourn for more than three days or move to another location without the approval of the other house.

Section 6. Privileges and Restrictions

1. Pay and Privileges

To strengthen the federal government, the Founders set congressional salaries to be paid by the United States Treasury rather than by members' respective states. Originally, members were paid $6 per day. Salaries for Senators and Representatives are $136,700.

The "immunity" privilege means members cannot be sued or be prosecuted for anything they say in Congress. They cannot be arrested while Congress is in session, except for treason, major crimes, or breaking the peace.

2. Restrictions

"Emoluments" means salaries. The purpose of this clause is to prevent members of Congress from passing laws that would benefit them personally. It also prevents the President from promising them jobs in other branches of the federal government.

Section 7. Passing Laws

1. Revenue Bills

"Revenue" is income raised by the government. The chief source of government revenue is taxes. All tax laws must originate in the House of Representatives. This insures that the branch of Congress which is elected by the people every two years has the major role in determining taxes. This clause does not prevent the Senate from amending tax bills.

2. How Bills Become Laws

A bill may become a law only by passing both houses of Congress and by being signed by the President. If the President disapproves, or vetoes, the bill, it is returned to the house where it originated, along with a written statement of the President's objections. If two-thirds of each house approves the bill after the President has vetoed it, it becomes law. In voting to override a President's veto, the votes of all members of Congress must be recorded in the journals or official records. If the President does not sign or veto a bill within 10 days (excluding Sundays), it becomes law. However, if Congress has adjourned during this 10-day period, the bill does not become law. This is known as a "pocket veto."

going to and returning from the same; and for any Speech or Debate in either House, they shall not be questioned in any other place.

2. No Senator or Representative shall, during the Time for which he was elected, be appointed to any civil Office under the Authority of the United States, which shall have been created, or the Emoluments whereof shall have been encreased, during such time; and no Person holding any Office under the United States, shall be a Member of either House during his continuance in Office.

Section 7

1. All Bills for raising Revenue shall originate in the House of Representatives; but the Senate may propose or concur with Amendments as on other bills.

2. Every Bill which shall have passed the House of Representatives and the Senate, shall, before it become a Law, be presented to the President of the United States; If he approve he shall sign it, but if not he shall return it, with his Objections, to that House in which it shall have originated, who shall enter the Objections at large on their Journal, and proceed to reconsider it. If after such Reconsideration two-thirds of that House shall agree to pass the bill, it shall be sent, together with the objections, to the other House, by which it shall likewise be reconsidered, and if approved by two-thirds of that House, it shall become a Law. But in all such Cases the Votes of both Houses shall be determined by Yeas and Nays, and the Names of the Persons voting for and against the Bill shall be entered on the Journal of each House respectively. If any Bill shall not be returned by the President within ten Days (Sundays excepted) after it shall have been presented to him, the Same shall be a Law, in like Manner as if he had signed it, unless the Congress by their Adjournment prevent its Return, in which Case it shall not be a Law.

▲ PREAMBLE OF THE CONSTITUTION

Visualizing History

▲ THE WORK OF CONGRESS Although some of the work of the legislature is done on the floor of Congress, most of it is done outside the chambers by committees. Each member of Congress has a staff of legislative assistants and other aides who research issues, draft bills, and organize the member's office. *How does a resolution differ from a bill?*

3. Every Order, Resolution, or Vote to which the Concurrence of the Senate and House of Representatives may be necessary (except on a question of Adjournment) shall be presented to the President of the United States; and before the Same shall take Effect, shall be approved by him, or, being disapproved by him, shall be repassed by two-thirds of the Senate and House of Representatives, according to the Rules and Limitations prescribed in the case of a Bill.

Section 8

The Congress shall have the Power

1. To lay and collect Taxes, Duties, Imposts and Excises, to pay the Debts and provide for the common Defence and general Welfare of the United States; but all Duties, Imposts and Excises shall be uniform throughout the United States;

2. To borrow money on the credit of the United States;

3. To regulate Commerce with foreign Nations, and among the several States, and with the Indian Tribes;

4. To establish an uniform Rule of Naturalization, and uniform Laws on the subject of Bankruptcies throughout the United States.

5. To coin Money, regulate the Value thereof, and of foreign Coin, and fix the Standard of Weights and Measures;

6. To provide for the Punishment of counterfeiting the Securities and current Coin of the United States;

3. Presidential Approval or Veto

The Framers included this paragraph to prevent Congress from passing joint resolutions instead of bills to avoid the possibility of a presidential veto. A bill is a draft of a proposed law, whereas a resolution is the legislature's formal expression of opinion or intent on a matter.

Section 8. Powers Granted to Congress

1. Revenue

This clause gives Congress the power to raise and spend revenue. Taxes must be levied at the same rate throughout the nation.

2. Borrowing

The federal government borrows money by issuing bonds.

3. Commerce

The exact meaning of "commerce" has caused controversy. The trend has been to expand its meaning and, consequently, the extent of Congress's powers.

4. Naturalization and Bankruptcy

"Naturalization" refers to the procedure by which a citizen of a foreign nation becomes a citizen of the United States.

5. Currency

Control over money is an exclusive federal power; the states are forbidden to issue currency.

6. Counterfeiting

"Counterfeiting" means illegally imitating or forging.

7. Post Office

In 1970 the United States Postal Service replaced the Post Office Department.

8. Copyrights and Patents

Under this provision, Congress has passed copyright and patent laws.

9. Courts

This provision allows Congress to establish a federal court system.

10. Piracy

Congress has the power to protect American ships on the high seas.

11. Declare War

While the Constitution gives Congress the right to declare war, the United States has sent troops into combat without a congressional declaration.

12. Army

This provision reveals the Framers' fears of a standing army.

13. Navy

This clause allows Congress to establish a navy.

14. Rules for Armed Forces

Congress may pass regulations that deal with military discipline.

15. Militia

The "militia" is now called the National Guard. It is organized by the states.

16. National Guard

Even though the National Guard is organized by the states, Congress has the authority to pass rules for governing its behavior.

17. Nation's Capital

This clause grants Congress the right to make laws for Washington, D.C.

18. Elastic Clause

This is the so-called "elastic clause" of the Constitution and one of its most important provisions. The "necessary and proper" laws must be related to one of the 17 enumerated powers.

Section 9. Powers Denied to the Federal Government.

1. Slave Trade

This paragraph contains the compromise the Framers reached regarding regulation of the slave trade in exchange for Congress's exclusive control over interstate commerce.

2. Habeas Corpus

Habeas corpus is a Latin term meaning "you may have the body." A writ of habeas corpus issued by a judge requires a law official to bring a prisoner to court and show cause for holding the prisoner. The writ may be suspended only during wartime.

3. Bills of Attainder

A "bill of attainder" is a bill that punishes a person without a jury trial. An "ex post facto" law is one that makes an act a crime after the act has been committed.

7. To establish Post Offices and post Roads;

8. To promote the Progress of Science and useful Arts, by securing for limited Times to Authors and Inventors the exclusive Right to their respective Writings and Discoveries;

9. To constitute Tribunals inferior to the Supreme Court;

10. To define and punish Piracies and Felonies committed on the high Seas, and Offenses against the Law of Nations.

11. To declare War, grant Letters of Marque and Reprisal, and make Rules concerning Captures on Land and Water;

12. To raise and support Armies, but no Appropriation of Money to that Use shall be for a longer Term than two Years;

13. To provide and maintain a Navy;

14. To make Rules for the Government and Regulation of the land and naval forces;

15. To provide for calling forth the Militia to execute the Laws of the Union, suppress Insurrections, and repel Invasions;

16. To provide for organizing, arming, and disciplining, the Militia, and for governing such Part of them as may be employed in the Service of the United States, reserving to the States respectively, the Appointment of the Officers, and the Authority of training the Militia according to the discipline prescribed by Congress;

17. To exercise exclusive Legislation in all Cases whatsoever, over such District (not exceeding ten Miles square) as may, by Cession of particular States, and the acceptance of Congress, become the Seat of Government of the United States, and to exercise like Authority over all Places purchased by the Consent of the Legislature of the State in which the Same shall be, for the Erection of Forts, Magazines, Arsenals, dock-Yards, and other needful Buildings;—And

18. To make all Laws which shall be necessary and proper for carrying into Execution the foregoing Powers, and all other Powers vested by this Constitution in the Government of the United States, or in any Department or Officer thereof.

Section 9

1. The Migration or Importation of such Persons as any of the States now existing shall think proper to admit, shall not be prohibited by the Congress prior to the Year one thousand eight hundred and eight, but a tax or duty may be imposed on such importation, not exceeding ten dollars for each Person.

2. The privilege of the Writ of Habeas Corpus shall not be suspended, unless when in Cases of Rebellion or Invasion the public Safety may require it.

3. No Bill of Attainder or ex post facto Law shall be passed.

▲ **INAUGURATION OF THE PRESIDENT** The inauguration is held on January 20 following a presidential election. Generally held on the steps of the Capitol, the ceremony centers on swearing into office the new President. *What does Article II, Section 1, Clause 5 describe?*

4. No capitation, or other direct, Tax shall be laid unless in Proportion to the Census or Enumeration herein before directed to be taken.

5. No Tax or Duty shall be laid on Articles exported from any State.

6. No Preference shall be given by any Regulation of Commerce or Revenue to the Ports of one State over those of another: nor shall Vessels bound to, or from, one State, be obliged to enter, clear, or pay Duties in another.

7. No Money shall be drawn from the Treasury, but in Consequence of Appropriations made by Law; and a regular Statement and Account of the Receipts and Expenditures of all public Money shall be published from time to time.

8. No Title of Nobility shall be granted by the United States:—And no Person holding any Office of Profit or Trust under them, shall, without the Consent of the Congress, accept of any present, Emolument, Office, or Title, of any kind whatever, from any King, Prince, or foreign State.

Section 10

1. No State shall enter into any Treaty, Alliance, or Confederation; grant Letters of Marque and Reprisal; coin Money; emit Bills of Credit; make any Thing but gold and silver Coin a Tender in Payment of Debts; pass any Bill of Attainder; ex post facto Law, or Law impairing the Obligation of Contracts, or grant any Title of Nobility.

4. Direct Taxes
The 16th Amendment allowed Congress to pass an income tax.

5. Tax on Exports
Congress may not tax goods that move from one state to another.

6. Uniformity of Treatment
This prohibition prevents Congress from favoring one state or region over another in the regulation of trade.

7. Appropriation Law
This clause protects against the misuse of funds. All of the President's expenditures must be made with the permission of Congress.

8. Titles of Nobility
This clause prevents the development of a nobility in the United States.

Section 10. Powers Denied to the States
1. Limitations on Power
The states are prohibited from conducting foreign affairs, carrying on a war, or controlling interstate and foreign commerce. States are also not allowed to pass laws that the federal government is prohibited from passing, such as enacting ex post facto laws or bills of attainder. These restrictions on the states were designed, in part, to prevent an overlapping in functions and authority with the federal government that could create conflict and chaos.

The Constitution of the United States   **85**

2. Export and Import Taxes

This clause prevents states from levying duties on exports and imports. If states were permitted to tax imports and exports they could use their taxing power in a way that weakens or destroys Congress's power to control interstate and foreign commerce.

3. Duties, Armed Forces, War

This clause prohibits states from maintaining an army or navy and from going to war, except in cases where a state is directly attacked. It also forbids states from collecting fees from foreign vessels or from making treaties with other nations. All of these powers are reserved for the federal government.

Article II. The Executive Branch

Section 1. President and Vice President
1. Term of Office

The President is given power to enforce the laws passed by Congress. Both the President and the Vice President serve four-year terms. The 22nd Amendment limits the number of terms the President may serve to two.

2. Election

The Philadelphia Convention had trouble deciding how the President was to be chosen. The system finally agreed upon was indirect election by "electors" chosen for that purpose. The President and Vice President are not directly elected. Instead, the President and Vice President are elected by presidential electors from each state who form the electoral college. Each state has the number of presidential electors equal to the total number of its senators and representatives. State legislatures determine how the electors are chosen. Originally, the state legislatures chose the electors, but today they are nominated by political parties and elected by the voters. No senator, representative, or any other federal officeholder can serve as an elector.

2. No State shall, without the Consent of the Congress, lay any Imposts or Duties on Imports or Exports, except what may be absolutely necessary for executing its inspection Laws: and the net Produce of all Duties and Imposts, laid by any State on Imports and Exports, shall be for the Use of the Treasury of the United States; and all such Laws shall be subject to the Revision and Controul of the Congress.

3. No State shall, without the Consent of Congress, lay any duty on Tonnage, keep Troops, or Ships of War in time of Peace, enter into any Agreement or Compact with another State, or with a foreign Power, or engage in War, unless actually invaded, or in such imminent Danger as will not admit of delay.

Article II

Section 1

1. The executive Power shall be vested in a President of the United States of America. He shall hold his Office during the Term of four years, and together with the Vice-President chosen for the same Term, be elected, as follows:

2. Each State shall appoint, in such Manner as the Legislature thereof may direct, a Number of Electors, equal to the whole Number of Senators and Representatives to which the State may be entitled in the Congress: but no Senator or Representative, or Person holding an Office of Trust or Profit under the United States, shall be appointed an Elector.

▲ **STATE OF THE UNION** Presidents use the annual State of the Union Address to outline yearly goals. *In which sections of the Constitution are the President's powers and duties defined?*

3. The Electors shall meet in their respective States, and vote by Ballot for two Persons, of whom one at least shall not be an Inhabitant of the same State with themselves. And they shall make a List of all the Persons voted for and of the Number of Votes for each; which List they shall sign and certify, and transmit sealed to the Seat of the Government of the United States, directed to the President of the Senate. The President of the Senate shall, in the Presence of the Senate and House of Representatives, open all the Certificates, and the Votes shall then be counted. The Person having the greatest Number of Votes shall be the President, if such Number be a Majority of the whole Number of Electors appointed; and if there be more than one who have such Majority, and have an equal Number of Votes, then the House of Representatives shall immediately chuse by Ballot one of them for President; and if no Person have a Majority, then from the five highest on the List the said House shall in like Manner chuse the President. But in chusing the President, the Votes shall be taken by States, the Representation from each State having one Vote; a quorum for this Purpose shall consist of a Member or Members from two-thirds of the States, and a Majority of all the States shall be necessary to a Choice. In every Case, after the Choice of the President, the Person having the greatest Number of Votes of the Electors shall be the Vice-President. But if there should remain two or more who have equal votes, the Senate shall chuse from them by Ballot the Vice President.

4. The Congress may determine the Time of chusing the Electors, and the Day on which they shall give their Votes; which Day shall be the same throughout the United States.

5. No person except a natural born Citizen, or a Citizen of the United States, at the time of the Adoption of this Constitution, shall be eligible to the Office of President; neither shall any Person be eligible to that Office who shall not have attained to the Age of thirty-five years, and been fourteen Years a Resident within the United States.

6. In Case of the Removal of the President from Office, or of his Death, Resignation, or Inability to discharge the Powers and Duties of the said Office, the same shall devolve on the Vice-President, and the Congress may by Law provide for the Case of Removal, Death, Resignation or Inability, both of the President and Vice-President, declaring what Officer shall then act as President, and such Officer shall act accordingly, until the disability be removed, or a President shall be elected.

7. The President shall, at stated Times, receive for his Services a Compensation, which shall neither be encreased nor diminished during the Period for which he shall have been elected, and he shall not receive within that Period any other Emolument from the United States, or any of them.

8. Before he enter on the execution of his office, he shall take the following Oath or Affirmation "I do solemnly swear (or affirm) that I will faithfully execute the Office of President of the United States, and will to the best of my Ability, preserve, protect and defend the Constitution of the United States.

3. Former Method of Election

This clause describes the original method of electing the President and Vice President. According to this method, each elector voted for two candidates. The candidate with the most votes (as long as it was a majority) became President. The candidate with the second highest number of votes became Vice President. In the election of 1800, the two top candidates received the same number of votes, making it necessary for the House of Representatives to decide the election. To prevent such a situation from recurring, the 12th Amendment was added in 1804.

4. Date of Elections

Congress selects the date when the presidential electors are chosen and when they vote for President and Vice President. All electors must vote on the same day. The first Tuesday after the first Monday in November has been set as the date for presidential elections. Electors cast their votes on the Monday after the second Wednesday in December.

5. Qualifications

The President must be a citizen of the United States by birth, at least 35 years old, and a resident of the United States for 14 years. See Amendment 22.

6. Vacancies

If the President dies, resigns, is removed from office by impeachment, or is unable to carry out the duties of the office, the Vice President becomes President. (Amendment 25 deals with presidential disability.) If both the President and Vice President are unable to serve, Congress has the power to declare by law who acts as President. Congress set the line of succession in the Presidential Succession Act of 1947.

7. Salary

Originally, the President's salary was $25,000 per year. The President's current salary of $200,000 plus a $50,000 taxable expense account per year was enacted in 1969. The President also receives numerous fringe benefits including a $120,000 nontaxable allowance for travel and entertainment, and living accommodations in two residences—the White House and Camp David. However, the President cannot receive any other income from the United States Government or state governments while in office.

8. Oath of Office

The oath of office is generally administered by the chief justice, but can be administered by any official authorized to administer oaths. All Presidents-elect except Washington have been sworn into office by the chief justice. Only Vice Presidents John Tyler, Calvin Coolidge, and Lyndon Johnson in succeeding to the office have been sworn in by someone else.

▲ THE PRESIDENT'S POWER As commander in chief of the United States armed forces, the President is the people's check on the power of the military. *What limits are placed on the President's power to make treaties?*

Section 2. Powers of the President

1. Military, Cabinet, Pardons

Mention of "the principal officer in each of the executive departments" is the only suggestion of the President's Cabinet to be found in the Constitution. The Cabinet is a purely advisory body, and its power depends on the President. Each Cabinet member is appointed by the President and must be confirmed by the Senate. This clause also makes the President, a civilian, the head of the armed services. This established the principle of civilian control of the military.

2. Treaties and Appointments

The President is the chief architect of American foreign policy. He or she is responsible for the conduct of foreign relations, or dealings with other countries. All treaties, however, require approval of two-thirds of the senators present. Most federal positions today are filled under the rules and regulations of the civil service system. Most presidential appointees serve at the pleasure of the President. Removal of an official by the President is not subject to congressional approval. But the power can be restricted by conditions set in creating the office.

3. Vacancies in Offices

The President can temporarily appoint officials to fill vacancies when the Senate is not in session.

Section 2

1. The President shall be Commander in Chief of the Army and Navy of the United States, and of the Militia of the several States, when called into the actual Service of the United States; he may require the Opinion, in writing, of the principal Officer in each of the executive Departments, upon any subject relating to the Duties of their respective Offices, and he shall have Power to Grant Reprieves and Pardons for Offences against the United States, except in Cases of Impeachment.

2. He shall have Power, by and with the Advice and Consent of the Senate, to make Treaties, provided two-thirds of the Senators present concur; and he shall nominate, and by and with the Advice and Consent of the Senate, shall appoint Ambassadors, other public Ministers and Consuls, Judges of the supreme Court, and all other Officers of the United States, whose Appointments are not herein otherwise provided for, and which shall be established by Law. But the Congress may by Law vest the Appointment of such inferior Officers, as they think proper, in the President alone, in the Courts of Law, or in the Heads of Departments.

3. The President shall have Power to fill up all Vacancies that may happen during the Recess of the Senate, by granting Commissions which shall expire at the End of their next Session.

Section 3

He shall from time to time give to Congress Information of the State of the Union, and recommend to their Consideration such Measures as he shall judge necessary and expedient; he may, on extraordinary occasions, convene both Houses, or either of them, and in Case of Disagreement between them, with respect to the Time of Adjournment, he may adjourn them to such Time as he shall think proper; he shall receive Ambassadors and other public Ministers; he shall take Care that the Laws be faithfully executed, and shall Commission all the Officers of the United States.

Section 4

The President, Vice-President and all civil Officers of the United States, shall be removed from Office on Impeachment for, and Conviction of, Treason, Bribery, or other high Crimes and Misdemeanors.

Article III

Section 1

The Judicial Power of the United States, shall be vested in one supreme Court, and in such inferior Courts as the Congress may from time to time ordain and establish. The judges, both of the supreme and inferior Courts, shall hold their Offices during good Behaviour, and shall, at stated Times, receive for their Services, a Compensation, which shall not be diminished during their Continuance in Office.

Section 3. Duties of the President

Under this provision the President delivers annual State-of-the-Union messages. On occasion, Presidents have called Congress into special session to consider particular problems.

The President's duty to receive foreign diplomats also includes the power to ask a foreign country to withdraw its diplomatic officials from this country. This is called "breaking diplomatic relations" and often carries with it the implied threat of more drastic action, even war. The President likewise has the power of deciding whether or not to recognize foreign governments.

Section 4. Impeachment

This section states the reasons for which the President and Vice President may be impeached and removed from office. (See annotations of Article I, Section 3, Clauses 6 and 7.)

Article III. The Judicial Branch

Section 1. Federal Courts

The term *judicial* refers to courts. The Constitution set up only the Supreme Court but provided for the establishment of other federal courts. There are presently nine justices on the Supreme Court. Congress has created a system of federal district courts and courts of appeals, which review certain district court cases. Judges of these courts serve during "good behavior," which means that they usually serve for life or until they choose to retire.

▲ **THE SUPREME COURT** Supreme Court proceedings are held in this room. The Constitution established the jurisdiction of the federal courts by defining the kinds of cases these courts may hear. **What is statute law?**

▲ JUSTICES OF THE SUPREME COURT Because we have judicial review, the Supreme Court is the official interpreter of the Constitution and has the final say in deciding what the Constitution means. *What is the term of office for a Supreme Court Justice?*

Section 2. Jurisdiction

1. General Jurisdiction

Use of the words *in law and equity* reflects the fact that American courts took over two kinds of traditional law from Great Britain. The basic law was the "common law," which was based on over five centuries of judicial decisions. "Equity" was a special branch of British law developed to handle cases where common law did not apply.

Federal courts deal mostly with "statute law," or laws passed by Congress, treaties, and cases involving the Constitution itself. "Admiralty and maritime jurisdiction" covers all sorts of cases involving ships and shipping on the high seas and on rivers, canals, and lakes.

2. The Supreme Court

When a court has "original jurisdiction" over certain kinds of cases, it means that the court has the authority to be the first court to hear a case. A court with "appellate jurisdiction" hears cases that have been appealed from lower courts. Most Supreme Court cases are heard on appeal from lower courts.

3. Jury Trials

Except in cases of impeachment, anyone accused of a crime has the right to a trial by jury. The trial must be held in the state where the crime was committed. Jury trial guarantees were strengthened in the 6th, 7th, 8th, and 9th Amendments.

Section 2

1. The judicial Power shall extend to all Cases, in Law and Equity, arising under this Constitution, the Laws of the United States, and treaties made, or which shall be made, under their Authority; to all Cases affecting ambassadors, other public ministers and consuls; to all cases of admiralty and maritime Jurisdiction; to Controversies to which the United States shall be a party; to Controversies between two or more states; between a State and Citizens of another State; between Citizens of different States; between Citizens of the same State claiming Lands under Grants of different States, and between a State, or the Citizens thereof, and foreign States, Citizens or Subjects.

2. In all Cases affecting Ambassadors, other public Ministers and Consuls, and those in which a State shall be Party, the supreme Court shall have original Jurisdiction. In all the other Cases before mentioned, the supreme Court shall have appellate Jurisdiction, both as to Law and Fact, with such Exceptions, and under such Regulations as the Congress shall make.

3. The trial of all Crimes, except in Cases of Impeachment, shall be by Jury; and such Trial shall be held in the State where the said Crimes shall have been committed; but when not committed within any State, the Trial shall be at such Place or Places as the Congress may by Law have directed.

Section 3

1. Treason against the United States, shall consist only in levying War against them, or in adhering to their Enemies, giving them Aid and Comfort. No Person shall be convicted of Treason unless on the Testimony of two Witnesses to the same overt Act, or on Confession in open Court.

2. The Congress shall have power to declare the Punishment of Treason, but no Attainder of Treason shall work Corruption of Blood, or Forfeiture except during the Life of the Person attainted.

Article IV

Section 1

Full Faith and Credit shall be given in each State to the public Acts, Records, and judicial Proceedings of every other State. And the Congress may by general Laws prescribe the Manner in which such Acts, Records, and Proceedings shall be proved, and the Effect thereof.

Section 2

1. The Citizens of each State shall be entitled to all Privileges and Immunities of Citizens in the several States.

2. A Person charged in any State with Treason, Felony, or other Crime, who shall flee from Justice, and be found in another State, shall on demand of the executive Authority of the State from which he fled, be delivered up, to be removed to the State having Jurisdiction of the crime.

3. No Person held to Service of Labour in one State, under the Laws thereof, escaping into another, shall, in Consequence of any Law or Regulation therein, be discharged from such Service or Labour, but shall be delivered up on Claim of the Party to whom such Service or Labour may be due.

Section 3

1. New States may be admitted by the Congress into this Union; but no new State shall be formed or erected within the Jurisdiction of any other State; nor any State be formed by the Junction of two or more States, or parts of States, without the Consent of the Legislatures of the States concerned as well as of the Congress.

2. The Congress shall have Power to dispose of and make all needful Rules and Regulations respecting the Territory of other Property belonging to the United States; and nothing in this Constitution shall be so construed as to Prejudice any Claims of the United States, or of any particular State.

Section 4

The United States shall guarantee to every State in this Union a Republican Form of Government, and shall protect each of them against Invasion; and on Application of the Legislature, or of the Executive (when the Legislature cannot be convened) against domestic Violence.

Section 3. Treason

1. Definition

Knowing that the charge of treason often had been used by monarchs to get rid of people who opposed them, the Framers of the Constitution defined treason carefully, requiring that at least two witnesses be present to testify in court that a treasonable act was committed.

2. Punishment

Congress is given the power to determine the punishment for treason. The children of a person convicted of treason may not be punished nor may the convicted person's property be taken away from the children. Convictions for treason have been relatively rare in the nation's history.

Article IV. Relations Among the States

Section 1. Official Acts

This provision insures that each state recognizes the laws, court decisions, and records of all other states. For example, a marriage license or corporation charter issued by one state must be accepted in other states.

Section 2. Mutual Duties of States

1. Privileges

The "privileges and immunities," or rights of citizens, guarantee each state's citizens equal treatment in all states.

2. Extradition

"Extradition" means that a person convicted of a crime or a person accused of a crime must be returned to the state where the crime was committed. Thus, a person cannot flee to another state hoping to escape the law.

3. Fugitive-Slave Clause

Formerly this clause meant that slaves could not become free persons by escaping to free states.

Section 3. New States and Territories

1. New States

Congress has the power to admit new states. It also determines the basic guidelines for applying for statehood. One state, Maine, was created within the original boundaries of another state (Massachusetts) with the consent of Congress and the state.

2. Territories

Congress has power over federal land. But neither in this clause nor anywhere else in the Constitution is the federal government explicitly empowered to acquire new territory.

Section 4. Federal Protection for States

This section allows the federal government to send troops into a state to guarantee law and order. The President may send in troops even without the consent of the state government involved.

Article V. The Amending Process

There are now 27 Amendments to the Constitution. The Framers of the Constitution deliberately made it difficult to amend or change the Constitution. Two methods of proposing and ratifying amendments are provided for. A two-thirds majority is needed in Congress to propose an amendment, and at least three-fourths of the states (38 states) must accept the amendment before it can become law. No amendment has yet been proposed by a national convention called by the states, though in the 1980s a convention to propose an amendment requiring a balanced budget had been approved by 32 states.

Article VI. National Supremacy

1. Public Debts and Treaties

This section promised that all debts the colonies had incurred during the Revolution and under the Articles of Confederation would be honored by the new United States government.

2. The Supreme Law

The "supremacy clause" recognized the Constitution and federal laws as supreme when in conflict with those of the states. It was largely based on this clause that Chief Justice John Marshall wrote his historic decision in *McCulloch* v. *Maryland*. The 14th Amendment reinforced the supremacy of federal law over state laws.

3. Oaths of Office

This clause also declares that no religious test shall be required as a qualification for holding public office. This principle is also asserted in the First Amendment, which forbids Congress to set up an established church or to interfere with the religious freedom of Americans.

Article VII. Ratification of the Constitution

Unlike the Articles of Confederation, which required approval of all thirteen states for adoption, the Constitution required approval of only nine of thirteen states. Thirty-nine of the 55 delegates at the Constitutional Convention signed the Constitution. The Constitution went into effect in June 1788.

Article V

The Congress, whenever two-thirds of both Houses shall deem it necessary, shall propose Amendments to this Constitution, or, on the Application of the Legislatures of two-thirds of the several States, shall call a Convention for proposing Amendments, which, in either Case, shall be valid to all Intents and Purposes, as part of this Constitution, when ratified by the Legislatures of three-fourths of the several States, or by Conventions in three-fourths thereof, as the one or the other Mode of Ratification may be proposed by the Congress; Provided that no Amendment which may be made prior to the Year One thousand eight hundred and eight shall in any Manner affect the first and fourth clauses in the Ninth Section of the first Article; and that no State, without its Consent, shall be deprived of its equal Suffrage in the Senate.

Article VI

1. All Debts contracted and Engagements entered into, before the Adoption of this Constitution, shall be as valid against the United States under this Constitution as under the Confederation.

2. This Constitution, and the Laws of the United States which shall be made in Pursuance thereof; and all Treaties made, or which shall be made, under the Authority of the United States, shall be the supreme Law of the Land; and the Judges in every State shall be bound thereby, any Thing in the Constitution or Laws of any State to the Contrary notwithstanding.

3. The Senators and Representatives before mentioned, and the Members of the several State Legislatures, and all executive and judicial Officers, both of the United States and of the several States, shall be bound by Oath or Affirmation, to support this Constitution; but no religious Test shall ever be required as a Qualification to any Office or public Trust under the United States.

Article VII

The Ratification of the Conventions of nine States shall be sufficient for the Establishment of this Constitution between the States so ratifying the same.

Done in Convention, by the Unanimous Consent of the States present, the Seventeenth Day of September, in the Year of our Lord one thousand seven hundred and Eighty-seven, and of the Independence of the United States of America the Twelfth. In Witness whereof We have hereunto subscribed our Names.

Signers

George Washington, **President and Deputy from Virginia**

New Hampshire
John Langdon
Nicholas Gilman

Massachusetts
Nathaniel Gorham
Rufus King

Connecticut
William Samuel Johnson
Roger Sherman

New York
Alexander Hamilton

New Jersey
William Livingston
David Brearley
William Paterson
Jonathan Dayton

Pennsylvania
Benjamin Franklin
Thomas Mifflin
Robert Morris
George Clymer
Thomas FitzSimons
Jared Ingersoll
James Wilson
Gouverneur Morris

Delaware
George Read
Gunning Bedford, Jr.
John Dickinson
Richard Bassett
Jacob Broom

Maryland
James McHenry
Daniel of St. Thomas Jenifer
Daniel Carroll

Virginia
John Blair
James Madison, Jr.

North Carolina
William Blount
Richard Dobbs Spaight
Hugh Williamson

South Carolina
John Rutledge
Charles Cotesworth Pinckney
Charles Pinckney
Pierce Butler

Georgia
William Few
Abraham Baldwin

Attest: William Jackson,
Secretary

Amendment I

Congress shall make no law respecting an establishment of religion, or prohibiting the free exercise thereof; or abridging the freedom of speech, or of the press; or the right of the people peaceably to assemble, and to petition the Government for a redress of grievances.

Amendment II

A well-regulated Militia, being necessary to the security of a free State, the right of the people to keep and bear Arms, shall not be infringed.

Amendment III

No soldier shall, in time of peace be quartered in any house, without the consent of the Owner, nor in time of war, but in a manner to be prescribed by law.

Amendment IV

The right of the people to be secure in their persons, houses, papers, and effects, against unreasonable searches and seizures, shall not be violated, and no Warrants shall issue, but upon probable cause, supported by Oath or affirmation, and particularly describing the place to be searched, and the persons or things to be seized.

Amendment 1.
Freedom of Religion, Speech, Press, and Assembly (1791)

The 1st Amendment protects the civil liberties of individuals in the United States. The 1st Amendment freedoms are not absolute, however. They are limited by the rights of other individuals.

Amendment 2.
Right to Bear Arms (1791)

The purpose of this amendment is to guarantee states the right to keep a militia.

Amendment 3.
Quartering Troops (1791)

This amendment is based on the principle that people have a right to privacy in their own homes. It also reflects the colonists' grievances against the British government before the Revolution. Britain had angered Americans by quartering (housing) troops in private homes.

Amendment 4.
Searches and Seizures (1791)

Like the 3rd Amendment, the 4th amendment reflects the colonists' desire to protect their privacy. Britain had used writs of assistance (general search warrants) to seek out smuggled goods. Americans wanted to make sure that such searches and seizures would be conducted only when a judge felt that there was "reasonable cause" to conduct them. The Supreme Court has ruled that evidence seized illegally without a search warrant may not be used in court.

Amendment 5.
Rights of Accused Persons (1791)

To bring a "presentment" or "indictment" means to formally charge a person with committing a crime. It is the function of a grand jury to see whether there is enough evidence to bring the accused person to trial. A person may not be tried more than once for the same crime (double jeopardy).

Members of the armed services are subject to military law. They may be tried in a court martial. In times of war or a natural disaster, civilians may also be put under martial law.

The 5th Amendment also guarantees that persons may not be forced in any criminal case to be a witness against themselves. That is, accused persons may refuse to answer questions on the ground that the answers might tend to incriminate them.

Amendment 6.
Right to Speedy, Fair Trial (1791)

The requirement of a "speedy" trial insures that an accused person will not be held in jail for a lengthy period as a means of punishing the accused without a trial. A "fair" trial means that the trial must be open to the public and that a jury must hear witnesses and evidence on both sides before deciding the guilt or innocence of a person charged with a crime. This amendment also provides that legal counsel must be provided to a defendant. In 1963, the Supreme Court ruled, in *Gideon* v. *Wainwright,* that if a defendant cannot afford a lawyer, the government must provide one to defend the accused person.

Amendment V

No person shall be held to answer for a capital, or otherwise infamous crime, unless on a presentment or indictment of a Grand Jury, except in cases arising in the land or naval forces, or in the Militia, when in actual service in time of War or public danger; nor shall any person be subject for the same offence to be twice put in jeopardy of life or limb; nor shall be compelled in any criminal case to be a witness against himself, nor be deprived of life, liberty, or property, without due process of law; nor shall private property be taken for public use, without just compensation.

Amendment VI

In all criminal prosecutions, the accused shall enjoy the right to a speedy and public trial, by an impartial jury of the State and district wherein the crime shall have been committed, which district shall have been previously ascertained by law, and to be informed of the nature and cause of the accusation; to be confronted with the witnesses against him; to have compulsory process for obtaining witnesses in his favor, and to have the Assistance of Counsel for his defence.

Visualizing
History

▲ **RIGHTS OF THE ACCUSED** Several amendments protect the rights of the accused. While awaiting trial, a defendant may be released by posting bail, a procedure regulated by the Eighth Amendment. *Which amendment guarantees the right to a speedy and fair trial?*

Amendment VII

In suits at common law, where the value in controversy shall exceed twenty dollars, the right of trial by jury shall be preserved, and no fact tried by a jury, shall be otherwise reexamined in any Courts of the United States, than according to the rules of common law.

Amendment VIII

Excessive bail shall not be required, nor excessive fines imposed, nor cruel and unusual punishments inflicted.

Amendment IX

The enumeration in the Constitution, of certain rights, shall not be construed to deny or disparage others retained by the people.

Amendment X

The powers not delegated to the United States by the Constitution, nor prohibited by it to the States, are reserved to the States respectively, or to the people.

Amendment XI

The Judicial power of the United States shall not be construed to extend to any suit in law or equity, commenced or prosecuted against one of the United States by Citizens of another State, or by Citizens or Subjects of any Foreign State.

Amendment XII

The Electors shall meet in their respective States and vote by ballot for President and Vice-President, one of whom, at least, shall not be an inhabitant of the same State with themselves; they shall name in their ballots the person voted for as President, and in distinct ballots the person voted for as Vice-President, and they shall make distinct lists of all persons voted for as President, and of all persons voted for as Vice-President, and of the number of votes for each, which lists they shall sign and certify, and transmit sealed to the seat of the government of the United States, directed to the President of the Senate;—The President of the Senate shall, in the presence of the Senate and House of Representatives, open all the certificates and the votes shall then be counted;—The person having the greatest number of votes for President, shall be the President, if such number be a majority of the whole number of Electors appointed; and if no person have such majority, then from the persons having the highest numbers not exceeding three on the list of those voted for as President, the House of Representatives shall choose immediately, by ballot, the President. But

Amendment 7.
Civil Suits (1791)

"Common law" means the law established by previous court decisions. In civil cases where one person sues another for more than $20, a jury trial is provided for. But customarily, federal courts do not hear civil cases unless they involve a good deal more money.

Amendment 8.
Bail and Punishment (1791)

"Bail" is money that an accused person provides to the court as a guarantee that he or she will be present for a trial. This amendment insures that neither bail nor punishment for a crime shall be unreasonably severe.

Amendment 9.
Powers Reserved to the People (1791)

This amendment provides that the people's rights are not limited to those mentioned in the Constitution.

Amendment 10.
Powers Reserved to the States (1791)

This amendment protects the states and the people from an all-powerful federal government. It provides that the states or the people retain all powers except those denied them or those specifically granted to the federal government. This "reserved powers" provision is a check on the "necessary and proper" power of the federal government provided in the "elastic clause" in Article I, Section 8, Clause 18.

Amendment 11.
Suits Against States (1795)

This amendment provides that a lawsuit brought by a citizen of the United States or a foreign nation against a state must be tried in a state court, not in a federal court. This amendment was passed after the Supreme Court ruled that a federal court could try a lawsuit brought by citizens of South Carolina against a citizen of Georgia. This case, *Chisholm* v. *Georgia*, decided in 1793, was protected by many Americans, who insisted states would lose authority if they could be sued in federal courts.

Amendment 12.
Election of President and Vice President (1804)

This amendment changes the procedure for electing the President and Vice President as outlined in Article II, Section 1, Clause 3.

To prevent the recurrence of the election of 1800 whereby a candidate running for Vice President (Aaron Burr) could tie a candidate running for President (Thomas Jefferson) and thus force the election into the House of Representatives, the Twelfth Amendment specifies that the electors are to cast separate ballots for each office. The votes for each office are counted and listed separately. The results are signed, sealed, and sent to the president of the senate. At a joint session of Congress, the votes are counted. The candidate who receives the most votes, providing it is a majority, is elected President. Other changes include: (1) a reduction from five to the three highest candidates receiving votes among whom the House is to choose if no candidate receives a majority of the electoral votes, and (2) provision for the Senate to choose the Vice President from the two highest candidates if neither has received a majority of the electoral votes.

The Twelfth Amendment does place one restriction on electors. It prohibits electors from voting for two candidates (President and Vice President) from their home state.

Amendment 13.
Abolition of Slavery (1865)

This amendment was the final act in ending slavery in the United States. It also prohibits the binding of a person to perform a personal service due to debt. In addition to imprisonment for crime, the Supreme Court has held that the draft is not a violation of the amendment.

This amendment is the first adopted to be divided into sections. It is also the first to contain specifically a provision granting Congress power to enforce it by appropriate legislation.

Amendment 14.
Rights of Citizens (1868)

The clauses of this amendment were intended 1) to penalize southern states that refused to grant African Americans the vote, 2) to keep former Confederate leaders from serving in government, 3) to forbid payment of the Confederacy's debt by the federal government, and 4) to insure payment of the war debts owed the federal government.

Section 1. Citizenship Defined By granting citizenship to all persons born in the United States, this amendment granted citizenship to former slaves. The amendment also guaranteed "due process of law." By the 1950s, Supreme Court rulings used the due process clause to protect civil liberties. The last part of Section 1 establishes the doctrine that all citizens are entitled to equal protection of the laws. In 1954 the Supreme Court ruled, in *Brown v. Board of Education* of Topeka, that segregation in public schools was unconstitutional because it denied equal protection.

Section 2. Representation in Congress This section reduced the number of members a state had in the House of Representatives if it denied its citizens the right to vote. This section

in choosing the President, the votes shall be taken by states, the representation from each state having one vote; a quorum for this purpose shall consist of a member or members from two-thirds of the states, and a majority of all the states shall be necessary to a choice. And if the House of Representatives shall not choose a President whenever the right of choice shall devolve upon them, before the fourth day of March next following, then the Vice-President shall act as President, as in the case of the death or other constitutional disability of the President.—The person having the greatest number of votes as Vice-President, shall be the Vice-President, if such number be a majority of the whole number of Electors appointed, and if no person have a majority, then from the two highest numbers on the list, the Senate shall choose the Vice-President; a quorum for the purpose shall consist of two-thirds of the whole number of Senators, and a majority of the whole number shall be necessary to a choice. But no person constitutionally ineligible to the office of President shall be eligible to that of Vice-President of the United States.

Amendment XIII

Section 1

Neither slavery nor involuntary servitude, except as a punishment for crime whereof the party shall have been duly convicted, shall exist within the United States, or any place subject to their jurisdiction.

Section 2

Congress shall have power to enforce this article by appropriate legislation.

Amendment XIV

Section 1

All persons born or naturalized in the United States, and subject to the jurisdiction thereof, are citizens of the United States and of the State wherein they reside. No State shall make or enforce any law which shall abridge the privileges or immunities of citizens of the United States; nor shall any State deprive any person of life, liberty, or property, without due process of law, nor deny to any person within its jurisdiction the equal protection of the laws.

Section 2

Representatives shall be apportioned among the several States according to their respective numbers, counting the whole number of persons in each State, excluding Indians not taxed. But when the right to vote at any election for the choice of electors for President and Vice-President of the United States, Representatives in Congress, the Executive and Judicial officers of a

▲ **POLITICAL PARTIES** The Constitution did not provide for the existence of political parties, which today play a major role in the election of the President and Vice President. ***What restrictions does the Twelfth Amendment place on electors?***

State, or the members of the Legislature thereof, is denied to any of the male inhabitants of such State, being twenty-one years of age, and citizens of the United States, or in any way abridged, except for participation in rebellion, or other crime, the basis of representation therein shall be reduced in the proportion which the number of such male citizens shall bear to the whole number of male citizens twenty-one years of age in such State.

Section 3

No person shall be a Senator or Representative in Congress, or elector of President and Vice-President, or hold any office, civil or military, under the United States, or under any State, who, having previously taken an oath, as a member of Congress, or as an officer of the United States, or as a member of any State legislature, or as an executive or judicial officer of any State, to support the Constitution of the United States, shall have engaged in insurrection or rebellion against the same, or given aid or comfort to the enemies thereof. But Congress may by a vote of two-thirds of each House, remove such disability.

was not implemented, however. Later civil rights laws and the 24th Amendment guaranteed the vote to African Americans.

Section 3. Penalty for Engaging in Insurrection The leaders of the Confederacy were barred from state or federal offices unless Congress agreed to revoke this ban. By the end of Reconstruction all but a few Confederate leaders were allowed to return to public life.

Section 4. Public Debt The public debt incurred by the federal government during the Civil War was valid and could not be questioned by the South. However, the debts of the Confederacy were declared to be illegal. And former slave owners could not collect compensation for the loss of their slaves.

Section 5. Enforcement Congress was empowered to pass civil rights bills to guarantee the provisions of the amendment.

Amendment 15.
The Right to Vote (1870)
Section 1. Suffrage for African Americans The 15th Amendment replaced Section 2 of the 14th Amendment in guaranteeing African Americans the right to vote, that is, the right of African Americans to vote was not to be left to the states. Yet, despite this prohibition, African Americans were denied the right to vote by many states by such means as poll taxes, literacy tests, and white primaries.

Section 2. Enforcement Congress was given the power to enforce this amendment. During the 1950s and 1960s, it passed successively stronger laws to end racial discrimination in voting rights.

Amendment 16.
Income Tax (1913)
The origins of this amendment went back to 1895, when the Supreme Court declared a federal income tax unconstitutional. To overcome this Supreme Court decision, this amendment authorized an income tax that was levied on a direct basis.

Amendment 17.
Direct Election of Senators (1913)

Section 1. Method of Election The right to elect senators was given directly to the people of each state. It replaced Article I, Section 3, Clause 1, which empowered state legislatures to elect senators. This amendment was designed not only to make the choice of senators more democratic but also to cut down on corruption and to improve state government.

Section 2. Vacancies A state must order an election to fill a senate vacancy. A state may empower its governor to appoint a person to fill a Senate seat if a vacancy occurs until an election can be held.

Section 4
The validity of the public debt of the United States incurred for payment of pensions and bounties for service, authorized by law, including debts in suppressing insurrections or rebellion, shall not be questioned. But neither the United States nor any State shall assume or pay any debt or obligation incurred in aid of insurrection or rebellion against the United States, or any claim for the loss or emancipation of any slave; but all such debts, obligations and claims shall be held illegal and void.

Section 5
The Congress shall have power to enforce, by appropriate legislation, the provisions of this article.

Amendment XV

Section 1
The right of citizens of the United States to vote shall not be denied or abridged by the United States or by any State on account of race, color, or previous condition of servitude.

Section 2
The Congress shall have power to enforce this article by appropriate legislation.

Amendment XVI
The Congress shall have power to lay and collect taxes on incomes, from whatever source derived, without apportionment among several States, and without regard to any census or enumeration.

Amendment XVII

Section 1
The Senate of the United States shall be composed of two Senators from each State, elected by the people thereof, for six years; and each Senator shall have one vote. The electors in each state shall have the qualifications requisite for electors of the most numerous branch of the state legislatures.

Section 2
When vacancies happen in the representation of any State in the Senate, the executive authority of such State shall issue writs of election to fill such vacancies: *Provided*, that the legislature of any State may empower the executive thereof to make temporary appointments until the people fill the vacancies by election as the legislature may direct.

Section 3

This amendment shall not be so construed as to affect the election or term of any Senator chosen before it becomes valid as part of the Constitution.

Amendment XVIII

Section 1

After one year from ratification of this article the manufacture, sale, or transportation of intoxicating liquors within, the importation thereof into, or the exportation thereof from the United States and all territory subject to the jurisdiction thereof for beverage purposes is hereby prohibited.

Section 2

The Congress and the several states shall have concurrent power to enforce this article by appropriate legislation.

Section 3

This article shall be inoperative unless it shall have been ratified as an amendment to the Constitution by the legislatures of the several States, as provided in the Constitution, within seven years from the date of the submission hereof to the states of the Congress.

Amendment XIX

Section 1

The right of citizens of the United States to vote shall not be denied or abridged by the United States or by any state on account of sex.

Section 2

Congress shall have power to enforce this article by appropriate legislation.

Amendment XX

Section 1

The terms of the President and Vice President shall end at noon on the 20th day of January, and the terms of the Senators and Representatives at noon on the 3rd day of January, of the years in which such terms would have ended if this article had not been ratified; and the terms of their successors shall then begin.

Section 3. Time in Effect This amendment was not to affect any senate election or temporary appointment until it was in effect.

Amendment 18.
Prohibition of Alcoholic Beverages (1919)

This amendment prohibited the production, sale, or transportation of alcoholic beverages in the United States. Prohibition proved to be difficult to enforce, especially in states with large urban populations. This amendment was later repealed by the 21st Amendment.

Amendment 19.
Women's Suffrage (1920)

This amendment, extending the vote to all qualified women in federal and state elections, was a landmark victory for the women's suffrage movement, which had worked to achieve this goal for many years. The women's movement had earlier gained full voting rights for women in four western states in the late nineteenth century.

Amendment 20.
"Lame-Duck" Amendment (1933)
Section 1. New Dates of Terms This amendment had two major purposes: (1) to shorten the time between the President's and Vice President's election and inauguration, and (2) to end "lame-duck" sessions of Congress.

When the Constitution first went into effect, transportation and communication were slow and uncertain. It often took many months after the election in November for the President and Vice President to travel to Washington, D.C., and prepare for their inauguration on March 4. This amendment ended this long wait for a new administration by fixing January 20 as inauguration day.

Section 2. Meeting Time of Congress

"Lame-duck" sessions occurred every two years, after the November congressional election. That is, the Congress that held its session in December of an election year was not the newly elected Congress but the old Congress that had been elected two years earlier. This Congress continued to serve for several more months, usually until March of the next year. Often many of its members had failed to be re-elected and were called "lame-ducks." The 20th Amendment abolished this lame-duck session, and provided that the new Congress hold its first session soon after the November election, on January 3.

Section 3. Succession of President and Vice President

This amendment provides that if the President-elect dies before taking office, the Vice President-elect becomes President. In the cases described, Congress will decide on a temporary President.

Section 4. Filling Presidential Vacancy

If a presidential candidate dies while an election is being decided in the House, Congress may pass legislation to deal with the situation. Congress has similar power if this occurs when the Senate is deciding a vice-presidential election.

Section 5. Beginning the New Dates

Sections 1 and 2 affected the Congress elected in 1934 and President Roosevelt, elected in 1936.

Section 6. Time Limit on Ratification

The period for ratification by the states was limited to seven years.

Amendment 21.
Repeal of Prohibition Amendment (1933)

This amendment nullified the 18th Amendment. It is the only amendment ever passed to overturn an earlier amendment. It remained unlawful to transport alcoholic beverages into states that forbade their use. It is the only amendment ratified by special state conventions instead of state legislatures.

Section 2

The Congress shall assemble at least once in every year, and such meeting shall begin at noon on the 3rd day of January, unless they shall by law appoint a different day.

Section 3

If, at the time fixed for the beginning of the term of the President, the President elect shall have died, the Vice President elect shall become President. If a President shall not have been chosen before the time fixed for the beginning of his term, or if the President elect shall have failed to qualify, then the Vice President elect shall act as President until a President shall have qualified; and the Congress may by law provide for the case wherein neither a President elect nor a Vice President elect shall have qualified, declaring who shall then act as President, or the manner in which one who is to act shall be selected, and such person shall act accordingly until a President or Vice President shall have qualified.

Section 4

The Congress may by law provide for the case of the death of any of the persons from whom the House of Representatives may choose a President whenever the right of choice shall have devolved upon them, and for the case of the death of any of the persons from whom the Senate may choose a Vice President whenever the right of choice shall have devolved upon them.

Section 5

Sections 1 and 2 shall take effect on the 15th day of October following the ratification of this article.

Section 6

This article shall be inoperative unless it shall have been ratified as an amendment to the Constitution by the legislatures of three-fourths of the several States within seven years from the date of its submission.

Amendment XXI

Section 1

The eighteenth article of amendment to the Constitution of the United States is hereby repealed.

Section 2

The transportation or importation into any State, Territory, or possession of the United States for delivery or use therein of intoxicating liquors, in violation of the laws thereof, is hereby prohibited.

Section 3

This article shall be inoperative unless it shall have been ratified as an amendment to the Constitution by conventions in the several States, as provided in the Constitution, within seven years from the date of the submission hereof to the States by the Congress.

Amendment XXII

Section 1

No person shall be elected to the office of the President more than twice, and no person who had held the office of President, or acted as President, for more than two years of a term to which some other person was elected President shall be elected to the office of the President more than once.

But this Article shall not apply to any person holding the office of President when this Article was proposed by the Congress, and shall not prevent any person who may be holding the office of President, or acting as President, during the term within which this Article becomes operative from holding the office of President or acting as President during the remainder of such term.

Section 2

This article shall be inoperative unless it shall have been ratified as an amendment to the Constitution by the legislatures of three-fourths of the several States within seven years from the date of its submission to the States by the Congress.

Amendment XXIII

Section 1

The District constituting the seat of Government of the United States shall appoint in such manner as the Congress may direct:

A number of electors of President and Vice President equal to the whole number of Senators and Representatives in Congress to which the District would be entitled if it were a State, but in no event more than the least populous State; they shall be in addition to those appointed by the States, but they shall be considered, for the purposes of the election of President and Vice President, to be electors appointed by a State; and they shall meet in the District and perform such duties as provided by the twelfth article of amendment.

Section 2

The Congress shall have power to enforce this article by appropriate legislation.

Amendment 22.
Limit on Presidential Terms (1951)

This amendment wrote into the Constitution a custom started by Washington, Jefferson, and Madison, whereby Presidents limited themselves to two terms in office. Although both Ulysses S. Grant and Theodore Roosevelt sought third terms, the two-term precedent was not broken until Franklin D. Roosevelt was elected to a third term in 1940 and then a fourth term in 1944. The passage of the 22nd amendment insures that no President is to be considered indispensable. It also provides that anyone who succeeds to the presidency and serves for more than two years of the term may not be elected more than one more time.

Amendment 23.
Presidential Electors for the District of Columbia (1961)

This amendment granted people living in the District of Columbia the right to vote in presidential elections. The District casts three electoral votes. The people of Washington, D.C., still are without representation in Congress.

Amendment 24.
Abolition of the Poll Tax (1964)

A "poll tax" was a fee that persons were required to pay in order to vote in a number of Southern states. This amendment ended poll taxes as a requirement to vote in any presidential or congressional election. In 1966 the Supreme Court voided poll taxes in state elections as well.

Amendment 25.
Presidential Disability and Succession (1967)

Section 1. Replacing the President The Vice President becomes President if the President dies, resigns, or is removed from office.

Section 2. Replacing the Vice President The President is to appoint a new Vice President in case of a vacancy in that office, with the approval of the Congress.

The 25th Amendment is unusually precise and explicit because it was intended to solve a serious constitutional problem. Sixteen times in American history, before passage of this amendment, the office of Vice President was vacant, but fortunately in none of these cases did the President die or resign.

This amendment was used in 1973, when Vice President Spiro Agnew resigned from office after being charged with accepting bribes. President Nixon then appointed Gerald R. Ford as Vice President in accordance with the provisions of the 25th Amendment. A year later, President Richard Nixon resigned during the Watergate scandal, and Ford became President. President Ford then had to fill the Vice Presidency, which he had left vacant upon assuming the Presidency. He named Nelson A. Rockefeller as Vice President. Thus both the presidency and vice-presidency were held by men who had not been elected to their offices.

Section 3. Replacing the President With Consent If the President informs Congress, in writing, that he or she cannot carry out the duties of the office of President, the Vice President becomes Acting President.

Amendment XXIV

Section 1
The right of citizens of the United States to vote in any primary or other election for President or Vice President, for electors for President or Vice President, or for Senator or Representative in Congress, shall not be denied or abridged by the United States or any State by reason of failure to pay any poll tax or other tax.

Section 2
The Congress shall have power to enforce this article by appropriate legislation.

Amendment XXV

Section 1
In case of the removal of the President from office or his death or resignation, the Vice President shall become President.

Section 2
Whenever there is a vacancy in the office of the Vice President, the President shall nominate a Vice President who shall take the office upon confirmation by a majority vote of both houses of Congress.

Section 3
Whenever the President transmits to the President pro tempore of the Senate and the Speaker of the House of Representatives his written declaration that he is unable to discharge the powers and duties of his office, and until he transmits to them a written declaration to the contrary, such powers and duties shall be discharged by the Vice President as Acting President.

Section 4
Whenever the Vice President and a majority of either the principal officers of the executive departments or of such other body as Congress may by law provide, transmit to the President pro tempore of the Senate and the Speaker of the House of Representatives their written declaration that the President is unable to discharge the powers and duties of his office, the Vice President shall immediately assume the power and duties of the office of Acting President.

Thereafter, when the President transmits to the President pro tempore of the Senate and the Speaker of the House of Representatives his written declaration that no inability exists, he shall resume the powers and duties of his office unless the Vice President and a majority of either the principal officers of the executive departments or of such other body as Congress may by law provide, transmit within four days to the President pro tempore of the Senate and the Speaker of the House of Representatives their written declaration that the President is unable to discharge the powers and duties of his office. Thereupon Congress shall decide the issue, assembling within forty-eight hours for that purpose if not in session. If the Congress within twenty-one days after receipt of the latter written declaration, or, if Congress is not in session, within twenty-one days after Congress is required to assemble, determines by two-thirds vote of both houses that the President is unable to discharge the powers and duties of his office, the Vice President shall continue to discharge the same as Acting President; otherwise, the President shall resume the power and duties of his office.

Amendment XXVI

Section 1
The right of citizens of the United States, who are eighteen years of age or older, to vote shall not be denied or abridged by the United States or by any State on account of age.

Section 2
The Congress shall have power to enforce this article by appropriate legislation.

Amendment XXVII
No law, varying the compensation for the services of Senators and Representatives, shall take effect, until an election of Representatives shall have intervened.

Section 4. Replacing the President Without Consent
If the President is unable to carry out the duties of the office but is unable or unwilling to so notify Congress, the Cabinet and the Vice President are to inform Congress of this fact. The Vice President then becomes Acting President. The procedure by which the President may regain the office if he or she recovers is also spelled out in this amendment.

Amendment 26.
Eighteen-Year-Old Vote (1971)
This amendment made 18-year-olds eligible to vote in all federal, state, and local elections. Until then, the minimum age had been 21 in most states.

Amendment 27.
Restraint on Congressional Salaries (1992)
Any increase in the salaries of members of Congress will take effect in the subsequent session of Congress.

Visualizing History

▲ VOTING RIGHTS The Twenty-sixth Amendment, ratified in 1971, extended the right and the responsibility of voting. *In what way did the amendment change voting eligibility?*

CHAPTER 3

★★

Launching the Republic
1789–1815

► CHEROKEE BEADED
SHOULDER BAG

Setting the Scene

Focus

With the ratification of the Constitution in 1789, a new national government set out to deal with the country's financial problems. As the United States developed politically, it faced new challenges in other ways. Between 1800 and 1815, the young republic doubled in size and found itself once more at war with Great Britain.

Concepts to Understand

★ How strong **leadership** brought stability to the new government

★ How **geographic expansion,** economic change, and conflict unified Americans and helped them form a national identity

Read to Discover . . .

★ some of the major issues faced by Presidents Washington and Adams during their terms of office.

★ the factors that caused the War of 1812.

Journal Notes

What were the personal characteristics and beliefs of the country's early leaders? Note details about them in your journal as you read the chapter.

HISTORY
Online

Chapter Overview
Visit the *American History: The Modern Era Since 1865* Web site at **me.glencoe.com** and click on *Chapter 3—Chapter Overviews* to preview chapter information.

CULTURAL	• **1789** *University of North Carolina founded*	• **1790** Columbia *is first American ship to circle globe*	• **1795** *Wooden-railed tramway built in Boston*
	1785	**1790**	**1795**
POLITICAL	• **1789** *George Washington is inaugurated*	• **1795** *Northwest Territory opens for settlement*	• **1797** *John Adams is inaugurated* • **1801** *Thomas Jefferson is inaugurated*

☆UNDER ☆MY ☆ ☆WINGS☆ ☆ ☆EVERY☆ ☆THING☆ ☆ ☆PROSPERS☆

History AND ART

A View of New Orleans
by John L. Boqueta de Woiseri, 1803

This aquatint of New Orleans was painted in celebration of the purchase of the Louisiana Territory from France in 1803. The American eagle holds what some called a prophetic banner.

◄ HOOKED RUG, 1790s

• **1804** *San Gabriel Mission is site of first California orange grove*

• **1807** *Inventor Robert Fulton perfects the steamboat* Clermont

• **1813** *Francis Scott Key writes "The Star-Spangled Banner"*

| 1800 | 1805 | 1810 |

• **1803** *Louisiana Purchase completed*
• **1807** *The* Chesapeake *is attacked*

• **1809** *Embargo Act is repealed*

• **1812** *War with Great Britain begins*
• **1815** *Treaty of Ghent ratified*

★★★

Organizing the Government

Guide to Reading

Main Idea

George Washington guided the new nation as its first president, while Alexander Hamilton brought financial stability to the new government.

Reading Strategy

Classifying Information   As you read about the new government, identify the key features of Hamilton's financial plan in a chart like the one shown here.

Hamilton's Financial Plan

Objectives

After studying this section, you should be able to

★ list the precedents set by Washington as first President.

★ discuss the key features of Hamilton's financial plan.

Key Terms

cabinet, protective tariff, revenue tariff, excise tax

▶ PRESIDENTIAL SEAL

---

*G*eorge Washington accepted the presidency reluctantly. On the day he left for his inauguration, he wrote in his diary:

❝ *About ten o'clock I bade adieu to Mt. Vernon, to private life, and to domestic felicity, and with a mind oppressed with more anxious and painful sensations than I care to express, set out for New York.* ❞

When Washington reached New York, the nation's capital, on April 23, 1789, he was rowed across the Hudson River on a barge built especially for the occasion. Most of New York's residents lined the wharves and cheered as the barge neared shore. Seven days later, Washington took the oath of office and gave the first Inaugural Address. Throughout the land there was public rejoic-ing for the man many believed to be the United States's greatest national asset.

■ Setting Precedents

Washington's background was as plantation manager and soldier. Because he lacked experience in government, he felt he was unprepared to be the chief executive. Although Washington doubted his own qualifications, many Americans regarded him with deep admiration. Such respect had its value to the new government. As a visible symbol of unity and power, Washington provided a focus for loyalty to the nation.

Washington as President

Washington proved to be a first-rate administrator. In the summer of 1789, Congress set up three executive departments: a

Department of State to take charge of foreign affairs, a Department of the Treasury to handle the nation's finances, and a Department of War to manage the military. Congress also created the position of attorney general to handle the government's legal matters. On important matters, Washington sought the advice of executive department heads, establishing what became known as the **cabinet,** a group of advisers to the President that continues to serve the same function today.

Creating a cabinet was only one of several precedents set by Washington in areas where the Constitution was silent or unclear. He determined that the Senate's approval power over presidential appointments did not extend to their removal from office. He took control of foreign affairs, limiting the Senate's role of advice and consent to ratifying or rejecting treaties only after they were made.

Although he headed the executive branch, Washington assumed leadership in legislative affairs as well. In written messages to Congress, Washington urged passage of laws he believed were in the public interest. With such encouragement, Congress almost invariably followed his lead. Later Presidents would follow suit and become what some have called "chief legislator."

The First Congress

Congress—both Senate and House of Representatives—met for the first time in April 1789. The Senate was a small, quiet, and formal body consisting of two members from each state elected by their state legislature. Senators dressed in powdered wigs, lace, and velvet. For its first five years, the Senate conducted its business in private. Not until 1794 was a gallery built for the public and the press.

▲ *THE WASHINGTON FAMILY* by Edward Savage, c. 1798 When Washington took the oath of office on April 30, 1789, the machinery of government did not exist. There were no federal laws, no federal courts, and no federal law-enforcement officials. *What was Washington's background before he became President?*

History AND ART

▲ *THE INSPECTION OF THE FIRST U.S. COINS* by John W. Dunsmore, 1914 The half disme [dime] was the first coin struck by the United States government in July 1792. *What debts did the new nation owe?*

The House was more informal. Elected by the people, the House welcomed the public and the press from the beginning. Debate was loud, and members often wore their hats inside the chamber. The House took the lead in legislative matters, especially in dealing with the nation's troubled finances.

Creation of the Judiciary

Congress also turned its attention to the judicial branch and passed the Judiciary Act of 1789, setting up the Supreme Court and lower courts. President Washington quickly named the first Supreme Court justices, deliberately choosing three from Northern and three from Southern states.

The Bill of Rights

Although a majority in both the Senate and the House had supported ratification of the Constitution, the Anti-Federalist minority insisted that Congress quickly provide the Bill of Rights promised during the ratifi-

cation campaign. In September 1789, after much debate, Congress proposed 12 amendments. Of these, 10 were ratified by the states and added to the Constitution in 1791. The Bill of Rights protected personal liberties, such as freedom of religion, freedom of speech, and trial by jury. It also protected the rights of the individual states.

■ Hamilton's Program

To pay for the country's expenses, Congress in 1789 passed a tariff, or tax on imports. Representatives from New England and the South at first wanted a **protective tariff**—a high tax on imports to protect their products from foreign competition. They finally agreed to a **revenue tariff,** a low tax on imports designed to provide income for the government rather than protection for private businesses.

Most of the money raised by the tariff was needed to pay off the national debt. The Continental Congress had borrowed money from foreign governments and individual

Americans to fight the Revolutionary War. The new government now wanted to honor these debts as well as make payments to the soldiers who had fought in the conflict.

The debate over national finances in 1790 and 1791 was dominated by 33-year-old Alexander Hamilton, the secretary of the treasury. Hamilton presented Congress with a financial plan that reflected his belief in a strong government that favored the wealthy classes and fulfilled its financial obligations.

In dealing with debts owed to foreigners and individual Americans, Hamilton called for the national government to pay its creditors in full. In doing so, he argued, the United States would tell its citizens and the world that it was a strong, independent nation whose promises were good. Congress responded by repaying foreign governments by 1796. It also enacted legislation to pay back American creditors.

Hamilton also proposed that the federal government pay the debts accumulated by individual states since the Revolution. The states had fought for the entire nation, he stated, so the cost of their help during the Revolution should be assumed by the national government. Most Southern states, however, had already paid their debts in full and did not want their taxes used to pay the debts of Northern states. A compromise, however, was finally worked out. The Southerners would back the federal government's assumption of state debts. In return, the nation's capital would eventually move to a new federal city on the Potomac River between Maryland and Virginia.

▲ MEMORIAL TANKARD

To help the government with its expenses, Hamilton favored an excise tax in addition to the tariff. An **excise tax** is a tax paid by the manufacturer of a product and passed on to those who buy the product. In 1791, Congress enacted the first excise tax—on whiskey.

A key element of Hamilton's proposals was that the federal government establish a national bank. The bank would be a place for the federal government to deposit its tax receipts, as well as a place where tax revenues and private deposits could be used for large loans to government and to businesses.

Most important, the proposed bank would issue paper money backed by gold and silver in the bank's vaults. The public could have confidence in this currency because it could be exchanged for coins on demand.

On the whole, Hamilton's plan had immediate success in restoring the credit of the United States. Most of his proposals had been enacted by Congress; however, the debate over many of them—especially the national bank—became bitter and divisive.

Section 1 ★ Assessment

Checking for Understanding

1. **Define** cabinet, protective tariff, revenue tariff, excise tax.

2. **Explain** the purpose and function of the national bank.

Critical Thinking

3. **Evaluating Performance** Given his lack of experience in government and politics, explain why Washington was able to head a new framework of government.

4. **Summarizing** Use a diagram like the one shown here to list the precedents George Washington set that are still practiced by presidents today.

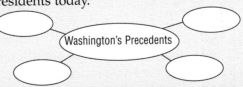

Washington's Precedents

INTERDISCIPLINARY ACTIVITY

5. **Government** Develop a chart that lists events that happen in your life and the way these events would be different without the Bill of Rights.

Planning Washington, D.C.

By using inspiration, imagination, and his skill in geometry, engineer Pierre Charles L'Enfant created the design for a national capital unlike any other. When L'Enfant, who fought in the Revolution, heard that Congress was planning a new national capital, he quickly offered his services. President Washington hired L'Enfant, and the President himself negotiated purchase from the farmers who owned the land where the capital was to rise.

▲ WASHINGTON, D.C., TODAY

▲ THE CAPITOL, 1824

Although L'Enfant's design was soon modified, his basic plan allowed a spacious, modern city to develop. He envisioned a rationally laid-out metropolis that would embody the new nation's republican ideals, with wide boulevards connecting the branches of government, national monuments, parks, and entry gates.

L'Enfant began by choosing the spots for the Capitol and President's house. The Congress building became the central point in a square grid of streets occupying the terrain between the Potomac and Anacostia rivers. The grid was slashed by avenues that radiated from the capitol hill like spokes on a wheel. These avenues provided a direct route to different parts of the city. At strategic spots, L'Enfant's unique blend of topography and geometric symmetry called for circular intersections to join three or more avenues.

Making the Math Connection

1. What geometric forms did L'Enfant use in planning the design of Washington, D.C.?

2. What are the advantages of locating a capital in a planned city? What might be some disadvantages?

3. What kinds of geometric shapes are used in the design of modern government buildings?

ACTIVITY

4. Make a map of your community. Include a compass rose, a scale, and a map legend that explains the symbols used on the map. Points of interest should include neighborhood stores, parks, community centers, or medical centers. Indicate any important geographic features.

★★★★★★★★★★★★★★★★★★★★★★★★★★★★★★★★★★★★

The Federalist Era

Main Idea

As the country developed, debate over the federal government's power led to the formation of the nation's first political parties.

Reading Strategy

Taking Notes As you read about the Federalist Era, use an outline form similar to the one shown here to list the nation's problems in the West as well as in the realm of foreign affairs.

I. Problems in the West
  A.
  B.
II. Foreign Affairs Problems
  A.
  B.

Objectives

★ Discuss the leaders and groups that opposed Hamilton's plan.
★ Describe the problems settlers faced during western expansion.
★ State how foreign affairs contributed to the growth of political parties.

Key Terms

enumerated power, implied power, nullification

▶ AMERICAN COINS, 1795–1796

*D*espite its merits, Alexander Hamilton's program encountered a good deal of opposition. Much of the opposition was led by Thomas Jefferson, Washington's secretary of state. These tensions between Hamilton and Jefferson involved a personal struggle for power in Washington's cabinet. In addition, their conflict also reflected larger differences in the vision each man had for the nation's future.

■ A Question of Power

Alexander Hamilton was a self-made man who called democracy "poison" and characterized the general public as selfish, unreasonable, and violent. He believed that a powerful central government was neces-sary to keep law and order. Also, he wanted to reduce the power of the states.

Thomas Jefferson, born to wealth and social position, believed that if people were given the opportunity, they would be decent and reasonable. A defender of liberty, Jefferson believed in a minimum of government and favored power at the local level. Because Jefferson could not block Hamilton in the executive branch, the conflict between the two men was played out in Congress, where Jefferson's ally, James Madison, represented Virginia.

When Congress debated the bill to establish a national bank, Madison attacked it on constitutional grounds. Congress had no right to set up a bank, he argued, because it was not among the **enumerated powers,** or powers mentioned specifically

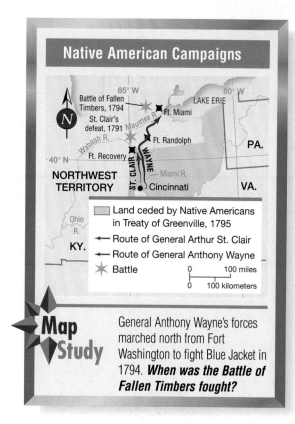

Native American Campaigns

Land ceded by Native Americans in Treaty of Greenville, 1795

← Route of General Arthur St. Clair

← Route of General Anthony Wayne

✴ Battle

Map Study

General Anthony Wayne's forces marched north from Fort Washington to fight Blue Jacket in 1794. *When was the Battle of Fallen Timbers fought?*

in the Constitution. Nor was it an **implied power,** a power that, while not directly stated in the Constitution, is suggested and does allow Congress to exercise its stated powers. If the federal government established a national bank, he feared there would be no limits to federal power.

Despite Madison's arguments, Congress passed the Bank Bill. Washington, however, hesitated to sign the bill, realizing that any action he took would set an important precedent. Instead, he asked Attorney General Edmund Randolph and Secretary of State Jefferson for written opinions on the constitutionality of a national bank. Each opposed it on the basis of Madison's argument that it was an overextension of federal power.

Washington passed these opinions on to Hamilton, who wrote a reply that convinced the President to sign the bill. In a classic statement of implied powers, Hamilton argued that because the bank's functions were among the powers given Congress, the Constitution gave Congress the right to choose any legal means to carry out those functions. In 1791 the Bank of the United States was established.

■ Problems in the West

While Americans debated the powers of the federal government, the nation faced continuing concerns about the western territories. The most immediate cause for alarm was conflict over land between western settlers and Native American nations.

Treaties and Settlement

South of the Ohio River, treaties were signed with the Cherokee in 1791 and the Chickamauga in 1794—and the Creek asked for federal government protection from settlers. The influx of settlers continued, however; and population increases enabled Kentucky and Tennessee to join the Union as states in the 1790s.

Northwest Conflicts

In November 1791, Native Americans in the Northwest Territory defeated United States regular troops and militia led by General Arthur St. Clair. The Native Americans demanded that all settlers north of the Ohio River leave the territory. Washington turned to Anthony Wayne, known for his military skills in the Revolutionary War. In August 1794, Wayne's force defeated Native Americans under Shawnee Chief Blue Jacket at the Battle of Fallen Timbers. A year later, in the Treaty of Greenville, the Native Americans agreed to surrender most of present-day Ohio.

The Whiskey Rebellion

Another western uprising occurred among farmers who opposed Hamilton's excise tax on whiskey. Because of the high cost of transportation, many farmers distilled their grain into whiskey and sold it or used it in place of scarce currency. Antitax sentiment drove farmers in western Pennsylvania to refuse to pay the tax and to attack revenue officers. Known as the Whiskey Rebellion, this revolt was put down by a strong federal government.

Developing a Multimedia Presentation

Suppose you want to present a research report on some aspect of the Colonial Era to your classmates, and you want to hold their attention. How do you do it? You might try using a variety of media.

Learning the Skill

A basic multimedia presentation involves using several types of media. Suppose you wanted to present a report on the Revolutionary War. You might present a taped reading of parts of the Declaration of Independence to explain why the colonists revolted. In presenting the war, you could display a detailed map of key battles along with photographs of important leaders. You might also show a video depicting important aspects of the conflict.

You can also develop a multimedia presentation on a computer. Multimedia, as it relates to computer technology, is the combination of text, video, audio, and animation in an interactive computer program.

In order to create multimedia productions or presentations on a computer, you need to have certain tools. These may include traditional computer graphics tools, draw programs, animation programs that make still images move, and authoring systems that tie everything together. Your computer manual will tell you which tools your computer can support.

Practicing the Skill

Ask yourself the following questions when developing a multimedia presentation:

1. Which forms of media do I want to include? Video? Sound? Animation? Photographs? Graphics? Other?

2. Which of these media forms does my computer support?

3. What kind of software programs or systems do I need? A paint program? A draw program? An animation program? A program to create interactive, or two-way, communication? An authoring system that will allow me to change images, sound, and motion?

4. Is there a "do-it-all" program I can use to develop the kind of presentation I want?

APPLYING THE SKILL

5. Using your answers to the questions above as guidelines, write a plan describing a multimedia presentation about a significant event from one of the first three chapters. Indicate what tools you will need and what steps you must take to put on a successful presentation.

The War of 1812

Guide to Reading

Main Idea
The United States and Britain went to war in 1812 over a number of issues that remained unresolved by the peace treaty they signed two years later.

Reading Strategy
Sequencing Information Create a time line like the one shown here to record key events, as you read about the War of 1812. Use the dates provided as a guide.

1812   1813   1814   1815

Objectives
After studying this section, you should be able to

★ describe the major campaigns of the War of 1812.

★ summarize the results of the War of 1812 and the Treaty of Ghent.

Key Terms
frigate, privateer

► AMERICAN MILITIA COAT, WORN DURING WAR OF 1812

On June 23, 1812, the British government ended its interference in neutral trade with Europe. British harvests had been poor, and the British desperately needed grain from the United States. The British move, however, came too late. The United States had declared war against Great Britain four days earlier.

The War in Canada

American military leaders believed that an attack on Canada would be an easy way to get back at the British. Canada was sparsely populated, and French Canadians were lukewarm toward their British rulers. The narrow strip of settlement along the St. Lawrence River and north of Lake Ontario was close to the United States and open to attack. Montreal, the strategic center of Canada, was only 30 miles (48 m) from New York State.

Lack of Preparation

The conquest of Canada stalled, however, because the military forces of the United States were unprepared. The regular army, numbering about 6,000 soldiers, was scattered throughout the frontier posts. The top commanders, veterans of the Revolution, were too old for warfare. There was no single commanding general and no overall strategy.

To compensate for the small size of the army, Madison called on the states to furnish militia. Some New England governors

▲ **WAR ON THE SEAS** On August 19, 1812, the United States frigate *Constitution* decisively defeated the British warship *Guerriere*. ***Why was it surprising that American ships were victorious in many early battles?***

refused to supply any troops because they were opposed to "Mr. Madison's War." Members of New York's militia refused to cross the Niagara River into Canada because they had enlisted only to defend their state from invasion.

Failures and Successes

The lack of preparation was evident when small but ably led Canadian forces took Detroit and two forts on Lake Michigan. An American attack across the Niagara River was turned back.

In 1813 matters improved at the western end of the war zone. Commodore Oliver Hazard Perry, having built a small fleet, won a brilliant victory over a British squadron and established American control of Lake Erie. Perry's victory made possible an invasion of Canada by way of Detroit. Kentucky volunteers under William Henry Harrison advanced into Canada and defeated a British army at the Battle of the

Thames, about 60 miles northeast of Detroit. In the East, however, attempted invasions of Canada from Sackett Harbor and Lake Champlain failed.

With the defeat of France in 1814, the British were free to strike hard at the United States. In late summer a powerful British army advanced southward from Montreal to invade New York. Blocking its way was an American army stationed at Lake Champlain. Although outnumbered nearly 3 to 1, American forces drove back the attacks, and the British retreated to Montreal. The northern border of the United States was safe.

• •

Footnotes to History

Step Lightly Sailors usually fought barefooted, a tactic attackers manipulated to their advantage. Cannons fired glass fragments and rusty nails at the enemy ship's deck. The *Constitution* used this tactic in its battle with the British ship *Guerriere*.

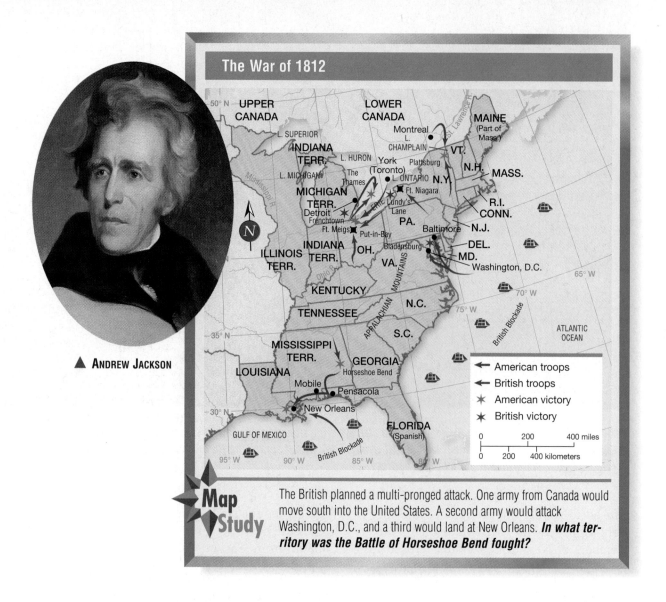

The War of 1812

UPPER CANADA
LOWER CANADA
MAINE (Part of Mass.)
L. SUPERIOR
INDIANA TERR.
Montreal
L. CHAMPLAIN
VT.
L. HURON
York (Toronto)
Platsburg
N.H.
MASS.
L. MICHIGAN
The Thames
L. ONTARIO
N.Y.
MICHIGAN TERR.
Ft. Niagara
Erie
Lundy's Lane
R.I.
CONN.
Detroit
Frenchtown
Ft. Meigs
Put-in-Bay
PA.
Baltimore
N.J.
ILLINOIS TERR.
INDIANA TERR.
OH.
Bladensburg
DEL.
MD.
Washington, D.C.
65° W
VA.
KENTUCKY
APPALACHIAN MOUNTAINS
70° W
TENNESSEE
N.C.
75° W
35° N
S.C.
ATLANTIC OCEAN
MISSISSIPPI TERR.
GEORGIA
Horseshoe Bend
British Blockade
LOUISIANA
Mobile
Pensacola
New Orleans
30° N
FLORIDA (Spanish)
GULF OF MEXICO
British Blockade
95° W
90° W
85° W
80° W

← American troops
← British troops
✴ American victory
✴ British victory

0   200   400 miles
0   200   400 kilometers

▲ Andrew Jackson

Map Study — The British planned a multi-pronged attack. One army from Canada would move south into the United States. A second army would attack Washington, D.C., and a third would land at New Orleans. *In what territory was the Battle of Horseshoe Bend fought?*

■ The British Offensive

In 1814 the British sent two other expeditions into the United States—one to attack Washington, D.C., and Baltimore, the other to take New Orleans.

Washington, D.C., and Baltimore

In August, a British army landed at Chesapeake Bay and marched into Washington, D.C. To retaliate against the American burning of York (now Toronto) in 1813, the British destroyed the Capitol and the White House. From Washington the British proceeded to Baltimore but were turned back by the forces guarding the city. During the bombardment of Fort McHenry in Baltimore harbor, Francis Scott Key wrote "The Star-Spangled Banner."

New Orleans

Unable to take Baltimore, the British army joined forces with the expedition attempting to capture New Orleans. Awaiting the British there was an American force under the command of Andrew Jackson of Tennessee. Jackson's army of regular soldiers and militia included two battalions of free African American volunteers. The British, advancing in the open, were no match for Jackson's soldiers, who were sheltered behind a barricade of cotton bales. The Battle of New Orleans was the greatest American victory of the war, but it was a useless slaughter. News traveled slowly in those days, and it was learned only after the battle that a peace treaty had been signed in Europe two weeks earlier.

■ The War at Sea

At the beginning of the war, the small navy of the United States appeared to be no match for the British fleet. During John Adams's term in office, however, half a dozen excellent **frigates**—medium-sized warships—had been built. These frigates had more firepower than any European ships of the same size and were speedy enough to escape from larger warships.

When war broke out, the frigates put to sea and within a few months had won a series of victories in battles with British vessels. On August 19, 1812, the U.S.S. *Constitution* decisively defeated the British ship *Guerriere* in the North Atlantic. British cannonballs bouncing off the solid planking of the *Constitution* provided the ship with its nickname, "Old Ironsides." Other American ships did equally well. In October the frigate *United States* destroyed the H.M.S. *Macedonian* in combat near the Canary Islands.

In addition to the frigates, the United States sent to sea more than 500 **privateers,** or armed private ships licensed to attack enemy shipping. The privateers captured more than 1,300 British vessels, some within sight of Britain.

As the war went on, however, American victories at sea grew fewer and fewer. With its superior numbers, the British fleet blockaded the entire Atlantic coast from Boston to Savannah. United States trade with other countries ceased, and the United States navy, bottled up in port, could not repeat its early successes.

■ The War's End

As the war dragged on, opposition grew, especially in New England. Public meetings were held to protest the conflict. Above all, they foresaw that the war would be damaging to their economies:

❝ *About three-fourths of our townsmen depend on the sea for the means of subsistence for themselves and their families. By the recent declaration of war more than one-half of that proportion is liable to fall into the hands of the enemy. . . . We feel therefore most strongly incumbent. . . . to seek a speedy termination of the present war.* ❞

In December 1814, delegates from New England met in secret at Hartford, Connecticut. The Hartford Convention did not insist that New England leave the Union, but it did demand seven constitutional amendments to increase the region's political power. The end of the war, however, undercut the purpose and work of the Convention.

The Treaty of Ghent ended the War of 1812, but it did not contain a word about neutral rights or impressment. Not a square mile of territory changed hands. The United States and Great Britain simply agreed to stop fighting, to restore the old boundaries, and to put other problems off for future settlement. Signed on Christmas Eve, 1814, the treaty was unanimously ratified by the Senate in February 1815.

Section 4 ★ Assessment

Checking for Understanding

1. **Define** frigate, privateer.
2. **Explain** why American troops failed to capture Canada.

Critical Thinking

3. **Analyzing Cause and Effect** Why was the Hartford Convention unsuccessful? Give reasons to explain your conclusions.

4. **Analyzing Issues** Use a chart like the one shown here to list the issues that the Treaty of Ghent left unresolved.

Unresolved Issues

INTERDISCIPLINARY ACTIVITY

5. **The Arts** Create a one-paragraph news bulletin about the Battle of New Orleans.

Using Vocabulary

For each term below, write a sentence explaining why it had either a unifying effect or a divisive effect on the new government.

protective tariff	**implied power**
revenue tariff	**nullification**
enumerated power	**judicial review**

Reviewing Facts

1. **List** the actions taken during Washington's presidency that reflected the Federalist principle of strong central government authority.

2. **Identify** the economic problems facing the nation in 1789, and tell how Hamilton's financial program addressed those problems.

3. **Outline** the causes that gradually led to the development of political parties.

4. **Explain** why *Marbury* v. *Madison* was a great victory for the Federalists and the judiciary.

5. **Describe** the military accomplishments of Andrew Jackson between 1813 and 1815.

Understanding Concepts

Leadership

1. Use a diagram like the one shown here to list some major features of President George Washington's leadership style.

Washington's Leadership Style

Geographic Expansion

2. When Jefferson doubled the size of the United States through the Louisiana Purchase, many people believed it was God's will that the United States should extend from sea to sea. Explain why Americans held this belief.

3. American expansion also occurred through the cession of Native American lands. Discuss how William Henry Harrison handled the conflict with the Native Americans.

Critical Thinking

1. **Drawing Conclusions** Washington was the first of several generals who later became President. Why do people think a good general will make a good President?

2. **Cause and Effect** What effects did the Louisiana Purchase have on the United States politically and economically?

3. **Analyzing Illustrations** Study the illustration below and answer the questions.
   a. What is happening?
   b. Does the artist express a point of view in this illustration?

▲ **IMPRESSMENT OF AMERICAN SAILORS**

History and Geography

The Barbary States

During the late 1700s and early 1800s, American ships were virtually driven from the Mediterranean Sea by the Barbary Coast States of Tripoli, Morocco, Algiers, and Tunis. These nations patrolled the Mediterranean, raiding the ships of nations that refused to pay them tribute, or protection money. The piracy ended when an American fleet of ships under Stephen Decatur, joined by warships of European nations, put an end to the practice. Study the map of the Barbary States and answer the questions.

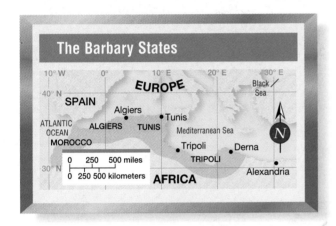

The Barbary States

1. **Location** In between approximately what lines of longitude do the Barbary States fall?

2. **Movement** In which direction would a traveler from Tunis go to reach Tripoli?

Cooperative Learning Interdisciplinary Activity: Economics

You and four class members will portray a banker and the following persons asking for a loan: (1) a New England manufacturer wanting to build a furniture factory, (2) a Western farmer wanting to buy 100 acres of land, (3) a Southern plantation owner wanting to acquire more land and enslaved persons, (4) a land speculator wanting to buy a million acres of land in the West. Each team member should por-tray a different person. After interviews are finished, decide together whether and why each of the loans should be granted or denied.

Practicing Skills

Developing a Multimedia Presentation

Working with another student, outline a plan for a multimedia presentation on the Lewis and Clark expedition. Consider the following questions to help guide you.

1. What specific examples would you use to depict the different aspects of the trip?

2. For each example, what form of media would you use?

Technology Activity

Using E-Mail Search the Internet to find out which member of the U.S. House of Representatives represents your community. Find the E-mail address of the representative. Then write and send an electronic letter to the representative suggesting action on a local or national issue you feel strongly about.

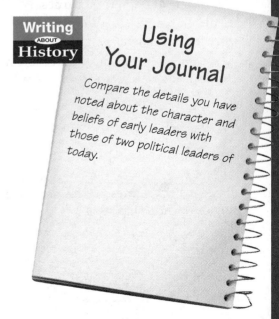

Writing ABOUT History

Using Your Journal

Compare the details you have noted about the character and beliefs of early leaders with those of two political leaders of today.

Cultural Kaleidoscope

Colonial Life

In The Kitchen

When Europeans first settled in America, they found no great treasures of gold or rare spices. From Native American peoples, however, they did gain something more vital for survival—plentiful foods and methods of cultivation. For early colonists, Indian corn, or maize, was the main food staple. Gradually, the colonists came to appreciate other native foods.

► Children performed chores to help prepare the day's meals. In many colonial households, children had no place at the table. They stood to eat and were not allowed to speak.

◄ New England farmers in the mid-1700s often grew apples, pears, peaches, and plums in orchards. They learned from Native Americans methods of grinding corn and recipes for cooking it.

▶ During the summer, maize was eaten green, but colonists usually allowed it to ripen and then ground it into cornmeal. Sometimes it was hulled and eaten whole as hominy.

▲ Cooking in the early 1700s was done over an open fire, and utensils for cooking necessarily had long handles. Metal was usually reserved for cooking tools. Utensils that today are made of metal, ceramic, or plastic were made of wood.

▶ Table, cutting board, and bowl

Standardized Test Practice

Directions: Choose the *best* answer to each of the following multiple choice questions. If you have trouble answering a question, use the process of elimination to narrow your choices. Write your answers on a separate piece of paper.

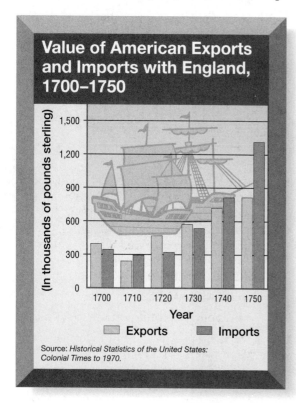

Value of American Exports and Imports with England, 1700–1750

Source: *Historical Statistics of the United States: Colonial Times to 1970.*

Use the graph to answer questions 1 and 2.

1. What was the value of imports from England in 1710?

A Almost 300 pounds sterling

B Almost 3,000 pounds sterling

C Almost 300,000 pounds sterling

D Almost 3,000,000 pounds sterling

Test-Taking Tip: Look at the information along the *bottom* and *sides* of the bar graph to fully understand what it represents. The bottom tells you the *years* as well as which color shows *exports* and which shows *imports*. Along the left side, it explains that the numbers represent *thousands of pounds sterling*. So all you need to do is add three zeroes to the numbers on the vertical axis.

2. In which year did the greatest difference between exports and imports occur?

F 1700

G 1720

H 1740

J 1750

Test-Taking Tip: Think about the words *greatest difference*. Does this mean that the two bars will be closest together or farthest apart?

3. Why did certain revolutionary figures such as John Hancock and Samuel Adams oppose the ratification of the Constitution?

A They thought that nine states were not enough to make a new country.

B They did not favor a Bill of Rights.

C They wanted to reunite with Great Britain.

D They feared a strong central government.

Test-Taking Tip: Eliminate answers that do not make sense. The American Revolution was based on the concept that individuals had basic rights. Therefore, it would be illogical for *revolutionaries* such as Hancock and Adams to oppose a Bill of Rights (answer B). It would also be illogical for revolutionaries to want to reunite with Great Britain (answer C).

4. **Why did the writers of the Constitution allow federal judges to be appointed for life?**

   F To ensure that Congress does not have the power to impeach them

   G To protect judges from being pressured by popular opinion

   H To reduce the expense of appointing new judges

   J To make sure that judges have time to rule on all of the cases they are asked to hear

   Test-Taking Tip: This question asks you to consider the *reason* the framers of the Constitution made this provision. If you are not sure, consider the opposite: What might happen if federal judges had to campaign for election to their positions every few years?

5. **During the American Revolution, the Loyalists were people who were loyal to**

   A George Washington.

   B King George III.

   C Marquis de Lafayette.

   D Queen Elizabeth I.

   Test-Taking Tip: This question requires that you remember who led Great Britain during the American Revolution. Use the process of elimination if you are unsure. Since George Washington was American, you can easily eliminate answer A.

6. **The "Great Compromise" was primarily a compromise between**

   F large states and small states.

   G Republicans and Democrats.

   H slave states and non-slave states.

   J Northern states and Southern states.

   Test-Taking Tip: Always read the question and all the answer choices carefully. Make sure you don't confuse the "Great Compromise" with the Missouri Compromise or the Compromise of 1850, which were both about slavery.

7. **The American colonists complained about having to pay British taxes while not being allowed to vote for members of the British Parliament. Which of the following quotations best expresses this complaint?**

   A "Don't tread on me."

   B "No taxation without representation."

   C "Hold your fire until you see the whites of their eyes."

   D "We must all hang together now, or assuredly we shall hang separately."

   Test-Taking Tip: The important words in this question are *taxes* and *vote*. Which quotation *best* matches this information?

UNIT TWO
FORGING A NATION
1815–1877

▲ BRASS CANDLESTICK, 1850s

 History AND ART

The Banjo Lesson
by Henry Tanner, 1893

American artist Henry Ossawa Tanner produced a number of realistic studies of American life. After he moved to Europe in the early 1900s, he found another source of inspiration—the Bible.

Why It's Important

The slavery issue dominated American life during much of the nineteenth century. During this period the country went to war, in part, over the issue of slavery. In the years following the Civil War, the nation began the long struggle to guarantee civil rights for African Americans.

To learn more about the growth of the nation in the nineteenth century, view the *Historic America: Electronic Field Trips* Side 1, Chapter 8; Side 1, Chapter 9; Side 1, Chapter 10; Side 2, Chapter 4; Side 2, Chapter 6 video lessons:

- *Gettysburg*
- *Frederick Douglass's Home*
- *The Alamo*
- *The Lowell Factories*
- *Seneca Falls*

▲ UNION SOLDIER

Themes

- American Democracy
- Civil Rights and Liberties
- Economic Development
- Geography and Environment
- Conflict and Cooperation

Key Events

- Missouri Compromise
- Seneca Falls Convention
- War with Mexico
- Compromise of 1850
- War Between the States
- Surrender of General Lee
- Reconstruction
- Compromise of 1877

PRIMARY SOURCES Library

See pages 858–859 for the primary source readings to accompany Unit 2.

◄ CONFEDERATE BUGLE

Portfolio Project

Use the library to locate sources about one of the important individuals, events, or developments discussed in this unit. Organize information about these sources to create an efficient reference guide for someone interested in writing an in-depth study of the subject.

Global Perspectives

The World

	1820		1840
Asia and Oceania	**1819** *Thomas Raffles obtains Singapore for Britain*		**1839** *Britain and China battle in First Opium War*
Europe	**1815** *Napoleon defeated at Waterloo*		◄**1837** *Victoria becomes Queen of Great Britain*
Africa		**1835** *Boer farmers start the "Great Trek"*	**1847** *Liberia becomes an independent republic*
South America	**1821** *Peru becomes independent of Spain*	**1824** *Simón Bolívar frees Peru and Bolivia from Spanish rule*	
North and Central America	**1823** *Monroe Doctrine proclaimed*	**1826** *Pan-Americanism gets under way at Panama*	**1840** *Act of Union unites Upper and Lower Canada*

The United States

	1820		1840
Pacific and Northwest	**1821** *California becomes a Mexican province*	**1830** *Fur traders open the Oregon Trail*	
Southeast	**1819** *Florida is purchased from Spain*	**1831** *Cyrus McCormick invents the reaper*	
Midwest			**1838** *Cherokee endure the "Trail of Tears"*
Southwest		◄**1836** *Battle of the Alamo fought*	**1845** *Texas annexed*
Atlantic Northeast	**1825** *Erie Canal completed*		**1839** *Charles Goodyear makes first vulcanized rubber*

Linking Across TIME

African Americans have made major contributions to our country's music. Gospel, an exuberant and joyous celebration of faith through music, grew out of the religious services held by enslaved African Americans. Blues, which grew out of work songs and chants, had a strong impact on the pioneers of rock 'n roll. Jazz, which some people consider the only new art form to be developed in the twentieth century, was influenced by both gospel and the blues.

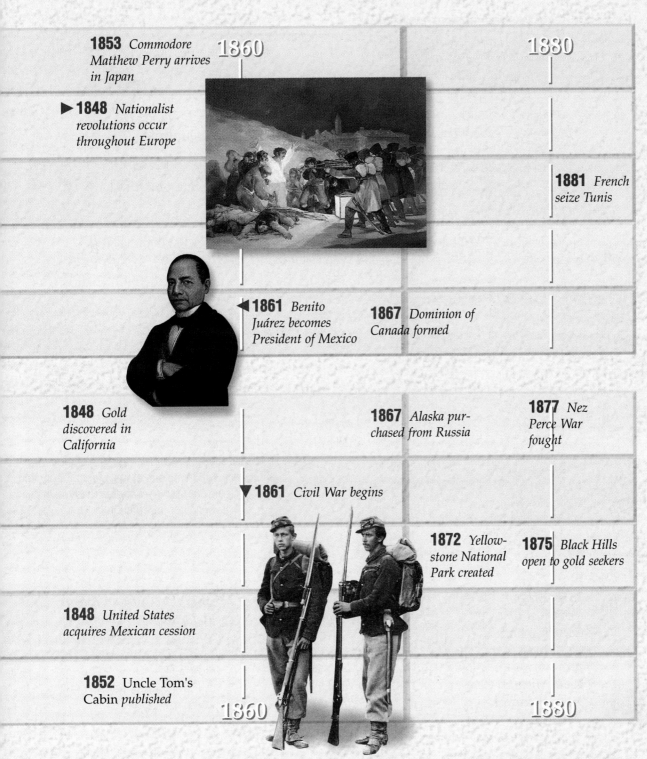

1853 *Commodore Matthew Perry arrives in Japan*

1860

1880

▶**1848** *Nationalist revolutions occur throughout Europe*

1881 *French seize Tunis*

◀**1861** *Benito Juárez becomes President of Mexico*

1867 *Dominion of Canada formed*

1848 *Gold discovered in California*

1867 *Alaska purchased from Russia*

1877 *Nez Perce War fought*

▼ **1861** *Civil War begins*

1872 *Yellowstone National Park created*

1875 *Black Hills open to gold seekers*

1848 *United States acquires Mexican cession*

1852 *Uncle Tom's Cabin published*

1860

1880

CHAPTER 4

★★★

Toward a Democracy
1815–1850

▶ CORNHUSK DOLL

Setting the Scene

Focus

The years after the War of 1812 until 1850 were a time of national optimism and the growth of democracy and the economy. Confident of their future, Americans experimented with social reform movements aimed at bettering society. At the same time, a strong sectional rivalry was developing. Each region wanted to further its own economic and political interests.

Concepts to Understand

★ What political, economic, and social factors affected national and regional feelings and **American democracy**

★ How **economic change** brought about the Industrial Revolution and changes in the workplace

Read to Discover . . .

★ how each section viewed the major issues faced by the nation.

★ in what ways Andrew Jackson was a symbol of his times.

★ how the spirit of reform affected various groups in American society.

Journal Notes

How did different regions respond to the idea of protective tariffs? Note details about how they responded in your journal as you read the chapter.

HISTORY Online

Chapter Overview
Visit the *American History: The Modern Era Since 1865* Web site at **me.glencoe.com** and click on **Chapter 4—Chapter Overviews** to preview chapter information.

CULTURAL	• **1816** *African Methodist Episcopal Church organized*	• **1821** *Emma Willard founds Troy Female Seminary*	• **1827** *First African American newspaper,* Freedom's Journal, *begins publication*
	1815	**1821**	**1827**
POLITICAL	• **1820** *Missouri Compromise reached*	• **1823** *Monroe Doctrine proclaimed*	• **1828** *Andrew Jackson elected President*

History AND ART

Morning Bell
by Winslow Homer, 1866

After the Civil War, Winslow Homer often painted scenes of everyday life. Homer's painting *Morning Bell* depicts young women going to work in a New England textile mill.

- **1833** *National Temperance movement founded*

- **1844** *First telegraph message sent*

- **1846** *Smithsonian Institution founded*

1833

1839

1845

- **1836** *Bank of the United States charter expires*

- **1840** *Whigs nominate Harrison*

- **1848** *First presidential election to be held on the same day in all states*

★★★

The Era of Good Feelings

Guide to Reading

Main Idea

After the War of 1812, a powerful spirit of nationalism dominated American life.

Reading Strategy

Organizing Information As you read about the "Era of Good Feelings," use a diagram such as the one shown here to list the events that demonstrated a spirit of nationalism.

Objectives

After studying this section, you should be able to

★ list events that showed a spirit of nationalism.

★ explain how the Supreme Court increased the national government's power.

Key Terms

nationalism, internal improvement, turnpike, toll, ultimatum

130
TO
WHEELING
to
Frostburgh
10

NATIONAL ROAD MILE MARKER ▶

Nationalism is a feeling of intense loyalty and devotion to one's country. It is a spirit that unifies into one nation diverse groups that share a geographic area. Nationalism can be demonstrated by people's actions, illustrated by such symbols as a flag, and expressed in a nation's art, literature, and music. In the United States, the spirit of nationalism increased significantly after the War of 1812. In 1816, James Monroe, a Virginia Republican, was elected President over New York Federalist Rufus King.

On a national goodwill tour, the new President promoted a spirit of unity everywhere he went. His warm reception by cheering crowds in Boston caused a local Federalist newspaper to proclaim that an "Era of Good Feelings" had begun. By 1820 the Federalists, discredited by their anti-war position during the War of 1812, had vanished from national politics, and President Monroe was reelected without opposition.

■ Nationalist Legislation

The new American nationalism was revealed in legislation as well as in politics. The War of 1812 had clearly demonstrated that Jefferson's ideal of a central government with strictly limited functions could not meet the needs of a nation in crisis. After the war, a Republican-controlled Congress passed a series of laws that seemed as though they had been written by Federalists.

The American System

Henry Clay of Kentucky and John C. Calhoun of South Carolina proposed an ambitious program called the "American System" based on a protective tariff and **internal improvements**—roads, canals, and other transportation needs. Clay and Calhoun also wanted to reinstate the national bank. Congress had refused to renew the charter of the First Bank in 1811 with disastrous results.

The notes of the Bank had been accepted everywhere as a national currency. State bank notes were generally accepted only in the locality where they were issued. Without a national bank, the federal government also had a difficult time borrowing money during the War of 1812. Clay and Calhoun argued that a national bank would create a national currency and encourage economic growth. They hoped that this nationalistic program would bring prosperity to all sections of the country and, to the nation, economic independence from the rest of the world.

A Second Bank

In 1816 Congress passed a bill to establish a second Bank of the United States that could issue currency and regulate state banks. Congress also responded with the Tariff of 1816. Unlike earlier revenue tariffs, which had provided income for the federal government, this tariff protected American manufacturers from foreign competition by placing high taxes on imports.

■ Supreme Court Nationalism

Nationalism also was demonstrated in a series of Supreme Court decisions by Chief Justice John Marshall. Between 1819 and 1824, Marshall ruled in three important Court cases that strengthened the power of the federal government over the states. Although opposed by defenders of states' rights, Marshall's decisions made the Constitution flexible enough to meet the nation's changing needs.

Implied Powers

In the landmark case *McCulloch* v. *Maryland* (1819), Marshall stated that the federal government possessed implied powers— that is, powers not specifically stated in the Constitution. In this instance, the Court ruled that Congress had the power to create the second Bank of the United States and that an attempt by Maryland to tax the bank

was unconstitutional. *McCulloch* v. *Maryland* established the superiority of federal power over state power in case of conflict.

Contract and Property Rights

In *Dartmouth College* v. *Woodward* (1819), the Court set out to protect contracts and property rights from state power. It was responding to efforts by New Hampshire to change the charter of Dartmouth College and make the private school a state institution. In the decision, Marshall noted that "the state legislatures were forbidden 'to pass any law impairing the obligation of contracts,' that is, of contracts respecting property." A college charter is a contract, he said, and a state had no right to interfere. Thus, the attempt to seize this private college was unconstitutional.

Interstate Commerce

In *Gibbons* v. *Ogden* (1824), the Court overturned a New York law that hindered out-of-state commercial steamboats from doing business in New York waters. Marshall

★★★ AMERICA'S FLAGS ★★★

The Flag of 1818 By 1818 the number of the states in the Union had reached 20. In April, President Monroe signed into law a bill that determined the basic design of the flag. Each newly admitted state would add a star to the field of blue—on the Fourth of July following the state's year of entry. The 13 stripes symbolizing the original states remained unchanged.

The Great Star Flag Congress did not stipulate how the stars should be arranged, so flagmakers used various designs. One  design had four rows of five stars each. The *Great Star Flag* placed the stars in the form of a five-pointed star.

★★★★★★★★★★★★★★★★★★★★★★★★

declared that the New York legislature had overstepped its power, because the Constitution gave the federal government control over interstate commerce. By establishing national power over interstate commerce, Marshall's opinion opened the way for easy trade between the states and national economic growth. It also provided the federal government with the constitutional basis for many of the broad and sweeping powers it exercises today.

■ Tying the Nation Together

After the War of 1812, the United States began to develop transportation systems. By the mid-1800s, roads, canals, steamboats, and railroads had created a truly national economy. People could now buy goods pro-duced in distant places. Information joined the flow of products as mail became deliverable throughout the nation. With the mail came newspapers, which brought national issues to the attention of the most remote rural communities.

Roads

In general, states or private businesses undertook improvements in overland transportation. State-chartered private companies constructed hundreds of miles of **turnpikes,** roads that were barricaded at intervals by poles that stopped travelers until they paid a **toll,** or fee. In the West, highways usually were constructed by the states themselves, at times with federal aid. From the sale of western lands, the federal government funded the National Road,

The Marshall Court and the National Interest

Case and Year	Issue and Decision
Marbury v. *Madison* (1803)	Declared an act of Congress unconstitutional. Court given power of judicial review and power to declare congressional and state legislation unconstitutional.
Fletcher v. *Peck* (Yazoo land fraud case, 1810)	Declared sanctity of contracts. Gave Supreme Court right to overturn state laws that ran counter to specific provisions of Constitution.
Martin v. *Hunter's Lessee* (1816)	Gave Supreme Court right to reverse decisions of state courts.
Trustees of Dartmouth College v. *Woodward* (1819)	Reaffirmed sanctity of contracts. Protected banks and corporations with state charters from meddling by state legislators.
Sturges v. *Crowninshield* (1819)	Tested constitutionality of state bankruptcy laws. Court determined that in absence of federal regulation, states were free to legislate.
McCulloch v. *Maryland* (1819)	Challenged constitutionality of Bank of the United States. Court said "implied powers" enabled Congress to enact any legislation within letter and spirit of Constitution.
Cohens v. *Virginia* (1821)	Tested constitutionality of Judiciary Act of 1789. Court said states gave up some sovereignty in ratifying Constitution, so state courts must accept federal jurisdiction.
Gibbons v. *Ogden* (1824)	Invalidated a state monopoly. Court gave Congress right to regulate interstate commerce, a decision of great importance for national development.

Source: *The Guide to American Law*, vol. 7 (1984).

Chart Study Chief Justice John Marshall dominated the Supreme Court until his death in 1835. The Marshall Court handed down a series of decisions that increased federal power over state governments. *What was significant about the* **McCulloch** *decision?*

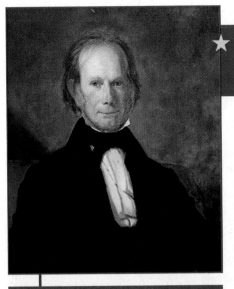

AMERICAN PORTRAITS

Henry Clay
1777–1852

Virginia-born and raised, Henry Clay moved to Kentucky, a state that kept him in Congress—and in the forefront of national politics—for nearly 50 years.

A fierce political rivalry soon developed between Clay and another Westerner, Andrew Jackson of Tennessee. The two first clashed in 1819 when Clay blasted Jackson's Florida invasion. The election of 1824 made them bitter enemies. Ignoring instructions from Kentucky to back Jackson for President, Clay supported John Quincy Adams, who appointed Clay secretary of state. Jackson's revenge came when he defeated Clay in the presidential election of 1832. Clay sought the presidency three more times before retiring. In 1849, however, he returned to Congress and put together a compromise between North and South that helped delay the Civil War.

which began in Cumberland, Maryland, and eventually reached Vandalia, Illinois. Great Conestoga wagons drawn by oxen or teams of 4, 6, or 8 horses moved westward along this route.

By 1840, roads crisscrossed the country, but they did not provide satisfactory transportation. David Stevenson described a journey by stagecoach along a typical route of the time in his book *Sketch of the Civil Engineering of North America*, published in 1838:

> *Sometimes our way lay for miles through extensive marshes, which we crossed by corduroy roads [roads having logs laid sideways across the roadbed]. . . . At others the coach stuck fast in mud, from which it could be extricated only by the combined efforts of the coachman and passengers; and at one place we traveled. . . . through a forest flooded with water, which stood to a height of several feet. . . . The distance of the route from Pittsburgh to Erie is 128 miles, which was accomplished* in forty-six hours . . . although the conveyance by which I traveled carried the mail, and stopped only for breakfast, dinner, and tea, but there was considerable delay by the coach being once upset and several times 'mired.'

Steamboats

Bulky goods, such as farm crops or manufactured goods, could not be quickly or profitably moved long distances by land. Far more important to commerce were America's inland waterways.

In 1807, Robert Fulton's steamboat, the *Clermont*, made its first voyages on the Hudson River from New York City to Albany. By demonstrating the usefulness of two-way river travel, Fulton launched the steamboat era. By 1850, nearly 800 steamboats regularly traveled the Mississippi River and its tributaries. Steamboats proved their ability to carry passengers and goods quickly and efficiently, but risks were high. The average life of a river steamboat was three to six years—not surprising considering the dangers presented by ice, bursting boilers, collisions, fires, and sandbars.

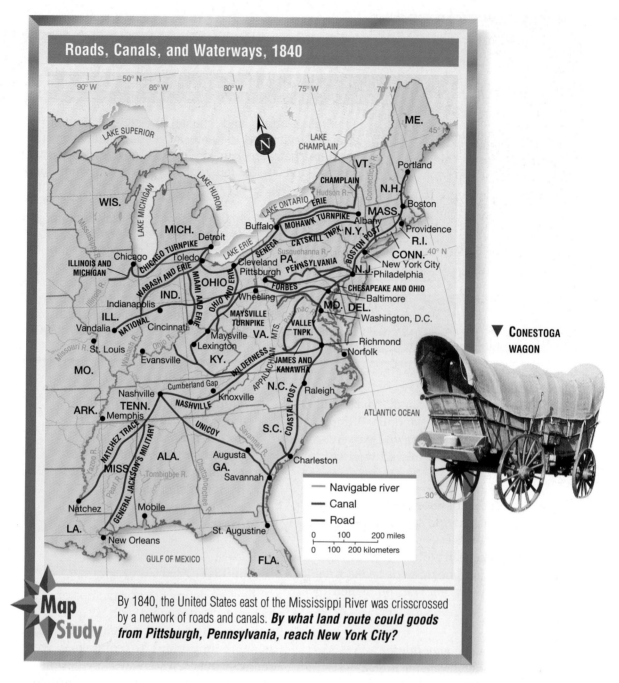

Roads, Canals, and Waterways, 1840

Navigable river
Canal
Road

0 100 200 miles
0 100 200 kilometers

▼ CONESTOGA WAGON

Map Study By 1840, the United States east of the Mississippi River was crisscrossed by a network of roads and canals. *By what land route could goods from Pittsburgh, Pennsylvania, reach New York City?*

Canals

For moving heavy goods, the thousands of miles of canals built during the first part of the 1800s were far more efficient than even the best roads. Most canals bypassed rapids and falls in rivers or linked natural waterways. The Erie Canal, completed in 1825, ran from Albany on the Hudson River to Buffalo on Lake Erie. The canal lowered the cost of moving goods and reduced travel time from 20 days to 6. It quickly made New York City the great port in America and brought prosperity to rural areas

upstate. The success of the Erie Canal encouraged other states, such as Pennsylvania, Ohio, and Indiana, to invest in canals.

Railroads

Railroads proved the most practical of all internal improvements. They were faster than roads and waterways and were passable in almost all weather. Nevertheless, railroads were slow to take hold, many because of opposition from state governments, which had heavy investments in roads and canals. Not until the second half of the 1800s would railroads dominate the nation's transportation systems.

■ Foreign Affairs

Domestic growth was accompanied by the search for peace abroad. Although the Treaty of Ghent had ended the War of 1812, bitter feelings remained between the United States and the two European powers who were allies in the war: Great Britain and Spain.

Easing of Tensions

Because of their strong trading ties, the United States and Great Britain recognized they had nothing to gain by continuing hostilities. Between 1815 and 1817, they worked out several of their disputes peacefully. The Rush-Bagot Agreement of 1817 removed all warships from the Great Lakes except for a few small vessels to control smuggling. The Convention of 1818 settled the United States-Canadian boundary at the forty-ninth parallel from the Lake of the Woods in Minnesota to the Rocky Mountains. Beyond the Rockies, the treaty provided "joint occupation" of the disputed Oregon Territory for 10 years.

The United States also reached agreement with Spain over Spanish Florida. American forces led by Andrew Jackson, in pursuit of Seminoles and Creeks who were battling Georgia settlers, had seized two Spanish settlements in Florida. President Monroe, at the urging of Secretary of State John Quincy Adams, issued an **ultimatum,** a demand that would have serious consequences if ignored, likely a resort to force. The Spanish were told either to govern Florida effectively or surrender it to the United States. Occupied with problems in its Latin American empire, Spain ceded Florida to the United States in the Adams-Onís Treaty of 1819. The treaty also set the boundary between the Louisiana Purchase lands and the Texas

▲ *On the River* by George Catlin Steamboats and canal boats speeded the movement of people and the transportation of goods. *How did New York City benefit from the Erie Canal?*

▲ THE MONROE DOCTRINE President Monroe consulted his cabinet before issuing the Monroe Doctrine. *What warning did the Doctrine contain?*

territory. The boundary was set at the western bank of the Sabine, Red, and Arkansas rivers to the Continental Divide. From there, the line followed the forty-second parallel west to the Pacific Ocean.

The Monroe Doctrine

In 1800, the United States was the only independent country in the Americas. European powers, such as Great Britain, France, the Netherlands, Portugal, and particularly Spain, ruled the rest of the hemisphere. Over the next two decades, however, many Latin American colonies revolted against Spain and declared their independence.

In the early 1820s, Spain gave signs of trying to regain its colonial empire. In 1823, Great Britain suggested to the United States that the two nations oppose intervention in Latin America by any power and that neither nation would acquire any part of Latin America for itself.

At that time, the Monroe administration was wrestling with another foreign-policy concern. Russia already claimed Alaska and was making aggressive moves on the Pacific coast. Reflecting the strong nationalism of the period, Monroe and Adams decided that the United States would act on its own, without consulting the British. In an address to Congress late in 1823, President Monroe set forth the policy that is now called the Monroe Doctrine. He declared that the Americas "are henceforth not to be considered as subjects for future colonization by any European powers" and that "we should consider any attempt on their part to extend their system to any portion of this hemisphere as dangerous to our peace and safety."

Throughout the 1800s, the European powers made few interventions in the Americas; however, it was the British navy, not the Monroe Doctrine, that made them back down. The significance of the Monroe Doctrine is in later events. Its bold warnings gained meaning only when the United States became a major sea power—a development that took nearly a century. Nor did the Monroe Doctrine restrict the nationalism, expansion, and intervention of the United States itself over the next 150 years.

Section 1 ★ Assessment

Checking for Understanding

1. **Define** nationalism, internal improvement, turnpike, toll, ultimatum.

2. **Describe** the chain of events that formed the background to the Monroe Doctrine.

Critical Thinking Activity

3. **Linking Past and Present** Roads, canals, and railroads were early transportation links between East and West. What major links tie different sections of the country together today?

4. **Analyzing Issues** Re-create the chart shown here, and explain how each decision increased the national government's power at the expense of state governments.

McCulloch v. Maryland	
Dartmouth College v. Woodward	
Gibbons v. Ogden	

INTERDISCIPLINARY ACTIVITY

5. **Geography** Trace a route from Savannah Georgia, to Indianapolis, Indiana, using the roads, canals, and waterways shown on the map on page 144. List the cities you will pass through on your journey.

★★★

Growth of Sectionalism

Guide to Reading

Main Idea

At the same time nationalism was spreading throughout the United States, a strong sectional rivalry also was beginning to develop.

Reading Strategy

Taking Notes As you read about the growth of sectionalism, use an outline like the one shown here to list the major characteristics of life in the North and in the South.

I. The North
  A.
  B.

II. The South
  A.
  B.

Objectives

After studying this section, you should be able to

★ discuss the impact of the Industrial Revolution on American life.

★ explain how industrialization contributed to wider acceptance of slavery in the South.

★ identify four areas of sectional conflict.

Key Terms

textile, closed shop, cotton gin, favorite son

COTTON GIN ▶

The late 1700s and early 1800s brought developments that would change life in all regions of the United States. With newly developed machines, goods could be produced more quickly and efficiently than ever before. The growth of industry—mainly in the North—brought new challenges that tested the resolve of the young nation.

■ The North

The Industrial Revolution spread from Great Britain to the United States during the late 1700s. In 1790, English-born businessman Samuel Slater opened America's first **textile**, or woven fabric, mill in Pawtucket, Rhode Island. More than 20 years later, the trade embargo against England in the War of 1812 gave a significant boost to the development of industry in northern areas of the United States.

Growth of Industry

New England became an early center of industry for a variety of reasons. The region boasted many swift-flowing streams, an abundant source of waterpower. New England's shippers were seeking additional opportunities in which to invest their profits. After the 1820s, European immigration to the region provided a large labor force. By 1840, 800 cotton mills and 500 woolen mills in New England employed nearly 50,000 workers. Shipping continued to thrive, and many small factories in the region were turning out such products as shoes, clocks, carriages, and paper.

Manufacturing also took hold in the Middle Atlantic states—Pennsylvania, New Jersey, and New York. Although textile mills thrived in this region, the area was better known for its coal and iron ore resources. Improved roads and the expansion of the

Visualizing **(H)istory**

▲ **RISE OF AMERICAN FACTORIES** As the Industrial Revolution spread, factories sprang up in many cities and towns in New England. *What types of products did these new factories produce?*

nation's railway systems opened markets in other regions, and increased the demand for machinery.

Social Changes

In the early 1800s, the North was still a region where families lived and worked together at farming, crafts, and home-based businesses. The Industrial Revolution, however, was gradually transforming the region to one in which people lived mostly in cities and earned their livings by working in factories. Industrialization created two new classes of people—the industrial capitalists who built and owned the factories and the industrial laborers who worked in them.

The Labor Movement

As machines replaced hand tools, jobs for skilled craftsworkers became scarcer, and many such workers were reduced to performing unskilled labor. In an effort to improve working conditions, workers organized into labor unions. In the United States, the first labor unions were formed by skilled craftspeople, such as carpenters, shoemakers, and printers. These unions, found in all major Northeastern cities, demanded higher wages, shorter hours, and the **closed shop**—a place of employment open only to union members.

Unskilled factory workers were less successful in forming unions. Strikes could be easily broken by employers who simply hired recent European immigrants to fill vacant factory positions. Incentive to organize was low, too, among textile workers, many of whom were young women from poor farms. By the early 1820s, however, some women had organized unions and were carrying out strikes to protest working conditions.

During the 1830s, an economic depression and widespread unemployment caused the collapse of many unions. In spite of setbacks, organized labor did secure some permanent gains during this period.

For example, several states limited the workday to 10 hours and placed restrictions on child labor.

■ The South

As textile mills produced cheaper goods for a worldwide market, the demand increased for raw cotton from the Southern states. To produce more cotton, Southern planters turned to the cotton gin, an invention developed in 1793 by a Northerner named Eli Whitney. The **cotton gin,** a machine that efficiently and cheaply cleaned the seeds from cotton fibers, made cotton increasingly profitable throughout the South.

Plantation Slavery

The invention of the cotton gin also strengthened the hold of slavery on the region. The planting, hoeing, picking, and ginning of cotton all required manual labor, and enslaved persons provided a fairly cheap source. Because the growing and harvesting of cotton continued throughout much of the year in the Deep South, there were no long periods of idleness. Thus, slave labor suddenly became profitable for cotton growers.

Cotton Is King

"Cotton is king" was a common Southern phrase that accurately reflected the importance of cotton to the South's economy. Because the South had few factories, cotton continued to be sent out of the region for manufacture. As the demand for raw cotton increased, and as constant replanting depleted soil fertility, the "cotton kingdom" moved westward into fertile areas of Mississippi, Alabama, and Arkansas.

▲ Eli whitney

Visualizing History

▲ THE PLANTATION SYSTEM The invention of the cotton gin by Eli Whitney helped make cotton the most important Southern agricultural product. Bountiful cotton harvests, particularly in the newer growing regions of Alabama and Mississippi, were the basis of the South's increasing prosperity. The cultivation of cotton, however, required intensive hand labor. *What tasks in cotton production did enslaved people perform?*

Class Structure

The profound influence of cotton on the South was reflected in the class structure of Southern society. At the top were a few wealthy planters, who enslaved 50 to 200 or more people and cultivated the best land. Below these rich owners was a larger class of less wealthy planters who owned medium-sized farms and usually had fewer than 20 enslaved persons. Then there were the owners of small farms, who made up a large majority of Southern farmers and owned either a few enslaved persons or none at all. Near the bottom of the social scale was a class of impoverished white people, who were usually illiterate and obtained food by hunting or farming the exhausted soils for which cotton planters had no use. Seen as lowest on this cotton-created scale were the African Americans. All but a few were enslaved, and nearly all performed heavy labor or menial tasks.

■ The West

Hostilities between settlers and Native Americans had limited settlement of the West until the end of the War of 1812. That war resulted in the breakup of Tecumseh's league and put an end to British support of the northern nations. Following the defeat of the Sauk (SAWK) leader, Chief Black Hawk, in 1832, the Native Americans were driven west of the Mississippi.

Perhaps the greatest lure of the Northwest was vast, fertile, and inexpensive land. Farmers poured in from northern and southern parts of the United States and from Europe. To meet farmers' needs for markets, merchandise, and transportation, merchants, storekeepers, and other suppliers gathered in towns, such as Cincinnati and Louisville, where cargo was transferred.

■ Sectional Rivalry

Because the regions were so different in geography, it is not surprising that Americans in these regions had different concerns and reacted differently to important issues.

Public Lands

One of the issues tackled by the country was public land policy. Western frontier farmers favored cheap land, rapid settlement, and the right of people to settle on whatever unoccupied acres they could find.

▶ IRON LADLES

Visualizing History

▲ THE TARIFF QUESTION Generally, Northeastern manufacturers and laborers favored protective tariffs while Southerners did not. *Why did the people of the Northwest support tariffs?*

Eastern manufacturers, on the other hand, opposed such policies for fear the West would draw off their labor supply. Eastern farmers believed that cheap Western lands would result in unfair competition.

Southerners were divided on this issue. Plantation owners wanted public lands opened for sale, but opposed people taking whatever unoccupied land they could find because these people might claim the best lands.

Protective Tariffs

Another controversial issue was protective tariffs. Northeastern manufacturers and laborers wanted protective tariffs to ensure that their factories could compete successfully with foreign manufacturers. Southerners, whose economy rested mainly on agriculture, opposed high tariffs because they would have to pay more for imported manufactured goods. Surprisingly, the Northwest, a farming region, was the section most completely in favor of protection. This was because many Northwesterners thought that high tariffs would provide revenue for new roads and canals and would increase urban markets for farm products.

Slavery

Among all the issues, the spread of slavery into Western territories raised feverish emotion. Because cotton production demanded the movement of plantations onto new lands and the plantation system depended on slave labor, Southerners insisted that they be allowed to take their enslaved workers with them anywhere except the free states. In the North and West, which were not economically dependent on slave labor, there was an increasing conviction that slavery was morally wrong. While allowing Southern states to maintain slavery where it already existed, Northerners did not want it extended to the territories. To Southerners, this meant that no new slave states could be formed, and the political power of the South would decrease.

■ The Missouri Compromise

The question of slavery's expansion became politically controversial in 1819 when Missouri applied for admission to the Union as a slave state. As soon as the bill reached the floor of Congress, Representative James Tallmadge of New York presented an amendment that stated, in part:

> ❝ ... That the further introduction of slavery or involuntary servitude be prohibited ... and that all children of slaves, born within [Missouri] shall be free. ... ❞

The Tallmadge Amendment would gradually end slavery in an area where it already existed. A new twist to the debate was introduced when Maine petitioned to be separated from Massachusetts and admitted to the Union as a free state. At this time slave and nonslave states were evenly represented in the Senate, although the North's population gave it a majority in the House.

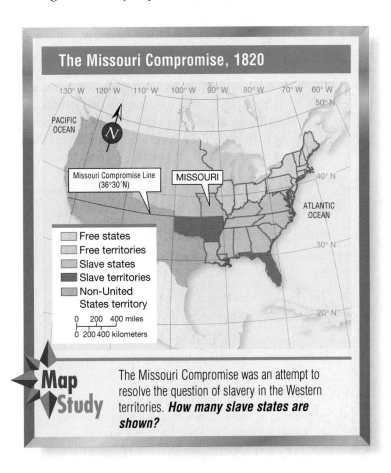

The Missouri Compromise, 1820

Missouri Compromise Line (36°30′N)

MISSOURI

PACIFIC OCEAN

ATLANTIC OCEAN

Free states
Free territories
Slave states
Slave territories
Non-United States territory

0   200   400 miles
0 200 400 kilometers

Map Study

The Missouri Compromise was an attempt to resolve the question of slavery in the Western territories. *How many slave states are shown?*

To maintain this balance of slave and non-slave states, a compromise was reached: Missouri and Maine would be admitted together. In the unsettled parts of the Louisiana Purchase, however, slavery would be forbidden north of the parallel 36°30', a line running west from the southern boundary of Missouri. The South agreed to this arrangement because of a widely held belief that the region west of the Mississippi was unfit for human settlement. When Southerners realized that this region was not "a great American desert," they began to demand changes in the Missouri Compromise.

■ Election of 1824

The election of 1824 reflected the growing sectionalism in American politics. In that election four Democratic-Republican candidates—John Quincy Adams, Henry Clay, William H. Crawford, and Andrew Jackson—ran for President. Each candidate was also a **favorite son**—a candidate supported by the political leaders from their own state and region. Each of the candidates was identified with regional interests; Jackson was the only one who showed strength ouside his own region, carrying Pennsylvania and New Jersey as well as most of the South and West. Although Jackson won a plurality (the largest number but less than half) of the popular vote, he failed to receive a majority of the electoral votes. Therefore, the House of Representatives had to choose

Visualizing **History** ▲ JOHN QUINCY ADAMS By the time of his election in 1824, John Quincy Adams was already an established figure in American political life. *Why was Adams's presidency not a successful one?*

the President from among the top three vote-getters. Clay was eliminated because he had placed fourth. He then threw his support to Adams, who was elected in February 1825.

When Adams named Clay secretary of state, Jackson's powerful supporters in Congress charged that the two men had made a "corrupt bargain." The denials of Adams and Clay, however, failed to remove suspicion. Jackson's supporters were determined that Adams's presidency should not succeed, and the President's ambitious federal programs received little support in Congress. The stage was set for Adams's defeat in the presidential election of 1828.

Section 2 ★ Assessment

Checking for Understanding

1. **Define** textile, closed shop, cotton gin, favorite son.

2. **Explain** the importance of cotton to the South and its effect on the region's way of life.

3. **Describe** the effects of the Industrial Revolution on the economy and lifestyles of the North.

Critical Thinking Activity

4. **Summarizing** Re-create the chart shown here, and explain how the different regions dis-

agreed over public lands, protective tariffs, and slavery.

Issue	Sectional Disagreement
Public Lands	
Protective Tariffs	
Slavery	

INTERDISCIPLINARY ACTIVITY

5. **Geography** Imagine you are a settler who is traveling to the Western frontier in the 1820s. List the 10 most essential items you would take with you.

▲ COTTON PICKERS BY ETHEL MAGAFAN

Songs of Slavery

Enslaved African Americans used music to help endure long, tedious hours of forced labor and to relax when they were released from chores. Although slaveholders forbade enslaved Africans from playing horns or drums, for fear that these could be used to send messages about planned rebellions, they were permitted to sing.

One kind of African American music that developed in the early 1800s was the spiritual. Sung in a lively style with strong rhythms and rich harmonies, the spirituals usually express themes of redemption from sin and from slavery and of a better life waiting in the future. Well-known spirituals include "Jacob's Ladder" and "Many a Thousand Gone."

The repertoire of songs African Americans sang was much more extensive than the slaveholders knew. It was not uncommon for African Americans to slip out of their quarters at night for secret meetings. In these secret gatherings, they poked fun at the slaveholders by telling folktales and singing songs such as "They Give Us the Husk."

They Give Us the Husk
We raise the wheat,
They give us the corn;
We bake the bread,
They give us the crust;
We sift the meal,
They give us the husk;
We peel the meat,
They give us the skin;
And that's the way
They take us in.

Making the Art Connection

1. Identify the "we" and "they" in this song.

2. What response might enslaved persons make to the idea that the slaveholders cared for them? Why do you think this is the case?

ACTIVITY

3. Do people still write and sing songs to give one another courage and hope in desperate situations? Name one such song, and tell its message in your own words.

★★★★★★★★★★★★★★★★★★★★★★★★★★★★

Age of Jackson

Main Idea

Elected president in 1828, Andrew Jackson promoted the supremacy of the federal government, fought sectionalism, and battled nullification.

Reading Strategy

Organizing Information As you read about the Age of Jackson, list democratic changes that developed during this period, using a diagram such as the one shown here.

Democratic Changes

Objectives

After studying this section, you should be able to

★ summarize the political career of Andrew Jackson.

★ list three democratic changes that developed during this period.

Key Terms

spoils system, pocket veto

ANDREW JACKSON'S DUELING PISTOLS ▶

During Adams's administration, the differences among the Jeffersonian Republicans had led to a split in party ranks. The group supporting Adams, known as National Republicans, wanted a strong federal government. The Jacksonians, soon to call themselves Democratic Republicans, or Democrats, favored a less powerful federal government.

 GOVERNMENT

■ Jacksonian Democracy

The party split made the presidential campaign of 1828 one of the bitterest in American history. In the end, Andrew Jackson won a sweeping victory—178 electoral votes to 83 for Adams. Jackson won every Southern and Western state and carried Pennsylvania and New York. For the first time, a candidate from the region west of the Appalachians was elected President. Jackson's victory was a major indication of the growing political power of the West.

The election of 1828 was also significant in that a large number of new voters participated. This turnout was partly because many states had lowered or eliminated property ownership as a voting qualification. Jackson appealed to many of the new voters, who believed that he defended the interests of the "common man." Although he was a dignified country gentleman, Jackson was born in a log cabin on the North Carolina frontier. His lowly beginnings made him a symbol of the growing power of democracy.

The People's Government

During Jackson's presidency, new voters made increasing demands on the government and learned the power of political organization. National issues became as much topics of conversation as local issues had always been. As national parties built stronger state and local ties, they began to rely upon a growing number of professional or career politicians. These changes helped to extend the **spoils system,** the practice of appointing people to government positions on the basis of party loyalty and party service.

Jackson actively influenced the rise of the new political system. He became the first President to oust large numbers of government employees in order to appoint his followers to office. Jackson often sought advice from several sources. As President, he had a group of personal friends, called by his enemies the "Kitchen Cabinet." This group advised him on all major decisions. He also increased presidential power by using the veto more than all previous Presidents. He was also one of the first Presidents to use the **pocket veto,** killing a bill by taking no action on it and waiting for Congress to adjourn.

Democracy made many advances under Jackson's presidency, but not all Americans shared in its benefits. In many states, women won the right to control property, but they did not yet have the right to vote. Native Americans and African Americans also did not achieve equal rights or freedom.

The "Trail of Tears"

In 1830, Jackson's supporters in Congress passed an act that called for moving the Native Americans in the East to lands west of the Mississippi River. One of the most

▲ *STUMP SPEAKING* by George Caleb Bingham, 1854–1855 Bingham's series of election paintings expresses faith in the democratic process. For nearly five years, the artist devoted his talent to illustrating the human aspect of the political process. ***What was significant about voter turnout in the election of 1828?***

powerful groups—the Cherokee—resisted this policy, and Jackson sent in the army. Forced to move from their homes to what is now Arkansas and Oklahoma, an estimated 4,000 Cherokee died of starvation, disease, or exposure on the march that became known as the "Trail of Tears."

By 1840, the United States government had moved all eastern Native Americans to western lands. The only exception was the Seminoles of Florida, some of whom settled deep in the Everglades after years of fighting American forces. Most citizens supported the harsh removal policy; only a few political and religious leaders raised their voices in protest.

"The Great Silence"

In the 1830s the cotton culture in the South had firmly established the institution of slavery, and criticism of the system became increasingly unacceptable to many people. In the South, those who spoke out against slavery risked physical harm. In the North, African Americans were free, but they were generally second-class citizens.

The debates of the 1820s leading to the Missouri Compromise had shown the slavery issue to be so explosive that a policy called "the great silence" began, and discussion of slavery as a national issue temporarily faded.

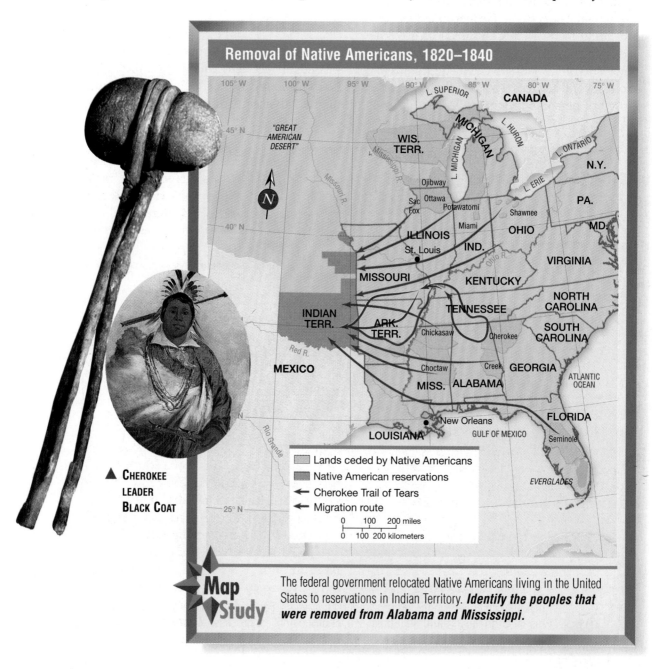

Removal of Native Americans, 1820–1840

▲ CHEROKEE LEADER BLACK COAT

Lands ceded by Native Americans
Native American reservations
Cherokee Trail of Tears
Migration route

0   100   200 miles
0 100 200 kilometers

Map Study — The federal government relocated Native Americans living in the United States to reservations in Indian Territory. *Identify the peoples that were removed from Alabama and Mississippi.*

▲ TRAIL OF TEARS by Robert Lindneux Native Americans who were forced from their land traveled west in the 1830s. **Why did the Cherokee call the forced march from their land the "Trail of Tears"?**

Political Controversies

During his term of office, Jackson made bold decisions on such issues as internal improvements, tariffs, and banking. Although a strong nationalist, Jackson opposed federal aid for roads. His stand, which dismayed Westerners and pleased Southerners, demonstrated his belief in a strict interpretation of the Constitution.

Tariff of 1828

Tariffs became a major issue during Jackson's presidency. Early in 1828, Congress had passed a law that increased tariff rates on foreign manufactured goods. This tariff aroused deep resentment in the South, especially in South Carolina where the cotton economy was depressed. South Carolina, however, held back from acting against the tariff because John C. Calhoun, the state's leading politician, was Andrew Jackson's running mate.

Calhoun anonymously wrote *The South Carolina Exposition*, in which he claimed that the Tariff of 1828 made the South a servant of Northern industrialists. He declared that a state could nullify, or reject, any law passed by Congress which the state believed had violated the Constitution.

Some supporters of nullification hoped to get Jackson on their side. They invited him to a dinner celebrating Jefferson's birthday on April 13, 1830. Jackson stood up to make a toast, raised his glass, looked at Calhoun, and solemnly said: "Our Federal Union: it must be preserved." Jackson's statement left no doubt that he would oppose nullification. Calhoun, pale and trembling, responded, "Our Union, next to liberty, the most dear."

The Nullification Crisis

In 1832, Congress passed another high-tariff act. South Carolina declared the tariff law "null, void, and no law." It threatened to secede, or leave the Union, if the government tried to collect duties in the state. In response, Jackson issued a proclamation in which he pointed out that nullification meant disunion and disunion meant treason. South Carolina's Senator Robert Y. Hayne resigned from the Senate to become governor of South Carolina, and Calhoun resigned the vice presidency to lead the fight in the Senate.

Upon Jackson's demand, Congress passed a force bill allowing him to use the armed forces to collect tariffs. At the same time, Senator Henry Clay of Kentucky pushed through a compromise tariff bill that provided for a gradual scaling down of tariffs. Thus Congress removed South Carolina's grievance about the tariff while denying its right to nullify a federal law. Jackson agreed to the compromise, but recognized that the issue of nullification had not been settled once and for all.

■ Jackson and the Bank

While the question of nullification was dividing the nation, Jackson was engaged in a dramatic struggle with the second Bank of the United States. Jackson believed that the Bank's vast powers threatened democratic government and distrusted its links with his political opponents.

A Campaign Issue

Jackson's opponents tried to make the Bank an issue in the election campaign of 1832. Henry Clay, Jackson's likely challenger for the presidency, introduced a bill to give the Bank a new charter even though the old one would not run out until 1836. Clay hoped to embarrass Jackson by forcing him either to sign a bill he disliked or to veto it. He did not believe that Jackson could defend a veto in the presidential campaign.

Disregarding controversy, Jackson proceeded to veto the bill after its passage by Congress. His veto message to Congress showed little knowledge of banking but great understanding of why many people disliked the Bank of the United States. Jackson wrote that the Bank favored the rich against the common people and that it was an overextension of federal power. The Constitution, he stated, nowhere explicitly granted the federal government the right to establish a central bank.

Destruction of the Bank

Winning an overwhelming victory in the 1832 election, Jackson took his triumph as a directive from the people to destroy the power of the Bank at once. In spite of initial opposition in his cabinet, Jackson had the government's deposits removed from the Bank and placed in strong state banks. In response, the Bank's president, Nicholas Biddle, called in loans and stopped lending. Biddle's move created such a scarcity of credit that hundreds of businesspeople were driven into bankruptcy and scores of banks failed. Factories closed down and workers were laid off.

After much public pressure, Biddle finally started extending easy credit to state banks. With money once again plentiful, the administration and Congress stimulated an economic boom by selling millions of acres of public lands and issuing surplus funds to the states for internal improvement projects. Worried by the free spending, reckless investments, and resulting inflation, Jackson then ordered that all payments for public lands be made in silver or gold. This drastic reversal of policy virtually stopped land sales, eliminated easy credit, and set the stage for a severe panic and depression in 1837.

Visualizing History ▲ **MARTIN VAN BUREN** Jackson used his influence to have Vice President Martin Van Buren nominated for President in 1836. *What economic woes struck the nation soon after Van Buren took office?*

Rise and Fall of the Whigs

The fight over the second Bank of the United States divided the nation. National Republicans and others opposed to Jackson's policies formed the Whig party. The Whigs, however, were so divided that they could not agree on a single candidate for President in 1836. They ended up nominating three candidates, hoping to divide the electoral college vote and throw the election into the Whig-controlled House of Representatives. Jackson's continuing popularity was enough to give the Democrats the election. Jackson's handpicked successor, Vice President Martin Van Buren, won 170 electoral votes against a combined total of 124 votes for all his Whig opponents.

Van Buren

Van Buren had hardly taken office when the country was hit by the Panic of 1837, one of the most severe depressions in history. Many people out of work turned to the government for help, but Van Buren refused all public aid. He believed in the laissez-faire idea that government should play the smallest possible role in American life. His only major legislative effort was to get the federal government entirely out of banking. Van Buren succeeded in having Congress approve an independent treasury system in which government funds in gold and silver would be stored in vaults throughout the country.

Harrison and Tyler

In 1840, the Democrats nominated Van Buren for reelection in spite of his unpopularity. The Whigs named the military hero of the Battle of Tippecanoe, General William Henry Harrison, for President, and chose former Senator John Tyler of Virginia as his running mate. Using the slogan, "Tippecanoe and Tyler too," Harrison stressed his colorful military career and portrayed himself as a simple frontiersman, although he had been born to wealth. Van Buren, on the other hand, was characterized as an aristocrat who had no concern for the people left without jobs by the depression. The result of the campaign was a decisive victory for Harrison—234 electoral votes to 60—although the popular vote was close.

▲ GENERAL WILLIAM HENRY HARRISON

After only a month in office, however, President Harrison died of pneumonia. John Tyler became the first Vice President to become President by the death of the incumbent. Having been placed on the Whig ticket simply to attract Southern support, Tyler favored states' rights and was opposed to most Whig programs that stressed a strong national government. As a result, he lost the support of leading Whigs, such as Henry Clay and Daniel Webster. Divided, without a program or leadership, the Whigs lost heavily in the congressional elections of 1842, and John Tyler became a President without a party.

Section 3 ★ Assessment

Checking for Understanding

1. **Define** spoils system, pocket veto.

2. **Describe** the role the Bank of the United States played in the election of 1832.

Critical Thinking Activity

3. **Inferring Values** At a celebration, President Andrew Jackson and Vice President John Calhoun exchanged toasts to the Union. In your own words, restate their implied messages.

4. **Examining Issues** Re-create the diagram shown here, and explain Jackson's position on these issues.

```
           Jackson's Position
          ┌──────┴──────┐
 Nullification Crisis   National Bank
```

INTERDISCIPLINARY ACTIVITY

5. **Government** Create campaign slogans for the presidential election in 1840 for the Whig and the Democratic candidates.

The Spirit of Reform

Guide to Reading

Main Idea

During the 1800s, several Americans tried to create a better society by promoting various social reforms.

Reading Strategy

Organizing Information As you read about the spirit of reform in America, list the areas which reformers addressed, using a diagram such as the one shown here.

Areas Addressed by Reformers

Objectives

After studying this section, you should be able to

★ identify social reform movements that were widespread during the early 1800s.

★ discuss the new values and beliefs that influenced educators, artists, and writers.

Key Terms

abolitionist, socialism

▶ **MINIATURE BOOKS OF THE 1830S**

*D*uring the early 1800s, many Americans began examining their society on the basis of ideas in the Declaration of Independence. In search of a better, more democratic world, they formed organizations to persuade others to their ways of thinking.

■ Advances in Education

In the 1820s and 1830s, as more Americans gained the right to vote, the need for free public education grew. In addition, it became necessary to educate the increasing number of immigrants who came to the United States in the mid-1800s. Democracy demanded an informed educated electorate, a goal not easy to achieve.

Free Public Education

In Massachusetts, the educator Horace Mann expanded public education in the late 1830s. As a result of Mann's efforts, Massachusetts quickly became the model for all other Northern states. By 1850, in spite of some initial resistance from taxpayers, most Northern states provided tuition-free elementary education.

Adult Education

While opportunities for formal higher education were limited for most people, there was a move toward adult education for the common person. Tax-supported libraries and privately supported learning societies began to take hold in many areas.

Interest in training teachers helped the cause of education for women. Although many men feared that higher education for women would disrupt home life, feminist leaders, such as Emma Willard, Catharine Beecher, and Mary Lyon, argued that chemistry could be used in cooking and math in household finance. Oberlin College in Ohio, the first coeducational school, saw its first female students graduate in 1841.

Oberlin College and Bowdoin College in Maine were the first institutions to allow African Americans to attend as students. Because African American men and women were generally barred from educational opportunities, there were fewer than 15 African American college students in the United States before 1840.

■ Struggle for Rights

During the Jacksonian period, many reformers called for action on such issues as care for the mentally ill, women's rights, and abolition of slavery. Their persistent efforts eventually awakened the United States to many of the needs of more than one-half of the population.

Treating Mental Illness

In the early 1840s, the reformer Dorothea Dix began visiting prisons, where she found many mentally ill persons who were being treated as criminals. Dix's findings led Massachusetts to pass a law establishing asylums where mental illness could be treated as a disease rather than as a crime. Largely as a result of Dix's influence, 20 more states founded insane asylums.

Women's Rights

In the early 1800s, women were considered "second-class citizens" in many ways. They could not vote and had no legal right to manage the affairs of their own children. They received less pay for work than men did. Almost all institutions of higher learning and most professional careers were closed to women.

Frustrated by limits on their actions, female reformers began a campaign for women's rights. In 1848 Lucretia Mott and Elizabeth Cady Stanton organized the Seneca Falls Convention. This gathering of female reformers drew up a "Declaration of Sentiments and Resolutions" that echoed the words of the Declaration of Independence:

❝ *We hold these truths to be self-evident: that all men and women are created equal; that they are endowed by their Creator with certain inalienable rights; that among these are life, liberty, and the pursuit of happiness. . . .* ❞

Most politicians were either indifferent or hostile to the issue of women's rights. Women did, however, gain relief from some of their worst legal handicaps. For example, many states passed laws permitting women to retain and manage their own property.

■ Antislavery Crusade

A glaring violation of democratic principles in the United States was African American slavery. It is not surprising, then, that the upsurge of democratic feeling in the Jacksonian period made the freeing of enslaved persons the dominant reform effort.

Abolitionists

Religious groups, such as the Quakers and the Baptists, had been the first to oppose slavery in the late 1700s. As slavery strengthened its hold over the South in the early 1800s, the voices of **abolitionists,** or those persons in favor of doing away with slavery, grew louder. Many abolitionists, such as the Massachusetts journalist William Lloyd Garrison, demanded immediate freedom for enslaved African Americans without compensation for slaveholders. They were willing to see the Union divided if necessary in order to rid the free states of the shame of being tied to the slave states.

Linking Past and Present

Surgical Tools

Early medicine depended a great deal on superstition and folklore. The doctors had only the most basic surgical tools.

Then

Basic Instruments

Early surgical instruments were simple. At best, a physician might carry in his saddlebag a set of amputating instruments, a trephine used to cut out sections of bone, and some crooked and straight needles. Some early physicians carried a scalpel or incision knife and a pair of forceps. Many physicians in the early 1800s had little training in surgical procedures.

Now

New Tools, New Methods

Modern technology has moved the practice of surgery forward. Clamps are used to close off blood vessels. Retractors hold back folds of skin. Lasers are used to make precise cuts in body tissues where using a scalpel would be impractical.

Infection during surgery was once a great danger. With the aseptic method of surgery, infection-causing germs are eliminated by cleaning and sterilizing all equipment used in the operating room.

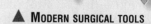

▲ **MODERN SURGICAL TOOLS**

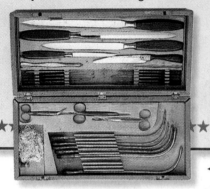

◄ **MEDICAL SURGEON'S KIT, 1800s**

The Underground Railroad

Another abolitionist leader who favored political action was Frederick Douglass. Self-educated and formerly enslaved, Douglass edited an abolitionist paper, *The North Star.* The title was meant to remind people of the Underground Railroad. This secret abolitionist organization, which had hiding places, or stations, throughout the Northern states and even into Canada, brought enslaved people out of the South. Moving at night, agents of the Underground Railroad, such as Harriet Tubman, had only Polaris, the fixed star in the northern skies, to guide them as they led enslaved people to freedom.

Southern Reactions

Southern slaveholders feared the influence of abolitionist ideas among enslaved African Americans. In 1831, Nat Turner, an African American preacher and enslaved person, led a rebellion in Virginia to free the slaves. Although unsuccessful, the revolt spread panic throughout the South, effectively ending the antislavery movement in the region.

As Southern hostility to abolition grew stronger, many Southerners demanded the suppression of abolitionist material as a condition for remaining in the Union. In 1836, under Southern pressure, the House of Representatives passed a "gag rule" providing that all abolitionist petitions should be shelved without debate. No prominent politician wanted to endanger the Union by attacking slavery where it was protected by law.

■ Arts and Sciences

During the 1830s and 1840s, many Americans wanted to prove that their culture was truly independent of Europe. This period saw many achievements by American writers, artists, and scientists.

American writers during the second quarter of the 1800s wanted Americans to feel proud of their country's heritage. James Fenimore Cooper's novels gloried in the drama of Native Americans and pioneers on the New York frontier. Nathaniel Hawthorne unfolded the Puritan history of New England in his novels and short stories. In *Moby Dick,* Herman Melville used his experience as a sailor to write a fascinating account of whaling that symbolized the human struggle itself.

American poets, too, turned from European to American subjects. Henry Wadsworth Longfellow immortalized the Native American hero Hiawatha. John Greenleaf Whittier in "Snow-Bound" described winter on a New England farm. Edgar Allen Poe wrote of the terrors that lurk in the world of the imagination.

Many American writers took an active part in reform movements. Whittier and Longfel-low joined the crusade against slavery, as did poet James Russell Lowell and poet and novelist Lydia Maria Child.

American painters and sculptors used European styles to portray the American scene. A group of landscape painters in the East was known as the Hudson River School. Their romantic paintings of the Catskill Mountains and Hudson River became highly prized. In architecture, Americans favored the "Federalist" and "Greek Revival" styles modeled on the classical buildings of ancient Greece and Rome.

Men and women in the United States also won fame in the field of science. The astronomer Maria Mitchell discovered a new comet and several groups of distant stars.

Matthew Maury, a naval officer, developed the science of oceanography. Dr. Crawford W. Long and Dr. W.T.G. Morton were the first physicians to use ether as an anesthetic during surgery.

► **FREDERICK DOUGLASS**

Visualizing History ▲ **MOVING TOWARD FREEDOM** Before the Civil War, thousands of enslaved people fled hundreds of miles and endangered their lives to reach the first station on the Underground Railroad. Frederick Douglass (inset) spoke on behalf of the emancipation of women as well as of enslaved people. *Why was Polaris important?*

■ Building a New World

During the early 1800s, new social, philosophical, and religious movements developed at this time that had a remarkable impact in transforming many areas of American society.

From Europe came a new idea—**socialism.** Socialists believed that business competition and individual ownership of property caused poverty and inequality. They proposed to substitute cooperation for competition and common ownership for individual ownership. Early followers of the idea started small, voluntary communities where their ideas could be put into practice. Among these communities was New Harmony, Indiana.

A great ferment in American religious life occurred in the first half of the 1800s. New religious groups arose, including some that practiced community living. Among these were the Church of Jesus Christ of Latter-day Saints, or the Mormon Church, and the Shakers.

In New England, new religious movements took separate paths from the region's Puritan heritage. The Unitarians rejected the doctrine of the Trinity and stressed the oneness of God and the perfectibility of human nature. The Transcendentalists emphasized the relationship between human beings and nature as well as the importance of the human conscience.

Protestantism experienced a renewal, a "Second Great Awakening." Throughout the country, beginning in New England and spreading westward, the growth of Protestant denominations was marked by great revival meetings, the building of new churches, and the founding of colleges and universities.

In cities a similar stirring of religious activity arose in the Catholic churches. In Boston and New York, for example, the Roman Catholic Church provided not only places of worship for Catholic European immigrants, but also schools, orphanages, and charitable organizations.

Among many Protestant groups the temperance movement developed in an effort to ban the use of alcohol. Temperance leaders wanted to do away with social evils, poverty, and crime that were often brought on by heavy drinking. In addition to trying to persuade people not to drink, temperance societies demanded laws to put an end to the sale of liquor. In 1851, Maine passed the first state prohibition law, an example followed by about a dozen states.

HISTORY Online

Student Web Activity

Visit the *American History: The Modern Era Since 1865* Web site at **me.glencoe.com** and click on *Chapter 4— Student Web Activities* for an activity about American painters.

Section 4 ★ Assessment

Checking for Understanding

1. **Define** abolitionist, socialism.

2. **List** four prominent American writers of the 1800s.

Critical Thinking Activity

3. **Analyzing Reform** The reform movements of the 1800s were initiated to extend rights and freedom of choice. What movement was an exception? What laws exist today that have similar goals to those of this movement?

4. **Summarizing** Re-create the chart shown here, and list the contributions of three key individuals to the antislavery movement.

Individuals	Contributions

INTERDISCIPLINARY ACTIVITY

5. **Government** Select a community issue you might want to research, such as landfills or recycling. Visit your library and find at least three resources for your topic.

BUILDING SKILLS

Critical Thinking Skills

Making Comparisons

Imagine that your young sister cannot decide between joining the debate team or playing basketball. She has limited free time, so she asks you to help her compare the two. You tell her that you cannot because that is "like comparing apples and oranges." Your friend hears this conversation and comes in to tell you that you can indeed compare the debate team to basketball.

▲ THE COUNTRY SCHOOL BY WINSLOW HOMER

Learning the Skill

To compare means to examine in order to identify similarities and differences. To be an accurate comparison, however, you must note at least one similarity and one difference.

In the example cited above, there are obvious differences between debating and basketball, yet there are at least two similarities. Both are group activities, and both are competitive in the nature in which points are scored.

No matter what you are comparing, there are steps that can help in making effective comparisons. They are:

- examine the information and take notes
- classify the information
- identify similarities and differences
- draw conclusions based on the comparisons you made

Read the two passages on this page. Then answer the questions that follow.

Passage A

. . . Give them a little spelling, a little ciphering [mathematics], *and a little handwriting, with a liberal sprinkling of the rod, and they'll have more than their fathers had before them. Did Tippecanoe Harrison graduate from a seminary? Did Old Hickory Jackson know any Latin or Greek?*

Passage B

Free public education is the mechanism by which democracy can be preserved. Horace Mann noted that education was the "great equalizer" and the "balance wheel of the social machinery." To Mann and his followers, education was the only way to "counterwork this tendency to the domination of capital and the servility of labor." A well-rounded éducation provides our citizens the means to better themselves.

Practicing the Skill

1. What is the topic of these passages?

2. In what ways are the passages similar? In what ways are they different?

3. What conclusions can you draw about the beliefs of the two writers?

Glencoe's **Skillbuilder Interactive Workbook, Level 2** provides instruction and practice in key social studies skills.

APPLYING THE SKILL

4. Examine the sections on the women's rights movement and the antislavery crusade on pages 161–162. Create a chart that shows their similarities and differences.

Using Vocabulary

Use each vocabulary term in a sentence about the growth of sectional conflict.

nationalism	cotton gin
internal improvement	spoils system
protective tariff	abolitionist

Reviewing Facts

1. **Explain** how the federal judiciary strengthened nationalism in key decisions between 1819 and 1824.
2. **Summarize** the changes that resulted from internal improvements in transportation.
3. **Identify** the important democratic changes that developed during the Jackson era.
4. **Compare** the effects of the Industrial Revolution on different sections.
5. **List** four issues on which the sections had major differences.
6. **Describe** the problems workers faced during the 1830s.
7. **Explain** why "cotton was king" in the South.
8. **Name** the plan that temporarily resolved sectional conflict over slavery.
9. **Summarize** advances in American education in the early 1800s.

Understanding Concepts

American Democracy

1. What political and democratic changes aided Andrew Jackson's election victory in 1828?
2. What reasons can you give for why both the abolitionist and temperance movements began among religious groups?

3. Re-create the chart shown here, and describe the status of each group during the period of Jacksonian democracy.

African Americans	
Native Americans	
Women	

Economic Change

4. What were some of the abuses of the free enterprise system that factory workers experienced? In what way did the government and citizens address these abuses?
5. In what ways did the Industrial Revolution divide the nation?

Critical Thinking

1. **Making Global Comparisons** Slavery was abolished in Great Britain, France, and Latin America before it was abolished in the United States. What economic and political differences probably accounted for this?
2. **Analyzing Fine Art** Study the painting on this page by artist James Hamilton entitled *Scene on the Hudson.* Then answer the questions that follow.

▲ *SCENE ON THE HUDSON* BY JAMES HAMILTON

CHAPTER 4 ★ ASSESSMENT

a. What captured your attention when you first looked at this painting?

b. What kind of mood is suggested by this painting?

c. What is your personal response to this painting?

3. Making Judgments Why would President Monroe want to issue the Monroe Doctrine independently of Great Britain? Was it possible for the United States during the Monroe administration to enforce this policy? Explain your reasoning.

4. Evaluating Policy Argue for or against the spoils system.

5. Analyzing Evidence What evidence can you find that at the beginning of the 1800s, European art and literature was considered superior to American art and literature?

History and Geography

The Nation and the Industrial Revolution

The Industrial Revolution affected each region of the country differently due to its physical characteristics. The North was rocky and mountainous with a short growing season, abundant moving water, and coal deposits. The South was lush and fertile with warm temperatures and a long growing season. The West had abundant fertile land but was distant from markets and separated from the rest of the country by rugged terrain.

1. Human/Environment Interaction How did the physical characteristics explain the economies that developed in each region?

2. Human/Environment Interaction How did workers and settlers adapt to their environment?

Cooperative Learning Interdisciplinary Activity: Government

Working in pairs, research the history of the government's and settlers' dealings with Black Hawk's nation. Imagine it is 1832 and Black Hawk has returned with his followers to reclaim Iowa lands that farmers now hold. You and your partner have been appointed by Jackson to recommend a solution. Agree on a fair plan and present it to your class.

Practicing Skills

Making Comparisons

Examine the paintings of the mill on page 139 and the factory on page 148. Then answer the questions that follow.

1. In what ways are the scenes the artists present similar? In what ways are the scenes different?

2. Compare the techniques of the artists. Which style of art do you prefer? Explain.

Technology Activity

Using a Word Processor

Use the Internet and other resources to find out more about a writer, artist, scientist or social reformer mentioned in this chapter. Organize your information and write a brief biographical sketch of the person. Present your report to the class.

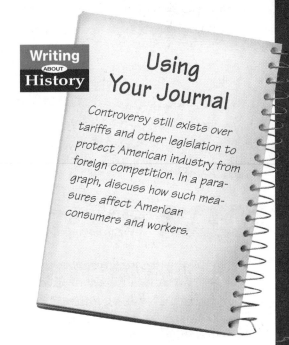

Writing ABOUT History

Using Your Journal

Controversy still exists over tariffs and other legislation to protect American industry from foreign competition. In a paragraph, discuss how such measures affect American consumers and workers.

CHAPTER 5

★★

The Civil War Era
1820–1865

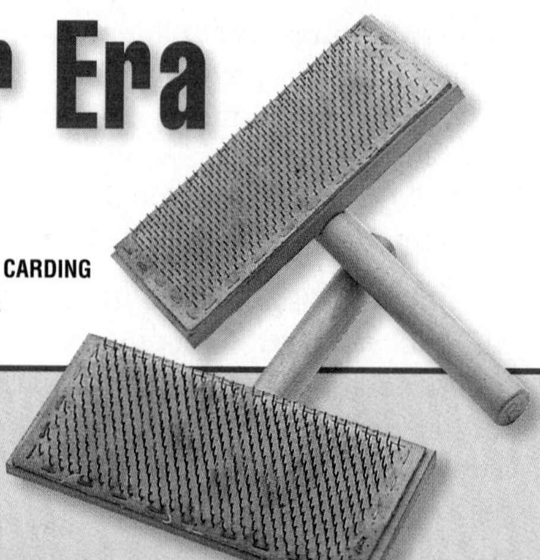

► COTTON CARDING PADDLES

Setting the Scene

Focus

During the mid-1800s, the United States used war and diplomacy to significantly expand its western territory. By 1850 thousands of settlers moved into this area to create new homes. Meanwhile, sectional divisions—especially concerning slavery—threatened the existence of the Union. Compromise at first seemed to work in holding the country together. With the election of an anti-slavery President in 1860, however, the South believed it had no choice but to leave the Union.

Concepts to Understand

★ How expansion was influenced by **geography and environment**
★ How political **conflict** over slavery and the nature of the Union led to secession

Read to Discover . . .

★ the causes and results of the Mexican War.
★ the events that led seven Southern states to secede from the Union.

Journal Notes

What contributed to division of the Union? As you read the chapter, record the events, decisions, acts, and other activities that answer the question.

HISTORY Online

Chapter Overview
Visit the *American History: The Modern Era Since 1865* Web site at **me.glencoe.com** and click on *Chapter 5—Chapter Overviews* to preview chapter information.

CULTURAL

• **1819** *University of Virginia founded*

• **1820** *Nation's population reaches 10 million*

• **1830** *Church of Jesus Christ of Latter-day Saints organized*

| 1810 | 1820 | 1830 |

POLITICAL

• **1818** *National Road reaches Wheeling*

• **1821** *Moses Austin receives land grant in Texas*

• **1836** *Texas wins independence*

History AND ART

View of Harpers Ferry
by Ferdinand Richardt, 1858

Danish artist Ferdinand Richardt captured a serene view of Harpers Ferry, Virginia—the location of the armory targeted for assault by abolitionist John Brown in 1859.

▲ FLAG OF THE
REPUBLIC OF TEXAS

- **1846** *Elias Howe patents sewing machine*

- **1852** *Harriet Beecher Stowe's* Uncle Tom's Cabin *published*

- **1861** *First transcontinental telegraph message sent*

1840	1850	1860

- **1846** *Mexican War begins*

- **1850** *Compromise of 1850 passed*
- **1854** *Kansas-Nebraska Act passed*

- **1860** *South Carolina secedes from the Union*
- **1865** *Civil War ends*

★★★★★★★★★★★★★★★★★★★★★★★★★★★★★★★★★★★★

Manifest Destiny

Guide to Reading

Main Idea

Embracing the notion of Manifest Destiny, Americans expanded the nation's borders during the first half of the 1800s.

Reading Strategy

Sequencing Information As you read about Manifest Destiny, create a time line of key events leading to the annexation of Texas by the United States.

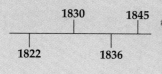

Objectives

After studying this section, you should be able to

★ describe American settlement of Oregon and Utah.

★ explain how Texas became part of the United States.

★ contrast the United States's short-term and long-range goals in the war with Mexico.

Key Terms

dark horse, joint resolution

▲ THE PRAIRIE HUNTER

*M*anifest Destiny developed from America's desire to settle new lands. Expanding the United States to the Pacific, however, meant taking land claimed or settled by other peoples. The United States, with limited military power, had to weigh carefully the possibility of hostilities with Native Americans on the plains, with Great Britain in Oregon, and with Mexico in Texas.

🌐 GEOGRAPHY

■ The Thirst for New Lands

The Oregon Territory extended from the Pacific Ocean to the Rocky Mountains, bordering Russian Alaska to the north and

California to the south. Four countries—the United States, Great Britain, Spain, and Russia—had originally claimed Oregon. By 1824, however, only the Americans and the British were left to compete for the vast Pacific Northwest territory.

Oregon

In the mid-1830s, American missionaries settled the Oregon Territory to convert Native Americans to Christianity. Their glowing reports of the land's fertility eventually brought a number of American pioneers, most of whom came by covered wagon over the Oregon Trail. By 1845, 5,000 Americans were living south of the Columbia River and demanding that their government take full possession of the Oregon Territory.

Utah

Another group of settlers moved west, not to expand United States territory but to escape from it. The Mormon Church and its founder Joseph Smith were forced to move several times to flee persecution. Many people resented the new religion because of its communal organization and Smith's teaching that a man could have more than one wife. After Smith's death at the hands of a mob, Brigham Young, the new leader, led the Mormons from Illinois—their latest place of settlement—to an isolated haven in territory that belonged to Mexico.

The move took place in 1847. The Mormons soon established flourishing settlements near the Great Salt Lake in Utah. They developed an advanced system for controlling the water supply in the semi-arid regions of the Far West. Around Salt Lake City, irrigation transformed the desert into a garden spot.

Texas

Texas—a vast, ill-defined area extending southwest from Louisiana to the Rio Grande and west to the foothills of the Rocky Mountains—belonged to Mexico. The original Spanish settlements in Texas were limited to a few hundred people and a dozen missions.

When Mexico broke away from Spain in 1821, its government sought migrants to come and develop Texas. In 1822 Stephen F. Austin, an American settler, took over a grant of land that the Spanish government had given his father. Mexican officials welcomed Austin and other Americans, provided they became Roman Catholics and accepted Mexican law.

Austin's settlement proved so successful that by 1830 Texas had attracted almost 30,000 Americans. In that year Mexico passed a law restricting further immigration because it was concerned about developments in Texas. Americans, knowing

▲ *Spirit of the Frontier* by John Gast, 1872 Driven by a sense of Manifest Destiny, Americans moved west. By 1848 the United States stretched unchallenged from sea to sea. *What role did Stephen Austin play in extending American settlement?*

that Mexico's law against slavery was not strictly enforced in Texas, had brought thousands of enslaved people. In addition, they had failed to become Catholics, and the flood of settlers now outnumbered local Mexicans 10 to 1.

Texas Independence

When the Mexicans abolished local rights, rebellion broke out in Texas. In 1835, Mexico's president General Antonio Santa Anna marched an army north to subdue the rebels. In February 1836, 2,000 Mexican troops besieged 188 Texans in the Alamo, a mission station in San Antonio. After two

▲ GENERAL SAM HOUSTON

weeks of resistance, the defenders of the Alamo were defeated.

The Mexican army pursued Sam Houston, the military leader of the Texans, and his troops toward the United States border. Then at San Jacinto (SAN juh•SIHN•tuh) Creek, Houston's forces turned and attacked. Crying "Remember the Alamo!" they surprised and defeated the Mexican troops. A captured Santa Anna signed a treaty recognizing the independence of Texas but renounced it as soon as he was free.

In 1836 Texas declared itself the Lone Star Republic and immediately sought admission to the United States. The United States government, however, refused to annex Texas because of Northern opposition to adding more slave territory to the Union and fears that admission of Texas would bring war with Mexico.

Election of 1844

As the presidential election of 1844 approached, the issue of territorial expansion took center stage. Former President Van Buren, a Democrat, and Henry Clay, a Whig, were expected to be the rival candidates. Then the unexpected happened: Van

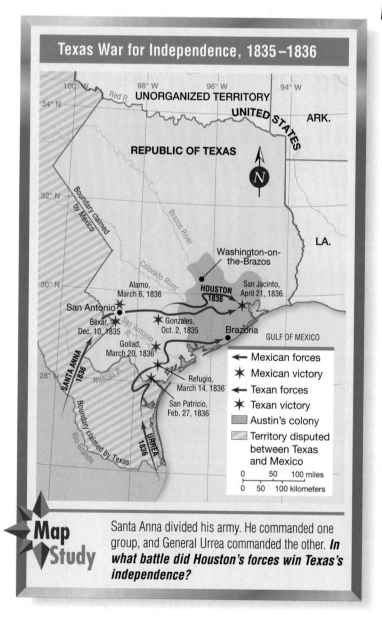

Map Study

Santa Anna divided his army. He commanded one group, and General Urrea commanded the other. *In what battle did Houston's forces win Texas's independence?*

Buren failed to receive the Democratic nomination. A group of Southerners who wanted Texas and Westerners who wanted Oregon nominated the first **dark horse,** or unexpected candidate, in the history of the presidency—James K. Polk of Tennessee.

Support for Expansion

Polk backed the annexation of both Oregon and Texas. Regarding Oregon, the Democrats' pro-expansion enthusiasm was dramatized by the campaign slogan "Fifty-four forty or fight!" (The parallel 54°40′ was the southern boundary of Alaska.) To counter this unexpected challenge, the Whigs had only Henry Clay's popularity. Although Clay had earlier opposed the admission of Texas, he issued a cautious statement accepting annexation if war could be avoided. Clay's hedging did not work, and Polk won the 1844 election by a slim margin.

Texas Statehood

President Tyler, who was still in office, asserted that Polk's victory was a mandate for the admission of Texas to the Union. He asked Congress to admit Texas by a **joint resolution** that would require only a simple majority, instead of a treaty that required a vote of two-thirds of the Senate.

In February 1845, both houses of Congress, by narrow majorities, passed the joint resolution. In December 1845, the Lone Star Republic became the twenty-eighth state. The boundary between Mexico and Texas remained undetermined, and the Mexican government threatened war.

■ Division of Oregon

The risk of war with Mexico put pressure on the United States to settle the Oregon question. It was one thing to shout, "Fifty-four forty or fight!" in an election campaign. It was quite another to take on Great Britain, the greatest sea power in the world, and prepare to fight Mexico.

Great Britain, however, was concerned about the large number of American settlers in Oregon who seemed willing to fight. Rather than losing all of the territory, the British were willing to relinquish the southern half. In 1846, Polk, now President, submitted to the Senate a British proposal to divide Oregon along the 49th parallel. In spite of the objections of Westerners, who accused the President of backing down on his demand for all of Oregon, the Senate approved the treaty, which was signed on June 15, 1846.

■ War With Mexico

The spark that finally ignited war between Mexico and the United States resulted from a dispute over the southern boundary of Texas. Mexico claimed it was the Nueces River, while the United States said it was the Rio Grande 130 miles to the south. Failing to reach a diplomatic settlement with Mexico, Polk ordered General Zachary Taylor to move his troops south to the Rio Grande. Taylor's troops were, in effect, looking for trouble, waiting for an incident justifying retaliation.

War Begins

Late in April 1846, Mexican soldiers crossed the Rio Grande and attacked a small group of United States cavalry. At Polk's urging, Congress declared war by overwhelming majorities in both houses. Although attacking Polk for starting the war, the Whigs in Congress supported it by voting for supplies and troops.

Many Americans, however, refused to support a war of aggression against a weaker neighbor. Even American soldiers had their doubts about the legitimacy of the war. In 1846 Colonel Ethan Allen Hitchcock wrote:

> 66 *I have said from the first that the United States are the aggressors. . . . We have not one particle of right to be here. It looks as if the government sent a small force on purpose to bring on a war, so as to have a pretext for taking California and as*

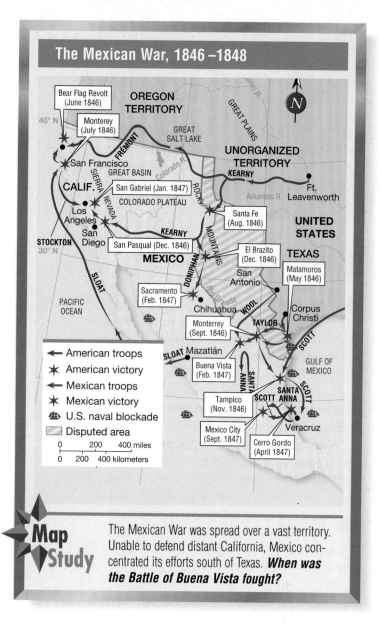

The Mexican War, 1846–1848

Bear Flag Revolt
(June 1846)

OREGON
TERRITORY

Monterey
(July 1846)

GREAT
SALT LAKE

GREAT PLAINS

San Francisco

GREAT BASIN

FREMONT

CALIF.

SIERRA NEVADA

Colorado R.

UNORGANIZED
TERRITORY

KEARNY

San Gabriel (Jan. 1847)

COLORADO PLATEAU

ROCKY MOUNTAINS

Arkansas R.

Ft.
Leavenworth

Los
Angeles

Santa Fe
(Aug. 1846)

UNITED
STATES

KEARNY

STOCKTON

San
Diego

San Pasqual (Dec. 1846)

MEXICO

DONIPHAN

El Brazito
(Dec. 1846)

San
Antonio

TEXAS

Matamoros
(May 1846)

SLOAT

PACIFIC
OCEAN

Sacramento
(Feb. 1847)

Chihuahua

Rio Grande

WOOL

Corpus
Christi

Monterrey
(Sept. 1846)

TAYLOR

SCOTT

American troops

American victory

Mexican troops

Mexican victory

U.S. naval blockade

Disputed area

0   200   400 miles

0   200   400 kilometers

SLOAT Mazatlán

Buena Vista
(Feb. 1847)

SANTA ANNA

GULF OF
MEXICO

Tampico
(Nov. 1846)

SCOTT

SANTA
ANNA

SCOTT

Mexico City
(Sept. 1847)

Veracruz

Cerro Gordo
(April 1847)

Map Study

The Mexican War was spread over a vast territory. Unable to defend distant California, Mexico concentrated its efforts south of Texas. **When was the Battle of Buena Vista fought?**

much of this country as it chooses, for, whatever becomes of this army, there is no doubt of a war between the United States and Mexico. . . . My heart is not in this business . . . but, as a military man, I am bound to execute orders. "

Polk's War Strategy

President Polk planned the military campaigns of the Mexican War as a three-part strategy. First, General Taylor and his troops invaded northern Mexico. By February

1847, they had penetrated nearly 300 miles into the country and won the Battle of Buena Vista.

As the second part of the strategy, a force under General Stephen Kearney took Santa Fe and marched to California, where they helped an American naval force defeat the Mexicans in Los Angeles. A local revolt in northern California, assisted by Americans, had already shaken off Mexican rule. Thus California came under United States control, and fighting in the West ended.

When Mexico still refused to make peace, Polk launched the third part of his war strategy, sending General Winfield Scott to conquer Mexico City. With a force of 10,000, Scott sailed south and landed at Veracruz. In September 1847, after six months of difficult fighting, he occupied the capital.

Treaty of Guadalupe Hidalgo

Working to the Americans' advantage was the disorganization of the Mexican government. After the capture of Mexico City, some months passed before a Mexican government could be organized to sign a peace treaty. Meanwhile, advocates of Manifest Destiny urged that the United States annex all of Mexico.

In February 1848, before the movement for total annexation had proceeded very far, a peace treaty was signed at Guadalupe Hidalgo, outside Mexico City. In spite of Polk's dissatisfaction with the agreement, he submitted the treaty to the Senate. After a round of expansionist arguments by those favoring annexation of all of Mexico, the Senate finally voted 38 to 14 in favor of the treaty.

Under the agreement, the United States gained full title to Texas (with the Rio Grande as the boundary). The United States also gained California and all of what was then called New Mexico. The nation paid $15 million outright for New Mexico and California and agree to pay some of the Mexican debt. Mexico lost only 1 percent of its population but half of its territory.

▲ ENTERING MEXICO CITY After six months of difficult fighting, General Winfield Scott forced his way into Mexico City. Scott's troops included young military officers Ulysses S. Grant and Robert E. Lee. *Why did some of the troops oppose the war?*

Further Expansion

In 1853, the United States completed expansion across the continent with the Gadsden Purchase for $10 million. This land provided a route where the land elevation was low enough to build a railroad across the southern part of the country to California.

Once the United States gained control of large areas of the West, Americans began moving into these regions in greater and greater numbers. In 1848, gold was discovered in California at Sutter's mill near Sacramento. Stories of instant riches led to a gold rush from the eastern United States and Europe.

In addition to gold, the acquisition of California gave the United States valuable ports from which to launch its Pacific trade. Along with the European powers, Americans secured trading privileges in China. By 1850, American clipper ships carried most of the Chinese tea exported to Europe. In 1854, a small United States fleet under Commodore Matthew C. Perry also persuaded isolationist Japan to open trade with the outside world.

Section 1 ★ Assessment

Checking for Understanding

1. **Define** dark horse, joint resolution.
2. **List** three rivals to American settlers for Western lands.
3. **Discuss** the results of the presidential election of 1844 and cite Polk's position on Texas annexation.

Critical Thinking

4. **Evaluating an Action** Imagine you are a newspaper editor in the mid-1840s. Write your opinion on whether the United States's actions to wage war against Mexico were justified.

5. **Analyzing Issues** Re-create the diagram shown here, and list the territories the United States won as a result of the war with Mexico.

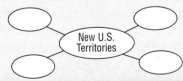

New U.S. Territories

INTERDISCIPLINARY ACTIVITY

6. **Government** Suppose you are a farmer wishing to settle in Texas in the early 1820s. Write a letter to Stephen F. Austin asking three questions about his colony.

★★★

Compromise and Growth

▶ CANNED FOODS AND MEDICINE, MID-1800s

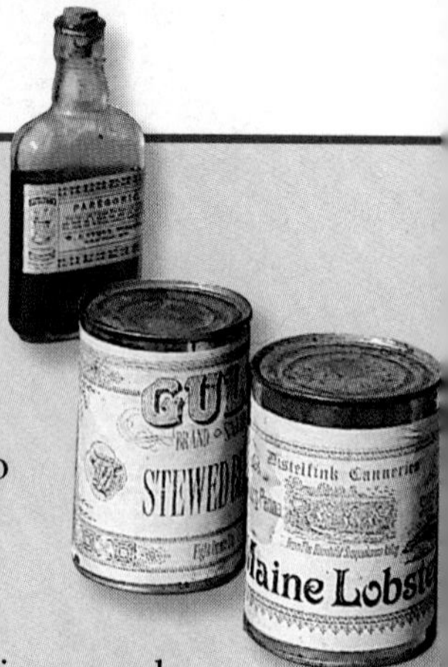

Guide to Reading

Main Idea

As the debate over the issue of slavery intensified, the country experienced a period of economic and social growth.

Reading Strategy

Classifying Information As you read about compromise and growth in America during the mid 1800s, use a chart such as this one to summarize the debate and compromise surrounding California's application for statehood.

Debate	Compromise of 1850

Objectives

After studying this section, you should be able to

★ explain why California's application for admission to the Union incited heated debates on the question of slavery.

★ explain how invention and increased immigration affected the economic growth of the United States.

Key Term

popular sovereignty

---

*E*ven before the war with Mexico had ended, growing antislavery sentiment in the North led the House of Representatives, with its Northern majority, to pass the Wilmot Proviso. This bill provided that all territory acquired from Mexico should be closed to slavery.

The Wilmot Proviso was defeated in the Senate, where the North and South were equally represented. Many Southern senators argued that Congress had no constitutional power to forbid slavery in the territories. If the representatives did outlaw slavery there, they would be denying slaveholders their rights as citizens.

■ Election of 1848

There seemed to be no way of reconciling these opposing views on the issues of slavery in the new territories. When the Polk administration ended in 1849, no steps had been taken to provide for civil government in New Mexico and California.

Democrats and Whigs

In the presidential election of 1848, both Northerners and Southerners took precautions to play down discussion of slavery. The Democrats, although controlled by their Southern wing, nominated a Northern senator, Lewis Cass of Michigan. Cass supported a compromise solution known as **popular sovereignty,** whereby voters within the territories would decide whether slavery would be permitted inside their borders. The Whigs, whose principal stronghold was in the North, nominated Zachary Taylor from Louisiana, a slaveholder himself. The Whigs avoided the issue of slavery by focusing on Taylor's military successes in the Mexican War.

The Free-Soil Party

Efforts to keep slavery out of the campaign failed, however. A third party emerged when various antislavery groups united with many Whigs and Democrats to form the Free-Soil party. Although the Free-Soil presidential candidate Martin Van Buren gained no electoral votes, he kept Cass from gaining New York's 36 electoral votes. This gave the election to Taylor with 163 electoral votes—exactly 36 more than Cass had.

■ The California Question

The issue of slavery in the new territories intensified after gold was discovered in California in 1848. By the end of 1849, an estimated 95,000 "forty-niners" from all over the world had settled in northern California.

Application for Statehood

With this tremendous growth in population came an urgent need to make California a state. In 1849, the newly established territorial government applied for admission to the Union as a free state in which slavery was forbidden. California's application for statehood touched off a long bitter debate. Admission of California would tip the balance of power in the Senate in favor of the free states, already in the majority in the House. If California were admitted as a free state, Southern leaders warned, their states would leave the Union.

Compromise of 1850

To deal with this alarming situation, Henry Clay, who had been in retirement since his defeat in the presidential election of 1844, successfully ran for reelection as senator. The Whig senator from Kentucky, a master of negotiation, proceeded to arrange his great compromise to save the Union. Clay's compromise was a series of measures intended to satisfy Northern and Southern demands. The principal provisions favoring the North were that California would be

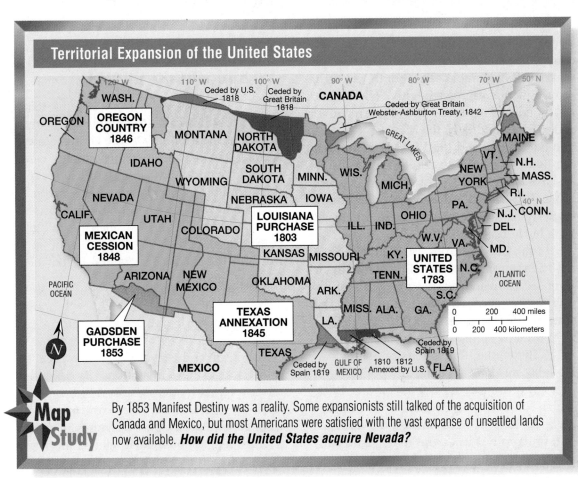

Territorial Expansion of the United States

Map Study By 1853 Manifest Destiny was a reality. Some expansionists still talked of the acquisition of Canada and Mexico, but most Americans were satisfied with the vast expanse of unsettled lands now available. *How did the United States acquire Nevada?*

▲ **COMMUNICATIONS AND TRANSPORTATION** Westward expansion created an urgent need for better connections between locations. A canal boom was ushered in with the completion of the Erie Canal. ***What innovations helped improve communications?***

admitted as a free state and that the slave trade—but not slavery—be forbidden in the District of Columbia. The South, in turn, would gain a stronger Fugitive Slave Law, designed to suppress the Underground Railroad. In addition, the Mexican Cession, gained at the end of the Mexican War, would be divided into two territories, Utah and New Mexico. The question of slavery there would be decided by popular sovereignty when the territories were organized with territorial legislatures.

At first, Clay's proposals failed to receive sufficient support to pass. President Taylor opposed Clay and offered proposals of his own. However, Taylor died suddenly in the summer of 1850. His successor, Vice President Millard Fillmore, favored the compromise. The young Illinois senator Stephen A. Douglas, a Democrat, skillfully put through the compromise as five separate bills, which Fillmore duly signed. The Compromise of 1850 averted immediate disaster but, unhappily, turned out to be just a temporary truce.

■ Economic and Social Growth

During the 20 years from 1840 to 1860, rapid growth became the dominant characteristic of the economy of the United States. Among the reasons for this growth were inventions and innovations, sufficient capital to build factories, and a class of businesspeople willing to start new enterprises. Other factors included an increase in agricultural productivity, a growing labor supply, and the increase in railroads that tied farms to factories.

Inventions and Industries

American industry grew partly because of a flood of new inventions. By 1861 the telegraph had made possible rapid communication throughout the continent and across the Atlantic. The rotary press allowed newspapers to publish far larger editions than ever before. Some inventions, such as the sewing machine, vulcanized rubber, and the steam engine, had the greatest impact on Northern industries.

Textile factories, powered by more efficient steam engines, increased in size as several operations were combined under a single roof. Techniques invented and developed by Eli Whitney and Simeon North for making interchangeable parts and breaking down manufacturing into simple operations now were applied in the mass production of clocks, watches, and farm machinery.

Advances in Agriculture

In spite of industrial advances, two-thirds of the nation's people in 1850 were still engaged in agriculture. Inventions, innovations, and government policies allowed agricultural productivity to keep pace with the nation's fast-growing industries.

The Midwest with its fertile plains attracted farmers from the northeastern United States and from Europe. Public lands there could be purchased for as little as 25 cents an acre. The development of a steel plow with replaceable parts enabled farmers to cut through tree roots in recently cleared forestland and to turn the tough sod of the prairies. With the new plows, farmers could plant more land than they could harvest. To solve this problem, Cyrus McCormick, a Virginia blacksmith, developed a mechanical "reaper," or grain harvester. These inventions were accompanied by still others: a mechanical drill to plant grain, the threshing machine, and the horsedrawn hay rake.

Although the West benefited more from these inventions than did the South, which still depended on slave labor, the Southern economy also improved. Increased demand for raw cotton by an efficient British textile

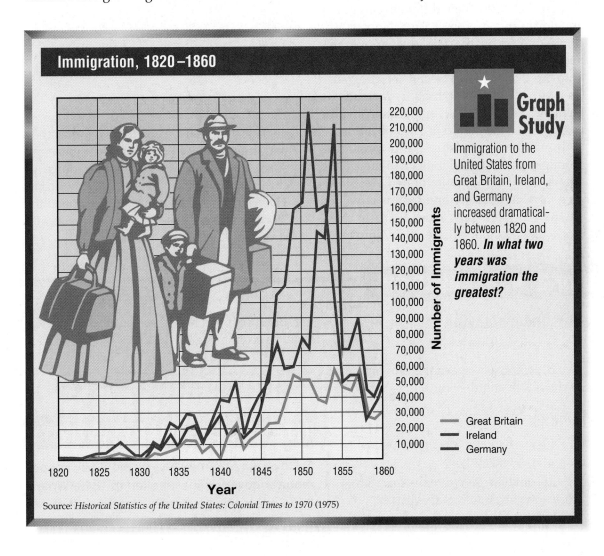

Immigration, 1820–1860

Graph Study

Immigration to the United States from Great Britain, Ireland, and Germany increased dramatically between 1820 and 1860. *In what two years was immigration the greatest?*

Number of Immigrants

220,000
210,000
200,000
190,000
180,000
170,000
160,000
150,000
140,000
130,000
120,000
110,000
100,000
90,000
80,000
70,000
60,000
50,000
40,000
30,000
20,000
10,000

— Great Britain
— Ireland
— Germany

1820 1825 1830 1835 1840 1845 1850 1855 1860

Year

Source: *Historical Statistics of the United States: Colonial Times to 1970* (1975)

industry brought prosperity to the Deep South. By 1860 seven-eighths of the world's supply of cotton came from the United States, and raw cotton comprised three-fifths of the nation's exports.

Increased Immigration

During the second quarter of the 1800s, a great migration from Europe to America began. Between 1840 and 1860, an average of more than 200,000 immigrants reached American shores each year. The reasons for this migration were both political and economic. Thousands of English, Irish, Scandinavian, and Dutch farmers and workers made the often perilous voyage to escape poverty and starvation. Others, like German thinkers and writers, came to avoid political persecution. By 1860, about one out of every eight Americans was foreign-born.

Some established Americans resented immigrants with their different languages, religions, and customs. Such bigotry was accompanied by the fear that immigrants would bring new and radical political ideas into the United States. Secret societies, such as the "Know-Nothings," formed to demand restrictions on immigration and the extension of the period of naturalization.

In spite of hardships and prejudice, immigrants continued to flock to the United States. Although some migrated West to its rich farmlands, many immigrants remained in the Northern port cities, such as New York and Boston, where their ships had

▲ "KNOW-NOTHING" SONG SHEET COVER

docked. One reason for this was that they had little money to continue their journeys. Also, the South already had a source of cheap labor—enslaved African Americans. The result was that immigrants supplied the North's growing industries with a steady stream of low-paid workers.

Section 2 ★ Assessment

Checking for Understanding

1. **Define** popular sovereignty.

2. **Identify** two differences between the economic systems of the North and the South.

Critical Thinking

3. **Evaluating Policies** Explain why abolitionists opposed popular sovereignty.

4. **Organizing Information** Re-create the diagram shown here, list the inventions of this period,

and briefly explain how they contributed to the nation's economic growth.

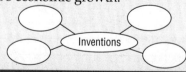

INTERDISCIPLINARY ACTIVITY

5. **Government** Imagine you are a newspaper reporter covering the election of 1848. Write three questions you want the presidential candidates to answer.

Industrial Innovation

"What is the North," asked a Southern writer during the 1850s, "but a conglomeration [group] of greasy mechanics, filthy operatives, small-fisted farmers, and moonstruck theorists?" Southerners may have looked scornfully at manufacturing in the North, but Europeans were fascinated by "Yankee notions" like machine-made clocks and buckets, canned food, and handguns with revolving chambers. These products were the result of Yankee ingenuity and the machine and tool industry, which mass-produced interchangeable parts.

The British called this industry "the American system of manufacturing," but "the Northeastern American system" would have been more accurate. More than half of America's 140,000 factories were concentrated between New York and Massachusetts, and they were the country's largest and most productive. The South had 20,000 factories, but they were small and concentrated on processing local products like cotton or tobacco rather than manufacturing.

In 1820 most manufacturing was done in homes or small shops. After 1820, however, the factory system began to take over. In factories the total process of manufacturing took place at one location. The need for a single location was due to the new sources of power—water and steam. The first factories used waterpower and were built in rural areas along rivers and streams.

Improved transportation and communication increased the importance of Northern cities as centers of trade. As city merchants grew wealthier, they sought investments that would further increase their business. Much of their capital, or investment money, went into new manufacturing industries.

▲ CRYSTAL PALACE, INDUSTRIAL EXHIBITION IN LONDON, 1851

Connecticut inventor Eli Whitney started the use of interchangeable parts. These were identical machine parts that could be quickly put together to make a complete product. Because all the parts were alike, they could be manufactured with less skilled labor, and they made machine repair easier.

Making the Economics Connection

1. Where did most manufacturing take place during this era?

2. What factors increased the growth of centers of trade?

3. How might the level of industrialization affect the ability of the North and the South to wage war?

ACTIVITY

4. Research specific developments that influenced economic growth during this period. Include these innovations in a chart using the following headings: Industry, Agriculture, and Transportation.

★★

The Approaching Conflict

Guide to Reading

Main Idea

As tensions grew between the North and South—mainly over the issue of slavery—the nation headed toward a breakup.

Reading Strategy

Organizing Information As you read about the approaching conflict, use a chart such as the one shown here to list events that might have prompted the South to secede.

Events Leading to Secession

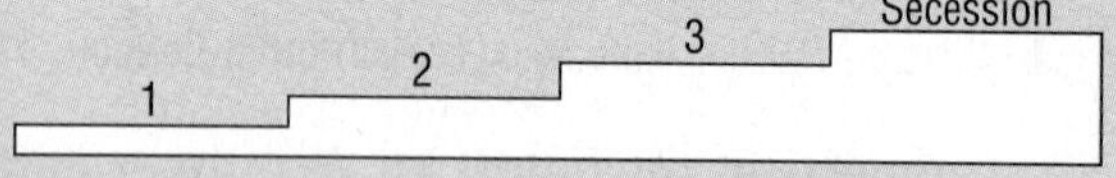

1
2
3
Secession

Objectives

After studying this section, you should be able to

★ discuss how most Southerners viewed and defended the institution of slavery.

★ explain the significance of the Kansas-Nebraska Act and the *Dred Scott* decision.

★ list the political events that led to the secession of seven Southern states.

Key Terms

platform, secession

▶ LINCOLN CAMPAIGN TORCH

HURRAH for LINCOLN

Southern legislatures made it increasingly difficult for slaveholders to emancipate their enslaved men and women. Some states decreed that free African Americans must either go somewhere else or be sold back into slavery. All African Americans, enslaved or free, had to carry identification passes when away from their homes. At night, patrols equipped with dogs and guns watched for runaways.

■ The South and Slavery

Although slavery was common in the South, the majority of people were not slaveholders. In addition, the bondage of African Americans assumed many different forms.

Some enslaved African Americans worked as house servants or were hired out to work in urban businesses. Most, however, worked on plantations and lived lives marked by hard labor, cruel discipline, and isolation. Marriages between enslaved persons were not legally recognized. Families could be broken up by sale. It was against the law to teach enslaved persons to read, although some white Southerners broke that law.

To support the system, many Southerners developed an elaborate defense of slavery. Southerners argued that slavery was necessary to provide an adequate labor supply and was "a positive good" because all the enslaved person's material needs were provided. Finally, defenders of slavery tried to use arguments from science and the Bible to show that slavery was acceptable.

The Rift Widens

For a few years it looked as though the Compromise of 1850 might provide a permanent solution to the slavery controversy. In the North, however, opposition to the stringent Fugitive Slave Law included in the Compromise of 1850 increased. Under this law, the word of a slaveholder, or even one who claimed to be, was taken as conclusive proof of identity of the runaway. A suspected runaway (who might in fact be a free person) had no right to testify on his or her own behalf. Any citizen might be required to join in pursuit of a runaway.

To fight this injustice, most free state legislatures passed personal liberty laws that nullified the Fugitive Slave Law by forbidding state officials to assist in the capture of runaways. Antislavery feeling in the North was also heightened by Harriet Beecher Stowe's *Uncle Tom's Cabin,* a novel portraying slavery at its worst. The book sold 300,000 copies in 1852, its first year of publication.

Kansas-Nebraska Act

In 1854, the political truce over slavery ended with the passage of the Kansas-Nebraska Act. Senator Stephen A. Douglas proposed the act to encourage the rapid settlement of the trans-Missouri region and the building of a transcontinental railroad with terminals at St. Louis and Chicago.

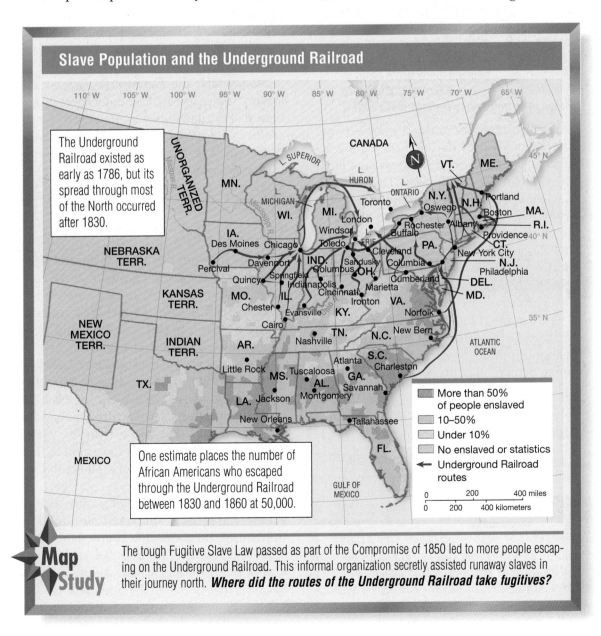

Slave Population and the Underground Railroad

The Underground Railroad existed as early as 1786, but its spread through most of the North occurred after 1830.

One estimate places the number of African Americans who escaped through the Underground Railroad between 1830 and 1860 at 50,000.

More than 50% of people enslaved
10–50%
Under 10%
No enslaved or statistics
Underground Railroad routes

0   200   400 miles
0   200   400 kilometers

Map Study The tough Fugitive Slave Law passed as part of the Compromise of 1850 led to more people escaping on the Underground Railroad. This informal organization secretly assisted runaway slaves in their journey north. *Where did the routes of the Underground Railroad take fugitives?*

▲ **HARRIET TUBMAN** One of the most successful Underground Railroad "agents" was Harriet Tubman. After making her own escape, she returned to the South again and again, freeing more than 300 others. *What book helped raise antislavery feelings in the North?*

Visualizing History

The act, however, opened intersectional controversy. It provided that the trans-Missouri region be divided into two new territories, Nebraska and Kansas. The question of whether or not slavery would exist in the new territories was to be decided by popular sovereignty. This part of the act negated the Missouri Compromise, because both territories lay above latitude 36°30'. A clause specifically repealing the Missouri ban on slavery north of that line was added.

The Kansas-Nebraska Act was criticized. The repeal of the Missouri Compromise was denounced in the North. The South continued to demand that the North recognize the rights of slaveholders in the territories.

Bleeding Kansas

Settlers started at once to move into the Kansas Territory. Because the slavery issue was to be decided by popular vote, a race developed to see whether the majority of settlers would come from slave or free states.

A bloody struggle between the proslavery and antislavery factions assumed the proportions of a civil war. The violence in "Bleeding Kansas" reached its peak on the eve of the presidential election of 1856.

Election of 1856

After the passage of the Kansas-Nebraska Act, the Whig party broke up over the slavery issue. To fill the void, a new party—the Republicans—appeared. In their **platform,** or statement of beliefs, the Republicans upheld the principle of "free soil," or keeping slavery out of the territories. Strongly organized in every northern state, the Republican party nominated General John C. Frémont.

Meanwhile, the Democrats dodged the slavery issue. To balance Southerners' dominance of the party, they nominated a Northerner, James Buchanan of Pennsylvania. With only a minority of the popular vote, Buchanan won the election with 174 electoral votes.

The *Dred Scott* Decision

In his Inaugural Address in March 1857, President Buchanan suggested that the controversy over slavery in the territories be left to the Supreme Court, which had recently heard a case on this question and was expected to render a decision soon.

Dred Scott was an enslaved man taken by a former master from the state of Missouri into territory closed to slavery by the Missouri Compromise and then brought back to Missouri again. For more than 10 years, Scott sued for freedom on the grounds that residence in a free territory released him from slavery.

On March 6, 1857, Chief Justice Roger Taney (TAW•nee) delivered an opinion upholding completely the Southern point of view that Scott had no right to sue in a federal court. Taney ruled against Scott because, he claimed, the founders of the United States did not intend for African

HISTORY Online **Student Web Activity**
Visit the *American History: The Modern Era Since 1865* Web site at **me.glencoe.com** and click on **Chapter 5— Student Web Activities** for an activity about fugitive slaves.

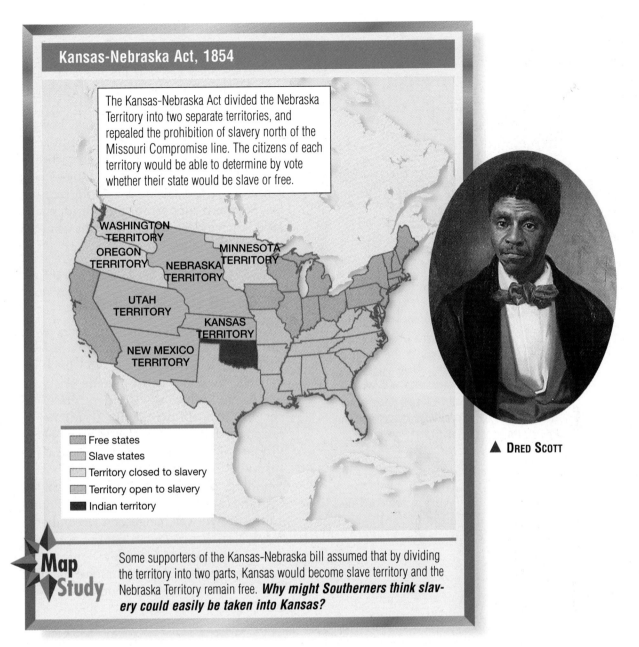

Kansas-Nebraska Act, 1854

The Kansas-Nebraska Act divided the Nebraska Territory into two separate territories, and repealed the prohibition of slavery north of the Missouri Compromise line. The citizens of each territory would be able to determine by vote whether their state would be slave or free.

WASHINGTON TERRITORY
OREGON TERRITORY
MINNESOTA TERRITORY
NEBRASKA TERRITORY
UTAH TERRITORY
KANSAS TERRITORY
NEW MEXICO TERRITORY

- Free states
- Slave states
- Territory closed to slavery
- Territory open to slavery
- Indian territory

▲ DRED SCOTT

Map Study Some supporters of the Kansas-Nebraska bill assumed that by dividing the territory into two parts, Kansas would become slave territory and the Nebraska Territory remain free. **Why might Southerners think slavery could easily be taken into Kansas?**

Americans to be citizens. The Missouri Compromise ban on slavery north of the 36°30′ line, the Court said, was unconstitutional because Congress had no right to ban slavery in the territories.

Instead of settling the slavery dispute, the *Dred Scott* decision made it more bitter. Many Northerners, especially Republicans, flatly opposed the decision. If the decision stood, the Republican party might as well go out of existence, because its basic principle—free soil—had been declared unconstitutional. Southerners, on the other hand, called on the North to obey the decision as the price of the South's remaining in the Union.

■ Lincoln and Douglas

The *Dred Scott* decision left the nation in a state of almost hopeless confusion about the principle of popular sovereignty. Did the decision forbid the people of a territory to decide whether or not they wanted slavery?

Stephen A. Douglas and Abraham Lincoln were rival candidates in the Illinois senatorial election in 1858. Douglas, a defender of popular sovereignty, was the most prominent Democrat in Congress and hoped to be elected President in 1860. Lincoln, on the other hand, had served only a single term in the House of Representatives. Although Lincoln was not an abolitionist,

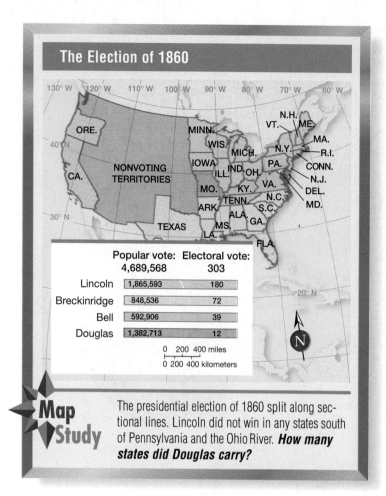

The Election of 1860

ORE.

MINN.

N.H.
VT. ME.

CA.

NONVOTING
TERRITORIES

WIS.
MICH.
IOWA
ILL IND. OH.
MO. KY.

N.Y.
PA.
MA.
R.I.
CONN.
N.J.
VA. DEL.
MD.

40° N

ARK.
TENN.
N.C.
S.C.

30° N

TEXAS

LA.

ALA.
MS.
GA.

20° N

FLA.

Popular vote:	Electoral vote:
4,689,568	303

	Popular	Electoral
Lincoln	1,865,593	180
Breckinridge	848,536	72
Bell	592,906	39
Douglas	1,382,713	12

0   200   400 miles
0 200 400 kilometers

N

Map Study

The presidential election of 1860 split along sectional lines. Lincoln did not win in any states south of Pennsylvania and the Ohio River. *How many states did Douglas carry?*

Freeport Doctrine

To solve this dilemma, Douglas formulated the so-called Freeport Doctrine. Douglas said he accepted the *Dred Scott* decision; however, a territory might effectively discourage slavery if it failed to pass laws to keep enslaved persons under control. By admitting that a territory could practically nullify the *Dred Scott* decision, Douglas won a narrow victory in the senatorial race but lost Southern support for the presidency in 1860. Lincoln lost the election but gained a national reputation.

■ John Brown's Raid

Tensions over the issue of slavery were further heightened by the actions of John Brown, a fiery abolitionist who believed that his mission was to liberate enslaved people and punish slaveholders. On October 16, 1859, Brown, with 21 followers, seized the federal arsenal at Harpers Ferry, Virginia, intending to free and arm the enslaved men and women of the surrounding countryside. The siege ended with the capture and trial of Brown. Found guilty, Brown was hanged on December 2. Many Northerners regarded him as a martyr to the cause of freedom. Southerners regarded Brown's punishment as just. They feared nothing so much as a slave revolt.

■ The Election of 1860

As the election of 1860 approached, Democrats split over the issue of slavery in the territories. A Northern wing of the party nominated Douglas for the presidency and backed popular sovereignty; a Southern wing nominated John C. Breckinridge of Kentucky and supported the *Dred Scott* decision. The Constitutional Union party, composed of former Southern Whigs, nominated John Bell of Tennessee and attempted to avoid the slavery issue.

With such division among their opponents, the door to the presidency stood open to the Republicans. They held that

he believed that if slavery were confined to its existing area, Southerners themselves might eventually abolish it.

Debates

During the campaign Lincoln and Douglas debated the issues. Douglas attempted to show that Republicans in general—and Lincoln, in particular—were abolitionists in disguise, bent on destroying the Union. During their debate at Freeport, Illinois, Lincoln asked Douglas if the people of a territory could exclude slavery. Douglas was trapped. If he answered "Yes," he would appear to support popular sovereignty, thereby opposing the *Dred Scott* decision. A "yes" answer would improve his chances for reelection as senator, but cost him Southern support for the 1860 presidency. A "no" answer would make it seem as if he had abandoned popular sovereignty, on which he had based his political career. This answer would be welcomed by the South but could cost him the senatorial election.

slavery should be left undisturbed where it existed, but that it should be excluded from the territories. They denounced John Brown's raid and also called for a protective tariff, free homesteads for settlers, and federal funds for internal improvements, including a railroad to the Pacific. Abraham Lincoln, the Republican candidate for President, gained a majority in the electoral college and carried nearly every free state. Breckinridge carried the Deep South, and Bell and Douglas divided the border states.

■ The South Secedes

The Republican victory caused great alarm in the Deep South. Many Southerners felt that they had no other recourse but to leave the Union. They believed that Lincoln's election meant abolition and rebellion by those who were enslaved. Mississippi senator Albert Gallatin Brown told a Southern audience:

❝ *The North is accumulating power, and it means to use that power [for emancipation]. . . . When that is done, no pen can describe, no tongue can depict, no pencil can point the horrors that will overspread this country. . . . Disunion is a fearful thing, but emancipation is worse.* ❞

■ The Confederacy

Between Lincoln's election in November 1860 and his inaugural in March 1861, seven states of the Deep South (South Carolina, Mississippi, Florida, Alabama, Georgia, Louisiana, and Texas) voted for **secession**—withdrawal from the Union. They drafted a constitution for their new alliance—the Confederate States of America—and called on the other slave states to join them.

When Lincoln reached Washington, D.C., in late February 1861, eight slave states remained in the Union. Although most Northerners believed that states did not have the right to leave the Union, few at first wished to fight to force them back in. In his Inaugural Address, Lincoln pleaded that the North and South be "not enemies, but friends" and said that "there need be no bloodshed or violence." Sadly, these hopes were soon dashed.

▲ REPUBLICAN CAMPAIGN POSTER

Section 3 ★ Assessment

Checking for Understanding

1. **Define** platform, secession.
2. **Distinguish** Northern and Southern reactions to the passage of the Kansas-Nebraska Act.

Critical Thinking

3. **Analyzing Choices** Compile a list of events, other than the election of Lincoln, that might have led to secession.

4. **Analyzing Issues** Re-create the chart shown here, and explain how the Kansas-Nebraska

Act and the *Dred Scott* decision undid the Missouri Compromise.

Kansas-Nebraska Act	*Dred Scott* decision

INTERDISCIPLINARY ACTIVITY

5. **Math** Create a bar graph that shows the electoral votes for the presidential candidates in the 1860 election. Write a caption that explains the election results.

Read to Discover

How did spirituals reflect the views of Christianity held by enslaved persons? In what ways did spirituals contribute to a unique African American culture?

Reader's Dictionary

drinking gourd	long-handled utensil; in the poem, it symbolizes the Big Dipper, which points to the North Star
smite	to strike
bondage	slavery

▼ CUMBERLAND LANDING, VIRGINIA, 1862

The struggles that tore the nation apart at mid-century were reflected in much of the period's writing. Spirituals—songs of salvation—provided the African Americans who wrote and chanted them not only with a measure of solace in bleak times but with a means for communicating secretly among themselves under their masters' watchful eye.

Follow the Drinking Gourd

When the sun comes back and the first quail calls,
Follow the drinking gourd,
For the old man is a-waiting for to carry you to freedom
If you follow the drinking gourd.

Follow the drinking gourd,
Follow the drinking gourd,

For the old man is a-waiting for to carry you to freedom
If you follow the drinking gourd.

The river bank will make a very good road,
The dead trees show you the way,
Left foot, peg foot traveling on
Follow the drinking gourd,
The river ends between two hills

Follow the drinking gourd,
There's another river on the other side,
Follow the drinking gourd,
Where the little river meets the great big river,
Follow the drinking gourd,
For the old man is a-waiting for to carry you to freedom
If you follow the drinking gourd.

Go Down, Moses

When Israel was in Egypt land,
Let my people go!
Oppressed so hard they could not stand,
Let my people go!

Chorus

Go down, Moses,
Way down in Egypt land
Tell ole Pharaoh,
Let my people go!
Thus say the Lord, bold Moses said,
Let my people go!
If not I'll smite your first-born dead,
Let my people go!
No more shall they in bondage toil,
Let my people go!
Let them come out with Egypt's spoil,
Let my people go!

▲ MUSIC ON THE PLANTATION

Swing Low, Sweet Chariot

Swing low, sweet chariot,
Coming for to carry me home,
Swing low, sweet chariot,
Coming to carry me home.
I looked over Jordan and what did I see
Coming for to carry me home,
A band of angels coming after me,
Coming to carry me home.
If you get there before I do,
Coming for to carry me home,
Tell all my friends I'm coming too,
Coming to carry me home.
Swing low, sweet chariot,
Coming for to carry me home,
Swing low, sweet chariot,
Coming to carry me home.

Responding to Literature

1. What is the message from one enslaved person to another in "Follow the Drinking Gourd"?

2. Which spiritual equates the plight of the African Americans with that of another group? Which group?

3. Describe the mood of the spirituals.

ACTIVITY

4. Prepare a table with the headings "Word or Phrase" and "Symbolizes." Under the first heading, list the following: *drinking gourd*, *old man*, *chariot*, and *home*. Under the second heading, write your ideas on what these words and phrases represent in these spirituals.

The Civil War

Guide to Reading

Main Idea
The Confederate attack on Fort Sumter began a long and bloody war between the North and the South.

Reading Strategy

Taking Notes As you read about the Civil War, identify and explain the significance of major battles in the East and the West, using the outline form shown here.

I. War in the East
   A.
   B.

II. War in the West
   A.
   B.

Objectives
After studying this section, you should be able to
★ explain the strategies of the North and the South.
★ identify and explain the significance of major battles of the war.

Key Terms
conscription, blockade

► UNION RECRUITMENT POSTER, 1861

The Civil War began on April 12, 1861, when Southern troops fired on Fort Sumter, a federally controlled military post in the harbor of Charleston, South Carolina. Both sides prepared for battle after the Fort Sumter clash. In the North, Lincoln requested 75,000 volunteers for 90 days to suppress the rebellion and preserve the Union; more responded than could be equipped or trained. In the South, four more states—Virginia, Arkansas, North Carolina, and Tennessee—left the Union and joined the Confederacy.

■ Strategies and Advantages

The Civil War was fought across the continent from southern Pennsylvania in the Northeast to New Mexico in the Southwest.

Almost 3 million soldiers wore the uniforms of the Union or the Confederacy. Countless other men and women supported these troops—on the farms, in the factories, on the battlefields, and behind the lines.

In many ways, the Civil War was the "last of the old wars and the first of the new." Still prominent were muzzle-loading rifles, horse cavalry, and chivalrous respect for the enemy. New were the use of railroads, the telegraph, ironclad ships, and observation balloons. The Civil War also saw the introduction of **conscription,** or the drafting of men for military service. It became the world's first major "total war" in which civilians as well as soldiers were directly affected.

The South's Leaders

The South had the better army, especially during the early years of the war. Because of a strong military tradition, many Confederate officers had attended the United States Military Academy at West Point in New York. Most of the top officers in the United States Army resigned their commissions to fight for the Confederacy, among them Robert E. Lee. After his native Virginia seceded, Lee decided that he could not "raise my hand against my relatives, my children, my home." He rejected Lincoln's offer to lead the Union armies and took command of Confederate forces in Virginia.

Northern and Southern Strategies

The Union's military strategy was simple: **blockade,** or close off, Confederate ports and ruin its economy; invade the South and split it into thirds at the Mississippi River and through Tennessee and Georgia; and capture the Confederate capital at Richmond, Virginia. Southern strategy was even simpler. Southerners would be fighting for their independence on familiar terrain. To win, the South did not have to do anything except hold out against enemy attacks.

Differences in Resources

The North was superior to the South in nearly every resource. The Union had most of the country's factories, railroads, banks, minerals, grain crops, and meat. The Confederacy had less than one-half as many people as the North, and more than one-third of these were enslaved persons. The Confederacy was open to attack along its land borders and its extensive coastline. In addition, with its stress on states' rights, the Confederate central government had difficulty getting troops and taxes from member states.

Wartime Diplomacy

The Union wanted to prevent European nations from supporting the Confederacy. The British and French governments, in particular, were openly sympathetic to Southern independence.

The South expected Britain's aid because British textile mills used Southern cotton. To prevent Britain and the South from developing closer commercial ties, President Lincoln ordered the blockade of Southern

ports. The South did not let the blockade go unchallenged. The Confederates built an ironclad—a floating fort with slanted sides of iron plates from a wooden frigate originally called the *Merrimac,* but renamed the *Virginia.* The Confederates unleashed the *Virginia* on the Union fleet in Norfolk Harbor. Union officials hurriedly built their own ironclad, the *Monitor.* The battle on March 9, 1862, was the first ever between ironclad warships. Neither ship was able to inflict much damage on the other, but the *Monitor* did keep the *Virginia* from destroying the rest of the Union fleet.

Unable to break the blockade militarily, Southern leaders tried diplomacy. They arranged for British shipyards to build and outfit Confederate warships to prey on Northern shipping. These vessels, however,

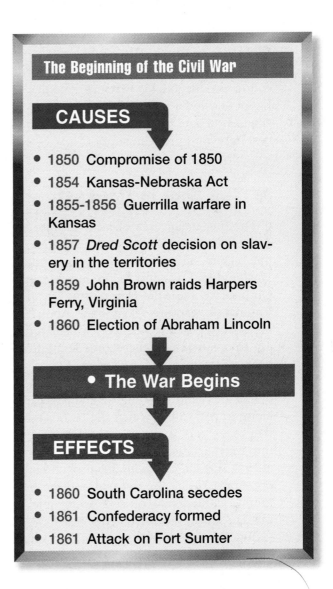

The Beginning of the Civil War

CAUSES

- 1850 Compromise of 1850
- 1854 Kansas-Nebraska Act
- 1855-1856 Guerrilla warfare in Kansas
- 1857 *Dred Scott* decision on slavery in the territories
- 1859 John Brown raids Harpers Ferry, Virginia
- 1860 Election of Abraham Lincoln

• The War Begins

EFFECTS

- 1860 South Carolina secedes
- 1861 Confederacy formed
- 1861 Attack on Fort Sumter

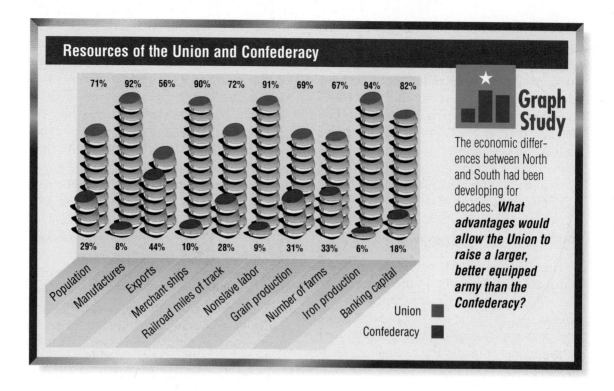

Resources of the Union and Confederacy

	Population	Manufactures	Exports	Merchant ships	Railroad miles of track	Nonslave labor	Grain production	Number of farms	Iron production	Banking capital
Union	71%	92%	56%	90%	72%	91%	69%	67%	94%	82%
Confederacy	29%	8%	44%	10%	28%	9%	31%	33%	6%	18%

Graph Study

The economic differences between North and South had been developing for decades. *What advantages would allow the Union to raise a larger, better equipped army than the Confederacy?*

could not break the Union blockade, nor could Britain's need for cotton. Increased cotton production by Britain's colonies in Egypt and India replaced the loss of Southern cotton and ended the Confederacy's best hope for European support.

■ The War in the East

The first major area of land warfare lay east of the Appalachians and centered on the region surrounding the two capitals, Washington, D.C., and Richmond, Virginia. On June 21, 1861, the Union army invaded Virginia to capture Richmond. About 30 miles from Washington, D.C., 30,000 Northern troops met a smaller Confederate force near a stream called Bull Run. Expecting victory and a quick end to the war, members of Congress and Washington civilians came along to picnic and watch the battle. What they saw was a confusing clash of two untrained armies. Union troops fought well at first, but the Confederates proved better organized. Using the railroad and the telegraph, Confederate officers were able to quickly supply reinforcements.

Together, panic-stricken Union soldiers and civilians fled back to Washington.

Indeed, Northern predictions of a quick war could have come true. "Give me 10,000 fresh troops, and I will be in Washington tomorrow," Confederate General Thomas "Stonewall" Jackson said after Bull Run. Jefferson Davis, the Confederate president, however, insisted on a defensive war, and the Union was saved.

After the Northern disaster at Bull Run, Lincoln replaced General Irvin McDowell with General George McClellan, who trained and reorganized the Union army. But in 1862 the Confederates turned back McClellan in several confrontations throughout Virginia.

Antietam

Confederate military success, however, did not extend onto Northern soil. Lee planned to attack Washington, D.C., from the north and destroy Northern morale. In September 1862, his 45,000 troops slipped into Maryland; and Lee split his army into two forces. McClellan, who was to protect Washington by keeping between Lee and the capital, frantically chased after his enemy.

Discovering Lee's plans, General McClellan attacked Lee on September 17, 1862, at Antietam (An•TEE•tuhm) Creek near

Sharpsburg, Maryland. In the bloodiest single day of the war, McClellan forced Lee to retreat back into Virginia. The Confederates suffered more than 11,000 casualties. McClellan lost even more, and his army was too damaged to pursue Lee and finish him.

Gettysburg

The following summer, Lee's army defeated Union forces at Chancellorsville. This victory encouraged Lee to head north into Pennsylvania. He was shadowed, however, by a Union army under General George G. Meade. An accidental clash between small units at Gettysburg developed into a bloody battle that marked the turning point of the war. As both armies gathered to do battle, Union troops took up positions on the crest of a low ridge. It became the Confederates' task to dislodge them from this high ground. Desperate

Confederate attacks—concluding on July 3 in a gallant but suicidal charge across an open field by General George Pickett's troops—were all but repulsed. After 3 days of fighting, Union casualties were more than 23,000. More than 28,000 Confederate soldiers were killed or wounded. "Do not let the enemy escape," Lincoln wired the victorious Meade.

On July 4, Lee retreated into Virginia. Once again, the Union army failed to pursue him. "Our army held the war in the hollow of its hand," a frustrated Lincoln said. "We had only to stretch forth our hands and they were ours. And nothing I could say or do could make the army move."

The Gettysburg Address

Although both sides suffered heavy casualties at Gettysburg, it was a devastating loss of life from which the sparsely populat-

▲ *BATTLE OF GETTYSBURG* Lithograph by L. Frang and Company The location of the Battle of Gettysburg was a matter of chance. Commanding officers did not decide on it, but some detached units clashed on the northern side of the town, and then Meade quickly concentrated his army there. *What was the result of the battle?*

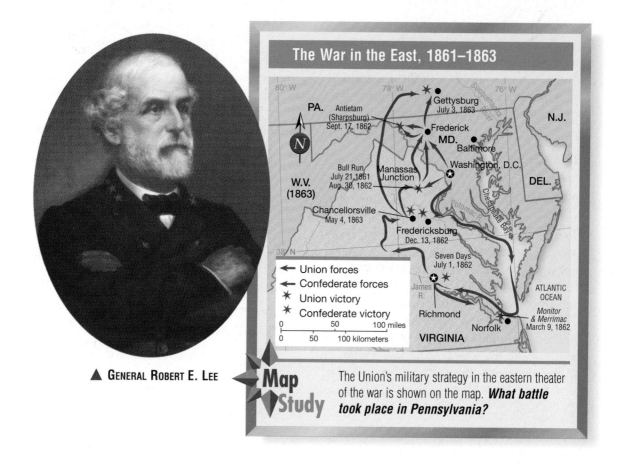

The War in the East, 1861–1863

Antietam (Sharpsburg) Sept. 17, 1862
Gettysburg July 3, 1863
Frederick
Baltimore
Washington, D.C.
Bull Run July 21, 1861 Aug. 30, 1862
Manassas Junction
Chancellorsville May 4, 1863
Fredericksburg Dec. 13, 1862
Seven Days July 1, 1862
Richmond
Monitor & Merrimac March 9, 1862
Norfolk

PA.
MD.
N.J.
DEL.
W.V. (1863)
ATLANTIC OCEAN
VIRGINIA

← Union forces
← Confederate forces
★ Union victory
★ Confederate victory

0   50   100 miles
0   50   100 kilometers

▲ GENERAL ROBERT E. LEE

Map Study

The Union's military strategy in the eastern theater of the war is shown on the map. *What battle took place in Pennsylvania?*

ed South could not recover. On November 19, 1863, President Lincoln visited Gettysburg to dedicate the battlefield cemetery and to honor the soldiers buried there. In this Gettysburg address, the President promised that "these dead shall not have died in vain." He also declared that soon the nation "shall have a new birth of freedom."

■ The War in the West

The second area of land warfare centered in the west, around the Mississippi River and its tributaries. In many ways, the west was critical to victory. If Union armies gained control of the Mississippi River, the Confederacy would lose its western food supplies.

The Union advance began in 1862 when General Ulysses S. Grant attacked Confederate positions at Fort Henry and Fort Donelson on the Kentucky-Tennessee border. When the Confederate commander at Fort Donelson tried to negotiate, Grant's reply created his reputation as a tough, no-nonsense

soldier: "No terms except unconditional and immediate surrender can be accepted."

The fall of Fort Donelson, with about 13,000 Confederate prisoners, opened the way for a Union advance south toward a railroad center at Corinth, Mississippi. From there Grant planned to move west along the railroad to capture Memphis, Tennessee, on the Mississippi River.

Shiloh

The Union advance was slowed in April 1862 by the bloody, two-day battle of Shiloh on the Tennessee-Mississippi border. Grant's forces were surprised by the Confederates under General Albert Sidney Johnston. The Union army escaped disaster only when reinforcements arrived and Johnston was killed. Grant lost 13,000 of his 63,000 troops, and Confederate casualties numbered 11,000 of 40,000. Impressed by the determination of his enemy, Grant later wrote that after Shiloh, "I gave up all idea of saving the Union except by complete conquest."

New Orleans

Meanwhile, Flag Officer David Farragut was ordered to capture New Orleans. To reach the city his warships had to move upriver from the Gulf of Mexico past 2 Confederate forts. After failing to destroy the forts, Farragut decided to pass under cover of darkness. As the maneuver began, the moon rose and Confederate forces opened fire. After a 90-minute battle, 20 of the 24 Union ships made it past the forts, and New Orleans surrendered without firing a shot.

By the end of 1862, Union armies occupied all of western Tennessee and were probing south into Mississippi. Other Union forces were advancing north from New Orleans. Only the strongly fortified city of Vicksburg blocked Union control of the river and success of the Union's western strategy.

Vicksburg and Chattanooga

After five attempts to capture Vicksburg failed, Grant began a daring campaign. After marching his army down the west bank of the Mississippi, below Vicksburg, he started inland. The Confederate commander at Vicksburg, thinking Grant was trying to trick him into the field, stayed behind his fortifications.

Moving quickly, Union forces reached Jackson, the capital of Mississippi, almost without opposition. Then Grant turned and fought his way back west to the outskirts of Vicksburg. In 17 days his troops marched 180 miles and won 5 battles against larger forces. Then he laid siege to Vicksburg.

With its citizens starving, Vicksburg finally surrendered on July 4. As a result of the Union capture of Vicksburg and other Mississippi River ports, Texas and Arkansas—the South's leading food producers—were cut off from the rest of the Confederacy.

Union forces then attempted to cut the Confederacy again—through eastern Tennessee and Georgia. The key was Chattanooga, a rail center on the Tennessee-Georgia border. In September 1863, a Union army under General William Rosecrans was

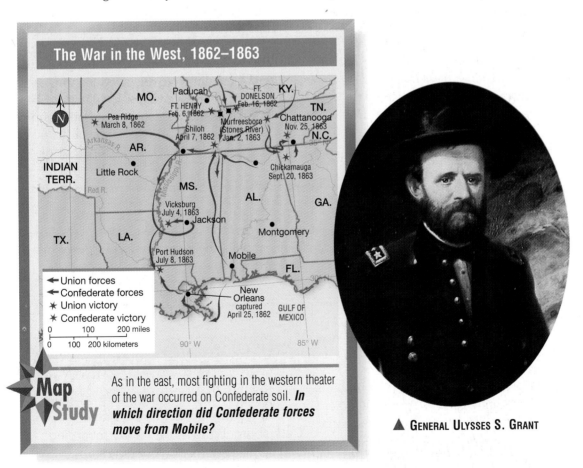

The War in the West, 1862–1863

- Pea Ridge March 8, 1862
- Paducah
- FT. HENRY Feb. 6, 1862
- FT. DONELSON Feb. 16, 1862
- Shiloh April 7, 1862
- Murfreesboro (Stones River) Jan. 2, 1863
- Chattanooga Nov. 25, 1863
- Chickamauga Sept. 20, 1863
- Little Rock
- Vicksburg July 4, 1863
- Jackson
- Montgomery
- Port Hudson July 8, 1863
- Mobile
- New Orleans captured April 25, 1862

MO. KY. TN. N.C. INDIAN TERR. AR. MS. AL. GA. TX. LA. FL. Arkansas R. Red R. Mississippi GULF OF MEXICO

90° W   85° W   30° N

← Union forces
← Confederate forces
✶ Union victory
✶ Confederate victory

0   100   200 miles
0   100   200 kilometers

Map Study
As in the east, most fighting in the western theater of the war occurred on Confederate soil. ***In which direction did Confederate forces move from Mobile?***

▲ GENERAL ULYSSES S. GRANT

▲ *OVERLOOKING CHATTANOOGA* by James Walker The Battle of Chattanooga was one of the few battles in which Confederate forces outnumbered Union troops, 70,000 to 56,000. At first, Confederate troops forced their foes to retreat to the city. *What was the significance of the Battle of Chattanooga?*

badly defeated by Confederate General Braxton Bragg at the Battle of Chickamauga in northwest Georgia. A Union officer described his army's retreat:

> *The march was a melancholy one. All along the road for miles, wounded men were lying. They had crawled or hobbled slowly away from the fury of the battle, become exhausted, and lain down by the roadside to die.* "

Rosecrans retreated to Chattanooga, where the Confederates attacked. The Union forces were saved when Grant arrived with reinforcements in late October and drove Confederate forces from the heights around the city. By the end of 1863, only four states—Georgia, South Carolina, North Carolina, and Virginia—remained to be subdued. In early 1864, Lincoln gave General William T. Sherman command in the west and summoned Grant to accomplish what none of his other generals could do—crush Robert E. Lee.

Section 4 ★ Assessment

Checking for Understanding

1. **Define** conscription, blockade.

2. **Discuss** the Battle of Gettsyburg and state why the battle was significant to the Union and Confederacy.

Critical Thinking

3. **Making Inferences** Bull Run changed people's perception of the war. From this reaction, what can you infer about the way people on both sides viewed the war before Bull Run?

4. **Comparing** Re-create the diagram shown here, and list the war strategies of the North and the South.

War Strategies	
North	South

INTERDISCIPLINARY ACTIVITY

5. **The Arts** Imagine that you are a Union or Confederate soldier at the Battle of Gettysburg. Write a diary entry recording that day's events and your emotions.

★★★★★★★★★★★★★★★★★★★★★★★★★★★★★★★

Behind the Lines

Guide to Reading

Main Idea
Both the Union and the Confederacy relied on their resources and citizens behind the lines in the war effort.

Reading Strategy

Classifying Information As you read about how the war affected everyday citizens, use a chart such as the one shown here to list the wartime roles each group played.

African Americans	
Native Americans	
Women	

Objectives

After studying this section, you should be able to

★ discuss behind-the-lines activity in the North and South.

★ explain the wartime roles played by women, African Americans, and Native Americans.

Key Terms

bounty, greenback, martial law, habeas corpus

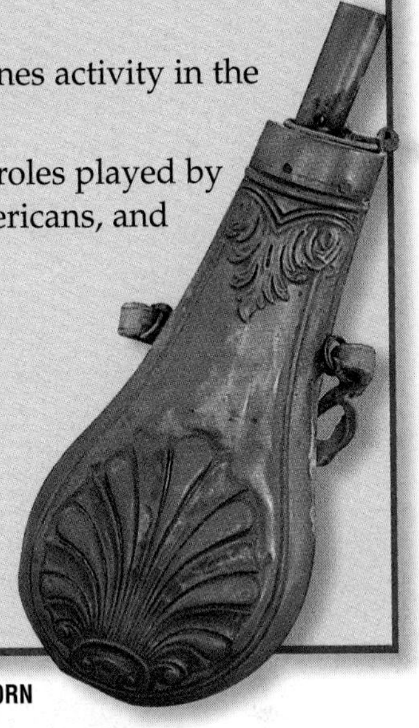

▶ **POWDER HORN**

The Civil War was the largest war ever fought on the North American continent. Of the 1.5 million Southern white males of fighting age, about 900,000 served in the Confederate armies. Of 4 million such males in the North, about half fought in the war. In addition, more than 200,000 African Americans fought and served in the Union military, and thousands more performed manual labor.

• •

Footnotes to History

The First Income Tax The North financed much of its war effort through taxes. Included was the nation's first income tax, passed in 1861. Individuals earning between $800 and $5,000 paid 5 percent; those with incomes between $5,001 and $10,000 paid 7.5 percent; and those with incomes above $10,000 paid 10 percent.

More Americans were killed in this war than in any other conflict in the history of the United States. Even in the early battles, the losses were shockingly high. As the war dragged on, the Union suffered terrible casualties but grew stronger. Confederate losses, however, gradually weakened the South's will to fight.

■ Wartime Government Powers

In a long war fought on a vast scale, victors are decided as much by government policies behind the lines as on the battlefield. Both the Union and Confederate governments exerted greatly increased powers in order to raise and supply the armies, finance the war, and suppress antiwar opinion.

Raising the Armies

At first, both North and South relied on volunteers and Lincoln's original 90-day volunteers were replaced by 3-year enlistments. But mounting casualties reduced enthusiasm for the war, and enlistments decreased. As the South's economy collapsed, and the scarcity of clothing and medicine was matched by shortages of food and shelter, Confederate desertions increased. Many Confederate soldiers saw no disgrace in going home to aid their suffering families.

The Draft

Both North and South were forced to draft men for military service. In April 1862, the South began drafting men aged 18 to 35 and later raised the upper age limit to 50. In March 1863, the United States Congress created a military draft in the North.

Draft laws were incomplete and discriminatory. A draftee could avoid service by hiring a substitute, and a Union draftee could buy his way out by paying the government $300. Such provisions aroused criticism that it was "a rich man's war and a poor man's fight."

▲ President Abraham Lincoln

In the South, some state governors helped their citizens evade the draft. In the North, opposition to conscription led to riots in New York City in July 1863. A resident reported that for four days:

> **"** . . . there were dreadful scenes enacted in the city. The police were successfully opposed; many were killed, many houses were gutted and burned: the . . . asylum was burned and all the furniture was carried off by women. . . . **"**

To those who enlisted, the North paid a **bounty,** or lump sum of money, of as much as $1,500 for a single 3-year enlistment. This led to the practice of "bounty jumping," whereby a man would enlist, collect his bounty and then desert, only to reenlist somewhere else.

Supplies

The Confederacy faced an uphill struggle to carry out its war effort. The Confederate government encouraged factories to supply troops with arms and ammunition, but the South lacked the industrial capacity to provide other necessities. The South had depended upon the North for, as one observer noted, "everything from a hairpin to a toothpick, and from a cradle to a coffin." As the war dragged on, shortages for the civilian population as well as the Confederacy's armies became commonplace.

The South ran out of almost everything. Shortages in feed for animals and salt for curing meant that little meat was available. Shortages in food were matched by shortages in clothing and medicine.

The North, on the other hand, had a strong industrial base, but the efforts of the Union government to supply its troops were hindered by overcharging and corruption. Army contractors sometimes supplied shoddy clothing, rotten meat, and defective shoes. The productivity of Northern factories was so great, though, that in spite of the graft, Union armies were better equipped than their enemy.

★★★★★★★★★★★★★★★★★★★★★★★★★★★★★★

$ ECONOMICS
Financing the War

The North was also far more successful than the South in financing the war. About one-fourth of the $4 billion the North needed came from taxation, and the rest from borrowing and issuing paper money. The Union government printed a large amount of currency, but not to the point where it became worthless. It issued $400 million worth of **greenbacks,** paper money that was not backed by gold or silver, but whose value rose and fell with the success of Union armies in the field.

The Confederacy was less able to finance the war than was the North. The South had intended to obtain money by selling cotton to Europe, but the Union blockade prevented this. To raise money, the Confederacy enacted an income tax and demanded 10 percent of all crops produced. Above all, it raised money by simply printing more of it. The Confederate government was able to operate only by forcing citizens of the South to accept its worthless currency in exchange for supplies. $

Civil Rights

Opposition to the war existed from the very beginning in both North and South. President Lincoln and President Davis each suppressed antiwar opinion by curtailing the civil rights of citizens. In parts of their territories, the two leaders declared **martial law,** a form of military rule that includes suspending constitutional guarantees of civil rights. They also put aside the right of **habeas corpus,** which requires that persons who are arrested be brought to court to show why they should be held. Lincoln, in particular, agonized over his decisions to deny citizens their civil rights. He believed, though, that the survival of the nation during an emergency overrode the Constitution.

■ The Emancipation Proclamation

When the Civil War began, there was not universal support in the North for a war to free enslaved persons. In many areas of the North there was open hostility to African Americans, and laws that limited their rights. Slavery still existed in Washington, D.C., and in five states that remained in the Union.

Lincoln, himself, declared that his goal in the war was "to save the Union . . . not either to save or to destroy slavery." While believing that slavery was a moral wrong, Lincoln recognized the constitutional guarantees for slavery and only opposed slavery's extension into the territories.

Pressure Mounts

As time passed, however, Lincoln came under increasing pressure to turn the war into a crusade against slavery. The abolitionists and a group of antislavery legislators in Congress known as Radical Republicans demanded that Southern slaveholders be punished for the war by loss of their property. As the number of battlefield casualties grew, Northerners increasingly began to feel that such bloodshed was justified only if it destroyed slavery. In addition,

AMERICAN PORTRAITS

Clara Barton
1821–1912

Clara Barton grew up loving sports and intended to make teaching her career. After 18 years in education, however, she went to work for the U.S. Patent Office. She was in the nation's capital when the guns of the Civil War started blazing.

Though lacking medical training, Clara Barton left her desk job to care for sick and wounded Union soldiers. Traveling to the sites of some of the worst carnage of the war, she even ventured deep into the Confederacy to assist federal forces laying siege to Charleston. She regularly risked her life by passing through the front lines to deliver supplies and nurse the wounded.

After the war—before she founded the American Red Cross in 1877—Clara Barton worked to identify thousands of soldiers who had perished at the Andersonville prison camp in Georgia.

Britain talked of mediating a settlement of the war. Lincoln realized that public opinion in Europe—and in Britain especially—was strongly opposed to slavery, and that no European government would defend the South in a war to end slavery.

Liberty Proclaimed

After Lee's defeat at Antietam in 1862, Lincoln announced that he would free enslaved people in the Confederate states on January 1, 1863. The Emancipation Proclamation, however, did not immediately free anyone, because it applied only to the areas held by the enemy. The Proclamation, however, turned the war into a moral crusade and aroused a new spirit in the North and among enslaved people themselves. As news of the Proclamation spread through the Confederacy, whenever Northern armies occupied Southern territory, thousands of African Americans poured into Union lines.

Slavery in areas where the Emancipation Proclamation did not apply remained a problem, however. About 800,000 enslaved persons lived in the slaveholding border states—Delaware, Maryland, Kentucky, and Missouri—that had remained in the Union. In addition, there were many more in areas of the South that the Union already had conquered. For these areas, Lincoln called for compensated emancipation—setting the enslaved free, but paying the slaveholders. Congress, however, adopted this idea only for the District of Columbia, which had about 3,000 enslaved people. Elsewhere, slavery was ended by the Thirteenth Amendment to the Constitution, ratified in 1865.

African American Soldiers

In the early years of the war, President Lincoln resisted appeals to enlist African Americans in the Union armies because he feared that such a policy would be resented in the border states. After the Emancipation Proclamation, the policy was changed. Nearly 200,000 African Americans enlisted for military service, and an additional 150,000 served in the quartermaster and engineering corps. African American soldiers were commanded by white officers, were paid less, and were segregated from white troops, who often resented them. Many African American regiments distinguished themselves in combat, however, and 23 soldiers won the Congressional Medal of Honor during the war.

Until the very end of the war, the South refused to accept African Americans for military service. Confederate armies, however, often used enslaved persons to dig fortifications, cook, drive wagons, and perform other labor.

Native Americans and the War

The war also dramatically affected Native Americans. The South acted quickly to gain support, sending commissioners to the Indian Territory to sign treaties. The Cherokee even fought on the Confederate side.

In 1864, the Union sent troops to restore its authority over the Native Americans. Federal victories over forces in Arkansas and in the Indian Territory showed the Native Americans the weakness of their Confederate allies. The North then renegotiated treaties with their nations and took land away from those who had fought for the Confederacy.

■ Women Behind the Lines

The demands the war placed on civilian populations created new roles for women. In both the North and the South, many women for the first time worked as government clerks and factory workers. Some women accompanied the armies in the field, cooking, sewing, and washing.

On Farms and Factories

Southern women were required to run plantations. On smaller farms, women plowed fields and handled other chores. Southern households became miniature factories, with spinning wheels and looms turning out clothing for the Confederacy.

In the North

Although most Northern women did not suffer from invading armies, they also were deeply affected by the war. In the North, the mechanical reaper and the sulky plow—where the operator rode on top of the plow itself rather than pushed it from behind—allowed women to take the place of husbands and sons. Industry's need for labor opened other opportunities in Northern factories. Many women needed such work to support their families.

On the Battlefield

Nurses were exposed to the worst horrors of war. Dorothea Dix became superintendent of female nurses in the Union army and in this position fought corruption and prejudice against her sex. Even more effective in widening the role of women in hospitals was Clara Barton, who later founded the American Red Cross.

Women also played a large part in America's first great private relief organization—the United States Sanitary Commission. This organization collected millions of dollars for projects to improve the living conditions of Union soldiers. It is little wonder that after the Civil War there was a renewed demand for woman suffrage.

Section 5 ★ Assessment

Checking for Understanding

1. **Define** bounty, greenback, martial law, habeas corpus.
2. **List** the contributions made by African Americans to the war effort on both sides.

Critical Thinking

3. **Cause and Effect** What effect do you think the war had on women's views about their status in society?
4. **Analyzing Issues** Re-create a diagram such as the one shown here, and list how both

Union and Confederate governments exerted increased powers to fight the war.

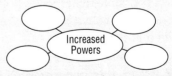

INTERDISCIPLINARY ACTIVITY

5. **The Arts** Create a recruitment poster calling for soldiers to enlist in either the Union or the Confederate army.

Analyzing Illustrations

▲ COMPANY E, 4TH U.S. INFANTRY

The photographs and illustrations that appear throughout this book contain special information. They aid in your understanding of each chapter. The pictures identify the focus of the material, and they make the book more interesting.

Learning the Skill

Look carefully at each picture to analyze its content. The steps you can take to analyze the picture are simple.

1. **Look** at the picture to get a general sense of what the subject is about.

2. **Read** the caption that goes with each picture or group of pictures.

3. **Decide** if the picture is a drawing, a painting, or a photograph. (Photography was not developed before the mid-1800s.)

4. **Decide**, if possible, whether or not a drawing or a painting was done by someone who lived at the time.

5. **Decide** whether a drawing is a posed portrait or an unposed photograph.

6. **Consider** the main theme and the general message of the picture.

7. **Identify** the main focus of the picture or the illustration.

8. **Consider** how the figures in the picture support the main theme.

9. **Consider** how the use of color or lack of color supports the theme of the picture.

10. **Decide** why you think the picture is used at its location in the book.

Practicing the Skill

1. When was this photograph taken? How do you know?

2. All of the figures in the picture are African American soldiers. What does this tell you about the makeup of the Union army?

3. Study the expressions and the postures of the soldiers. What information does this give you?

Glencoe's **Skillbuilder Interactive Workbook, Level 2** provides instruction and practice in key social studies skills.

APPLYING THE SKILL

4. Create a collage of Civil War paintings and photographs. Write a caption that identifies each illustration's main theme.

★★★★★★★★★★★★★★★★★★★★★★★★★

Ending the War

Guide to Reading

Main Idea

Ulysses S. Grant dealt the final blow to the Confederacy and its commanding general, Robert E. Lee.

Reading Strategy

Sequencing Information   As you read about the end of the war, make a time line of key events leading up to the South's surrender. Use the dates provided as a guide.

Sept. 1864   April 1865

May 1864   Nov. 1864

Objectives

After studying this section, you should be able to
★ explain the changes in Union military strategy after Grant took command.
★ discuss the issues in the election of 1864.

Key Term

forage

► CONFEDERATE ARMY HAT

General Grant determined that to win the war he would utilize the Union's biggest advantages over the South—its overwhelming superiority in population and in production capacity. To end the South's ability to fight, he would not only defeat Confederate armies, but would destroy them. To end the South's will to fight, he would engage in "total war"—war against civilians and resources as well as against armies.

■ Grant in the East

Moving south into Virginia, in May and June 1864, Grant's force of 120,000 engaged the Confederate army of 60,000 almost continuously. At the Battle of the Wilderness, Lee stopped Grant in a forest where the fighting was so heavy that the woods caught fire, trapping the wounded in the flames and burning them to death. But instead of retreating after a defeat, as previous Union commanders had done, Grant

kept advancing. He attacked Lee at Spotsylvania in a bloody battle that one soldier called "the most terrible twenty-four hours of our service in the war." In early June, Grant attacked Lee again, at Cold Harbor, where he ordered suicidal charges against fortified Confederate positions.

In less than a month, Union forces had suffered casualties greater in number than Lee's entire army. A Union officer protested that "our men have, in many instances, been foolishly and wantonly sacrificed." Grant knew that he could replace his losses while his enemy could not, and he promised "to fight it out along this line if it takes all summer."

In mid-June Lee retreated to Petersburg, south of Richmond, where Grant surrounded the Confederates and their capital and laid siege to the city. In July Lee attempted to break the siege by instructing General Jubal Early to move through Virginia's Shenandoah River valley to threaten Washington, D.C. Grant dispatched the Union cavalry under General Philip Sheridan to drive the Confederates from the area and told him "nothing should be left to invite the enemy to return." He ordered Sheridan to make the valley "a barren waste." By March 1865, Sheridan had carried out his orders so well, he reported to Grant, that a crow flying across the valley would have to carry its food. Meanwhile, Grant continued his siege of Richmond.

Sherman's March

In May 1864, as Grant invaded Virginia, he ordered General William T. Sherman and his 100,000 troops posted in Chattanooga, Tennessee, to engage and destroy the Confederate army in the west. The Confederates were forced to retreat toward Atlanta, Georgia, which Sherman captured in September and occupied until November, when he ordered the city evacuated and destroyed. City officials begged that Atlanta be spared, but Sherman replied:

◀ **HISTORIC DISTRICT, RICHMOND TODAY**

Visualizing Ⓗ*istory*

▲ **DESTRUCTION IN THE SOUTH** By April 1865 many major cities of the Confederacy, including Atlanta and the capital city of Richmond (above), had felt the full force of war. *Why did Sherman burn Atlanta?*

❝ *You might as well appeal against the thunderstorm as against these terrible hardships of war. They are inevitable, and the only way the people of Atlanta can hope once more to live in peace and quiet at home, is to stop the war. . . .* ❞

To divide the South a second time, Sherman adopted Grant's tactics before Vicksburg—strike into enemy territory and **forage,** or live off the land. His army marched southeast and for a month carved a path of destruction 60 miles wide through one of the richest agricultural regions of the South. Sherman reached the Atlantic coast at Savannah, Georgia, and reported to Grant that he had destroyed $100 million worth of property in Georgia—$20 million in military damage and "the remainder is simply waste and destruction."

As he entered Savannah on December 20, 1864, Sherman learned that five days before, outside Nashville, Tennessee, General George Thomas had destroyed the Confederates' western army. The war in the west was over. In February 1865, Sherman left Savannah and marched north through the Carolinas, destroying everything in his path and planning to link up with Grant at Richmond.

The Election of 1864

Throughout the war, federal, state, and city elections continued to be held in the North, but the war divided both major parties into War Democrats and Peace Democrats, Radical Republicans and Conservative Republicans. In the presidential election of 1864, the Republican party temporarily changed its name to the Union party to attract Democrats who supported the war.

The Unionists renominated Lincoln for President and chose a War Democrat for Vice President, Andrew Johnson, military governor of Tennessee. The Democrats nominated George McClellan, the popular general whom Lincoln had twice removed from command. But the Democrats drew up a peace platform that branded the war a fail-

Linking Past and Present

Mess Call

Feeding the troops has always been a problem of warfare. Various means have been tried to provide soldiers nourishment efficiently.

Then

Pork and Hardtack

One of the more unpleasant features of life in the Civil War was the food. Neither the Confederacy nor the Union enlisted cooks and no training was available to those who received the mess assignment.

When in quarters, a company would receive a government issue of flour, pork, beans, potatoes, and coffee. Initially, six or eight recruits would form a mess team and take turns cooking.

On the march, rations typically consisted of dried salt pork, hardtack (a saltless hard biscuit made from flour), and coffee. Southern soldiers usually went without coffee, and cornmeal was substituted for hardtack. Veteran soldiers found fresh hardtack palatable enough. With age, however, it could become infested with weevils. Some soldiers thought it better to eat it in the dark. Soldiers from both armies frequently supplemented meager rations by stealing crops and livestock from nearby farms.

Now

Prepackaged Meals

Rations for the modern soldier are far different. Combat rations, popularly known as C-rations, were first developed in 1940. They consisted of 6 cans of food—3 meat units and 3 carbohydrate units—as well as a powdered drink.

MREs, or Meals Ready to Eat, were distributed to soldiers during the Persian Gulf War. MREs consist of prepackaged foods in airtight containers that are pasteurized by irradiation. Soldiers in combat areas can add hot water to these dehydrated foods to make them edible.

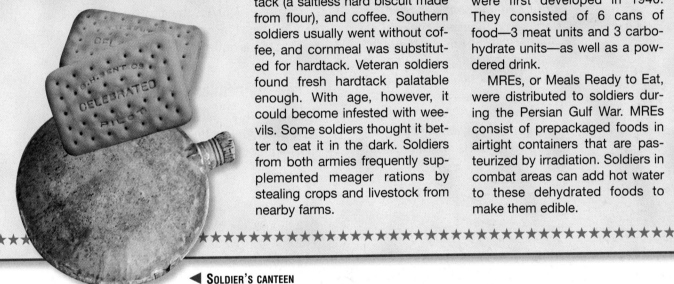

◄ SOLDIER'S CANTEEN

ure and called for the immediate restoration of the Union.

Lincoln's chances for victory largely depended on the fortunes of the Union armies in the field. In mid-1864 the war was going badly, and Lincoln was certain that he would be defeated. But Sherman's capture of Atlanta in September, coupled with McClellan's refusal to support his party's platform, gave Lincoln the victory. The voters had decided that "it was not best to swap horses while crossing the river," Lincoln said.

In his second Inaugural Address in March 1865, Lincoln reviewed the causes of the war and hoped for a peace without bitterness. Both sides "read the same Bible and pray to the same God," he noted, so "let us judge not that we be not judged." It may be, Lincoln said, that the war was divine vengeance on both North and South for two centuries of wrong to African American people.

Lincoln concluded his short address by extending charity to the defeated South. He directed his generals to offer the Confederate armies the most liberal terms of surrender and asked Northerners:

> 66 *With malice toward none, with charity for all . . . let us strive on to finish the work we are in, to bind up the nation's wounds, . . . to do all which may achieve and cherish a just and lasting peace among ourselves and with all nations.* 99

In the four years since the untried prairie lawyer delivered his first Inaugural

Address, his stock had risen. In spite of violent attacks in Congress and in the press, Lincoln inspired affection and trust, as shown by the nicknames "Uncle Abe" and "Father Abraham." Many people had begun to appreciate the ability and strength of character hidden behind Lincoln's homely exterior. One of these was the novelist Nathaniel Hawthorne, who wrote about the President:

> *There is no describing the lengthy awkwardness nor the uncouthness of his movement; and yet it seemed as if I had been in the habit of seeing him daily, and had shaken hands with him a thousand times in some village street . . . If put to guess his calling and livelihood, I should have taken him for a country schoolmaster as soon as anything else . . . [Yet, I like his appearance] . . . and, for my small share in the matter, would as [soon] have Uncle Abe for a ruler as any man whom it would have been practicable to put in his place.* "

■ The Final Days

While Lincoln was delivering his second Inaugural Address in March 1865, Grant was pressing in on Richmond and Sherman was marching through the Carolinas. Aware that the situation was hopeless, General Lee advised President Davis that he could no longer defend Richmond. The Confederate government fled south, and Lee's army finally evacuated the city. By April 4, 1865, President Lincoln was able to walk through the streets of the former Confederate capital.

Lee Surrenders

Just days later, Grant's forces cut off Lee's troops as they attempted to unite with other Confederate armies. Grant urged Lee

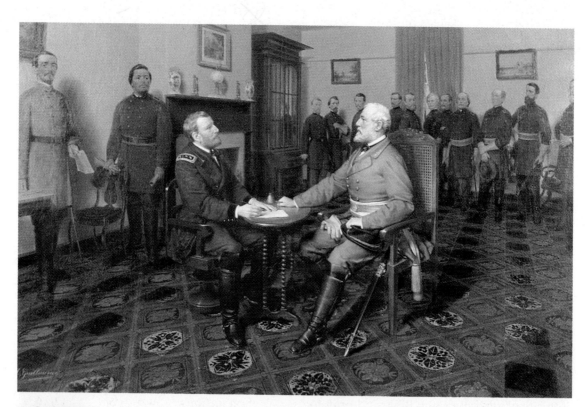

Visualizing History

▲ LEE (RIGHT) SURRENDERS TO GRANT AT APPOMATTOX COURT HOUSE Grant ordered Union troops not to celebrate. "The war is over," he said, "the rebels are our countrymen again." *How did Grant's surrender terms compare with Lincoln's attitude toward the South?*

to surrender in order to prevent "further effusion of blood." On April 9, 1865, the two men met at Appomattox Court House in central Virginia. Grant offered Lee generous terms: Southern soldiers could go home if they pledged not to fight again. The officers would keep their pistols and the men their horses.

When Lee's army came to lay down their arms, Union troops saluted each division as it appeared. As the Confederate forces marched before them, the Union troops watched silently, with "not a cheer, nor a word, nor whisper of vainglory," one Union officer described it, "but an awed stillness rather, a breath-holding, as if it were the passing of the dead."

Defying orders from President Davis, by June, all other Confederate generals also surrendered. The long, bitter struggle that split the nation finally came to an end.

Lincoln Is Assassinated

President Lincoln did not live to see the end of the war, however. On April 14, 1865, just five days after Lee's surrender, Lincoln was assassinated by John Wilkes Booth, a fanatical Confederate sympathizer. Booth's deed was a tragedy for both North and South, for it removed the one person best equipped to "bind up the nation's wounds." A Richmond newspaper called Lincoln's death "the heaviest blow which has ever fallen upon the people of the South." A young

Southern woman confided to her diary, "The most terrible part of the war is now to come."

▶ JOHN WILKES BOOTH (BELOW) AND WANTED POSTER

▲ President Lincoln was shot and killed while attending a play at Ford's Theater in Washington, D.C. An eyewitness later recalled that the theater was filled with "the shouts, groans, curses, smashing of seats, screams, and cries of terror." The items shown below the wanted poster and Booth's photo are the contents of Lincoln's pockets the day he died. *Why did many Southerners as well as Northerners mourn the loss of the President?*

Section 6 ★ Assessment

Checking for Understanding

1. **Define** forage.

2. **Explain** the strategy that Grant adopted to defeat the Confederacy.

Critical Thinking

3. **Analyzing a Quotation** To explain his reelection, Lincoln stated, "It was not best to swap horses while crossing the river." Explain the meaning of Lincoln's quotation and how it applied to him.

4. **Organizing Information** Re-create the chart below to list the targets of the Union's "total war" strategy and provide an example of each.

Total War	Example

INTERDISCIPLINARY ACTIVITY

5. **The Arts** Write a one-paragraph news bulletin describing Robert E. Lee's surrender to Ulysses S. Grant at Appomattox. Include a headline.

Using Vocabulary

Photography was first used extensively to record history during the American Civil War. Regard each of the terms below as captions for a pictorial history of the Civil War era. After each term, describe a photograph that would explain the concept or identify the term.

secession martial law
conscription forage

Reviewing the Facts

1. Specify both agrarian and commercial reasons that promoted Manifest Destiny.
2. Name two important events in the Texas independence movement.
3. Explain the reasons for the war between the United States and Mexico.
4. Classify the provisions of the Compromise of 1850 into those that appealed to Southern states and those that appealed to Northern states.
5. Explain why the Kansas-Nebraska Act resulted in renewed fighting between slavery and anti-slavery forces.
6. State three reasons why large numbers of immigrants came to the United States between 1830 and 1860.
7. Summarize the *Dred Scott* decision.
8. Relate the issue of popular sovereignty to the Lincoln-Douglas debates.
9. List two Southern military advantages and two Northern military advantages at the beginning of the Civil War.
10. Summarize the effects the Emancipation Proclamation had on the war.

Understanding Concepts

Geography and Environment

1. Explain the role of geography in supporting the belief that it was "natural" for the United States to expand to the Pacific Ocean.

Conflict

2. Re-create a chart such as the one shown here, and explain the conflict regarding each scenario as well as the compromise that was reached.

Scenario	Conflict	Compromise
California applies for statehood		
Settlement of trans-Missouri region		

Critical Thinking

1. **Linking Past and Present** What are some issues today that divide Americans? What distinguishes a divisive issue from one that can be solved through compromise?

2. **Analyzing Fine Art** Study the painting on this page entitled *October, 1867* by John Whetton Ehninger and answer the questions that follow.

   a. What does the painting tell you about these individuals and the period in which they lived?

   b. What is your emotional reaction to the painting?

▲ *OCTOBER, 1867* BY JOHN WHETTON EHNINGER

CHAPTER 5 ★ ASSESSMENT

History and Geography

The Civil War, 1864–1865

Study the map of the final campaigns of the Civil War. Then answer the questions that follow.

1. **Movement** In which direction did Union forces move after the occupation of Atlanta?

2. **Location** In what state is Appomattox located?

Cooperative Learning Interdisciplinary Activity: Political Science

Was President Polk a shrewd and visionary leader who expanded the power and borders of the United States, or was he a bully who took what he wanted without regard for other people's rights? You and a partner will evaluate Polk's presidency to answer this question. One of you will be a Polk supporter and the other an opponent. First, work together to compile a list of Polk's achievements. Then work separately and write an evaluation of each action according to your role of supporter or opponent. When you have fin-ished writing, exchange and discuss each other's evaluations. Then present your findings to the class.

Practicing Skills

Analyzing Illustrations

Study the illustration of Harpers Ferry on page 169. Then answer the questions that follow.

1. Is the illustration a drawing, a painting, or a photograph?

2. What mood or feeling is communicated in this illustration?

Technology Activity

Building a Database

Search the library, the Internet, and other resources for information about a Civil War battle. Then create a database about the battle by organizing its key information in a structured fashion. Include such items as where it was fought, who led each army, how many soldiers died on each side, and other aspects you consider to be significant.

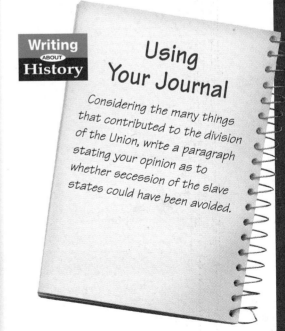

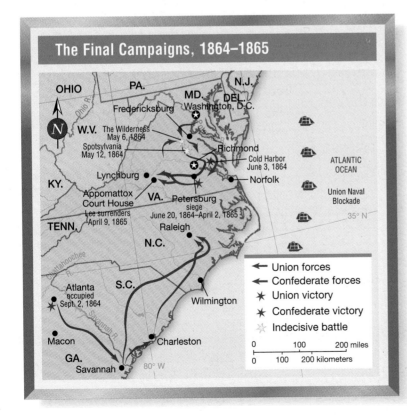

The Final Campaigns, 1864–1865

OHIO
PA.
N.J.
MD.
Washington, D.C.
DEL.
Fredericksburg
W.V. The Wilderness May 6, 1864
Spotsylvania May 12, 1864
Richmond
Cold Harbor June 3, 1864
ATLANTIC OCEAN
Lynchburg
Norfolk
KY.
Appomattox Court House
Lee surrenders April 9, 1865
VA.
Petersburg siege June 20, 1864–April 2, 1865
Union Naval Blockade
35° N
TENN.
Raleigh
N.C.
Atlanta occupied Sept. 2, 1864
S.C.
Wilmington
Macon
Charleston
GA.
80° W
Savannah

← Union forces
← Confederate forces
★ Union victory
★ Confederate victory
✳ Indecisive battle

0   100   200 miles
0   100   200 kilometers

Writing ABOUT History — Using Your Journal

Considering the many things that contributed to the division of the Union, write a paragraph stating your opinion as to whether secession of the slave states could have been avoided.

CHAPTER 6

★★★★★★★★★★★★★★★★★★★★★★★★★★★★★★★★

Reconstruction
1865–1877

► **ELECTION CAMPAIGN RIBBON, 1868**

Setting the Scene

Focus

Confederate war veterans who returned home after the war found their land devastated. African Americans quickly discovered that freedom did not mean equality. The first order of business for the federal government, however, was to readmit the Southern states to the Union. This proved difficult because white Southerners were bitter and Radical Republicans in Congress worked to keep their party in power.

Journal Notes

As you read the chapter, note how racial equality was inhibited during Reconstruction. Write your findings in your journal.

Concepts to Understand

★ Why **adaptation** to new social conditions was necessary for newly freed men and women and white planters

★ How different groups sought to exercise **power and authority** during the Reconstruction era

Read to Discover . . .

★ why Reconstruction policies differed.

★ what the Compromise of 1877 established.

HISTORY Online

Chapter Overview
Visit the *American History: The Modern Era Since 1865* Web site at **me.glencoe.com** and click on **Chapter 6—Chapter Overviews** to preview chapter information.

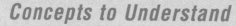

CULTURAL

● **1866** *Fisk School, later Fisk University, founded in Nashville, Tennessee*

● **1871** *P. T. Barnum opens circus in Brooklyn, New York*

1865 | **1869**

● **1868** *President Johnson impeached by House; Senate fails to convict him*

● **1869** *Federal government completes Great Western Survey*

POLITICAL

TOY WHEELED HORSE, LATE 1800s

History AND ART

Dog Swap
by R.N. Brooke

Artist R.N. Brooke skillfully captured the details of daily life during Reconstruction.

• **1876** *Alexander Graham Bell transmits message on telephone*

• **1879** *The Church of Christ, Scientist, chartered*

1873

1877

• **1873** *New York Stock Exchange closes for 10 days after economic panic begins*

• **1877** *Compromise of 1877 completed*
• **1881** *Kansas passes a prohibition law*

After Slavery

Main Idea

The North's victory in the Civil War brought an end to slavery—but African Americans still faced problems.

Reading Strategy

Organizing Information As you read about life in the South after slavery, use a diagram similar to the one shown here to list the changes that freedom brought to African American families.

African American Families

Objectives

After studying this section, you should be able to

★ explain the changes in Southern society that occurred after the Civil War.

★ discuss the changes that freedom brought to African American families.

Key Terms

tenant farmer, sharecropper

▶ **BADGE WORN BY FREED AFRICAN AMERICANS**

When Confederate veterans—tired, ragged, and hungry—went home at the end of the Civil War, they returned to a ravaged land. Large areas of land had been systematically laid to waste by the armies of Sherman and Sheridan. One Mississippi woman remembered her father's homecoming after the war:

> ❝ *He had come home to a house stripped of every article of furniture. The plantation was stripped of the means of cultivating any but a small portion of it. A few mules and one cow made up the stock. . . . He owned nothing that could be turned into money without great sacrifice but five bales of cotton.* ❞

The wreckage stretched from South Carolina's Atlantic coast in the east to Tennessee in the west and from Virginia's Shenandoah Valley in the north through Georgia in the south. It was not only the land that was in ruin, however. Economically, politically, and socially, the South was in total disarray. Confederate money was worthless, and Southern banks were ruined. Government at every level had all but disappeared. There were no courts, no judges, no sheriffs, and no police—no law or authority except when groups of people took matters into their own hands. The war also left the South's transportation system in complete disorder. Roads were impassable, bridges had been destroyed or had washed away, and railroad tracks had been rendered unusable. For planters, the greatest economic blow was the loss of their enslaved workers, an investment worth more than $2 billion. When the workers were freed, the plantation system collapsed.

■ New Ways of Life

The devastation of war affected all levels of Southern society. For landowners it meant that their old way of life had been swept away.

The Plight of the Landowners

After his regiment surrendered at Appomattox, the planter Harry Hammond said he had "a pipe, some tobacco, and literally nothing else." Although Hammond owned a large plantation, he could find no one who could afford to buy his land when he put it up for sale. Hammond was saved from total ruin when most of the 300 African Americans on the plantation agreed to stay and work the land. In return for their labor, Hammond provided his formerly enslaved workers with housing, firewood, weekly food allotments, every other Saturday off, and $15 a year in cash after the crops were harvested. Hammond also agreed to provide the loan of a mule and a plow so that the workers could grow their own crops.

Not every planter was so fortunate. Southerners who had invested heavily in Confederate currency and bonds were wiped out financially when Confederate funds became worthless after the war. Many lost their land because of taxes or other debts they could not pay. Some sold their acres to anyone who could pay the outrageously low prices for which Southern farms and plantations were advertised in Northern newspapers. On other plantations and on small farms throughout the South, war widows struggled to hold on to their property and keep it producing.

★★★ AMERICA'S FLAGS ★★★

The 37-Star Flag By 1866 Nebraskans had ratified their state's constitution in accordance with the U.S. Constitution, and the state was admitted into the Union on March 1, 1867.

★★★★★★★★★★★★★★★★★★★★★★

The Plight of Workers

Poor African Americans and whites realized that social and economic status in the South was tied to the land, but few had money to buy land, even at such low prices. So some became **tenant farmers,** farming land that they rented. The landowners usually received a part of the crop as rent. Some landowners provided the farming tools, seeds, and supplies in order to receive an even larger portion of the crop. Even tenant farming, however, was beyond the means of many poor Southerners, and more often they became **sharecroppers,** persons who worked the owner's land—sometimes using the owner's tools, animals, and seed—and received a share of the crops in return.

Although these arrangements seemed a solution that would provide a living for both workers and landowners, the system contained serious defects. For example, debt-ridden landowners wanted to get the highest possible return, so they pressured tenants to grow only cotton or tobacco, cash crops that paid the most. To prevent depletion of the soil, however, tenants should have planted a variety of crops, including food crops.

Tenants, black and white alike, usually had to buy seed, fertilizer, work animals, and food on credit, at interest rates as high as 40 percent. Thus, no matter how hard they worked, many tenants fell deeply into debt and remained trapped on the land until they paid those debts—no freer to leave than enslaved workers had been. The system often put poor farmers into debt from which they were unable to escape. Nevertheless, the tenant system expanded during these years. As late as 1907, a federal investigator estimated that one-third of the farms in the Cotton Belt depended on the labor of tenants tied to the land by their debts. Years later a former enslaved person recalled the frustration that many African Americans felt about the system:

❝ *Lincoln got praise for freeing us, but did he do it? He gave us freedom without giving us any chance to live to ourselves and we still had to depend on the*

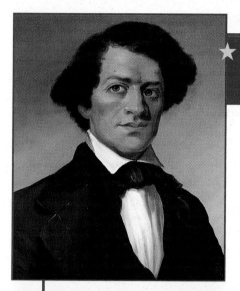

AMERICAN PORTRAITS

Frederick Douglass
1817–1895

Born enslaved, Frederick Douglass escaped (after one failed attempt) in 1838 and quickly emerged as a leading abolitionist. During the Civil War, he prodded President Lincoln to free African Americans, and he helped organize them to fight for freedom.

After Lincoln was assassinated, Douglass strongly opposed the Reconstruction program of President Johnson. Instead he backed the Radical Republican plan. He used his oratorical ability to insist on full equality for African Americans in all parts of the nation, and he was a vigorous backer of the Fourteenth Amendment. He was particularly outspoken in support of the Fifteenth Amendment, guaranteeing African American men the right to vote. To Douglass, being able to vote meant that African Americans would not only be full citizens but would also have a weapon to protect their rights.

southern white man for work, food, clothing, and he held us through our necessity and want in a state of servitude but little better than slavery. ”

From Slavery to Freedom

Even before the end of the war, some slaveholders noticed a change in the attitude of African Americans as they sensed freedom close at hand. Other planters were stunned, however, when enslaved workers they thought were content left without a word to try to reach the Union lines.

Freedom strengthened African American family ties. Families that had been separated were now reunited. Newspapers carried advertisements from African Americans seeking information about missing relatives:

“ *$200 reward. During the year 1849, Thomas Sample carried away from this city, as his slaves, our daughter Polly, and son, Geo. Washington, to the State of Mississippi, and subsequently to Texas. . . . We will give $100 each for them, to*

any person who assist them, or either of them, to get to Nashville, or get word to us of their whereabouts, if they are alive. ”

Freed men and women, many of whom had only first names, now went about choosing family names. Some chose the name of an ancestor or the name of a hero, like Lincoln. Some adopted their former slaveholder's family name, but many African Americans rejected such an idea. "That's my old rebel master's title," said one young man, "and I don't see any use in being called for him."

Leaving the Plantation

Newly freed workers who remained on the plantations as paid laborers usually refused to live in their old quarters. They objected to the common areas for cooking and washing and sought the privacy of separate cabins. For others, freedom meant leaving the plantation and their former masters and starting a new life. Some settled on the Great Plains and farmed land of their own. Others headed for large cities, hoping to find jobs there.

The Freedmen's Bureau

At the close of the war, Congress had created within the War Department a Bureau of Refugees, Freedmen, and Abandoned Lands, which became popularly known as the Freedmen's Bureau. Led by General O. Howard, the Bureau at first gave food and clothing to all families in the war-ravaged South. Its primary mission, however, was to help African Americans adjust to their new freedom. In addition, the Bureau provided medical help and founded 45 hospitals in 14 states.

Education

The Bureau was especially active in the field of education. Sponsored by the Freedmen's Bureau and the American Missionary Association, hundreds of Northern school teachers went South after the war. Many were young women who had been active in the antislavery and women's rights movements, who now dedicated themselves to educating the newly freed African Americans. The teachers frequently found their students just as dedicated to getting an education. One African Ameri-can teacher from Philadelphia who taught school in Georgia noted that many of her students worked in the fields in the morning and came to class "after their hard toil in the hot sun, as bright and as anxious to learn as ever." At the end of the day, these same classrooms were filled with adults, equally hungry for the education that had been denied to them. The Freedmen's Bureau also worked to establish colleges to train African American teachers, contributing to the founding of Howard University, Hampton Institute, Fisk University, and other colleges for African Americans.

Jobs

In addition, the Freedmen's Bureau tried to find jobs for formerly enslaved workers. It encouraged them to sign labor contracts with planters to provide work in return for wages or a share of the crops. Because most formerly enslaved men and women could neither read nor write, Bureau agents tried to prevent them from being cheated in these contracts, but the Bureau never had enough agents to do this job fully.

Visualizing History

▲ FREEDMEN'S BUREAU SCHOOL The Freedmen's Bureau set up hundreds of schools in the South for African American children and adults. *In what other ways did the Bureau help African Americans adjust to a new life?*

▲ **A RESETTLEMENT PLAN** After the Civil War, federal commissioners resettled a portion of the freed African Americans on abandoned and confiscated southern land, including the Sea Islands (shown above). *Why were the new tenants forced from the land?*

Land

The dream of most freed men and women was to own land. During the war Union troops had seized large amounts of land from Southern planters, and Congress decided to distribute some of this land to formerly enslaved workers. On the Sea Islands of South Carolina, the Freedmen's Bureau was permitted to sell or lease confiscated land in parcels of up to 40 acres. Many newly freed African American families hoped that 40 acres and a mule would help them start their lives anew. However, when President Andrew Johnson decided

to pardon Confederates, he restored their property rights. If their land had been distributed to African Americans, it was returned to its former owners.

General Howard went to the Sea Islands to tell African American farmers that their land was being returned to pardoned Confederates. He urged them to sign labor contracts to work on the land they briefly had owned. Most of the farmers refused to sign contracts, and a large number refused to give up their land. They were evicted against their will—some at bayonet point—by Union troops.

Section 1 ★ Assessment

Checking for Understanding

1. **Define** tenant farmer, sharecropper.

2. **List** three drawbacks to tenant farming.

3. **Describe** the efforts made by the Freedmen's Bureau in the field of education and labor.

4. **Explain** efforts to provide land to the newly freed African Americans and the outcome of these efforts.

Critical Thinking

5. **Analyzing Issues** Re-create the chart shown here, and explain how the war changed

the lives of both landowners and workers in the South.

Landowners	Workers

INTERDISCIPLINARY ACTIVITY

6. **The Arts** Many freed African Americans placed newspaper advertisements to locate members of their families who had been sold. Write such an ad of at least 50 words that includes pertinent details.

★★★

Reconstructing the South

Guide to Reading

Main Idea
After the war, Northern leaders differed over the best way to rebuild the nation.

Reading Strategy

Classifying Information As you read about the reconstruction of the South, highlight aspects of the various rebuilding plans in a chart such as the one shown here.

Lincoln's Plan	Johnson's Plan	Radicals' Plan

Objectives

After studying this section, you should be able to

★ compare the Lincoln and Johnson plans for Reconstruction with the plans of the Radical Republicans.

★ explain how the black codes and the return of former Confederates to power affected Reconstruction.

Key Terms

amnesty, mandate, disenfranchise, impeach

▶ TICKET TO IMPEACHMENT TRIAL

Reconstruction did involve much more than merely rebuilding and repairing the war damage inflicted on the South. It also meant restructuring Southern society by granting rights to formerly enslaved persons and restoring the nation by readmitting Southern states to the Union.

■ Presidential Reconstruction

Before the end of the war, Congress and President Lincoln struggled with, and frequently clashed over, Reconstruction policies and programs.

Some believed that the South should be punished. President Lincoln argued that the task before the country was to restore the Union.

Lincoln's Plan

Before the war ended, Lincoln began to plan for the peace that would follow the war. Because his primary goal was to restore the Union as quickly as possible, the President favored a generous policy. Except for a few high-ranking Confederate officials, he offered **amnesty,** or pardon, to all Southerners who pledged an oath of loyalty to the United States. Lincoln proposed that when 10 percent of a state's voters in the 1860 presidential election had taken this oath, Congress would readmit the state to the Union.

Lincoln's plan did not address the plight of the newly freed African Americans. Although Lincoln strongly supported the Thirteenth Amendment, for a long time he personally had favored colonization of free African Americans in Africa and the Caribbean. He was willing, though, to let the

South handle the matter. The President urged, however, that African Americans who could read and write and those who had served in the Union army be allowed to vote.

The Radical Republicans' Plan

Resistance to Lincoln's plan surfaced at once from his Radical Republican opponents in Congress. The Radicals' alternative to Lincoln's plan came in the Wade-Davis Bill of 1864. This legislation proposed putting the South under military rule and required a majority of a state's electorate to take the loyalty oath as a condition for the state's readmission. Lincoln killed this bill with a pocket veto—he let the session of Congress expire without signing the legislation. However, when the states of Arkansas, Tennessee, and Louisiana met the conditions of Lincoln's plan, Congress refused to readmit them to the Union. The President then realized that a peace based on "malice toward none and charity for all" was not possible, and he began to negotiate with Radical congressional leaders. At this critical point, Lincoln was assassinated.

Johnson's Program

Andrew Johnson, who succeeded to the presidency, attempted to carry out Lincoln's Reconstruction policies. He was hampered in this effort because, as an unelected President, he had little popular following. In addition, as a former Democrat, he could not command the support of the Republican majority in Congress, and as a Tennessean and former slaveholder, he offended the Radicals. If these handicaps were not enough, he was viewed by his critics as being self-righteous, hot-tempered, stubborn, and crude.

In the summer of 1865, with Congress in recess, Johnson began to implement his Reconstruction program. His conditions for readmission were that each Southern state abolish slavery, repeal its ordinance of secession, and repudiate its war debts. When Congress returned in December, every state except Texas had followed Johnson's formula and asked to return to the Union. The Radicals, however, expressed alarm because the leniency of Johnson's plan allowed the return of traditional leadership in each of

▼ CARPETBAG

Visualizing History

▲ CONGRESSIONAL ACTION Controlled by the Radical Republicans, the Joint Committee on Reconstruction maintained the authority of Congress over Reconstruction. *What was the goal of the Civil Rights Bill of 1866?*

Honoring the Nation's Military Heroes

Since the beginning of history, heads of state have awarded decorations and medals to individuals for bravery or merit during times of war. Until the Civil War, the United States did not have any permanent national military decorations or medals.

Then

The Medal of Honor

Congress authorized the first permanent U.S. military medal—the Medal of Honor—during the Civil War. Often called the Congressional Medal of Honor, it is the nation's highest military decoration for bravery and valor by men and women in the armed forces.

Campaign medals, also known as war service medals, have been awarded to all ranks of the military for service in every war fought by the United States from the Civil War to the present. The U.S. War Department authorized the Army Civil War Campaign Medal in 1907—42 years after the conflict ended.

Since the inception of the Medal of Honor, more than 3,400 have been awarded. Recipients receive $200 per month for life and a right to burial at Arlington National Cemetery. Nearly one-half of the Congressional Medals of Honor have been awarded to soldiers who fought in the Civil War.

Now

Military Decorations and Medals

During the twentieth century, the United States has instituted other awards, including the Silver and Bronze stars, dating from World Wars I and II respectively, and the Distinguished Service Medal of the army, navy, and air force.

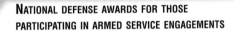

NATIONAL DEFENSE AWARDS FOR THOSE PARTICIPATING IN ARMED SERVICE ENGAGEMENTS

---

these states, and Southern voters elected former Confederate officials to power. As a result, Congress refused to seat members from the Southern states.

White Men and Black Codes

The Radicals were also concerned about the status of African Americans in the South. Like Lincoln, President Johnson believed that this was a state matter and that federal jurisdiction stopped with the abolition of slavery. Consequently, the new Southern state governments endorsed the principle stated by the governor of Mississippi, "Ours is and ever shall be a government of white men."

The new Southern state legislatures passed a series of laws known as "black codes" that severely limited the rights of African Americans and made it plain that African Americans were still to have a subordinate status in the South. State governments made few provisions for African Americans' schools.

In no Southern state were African Americans permitted to vote, testify against whites, handle weapons, or serve on juries. In some states, all African Americans were required by law to have steady work. Those who did not were arrested as vagrants and their labor sold to the highest bidder. Some states permitted African Americans to work only as farmers and servants and denied them many of the rights enjoyed by whites.

The North Responds

Northerners were outraged by the black codes, and even Johnson's supporters were alarmed by the actions of the Southern states. Their fears proved well founded. Events in the South increasingly led moderate Northerners to support the Radicals in Congress against the President.

In 1865, House and Senate leaders created a Joint Committee on Reconstruction to set congressional policy for restoring the Union. The Joint Committee proposed bills providing economic aid for African Americans and protection of their civil rights. Congress passed these bills, but President Johnson vetoed each one. Finally, in April 1866, Congress passed the Civil Rights Bill, which granted citizenship to African Americans and gave the federal government the power to intervene to protect the rights of freed men and women. When Johnson also vetoed this bill, Congress overrode his veto.

The Fourteenth Amendment

Fearing that the Civil Rights Act might be overturned in court, however, Congress passed the Fourteenth Amendment to the Constitution in June 1866. The amendment defined citizenship to include African Americans and required that no state deny any person "the equal protection of the laws." In addition, the amendment barred many Confederate political leaders from holding public office and prohibited any state from paying Confederate war debts.

President Johnson attacked the Fourteenth Amendment and campaigned against its ratification. As the 1866 congressional elections neared, it was clear that they would reveal whether the President or Congress would control the direction of Reconstruction.

The November election provided an overwhelming victory for the Radicals, who gained control of both the House and Senate. They now had the strength to override any presidential veto and could claim that they had been given a **mandate,** or command, from the public to enact their own Reconstruction program.

■ Radical Reconstruction

Now firmly in control, the Radical Republicans began implementing their policies for Reconstruction.

One goal was to sweep away the new state governments in the South and to replace them with military rule. Other goals were to ensure that former Confederate leaders would have no role in governing the South and that the freed African Americans' right to vote was protected.

Reconstruction Plans

Radical plans were inspired by self-interest as well as by concern for the freed African Americans and a desire to punish the South. The Radicals expected that African Americans would express their gratitude for freedom by voting Republican. Radical plans also were supported by Northern business leaders, who feared that a Congress controlled by Democrats might lower tariffs or destroy the newly established national banking system.

Many Radicals genuinely cared about the plight of the freed men and women, of course. They had been abolitionists and had pushed Lincoln into making emancipation a goal of the war. They believed in a right to equality and that government must rest on the consent of the governed. Senator Henry Wilson of Massachusetts summarized their position by saying:

> 66 [Congress] must see to it that the man made free by the Constitution is a freeman indeed; that he can go where he pleases, work when and for whom he pleases . . . go into the schools and educate himself and his children; that the rights and guarantees of the common law are his, and that he walks the earth proud and erect in the conscious dignity of a free man. 99

Reconstruction Legislation

In March 1867, Congress passed a Reconstruction Act that abolished the South's new state governments and put them under military rule. Except for Tennessee, the former Confederacy was divided into five military districts, each under command of a Union general. To be restored to the Union, each of the states was required to hold a

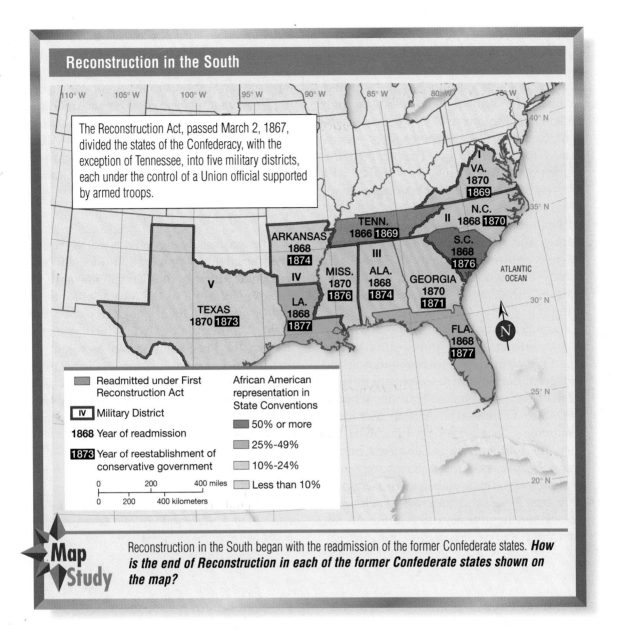

Reconstruction in the South

The Reconstruction Act, passed March 2, 1867, divided the states of the Confederacy, with the exception of Tennessee, into five military districts, each under the control of a Union official supported by armed troops.

I VA. 1870 1869

N.C. II 1868 1870

TENN. 1866 1869

ARKANSAS 1868 1874

III

S.C. 1868 1876

MISS. 1870 1876

ALA. 1868 1874

GEORGIA 1870 1871

IV

V

LA. 1868 1877

TEXAS 1870 1873

FLA. 1868 1877

ATLANTIC OCEAN

N

Readmitted under First Reconstruction Act

IV Military District

1868 Year of readmission

1873 Year of reestablishment of conservative government

0 200 400 miles
0 200 400 kilometers

African American representation in State Conventions

50% or more
25%–49%
10%–24%
Less than 10%

Map Study Reconstruction in the South began with the readmission of the former Confederate states. *How is the end of Reconstruction in each of the former Confederate states shown on the map?*

constitutional convention with delegates elected by all adult males and to frame a state constitution that gave African Americans the right to vote. If the voters ratified the constitution, a state government could be elected. Finally, if Congress approved the constitution, if the state legislature ratified the Fourteenth Amendment, and if the amendment became a part of the Constitution, then the state would be readmitted to the Union. By 1868 Louisiana, Alabama, Arkansas, Florida, North Carolina, and South Carolina had met these requirements and regained statehood.

In 1869 Congress protected African American suffrage by passing the Fifteenth Amendment to the Constitution, providing

that the right to vote "shall not be denied . . . on account of race, color, or previous condition of servitude." Congress required that states not yet complying with the Reconstruction Act—Virginia, Georgia, Mississippi, and Texas—ratify the Fifteenth Amendment as a further condition for readmission to the Union.

■ Carpetbag Government

By 1870 each of the 10 states under military rule had been readmitted to the Union. However, Radical Reconstruction had **disenfranchised**—or taken the right to vote from—many former Confederates. In addition, many other Southern white men boycotted elections. As a result, government in the Southern states was left to two small groups. One was a group of white Southern Union sympathizers whom Southerners nicknamed "scalawags." Northerners who came South—called "carpetbaggers"—comprised the other group. They gained this derogatory name because they arrived with all their belongings in cheap suitcases made of carpet fabric.

Some carpetbaggers were respectable, honest, and sincerely devoted to the public interest. However, enough of them were greedy and self-seeking so as to give the phrase "carpetbag governments" a reputation for graft, fraud, and waste.

Carpetbag rule was not without achievement, however. Most public funds were spent honestly to encourage rebuilding and industrial development. Carpetbag governments also established public schools, including facilities for African American children.

Many Southern whites despised carpetbag governments. African American voters, however, saw the carpetbag governments as their best hope, and they overwhelmingly voted for Republican candidates. At the height of Radical Reconstruction, 700,000 African Americans could vote in the South compared to 625,000 whites. Even so, no African Americans were elected governors, and only in South Carolina did a state legislature have a majority of African American members. Fifteen African Americans were elected to the House of Representatives during Reconstruction, and two African American men served as United States senators.

The Radicals in Power

The Radicals were determined to reduce the presidential power that Lincoln had assumed during the Civil War and to remove Johnson as an obstacle to their plans. In March 1867, Congress passed the Army Appropriation Act, which severely limited the President's power as commander in chief. Accompanying this legislation was the Tenure of Office Act, which required Senate approval for the President to remove any government official whose appointment had required its consent.

Challenging the Tenure Law

The Radicals knew that President Johnson wanted to remove Edwin Stanton, Lincoln's secretary of war, who remained in

 Visualizing History

▲ **MEMBERS OF CONGRESS** The first African American members of Congress are shown in this Currier and Ives print. The first African American senator, Hiram R. Revels, is at the far left. *What were the major achievements of Southern governments during this period?*

Johnson's cabinet but who openly sided with the Radicals. Characteristically, Johnson ignored these warnings. He continued trying to block Radical Reconstruction. Johnson also removed commanders in the Southern military districts who supported the Radicals and, while Congress was in recess, he fired Stanton.

To replace Stanton, Johnson appointed General Grant, but when the Senate reconvened it rejected Grant's nomination, and Grant resigned in favor of Stanton. Outraged, Johnson fired Stanton again—on February 21, 1868—this time replacing him with General Lorenzo Thomas. In answer, Stanton barricaded himself inside his office and refused to leave.

Johnson Impeached

The Radicals came to Stanton's support. Three days later, the House of Representatives voted to **impeach,** or charge, Johnson with "high crimes and misdemeanors" in office. As provided in the Constitution, the President was tried by the Senate. A two-thirds majority vote was needed for a conviction.

For more than two intense months, the Senate debated the President's fate. Radical members of the House, led by Thaddeus Stevens, presented the case against Johnson. Johnson's lawyers argued that Lincoln, not Johnson, had appointed Stanton to the Cabinet and, therefore, that the Tenure of Office Act did not apply.

On May 16, 1868, the Senate voted 35 to 19 to find Johnson guilty, just 1 vote short of conviction. Seven Republican senators were not able to find honest evidence that Johnson was guilty. Although Johnson remained in office for the last few months of his term, he was powerless to challenge the Radicals' policies.

The 1868 Election

The Radical Republicans sought a candidate in the 1868 presidential election who could sweep the country and keep them in power. They chose General Grant. The Democrats nominated Horatio Seymour, former governor of New York, and their platform condemned Radical Republican actions.

Although Grant won easily, by a vote of 214 to 80 in the electoral college, a small shift in the popular vote in key states would have given Seymour the election. Grant won because he was supported by the carpetbag governments of the South and because three Southern states had not yet been readmitted.

Student Web Activity
Visit the *American History: The Modern Era Since 1865* Web site at **me.glencoe.com** and click on *Chapter 6—Student Web Activities* for an activity about the impeachment.

Section 2 ★ Assessment

Checking for Understanding

1. **Define** amnesty, mandate, disenfranchise, impeach.
2. **List** two objections the Radicals had to Lincoln's Reconstruction plans.

Critical Thinking

3. **Determining Cause and Effect** How do congressional elections during a President's term of office act as a barometer of presidential policies and popularity? Give specific examples.

4. **Summarizing** Re-create the diagram shown here, and list what rights African Americans were denied under the black codes.

Rights Denied African Americans

INTERDISCIPLINARY ACTIVITY

5. **Government** Create a time line that shows important political events during the Reconstruction era.

BUILDING SKILLS
Technology Skills

Using an Electronic Spreadshseet

People use electronic spreadsheets to manage numbers quickly and easily. You can use a spreadsheet any time a problem involves numbers and other information that you can arrange in rows and columns.

Learning the Skill

A spreadsheet is an electronic worksheet. All spreadsheets follow a basic design of rows and columns. Each column (vertical) is assigned a letter or a number. Each point where a column and row intersect is called a *cell*. The cell's position on the spreadsheet is labeled according to its corresponding column and row—Column A, Row 1 (A1); Column B, Row 2 (B2), and so on.

Spreadsheets use standard formulas to calculate the numbers. You create a simple mathematical equation that uses these standard formulas, and the computer does the calculations for you.

Practicing the Skill

Suppose you want to know how many votes the Republican and Democratic candidates received across five states in the 1868 presidential election. Use these steps to create a spreadsheet that will provide this information:

1. In cells B1 and C1, type a candidate's name or political party. In cell D1, type the term *total*.

2. In cells A2–A6, type the name of a state. In cell A7, type the word *total*.

3. In row 2, enter the number of votes each candidate received in the state named in cell A2. Repeat this process in rows 3–6.

4. Create a formula to calculate the votes. The formula for the equation tells what cells (2B + 2C) to add together.

5. Copy down the formula in the cells for the other five states.

6. Use the process in steps 4 and 5 to create and copy a formula to calculate the total number of votes each candidate received.

APPLYING THE SKILL

7. Use a spreadshseet to enter your test scores and your homework grades. At the end of the grading period, the spreadsheet will calculate your average grade.

★★

Restoring Southern Power

Guide to Reading

Main Idea

As Reconstruction ended, many former Confederates regained power in the South.

Reading Strategy

Taking Notes   As you read about the restoration of the old power structure in the South, outline the provisions of the Compromise of 1877 in the form shown here.

I. Republican Gains
  A.
  B.

II. Democratic Gains
  A.
  B.

Objectives

After studying this section, you should be able to
★ describe Southern resistance to Reconstruction.
★ discuss political and economic change in the South after Reconstruction.

Key Term

segregation

▶ **PLOW USED BY SHARECROPPER, 1860S**

Unable to strike openly at the federal government, opponents of Reconstruction organized secret resistance societies. The largest of these groups was the Ku Klux Klan. Started in Tennessee in 1866, the Klan spread throughout the former Confederacy. Hooded, white-robed Klan members rode in bands at night and threatened carpetbaggers, teachers in African American schools, and African Americans themselves. Using beatings, murder, and other violence to back up their threats, Klansmen broke up Republican meetings, tried to drive Freedmen's Bureau officials out of their communities, and tried to keep freed African Americans from voting.

Although by 1872 it had been greatly suppressed by federal troops, the Klan and similar organizations contributed to the establishment of Southern governments opposed to the Radicals. Democrats, often called "Redeemers," gained control of one Southern state after another, until by 1876 only South Carolina, Florida, and Louisiana did not have governments controlled by white Democrats, many of whom were former Confederates.

One reason for these Democratic successes in the South was that Northerners were becoming weary of Radical Reconstruction. In 1872 a group called the Liberal Republicans, including several prominent Republican leaders, opposed the Radicals and refused to support Grant for reelection because they considered him unfit for the presidency. The Liberal Republicans joined with the Democrats to nominate newspaper publisher Horace Greeley for President. Although Grant won reelection, the Radicals' power was weakened, and Grant's administration loosened its controls over the South. As fewer troops were sent to protect African American voters during Southern elections, white political power was restored.

■ The Compromise of 1877

The presidential election of 1876 brought the end of Radical Reconstruction. In the campaign the Republicans "waved the bloody shirt," or attempted to stir up bitter memories of the war. Democrats countered by attacking the excesses of Radical Reconstruction and the corruption they claimed was rampant in the Grant administration.

On Election Day, Democratic candidate Samuel J. Tilden, governor of New York, polled 250,000 more popular votes than the Republican Rutherford B. Hayes, Ohio's governor. Tilden was a vote short of a majority in the electoral college, but 20 electoral votes were disputed. One of these electoral votes was from Oregon, and it was challenged on a technicality. The other 19 involved disputed results from the 3 Southern states still under carpetbag rule—Florida, South Carolina, and Louisiana—where charges of massive voting fraud flew.

Electoral Commission

Republicans complained that Democrats had prevented African Americans from voting, and Democrats accused Republicans of using federal troops to raise its vote totals. These 3 states each filed 2 sets of election returns, 1 for Tilden and another for Hayes.

Because the Constitution did not provide for settling such a dispute, Congress appointed a commission of 5 members each from the House, the Senate, and the Supreme Court to settle the matter. Tilden needed only 1 of the disputed electoral votes to become President, but Hayes needed all of them. Voting strictly along party lines, the commission awarded all 20 disputed electoral votes to Hayes. Congress accepted the verdict on March 2, 1877, 2 days before the inauguration.

Reaching an Agreement

The Democrats were outraged at the commission's decisions, and they were determined not to be defrauded. There were threats of civil war and talk of blocking Hayes's inauguration. The Republicans were just as determined to keep control of the presidency, and they began to talk about a compromise. After negotiations between party leaders, the Democrats agreed to accept the election results and the Republicans agreed to several demands. Democrats were assured that a Southerner would become postmaster general, an important position because of the many federal jobs it controlled. Republicans also promised federal funds for internal improvements in the South. Most important, Republicans agreed to withdraw the remaining federal troops from the South. Without soldiers to protect them, the three remaining carpetbag governments collapsed and Reconstruction officially came to an end.

■ After Reconstruction

In many ways, the South after Reconstruction was similar to the South before the Civil War. As white Southern Democrats returned to power, African Americans lost many of their civil rights.

● ●
Footnotes to History

Popular Vote   Three times in American history—in the elections of John Quincy Adams in 1824, Rutherford B. Hayes in 1876, and Benjamin Harrison in 1888—the candidate who lost the popular vote won the election.

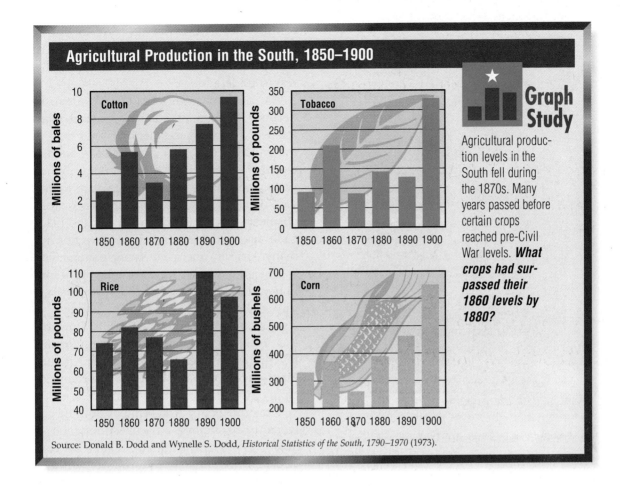

Agricultural Production in the South, 1850–1900

Cotton (Millions of bales) — 1850, 1860, 1870, 1880, 1890, 1900

Tobacco (Millions of pounds) — 1850, 1860, 1870, 1880, 1890, 1900

Rice (Millions of pounds) — 1850, 1860, 1870, 1880, 1890, 1900

Corn (Millions of bushels) — 1850, 1860, 1870, 1880, 1890, 1900

Graph Study

Agricultural production levels in the South fell during the 1870s. Many years passed before certain crops reached pre-Civil War levels. *What crops had surpassed their 1860 levels by 1880?*

Source: Donald B. Dodd and Wynelle S. Dodd, *Historical Statistics of the South, 1790–1970* (1973).

Segregation

For years, in the North as well as the South, **segregation,** or the practice of separating people on the basis of race, had been an accepted way of life. Even before the Civil War, custom in the North had separated African American and white travelers on railroads, coaches, and steamboats and in hotels. Such segregation also existed in Northern schools, churches, hospitals, and cemeteries. After Reconstruction, however, the South began to pass "Jim Crow" laws, which legally segregated blacks from whites in daily life.

Where possible, African Americans protested segregation. These protests helped to integrate the streetcar lines of Washington, D.C.; Richmond, Virginia; and Charleston, South Carolina. In 1875 Congress passed a Civil Rights Act requiring that all people have equal access to public places and transportation facilities. In 1883, however, the Supreme Court ruled that the act was unconstitutional, and by the 1890s Jim Crow laws were common throughout the South.

The "New South"

Despite the South's return to white supremacy, by the late 1870s there was increasing talk of a "New South." An alliance between powerful white Southerners and Northern financiers brought about the economic rebuilding of the South. Northern capital helped to build railroads, and by 1890 the South had twice the railroad mileage that it had had in 1860.

Better transportation encouraged the industrialization of the South. A growing iron and steel industry developed around Birmingham, Alabama, and in North Carolina tobacco processing became big business. Cotton mills appeared in countless small towns throughout the South. Nevertheless, far from populous Northern markets and paying high freight rates, Southern industries faced serious problems. To compete, Southern factory owners generally paid lower wages than did factories in the North.

With these developments in transportation and industry and with the spread of

▲ AFRICAN AMERICAN CHILDREN ATTENDING FREE SCHOOL

century. Reconstruction also provided only limited and temporary help to Southern African Americans, whose rights it professed to defend.

As time passed, abolitionist idealism declined, and many Radicals proved more interested in African American votes than in the welfare of African Americans. Congress closed the Freedmen's Bureau after only five years, and it made no long-range plans to provide what the freed African Americans needed most—land and education. As the black codes revealed, without federal protection, for many African Americans emancipation merely meant a new kind of slavery—continued attachment to the white power structure as sharecroppers and tenant farmers.

Although immediate efforts to improve the lives of Southern African Americans failed, the Fourteenth and Fifteenth Amendments wrote into the Constitution the principle of equality for all people.

The Fourteenth Amendment defined citizenship to include African Americans. It also said that no state could take away a citizen's life, liberty, or property without due process of law, and that every citizen was entitled to equal protection of the laws. The Fifteenth Amendment stated that the right to vote "shall not be denied . . . on account of race, color, or previous condition of servitude."

For many years these amendments remained almost a dead letter, but in the 1900s they provided the legal basis and, in part, the inspiration for movements to obtain for African Americans their full rights as citizens.

sharecropping in agriculture, the South's economy gradually revived. By 1900 Southern industrial production was four times what it had been in 1860.

Few Gains for African Americans

In many ways, Reconstruction aided the South. However, it also caused much bitterness in that region, helping to create the "Solid South"—a voting bloc dominated by the Democrats that did not break up for a

Section 3 ★ Assessment

Checking for Understanding

1. **Define** segregation.
2. **Describe** the strategies and tactics used by the Ku Klux Klan.

Critical Thinking

3. **Distinguishing Fact From Opinion** Describe the images of the South created by motion pictures and novels. What facts from the era refute these images?

4. **Summarizing** Describe the political and economic changes in the South after Reconstruction, using a chart such as the one shown here.

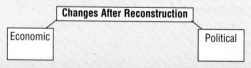

Changes After Reconstruction

Economic   Political

INTERDISCIPLINARY ACTIVITY

5. **The Arts** Create a display of photographs or drawings that illustrate the Fourteenth and Fifteenth Amendments.

▲ FOUNDRY, BIRMINGHAM, ALABAMA, 1887

Growth of Southern Manufacturing

Many factors pushed the postwar South toward industrialization. Most important, however, was the surplus labor supply. Widows, orphans, and displaced formerly enslaved workers needed work, and agriculture could not employ them all. This meant there was a large pool of cheap labor. In addition, Northerners and Europeans invested capital in fledgling Southern industries, as did a number of Southerners themselves.

Two industries that made spectacular advances in the postwar South were textiles and tobacco processing. Cotton mills sprang up in the major cotton-growing areas of the South. By 1900 there were 400 mills in operation. The postwar demand for a new product—cigarettes—and the invention of the cigarette-rolling machine in 1880 were the catalysts that fueled the development of the tobacco-processing industry.

▶ SEWING MACHINE, MID-1800S

Other industries based on agriculture or minerals also developed, such as steel manufacturing and making cottonseed oil. Still, despite gains in industrialization, the South remained primarily rural and agricultural until the industrial advances of the mid-twentieth century.

Making the Economics Connection

1. What factors led to the development of industry in the postwar South?

2. What Southern cities of the 1900s are noted as industrial centers?

ACTIVITY

3. Create a table that lists innovations during your lifetime and describes their effects on the economy.

229

Self-Check Quiz

Visit the *American History: The Modern Era Since 1865* Web site at **me.glencoe.com** and click on *Chapter 6—Self-Check Quizzes* to prepare for the chapter test.

Using Vocabulary

Create a classification system that demonstrates how these words below are related. First, write *Reconstruction* as your main heading. Under the main heading create several smaller categories. Challenge yourself to see how many different classifications you can devise.

tenant farmer	sharecropper
segregation	black codes
amnesty	carpetbagger
mandate	disenfranchise
impeach	

Reviewing Facts

1. **Cite** two reasons why tenant farming and sharecropping were used in the South.

2. **Explain** how black codes prevented African Americans from achieving equality.

3. **List** three motives of the Radical Republicans in Congress.

4. **Name** three sectors of the Southern economy that improved after the Civil War.

Understanding Concepts

Adaptation

1. Re-create the diagram shown here, and list the efforts made by the Freedmen's Bureau to improve the lives of freed slaves.

Freedmen's Bureau

2. Explain why freedom did not automatically lead to equality for African Americans after the Civil War.

Power and Authority

3. What are the significant reasons that explain how the power of the Radical Republicans first grew and later diminished?

Critical Thinking

1. **Identifying Central Issues** The 1860s were a time of radical change. Summarize the string of events that caused so much political and social turbulence during the 1860s.

2. **Analyzing Fine Art** Study the painting on this page, entitled *A Visit from the Old Mistress* by Winslow Homer, and answer the questions that follow.

   a. Identify the two main figures.

   b. How does the artist contrast these figures?

   c. What idea do you think the artist is expressing?

3. **Making Comparisons** During Reconstruction, white Americans knew very little about the African continent. Africa at this time had hundreds of different ethnic groups, each with its own language and customs. How did Americans' ignorance about African culture affect their attitudes toward African Americans?

4. **Drawing Conclusions** Do you think Lincoln would have suffered the same fate as Johnson had he lived?

5. **Analyzing Alternatives** If you had been in the Senate, would you have voted for or against conviction of President Johnson? Explain.

6. **Recognizing Bias** Study the following statements and decide which ones show evidence of emotional bias and which ones show an attempt to be objective. Explain your choices.

   a. "The real human tragedy is the upward striving of downtrodden men, the groping for light among people born in darkness. . . ." (W.E.B. DuBois on Reconstruction)

   b. "If the question was, Is Andrew Johnson a fit person for President? I should answer, no; but it is not a party question, nor upon Andrew Johnson's deeds and acts, except so far as they are made to appear in the record, that I am to decide." (Senator Lyman Trumbell on Johnson's impeachment)

History and Geography

Reconstruction in the South

Study the map on Reconstruction on page 221. Then answer the questions that follow.

1. **Region** What two geographic divisions of the South are shown on the map?

2. **Place** Which state had the largest number of African American members in its convention? Which state had the smallest?

Cooperative Learning ## Interdisciplinary Activity: Government

You belong to a group analyzing Reconstruction policies. Each member of your group will assume one of these roles: a Southern landowner, a Northern carpetbagger, and an African American sharecropper. Your goal is to write two Reconstruction laws that are acceptable to all. Write one law on voting rights for African Americans and a second law on the treatment of former Confederate soldiers.

Practicing Skills

Using an Electronic Spreadsheet

Working with another student, use an electronic spreadsheet to track the weather in your community. Enter the daily high, average, and low temperatures in your community for four weeks. At the end of this period, calculate your average local temperature. Then use the spreadsheet to make line graphs showing the monthly high temperatures, average temperatures, and low temperatures. Use the following points to help guide you.

1. Assign each column (vertical) a letter or a number.

2. Label each cell according to its corresponding row and column.

Technology Activity

Using a Word Processor

Use the Internet and library sources to find out more about the impeachment of President Johnson. Imagine you are a reporter back then, and write a story about a particular aspect of the process.

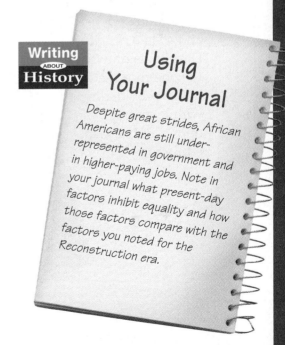

Writing ABOUT History

Using Your Journal

Despite great strides, African Americans are still underrepresented in government and in higher-paying jobs. Note in your journal what present-day factors inhibit equality and how those factors compare with the factors you noted for the Reconstruction era.

Cultural Kaleidoscope

Education

The One-Room Schoolhouse

Until education became widespread, many children learned to read and write in one-room schoolhouses. The backbone of the curriculum was the three R's—reading, writing, and arithmetic. Children of all ages learned mostly by rote—one group recited while the rest studied their lessons. Students today might view the one-room schoolhouse as primitive. Chalkboards and maps were rare, and students, lacking even paper and pen, used a slate and a slate pencil. Despite its drawbacks, the one-room schoolhouse provided many with their only opportunity for an education.

▲ Many American leaders saw in public schools a means of promoting national spirit.

▼ The hornbook for learning the alphabet was still in use during the 1800s in many schoolhouses.

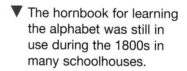

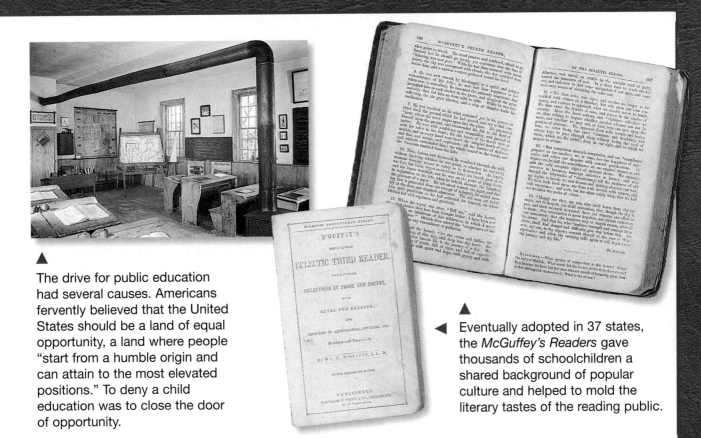

The drive for public education had several causes. Americans fervently believed that the United States should be a land of equal opportunity, a land where people "start from a humble origin and can attain to the most elevated positions." To deny a child education was to close the door of opportunity.

◄ Eventually adopted in 37 states, the *McGuffey's Readers* gave thousands of schoolchildren a shared background of popular culture and helped to mold the literary tastes of the reading public.

▲ More and more schools provided desks in the 1800s. Earlier, students sat on backless wooden benches. The teacher's desk was often on a raised platform.

◄ Even where there was a will to establish schools, the widely separated homesteads in rural areas made large schools impractical. The one-room schoolhouse filled a vital need.

Standardized Test Practice

Directions: Choose the *best* answer to each of the following multiple choice questions. If you have trouble answering a question, use the process of elimination to narrow your choices. Write your answers on a separate piece of paper.

1. **Many Northerners saw John Brown as a martyr to the cause of freedom and the abolition of slavery. Southerners were afraid of John Brown because they felt he might**

   A increase the chances of electing a Republican President.

   B encourage a slave revolt.

   C destroy the Underground Railroad.

   D convince Native Americans to fight against the South in the Civil war.

   > **Test-Taking Tip:** Look for clues *in the question* to help you find the answer. For example, if John Brown believed in *freedom* and the *abolition of slavery*, it is unlikely that he would have destroyed the Underground Railroad (answer C).

2. **The Fourteenth Amendment, passed in 1866, redefined citizenship in the United States and was largely a reaction to**

   F Lincoln's offer of amnesty to former Confederate soldiers.

   G the "black codes" passed by Southern state legislatures.

   H the large number of carpetbag governments in the South.

   J President Johnson's dismissal of Edwin Stanton, Secretary of War.

   > **Test-Taking Tip:** This question requires that you remember the provisions of the Fourteenth Amendment. A clue to help you remember is stated in the question: it *redefined citizenship in the United States.* Eliminate answers that aren't related to *citizenship*. For example, although carpetbag governments were often corrupt, they did not usually threaten citizen's rights. Therefore, you can eliminate answer H.

3. **The Radical Republicans' plans for Reconstruction were intended to do all of the following EXCEPT**

   A prevent all former Confederate leaders from taking new positions in government.

   B ensure that African Americans had the right to vote.

   C ensure that women had the right to vote.

   D prohibit states from paying Confederate war debts.

   > **Test-Taking Tip:** Be careful—overlooking the word EXCEPT is a common error. Choose the answer that does NOT fit with the question. The other three will be correct. The Radical Republicans *were* concerned about preventing former Confederate leaders from returning to power (choice A), the rights of African Americans (answer B), and prohibiting states from paying war debts (choice D). Therefore, choice C must be correct.

4. **What was the Underground Railroad?**

   F The first subway system in the United States

   G A network of people that helped enslaved persons escape

   H A network of people who returned fugitive slaves to their owners in the South

   J A movement destroyed by John Brown in 1859

   > **Test-Taking Tip:** Think about the meaning of the word *underground*. It either means, literally, "under the ground," or, metaphorically, "in secret." People who returned fugitive slaves would *not* have needed to do so "under the ground" or "in secret," so answer H can be eliminated.

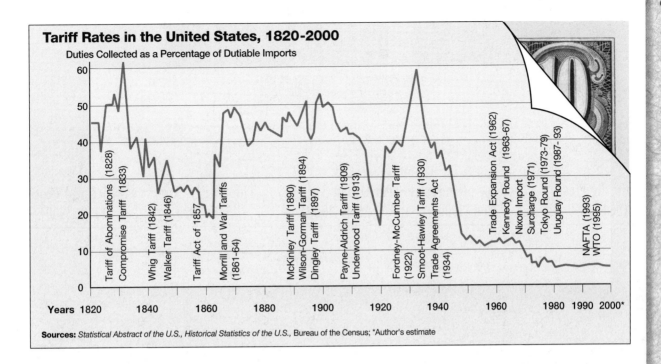

Tariff Rates in the United States, 1820-2000

Duties Collected as a Percentage of Dutiable Imports

Labels on graph:
- Tariff of Abominations (1828)
- Compromise Tariff (1833)
- Whig Tariff (1842)
- Walker Tariff (1846)
- Tariff Act of 1857
- Morrill and War Tariffs (1861-64)
- McKinley Tariff (1890)
- Wilson-Gorman Tariff (1894)
- Dingley Tariff (1897)
- Payne-Aldrich Tariff (1909)
- Underwood Tariff (1913)
- Fordney-McCumber Tariff (1922)
- Smoot-Hawley Tariff (1930)
- Trade Agreements Act (1934)
- Trade Expansion Act (1962)
- Kennedy Round (1963-67)
- Nixon Import Surcharge (1971)
- Tokyo Round (1973-79)
- Uruguay Round (1987-93)
- NAFTA (1993)
- WTO (1995)

Years 1820 1840 1860 1880 1900 1920 1940 1960 1980 1990 2000*

Sources: *Statistical Abstract of the U.S., Historical Statistics of the U.S.,* Bureau of the Census; *Author's estimate

5. What is the primary reason that large numbers of settlers came to California in the late 1840s?

A China and Japan were opened to American trading ships.

B Settlers were given free land in California.

C Settlers wanted to help fight in the Mexican War.

D Gold was discovered in California.

Test-Taking Tip: This question asks for the *primary reason* that settlers came to California. Although it is true that California ports gave merchants access to China and Japan, it is not the *primary reason* that large numbers of settlers moved to California. Therefore, you can eliminate answer A.

6. Protective tariffs are sometimes used to raise the prices of imported goods so that they cannot compete with domestic products. Based on the graph above, which of the following is true?

F The United States imports many products.

G The Compromise Tariff was the highest in world history.

H Tariff rates in the United States have fluctuated greatly.

J Tariffs were higher in 1860 than in 1820.

Test-Taking Tip: Use the information *on the line graph* to support your answer. While it may be true that the United States imports many products from other countries (answer F), that information cannot be found on the graph. Nor does the graph cover world history, which eliminates answer G.

UNIT THREE
NEW HORIZONS
1860–1900

★★★

History AND ART

Miners in the Sierra
by Charles Nahl and Frederick August
Wenderoth, 1851–1852

An abundance and variety of natural resources
were utilized for industrial production.

▲ HORATIO ALGER COVER

Why It's Important

This was an age of optimism, coupled with a belief in the certainty of human progress. As settlers continued to spread across the continent, a wave of immigrants flocked to the nation's industrial centers. Today, the children and grandchildren of these immigrants play a prominent role in many aspects of American society—from business to politics—and are part of the nation's diverse cultural makeup.

To learn more about the development of the nation in the years following the Civil War, view the *Historic America: Electronic Field Trips* Side 2, Chapter 3; Side 2, Chapter 5; Side 2, Chapter 7 video lessons:
- *Little Big Horn*
- *Thomas Edison's Lab*
- *Ellis Island*

Themes

- Geography and Environment
- Conflict and Cooperation
- Influence of Technology
- Cultural Diversity

Key Events

- First transcontinental railroad
- Interstate Commerce Act
- American Federation of Labor formed
- Sherman Antitrust Act
- Battle at Wounded Knee
- Populist party formed

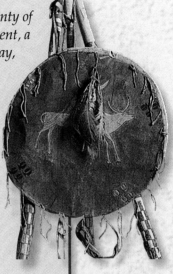

▲ CHEYENNE SHIELD OF PAINTED BUFFALO HIDE

▲ EARLY PHONOGRAPH

PRIMARY SOURCES Library See pages 860–861 for the primary source readings to accompany Unit 3.

▼ SULKY PLOW

Portfolio Project

Design a political cartoon that shows the contrasting sides of one of the divisive issues of this era; for example, Native American and settler, labor and big business, or political machine and reformer.

Global Perspectives

The World

	1860		1875
Asia and Oceania			
Europe			
Africa			
South America			
North and Central America			

1870 *Germany unifies under Bismarck*

1867 *Diamond fields discovered in South Africa*

1861 *Gabriel Moreno becomes president of Ecuador*

The United States

	1860		1875
Pacific and Northwest			
Southeast			
Midwest			
Southwest			
Atlantic Northeast			

1869 *First transcontinental rail route is completed*

▲ **1876** *Sioux nation defeats Custer at Little Bighorn*

1870 *H. R. Revels of Mississippi becomes the first African American in Congress*

1860 *The Pony Express is established*

◄ **1878** *First electric light company is established*

Linking Across TIME

There has been a Jewish presence in North America for hundreds of years. Jews tended to gravitate to areas where they met little prejudice—Rhode Island, Pennsylvania, and South Carolina, for example. By the mid-1700s the largest concentration of Jews was found in South Carolina's major city, Charleston. The Jewish population in the United States remained relatively small until the late 1800s, when there was an influx of Jews from central and eastern Europe. Today, the United States has the largest Jewish population in the world.

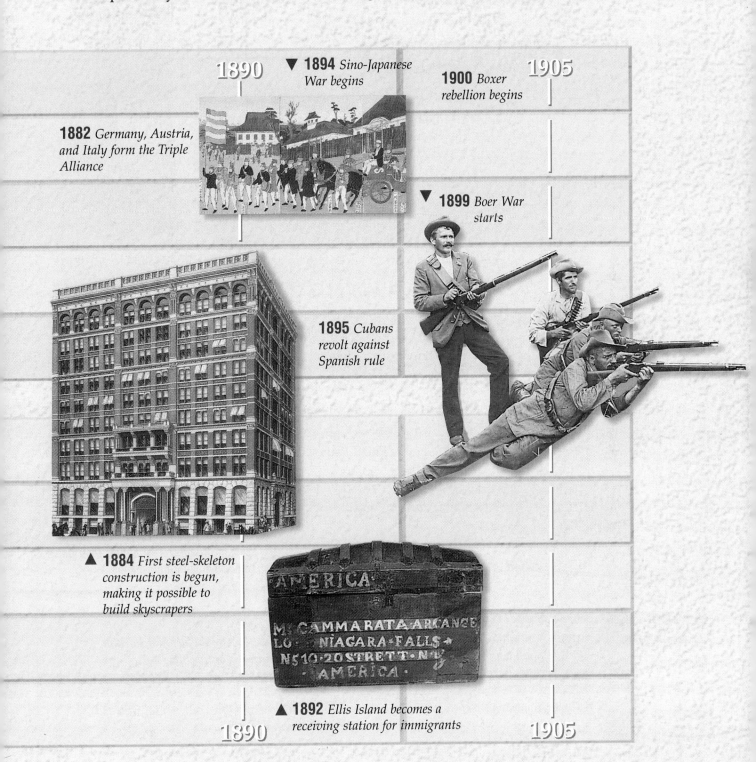

1890

▼ **1894** *Sino-Japanese War begins*

1900 *Boxer rebellion begins*

1905

1882 *Germany, Austria, and Italy form the Triple Alliance*

▼ **1899** *Boer War starts*

1895 *Cubans revolt against Spanish rule*

▲ **1884** *First steel-skeleton construction is begun, making it possible to build skyscrapers*

▲ **1892** *Ellis Island becomes a receiving station for immigrants*

1890

1905

CHAPTER 7

★★

Into the West
1860–1900

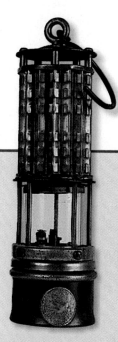
▲ LANTERN, LATE 1800S

Setting the Scene

Focus

The settlement of the Far West frontier was filled with hardships and tragedy as well as adventure. For Native Americans, the slaughter of the buffalo and gradual expansion of white settlement meant the end of their way of life. For miners, ranchers, and farmers, life on the Great Plains meant long hours of work, a harsh climate, and isolation.

Concepts to Understand

★ How **conflict** between the Plains peoples and settlers led to the destruction of Native American society

★ Why national **expansion** developed in the Great Plains region

Read to Discover . . .

★ the role of the railroads in the settlement of the Great Plains.

★ how life on the Great Plains measured up to settlers' expectations.

Journal Notes

What geographic and environmental features created hardships for those who settled and farmed the West? Make notes in your journal as you read the chapter.

HISTORY
Online

Chapter Overview
Visit the *American History: The Modern Era Since 1865* Web site at **me.glencoe.com** and click on **Chapter 7—Chapter Overviews** to preview chapter information.

CULTURAL		
● **1866** *First major "long drive" moves Texas longhorns to Missouri*	● **1872** *Yellowstone National Park is created in Wyoming Territory*	
1860	**1870**	
● **1862** *Homestead Act passes*	● **1869** *First transcontinental railroad is constructed*	
POLITICAL		

Last Stand of the Patriarch
by Henry Francis Farny, 1905

With the movement of white settlers to the West, Native American life began to change.

◀ SIOUX ORNAMENT
WITH QUILLWORK
AND FEATHERS

• **1883** *"Buffalo Bill" Cody opens his first wild west show*

• **1895** The Red Badge of Courage *published*

1880

1890

• **1884** *United States government prohibits Native American Sun Dance*

• **1890** *Census Department declares the frontier closed*

★★★★★★★★★★★★★★★★★★★★★★★★★★★★★★★★★★★★★★

People of the Plains

Guide to Reading

Main Idea

The way of life of Native Americans on the Great Plains began to disappear as a growing number of settlers moved west.

Reading Strategy

Taking Notes As you read about Native Americans of the Great Plains, briefly describe their way of life, using an outline like the one shown here.

> Native Americans of the Plains
> I. Nomadic Life
>   A.
>   B.
> II. Settled Life
>   A.
>   B.

Objectives

After studying this section, you should be able to

★ describe the Plains peoples' way of life.

★ give three reasons the Plains peoples' way of life came to an end.

Key Term

nomadic

▶ **OMAHA HIDE WAR SHIRT**

The United States government had assigned Major Stephen H. Long the exploration of the region beyond the Mississippi River in 1820. In his report, Long used the term "Great American Desert" to describe the territory—a term that soon appeared on nearly all the maps of the West. Believing the land to be completely desolate, many settlers who ventured to California and Oregon completely avoided it, choosing to travel by clipper ship around Cape Horn at the tip of South America.

■ A Nomadic Life

The territory that early European explorers believed to be a desert was home to countless species of wildlife. Hundreds of millions of jackrabbits and prairie dogs, millions of wolves and coyotes, and an estimated 12 to 15 million American bison—usually called buffalo—roamed the Great Plains.

The region was also home to many different Native American nations. Some, like the Omaha and the Osage nations, lived in communities as farmers and hunters. Most of the Native Americans, however, including the Sioux [SOO], the Comanche [kuh•MAN•chee], and the Blackfeet, were **nomadic** peoples. They roamed vast distances, following their main source of food: the great herds of buffalo that lived on the plains.

For generations the nomadic peoples of the plains had only dogs to haul their possessions as they traveled from one hunting area to another. In the 1600s, horses, either traded or stolen from Spanish settlers in the Southwest, changed the Plains peoples' way of life. By the mid-1750s, almost every Plains people rode on horseback. Horses became a vital part of their social, economic, and political life. The Comanche were perhaps the best riders, but the Sioux, Cheyenne [shy•AN], Pawnee, Blackfoot, and Crow nations were nearly as skilled. In the deserts of the region that are the present-day states of Arizona and New Mexico, the Apache [uh•PA•chee] and Navajo [NA•vuh•hoh] captured horses to sell to northern peoples.

The horse made the Plains people much more effective hunters than they had been on foot. It became easier to follow the buffalo, which provided the main source of food, skins for clothing and shelter, and bones for tools. The buffalo hunt not only yielded life's necessities, it also provided sport, ritual, worship, and training for war. Fighting from horseback, Native American warriors were better able to resist the encroachments of settlers and railroads.

◼ Railroads Open the West

A Dakota newspaper editor wrote, "Without the railroad it would have required a century to accomplish what has been done in five years." What was "accomplished" was the killing of nearly all the buffalo and other prairie life, obstruction of the Plains peoples' way of life, and removal of any surviving peoples to reservations.

First Transcontinental Railroad

Railroad building in the West began at a furious pace during the Civil War. The most dramatic achievement was the completion of the first transcontinental line in 1869. Discussion of this project started when gold was discovered in California in 1848.

During the 1850s at least 10 routes were surveyed, and the Gadsden Purchase was acquired from Mexico principally because the Gila River valley provided the easiest route across the western plateau. Congress wanted to finance this gigantic project, but

▼ **APACHE LEADER**

▲ **PLAINS LIFE** Native Americans faced many hardships on the plains. *How did the extinction of the buffalo affect the Plains peoples' way of life?*

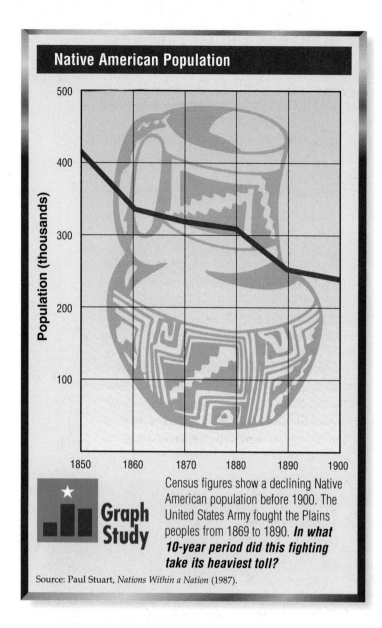

Native American Population

Population (thousands)

500
400
300
200
100

1850　1860　1870　1880　1890　1900

Graph Study

Census figures show a declining Native American population before 1900. The United States Army fought the Plains peoples from 1869 to 1890. *In what 10-year period did this fighting take its heaviest toll?*

Source: Paul Stuart, *Nations Within a Nation* (1987).

Construction proceeded rapidly as the 2 lines raced to get more government money and land. At the height of the competition, the Union Pacific builders employed 10,000 workers. Irish immigrant crews working for the Union Pacific and Chinese immigrants working for the Central Pacific sometimes laid as much as 10 miles of track a day—a remarkable feat because the digging and grading were done by hand. The Central Pacific had a difficult time in the Sierra Nevada ranges with snow that sometimes collected in drifts 60 feet deep. Its heavy equipment was carried from the East 19,000 miles around Cape Horn to California by a fleet of 30 ships.

On May 10, 1869, the "wedding of the rails" took place at Promontory Point, Utah. The whole country celebrated as a transcontinental telegraph reported the blow of a silver sledgehammer driving a golden spike to complete the railroad. A magnetic ball dropped from a pole on the top of the Capitol in Washington, D.C.; in Chicago a seven-mile procession paraded through the streets; in small towns citizens rang church bells.

Other Railroads

The first transcontinental line was soon followed by others—the Northern Pacific; the Atchison, Topeka and Santa Fe; the Southern Pacific; and the Great Northern. Like other big businesses, the railroads needed people of ability, imagination, and drive. The greatest of the Western builders was James J. Hill, a small, short-tempered, red-bearded man of enthusiasm and energy. Beginning in 1879, Hill built the Great Northern, connecting the state of Minnesota and the Washington Territory, without government help. By encouraging settlement as soon as the rails were laid, Hill ensured that his line would have customers. He offered free transportation from Eastern ports, credit, farm machinery, and even free advice on how to improve crops. Hill's careful construction of the Great Northern kept maintenance costs down and enabled him to charge lower rates. As a result, his railroad became the leading carrier in the Northwest.

sectional rivalry caused delays. The South preferred that the eastern terminal be located at New Orleans; the North argued for St. Louis or Chicago. In 1862, with Southern representation temporarily withdrawn from Congress, the government passed an act to encourage the building of a Pacific Railroad.

The Union Pacific Company was to build west from Omaha, while the Central Pacific Company was to run lines east from Sacramento. The federal government loaned money to both companies at the rate of $16,000, $32,000, or $48,000 per mile, according to the terrain. Each company also received land grants along the right-of-way averaging 640 acres per mile.

Believing passionately in the life of the farmers on the plains, Hill wanted to promote maximum settlement. He expressed the idea that

> *Population without the Prairie is a mob, and the Prairie without Population is a desert.*

Killing of Buffalo

The railroads played a major role in the extermination of the buffalo. Though buffalo had formerly ranged eastward as far as Pennsylvania and the Carolinas, their natural habitat was the Great Plains, where they migrated north and south with the seasons. The Union Pacific Railroad effectively cut the huge herds in half. At first buffalo hunting supplied meat for railroad workers, but later it became "sport" for city vacationers to shoot the animals from train windows. In 1871 it was discovered that buffalo leather could be sold at a profit. Professional hunters killed millions for their hides. Trainloads of bones were shipped east to make fertilizer or charcoal. By 1886 only a few hundred buffalo were left, deep in the Canadian woods.

■ Plains Wars

To protect their lands and to stop the waste of the buffalo, Plains people had to fight. For two and one-half centuries they had maintained their way of life against Spanish, English, French, and American invaders. The last battles against overwhelming forces proved futile. The military effort to remove Native Americans from the plains was relentless, with the United States spending an estimated million dollars for each adult male Native American killed.

Taking of Native American Land

The first concentrated fighting broke out in Colorado just after the Civil War started in the East. Government officials tried to

Linking Past and Present

Native American Survival

Millions of Native Americans lived in the Americas when Columbus arrived. Scattered across the North American continent were hundreds of different groups.

Then_____

A Shrinking Population

The well-being and longevity of the Native Americans experienced a steady decline with the arrival of the Europeans. The Europeans carried

diseases such as smallpox and measles, for which the Native Americans had no immunity. The Native American population in the United States reached its low point in 1890. By the end of the 1800s, many tribes had been extinguished.

Now_____

Toward Well-Being

Recent history shows a strong reversal of many measures of decline. Life expectancy for Native Americans has increased to 72 years—a jump of more than 10 years from 1970 levels. Native Americans are now a rapidly growing minority group. The number of American Indian, Inuit, and Aleut peoples has surpassed

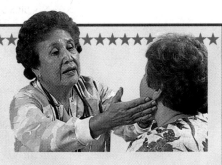

2 million, and projections forecast more than 4 million by the year 2050.

Campaigns at both the government and grassroots levels have brought results. The Indian Health Service provides both curative and preventive services to more than 1 million Native Americans residing in counties within or near reservations in 33 states. Leaders such as Cecilia Fire Thunder of the Oglala Sioux and Susie Yellowtail of the Crow have worked to promote wellness programs for Native Americans.

▲ *THE OUTLIER* by Frederic Remington, 1909
Artist Frederic Remington captured dramatic and compelling images of the vanishing Western frontier. **Why did the Dawes Act fail?**

[oh•GLA•lah] Sioux became enraged at the territorial government's plans to build a road through their sacred lands. Led by Red Cloud, they successfully resisted for several years. In the end, however, the Sioux lost their land to miners searching for gold in the Black Hills.

Efforts Toward Peace

After the bloody war with the Sioux, humanitarians in the East called for a change of government policies. The United States divided responsibility for the Native Americans between the Department of the Interior and the War Department. The Department of the Interior first was to placate Native Americans with gifts and to establish reservations; the War Department was to make war on those who resisted.

In 1867 the federal government sent a peace commission to meet with representatives of several nations, including the Comanche, Kiowa [KY•uh•WAW], Cheyenne, and Arapaho. This effort to end the constant warfare produced agreements that stipulated that the Native Americans were to live on two major reservations on the Great Plains, one in Oklahoma and one in the Dakota Territory. Not all nations were involved, however, so conflicts between Native Americans and the army continued.

Hostilities Resume

With the discovery of gold in the Dakota Territory in 1874, miners flooded into Sioux and Cheyenne lands. Two years later the Sioux, led by Chiefs Sitting Bull and Crazy Horse, attacked the miners and settlers. The conflict came to a climax in June 1876 at the Little Bighorn River, where a large group of Cheyenne and Sioux were camped. General George Custer attacked, but the Native Americans killed Custer and all of his troops at the Battle of the Little Bighorn. The Sioux victory meant only a brief reprieve. In 1881 they surrendered for a final time to the United States Army.

The final clash occurred at Wounded Knee, South Dakota, in December of 1890, where more than 190 unarmed Native

force the Arapaho and Cheyenne from an area that had been granted to them "forever" 10 years earlier. Warfare continued for 3 years until Black Kettle, the Cheyenne chief, was trapped at Sand Creek in eastern Colorado by Colonel John Chivington. The militia ignored Black Kettle's repeated attempts to surrender and killed men, women, and children.

In 1862 the Santee Sioux of Minnesota attacked a group of settlers who had moved into their hunting lands. After the militia defeated them, the Sioux were forced to move to reservations in the Dakota Territory. A short time later, the Oglala

Americans were killed. With this tragic encounter, the wars came to an end.

Although Plains nations fought hundreds of battles from 1860 to 1890, their cause was doomed because they were dependent on the buffalo for food, clothing, fuel, and shelter. When the herds were wiped out, resistance became impossible. In spite of some victories and heroic deeds, such as the 1,500-mile march of the Nez Perce (NEHZ PUHRS) under Chief Joseph in 1877 to avoid capture, the result was inevitable. Chief Joseph's speech at his surrender summarized the hopelessness of the cause:

66 *Our chiefs are killed. . . . The little children are freezing to death. My people . . . have no blankets, no food. . . . Hear me, my chiefs; I am tired; my heart is sick and sad. From where the sun now stands, I will fight no more forever.* 99

The Dawes Act

In 1887, three years before Wounded Knee, Congress passed the Dawes Act, which broke up Native American nations, even on the reservations. The Dawes Act gave each family 160 acres to cultivate. After a probation period of 25 years, Native Americans would be granted ownership of the land and United States citizenship.

The Dawes Act was the result of humanitarian opposition to the United States Army's extermination policy. In 1881 Helen Hunt Jackson had written *A Century of Dishonor,* a book that criticized the government policy toward Native Americans. Unfortunately, the new legislation did more harm than good. Plains peoples were nomads whose way of life was based on the buffalo hunt. They did not understand legal technicalities of land ownership, knew little about farming, and were demoralized by reservation life. Between 1887 and 1943, Native Americans lost to real estate speculators and dishonest government agents an estimated 86 million acres of the 138 million acres that had been set aside for them.

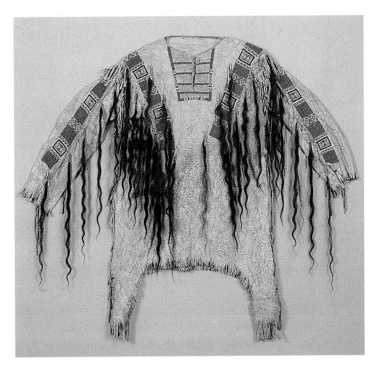

▲ PLAINS BEADED AND FRINGED HIDE SHIRT

Section 1 ★ Assessment

Checking for Understanding

1. **Define** nomadic.
2. **Explain** how the expansion of the railroads benefited some people at the expense of others.

Critical Thinking

3. **Analyzing Issues**   Use a diagram such as the one shown here to list the events that brought an end to the Plains peoples' way of life.

INTERDISCIPLINARY ACTIVITY

4. **The Arts** Research the Sioux people during the late 1800s and create a Sioux pictorial time line.

BUILDING SKILLS

Social Studies Skills

Interpreting Climate Maps

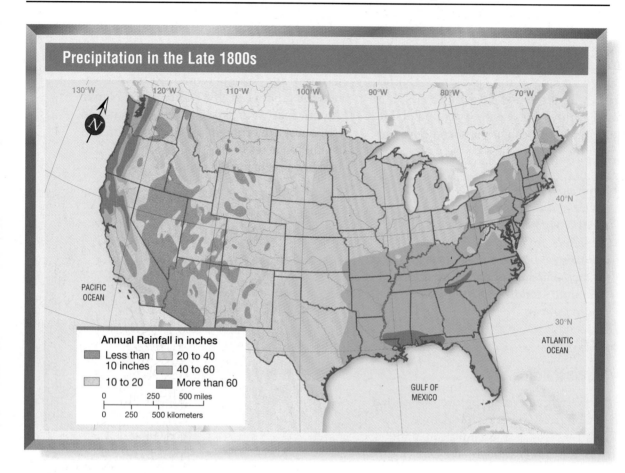

Precipitation in the Late 1800s

Annual Rainfall in inches
- Less than 10 inches
- 10 to 20
- 20 to 40
- 40 to 60
- More than 60

0   250   500 miles

0   250   500 kilometers

PACIFIC OCEAN

ATLANTIC OCEAN

GULF OF MEXICO

Climate plays an important role in determining the way of life in any geographic region. It affects what plants and animals thrive in the region. It also affects how people work, dress, and eat.

Learning the Skill

Climate maps may show differences in precipitation, temperature, or both. Steps to follow in reading a climate map include:

- **Read** the map title to identify the climatic factors that are shown on the map.
- **Study** the legend to identify the meaning of the colors or symbols on the map.
- **Use** the colors or symbols shown in the key to interpret the information on the map.
- **Draw** conclusions about the climate similarities and differences among regions.

Practicing the Skill

1. What information is shown?
2. Which part of the country generally received more rain?
3. How much precipitation could a Wisconsin farmer expect?

Glencoe's **Skillbuilder Interactive Workbook, Level 2** provides instruction and practice in key social studies skills.

APPLYING THE SKILL

4. Create a table that lists these two climate headings: Mild, rainy winters and hot, dry summers; Hot summers and cold winters with little rain. Under each heading, predict how that particular climate might affect the economy, recreation, dress, food, and housing.

★★★

Ranching and Mining

Guide to Reading

Main Idea
The settlement of the West opened up the era of cattle ranching and mining.

Reading Strategy

Organizing Information As you read about life in the West, use a diagram such as the one shown here to list the everyday realities that inspired the myths of the "Old West."

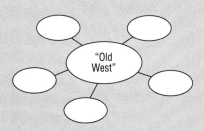

"Old West"

Objectives

After studying this section, you should be able to

★ explain the role of the environment in the rise and fall of the long drive.

★ identify the realities behind the myths of the Old West.

Key Terms

maverick, long drive, vigilance committee, vaudeville, "Western"

▶ **NAT LOVE**

The open-range cattle industry started in Spanish Texas. The Spanish brought the techniques of herding on horseback, roping, and the roundup to the Americas. From the Spanish, too, came the distinctive dress and equipment of the cowhand. The cattle in Texas were mainly Spanish in origin, although some were brought by American and French settlers to Texas when it was part of Mexico. The Great Plains, with its vast open grasslands, was well suited for raising cattle. Faced with such an opportunity, ranchers rapidly moved into the last frontier.

■ The Cattle Kingdom

After the Texas Revolution in 1836, **mavericks,** or unbranded cattle, multiplied on the open range. An estimated 330,000 head of cattle in 1850 grew to between 3 and 4 million head by 1860. There were so many that they could be bought for as little as $3 or $4 a head in Texas.

Cattle Drives

After the Civil War, opportunity developed for great profit in the cattle industry as growing cities of the North provided huge markets for meat. There were, however, no direct railroad lines from Texas to the North. The result was the **long drive.** As the spring of 1866 turned the grasslands green, cowhands drove herds of steers to railroad shipping centers in Missouri and Kansas. The routes of the long drives became known as trails—such as the Chisholm Trail from near San Antonio to Abilene, a station on the Kansas Pacific Railroad.

A single herd might number 2,500 and be attended by 8 to 10 cowhands, a trail boss, and wranglers to care for the horses. The life of a cowhand on the trail demanded discipline, endurance, and courage, but it paid well to those who survived. More than 30,000 cowhands may have ridden the trails

to deliver cattle from Texas to the North. Several thousand of these were African Americans, free to earn their first wages after the Civil War.

Life in the cattle towns was exciting, but many cowhands told exaggerated tales of daring that multiplied as dime novels— books of stories that sold for a dime— spread the myths of the "Wild West" in Eastern towns and cities. A typical tale was *The Life and Adventures of Nat Love: Better Known in the Cattle Country as "Deadwood Dick"—By Himself.* Love was an authentic African American cowboy whose story became part of the romance of the West.

For the investor, the profits obtained from a successful cattle drive were enormous.

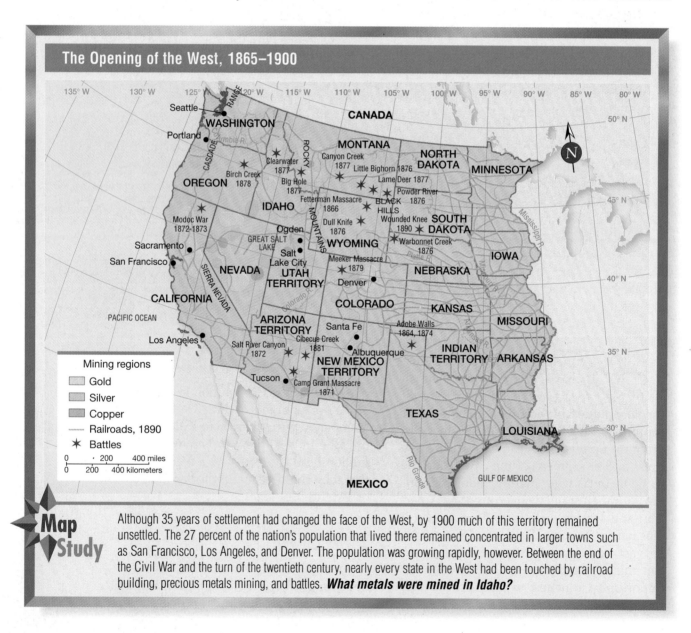

The Opening of the West, 1865–1900

Map Study

Although 35 years of settlement had changed the face of the West, by 1900 much of this territory remained unsettled. The 27 percent of the nation's population that lived there remained concentrated in larger towns such as San Francisco, Los Angeles, and Denver. The population was growing rapidly, however. Between the end of the Civil War and the turn of the twentieth century, nearly every state in the West had been touched by railroad building, precious metals mining, and battles. **What metals were mined in Idaho?**

As the buffalo were cleared from the plains, the Cattle Kingdom expanded northward until, by 1885, it covered an area half as large as Europe, extending from Texas to Montana.

Decline of the Cattle Industry

Although offering vast profits, the industry was beset by difficulties. Steers could go blind from drought, drown in flash floods, die in stampedes, or get infected by the dreaded Texas fever. They might be stolen by rustlers or shot by angry homesteaders trying to protect their crops. The open-range cattle industry collapsed even more rapidly than it had risen. Too many animals were put on the ranges, and overgrazing resulted. Overproduction drove prices down. Sheepherders and homesteaders competed with the cattle ranchers for land.

Nature helped to end the long drives. The cold winter of 1885 and 1886 was followed by a summer so dry that the grass withered and streams disappeared. In the winter of 1886–1887, terrible blizzards covered the ground with snow so deep that the cattle could not paw down to grass. Next came an unprecedented cold spell, with temperatures ranging as low as –60°F. "When spring finally came," wrote historian Ray Allen Billington, "cattlemen saw a sight they spent the rest of their lives trying to forget. Carcass piled upon carcass in every ravine, gaunt skeletons staggering about on frozen feet, trees stripped bare of their bark. . . ."

The cattle industry survived this terrible blow, but the day of the open range was over.

■ The Mining Frontier

The discovery of gold in California was just the beginning of prospecting in the West. Inspired fortune seekers moved to California.

· ·

Footnotes to History

A Growing Industry Some cattle ranches in the West were enormous, covering more land than Massachusetts and Vermont together. On these ranches, hundreds of thousands of cattle were raised for far-off markets.

Mining and Mining Towns

From California the fortune seekers spread east into the Great Basin and Rocky Mountain regions. A gold strike in Colorado in 1858 set off a stampede to the region the next year.

❝ *The first breath of spring started the hordes westward. Steamboats crowded to the rails poured throngs of immigrants ashore at every Missouri River town. . . . All through April, May, and June they left the jumping-off places in a regular parade of Conestoga wagons, hand carts, men on horseback, men on foot— each with "Pikes Peak or Bust" crudely pinned on their packs and wagon canvas. . . . By the end of June more than 100,000 "fifty-niners" were in the Pikes Peak country.* ❞

The Colorado strike was followed by many other finds: gold in the Black Hills of South Dakota, copper in Montana, and silver in many places. The Comstock Lode at Virginia City, Nevada, yielded about $300 million worth of silver ore between 1859 and 1877. These discoveries attracted swarms of fortune seekers, and new mining towns appeared overnight.

The discovery of precious metals brought thousands of miners into a single area, giving rise first to makeshift camps and later to towns and cities. People from a variety of backgrounds mingled in these places. A study of one Western camp revealed that the population consisted of 37 from China, 35 from Great Britain, 29 from Mexico, 24 from other nations, and 81 from other parts of the United States. In addition, other newcomers, including a substantial number of women, set up businesses to serve the miners.

Despite differences in background, all of the miners shared one goal: an unbending desire to mine that lucky strike that would bring them wealth. After the minerals in one area were exhausted, miners would leave town, and a once-lively center of trade and commerce would become a deserted ghost town almost overnight. While the wealth lasted, however, mining communities could be spirited—as well as dangerous—places. One observer described one such mining town in this way:

> This human hive, numbering at least 10,000 people, was the product of 90 days. Into it were crowded all the elements of a rough and active civilization. . . . [F]illed with gambling tables and gamblers, and the miner who was bold enough to enter one of them with his day's earnings in his pocket seldom left until thoroughly fleeced. . . . Not a day or night passed which did not yield its full fruition of fights, quarrels, wounds or murders. . . . Street fights were frequent . . . and everyone was on his guard against a random shot.

Human life was cheap in these communities of tents and crude dwellings, with their rows of saloons and gambling houses. There was a vital need for law enforcement agencies to settle disputes over mining claims and to punish or prevent crime. Self-appointed volunteers called **vigilance committees** sometimes provided law and order. Other times mass meetings drew up their own rules and elected their own officials.

Soon the different communities of a region such as Colorado or Nevada would band together and demand territorial status or statehood. Usually the actual grant of statehood came after the arrival of homesteaders and miners, because cattle raisers were too nomadic to provide stable government.

The "Wild West"

The "Wild West" captured the imagination of Americans immediately. Dime novels and popular ballads spread the adventures of Wild Bill Hickok, Billy the Kid, and Jesse James. A Wild West Show became part of Barnum and Bailey's circus; and Annie Oakley, the sharpshooter, appeared on **vaudeville,** or live variety show, stages everywhere. The Wild West period lasted

Charles M. Russell
1864–1926

AMERICAN PORTRAITS

Born in St. Louis, Charles Russell much preferred to watch the fur traders and men who worked along the Mississippi River than to attend school.

In 1880, at the age of 16, Russell set out for Montana to work as a cowhand and to observe Native American life. He began to paint life as he saw it, creating realistic scenes of the untamed West. Among Russell's favorite subjects were cowhands riding bucking broncos, Native Americans hunting buffalo, and outlaws holding up stagecoaches.

Little realizing the value of his paintings, he often gave them away. By the early 1890s, however, Russell was able to stop cowpunching and devote himself solely to art. By 1920 Russell's portrayals of "cowboys and Indians" commanded high prices, and he was recognized as one of the finest artists of the American West.

▲ **MINING TOWNS** The discovery of gold in Colorado and silver in Nevada started a rush to the West. Thousands flocked into "boom towns" like Creede, Colorado, to strike it rich. *How many "fifty-niners" went to Pikes Peak country?*

little more than 30 years, yet its fascination has continued in storybooks and comics, Western songs and costumes, and **"Westerns"**—movies produced by Hollywood and shown at movie theaters or on television.

The romance of the Wild West conceals some of the truth. The conquest of the plains and the Rockies by the invading cattle ranchers, miners, and homesteaders destroyed natural resources, wildlife, and human beings. Charles Marion Russell, a frontier artist, gave this sobering message in a speech to "forward-looking citizens" in Helena, Montana:

" *I have been called a pioneer. . . . [A] pioneer is a man who comes to a virgin country, traps off all the fur, kills off all the wild meat, cuts down all the trees, grazes off all the grass, plows the roots up, and strings ten million miles of wire. A pioneer destroys things and calls it civilization. I wish to God this country was just like it was when I first saw it and that none of you folks were here at all.* "

Section 2 ★ Assessment

Checking for Understanding

1. **Define** maverick, long drive, vigilance committee, vaudeville, "Western."

Critical Thinking

2. **Summarizing** Re-create a diagram such as the one shown here, and use it to explain the rise and the fall of the open-range cattle industry.

Open-Range Cattle Industry	
Rise	Fall

3. **Predicting Outcomes** Had the open-range system continued, what conflicts could have developed as the farmers settled the plains?

INTERDISCIPLINARY ACTIVITY

4. **The Arts** Find paintings by such artists as Frederic Remington, Charles Russell, or George Catlin. Write a paragraph on one of these artists answering the question: Is the artist's style realistic or romantic?

The Civil War shattered the illusions of many Americans, including writers. They had little use for the idealism of antebellum books. This postwar generation of writers depicted events and characters in the hard, cold light of reality. One master of the new realism was Mark Twain.

Read to Discover

In this excerpt, Mark Twain applies a light touch to his account of a journey to Carson City with two miners. As you read, determine what the author is implying about human nature.

Reader's Dictionary

circussing	creating frenzied activity and confusion
stealthy	deliberate and secret
sinister	evil

_R_oughing It (excerpts)

The snow lay so deep on the ground that there was no sign of a road perceptible, and the snowfall was so thick that we could not see more than a hundred yards ahead, else we could have guided our course by the mountain ranges. The case looked dubious, but Ollendorff said his instinct was as sensitive as any compass, and that he could "strike a beeline" for Carson City and never diverge from it. . . . For half an hour we poked along warily enough, but at the end of that time we came upon a fresh trail, and Ollendorff shouted proudly:

"I knew I was as dead certain as a compass, boys! Here we are, right in somebody's tracks that will hunt the way for us without any trouble. Let's hurry up and join company with the party."

So we put the horses into as much of a trot as the deep snow would allow, and before long it was evident that we were gaining on our predecessors, for the tracks grew more distinct. We hurried along and at the end of an hour the tracks looked still newer and fresher—but what surprised us was, that the number of travelers in advance of us seemed to steadily increase. We wondered how so large a party came to be traveling at such a time and in such a solitude. . . . Presently [Ballou] stopped his horse and said:

"Boys, these are our own tracks, and we've actually been circussing round and round in a circle for more

▲ COLORADO GHOST TOWN

than two hours, out here in the blind desert! By George this is perfectly hydraulic!". . . .

All agreed that a campfire was what would come nearest to saving us, now, and so we set about building it. We could find no matches. . . . This was distressing, but it paled before a greater horror—the horses were gone! I had been appointed to hold the bridles, but in my absorbing anxiety . . . I had unconsciously dropped them and the released animals had walked off in the storm. . . .

We were miserable enough, before; we felt still more forlorn, now. . . . At this critical moment Mr. Ballou fished four matches from the rubbish of an overlooked pocket. . . . when Mr. Ballou prepared to light the first match, there was an amount of interest centered upon him that pages of writing could not describe. The match burned hopefully a moment, and then went out. It could not have carried more regret with it if it had been a human life. The next match simply flashed and died. The wind puffed the third one out just as it was on the imminent verge of success. We gathered together closer than ever . . . as Mr. Ballou scratched our last hope on his leg. It lit, burned blue and sickly, and then budded into a robust flame. Shading it with his hands, the old gentleman bent gradually down and every heart went with him. . . . The flame touched the sticks at last, took gradual hold upon them . . . held its breath five heartbreaking seconds, then gave a sort of human gasp and went out.

Nobody said a word for several minutes. It was a solemn sort of silence; even the wind put on a stealthy, sinister quiet, and made no more noise than the falling flakes of snow. . . .

Then [next morning] came a white upheaval at my side, and a voice said, with bitterness: "Will some gentleman be so good as to kick me behind?" It was Ballou—at least it was a tousled snow image in a sitting posture, with Ballou's voice.

I rose up, and there in the gray dawn, not fifteen steps from us, were the frame buildings of a stage station and under a shed stood our still saddled and bridled horses!

▼ IDEALIZED SCENE OF MINING CAMP

Responding to Literature

1. Were the men in *Roughing It* experienced Western travelers? Explain.

2. Why does the narrator find the group's situation humiliating?

3. How does Twain's tone in this selection contribute to its humor?

ACTIVITY

4. Mark Twain is referred to as a realist. A realist is often described as one who views the world as it is, while an idealist views the world as it should be. Name historical and political figures and categorize them as realists or idealists. Write your opinion about which type of person makes a better leader.

★★

Farming Moves West

Guide to Reading

Main Idea

Spurred on by technological advancements and the opportunity for profit, settlers worked to turn the Great Plains into farmland.

Reading Strategy

Classifying Information As you read about farming in the West, use a chart such as the one shown here to list the problems plains farmers faced.

Problems for Plains Farmers

Objectives

After studying this section, you should be able to

★ list three factors that made farming the plains possible.

★ summarize the problems faced by plains farmers.

Key Terms

meridian, commodity

McCormick **HARVESTING MACHINE** ▶

*I*n 1862 Congress passed the Homestead Act, enabling a head of a family to acquire a 160-acre farm for $10. To ensure that the land went to actual settlers, the act required that the owner must reside on or cultivate the land for 5 years. The act was passed as a result of nearly half a century of agitation by Western farmers and Eastern laborers.

■ Farming the Great Plains

The Homestead Act did not work out as planned. Through fraud, speculators rather than actual settlers gained possession of much land. The law required that a would-be homesteader put up a home and cultivate the land. Speculators paid relatives or employees to lay down a few logs as a "foundation" and scatter a few grains of corn. After five years they collected title to a large tract. A more important reason for the ineffectiveness of the Homestead Act was that much of the most desirable land near the railroad lines was usually controlled by the railroad companies themselves.

Technology

Before the plains could be settled, farmers had to be convinced that they could overcome the disadvantages of the dry environment. In the East a farmer could get water from a stream or by digging a well 10 to 20 feet deep. In the plains few streams ran year-round, and underground water was 30 to 300 feet down. The American farmer had always depended on trees for fuel, buildings, and fences. On the plains, trees were found only in the bottomlands near rivers.

Some of the difficulties of farming the plains were overcome by technology from the Industrial Revolution. Cheap iron and steel made possible the iron-encased, drilled well and the cast-iron windmill. Joseph Glidden sold his first barbed wire in 1874, making up for the lack of wooden fence rails.

Improved agricultural machinery cut the cost of raising crops. The reaper, in general use by 1865, was followed by the mechanical binder, which tied the grain into sheaves as fast as it was cut. By the 1880s, 2 people and a team of horses could harvest and bind 20 acres of wheat a day. The steam-driven threshing machine also came into general use. In addition to solving technical problems, the Industrial Revolution created a vast new urban population and expanded the market for food, both in America and Europe.

Railroads

The ineffectiveness of the Homestead Act provided Westerners with a grievance but did not interfere with settlement. Although railroads sometimes discouraged the acqui-sition of free land, they actively promoted the sale of their own. They did not charge high prices because they wanted settlers to get the land into production. In fact, the most important factor in promoting settlement was the railroad.

Land-grant railroads had "Bureaus of Immigration" to persuade farmers to settle along their lines. They maintained offices in the principal European cities and agents in Eastern seaports to meet immigrants as they left the boat. Steamship companies and Western states advertised the region as so healthy that it cured all known diseases. The industrious person could expect to become wealthy; an $8,000 investment, it was claimed, might soon result in a steady income of $11,000 per year—an enormous sum considering that a 160-acre farm was homesteaded for $10. The West was pictured as a place where unmarried women would easily find husbands. "When a daughter of the East is once beyond the Missouri," said one railroad advertisement, "she rarely recrosses it except on a bridal tour."

Visualizing History

▲ **LIVING ON THE PLAINS** Lack of trees on the Great Plains forced homesteaders to build homes from materials other than wood. One of the most common was sod cut from the grassy turf. *What were the environmental realities that farmers on the plains faced?*

▲ **BARBED WIRE** The introduction of barbed wire, perfected in 1874, was a blessing for farmers. Previously farmers had made do with earth embankments and hedges to keep cattle out of their crops. ***What equipment and materials were needed to farm on the plains?***

To offset the myth of the "Great American Desert," a new myth was created. Some "experts" said that rainfall on the Great Plains would increase with the planting of trees or with simple cultivation.

As the plains were opened, the production of wheat—centering in Minnesota, the Dakotas, Kansas, and Nebraska—quadrupled. Wisconsin, too far from the market to send fresh dairy products, used its surplus milk for cheese production. Near every great city, truck gardens provided supplies of fresh vegetables.

🌐 **GEOGRAPHY**
■ Sod House Reality

The life of a Great Plains farmer seldom approached the railroad agents' glowing reports and prophecies. The realities of the

• •

Footnotes to History

Fencing Costs In 1871 the cost of fencing a 160-acre homestead on the Great Plains, with wood brought in from Wisconsin, was estimated at $1,000. The homestead itself would have cost $20 in land-office fees.

weather, economic conditions, and other hardships combined to make life on the plains difficult.

Weather

The climate that was supposed to cure all known diseases turned out to be severe. In the summer the temperature might go over 100°F for days at a time. In winter there were periods of extreme cold, and terrible blizzards drove the snow through every chink in doors and windows. Families could be stranded in sod houses for many days.

Prairie fires were a constant danger in the spring and fall. Sometimes grasshoppers appeared in huge numbers and destroyed the crops.

Worst of all disasters was drought. The normal rainfall of the plains region was markedly less than that of the wooded East, dropping from about 30 to 40 inches per year along the 98th **meridian,** or line of longitude, to 10 inches just east of the Rockies.

The greatest push westward into the Great Plains took place in the early 1880s, during a cycle of wet years that offered false promises of abundant crops. In the late 1880s, drought returned to drive thousands back east in despair. In spite of all the difficulties, most settlers managed to adjust to

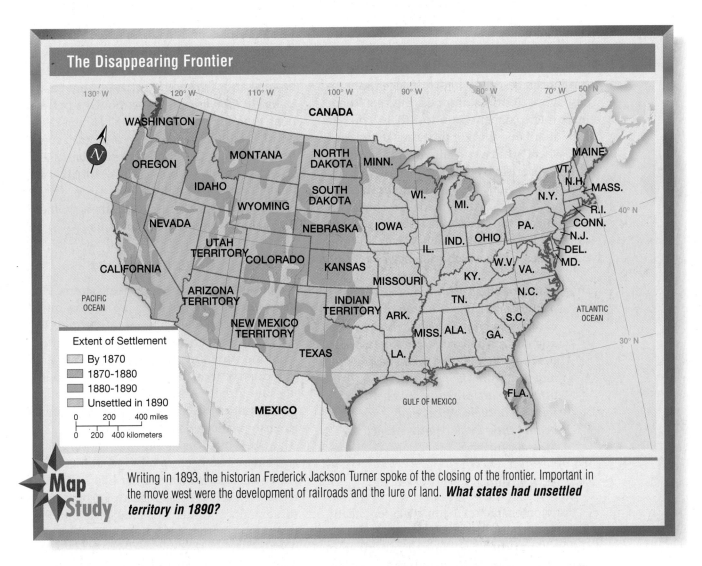

The Disappearing Frontier

Extent of Settlement
- By 1870
- 1870-1880
- 1880-1890
- Unsettled in 1890

0   200   400 miles

0   200   400 kilometers

Map Study

Writing in 1893, the historian Frederick Jackson Turner spoke of the closing of the frontier. Important in the move west were the development of railroads and the lure of land. *What states had unsettled territory in 1890?*

their physical environment. Water from deep wells enabled them to plant gardens and trees around their homes. Railroads brought lumber and brick for houses to replace sod huts and coal to replace cornstalks or hay as fuel.

Economics

Plains farmers faced a second problem at least as frustrating as the weather. They were in the grip of economic forces beyond their control. Formerly, out of necessity as subsistence farmers, they had produced almost everything they needed. The independent farmer was admired in literature and melodramas, especially when contrasted with unhappy factory hands, the idle rich, or "city slickers." With the opening of great urban markets, however, farmers tended to specialize. Some farmers grew a single cash crop, such as wheat or corn; others might specialize in dairy production or cattle raising. Their incomes went up, but so did their expenses. Large-scale farming required a great deal of agricultural machinery. The need to buy clothing and food made farmers less independent.

A farmer's prosperity, perhaps even the ownership of the farm, might depend on the unpredictable price of grain in an international market. Farmers also became dependent on the railroad, which carried their crops to market, on the commission merchant who marketed it, and on the owners of grain elevators who stored it. Farmers who raised hogs or beef cattle were in a similar situation; they had little bargaining power and were forced to take whatever the meat packers paid.

Farming on the plains demanded large investments of money to drill wells, put up windmills, enclose fields in barbed wire, and buy machinery. Because few farmers could pay with cash, they had to borrow by mortgaging their land. Then, to pay interest on the mortgages, they had to concentrate on cash crops. If prices dropped, they could not meet their payments and lost their land. By 1900 about one-third of the farms in the corn and wheat areas were cultivated by tenants.

Not surprisingly, farmers protested. Even though they supplied the **commodities,** or economic goods, that paid for European investments, the wealth they created seemed to be siphoned off to others. Their attitude was expressed by a Nebraska newspaper:

> *There are three great crops raised in Nebraska. One is a crop of corn, one a crop of freight rates, and one a crop of interest. One is produced by farmers, who sweat and toil, from the land. The other two are produced by men who sit in their offices and behind their bank counters and farm the farmers.*

The Plains Women

For women, life on the plains often meant solitude and drudgery. "Born and scrubbed, suffered and died," is the epitaph given a woman in one of Hamlin Garland's poems. Yet the settlement of the West owed much to the endless toil of frontier women.

Women have written some of the best accounts of plains life, such as *Cimarron* by Edna Ferber and *My Antonia* by Willa Cather. While not minimizing the sufferings, these novels reveal how much easier life became after the sod house days were past.

In *My Antonia* Cather mentioned a prominent building in Black Hawk, Nebraska, a new brick high school. As soon as farm communities had the funds, they established churches and schools. The Morrill Act helped states to establish universities. These were open to women as well as men; women had gained a new position of equality.

Declining Status of Farmers

Farmers, however, were losing status. For years they had been held up as the most admirable and the happiest of people. By the 1880s power and prestige had shifted from the rural areas to the cities. "Captains of industry" won the admiration of the public, and urban America regarded country people not as the backbone of the nation but as unsophisticated and backward.

In 1890 the Census Bureau reported that settlement had been so rapid "that there can hardly be said to be a frontier line." In reality, much land was still unoccupied, and new settlement continued at a brisk pace into the twentieth century, but the news that the frontier was closing encouraged prophets of doom, who saw the end of an era. They believed that the existence of unoccupied land at the frontier had provided a "safety-valve of social discontent," the idea that Americans could always make a fresh start.

Section 3 ★ Assessment

Checking for Understanding

1. **Define** meridian, commodity.
2. **Explain** the role of the railroads in settling the Great Plains.

Critical Thinking

3. **Understanding Cause and Effect** What geographic features of the Great Plains created needs for new agricultural technology? How did technology answer these needs?

4. **Analyzing Issues** Re-create the chart shown here, and describe how each factor helped make farming in the West more attractive and profitable.

Improved Machinery	
Growing Urban Population	
Railroads	

INTERDISCIPLINARY ACTIVITY

5. **The Arts** Create a pictorial display that shows the three machines and tools from the late 1800s you consider most essential for farming the Great Plains.

The Great American Desert

To Americans accustomed to well-watered, timbered lands east of the Mississippi River, the Great Plains seemed a vast and forbidding desert. The 100th meridian marked the line west of which annual rainfall was less than 20 inches. Farther west the annual rainfall was even less. Aquifers—strata of water-bearing rock—lay much farther below the surface than they did in the East, making hand-dug wells impractical.

The general aridity of the Great Plains region had caused explorers to label the area a desert. Major Stephen Long, leading an army expedition to explore the Great Plains in 1820, stated that ". . . it is almost wholly unfit for cultivation. . . . The scarcity of wood and water, almost uniformly prevalent, will prove an insuperable obstacle in the way of settling the country." Long prepared a map, labeled the region the Great American Desert, and influenced Americans' perception of the plains for decades.

Almost every map published between 1820 and 1860 used Long's label. Americans' misconception about the plains delayed settlement until new technology—drilling machines and the windmill—tapped deep aquifers. Until the water runs out, technology has conquered geography.

▲ THE CHRISMAN SISTERS AT THEIR NEBRASKA HOMESTEAD

▲ NEBRASKA WHEAT FIELD

Making the Geography Connection

1. The absence of which resources led people to think of the Great Plains as a desert?

2. In what ways could settlers adapt to the environment?

3. How might the "mining" of aquifers affect people on the Great Plains today?

ACTIVITY

4. Create a cartoon that illustrates in a humorous way one aspect of life on the Great Plains.

Using Vocabulary

Explain why each of these terms is used in a chapter about opening the West.

nomadic	maverick
long drive	vigilance committees
"Western"	meridian
commodity	vaudeville

Reviewing Facts

1. **Describe** the lives of the nomadic Plains peoples.

2. **Give** reasons why the Plains peoples' way of life came to an end.

3. **List** the factors that drew settlers to the West.

4. **Contrast** the open-range cattle industry with the system that replaced it.

Understanding Concepts

Conflict

1. Explain the conflicts between Native Americans and settlers. What groups today might oppose unrestrained development and fencing of wilderness areas?

Expansion

2. Re-create the diagram shown here, and list the ways in which settlers gained control of the harsh environment of the Great Plains.

Settlers Control Environment

Critical Thinking

1. **Recognizing Effects** How did the railroads benefit from encouraging farmers and immigrants to settle near their rail lines?

2. **Analyzing Art** Study the rendering on this page of a Kiowa calendar. Unique among Native Americans on the plains was the Kiowas' practice of recording time by painting pictures and symbols on animal hides. Winters on these historical calendars were recorded by black bars, which represented plants without leaves. Summers were recorded by a drawing of the sun-dance medicine lodge. On long winter nights, the painted hides were used to recite the group's history, keeping alive its memories.

   a. Why is the calendar important to the Kiowa?

   b. List other ways in which an artist might represent the seasons.

▲ **KIOWA CALENDAR**

3. **Assessing Change** How did the change from a nomadic to a reservation lifestyle affect Native Americans?

4. **Correcting Stereotypes** Imagine that you have been asked to direct the making of a Western film. What ideas would you recommend to correct some false notions about the Old West?

5. **Understanding Cause and Effect** What was the intention of the Dawes Act? What were its consequences for Native Americans?

6. **Point of View** In the 1870s, crossing the plains was still an adventure because the area was sparsely settled and government was just beginning to establish control and order. Write a day's entry in the diary of a 17-year-old traveling west by rail in 1870. Include details about the geographic features, the hardships, and the traveler's reactions.

History and Geography

Westward Movement

In the 1800s settlers moved west and established farms, towns, and cattle ranches. Settlement and development accelerated rapidly after the building of the railroads.

1. **Movement** What geographic features attracted people to move west?

2. **Human/Environment Interaction** Why did the building of the railroad accelerate the movement of people to the West?

Cooperative Learning Interdisciplinary Activity: Dramatic Arts

In groups of 4–5 students, research the details of life during the days of the open-range cattle industry. Divide the research assignments so that each group member is responsible for reporting on a different aspect of life during this period.

Two good sources that provide an accurate account of life during the days of the open-range cattle industry are *Cowboys of the Wild West* by Russell Freedman and *The Day of the Cattleman* by Earnest Staples Osgood.

After each group has completed its research and written notes, your group should create two dramatizations of an event during a roundup or a long drive. Remember that the long drive usually culminated in a railroad town such as Abilene, Dodge City, or Sedalia, where cowhands sold their cattle to buyers from the larger cities.

Shape the first dramatization to depict the event as it may have been shown in a Western. The second dramatization should present it as it might have happened in real life. Each dramatization should last from four to six minutes. After rehearsing, present your dramatizations to the class.

Practicing Skills

Interpreting Climate Maps

Find a precipitation map of the United States in your local newspaper or in a national magazine. Use the map to answer the questions that follow.

1. What data is shown on the map?

2. Does the map include a legend? What categories are included?

3. What does the map predict about the area where you live?

Technology Activity

Using a Word Processor Use the Internet and other library sources to find out more about a famous person (e.g., Annie Oakley, Jesse James) or an event—such as a gunfight—associated with the "Wild West." Write a brief biography of the person or a description of the event.

Writing ABOUT History

Using Your Journal

Compare and contrast the hardships for the settlers in the West with those faced by the colonists in the 1600s.

CHAPTER 8

★★

The Rise of Industry
1860–1900

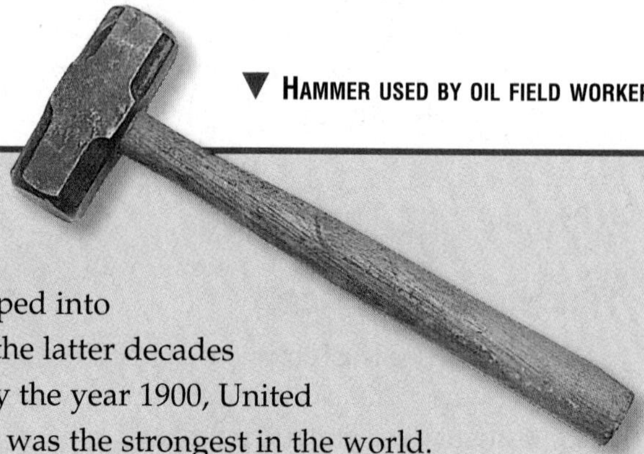

▼ HAMMER USED BY OIL FIELD WORKERS

Setting the Scene

Focus

The United States developed into a great industrial power in the latter decades of the nineteenth century. By the year 1900, United States industrial production was the strongest in the world. This remarkable growth was the result of many different factors—cheap labor, abundant raw materials, new technology—but also of new forms of business organization.

Concepts to Understand

★ Why business leaders believed that **individual initiative** benefited all of society

★ How **government restriction** and other forces affected economic development

Read to Discover . . .

★ what factors caused American industry to grow so rapidly.

★ how Andrew Carnegie and John D. Rockefeller were able to become industrial giants.

Journal Notes

When you read about Rockefeller and Carnegie, look for instances when they gave away some of their wealth. Note these instances in your journal.

HISTORY Online

Chapter Overview
Visit the *American History: The Modern Era Since 1865* Web site at **me.glencoe.com** and click on *Chapter 8—Chapter Overviews* to preview chapter information.

CULTURAL		
• **1869** *Mark Twain publishes* Innocents Abroad	• **1879** *Thomas Edison invents the first practical electric light*	
1860	**1870**	
• **1865** *Civil War ends*	• **1873** *Panic of 1873 strikes*	
POLITICAL		

Factory Chimneys
by Maximillian Luce, 1896

Mass production—production of large quantities of goods at low cost—was the heart of the new industrial system.

◀ INVENTOR THOMAS ALVA EDISON

• **1882** *Standard Oil Trust formed*

• **1893** *First successful gasoline-powered car operated*

1880	1890

• **1884** *Congress establishes the Federal Bureau of Labor*

• **1893** *Colorado grants women the right to vote*

★★

Industrialization Takes Hold

Main Idea

In the years following the Civil War, the nation experienced a surge of industrial growth.

Reading Strategy

Organizing Information As you read about industrialization taking hold in America, use a diagram such as the one shown here. List the causes for industrial growth on the diagonal lines.

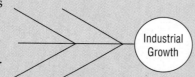

Industrial Growth

Objectives

After studying this section, you should be able to

★ identify and explain the factors that encouraged industrial growth.

★ discuss the railroad's role in the growth of industry.

Key Terms

entrepreneur, economies of scale

▶ CASH REGISTER, 1878

*U*nlike the South, the North emerged virtually undamaged by the Civil War, its railroads and factories intact. Furthermore, the war and Reconstruction eliminated Southern planters as rivals to Northern industrialists for political power, allowing industrial growth to proceed at an even greater pace. Although interrupted by depressions from 1873 to 1878, 1882 to 1884, and 1893 to 1896, America's industrial production doubled every 12 to 14 years. By the 1880s the United States had overtaken Great Britain as the world's industrial leader.

■ Resources

The change from a primarily agricultural society to an industrial one was possible because the United States had the means necessary for a changing and growing economy.

Among these were an abundance and variety of natural resources and large numbers of workers to turn raw materials into goods.

A Wealth of Natural Resources

Before the war, natural resources such as coal, iron ore, and petroleum had scarcely been touched. By the 1860s, however, methods for extracting and utilizing these resources were well developed.

As a result, the amount of coal mined in the United States more than doubled in every decade between 1840 and 1890. By the 1870s, vast deposits throughout the Appalachians from Pennsylvania to Alabama were being mined. Completion of the Soo Canal between Lake Superior and Lake Huron in 1855 allowed ships to move iron ore mined in Michigan and Wisconsin to iron and steel mills on the lower Great Lakes.

The American oil industry got its start in 1859 in western Pennsylvania when the first successful well was drilled. By 1900 oil fields extended as far west as Texas. Production had risen from 2,000 barrels per year in 1859 to 64 million barrels per year in 1900.

A Growing Labor Force

The human resources available to American industry were as important as the mineral resources. Workers came to new jobs in cities the way pioneers moved to new lands.

Between 1860 and 1890, America's population more than doubled, rising from 31 million to nearly 75 million. The flood of immigration that had begun in the 1840s continued, contributing to this growth. Pulled by opportunities in America—and pushed out by the lack of them at home—14 million immigrants arrived between 1860 and 1900, more than twice the number of the previous 40 years. Many of these immigrants were adult males eager to find employment. These newcomers enlarged the labor pools that accumulated wherever jobs were available, and that helped keep industrial wages low.

■ Public Policies and Private Investment

American industry developed within a free enterprise system. Americans embraced a philosophy of laissez-faire, which comes from the French phrase meaning "let alone." As a result, American industries developed with few government restraints. In fact, some government policies actually encouraged industrialization. **Entrepreneurs,** or business organizers, sought and received special favors from Congress. Liberal immigration laws ensured a steady supply of cheap labor. High protective tariffs encouraged American

▲ OFFICE SECRETARY IN THE LATE 1800S

industries and raised manufacturers' profits by keeping out foreign goods. The federal government sold public lands containing vast mineral resources for a small proportion of their true value and assumed about one-third of the cost of building Western railroads. It gave railroads grants of money totaling more than $700 million and gave them public lands throughout the West equaling the size of Texas.

While European entrepreneurs often retired when they acquired enough money to buy their way into the upper class, Americans regarded moneymaking itself as a worthwhile goal. "Such opportunities for making money," wrote Thomas Mellon, a Pittsburgh judge who later became a banker, "never existed before in all my former experience."

The money to be made in American manufacturing and transportation attracted private investors. The savings of New Englanders—accumulated from the West Indies and China trade, from clippers and whalers, from textile mills and shoe manu-

- -
Footnotes to History

Wages Working-class incomes varied greatly during the late 1800s. In 1889 a carpenter earned $680 annually, a laborer, $380, and a woman in a silk mill, $130.

HISTORY Online

Student Web Activity
Visit the *American History: The Modern Era Since 1865* Web site at **me.glencoe.com** and click on *Chapter 8— Student Web Activities* for an activity about immigration.

factures—helped build hundreds of factories and thousands of miles of railroad track. An equally important source of private capital was Europe, especially Great Britain. By 1900 British investors owned $2.5 billion in American railroad securities—more than twice the national debt of the United States.

■ Science and Technology

A flood of important inventions helped increase America's productive capacity and improved the network of transportation and communications that was vital to the nation's industrial growth. As American universities extended their activities beyond teaching, they became important centers of scientific research.

The Typewriter and the Telephone

The American public knew little of the university professors who extended the boundaries of science. People were greatly impressed, however, with inventors such as C. Latham Sholes, a Wisconsin printer whose idea for a typewriter in 1868 revolutionized business communications.

Equally inventive was Alexander Graham Bell, an immigrant from Scotland. Bell's profession was teaching deaf children to speak. He applied his speech training to developing the principles upon which the telephone is based. In 1876 he sent the first telephone communication to his laboratory assistant in the next room: "Mr. Watson, come here; I want you."

A year later he demonstrated the commercial value of his invention by sitting in Boston and talking with Watson in New York City—and the Bell Telephone Company was founded. By 1886 more than 250,000 phones were in use, mostly in businesses. This rapid growth created jobs for thousands of women as switchboard operators. By 1900 telephone rates had been lowered, and telephones increasingly began to appear in American homes.

Edison's Contributions

Perhaps even more famous than Bell was Thomas Alva Edison, who has been erroneously credited with inventing the electric light and moving pictures. Edison actually made few original discoveries. Instead, he was a great innovator who put the inventions of others to practical use. For example, Edison's redesign of Sholes's typewriter

▲ CANDLESTICK TELEPHONE, 1890s

Visualizing History

▲ OFFICE WORK Among new opportunities for women living in the big cities were positions as secretaries, stenographers, and switchboard operators. Many women were able to find employment and earn a living. *What innovations helped create new jobs?*

The Camera

For centuries scientists and inventors experimented with recording images in a lasting way. A French inventor produced the world's first photograph—a blurry farmyard view—by coating a metal plate with a light-sensitive chemical.

Then

Pictures for the Masses

Although the first true camera was not developed until 1826, improvements followed rapidly. Scientific and technical discoveries aided in reducing the exposure time to 1/25 of a second by the 1870s. The development of negative film and specialized lenses also proved beneficial. Yet because photography required competent understanding of scientific and chemical processes, few Americans other than professional photographers owned cameras.

In 1888 George Eastman introduced the Kodak box camera, the first camera designed for amateur use. Lightweight and easy to operate, the Kodak put photography into the hands of millions.

Let the Children Kodak

For after all the home pictures are what count. We all enjoy the personal pictures that tell of our travels and our vacations—but the intimate home pictures of the children and by the children—those are the pictures that are most cherished as the years go by.

And with a Kodak or a Brownie it's all very simple. The youngsters, even from their kindergarten days, have no trouble in mastering the Brownie or one of the smaller Kodaks. Every step in picture making has been made easy and inexpensive by the Kodak system. Brownie cameras at one to twelve dollars, and Kodaks from five dollars up, offer a wide variety to suit all pockets and purposes.

EASTMAN KODAK COMPANY,
ROCHESTER, N. Y., *The Kodak City.*

◄ **Turn-of-the-century advertisement**

▲ **Modern Camera, 120 mm Hasselblad**

Now

The Photographic Revolution

Photography progressed rapidly during the 1900s. Significant technical advances include color film, instant cameras, and the flash synchronization system. Today, a person can take a picture simply by pressing a button. An instant camera can produce a photo in about 15 seconds.

---

permitted people to type faster than they could write. His improvement of Bell's telephone allowed voices to be transmitted longer distances. His work on improving the telegraph led to one of his few actual inventions, the phonograph.

The incandescent electric light had been demonstrated in Britain in 1840. But it was Edison who, in 1879, developed cheap methods of supplying power and wire, as well as filaments that lasted more than just a few minutes. The incandescent bulb lighted America's cities and made industrial production possible 24 hours a day.

The Canning Industry

During the Civil War, soldiers in the Union army had received some rations in cans, an innovation that demonstrated the value of canned food. After the war the canning industry improved its methods, and by 1900 machines had been designed to make, fill, and seal cans. A large variety of canned foods began to appear on the shelves of the nation's stores.

Textiles, Clothing, and Shoes

America's textile industry had long depended on machines to turn fibers into cloth. In 1893 the invention of the Northrup automatic loom led to the manufacture of cloth at an even faster rate. Bobbins, which had previously been changed by hand while the loom was stopped, were now changed automatically without stopping the loom.

Great changes also occurred in the clothing industry. Standard sizes, developed from measurements taken of Union soldiers during the Civil War, were used in the manufacture of ready-made clothes. The use of power-driven sewing machines and cloth cutters moved the clothing business from small tailor shops to large factories.

Similar changes took place in the shoe-making industry. New processes and inventions made **economies of scale** possible. In other words, large factories could mass-produce shoes more cheaply and efficiently than smaller companies. These factories could also pass these savings on to their

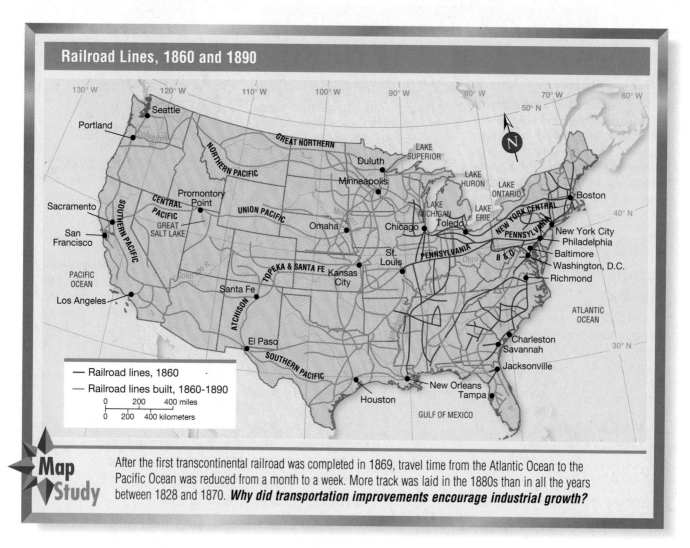

Railroad Lines, 1860 and 1890

Railroad lines, 1860
Railroad lines built, 1860-1890

0   200   400 miles
0   200   400 kilometers

Map Study After the first transcontinental railroad was completed in 1869, travel time from the Atlantic Ocean to the Pacific Ocean was reduced from a month to a week. More track was laid in the 1880s than in all the years between 1828 and 1870. *Why did transportation improvements encourage industrial growth?*

customers in the form of lower prices. By the turn of the century, local cobblers had nearly disappeared.

Steel, Oil, and Trains

Industrial growth was tied to advances in specific industries. The Bessemer process revolutionized American steelmaking in the 1870s. As steel was increasingly used for products such as machines, rails, and building beams, industry in general began to expand. The boom in the oil industry, along with the development of oil-lubricated machine tools—metal lathes, punches, and drill presses used to make other machines—brought tremendous growth in industrial capability.

New technology also stimulated the growth of the railroad industry. The Bessemer process was a factor in the expansion of railroad operations. This process allowed

the railroad companies to replace iron rails with steel, which held up better and was able to carry heavier loads.

Another innovation was the Westinghouse air brake. The brake allowed the cars and locomotives to stop simultaneously—another factor making longer trains and heavier loads possible. Kerosene lamps, and later electric lights, provided better headlights for nighttime travel.

■ Railroad Building

Perhaps no other single factor was more responsible for the growth of industry in the United States than the expansion of the nation's railroads. At the end of the Civil War, there were 35,000 miles of railroad track in the United States. The tracks were of various gauges, or widths between the two rails.

Standardization and Consolidation

By the mid-1870s the amount of track had doubled, and by 1890 it had more than doubled again. In 1900 passenger and freight trains steamed along almost 200,000 miles of rails. By then track also was laid according to a standard gauge—4 feet, 8½ inches wide—so that freight could move from line to line without having to be unloaded from one car and reloaded onto another. This standardized railroad network bound all sections of the country into one market and one nation. Trains could carry bulky products long distances quickly and cheaply, making it possible for businesses to sell their goods across the continent. In 1860 railroads carried less than half as much freight as inland waterways. By 1890 railroads carried five times as much.

Railroads were not only the biggest shippers of industrial products; they were also American industry's best customers. In the mid-1880s, for example, rails were the single most important product of American steel companies. In addition, construction and operation of railroads required huge amounts of coal to power locomotives, lumber for ties and cars, iron for bridges, and petroleum products to lubricate moving parts.

Consolidating of smaller lines in the Midwest, East, and South was as important to development as the building of railroads spanning the West. Railroad building in the East was intended to promote specific cities or to serve local needs. As a result, hundreds of unconnected small lines, with tracks of varying gauges, were in use. The South had more than 400 railroads averaging less than 40 miles each. The challenge facing Eastern capitalists was to create a single rail system from this maze of small companies.

Railroad consolidation proceeded rapidly from the end of the Civil War to the turn of the century. By 1890 the Pennsylvania Railroad was a consolidation of 73 smaller companies with more than 5,000 miles of track. The Southern Pacific Railway had pieced together companies with 8,500 miles of lines. Eventually most rail traffic was controlled by 7 giant systems with terminals in major cities and scores of branches reaching into the countryside.

▲ *ACROSS THE CONTINENT* by Currier and Ives, 1868 Currier and Ives produced America's most popular and successful prints of the 1800s. *Why did rail transport surpass water transport in the late 1800s?*

Getting a "Share of the Business"

In gaining and using such power, many railroad builders became tough, ruthless, and unethical competitors who amassed fortunes in the course of their activities. Railroad consolidator Jay Gould sold small lines that he owned to large railroads that he controlled at prices far above the small railroads' actual worth. When railroad builder Collis Huntington remarked, "It takes money to fix things," he meant bribing government officials, not repairing equipment! In describing his industry, railroad executive Charles Francis Adams, Jr., observed:

> *Honesty and good faith are scarcely regarded. Certainly they are not tolerated at all if they interfere with a man's getting his "share of the business." Gradually this demoralizing spirit of low cunning has pervaded the entire system. Its moral tone is deplorably low. . . .*

Cornelius Vanderbilt

One of the most successful railroad consolidators was Cornelius Vanderbilt, who built the New York Central system. By the mid-1850s, he had built the largest steamboat fleet in America. Yet Vanderbilt saw that the future of transportation was in railroads. So at age 73 he merged 3 short New York railroads he had purchased to form the New York Central, which ran from New York City to Buffalo. Within 4 years Vanderbilt extended his control over lines all the way to Chicago. In addition to bringing many lines under one management, Vanderbilt made great improvements in service. He was one of the first to use the Westinghouse air brake and the very first to lay a four-track main line—two tracks for freight and two for passenger traffic.

Benefits

Vanderbilt, like other railroad tycoons, was a combination of shrewd speculator, ruthless competitor, and visionary. Yet Vanderbilt and other railroad entrepreneurs provided great benefits, too. Standard-gauge track was universally accepted, and standard time zones were established to simplify scheduling.

The big systems were able to improve equipment, to shift cars from one section of the country to another according to seasonal needs, and to speed long-distance transportation. They made railroad operation so much more efficient that the average rate per mile for a ton of freight dropped from 2 cents in 1860 to less than 1 cent in 1900. The railroad executives also showed entrepreneurs how to operate large companies across great distances.

Section 1 ★ Assessment

Checking for Understanding

1. **Define** entrepreneur, economies of scale.
2. **Explain** the contribution of the railroad in the growth of industry.

Critical Thinking

3. **Applying Ideas** One writer noted that "This standardized railroad network bound all sections of the country into one market and one nation." Explain what the writer meant.
4. **Analyzing Issues** Re-create the chart shown here, and add descriptions of how each technology accelerated the growth of industry in the United States.

Typewriter/Telephone	
Electric Lighting	
Power Machines	

INTERDISCIPLINARY ACTIVITY

5. **Science** Research a modern-day invention, such as the computer, laser, or optic fiber. Create a visual display that presents information about how the invention has changed people's lives.

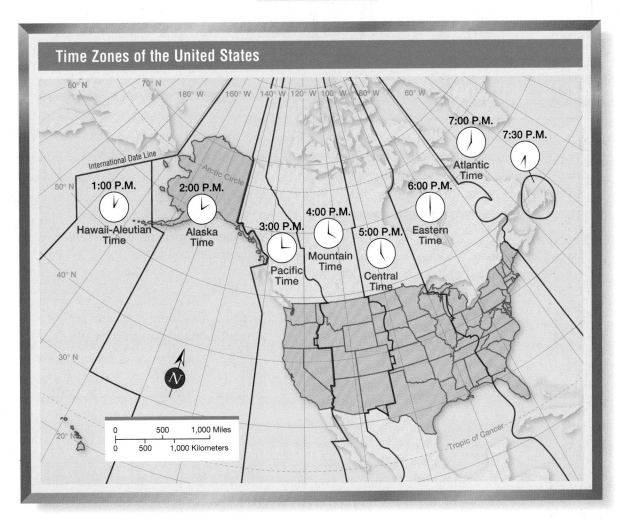

Time Zones of the United States

Standard Time Zones

Throughout most of the nineteenth century, few Americans could agree on the time of day because every community determined its own time by the position of the sun. Railways, however, required a single standard of time for scheduling and routing. In 1883 American and Canadian railroads established standardized time zones.

In 1884 delegates from 27 nations met in Washington, D.C., and divided the earth into 24 time zones. The base time zone was established with the Prime Meridian (0° longitude) as its midpoint. Since the Prime Meridian ran through Greenwich in Britain, the time in the base zone became known as Greenwich time.

Making the Geography Connection

1. Why did standardized time zones become necessary in the 1800s?

2. If you traveled from Detroit, Michigan, to Tucson, Arizona, what time zones would you cross?

ACTIVITY

3. If it is 6 A.M. in Omaha, Nebraska, what time is it in Jacksonville, Florida; Butte, Montana; and Anchorage, Alaska? Put your answers in the form of a table or a visual display.

★★★

Growth of Big Business

Guide to Reading

Main Idea

The late 1800s saw the rise of "Big Business," gigantic companies owning scores of plants and generating huge profits.

Reading Strategy

Organizing Information As you read about the growth of "Big Business," use the chart shown here to list various ways businesses can be organized.

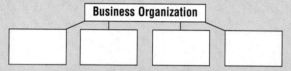

Business Organization

Objectives

After studying this section, you should be able to

★ discuss the methods big business used to become successful.

★ explain why incorporation encouraged business growth.

Key Terms

corporation, holding company, trust, horizontal integration, vertical integration

---

The railroads were America's first "Big Business." Founding a major railroad consumed larger sums of money than any previous American enterprise. The investment required was so great that no one individual could make it. Instead, a large railroad line was organized as a **corporation**—a company formed by a group of investors who each receive a share of ownership in proportion to the amount they invested. Investors also enjoyed the protection of limited liability: they risked only the amount of their investment, even if the corporation went bankrupt and could not pay its bills.

The expansion of the railroads, along with other improvements in transportation and communication, created the mass market. No longer were manufacturers limited to local or regional sales. The mass market made mass production practical.

■ Benefits of Big Business

Corporate structure allowed entrepreneurs in many industries to raise the money they needed to launch or expand companies as opportunities arose. Big business enjoyed many advantages.

Efficiency in Production and Labor

Large companies could manufacture enough products to meet the demands of a national market. They produced better products at lower cost than their smaller competitors through the economies of scale that resulted from using the newest processes and combining operations formerly performed by separate companies. High salaries were offered in order to get expert managers. At the same time, they increased efficiency by establishing separate departments for specialized functions such as purchasing, production, research, distribution, and sales.

In conducting their operations, big companies organized work to gain maximum production from their employees. A steel company engineer, Frederick W. Taylor, developed a system to study and time workers and to make changes so their jobs could be performed more efficiently. Such studies even included counting the steps a worker took in moving from one place to another on the job and determining what size shovels were best for shoveling coal, rice, and iron ore!

The Big Business of Meatpacking

The advantages of big business were shown dramatically by the development of large meatpacking companies. In the past, fresh meat had been slaughtered locally, and every town had at least one slaughterhouse. When the refrigerated railroad car made it possible to ship fresh meat over long distances, huge companies such as Swift and Armour appeared, selling their products throughout the country. The big packers were so highly organized and efficient that they could sell meat at a loss and make their profit from the rest of the carcass. Chicago humorist Finley Peter Dunne, writing under the name of the fictional Irish saloon keeper "Mr. Dooley," hardly exaggerated about Armour when he noted:

"A cow goes lowin' softly into Armour's an' comes out glue, gelatin, fertylizer, celooloid, joolry, sofy cushions, hair restorer, washin' sody, soap, lithrachoor an' bed springs so quick that while aft she's still cow, for'ard she may be anything fr'm buttons to pannyma hats."

Big Business

Because of their efficiency, organization, and size, large businesses were frequently in a position to take advantage of their competitors and sometimes of the public. Big companies could demand volume discounts from shippers. They could sell their products in an area at a loss until local competitors were forced to shut down or sell out. If a large company succeeded in getting a monopoly in its industry, it could raise consumer prices and pay less to suppliers of raw materials.

Big business in the late nineteenth century resulted from the vision of people who recognized great opportunities for wealth and were willing to take risks to get it. The companies they organized—American Tobacco, General Electric, and United

AMERICAN PORTRAITS

Gustavus Swift
1839–1903

At the age of 16, Gustavus Swift borrowed $25, bought a cow, slaughtered it, and sold the beef at a $10 profit. From that point on, Swift devoted his life to making money from meat.

Swift first opened several butcher shops. With a talent for buying only the best cattle, he next moved to Chicago—capital of the cattle market—and went into business shipping livestock by rail to Eastern cities. He soon realized, however, that he could

make more money butchering the cattle in Chicago and shipping the meat.

At first, to prevent spoilage, Swift could ship only during winter months. But then he hired an engineer who developed a refrigerated railroad car that made it possible to ship year-round. As hungry workers swelled the size of Eastern cities, Swift & Co. made great profits by shipping huge quantities of meat to feed them.

▲ **MARKETING GOODS** Mass production of consumer goods, such as hats, combined with transportation improvements inspired entrepreneurs to print merchandise catalogs and open mail-order stores. *Why were big businesses able to sell for less than local companies?*

Fruit, among them—came to dominate their industries and sold products not just nationwide but to the entire world.

Business Tactics

In attaining success, however, many entrepreneurs showed few scruples in driving competitors out of business. Their tactics included evading the law, bribing officials, destroying labor unions, and devastating the environment. Some entrepreneurs commonly sold products at below their cost until local businesses were forced to close down or sell out.

Mixed Feelings Toward Big Business

The American public, therefore, had mixed feelings about big business and its leaders. Americans worried about the corrupting influence of wealth and power. Yet others admitted that they benefited from big business's efficiency, its lower prices, and the jobs it created. Historian Vernon L. Parrington said of the entrepreneurs:

❝ *These new Americans were primitive souls, ruthless, predatory,*

capable, single-minded men; rogues and rascals often, but never feeble, never hindered by petty scruples, never given to puling [whimpering] or whining. . . . Analyze the most talked-of men of the age and one is likely to find a splendid audacity coupled with immense wastefulness. A note of tough-minded-ness marks them. . . . They fought their way encased in rhinoceros hides. ❞

Rags to Riches

Success in business became a best-selling theme in popular fiction. Horatio Alger became wealthy himself when he wrote novels like *Mark the Match Boy, Tattered Tom,* and more than 100 others—all "rags-to-riches" stories of young men who became successful in business because of hard work and lucky breaks.

■ The Role of Corporations

American law allowed the formation of business corporations, and conditions in the United States encouraged their existence.

As a business form, the corporation offered a number of advantages over a partnership or a sole proprietorship. The corporation had a permanence that lasted beyond the lives of its owners or stockholders. That meant company managers could confidently plan far into the future.

Kinds of Companies

By selling stocks and bonds, a corporation could raise the capital, or investment money, for its operations. Small amounts of capital from many individual investors could be pooled into the huge sums needed to start or expand a large company. In that way no one investor would have to take a big financial risk. To reduce risk even more, investors could spread it out by purchasing stock in several corporations. One specialized form of corporation, the **holding company,** became very popular. Holding companies manufactured no products and had no customers. They existed only to own stock in other corporations. Through holding companies, wealthy capitalists could own controlling interests in many businesses.

Other companies were organized into trusts. A **trust** was formed when several companies gave control of their operations to a single board of trustees. The shareholders of each individual company continued to own it and keep its profits, but management of all companies in the trust was in the same hands. Through holding companies and trusts, entrepreneurs formed the huge business combinations that dominated the late nineteenth century. Some combinations were able to restrict or prevent competition among their members.

Ways to Combine Companies

Business consolidation—combining companies into one unit—took various forms. Sometimes companies were consolidated by **horizontal integration,** in which several firms engaged in the same kind of business were joined together. If a horizontal combination became large enough, it could achieve a monopoly of that industry.

Companies also were consolidated by **vertical integration,** which joined businesses engaged in different but related activities. A vertical combination, for example, might include under the same ownership individual companies that provided raw materials, transported those raw materials to factories, manufactured a product from those raw materials, and distributed and sold the finished product.

A horizontal combination, once established, was able to expand vertically because of the control its size gave it over both suppliers and distributors. Similarly, a vertical combination could become so efficient that it expanded horizontally by buying its competitors, forcing them into trusts, or driving them out of business.

Section 2 ★ Assessment

Checking for Understanding

1. **Define** corporation, holding company, trust, horizontal integration, vertical integration.

Critical Thinking

2. **Contrasting** Re-create the diagram shown here, and describe the practices that made businesses both successful and the objects of criticism.

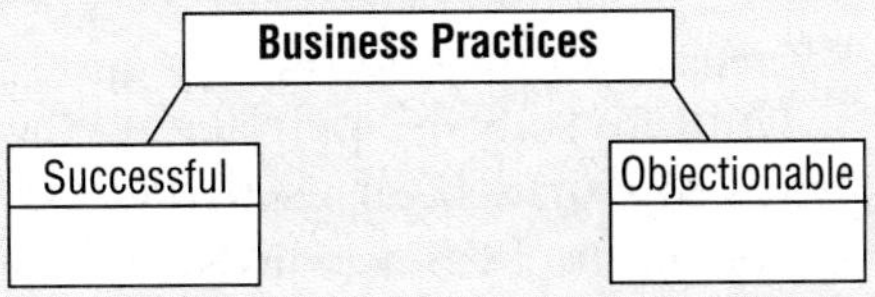

Business Practices
- Successful
- Objectionable

3. **Evaluating Change** How might the shift to the prevalence of big business work to the advantage or disadvantage of a consumer?

INTERDISCIPLINARY ACTIVITY

4. **Economics** Keep track of all the purchases you make for one week. List the name of the businesses that sold them to you. Indicate whether you think each business is small, medium, or large.

★★

Captains of Industry

Guide to Reading

Main Idea

In an era of business tycoons, two men stood out—John D. Rockefeller and Andrew Carnegie.

Reading Strategy

Taking Notes As you read about the giants of the business world, explain why these men embraced the notion of social Darwinism, using an outline like the one shown here.

I. Rockefeller
   A.
   B.

II. Carnegie
   A.
   B.

Objectives

After studying this section, you should be able to

★ compare the methods used by Carnegie and Rockefeller to achieve success.

★ explain social Darwinism.

Key Terms

rebate, social Darwinism, philanthropy

▶ COVER OF *MCCLURE'S MAGAZINE*

Although giant combinations arose to control the beef, flour, whiskey, tobacco, lead, and sugar industries, as well as many others, by 1900 the American economy ran on oil, and its backbone was steel. No industrialists exemplified the principles of doing "big business" in late-nineteenth-century America more than the entrepreneurs who dominated these two basic industries—John D. Rockefeller in oil and Andrew Carnegie in steel.

■ Rockefeller and the Standard Oil Trust

The most successful example of horizontal consolidation was the Standard Oil Trust, which gained a near monopoly of oil refineries and pipelines. The guiding genius behind Standard Oil was John D. Rockefeller, who during his 98 years, from 1839 to 1937, amassed what was at the time the world's largest fortune—almost $1 billion.

The Early Years

Rockefeller went to work at age 16 as a bookkeeper in a wholesale commission and produce company in Cleveland, Ohio. Dominated by the idea that he was "bound to be rich," he saved $800 in 3 years on a salary of $15 per week. At 19 he left his job and opened his own commission house. In only 4 years he increased his capital to about $100,000. Then in 1862, at age 23, he put all his money into a new and growing industry—petroleum refining.

Until the 1850s, petroleum, then called "rock oil," had been used only as a patent medicine. In 1855 scientists discovered that petroleum, when refined into kerosene, gave better light than whale oil in lamps and made a much better lubricant than animal fat.

The first oil well, drilled in 1859, set off a stampede to western Pennsylvania much like the California gold rush of 1849. Land values jumped from a few dollars an acre to hundreds of dollars a square foot, new towns appeared overnight, and the demand for kerosene spread worldwide. In spite of the Civil War, the petroleum industry grew so fast that by 1865 oil products had risen to fourth place among American exports.

Drilling for oil was always a big gamble, and Rockefeller realized oil refining was a safer investment. The entire oil business was highly disorganized, however. Fortunes were made and lost overnight as the price of oil fluctuated wildly. Rockefeller believed such unstable conditions resulted from competition among thousands of small producers and hundreds of small refiners.

Standard Oil Becomes a Giant

By 1870 Rockefeller's firm, the Standard Oil Company of Ohio, was the largest of 26 refineries in Cleveland, processing 2 or 3 percent of the crude oil produced in the United States. Over the next 9 years, Rockefeller gained control of more than 90 percent of the nation's refining business and brought order to a chaotic industry. But to achieve stability and efficiency in the oil business, Rockefeller used methods so shrewdly brutal that when they were revealed he became one of the most hated men in America.

One of Standard Oil's major weapons was the **rebate,** or discount, on freight charges. In 1872 the company offered to give certain railroads all its shipping business if those railroads secretly agreed to charge Standard Oil 25 to 50 percent less than they charged its competitors. In return for its business, these railroads also promised to tell Rockefeller the destinations of all his competitors' shipments. This information gave him valuable insights into his rivals' business dealings. These secret arrangements gave Standard Oil such an advantage over other Cleveland refineries that within 3 months all but 5 were forced

to sell out to Rockefeller. Once it controlled oil refining in Cleveland, Standard Oil moved rapidly toward a nationwide monopoly by allying with the strongest companies throughout the industry. In 1880 a committee of the New York legislature reported on the extent of Standard Oil's domination of the oil business:

❝ *It owns and controls the pipe lines of the producing regions that connect with the railroads. It controls both ends of these roads. It ships 95 percent of all oil. . . . It dictates terms and rates to the railroads. It has bought out and frozen out refiners all over the country. By means of the superior facilities for transportation which it thus possessed, it could overbid [its competitors for crude oil] in the producing regions and undersell [its competitors] in the markets of the world.* ❞

▲ JOHN D. ROCKEFELLER Although he was ruthless in business dealings, John D. Rockefeller always carried dimes in his pockets to give to small children he encountered on the street. *What change did Rockefeller bring to the oil industry?*

▲ IDA TARBELL Ida Tarbell was one of several American writers who played a major part in exposing social problems. *What company did Tarbell target in her series of articles for McClure's Magazine?*

By a secret agreement that became known as the Standard Oil Trust, Rockefeller moved in 1882 to consolidate his control of the oil industry further by combining 40 companies under a single management. Once in control of most of the refining and transportation of oil in the United States, Standard Oil expanded vertically. It gained control of oil fields to have an independent supply source, and it marketed natural gas. At the other end of the production process, Standard Oil moved into the distribution of petroleum products, both in the United States and overseas. Eventually Standard Oil controlled a fleet of oceangoing tankers and door-to-door delivery wagons in Europe. It even manufactured and sold cooking stoves to increase the demand for kerosene!

Following Standard Oil's Lead

Standard Oil's spectacular success led others to establish horizontal combinations of companies in industries as varied as whiskey, bituminous coal, and rope. The

purpose of these combinations was mainly to prevent overproduction and to keep prices up. Yet it was difficult to control an entire industry and to keep new firms out of the market. Such efforts to obtain monopolies were greatly resented by small business people and consumers. Vertical combinations, on the other hand, were not monopolistic. The savings that resulted from the economies they brought to production were passed on to consumers in lower prices. Vertical combination thus became a common form of business organization.

Business Tactics Exposed

Although Rockefeller's rivals in the oil industry were painfully aware of his ruthless methods, it was an investigative journalist who exposed them to the public. This courageous woman was Ida Tarbell.

In 1903, in a series of brilliant articles in *McClure's Magazine,* Tarbell revealed Rockefeller's secret deals and his high-pressure tactics. She explained how companies controlled by Standard Oil continued to do business under their former names. She documented how, to conceal his control of these companies, Rockefeller appointed "dummy directors," who were sometimes employees such as errand-runners or secretaries.

Rockefeller, a devout churchgoer and Sunday school teacher, did not think that his actions were wrong. He pointed out that what he had done to destroy his competitors had not been illegal when he first did it. Rebates, for example, were granted by railroads to big shippers in many other industries. When buying out his competitors, Rockefeller offered to pay them in either cash or Standard Oil stock, advising them to take the stock. Those who took his advice became rich.

Much of Rockefeller's advantage over competitors came from his passion for efficiency and his hatred of waste. Standard Oil continuously improved its product. The company had few labor troubles because it paid its workers well. It tried to protect their jobs in times of depression and was one of the first companies to pay old-age pensions.

■ Andrew Carnegie, Master of Steel

The most remarkable example of the creation of a vertical combination was the giant steel corporation built by Andrew Carnegie.

Coming to Pittsburgh from Scotland at the age of 13, Carnegie went to work in a cotton factory where he earned $1.20 for working a 72-hour week. He saw an opportunity to grow with the railroad, however, and in 1853 he went to work as a clerk and telegraph operator for the Pennsylvania Railroad. His ability, energy, and ambition were so great that at age 23 he became superintendent of the railroad's western division.

Looking to the Future

While working for the railroad, Carnegie wisely invested his earnings in iron companies. As the railroads grew, Carnegie foresaw his opportunity for personal success in the increasing demand for rails, bridges, and locomotives. By age 30, when he left the railroad to manage an iron bridge company, his investments were producing an annual income of nearly $50,000.

After seven years making iron bridges, Carnegie again looked at the future and saw it was in steel. In 1873 he formed a group of investors to build the largest and most modern steel mill in the world near Pittsburgh. Carnegie was the first person in the United States to use two new ways of making steel—the Bessemer process and the open-hearth process. These processes enabled him to produce steel so cheaply that it could now be used for rails and construction girders, as well as for cutlery and precision machines.

Another Giant Is Born

Almost overnight Carnegie changed the character of the industry. Previously iron and steel had been manufactured at hundreds of small furnaces all over the country. But Bessemer converters and open-hearth furnaces required heavy investments of capital and huge amounts of coke and ore to keep them going. Small companies were soon forced out of business by big ones.

In less than 20 years, Carnegie was the greatest steelmaker in the world. One reason for his phenomenal success was that he took the guesswork out of making steel by getting the best technical and scientific experts he could find. Carnegie liked to boast that he "was smart enough to surround himself with men far cleverer than himself." For example, his managers were able to determine almost to the penny what it cost to produce a ton of steel. With this knowledge, Carnegie could set prices below his competitors and still make a profit. His chemists found uses for by-products previously considered to be industrial waste, and they discovered how to use low-grade ores.

History AND ART

▲ *THE STEEL MILL* by Maximillian Luce, 1895 Although the growth of the oil industry after the Civil War was phenomenal, the steel industry achieved even greater growth. ***What benefits did the success of these industries bring to the nation?***

In his constant effort to be more efficient, Carnegie combined all of the processes required for making steel into one great vertical combination. In addition to blast furnaces and steel mills, the Carnegie Steel Company controlled rich iron ore deposits near Lake Superior, fleets of ships to carry the ore over the Great Lakes, a railroad to carry the ore from the Lake Erie region to Pittsburgh, coal mines in Pennsylvania to fire the blast furnaces, and factories for producing finished steel products such as wire.

Crushing Labor and Gobbling the Competition

Seeking out the ablest people in the industry, Carnegie bought their loyalty by making them partners. Equally alert for ability inside his companies, he rapidly promoted exceptional employees. Common laborers in his mills fared less well, however, as he drove wages down and hours up. In 1892, with his partner, Henry C. Frick, he crushed the steelworkers' union, so that the 12-hour day remained standard for many years.

During the three major depressions of the late 1800s, while other steel companies closed down, Carnegie expanded. He rebuilt his factories to be even more efficient and acquired his weakened competitors.

■ Social Darwinism and the Industrialists

Andrew Carnegie was making $25 million a year at a time when there was no income tax. His workers, on the other hand, earned $8 or $9 a week. He made steel so cheaply and competed so mercilessly that remaining steel companies faced bankruptcy. Carnegie and most other great industrialists found justification for these actions and their consequences in a philosophy known as **social Darwinism,** which applied the biological theories of naturalist Charles Darwin to human society.

Darwin believed that in nature a competition exists in which only the fittest—the strongest, most clever, most efficient—

plants and animals survive. The weak individuals die out, and each species thereby remains strong and healthy. Philosophers such as Yale professor William Graham Sumner argued that this competition also operated in human society, and that industrialists like Rockefeller and Carnegie had succeeded because of their rare talents. "The millionaires are a product of natural selection," Sumner wrote. "They get high wages and live in luxury, but the bargain is a good one for society." Not surprisingly, Andrew Carnegie and John D. Rockefeller both believed wholeheartedly in the philosophy of social Darwinism. Carnegie called it a method better than elections for selecting leaders. "By a process of pitiless testing we discover who are the strong and who are the weak," he wrote. "To the strong we give power in the form of the autocratic control of industry and of wealth." Rockefeller told his Sunday school class that his business practices merely demonstrated "the survival of the fittest . . . a law of nature and a law of God."

Visualizing (H)istory ▲ **ANDREW CARNEGIE** If any entrepreneur symbolized the rags-to-riches legend, it was Andrew Carnegie. The son of poor immigrants, Carnegie built a company that by 1900 was making one-fourth of the nation's steel and serving a world market. *What caused Carnegie to believe the future was in iron and steel?*

▲ *THE SITWELL FAMILY* by John Singer Sargent Wealthy families lived in elegant homes staffed by scores of servants. While some of the wealthy were given to showy displays, others used their wealth and position to help others. ***What is philanthropy?***

But for Carnegie the achievement of great power and wealth was not enough. He looked beyond success to question whether those who profited from society owed anything to it in return.

Writing in the *North American Review* in 1889, Carnegie maintained that a wealthy person should:

❝ . . . [C]onsider all surplus revenues which come to him simply as trust funds, which he is called upon to administer . . . in a manner which, in his judgment, is best calculated to produce the most beneficial results for the community . . . becoming the mere agent and trustee for his poorer brethren, bringing to their service his superior wisdom, experience, and ability to administer, doing for them better than they would or could do for themselves. ❞

Carnegie practiced what he preached. In 1901 he sold his steel properties to the newly formed United States Steel Corporation for $250 million and withdrew from business to devote the rest of his life to **philanthropy** (fuh•LANT•thruh•PEE), or actions benefiting society. By the time he died in 1919, he had donated $350 million—mostly to building public libraries, improving education, and promoting research. Rockefeller also returned much of his fortune to society in gifts that totaled more than $500 million.

Sherman Antitrust Act

In 1881 *The Atlantic Monthly* published an article entitled "The Story of a Great Monopoly," by Henry Demarest Lloyd, telling how the Standard Oil Company had monopolized the oil-refining business. The article caused such a sensation that the magazine had to print three times as many copies as usual. Throughout the next decade, as it was revealed that many industries were in danger of being monopolized, demands for federal regulation came from many groups—small businesses, farmers, consumers, laborers, and even some big businesses.

Even officials of the great corporations began to have concerns about growing public cries for reform. Henry O. Havemeyer, head of the American Sugar Refining Company, which controlled a trust producing more than 90 percent of the nation's sugar, urged that manufacturers of products in general use should submit to some federal regulation.

In the election of 1888, both the Democratic and the Republican political parties promised action. Then in 1890, with only one dissenting vote, Congress passed the Sherman Antitrust Act. The Sherman Act wrote into federal law a traditional principle of English common law. This is the idea that private monopolies and artificial restrictions on trade were wrong. In the words of the act:

" *Every contract, combination, in the form of trust or otherwise, or conspiracy, in restraint of trade or commerce among the several states or with foreign nations, is hereby declared to be illegal."* "

The Sherman Act had little effect on preventing business consolidation. It was not strictly enforced and was so loosely worded that its meaning was doubtful. Did the law mean, for example, that all mergers were unlawful, that all business transactions must be open and public, that any contract that permitted one company to take business from another was illegal?

Under the Constitution, the answers to such questions are left to the federal courts, which in the 1890s were probably more favorable to business interests than at any other time in the history of the United States. In *United States* v. *E. C. Knight Company,* the Supreme Court in 1895 agreed that the American Sugar Refining Company was a trust and that it enjoyed a near monopoly in the manufacture of sugar. The Court ruled, however, that the company's activities did not violate the Sherman Act because manufacturing was not interstate commerce.

The Supreme Court's decision in the *United States* v. *E.C. Knight Company* case was followed by one of the greatest periods of business consolidation in American history. In 1890 there had been 24 trusts worth a total of $436 million. In 1900 there were 183 huge combinations with a total worth of more than $3 billion. At the same time, big business simply turned away from trusts and toward holding companies in creating combinations.

In spite of its early failures, the Sherman Act was an important law. It signaled to large corporations to be more aware of how their activities looked to the public. As a result, corporate image and public relations became important business concerns. Later regulation of big business and industry would depend on additional legislation, on the interpretations of future courts, and on attitudes in the executive branch about enforcement.

Section 3 ★ Assessment

Checking for Understanding

1. **Define** rebate, philanthropy.

2. **Explain** the philosophy of social Darwinism.

Critical Thinking

3. **Judging Actions**   Would the United States have been better off without industrial giants such as John D. Rockefeller? Explain.

4. **Comparing**   Re-create the chart shown here, and list the methods that both Rockefeller and Carnegie used to build their industrial empires.

Methods of Carnegie and Rockefeller

INTERDISCIPLINARY ACTIVITY

5. **Economics**   Write a one-page editorial in which you argue that government regulation either helps or hinders economic activity and the public welfare.

Reading Line Graphs

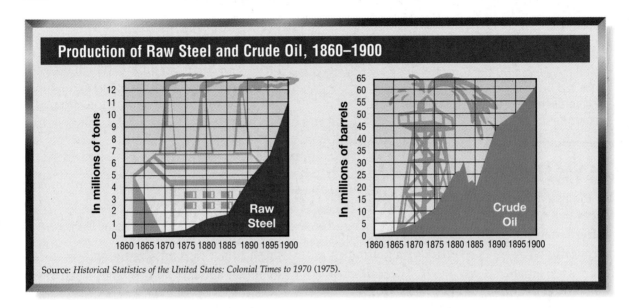

Production of Raw Steel and Crude Oil, 1860–1900

Source: *Historical Statistics of the United States: Colonial Times to 1970* (1975).

When historical information involves numbers and statistics, it often is presented on a graph. Graphic data can be presented in the form of circle graphs, bar graphs, or line graphs.

Learning the Skill

Graphs are a good way to present data in a form that readers can grasp easily and quickly. One type of graph is a line graph. Line graphs show data moving through a fixed period in time, which is good for showing trends and making predictions.

A line graph charts information about two variables. Line graphs typically show how one variable, depicted on the vertical axis, changes over time. Time, the second variable—whether minutes, hours, days, or years—is recorded on the horizontal axis.

To read a line graph, follow these steps:

- **Read** the title to get a general idea of what the graph shows.

- **Examine** the labels. Labels define the two variables and explain what the lines and/or points on the graph represent. Labels also specify the units of measurement.

- **Analyze** the graph. Look for increases, decreases, and sudden shifts. Analyze the *amount* and the *rate* of change.

- **Draw** conclusions or generalizations from the statistics presented on the graph. What trends or patterns appear?

Practicing the Skill

1. What is measured on these graphs? Over what time period?

2. Explain why the statistics are shown on two different graphs.

3. What generalizations can be made about steel and oil production between 1860 and 1875?

 Glencoe's **Skillbuilder Interactive Workbook, Level 2** provides instruction and practice in key social studies skills.

APPLYING THE SKILL

4. Keep track of the time you spend on homework each day over a one-week period. Chart the information on a line graph.

Self-Check Quiz

Visit the *American History: The Modern Era Since 1865* Web site at **me.glencoe.com** and click on *Chapter 8—Self-Check Quizzes* to prepare for the chapter test.

Using Vocabulary

Use the listed vocabulary words to complete the sentences that follow.

entrepreneurs	**horizontal integration**
corporations	**vertical integration**

1. Businesses organized as _____ can raise capital from a number of investors.
2. When governments practice laissez-faire policies, _____ can run businesses with very little government regulation.
3. Carnegie and Rockefeller consolidated a number of businesses using both _____ and _____ .

Reviewing Facts

1. **Enumerate** the factors that boosted industrial growth in the United States.
2. **State** the roles played by the railroad in the growth of American industry.
3. **List** all the types of business organizations, big and small, that companies could form.
4. **Describe** the provisions of the Sherman Antitrust Act and its effects.
5. **Cite** at least three industries that big business controlled during this era.

Understanding Concepts

Individual Initiative

1. Re-create the diagram shown here, and list the common elements of the business strategies of Rockefeller, Carnegie, and Vanderbilt.

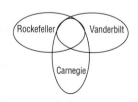

2. Cite examples of individuals and how they used their initiative to shape industrial growth.

Government Restriction

3. Lack of government restriction benefited some businesses and hurt others. Which types of businesses benefited, and which might have been more successful with some protection?

Critical Thinking

1. **Judging Effects** Discuss how a big company manufacturing products high in both quantity and quality benefits the consumer and the company.
2. **Analyzing Political Cartoons** Study the cartoon that appears on this page. Then answer the questions that follow.
   a. What figures are shown?
   b. Who or what does the octopus symbolize?
   c. What does the cartoon suggest about big business?
   d. What title would you give this cartoon?

3. **Analyzing Cause and Effect** Why do you think the United States developed economically at a faster rate than most other countries?
4. **Drawing Conclusions** Do you think that it is still possible today to go from "rags to riches"? Explain your answer.

5. **Demonstrating Reasoned Judgment** Do the doctrines of laissez-faire and social Darwinism have any following today? Explain.

History and Geography

The Nation Industrializes

The period from the end of the Civil War to 1900 was an era of unmatched economic growth in the nation. The key to this growth was industrialization.

1. **Human/Environment Interaction** What natural resources helped U.S. industry grow?

2. **Human/Environment Interaction** How did technology help to develop the resources of production?

Cooperative Learning Interdisciplinary Activity: Economics

Meet in groups of four to discuss how to get capital to start a business. To begin, prepare a business plan. It should describe your product or service and explain why the product or service is needed, how you plan to make or provide it, how your business will be run, what resources you need, and how you plan to use the capital. Write your plan, then present it to the class.

Practicing Skills

Reading Line Graphs

Study the graph on this page, then answer the questions that follow.

1. What is measured on this line graph?

2. What period of time does the graph cover?

3. When did production surpass 100 million tons?

4. Does the graph show any decreases over time?

Technology Activity

Using a Spreadsheet

Imagine you are a shareholder in a corporation. Choose a company from the stock market section of your local newspaper, and follow the movement of its stock for a two-week period. Track the performances of the stock on a spreadsheet by marking daily increases and decreases in its share prices. Compare your results with those of your classmates, and decide whether you made a good investment.

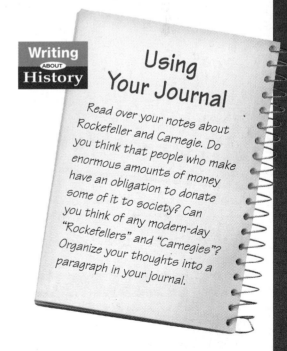

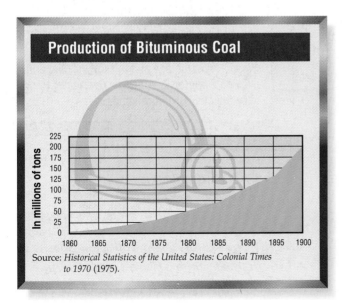

Production of Bituminous Coal

In millions of tons

225
200
175
150
125
100
75
50
25
0

1860 1865 1870 1875 1880 1885 1890 1895 1900

Source: *Historical Statistics of the United States: Colonial Times to 1970* (1975).

Writing ABOUT History

Using Your Journal

Read over your notes about Rockefeller and Carnegie. Do you think that people who make enormous amounts of money have an obligation to donate some of it to society? Can you think of any modern-day "Rockefellers" and "Carnegies"? Organize your thoughts into a paragraph in your journal.

CHAPTER 9

★★

An Urban Society
1860–1900

▶ Union symbol

Setting the Scene

Focus

One factor supporting industrialization in the late nineteenth century was the abundant labor supply. For workers, poor pay and working conditions led to a renewed interest in labor unions. Efforts by unions such as the Knights of Labor to improve conditions, however, were only modestly successful. The union movement was also influenced by the influx of millions of immigrants. These new arrivals crowded into America's cities and brought with them the cultural heritage of their old world.

Concepts to Understand

★ How **unity** among workers led to the growth of unions

★ How **conflict** between workers and employers resulted in unrest

Read to Discover . . .

★ the difficulties experienced by labor unions in the late 1800s.

★ the major factors behind the migration to American cities.

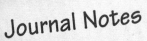

Journal Notes

What were some of the major obstacles facing immigrants coming to the United States in the late 1800s? Note examples as you read the chapter.

HISTORY Online

Chapter Overview
Visit the *American History: The Modern Era Since 1865* Web site at **me.glencoe.com** and click on ***Chapter 9—Chapter Overviews*** to preview the chapter information.

CULTURAL

• **1868** *Immigration drops to 130,000*

• **1876** *Central Park opens in New York City*

| 1860 | 1870 |

• **1867** *Great Western Surveys begin*

• **1872** *Victoria Claflin Woodhull, first woman presidential candidate, is nominated*

POLITICAL

◀ **FAMILY AT ELLIS ISLAND, EARLY 1900S**

History AND ART

Hester Street
by George Luks, 1905

Hester Street in New York City—part of a Jewish immigrant neighborhood—was filled with vitality and color.

• **1883** *Brooklyn Bridge in New York City is completed*

• **1893** *Columbian Exposition opens in Chicago*

1880

1890

• **1886** *Haymarket Square riot takes place in Chicago*

• **1892** *Steelworkers' strike put down at the Homestead mill*
• **1894** *Pullman strike ends*

★★

The Workers' Plight

▶ COAL MINER'S HELMET

With the growth of industry, the number of factory workers rose from about 900,000 in 1860 to more than 3.2 million in 1890. Industrialization affected various aspects of workers' lives—where they worked and lived, the size of the workforce, and the nature of work itself. Many workers were forced to make the transition from skilled to semiskilled or unskilled labor. The experience and skill of such artisans as carpenters, silversmiths, and furniture makers no longer gave them any advantage over the unskilled. It took little training to tend a machine.

■ Problems

With machines taking the place of human skills, work became monotonous. Workers concentrated on highly specific, repetitive tasks and could take little pride in the fruits of their labor. As factories increased the efficiency of production, more and more people worked for fewer and fewer employers. The workers began to feel like "cogs in a wheel." Machines were designed to work at a given pace, and the workers were forced to try and keep up.

Unfair Conditions of Employment

Low wages and long hours posed additional burdens for industrial workers. Workdays of 10 to 14 hours were common. Although **real wages**—wages adjusted for inflation—rose more than 10 percent between 1870 and 1900, the average income remained inadequate. Most industrial workers earned between $400 and $500 a year during the 1890s; $600 was the minimum annual income needed to maintain a decent standard of living.

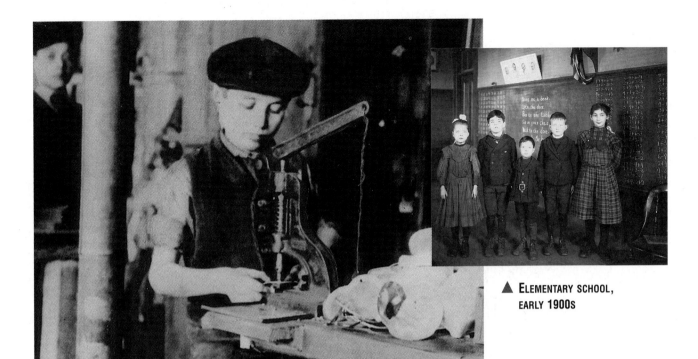

▲ ELEMENTARY SCHOOL, EARLY 1900s

▲ CHILD LABOR Children were often employed in small, makeshift factories in which workers were hired on a piecework basis. *How were state labor laws evaded?*

In some industries workers were required to live in **company towns,** built and run by the companies. The best known was the town of Pullman, Illinois, where every citizen worked for the Pullman Palace Car Company. The usual practice was for companies to deduct money from the workers' pay for rent and advances to the company store as well as medical and fuel fees. Some companies paid their workers in **scrip,** or company money, that could be redeemed only at the company store. This store usually charged higher prices than did stores in other towns, and many workers remained in constant debt.

Health and Safety Hazards

Factory work was unhealthful as well as dangerous. Miners breathed coal dust all day. Factory workers breathed sawdust, stone dust, cotton dust, or toxic fumes. Heavy machines, grouped together on shop and mill floors for the sake of efficiency, caused an appallingly high injury rate among workers. An 1884 government report described working conditions for women in a small factory in Boston:

❝ *The work is dangerous . . . [they] are liable to get their fingers jammed under the bench, or caught in the die when it comes down to press the parts of the buttons together.* ❞

Child Labor

Children, some as young as six, were regularly employed as factory workers. Throughout the 1800s there were some efforts to restrict child labor, but state laws were usually worded in such a way that they could be easily evaded both by employers and by parents who needed the income. In 1885 in New Jersey, there were 340,000 children of school age. About 90,000

HISTORY Online

Student Web Activity
Visit the *American History: The Modern Era Since 1865* Web site at **me.glencoe.com** and click on *Chapter 9— Student Web Activities* for an activity about child labor.

of them did not attend school; most worked full-time jobs. Industrial work was neither less difficult nor less dangerous for children than it was for adults. As a Pennsylvania newspaper, the *Luzerne Union,* reported in January 1876:

> 66 *During the past week, nearly one boy a day has been killed, and the public has become so familiar with these calamities that no attention is given them after the first announcement through a newspaper or friend.* 99

Job Insecurity

Always looming was the threat of pay cuts or layoffs. Workers were vulnerable to the **business cycle**—a recurring sequence of change in business activity. Beginning with a period of prosperity, business activity declines until a low point, or depression, is reached. A period of recovery follows when business conditions become more active. A period of prosperity is again reached. The cycle is then repeated.

In the late 1800s, business went through many such cycles. During slack periods employers kept their costs down by reduc-

▲ ORGANIZING THE WORKERS Union leaders hoped to improve conditions for workers, such as these immigrants working at home. *What were the difficulties that unions encountered in organizing immigrants?*

ing wages or laying off workers. Millions of people lost their jobs or had their wages slashed during the depressions of 1873, 1882, and 1893. Workers looked to labor unions for protection.

■ The Revival of Labor Unions

The growth of labor unions during the early 1800s had been halting and sporadic, but conditions during the Civil War spurred the revival of unionism. With hundreds of thousands of workers not available while serving in the army, unions were in a strong position to demand better pay. During the war the number of local unions rose dramatically. To strengthen local unions, labor also began to organize on a national scale.

Problems With Organizing

Labor unions faced serious difficulties in organizing because of the mobility and diversity of the American labor force. Workers who did not "stay hitched," but moved from job to job were difficult to organize. The constant influx of large numbers of immigrants—averaging more than one-third of a million a year between 1870 and 1900—also presented a problem. Differences in language, religion, and customs among the immigrants made it hard to unite them into an effective union.

Another problem was that different labor leaders had different goals. Some leaders envisioned uniting all workers into one large union in order to promote widespread reforms. Others believed that unions should be organized by particular crafts or industries and work only for short-term benefits.

Unions also faced strong opposition from employers. Workers were often required to take oaths swearing they would not join a union. If found to have been involved in union activity, a worker would be fired and often could not get another job because of **blacklists,** or records of "troublemakers" kept by employers. Once blacklisted, a laborer could get a job only by changing residence, trade, or even name. Another way employers

Visualizing History

▲ RAILWAY STRIKE The railway strike of 1877 resulted in one of the most violent upheavals in the history of American labor. *How did the strike start?*

retaliated against union organizing in a workplace was the **lockout**—whereby the factory was shut down—or by firing union members and hiring **scabs,** or replacement workers. In any lockout or strike, the odds favored employers. Few unions had enough money to support their members through the long period of unemployment caused by a strike.

Problems With Public Image

Labor unions also had to fight public opinion. Many Americans viewed fixing wages and hours by **collective bargaining**—negotiation between an employer and a labor union—as violating the right of an individual to deal personally with the employer. Only infrequently did public opinion condemn employers when labor disputes resulted in violence. This happened during the Homestead lockout in 1892 when the Carnegie Steel Company hired a private army of 300 Pinkerton detectives armed with repeating rifles. Generally, however, labor unions were held responsible when disorder occurred.

Another problem for unions was that law enforcement agencies usually sided with the employers. Employers suffered no penalties for lockouts and blacklists. Union strikes and boycotts, on the other hand, were judged to be "conspiracies in restraint of trade" for which labor leaders might be jailed or fined. Contracts between employers and unions were not usually enforceable by law. When violence occurred, or was even threatened, the police—and sometimes armed troops—were sent to the aid of employers.

■ Railroad Strike of 1877

Despite these obstacles labor unions survived—sometimes just barely. Membership in the union fluctuated according to business conditions. Following the depression of 1873, 5,000 businesses closed, causing widespread unemployment and homelessness.

Union membership dropped from more than 300,000 to 50,000. Three million workers were unemployed. At this time there were no unemployment or relief benefits available from either the state or federal government. Tramps and hobos roamed the countryside; workers' rallies to demand relief were stopped or suppressed by mounted police.

Labor Responds to Wage Cuts

The hard times of the 1870s reached a climax in the railroad strike of 1877, which shook the nation as no labor conflict in its history had done before. After years of prosperity, railroad companies were hit hard by economic woes. They turned to drastic measures to cut their losses. Some railways cut workers' pay as much as 35 percent. Workdays were lengthened up to 15 and sometimes even 18 hours. Companies discontinued the "free ride" policy that had allowed workers to travel free to and from their jobs. These measures made railway workers bitter and angry.

In 1877 wages were cut another 10 percent by the Pennsylvania Railroad and then by the Baltimore and Ohio (B & O) line. Workers threatened to walk off the job if nothing was done. Management refused to budge, certain that replacements for the strikers could be found. On July 16 about 40 B & O workers held a work stoppage. The trains rolled anyway, but down the line at Martinsburg, West Virginia, the firemen, those who tend the furnace and supply it with fuel, abandoned the trains. Strikers soon took over the town. The governor of West Virginia, at the urging of a B & O vice president, sent two companies of state militia to Martinsburg. It took federal troops, however, to regain control of the town.

The scene at Martinsburg was only the beginning. Troops and workers clashed in the streets of Pittsburgh, Buffalo, San Francisco, and Toledo. In late July, 20 persons were killed in Philadelphia, and, in another Pennsylvania city, Reading, 11 were killed. At the height of the strike, more than one-half of the freight on the nation's 76,000 miles of track had stopped running. Although the clashes were usually spontaneous, newspapers viewed them collectively as

> 66 ... an insurrection, a revolution, an attempt of Communists and vagabonds to coerce society and endeavor to undermine American institutions. 99

Management Gains a Costly Victory

In several cities order was restored only after President Rutherford B. Hayes had sent in federal troops. Hayes himself, however, was troubled. He felt railroad officials had brought on the crisis by their own ruthless actions. The President confided in his diary, "Shall the railroads govern the country or shall the people govern the railroads?"

When the railroad strike was over, more than 100 persons were dead, 1,000 had been jailed, and 100,000 workers had gone on strike. In addition there was such fear of violent revolution that state militia were reorganized. National Guard armories were built in many large cities as fortresses, where troops could hold out against strikers if necessary. Union leaders learned from the strike that they were not united or strong enough to defeat the powerful combination of business and government.

Section 1 ★ Assessment

Checking for Understanding

1. **Define** real wages, company town, scrip, business cycle, blacklist, lockout, scab, collective bargaining.

2. **Discuss** the hardships facing industrial workers during the late 1800s.

Critical Thinking

3. **Summarizing** Re-create the diagram shown here, and list the problems American unions faced in trying to achieve their goals during the late 1800s.

Union Difficulties			

INTERDISCIPLINARY ACTIVITY

4. **The Arts** Imagine you are a reporter assigned to cover the railroad strike of 1877. Write an article describing the scene of the strike as you arrive.

Summarizing

Imagine that you have received an expensive camera for your birthday. The instructions are long and complicated. The more you read, the more confused you become. Finally, you discover a *summary* of the main steps, and your confusion disappears.

Learning the Skill

Summarizing is the process of recapping main ideas by bringing together the major points and excluding the minor ones. A summary does not use examples except to clarify main ideas or concepts that may be new to you or to your audience. Knowing how to summarize is a useful skill for you when you have to answer essay questions, take notes, and write research papers.

Read the following material carefully. Then answer the questions that follow.

During the late 1800s, the United States, like other modernized nations, was experiencing societal changes brought on by the shift from an agriculture-based economy to one based on industrial production. American life up to this time had been based on a rugged self-determinism, a belief that one should take care of one's self and family. This was largely done through owning and farming land.

To encourage settlement in the frontier, Congress passed laws that provided land to settlers who would cultivate it and pay a fee. More land was occupied and improved in the closing years of the 1800s than had been occupied and improved during the first 250 years of American history.

The growth of industry lured many people to the cities and into jobs that required a new set of values. People in the industrial labor force faced profound changes in their lives. Often a man did not so much work for his family as he did for his boss. Further, working conditions and pay were often a source of discontent.

▲ MOVING ASSEMBLY LINE, HIGHLAND PARK, MICHIGAN

Long hours were another burden to workers. During the late 1800s, 65- and 70-hour workweeks were common. Labor unions began to organize, and although their intent was to lend support to exploited employees, it often made workers feel they were helpless to take care of themselves.

Practicing the Skill

1. Locate and list in order of appearance the main ideas expressed in the material.

2. Summarize the text by rewriting the main ideas in your own words.

Glencoe's **Skillbuilder Interactive Workbook, Level 2** provides instruction and practice in key social studies skills.

APPLYING THE SKILL

3. Reread the material under the heading "Railroad Strike of 1877" on page 293. Then, following the guidelines suggested in the example, list the main ideas of the material and write a short summary of the material presented.

★★★

The Rise of New Unions

Guide to Reading

Main Idea

Despite the difficulties they faced, unions grew in number and strength during the late 1800s.

Reading Strategy

Classifying Information As you read about the rise of unions, use a chart such as the one shown here to identify the membership and goals of the nation's two strongest labor unions.

Unions	Membership	Goals
Knights of Labor		
AFL		

Objectives

After studying this section, you should be able to

★ identify two of the strongest labor unions of the late 1800s.

★ evaluate the gains labor unions achieved during this period.

Key Terms

arbitration, industrial union, injunction

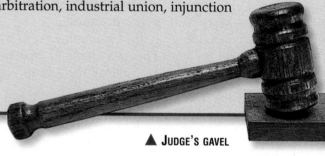

▲ JUDGE'S GAVEL

As industrialization was an urban phenomenon, so too were unions. Those states with the highest percentage of workers in industry had the greatest urban populations. It was in these industrial areas of the North and the Midwest that a score of new labor organizations were established in the late 1860s.

■ The Knights of Labor and the AFL Unions

By far the most influential labor organization was the Noble Order of the Knights of Labor. Founded in 1869, the Knights of Labor attempted to bring all laboring people—skilled and unskilled, black and white, men and women, white-collar and blue-collar—into one big union.

The Desire for Widespread Reform

Terence V. Powderly, an immigrant and a former railway switchtender, led the Knights of Labor after 1879. An eloquent speaker and a tireless organizer, Powderly believed a single, powerful union was the best means of gaining concessions from employers for better working conditions.

Powderly persuaded the Knights to support equal pay for women, temperance, abolition of child labor and, above all, establishment of cooperatively owned industrial plants. A man of peace, he opposed strikes and wished to submit labor disputes to **arbitration**—a process whereby an impartial third party helps workers and management reach an agreement.

Membership in the Knights grew rapidly in the early 1880s—especially after the striking Knights won the dispute against Jay Gould's Wabash Railway. Membership in the Knights soared from 100,000 in 1885 to 700,000 in less than a year. Some newspapers feared that Powderly would become stronger than the President.

The Knights of Labor, however, were soon swamped with troubles. The union had wasted its funds in unsuccessful attempts to set up cooperative businesses. Moreover, the effort to unite different kinds of labor into one big union had failed. Workers in different crafts and industries often had little in common with one another and little interest in working for the same goals.

Haymarket Square Riot

The decline of the Knights was hastened by the Haymarket Square riot in Chicago on May 4, 1886. This event followed a peaceful meeting of some 3,000 workers who gathered together to protest the shooting of striking McCormick Harvester Company workers by the police. As the meeting was

breaking up, someone threw a bomb into a group of police officers. Seven persons were killed and more than 60 were injured. Although the identity of the bomb-thrower was never established, 8 anarchist leaders were arrested and found guilty of taking part in the crime. Four were later executed for murder. Although the Knights of Labor could in no way be held responsible for the Haymarket affair, it became identified with radicals and violence. From then on the Knights of Labor declined rapidly.

Foundation of the AFL

In 1886, the year the Knights began to decline, the American Federation of Labor (AFL) was organized. In its principles as well as its structure, the AFL differed greatly from the Knights. While the Knights had accepted a large number of unskilled workers, the AFL accepted only skilled workers. This policy indicated the reluctance of the

 Visualizing History ▲ TROUBLE AT THE HAYMARKET On the night of May 4, 1886, a crowd gathered in Chicago's Haymarket Square to protest police violence. As the meeting was breaking up, a bomb was thrown into a group of police and the police fired into the crowd. *What effect did the Haymarket affair have on the labor movement?*

AFL to accept women, African Americans, and immigrants—the majority of whom were unskilled—into their union. Also, the AFL organized workers into separate unions, each covering a particular craft.

Each union managed its own affairs with only occasional help from the national organization. The AFL's fees were relatively high, in order to restrict membership, build up strike funds, and provide benefits to members and their families in cases of sickness, unemployment, or death.

The AFL might never have enjoyed the success it did were it not for Samuel Gompers, its president for 37 years. Born in London, Gompers adapted some ideas of British trade unions, the best established in the world. Gompers, who prided himself on being practical, was interested only in day-to-day gains of AFL members—higher wages, shorter hours, and benefits for disabled workers.

So effective was the organization and leadership of the AFL that when hard times hit again in 1893, its member unions not only survived but thrived. Between 1890 and 1900, when other labor organizations lost members, AFL membership rose from 190,000 to 500,000.

■ The Pullman Strike

To address the needs of unskilled and semiskilled labor—and yet avoid the "one big union" approach—a new type of labor organization developed. This was the **industrial union,** in which all classes of workers in a single industry are joined together. Among those who saw the advantages of an industrial union was Eugene V. Debs, an officer of the Brotherhood of Locomotive Firemen, one of several railway unions. He felt that the separation of railway workers into different unions weakened their power. Conductors and engineers, the "aristocracy of labor," looked down on less skilled and lower paid workers, and the unskilled had no organization at all. Debs, therefore, started a new organization in 1893—the American Railway Union. This union included all types of railroad workers—from conductors, firemen, and engineers to telegraph opera-

tors and station clerks. By 1894 the American Railway Union was powerful enough to force James J. Hill, the owner of the Great Northern Railway, to restore wage cuts.

Protest Leads to Walkout

Hardly had the Great Northern strike ended than the Pullman strike began in Pullman, Illinois, the company town built by George M. Pullman for his workers. Losing profit because of a reduced demand for its railroad cars, the Pullman Palace Car Company laid off two-thirds of its employees and cut the wages of the rest. It did not, however, reduce either the dividends it paid to stockholders or the rents charged to workers in the town. When a delegation of workers met with Pullman to protest the pay cuts, they were fired. At noon the following day, 10,000 Pullman workers walked off the job.

The American Railway Union took up the Pullman workers' cause. Debs's first move was to propose that the dispute be referred to arbitration. Pullman, however, replied, "There is nothing to arbitrate." Realizing that negotiating with Pullman was futile, the union called for members to refuse to work

▲ RIDING IN LUXURY—THE PULLMAN CAR

on any train that included a Pullman car. Railway workers answered the union's call. Within 5 days 100,000 railroad workers had walked off the job. Railway traffic west of Chicago was almost paralyzed. Debs warned his followers not to interfere with the mail and appealed to them to be "orderly and law-abiding." A few mail trains were delayed, but there were few disturbances.

Federal Intervention Turns the Tide

Quickly, President Grover Cleveland stepped in. Over protests by the mayor of Chicago and the governor of Illinois, President Cleveland sent federal troops to guard mail trains. Immediately, rioting broke out as angry mobs, sympathetic to the strikers, taunted the soldiers. Members of the American Railway Union kept out of trouble but nevertheless received the blame. Even before the troops had arrived, the federal government obtained an **injunction,** or court order, forbidding the union to continue the strike. Debs refused to obey the injunction and was imprisoned.

Without Debs's leadership, the Pullman strike collapsed and with it the American Railway Union. From that point on, employers used the injunction as a means of breaking up strikes.

Although labor unions lost more disputes than they won, and most workers remained unorganized (only 4 percent of American workers belonged to unions in 1900), workers made some gains in the late 1800s. Fed-

Visualizing History ▲ **LABOR LEADER** The only major labor union to endure into the 1900s was the American Federation of Labor, or AFL. It was founded in 1886 by an immigrant cigar maker named Samuel Gompers. *What were the goals of the AFL?*

eral and state legislation reflected the growing political influence of labor. Wages began to increase slowly, and the workday was shortened. Moreover, nearly every state passed laws regulating working conditions and requiring minimum standards of health and safety.

Section 2 ★ Assessment

Checking for Understanding

1. **Define** arbitration, industrial union, injunction.

2. **Summarize** the difficulties faced by the Knights of Labor and the American Railway Union.

Critical Thinking

3. **Analyzing Issues** Re-create the diagram shown here, and list the achievements of

labor unions in the United States during the late 1800s.

Union Achievements

INTERDISCIPLINARY ACTIVITY

4. **Economics** Create a collage of the American labor force from media pictures of people at work.

★★★

Patterns of Immigration

Guide to Reading

Main Idea

Looking to start new lives, millions of immigrants, mostly from Europe, journeyed to American during the late 1800s.

Reading Strategy

Organizing Information As you read about the wave of immigration in the United States, use a diagram such as the one shown here to explain the difference between "old" and "new" immigration.

```
Immigration to the U.S.
   ┌──────────┴──────────┐
 "Old"                 "New"
 ┌────┐               ┌────┐
 │    │               │    │
 └────┘               └────┘
```

Objectives

After studying this section, you should be able to

★ identify the reasons that immigrants came to the United States.

★ distinguish between the "old" and the "new" immigration.

Key Terms

pogrom, anarchism

▶ **ADVERTISEMENT URGING IMMIGRATION TO AMERICA**

The thirteen colonies had been settled mainly by English settlers. Other settlers from Holland, Sweden, France, Scotland, Ireland, and Germany came later. After 1815, however, increasing numbers of immigrants started to arrive from Ireland. During these early years, a total of only about 400,000 immigrants had come to America. Beginning in the 1850s and continuing after the Civil War, immigration rose sharply.

■ The "Old Immigration"

During the period of "Old Immigration," which started in the 1830s and reached a high point in the 1840s, there was a great wave of immigration to America's shores. Between 1840 and 1850, an additional 1.5 million newcomers journeyed to the United States. Nearly one-half were from Ireland, which was suffering from a potato famine. Between 1846 and 1860, about 1.5 million Irish immigrated to America, settling in New York and Boston, which functioned as ports of entry into the United States.

In the 1840s large numbers of Germans also began to come to America. Some left their homeland because of crop failures. Others came to escape political persecution after the failure of the Revolution of 1848. Still others were German Jews seeking religious freedom. Large numbers of German immigrants settled on farms and in cities in the Midwest—areas that were rapidly growing and had job opportunities. The Germans gave a distinctive flavor to such cities as Cincinnati, Milwaukee, and St. Louis. Then, in the 1850s, after the Gold Rush, Chinese immigrants began to come to the Pacific Coast. Many were hired to help build the railroads. About 100,000 Chinese had settled in the West by the mid-1870s.

During the colonial period, most immigrants were readily accepted. Workers were badly needed in all the colonies.

European agents of railroad companies and steamship lines described America as a land where riches could be had almost for the asking. Perhaps the most persuasive arguments for others to come to this country were the "America letters" written by recent immigrants to their family and friends. "If you wish to be happy and independent, then come here," wrote a German farmer from his new home in Missouri. In the 1840s and 1850s, however, some native-born Americans began to resent the newcomers, especially the Irish immigrants. Some Americans resented them because they dressed and sounded "different" and because they were Catholics.

■ The "New Immigration"

Until the 1880s most newcomers had come from the nations of northern and western Europe. After 1885, however, large numbers came from nations of southern and eastern Europe. The new immigrants were from Italy, Russia, and Poland as well as from the nations of the Austro-Hungarian Empire.

Italians were one of the largest groups of new immigrants. Many came from Sicily and the southern part of Italy. People in this region faced economic misfortune. Unemployment and overpopulation made existence perilous. As a result, millions of Italian Catholics chose to go to America.

Eastern European Jews were another sizable group of new immigrants. Although scattered throughout many countries, the

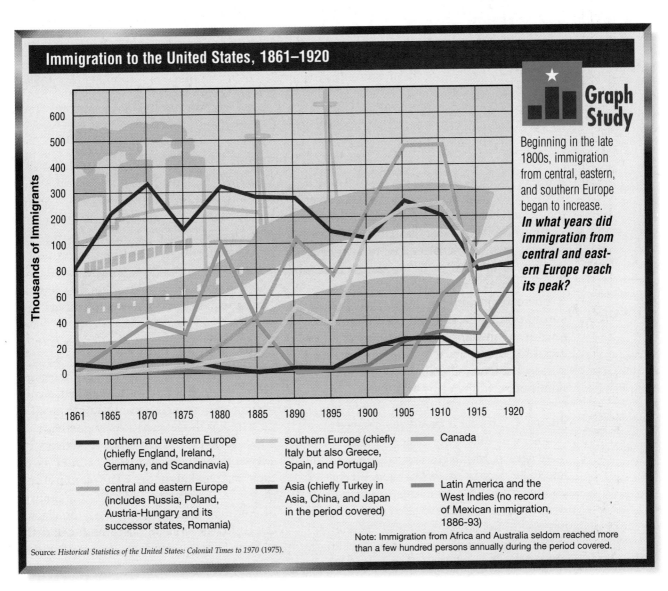

Immigration to the United States, 1861–1920

Graph Study

Beginning in the late 1800s, immigration from central, eastern, and southern Europe began to increase. *In what years did immigration from central and eastern Europe reach its peak?*

Thousands of Immigrants (vertical axis: 600, 500, 400, 300, 200, 100, 80, 60, 40, 20, 0)

(horizontal axis: 1861, 1865, 1870, 1875, 1880, 1885, 1890, 1895, 1900, 1905, 1910, 1915, 1920)

Legend:
- northern and western Europe (chiefly England, Ireland, Germany, and Scandinavia)
- central and eastern Europe (includes Russia, Poland, Austria-Hungary and its successor states, Romania)
- southern Europe (chiefly Italy but also Greece, Spain, and Portugal)
- Asia (chiefly Turkey in Asia, China, and Japan in the period covered)
- Canada
- Latin America and the West Indies (no record of Mexican immigration, 1886-93)

Note: Immigration from Africa and Australia seldom reached more than a few hundred persons annually during the period covered.

Source: *Historical Statistics of the United States: Colonial Times to 1970* (1975).

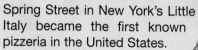

Linking Past and Present

Italian Cuisine

Between 1890 and 1910 about 2.7 million southern Italians immigrated to the United States. Among their contributions to America was a rich and varied cuisine.

Then_____

Pizza and Pasta

Italian bakery ovens produced the first pizzas, which had been a strictly Neapolitan item in Italy. Opening in 1905, "G Lombardi" on Spring Street in New York's Little Italy became the first known pizzeria in the United States.

Other Italian dishes became lasting contributions to American cuisine. Many people came to love Italian pasta. Macaroni, manicotti, spaghetti, and lasagna were first introduced to Americans by the little shops nestled among the blocks of big-city tenements.

Now_____

A Continuing Heritage

Americans continue their love affair with Italian food today both at home and when eating out. Entire cookbooks are devoted to Italian cooking. When polled by a culinary news magazine, Americans selected Italian food as the second favorite restaurant fare. Among fast-food chains, Pizza Hut ranks fourth and Domino's Pizza ranks seventh in total sales.

Jews of eastern Europe were confronted with many common problems wherever they lived. For one thing they were often the victims of religious discrimination. In many regions Jews were not allowed to own land, work in certain trades, or move out of areas that had been set aside for them.

These limitations on Jews created widespread poverty. In addition eastern European Jews lived in danger of **pogroms,** or organized massacres. Jewish immigrants seeking personal safety, religious freedom, and economic opportunity came to America.

Slavs made up a third group of new immigrants. "Slavs" is a broad label given to a people, generally from eastern Europe, who have similar languages and customs. In the late 1800s, large numbers of Slavs left Russia, Poland, and other countries to escape economic woes. Many Slavs also came in search of political freedom.

These newcomers were, for the most part, poor. They hoped to find a better life in America. In part it was their labor that made the rapid industrialization of the United States possible. For many people, immigrating to the United States was the only way for them to escape persecution in their homeland. One Jewish immigrant noted that "the only hope for the Jews in Russia is to become Jews out of Russia."

Ethnic Neighborhoods

The new immigrants flocked to the cities. There they lived together in ethnically homogeneous neighborhoods such as "Little Italy" or the Jewish "Lower East Side" in New York City. There they practiced the ways of life they were used to and spoke their native languages. The communities they established revolved around a number of traditional institutions. They re-created the churches, synagogues, clubs, and newspapers of their homeland and adapted them to their new environment.

Public Resentment

This huge influx of immigrants created special social problems. Because immigrants lived in their own neighborhoods, practiced their own customs, and spoke their own languages, many Americans wondered if they could ever be assimilated into American life. Some people, especially workers, blamed them for low wages. Others resented that many immigrants were Catholics or Jews.

The railroad strike of 1877 and the Haymarket Square riot of 1886 resulted in many people's fear of immigrants who, it was thought, believed in socialism or even **anarchism,** a belief in no direct government authority over society. A few politicians, notably Senator Henry Cabot Lodge of Massachusetts, were strongly reactionary in their response to the issue of immigration. They wanted immigration from southern and eastern Europe to be stopped completely. In 1896, Senator Lodge argued for a bill that would exclude all prospective immigrants who could not read or write at least 25 words of the United States Constitution in some language. Lodge concluded that such a test would

" *. . . bear most heavily upon the Italians, Russians, Poles, Hungarians, Greeks, and Asiatics . . . races most affected by the test are those who[m] emigration has . . . swelled rapidly . . . and who are most alien to the great body of the United States.* "

In the late 1800s, hostility grew toward many of the new racial and ethnic groups coming into the new country. The differences in customs, dress, and language of the new arrivals created a basic distrust of the foreign born by many native-born Americans. Some historians believe that this reaction was a response to the rapid changes occurring in America because of industrialization. For those native-born Americans who were uncertain and disturbed by social change, immigrants became easy targets of hostility.

Organized Opposition

Some Americans formed groups to counter what they considered the immigrant threat. One of these groups, the American Protective Association, was founded in 1887

Visualizing History

▲ THE NEW IMMIGRANTS During the late 1800s, new immigrants poured into the United States, braving the long and difficult journey to start a new life. *Why did many people view these newcomers as a threat?*

to protest the large number of Catholic immigrants. In some parts of the country, local laws were passed that prohibited immigrants from holding certain kinds of jobs and denied them other rights. Jewish immigrants, for example, were denied admission to some universities. In addition the immigrants faced actual physical attacks.

The anti-immigration movement was not limited to groups such as the American Protective Association. Some well-known scholars of the time were susceptible to these feelings as well. Historian and future President Woodrow Wilson and frontier historian Frederick Jackson Turner lamented the lessening flow of immigration from northern Europe and the rise in numbers of "inferior stocks" coming to America. One writer considered the new immigration a plot by European governments to "unload the sweepings of their jails and asylums."

Anti-Chinese Sentiment

Public resentment was not limited to newcomers from Europe, however. The Chinese, too, suffered discrimination on the Pacific Coast. The discovery of gold in 1849 and the subsequent demand for cheap labor first brought the Chinese to California. Many found work in the gold fields or on the construction of the Central Pacific Railroad. By 1852 there were some 25,000 Chinese men, women, and children living on the Pacific Coast and thereafter they came at

▲ CHINESE FAMILY IN CALIFORNIA, EARLY 1900S

the rate of 4,000 a year. By the end of the 1870s, there were almost 75,000 Chinese in California alone. Their willingness to work for low wages prompted a violent anti-Chinese movement among the white workers of California. Such feelings intensified during hard economic times. During the depression that followed the Panic of 1873, unemployed workers in California attacked the Chinese. Some Americans began to demand that Chinese immigrants be excluded from the United States.

In 1879 Congress forbade the importing of foreign workers under contract—a law aimed primarily at the Chinese. Then, in 1882, Congress, responding to pressure from the western states, suspended nearly all immigration from China for 10 years.

Section 3 ★ Assessment

Checking for Understanding

1. **Define** pogrom, anarchism.

2. **Identify** two attempts that were made to decrease immigration to the United States.

Critical Thinking

3. **Identifying Causes** Re-create the diagram shown here, and list reasons why Europeans migrated to the United States.

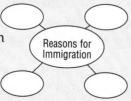

Reasons for Immigration

4. **Understanding Cause and Effect** How did religious prejudice create problems for some immigrants?

INTERDISCIPLINARY ACTIVITY

5. **The Arts** Find out what groups of immigrants settled in your local area. Present a graphic display using photographs or your own sketches on the cultural influences these people have had on your town or city.

★★

City Life and Problems

Guide to Reading

Main Idea
As people flocked to the cities to find jobs, the nation's urban centers encountered a host of new problems.

Reading Strategy

Taking Notes As you read about city life and its problems, list the factors that led to the growth of cities during the late 1800s. Use an outline form such as the one shown here.

I. Movement
   A.
   B.
II. Attractions
   A.
   B.

Objectives
After studying this section, you should be able to
★ identify the factors that led to the growth of cities during the late 1800s.
★ list the problems resulting from an increase in the urban population.

Key Term
merchandising

► **BOOK ON URBAN LIFE BY JACOB RIIS**

All over the nation—but especially in the Northeast—cities were growing rapidly. This urban growth was a result of industrialization. In 1840, 1 out of every 12 Americans lived in a city with a population of more than 8,000. By 1900, however, 1 out of every 3 Americans lived in a large city.

Why were so many people attracted to the cities? One reason was that rising new industries held out the promise of jobs and opportunity. Where else could immigrants—or other Americans, for that matter—fulfill the "rags to riches" dream of making a fortune overnight? The cities of the 1890s held the promise of excitement and activity, in contrast to the isolation of rural farm life. There was running water, modern plumbing, museums, libraries, theaters, shops, convenient transportation, and countless things to see and do.

■ Urbanization

Between 1860 and 1900 American urban areas grew twice as fast as the total population. Chicago, which in the 1830s had been a frontier town with a few hundred residents, became a vast metropolis of almost 2 million people. New York became the second-largest city in the world. During the same span of years, Philadelphia grew from less than 600,000 people to about 1.3 million. Both Boston's and Baltimore's populations increased from about 200,000 to more than one-half million.

Industrial cities were essentially the product of mines, factories, steamships, and railroads. New cities appeared, or old ones mushroomed, near coal and iron deposits (Birmingham, Alabama, and Pittsburgh), sources of water power (Lowell and Lawrence, Massachusetts), shipping centers

Jane Addams
1860–1935

By the time the guns of World War I began blazing in 1914, Jane Addams was already famous as the founder of Hull House—the settlement house that served Chicago's immigrants and urban poor. By then peace had become her passion.

In 1915 Addams urged European leaders to find a way to end the mounting carnage. When the United States entered the war, she was labeled unpatriotic for holding true to her pacifist ideals. After the war ended in 1918, Addams worked to ensure no repetition of the "war to end all wars."

Addams was elected president of the Women's International League for Peace and Freedom in 1915 and held that office until 1929. Her devotion to world peace was recognized in 1931 when she was named corecipient, with educator Nicholas Murray Butler, of the Nobel Peace Prize.

(Baltimore and New York City), and at railroad centers (Omaha and Chicago). Industrial cities, especially in the Northeast, had the greatest growth, but cities in all regions experienced rapid growth. Between 1860 and 1900, Nashville grew from 16,000 to more than 80,000, Minneapolis from 2,500 to more than 200,000, and Los Angeles from 4,000 to more than 100,000.

Once established, cities seemed to generate their own growth. To serve industry such facilities as banks, insurance companies, docks, and warehouses developed. These, in turn, attracted more industry and workers. Immigrants could often find employment only in urban industrialized areas. Yet an even greater number of new workers came from rural areas of the United States.

■ Problems of City Life

The modern industrial city confronted many people with an unfamiliar and often unattractive environment. The new cities were built with less concern for the comforts of the inhabitants than for the profits of builders and real-estate speculators. People poured into the cities faster than housing could be built to accommodate them. Many had no choice but to live in tenements, poorly constructed and cramped five- or six-story buildings, which housed many families. Many of the rooms and tenements had no windows and were often dark, narrow, and airless.

As more and more people were crowded together and the buildings began to deteriorate, city slums developed. Lacking proper sanitation, tenements became foul-smelling and vermin-infested. Typhoid and other diseases often spread rapidly.

Lack of Social Services

Besides inadequate housing, there was a shortage of police and firefighters. City water was impure and sewers were often clogged. Garbage collection was sporadic. In addition there were no attempts at city planning. Little was done to provide for open spaces, parks, and playgrounds or to take advantage of rivers and other natural features. The few open spaces were often used as garbage dumps or left vacant with a scanty growth of grass and weeds competing with cinders and tin cans.

Rivers and harbors were polluted by sewage and factory wastes, and the air was fouled by smoke from thousands of chimneys. The new environment cut off people from sun, air, and natural beauty.

New Concerns Arise

The growth of cities created a demand for new sources of water because wells and brooks provided too scanty a supply and were often polluted. New York City, the first of the major cities to meet this problem head-on, built the Croton Aqueduct 25 miles outside the city limits.

Cities also had to come up with more efficient means of intercity transportation. This was accomplished by the horse car and later by the elevated railway, the trolley car, and the subway. The demand for space in preferred localities such as Wall Street in New York or the Loop in Chicago resulted in the creation of huge skyscrapers, which, in turn, added a vertical dimension to transportation—in the form of the elevator.

Rise in Crime

An unexpected problem of urban life, however, was the increase in crime. There had always been occasional violence and theft, but never on a scale demanding an organized police force. There had been nothing resembling modern police until the formation of the Metropolitan Police of London, known as "bobbies," around 1830.

Because the problems experienced by growing urban centers were new, old solutions could not be relied upon. It seemed as if the answers were as varied as the problems. Some people looked back to an earlier morality and sought to enforce the Puritan Sabbath as a means of regenerating the city. As a result restaurants and amusement places were closed. There were even efforts to forbid the running of trains and streetcars.

Public Awareness Spurs Legislation

One who faced the realities of life in factories, shops, and slums was Jacob A. Riis (REES), a Danish American police reporter

▲ **URBAN PROBLEMS** Poverty and overcrowding brought on many social problems in large cities throughout the United States. *What problems did residents of tenements in the nation's larger cities face?*

▲ **A NATION OF CITIES** As the United States became a nation of cities, public services expanded to serve the needs of the people. Paved roads, electric street lights, and streetcars improved transportation. *What did critics say about the appearance of cities?*

for New York newspapers. In the course of his work, Riis had seen again and again the connection between slums and human degradation. In 1890 he focused public attention on the problem in a best-selling book, *How the Other Half Lives.* By appealing to public conscience, Riis secured legislation that reduced the worst slum conditions, along with other measures that improved the lives of city dwellers, such as playgrounds for schools. Among his close friends was a rising young Republican politician, Theodore Roosevelt, whom he "educated" by taking him into tenements, sweatshops, and jails.

Footnotes to History

Wages and Prices In 1900 the average American worker earned 22 cents an hour, or $12.98 a week based on the typical 59-hour workweek. A tailor-made suit cost $10; a skirt $4. Prices for meat at the local market were 7 cents a pound for chicken, 10 cents for beef, and 12.5 cents for sausage. The average price for an automobile—$1,550 and out of reach for most—meant Americans continued to rely on the horse and buggy and streetcars. In any case, the nation had just 150 miles of paved roads.

Settlement Houses Assist Communities

The year before *How the Other Half Lives* was published, Jane Addams founded, in a Chicago slum, the most famous settlement house in the United States, Hull House. About this neighborhood, Addams wrote:

" *[T]he streets were inexpressibly dirty . . . the street lighting bad. . . . Many houses have no water save the faucet in the back yard; there are no fire escapes. . . .* "

Addams, a deeply religious woman, was inspired by a passionate desire to put her faith to work. Modeling her endeavor on Toynbee Hall, a settlement house in England, Jane Addams was determined to improve the life of the "other half." Hull House soon had activities as varied as an art gallery and a gymnasium as well as hot lunches for factory workers and classes in English. Above all, Addams was interested in helping children, believing that "a fence at the top of a precipice is better than an ambulance at the bottom." Addams surrounded herself with young people who were glad to enlist in a war against human suffering.

Similar convictions were the motivating forces behind the founding of other settlement houses, including the Henry Street Settlement in New York City, the Santa Maria Institute in Cincinnati, and the South End House in Boston. In addition to providing immediate services to neighborhood people, settlement houses were schools where hundreds of men and women learned social responsibility.

Many of these people later helped to promote reform legislation, either as political lobbyists or officeholders. "Graduates" of Hull House, for example, were instrumental in securing the first playgrounds in Chicago, better garbage collection, and the first Illinois factory inspection law. Frances Perkins, trained in a New York settlement house, embarked on a political career that led to her appointment as secretary of labor, the first woman to serve on a presidential cabinet.

■ Beautifying the City

Among the indictments against sprawling industrial cities were their ugliness and their lack of provision for rest and recreation. Architects and landscape designers were among those who sought remedies.

Public Buildings and Open Spaces

In 1876 New York City opened Central Park, designed by Frederick L. Olmsted and Calvert Vaux, as "a great breathing space for the toiling masses." Olmsted was the first person to use the term *landscape architect* as the name of this kind of work. Olmsted also designed Prospect Park in Brooklyn. Many other cities followed New York's example. In 1892 and 1893 Chicago hosted a World's Fair on fairgrounds designed by Olmsted, with buildings in the classical style surrounded by lagoons and landscaped grassy areas.

The Chicago World's Fair revealed that American architecture was dynamic and original. The best architects now thoroughly understood European styles and adapted them for modern use. The firm of McKim, Mead, and White used the Italian Renaissance style in their design for the Boston Public Library. Henry Richardson adapted Romanesque style in his design for churches, libraries, warehouses, and even department stores.

New Functional Architecture

The Transportation Building at the Chicago Fair, designed by Louis Sullivan, however, was based on a new concept: form follows function. Sullivan believed an architect should create designs that reveal a building's purpose and method of construction. He was one of the first architects to design skyscrapers. His influence, both directly and later through the work of his pupil Frank Lloyd Wright, reached worldwide.

The finest example of a structure in which form expressed function was the Brooklyn Bridge. Completed in 1883, 16 years after it was begun, it was the largest suspension bridge in the world at that time. Hung from great steel cables with a span half again as long as that of any previous bridge, it was designed and constructed by two German Americans, John Roebling and his son Washington Roebling. During the project, John was killed on the job. His son continued directing the work until he himself was injured. The work was then taken over by John's wife who, with her son's direction, completed the project.

Public Libraries

For those who wished to continue their education, American cities provided opportunities that had never existed before. In 1876 the American Library Association was founded to encourage "the best reading for the largest number at the least expense." By 1900 the public libraries, which receive support from taxes, revenues, and private donations, came to be recognized as "no less important than the schoolhouse in the system of popular education."

Downtown Shopping Districts

New means of **merchandising,** or the buying and selling of goods, were created to meet the growing needs of urban populations. One striking example was the department store. Stores such as A. T. Stewart and John Wanamaker were retail centers where nearly all kinds of goods were sold in one location. These stores had an enormous appeal to people of all classes. As a result the downtown areas of cities became centers where

▶ **FLATIRON BUILDING, NEW YORK CITY**

people came to shop. Merchants who wanted this new business were active in making sure that the areas were kept clean and attractive. New streets, sidewalks, and buildings were constructed.

Despite some setbacks, citizens made progress solving some of the problems facing the major cities. The availability of electricity enabled shops and factories to remain open after dark and thus stimulated urban nightlife as well.

Efforts by Municipal Governments

Throughout the late 1800s, city governments turned their efforts toward providing the services needed for their citizens. Steps were taken by city leaders to reduce crime, to improve recreational opportunities and living conditions, and to solve some of the public health problems that accompanied the rapid growth of the cities. Methods of identifying criminals, such as the use of photographs, were improved. Electric streetlights added a large measure of safety on city streets.

Many parks were built, usually toward the edges of already congested cities. Public utilities provided electricity, clean water, and sewage services for many urban areas. By 1898 approximately 350 communities had built publicly owned electric light companies, and by 1900 more than 3,500 public waterworks had been constructed nationwide.

The need for better communication spurred the use of a new innovation, the telephone. Within a few years after the telephone was invented in 1876, telephone exchanges were established in more than 80 cities. Within 20 years nearly 800,000 telephones were in use throughout the United States, twice as many as were in use in Europe. The impact of the telephone upon American life was enormous, linking many of the urban and rural areas of the nation almost instantly.

Despite these changes for the better, many social reformers felt that this was only a start. They contended that it was essential to find solutions for problems before the problems ever occurred. More and more reformers urged government to deal with the causes of social and economic problems. Jacqueline Shaw Lowell, the founder of the New York Charity Organization Society, expressed this attitude about the city's problems when she noted:

" [There are] five hundred thousand wage earners in this city, 200,000 of them women, and 75,000 of those working under dreadful conditions. . . . If the working people had all they ought to have, we should not have the paupers and the criminals. . . . It is better to save them before they go under than to spend your life . . . taking care of them afterwards. "

Section 4 ★ Assessment

Checking for Understanding
1. **Define** merchandising.
2. **Describe** the efforts made to improve life and conditions in the cities.

Critical Thinking
3. **Understanding Analogies** How does Jane Addams's theory that "a fence at the top of a precipice is better than an ambulance at the bottom" explain her focus on children?
4. **Organizing Information** Re-create the diagram shown here, and list the problems that

cities encountered as their populations grew in the late 1800s.

Cities' Problems

INTERDISCIPLINARY ACTIVITY

5. **Government** Create a public service announcement to inform new residents about community services provided by local agencies.

Urban Pollution and Public Health

Citizens who complain about air pollution, poor water quality, and inadequate garbage disposal in modern cities might feel at home if transported to the New York City of 1866. A report on the sanitary conditions of the city in that year identified the following problems:

(1) filthy streets; (2) neglected garbage and domestic refuse; (3) obstructed and faulty sewers and drains; (4) neglected privies and stables; (5) cattle pens and large stables in the more populous districts; (6) neglected and filthy markets; (7) slaughterhouses and hide and fat depots in close proximity to populous streets; (8) droves of cattle and swine in crowded streets; (9) swill-milk stables; . . . (10) bone boiling, fat melting . . . within the city limits; (11) . . . offensive exhalations . . . in gas manufacture; . . . (12) . . . dumping grounds and manure yards in vicinity of populous streets; (13) . . . management of refuse and junk materials; . . . (14) overcrowding of . . . public conveyances; . . . (15) neglect of dead animals in the streets and gutters of the city.

Such urban problems were not new. Examples can be found even in ancient times. Many cities, having become centers for trade, government, and religion, were large and crowded. Some historians place Rome's population at more than 1 million by the start of the first century A.D. Within 100 years overcrowding resulted in many of Rome's citizens living in apartment houses. Some apartments were 5 or 6 stories high and sheltered about 200 people each. Many of the city's residential structures were flimsy and poorly constructed, and living conditions paralleled those in the impoverished sections of nineteenth-century New York.

The living conditions of the urban poor left a great deal to be desired. Life in the crowded tenements was hazardous at best. Fires were an ever-present threat. In the late 1800s, the amount of damage from urban fires was on the

▲ CITY STOREFRONT, C. 1910

rise. Much of Chicago's downtown area burned in 1871, and two years later Boston experienced a devastating fire.

Another threat was illness. One reason for this was poor diet. Another was unsanitary conditions. Most tenement houses had neither indoor plumbing nor good ventilation.

Making the Geography Connection

1. Categorize the pollution problems under air, soil, and water.

2. Why do you think the speed of urban growth contributes to environmental problems?

ACTIVITY

3. Identify an environmental problem in your state. Write a letter to your state legislator expressing your concerns. Ask whether solving this problem should take precedence over business considerations that might be involved.

311

CHAPTER 9 ★ ASSESSMENT

Self-Check Quiz

Visit the *American History: The Modern Era Since 1865* Web site at **me.glencoe.com** and click on *Chapter 9—Self-Check Quizzes* to prepare for the chapter test.

Using Vocabulary

Use the following terms in sentences or short paragraphs. Relate them by using two or more of the terms in each sentence or paragraph.

real wages   company town
lockout   collective bargaining
arbitration   industrial union
injunction   tenement

Reviewing Facts

1. Discuss the hardships and problems that plagued industrial workers in the late 1800s and early 1900s.

2. Report on the problems facing labor unions in the late 1800s.

3. Summarize the achievements of labor unions during the late 1800s.

4. List the reasons why people immigrated to the United States.

5. Cite reasons for the growth of cities during the late 1800s.

Understanding Concepts

Unity

1. Use a diagram like the one shown here to describe the poor working conditions that labor organizers hoped unions could improve.

Poor Working Conditions

Conflict

2. With what groups did labor unions have conflict once they were organized? What were some of the reasons for the conflict? Explain how the conflict was resolved.

Critical Thinking

1. **Understanding Stereotypes** What stereotypes of labor unions were created because of the actions of a few union members or nonunion strikers? How did they work against the efforts of organized labor?

2. **Analyzing Photographs** Study the photograph on this page of children on a New York City street in the early 1900s and answer the questions that follow.

   a. What are the individuals in the photograph doing?

   b. What evidence do you see that conveys economic conditions?

   c. What title would you give this photograph?

▲ CHILDREN ON MULBERRY STREET, NEW YORK CITY

3. **Determining Cause and Effect** Explain how technology and industrialization created wealth among business owners. How did the same technology and industrialization create poverty among workers?

History and Geography

Urbanization

A new America emerged during the late 1800s. This new America was shaped by an urban environment that replaced an older agrarian setting.

1. **Human/Environment Interaction** Why did many rural residents move to the cities?

2. **Human/Environment Interaction** How did immigrants try to adjust to life in the United States?

Cooperative Learning — Interdisciplinary Activity: Labor History

Work with a partner to research a major strike that occurred in the United States within the last five years. Find information on the workers' grievances and on the company's position in the strike. Use this information to take turns as a union representative and a company representative questioning one another during an arbitration meeting.

Practicing Skills

Summarizing

The following excerpt details the Homestead Steel Strike of 1892. Read the material carefully. Then answer the questions that follow.

Strikes did not cease following the tragedy at Haymarket Square. Andrew Carnegie's Homestead Steel Plant in Pennsylvania was the scene of more violence.

The 25,000-member Amalgamated Association of Iron & Steel Workers had negotiated a contract for Homestead workers in 1889. When the union sought to renew the contract in 1892, the company refused. Homestead officials contended that the union had no right to negotiate for all workers. The company refused a pay raise and countered with an 18 to 26 percent cut for all workers.

As a result, Homestead's 3,000 unskilled workers joined the plant's 800 union members in a strike. The company manager, Henry Frick, ordered a lockout and called in strikebreakers. The strikers formed picket lines around the plant.

The company hired the Pinkerton Private Detective Agency to ensure the safety of the strikebreakers. When 300 Pinkerton guards arrived on the morning of July 6, they were met by armed strikers ready for battle. The Pinkertons were forced to surrender and were returned to Pittsburgh. Three guards and seven strikers were killed.

Pennsylvania Governor Robert Pattison responded by sending the Pennsylvania National Guard to Homestead. By July 26 the New York Times *could report that "the Homestead Strike has had its back broken." The company took legal action against some of the strike leaders for murder and conspiracy. Amalgamated, once the most powerful trade union in the AFL, was crushed.*

Practicing the Skill

1. List in order of occurrence the major events and main ideas expressed in the material.

2. Summarize the text by rewriting the major events and main ideas in your own words.

Technology Activity

Using the Internet Use the Internet to research various countries, and choose one in which you would like to live. Provide reasons for your choice in a brief report.

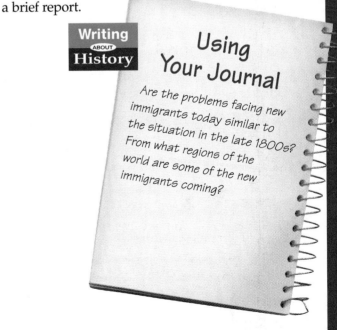

Writing ABOUT History

Using Your Journal

Are the problems facing new immigrants today similar to the situation in the late 1800s? From what regions of the world are some of the new immigrants coming?

CHAPTER 10

★★★ ★★★

The Gilded Age
1865–1900

► TIFFANY LAMP

Setting the Scene

Focus

American political life reached a low point between 1865 and 1900. Corruption in the form of graft and bribery became almost routine in local, state, and national governments. Both the Democratic and Republican parties came under the influence of lobbyists and other special interests. Neither party was ready for change, although the assassination of President Garfield prompted civil service reform.

Concepts to Understand

★ How the spoils system and lobbyists fostered **corruption** in government

★ How **public protest** by a free press worked to end political corruption

Read to Discover . . .

★ the major forms of political corruption.

★ new forms of leisure pastimes and amusements that attracted the interest of Americans before 1900.

Journal Notes

As you read the chapter, note the types of corruption and questionable ethics in government during the Gilded Age.

HISTORY Online

Chapter Overview
Visit the *American History: The Modern Era Since 1865* Web site at **me.glencoe.com** and click on *Chapter 10—Chapter Overviews* to preview chapter information.

CULTURAL

• **1873** *One of the first schools of nursing opens at Bellevue Hospital in New York*

• **1876** *National Baseball League formed*
• **1883** *Joseph Pulitzer buys the* New York World

| 1865 | 1875 |

POLITICAL

• **1872** *Crédit Mobilier scheme uncovered*

• **1883** *Pendleton Act passes*
• **1884** *Cleveland elected President*

Sunset Hour on the West Lagoon
by Williard L. Metcalf

This painting depicts a scene at Chicago's first world's fair, the Columbian Exposition of 1893. The striking beauty of the buildings and grounds spurred beautification programs in many cities.

◀ CROQUET DRESS, LATE 1800s

• **1890** *Reporter Nelly Bly circles globe by train and steamship in 72 days*

• **1895** *William Randolph Hearst purchases the* New York Morning Journal

1885	1895

• **1890** *McKinley Tariff passes*

• **1896** *McKinley elected President*

★★★★★★★★★★★★★★★★★★★★★★★★★★★★★★★★★★★★

A Tarnished Image

Guide to Reading

Main Idea

During the late 1800s, political scandals plagued many city governments as corrupt politicians sought to increase their wealth and power.

Reading Strategy

Organizing Information As you read about politics' tarnished image, use a diagram such as the one shown here to list causes of increased political corruption during this period on the diagonal lines.

Corruption

Objectives

After studying this section, you should be able to

★ identify the major causes of increased political corruption.

★ give examples of corruption at local, state, and national levels.

Key Terms

graft, political machine, kickback, ward, lobbyist, township

BOSS WILLIAM TWEED ▶

The Gilded Age was a phrase coined by two authors of the period—Mark Twain and Charles Dudley Warner—in a novel about the corruption of the Grant administration. In the years following the Civil War, the quality of American government left much to be desired. Politicians were irresponsible, loyalties were shallow, and money was tainted.

In this post-Civil War period, the most ambitious and talented people were no longer attracted to politics but to business. Indeed, politics itself became something of a business. The goal of political entrepreneurs was to achieve power and position through political office. Often politicians were able to line their pockets with money. Corruption seemed to flourish at every level of government. At first the corruption was not apparent. Material progress had produced a society that appeared to be bright and attractive. Society and government were not what they appeared to be on the surface, however.

■ Political Machines

Some of the most outrageous examples of **graft,** or thievery in office, were those at the grassroots level of city government. A factor that contributed to corrupt city government was the rapid growth of cities.

Growth of Cities

In 1840 there were only 131 cities in the United States; by 1880 there were 939. In addition cities often doubled, tripled, or even quadrupled in size within a decade. Services for these large populations had to be expanded at a rate never experienced before. Providing increased police and fire protection, water supplies, and sewage disposal was a daunting task for what often were untrained and ill-paid city officials. At the same time, businesses were eager to get lucrative contracts for paving streets and building new schools. An alliance between business and politics that fostered corruption resulted.

Maintaining Control

The usual democratic restraints on abuses of power did not work well in the cities of this era. Large portions of the population of cities were immigrants who had little or no experience with urban living or with democratic government. Many were accustomed to corruption in government. Both poor immigrants and native-born residents had little time to worry about abstract notions of government. They worked from dawn to dusk just to keep food on the table. Those more well-off, who might have gone into politics, were busy making money in business and real estate. As a result, almost every major city was dominated by a **political machine**—a party-linked political organization that maintained power by controlling votes, controlling the courts, and controlling the police as well.

The strength of a political machine came from the bottom up, not from the top down. Local politicians took care of the needs of their voters. They often provided groceries to families who were needy, organized free celebrations on important national holidays, attended ethnic religious and social events, and even helped get people out of jail. In this way politicians earned the loyalty of their neighborhood citizens. When election time came around, the votes were always there, keeping the helpful politicians in power.

The "Tweed Ring"

The most notorious city machine was the "Tweed Ring" in New York City. In 1868 "Boss" William M. Tweed gained control of New York's Democratic machine, known locally by the name of its central meeting place—Tammany Hall. For the next 3 years, he and his underlings managed to steal millions of dollars of city funds. The usual way this was done involved a process known as the "kickback." A **kickback** was an arrangement whereby contractors would pad, or increase, the amount of their bills for city work and pay or "kick back" a percentage of that amount to politicians in the ring. In one example a county courthouse that should

▲ THE TRUSTS Powerful trusts dominate the United States Senate in this 1889 cartoon by Joseph Keppler. The people's entrance to the Senate chambers (upper left) is shown bolted shut. *How did the trusts influence senators?*

Visualizing History

▲ **Nast and Tweed** Thomas Nast (left) entertained Americans with biting political cartoons in the late 1800s. The most well-known political machine was run by "Boss" William M. Tweed (right). ***Why did corruption in the federal government spread during the Grant administration?***

have cost taxpayers $250,000 actually cost $11 million. One plastering contractor was paid almost $3 million for 9 months' work.

In 1871 the *New York Times* published evidence of Tweed's rampant greed. At the same time, Thomas Nast, a brilliant political cartoonist, ridiculed Tweed in his cartoons for *Harper's Weekly.* Nast's cartoons found their mark and were devastating. Tweed was driven to complain: "I don't care a straw for your newspaper articles: my people don't know how to read, but they can't help seeing them . . . pictures." Tweed and his cronies were convicted of criminal conduct and driven from office.

Footnotes to History

The National Equal Rights Party New parties entered the political scene during this era. In 1884 suffragist leaders formed the National Equal Rights party. The party convention chose as its presidential candidate Belva A. Lockwood, a noted attorney and the first woman admitted to practice before the Supreme Court. Renominated in 1888, Lockwood was the first woman candidate for the presidency.

In spite of Tweed's removal, Tammany Hall continued to be an active influence in New York politics. This was true because local machine leaders drew their power from the local neighborhoods that they served 24 hours a day. A good deal of the graft, however, was used to help needy residents of the neighborhood **wards,** small administrative divisions of a city.

Occasionally city graft became so flagrant that voters were driven to "throw the rascals out" and put in a reform administration. Such movements often failed. Reform candidates focused on economy and honest administration but failed to understand the reasons why the political machines commandeered so much loyalty and met with such success.

Widespread Corruption

Corruption was not limited to local governments. It also occurred at the state and federal levels. In addition to the corruption, government in the late 1800s was affected by a marked lack of leadership. Neither Congress nor the President provided the direction the nation needed.

In State Government

Politics at the state level was nearly as corrupt as in the cities. In many states big business stood to gain or lose large amounts of money as a result of legislative votes on various matters, such as tax rates and internal improvements. Thus, companies spent large sums to influence votes.

In pre-Civil War times, businesspeople influenced politicians by writing letters and inviting them to expensive dinners. After the war the demands on government increased to the point that the amount of money spent by state governments was huge, and the stakes for those seeking state contracts were high. Businesses now began to employ **lobbyists**—people paid to represent a company or a special interest group. Sometimes they tried to influence votes by offering money in the form of campaign contributions. If it was unclear who would win a race, contributions were given to both parties. Such payments were regarded by legislators and lobbyists alike as "insurance" against unfavorable legislation.

At other times money was offered in the form of outright bribes. When Jay Gould controlled the Erie Railroad, he was reported to have spent $500,000 in bribes during a single session of the New York state legislature. Of the relations between the Standard Oil Company and the government of Pennsylvania, one observer wrote, "The Standard has done everything with the Pennsylvania legislature except to refine it."

In Federal Government

In general there was more corruption in state and local politics than in national politics. By far the worst misconduct in the federal government occurred when Grant was President.

Grant had been a great general, but he was a poor President. Although he was personally honest, he seemed unable to distinguish decent people from the dishonest. Dazzled by wealth, he fell under the sway of financial speculators James J. Fisk and Jay Gould, who reaped millions of dollars from their relationship with the President. Members of Grant's family, personal staff, and cabinet peddled influence and jobs in return for cash. At one time Grant's brother managed to hold four jobs by farming out the duties to other men.

Crédit Mobilier

In 1872 the scandals spread to Congress as well. A New York newspaper revealed that officers of the Union Pacific Railroad had formed their own construction company called the Crédit Mobilier. The contracts this company received enabled the railroad officers to reap enormous personal profits. To forestall investigation, the company distributed shares of stock "where it would do the most good." Grant's Vice President and several prominent members of Congress turned out to have accepted these thinly disguised bribes.

When the graft in his administration was uncovered, Grant declared that he would "let no guilty man escape." However, he

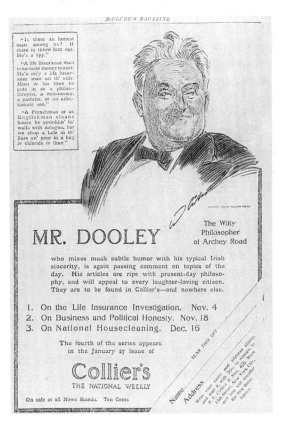

▲ **Mr. Dooley** Humorist Finley Peter Dunne's creation, Mr. Dooley, was a shrewd observer of political events. *Which political party were new immigrants likely to join?*

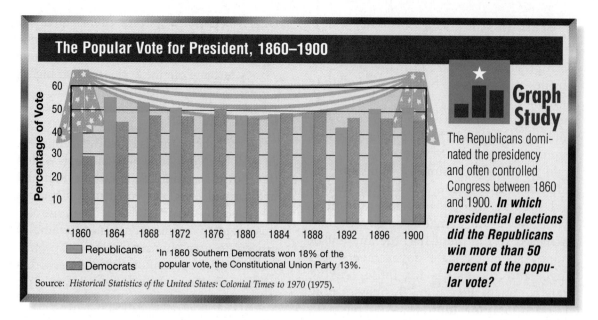

The Popular Vote for President, 1860–1900

Percentage of Vote

*1860 1864 1868 1872 1876 1880 1884 1888 1892 1896 1900

Republicans

Democrats

*In 1860 Southern Democrats won 18% of the popular vote, the Constitutional Union Party 13%.

Source: *Historical Statistics of the United States: Colonial Times to 1970* (1975).

Graph Study

The Republicans dominated the presidency and often controlled Congress between 1860 and 1900. *In which presidential elections did the Republicans win more than 50 percent of the popular vote?*

protected many accused of wrongdoing from both investigation and punishment.

■ Postwar Political Parties

Even political analysts often found it difficult to explain the positions Democrats and Republicans took on major issues such as the tariff and railroad regulation. English writer James Bryce wrote:

> *Neither party has, as a party, anything to say on these issues, neither party has any clean-cut principles. . . . All has been lost except office or the hope of it.*

Issues Split Parties

One reason that parties seemed so similar was that they both reflected sectional differences so accurately. At every level, from wards to **townships,** or smaller divisions of a county broken up into local government districts, political parties were popular, and democratic participation was high. They did not avoid any of the issues; rather they were split internally on most of them. In the Northeast, for example, with its strong banking system, both parties favored the gold standard. In the Midwest both parties favored increasing the amount of money in circulation. Republicans in the developing Midwest were protariff, while Southern

Democrats were antitariff. Both parties in the Northeast were divided on the tariff issue.

The humorist "Mr. Dooley," created by Finley Peter Dunne, described a hypothetical candidate for President as someone who was pulled in different directions by varied interests and needed to be all things to all people.

> *Wanted: a good, active Dimmy-crat, sthrong iv lung an' limb; must be . . . a sympathizer with th' crushed an' down throdden people but not be anny means hostile to vested inthrests; must advocate sthrikes, gover'mint be injunction, free silver, sound money, greenbacks, a single tax, a tariff f'r rivinoo . . . at home in Wall sthreet an' th' stock yards, in th' parlors iv th' r-rich an' th' kitchens iv th' poor.*

Although fairly evenly matched in strength, the two parties were hardly identical. Though both parties received support from people in every walk of life, each had a distinctive base of support.

Republicans

The Republicans were supported by Western farmers and merchants, who benefited from Republicans' internal improvements and liberal land policies, and Eastern businesspeople, who benefited from high tariffs and national banks. The Republicans tended to be old-immigrant Protestants—Presbyterians, Methodists, Congregationalists, or Baptists. The Republicans' problem was to keep together its Eastern and Western wings, which differed on such issues as greenbacks, free silver, tariffs, and banking.

The Republicans' "patron saint" was Abraham Lincoln. As the party that had led during the Civil War, they had great prestige in the North and the West. "The party that saved the nation must rule it," they proclaimed.

While critics attacked the Republicans for keeping alive war hatreds by "waving the bloody shirt," appeals to the memory of the Civil War were much more than that. Republican strength came from genuine devotion to the idea of the United States as a nation rather than as a federation of states. Many Republicans continued to be inspired by the party's early idealism. They felt that government existed to advance the public good.

Democrats

Democrats, too, looked back to the Civil War. From the end of Radical Reconstruction until well into the twentieth century, Southern states formed the "Solid South," never wavering in its allegiance to the Democrats.

The Democrats could not have remained a national party with only Southern support, however. The party depended on an alliance between white Southerners and Northern city machines. Democrats tended to get the support of recent immigrants, many of whom were Catholics or liturgical Protestants, such as Lutherans or Episcopalians. Their religious and cultural background was quite different from that of evangelical Protestants, such as Methodists and Baptists, who formed the core of the Republican party. The Democrats had allies among Western farmers, especially when crop prices were low, and among certain groups of businesspeople and owners of import companies who favored a lower tariff.

The Democratic party had two "patron saints"—Thomas Jefferson and Andrew Jackson. Like these leaders the Democrats claimed to represent the interests of ordinary Americans. In contrast to the Republicans' view that the federal government should take an active role in helping the needy and shaping national growth, the Democrats wanted to keep the federal government on a skimpy allowance and a short leash. "That government governs best which governs least" remained their motto.

During the entire period from 1865 to 1900, Democrats held the presidency for only two terms. Although they usually lost the White House, the Democrats were seldom far out of the running. Democratic candidates often got almost as many popular votes as their victorious opponents, and it was rare that the Republicans did not have to deal with Democrats in control of at least one house of Congress.

Section 1 ★ Assessment

Checking for Understanding

1. **Define** graft, political machine, kickback, ward, lobbyist, township.

2. **State** how the Republican and Democratic parties differed concerning the role of the federal government.

Critical Thinking

3. **Summarizing** Re-create the diagram shown here, and list examples of corruption that existed in government.

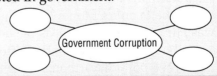

Government Corruption

INTERDISCIPLINARY ACTIVITY

4. **Government** Assume the role of an American living in one of the nation's largest cities during the late 1800s. Write a letter to the mayor of your city expressing your concerns over overcrowdedness.

Interpreting Political Cartoons

Political cartoons are drawings that express a favorable or unfavorable opinion or point of view. They usually focus on public figures, political events, or economic or social conditions. Benjamin Franklin reportedly drew the first American editorial cartoon in 1754. Since that time, the editorial cartoon has been a regular part of most newspapers.

▲ *WHO STOLE THE PEOPLE'S MONEY? 'TWAS HIM.*

Learning the Skill

Editorial cartoons reveal a glimpse of the past. They show how a character or an event was viewed at the time it was drawn.

Each cartoon contains useful clues to its meaning. These clues may come from labels or captions, the appearance and action of figures, or the use of symbols—pictures that represent ideas or concepts.

The creator of this cartoon, Thomas Nast, pioneered the use of cartoons to comment on significant political issues of the day. None of William "Boss" Tweed's critics leveled more scathing attacks at his notorious Tammany Hall machine than did Nast. In this cartoon, "Who Stole the People's Money?" the answer is "'Twas Him." Tweed appears as the heavy-set man in the left foreground of the cartoon.

To interpret a political cartoon, follow these steps:

• **Read** the caption and any other words printed in the cartoon.
• **Analyze** each element in the cartoon.
• **Identify** the clues. What is happening in the cartoon? Who or what is represented by each part of the drawing? What or who do the figures represent? To what do the symbols refer? Studying the clues helps you to understand the cartoonist's point.
• **Synthesize** these elements to decide the point the cartoonist is making.

Practicing the Skill

1. What is going on in this picture?
2. What words give clues to the cartoon's meaning?
3. What symbols are depicted? What do these symbols represent?
4. What point is the cartoonist making?

 Glencoe's **Skillbuilder Interactive Workbook, Level 2** provides instruction and practice in key social studies skills.

APPLYING THE SKILL

5. Cut out and mount on construction paper a series of current political cartoons. Write down the message of each cartoon.

★★★

Calls for Good Government

Guide to Reading

Main Idea

Amid calls from reformers to clean up government, a slow and steady movement away from political abuse began.

Reading Strategy

Sequencing Information   As you read about attempts at government reform, create a time line like the one shown here to list key events relating to the reform of government. Use the dates provided as a guide.

1877 ————————————————————— 1883
      └—————————————————————┘
                            1884

Objectives

After studying this section, you should be able to

★ identify the reforms made during the 1870s and the 1880s.

★ describe the tariff controversy.

Key Terms

patronage, rider, free-trader, protectionist

STATE POLITICAL PARTY BANNER, 1890s ▶

---

efore the administration of Rutherford B. Hayes, one of the common practices had been **patronage**—the assumed right of elected officials to control political appointments to unelected positions. Patronage employees made the federal government the epitome of apathy and astonishingly idle.

 GOVERNMENT
■ Civil Service Reforms

With the election of Hayes, a spirit of reform entered the White House.

Hayes Begins Reforms

After his inauguration in 1877, Hayes named Carl Schurz, owner of a German-language newspaper in St. Louis, Missouri, and United States senator from Missouri, to take charge of the Department of the Interior, which had previously been the scene of some of the worst examples of patronage. This practice was soon curbed. Hayes also forbade the practice of "shaking down" federal workers—forcing them to make political campaign contributions.

Hayes also defied congressional leaders by blocking important appointments favored by individual members of Congress. In addition he refused to sign otherwise acceptable legislation if Congress had attached **riders**—irrelevant amendments—of which he disapproved. He vetoed several appropriations bills with riders attached and finally won a clear-cut victory. Through his actions Hayes not only cut down on corruption but began to restore the balance of power between Congress and the President.

Election of 1880

Hayes's reforms brought him enemies among the Stalwarts, a group of Republican machine politicians who strongly opposed civil service reform. After Hayes declined to run for a second term, the party became divided between the Stalwarts, who wanted to nominate Grant for a third term, and the "Halfbreeds," who opposed Grant. After a prolonged deadlock at the national convention, the Republicans nominated dark horse James A. Garfield, a former Union general.

To blunt the old charge of disloyalty in wartime, the Democrats nominated General Winfield S. Hancock, a Union hero of the Battle of Gettysburg. The intellectual level of the ensuing campaign may be judged by the following excerpt from the speech of a Republican orator:

> *I belong to a party that believes in good crops; that is glad when a fellow finds a gold mine; that rejoices when there are forty bushels of wheat to the acre. . . . [T]he Democratic party is a party of famine; it is a good friend of an early frost; it believes in the Colorado beetle and in the weevil.*

Despite such inflammatory rhetoric, Garfield narrowly won the election by a margin of less than 10,000 votes.

The Pendleton Act

Under Hayes and Garfield, government was cleaner than it had been during the Grant administration, but the spoils system remained a constant source of inefficiency and graft. Disputes over patronage poisoned the relationship between the President and Congress. There was little momentum for reform.

In July 1881, however, as President Garfield entered the Washington, D.C., railroad station, he was shot by a disappointed office seeker. The unbalanced man cried, "I am a Stalwart and Arthur is President now." Garfield clung to life for two months, but in September Vice President Chester A. Arthur, a New York Stalwart, succeeded to the presidency.

Garfield's assassination excited opinion against the spoils system. In 1883 Congress passed the Pendleton Act, which has been called (with some exaggeration) "the Magna Carta of civil service reform." This law allowed the President to decree which federal jobs would be filled according to rules set by a bipartisan Civil Service Commission.

Visualizing History

▲ **ASSASSINATION OF THE PRESIDENT** President Garfield was shot only four months after his inauguration by a frustrated patronage seeker, Charles J. Guiteau. The assassination raised a cry against the spoils system. ***After Garfield's death, who became President?***

Susan B. Anthony
1820–1906

From her Quaker upbringing, Susan B. Anthony learned that men and women were equal before God. She spent most of her 86 years trying to convince others of that equality.

After teaching school for several years, Anthony returned home to help run the family farm. While living in her father's house, she began to focus on the great reform movements of the day. Anthony first joined a temperance group and experienced gender discrimination firsthand when she was refused permission to speak at a temperance rally. Realizing that as long as women were propertyless and voteless they would also remain powerless, Anthony began devoting her considerable energies to securing equal rights for women. Throughout the four decades from the end of the Civil War to her death, she was the nation's foremost crusader for a woman's right to vote.

Candidates competed for these jobs through examinations. Appointments could be made only from the list of those who took the exams. A civil service official could not be removed for political reasons.

Although President Arthur was a veteran of machine politics, he supported the Pendleton Act, placing 14,000 jobs (about one-tenth of the total) under the control of the civil service. The federal government had finally begun a shift away from the spoils system.

Cleveland in Office

The reform movement begun by Hayes and continued by Garfield and Arthur did not stop. Thus, the major theme of the presidential election of 1884 was honesty in politics.

Election of 1884

The Republican nominee, Representative James G. Blaine, was a man of great ability and personal charm. However, his reputation was clouded by charges that he had taken money for helping a railroad. As a result some independent reformers in the Republican party, called "Mugwumps," did not support him. The Democrats won Mugwump support by nominating Grover Cleveland, who earned a reputation for integrity as mayor of Buffalo and governor of New York.

The campaign of 1884 was a negative one, focusing less on issues and more on character assassination. Blaine was portrayed as a "tattooed man" with railroad stocks and bonds indelibly engraved on his skin. Cleveland was attacked on the grounds that he had hired a substitute to fight for him in the Civil War and that he had fathered an illegitimate child. Republicans chanted:

> Ma! Ma! Where's my pa?
> Gone to the White House,
> Ha! Ha! Ha!

To which the Democrats countered:

> Blaine, Blaine, James G. Blaine,
> The continental liar from the
> State of Maine.

Cleveland won the election by a narrow margin, becoming the first Democratic President elected since 1856. Balloting in New York was close. Had 600 voters switched to Blaine, he would have won the state—and the presidency. The Republicans retained control of the Senate, but the Democrats gained a majority in the House of Representatives.

▲ GROVER CLEVELAND

Reforms Continue

Unskillful in political maneuvering, Cleveland often met defeat in his dealings with Congress. Nevertheless, his devotion to the public good did much to restore the prestige of the presidency. Cleveland's first problem was to deal with the Democratic office seekers who swarmed to Washington seeking the fruits of his victory. If he were to make appointments on merit alone, he would split his party wide open. If he were to give in to the spoils system, he would lose the support of the Mugwumps and other reformers who had played a decisive part in electing him. As a compromise Cleveland appointed many "deserving Democrats" to office. He also made every effort to see that the new appointees were qualified.

Cleveland entered office with a weak understanding of most national issues but worked intensely at the job. Few Presidents have put in more study to determine what course of action to follow. His Republican predecessors, for example, had signed hundreds of private bills giving pensions to veterans unable to qualify under regular laws. Examining such bills with care, Cleveland found many of them fraudulent. One veteran, for example, asked for a pension for an injury suffered while *intending* to enlist. Cleveland disapproved of so many pension bills that his vetoes totaled more than those of all previous Presidents.

Cleveland worked to improve government efficiency and integrity. He supported the Presidential Succession Act, which established a line of succession to the presidency in the event of the death of the Vice President. He also won repeal of the Tenure of Office Act, which strengthened presidential independence. Interested in preserving public lands, Cleveland reclaimed land from private companies that had not lived up to the terms of their land grants.

$ ECONOMICS

■ Tariffs and the Election of 1888

The public question that Cleveland studied most seriously was the tariff. During the Civil War, duties had been raised from an

▼ POLITICAL CARTOON ON 1888 CAMPAIGN

average of 19 percent in 1861 to more than 40 percent in 1865.

Different Views on Tariffs

High tariff rates, which benefited manufacturers, were constantly attacked by farmers, consumers, shippers, and importers. These **free-traders** argued that a protective tariff was unfair government interference with the normal laws of supply and demand. Tariffs, they said, were subsidies paid to manufacturers out of the pockets of consumers.

Protectionists, on the other hand, defended the tariff as a means of nurturing fledgling industries in the United States. They argued that tariffs kept wages high by shielding them from competition with cheap foreign labor. Previous bills to lower the tariff had been defeated.

Shortly after Cleveland took office, Carl Schurz asked him about his views on the tariff issue. "You know I really don't know anything about it," replied the President. Cleveland investigated the problem thoroughly. His studies convinced him that the existing tariff was responsible for the treasury's large surplus. Cleveland argued that the surplus was a sign of overtaxation. He proposed a reduction of the tariff—not because he was a free-trader, but because he was in favor of limited government. Excess money in the treasury, he said, was not good for the economy; it was a temptation to Congress, which was apt to spend it wastefully. The President's dramatic effort to lower the tariff was blocked by House Republicans.

Harrison Elected President

The tariff became the major issue in the presidential election of 1888. Openly avowing protection for the first time, the Republicans collected a record-breaking campaign fund. "Put all the manufacturers of Pennsylvania under the fire," said a Republican campaign manager, "and fry that fat out of them." The Republicans revived Henry Clay's name for the protective tariff, calling their economic program the "American system." Renominating Cleveland, the Democrats campaigned against unnecessary taxation. As in 1880 and 1884, the result was

extremely close. Although he got fewer popular votes than Cleveland, the Republican candidate, Benjamin Harrison, won a majority in the electoral college.

The new President was a quiet, reserved man, whom one observer called a "human iceberg." Harrison was too reserved to make a good Gilded Age politician. Still, he had an able legal mind and a distinguished career as an attorney in Indiana. He had been elected to the Senate in 1881.

Harrison had fought under Sherman at Atlanta and was not shy about "waving the bloody shirt" for votes. An ardent protectionist, he was conservative in fiscal policy and liberal when it came to veterans' pensions.

Treasury Surplus and the Tariffs

Once in office the Republicans promptly disposed of the treasury surplus by spending it, and it was the last time in history that the government held a surplus. Within two years the "Billion-Dollar Congress" had

 Visualizing History

▲ **PRESIDENT HARRISON** Unlike Cleveland before him, President Benjamin Harrison favored attempts to freely spend the mounting treasury surplus. *How long did it take the "Billion-Dollar Congress" to convert the surplus into a deficit?*

created a deficit, mostly through handouts to special-interest groups. The number of Civil War pensioners increased by more than half—many of them the same ones whom Cleveland had turned down.

Moving on to the election-winning tariff issue, the Republicans passed the McKinley Tariff of 1890, which was the highest in the country's history. It dried up revenue by levying rates so high that some foreign products were kept entirely out of the country.

Nearly every foreign product that competed with American-made products was heavily taxed, including such items as food, clothing, furniture, and tools. Western silver states supported the tariff in exchange for the passage of the Sherman Silver Purchase Act, which authorized the federal government to buy up 4.5 million ounces of silver a month.

Millions of dollars were spent on the improvement of waterways, coastal defenses, federal buildings, and naval expansion. Congress also passed the Sherman Antitrust Act and provided for admission to the Union of North and South Dakota, Montana, Washington, Idaho, and Wyoming. $

Several Issues Hurt Republicans

The Republicans' position on protective tariffs, which had helped them win the presidency in 1888, hurt them two years later. Because there was little competition in the market, prices generally were falling; thus, debts were harder to repay.

Republicans also were hurt nationally by local Republicans in such states as Wisconsin and Massachusetts, who supported compulsory school attendance where instruction was in English. Many Catholic and Lutheran immigrant families in these states wanted public funding for their parochial schools, in which students were taught in their first language. Republicans also pushed Prohibition at the grassroots level.

Democrats used these issues, together with that of a backfiring tariff, to attack the Republicans. The congressional elections of 1890 resulted in a Democratic landslide.

By 1892 the Republicans' position was even worse. Dispiritedly, they renominated Harrison, and the Democrats nominated Grover Cleveland again. Popular discontent with the Republicans was so high that for the first time since before the Civil War Democrats won not only the White House but both houses of Congress.

This time, however, Cleveland won by more than 350,000 popular votes and an electoral majority of 277 to 145. Cleveland became the only President in American history to serve two nonconsecutive terms.

Of larger importance than Cleveland's margin of victory was the support given to a third-party candidate, James B. Weaver. Weaver, who had been the candidate for the Greenback party in 1880, ran in 1892 under the banner of the new People's party, better known as the Populist party. By this time, many Americans were already responding to the Populist philosophy.

Section 2 ★ Assessment

Checking for Understanding

1. **Define** patronage, rider, free-trader, protectionist.

2. **Explain** the controversy over raising or lowering the tariff.

Critical Thinking

3. **Evaluating Reforms** How could the civil service system limit the patronage system and cut down on corruption?

4. **Analyzing Issues** Re-create the chart shown here, and describe the political reforms made during the 1870s and 1880s.

Political Reforms

INTERDISCIPLINARY ACTIVITY

5. **Government** Prepare a time line showing the Presidents of the United States from 1876 to 1900.

★★★★★★★★★★★★★★★★★★★★★★★★

Cultural Life

THE BATH BY MARY CASSATT ▶

Guide to Reading

Main Idea

America's cultural scene changed rapidly after the Civil War.

Reading Strategy

Organizing Information As you read about cultural life in America, use a diagram such as the one shown to list the kinds of recreations Americans pursued during this era.

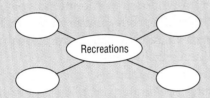

Recreations

Objectives

After studying this section, you should be able to

★ discuss developments in literature, art, and higher education.

★ describe how various leisure activities expanded.

Key Terms

antebellum, realism, expatriate, yellow journalism

---

he United States was quickly becoming an urban, industrialized society. It needed citizens who could understand complex political and economic questions, and it needed literate workers and managers who could staff its offices, shops, and factories.

■ Education

In the late nineteenth century, the nation reformed its educational system. Public education and higher education benefited from the reforms.

Public Education

By 1900 many states had or were working toward compulsory school attendance. In cities, graded schools replaced one-room schoolhouses. The school year, which had traditionally been squeezed in between fall harvest and spring planting, was lengthened. Many cities also introduced free secondary education, and the number of public high schools increased from a few hundred in 1860 to more than 2,500 in 1890. Yet there remained much room for improvement. In 1900 the average child received only 5 years of schooling.

Private Colleges and Universities

The most far-reaching development in education during the late 1800s was the expansion of higher education. At mid-century most colleges and universities in the United States had poor equipment, scanty libraries, and ill-trained, overworked faculties. Fixed curricula that emphasized ancient Greek and Roman thought included little training in modern languages, history, or science. There were no first-rate graduate schools in law, medicine, or the liberal arts. No American scientific school compared well with the best in Europe.

By 1900 these weaknesses had been vigorously attacked. Responding to the need for more practical education, colleges in the United States reformed their fields of study. Courses in the social and natural sciences were made available, and the elective system, first introduced at Harvard, made it possible for students to choose an individual course of study.

Young scholars from the United States who were trained in the world's best universities—in Germany—brought back higher standards of scholarship and scientific research. Existing private universities were greatly expanded, and new ones were founded—most with the aid of wealthy businesspeople who supported the trend toward making education more useful. More than two dozen new schools were devoted specifically to technical training. The Massachusetts Institute of Technology and others like it supplied industry with highly trained engineers, metallurgists, and chemists. Also during this period the first graduate schools of business, such as the Wharton School of Finance, were established.

State Universities

Along with the growth of privately endowed universities and technical schools came an expansion of state universities. Such institutions owed a great deal to the Morrill Act of 1862, which gave public lands to each state as a grant to finance the endowment of colleges. While the main goal of these schools was to extend knowledge of "agriculture and mechanic arts," they were funded to teach science and classical studies as well. The University of California, Texas A&M, and most of the large state universities of the Midwest began as land-grant colleges.

Universities in the Midwest also played an important role in opening higher education to women for the first time. In the pre-Civil War era, women had been admitted to Oberlin and Antioch colleges in Ohio. After the war, coeducation became common west of the Appalachians. In the more conservative East, women founded private colleges of their own, such as Mount Holyoke, Vassar, Smith, Radcliffe, and Bryn Mawr. These colleges shared the same educational goals as all-male institutions.

The adult public also cried out for more learning. Beginning in 1874 as a summer program to train Sunday school teachers, the

History AND ART

▲ *SNAP THE WHIP* by Winslow Homer, 1872 Winslow Homer's painting captures the joy of a school recess. Homer is known for his vivid use of color and attention to detail. *What subjects did realist artists seek to portray?*

Linking Past and Present

The Summer Olympic Games

The first Olympics were held in 776 B.C. to celebrate amateur sports. Resumed in 1896, the first modern games were held in Athens, Greece.

Then

The First Modern Games

The first Olympic Games of the present cycle were held in the rebuilt stadium of Athens. Nearly 290 athletes representing 13 nations participated. The American team dominated the track and field events, winning 9 of the 11

events. Thomas Burke captured the 100-meter dash with a time of 12 seconds. Ellery Clark set the high jump standard at 5'11" and James Connolly's 45' was the best mark for the triple jump. The Games proved a success, and organizers made plans to hold the Games in Paris in 1900.

Now

Bigger, Stronger, and Faster

After a century, the Olympic Games bear little resemblance to the games of 1896. Men and women athletes representing 197 nations competed in 271 events at the Atlanta Games in 1996. Modern performances leave little doubt that today's athletes are stronger and faster. Donovan Bailey of

▲ FLORENCE GRIFFITH-JOYNER

Canada holds the Olympic record for 100 meters with a time of 9.84. Florence Griffith-Joyner of the United States holds the women's record with 10.49 seconds. High jump competitors regularly clear 7' and more. The record for the triple jump is over 60'.

▲ ATHLETE AT THE FIRST MODERN GAMES

Chautauqua (shuh•TAW•kwuh) Institute in western New York sparked a movement that provided the masses with instruction in such subjects as literature, economics, science, and government through summer school instruction and correspondence school.

■ Literature

United States writers responded to the post-Civil War era in different ways. One popular school of postwar writers looked backward, striving to capture the romance of vanishing rural traditions. A center of such "local-color" writing was the South. Civil War and Reconstruction had swept away an entire way of life, leaving poverty and destruction in its wake. In the 1870s and the 1880s, Southern local colorists wrote nostalgically about **antebellum**—or pre-Civil War—manners, customs, and institutions.

Local colorists also wrote of vanishing ways of life in the small towns and fishing villages of New England, on the farms of the Midwest, on the ranches of the plains, and in the mining camps and boomtowns of the Wild West.

One of America's greatest writers was a local colorist named Samuel Clemens who wrote under the name Mark Twain. Twain wrote vivid and hilarious stories about his travels in the West. His most enduring works—*The Adventures of Tom Sawyer* and *The Adventures of Huckleberry Finn*—are tales of his boyhood home on the Mississippi River. Twain's books were not only acclaimed by critics but loved by the public. He combined shrewd observation and irreverent wit.

Twain's writing bridged the gap between popular and highbrow literature, between ordinary local-color writing and **realism,** a European-influenced movement that strove for accurate representation.

Realist writers wanted to get away from the emotional preoccupations of the romantic movement and the pretty, sentimental themes of popular literature. Realist writers took a close look at real people's lives and problems. William Dean Howells declared that novels should "speak the dialect, the language, that most Americans know." In *The Rise of Silas Lapham*, Howells depicted a crude but likable bumpkin—the new American millionaire. In *The Red Badge of Courage*, Stephen Crane depicted a Union soldier's fear and cowardice under fire. Other realists exposed the seamy underside of urban life. Critics of realism argued that realistic fiction was not uplifting, that its subject matter was often ordinary or even ugly, and that its characters' misdeeds were not always suitably punished.

History AND ART

▲ *The Little White Girl* by James Abbott McNeill Whistler, 1864 James Whistler adapted the concepts of Japanese color prints to his own style. **What subjects did realist artists seek to portray?**

■ Art and Architecture

Realism was also an important force in American painting during the Gilded Age. Rejecting the classicism and romanticism of the first half of the century, realist painters portrayed ordinary people in everyday activities. Winslow Homer moved from painting Civil War scenes to subjects such as a schoolyard full of boys playing a rowdy game, a hunter and his dogs, or sailors at sea. Of another great realist painter, Walt Whitman said:

❝ *I never knew of but one artist, and that's Tom Eakins, who could resist the temptation to see what they thought ought to be rather than what is.* ❞

Some of America's greatest painters, however, became **expatriates**—people who choose to live outside their native country. John Singer Sargent, a portraitist of Europe's upper classes, lived in England. James Abbott McNeill Whistler and Mary Cassatt also lived in Europe. Cassatt was influenced by a style of painting called impressionism. Impressionists tried to capture the play of light, color, and pattern as they made immediate impressions on the senses.

The architecture of the Gilded Age was heavy and ornate. It is often called "Victorian," after Queen Victoria of Great Britain who reigned from 1837 to 1901. On the outside, Victorian houses had turrets, towers, porches, and gables. The development of better woodworking machines made it possible to add elaborate "gingerbread" decorations to roofs and porches of houses. The interior decor was similarly ornamented. Rooms were crowded with dark, thickly carved furniture, plush carpeting, heavy curtains, and countless knickknacks on ornate shelves.

Some dismissed the Victorian style as vulgar—a symbol of greed that characterized the Gilded Age. Others have celebrated the gaudiness as a symbol of the period's vitality and exuberance.

■ The Yellow Press and the Dime Novel

The Industrial Revolution brought some Americans unaccustomed leisure time. As machines took over the work of more and more hands, the time required to produce a shirt, a bucket, a pin, or a table was reduced to a fraction of what it had been. Hours of work, although still long by the standards of the twentieth century, were gradually reduced. As leisure time increased, new forms of entertainment developed.

◄ JOURNALIST NELLY BLY

Penny Newspapers

Journalism took new forms. In the late 1800s, improvements in papermaking and printing made it possible to produce newspapers more cheaply than before. At the same time, newspapers could make their profits entirely from advertisers. Copies were sold below cost to attract the greatest number of readers. These penny newspapers strove to amuse readers as much as to inform them. Their intended audience was not the educated middle and upper classes but clerks, laborers, and homemakers.

The pioneer among the penny newspapers was the *New York World*, purchased by Joseph Pulitzer in 1883. In 15 years its circulation rose from 15,000 to more than 1 million. Pulitzer, dedicating his paper "to the cause of the people rather than the purse-proud potentates," attacked unfair employers and grafting politicians with vigor. The real source of Pulitzer's success, however, was not politics but sensationalism. He was one of the first to use "scare headlines" like "Baptized in Blood" and "Death Rides the Rails." He also introduced the colorized Sunday supplement and the serialized comic strip. From the yellow ink he used in his comics came the term **"yellow journalism,"** which critics applied to the subject matter and style of the *World* and all its imitators. If he could not find news, Pulitzer made it. Once he sent a young reporter, Nelly Bly, to travel around the globe in less time than it took the hero of Jules Verne's popular novel, *Around the World in Eighty Days.*

Dime Novels

Another form of reading matter produced for a mass market was the dime novel, which was designed especially to interest boys. These were adventure stories where heroes such as Mustang Sam and Deadwood Dick fought cattle rustlers and outlaws. Dime novels also portrayed the worlds of business and crime. Moralists suspected that these early paperbacks would corrupt the young. Defenders pointed out, however, that because dime novels were not the work of realists, no bad deed ever went unpunished; no good boy went without his just reward.

Footnotes to History

The Appeal of the Gridiron Football became a popular spectator sport during the Gilded Age, with college competition proving to be the biggest draw. Rutgers and Princeton played in the first collegiate contest in 1869. Throughout the late 1800s, three big eastern universities—Harvard, Yale, and Princeton—dominated the sport.

HISTORY Online

Student Web Activity

Visit the *American History: The Modern Era Since 1865* Web site at **me.glencoe.com** and click on *Chapter 10— Student Web Activities* for an activity about baseball.

■ Sports and Entertainment

As work became less strenuous, many looked for leisure activities that involved physical exercise. Golf, croquet, and lawn tennis from Great Britain were popular sports with the middle and upper classes. College students brought in other British sports, including rowing, track, and rugby (from which American football was derived).

Baseball, however, was a truly American invention—its earliest form was played before the Civil War. College and club teams sprang up all over the country in the late 1800s. The first professional team was the Cincinnati Red Stockings in 1869; in 1876 the National League was organized. Professional baseball found a ready audience and loyal fans in crowded urban areas where working-class people had little money for entertainment.

The enthusiasm for baseball had started during the Civil War. In the years that followed, thousands played and many more watched the game. It became known as "America's favorite pastime."

After the modern safety bicycle was substituted for the dangerous "high wheeler," bicycling became a craze. There were hundreds of bicycle clubs; special trains carried cyclists into the country on Sundays, and special bicycle paths were built in parks and suburbs. A transcontinental bicycle route was wanted.

Cities became centers of cultural life. In a day when the motion picture had not yet been invented, theater and vaudeville shows enjoyed great popularity. Large cities boasted opera companies and symphony orchestras, theaters, and museums of fine art.

In 1891 Peter Tchaikovsky, the Russian composer, came to America and conducted one of his own works at the new Carnegie Music Hall in New York City. He wrote home that everything went wonderfully, and that he was received with even greater enthusiasm than he had been in his native land.

HONUS WAGNER OF THE PITTSBURGH PIRATES ▶

Section 3 ★ Assessment

Checking for Understanding

1. **Define** antebellum, realism, expatriate, yellow journalism.

Critical Thinking

2. **Supporting Opinions** Argue for or against compulsory education in a democratic society. Support your opinion with facts or arguments that show how your position supports democratic goals.

3. **Analyzing Issues** Use a chart similar to the one shown here to describe the cultural styles at work during the late 1800s.

Literature	
Art	
Architecture	

INTERDISCIPLINARY ACTIVITY

4. **The Arts** Create a collage comparing modern American art and art of the late 1800s.

Improvements in Printing

During the late 1800s, improvements in printing led to the inexpensive mass production of newspapers, magazines, and books. In 1863 American inventor William A. Bullock produced the first web-fed press. This press printed on huge rolls of paper rather than single sheets. Printer Richard March Hoe perfected the continuous-roll press in 1871. This device made it possible to produce up to 12,000 full newspapers an hour.

In 1886 linotype typesetting machines cut the time required to set type to a fraction of that required to set it by hand. The linotype operator sat at a keyboard. When the operator touched a letter on the keyboard, a lead mold was placed in line with other letters. Each complete line of type was molded onto a single slug, and the slugs were made into printing plates. The linotype allowed text to be assembled much faster into columns and pages.

Improved printing technology led to rapid growth of the publishing industry. It also led to increased competition among newspaper publishers to get out the "latest edition."

Improvements in printing also aided the magazine industry. For nearly 20 years after the Civil War, the magazine industry was limited by technology. For the most part, magazines were monthlies or weeklies that reached a small readership. The leaders in the field included the *Atlantic Monthly* and *Harper's Magazine*.

Improvements in the printing process, however, led to a new form of magazine in the 1880s. Such popular magazines as the *Ladies' Home Journal* and the *Saturday Evening Post* reached larger audiences.

Another development leading directly from improvements in printing concerned the Sunday edition. Throughout the country major city newspapers created Sunday papers of 50 or more pages. Comic strips, which began as Sunday features, were moved into separate colored supplements. By 1900 the formula of the American newspaper—daily and Sunday—was in place. In addition the new techniques helped magazines such as *McClure's* and the *Saturday Evening Post* achieve mass circulation.

▲ NEWSBOY IN THE EARLY 1900S

Making the Science Connection

1. What is a linotype machine?

2. How did improved methods of printing and typesetting affect the publishing industry?

3. How is most publishing done today?

ACTIVITY

4. Create a collage from newspapers and newsmagazines that depicts creative use of artwork, color, and design.

Using Vocabulary

Each term below has one of the following connotations: *political, economic,* or *cultural.* Classify each term under its respective connotation. Write a sentence that explains the connection between the term and its connotation.

antebellum	political machine
expatriate	protectionist
free-trader	realism
graft	rider

Reviewing Facts

1. Explain the increase in political corruption following the Civil War.
2. Name the Presidents who introduced reform or resisted corruption in government.
3. List some political reforms made during the 1870s and the 1880s.
4. List changes in higher education.

Understanding Concepts

Corruption

1. What legitimate purpose do lobbyists serve? What restrictions should be placed on them to avoid wrongdoing?

Public Protest

2. Re-create the diagram shown here, and list the events in this chapter which suggest that a free press can inspire public protest to corruption in government.

Events

Critical Thinking

1. **Linking Past and Present** What businesses today depend on people having leisure time? Would all these businesses exist if work hours had not been shortened? Explain.

2. **Analyzing Illustrations** Study the advertisement on this page and answer the questions that follow.

   a. What is the product that is featured in the advertisement?

   b. This advertisement appeared in 1885. In what ways would a modern advertisement differ from this example? In what ways would the ads be similar?

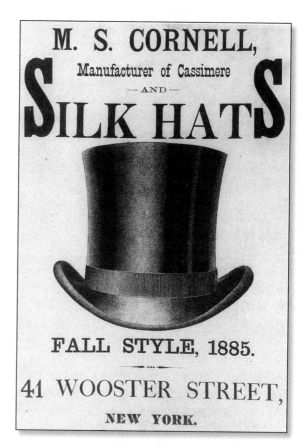

3. **Determining Cause and Effect** Throughout most of the nation's history, government workers and officeholders have earned substantially less than people in business with comparable ability and responsibility. How might this imbalance lead to corruption in government?

History and Geography

Changing Regions

With rapid growth and industrialization came change in the way people lived as well as growing differences in regional issue interests.

1. **Human/Environment Interaction** How did the growth of cities and urban overcrowdedness affect community services?

2. **Region** Why did Western farmers tend to support the Republican party?

Interdisciplinary Activity: Journalism

Work with a partner to act out an interview between a newspaper reporter and a local political boss or a machine politician. The reporter should review information on corrupt government practices as were presented in the chapter. The politician should review information on party machines. After the interview, both of you should list what were the most pertinent points brought out in the interview. Compare your findings with those of other groups.

Practicing Skill

Interpreting Political Cartoons

Study the cartoon on this page. Then answer the questions that follow.

1. What is happening in the picture?

2. What words give clues to the cartoon's meaning?

3. Who are the figures in the cartoon?

4. What point is the cartoonist making?

Technology Activity

Using a Word Processor Use the Internet and other library resources to find out more about the life of one of the writers, artists, journalists, or musicians discussed in the chapter. Prepare a one-page biography of that person and present it to the class.

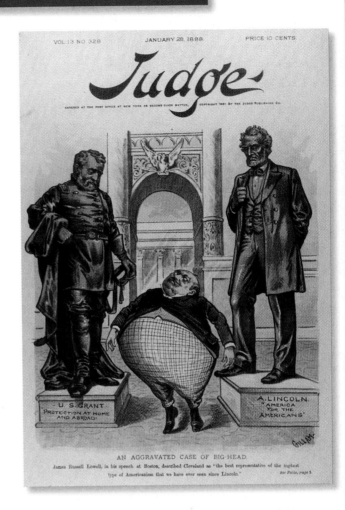

VOL. 13. NO. 328   JANUARY 28, 1888.   PRICE 10 CENTS.

Judge

AN AGGRAVATED CASE OF BIG-HEAD.

James Russell Lowell, in his speech at Boston, described Cleveland as "the best representative of the highest type of Americanism that we have ever seen since Lincoln."

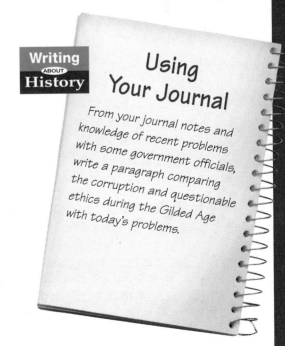

Writing ABOUT History

Using Your Journal

From your journal notes and knowledge of recent problems with some government officials, write a paragraph comparing the corruption and questionable ethics during the Gilded Age with today's problems.

CHAPTER 11

★★★

Politics and Protest
1865–1900

► **POLITICAL CAMPAIGN BUTTONS**

Setting the Scene

Focus

In the late nineteenth century, most Americans continued to live on the farm. By the 1880s, however, agriculture was in crisis. Farmers blamed their difficulties on abuses by the railroads, greedy bankers, and Eastern industrialists. Farmers began to band together to fight these problems, which in turn led to the creation of a new political party, the Populists. Populism shared some goals with a larger movement aimed at redistributing the wealth and political power in the United States.

Concepts to Understand

★ Why **economic inequity** developed between farmers and urban workers

★ Why many reformers believed that **social change** would result in a more just and equitable society

Read to Discover . . .

★ some of the problems that American farmers faced in the 1880s.

★ what were the major goals of the Populist party.

Journal Notes

As you read the chapter, note in your journal the answers to these questions: Why was the Democratic party divided in 1896? What effect did this division have on the presidential election?

HISTORY Online

Chapter Overview
Visit the *American History: The Modern Era Since 1865* Web site at **me.glencoe.com** and click on **Chapter 11—Chapter Overviews** to preview chapter information.

CULTURAL	• **1874** *National Woman's Christian Temperance Union formed in Cleveland*	• **1881** *Clara Barton founds the American Red Cross*

	1865	1875

POLITICAL	• **1871** *Civil Service Reform Act passes*	• **1877** Munn *v.* Illinois • **1878** *Bland-Allison Act passes*

▲ RAILROAD CONDUCTOR'S BADGE

• **1891** *Hamlin Garland publishes* Main-Travelled Roads

• **1896** *Henry Ford builds his first automobile*

1885

1895

• **1892** *Populist national convention held in Omaha*

• **1896** *William J. Bryan delivers "Cross of Gold" speech*

★★★★★★★★★★★★★★★★★★★★★★★★★★★★★★★

Agrarian Unrest

Guide to Reading

Main Idea

Despite America's industrial boom, farmers continued to struggle—prompting a wave of unrest.

Reading Strategy

Organizing Information As you read about agrarian unrest, use a diagram similar to the one shown to highlight the Grange's rise and fall.

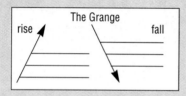

Objectives

After studying this section, you should be able to

★ identify the problems farmers faced during the late 1800s.

★ discuss the rise and fall of the Grange.

★ analyze the impact of the Interstate Commerce Act.

Key Terms

pooling, cooperative

► **HARVESTING MACHINE AD, LATE 1800S**

There appeared, as if from nowhere, a plague of grasshoppers that destroyed not only the wheat but the morale of farmers on the Great Plains. The Norwegian American writer, Ole Rölvaag, described the coming of the grasshoppers in his novel *Giants in the Earth:*

> **They actually hurt me as they flew against my face and hands. The wagon . . . was literally filled with them. The road was seething. . . . I saw Father standing almost in despair. So thick were the grasshoppers in the cornfield of which both of us had been so proud, that not a spot of green was left to be seen. And within two hours . . . not a leaf was left. . . .**

The grasshoppers ate anything green, choked wells to the brim, broke the branches off fruit trees by their weight, and even devoured harnesses and tool handles. They came in clouds that darkened the sky and covered the ground.

■ The Plight of the Farmers

Even clouds of grasshoppers were only one of the hazards of life on the plains. There was always the threat of prairie fires, dust storms, and, worst of all, drought, which combined with hot winds and temperatures over 100°F to bake crops in the ground and to cake farmers' faces with the salt of their sweat.

Farm prices began to decline in the 1880s; the price of wheat fell from 91 cents a bushel in 1883 to 69 cents in 1886. This decline was largely the result of overproduction of crops. New inventions, such as steam-powered harvesting and threshing machines, had improved crop yields, and more efficient techniques greatly increased farm production. As prices declined farmers had to borrow more and more money. Costs of the new farm machinery that assisted with large harvests were high. Often farmers could afford such equipment only on a mortgage. High, too, were the costs of shipping crops to market. The more farm prices fell, the harder it became for farmers to pay back their loans.

Even farmers who were not investing in mechanized equipment frequently had to borrow money. They had to live for a full year on the payments they received for their crops in the fall. If the money did not last, they were forced to borrow. This meant they were at the mercy of interest rates. It also meant that farmers were pretty much forced to sell their crops as soon as they came in. At that time, of course, because of the large supply, prices were always low. This is why farmer organizations, most notably the Southern Alliance, began to look for other ways to finance and market crops. Many farmers also began to call for railroad regulations for a variety of reasons.

■ Railroad Abuses

Railroads opened vast stretches of the West to settlement, making it possible for farmers to get their crops to markets and to get manufactured goods from the East. Huge sums of money were required to finance the building of a railway system. The promise of quick profits made the railroad an attractive investment for shrewd business leaders. Millions of dollars were raised through the sale of stock to private investors, both American and European.

Because a railroad promised growth and prosperity for those along its path, state and local governments offered loans and land grants in order to obtain railroad connections. Not all the dealings were legal, however.

Unethical Business Practices

Some railroad companies spent millions of dollars in bribes to state legislators and other public officials in exchange for special favors, such as land grants, cash subsidies, pro-railroad laws, and tax exemptions. But they often evaded laws designed to make them provide services in return for the benefits they were granted.

Farm Prices, 1860–1900

Graph Study

Farm prices peaked during the Civil War. *What was the price of wheat in 1900?*

Price of Crops: 3.00, 2.80, 2.60, 2.40, 2.20, 2.00, 1.80, 1.60, 1.40, 1.20, 1.00, .80, .60, .40, .20

1860, 1870, 1880, 1890, 1900

Wheat (price per bushel)
Corn (price per bushel)
Cotton (price per lb.)

Source: *Historical Statistics of the United States: Colonial Times to 1970* (1975).

▼ Fighting grasshoppers in Kansas, 1875

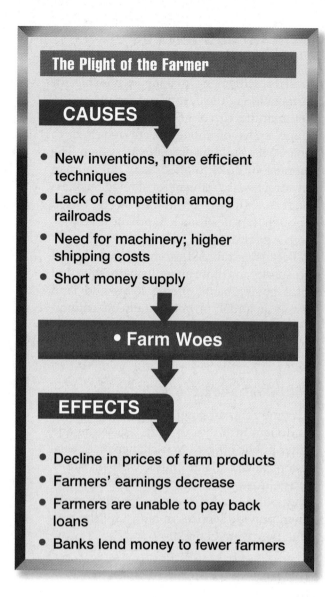

The Plight of the Farmer

CAUSES

- New inventions, more efficient techniques
- Lack of competition among railroads
- Need for machinery; higher shipping costs
- Short money supply

• Farm Woes

EFFECTS

- Decline in prices of farm products
- Farmers' earnings decrease
- Farmers are unable to pay back loans
- Banks lend money to fewer farmers

Another abuse was called "stock watering," the practice of increasing the number of shares of a company without adding to the company's assets. Such action cheated all the stockholders. It also hurt the public because the railroads had to keep their rates high to pay dividends.

Unfair Pricing

In a day when trucks and highways were not yet dreamed of, railroads often enjoyed a natural monopoly; that is, in certain places there was no competition for services. Railroads took advantage of this situation by charging more for short hauls where they had a monopoly than for long hauls where they faced competition from other railroad lines. Thus, it cost shippers more to send goods from Poughkeepsie, New York, to New York City than to send goods from Chicago to New York City.

Sometimes competing railroad lines divided up traffic serving the same route, a practice known as **pooling.** Railroads pooled to make sure each line had enough traffic to pay costs and debts.

■ The Grange

Feelings against railroad abuses were especially strong in the West where there was almost no competition from other forms of transportation. This was because railroads had been favored by huge government subsidies in the form of land. Business owners and workers in the cities as well as farmers resented the railroads.

It was a nationwide farm organization, however, that began a movement against the unfair practices of the railroads. This organization tried to end railroad abuses with laws passed by state legislatures.

From Social Support to Political Action

The Patrons of Husbandry, commonly called the Grange, was an early national farm organization. It was founded in 1867 by Oliver Hudson Kelley. At first the main purpose of the Grange was to relieve the isolation and loneliness in the lives of farm families by providing social activities. Also, recognizing the importance of women on the farm, the Grange was the first fraternal organization to admit women on an equal basis.

The panic of 1873, however, turned the Grange into a reform lobby. As crop prices fell and credit became scarce, farmers began to talk about how to solve their common problems. Local Grange organizations pooled farmers' resources to set up mills, factories, banks, insurance companies, grain elevators, and **cooperatives,** or nonprofit stores owned by farmers. The local Granges involved themselves in politics and pressed for state laws to help farmers.

By 1874 the Grange had 1.5 million members in states throughout the Midwest, the South, and the West. Its solidarity met with such success that several states passed "Granger laws" that fixed maximum freight and passenger rates, forbade railroads to discriminate between places or shippers, and attempted to regulate monopolies of such farmer necessities as grain elevators and warehouses.

Granger Laws Versus Business Interests

Private businesses protested loudly against the Granger laws. Their main argument was that government should not interfere with private enterprise. Railroad lawyers argued that Granger laws were unconstitutional because the Fourteenth Amendment forbade a state to "deprive any person of life, liberty, or property, without due process of law." They viewed a railroad corporation as a legal "person" that should not be deprived of its property by being forced to lower its rates.

Defenders of the Granger laws said railroads that had accepted generous aid from government should not claim to be devotees of laissez-faire capitalism. Further, they argued that laissez-faire rules did not apply to natural monopolies because there was no competition to keep prices down. The Grangers maintained that government must regulate railroads and other such monopolies in order to protect the public.

Supreme Court Decisions

In 1877 the Supreme Court decided in favor of the Granger laws in the case of *Munn* v. *Illinois*. The Court stated that common carriers, such as railroads, and public utilities, such as grain elevators, "stand in the very gateway of commerce" and "take toll of all who pass." Therefore these carriers must "submit to being controlled by the public for the common good."

In spite of such Court decisions, the Granger laws were unsuccessful. The railroads fought the laws by cutting services or threatening to lay no more track until the acts were repealed. Moreover, in the late 1870s, membership in the Grange declined and so did its political activity. The main cause of the Grange's collapse was its venture into business activities. The Grange set up plow and reaper factories, grain elevators, packing plants, and banks. Bitterly opposed by private companies and often not well run, these

★★★ AMERICAN PORTRAITS

Willa Cather
1873–1947

Life on the prairie was a memorable experience for a young girl in the 1880s and the 1890s. The beauty of the land and the hardy determination of the pioneers lasted long in the memory of Willa Cather.

Born in Virginia in 1873, Willa moved with her family to a farm near Red Cloud, Nebraska, at the age of nine. The next eight years would provide the reflections for several novels, written years later.

Cather tried her hand at writing while teaching school in Pittsburgh in 1901 and then became an editor for *McClure's Magazine*. However, her real success did not begin until she started writing about life on the plains. Many of her famous novels, such as *O Pioneers!* (1913), tell of the tough, yet sensitive, nature of the immigrants who matched their determination against the demanding and lonely life on a plains farm.

Granger businesses usually failed. Their collapse discredited the Grange, and by 1880 its membership was less than one-fourth of what it had been in 1874.

The remaining Granger laws were dealt a mortal blow in 1886. In the *Wabash Railway* decision, the Supreme Court held that the states could control railroad traffic only within each state's own borders. They did not have the power to regulate railroad traffic that crossed state borders. Because most railroad traffic crossed state boundaries, the Court's decision effectively wiped out states' regulation of railroad rates.

The fall of the Grangers did not stop other organizations from forming. One especially important local group was started in Texas in the mid-1870s. This group, guided by Dr. C.W. Macune, soon joined with similar groups in Arkansas and Louisiana to form a national alliance. It was called the National Farmers' Alliance and Industrial Union and was referred to as the Southern Alliance.

■ Interstate Commerce Act

The Supreme Court's ruling in the *Wabash* decision made it clear that regulation would have to come at the national level. In 1887 Congress passed the first federal law to regulate interstate commerce. The Interstate Commerce Act declared that the rates that railroads charged must be "reasonable and just"; it forbade pooling, rebates, and higher rates for short rather than long hauls.

The railroad companies were required to publish rates, give advance notice of all rate changes, and make annual financial reports available to the federal government. Enforcement of the law was placed under the Interstate Commerce Commission (ICC), a five-member panel appointed by the President.

As far as its immediate purpose was concerned, the Interstate Commerce Act was a failure. The ICC, lacking power to set rates, could only make recommendations or bring suits in the federal courts. Of 16 such cases that reached the Supreme Court, the Court held for the railroads in 15.

In 1892 Richard Olney, a corporate lawyer who later served as attorney general and secretary of state, wrote to a railroad official urging him not to advocate repeal of the Interstate Commerce Act. "It satisfies popular clamor for government supervision of the railroads," observed Olney, "at the same time that such supervision is almost entirely nominal."

In retrospect, though, the Interstate Commerce Act was a very important law. It established the precedent that the federal government might control large-scale private enterprise if the public good seemed to require it. It also provided a model for the regulatory commissions of today.

Section 1 ★ Assessment

Checking for Understanding

1. **Define** pooling, cooperative.

2. **Analyze** the short-term and long-term effects of the Interstate Commerce Act.

Critical Thinking

3. **Applying Principles** State in your own words the law of supply and demand. Then explain how the law worked against farmers.

4. **Analyzing Issues** Re-create the diagram shown here, and list the reasons why farmers' failed to share in the American economy's prosperity.

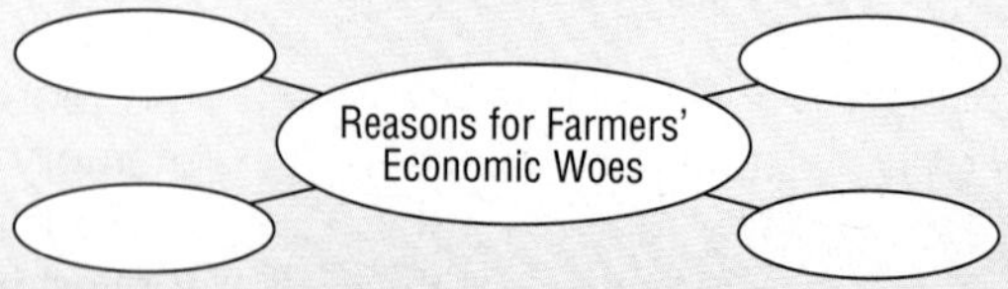

Reasons for Farmers' Economic Woes

INTERDISCIPLINARY ACTIVITY

5. **The Arts** Imagine you are a farmer in the late 1800s. Write a letter to the editor of your local newspaper detailing your proposals for dealing with railroad abuses.

★★★

Rise and Fall of Populism

Guide to Reading

Main Idea

After the Grange's collapse, farmers formed new organizations that became the basis of a new national political party.

Reading Strategy

Classifying Information As you read about the rise and fall of Populism, use a chart such as the one shown here to list the groups that supported each currency standard and to explain the reasons for their support.

Currency Standard	Groups in Support	Reasons
Greenbacks		
Free Silver		

Objectives

After studying this section, you should be able to

★ explain the motivations of the groups that supported greenbacks and free silver.

★ describe the campaign and results of the election of 1896.

★ discuss the Populist movement.

Key Terms

inflation, deflation, gold standard, third party

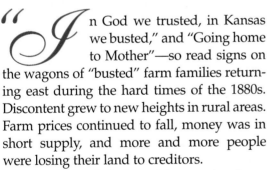

► GRANGE FARMER

"*I*n God we trusted, in Kansas we busted," and "Going home to Mother"—so read signs on the wagons of "busted" farm families returning east during the hard times of the 1880s. Discontent grew to new heights in rural areas. Farm prices continued to fall, money was in short supply, and more and more people were losing their land to creditors.

Many blamed their problems not only on the drought but on human forces as well: greedy bankers, industrialists, and railroad companies that were accused of controlling government policies and bleeding rural areas dry. Like the Grangers, these men and women turned to politics to solve the problems caused by rapid economic change. The farmers' alliances, which spawned the Populist party, succeeded beyond the dreams of the Grangers.

Greenbacks and Free Silver

If there was anything that farmers in the late 1800s demanded more strongly than the regulation of natural monopolies or the reduction of the marketers' profits, it was "cheap money." The value of money, like that of any other commodity, changes according to the supply. If the number of dollars in circulation increases while there is no increase in the amount of goods and services for sale, the dollar buys *less,* and prices go up. This situation is called **inflation.** On the other hand, if the number of dollars in circulation decreases while there is no decrease in the amount of goods and services for sale, the dollar buys *more,* and prices go down. This situation is called **deflation.** In the three decades after the

Civil War, the production of agricultural staples, such as wheat and cotton, nearly quadrupled while the supply of money increased very little. Thus, the prices received by farmers dropped by nearly two-thirds.

The Gold Standard

In 1865, with the value of currency inflated by the wartime issuance of United States notes, or greenbacks, there was $10.60 in circulation for every person in the country. By 1895 per capita circulation had sunk to $4.50. This was partly the result of a movement toward adoption of the **gold standard**. A country that adopted the gold standard made all its currency convertible into gold. Formerly, most countries had been on a bimetallic standard of both gold and silver.

▲ *A PRAYER FOR RAIN* by A.B. Frost, 1894 On the Great Plains, farming had its agonies. Bumper crops brought low prices, and drought brought no crops. *What was the goal of the Populist party?*

The difficulty with the gold standard in the late nineteenth century was that world production of gold did not increase as fast as world production of goods. This restricted the currency supply and drove prices down. Deflation was hard on farmers, who borrowed money more heavily than ever before. This resulted in thousands of farm owners losing their land.

As soon as greenbacks began to be called in during the late 1860s and prices began to drop, farmers started to demand inflation. They protested that bankers and bondholders had lent "50-cent dollars" during the war; they now wanted to be repaid in 100-cent dollars. In the midterm election of 1878, a Greenback party polled more than 1 million votes, electing 15 members to Congress.

The Demand for Free Silver

The Greenback movement declined after the mid-1870s as inflationists turned to free silver. Ever since the gold rush of 1849 had lowered the price of gold, silver miners had sold their silver commercially rather than selling it to the Treasury. In 1873 Congress, unaware of the potential of new silver mines, decided to stop coining silver money and adopted the gold standard. Six years later, after building up a gold reserve, the federal government resumed specie, or coin, payments. These events caused a howl of protest from Western silver miners because new mines, especially the famous Comstock Lode, produced a flood of silver that would no longer be coined. Denouncing what they called "the Crime of '73," silver miners demanded a policy of free silver, meaning that the government should coin all silver brought to the mint. They were joined by farmers of the West and the South who expected that free silver would mean a cheaper dollar and higher prices.

The strength of the silver movement was shown by the Bland-Allison Act of 1878, which was passed over President Hayes's veto. This law required that the Treasury buy from $2 million to $4 million worth of silver a month and issue currency against it. Although adding to the money supply, the Bland-Allison Act did not halt deflation.

■ The Populist Movement

The election of 1892 was notable because for the first time since 1860, a **third party,** a minor political party, won electoral votes. The new organization, the People's, or Populist party, was principally an expression of farmers' grievances.

Government Policies

Ever since the Civil War, federal policies had favored industry over agriculture and the city over the country. In spite of the clamor for a cheaper dollar, the United States remained on the gold standard—to the advantage of creditors—and farm prices went steadily down—to the advantage of urban consumers. The protective tariff raised the price of the goods farmers bought, to the advantage of manufacturers, but American agricultural staples were sold overseas in an unprotected market. Legislation that favored agrarian, or farming, interests proved ineffective. State and federal regulation of railroads had been frustrated by adverse judicial decisions. When drought hit the Great Plains region in the late 1880s, the farmers were in a rebellious mood. In the West in general, economic distress was widespread; after the depression of 1893, feelings became so bitter that many citizens feared a revolution.

Forming a Party

The Populist party originated from two great farmers' organizations, which were formed after the decline of the Grange—the Southern Alliance, which covered the cotton and tobacco belt, and the Northern Alliance, especially strong in the plains region. Although the two alliances failed to merge,

· ·

Footnotes to History

Populist Leaders Tom Watson from Georgia captured the essence of the new party when he declared that the Populists' chief target was "monopoly—not monopoly in the narrow sense of the word—but monopoly of power, of place, of privilege, of wealth, of progress."

they made similar demands—free silver, more paper money, cheaper credit, government ownership of railroads, and the restoration of railroad bounty lands to the federal government. After several congressional election successes and conferences in Cincinnati in 1891 and St. Louis in February 1892, a new political party was formed. The People's party held a national convention in Omaha in July 1892. Although mostly from farm organizations, delegates also represented the Knights of Labor and the followers of social reformers Henry George and Edward Bellamy.

Following the custom of the time, the convention nominated for President a Civil War veteran, James B. Weaver. There was nothing customary, however, about the Populist party's platform.

▲ POPULIST LEADER
MARY ELIZABETH
LEASE

The Omaha Platform

The preamble of the Omaha platform expressed indignation at the existing political and economic conditions. It condemned the political corruption, the newspapers dominated by business interests, the mortgage burden, and the condition of labor. The influence of social reformers was seen in the statements that "the land is concentrating in the hands of the capitalists" and that governmental injustice breeds "two great classes—tramps and millionaires." Turning to money and banking, the Populists characterized worldwide adoption of the gold standard as "a vast conspiracy against mankind . . . organized on two continents."

The following was perhaps the most zealously radical statement in the preamble of the Omaha platform:

❝ *We believe that the powers of government—in other words, of the people—should be expanded . . . as rapidly and as far as the good sense of an intelligent people and the teachings of experience shall justify.* ❞

The Omaha platform revealed that it was the agriculturalists—not organized labor—who dominated the Populist party.

The demands of organized labor were given a subordinate position. Excluded from the platform proper, labor's demands were placed among a miscellaneous list of resolutions that were given the title "Expression of Sentiments."

The Omaha platform seems less radical now than it did at that time. The Populists proposed not to overthrow the capitalist system but simply to change the rules. They aimed to achieve their ends not through revolution but through the orderly process of free elections. The Populist platform reveals an important function of third parties in the United States—to bring to public attention measures that the major parties later adopt as their own.

Election of 1892

The Populists' enthusiasm as they entered the campaign of 1892 had a religious tone. They adapted revival meeting hymns as party songs. Huge rallies were addressed not only by men but also by "women with skins tanned to parchment by the hot winds, with bony hands of toil, and clad in faded calico." The balloting revealed the distinct character of various regions in the People's party. All of its 22 electoral votes came from states lying west of the Mississippi River. In the South sympathy with Populist aims was widespread, but there was fear that the new party might divide the Democratic vote and let the Republican party back into power. Southern Democrats with Populist principles—"Popocrats"—nonetheless helped elect their own party's candidate, Grover Cleveland.

▲ BRYAN AND SILVER The British humor magazine *Puck* shows candidate William Jennings Bryan as a puppet being controlled by the silver-mine owners. ***Besides the mine owners, who supported free silver?***

348 UNIT 3 New Horizons: 1860–1900

■ Cleveland's Second Term

Cleveland's second term proved difficult. Inheriting a treasury deficit from the Harrison administration, he had scarcely taken office when the panic of 1893 burst upon the country. Although Cleveland could not have prevented this disaster, he was blamed for it. Furthermore, he managed to antagonize almost every element in his party. For example, he angered "machine" politicians by putting 120,000 civil service jobs on the merit system. Cleveland also infuriated workers by using troops in the 1894 Pullman strike.

Cleveland Loses Democratic Support

Above all, Cleveland antagonized farmers by defending the gold standard. Fearful that the Sherman Silver Purchase Act would flood the United States Treasury with so much silver that it could not be redeemed in gold, he called a special session of Congress in 1893 and forced repeal of the law. Because most Western and Southern Democrats opposed him, he was able to do this only with Republican support. Even after federal buying of silver ceased, the gold standard was endangered because it was difficult for the government to keep an adequate gold reserve in the treasury. To obtain the precious metal, the Treasury Department sold United States bonds.

In one transaction J. Pierpont Morgan, the most powerful banker on Wall Street, obtained federal bonds so far below their market value that he and the bankers associated with him made $1.5 million. Western fury at the Morgan bond transaction was unbounded. The gold standard was bad enough, but to pay bankers to preserve it seemed to them almost treasonable.

The President's hope of lowering the prohibitive duties of the McKinley Tariff faded when a few Democratic senators joined the Republicans in tacking 633 amendments on a new tariff bill, thereby keeping rates almost at former levels. Cleveland let the resulting Wilson-Gorman Tariff of 1894 become a law without his signature, but he denounced the action of the rebellious senators as "a piece of party perfidy and dishonor."

▲ President Grover Cleveland

Republicans Nominate McKinley

Meanwhile the Republicans had become, more than ever, identified with business interests. A dominant figure in the party was Mark Hanna, an Ohio businessman-politician. Big, bluff, and low-browed, Hanna became, perhaps unjustly, a symbol of the alliance between corporate wealth and politics. In 1896 Hanna used his great organizing talents to secure the Republican nomination for his friend William McKinley on a platform pledging high tariffs and maintenance of the gold standard.

Democrats Nominate Bryan

The Democratic national convention opened with such a bitter fight between Gold Democrats and Silver Democrats that it was almost impossible to keep a semblance of order. Then, with dramatic suddenness,

HISTORY Online

Student Web Activity
Visit the *American History: The Modern Era Since 1865* Web site at **me.glencoe.com** and click on *Chapter 11— Student Web Activities* for an activity on political cartoons.

the party found a leader in a rather obscure presidential candidate, William Jennings Bryan of Nebraska. Bryan combined a romantic devotion to free silver with a personality, voice, and presence that made him literally a spellbinder.

Speaking at the convention, Bryan used images that seemed to identify the gold standard with evil itself:

> 66 *You shall not press down upon the brow of labor this crown of thorns—you shall not crucify mankind upon a cross of gold!* 99

This speech contained hardly a single fact-based argument for a bimetallic standard. It was so charged with emotion that it made free silver a crusade—with Bryan as its standard bearer. Although only 36 years old, he received the Democratic nomination. Most Populists also agreed to support Bryan.

The Campaign for the Presidency

Breaking with tradition, which held that political campaigning was beneath the dignity of one who aspired to the presidency, Bryan traveled the country in search of support. In spite of all his efforts, though, Bryan's cause was doomed. Most large Democratic newspapers abandoned him; the Gold Democrats deserted the Democratic party and ran a separate candidate. Collecting an immense campaign fund, Hanna hired speakers and issued pamphlets aimed at countering the free silver arguments. McKinley was helped by the fact that prices of grain and cotton rose.

The most serious weakness in Bryan's campaign was that free silver was a poor issue on which to base an entire campaign. No one knew what the result of free coinage of silver would be; it would not have ended fluctuation in the value of money, and it might have caused a business panic.

McKinley Wins

The Republicans won the election of 1896 by a decisive margin, carrying all the thickly populated states of the Northeast and Midwest. It was a victory for industry over agriculture, city over country, North and East over West and South.

After their defeat in the election of 1896, the Populists ceased to be a force in politics. Though many at the time felt that all their efforts had failed, those who lived long enough saw most of the planks of their party's platform signed into law.

Section 2 ★ Assessment

Checking for Understanding

1. **Define** inflation, deflation, gold standard, third party.

2. **Outline** the issues in the presidential election campaign of 1896.

Critical Thinking

3. **Recognizing Common Goals** The alliance between laborers and farmers was hampered by each group's different interests. What did the two groups have in common that encouraged such an alliance?

4. **Analyzing Issues** Re-create the diagram shown here, and list two important objectives of the Populist party.

Populist Party Objectives

INTERDISCIPLINARY ACTIVITY

5. **Government** Make a poster of newspaper and magazine ads that advertise political issues or candidates. Write a caption for each illustration that discusses the message that the ad presents.

Folk Songs of Protest

Songs of protest are threaded throughout American history. In 1777 Americans marched to battle at Saratoga singing "Yankee Doodle." During the 1960s protesters marched for civil rights singing "We Shall Overcome." In the 1890s, too, Populists sang a protest song against bankers called "The Kansas Fool."

THE KANSAS FOOL

We have the land to raise the wheat
And everything that's good to eat;
And when we had no bonds or debt,
We were a jolly, happy set.
With abundant crops raised everywhere,
'Tis a mystery, I do declare,
Why farmers all should fume and fret,
And why we are so deep in debt.

The bankers followed us out west,
And did in mortgages invest;
They looked ahead and shrewdly planned,
and soon they'll have our Kansas land.

CHORUS

Oh Kansas fools! Poor Kansas fools!
The banker makes of you a tool;
I look across the fertile plain,
Big crops—made so by gentle rain;
But twelve-cent corn gives me alarm,
And makes me want to sell my farm.

Other works expressed a tone that was partly serious and partly humorous.

STARVING TO DEATH ON MY GOVERNMENT CLAIM

My name is Tom Hight,
An old bach'lor I am;
You'll find me out west
   in the county of fame,
You'll find me out west
   on an elegant plain,
Starving to death
   on my government claim.

Hurrah for Green County!
   the land of the free;
The land of the bedbug,
   grasshopper, and flea;
I'll sing of its praises,
   I'll tell of its fame,
While starving to death
   on my government claim.

Making the Art Connection

1. What complaints do farmers make in the first song?

2. How do these protest songs reflect the fears and concerns of farmers that organized interests were acting against them?

ACTIVITY

3. Write the verses of a current protest song on poster board. Use newspaper and magazine clippings to illustrate the song's message.

★★

Other Forces for Reform

Guide to Reading

Main Idea

In addition to Populism, other reform movements emerged during the Gilded Age.

Reading Strategy

Sequencing Information As you read about reforms which occurred during the late 1800s, create a time line like the one shown to list key events relating to the temperance and women's rights movements. Use the dates provided as a guide.

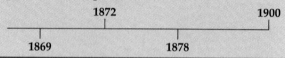

Objectives

After studying this section, you should be able to

★ trace women's involvement in the temperance and suffrage movements.

★ discuss the political ideas of Karl Marx and Henry George.

Key Term

conspicuous consumption

► **CARRIE NATION,**
FIGHTER FOR PROHIBITION

*R*eforms of the Civil War and Reconstruction periods encouraged people in the United States to look to government as the agent of social change. In the years of its unquestioned dominance, the Republican party had freed slaves, imposed a new way of life on the South, and opened the West to settlement. After the war, reformers who were dissatisfied with various aspects of life in the Gilded Age also looked to the government for action.

■ Temperance and Women's Rights

The period after the Civil War was not just a time of industrial progress, urban growth, and agrarian and labor discontent. Like the Jacksonian period, it also produced reforms designed to cure the ills of the new industrial society of the United States.

The Temperance Movement

Several reform movements that had begun earlier continued to reach toward their goals. Supporters of Prohibition, for example, formed a national political party in 1869; in 1872 they ran a presidential candidate. The temperance movement had never been more active.

Most effective were two national organizations that waged a ceaseless campaign against the evils of liquor and the saloon: the Anti-Saloon League and the Woman's Christian Temperance Union (WCTU). The WCTU revealed that women were learning the techniques of large-scale organization. Frances Willard, the head of the WCTU, made her group an effective force for causes other than temperance, such as prison reform and protective labor laws. Because women were far more likely than men to favor temperance, temperance advocates usually favored woman suffrage.

Woman Suffrage

Woman suffrage had its beginnings in the antebellum period; its first leaders were female abolitionists like Elizabeth Cady Stanton, who decided to put the antislavery cause ahead of their own. After the war woman suffrage was championed with renewed vigor.

In 1878 Susan B. Anthony of the National Woman Suffrage Association (NWSA) persuaded a sympathetic senator to propose the first woman suffrage amendment to the Constitution. It was voted down many times in the next 40 years. These defeats reflected the opinion of the majority of the people at the time, both male and female.

At the state level, suffragists had better success. By 1900 about half the states allowed women to vote on school issues, where their special knowledge of children was presumed to be a benefit. On the frontier, where women shared the hardships and dangers equally with men, support for woman suffrage was more widespread. By 1900, four states—Colorado, Wyoming, Utah, and Idaho—had granted women the right to vote.

Women and Unions

Women workers especially suffered exploitation during the new industrial age. By 1900 almost 5 million women were employed in the United States. It was not uncommon for women to work in "sweat shops" for 10 to 14 hours a day, often for less than $4 a week. Most unions, however, refused to accept women as members. One exception, the International Ladies' Garment Workers Union, had women leaders as well as women members. In 1903 a group of women formed the National Women's Trade Union League to campaign for better working conditions.

■ Socialism

Wherever industrialism appeared, there were people driven toward extreme solutions for the problems it created. Something seemed wrong with a system that produced

▼ Elizabeth Cady Stanton

▲ **Women and the vote** Thousands marched to demonstrate their support for woman suffrage. Suffragists maintained that their votes could strike a blow against political machines. *What states provided woman suffrage by 1900?*

both the idle rich, who lived in mansions, and the unemployed poor, who lived in slums. Some were impelled toward socialism.

Experiments in Socialism

Socialists in the early 1800s did not attempt to change the economic system by gaining control of the government. Instead they tried to effect change by experimenting with cooperative communities. Robert Owen brought his idea of cooperative control of industry from England to New Harmony, Indiana, in 1825. Such socialist communities reached their peak in America in the 1840s.

Karl Marx and Socialism

Socialists of the late nineteenth century were dedicated to changing the entire social and political system, partly because of the influence of Karl Marx. Marx had been a student at the University of Berlin during the emergence of a new philosophical and literary movement that questioned established values. Searching for meaning in history, Marx finally wrote his economic philosophy in *The Communist Manifesto* in 1847 and in *Das Kapital*, the first volume of which was published in 1867. Marx predicted that capitalism was doomed. Fewer and fewer capitalists, he said, would control all wealth, while the mass of the people would be pushed into the ranks of the proletariat (people without property). Eventually the proletarians would rise and overthrow their masters. History, said Marx, had seen continual class struggles, but the conflict between industrial workers and capitalists would be the last. When the workers eventually took control of society, Marx believed they would establish a classless society.

Marxist socialism appealed to many workers in the industrial countries of Europe. In the United States, however, it gained only a small following.

The American Socialist Party

Eugene V. Debs became a lifelong convert to socialism because of unjust treatment after his imprisonment in an Illinois jail during the Pullman strike. Declaring that in a democracy workers could gain control of the government and use it to change the free enterprise system, he organized the American Socialist party.

■ Dissenting Voices

Socialism was not the only remedy proposed at the time. Other solutions to fix society's ills included a single tax on land and a classless society.

Visualizing History

▲ **AT THE OFFICE** In the early 1900s, professional careers were largely reserved for men, while secretarial jobs were thought to be women's work. *How many women were employed by 1900?*

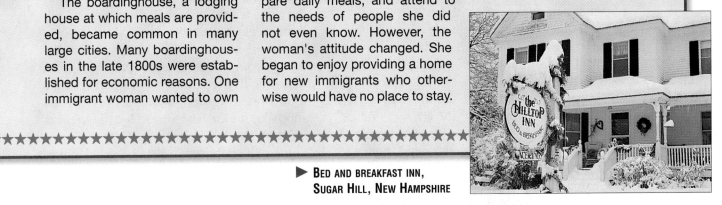

Linking Past and Present

A Home Away from Home

The bed and breakfast way of travel has long been a part of the American landscape—going back to the 1600s when taverns and inns provided shelter for weary tourists.

Then

The Boardinghouse

The boardinghouse, a lodging house at which meals are provided, became common in many large cities. Many boardinghouses in the late 1800s were established for economic reasons. One immigrant woman wanted to own

▶ **RIDGE STREET, NEW YORK CITY**

her own home in America. Having difficulty just making ends meet shortly after she arrived in the United States, she cooked for four boarders. Initially she resented having to share her home, prepare daily meals, and attend to the needs of people she did not even know. However, the woman's attitude changed. She began to enjoy providing a home for new immigrants who otherwise would have no place to stay.

Now

Bed and Breakfast

A modern form of the boarding-house is the bed and breakfast home (B&B). A bed and breakfast home is a private residence that is used to accommodate paying guests overnight. Breakfast is provided. B&B is the perfect offering for travelers who prefer a relaxed atmosphere of hospitality and comfort to the more impersonal offerings of hotels or motels.

▶ **BED AND BREAKFAST INN, SUGAR HILL, NEW HAMPSHIRE**

Henry George and the Single Tax

Another writer with a proposal for remaking society was Henry George, whose major work *Progress and Poverty* was published in 1879. George attacked the central problem posed by the socialists: Why should the advance of the industrial revolution, with more and more machinery for producing wealth, apparently result in more poverty? George said the problem was that ownership of land—the source of all wealth—was being concentrated in the hands of speculators. These speculators did not put the land to use. They merely waited for it to increase in value, meanwhile charging high rents that drove down wages and business profits. George criticized the growing gap between rich and poor:

“ *We need not look far from the palace to find the hovel. When people can charter special steamboats to take them to watering places . . . build marble stables for their horses and give dinner parties which cost . . . a thousand dollars a head, we may know that there are poor girls on the street . . . [facing] starvation.* ”

George did not propose socialism as a remedy. Instead he urged what he called the "single tax" on land values. The rate of the single tax would be based not on existing value but on *potential* value if the land were used efficiently. Thus there would be no profit in keeping land out of use and waiting for it to increase in worth; owners would either have to develop it themselves or sell it to someone else who would do so. George argued that this would cause prosperity by promoting maximum productivity and by plowing the profits of the land monopoly back into society. Although George's ideas had great appeal, the single-tax idea was too radical a change to be accepted completely. However, it did influence methods of taxation both in this country and abroad.

Thorstein Veblen and "Conspicuous Consumption"

Another widely read book, *The Theory of the Leisure Class,* was published in 1899 by Thorstein Veblen. The son of Norwegian immigrants, Veblen had been influenced by Populism in his early days in Wisconsin. Attending Yale and Johns Hopkins University, he became interested in the social sciences, especially economics. His appreciation for science led him to write with the cool detachment of an observer.

Influenced by Darwin's theory of evolution, Veblen believed in the process of natural selection. He contended that the "leisure class," which was made up of those people who had great wealth, was *not* an example of the most fit. In fact Veblen argued that the leisure class hindered progress and evolution. Veblen believed that, like the dinosaur, the leisure class would eventually disappear.

Veblen used the phrase **conspicuous consumption** to describe the life of the upper class. Veblen described conspicuous consumption as the use of vast resources just for show. The phrase had deep meaning because the contrast between wealth and

poverty was not hidden. The mansions that lined the streets of cities like New York and Chicago were within a few blocks of immigrant ghettos. However, Veblen's vision of a community of equals governed by an elite group of social planners was judged impractical by most Americans of his time.

Limited Support for Radical Changes

Probably the reason why radical formulas for altering society did not gain wide support was that many Americans did not want change. Even those at the bottom rung of the economic ladder often felt they had bettered their position from an earlier time.

A New England farm boy might find drawing wages of a dollar a day for a 60-hour week in a factory preferable to working from dawn to dark trying to make a living from a rocky farm. An immigrant might be living with her family in a single room and working in a windowless sweatshop, but for the first time in her life she was wearing shoes.

Even the poorest workers believed that in time they would also be able to "get ahead" and become property owners. They fervently believed in the "rags-to-riches" story and felt, like the heroes of the Horatio Alger series, that they could by work, perseverance, and luck rise to a higher station in life. If property rights were destroyed, what would happen to the American dream?

Section 3 ★ Assessment

Checking for Understanding

1. Define conspicuous consumption.
2. Describe the movements to gain voting rights for women.

Critical Thinking

3. **Arguing an Opinion** Why did many states refuse women the right to vote? What arguments would you propose to justify women's right to vote in the late 1800s?
4. Comparing Re-create a spider map such as the one shown here. Write *Marx, George,* and

Veblen on the vertical lines. Fill in each thinker's social solutions on the horizontal lines.

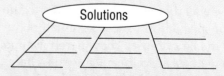

Solutions

INTERDISCIPLINARY ACTIVITY

5. **Government** Create a table comparing major reform issues of the late 1800s with those of today.

BUILDING SKILLS

Technology Skills

Building a Database

Have you ever cataloged your CD collection or tried to maintain a list of the names and addresses of your friends and relatives? If you have collected information and kept some sort of list or file, then you have created a database. This skill will help you learn more about databases.

Learning the Skill

An electronic database is a collection of facts that are stored in files on the computer. The information is organized in fields.

A database can be organized and reorganized in any way that is useful to you. By using a database management system (DBMS)—special software developed for record keeping—you can easily add, delete, change, or update information in your database. You give commands to the computer, telling it what to do with the information, and it follows your commands. When you want to retrieve information, the computer searches through the files, finds the information, and displays it on the screen.

▲ ELIZABETH CADY STANTON (LEFT) AND SUSAN B. ANTHONY

Practicing the Skill

Portions of this chapter discussed the efforts of Susan B. Anthony and other leaders who sought greater social and political rights for women. Using the following steps, build a database of the events relating to women's attempts to achieve greater equality.

1. Determine what facts you want to include in your database.

2. Follow instructions in the DBMS you are using to set up fields. Then enter each item of data in its assigned field.

3. Determine how you want to organize the facts in the database—chronologically by the date of the event, or alphabetically by the name of the event.

4. Follow the instructions in your computer program to place the information in order of importance.

5. Check your database for accuracy. If necessary, add, delete, or change information or fields.

APPLYING THE SKILL

6. Bring to class current newspapers with articles about an ongoing news story in your community. Using the steps just described, build a database containing the information from the newspapers. Explain to a partner why the database is organized the way it is and how it might be used in this class.

HISTORY *Online*

Self-Check Quiz
Visit the *American History: The Modern Era Since 1865* Web site at **me.glencoe.com** and click on **Chapter 11—Self-Check Quizzes** to prepare for the chapter test.

Using Vocabulary

Use each of the following terms in a statement that might have been made by each of the following:

Railroad owner: pooling
Farmer: cooperatives
Banker: inflation

Reviewing Facts

1. **Summarize** the factors that created financial hardships for farmers in the late 1800s.
2. **List** three purposes of the Granger laws.
3. **Specify** what the Interstate Commerce Act required of the railroads.
4. **Explain** why deflation hurt the farmers.
5. **Describe** the gold standard and its effect on the money supply.
6. **State** the reforms the Populists demanded in their platform.

Understanding Concepts

Economic Inequity

1. In the farmers' view, what groups enriched themselves at the farmers' expense?

Social Change

2. Re-create the diagram shown here, and list those groups and persons who fought for the poor disenfranchised members of society.

```
         Champions of Poor
        /                 \
   Groups              Persons
```

Critical Thinking

1. **Understanding Cause and Effect** Explain how new agricultural technology helped the farmers. How did it financially hurt some farmers?
2. **Comparing Fine Art** Study the two paintings on this page by artist John Singer Sargent. Then answer the questions.
   a. What is the mood in each of these works?
   b. What adjectives would you use to describe these paintings?
   c. Compare the use of color and light in these paintings.
   d. Which painting do you prefer? Explain.

History and Geography

Regionalism and the Election of 1896

The Republican party nominated William McKinley for President in 1896. The Democrats nominated William Jennings Bryan. The Republican platform endorsed the protective tariff, opposed the free coinage of silver, and did not deal with the issues of railroad and trust abuses and labor injunctions. The Democratic platform demanded tariff reduction,

called for free silver, and pledged stricter control of trusts and railroads. The map below shows how the nation divided geographically in the election.

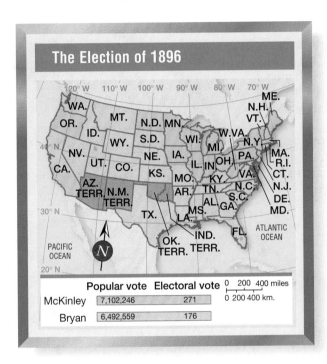

The Election of 1896

	Popular vote	Electoral vote
McKinley	7,102,246	271
Bryan	6,492,559	176

1. **Region** Why was Bryan's main support in the South and West?

2. **Place** In which of the states was the electoral vote divided?

3. **Region** Which candidate received stronger support in the Northeast?

4. **Region** Can you conclude from the map what regions of the nation were likely to support restrictions on industry? Explain.

Cooperative Learning Interdisciplinary Activity: Economics

You will be part of a discussion between four people meeting in a Great Plains town in the year 1886. Divide the following roles among yourselves: a farmer, a banker, a railroad owner, and a politician. The purpose of this meeting is to discuss the problems of the farmer. The farmer will begin the meeting by stating his or her main concerns. The other members should discuss ways to answer the farmer's problems, although each individual should be prepared to argue why he or she cannot agree to a recommended change. End the meeting by having all members agree on two recommendations for helping the farmer.

Practicing Skills

Building a Database

Prepare a database of the rise and fall of the Populist movement. Use the Internet and other research materials from your local library to find information about the movement's leaders as well as statistics about the Populist party's political performance. Share your database with the rest of the class.

Technology Activity

Using a Word Processor

Use the Internet and other resources to find out more about the status of farmers today. Focus on the farmers in your community or state. Compile your information into a brief report and share it with the class.

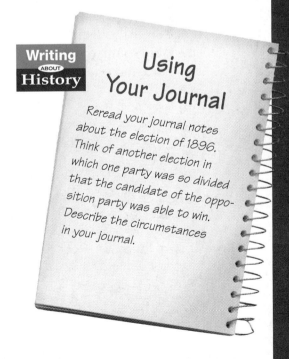

Writing ABOUT History

Using Your Journal

Reread your journal notes about the election of 1896. Think of another election in which one party was so divided that the candidate of the opposition party was able to win. Describe the circumstances in your journal.

Cultural Kaleidoscope

Life in the West

ON THE RANGE

The West and life on the range have always had a special mystique. Television, books, and the movies have kept alive the legend of the Western hero, but the reality of life on the range is overlooked. The work was hard, sometimes boring, and often dangerous. Determination, bravery, and endurance were required to tend great herds of restless and stubborn cattle or to prod a herd great distances on the long drive. Life on the range seems romantic in retrospect, but to the cowhands it was hard and often hazardous.

▶
The rope, or lariat, was an important tool in the hands of a skilled roper. Cowhands used the lariat to rope cattle, pull cattle out of mud, and haul wood to the campfire.

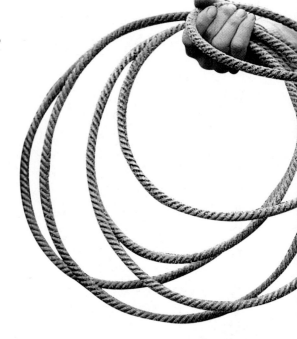

▼
The cowhand's clothing served a useful purpose. Chaps protected the legs during the long hours in the saddle.

◀
The cowhand took special care of the tack, equipment, and grooming tools for the horse. One important piece, the bridle, is used to control the movements of the horse by straps and metal pieces placed on the head and in the mouth of the animal.

▲ *TURN HIM LOOSE, BILL* by Frederic Remington
Few cowhands owned their own horses. The cowhand chose his horse from the herd of available horses.

► Cattle owners kept track of who owned an animal by branding it. Each ranch had its own easily recognizable brand.

► A cowhand wore boots with tapered high heels to make sure his feet did not slip through the stirrups when riding.

THE PRINCETON REVIEW

Standardized Test Practice

Directions: Choose the *best* answer to each of the following multiple choice questions. If you have trouble answering a question, use the process of elimination to narrow your choices. Write your answers on a separate piece of paper.

1. Which of the following was NOT a result of the westward expansion of the railroad?

A Improved living conditions for Native Americans

B The near-extinction of the buffalo

C Increased immigration from Ireland and China

D New settlements in western territories.

> **Test-Taking Tip:** Be careful— overlooking the words NOT or EXCEPT in a question is a common error. Read through all the answer choices and choose the one that does NOT fit. The other three will be correct. For example, you may remember that many of the railroad workers were Irish and Chinese immigrants. Immigration increased from these countries as people came to the U.S. looking for railroad jobs. Therefore, this answer cannot be the correct choice.

2. The Great Plains were originally thought to be impossible to farm, due to the dry weather and lack of natural resources. New technology helped to solve this problem. Which of the following is NOT an example of new technology that helped farmers on the plains?

F Barbed wire was used in place of wood fences.

G New machines made harvesting crops more efficient.

H The Homestead Act distributed land to potential farmers.

J Deeper wells were dug to increase access to water.

> **Test-Taking Tip:** The important word in this question is *technology*. Three of these answer choices refer to some type of *technology*. Which one does *not*?

3. The intent of the Sherman Antitrust Act was to regulate big business. The Act sought to

A encourage philanthropy on the part of wealthy factory owners.

B instruct businesses in how best to combine and consolidate.

C reduce the amount of yellow journalism in the U.S.

D prevent monopolies in important industries.

> **Test-Taking Tip:** Notice that the question itself gives you a clue. If the intent of this Act was to *regulate big business*, then *yellow journalism* (answer C) is unlikely to be the answer.

4. After years of fighting with Western settlers, many Native Americans were relocated to reservations in Oklahoma and the Dakota Territory in the 1860s. What caused the fighting to begin again in the 1870s?

F Long-standing tribal conflicts between the Sioux and the Cheyenne

G The arrival of miners who wanted to dig for gold in the Dakota Territory

H The passage of the Dawes Act

J The completion of the first transcontinental railroad line

> **Test-Taking Tip:** Eliminate answers that don't make sense. Conflict between the Sioux and Cheyenne is not likely to affect relations with white settlers. Therefore, you can eliminate answer F. Although the Dawes Act greatly altered traditional Native American cultures by encouraging farming among peoples who were originally nomadic hunters, it did not cause battles in Oklahoma and the Dakota Territory. Therefore, answer H also can be eliminated.

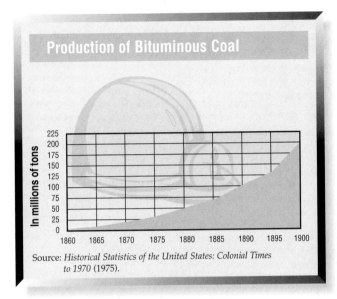

Production of Bituminous Coal

In millions of tons

225
200
175
150
125
100
75
50
25
0

1860 1865 1870 1875 1880 1885 1890 1895 1900

Source: *Historical Statistics of the United States: Colonial Times to 1970* (1975).

Use the graph <u>and</u> your knowledge of American history to answer question 5.

5. Acording to the graph above,

A the production of bituminous coal decreased steadily throughout the late 1800s.

B the production of bituminous coal first surpassed 100 million tons in 1880.

C 1895–1900 was the five-year period during which production of bituminous coal increased most rapidly.

D the greatest production of bituminous coal occurred during the Civil War.

Test-Taking Tip: Read the title and look at the information along the side and bottom of the line graph to understand what it represents. Double check each answer choice against the information on the graph to make sure you have chosen the *best* answer. If you remember that the Civil War occurred during the first five-year period on the graph you can eliminate answer D. Since the line rises steadily throughout the time period covered on the graph you can also eliminate answer A.

6. During the election of 1888, imposing a tariff on foreign goods was a major issue. Whom did the tariff benefit most?

F American farmers

G American consumers

H American importers

J American manufacturers

Test-Taking Tip: Think about what a *tariff* does. It is a type of tax—and it increases the price of goods on which it is imposed. If *foreign goods* became more expensive, then consumers probably bought more domestic products. Which group of people would benefit the most?

7. Many immigrants came to the United States because

A they could not find jobs in their home countries.

B they wanted to escape religious persecution.

C they sought political freedom.

D All of the above

Test-Taking Tip: This question requires you to use your knowledge of immigration history. Think about conditions in other regions of the world during the late 1800s. For example, you may remember that there were pogroms in Russia. Make sure that you read through *all* of the answer choices before choosing the *best* one.

UNIT FOUR
ENTERING A NEW CENTURY
1867–1920

★★★

▲ BANJO, LATE 1800s

History AND ART

Cliff Dwellers
by George Wesley Bellows, 1913

Bellows's works often show elements of humor and adventure. His favorite themes, which include landscapes and athletic events, mark him as a uniquely American painter.

Why It's Important

In an age of optimism, United States foreign policy shifted away from isolationism, and the nation became a major power in international affairs. Americans also took a look at their political institutions and concluded that change was necessary. Progressive-minded reformers sought a more democratic government while working to end a host of social ills. These citizens put in place reforms that have helped make America a safer, more just society.

To learn about women's struggle for equal rights in the years before the Progressive Era, view the *Historic America: Electronic Field Trips* Side 2, Chapter 6 video lesson:
- *Seneca Falls*

Themes
- American Democracy
- Economic Development
- The Individual and Family Life
- U.S. Role in World Affairs

Key Events
- Purchase of Alaska and annexation of Hawaii
- Spanish-American War
- Building of the Panama Canal
- States institute direct primary, initiative, and referendum
- Formation of the National Association for the Advancement of Colored People
- Income taxes enacted
- "Bull Moose" party formed
- Federal Reserve System created
- Federal Trade Commission established

▼ PRIMARY SOURCES
Library

See pages 862–863 for the primary source readings to accompany Unit 4.

▲ TRAVEL TRUNK

◄ CHILD'S TOY, EARLY 1900S

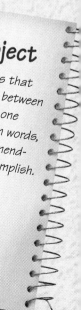

Portfolio Project

Read the amendments that passed during the time between 1867 and 1920. Choose one and rewrite it in your own words, making clear what the amendment is expected to accomplish.

Global Perspectives

The World

	1875		1890	
Asia and Oceania	1875		1890	**1894** *Sino-Japanese War begins*
Europe	**1870** *Franco-Prussian War begins*			◀ **1893** *New Zealand becomes first nation to grant woman suffrage*
Africa	**1869** *Suez Canal opens*			
South America			▶ **1889** *Brazil becomes a republic*	
North and Central America				

ONE MILLION WOMEN OF THIS STATE WANT THE VOTE WE KNOW BECAUSE WE HAVE CANVASSED THEM *The largest number of men ever registered at any election was 1,800,000.* A MILLION WOMEN IS A BIG MAJORITY VOTE *ON THE WOMAN SUFFRAGE AMENDMENT* YES NOV. 2

The United States

	1875		1890	
Pacific and Northwest				**1894** *Hawaii becomes a republic*
Southeast		◀ **1881** *Booker T. Washington founds Tuskegee Institute*		
Midwest				
Southwest				
Atlantic Northeast	1875	▲ **1886** *Statue of Liberty dedicated*	1890	

366   UNIT 4 Entering a New Century: 1867–1920

Linking Across TIME

A trip to the grocery store gives an indication of the Italian influence on American life. Foods like pizza, spaghetti, macaroni, minestrone, parmesan cheese, broccoli, and zucchini are all part of the American diet. However, they were all introduced by the Italian immigrants who came to the United States around the turn of the century.

▶ **1904** *Russo-Japanese War begins*

1905

1920

◀ **1908** *Belgium establishes control over the Congo*

1898 *Battleship* Maine *explodes; Spanish-American War begins*

▲ **1914** *Panama Canal opens*

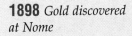
1898 *Gold discovered at Nome*

▼ **1903** *Wright brothers' first flight*

▶ **1908** *Model T Ford produced*

1912 *New Mexico and Arizona become states*

1905

1920

CHAPTER 12

★★

Imperialism
1867–1908

▼ RED LEATHER BOOTS
AND BUTTON HOOK

Setting the Scene

Focus

Foreign policy before the late nineteenth century had been dominated by two ideas. The first was President Washington's isolationist warning against entering into "entangling alliances." The second was President Monroe's warning to Europe against interference in the Americas. War with Spain, however, resulted in a more aggressive foreign policy and the acquisition of overseas colonies. Suddenly, the United States had become a major world power.

Concepts to Understand

★ How increased United States **economic and political power** led to the acquisition of an overseas empire

★ How **confrontation** with Spain resulted in war over Cuba

Read to Discover . . .

★ why Americans moved away from a policy of isolationism.

★ the problems and responsibilities that victory in the Spanish-American War brought the United States.

Journal Notes

Why did the United States become involved in the affairs of other countries? Record each country and the reasons for each as you read this chapter.

HISTORY Online

Chapter Overview
Visit the *American History: The Modern Era Since 1865* Web site at **me.glencoe.com** and click on **Chapter 12—Chapter Overviews** to preview chapter information.

CULTURAL

• **1880** *"General" William Booth organizes the Salvation Army*

• **1891** *University of Chicago founded*
• **1893** *World's Columbian Exposition is held in Chicago*

| 1875 | 1885 |

• **1882** *Chinese Exclusion Act is passed*

• **1893** *Queen Liliuokalani of Hawaii is overthrown*

POLITICAL

ADVERTISEMENT FOR CARIBBEAN CRUISE, EARLY 1900s

History AND ART

The Return of the Conquerors
by Edward Moran, 1898

Edward Moran painted this work to commemorate the American victory over Spain in the Spanish-American War. In the foreground is Admiral Dewey's flagship *Olympia.*

•**1903** The Great Train Robbery *motion picture produced; first to have a fully developed plot*

•**1910** *Women make up 21 percent of the workforce*

1895

1905

•**1898** *Spanish-American War begins*
•**1899** *Hay initiates Open Door policy*
•**1900** *Boxer Rebellion in China*
•**1904** *Roosevelt Corollary announced*

•**1905** *Roosevelt arbitrates Russo-Japanese War*

★★

America Looks Abroad

Guide to Reading

Main Idea

By the mid-1800s, America had begun looking beyond its continental borders to add territory.

Reading Strategy

Organizing Information As you read about how the United States expanded its role in the world, use a diagram similar to the one shown here to list examples of the nation's emergence from isolationism.

Emergence From Isolationism

Objectives

After studying this section, you should be able to

★ discuss the emergence of the United States from isolationism.

★ cite two examples of arbitration averting war.

Key Terms

imperialism, isolationism, reciprocity, arbitration

▶ QUEEN LILIUOKALANI OF HAWAII

European colonialism was motivated by trade and adventure, power and profit, idealism and national patriotism. These nations also believed they had a "civilizing mission" toward nonwhite populations. The Industrial Revolution generated a need for markets for manufactured goods and new sources of raw materials. **Imperialism**—the policy of establishing colonies and building empires—answered these needs.

Isolationism, or separation from the political affairs of other countries, was a policy established by George Washington. In his Farewell Address, he warned against entangling alliances. Later the Monroe Doctrine emphasized the United States's desire to keep the Americas separate from Europe. Another factor affecting American foreign policy was the Declaration of Independence—the idea that people had the right to govern themselves.

■ Securing an American Continent

European control of parts of North America by France and Russia ended in the 1860s. The United States challenged a French expansion effort in 1861 and bought Russian territory in 1867.

End of French Expansion

Mexico's reform government under Benito Juárez (HWAHR•uhs) stopped payment of its foreign debts. French, Spanish, and British troops entered the country to force payment. The debts were collected and Spain and Britain left, but the French remained and quickly occupied Mexico City. Ignoring the Monroe Doctrine and taking advantage of the American Civil War, the French emperor Napoleon III overthrew

▲ **MINING GOLD IN THE YUKON** Many settlers and prospectors came to Alaska after gold was discovered in the region in the late 1800s. *Why did Russia decide to sell Alaska to the United States?*

the Republic of Mexico. In 1864 Napoleon III installed Austrian prince Maximilian as Mexico's emperor.

The United States protested and, after the Civil War, sent nearly 50,000 troops to the border at the Rio Grande. Napoleon's forces withdrew. The Mexicans promptly defeated Maximilian's army and executed Maximilian. The United States proved its willingness to back the Monroe Doctrine with force.

🌐 GEOGRAPHY

Acquisition of Alaska

Secretary of State William H. Seward believed in Manifest Destiny. He envisioned a great empire and wanted to annex Canada, Hawaii, and several Caribbean islands.

• • • • • • • • • • • • • • • • • • • •

Footnotes to History

North to Alaska   In August 1896 news spread across the nation that gold had been discovered in the Canadian Yukon Territory, sparking one of the great gold rushes in United States history. Despite the distance and dangers, an estimated 100,000 Americans set out for the Klondike over the next two years. Excavation along the dozen miles along the shore of the Bering Sea yielded the richest tidewater diggings in history.

Seward's only major achievement along this line was the purchase of Alaska in 1867. The undeveloped territory of Alaska, twice the size of Texas, was held by Russia, but the czar saw little value in the territory.

In 1867, when the Russian minister to the United States informed Seward that the czar wanted to sell Alaska, the secretary of state jumped at the chance. In a few hours, Seward arranged a treaty in which the United States would buy Alaska for $7.2 million—less than two cents an acre. After four months of selling the idea to Congress, the transaction was completed. 🌐

▪ Empire Building

At one time the United States had little need to look beyond its own borders for growth. Raw materials were abundant, and the home market was immense. By the 1890s, the country had developed into a great industrial nation, able to compete with European producers.

Reciprocity

James G. Blaine, secretary of state under Presidents Garfield and Harrison, wanted to open up new markets not by taking on colonies, but by increasing American trade

▲ ANCHORAGE, ALASKA

▲ **ALASKA** The wealth of resources found in this scenic state proved Alaska's worth, even though its purchase was originally called Seward's Folly. *Why did some Americans call for the annexation of Hawaii?*

through **reciprocity**—the mutual lowering of tariff barriers. He tried, without much success, to include reciprocity provisions in the McKinley Tariff of 1890. He was able to chair a Pan-American Congress in Washington, D.C., in 1889. The goal of the group, which later became the Pan-American Union, was to promote economic cooperation and trade among the Americas. Success was limited, however, because the United States intervened, often forcibly, in Latin American affairs.

Should Hawaii Be Annexed?

American missionaries and traders first ventured to Hawaii in the early 1800s. American sugar growers followed. By the 1890s Hawaii was closely connected to the United States through commerce and the many Americans living there.

While many nationalities lived in Hawaii, native Hawaiian rulers were controlled by the American business community until the Hawaiian Queen Liliuokalani (lih•LEE•uh•woh•kuh•LAH•nee) came into power in 1891. She was determined to return control to her own people. In response, some American business leaders, with the help of marines from the cruiser *Boston*, took over the government.

The American minister to Hawaii wrote the Department of State that Hawaii was ready to annex. President Cleveland dis-

agreed. He decided that the use of American troops to overthrow the Hawaiian government was a violation of "national honesty." Despite criticism, Cleveland withdrew American soldiers from Hawaii. He also tried, but failed, to oust the revolutionary provisional government and put Liliuokalani back on her throne.

■ Challenging Great Britain

After the Civil War, the United States appeared ready to take a position among the powers of the world. Twice the United States forced Britain to submit to **arbitration,** or the settlement of a dispute by an impartial group.

Civil War Damages

In 1868 Charles Sumner, head of the Senate Foreign Relations Committee, claimed that Great Britain owed the United States more than $2 billion in damages for allowing Confederate ships to use British ports during the Civil War. If the British would not pay, Senator Sumner declared, the United States should take British-controlled Canada.

In 1871 Secretary of State Hamilton Fish arranged for arbitration. Britain did not want to risk war in Canada and feared that a hostile United States might supply Britain's enemies with warships. The United States backed down on its demand for "indirect" damages. In the Treaty of Washington, the United States was awarded $15.5 million, which Britain paid.

Venezuela Border Dispute

President Cleveland requested that the British put a long-standing Venezuela–British Guiana boundary dispute to arbitration. In July 1895 Secretary of State Richard Olney wrote the British government that their refusal to arbitrate violated the Monroe Doctrine. He warned:

" *The United States is practically sovereign on this continent and its fiat is law upon the subjects to which it confines its interposition.* "

Britain answered that the Monroe Doctrine had no standing in international law and did not apply to the situation.

Aware of the possibility of war, President Cleveland asked Congress for authorization to appoint a commission to determine the boundary without consulting Britain. Americans responded with excitement, but Britain thought it "monstrous and insulting." For a few days, war seemed a strong possibility.

Fortunately, the British government backed down. Early in January 1896, Britain's attention was diverted from Venezuela by a dispute with Germany involving South Africa. Seeking to improve relations with the United States, Britain agreed to arbitration.

The boundary settlement turned out in Britain's favor and a new era of Anglo-American understanding emerged.

■ Strengthening the Navy

The Venezuelan crisis called attention to the fact that the United States had only three modern battleships. The crisis also popularized the writings of American naval officer Alfred T. Mahan. Mahan believed that as America developed its industry, the nation should look outward. Great nations of the past had built up foreign markets, expanded their merchant fleets, constructed navies to protect their commerce, and planted colonies. Mahan argued that a modern nation needed sea power in order to become great.

At first Mahan had more influence abroad. Kaiser (Emperor) Wilhelm II of Germany studied his books and instructed German naval officers to read them. In Great Britain Mahan was showered with honors. Mahan influenced rising American leaders such as Senator Henry Cabot Lodge and Theodore Roosevelt and helped to shape United States naval policy.

Congress established a Naval Advisory Board in 1881 that pressed for larger naval appropriations. In 1883 Congress authorized construction of 1 more cruiser and 3 battleships. By adding 3 heavier and more powerful ships in 1890 and by voting for 13 new ships in 1895, Congress made it clear that it intended to have a navy capable of matching any enemy on the high seas.

Section 1 ★ Assessment

Checking for Understanding

1. **Define** imperialism, isolationism, reciprocity, arbitration.

2. **Show** how the French challenged the Monroe Doctrine in 1861.

Critical Thinking

3. **Understanding Cause and Effect** How did the writings of Captain Alfred T. Mahan lead to expanding the American navy?

4. **Analyzing Issues** Re-create this diagram, and describe two instances where arbitration settled U.S.-British disputes.

Confrontation	Arbitration

INTERDISCIPLINARY ACTIVITY

5. **Government** Construct a time line that shows American involvement in Mexico, Alaska, Hawaii, and Venezuela during this era.

Coaling Stations and Colonies

By the end of the 1800s, Americans began to think in terms of a different and broader Manifest Destiny. The original concept was changed to include overseas as well as westward expansion. The idea that it was the fate of the United States to extend its boundaries beyond the seas has been called the new Manifest Destiny.

The change in attitude toward foreign affairs was due to certain ideas and developments that occurred in the late 1800s. One such development was imperialism. Nations began to establish empires around the globe to build important new sources of raw materials and provide new avenues for investment.

More justification for imperialism was provided by Captain Alfred Thayer Mahan. Mahan believed that for a country to become a major sea power, its ships needed remote sources of supplies that could not be carried for an entire voyage. While commercial shipping required these supply stations, an armed navy needed them even more. The supplies, according to Mahan, were "first, fuel; second, ammunition; last of all, food."

Fuel became essential to shipping as nations switched from sail to steam power at the turn of the century. No ship could steam away from its home port for any great distance without refueling. A fleet that wanted to trade or fight very far beyond its home waters needed coaling stations in distant lands.

Mahan did not favor unchecked expansionism. Too many supply and fueling bases in foreign lands, he warned, could drain the resources

▲ U.S.S. *IOWA*, C. 1900

of the parent country and could become "a source of weakness, multiplying exposed points, and entailing division of force."

The United States had made some strides earlier in the century. One of these was the development of ironclad ships during the Civil War. However, after the war, the United States allowed its navy to deteriorate.

Mahan's ideas provided a real impetus for change. Influenced by Mahan's concepts, Congress passed the Naval Act of 1890, which appropriated additional money for battleships. By 1900 the United States had the naval power it needed to back up an expanded role in foreign affairs.

Making the Science Connection

1. What supplies did coaling stations provide?

2. How did new technology influence American foreign policy?

3. What was the danger of having too many supply and fueling bases?

ACTIVITY

4. Create a poster that displays examples of twentieth-century technology that have benefited trade and transportation.

★★★

The Spanish-American War

Guide to Reading

Main Idea

Seeking to support the Cuban people's independence effort—and to expand its own empire—America went to war with Spain.

Reading Strategy

Sequencing Information As you read about the Spanish-American War, use a diagram similar to the one shown here to list the events leading up to the war with Spain.

event		event

| event |

Objectives

After studying this section, you should be able to

★ list the events that led to the United States's involvement in the Spanish-American War.

★ explain the reason for the involvement of the Philippines in the war.

Key Term

neutrality

► TIN TRAY WITH LIKENESS OF THEODORE ROOSEVELT

Americans were outraged when they found that the Spanish Governor-General Valeriano Weyler had ordered Cuban men, women, and children into "reconcentration camps." Weyler, unable to tell civilians from rebels, had set up the camps where 200,000 Cubans, an estimated one-eighth of the population, died of illness and starvation. Some leaders of the Cuban independence movement were naturalized American citizens who had returned to work in Cuba. When captured by Spanish authorities, they demanded protection by the United States.

Not all sentiment supported the Cubans, however. American business interests had invested more than $30 million in Cuba—mostly in sugar plantations—and wanted the revolt to end. Some plantation owners, doubting the capacity of the Cubans for self-government, favored the restoration of Spanish rule. The force of public opinion, however, caused many in the business community to change their minds.

Drawn Into War

Although President Cleveland preserved strict **neutrality,** or the refusal to take sides, in the Cuban struggle, he warned that if "the useless sacrifice of human life" went on, the United States might have to abandon the policy of "patient waiting." President McKinley, who came into office in the middle of the conflict, was also committed to neutrality. He even offered to buy Cuba, but was rejected. A peaceful solution seemed possible when Spain recalled General Weyler and offered Cuba a measure of local self-government. Assistant Secretary of the Navy Theodore Roosevelt was impatient

▲ THE *MAINE* Coverage of sinking of the *Maine* raised American anger against Spain. **Who was responsible for sinking the ship?**

with McKinley's negotiation with Spain and described the President as having "no more backbone than a chocolate eclair." William Randolph Hearst's *New York Journal* and Joseph Pulitzer's *New York World* fanned public anger with exaggerated and sometimes fabricated stories of Spanish atrocities in Cuba. This "yellow journalism" helped sell papers and encouraged war:

> *How long are the Spaniards to drench Cuba with the blood and tears of her people? . . . How long shall old men and women and children be murdered by the score, the innocent victims of Spanish rage against the patriot armies they cannot conquer?*
> *. . . How long shall the United States sit idle and indifferent?*

"Remember the *Maine!*"

Public sentiment in favor of war was growing when, on February 9, 1898, the *Journal* printed a private letter written by Enrique Dupuy de Lôme, the Spanish ambassador to the United States, in which he called McKinley "weak and a bidder for the admiration of the crowd. . . . " This comment was a national insult. The ambassador resigned, but the damage to United States–Spanish relations was done.

Six days later the United States battleship *Maine,* anchored off the Cuban capital, Havana, exploded, killing 260 crew members. United States naval experts declared that the explosion came from outside the ship. Spanish experts replied that there were no mines.

The "yellow press" in 1898 expressed no indecision. Papers promptly blamed Spain and even printed diagrams showing just how the deed was done. "Remember the *Maine!*" became the battle cry throughout the United States.

Preparing for War

Congress responded to a torrent of public indignation against Spain by allocating $50 million for war preparations. McKinley, meanwhile, demanded that Spain give Cuba independence. Although at the last moment Spain claimed it was trying to comply, McKinley nevertheless delivered a warlike message to Congress. Congress demanded that Spain evacuate the island. When no reply to this ultimatum was received, Congress declared war on April 25.

While expansionists were excited about the prospects of gaining Cuba, humanitarian forces in Congress attached the Teller Amendment to the declaration of war. In it Congress pledged "to leave the government and control of the Island to the people" as soon as peace was established there.

■ "A Splendid Little War"

While the army prepared to invade Cuba, the conflict, called by Secretary of State John Hay a "splendid little war," began in the Pacific. Although the McKinley administration had no thought of expanding the territories of the United States, some officials believed that this was a prime opportunity to do so. One such person was Theodore Roosevelt.

The Philippine Connection

When John D. Long, secretary of the navy, was out of his Washington office, Roosevelt took charge. On February 25, 1898, he ordered on his own authority a Pacific squadron stationed in Hong Kong to sail for the Philippine

Islands, a Spanish colony for 300 years, if war broke out. Commodore George Dewey, commander of the United States fleet, would try to prevent a Spanish fleet in Manila Bay from going to sea. As soon as war was declared, Dewey's fleet set sail; it penetrated Manila Bay on May 1 and rapidly destroyed the weaker Spanish fleet. The quick victory surprised the President, and an army of occupation was hastily organized to sail from San Francisco to the Philippines.

A native Filipino, Emilio Aguinaldo (AH•gee•NAHL•doh), had led an uprising against Spanish rule of the Philippines in 1896. Aguinaldo was exiled in Hong Kong, where Dewey met him and provided supplies so he could lead a revolt against the Spanish forces that remained in the islands. By the time the American army arrived in the

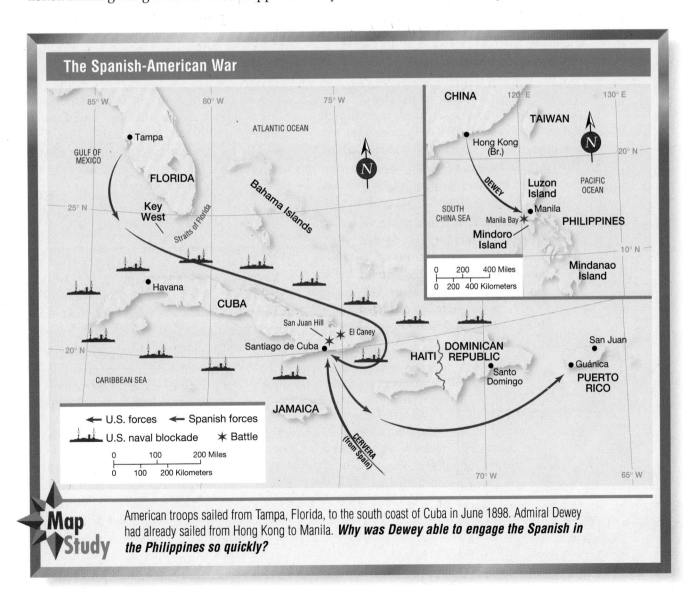

The Spanish-American War

Map Study
American troops sailed from Tampa, Florida, to the south coast of Cuba in June 1898. Admiral Dewey had already sailed from Hong Kong to Manila. *Why was Dewey able to engage the Spanish in the Philippines so quickly?*

Philippines, Aguinaldo's forces controlled all the territory except the city of Manila. When the Spanish surrendered and turned the Philippines over to the United States Army, it left unanswered the question of who would rule the islands after the war.

Fighting in Cuba

When war was first declared, McKinley had called for 200,000 volunteers to supplement the regular army, which numbered only 28,000. The War Department was inefficient. Nevertheless, 17,000 troops were declared ready to sail from Tampa, Florida, to Cuba by the middle of June. To fight a war in the tropics, they were issued heavy woolen uniforms left over from the western wars against the Plains peoples. Their ammunition was out-of-date; there were almost no medical supplies; and rations included inedible meat that the soldiers nicknamed "embalmed beef."

After landing on the south coast of Cuba, the Americans advanced on the city of Santiago. One regiment was called the "Rough Riders"—an assortment of college athletes, cowboys, miners, and law officers—led by Theodore Roosevelt, who had resigned from the Navy Department in order to join the fight. On foot because their horses were still in Florida, they charged up San Juan Hill. By securing the heights overlooking Santiago, they helped capture the city.

The Rough Riders were not alone in this attack. Among the other regiments was the all-black 10th Cavalry Regiment. Many African Americans had responded to the call for soldiers both because they identified with the Cubans' struggle for freedom and because they hoped it would improve their own lot. At least four of these African American soldiers were awarded the Congressional Medal of Honor.

Naval Encounters

At the outbreak of hostilities, an American squadron of new battleships under Admiral William T. Sampson was given the task of intercepting a Spanish squadron under Admiral Pascual Cervera (pahs•KWAHL suhr•VEHR•uh). Knowing that Cervera had left the Cape Verde Islands off the west coast of Africa in April, Americans feared he would attack the undefended Atlantic coast of the United States. They canceled hotel reservations at seaside resorts and prepared for defense, but Cervera headed directly for Santiago harbor.

Joseph Pulitzer
1847–1911

★★★★AMERICAN PORTRAITS

After emigrating from Hungary, Joseph Pulitzer made publishing history—and a personal fortune—by creating a new form of newspaper journalism.

As a soldier during the Civil War, Pulitzer noted how Americans loved to read newspapers. After the war, he bought and merged two St. Louis newspapers. Circulation soared as he filled his paper with scandals and attacks on big business. He later bought two New York papers, bringing to them the same successful recipe—sensationalism and controversy. He won a mass audience by running comic strips and covering fashions and sports.

After retiring, he saw his papers engage in "yellow journalism" to compete with William Randolph Hearst's flag-waving newspapers. Pulitzer took back control and returned his newspapers to their flamboyant investigative style.

▲ MANILA BAY United States naval ships in the Pacific, under Commodore George Dewey, sailed into Manila Bay on May 1, 1898. *When did Spain and the United States agree to an armistice?*

Sampson's superior force found the Spanish fleet at Santiago and blockaded the harbor. Once the American army took the heights overlooking Santiago, Cervera could surrender or try to break the blockade. On July 3, with little hope of victory, Cervera ordered his ships out of Santiago harbor. In the ensuing battle, all Spanish vessels were sunk. Only one American was killed and one was wounded. Effective Spanish resistance in Cuba ceased with the surrender of Santiago two weeks later. American troops went on to occupy another Spanish possession, the island of Puerto Rico. On August 12 Spain and the United States agreed to an armistice.

The "splendid little war" cost 5,000 American lives, mostly due to disease and food poisoning. The flag of the United States, an emerging world power, flew over distant islands. Had American isolationism ended?

Section 2 ★ Assessment

Checking for Understanding

1. **Define** neutrality.
2. **State** the importance of the naval battle between Sampson and Cervera.

Critical Thinking

3. **Making Judgments** How did the United States justify going to war with Spain given a previous policy of noninvolvement?
4. **Sequencing Information** Create a time line like the one shown, and use it to list key events relating to the Spanish-American War. Use the dates provided as a guide.

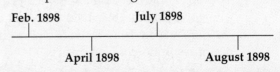

INTERDISCIPLINARY ACTIVITY

5. **Government** Create a table that compares the Spanish-American War and the Civil War. Compare length of war, methods of fighting, and battle sites.

★★

Becoming a World Power

Guide to Reading

Main Idea

After the Spanish-American War, America began to acquire overseas territories.

Reading Strategy

Classifying Information As you read about how America became a world power, create a chart similar to the one shown here to list the arguments for and against annexing the Philippines.

Annexing Philippines	
For	Against

Objectives

After studying this section, you should be able to

★ explain why the Philippine Islands were difficult to govern.

★ discuss the constitutional difficulties involved in colonization.

Key Term

protectorate

▶ MILITARY RECRUITMENT POSTER

The Spanish-American War and the prospect of expanding in the Pacific brought a change of policy toward the Hawaiian Islands. Cleveland had resisted a move to annex them in 1893, and in 1897 the Senate had turned down an annexation treaty presented by McKinley. Hawaii, the halfway point between California and the Philippines, would be valuable as a naval base, however. In July 1898, before the war ended, the Hawaiian Islands were annexed by a joint resolution of Congress.

■ The Philippines

The armistice left Americans in control of the Spanish-owned Philippine Islands. The debate over whether to acquire and annex the Philippines was a stormy one.

Arguments For and Against Annexing the Philippines

Before entering the Spanish-American War, most Americans had no idea of annexing territory, particularly a territory 6,000 miles from the Pacific coast. McKinley confessed that before Dewey's victory he could not have come within 2,000 miles of placing the Philippine Islands on a map. Once he said, "If old Dewey had just sailed away when he smashed that Spanish fleet, what a lot of strong feelings he would have saved us."

Strong feelings developed against acquiring the islands. Several leading Democrats, including former President Grover Cleveland, were opposed. Many influential private citizens agreed with them. Prominent Republicans such as Speaker of the House Thomas B. Reed and several senators fought annexation as a violation of American tradition.

Senator Henry Cabot Lodge spoke for those who wanted a larger American role in world affairs. Business interests thought of new markets and fields of investment. Public opinion was excited by the prospect of acquiring an empire. Patriotism merged with belief in social Darwinism, or the belief in the "survival of the fittest." If the United States was the most fit to govern the Philippines, why should it haul down the Stars and Stripes and allow Japan or Germany or some other power to step in and take them?

For others, like Reverend Josiah Strong, there was a sense of mission based on racial and religious bias. Strong, in his book *Our Country*, blended social Darwinism with his interest in spreading Christianity. He felt the nationality groups were in a competition from which Anglo-Saxons were destined to emerge victorious.

Settlement With Spain

McKinley, a deeply religious man, wrestled with the problem, then reported that through prayer he had decided to:

> *... [E]ducate the Filipinos, and uplift and civilize and Christianize them, and by God's grace, do the very best we could by them, as our fellow men for whom Christ died.*

Actually, Catholic missions had been started in the Philippines in the 1500s. McKinley instructed his peace commissioners to ask for all of the Philippine Islands. When Spain resisted, the United States offered to pay $20 million for them. In the treaty, signed December 10, 1898, Spain gave up control over Cuba and surrendered Puerto Rico, the Pacific island of Guam, and the Philippine Islands. Anti-imperialist feeling in the Senate was so strong that the treaty was ratified by only a two-vote margin. A Senate resolution promising eventual independence to the Filipino people was defeated only by the tie-breaking vote of the Vice President.

The United States encountered problems in trying to govern the Philippines. The

▲ **THE BIG STICK** To many people around the world, the United States in the late 1800s and early 1900s used its power to spread its influence. *Why did the United States encounter difficult problems in trying to govern the Philippines?*

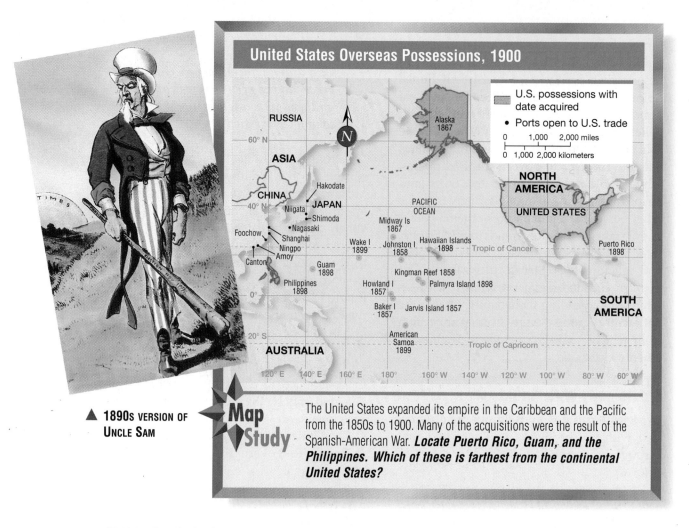

United States Overseas Possessions, 1900

RUSSIA

ASIA

60° N

CHINA

Hakodate

JAPAN

40° N

Niigata

Shimoda

Nagasaki

Foochow

Shanghai

Ningpo

Amoy

Canton

Guam
1898

Philippines
1898

0°

20° S

AUSTRALIA

Alaska
1867

PACIFIC
OCEAN

Midway Is
1867

Wake I
1899

Johnston I
1858

Hawaiian Islands
1898

Kingman Reef 1858

Howland I
1857

Palmyra Island 1898

Baker I
1857

Jarvis Island 1857

American
Samoa
1899

Tropic of Capricorn

NORTH
AMERICA

UNITED STATES

Tropic of Cancer

Puerto Rico
1898

SOUTH
AMERICA

120° E   140° E   160° E   180°   160° W   140° W   120° W   100° W   80° W   60° W

U.S. possessions with
date acquired

• Ports open to U.S. trade

0   1,000   2,000 miles

0   1,000 2,000 kilometers

**1890s VERSION OF
UNCLE SAM**

Map Study

The United States expanded its empire in the Caribbean and the Pacific from the 1850s to 1900. Many of the acquisitions were the result of the Spanish-American War. *Locate Puerto Rico, Guam, and the Philippines. Which of these is farthest from the continental United States?*

7,100 islands had 7.5 million people, who were divided into 43 ethnic groups speaking 87 different languages and dialects. The Filipinos ranged from people living in the forests to highly literate city dwellers.

Filipino Resistance

Filipino patriots had helped the American forces capture the islands. Once it became clear that the United States intended to annex the Philippines, however, a new uprising broke out—this time against the Americans. Feeling that they had been cheated out of their independence, Filipino

Student Web Activity
Visit the *American History: The Modern Era Since 1865* Web site at **me.glencoe.com** and click on *Chapter 12—Student Web Activities* for an activity about imperialism.

soldiers took to the hills. A revolutionary government was set up under Emilio Aguinaldo. Its leaders adopted a republican constitution. Aguinaldo and the other Filipino leaders knew that if the republic were to succeed, they must gain the loyalty of the people and set up diplomatic relations with other countries.

Fighting between Filipino and United States forces broke out in February 1899. Within two months, the Filipinos had been driven from their capital city, and the government fled. Aguinaldo continued to carry on guerrilla operations that produced some success. Aguinaldo's capture in March 1901, however, for all practical purposes ended the Filipinos' military efforts. More than 60,000 troops—four times the number sent to Cuba—and three years of fighting were required to suppress the Filipino patriots and put down the revolt. The Philippines remained a territory of the United States until 1946.

Many Americans were distressed to find their country at war with an independence movement. Mark Twain suggested that Old Glory should have its white stripes painted black and its stars replaced with skull and crossbones.

Even before the Filipino uprising was put down, President McKinley declared that American policy toward the islands would be for the good of the Filipinos. The President stated,

" *The Philippines are ours, not to exploit but to develop, to civilize, to educate, to train in the science of self-government.* "

President McKinley sent two commissions to investigate the conditions in the Philippines and set up a civil government.

There were several changes during the first years of United States rule in the Philippines. The English language replaced Spanish as the language of general usage. The number of American business enterprises grew quickly, largely because Americans were permitted to sell their goods tariff-free in the Philippines. Street names were Americanized.

Resentment against American rule in the Philippines was moderately relieved in 1901 when President Theodore Roosevelt appointed William Howard Taft as the first civilian governor. Genuinely devoted to the interests of the island people, Taft started a program to prepare the Filipinos for self-government, and public schools were established. The United States bought out large foreign landowners and passed laws to keep property in the hands of the Filipinos.

Taft did not believe that the Philippines would be ready for independence for many years, though. In 1907 an elective legislature was set up, and in 1916 the United States promised that the Philippines would have independence eventually. That independence was finally granted in 1946.

Linking Past and Present

The Sound of Music

The late 1800s produced the first craze of popular music in the United States. Among the reasons for this phenomenon was Edison's phonograph. In 1900 over 150,000 phonographs and 3 million records were bought by the public.

Then

Talking Machines

The phonograph, fondly called the talking machine, was one of the leading sources of entertainment. The phonograph and its accessories were decorated in the popular art of the day. Phonograph records—only 78 rpm were in use—used expendable needles, which were sold in multicolored tin boxes. Many phonograph companies also made a startling number of amplifying horns—the speakers of the day—as well as record turntables and picture records.

Now

Cassettes and Discs

By the 1980s new technology was transforming the industry. The major agents of change were the cassette and the compact disc, often called the CD. The cassette is a plastic cartridge containing magnetic tape on which the music is recorded. The CD is a round, flat platter on which the music is stored by digital code. By the mid-1990's compact discs accounted for more than 60 percent of total sales, cassettes for 36 percent, and records for less than 1 percent.

▲ COMPACT DISCS AND PLAYER

◀ EARLY PHONOGRAPH

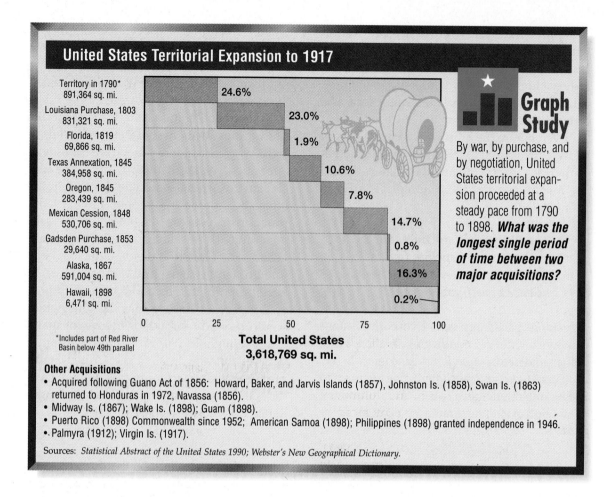

United States Territorial Expansion to 1917

Territory	Percentage
Territory in 1790* 891,364 sq. mi.	24.6%
Louisiana Purchase, 1803 831,321 sq. mi.	23.0%
Florida, 1819 69,866 sq. mi.	1.9%
Texas Annexation, 1845 384,958 sq. mi.	10.6%
Oregon, 1845 283,439 sq. mi.	7.8%
Mexican Cession, 1848 530,706 sq. mi.	14.7%
Gadsden Purchase, 1853 29,640 sq. mi.	0.8%
Alaska, 1867 591,004 sq. mi.	16.3%
Hawaii, 1898 6,471 sq. mi.	0.2%

0   25   50   75   100

Total United States 3,618,769 sq. mi.

*Includes part of Red River Basin below 49th parallel

Graph Study

By war, by purchase, and by negotiation, United States territorial expansion proceeded at a steady pace from 1790 to 1898. *What was the longest single period of time between two major acquisitions?*

Other Acquisitions
- Acquired following Guano Act of 1856: Howard, Baker, and Jarvis Islands (1857), Johnston Is. (1858), Swan Is. (1863) returned to Honduras in 1972, Navassa (1856).
- Midway Is. (1867); Wake Is. (1898); Guam (1898).
- Puerto Rico (1898) Commonwealth since 1952; American Samoa (1898); Philippines (1898) granted independence in 1946.
- Palmyra (1912); Virgin Is. (1917).

Sources: *Statistical Abstract of the United States 1990; Webster's New Geographical Dictionary.*

■ Problems of an Overseas Empire

The new possessions posed constitutional problems summarized in the question, "Does the Constitution follow the flag?" Congress, according to the Constitution, may not set tariff duties on goods carried from one part of the United States to another. Did this mean that no duties would be laid on goods from American colonies? The Constitution guarantees to all American citizens certain civil rights. Did constitutional guarantees of civil rights extend to the people of the new colonies who knew nothing of American justice?

The Supreme Court decided that the Constitution did not cover overseas possessions. Puerto Rico, the Court ruled, was a dependency; therefore Congress could set tariffs on its products. Other decisions determined that inhabitants of dependencies enjoyed full civil rights only if granted them by congressional legislation.

Cuba

According to the Teller Amendment, the United States pledged to withdraw from Cuba when order was restored. After three years of civil war, however, the island was in terrible condition. The United States Army remained in Cuba to set up a republican government, oversee Cuban finances, and establish public health programs.

In 1901, to protect its interests in Cuba, the United States Congress added the Platt Amendment to an army bill. This amendment, which governed the relations between Cuba and the United States for 33 years, provided that: (1) Cuba should not make any treaty with another nation that weakened its independence; (2) Cuba should allow the United States the right to buy or lease naval stations; (3) Cuba's public debt should not exceed its capacity to pay; and (4) the United States should have the right to intervene to protect Cuban independence and keep order. These conditions, written into Cuba's constitution and into a treaty with the United

States, made Cuba an American **protectorate**—a nation or region controlled by a stronger state. The attitude that Cuba was part of "the white man's burden" was reflected in an editorial by William Allen White in Kansas's *Emporia Gazette*:

66 *Only Anglo-Saxons can govern themselves. The Cubans will need despotic government . . . to restrain anarchy until Cuba is filled with Yankees.* 99

For almost four years, Cuba was under military rule directed by General Leonard Wood. The greatest achievement of Wood's administration was the suppression of yellow fever. An American medical team under Dr. Walter Reed proved the theory of a Cuban physician, Carlos J. Finlay: that yellow fever is transmitted by the stegomyia mosquito. American doctors and volunteers allowed themselves to be bitten by mosquitoes, and some of them died as martyrs to medical progress. Major William C. Gorgas, an Army doctor, carried on a campaign to eliminate mosquitoes from Havana. By 1901, for the first time in centuries, there was no yellow fever in the Cuban capital.

Puerto Rico

The United States had made no prior commitment to withdraw from Puerto Rico as it had done in Cuba. That island's cultural ties with Spain and Latin America through the

Visualizing History

▲ **AN OVERSEAS EMPIRE** As in most wars, the civilians suffered many hardships. Thousands of Filipinos perished from sickness, starvation, and other indirect effects of war. The Philippines gained independence in 1946. *When was Puerto Rico granted territorial status?*

Roman Catholic Church, the Spanish language, and other traditions had existed for nearly 300 years. Yet, the United States chose to keep the island as its territory.

After a brief period of military rule, Congress gradually allowed Puerto Rico a degree of self-government. The Puerto Rican people demanded either independence or complete self-rule under the American flag. In 1917 they were granted territorial status and made citizens of the United States.

Section 3 ★ Assessment

Checking for Understanding

1. **Define** protectorate.
2. **Describe** how problems with Cuba and Puerto Rico were resolved.

Critical Thinking

3. **Making Decisions** Analyze the reasoning of the Supreme Court on constitutional guarantees for overseas possessions. Do you agree?
4. **Examining Issues** Re-create the diagram shown here, and list the ways in which the

United States resolved annexation difficulties in the Philippines.

Resolutions

INTERDISCIPLINARY ACTIVITY

5. **The Arts** Research the origins of these names: *Puerto Rico, Venezuela,* and *the Philippines.* Compare your findings with the findings of other students.

Using the Internet

◄ ONE OF THE PANAMA
CANAL'S GIANT LOCK GATES

Are you one of many people worldwide who would like to surf the Net? Using the Internet can give you the chance to find information on many subjects.

Learning the Skill

The Internet is a global computer network that offers many features, including electronic mail, information, and on-line shopping.

Before you can connect to the Internet and use its services, however, you must have three things: a computer, a modem (a device that lets your computer send and receive data over a telephone line), and a service provider. A service provider is a company that, for a fee, gives you entry to the Internet.

Once you are connected, the easiest and fastest way to access sites and information is to use a "browser," a program that lets you view and explore information on the World Wide Web. The Web consists of many documents called "Web pages," each of which has its own address, or Uniform Resource Locator (URL). Many URLs start with the keystrokes *http://*.

Practicing the Skill

This chapter focuses on American expansion beyond its borders, including its role in the construction of the Panama Canal. Surf the Internet to learn more about the building of this engineering marvel.

1. Log on to the Internet and access one of the World Wide Web search tools, such as *Yahoo!*, *Lycos*, or *WebCrawler*.

2. Search by category or by name. If you search by category in *Yahoo!*, for example, click on *Panama*. To search by name, type in *Panama Canal*.

3. Scroll the list of Web pages that appears when the search is complete. Select a page to bring up, and read or print it. Repeat the process until you have enough information you can use to develop a short report on the construction of the Panama Canal.

APPLYING THE SKILL

4. Using the steps just described, search the Internet for information on any other topic in this chapter that interests you. Based on the information, write an article for your school newspaper or magazine.

★★★★★★★★★★★★★★★★★★★★★★★★★

A New Arena

Guide to Reading

Main Idea
Under President Roosevelt, the United States expanded its role in world affairs.

Reading Strategy
Organizing Information As you read about the nation's increasingly aggressive foreign policy, use a diagram similiar to the one shown here to list examples of Roosevelt's "Big Stick" diplomacy.

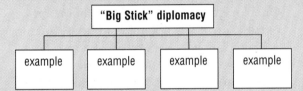

"Big Stick" diplomacy

example | example | example | example

Objectives
After studying this section, you should be able to

★ give examples of Roosevelt's "Big Stick" diplomacy.

★ discuss the goals and results of the "Open Door" policy in China.

★ discuss America's concerns over the Russo-Japanese War.

Key Terms
anarchist, corollary, partitioned, sphere of influence, indemnity

▶ THEODORE ROOSEVELT, BRONZE RELIEF

*I*n the Western Hemisphere, the acquisition of Puerto Rico and the establishment of a protectorate over Cuba gave the United States a new interest in this region. American expansion into the Pacific brought closer contact with East Asian nations, particularly China. Several European countries, along with Japan, were fiercely competing for trading rights in China. The United States entered a new and complex arena of international politics.

■ The Election of 1900

In 1900 William Jennings Bryan, again the Democratic candidate, attempted to make imperialism the paramount issue of the presidential campaign. The Republicans again nominated McKinley for President. Theodore Roosevelt, who had become governor of New York, received the nomination for Vice President. As much as possible, the Republicans avoided discussion of imperialism because they were divided. The result was an even greater Republican victory than that in 1896.

Six months after his second inauguration, McKinley spoke of the United States's new position in the world. Previously a strong supporter of isolationism, he announced a change of heart, saying:

❝ *Isolation is no longer possible or desirable. God and man have linked the nations together. No nation can longer be indifferent to any other. . . .* ❞

President McKinley explained that America's diversity of products and its efficiency in producing them had so increased that there was an urgent need for more markets. He proposed reciprocity treaties with foreign nations, providing for mutual lowering of tariffs.

McKinley did not live to put his new policy into effect. The day after delivering his speech he was shot by an **anarchist,** one who opposes all forms of government. Just short of 43 years old, Roosevelt became the youngest President.

■ The Big Stick

Theodore Roosevelt had a genius for the dramatic gesture. He told young men, "Don't flinch, don't foul, hit the line hard." Roosevelt's actions were sometimes impulsive, sometimes unwise, but he firmly believed that power imposed responsibility. One of Roosevelt's mottoes in foreign policy was a West African saying, "Speak softly and carry a big stick."

The Panama Canal

The "Big Stick" was most in evidence in the Caribbean. Roosevelt and others believed that in addition to saving time for commercial shipping, a canal would answer the strategic need to shuttle warships between the Atlantic and the Pacific oceans.

This was clearly demonstrated during the Spanish-American War. The battleship *Oregon,* ordered from Puget Sound to Cuba,

• •
Footnotes to History

Digging the Canal   The route of the Panama Canal ran through hills of soft volcanic material. As a shovelful of dirt was removed, more soil slid into place. Massive landslides occurred as the heavier hilltops lost the support of their subsoil. To keep digging was the only solution: First the hilltops were dug away, then the lower layers of soil. Crews dug more than 211 million cubic yards (161 million cu. m) of dirt before the canal was completed.

was forced to steam 14,000 miles around Cape Horn—3 times as far as if there had been a canal.

In the 1800s a French company had made a vain and costly effort to cut through Panama. Early in the 1890s, an American company started to dig a canal through Nicaragua but soon abandoned the attempt. In 1901 Britain, which also had an interest in the canal, agreed that the United States could build, control, and fortify a canal, provided that ships of all nations were charged an equal toll.

Immediately, Secretary of State John Hay offered Colombia, which controlled Panama, $10 million and a yearly rent of $250,000 for the right to construct a canal through Panama and control a narrow strip of land on either side. However, feeling that the price was too low and fearful of losing control of Panama, the Colombian senate unanimously refused to ratify the agreement.

Roosevelt was furious. He let it be known that he would not mind if Panama revolted. On November 3, 1903, a revolution broke out, and an independent Republic of Panama was proclaimed. On November 6 the United States recognized Panama's independence. Less than two weeks later the United States and Panama signed a treaty for the canal.

Roosevelt defended his Big Stick diplomacy in Panama on the ground that he advanced "the needs of collective civilization" by speeding up the building of an inter-ocean canal. His action was widely condemned in the United States as unjustifiable aggression. In Latin America it aroused dislike and distrust of the United States.

The engineering difficulties involved in cutting through the Isthmus of Panama were enormous and were compounded by the tremendous health problems encountered in the tropics. In 1885 an English writer wrote of Panama:

❝ *In all the world there is not perhaps now concentrated in any so much foul disease. . . . The Isthmus is a damp, tropical jungle, intensely hot, swarming with mosquitoes . . . the home, even as Nature made it, of yellow fever, typhus, and dysentery.* ❞

George W. Goethals, a colonel in the Corps of Engineers, directed the engineering feat that completed the canal in 1914. Dr. William C. Gorgas, who had cleaned up Havana, reduced the health threats in Panama.

Venezuela

Roosevelt, like Cleveland, defended Venezuela from possible European aggression, strengthening the Monroe Doctrine. By 1902 Venezuela owed money to citizens of several European countries. Cipriano Castro, the Venezuelan dictator-president, refused either to pay the debts or submit them to arbitration. Roosevelt said the Monroe Doctrine did not protect Latin American nations against punishment for misbehavior.

After consultation with the American State Department, Great Britain and Germany, Venezuela's two principal creditors, blockaded Venezuelan ports to force payment. The blockade was very unpopular in the United States because it was perceived as a violation of the Monroe Doctrine. Feeling was intensified when Venezuelan gunboats were sunk and Venezuelan ports bombarded. Public anger moved Roosevelt to press for an end of the blockade and the submission of the dispute to arbitration. Although both parties agreed to arbitration, Great Britain was quicker to respond than Germany was. This added to Roosevelt's distrust of the rising German empire.

Roosevelt Corollary

In 1903 Argentine foreign minister Luis Drago urged that forcibly collecting debts from bankrupt countries be made a violation of international law. If the United States opposed Drago and allowed foreign nations to block the coasts and bombard the cities of defaulting Latin American nations, the door was left open to further aggression. If, however, the United States outlawed forcible collection of debts, it might be pushed into defending financial dishonesty. The President's reply to the Drago Doctrine became known as the Roosevelt **Corollary,** or addition, to the Monroe Doctrine. Whenever an American republic was guilty of "chronic

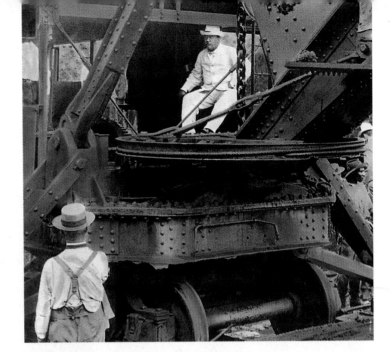

Visualizing History ▲ THE PANAMA CANAL Work on the Panama Canal began in 1904 and lasted 10 years. *What difficulties were encountered?*

wrongdoing," said Roosevelt, the United States might have to intervene itself.

Dominican Republic

The Roosevelt Corollary was first applied in the Dominican Republic. In 1905 the United States assumed the responsibility of collecting Dominican customs. The United States Marine Corps collected the duties and divided them to support the Dominican government and to pay that nation's debts to European countries.

Roosevelt's successor, President William Howard Taft, continued Roosevelt's policies but with a shift of emphasis. Taft's secretary of state, Philander C. Knox, promoted American business interests abroad with the slogan, "Every diplomat a salesman." In Latin America this "dollar diplomacy" resulted in increased sales of United States goods—including warships—and in efforts to increase American investments there.

Although Taft described his brand of diplomacy as "substituting dollars for bullets," sometimes he used both. In 1912 he sent marines to Nicaragua to install a more friendly government and to force acceptance of a loan from New York bankers. Such policies increased the unpopularity of the United States in Latin America.

▲ SPHERES OF INFLUENCE Cities in China grew into centers of trade. Major international powers divided China into spheres of influence. *What clash of interest led to the Russo-Japanese War?*

■ The Balance of Power in East Asia

Roosevelt realized that the position of the United States in East Asia was weak. He called the Philippines the "Achilles' heel" of American defense; they were easily vulnerable to attack by Japan. China and Russia also posed problems.

China and the Open Door

At the close of the nineteenth century, it looked as though China, like Africa, would be **partitioned,** or divided, among stronger powers. In 1898 and 1899, Russia, Germany, France, and Great Britain forced China to lease its ports, some of them for 99 years. Each "leasehold" was expected to become the center of a **sphere of influence**—an area where a European nation controlled economic development.

The United States and Great Britain, in order to ensure open avenues of trade with China, decided to oppose the parceling out of Chinese territory. Early in 1898 the British government proposed a joint declaration with the United States in favor of the "Open Door"—with the goal of preserving equal trading opportunities in China for all foreign nations. At that time the United States was cool to the idea, but its annexation of the Philippines changed the American attitude.

John Hay, secretary of state, thought that the days of American isolationism must end. Having defended the acquisition of an overseas empire, he agreed with Great Britain on the policy of an Open Door in China. In September 1899, Hay sent notes to countries with leaseholds in China asking that they keep the ports open to vessels of all nations on equal terms.

Boxer Rebellion

While foreign countries debated control of China, Chinese secret societies were organizing to oust foreign control. One of these was called "the Boxers" by Westerners because of the physical exercises they practiced.

When a falsified story was printed in America suggesting that Westerners were negotiating the dismantling of a Chinese monument, the Boxer Rebellion broke out. With secret aid from the Chinese government, the Boxers intended to wipe out "foreign devils" and their Christian converts. They killed more than 200 foreigners, mostly missionaries and their families. For 7 weeks the Boxers laid siege to foreign embassies in Beijing.

During this crisis Hay worked to prevent full-scale retaliation and war against China and to persuade the leaseholding powers not to use the Boxer Rebellion as an excuse to partition the country. In July 1900, he sent a second set of Open Door notes. This time he declared that the policy of the United States was to seek ways to "preserve Chinese territorial and administrative entity."

The United States lacked sufficient military power to enforce Hay's Open Door notes of 1899 and 1900. Equal trading opportunities in China and the preservation of China's territorial integrity lay in maintaining a "balance of power" among the nations with ambitions in East Asia.

Russo-Japanese War

China's two closest neighbors, Japan and Russia, were especially threatening. In 1893 Japan established a protectorate over the independent kingdom of Korea and obtained Formosa and other islands off China's northeast coast. Japan had designs on the resource-rich Chinese province of Manchuria, in which Russia was already established. The Russians hoped to move into Korea. This clash of interests led to the Russo-Japanese War in 1904.

Japan won victories over Russia on both land and sea. By the summer of 1905, both countries were ready to make peace. The Japanese secretly asked Roosevelt if he would serve as go-between. After consulting the czar, Roosevelt formally offered to help make peace. Both nations accepted the President's proposals and sent diplomats to a peace conference in Portsmouth, New Hampshire, in August 1905.

Treaty of Portsmouth

The President induced Japan to give up claims for a money **indemnity,** or payment for damages, and Russia to give up the southern half of the island of Sakhalin (SA•kuh•LEEN). Japan also took over Russian interests in southern Manchuria.

The war altered the balance of power in East Asia. Now it was no longer Russian expansion that was most to be feared, but Japanese. Roosevelt himself believed that there was potential danger of war.

Roosevelt arranged a compromise in 1907 and 1908, known as the Gentlemen's Agreement. In a complicated series of maneuvers, he soothed Japanese anger and showed the Japanese that he was not afraid of them. To check Japanese expansion toward the Philippines, Roosevelt recognized Japan as dominant in Korea and Manchuria.

The resolution of the Russo-Japanese War was an example of Roosevelt's efforts to use arbitration rather than war to settle controversies. Although he upgraded America's military power, he believed that the United States had an obligation as a leader of an interdependent world to act responsibly.

Section 4 ★ Assessment

Checking for Understanding

1. **Define** anarchist, corollary, partitioned, sphere of influence, indemnity.
2. **Indicate** how President Roosevelt acted as peacemaker in the Russo-Japanese War.
3. **Explain** how Big Stick diplomacy led to ill feeling against the United States.

Critical Thinking

4. **Analyzing Issues** Re-create the diagram shown here, and identify the goal and results of the "Open Door" policy that the United States adopted in its relations with China.

INTERDISCIPLINARY ACTIVITY

5. **The Arts** Create a cartoon that illustrates your opinions regarding America's "Big Stick" policy.

Self-Check Quiz

Visit the *American History: The Modern Era Since 1865* Web site at **me.glencoe.com** and click on **Chapter 12—Self-Check Quizzes** to prepare for the chapter test.

Using Vocabulary

Assume that you are a reporter for an antiadministration newspaper covering the Latin American situation in 1903. Write a feature article describing Theodore Roosevelt's policies using the following vocabulary terms.

imperialism   protectorate
isolationism   corollary

Reviewing Facts

1. **Explain** how confrontation with Great Britain in 1895–1896 led to strengthening the American navy.

2. **List** three reasons America went to war over Cuba. Which was most important?

3. **Discuss** why many Americans favored an Open Door policy in China.

4. **Indicate** why the United States needed to build the Panama Canal.

Understanding Concepts

Economic and Political Power

1. How did the use of the Big Stick in Latin America increase American wealth and political power?

Confrontation

2. Re-create the diagram shown here, and list the reasons why the United States was unable to avoid military confrontation with Cuba.

Military Confrontation

Critical Thinking

1. **Recognizing Stereotypes** How did adherence to social Darwinism cause the United States to stereotype people who lived in countries under their possession? In what ways did stereotyped thinking influence political and economic policies toward these territories?

2. **Analyzing Fine Art** The painting on this page, *Charge of San Juan Hill*, by Frederic Remington depicts the bravado of the Rough Riders. Analyze the painting and answer the questions that follow.

   a. What is happening in the painting?

   b. What details do you see in this scene?

   c. Do you think Remington has captured the reality of battle? Why or why not? Give reasons to support your answer.

▲ CHARGE OF SAN JUAN HILL BY FREDERIC REMINGTON

History and Geography

The Panama Canal

The building of the Panama Canal was regarded as one of the great engineering feats of the time. Many nations attempted to build a canal across Panama. The project, which cost more than $365 million, took seven years to complete. Study the map of the canal, then answer the questions that follow.

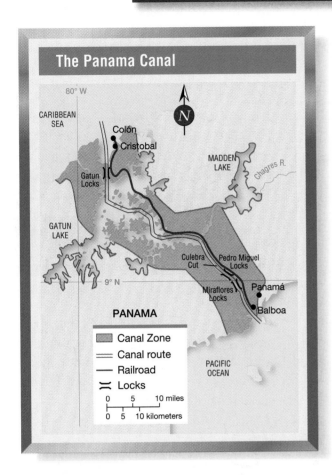

The Panama Canal

CARIBBEAN SEA

Colón
Cristobal

MADDEN LAKE

Chagres R.

Gatun Locks

GATUN LAKE

Culebra Cut

Pedro Miguel Locks

9° N

Miraflores Locks

Panamá

Balboa

PACIFIC OCEAN

PANAMA

- Canal Zone
- Canal route
- Railroad
- ⊃⊂ Locks

0   5   10 miles
0   5   10 kilometers

80° W

1. **Location** What cities are located near the path of the canal?

2. **Movement** In what direction would a ship on route to Cristobal from Balboa travel?

3. **Human/Environment Interaction** What military and economic benefits would a canal through Panama provide?

Cooperative Learning — Interdisciplinary Activity: Geography

Work in a group of three or more to plan a trip from where you live to one of the following cities: Mexico City, Mexico; San Juan, Puerto Rico; Toronto, Canada; Fairbanks, Alaska.

Each member of your group will do one of the following: (a) find historic places to visit; (b) draw the route to follow on a map; or (c) make a list of provisions and clothes to bring. Combine your findings in a travel information packet. Share your trip with the rest of the class.

Practicing Skills

Using the Internet

Go through the steps described on page 386 for searching the Internet, and collect information about a modern-day topic that interests you, such as music or sports. Write an article for the school newspaper or magazine based on this information you retrieved.

Technology Activity

Using a Word Processor

Use the Internet and other library resources to find out what another country thinks about the United States. Determine if that country's view is positive or negative and what reasons the nation provides for its opinion. Use this information to write a brief report and present it to the class.

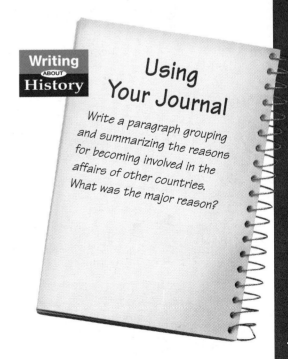

Writing ABOUT History

Using Your Journal

Write a paragraph grouping and summarizing the reasons for becoming involved in the affairs of other countries. What was the major reason?

CHAPTER 13

★★★

The Progressive Era
1893–1920

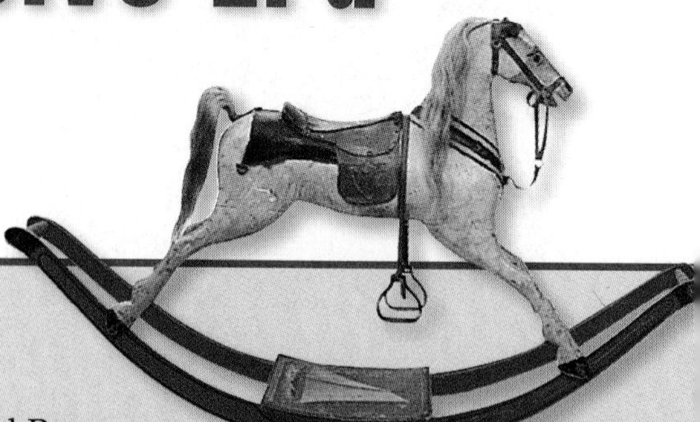

▲ **WOOD AND LEATHER ROCKING HORSE**

Setting the Scene

Focus

In the late 1800s, the Grangers and Populists had sought to resist corrupt government and unfair business practices. By 1900 their stalled efforts were given fresh life by a new group of reformers—the progressives. These optimistic, largely urban, middle-class reformers were confident in their ability to improve government and the quality of life. Their reforms were based not only on traditional democratic values but also on the new philosophy of pragmatism and study of the social sciences.

Journal Notes

Note in your journal, as you read the chapter, how women continued to push for the right to vote.

Concepts to Understand

★ Why **reform** efforts were successful in correcting the worst abuses of big business and government

★ How **values and beliefs** shaped the program of the Progressive Era

Read to Discover . . .

★ the types of reform that progressive leaders advocated.

★ the limitations of progressivism.

HISTORY Online

Chapter Overview
Visit the *American History: The Modern Era Since 1865* Web site at **me.glencoe.com** and click on **Chapter 13—Chapter Overviews** to preview chapter information.

CULTURAL

• **1890** *Census shows population of the United States at 63 million*

• **1897** *The first subway system is completed in Boston*

1890 — 1900

POLITICAL

• **1890** *Sherman Silver Purchase Act passes*

• **1902** *Oregon adopts the initiative and referendum*

History AND ART

The Lone Tenement
by George Wesley Bellows, 1909

This urban scene displays the artist's vigorous and spontaneous style. Bellows is also remembered for his sports paintings, particularly prizefights.

●**1909** *National Association for the Advancement of Colored People (NAACP) is formed*

●**1920** *Sinclair Lewis's* Main Street *is bestseller*

1910

1920

●**1917** *United States declares war on Germany*

●**1920** *Ratification of woman suffrage*

★★

Sources of Progressivism

Guide to Reading

Main Idea
Reformers of the early 1900s proposed a variety of changes designed to improve the quality of life in the nation's cities.

Reading Strategy
Taking Notes As you read about the sources of progressivism, list the general characteristics of the persons considered to be progressives. Use an outline form similar to the one shown here.

Characteristics of Progressives
I. Profession
   A.
   B.
II. Political Affiliation
   A.
   B.

Objectives
After studying this section, you should be able to

★ discuss the role of the muckrakers in identifying social ills and promoting social change.

★ explain how methods and strategies used in business and education influenced social reform.

Key Terms
social gospel, pragmatism

► **LABOR UNION POSTER**

Despite widespread social, political, and economic change in the late 1800s, the Gilded Age produced no broad effort to improve society. Populism was a large movement, but it was farm based and did not attract urban workers to its goals. The labor movement was also large, but it involved itself primarily with issues related to workers' jobs, wages, and working conditions.

Alternating periods of prosperity and depression accompanied industrialization in the late nineteenth century. Economic contractions shook the United States in the mid-1870s and well into the mid-1880s. The depression that followed the Panic of 1893, however, was the worst the nation had yet seen. As the split between rich and poor became too wide to ignore, Americans of all classes began to ask hard questions about the nation's political and economic systems.

$ **ECONOMICS**

■ Inequality in America

Not until the 1890s did Americans begin to show widespread concern about the direction in which their society was moving. Increasing poverty was one area of concern.

The Gap Between the Rich and Poor

Millions of American laborers worked long hours for low wages in the late 1800s. Wages of industrial workers averaged $10 to $12 for a 60- to 80-hour week. One of every

5 women worked, frequently for as little as $6 to $8 a week, and children received even less. If workers were injured in industrial accidents, were laid off when business slowed, or became unemployed for any reason at all, their income completely stopped. At the other end of the scale were the immensely rich, the people who owned huge yachts, palatial estates, private railroad cars, and summer retreats covering thousands of acres. In 1900, when Andrew Carnegie earned $25 million from his steel company, the average worker made $500.

While 20 percent of the nation's families lived in comfort, 80 percent barely subsisted. A 1904 study estimated that 10 million Americans—12 percent of the nation's population—were "underfed, underclothed, and poorly housed." Relief for the poor was of little help because it was local, unsystematic, and largely dependent on private charity for funds.

It was not just the disparity of wealth that was alarming but also the distribution of political power. Wealthy industrialists appeared to dominate government. With such vast wealth and power at the top of society and such grinding poverty at the bottom, many Americans feared revolution. $

Socialist Solutions

Some Americans turned to socialism as the answer. Edward Bellamy's 1887 novel *Looking Backward 2000–1887* made socialism seem an attractive alternative to the existing industrial society. His book tells the story of a nineteenth-century person in the United States who awakens from a prolonged hypnotic trance to find himself alive in a socialist paradise in the year 2000. All business has been merged into one big trust run by the people themselves; there is work and leisure for all without a trace of poverty or crime. Bellamy's vision of a socialist utopia made such an impact that his book sold 1 million copies, and numerous Nationalist Clubs were founded to advance his ideas.

Bellamy had no real program for action, however, and his followers eventually drifted toward other reform movements. Bellamy's influence, though, was reinforced by other socialist writers. Socialist ideas were widely circulated by popular authors such as Jack London and Upton Sinclair.

Popular labor leader Eugene V. Debs also lost faith in capitalism after being jailed during the Pullman strike of 1894. Declaring that in a democracy workers could gain control of the government and use it to change the free enterprise system, he organized the American Socialist party.

Opposed to Debs and other moderates were radical socialists such as Daniel De Leon, who preached that democratic reform was useless. "We Socialists are not reformers; we are Revolutionists," he

Weekly Wages in the Woolen Industry

Occupation and Location	Men 1890	Men 1900	Women 1890	Women 1900
New England Bobbin hands, doffers, and filling and roving carriers	4.50	5.00	3.00	4.00
Dresser tenders and beamers	12.00	8.00	6.00	6.50
General hands, helpers, and laborers	6.50	7.00	5.00	5.50
Loom fixers	12.50	13.50	—	—
Overseers and foreman	19.50	19.50	—	—
Spinners	7.50	9.50	5.50	6.00
Weavers	7.50	9.00	6.50	7.50
All Occupations	7.50	8.00	6.50	6.50
Middle States All Occupations	7.50	9.00	5.00	5.00
Southern States All Occupations	6.50	6.50	3.50	3.50
Central States All Occupations	8.50	8.00	4.00	4.00
Pacific States All Occupations	9.50	9.50	5.00	5.00
All Sections All Occupations for workers under 16	3.00	3.50	3.00	3.50

Median weekly rates in dollars

Source: Twelfth Census of the United States, 1900 *Special Reports: Employees and Wages (1903).*

Chart Study Note the differences in pay rates for skilled and unskilled labor for men and women, the regional variations in pay, and the lower wages for children. ***Why are no rates shown for female supervisors?***

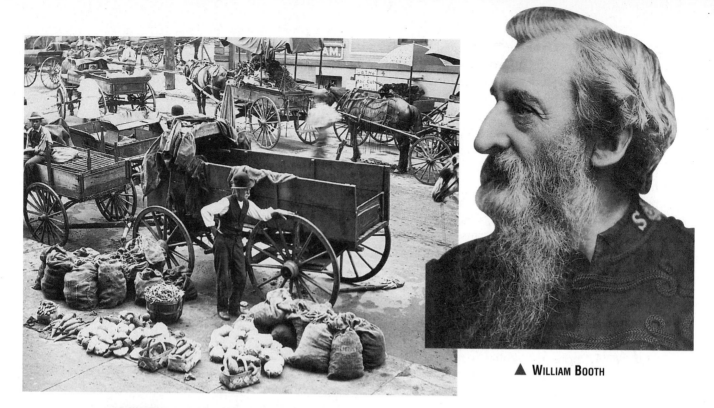

▲ WILLIAM BOOTH

▲ THE SOCIAL GOSPEL The Salvation Army, after being established in England by General William Booth, was organized in the United States in 1880. It helped provide food, lodging, and hope for the urban needy. *What else did the Salvation Army provide?*

declared. "We care nothing for forms. We want a change of the inside of the mechanism of society. . . ." De Leon argued that even labor unions were traitors to the working class because they compromised with the industrialists. He proposed to organize all workers into new industrial unions that would eventually take over American business.

The Wobblies

Debs and De Leon briefly cooperated in 1905 in founding such a labor union, the Industrial Workers of the World, or "Wobblies." Debs soon withdrew, however, and the IWW rejected De Leon in favor of more radical leaders who preached murder and sabotage. The preamble of the IWW's constitution declared, "The working class and the employing class have nothing in common. There can be no peace so long as hunger and want are found among millions of working people. . . ."

Wherever the IWW existed, there were confrontations, strikes, sabotage, and often violence. The IWW remained strong, however, until after World War I, when Americans rejected radical politics.

More Moderate Voices

Most socialists were more moderate than the Wobblies, however, and the socialist movement gained strength throughout the early 1900s. At its height in 1912, Debs polled nearly 1 million votes as the Socialist party candidate for President. Although this was less than 10 percent of the total votes cast, the socialist movement had an importance greater than its numbers indicated. Other more moderate reformers called "progressives" owed much of their success to a growing public feeling that the only way to save the capitalist system was to improve it.

■ Progressive Leadership

The Progressive Era occupied the first 15 years of the twentieth century. Although the reforms of this period are sometimes called the Progressive movement, that label can be misleading. Unlike the Populists, the progressives were not a political party.

Who the Progressives Were

Although a Progressive party was formed in 1912, progressives also were found in both major parties. Nor were progressives united by a geographic section or by an occupation. Instead, they were a broad and largely unorganized group of reformers who often worked independently, each seeking solutions to a specific problem. Some were local reformers, while others worked for change at state or national levels. The reforms progressives advocated sometimes even conflicted.

Also unlike the Populists, the progressives were generally not the victims of existing conditions. They were mostly urban middle-class professionals who worked as journalists, social workers, educators, and clergy. Although they themselves were not suffering, they sympathized with those who were.

The Social Gospel

Progressives among Catholic priests, Jewish rabbis, and Protestant ministers began to preach a new **social gospel:** that religious organizations should work to improve society as well as to meet the spiritual needs of their congregations. Leaders such as Washington Gladden, Josiah Strong, and Walter Rauschenbush were concerned about social problems. Rauschenbush explained his view:

> " *Our business is to make over an antiquated and immoral economic system. . . . Our inherited Christian faith dealt with individuals; our present task deals with society.* "

In 1908 the National Council of the Churches of Christ was founded to support social reform. In every large city the Salvation Army—a religious group devoted to helping the needy—provided food, lodging, and hope for the despairing and poor. Like the settlement houses of the late 1800s, urban churches began to consider the whole person by providing recreational facilities, adult-education classes, nurseries, and counseling.

Women Reformers

Women also became a driving force for progressive reform. That women figured so largely in the Progressive movement was an indication that their status was improving.

Ida Tarbell
1857–1944

AMERICAN PORTRAITS

After teaching school briefly, Ida Tarbell made her career as a writer and editor. She wrote hundreds of articles and many books, but her reputation as a "muckraker" rests on one book, *The History of the Standard Oil Company,* initially published as articles in *McClure's Magazine.*

Her interest in Standard Oil was deeply personal. Her father claimed that the company had forced him out of the oil tank business and had caused his partner to commit suicide. *McClure's* asked her to write about Standard Oil because of her knowledge of the oil business and because of her flair for writing.

For two years she researched Standard Oil's practices. Her revelations created such a popular furor that Standard Oil was investigated and eventually broken up by the Supreme Court for violating federal antitrust laws.

By 1900 women's colleges in the North and East had been turning out well-trained graduates for two generations. These women were aware of and interested in the various issues of the day. National women's clubs devoted to the study of such issues were common. By 1910 these clubs had nearly 1 million members.

Furthermore, the rights of women were expanding. By 1900 every state recognized the right of women to make a will. Most states recognized the right of women to dispose of their own wages, and some states had given them the right to equal guardianship of children. More importantly, five Western states had adopted woman suffrage.

The settlement-house movement, which women continued to lead, expanded into broader areas of reform such as slum clearance and legislation to limit working hours and outlaw child labor. Florence Kelley left Jane Addams and Hull House in Chicago and founded the National Consumers League, where she organized boycotts of goods produced by children or by workers in unsafe or unhealthful conditions. Another former Hull House social worker, Julia Lathrop, became the first head of the federal Children's Bureau, created in the Department of Labor in 1912 and now part of Health and Human Services. Other female progressives included Carrie Chapman Catt, widely known for her work in the woman suffrage movement. Elizabeth Platt Decker headed the General Federation of Women's Clubs, which attracted nearly 1 million women in the early 1900s to promote the arts, education, and community health.

Striving for Big-Business Efficiency

Ironically, progressive reformers owed a great debt to the big businesses that so many of them detested. Unlike Populists, who believed that common people could solve society's problems, progressives put their faith in experts. Although critical of the methods and power of business leaders, progressives admired their ability to run large companies smoothly and efficiently. Progressives were confident that just like the trained managers, scientists, and efficiency experts who solved business problems, expert reformers could analyze and solve problems that kept society from running smoothly.

■ Educators and Investigators

In the mid-1800s, most American colleges were small, church-supported institutions less concerned with knowledge than with shaping the character of their students. Graduates who wanted to pursue further studies often went to Germany, where universities awarded an advanced degree, the Ph.D. These students brought back to America a learning style that emphasized questioning and research instead of memorizing facts. They pioneered changes in American colleges.

The Influence of Pragmatism

Coupled with educational reform was a new way of thinking known as **pragmatism,** an approach to problem solving that was popularized by Harvard philosopher William James. Pragmatists questioned the absolute truth of science. They believed that scientific laws stated only what was *probably* true and that ideas must be tested to see if they worked.

By the late 1800s many American colleges offered courses in social work, economics, political science, and sociology and granted advanced degrees. Professors such as social scientist Richard Ely at the University of Wisconsin taught students to solve problems pragmatically. At Johns Hopkins University, historian Henry Adams taught students how to do research and told them, "By the instrumentality of scholars great improvement of society is to be made." American colleges thus provided a core of reformers to study society and change it.

Pragmatist John Dewey, who taught at the University of Chicago, argued that the value of government actions should be measured by the good they do. Harvard Law School professor Oliver Wendell Holmes, Jr., was a pragmatist. In his book *The Common*

Law, he wrote that law should not be an absolute set of principles but a tool to meet the needs of society. When Holmes was appointed to the Supreme Court in 1902, his ideas began to influence its decisions.

The Muckrakers

Other, more popular, writers played a major role in investigating and exposing a variety of social problems. President Theodore Roosevelt compared these writers to a character in John Bunyan's book, *Pilgrim's Progress,* who constantly looked downward and raked filth, and he labeled them "muckrakers."

Most muckrakers were journalists who wrote for popular magazines like *McClure's Magazine, Cosmopolitan,* and *Collier's.* Although similar to the "yellow journalism" of the period, these articles were not written to boost sales but to expose conditions the writers had found deeply disturbing. For example, in 1902 Lincoln Steffens wrote a series of articles for *McClure's Magazine* that described shocking graft and corruption in city governments across the nation. He was followed in the same magazine by Ida Tarbell's exposé of the corrupt business practices of the Standard Oil Company. In 1906 David Phillips shocked the nation with a series in *Cosmopolitan* about links between big business and 75 United States senators.

Other muckrakers revealed the results of their investigations in books. In 1906 John Spargo's *The Bitter Cry of the Children* wrote about abuses of child labor, and two years

Visualizing History ▲ **THE MUCKRAKERS** The investigative reporting of journalists such as Ida Tarbell, Ray Stannard Baker, and Lincoln Steffens (above) made them frequent contributors to national magazines. *Why did President Roosevelt call such reporters "muckrakers"?*

later, Ray Stannard Baker's *Following the Color Line* revealed the long pattern of discrimination against African Americans in both the North and the South. Still other muckrakers were novelists who used fiction to criticize existing social conditions. In *The Octopus,* Frank Norris told how railroads dominated wheat farmers in a rich Western valley. Despite their revelations of society's ills, most muckrakers were not activists. They merely identified problems and argued for reform but counted on others to accomplish it.

Section 1 ★ Assessment

Checking for Understanding

1. **Define** social gospel, pragmatism.

Critical Thinking

2. **Understanding Cause and Effect** What relationship do the ideas of philosophy professor William James have to progressive reform?

3. **Summarizing** Re-create the diagram shown here, and list five problems in American society that muckraking journalists described in their writing.

Problems

INTERDISCIPLINARY ACTIVITY

4. **Economics** Write a letter to a 1910 newspaper that tells why you believe government should or should not get involved in wage reform.

Read to Discover

Why did naturalism, harsh and uncompromising, gain momentum during the years when the United States experienced a population boom? Read how Dreiser describes urban living. The city, with its immense presence and its disregard for the individual, proved the perfect backdrop for naturalistic literature.

Reader's Dictionary

novel   new; original
tacitly   expressed without words
shanty   crudely built dwelling or shelter

▲ THEODORE DREISER

A major literary development in the late nineteenth century was naturalism, which developed out of realist fiction. Naturalist writers carried the vivid detail of realism a step further by depicting environmental factors. In his first novel, *Sister Carrie*, published in 1900, Theodore Dreiser describes the compelling attraction as well as the cold indifference of life in growing cities.

Sister Carrie (excerpts)

To Carrie, the sound of the little bells upon the horse-cars, as they tinkled in and out of hearing, was as pleasing as it was novel. She gazed into the lighted street when Minnie brought her into the front room, and wondered at the sounds, the movement, the murmur of the vast city which stretched for miles and miles in every direction.

Mrs. Hanson, after the first greetings were over, gave Carrie the baby and proceeded to get supper. Her husband asked a few questions and sat down to read the evening paper. He was a silent man, American born, of a Swede father, and now employed as a cleaner of refrigerator cars at the stock-yards. . . . His one observation to the point was concerning the chances of work in Chicago.

"It's a big place," he said. "You can get in somewhere in a few days. Everybody does."

It had been tacitly understood beforehand that she was to get work and pay her board. He was of a clean, saving disposition, and had already paid a number of monthly installments on two lots far out on the West Side. His ambition was some day to build a house on them. . . .

"You'll want to see the city first, won't you?" said Minnie, when they were eating. "Well, we'll go out Sunday and see Lincoln Park."

Carrie noticed that Hanson had said nothing to this. He seemed to be thinking of something else.

"Well," she said, "I think I'll look around tomorrow. . . . Which way is the business part?"

Minnie began to explain, but her husband took this part of the conversation to himself.

"It's that way," he said, pointing east. "That's east." Then he went off into the longest speech he had yet indulged in, concerning the lay of Chicago. "You'd better look in those big manufacturing houses along Franklin Street and just the other side of the river," he concluded. "Lots of girls work there. You could get home easy, too. It isn't very far." . . .

In 1889 Chicago had the peculiar qualifications of growth which made such adventuresome pilgrimages even on the part of young girls plausible. . . . It was a city of over 500,000, with the ambition, the daring, the activity of a metropolis of a million. Its streets and houses were already scattered over an area of seventy-five square miles. Its population was not so much thriving upon established commerce as upon the industries which prepared for the arrival of others. The sound of the hammer engaged upon the erection of new structures was everywhere heard. . . .

The entire metropolitan center possessed a high and mighty air calculated to overawe and abash the common applicant, and to make the gulf between poverty and success seem both wide and deep.

Into this important commercial region the timid Carrie went. She walked east along Van Buren Street through a region of lessening importance, until it deteriorated into a mass of shanties and coal-yards, and finally verged upon the river. She walked bravely forward, led by an honest desire to find employment and delayed at every step by the interest of the unfolding scene, and a sense of helplessness amid so much evidence of power and force which she did not understand. . . .

Through the open windows she could see the figures of men and women in working aprons, moving busily about. The great streets were wall-lined mysteries to her. . . .

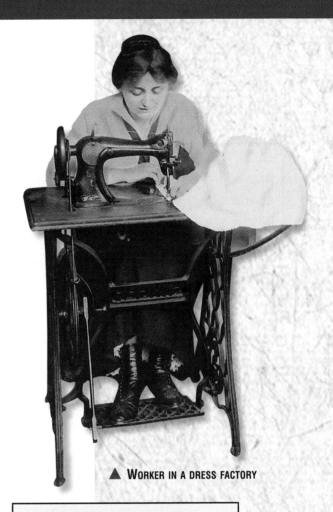

▲ **WORKER IN A DRESS FACTORY**

Responding to Literature

1. Why do you think Carrie came to live with her sister?

2. What kind of attitude about life in the city does Mr. Hanson demonstrate?

3. Do large cities today hold the attraction that they held for Carrie and other ambitious men and women at the turn of the century? Why or why not?

ACTIVITY

4. Create a table that shows the advantages and the disadvantages of living in a large city as opposed to a small town or rural living.

★★

Progressive Reforms

Guide to Reading

Main Idea
Progressives helped reform government, guarantee consumer rights, improve education, and protect workers.

Reading Strategy

Organizing Information As you read about progressive reforms, use a diagram similar to the one shown here to describe what reforms helped protect adult and child workers.

Improvements for Workers

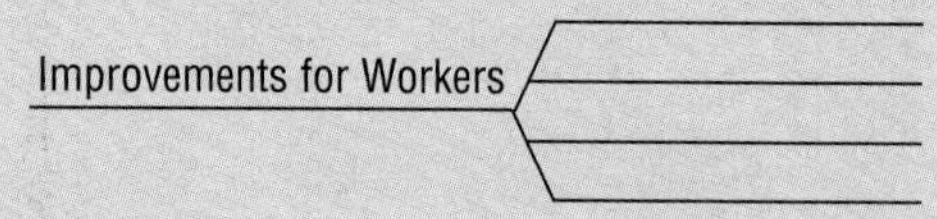

Objectives
After studying this section, you should be able to

★ explain how reforms strengthened democracy.

★ describe the advances made by social reformers and government in protecting adult and child workers.

Key Terms
direct primary, initiative, referendum, recall

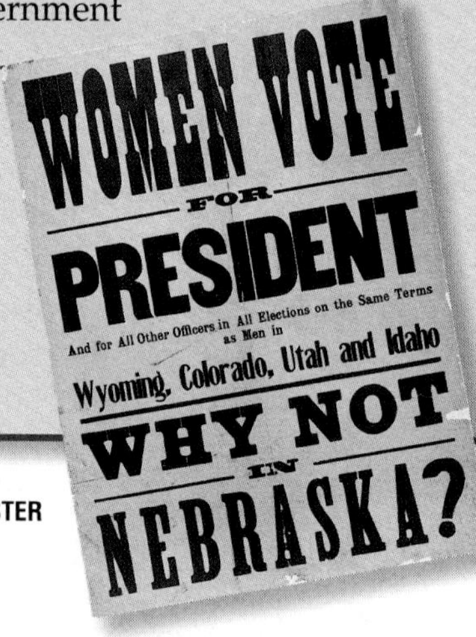

▶ **WOMAN SUFFRAGE POSTER**

WOMEN VOTE FOR PRESIDENT
And for All Other Officers in All Elections on the Same Terms as Men in
Wyoming, Colorado, Utah and Idaho
WHY NOT IN NEBRASKA?

---

*I*t is fitting that the earliest evidence of progressive activism dealt with cities. Being primarily city residents, progressives were viewed as representative of the increasing importance of the nation's urban centers. What is perceived as the initial progressive reform came even before the muckrakers began to write. This reform was inspired not by a book or a magazine article but by a natural disaster.

■ Reforms in Government

In 1900 a hurricane roared in from the Gulf of Mexico and devastated the coastal city of Galveston, Texas. When the political machine that controlled city government proved incapable of responding to the disaster, local reformers and business leaders convinced the state legislature to allow them to take control. In April 1901, the mayor and city council were replaced by five commissioners chosen in a nonpartisan election. Four of the commissioners were local business leaders who applied their management experience to running the city, and it quickly recovered. Reformers in other cities were impressed. Galveston's experience demonstrated the benefits of running a city like a business.

Changes in City Government

From the commission plan developed another progressive reform—the city-manager plan. In this reform an elected city council hired a professional manager to run city government, much as the directors of a business would hire a superintendent to run a factory.

Early city managers often were engineers, because much of the business of running a modern city—such as sewage disposal, water supply, and paving streets—was technical. By 1915 more than 400 cities had adopted commission or city-manager plans.

Even in cities where progressives could not reshape government, reform mayors fought powerful combinations of political bosses, unethical business leaders, and corrupt city officials. Reform mayors such as Tom Johnson in Cleveland, Samuel "Golden Rule" Jones in Toledo, and Hazen Pingree in Detroit gained national attention. All three left successful businesses to battle corruption in city government and to force streetcar lines, electric companies, and other utilities to behave in the public interest.

Voting Reforms

At the state level, political reform was first achieved in Wisconsin. Robert La Follette, after twice failing to become Republican

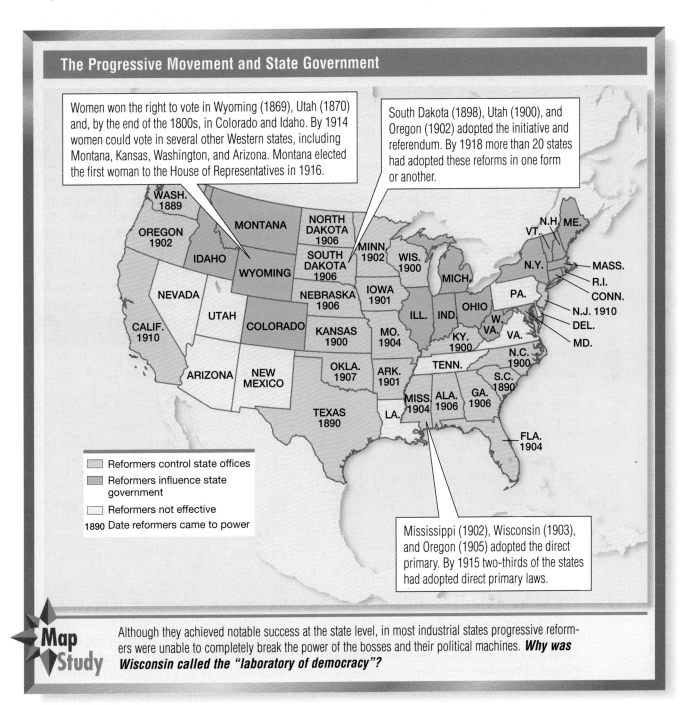

The Progressive Movement and State Government

Women won the right to vote in Wyoming (1869), Utah (1870) and, by the end of the 1800s, in Colorado and Idaho. By 1914 women could vote in several other Western states, including Montana, Kansas, Washington, and Arizona. Montana elected the first woman to the House of Representatives in 1916.

South Dakota (1898), Utah (1900), and Oregon (1902) adopted the initiative and referendum. By 1918 more than 20 states had adopted these reforms in one form or another.

Mississippi (1902), Wisconsin (1903), and Oregon (1905) adopted the direct primary. By 1915 two-thirds of the states had adopted direct primary laws.

WASH. 1889
OREGON 1902
MONTANA
NORTH DAKOTA 1906
MINN. 1902
VT.
N.H. ME.
IDAHO
WYOMING
SOUTH DAKOTA 1906
WIS. 1900
N.Y.
MASS.
NEVADA
NEBRASKA 1906
IOWA 1901
MICH.
PA.
R.I.
CONN.
UTAH
COLORADO
ILL. IND. OHIO
W. VA.
N.J. 1910
DEL.
CALIF. 1910
KANSAS 1900
MO. 1904
KY. 1900
VA.
MD.
ARIZONA
NEW MEXICO
OKLA. 1907
ARK. 1901
TENN.
N.C. 1900
TEXAS 1890
LA.
MISS. 1904
ALA. 1906
GA. 1906
S.C. 1890
FLA. 1904

Reformers control state offices
Reformers influence state government
Reformers not effective
1890 Date reformers came to power

Map Study

Although they achieved notable success at the state level, in most industrial states progressive reformers were unable to completely break the power of the bosses and their political machines. **Why was Wisconsin called the "laboratory of democracy"?**

candidate for governor, finally was elected in 1900. He used his office to attack the tradition of party nominating conventions. Because party bosses controlled the selection of convention delegates, they also controlled the selection of election candidates. From his own experience, La Follette knew that reformers had little chance of being chosen to run for office. In 1903 he pressured the state legislature to require that each party hold a **direct primary,** a preliminary election in which voters choose candidates for the general election. This reform took the nomination of party candidates from the bosses and their political machines and gave it to the people.

To reduce the control that big business and the party bosses had over state legislators, La Follette introduced three other reforms. The **initiative** allowed a group of citizens to introduce legislation and required the legislature to vote on it. The **referendum** allowed proposed legislation to be submitted to the voters for approval, and the **recall** allowed voters to remove an elected official from office by holding a special election. Although none of these ideas originated in Wisconsin, La Follette's great success in enacting them there gave the state a reputation as "the laboratory of democracy," and progressives in other states copied Wisconsin's reforms.

The most significant political reform that the progressives accomplished at the national level was the direct election of senators. Because they were chosen by their state legislatures, senators were shielded from direct public pressure. Progressive reformers felt that if its members were elected, the Senate would be more responsive to the public will and less influenced by powerful business interests. The call for this reform became so great that in 1913 the Seventeenth Amendment to the Constitution provided for direct election of senators.

Slow Progress for Women

It was difficult to argue that the people should have a greater voice in government affairs without including women, especially because they were increasingly holding jobs in factories, business offices, and schools, as

Visualizing History

▲ THE RIGHT TO VOTE Women parade for the right to vote in New York. *Which region of the nation was first to grant woman suffrage?*

well as taking prominent roles in reform movements. In addition, some progressives believed that if women gained the right to vote, their influence would help push through other reforms. By 1914, 11 Western states had granted women full suffrage. In the East, women promoted their cause by holding parades and circulating petitions. Many women believed, however, that a constitutional amendment would be needed to gain the vote nationwide.

■ Consumer Protection

A basic principle that American business inherited from Great Britain was *caveat emptor,* Latin for "let the buyer beware." This meant that people who purchased worthless life insurance, bread made with sawdust, or colored water labeled as medicine had only themselves to blame for not being more careful. Progressives argued that consumers had no way of knowing when meat was prepared under unsanitary conditions, children's cough syrup was dosed with opium, or other products were similarly misrepresented.

Regulating the Insurance Industry

In 1905 Charles Evans Hughes, a lawyer who worked for the New York legislature, investigated the insurance industry. He uncovered bribery of elected officials and huge salaries insurance executives paid to themselves and to family members they hired. Consequently, New York—and later other states—passed laws to regulate insurance companies and to protect the interests of policyholders.

Making Buildings Safer

At the local level, protection for consumers often came in the form of city zoning laws. The laws regulated how land and buildings could be used. Building codes prohibited some of the worst features of tenements by setting minimum requirements for light and air, fire escapes, room size, and sanitation.

Ensuring the Safety of Food and Medicine

Passage of pure food and drug laws demonstrated the effectiveness of the muckrakers in influencing consumer protection. Articles in *Collier's* about harmful medicines in 1906 convinced the chief chemist of the Department of Agriculture to perform experiments on himself and then to call for regulation. Even more sensational was the publication in 1906 of Upton Sinclair's best-selling book, *The Jungle,* a fact-based novel that portrayed horribly unsanitary conditions in slaughterhouses:

> *There would be meat that had tumbled out on the floor, in the dirt and sawdust, where workers had tramped and spit uncounted billions of [tuberculosis] germs. There would be meat stored in great piles in rooms; and the water from leaky roofs would drip over it, and thousands of rats would race about on it.*

An outraged President Theodore Roosevelt demanded reform, and Congress responded with legislation. The Pure Food and Drug Act established a government agency, the Food and Drug Administration, to protect consumers from unsafe medicines and foods. The Meat Inspection Act was passed on the same day in 1906. These laws regulated the content and inspection of food, prohibited the use of addictive drugs in nonprescription medicines, and required accurate labels on food and drug products. State governments followed with similar legislation to regulate food and drugs that did not cross state lines.

■ Protecting Workers

"I aimed at the public's heart," Upton Sinclair complained, "and by accident I hit

Visualizing History ▲ CHILD LABOR One concern for reformers was protecting children, such as these workers in a Pennsylvania coal mine. *How was child labor reform achieved?*

Child Labor

CAUSES

- Young children worked 10-hour days in poor conditions
- Children had to work because their families could not survive without extra income

• Reform

EFFECTS

- A national child labor committee was formed to promote abolition of child labor
- John Spargo wrote *The Bitter Cry of the Children*
- By 1914 nearly every state had set minimum age of employment
- The Children's Bureau was established as a branch of the Department of Labor

it in the stomach." Sinclair did not intend *The Jungle* to focus public attention on impure food. Instead he wanted to expose the terrible working conditions in slaughterhouses. One of the grim realities of industrialization was the frequency of industrial accidents.

Workers' Compensation

Workers who suffered industrial accidents had little protection. Employers argued that industrial accidents were not caused by unsafe conditions but by carelessness, and they often fired employees who were seriously disabled. Progressives joined labor union leaders to pressure state legislatures for workers' compensation laws. These laws established insurance funds into which employers made payments. Workers who were injured by industrial accidents were paid from the fund. In 1902 Maryland was first to pass such legislation, and by 1911 10 of the states had workers' compensation laws on the books. Workers' compensation laws not only helped injured workers, they improved working conditions for all workers because employers with low accident rates paid lower insurance premiums. Related progressive legislation established state agencies to inspect factories, limited workers' hours, and attempted to end crowded, unsanitary work environments.

Protecting Women: *Muller* v. *Oregon*

Many progressives were especially interested in improving working conditions for women. By 1900 about 20 percent of all workers were women, and progressive reformers believed women workers needed special protection. In 1903 Oregon passed a law limiting female factory workers to a 10-hour day. Employers challenged the law as violating a woman's civil right to work as long as she chose, and in 1908 the case was appealed to the Supreme Court.

To defend the law in *Muller* v. *Oregon*, progressive attorney Louis D. Brandeis presented research that convinced the Court that long working hours damaged women's health, and the Oregon law was upheld. After the *Muller* decision, several other states quickly passed similar laws.

Muller v. *Oregon* was a revolutionary legal decision. For the first time, the Court looked beyond legal principles and precedents and applied pragmatism to the law. The Court began to weigh what was best for society when it decided cases. In so doing, it took the first step toward becoming an instrument of social reform.

Protecting Children

Probably the most emotional progressive labor reform was the campaign against

Scouting

While many progressive reformers often focused on social issues, others concentrated on providing organized activities for boys and girls.

Then

Beginnings

Organizations such as the Boy Scouts of America (founded in 1910) and the Girl Scouts of America (1912) arose to provide supervised activities that stressed traditional values.

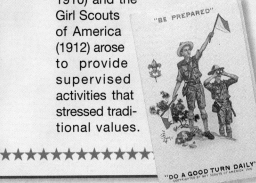

"BE PREPARED"

"DO A GOOD TURN DAILY"
COPYRIGHTED BY BOY SCOUTS OF AMERICA, 1916

Scouts hiked during the school year, camped in the summer, and attended weekly meetings packed with instructions, drills, and games. Scouting channeled adolescent energy into the wholesome pursuit of specialized merit badges acquired by passing tests on woodcraft, reconnaissance, and citizenship skills.

Now

The Growth of Scouting

The scouting program of work, play, and companionship continues today. The program is part of an international organization, encompassing members in more than 100 nations. Currently, in the United States, about 10 million individuals hold membership in the

▲ ORDER OF THE ARROW, BOY SCOUTS

Boy Scouts and Girl Scouts. Scouting has touched the lives of a wide and very diverse group of individuals. More than 90 pilots and scientists selected as astronauts and mission specialists, including Neil Armstrong and Dr. Anna Fisher, were active in scouting. Others with backgrounds in scouting include baseball great Henry Aaron and John F. Kennedy, the first scout to become President.

child labor. Although children had always worked on family farms, urban children found factory work dangerously monotonous and conditions often unhealthy or unsafe. Reformers established a National Child Labor Committee in 1904 to campaign for the abolition of child labor.

Muckraker John Spargo's 1906 book, *The Bitter Cry of the Children,* presented detailed evidence of the conditions of child labor in America. He told of anthracite coal mines, where thousands of "breaker boys" were hired at age 9 or 10 to pick slag out of coal and were paid 60 cents for a 10-hour day. He described how the work permanently bent their backs and often crippled their hands. He revealed that in textile mills more than one-eighth of the employees were less than 16 years old and that some children entered cotton factories at age 7 or 8. Public opinion was so stirred by such information that by 1914 all but one state set a minimum age for employment and many established other limits on

child labor as well. At the federal level, the newly established Children's Bureau had few powers, but it investigated and published information that helped the campaign to improve the well-being of child workers.

■ Varieties of Reform

In addition to reforming labor practices, many progressives insisted that business be regulated. Because of their great influence and power, large corporations commonly gained tax breaks from state legislatures.

HISTORY Online

Student Web Activity
Visit the *American History: The Modern Era Since 1865* Web site at **me.glencoe.com** and click on *Chapter 13— Student Web Activities* for an activity about child labor.

Robert La Follette, the governor of Wisconsin, determined that railroads paid less than half the property taxes of other businesses. He obtained reform laws to tax railroads on a more equal basis. La Follette also established a commission to regulate the railroads in the state.

On the federal level, Congress began to tax corporate profits in 1909. Although the Supreme Court in 1895 had declared an income tax unconstitutional, in 1913 the Sixteenth Amendment empowered the federal government to levy such a tax.

Public Utilities

The Progressive Era also was a time when reformers called for regulation of public utilities such as streetcar lines, waterworks, and electric-light companies. Many states set up public service commissions with the power to control the rates charged by public utilities. Some city reformers called for city governments to buy them out and run the utilities directly. By 1915, for example, all but 1 of the 36 largest cities owned or operated their own waterworks.

Health, Recreation, and Education

Progressive reform was also felt in other areas. It resulted in playgrounds and dental clinics for children. Private charities multiplied and broadened their social usefulness. Progressives also began to show concern about America's natural resources. State and federal governments passed conservation laws and set aside public recreation areas.

The reform impulse also resulted in great progress in education. Many states passed laws requiring children to attend school, and the number of high schools more than doubled between 1900 and 1920. The school year was lengthened and the curriculum enriched by courses in music, art, home economics, and industrial arts.

The Fight Against Alcohol Use

Long at the forefront of the temperance movement was the Woman's Christian Temperance Union (WCTU), founded in 1874. By 1890, it already had 150,000 members.

Like so many progressive reforms, temperance was first accomplished at the local level. By 1914 nearly half the people of the United States lived in areas where the sale of alcohol was illegal, and 12 states had passed statewide Prohibition laws. In 1919 Prohibition became nationwide when the Eighteenth Amendment was added to the Constitution. It declared that the manufacture or sale of liquor in the United States "is hereby prohibited."

Section 2 ★ Assessment

Checking for Understanding

1. **Define** direct primary, initiative, referendum, recall.

2. **Describe** the commission plan as a form of city government.

Critical Thinking

3. **Understanding Cause and Effect** Explain why progressive reforms strengthened the cause of woman's suffrage.

4. **Analyzing Issues** Re-create the diagram shown here, and list three reforms that came out of the Progressive movement and promoted citizen involvement in government.

INTERDISCIPLINARY ACTIVITY

5. **Government** Identify reforms that are being demanded today. On a chart, compare these with reforms sought by progressives in terms of who will benefit from the reforms, who opposes them and why, and overall goals.

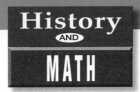
Urbanization

Demography is the study of population. Demographers measure population density (how many people live in a given area), distribution (where people live), and migration patterns (movement from one place to another). They collect and examine other information about people—births and deaths, marriages, ages, and national backgrounds. Their findings

The greatest growth occurred in the industrial cities of the Northeast, but cities in all regions experienced rapid growth. Nashville went from just less than 17,000 people to more than 80,000, Minneapolis from 2,500 to more than 200,000, and Los Angeles from 4,400 to more than 100,000. Cities such as Detroit, Cleveland, Buffalo, Milwaukee, Indianapolis, Columbus, Toledo, Omaha, and Atlanta doubled, or even tripled, in size.

Urban Population, 1860–1920

Year	Percent Rural	Percent Urban	Cities 2,500 to 50,000	Cities over 50,000
1860	80.2	19.8	376	16
1870	74.3	25.7	638	25
1880	71.8	28.2	904	35
1890	64.9	35.1	1290	58
1900	60.3	39.7	1659	80
1910	54.3	45.7	2153	109
1920	48.8	51.2	2578	144

often explain how changes in a society have affected people.

The table on this page shows demographic information for the period from 1860 through 1920. During this period, great cities became an important part of the national scene. Cities were vital centers of physical, social, and cultural change during this period. One of the most obvious changes was their sheer growth.

Urban growth was not new. Most American cities had been growing steadily since colonial times, and New York City already had more than 1 million residents by 1860. The rate of growth, however, rose significantly. By 1900 New York's population had more than tripled.

During the same span of years, Chicago's population rose from 440,000 to about 1.7 million, Philadelphia grew from 565,000 people to approximately 1.3 million, while population in both Boston and Baltimore increased from about 200,000 to more than 500,000.

Not only was there a growth in city population, but the entire nation was undergoing urbanization—a rise in the proportion of the total population living in urban settings. In 1860, less than 20 percent of the population of the United States lived in towns and cities with populations of 2,500 or more. By 1900 that figure had reached about 40 percent. By 1920, a majority of Americans would be city dwellers.

Making the Math Connection

1. According to the table, when did urban dwellers first outnumber rural dwellers?

2. What percentage of Americans in 1880 lived in rural settings?

ACTIVITY

3. Create a bar graph that shows urban growth from 1860 through 1920.

★★

Limits of Progressivism

Guide to Reading

Main Idea
While progressivism resulted in many lasting changes, not all Americans enjoyed the benefits of reform.

Reading Strategy

Organizing Information
As you read about the limits of progressivism, use a diagram similar to the one shown here to describe progressive attitudes toward immigrants and racial minorities.

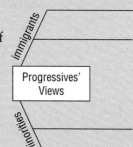

immigrants

Progressives' Views

minorities

Objectives
After studying this section, you should be able to

★ describe progressive attitudes about immigrants and racial minorities.

★ explain why African American leadership changed.

Key Term
literacy test

▶ WOODEN ICE SKATES, EARLY 1900S

he achievements of progressive reform at the national level were less far-reaching than its successes at local and state levels. It was more difficult to create nationwide demands for reform than to organize effective campaigns on a smaller scale. The federal government also was more difficult to prod into action. The Senate, chosen by boss-dominated state legislatures until 1913, was a highly conservative body. In the House of Representatives, powerful figures such as committee heads and the speaker usually resisted change.

The Supreme Court became somewhat less conservative than it had been in the 1890s, as progressives Oliver Wendell Holmes (1902), Charles Evans Hughes (1910), and Louis D. Brandeis (1916) were appointed to the Court. Yet the majority of justices seldom were willing to extend federal power into new areas.

Partly because of the attitude of the courts, many of the evils described by the muckrakers were considered outside the constitutional sphere of the federal government's powers, making national reform nearly impossible.

The benefits of progressivism were spread unevenly in other ways, too. Many middle-class progressives feared labor unions almost as much as they did trusts. So although progressives worked with labor leaders to improve working conditions, few objected when businesses organized effectively to prevent unions in their plants—often with cooperation from local courts and police. Therefore, wage gains during the Progressive Era went only to skilled workers. The earning power of unskilled workers actually dropped because prices increased more rapidly than their rates of pay.

■ Reformers and Immigrants

Among the many factors that held down the wages of unskilled workers was the continuing flood of immigrants to the United States, averaging one million a year during the Progressive Era—largely from southern and eastern Europe. This "New Immigration" caused widespread alarm, as immigrant men and women competed for unskilled jobs in American mines, mills, and factories.

In addition, the newcomers seemed to have more difficulty fitting in to established American culture than the "old immigrants" from northern and western Europe. Pressure from labor-union leaders and such organizations as the Immigration Restriction League persuaded Congress in 1897, 1913, and 1915 to enact laws requiring all immigrants to pass **literacy tests,** tests to show they could read English. All three laws were vetoed, but such a law passed over President Woodrow Wilson's veto in 1917.

Reform and Immigrant Cultures

Many progressives feared the socialist ideas that immigrants brought from Europe. As middle-class reformers, progressives wanted to change capitalism, not abolish it. Many also worried about preserving existing values and culture. Therefore, many progressive reforms were aimed at weakening the political strength of immigrant numbers and instilled in newcomers what reformers thought were proper American values.

In calling for reform of city government, one writer complained about:

>   *[t]he mass of ignorant voters, who now help the vicious bosses to govern our cities. . . . A colony of Italians, Scandinavians, Germans, or Irish, preserving their national language and their national ideas, and living as foreigners among us is very difficult to reach, but their votes count just as much as the votes of the most highly educated men among us.*

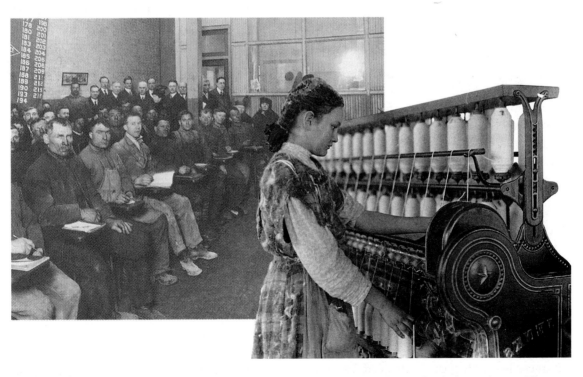

Visualizing History

▲ **ADULT CLASSES** Many businesses organized English classes for their employees. The classes were held in the plant so that workers could attend at the end of their shift. *Why would employers consider learning English important?*

▲ **STRIVING FOR JUSTICE** Booker T. Washington (right) and W.E.B. Du Bois were among the most important African American leaders of the period. Both men had the same goals, but they took different approaches to those goals. ***What organization did Du Bois help form?***

When progressives reformed government by defeating political bosses and machines, they also destroyed the system that provided immigrant groups with a political voice, political jobs, and political power.

Education and Resistance

As reformers obtained child labor laws and school attendance laws, they forced immigrant children out of factories and into classrooms. Many states made the study of American history a required course in public schools during the Progressive Era. Educator John Dewey advised that it was essential to teach students to be good citizens.

With the great increase in immigration in the late 1800s, other functions were thrust upon the schools. Besides teaching intellectual skills and citizenship, the schools taught patriotism and gave Americans a sense of unity. In this way, schools assisted in the work of assimilating newcomers into American culture by teaching the English language and stressing American values.

In the late 1800s American education was rapidly becoming free, public, and almost universal. In fact, by 1900 most states had compulsory education laws. These laws required that children attend school for a certain part of each year.

As a result, enrollment increased. In 1870 less than 60 percent of all children ages 5 to 17 were enrolled in elementary and secondary schools. By 1900 the figure was over 72 percent. The number of public high schools increased from about 150 in 1870 to nearly 6,000 by 1900. The greatest growth occurred in the Northeast and the Midwest.

The benefits of public school education, however, were not shared by everyone. Most pupils were middle- and upper-class children who chose to go to a public school rather than to be privately educated. Many immigrant children did not complete their schooling. Many poor immigrants needed their children to work to add to the family income. Forced to work at an early age, they sometimes did not even finish elementary school.

■ Progressives and Race

The most conspicuous limit to progressivism was its attitude about race. Like most white Americans at that time, most progressives believed that nonwhite races were inferior. Therefore, reformers did not object to the segregation of Japanese Americans in San Francisco schools in 1906, nor did they oppose sharp cuts in Japanese immigration that began in 1907.

Ignoring the Problems of African Americans

In addition, progressives accepted widespread discrimination against African Americans. Although many progressives sympathized with their plight, most reformers agreed with Theodore Roosevelt, who stated that Africans "as a race and in the mass are altogether inferior to whites."

Few progressives objected to the Jim Crow laws that Southern states had passed after Reconstruction to restore segregation. In 1896, when the Supreme Court ruled in *Plessy* v. *Ferguson* that segregation was constitutional as long as separate facilities were equal, no progressive campaign was launched for reform. While Southern whites were lynching African Americans and barring them from voting or holding public office, progressives were crusading for primary elections, direct election of senators, and other reforms to spread democracy. Like most whites, progressives generally accepted the South's Jim Crow system, partly because of indifference and partly because African Americans in the North also were restricted to low-paying jobs, segregation, and inferior social status.

The Struggle for Equality Continues

These circumstances help explain a shift in African American leadership during the Progressive Era. At the turn of the century the most influential African American leader

• •

Footnotes to History

Separate but Equal For nearly 50 years after the *Plessy* decision, the separate but equal doctrine was used to justify segregation in the United States. In the late 1930s and the 1940s, the Supreme Court began to challenge the doctrine in a series of decisions that have had far-reaching implications. The most important decision came in 1954 involving African American students in Topeka, Kansas.

was Booker T. Washington. Formerly enslaved, Washington founded Alabama's Tuskegee Institute in 1881 to train African Americans in 30 trades. Washington argued that equality would be achieved not through campaigns for reform but when African Americans gained the education and skills to become valuable members of their communities. In 1895 he spelled out this view:

" ... [T]he agitation of questions of social equality is the extremist folly. . . . [P]rogress in the enjoyment of all privileges that will come to us must be the result of severe and constant struggle rather than of artificial forcing. No race that has anything to contribute to the market of the world is long in any degree ostracized. "

Yet as the great changes in society that accompanied progressive reform bypassed African Americans, a new leadership arose that rejected Washington's approach to achieving equality. The most prominent new African American leader was W.E.B. Du Bois,

Visualizing History

▲ EDUCATION Progressives believed in compulsory public education to keep children out of factories and to provide them with proper values. *Why did many states require high school students to study American history?*

▲ **IN THE CITIES** The rapid growth of cities led to a push for building codes and zoning laws. Other areas of progressive reform included child labor and foods. *In what other areas did progressives help change American society?*

a Harvard-educated history professor at Atlanta University. Du Bois argued that suffrage was the way to end white supremacy, stop the lynching of African Americans, and gain better schools. In 1905 Du Bois and 28 other leaders convened at Niagara Falls to demand full political rights and responsibilities for African Americans as well as an end to racial discrimination.

This call resulted in the founding of the National Association for the Advancement of Colored People (NAACP) in 1909. "The power of the ballot we need in sheer self-defense," Du Bois said, "else what shall save us from a second slavery?" Du Bois edited the NAACP's magazine, *The Crisis*. In fiery editorials he called for African Americans to fight openly against injustice and discrimination.

The End of the Progressive Era

Despite the failure of most progressives to be concerned about such questions, progressive reform helped change American society in a number of ways. Although they excluded large groups from their efforts, the progressives expanded democracy, reformed the education system, and improved the quality of life for millions of men, women, and children.

Except for the two amendments to the Constitution in 1919 and 1920, progressivism in America ended as the United States entered World War I. Americans turned from reforming their own society to a crusade to "make the world safe for democracy."

Section 3 ★ Assessment

Checking for Understanding

1. **Define** literacy test.

2. **Describe** how some progressive reforms worked to limit the political power of immigrants.

3. **Discuss** the status of African Americans during the Progressive Era.

Critical Thinking

4. **Comparing** Re-create the chart shown here, and compare the methods Booker T.

Washington and W.E.B. Du Bois favored to increase African Americans' participation in society.

Booker T. Washington	W.E.B. Du Bois

INTERDISCIPLINARY ACTIVITY

5. **The Arts** Create a poster that illustrates three Progressive Era accomplishments.

BUILDING SKILLS
Critical Thinking Skills

Making Inferences

▲ A GROUP OF IMMIGRANT WOMEN AT WORK

When you use the facts an author presents to draw a conclusion that is not explicitly stated, you are making an inference.

Learning the Skill

To make an inference, follow these steps:

- Read carefully for stated facts and ideas.
- Summarize the information and list the important facts.
- Decide what conclusions might be drawn beyond what the author has said directly.
- Examine each inference critically to make sure that it is based on careful analysis of the information you have. Ask: On what evidence do I base this inference?

Read this excerpt, then answer the questions that follow.

In unaired rooms, mothers and fathers sew by day and by night. Those in the home sweatshop must work cheaper than those in the factory sweatshops. . . . And the children are called in from play to drive and drudge beside their elders. . . .

All the year in New York and in other cities you may watch children radiating to and from such pitiful homes. Nearly any hour on the East Side of New York City you can see them—pallid boy or spindling girl—their faces dulled, their backs bent under a heavy load of garments piled on head and

shoulders, the muscles of the whole form in a long strain . . . [w]hile in the same city, a pet cur is jeweled and pampered on a fine lady's velvet lap on the beautiful boulevards.

Practicing the Skill

Based on this passage, which of the following inferences might be made about the author's views?

1. Workers would be better off if they moved out of the city.
2. Efforts are needed to remedy working and living conditions for the poor.
3. The work has a harmful effect on the children's health.
4. Wealthy people should try to alleviate working conditions for the poor.

Glencoe's **Skillbuilder Interactive Workbook, Level 2** provides instruction and practice in key social studies skills.

APPLYING THE SKILL

5. Paste a political cartoon from a newspaper or magazine on a piece of paper or posterboard. List three valid inferences based on the work.

Using Vocabulary

Imagine that you are a muckraker who is investigating the need for urban reform. Use the following words to write an article summarizing the corruption and stating your recommendations.

social gospel	referendum
recall	pragmatism

Reviewing Facts

1. **Discuss** the role of the muckrakers in promoting social change.

2. **Describe** the inequalities that existed between the upper and lower classes of society.

3. **Explain** why reform was more successful at state and local levels than at the national level.

4. **State** the connection between progressive reform and big business management methods.

Understanding Concepts

Reform

1. Re-create the diagram shown here, and list how reform in government extended democracy in the Progressive Era.

```
              Extended Democracy
              ┌──────────┴──────────┐
     ┌─────────────┐        ┌─────────────┐
     │             │        │             │
     └─────────────┘        └─────────────┘
```

Values and Beliefs

2. Describe the values of the people who preached the social gospel and pioneered social programs.

3. How did progressives' beliefs about immigrant cultures influence their reform activities?

Critical Thinking

1. **Understanding Cause and Effect** To what extent were progressive reformers inspired by the Populists? Consider the membership, goals, and approach to problem solving of each group.

2. **Analyzing Artifacts** Study the picture on this page from *Harper's Weekly* and answer the questions that follow.

   a. What is the purpose of this picture?

   b. What is the central focus of the picture?

   c. Do you think this picture is effective? Explain your answer.

3. **Making Comparisons** Compare the commission plan of government to the city-manager plan and explain how each expressed the progressive approach to government.

History and Geography

The Progressive Movement in America

Use the map on page 405 and information from Chapter 13 to help you answer each of the following questions.

1. **Location** In what year did reformers gain control of state offices in Oklahoma?

2. **Region** In what states in the western and southwestern United States did Progressives have little impact?

3. **Human/Environment Interaction** Which progressive reforms were specifically designed to help
   a. rural residents
   b. urban residents
   c. both rural and urban residents

Cooperative Learning Interdisciplinary Activity: Health

Worker safety was an important part of the progressive program. Reformers realized that safety and accidents can touch every aspect of daily living. Although many accidents occurred at home, the workplace also posed a threat to safety. Organize into groups of four to complete the following activity on worker safety.

Research and compile information on three of your state's workers' safety laws. Include information on when the laws were passed and their intended goals. Include, if possible, information or statistics on worker safety. Conclude from your research whether the laws have been beneficial in promoting worker safety.

Have members of your group who are employed list and illustrate specific safety measures that are taken at their workplaces. Discuss why employers place so much emphasis on safety.

Share your findings with the other students. Display the information on the class bulletin board.

Practicing Skills

Making Inferences

When making inferences apply your own knowledge, experience, and opinions to form conclusions. Reread the material on consumer protection on page 407, then answer the questions that follow.

1. Many men and women worked to protect consumers. What inference can you make about their motivations?

2. What inference can you make about the effects of the book *The Jungle* on consumer protection efforts?

3. Is the following statement a valid inference: "Progressive reform made great inroads in many areas, but perhaps its strongest influence occurred in the regulation of building codes." Why or why not?

Technology Activity

Using E-Mail Research the names of five organizations that have some of the same goals as the progressive reformers of the late 1800s and early 1900s. Choose one organization that interests you and make contact through E-mail to get more information about the group.

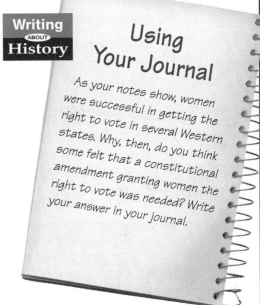

Writing ABOUT History

Using Your Journal

As your notes show, women were successful in getting the right to vote in several Western states. Why, then, do you think some felt that a constitutional amendment granting women the right to vote was needed? Write your answer in your journal.

CHAPTER 14

★★

White House Reformers
1900–1914

► EARLY TELETYPEWRITER

Setting the Scene

Focus

After the turn of the century, progressive reforms at the national level were aided by three strong-minded Presidents: Theodore Roosevelt, William Howard Taft, and Woodrow Wilson. These Presidents had different political philosophies, styles, and temperaments. Yet each worked to control big business, gain protection for workers, and protect the American people from social ills.

Concepts to Understand

★ How **interests and positions** of the progressives were translated into federal legislation
★ How business practices worked to limit **economic competition**

Read to Discover . . .

★ in what ways Roosevelt was successful or disappointing as a progressive leader.
★ what progressive reforms were achieved by Wilson as President.

Journal Notes

Note instances in your reading where Presidents appealed directly to the nation in order to gain support for new or controversial programs.

HISTORY Online

Chapter Overview
Visit the *American History: The Modern Era Since 1865* Web site at **me.glencoe.com** and click on *Chapter 14—Chapter Overviews* to preview chapter information.

CULTURAL
- **1902** *First Rose Bowl game played*
- **1903** *Orville Wright flies first heavier-than-air airplane*

- **1906** *San Francisco earthquake causes extensive damage*
- **1907** *Electric washing machine invented*

| 1900 | 1904 |

POLITICAL
- **1901** *Theodore Roosevelt becomes President*

- **1906** *Pure Food and Drug Act passed*

History AND ART

The Grand Canyon of the Yellowstone
by Thomas Moran, 1872

On a government expedition to the West, Moran made sketches for a series of paintings. His work prompted Congress to designate Yellowstone a national park.

- **1908** *First Model T Ford automobile produced*

- **1913** *Congress designates Mother's Day as the second Sunday in May*

1908	1912

- **1908** *William Howard Taft elected President*

- **1912** *Woodrow Wilson elected President*
- **1912** *Progressive party is formed*
- **1913** *Federal Reserve System created*

★★★★★★★★★★★★★★★★★★★★★★★★★★★★★★★★★★★

The Square Deal

Guide to Reading

Main Idea

To make government more responsive to citizens, President Theodore Roosevelt proposed a series of reform initiatives known as the "Square Deal."

Reading Strategy

Organizing Information As you read about Roosevelt's "Square Deal," use a diagram similar to the one shown here to list the key events that led to the settlement of the 1902 coal strike.

Objectives

After studying this section, you should be able to

★ explain why Theodore Roosevelt became known as a "trustbuster."

★ identify the series of events that led to settlement of the 1902 coal strike.

★ examine Roosevelt's efforts for conservation of wilderness areas.

★ discuss Roosevelt's legacy to the United States.

Key Term

conservation

▶ **INDUSTRIAL FLATIRON**

When Theodore Roosevelt received the Republican vice-presidential nomination in 1900, the powerful Republican leader Mark Hanna warned that there would be only one life between "that cowboy" and the White House. After McKinley's assassination in 1901, Theodore Roosevelt—the "cowboy," the reformer, the progressive—did indeed become President of the United States.

🏛 GOVERNMENT

■ The Trustbuster

Roosevelt described his approach to social problems as the "Square Deal," a belief that all people should have an equal opportunity to succeed through strong personal ethics, a sense of fairness, and adherence to the spirit of the law. Roosevelt also promised America that he would continue McKinley's policies unbroken. Not having become President by election, Roosevelt felt he did not have the authority to push a general program of reform through Congress. During this time, however, industries were merging at an all-time high rate. This rash of mergers prompted Roosevelt to urge Congress to pass legislation regulating big business.

Popular Support for Regulation

When Congress did not respond, Roosevelt turned to the American people to garner support for his program. The response was overwhelming. Government leaders responded with a series of moves designed to limit the trusts. First, the attorney general took the Northern Securities Company to court. In 1904 the Supreme Court overturned previous court decisions and ruled that Northern Securities, which had tried to attain a monopoly of northwestern railroads, had violated the Sherman Act.

Legislation to Assist Antitrust Suits

Roosevelt was not opposed to all trusts. He believed the government should leave honest corporations alone. Only the trusts that damaged the public or worked outside the law should be regulated or broken up. In his own words, "We draw the line against misconduct, not against wealth."

Roosevelt also understood that trust-busting suits could not prevent monopolies. Well-considered cases brought to court at the appropriate time, however, could force even the most powerful trust to obey the law. Roosevelt's reputation as a trustbuster grew.

Eventually, Congress followed Roosevelt's lead and, in 1903, passed the Expedition Act, which gave federal antitrust suits precedence on the dockets of circuit courts. An act of Congress also established the Department of Commerce and Labor, empowered to investigate interstate commerce. In addition, the Department of Justice started more trust-busting suits against corporations than they had at any time during the three previous administrations.

■ The Coal Strike of 1902

One of the most prolonged strikes in United States history started in May 1902, when nearly 150,000 workers walked out of the anthracite mines of eastern Pennsylvania. Terrible conditions precipitated this strike: low wages, frequent layoffs, and the requirement to live in cheaply built company towns. The strikers drew widespread public support.

Visualizing History

▲ **ON STRIKE** The major weapon for men and women workers against management was the strike. Coal miners at Shenandoah, Pennsylvania, demonstrate to win better pay and working conditions during the 1902 coal strike. ***How was the strike settled?***

▲ FACTORY WORKERS ON STRIKE

Management and Labor in a Deadlock

John Mitchell, who represented the United Mine Workers, asked mine operators to consider allowing an independent party to determine whether miners' wages were adequate. But George F. Baer, principal spokesperson for the mine employers, refused Mitchell's suggestion, saying that "anthracite mining is a business and not a religious, sentimental, or academic proposition." Baer further alienated a public already sympathetic to the workers when he refused to listen to the miners' complaints, to submit to arbitration, or to recognize the United Mine Workers as the true representative of the mine workers. This attitude and the strong conviction behind the miners' position caused the strike to drag on, with no prospect of settlement. Appeals for action poured in to the President.

Presidential Action Helps Resolve the Strike

Roosevelt had no power to force an agreement, yet he resolved to use whatever influence he had to end the strike. Early in October, Roosevelt invited representatives of the operators to meet union representative Mitchell at the White House. Nothing was accomplished in a stormy session, but public opinion soured even more toward the employers.

Faced with this deadlock, Roosevelt considered a legally questionable seizure of the mines by federal troops, but after a conference between Elihu Root, the President's representative, and J. Pierpont Morgan, whose banking firm indirectly controlled most of the anthracite mines, Morgan was able to put enough pressure on the operators to force them to back down. Morgan's action was apparently prompted by concern that United States businesses would suffer if the strike continued. Roosevelt's action in using the prestige of his office and his personal influence to settle the strike was recognized in this country and abroad as an important precedent. The London *Times* commented:

> ❝ *The President has done a very big and entirely new thing. We are witnessing not merely the end of the coal strike, but the definite entry of a powerful government on a novel sphere of operation.* ❞

■ Efforts at Conservation

Even before Theodore Roosevelt became President, the nation was adopting a policy of **conservation,** the planned management of natural resources to prevent destruction or neglect. In 1872 an act of Congress created Yellowstone National Park, and the 1890s saw the establishment of four more national parks. In 1891 Congress enacted the Forest Reserve Act, empowering Presidents to set aside land for national forests and withdraw forest lands from the public domain. In this way, land could be set aside for preservation rather than left available for private claim or purchase.

Action Based on Personal Commitment

Roosevelt's efforts to preserve the nation's natural resources stemmed from a deep love for America's wilderness. His beliefs made conservation popular. He stimulated public

▲ CONSERVATION Theodore Roosevelt was an avid supporter of the conservation movement. Roosevelt worked to protect wildlife and scenic areas. **What was the purpose of the Newlands Act?**

interest in the subject by writing, by taking publicized holiday trips to the West, and by constantly pushing for better conservation laws. Roosevelt also used the power and prestige of the presidential office to promote the cause.

Laws to Preserve Our Natural Legacy

The Newlands Act of 1902, supported by Roosevelt, provided federal aid to irrigation projects in arid states. He also enforced laws against the illegal occupation of public lands. Using the Forest Reserve Act, Roosevelt more than tripled the amount of land previously set aside for national forests.

Roosevelt also enlisted states' aid in the conservation effort. In May 1908 he called a national conference on conservation that resulted in the creation of more than 40 state conservation commissions and a National Conservation Commission, which began an inventory of the nation's natural resources.

Wisconsin senator Robert La Follette, though often critical of Roosevelt, predicted that future historians would conclude that Roosevelt's greatest achievement was not the Square Deal, but the preservation of the nation's natural resources for the benefit of all.

■ Further Regulation

As the presidential election of 1904 approached, the "Old Guard" of the Republican party was unhappy at the prospect of four more years of the Rough Rider in the White House. The New York *Sun* accused Roosevelt of "bringing wealth to its knees" and "putting labor unions above the law." It seemed possible that Mark Hanna might try to block Roosevelt's nomination, but Hanna died in February 1904. Roosevelt had popular opinion behind him and was, as even his enemies admitted, the ablest politician of the day. He received the unanimous nomination from the Republican national convention.

After being elected to a full term in 1904, Roosevelt felt confident enough to respond to the growing public clamor for stricter regulation of the railroads. The Interstate Commerce Commission had only limited success in controlling the unfair practices and political influence of these powerful businesses.

HISTORY
Online

Student Web Activity
Visit the *American History: The Modern Era Since 1865* Web site at **me.glencoe.com** and click on **Chapter 14—Student Web Activities** for an activity on conservation.

Some leaders proposed that the railroads be owned and operated by the government. Thinking such a step would lead to far-reaching disaster, Roosevelt urged tighter regulation as an alternative. As a result of popular support, clever politics, and willingness to compromise, Roosevelt was able to push the Hepburn Bill through the Senate 18 months after he urged Congress to act.

The Hepburn Act of 1906 strengthened the Interstate Commerce Act of 1887 in several ways. It abolished the "free pass" that railroads granted to politicians and other influential people. It widened the jurisdiction of the Interstate Commerce Commission to include express companies, pipelines, and sleeping-car companies. Railroad corporations were restrained from operating other businesses.

Most important of all, the Interstate Commerce Commission was granted power to fix rates, although its decisions could be appealed to the courts. Complaints to the commission soon multiplied 40 times, and a great many rates were lowered.

Roosevelt also urged legislation to address abuses in the food and meatpacking industries. The Meat Inspection Act of 1906 gave government the right to inspect meats sold in interstate commerce and the right to enforce cleaner conditions in meatpacking plants.

■ Assessing Roosevelt's Progressive Policies

In spite of Roosevelt's many accomplishments, Congress offered much resistance to his ideas. His legislative achievement was so unimpressive that some critics accused Roosevelt of producing "more noise than accomplishment."

Roosevelt and Politics

Roosevelt failed to effect a revision of the tariff, regarding the issue as "political dynamite." He did use the issue to his advantage, however, occasionally threatening to bring it up unless congressional leaders supported other legislative measures. Roosevelt also never seriously supported long-overdue efforts to make the banking system more stable and the currency system more flexible.

One reason for the failure to produce much reform legislation was Roosevelt's feeling that politics was "the art of the possible." His philosophy of reform was one of gradualism: he was willing to accept half a loaf if he could not get the whole. Furthermore, the Republican leaders in Congress, carryovers from the McKinley-Hanna period, were unsympathetic to progressive legislation.

Roosevelt and History

Although Roosevelt accomplished less than he seemed to promise, he restored the people's faith in the power of the federal government to serve their interests. Through his Square Deal philosophy, he promoted the idea that the cure for the evils of unrestrained individualism was not socialism but moderate reform. Above all he created a demand for reform. According to one historian, "Roosevelt was the best publicity man progressivism ever had."

Section 1 ★ Assessment

Checking for Understanding

1. **Define** conservation.
2. **Explain** why Roosevelt preferred regulation to trust-busting.
3. **State** Roosevelt's conservation policies.

Critical Thinking

4. **Summarizing** Use a chart such as the one shown here to list Roosevelt's progressive achievements. Include a brief assessment of each achievement.

Roosevelt's Progressive Achievements

INTERDISCIPLINARY ACTIVITY

5. **The Arts** Draw a political cartoon that illustrates Roosevelt's "Square Deal."

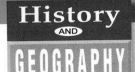

The Conservation Movement

By the beginning of the twentieth century it was becoming clear that the natural resources Americans had long taken for granted were—in fact—in danger of being used up. Theodore Roosevelt, a champion of conservation, made an effective case for the wise and scientific use of natural resources by people of all ages.

To the Society of American Foresters in 1903, Roosevelt said, "First and foremost, you can never afford to forget for one moment what is the object of forest policy. . . . Your attention should be directed not to the preservation of the forests as an end in itself, but as the means for preserving and increasing the prosperity of the nation."

Roosevelt's 1907 Arbor Day message to schoolchildren said in part, "Within your lifetime the nation's need for trees will become serious. . . . You will want what nature once so bountifully supplied and man so thoughtlessly destroyed; and because of that want you will reproach us, not for what we have used, but for what we have wasted. . . ."

Roosevelt abhorred the way the country's national resources were being exploited. For example, irreplaceable resources such as natural gas were wasted, and fires and floods, caused by poor management of land and water services, were common. Roosevelt wanted not only to protect wildlife and scenic areas, but also to ensure efficient use of soil, minerals, and forests.

The National Reclamation Act, also known as the Newlands Act of 1902, was the first major conservation law passed under Roosevelt. It provided for replacing natural services and set aside funds from public land sales for irrigation projects in the West.

During Roosevelt's terms, the size of the national forests were increased from about 40 million acres to more than 190 million acres. Roosevelt also worked to preserve other valuable lands as well. At his direction, the Department of the Interior set aside 80 million acres of coal lands.

▼ ARAPAHO NATIONAL FOREST, COLORADO

Making the Geography Connection

1. What did Roosevelt suggest was the object of forest policy?

2. How did Roosevelt's conservation program relate to the Square Deal?

ACTIVITY

3. Imagine you are a reporter researching environmental issues in the United States. Use your text and other resources to decide which issues you will address. Write a newspaper story in which you discuss how you think these issues will continue to affect the nation.

★★★★★★★★★★★★★★★★★★★★★★★★★★★★★★★★★★★★★★

The Taft Presidency

Guide to Reading

Main Idea

President Taft supported Roosevelt's progressive policies but lacked the leadership to implement them.

Reading Strategy

Organizing Information As you read about the Taft presidency, use a diagram similar to the one shown here to summarize the provisions of the Payne-Aldrich Tariff and to describe its effect on the public.

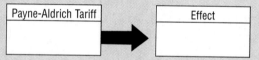

Payne-Aldrich Tariff	➡	Effect

Objectives

After studying this section, you should be able to

★ explain the impact of the Payne-Aldrich Tariff.

★ examine the public reaction to the Ballinger-Pinchot controversy.

★ describe the reactions of Roosevelt and the public to Taft's leadership.

Key Term

income tax

▶ ROOSEVELT AND TAFT IN CONFLICT

Although a distinguished public servant, having served as a judge, as governor of the Philippines, and as Roosevelt's secretary of war, Taft was a reluctant President. His true ambition lay in the judicial, not the executive, branch of government. Remarking on the snow, sleet, and rain that pelted the people coming to his Inaugural Address, Taft said, "Even the elements do protest."

■ Taft in Difficulty

Taft began his term as President by addressing the tariff issue, largely ignored during Roosevelt's eight-year term. Since passage of the Dingley Tariff of 1897, prices had advanced more rapidly than wages, and many blamed the resulting high cost of living on unduly high tariff rates. Some, including Taft, also believed that high rates encouraged monopoly.

Subversion of Tariff Reform

Congress met in March 1909, and within less than a month the House of Representatives passed a measure, introduced by Sereno Payne of New York, that provided for substantial reductions in the tariff without abandoning the principle of protection. Under the leadership of conservative Senator Nelson W. Aldrich of Rhode Island, however, more than 800 amendments were tacked onto the House bill. Many of these amendments were designed to conceal higher rates, such as changing a duty on certain small articles from so much "per hundredweight" to so much "per hundred."

When Aldrich attempted to railroad the amended bill through the Senate, he was met with resistance in his own party. Several Republican senators, nicknamed "the Insurgents," used their privilege of unlimited debate to reveal the way Aldrich and his allies were carrying out the demands of high-tariff lobbyists instead of the people. Too late, Taft attempted to persuade the Old Guard leaders to reduce the rates, but they made only slight concessions before the bill received Senate approval.

By the time the bill reached Taft's desk, the Payne-Aldrich Tariff contained high duties on iron ore, coal, and hides and increases on other materials. The bill, however, allowed for a corporation tax, established a tariff commission to make a scientific study of rates, and provided for some flexibility in rates at the discretion of the President. For these reasons, and because he feared a split between the Old Guard and the Insurgents in his own party, Taft signed the bill despite its weaknesses.

Continuing Controversy

Another blow was dealt to Taft's popularity when a conflict developed between Taft's secretary of the interior, Richard A. Ballinger, and the chief forester, Gifford Pinchot. Ballinger reopened for private purchase certain lands in Montana, Wyoming, and Alaska that had been withdrawn while Roosevelt was President. Pinchot, a well-known conservationist, protested these actions and publicly accused Ballinger of fraud. Taft, convinced of Ballinger's innocence—later confirmed by a congressional investigating committee—dismissed Pinchot for insubordination. But the public viewed Taft's action as a move against the conservation effort begun by Roosevelt, and Taft's popularity plummeted. Even though Ballinger was exonerated of the charges, he eventually resigned his post.

Immediately following the Ballinger-Pinchot controversy came an outbreak of Insurgent Republicanism in the House of Representatives, which took the form of an attack on the Old Guard speaker of the House, Joseph G. "Uncle Joe" Cannon. The speaker had come to enjoy a power over

legislation greater in some ways than that of the President. He appointed all committees, he decided what bills should be referred to which committees, and by almost absolute control over debate he could push some measures through without discussion and see that others never reached the floor.

The conservative Cannon used the powers of this office to hold up progressive legislation. He also cooperated with Aldrich during the tariff debacle in 1909. Furthermore, Cannon had long been an opponent of conservation. With the motto "Not one cent for scenery," he had stalled the creation of national parks and forests.

Finally, in March 1910, a coalition of Democrats and Republican Insurgents forced a change in the rules of the House that stripped the speaker of much of his power. This attack on Cannon hurt Taft, who in order to keep party harmony aligned himself with

Visualizing History

▲ ROOSEVELT AND TAFT In this cartoon, a smiling Roosevelt celebrates with Taft, his chosen successor. Soon, however, Roosevelt and Taft found themselves at odds. *Why did Taft dismiss Gifford Pinchot?*

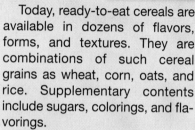

Breakfast Cereals

Early attempts to make a ready-to-eat dry breakfast cereal resulted in tasteless fare. These failures did not discourage two brothers, Will and John Kellogg, who ran a sanitarium in Battle Creek, Michigan. While there, the brothers experimented with a variety of grains and textures.

Then

Growth and the Cereal Industry

Success came with flavoring and roasting very thin flakes of grain. Almost immediately, the brothers recognized its sales potential. In 1906 Will Kellogg

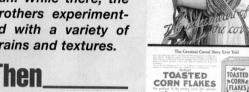

organized the Kellogg Company to manufacture cereal products as breakfast foods. The company became a huge success, partly because of its innovative advertisements and promotions. It was the first cereal company to aim its advertising directly at children, sparking a host of imitators. A patient at the sanitarium, C.W. Post, decided to start his own cereal company. Its products included a cereal first called Elijah's Manna, which was later renamed Grape-Nuts. To differentiate it from the more than 40 other cereal companies based in Battle Creek alone, Kellogg had his own signature printed on each package.

Now

20 Billion Bowls

Today, ready-to-eat cereals are available in dozens of flavors, forms, and textures. They are combinations of such cereal grains as wheat, corn, oats, and rice. Supplementary contents include sugars, colorings, and flavorings.

These ingredients are cooked together under pressure; dried; ground, flaked, or shredded; then toasted and packaged. To make puffed cereals, grains are heated in a pressure chamber. When the pressure is released, water vapor expands each grain to many times its original size.

People in the United States eat more than 20 billion bowls of cereal yearly.

---

the speaker. Thus, by signing the Payne-Aldrich Tariff, by supporting Ballinger against Pinchot, and by backing Cannon, Taft gave the impression that he had "sold the Square Deal down the river." An Insurgent senator described Taft as "a large good-natured body entirely surrounded by people who know exactly what they want." Popular indignation was so great that the congressional elections of 1910 resulted in a sweeping Democratic victory, with Democrats taking the majority in the House and Democrats and Republican Insurgents wresting control of the Senate from the Old Guard.

■ "New Nationalism"

During his retirement Roosevelt tried hard to maintain faith in the man he had chosen as his successor, but he found public

opinion toward Taft had worsened. In spite of Roosevelt's intention to remain out of politics, Taft's disappointing performance as President soon drew Roosevelt back into the political arena.

Roosevelt aligned himself with the Insurgents in the Republican party, who had started to call themselves "Progressive Republicans," or simply "Progressives." In a speech at Osawatomie, Kansas, during the congressional election of 1910, Roosevelt spoke of a new set of policies that he called the "New Nationalism." In words that recalled the Populist platform of the 1890s and foreshadowed the New Deal of the 1930s, Roosevelt said:

❝ *We are face to face with new conceptions of the relations of property to human welfare. . . .*

The man who wrongly holds that every human right is secondary to his profit must now give way to the advocate of human welfare, who rightly maintains that every man holds his property subject to the general right of the community to regulate its use to whatever degree the public welfare may require it. 99

In his New Nationalism speech, Roosevelt outlined a much more radical program of action than he had ever proposed while in the presidency. He favored both state and federal legislation to actively promote human welfare, including laws to protect women and children in the labor force and workers' compensation for those injured on the job.

Attacking the courts for declaring certain progressive legislation unconstitutional, Roosevelt suggested that state judges be subject to recall and that Supreme Court decisions be reversible by popular vote. By taking such stands, Roosevelt established his position as the natural leader of the Progressive Republicans.

■ Taft's Successes

Despite Taft's political problems, his administration experienced several successes. Although it was Roosevelt who was nicknamed the "trustbuster," Taft actually prosecuted twice as many antitrust cases in four years as his predecessor had in seven. Taft established the Tariff Board to investigate tariff rates, and under his leadership a federal budget began to take shape. Taft also supported the Sixteenth Amendment, giving Congress power to collect **income taxes**, or taxes on the income of individuals and companies, and the Seventeenth Amendment, calling for direct election of United States senators. In addition, during his administration two new states—New Mexico and Arizona—were admitted to the United States.

Taft genuinely supported Roosevelt's Square Deal policies, but unlike Roosevelt, who claimed an executive right to do anything not forbidden, Taft's judicial background allowed him to use "only those powers expressly authorized by law." Taft also lacked his predecessor's gift for dramatizing issues and enlisting public support. To some degree, Taft brought his political troubles on himself. He had a very different temperament from other politicians, and he had a hard time keeping up with the incessant work of the office. He did not really want to be President; his greatest ambition—later fulfilled—was to sit on the Supreme Court. In the end, Taft's administration would be remembered for its failures rather than its achievements.

Section 2 ★ Assessment

Checking for Understanding

1. **Define** income tax.

2. **Explain** Theodore Roosevelt's New Nationalism program.

Critical Thinking

3. **Making Judgments** Analyze how Taft's leadership led to increasing the power and authority of the federal government.

4. **Examining Issues** Re-create the diagram shown here, and list the reasons the public thought Taft was destroying the Square Deal.

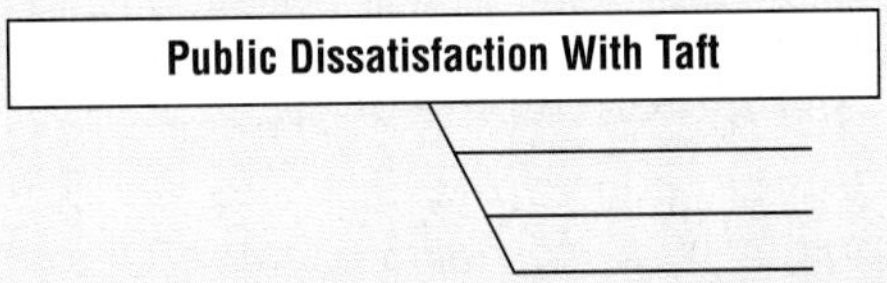

Public Dissatisfaction With Taft

INTERDISCIPLINARY ACTIVITY

5. **Government** Ask various people in your community how they feel about the current President's performance on one issue. Report your findings to the class.

★★

The Election of 1912

Guide to Reading

Main Idea
The presidential campaign of 1912 featured the rise of a third political party and the return of Theodore Roosevelt.

Reading Strategy
Classifying Information As you read about the election of 1912, use a chart similar to the one shown here to list the election's major candidates and their respective parties.

Candidate	Party

Objectives
After studying this section, you should be able to

★ relate the events that led to the formation of the Progressive party.

★ explain how a split in the Republican party helped lead to Woodrow Wilson's election in 1912.

Key Term
inheritance tax

▶ POLITICAL CARTOON, 1912 PRESIDENTIAL ELECTION

Senator Robert La Follette, a man of great ability and a leader of the recently formed National Progressive Republican League, had the support of many Progressive Republicans for the 1912 presidential nomination. When La Follette suffered a temporary nervous collapse, however, the Progressives turned to Roosevelt. Explaining that his no-third-term pledge referred to a third consecutive term, Roosevelt declared himself a candidate against Taft for the Republican nomination.

■ Roosevelt Challenges Taft

The heated, emotional struggle for control of the Republican party reached its climax at the national convention in June. Conservatives rallied behind Taft, as did many former supporters of the Square Deal who thought Roosevelt too radical or who disliked his running for a third term. Except for some devoted followers of La Follette, the Progressive Republicans lined up for Roosevelt. In states where convention delegates were chosen in primary elections, Roosevelt was generally the choice of the voters.

The Taft forces, however, had the immense advantage of controlling the party machinery. The convention chairperson Elihu Root kept such a tight hold on proceedings that he was accused of driving a steam roller over the Roosevelt forces. The convention's Credentials Committee gave 235 of 254 convention seats to Taft. When Taft received the nomination on the first ballot, Roosevelt charged the Republican party leaders with stealing the nomination. He stood ready, he said, to carry on the battle for progressive principles outside the party.

Formation of Progressive Party

In August a convention met in Chicago to found a new political party—the Progressive party. The delegates were a curious mixture—college professors, social workers, newspaper editors, former Rough Riders, wealthy people motivated by social conscience, and some professional politicians.

Senator Albert J. Beveridge, who had followed Roosevelt out of the Republican party, called on the new party to work for a nobler America. The Progressives, said Beveridge, stood for "social brotherhood" as opposed to "savage individualism," for a "representative government that represents the people," as opposed to invisible government controlled by corrupt bosses and the "robber interest."

The Progressive platform demanded reforms such as a more direct democracy through such means as the initiative and referendum, for conservation of natural resources for the general welfare, for woman suffrage, and for labor reforms such as the prohibition of child labor.

In addition, Progressives called for revision of the currency system and the introduction of an **inheritance tax,** which would be a percentage of the value of an inheritance, levied on the privilege of an heir to receive this property.

The party nominated Theodore Roosevelt for the presidency and immediately acquired a party symbol when the former President announced that he felt "as strong as a bull moose." The Progressive party had a strong enthusiasm and one of the most popular individuals in public life. It also had abundant campaign funds, supplied by wealthy businesspeople who believed that capitalism could survive only if it was reformed.

The Bull Moose crusade was a forlorn hope, however. Most of the Progressives were amateurs with little or no knowledge of practical politics. Party machinery could not be set up in thousands of election districts overnight. All that Roosevelt accomplished by bolting from the Republican party was to give control of the Republican party to the Old Guard, and to ensure the election of a Democratic President.

"Look up, not down—
Look out, not in—
Look forward, not backward—
And lend a hand."

Founders' Day
October 27, 1912
THE
Progressive Party

Visualizing **History**

▲ ROOSEVELT THE CAMPAIGNER
Theodore Roosevelt was a vigorous and effective campaigner. The Progressive party platform included a minimum-wage law for women, workers' compensation laws, and strong regulation of child labor. *Who were the Republican and Democratic candidates in the 1912 election?*

The New Freedom

When the Democratic convention met at Baltimore in June 1912, there was discord between the progressive wing, to which William Jennings Bryan belonged, and the conservative wing, whose delegates represented city political machines. Although disclaiming any desire for another nomination,

▲ TAFT AND SONS Theodore Roosevelt once said, "Taft has the most lovable personality I have ever come in contact with." Their friendship was wrecked, however, on the realities of politics and ambition. ***On what ballot was Taft nominated in 1912?***

Bryan was influential in seeing that the Democratic platform was as progressive as that of the Bull Moose party itself. After a protracted struggle, Woodrow Wilson, who had won national fame as a reform governor of New Jersey, received the nomination on the 46th ballot, partly through the help of Bryan.

Two Progressive Platforms

In the campaign Taft was not active, privately expressing the opinion that Wilson was sure to win. The real battle took place between Roosevelt and Wilson. Both men supported progressivism, although under different labels. Wilson countered Roosevelt with what he called the "New Freedom."

Although there appeared to be little distinction between the philosophies of the two candidates, they did in fact differ. Roosevelt's New Nationalism accepted big business as a fact of life and proposed a more powerful federal government and a strong executive to keep it under control. Wilson's New Freedom viewed monopolies as enemies of free competition. He also advocated the use of federal power to ensure more equality of opportunity.

The differences between Wilson and Roosevelt were striking. Roosevelt had long been the best-known political figure in the United States. Wilson, a former university president and college professor, had been active on the American political scene for only three years. Roosevelt, the former Rough Rider, was thought of by the public as a strong fighter in a war on privilege. While Roosevelt enjoyed mixing with all sorts of people, Wilson was aloof.

One writer likened Roosevelt to a great national spectacle, like Niagara Falls. People jammed the halls when he spoke, but it is not certain that they came so much to listen as to gape.

On the campaign platform Wilson's tall, angular figure displayed an ease of manner and his homely face exhibited a warmth he often lacked in personal relations. From his early teens, he had often dreamed of persuading people through eloquence. Even his strongest enemies admitted that he

★★★ AMERICA'S FLAGS ★★★

The Twenty-fifth Flag Statehood for both Arizona and New Mexico increased the number of stars to 48 in 1912. This flag served as the American flag from 1912 to 1959, more years than had any other flag.

★★★★★★★★★★★★★★★★★★★★★★★

could be very persuasive. Although Wilson lacked the magnetism of his rival Roosevelt, he knew how to touch people's conscience and appeal to their sense of reason.

An attempt to assassinate Roosevelt gave him an opportunity to demonstrate his courage and self-possession. On his way to deliver a speech in Milwaukee he was shot in the chest. Pausing only long enough to make sure that his assailant received protection of the police, Roosevelt insisted on delivering his speech before receiving medical attention. Not seriously wounded, he was later able to resume his campaign at full speed.

Results of the Election

The results of the election fulfilled Taft's prediction of victory for Wilson. Although he won the presidency, Wilson actually had fewer popular votes than Roosevelt and Taft combined. Because of the split in the Republican vote, however—and also a surprisingly strong Socialist party vote—Wilson carried 40 of the 48 states, with a total of 435 electoral votes; his opponents together received only 96 electoral votes. So, for the first time since Grover Cleveland's election in 1892, a Democrat became President of the United States.

Wilson's Previous Career

Woodrow Wilson had gained national prominence as a foe of privilege and as an individual with strong powers of leadership. During eight years as president of Princeton University, he not only raised standards and improved teaching, but also fought social privilege as represented by social clubs. As governor of New Jersey he fought political bosses who represented special interests, not the interests of the people as a whole. Under his leadership, the New Jersey legislature enacted an elaborate program of progressive measures.

The extraordinary successes gained by the "scholar in politics" can be explained partly by the fact that from childhood he had been ambitious to hold high office. Not only had he trained himself in public speaking, but he had also devoted much of his life to studying the techniques of effective political leadership. A long-time admirer of the British government, he developed the theory that the President, like the British prime minister, should take the initiative in guiding and promoting legislation. The President alone, in his opinion, stood for the interests of the entire nation.

In addition to books on government, Wilson had written a history of the United States and many articles, mostly on political topics. He was well informed on domestic issues, especially the tariff. A Southerner who had lived his adult life in the North, a Democrat who admired Alexander Hamilton as well as Thomas Jefferson, a scholar who knew the past as well as the present, Wilson was able to see public questions in perspective.

Section 3 ★ Assessment

Checking for Understanding

1. Define inheritance tax.
2. Explain why Roosevelt left the Republicans and helped form the Progressive party.

Critical Thinking

3. Recognizing Stereotypes   Analyze whether supporters of the Progressive party were radical reformers or dreamers.
4. Summarizing   Re-create the diagram shown here, and list the details of the Progressive party platform. Give your position on each of the issues.

> Progressive Party Platform

INTERDISCIPLINARY ACTIVITY

5. Government Imagine you are a volunteer working for one of the presidential candidates in the 1912 election. Prepare a poster that explains your candidate's position on one major issue.

BUILDING SKILLS
Critical Thinking Skills

Supporting Generalizations

A generalization is a statement that offers a general characteristic rather than a specific one. Sometimes when making a point or offering an interpretation, an author may make a generalization and then give supporting statements. At other times, however, you may be given only a generalization without supporting statements, or supporting statements without a generalization. In such cases you will need to supply what's missing.

Learning the Skill

As a historian, it is important to back up generalizations with supporting statements or evidence. Here are guidelines for making supporting statements.

- Supporting statements must relate directly to the generalization.
- They must be logical.
- They must be based on fact.

Study the map of the election of 1912, noting how the guidelines have been applied to the following generalizations.

Generalization:
- The Southern states had a great influence on the election of the Democratic candidate, Woodrow Wilson.

Supporting statement:
The election map shows that all electoral votes from the Southern states went to Woodrow Wilson. (This statement relates directly to the generalization, is logical, and is based on fact.)

Generalization:
- Those who voted preferred Woodrow Wilson.

Supporting statement:
Woodrow Wilson won the election of 1912. (This statement relates directly to the generalization and is logical, but it is not based on fact. The majority of citizens who voted did not vote for Wilson.)

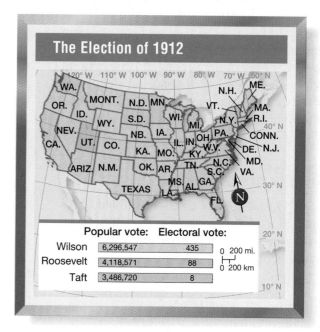

The Election of 1912

	Popular vote:	Electoral vote:
Wilson	6,296,547	435
Roosevelt	4,118,571	88
Taft	3,486,720	8

Practicing the Skill

1. Write a supporting statement for the following generalizations.

   a. Despite his popularity with the public, Theodore Roosevelt often had great difficulty getting "Square Deal" measures through Congress.

   b. Taft continued Roosevelt's reform program, but the public lost confidence in his leadership.

Glencoe's **Skillbuilder Interactive Workbook, Level 2** provides instruction and practice in key social studies skills.

APPLYING THE SKILL

2. Review information in Section 3 about Theodore Roosevelt's reentry into the national political arena. Write a generalization about the goals and objectives of the Progressive party. Then support your generalization with facts.

436

Wilson's Progressivism

Guide to Reading

Main Idea

As President, Woodrow Wilson worked to further the cause of progressive reform.

Reading Strategy

Organizing Information As you read about the presidency of Woodrow Wilson, use a diagram similar to the one shown here to list Wilson's accomplishments.

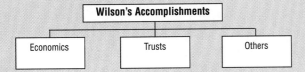

Wilson's Accomplishments

Economics — Trusts — Others

Objectives

After studying this section, you should be able to

★ explain why Wilson had congressional support for his programs.

★ list the accomplishments of Wilson's domestic program, including legislation on tariffs and on trusts.

Key Terms

rediscount, price-cutting, interlocking directorate

▶ **NUTCRACKER IN LIKENESS OF WOODROW WILSON**

The new President entered office with several handicaps. He was a minority President, chosen by only 42 percent of the voters. With no experience in national politics, he knew few Democratic party leaders. In addition, the Democratic party at the time comprised a loose alliance of local interests not expected to work well together. Long out of office, the Democrats lacked people with experience in government at the federal level.

Wilson and Congress

Although inexperienced in national politics, Wilson enjoyed certain advantages upon entering office. The 1912 election results sent Congress a clear message that most Americans demanded progressive legislation. If the Democrats did not support the President in the creation of this legislation, warned a

member of Congress, they would be "turned into the wilderness for 40 years more." No prominent Democratic leaders opposed Wilson, as Republicans Cannon and Aldrich had thwarted Taft. On the contrary, Wilson enjoyed the loyal support of most Democrats—including Bryan, the most influential man in the party, whom Wilson appointed secretary of state.

Wilson's first Inaugural Address was one of the shortest and most eloquent ever delivered. He began by asking the meaning of the Democratic triumph at the polls. His answer was that it meant little "except when the Nation is using that party for a large and definite purpose." To Wilson, the purpose was to do away with the evils that, along with many blessings, industrialism had brought. The President described these evils as the "inexcusable waste" of natural resources, the "human cost" of unrestrained individualism, and the use of government "for private and selfish purposes." Wilson

▲ **INAUGURATION OF A NEW PRESIDENT** The shortcomings of industrial America were widely recognized when Woodrow Wilson became President in March 1913, so it was no surprise that his brief Inaugural Address was devoted to domestic reform. ***What goals did Wilson set forth in his Inaugural Address?***

also stated his goals—not, he said, Democratic or Republican goals but goals for all the nation. After calling for reform of tariffs and banking, equality of business opportunity, improvements in agriculture, and conservation of natural resources, he concluded:

❝ *This is not a day of triumph. It is a day of dedication. Here muster not the forces of party, but the forces of humanity. . . . I summon all honest men, all patriotic, all forward-looking men to my side. God helping me, I will not fail them, if they will but counsel and sustain me!* ❞

■ The Underwood Tariff

The President lost no time in embarking on his program of reform. Like Taft, Wilson at once called Congress into special session. Appearing in person before Congress—the first President to do so in 100 years—he delivered a special message on the tariff. This short speech made headlines nationwide and illustrated Wilson's long-standing belief that the President's greatest power lay in focusing public attention on important issues.

Wilson's message charged that high tariffs had:

❝ *. . . built up a set of privileges and exemptions from competition behind which it was easy . . . to organize monopoly; until . . . nothing is obliged to stand the tests of efficiency and economy.* ❞

Lower rates, he claimed, would help businesses by putting them under "constant necessity to be efficient, economical, and enterprising. . . ." Opening the American market to foreign products would at the same time open foreign markets to American goods. Wilson warned, however, against undue haste, making it clear that he did not favor removing protective duties entirely.

The House of Representatives soon passed a bill, sponsored by Alabama representative Oscar W. Underwood, embodying the President's recommendations. The real fight occurred in the Senate, where previous attempts to lower the tariff had foundered, and where the Democrats had only a six-vote majority. Lobbyists swarmed to Washington, pressuring senators to alter the bill. But before senatorial opposition could crystallize, Wilson again appealed to the people. He denounced the "insidious" lobbyists and asked an aroused public to insist that Congress put an end to "this unbearable situation." The President then held personal conferences with Democratic senators and wrote letters to those threatening to oppose him. Under such varied and unrelenting pressure from the executive office, the Senate voted to accept the House bill with little change.

The Underwood Tariff Act represented the first substantial drop in import duties since 1857. It attempted to fix duties at a level where costs of production in the United States and abroad would be equalized, thus lowering the duty paid on almost 1,000 articles. It removed protection entirely from industries that already competed successfully with foreign producers.

A most important section of the Underwood Tariff Act was the provision for levying an income tax, now legalized by the Sixteenth Amendment. Originally introduced merely to make up for losses in revenue created by lower tariffs, the income tax became the federal government's chief source of revenue in a very short time.

■ The Federal Reserve Act

As the tariff debate reached a crescendo, Wilson appeared before Congress to introduce the second major item in his reform program: a revision of the banking and currency system. The purpose of the revision was to provide businesses with cheaper and more available credit. Like the tariff message, Wilson's speech was so brief that many influential newspapers published the entire text.

Flaws in the Banking System

In 1907 a sharp panic had revealed serious weaknesses in the American banking and currency system. There were runs on banks, many of which closed or stopped lending as a result. In 1908 Congress set up the National Monetary Commission, headed

◀ FEDERAL RESERVE SYMBOL

Visualizing History

▲ STRUCTURE OF THE FEDERAL RESERVE By 1994 the United States had more than 11,000 commercial banks. Nearly 40 percent of these were member banks that belonged to the Federal Reserve System. *What flaws in the banking system was the Federal Reserve System set up to correct?*

by conservative Senator Aldrich, to investigate the situation and propose change. After four years of study, the Aldrich Commission reported that the financial organization of the United States was flawed in four respects.

First, American banking lacked stability in times of crisis. Banks did not keep enough money on reserve to cover sudden withdrawals, and there was not enough cooperation between banks.

Second, America's currency was inflexible. The amount of money in circulation was based on the amount of gold and silver in the treasury, plus the bonds held by the national banks. The present system provided no way to increase or decrease the supply of money according to the investment needs of the country.

Third, there was no central control of banking practices. In other modern industrialized countries, central banks, such as the Bank of England and the Bank of France, directed banking policy. Nothing similar had existed in this nation since Andrew Jackson had destroyed the second Bank.

Finally, the commission found that too much bank capital was concentrated in New York City and on Wall Street. Meanwhile, other parts of the country, especially isolated rural districts, often suffered from a lack of adequate banking facilities and credit.

Although few questioned the list of ills in the banking and currency system, government leaders disputed the cure. Bankers favored a great central bank, privately controlled, like the first and second Banks of the United States. Many progressives, especially Bryan, called for strict federal control of banking and credit. It was Wilson's difficult task to select a plan that would work and at the same time win support from both bankers and Bryan's followers.

Central Banking Authority

The plan Wilson finally chose was called the Federal Reserve Act. Again, under constant pressure from the President, Congress finally passed the law in December 1913. The Federal Reserve Act promptly became one of the most important and useful pieces of legislation in United States history.

The new system provided for 12 Federal Reserve Banks situated throughout the country. All national banks were required to join them, and other banks could join if they wished. The Federal Reserve did not deal directly with individuals but instead serviced member banks. These "banks for bankers" concentrated reserves, so they could provide support to individual banks in times of temporary difficulty such as a "run." They also provided for local investment needs and made it easier to move funds from one part of the country to another.

The Federal Reserve Act provided a compromise between private and public control. The Federal Reserve Banks themselves were privately owned, a majority of their directors being elected by the member banks. Overall control of the Federal Reserve Banks, however, remained in the hands of a Federal Reserve Board, whose 7 members were appointed by the President, subject to approval by the Senate, for 14-year terms. Thus the center of the nation's financial power moved from Wall Street in New York City to Washington, D.C.

Flexible Money Supply

Before passage of the Federal Reserve Act, local banks frequently lacked funds to make sound loans to businesspeople and farmers. For want of adequate funds, stores and factories closed, and crops rotted. The Federal Reserve Act greatly improved this situation by providing for a new form of "flexible" currency known as Federal Reserve notes. The new money went into circulation when local banks needing cash brought businesspeople's promissory notes to Federal Reserve Banks. In return, the Federal Reserve Bank issued Federal Reserve notes, assessing the member bank a small fee called a **rediscount.**

When a Federal Reserve Bank bought promissory notes, it could print and issue more paper money, using those notes as part of the security, or collateral, thereby protecting the value of the currency. Then, when the notes were paid and the money came back to the Bank, the currency was retired.

The Federal Reserve Banks also controlled the amount of money in circulation by raising or lowering the rediscount rate, or the rate at which they charged for rediscounting. Raising the rate discouraged banks from lending and so "contracted" the currency; lowering the rate encouraged lending and "expanded" the currency. Thus currency and credit in any Federal Reserve District expanded or contracted according to the economic needs of that region.

On the whole, the Federal Reserve Act made the banking system responsive to the needs of a great industrial nation. It succeeded in its first great test, during World War I, when it assisted industrial expansion and helped finance the war effort.

■ Wilson Regulates Trusts

Shortly after signing the Federal Reserve Act, Wilson asked Congress to pass an antitrust law more effective than the Sherman Antitrust Act. Denying any desire to interfere with legitimate business activities, his message to Congress proposed various methods of preventing the "indefensible and intolerable" abuses of private monopoly.

Federal Trade Commission

Late in 1914, Congress responded to Wilson's requests by passing two laws. The first, the Federal Trade Commission Act, established a Federal Trade Commission to

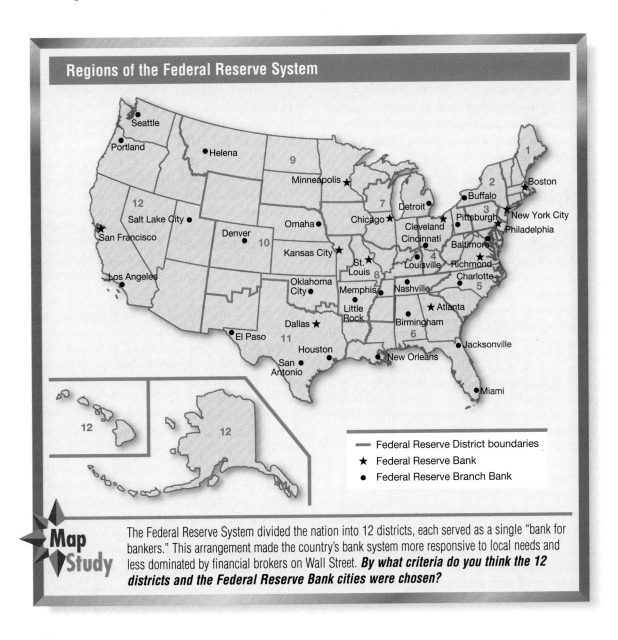

Regions of the Federal Reserve System

- ▬▬▬ Federal Reserve District boundaries
- ★ Federal Reserve Bank
- ● Federal Reserve Branch Bank

Map Study

The Federal Reserve System divided the nation into 12 districts, each served as a single "bank for bankers." This arrangement made the country's bank system more responsive to local needs and less dominated by financial brokers on Wall Street. *By what criteria do you think the 12 districts and the Federal Reserve Bank cities were chosen?*

AMERICAN PORTRAITS

W.E.B. Du Bois
1868–1963

The first African American to receive a Harvard Ph.D., W.E.B. Du Bois was a distinguished educator who refused to accept racial inequality. Du Bois initiated the Niagara Movement in 1905 to fight racial discrimination against African Americans in the United States.

For 24 years, Du Bois served as editor of the NAACP's journal, *The Crisis*, using it as a tool to assert demands for racial justice and equality. Between 1910 and 1930, his influence shaped not only the NAACP but a generation of African American intellectuals and activists.

In 1919 he organized the first Pan-African Congress, which promoted the idea that all people of African descent throughout the world should work together to combat the effects of discrimination. *Pan-Africanism* is still strong today among nations in Africa, where Du Bois moved in 1961.

---

investigate and regulate business practices. The commission had power to order companies to "cease and desist" from unfair conduct. In actual practice, though, Wilson's appointees to the commission failed to take strong actions against trusts.

Clayton Antitrust Act

In October 1914, less than a month after passage of the Federal Trade Commission Act, Congress passed the Clayton Antitrust Act. This act forbade several practices that destroyed competition or prevented new businesses from being developed. These practices included ruinous **price-cutting,** whereby a large company deliberately sold goods at a loss to drive weaker competitors out of business; "tying" of contracts, whereby a purchaser of goods from a particular company had to agree not to trade with its competitors; and intercorporate investment, whereby a company bought part ownership in a rival concern. The act also outlawed **"interlocking" directorates** between large corporations and banks, whereby the same people acted as directors in many different companies.

The Clayton Act also contained two sections favorable to trade unions. As noted earlier, the Sherman Act, by forbidding conspiracies, had proven more effective against labor unions than against business monopolies. In the Danbury Hatters' case, fought out in the federal courts from 1903 to 1915, a union had been ruined financially by being forced to pay triple damages to a business concern whose product had been boycotted. To discourage such use of antitrust laws, the Clayton Act stated that "nothing in the antitrust laws shall be construed to forbid the existence and operation of labor . . . organizations."

In addition, ever since the jailing of Eugene V. Debs for contempt of court in the 1894 Pullman strike, labor unions had protested the use of court injunctions forbidding strikes and boycotts. In answer to their protests, the Clayton Act forbade federal courts to issue injunctions against peaceful strikes, picketing, boycotts, or union meetings.

The Clayton Antitrust Act lost most of its effectiveness because of loose wording and unfavorable interpretations by the federal courts. The protection of labor unions from suits under the Sherman Act was limited to unions pursuing their "legitimate" purposes—and it was the courts that defined the word *legitimate.* Injunctions might still be issued when "necessary to prevent irreparable damage to property or to a property right," which again left a large loophole for conservative judges.

■ Wilson's Other Accomplishments

The Clayton Act completed the legislative program that Wilson had originally promoted. Wilson, however, did not stop there, turning his attention to other domestic issues.

Domestic Legislation

Additional legislation passed during his first term included the establishment of 12 regional Federal Farm Loan Banks, endowed with public funds in order to provide loans for agriculture. A Federal Highways Act, designed to help farmers get their produce to market, allotted federal funds to states for road construction and development. Wilson also supported the Keating-Owen Child Labor Act, which prohibited the employment of children under age 14 in factories producing goods for interstate commerce. The Adamson Act, passed under threat of a nationwide tie-up in transportation, established an 8-hour day for railroad workers.

Under Wilson's directed eye, much constructive legislation had been passed quickly. Wilson supplied a skillful and dynamic leadership, sometimes keeping Congress in session throughout the hot summer months. Chauncey Depew, a noted conservative Republican, said that for a man regarded as a mere theorist, Wilson had accomplished "the most astonishing practical results."

Segregation in the Capital

The reforms Wilson achieved did not have "practical results" for African Americans, however, as the President brought Jim Crow to Washington. The nation's capital had been desegregated since Reconstruction, but Wilson strongly believed in separating the races. His administration segregated drinking fountains, rest rooms, and lunch counters in government office buildings and assigned jobs according to race.

A number of prominent African American leaders like W.E.B. Du Bois, who had supported Wilson in 1912, turned against him. African American newspaper editor William Monroe Trotter blamed Wilson's New Freedom for a "new slavery for your Afro-American fellow citizens." Yet the President exemplified the racial prejudice of many other progressive reformers.

Wilson also opposed woman suffrage at first. Later, however, he modified his position. During this second term, the Nineteenth Amendment gave women the right to vote.

Wilson's efforts during the beginning of his first term focused almost exclusively on domestic matters. In fact, foreign affairs did not even receive mention in his first Inaugural Address. But by the end of his term, world events overshadowed these domestic achievements. Wilson's role as architect and promoter of progressive legislation was all but forgotten. It was obscured by growing tensions in foreign affairs that resulted in tragedy for him and for the world.

Section 4 ★ Assessment

Checking for Understanding

1. **Define** rediscount, price-cutting, interlocking directorate.
2. **Explain** why Wilson had congressional support for his programs.

Critical Thinking

3. **Making Judgments** Evaluate the effect of Wilson's antitrust legislation and the creation of the Federal Reserve System on the economy.
4. **Examining Issues** Re-create the diagram shown here, and list the provisions of the Clayton Antitrust Act that limited the power of monopolies in the United States.

Clayton Antitrust Act Provisions			

INTERDISCIPLINARY ACTIVITY

5. **Government** Create a table using the headings: Work, School, and Housing. Under each, state how life would be different in a segregated society.

Using Vocabulary

Write a paragraph describing Wilson's New Freedom program. Use the following terms:

progressivism   **labor**
antitrust   **monopoly**

Reviewing Facts

1. Describe the progressive beliefs of Theodore Roosevelt.
2. Cite two important achievements of William Howard Taft's administration.
3. Compare the progressivism of Woodrow Wilson and Theodore Roosevelt based on their respective programs.

Understanding Concepts

Interests and Positions

1. Show how Taft's policies seemed to go against Roosevelt's Square Deal.

Economic Competition

2. Re-create the diagram shown here, and list various big-business practices and tactics in the early 1900s and how each slowed or inhibited economic competition.

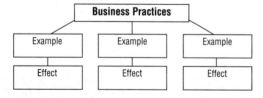

Critical Thinking

1. **Linking Past and Present** Compare Theodore Roosevelt's approach to conservation of natural

resources with those of Presidents during the 1980s and 1990s.

2. **Analyzing Political Cartoons** Study the cartoon on this page showing President Woodrow Wilson, then answer the questions that follow.
   a. Do you think the cartoonist has a favorable or unfavorable view of Wilson? Explain.
   b. What point is the cartoonist making?
   c. Write a title for the cartoon.

History and Geography

Conservation and the Environment

Review the information on conservation in the chapter, then answer the questions that follow.

1. **Human/Environment Interaction** When was the National Reclamation Act passed? What was its purpose?

2. **Human/Environment Interaction** What efforts did state government make to promote conservation?

Imports and Tariff Duties

Year	VALUE OF IMPORTS (Millions of dollars)			DUTIES COLLECTED		
	Total	Free	Dutiable		(Millions of dollars)	(Percent of total value of imports)
1880	$ 628	$ 208	$ 420		$ 183	29.1%
1885	$ 579	$ 192	$ 387		$ 178	30.8%
1890	$ 766	$ 258	$ 508		$ 227	29.6%
1895	$ 731	$ 377	$ 354		$ 149	20.4%
1900	$ 831	$ 367	$ 464		$ 229	27.6%
1905	$1,087	$ 517	$ 570		$ 258	23.8%
1910	$1,547	$ 761	$ 786		$ 327	21.1%
1915	$1,648	$1,033	$ 616		$ 206	12.5%
1920	$5,102	$3,116	$1,986		$ 326	6.4%

Source: *Historical Statistics of the United States: Colonial Times to 1970* (1975).

Cooperative Learning Interdisciplinary Activity: Mathematics

With a partner, use almanacs, magazines, and other reference books to obtain information about the salaries of professional athletes, business leaders, college presidents, governors, and the President of the United States. Present your findings in the form of a bar graph. Then write a paragraph indicating the President should earn more or less money than others on the graph.

Practicing Skills

Supporting Generalizations

Use what you have learned about supporting generalizations to examine the data in the table above and to answer the questions below.

1. What is the subject of this data?

2. Explain the trend in the total value of imports represented on this table.

3. Explain the trend in total duties collected in the time period covered by the table.

4. Write generalizations with supporting statements on the value of American imports and on the amount of duties collected from 1880 to 1920.

Technology Activity

Building a Database Use information from the chapter and other resources to create a database of the progressive achievements of Presidents Roosevelt, Taft, and Wilson.

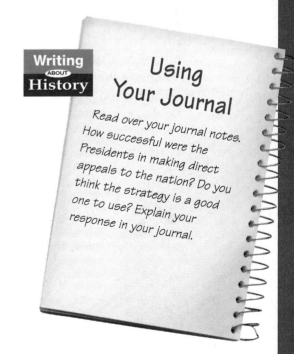

Writing ABOUT History

Using Your Journal

Read over your journal notes. How successful were the Presidents in making direct appeals to the nation? Do you think the strategy is a good one to use? Explain your response in your journal.

Cultural Kaleidoscope

Transportation

Moving Into The Fast Lanes

As America evolved into a world power at the turn of the twentieth century, it also began to look differently at itself. The frontier was nearly gone and in its place, from 1880 to 1914, booming industrial expansion became a hallmark of American culture. No symbol better expresses this period than the automobile. Although the auto was invented in the nineteenth century, it is truly a twentieth-century phenomenon that touched and changed the way Americans lived.

► Beginning in 1908, the Ford Model T reached unparalleled sales, justifying its nickname of the car that put the world on wheels.

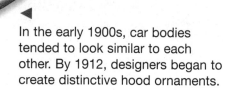

◄ In the early 1900s, car bodies tended to look similar to each other. By 1912, designers began to create distinctive hood ornaments.

◄ Some automakers outfitted their vehicles with horns operated by hand or by foot. Some luxury cars included two horns—a quiet one for use in the city and a louder one for country driving.

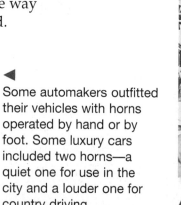

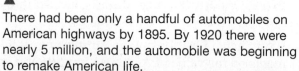

▲ There had been only a handful of automobiles on American highways by 1895. By 1920 there were nearly 5 million, and the automobile was beginning to remake American life.

446

▶
No better proof of the impact of the automobile exists than in the popular songs of the day.

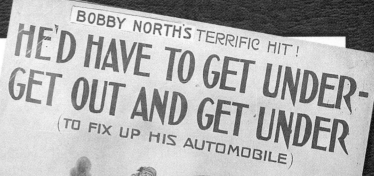

▲
Headlights were once called headlamps and were typically constructed of brass.

▼
Modern cars still have four wheels and run on gasoline. Yet they look very different from cars of 80 years ago. Shown is the front compartment of the 1914 Mercer Raceabout.

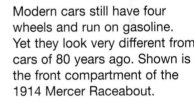

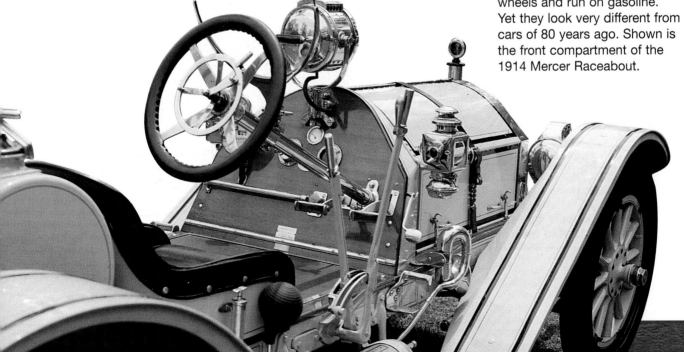

Standardized Test Practice

Directions: Choose the *best* answer to each of the following multiple choice questions. If you have trouble answering a question, use the process of elimination to narrow your choices. Write your answers on a separate piece of paper.

Read the quotation below and answer the question that follows.

"If a nation expects to be ignorant and free, it expects what never was and never will be."

—Thomas Jefferson

1. These words reflect the belief that

A freedom is an unattainable goal.

B the people of this nation are ignorant.

C a system of laws is necessary to maintain freedom.

D freedom is not possible when people are uneducated.

> **Test-Taking Tip:** Make sure that your answer choice is strongly supported by the quotation. Some of the answer choices make sense on their own, but only *one* choice matches the main idea of the quotation.

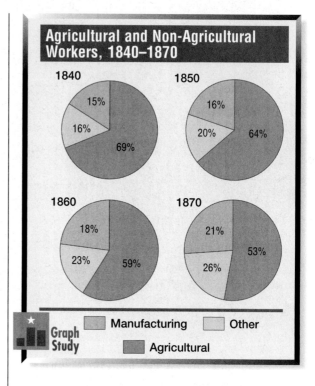

Agricultural and Non-Agricultural Workers, 1840–1870

1840: 15%, 16%, 69%
1850: 16%, 20%, 64%
1860: 18%, 23%, 59%
1870: 21%, 26%, 53%

Graph Study

Manufacturing · Other · Agricultural

Use the graph <u>and</u> your knowledge of American History to answer questions 2 and 3.

2. Between 1840 and 1870, the percentage of agricultural workers

F more than doubled.

G declined.

H remained the same.

J increased slightly.

> **Test-Taking Tip:** You will need to use the graph for this question. Do *not* rely only on your memory. Remember that all the wedges in a pie graph have different sizes for a reason. Compare the wedges for agricultural workers in the two years under question.

3. What was one reason for this change?

A Crop failures caused many to abandon their farms.

B Many farms became unnecessary as inexpensive imports became available.

C Many farmers moved to cities to work in factories.

D Immigrants from Europe brought new farming techniques.

> **Test-Taking Tip:** This question requires that you use the graph *and* your knowledge of history. Look at the other wedges in the pie graphs. The percentage of workers in manufacturing increased. What do you think the relationship of this change to the change in agricultural workers might be? Who might have taken the increased number of manufacturing jobs?

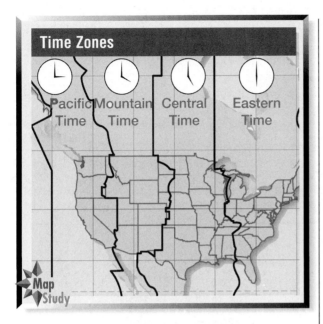

Time Zones

Pacific Time · Mountain Time · Central Time · Eastern Time

Map Study

4. Until the late 1800s, every community determined its own time by the position of the sun. Railroads, however, required a single standard time for scheduling and routing. In 1883, the railroad companies divided the U.S. into 4 standard time zones. Congress made them official in 1918.

According to the map, if it is 12:00 P.M. in Texas, what time is it in Washington State?

F 10:00 A.M.

G 11:00 A.M.

H 1:00 P.M.

J 2:00 P.M.

> **Test-Taking Tip:** Remember that time zones get progressively earlier as you move west. Therefore, you can eliminate choice H and J, even if you are not sure how to figure out what the time difference is exactly. 12 P.M. is the same as noon.

5. All of the following were progressive reforms in the early 1900s EXCEPT

A protecting consumers from unsafe food and drugs.

B passing child labor laws.

C regulating public utilities.

D promoting the equality of African Americans.

> **Test-Taking Tip:** This question requires you to place historical events in their proper time period. Only three of these reforms were promoted *in the early 1900s*. The civil rights movement related to African Americans did not become prominent until World War II and after.

6. In contrast to Booker T. Washington, W.E.B. Du Bois argued that to achieve equality African Americans primarily needed to

F learn valuable trades.

G gain the right to vote.

H gain access to better schools.

J be in segregated schools.

> **Test-Taking Tip:** Eliminate answers that you know are wrong. Booker T. Washington believed that African Americans primarily needed to learn valuable trades in order to achieve economic equality. Since W.E.B. Du Bois's ideas were *in contrast* to Washington's, you can eliminate answer F.

STOP

UNIT FIVE
CRUSADE AND DISILLUSION
1914–1932

★★★

▼ WALL TELEPHONE

▲ DUSTER COAT

History AND ART

Third Avenue
by Charles Goeller, 1933–1934

Scenes of city life during the Great Depression were important themes for many artists.

Why It's Important

The spirit of progressive reform dwindled as the United States drifted into World War I. Once the war ended, the national mood was no longer one of progress and optimism. The nation turned inward during the 1920s, as it enjoyed a cultural and economic boom. Good times soon ended, however, with the onset of worldwide depression. From World War I to the global economic crisis, the events of the early twentieth century foreshadowed a larger role for the United States in world affairs.

To learn more about immigration, an issue that Americans continued to grapple with throughout the early twentieth century, view the *Historic America: Electronic Field Trips* Side 2, Chapter 7 video lesson:

- *Ellis Island*

Themes

- Conflict and Cooperation
- Influence of Technology
- The Individual and Family Life
- United States Role in World Affairs

Key Events

- World War I begins in Europe
- Congress declares war on Germany
- The Senate rejects the Treaty of Versailles and the League of Nations
- Teapot Dome oil scandal
- Stock market crash
- Bonus Army marches on Washington

▲ GOVERNMENT POSTER, WORLD WAR I

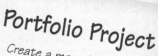

PRIMARY SOURCES Library See pages 864–865 for the primary source readings to accompany Unit 5.

◀ GERMAN HELMET, EARLY 1900S

Portfolio Project

Create a map of Latin America indicating the affairs that involved the United States in the region from 1914 to 1932.

Global Perspectives

★★★★★★★★ ★★

The World

	1910	1920
Asia and Oceania		
Europe	**1914** World War I begins	**1919** Treaty of Versailles signed ▲ **1922** Mussolini and his Fascists march on Rome **1917** Russian Revolution begins
Africa		◄ **1922** Egypt becomes independent
South America		
North and Central America	**1912** U.S. Marines land in Nicaragua	**1916** U.S. Marines land in Dominican Republic; Mexico warns U.S. not to invade

The United States

	1910	1920
Pacific and Northwest		
Southeast		
Midwest		◄ **1920** Prohibition begins nationwide
Southwest		
Atlantic Northeast		◄ **1917** U.S. declares war on Germany and Austria-Hungary

SPIRIT of 1917

JOIN THE
UNITED STATES MARINES
AND BE
FIRST IN DEFENSE ON LAND OR SEA
APPLY AT
24 East 23rd Street   New York, N.Y.

Linking Across TIME

While the great migration of Eastern Europeans to the United States came at the end of the 1800s, the first Eastern European immigrants arrived nearly 200 years before. John Smith, the leader of Jamestown, wanted to exploit the colony's pine trees for pitch and turpentine. So he sent to Poland, where the manufacturing of naval stores was well established, for skilled workers. The first Polish artisans arrived in 1608, probably as indentured servants. Colony records listed them as free members of the community some 11 years later.

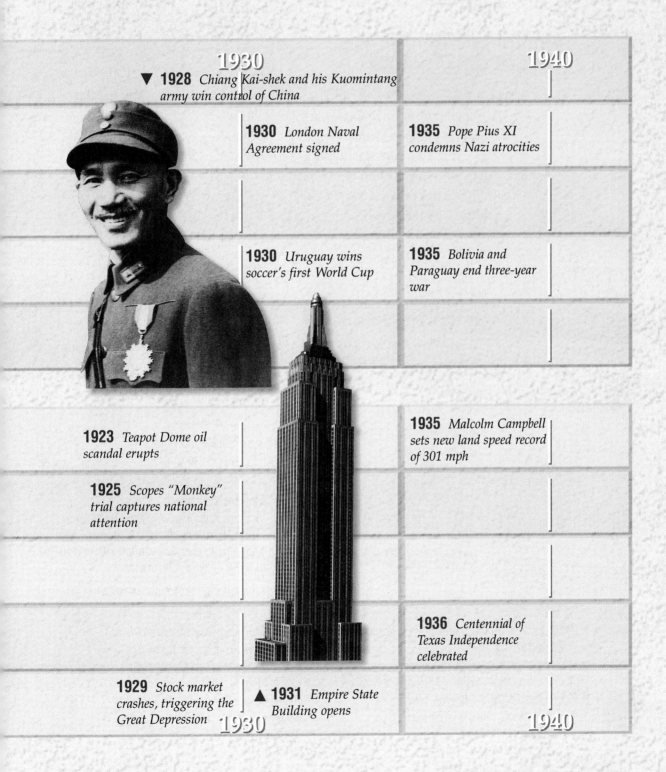

1930

▼ **1928** *Chiang Kai-shek and his Kuomintang army win control of China*

1930 *London Naval Agreement signed*

1930 *Uruguay wins soccer's first World Cup*

1923 *Teapot Dome oil scandal erupts*

1925 *Scopes "Monkey" trial captures national attention*

1929 *Stock market crashes, triggering the Great Depression*

▲ **1931** *Empire State Building opens*

1940

1935 *Pope Pius XI condemns Nazi atrocities*

1935 *Bolivia and Paraguay end three-year war*

1935 *Malcolm Campbell sets new land speed record of 301 mph*

1936 *Centennial of Texas Independence celebrated*

1930

1940

CHAPTER 15

★★★

World War I Era
1914–1920

► CONGRESSIONAL
MEDAL OF HONOR

Setting the Scene

Focus

When Europe went to war in 1914, the United States sought to stay out of the conflict. Both sides disregarded American neutrality. Germany's use of unrestricted submarine warfare and economic ties to Great Britain eventually led the United States into the bloody struggle. Mobilization called for many sacrifices by the American people. The Senate, however, rejected Wilson's proposed peace settlement, and wartime fervor led to intolerance.

Journal Notes

What was the general attitude of the American people during World War I? Record your observations as you read the chapter.

Concepts to Understand

★ How **conflict** became evident in American society during and after World War I

★ How Wilson's idealism and American **economic interests** led to controversy over foreign policy

Read to Discover . . .

★ why the United States declared war on the German Empire in 1917.

★ why the United States did not join the League of Nations.

HISTORY Online

Chapter Overview
Visit the *American History: The Modern Era Since 1865* Web site at **me.glencoe.com** and click on *Chapter 15—Chapter Overviews* to preview chapter information.

CULTURAL

● **1915** *First transcontinental telephone is hooked up*

● **1917** *Temperance movement leads to prohibition laws in 29 states*

1914 | **1916**

● **1914** *World War I begins when Austria-Hungary declares war on Serbia*

POLITICAL

● **1916** *Germany agrees to restrict submarine warfare*
● **1917** *United States declares war on Germany*

History AND ART

Allies Day
by Childe Hassam, 1916

Hassam depicts a vision of the Avenue of the Allies in red, white, and blue brush strokes.

▲ WORLD WAR I POSTERS

• **1918** *Daylight saving time is first adopted*

1918

• **1918** *Wilson proclaims his Fourteen Points*

• **1919** *Sherwood Anderson publishes* Winesburg, Ohio

1920

• **1919** *Versailles peace conference is held*
• **1920** *Nineteenth Amendment is ratified*

Prelude to War

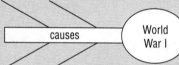
▶ *REVOLUTION* BY JOSÉ CLEMENTE OROZCO, 1920

President Wilson's focus on domestic issues was demonstrated in his first Inaugural Address in 1913. He was comfortable with and well-informed on matters such as the tariff and banking. But in foreign affairs neither Wilson nor those he counted on for advice were experienced.

■ Wilson's Moral Diplomacy

As President, Wilson resolved to "strike a new note in international affairs" and to see that "sheer honesty and even unselfishness . . . should prevail over nationalistic self-seeking in American foreign policy." However, other forces at work at home and abroad frustrated his hope to lead the world by moral example.

Political Unrest in Mexico

For nearly 30 years, Mexico had been ruled by a dictator, Porfirio Díaz (pawr•FEE•rih•oh DEE•AHS). He brought stability and encouraged foreign investment in Mexico's economic development. When Díaz was overthrown in 1911, Mexico entered a period of political chaos.

Francisco Madero (frahn•SEES•koh muh•DEHR•oh) came to power. Investors in Mexico feared that the new president would confiscate all property owned by foreigners. Businesspeople and foreign diplomats plotted with units of the Mexican army to overthrow Madero. Before Wilson took office, General Victoriano Huerta (veek•toh•ree•AH•noh WEHR•tuh) seized power, and Madero was murdered—presumably on Huerta's orders.

American capitalists supported Huerta in the belief that he would support business interests. Other countries with large Mexican investments recognized the new ruler. Repulsed by Huerta's brutality, Wilson refused to recognize the new government. He was convinced that without United States support "the unspeakable Huerta" would be overthrown.

Wilson Intervenes

Because Huerta remained in power, Wilson looked for a reason to intervene. In April 1914, American sailors on shore in the city of Tampico (tam•PEE•koh) clashed with Mexican authorities. Seeing a chance to overthrow Huerta, Wilson sent marines to seize the Mexican port of Veracruz (VEHR•uh•KROOZ). Although Wilson expected the Mexican people to welcome his action, anti-American riots broke out in Mexico and throughout Latin America. The President's intervention also was condemned in the European press.

Shocked by world reaction, Wilson accepted an offer from the ABC powers (Argentina, Brazil, and Chile) to mediate the dispute. The ABC powers supported Wilson by recommending that Huerta go into exile.

Venustiano Carranza (vay•noos•TYAH•noh kuh•RAN•zuh) was installed as Mexico's president.

Yet trouble continued between the United States and Mexico. Mexican forces opposed to Carranza conducted raids into the United States. Led by Pancho Villa (PAHN•choh VEE•yuh), guerrillas burned the town of Columbus, New Mexico, and killed 18 Americans. Wilson sent 6,000 troops under General John J. Pershing across the border to find and capture Villa. A year-long expedition failed to capture the guerrillas and resulted in a clash with the Mexican army. Tensions eased in January 1917 when Wilson's growing concern over the war in Europe caused him to recall the troops.

In the Caribbean

Wilson followed Roosevelt's example by ordering marines in Nicaragua, Haiti, and the Dominican Republic to preserve order and set up governments viewed by Americans as more stable than those in control. In 1917 the United States expanded its naval power in the Caribbean by purchasing Denmark's strategically valuable Virgin Islands.

Visualizing History ▲ **MARINES IN VERACRUZ** In April 1914 President Woodrow Wilson ordered American forces into Mexico to seize the port of Veracruz. *How did Latin American nations respond to American intervention?*

■ War in Europe

While Wilson was dealing with problems in Mexico and the Caribbean, Europe began one of the bloodiest wars in its history.

🌐 GEOGRAPHY
Setting the Stage for War

In the late 1800s, as Europe became industrialized and nations sought to establish empires, tensions arose among colonizing nations. Within Europe itself, nationalism also heightened rivalries and tension. Much of central and eastern Europe was ruled by empires that included several nationality groups, each with its own language. Many of these groups wanted to form independent nations by joining with similar groups in other nations. In Austria-Hungary, for example, Slavic groups resented being ruled by the Germans and Magyars (Hungarians). They wanted to join other Slavic peoples to form a South Slav, or Yugoslav, nation in the Balkans.

The Balkans were an area of Slavic peoples in southeastern Europe that for decades had been fought over by three major powers—Russia, Austria-Hungary, and the Ottoman Empire (Turkey and its provinces). In 1908 Austria-Hungary annexed two Balkan territories once ruled by the Turks, Bosnia and Herzegovina (HEHRT•suh•goh•VEE•nuh). Serbia, a Balkan nation on Austria-Hungary's border, called on Russia, its historic protector, for help. The Russians, weakened from their defeat by Japan in 1905 and wanting the Balkans for themselves, did nothing.

This instability and the complex rivalries led to an arms race as each country sought to defend itself. The arms race generated more mistrust and helped military leaders achieve more power and influence in European governments. 🌐

Formation of Alliances

The European nations made alliances with one another for mutual self-defense. The Triple Alliance drew together Germany, Austria-Hungary, and Italy. Fearing isolation

▲ PANCHO VILLA Many Americans viewed Pancho Villa as nothing more than a bandit. To Mexico's poor, however, he was a democratic savior. *What action did Wilson take against Villa?*

in Europe, France and Russia agreed to help each other if either became involved in war with Germany or Austria-Hungary. France arranged a separate partnership with Great Britain known as the Entente Cordiale (AHN•TAHNT KAWR•DYAHL), meaning "cordial understanding." After Russia's defeat in 1905 reduced Britain's fear of Russian power, all three nations came together to form the Triple Entente.

War Begins

Tensions were high in June 1914, when Archduke Franz Ferdinand, heir to the throne of Austria-Hungary, visited Bosnia. His assassination by Slavic nationalist Gavrilo Princip provided the incident that ignited Europe into war. Austria-Hungary declared war on Serbia on July 28, 1914.

One month after the assassination, war exploded in Europe. To protect its status as a European power, Russia felt it had to defend Serbia. Believing that Germany would aid Austria-Hungary, Russian armies mobilized along the borders of both nations. Germany demanded that Russia halt its threatening acts and that France pledge neutrality in the event of a war between Russia and Germany. Both Russia and France rejected Germany's demands. On August 1 Germany declared war on Russia;

on August 3 it declared war on France. The German army crossed neutral Belgium on its way to invade France.

Responding to the invasion of Belgium, Great Britain declared war on Germany. Europe was divided into two camps. Those fighting for the Triple Entente were called the Allies. Italy (which switched sides in 1915), France, Russia, and Great Britain formed the backbone of the Allies. What remained of the Triple Alliance—Germany and Austria-Hungary—joined with the Ottoman Empire and Bulgaria to form the Central Powers.

■ United States Neutrality

As war consumed Europe, Americans hoped the vast Atlantic Ocean would keep them out of the conflict. President Wilson stated that this was "a war with which we had nothing to do."

Taking of Sides

Despite a neutral stance, America could not help but take sides. Immigrants of European nationality groups gave many Americans roots that influenced their opinions. Many of the 8 million German Americans were sympathetic to their homeland. Many Irish Americans, seething from British domination of Ireland, also hoped for a German victory. In general, however, the common heritage shared by the United States and Britain, and America's historic links with France, put American public opinion on the side of the Allies.

Both Sides Strain Neutrality

America's neutrality did not protect it from either the Allies or the Central Powers. The British imposed a blockade on the Central Powers. They planted mines in the North Sea, forced neutral ships into port for inspection, opened American mail, and redefined **contraband,** or prohibited materials, so that not even food could be shipped to Germany. Trade between the United States and the Central Powers shrank.

At the same time, exports from the United States to the Allies nearly quadrupled, as war materials and food from America helped the Allies. Ties between the United States and the Allies became closer when the United States government lent the Allies $2 billion. The American public purchased another $2 billion in British and French war bonds.

To retaliate against the British blockade, cut off Britain's war supplies, and starve Britain into submission, the Germans relied on a new weapon—the submarine. The "U-boat" broke long-established rules of warfare by sinking unarmed ships. International law required that unarmed ships not be sunk without providing for the safety of passengers and crews.

In 1915 the British passenger liner *Lusitania* was sunk. Nearly 1,200 passengers drowned—including 128 Americans. Some Americans felt that this act was grounds for war. But others thought that people who traveled on ships of warring nations did so

Visualizing History

▲ **ASSASSINATION AT SARAJEVO** The assassination of Archduke Ferdinand and his wife proved to be a fateful event. Within a month, the continent of Europe was ablaze with war. *How did the United States react to the start of war?*

▲ **WAR ON THE SEAS** United States neutrality was put to a test when German submarines attacked American vessels in the Atlantic. *Why were submarine attacks considered a barbaric act of war?*

at their own risk, especially when Germany had taken out newspaper ads warning Americans not to travel on the *Lusitania*.

The Sussex Pledge

Wilson steered a middle course on the issue of the U-boats. He refused to take extreme measures against Germany. However, he sent several messages to Germany insisting that its government safeguard the lives of noncombatants in the war zones.

Late in March 1916, Wilson's policy was tested when a U-boat torpedoed the French passenger ship *Sussex*, injuring several Americans on board. Although Wilson's advisers favored breaking off relations with Germany, the President chose to issue a final warning. He demanded that the German government abandon submarine warfare or risk war with the United States. Germany did not want to strengthen the Allies by drawing the United States into the war. So it offered to compensate Americans injured on the *Sussex* and promised with certain conditions to sink no more merchant ships without warning. The Sussex Pledge, as it was called, met the foreign-policy goals of both Germany and the President by keeping the United States out of war a little longer.

Section 1 ★ Assessment

Checking for Understanding

1. **Define** contraband.

2. **Cite** two causes of World War I.

3. **What** did President Wilson consider to be the basis of his foreign policy in Latin America?

Critical Thinking

4. **Evaluating Tactics** Can German U-boat attacks on the *Lusitania* and *Sussex* be justified? Explain.

5. **Analyzing Issues** Re-create the diagram shown here, and list two trends that made American neutrality difficult.

Trends

INTERDISCIPLINARY ACTIVITY

6. **Government** Check sources such as local newspapers and municipal reports to see how people in your community reacted to the beginning of World War I.

BUILDING SKILLS
Social Studies Skills

Interpreting a Political Map

The ability to read and understand a map is a skill that may be applied in many areas; it is particularly useful in the study of history. There are many kinds of maps in use today: historical, physical, thematic, and political.

Learning the Skill

Historical maps show places and events from the past. Physical maps show natural features such as mountains, valleys, plains, and bodies of water. Thematic maps deal with specialized information, often on a single topic such as population density or land use.

A political map shows the political boundaries or borders of a state, country, and/or region. Political maps change whenever political borders change. A political map of the world today looks very different from one only 10 years old.

Follow these procedures when you evaluate a political map:

• **Determine** the time period covered by the map. This may be given in the title, although some political maps supply the date in the copyright.

• **Read** the map title and scale.

• **Examine** the legend. What information is provided by the map?

• **Analyze** the lines of latitude and longitude. These lines do not change. Use them when you compare change in boundaries over time. Boundaries are usually represented by a solid dark line.

Practicing the Skill

Apply the information from the chapter and the guidelines shown as you analyze the map of Europe in 1914.

1. What countries shown on this map maintained neutrality during World War I?

2. How might location have influenced neutrality?

3. Explain this statement: In 1914 the borders of the United Kingdom were determined by geography, not just politics.

4. Compare the map on this page with the map of Europe on page 474. What became of Austria-Hungary? What happened to Serbia? To the Baltic Provinces?

Glencoe's **Skillbuilder Interactive Workbook, Level 2** provides instruction and practice in key social studies skills.

APPLYING THE SKILL

5. Make a map of the county in which you live. Include your community and other cities as well as important physical features. Make a legend that shows the symbols or colors used on the map and what they mean.

Europe in 1914

Legend:
- Allies
- Central Powers
- Neutral nations

0   250   500 miles
0 250 500 kilometers

ICELAND, NORWAY, SWEDEN, FINLAND, DENMARK, BALTIC SEA, BALTIC PROVINCES, UNITED KINGDOM, NETHERLANDS, RUSSIA, IRELAND, ATLANTIC OCEAN, BELGIUM, GERMANY, POLAND, UKRAINE, SWITZERLAND, AUSTRIA-HUNGARY, ROMANIA, PORTUGAL, FRANCE, ITALY, SERBIA, BLACK SEA, BULGARIA, SPAIN, MEDITERRANEAN SEA, MONTENEGRO, TURKEY, AFRICA, ALBANIA, GREECE

★★★

America Enters the War

Guide to Reading

Main Idea
After struggling to remain neutral, the United States eventually entered World War I on the side of the Allies.

Reading Strategy
Organizing Information As you read about U.S. involvement in World War I, use a diagram like the one shown here to list the events that pushed America into the conflict.

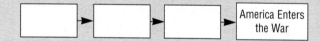

America Enters the War

Objectives
After studying this section, you should be able to

★ identify the events that led the United States to enter World War I.

★ describe the role of the United States in helping the Allies to achieve victory over the Central Powers.

Key Term
armistice

▶ **DISTINGUISHED SERVICE CROSS**

*I*n 1916 Wilson ran for reelection on a peace ticket under the slogan "He kept us out of the war." Although Wilson never used the slogan himself, he emphasized that he had kept "peace with honor."

Wilson defeated the Republican candidate Charles Evans Hughes in a close election. Following his reelection, Wilson devoted his energies to finding a peaceful solution to the war. The President realized the only sure way to keep Americans out of the European conflict was to end this terrible war altogether.

Student Web Activity
Visit the *American History: The Modern Era Since 1865* Web site at **me.glencoe.com** and click on *Chapter 15—Student Web Activities* for an activity on trench warfare.

A quick victory eluded both sides, as defensive weapons proved superior to offensive tactics. The war was especially gruesome. The use of poison gas and such other new weapons as the tank and the machine gun, along with enormous casualty lists, ended the optimism that had pervaded western Europe before the war.

■ "Peace Without Victory"

On December 18, 1916, Wilson asked the warring nations to state their peace terms. As a neutral party, he hoped to negotiate a settlement, but both sides responded with terms that their opponents would not accept. In spite of these replies, Wilson addressed the Senate on January 22, 1917, calling for "peace without victory."

Submarine Warfare Resumes

The Germans soon dashed Wilson's hope of mediating an end to the war. German losses on the battlefield and the shortages caused by the British blockade forced Germany to resume unrestricted submarine warfare. German naval commanders claimed they could starve Britain into submission in five months if the German government gave U-boats permission to sink ships on sight. The Germans felt that even if this violation of their Sussex Pledge drew the United States into the war, the Americans could not raise an army and transport it to Europe in time to prevent the Allies from collapsing. Therefore, on January 31, 1917, Germany announced that all vessels near Great Britain, France, and Italy would be sunk without warning.

On February 3, 1917, Wilson responded by breaking off diplomatic relations with Germany. When goods piled up in American ports because ships feared to sail, he asked Congress for the power to arm merchant ships. This measure passed the House of Representatives easily but stalled in the Senate. Finding the authority in a 1797 law, Wilson armed the merchant ships.

Drawn Into War

Meanwhile, other events caused the nation's antagonism toward Germany to mount. The British government revealed that it had intercepted a cable from the German foreign minister, Arthur Zimmermann, to the German ambassador in Mexico. Zimmermann instructed the ambassador to arrange an alliance between Mexico and Germany in the event that the United States entered the war. To encourage Mexico's cooperation, Germany promised that Mexico would regain Texas, Arizona, and New Mexico upon a German victory. American newspapers published the Zimmermann Note, outraging the public. Then, between March 12 and March 19, four American merchant ships were sunk without warning. Two days later Wilson called a special session of Congress to consider "grave questions of national policy."

On April 2, 1917, Wilson appeared before Congress with a heavy heart. In one of the most eloquent speeches ever delivered in the Capitol, the President asked the members of Congress to declare war on Germany:

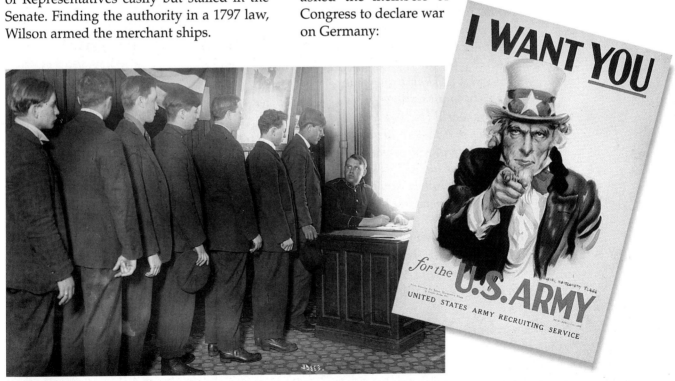

▲ **PREPARING FOR WAR** Americans register for the draft. The World War I era produced this classic recruitment poster, which has been used ever since. **What events drew the United States into the war?**

▲ JOHN J. PERSHING

Visualizing History ▲ **TRENCH WARFARE** Much of World War I was fought from trenches where soldiers spent days, or even weeks, in mud and unsanitary conditions. *What was the status of the conflict when the United States entered the war?*

" *It is a fearful thing to lead this great, peaceful people into war, into the most terrible and disastrous of all wars, civilization itself seeming to be in the balance. But the right is more precious than peace, and we shall fight for the things which we have always carried nearest our hearts—for democracy, for the right of . . . free peoples as shall bring peace and safety to all nations and make the world itself at last free. To such a task we dedicate our lives and our fortunes, everything we have. . . . [T]he day has come when America is privileged to spend her blood and her might for the principles that gave her birth and happiness and the peace which she has treasured. God helping her, she can do no other.* "

In his war message, the President insisted that the United States's quarrel was only with the "military masters" of Germany, and he expressed friendship for the German people. Maintaining that the United States had "no selfish ends to serve," Wilson stated that the people of the United States would be fighting to make the world "safe for democracy" and to promote "peace and safety to all nations." Four days after Wilson's message, Congress, after a spirited debate, declared war on Germany by the overwhelming margins of 82 votes to 6 in the Senate and 273 to 50 in the House.

■ Status of the Allies

When the United States entered the war, the Allies seemed in danger of defeat. U-boats were sinking ships at a rate that threatened to wipe out the entire merchant tonnage of the world; the British Isles had only a two-month supply of food with no relief in sight. Late in 1917 the Italians suffered a severe defeat at the village of Caporetto. Russia's military effort slackened and then ceased after the overthrow of the czar and the Bolshevik, or communist, revolution. In March 1918, Russia signed the Treaty of Brest-Litovsk, surrendering to Germany immense areas of land including Ukraine.

With one of the richest grain-growing areas in the world now in its possession, Germany hoped to relieve severe food shortages. Russia's withdrawal from the conflict also freed German armies to fight on the Western Front—the area along the French-German border where the war had been stalemated for nearly four years.

The World at War: World War I

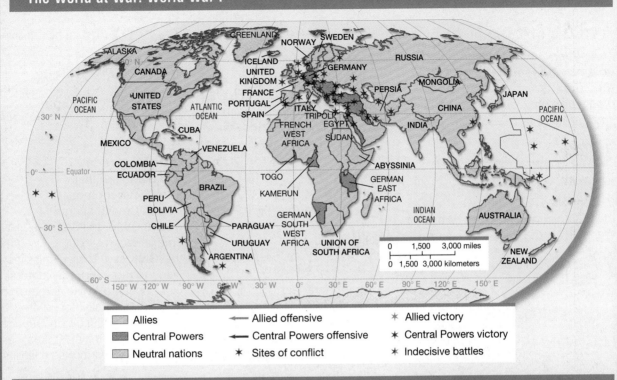

Allies	← Allied offensive	✳ Allied victory
Central Powers	← Central Powers offensive	✳ Central Powers victory
Neutral nations	✳ Sites of conflict	✳ Indecisive battles

The Western Front   The Eastern Front

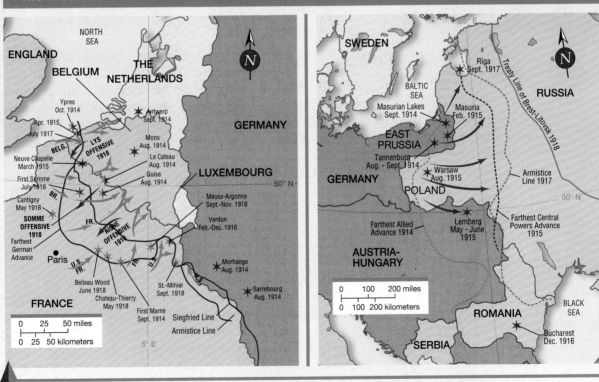

Map Study

Although most action in World War I occurred in Europe, it was truly a world conflict. Note the battles outside Europe, the intercontinental alliances, and Europe's division of Africa. **When did the Battle of Belleau Wood take place?**

Aerial Warfare

Aviation technology opened up a new dimension to war. For the first time combat took place not only on land and at sea, but also in the air.

Then_____

Flaming Coffins

Controlled air flight was less than 20 years old when World War I broke out. Fire was such a constant danger that airplanes were often referred to as "flaming coffins."

At first, the planes were used for reconnaissance, surveying and scouting, and for photographing enemy positions. Later, they were used for bombing. Both the Allies and the Central Powers developed a machine gun that was synchronized to fire through the whirling propeller of a flying plane.

Now_____

The Stealth and Missiles

An important part of modern warfare strategy is the use of stealth aircraft and missiles to strike at the enemy's air defense. Stealth is a name for military aircraft, both fighters and bombers, that are difficult for radar to detect. Stealth aircraft were used for the first time in warfare during the Gulf War. Cruise missiles, flying too low for radar detection, were used to strike targets considered too risky for piloted aircraft. In the assault on Baghdad, some of the initial strikes came from Tomahawk cruise missiles.

▼ STEALTH FIGHTER-BOMBER

▼ AMERICAN FLYING ACE
EDDIE RICKENBACKER

■ Raising an Army

The Allies did not expect the United States to participate in combat because in the spring of 1917 American forces numbered only 200,000. In addition, the army possessed only 1,500 machine guns, 55 obsolete airplanes, and no heavy artillery.

The Draft

Although these numbers looked discouraging, the United States mobilized rapidly. On May 18, 1917, Congress passed the Selective Service Act, requiring all men between the ages of 21 and 30 to register for military service. In June nearly 10 million young men signed up. The draft eventually extended to all men between 18 and 45 and resulted in the induction of 2.8 million men into the armed forces. Another 2 million men and women volunteered for military service.

Twelve weeks after war had been declared, the first United States soldiers landed in France. On July 4, symbolically recalling the American-French partnership during the American Revolution, Colonel Charles E. Stanton stood at the tomb of France's great war hero, Marquis de Lafayette, and said, "Lafayette, we are here." More than 2 million American soldiers comprising 42 infantry divisions reached France before the war ended. This vast new reservoir of military strength was an important factor in the Allied victory.

African Americans

Among those drafted to serve in the war were some 370,000 African Americans; of these, 200,000 served overseas. African American soldiers encountered rampant discrimination and prejudice in the army, where their units were completely segregated from white units. In addition, African Americans were not allowed to serve in the Marine Corps, and the 10,000 in the navy were restricted to the lower ranks.

Still, in the bitter battles along the Western Front, African American soldiers fought valiantly, winning praise from both the French commander, Marshal Henri Pétain (ahn•REE pay•TAN), and the United States commander, General John Pershing. African American soldiers in one infantry regiment won 21 American Distinguished Service Crosses and 68 French military decorations. The entire 369th Infantry won the highly prized French decoration, the Croix de Guerre (KRWAH dih GEHR), for gallantry.

■ Victory on Land and Sea

In the spring and early summer of 1918, Germany made a last desperate effort to win the war and nearly succeeded. Starting in March, the Germans almost penetrated the British lines; a second drive in June threatened Paris. United States troops helped to stop the advance, distinguishing themselves in a counterattack at Château-Thierry (SHA•TOH TYEH•REE), a town less than 50 miles from Paris.

The tide turned in mid-July as Marshal Ferdinand Foch (FAWSH), supreme commander of the Allied armies, ordered a great counteroffensive along the Western Front close to the German border. Pershing requested that American troops be assigned a section of the front for themselves—an area near Verdun. In mid-September 550,000 "doughboys"—the nickname given American soldiers—won an overwhelming victory at St.-Mihiel (san mee•yehl). Then an even larger force drove toward the key city of Sedan, breaking through well-defended portions of the German lines.

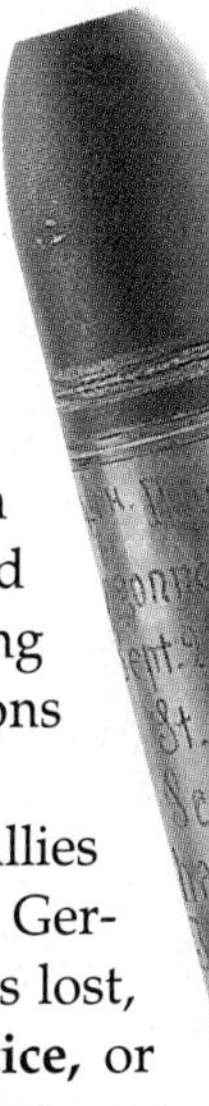

By early November, the Allies were poised to advance onto German soil. Realizing the war was lost, the Germans signed an **armistice,** or temporary stop to the fighting, on November 11, 1918.

American naval forces joined the British in waging war against Germany's deadly U-boats. The invention of the depth charge, an underwater explosive, provided the Allies with a new weapon, but its effective use demanded hundreds of patrol vessels to watch for U-boats and protect Allied ships by escorting them out of dangerous areas. So, in addition to 79 destroyers, the United States supplied more than 100 small "sub-chasers" plus a variety of former yachts, tugs, and fishing boats—"almost any craft which could carry a wireless, a gun, and depth charges was boldly sent to sea." By the end of 1917, the number of U-boat casualties was slashed in half. In 1918 the United States Navy took the principal role in laying mines across the North Sea, which prevented U-boats from reaching the Atlantic Ocean and isolated those already at sea from ports and supplies.

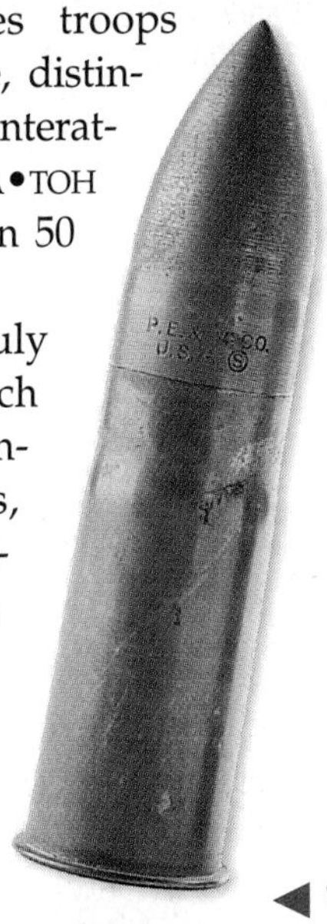

◀ WORLD WAR I SHELL

Section 2 ★ Assessment

Checking for Understanding

1. **Define** armistice.

2. **Explain** the meaning of the phrases "peace without victory" and "Lafayette, we are here."

Critical Thinking

3. **Assessing Outcomes** Would Germany have won if the United States had not entered the war? Explain your position.

4. **Summarizing** Re-create the chart shown here, and list the ways in which the United States helped the Allies achieve victory in the war.

U.S. Troops	U.S. Navy

INTERDISCIPLINARY ACTIVITY

5. **The Arts** Prepare the text for a radio news broadcast on one of the major battles of World War I.

★★

War on the Home Front

Guide to Reading

Main Idea
Victory in World War I was due, in large part, to the efforts and sacrifices made on the home front.

Reading Strategy
Organizing Information As you read about how the war affected the home front, use a diagram like the one shown here to list the steps that Americans took to support the war effort.

Step 3

Step 2

Step 1

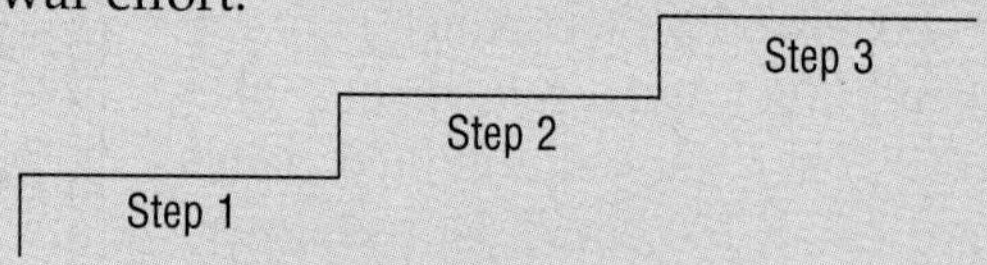

Objectives
After studying this section, you should be able to
★ explain how the war was financed.
★ describe how public opinion was shaped by the government.

Key Term
victory garden

WAR GARDENS OVER THE TOP

► WORLD WAR I POSTER

The United States found itself ill-equipped for battle when it entered World War I. The most immediate domestic concern that Congress faced was to keep the United States and Allied armies supplied by gearing United States industry to the war machine. In addition, the federal government needed to raise money to pay for the war and to mobilize the American people to support the war effort.

■ Mobilizing the Economy

To accomplish these goals, Wilson and Congress applied the Progressive Era's ideals of efficiency, control, and conformity in society to the war effort at home. "It is not an army that we must shape and train for war," said the President, "it is a nation."

Organizing Industries

The government's solution to the problem of supplying the troops was to place most industries under the control of federal agencies. The most important of these—the War Industries Board—handled purchasing for both the Allies and the United States. Under the leadership of Bernard Baruch, a Wall Street stockbroker, the War Industries Board attempted "to operate the whole United States as a single factory dominated by one management." Enlisting the most able businesspeople in America to direct the war effort, the government received the cooperation of business to convert factories to war production. Federal officials determined how raw materials would be allocated and what prices should be fixed.

The Fuel Administration was in charge of boosting coal and oil production, while encouraging people to conserve. The agency introduced such conservation methods as daylight savings time and shortened workweeks for nonwar-related factories. The Railroad Administration took charge of the railroads and ran them as a single system. The War Labor Board worked to prevent labor disputes.

Labor unions generally supported the war effort, hoping that cooperation would result in goodwill from the government and big business. Union leaders saw in the war opportunities for higher pay, better working conditions, and the right to organize and bargain collectively. Membership in unions doubled, and unions won concessions, such as the eight-hour day that industries had long opposed.

Involvement of Women

Wartime also meant increased opportunities for American women. Millions of jobs given up by men who volunteered or were drafted were filled by women. For the first time, women were welcomed in many occupations. Female workers became an essential part of the nation's war effort in war industries and defense plants.

Despite the progress toward social and economic equality the war offered them, many women wondered how the United States could be fighting to save democracy and still deny them the vote at home. Activists for woman suffrage continued to work during the war.

Involvement of African Americans

African Americans might well have asked similar questions because Southern states continued to deny them the right to vote. Also, African American soldiers fighting in Europe encountered far less discrimination from Europeans than they had experienced in their own country.

Nevertheless, the war offered new opportunities for African Americans at home. Job opportunities and high wages during the

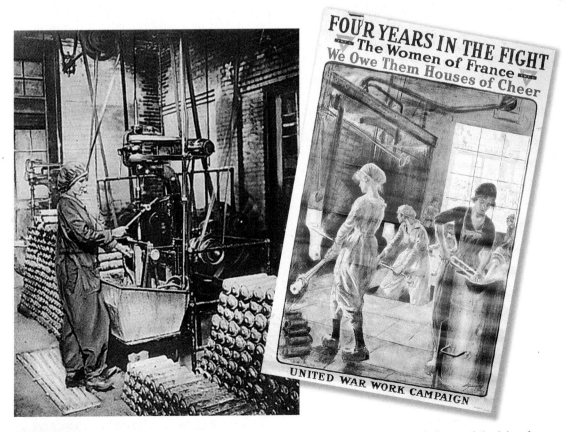

▲ **At Home** During the war more and more women became a vital part of the labor force. In addition, women volunteered for noncombat duty on the war front or for a military Home Guard in the United States. ***What happened to the suffrage movement during the war?***

▲ Poster supporting bonds

Impact of War on Civilians

The war had a great impact on the lives of all American civilians. Using the slogan "Food Will Win the War—Don't Waste It," the Food Administration, directed by Herbert Hoover, supervised efforts to reduce food consumption. Families were encouraged to "Hooverize" by "serving just enough" and by having Wheatless Mondays and Meatless Tuesdays.

Citizens were also encouraged to plant **victory gardens,** gardens for raising their own vegetables. To increase wheat production, the federally financed Grain Corporation guaranteed farmers first $2.00, then $2.26 per bushel. In 1918 it bought the entire American wheat crop. The combined efforts of the Food Administration and the American public were tremendously successful.

The Cost of War

World War I was costly. By its end the United States was spending about $44 million a day, or a total of about $33 billion. Of that amount, $10 billion went to the Allies as loans. The government raised about one-third of the money to finance the war through taxation. Income taxes were increased, although only wealthier families paid income taxes at that time. Corporations also paid higher taxes, including an "excess profits" tax, designed to return war profits to the government. The government also levied excise duties on items as varied as theater tickets, chewing gum, and phonograph records.

The government borrowed the rest of the money—more than $20 billion—from the American people by selling four issues of Liberty Bonds and a postwar issue of Victory Bonds. Posters, rallies, and "Liberty Loan sermons" encouraged people to buy the bonds.

Purchasing bonds became an act of patriotism. Even children were urged to use their pennies to buy War Savings Stamps. Boy Scouts sold the stamps under the slogan "Every Scout to Save a Soldier." Twenty-one million people—more than one-fifth of the nation's population—subscribed to the Fourth Liberty Loan.

war pulled 500,000 African Americans from Southern farms to munitions-producing Northern factories. Most were offered only unskilled or semiskilled jobs, but by war's end, more than 100,000 African Americans held jobs as skilled workers or factory supervisors.

Although discrimination against African American workers led to race riots in 26 Northern cities in 1919, African Americans in the North made significant economic gains during the war. As a result, migration northward continued after the war ended. One African American wrote a letter to a Chicago newspaper explaining this "great migration." African Americans, he said, were

" *... compelled to go where there is better wages and sociable conditions, believe me ... many places here in [Alabama] the only thing that a black man gets is a peck of meal and from 3 to 4 lbs. of bacon per week, and he is treated as a slave.* "

GOVERNMENT

■ Controlling Public Opinion

Success of the war effort depended on voluntary civilian cooperation. Therefore, the government wanted to make sure that Americans supported the nation's war aims.

Selling the War to Americans

The Committee on Public Information under the leadership of journalist and author George Creel was established to "sell" the war to America. Creel described his job as "the world's greatest adventure in advertising." He recruited advertising people, commercial artists, authors, songwriters, entertainers, public speakers, and motion-picture companies to help him.

Pamphlets were distributed explaining the causes and aims of the war. "Four-minute men" spoke at movie theaters and public halls and gatherings in support of the war effort. Although this flood of propaganda reinforced the President's image of the war as a moral crusade, it also helped promote widespread intolerance.

Control of War Protesters

To prevent spying and resistance to the war effort, Congress passed the Espionage and Sedition acts. Severe penalties imposed by these laws silenced most war opposition. Loyalty Leagues, organized by Creel, encouraged Americans to spy on their neighbors and to report those who might be "disloyal." In addition, the postmaster general was given authority to ban certain newspapers, magazines, and pamphlets from the mail. Thousands of people were imprisoned, sometimes for opinions expressed in private conversations. People were arrested for criticizing the President, for questioning the American form of government, for criticizing the army or even military uniforms. Socialist leader Eugene Debs was arrested and sentenced to 10 years in prison for merely telling an audience to "resist militarism, wherever found." People were even jailed for criticizing the Red Cross and the YMCA.

War fever was responsible for the vigorous enforcement of these laws, and the courts generally upheld the principle behind them. About 3,000 cases involving convictions under the Espionage and Sedition acts were heard on appeal in federal courts. After the war some of these cases

★★★★★★★★★★★★ AMERICAN PORTRAITS

George M. Cohan
1878–1942

By the time he wrote "Over There"—the most popular song of World War I—George M. Cohan was already one of America's biggest stars. At the age of 14, he was creating songs and skits for his family's vaudeville act. By his early 20s, he was writing, producing, and starring in hit Broadway shows.

Claiming that he had been born on the 4th of July (actually July 3), Cohan discovered early in his career that he could excite crowds with such patriotic appeals as his "I'm a Yankee Doodle Dandy."

When American troops left for France in 1917, he quickly penned "Over There," touching the chord of nationalistic fervor sweeping the country. His song became America's war anthem. In 1940 Congress awarded Cohan a Medal of Honor for "Over There" and "You're a Grand Old Flag," another patriotic song.

reached the Supreme Court. In the landmark case *Schenck* v. *United States* (1919), Justice Oliver Wendell Holmes, writing for a unanimous Court, stated:

> *When a nation is at war, many things that might be said in time of peace are such a hindrance to its efforts that their utterance will not be endured so long as [soldiers] fight and that no Court could regard them as protected by any constitutional right. . . .*

The Court refused, however, to support punishment when no "clear and present danger" of hurting the United States existed or when the accused was jailed for unpopular political beliefs.

Persecution of Germans

War fever was also to blame for the mistreatment and persecution of German Americans. Despite Wilson's insistence that Americans were "the sincere friends of the German people," anti-German sentiment ran high. Many school systems banned the teaching of the German language, and orchestras stopped performing the music of Beethoven, Schubert, and Wagner.

■ Wilson's Fourteen Points

While the war was foremost in the President's mind, Wilson never ceased to think

◀ LIBERTY LOAN POSTER

ahead to peace. In January 1918, Wilson went before Congress to present his goals for a lasting peace. With his Fourteen Points (see Appendix), the President hoped to establish a new world order.

The Fourteen Points were based on "the principle of justice to all peoples." The President proposed to eliminate the general causes of war through disarmament, freedom of the seas, and open diplomacy instead of secret agreements. Wilson also addressed the right of peoples to live under a government of their own choosing. Finally, he proposed an international peacekeeping organization.

Although Wilson's words appealed to a world weary of war, other Allied leaders did not support him. They wanted German territory and to punish Germany. A formidable challenge lay ahead for the President if he were to see his dream of peace realized.

Section 3 ★ Assessment

Checking for Understanding

1. **Define** victory garden.

2. **List** the two ways the government raised money for the war.

Critical Thinking

3. **Defending an Opinion** Was government action to suppress opposition to the war justified? Explain your reasoning.

4. **Analyzing Issues** Re-create the diagram shown here, and list how the government tried to silence war opposition.

INTERDISCIPLINARY ACTIVITY

5. **Government** Write a law that specifies who is eligible to be drafted in wartime and what to do about people who refuse to serve.

★★★★★★★★★★★★★★★★★★★★★★★

After the War

Guide to Reading

Main Idea

President Wilson sought to establish a grand peace plan after the war, but opposition to the plan at home and infighting among the Allies doomed his effort.

Reading Strategy

Sequencing Information As you read about the war's aftermath, re-create this diagram, and list the chain of events that led to the defeat of the Treaty of Versailles in America.

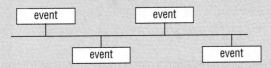

Objectives

After studying this section, you should be able to

★ describe the outcome of the Versailles peace conference.

★ explain why the Senate rejected the Treaty of Versailles.

★ identify domestic problems that arose after the war.

Key Terms

covenant, deport

▶ WORLD WAR I HELMET

Midterm elections in the United States in November 1918 showed a changing attitude toward Wilson and his policies. Realizing that Democrats faced heavy losses in the elections, the President appealed to voters to show support for his peace program by returning Democrats to Congress. Instead, voters elected Republican majorities in both houses.

■ The Peace Plan Opposed

Shortly after the election, Wilson announced his intention to head the American delegation to the peace conference. His decision was not received well by those who thought that as President his place was at home. Wilson faltered again when he failed to include any prominent Republicans in the American delegation to the conference.

Peace Conference

The peace conference opened at the palace of Versailles in January 1919, but most of the sessions took place in Paris. Delegates from 27 nations attended. The proceedings, however, were dominated by the leaders of the three most powerful nations—the United States's President Wilson, Britain's Prime Minister David Lloyd George, and France's Premier Georges Clemenceau (KLEH•muhn•SOH). With Vittorio Orlando, the Italian premier, these men became known as "the Big Four." Because their meetings were held in secret, Wilson was robbed of an effective weapon—direct appeal to public opinion. Secrecy also seemed to violate the Fourteen Points, which pledged "open covenants openly arrived at." Nevertheless, the President scored an immediate triumph by forcing plans for a League of Nations into the

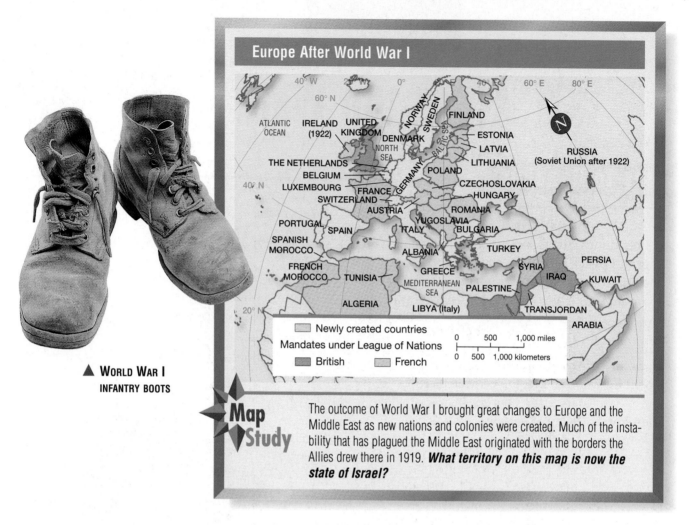

Europe After World War I

The outcome of World War I brought great changes to Europe and the Middle East as new nations and colonies were created. Much of the instability that has plagued the Middle East originated with the borders the Allies drew there in 1919. **What territory on this map is now the state of Israel?**

▲ **WORLD WAR I INFANTRY BOOTS**

peace treaty. In mid-February the **covenant,** or charter, of the League, written by Wilson himself, was accepted by the conference.

Opposition Grows

During Wilson's absence his political influence in the United States weakened alarmingly. The likelihood that Wilson's peace program would fail became evident when 39 Republican senators and senators-elect—far more than enough to prevent ratification of a treaty—signed a statement opposing the League of Nations. Instead of trying to repair the rift, however, Wilson publicly denounced the "narrow, selfish, provincial purposes" of his opponents and insisted that the League be part of the peace treaty. At the peace table, he tried to appease his critics at home by calling for changes designed to protect American interests. To accept such changes, the Allies required Wilson to make further concessions in their favor.

Treaty of Versailles

Despite Wilson's hopes, it was a victor's peace. In the Middle East, the Ottoman Empire lost territory. In Europe, Austria-Hungary was split up. The greatest humiliation was reserved for the Germans, however. Germany lost territory and was stripped of its colonies. In addition, Germany was required to pay for damage it had done in Europe and to repay the Allies for the cost of the war. Although many of the Fourteen Points were ignored, Wilson trusted the League of Nations to right injustices after the desire for revenge subsided.

Difficulty at Home

The peace settlement complete, in July 1919 President Wilson came home to face his foes. Although he hoped Americans would support the treaty, they criticized it from all sides. In Congress a small group of senators branded the League a "treacherous and treasonable scheme," while a much larger group wanted the Senate to ratify the treaty but with amendments that would preserve the nation's freedom to act independently.

Instead of compromising, Wilson insisted that the Senate ratify the treaty without changes. Convinced that he could defeat his opposition by appealing to public opinion, Wilson went directly to the people. Starting in Ohio in September, he traveled 8,000 miles and made 37 major speeches in less than a month on behalf of the treaty. Almost everywhere his reception was warm; he seemed to be regaining popular support. Had his strength held out, he might have won the battle, but the physical strain proved too great for the President. He collapsed in Colorado on September 25 and was forced to abandon his speaking tour. Shortly after returning to the White House, Wilson suffered a stroke that paralyzed one side of his body and impaired his speech. He was bedridden for months, isolated from even his closest advisers.

With the President silenced, in November 1919, and again in March 1920, the Senate refused to ratify the Versailles treaty. Instead, the United States negotiated a separate peace treaty with each of the Central Powers in 1921.

■ America's Postwar Problems

The fate of the treaty was only one of the problems the United States faced after World War I. Demobilizing the armed forces, returning to a peacetime economy, and coping with fears of espionage presented the country with serious challenges.

Demobilization

The United States began to demobilize as soon as the hostilities ended. Within a short time, the army was reduced to less than 500,000, and economic controls were lifted. The businesspeople left Washington, D.C., and industry converted to peacetime production. With Wilson preoccupied with the peace treaty and later incapacitated, the nation received little overall direction. Industry enjoyed a brief postwar boom, resulting from the increased demand for consumer goods that had been scarce during the war. Unfortunately, government spending during the war brought inflation that nearly doubled the cost of living by 1919, and prices rose to a point where many consumers could not afford to pay for new items. Consequently, after 1920 business activity slowed. Farmers were especially hard-hit. Slackening demands for food and the end of government price guarantees caused agricultural prices to plummet. Many farmers who took advantage of high wartime crop prices and went into debt to expand their farms now faced bankruptcy.

▲ *SIGNING OF THE TREATY OF VERSAILLES* by John Johansen, 1919 The greatest obstacle at the peace conference was that many countries were interested chiefly in gaining territory and inflicting punishment on Germany. ***Who played major roles in treaty negotiations?***

▲ **ANTI-IMMIGRANT SENTIMENT** A 1920 cartoon shows immigrants taking jobs from Americans. *How did many Americans view labor leaders?*

Labor Unrest

High prices also contributed to labor unrest after the war, and when the War Labor Board disbanded, the truce between employers and organized labor ended. A record number—3,600—strikes occurred in 1919, most meeting with little success. Four of them—the Seattle general strike, the Boston police strike, the steel strike, and the coal strike—were highly disruptive and had effects that lasted well into the 1920s.

In January 1919, only 2 months after the armistice, 35,000 shipyard workers from Seattle, Washington, went on strike to gain an increase in their wages. The next month union workers in all Seattle industries walked off their jobs in support of the shipyard strikers. Many city residents viewed the strike as revolutionary. They responded by hoarding food and fuel and by purchasing guns. Seattle's mayor blamed the situation on dangerous radicals and after 5 days used the state militia to break the strike.

In September 1919, another major city was hit by labor unrest as Boston's police force went on strike for better wages and working conditions. Looters soon were in the streets, smashing windows and stealing goods. When the mayor was unable to restore order, Massachusetts governor Calvin Coolidge

called out the state guard. A new police force was hired, and Coolidge received national acclaim for his view that "There is no right to strike against the public safety by anybody, anywhere, anytime."

Later that month more than 350,000 steelworkers went on strike across the nation, demanding better wages, an 8-hour rather than a 12-hour day, and the right to join a union. Two-thirds of the strikers were immigrants. Most of the office workers and supervisors who refused to join the strike were American-born. The companies blamed the strike on radicals who told "these foreigners . . . that if they would join the union they would get Americans' jobs." When the companies hired replacement workers, violence broke out, and federal troops were called in to protect them. After 4 months, the strikers gave up with no gains.

While the steel strike was under way, 450,000 coal miners walked off their jobs nationwide. Overworked and underpaid, the strikers demanded a 60 percent pay increase and a 30-hour week. Since at the time coal was the nation's major energy source, the government responded quickly. Obtaining a court order, it forced the strikers back to work. Eventually, however, coal miners won a large pay increase to an average of $7.50 a day.

Red Scare

Many Americans had long suspected a link between labor unrest and political radicalism. The strikes of 1919 helped fuel a larger "Red Scare" than the United States experienced after the war. When the Bolsheviks seized power in Russia in 1917, they called on workers everywhere to revolt. In 1919 communism seemed to have great appeal among the poverty-stricken peoples of war-torn Europe. Although the overwhelming majority of American labor leaders were not allied with the Communists, nevertheless, many Americans suspected them of planning revolution.

The same laws used to quiet opposition and suppress civil liberties during the war were now turned against radicals. Immigrants—especially those with Russian names—came under suspicion. Attorney General A. Mitchell Palmer rounded up 6,000 immigrants that the government suspected of being Communists and **deported**—expelled from the country—nearly 600 of them. Some of the immigrants deported had become American citizens, and some were deported without trials.

Racial Tension

Accompanying the Red Scare was a wave of racism. Racial tensions rose as white soldiers returning from Europe found themselves competing for jobs and housing with African Americans who had come north during the war. During the summer of 1919, race riots broke out in many Northern cities. The worst was in Chicago, where nearly 40 people were killed and more than 500 injured. One journalist described the scene:

> *During this wild week mobs of whites pursued and beat and killed [African Americans]. Other mobs of [African Americans] pursued and beat and killed whites. . . . Armed bands in motor trucks dashed wildly up and down the streets, firing into houses. . . .*

Few cities in the United States escaped racial violence in the early 1920s. Even after the Red Scare died down, racial intolerance lived on in organizations such as the Ku Klux Klan, which spread from the South to become a powerful national force.

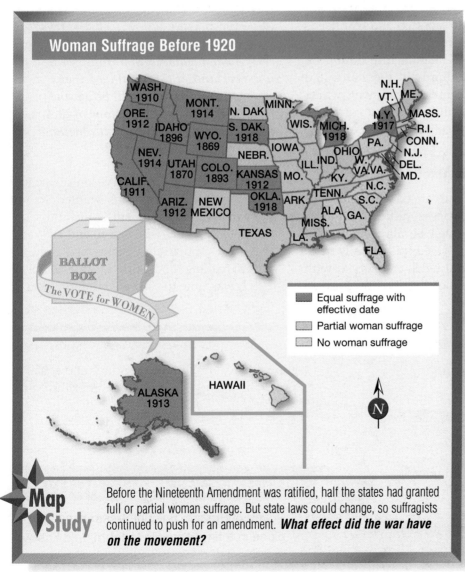

Woman Suffrage Before 1920

WASH. 1910
ORE. 1912
MONT. 1914
N. DAK.
MINN.
N.H.
VT. ME.
IDAHO 1896
WYO. 1869
S. DAK. 1918
WIS.
MICH. 1918
N.Y. 1917
MASS.
R.I.
NEV. 1914
UTAH 1870
COLO. 1893
NEBR.
IOWA
ILL. IND. OHIO
PA.
CONN.
N.J.
DEL.
MD.
CALIF. 1911
KANSAS 1912
MO.
KY.
W. VA. VA.
ARIZ. 1912
NEW MEXICO
OKLA. 1918
ARK.
TENN.
N.C.
S.C.
TEXAS
MISS.
ALA.
GA.
LA.
FLA.

BALLOT BOX
The VOTE for WOMEN

ALASKA 1913

HAWAII

N

- Equal suffrage with effective date
- Partial woman suffrage
- No woman suffrage

Map Study
Before the Nineteenth Amendment was ratified, half the states had granted full or partial woman suffrage. But state laws could change, so suffragists continued to push for an amendment. *What effect did the war have on the movement?*

ONE MILLION WOMEN OF THIS STATE WANT the VOTE WE KNOW BECAUSE WE HAVE CANVASSED THEM The largest number of men ever registered in New York was 1,800,000 A MILLION WOMEN IS A BIG MAJORITY. VOTE ON THE WOMAN SUFFRAGE AMENDMENT YES NOV. 2

▲ MARCHING FOR THE VOTE

■ Wilson's Legacy

Despite a lack of presidential leadership as Wilson's second term drew to a close, Congress and the states implemented important laws. However, Congress would not approve joining the League of Nations.

In 1920 Congress passed the Esch-Cummins Act, which turned the operation of railroads back to their owners. This statute gave the Interstate Commerce Commission almost complete power to fix rates as well as to regulate railroad financing.

Prohibition

World War I helped to add two amendments to the Constitution. Prohibition, which had made gains before the war began, made even greater advances during the war. "Hooverizing" put American citizens in the mood to sacrifice, and war needs compelled the federal government to forbid the use of grain to manufacture liquor. By January 1919, two-thirds of the states had ratified the Eighteenth Amendment, which prohibited "the manufacture, sale, or transportation" of intoxicating beverages.

The Nineteenth Amendment

The war also advanced the cause of women's rights. It was difficult to deny demands that women be allowed to vote after they had performed traditionally male jobs in factories and fields and served with courage and devotion behind the lines in Europe. On the eve of the 1920 presidential election, after decades of struggle, women gained suffrage when the Nineteenth Amendment was ratified.

A Warning

Wilson's final year and a half in office left the country virtually leaderless. The President had recovered sufficiently to transact routine business, but his energies still were focused on getting the United States into the League of Nations. Retaining a belief that the American people would not retreat from world leadership, he urged that the election of 1920 be a "great and solemn referendum" on the League issue.

The 1920 election saw Wilson's party and the League repudiated at the polls. The country wanted to turn its back to world responsibilities. In 1923, shortly before he died, Wilson warned:

> ❝ *I can predict with absolute certainty that within another generation there will be another world war if the nations of the world do not concert the method by which to prevent it.* ❞

Few people listened to Wilson's warning, however. Most Americans wanted to put their memories of war, suffering, and sacrifice behind them. "The war to end all wars" was over. The United States had done its part in making the world "safe for democracy." It was time to start enjoying the peace.

Section 4 ★ Assessment

Checking for Understanding

1. **Define** covenant, deport.

2. **List** the provisions of the Versailles treaty.

Critical Thinking

3. **Analyzing Motives** Explain why "peace without victory" was so difficult to achieve at Versailles.

4. **Examining Issues** Re-create the diagram shown here, and list the economic and social problems that plagued America after the war.

Economic		Social
	Postwar Problems	

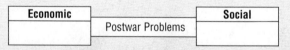

INTERDISCIPLINARY ACTIVITY

5. **Science** Prepare a list of items you would place in a time capsule to let people know in 300 years about the World War I era.

Changing the Map of Europe

Part of President Wilson's peace program following World War I called for self-determination of nations. Before the war Europe was a complex mosaic, or pattern, of distinct ethnic groups. Many of these groups lived within the borders of nations dominated by other ethnic groups. Wilson believed that national boundaries should be drawn to give each ethnic population its own nation.

Other powers at the Versailles peace conference, however, had their own plans. Allied leaders wanted to weaken the Central Powers by dividing their land. Some Allies also wanted their enemies' territory for themselves.

Germany's land area was greatly reduced. Germany's colonies were given over to the Allies as mandates, territories ruled by the Allies with the approval of the League of Nations. Alsace and Lorraine were returned to France. The French also received control of the coal-rich Saar Basin for 15 years.

The Allies signed individual peace treaties with other nations, most of them centering on territorial topics that focused on partitioning the Austro-Hungarian Empire. With the end of the Hapsburg dynasty, Hungary became independent, and Austria was left a small, economically weak country.

From the ashes of the old Russian and Austro-Hungarian empires, new nations emerged in eastern Europe. Among these countries were Finland, Estonia, Lithuania, Latvia, Poland, Czechoslovakia, and Yugoslavia.

▲ THE BIG FOUR MEET AFTER WORLD WAR I

Wilson's secretary of state, Robert Lansing, noted that the boundaries created after the war were artificial and did not follow ethnic population patterns. Lansing stated that they would last only as long as dissatisfied nations were too weak to change them. He believed that when one nation became confident of its strength and began to seek to remedy these boundaries, a new war would take place. Twenty years later that became the case.

Making the Geography Connection

1. How did Wilson think national boundaries should be determined in Europe after World War I?

2. What new nations were created in eastern Europe after the war?

ACTIVITY

3. Select a European nation and create a time line showing important events in its history from 1900 to 1920.

Using Vocabulary

Imagine that you have kept a diary of events of World War I. Write headlines of three diary entries using each of the following terms in a headline.

covenant   deport
armistice   victory garden

Reviewing Facts

1. **Discuss** Wilson's foreign-policy views and how they related to his actions in Latin America.

2. **State** how nationalism and alliances created the conditions that led to World War I.

3. **Identify** two reasons the United States declared war on Germany.

4. **List** two actions taken by the American military that helped win the war.

5. **Describe** the terms of the Versailles treaty.

Understanding Concepts

Conflict

1. Explain how Wilson's ideals influenced his actions and made compromise difficult.

Economic Interests

2. Re-create the diagram shown here, and describe the economic and political interests in the United States that made maintaining neutrality in World War I impossible.

Economic		Political
	⟨ Factors Against Neutrality ⟩	

Critical Thinking

1. **Evaluating Foreign Policy** Consider the United States's neutrality policy before entering the war. Evaluate the feasibility of this policy. Consider the events that forced the United States to abandon neutrality and enter the war.

2. **Expressing Viewpoints** During World War I the government worked to control public attitudes about the war. In your opinion, was it necessary for the government to take such actions? Explain your viewpoint.

3. **Analyzing Fine Art** Study the mural by José Clemente Orozco entitled *Revolutionists* on this page, then answer the questions that follow.

   a. What themes are illustrated?

   b. What was happening in Mexico in the early 1900s that may have inspired this work?

   c. Why would a wall mural be a good way to spread a message?

4. **Analyzing Graphs** Study the graph on page 481, then answer the questions that follow.

   a. What was the first month that the United States had 1 million troops in the army? By what month were there 1 million American soldiers in Europe?

b. About what percentage of the United States Army was in Europe by the end of 1917? By the armistice a year later?

c. What information does this graph provide about the efficiency of America's mobilization?

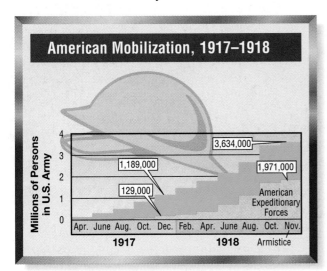

American Mobilization, 1917–1918

Millions of Persons in U.S. Army

3,634,000

1,189,000

1,971,000

129,000

American Expeditionary Forces

Apr. June Aug. Oct. Dec. Feb. Apr. June Aug. Oct. Nov.

1917   **1918**   Armistice

History and Geography

World War

War in Europe engulfed many nations. Review the chapter and the maps on page 465 to help you answer these questions.

1. **Movement** In which direction did forces of the Central Powers advance into Russia?

2. **Region** Which nations in South America sided with the Central Powers? The Allies?

3. **Location** What major battles were fought in France in 1915?

Cooperative Learning

Interdisciplinary Activity: Journalism

Work with a partner to write two newspaper editorials on the United States government's methods of controlling public opinion during World War I—one supporting the government's policies and the other opposing them. Before writing, collaborate on a list of pros and cons about the government's activities, including the Espionage and Sedition acts and the Committee on Public Information.

Then each of you should take opposite positions and write an editorial. Exchange your editorials and write a "letter to the editor" as a rebuttal to your partner's position.

Practicing Skills

Interpreting a Political Map

Study the map that appears on page 474, then answer the questions that follow.

1. Of these nations, which one was newly created after the war: Spain, Poland, or Syria?

2. Do you agree with the following assessment: Newly created nations were generally located in western Europe. Explain.

Technology Activity

Using a Word Processor

Use the Internet and other library resources to find out more about one World War I battle. Compile a variety of information about the battle and write a brief report to share with the class.

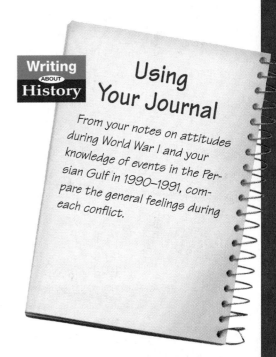

Writing ABOUT History

Using Your Journal

From your notes on attitudes during World War I and your knowledge of events in the Persian Gulf in 1990–1991, compare the general feelings during each conflict.

CHAPTER 16

★★★

The Decade of Normalcy
1920–1928

▶ THE CLOCHE, POPULAR WOMAN'S HAT OF THE 1920S

Setting the Scene

Focus

The decade that followed World War I differed considerably from the Progressive years that came before it. Voters turned to conservative leaders who promised to turn the country away from European affairs and inward to "normalcy." For many Americans this shift meant preserving the values of rural America and enjoying prosperity. For others it meant a fascination with a dazzling new assortment of consumer goods, entertainment, and changing fashions.

Concepts to Understand

★ Why shifts in government policies and increased production resulted in **economic change**
★ How **social change** affected the arts, the role of women, and minorities

Read to Discover . . .

★ ways United States involvement in international relations changed following World War I.
★ what signs of social tension were evident in the 1920s.

Journal Notes

What was the Harlem Renaissance? Jot down details about it as you read the chapter.

HISTORY Online

Chapter Overview
Visit the *American History: The Modern Era Since 1865* Web site at **me.glencoe.com** and click on *Chapter 16—Chapter Overviews* to preview chapter information.

CULTURAL	• **1920** *First commercial radio broadcast is aired* • **1922** *Lincoln Memorial is dedicated*	• **1925** *John Scopes trial over teaching evolution in Dayton, Tennessee, occurs*
	1920	**1923**
POLITICAL	• **1920** *Warren Harding is elected* • **1921** *Washington Conference is held*	• **1923** *Calvin Coolidge becomes President after Harding's death*

▲ TROMBONE USED IN JAZZ GROUP, 1920S

History AND ART

Dance Hall
by Thomas Hart Benton, 1930

Thomas Hart Benton excelled at mural painting, concentrating on Midwestern legend, history, and daily life.

• **1927** *First "talking" motion picture,* The Jazz Singer, *is released*

• **1929** *Chicago mobsters murder seven rival gang members in the St. Valentine's Day Massacre*

1926	1929

• **1926** *United States intervenes in Nicaragua*

• **1928** *Kellogg-Briand Pact is negotiated*

• **1929** *Herbert Hoover becomes President*

★★★

The Harding Years

Main Idea

After World War I, Americans turned away from the rest of the world and enjoyed an era of prosperity.

Reading Strategy

Classifying Information As you read about the Harding years, use a chart such as the one shown here to explain the provisions as well as the intent of the National Origins Act.

National Origins Act	
Provisions	Intent

Objectives

After studying this section, you should be able to

★ describe foreign policy issues following World War I.

★ explain the provisions of the National Origins Act.

★ describe the scandals in the Harding administration.

Key Terms

reparation, technological unemployment, open shop, welfare capitalism

▶ **1920 REPUBLICAN CAMPAIGN PIN**

The end of the war created new problems for the United States. After the dismantling of the War Industries Board, business lost the profitable military contracts of the war years. Four million recently demobilized service men and women needed work. In 1920 and 1921, unemployment soared, as did prices. Labor unrest was reflected in the United States Steel strike and the Boston police strike of 1919.

■ The Election of 1920

Several prominent men sought the Republican nomination in 1920, the prize going to a dark horse, Ohio senator Warren G. Harding. Harding's running mate was Massachusetts governor Calvin Coolidge. To oppose Harding, the Democrats chose Ohio governor James M. Cox, a loyal Wilson supporter. Cox's running mate was Franklin D. Roosevelt, who, like his distant cousin, Theodore, had served as assistant secretary of the navy. The strategy chosen by Cox was as Wilson desired—to campaign for the League of Nations.

The Republicans were divided on the issue. Harding said he favored "a society of free nations" to keep peace. Most prominent Republicans took this to mean that Harding supported their decision to join the League, but anti-League Republicans seemed certain that Harding opposed it. Thus, as journalist Walter Lippmann pointed out, Harding received support from "men and women who thought a Republican victory would kill the League, plus those who thought it was the most practical way to procure the League."

The election was an overwhelming Republican victory. Harding carried every northern and western state and even broke the Democratic Solid South by carrying Tennessee. A key to the election results may be found in the President's reassuring slogan—"a return to normalcy"— coined by Harding during his campaign. It suggested a return to "the good old days," to the conditions that prevailed before the shocks of World War I.

■ Postwar Foreign Policy

After his election, Harding announced that his administration would not lead the United States into the League of Nations "by the side door, back door, or cellar door." The United States was too powerful, too economically interconnected, and too widely involved in world affairs to retreat into isolationism, however, and participated actively in many League conferences.

War Debt

One international problem that demanded a solution was $10.3 billion in Allied war debts owed to the United States for food and war materials. The debtor nations had difficulty meeting their payments. They argued that high American tariffs had closed the United States market to their imports and slowed their economic recovery. Furthermore, debtor nations argued, because the United States had lost fewer people in the war than the other Allies, it should be willing to pay more of the financial cost. The United States government, however, took the position that the Allies had gained territory and **reparations,** or payments for damages, as a result of the victory while the United States had claimed no reward, and that to cancel these debts would destroy faith in international agreements.

Eventually the United States made agreements with 17 of the 20 debtor nations, reducing the debts by 30 to 80 percent. Most of the money the Allies paid actually came from Germany. To pay its reparations, Germany obtained private bank loans from other countries—especially the United States.

The Washington Conference

At the time of the Harding administration, the United States, Great Britain, and Japan were experiencing costly and competitive naval buildups that originated during the war. There was also friction in East Asia, caused mainly by conflicts over commercial rights in China and by Western suspicion of Japan's recent territorial gains. After World War I, Japan had acquired all of Germany's Pacific islands north of the equator as well as the Chinese port of Kiaochow (jee•OW•JOH). Japan also treated the rest of the Chinese province of Shantung as its own.

In the hope of resolving these problems, the administration hosted an eight-nation conference in Washington, D.C. The negotiations, which lasted from November 1921 to February 1922, led to three important treaties.

The Four-Power Treaty

The Four-Power Treaty, signed by the United States, Great Britain, France, and Japan, was an agreement among the four

 ▲ NOT ROOM FOR BOTH By showing the League of Nations agreement trying to replace the Constitution in ruling the nation, this artist expressed concern that joining the League would deprive the United States of the freedom to set its own policies. *What role did the 1920 election play in resolving this issue?*

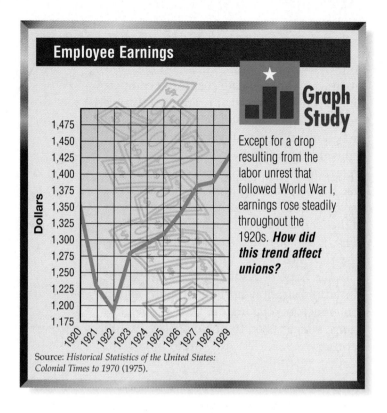

Employee Earnings

Graph Study

Except for a drop resulting from the labor unrest that followed World War I, earnings rose steadily throughout the 1920s. *How did this trend affect unions?*

Dollars

1,475
1,450
1,425
1,400
1,375
1,350
1,325
1,300
1,275
1,250
1,225
1,200
1,175

1920 1921 1922 1923 1924 1925 1926 1927 1928 1929

Source: *Historical Statistics of the United States: Colonial Times to 1970* (1975).

---

policies of John Hay into a treaty. The signers agreed to preserve equal commercial rights in China and to refrain from "taking advantage of conditions in China to seek special rights or privileges." Following this policy, Japan soon withdrew from the province of Shantung.

Although the immediate results of the Washington Conference were encouraging, the conference failed to reach an agreement limiting military forces on land. Moreover, the treaties had notable shortcomings. Under the Five-Power Treaty, naval powers could still build unlimited numbers of smaller combat vessels, such as submarines and destroyers. In addition, the Four-Power Treaty did not commit the signers to active military defense of their allies; indeed, such a commitment might have been unacceptable to the United States. The Nine-Power Treaty made no provision for enforcement of the Open Door policy.

great powers to respect one another's Pacific holdings. In case of disagreements or a threat from another nation, the signers also agreed to confer "fully and frankly."

The Five-Power Treaty

Under the Five-Power Treaty, the 5 naval powers of the United States, Great Britain, Japan, France, and Italy agreed to freeze their navies at 1921 levels and thus avoid the financial strain of further naval buildups. The signers further agreed to halt the building of large warships for 10 years; some ships under construction would even be scrapped. The treaty also included an agreement by the United States and Great Britain not to build new fortifications or naval bases in the western Pacific. This provision gave Japan control of nearby waters in exchange for agreeing to remain at inferior naval strength.

The Nine-Power Treaty

The Nine-Power Treaty—signed by the United States, France, Great Britain, Japan, Italy, Belgium, China, the Netherlands, and Portugal—put the "Open Door" China

■ Business Normalcy

From the start, Harding's handling of domestic problems made it apparent that normalcy meant a general retreat from government regulation of business. Although the federal government actively aided businesses by levying protective tariffs, promoting foreign trade, and breaking strikes, its policy in other matters was laissez-faire. There was little effort to enforce the antitrust laws that regulated business mergers. Reflecting the dominant feeling of the time, regulatory agencies such as the Interstate Commerce Commission and the Federal Trade Commission were largely unsympathetic to policies restricting private enterprise.

The Fordney-McCumber Act

The new trend was immediately seen in the tariff laws. In 1922 Congress passed the Fordney-McCumber Act, raising import duties to high levels. This protected agriculture as well as certain young industries, such as rayon, china, and the optical-glass and chemical products for which the United States seized patents from Germany during the war. Because the Fordney-McCumber Act authorized the President to raise or lower duties by as much as 50 percent, rates often went still higher.

Creating the Bureau of the Budget

Because World War I had raised the national debt from less than $10 per person to over $200, the Harding and Coolidge administrations attempted to lower this burden by making the government more fiscally responsible. In 1921 Congress created the Bureau of the Budget in the Treasury Department.

The efforts of the Bureau of the Budget to introduce savings were especially supported by Coolidge, who felt so strongly about curbing the nation's expenditures that he devoted serious attention to routine federal purchases such as lead pencils and typewriter ribbons. After the Washington Conference, there was no threat of war on the horizon, and even military expenditures were greatly lowered.

Changes in Taxation

Andrew Mellon, secretary of the treasury from 1921 to 1932 and a wealthy man, believed that heavy taxes on excess profits "penalized success" and discouraged investment in productive enterprise. At Mellon's insistence, Congress abolished the wartime excise and excess profits taxes and reduced tax rates on incomes by nearly two-thirds. Even with these cuts, the nation's prosperity produced enough tax revenue to reduce the national debt by $8 billion between 1921 and 1929.

■ Labor and Labor Unions

Between 1921 and 1928, the average annual wage for workers rose from $1,227 to $1,384. However, new manufacturing caused **technological unemployment**—jobs lost when occupations become obsolete. Although people replaced by machines usually found jobs elsewhere, the transition was sometimes difficult. Not only were they often forced to leave home to find employment, but they also frequently lost the benefit of long years spent learning a particular skill.

The introduction of jukeboxes and sound films, to cite an extreme example, caused widespread unemployment among musicians. Although the assembly line lowered the costs of production, many laborers could not stand the monotony and nervous tension caused by working at a speed set by the machine.

Union Decline

The "prosperity decade" saw labor unions decline in strength. Even the American Federation of Labor, one of the largest organizations, had difficulty holding its members in the face of antiunion activities. Employers joined to promote the **open shop**—a shop where workers do not have to

Visualizing History

▲ **KKK** Members of the Ku Klux Klan parade down Pennsylvania Avenue in Washington, D.C., in September 1926. The KKK spread from the South to gain national power in the 1920s. *How did the Klan as well as many other Americans react to increased immigration after World War I?*

join a union. Labeled the "American Plan," in practice the open shop meant a shop closed to union members. To further reduce the power of unions, companies promoted **welfare capitalism,** a system to make employees feel more a part of the business by enabling them to buy shares of stock, by instituting profit sharing, and by providing such fringe benefits as medical care, retirement pensions, and recreational facilities. Moreover, wages and conditions improved somewhat during the 1920s. With some improvement in their standards of living and the relative weakness of unions, striking seemed pointless to many workers.

Strikebreaking

Although Herbert Hoover, secretary of commerce, persuaded President Harding to make a successful personal appeal to the leaders of the steel industry to abandon the 12-hour day, the federal government was usually on the side of the employers. Thus Attorney General Harry M. Daugherty helped to break railroad and coal strikes in 1922 by obtaining injunctions that prohibited every conceivable union activity, including picketing, making public statements to the press, and jeering at strikebreakers. In 1919 the Indiana State Guard—and eventually federal troops—protected strikebreakers at United States Steel. In addition, the Supreme Court continually whittled away at the protections that unions thought they had secured by the Clayton Act of 1914. Once again, injunctions were freely used to stop strikes and boycotts.

■ Restricting Immigration

In the decade before World War I, approximately 1 million persons a year came to live in the United States, over two-thirds of these from countries in southern and eastern Europe. To slow down this tide of immigration, Congress passed in 1917 an act requiring a literacy test, designed to exclude large numbers of immigrants.

The act, however, had little effect. New immigrants congregated in such cities as New York and Chicago, where opportunities for employment were greatest. Established immigrants resented the new immigrants' increasing political power. Even more, they

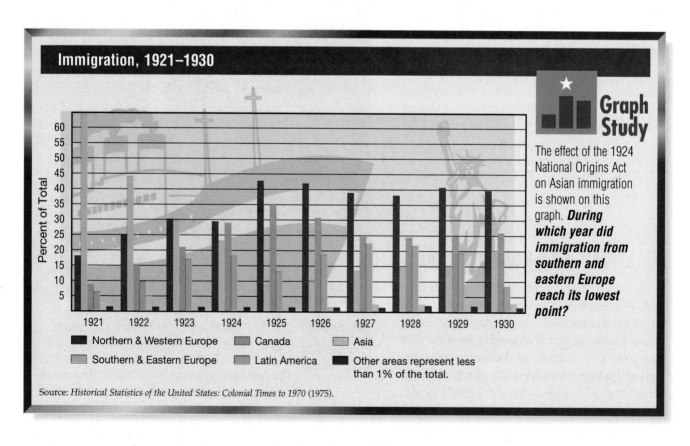

Immigration, 1921–1930

Graph Study

The effect of the 1924 National Origins Act on Asian immigration is shown on this graph. *During which year did immigration from southern and eastern Europe reach its lowest point?*

Percent of Total

Northern & Western Europe Canada Asia
Southern & Eastern Europe Latin America Other areas represent less than 1% of the total.

Source: *Historical Statistics of the United States: Colonial Times to 1970* (1975).

feared that the newcomers, most of whom were Catholic, would overthrow traditional Protestant values. Conservative labor unions were angered by the willingness of poor immigrants to work for very low wages. Employers, who had previously favored unrestricted immigration as a means of hiring cheap labor, now came to fear that the new immigrants were radicals who would fight for a communist revolution.

The National Origins Act

During and after World War I, feeling against "hyphenated-Americans" was stimulated by anti-German hysteria, by the Red Scare, and by the Ku Klux Klan. When immigrants came to the United States, fleeing their war-torn countries in the hopes of finding wealth and opportunity, Congress took quick action. In 1921 Harding signed the Emergency Quota Act, which cut the number of people admitted to the United States. According to this act, only 3 percent of the total number of people in any national group already living in the United States in 1910 would be admitted during a single year.

Three years later the National Origins Act made restriction a permanent policy. This 1924 law temporarily reduced the quota still further. It also provided that after 1927 a total of only 150,000 immigrants would be admitted to the United States per year, their nationalities apportioned on the basis of the 1920 census. This meant that more than 85 percent of the new immigrants would be from Europe—mainly from Great Britain, Ireland, Germany, and Scandinavia.

The intention of the National Origins Act was clearly to discriminate against certain nationalities and races. This became even more apparent when immigrants from Asia and Africa were either assigned very small quotas or barred entirely. Japanese immigration was completely excluded. The Japanese regarded the law as a national insult, and the day it went into effect was declared a day of public mourning and national humiliation in Japan. The incident discredited moderate Japanese politicians who sought to cooperate with the United States and advanced the cause of reactionary militarists in Japan.

 History AND ART

▲ *The Passion of Sacco and Vanzetti* by Ben Shahn, 1932 Many Americans rallied to the defense of Nicola Sacco and Bartolomeo Vanzetti. **Why did this case arouse controversy?**

Sacco and Vanzetti

An event that for many came to symbolize mistrust of immigrants in the United States was the trial of Nicola Sacco and Bartolomeo Vanzetti. These two Italian immigrants and anarchists were accused in 1921 of killing two men during a robbery in Massachusetts. They were convicted, but many thought they never received a fair trial. It was believed that the trial judge was prejudiced against the defendants because of their ethnic backgrounds and political beliefs. For years attempts were made to obtain a retrial, but in 1927 Sacco and Vanzetti were executed. In his final statement in court, Vanzetti continued to maintain his innocence of the crime, saying:

> " . . . [M]y conviction is that I have suffered for things that I am guilty of. I am suffering because I am a radical and indeed I am a radical; I have suffered because I was an Italian and indeed I am an Italian. . . . "

The question of the guilt or innocence of Sacco and Vanzetti has never been answered with certainty. Their trial made many people think critically about the American justice system, however.

■ Scandals Among Harding's Advisers

Although President Harding was personally honest, there was more corruption in his administration than in any previous one. Harding's poker-playing friends, known as "the Ohio Gang," used their ties to the President and the attorney general to sell government appointments, pardons, and immunity from prosecution.

Less than 18 months after Harding took office, his administration was racked by scandal. It was discovered that Charles R. Forbes, the director of the Veterans Bureau and a close friend of Harding, had made illegal deals that had netted him hundreds of thousands of dollars in commissions. When this fact became public, the attorney for the Bureau, who was also involved, shot himself. His suicide was closely followed by that of Jesse Smith, a close friend of Attorney General Harry M. Daugherty, who himself was later accused of corruption while in office.

The worst scandal involved Harding's secretary of the interior, Albert B. Fall, who secretly leased to private interests some oil lands, which had been set aside for the navy at Teapot Dome, Wyoming, and Elk Hills, California. In return Fall received bribes totaling more than $300,000. Eventually the Senate investigated the Teapot Dome scandal, and Secretary Fall went to prison.

When Harding learned what was going on, he complained privately that he had been betrayed. He said that he had no troubles with his enemies, but his friends—they were a different story. In the summer of 1923, Harding traveled to Alaska, deeply concerned and depressed over the scandals in his administration. On his return he became severely ill. He died on August 2, shortly before news of the scandals broke to the public.

Section 1 ★ Assessment

Checking for Understanding

1. **Define** reparation, technological unemployment, open shop, welfare capitalism.
2. **Explain** two foreign-policy problems the United States faced after the war.

Critical Thinking

3. **Analyzing Changes** Explain why Harding's election fit America's mood and how this mood had changed since 1917.

4. **Summarizing** Re-create the diagram shown here, and describe the scandals in the Harding administration.

Harding Administration
Scandals

INTERDISCIPLINARY ACTIVITY

5. **Math** Select one of the years shown on the graph on page 488. Display the information for that year in a circle graph.

Household Technology

". . . [T]he wise woman," proclaimed a 1920s electric company ad, "delegates to electricity all that electricity can do." Inventions such as electric irons, vacuum cleaners, and washing machines changed the lives of urban middle-class housewives in the decade of the 1920s. But these devices changed only the way women spent their time, not how much time they spent.

One study revealed that upper middle-class homemakers employed only half as many full-time servants as their mothers had. These women did work their mothers had hired others to do. Although some women found that laborsaving devices gave them more leisure time, others said that the dirt and soot caused by automobile traffic and nearby factories made their homes dirtier than those of the previous generation. Most of the women surveyed said they spent less time on housework than their mothers, but parenting and other demands had increased. "So many things our mothers didn't know about, we feel that we ought to do for our children," said one woman.

The technological innovations were developed by such creative individuals as Charles Steinmetz. Steinmetz gained recognition in electrical science, and General Electric offered him a job with an excellent salary and superb research facilities.

Known as the "Electrical Genius of GE," Steinmetz made contributions to science and science engineering that sped the nation into an age of electricity. More than 200 patents flowed from his work, which included the study, explanation, and harnessing of alternating current. Before Steinmetz, it had been impossible to transmit electricity more than 3 miles without using multiple generators.

▲ VACUUM CLEANER ADVERTISEMENT, 1920S

Making the Science Connection

1. What laborsaving devices aided American housewives during the 1920s?

2. What benefits were derived from the work of Charles Steinmetz?

ACTIVITY

3. Find a photo or drawing of a household innovation that in your opinion has provided the greatest benefits. Write a paragraph explaining your reasons for choosing that particular item.

★★★★★★★★★★★★★★★★★★★★★★★★★★★★★★

The Coolidge Era

Guide to Reading

Main Idea
President Coolidge maintained a conservative approach to government as the nation's economy continued to soar.

Reading Strategy

Organizing Information As you read about the Coolidge years, use a diagram like the one shown here to explain the Model T's impact on both industry and society.

Impact on Industry	Model T	Impact on Society

Objectives

After studying this section, you should be able to

★ discuss the changes to industry Henry Ford introduced.

★ outline the problems of farmers and the government's response.

★ describe the background and details of the Kellogg-Briand Pact.

Key Term

domestic market

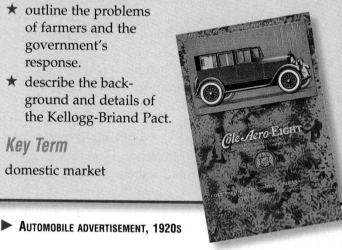

▶ AUTOMOBILE ADVERTISEMENT, 1920s

Coolidge had traits often associated with small-town America. He was conservative, cautious, and given to few words. In public speeches and magazine articles, he preached the old-fashioned virtues of honesty, thrift, and hard work. His philosophy of government was simple: economy and laissez-faire. To take as little action as possible was with Coolidge almost a principle of life; he once said, "Four-fifths of all our troubles in this life would disappear if we would only sit down and keep still."

■ The Election of 1924

By 1924 the scandals of the Harding administration had surfaced, hurting the Republican party. This presented the Democratic party with a ready-made issue for the presidential campaign.

The Democrats Are Divided

The Democrats threw away their chances for victory at their national convention, however. The party was deeply divided over two issues: Prohibition—which the rural regions favored and the cities opposed—and more importantly, the Ku Klux Klan.

This secret society, which took its name and ritual from the Southern organization of Reconstruction times, was designed to intimidate African Americans, Catholics, Jews, immigrants, and "foreign ideas," such as the League of Nations. By the mid-1920s the Klan had become a force in American politics, despite its willingness to use terror and violence.

At the 1924 Democratic convention, the rivals for the nomination were William G. McAdoo of California and Governor Alfred E. Smith of New York. McAdoo favored Prohibition and received most of his support from the western and southern regions of the United States. Governor Smith was a Roman Catholic and opponent of Prohibition. His strongest backing came mostly from urban areas of the Northeast. Smith's supporters wanted an outright condemnation of the Ku Klux Klan, a move that Southern and Western delegates blocked.

The two candidates were deadlocked for so long that the cowboy-humorist Will Rogers suggested that the eventual nominee might be born at the convention. By the time a compromise candidate—John W. Davis of West Virginia—was nominated on the one-hundred-and-third ballot, the Democrats had lost all chance of winning the election.

The Republicans Win

The Republicans campaigned on the slogan "Keep Cool with Coolidge"; the way to keep business thriving, they said, was not to "rock the boat" but to keep in power the party that favored business. This strategy was successful. In an election that attracted only half the eligible voters to the polls, Coolidge won easily.

■ Business

During the 1920s many Americans went almost dizzy with prosperity. As business boomed and wages rose, former luxuries became necessities. A combination of increased leisure time for both men and women, new gadgets, new amusements, and more money to spend resulted in something approaching glorification of wealth and of the material comforts that went with it.

The Impact of the Automobile

The outstanding symbol of the new age was the automobile. In the early twentieth century, when the manufacture of automobiles in the United States was just beginning, driving cars was a sport for the wealthy. It was Henry Ford who almost single-handedly changed the automobile from a toy of the wealthy to a necessity for all. Ford's famous "Model T"—affectionately known as the "Tin Lizzie"—was so cheap that most families could afford it. Ford applied many of the familiar techniques of successful industrialists, such as the use of standardized parts and the formation of a vertical organization to combine different

AMERICAN PORTRAITS

Will Rogers
1879–1935

Part Native American, Will Rogers grew up in the West and became a cowboy while in his teens. He landed jobs with Wild West shows, where he would mix in a few jokes while doing his rope-twirling act. Aiming good-natured barbs at famous people, he became known as the "cowboy philosopher."

By 1920 Will Rogers was a star of both stage and screen. Starting in 1926, his daily newspaper column spread his humorous views of life and politics throughout the nation. Claiming "I don't make jokes—I just watch the government and report the facts," he always poked fun in a lighthearted way and was never hostile; one of his favorite sayings was "I never met a man I didn't like."

By the late 1920s audiences were listening to his commentary on radio. To Americans, Rogers had become a national treasure.

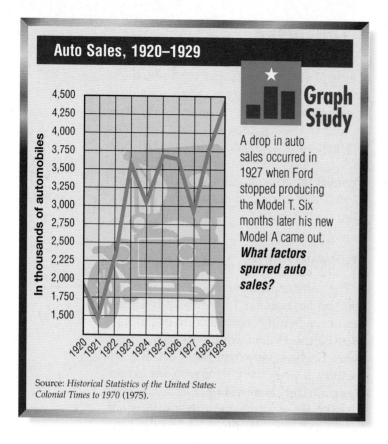

Auto Sales, 1920–1929

In thousands of automobiles

4,500
4,250
4,000
3,750
3,500
3,250
3,000
2,750
2,500
2,225
2,000
1,750
1,500

1920 1921 1922 1923 1924 1925 1926 1927 1928 1929

Graph Study

A drop in auto sales occurred in 1927 when Ford stopped producing the Model T. Six months later his new Model A came out. *What factors spurred auto sales?*

Source: *Historical Statistics of the United States: Colonial Times to 1970* (1975).

and the simplicity of the formula spawned imitators. By the mid-1920s other great trusts, notably General Motors and Chrysler, were competing successfully with Ford.

The impact of the automobile on life in the United States was revolutionary. Although small businesses generally continued to decline, new fields for small enterprises—garages, gas stations, diners, and tourist homes—appeared. Draft animals disappeared from farms as tractors took their places. The isolation of rural areas lessened, as cars put towns within easy reach of many farmers, and put the country within reach of city dwellers.

The Growth of Big Business

It seemed that Americans had discovered a magic formula for producing wealth and fulfilling human wants on a scale never before thought possible. Its ingredients were mass production, standardized products, and a nationwide market. This formula tended to favor big businesses over small because only big businesses could set up assembly lines, do the research necessary for constant development of new products, and afford nationwide advertising. It was natural then that the 1920s should see much concentration of industry. Mergers and holding companies helped to concentrate industry by reducing competition. The chain store soon became a familiar sight on Main Street, capturing one-fourth of the grocery business by 1929.

Whereas many Americans had formerly regarded big business as an enemy, they now relied on it both to supply cheap products and to create new opportunities for wealth. The stock market provided striking evidence of this when, for the first time in history, some members of the general public began to buy securities. The prices of shares of stock, especially those connected with new industries, mounted to dizzying heights. More and more purchasers "invested in the future."

With wealthier Americans speculating in the stock market, money to run business came from more and more diverse sources. Business, on the other hand, was becoming

operations. But Ford's greatest achievement was the assembly line, which divided operations into such simple tasks that most of the work could be done by unskilled labor. Furthermore, by bringing the parts to the workers, assembly lines sped up production so fast that Ford could boast that:

> " . . . [R]aw iron ore at the docks at 8:00 Monday morning could be marketed as a complete Ford car on Wednesday noon, allowing 15 hours for shipment. "

Ford's economies so reduced costs that an American automobile, which sold for an average price of $2,123 in 1907, could be bought for as little as $290 in 1924. While reducing costs, he staved off unionization by nearly doubling wages in 1914 to $5 a day. Other employers resented Ford because his pay scale was so high that it caused discontent among their own workers. It was Ford's belief that mass-production methods and low prices would produce an immense market for goods. This turned out to be correct, more and more concentrated. One device used by businesspeople to concentrate financial power was the "pyramiding" of holding companies, whereby it was possible—with a relatively small outlay of capital—for businesspeople to gain control of immense industrial properties.

■ The Plight of Agriculture

Farmers were the one great economic group that did not share in the Coolidge prosperity. The average income for farmers in 1929 was less than one-third of the average income for the rest of the country.

Falling Prices and Shrinking Markets

Technological advances led to greater production, which caused a slump in farm prices even while farmers' costs mounted. As one account puts it:

❝ *Freight rates, wages, taxes, farm implements, and the like, all of which went into the farmers'* *cost of production, remained high or came down via the stairway, while farm prices took the elevator.* ❞

Farm prices took disastrous slides in 1920 and 1921 and did not recover. Wheat went from almost $2.50 a bushel to less than $1.50. The foreign market dwindled because the United States had changed from a debtor to a creditor nation. Before World War I, foreign investments in the United States exceeded American investment abroad; the principal means of making up this unfavorable credit balance was for the United States to export agricultural staples, such as wheat and cotton. During the war the balance shifted the other way, principally because of United States loans to the Allies. With the return of peace, countries owing the United States money preferred not to buy its products. Great Britain, for example, often bought wheat from Argentina or Canada, especially after the Fordney-McCumber Tariff reduced the American market for British goods.

The **domestic market,** the market composed of buyers and sellers within the country, also diminished. New fabrics such as rayon lessened the demand for cotton; the

Visualizing History

▲ ON THE ASSEMBLY LINE Finishing touches are put on a Model A at a Ford plant in Dearborn, Michigan. *What effect did assembly-line production have on the price of automobiles?*

History AND ART

▲ *WHEAT* by Thomas Hart Benton, 1967 During his later career, Thomas Hart Benton chronicled America's past. *Why did the domestic market for agricultural products diminish during the 1920s?*

substitution of tractors and trucks for draft animals reduced the need for fodder. Faced with decreasing demands for the traditional staples, farmers might have been expected to shift to other products—but that was easier said than done. A Southern tenant farmer usually had no skill at anything but raising cotton. A Dakota wheat farmer usually lacked the capital and the knowledge to change, say, to dairy farming, which in any case was not well suited to that region. Moreover, many farmers had borrowed heavily during the war to buy new land at inflated prices. The only obvious way to pay off the debt was to raise more crops. But more crops meant unsalable surpluses; unsalable surpluses meant low prices. Low prices made the debt burden even heavier.

The Influence of the Farm Bloc

Early in Harding's administration, members of Congress from the Midwest and Plains states formed the Farm Bloc. It included about 25 senators and 100 representatives from both parties. Strong enough to hold a balance of power in Congress, the Farm Bloc forced through several laws favoring farmers. The Capper-Volstead Act of 1922 made farm cooperatives free of antitrust laws; the Intermediate Credits Act of 1923 set up federal banks to make loans to aid farm cooperatives.

None of the laws, however, dealt with the farmers' major problem: surpluses they could not sell. If wheat farmers were to benefit from the 42-cent-a-bushel protective tariff, which eliminated foreign competition, they somehow had to limit the amount of wheat put on that market.

The Farm Bloc supported the McNary-Haugen Bill. This bill proposed that the federal government buy crop surpluses and sell them abroad, while protecting the United States market with a high tariff. This would immediately raise the domestic price. Whatever losses the government suffered would be covered by an equalization fee—a tax

▲ FARM LANTERN, 1920s

charged against producers. Supporters of the bill claimed that it would help farmers as the tariff helped manufacturers.

Twice the bill passed Congress, but both times President Coolidge vetoed it. The idea would not work, he insisted, and furthermore, a "healthy economic condition is best maintained through a free play of competition." Thus, farmers failed to obtain protections similar to those many businesses received at the time.

■ Foreign Affairs

During the 1920s both Republican Presidents worked to promote world peace through individual agreements. During Coolidge's administration, France and the United States took the lead in promoting a treaty that attempted to "outlaw war." Called the Kellogg-Briand Pact after the American secretary of state and the French foreign minister who proposed it, the treaty was eventually ratified by 64 nations, each agreeing to abandon war "as an instrument of national policy" and to settle disputes by peaceful means.

A serious weakness of the pact was that it had no means of enforcement. No provisions were set down in the event there were acts of aggression among signer nations.

Although the United States generally participated in talks and treaties with European and Asian nations during this period, its manner toward Latin America remained protective. The Harding and Coolidge administrations—following the Roosevelt Corollary to the Monroe Doctrine—occasionally sent troops to "preserve order" in Caribbean countries. They became increasingly aware, however, that the Latin American people acutely resented such intervention. Although not willing to give up the right to intervene, Secretary of State Charles Evans Hughes believed troops should be sent to Latin America only to promote political stability, not to assist American investors. Accordingly, in the mid-1920s, United States Marines withdrew from the Dominican Republic and Nicaragua, where they had been sent in the previous decade to maintain order.

Read to Discover

Edna St. Vincent Millay captures the tireless energy of youth and the fun of being young and in love in New York City. Langston Hughes absorbed the poetry of everyday language and uses rhythms of the jazz age to reflect the pride of African Americans.

Reader's Dictionary

wan	weak; dim or faint
shawl	a fabric garment used to cover the head or shoulders
boogie-woogie	percussive style of playing blues music featuring inventive melodic variations

▲ EDNA ST. VINCENT MILLAY

After World War I, divergent movements in American literature grew up in New York's Harlem and Greenwich Village and in the nation's heartland. Two poets who typify these movements are Edna St. Vincent Millay and Langston Hughes.

▲ LANGSTON HUGHES

*R*ecuerdo

by Edna St. Vincent Millay

We were very tired, we were very merry—
We had gone back and forth all night on the ferry.
It was bare and bright, and smelled like a stable-
But we looked into a fire, we leaned across a table,
We lay on a hill-top underneath the moon;
And the whistles kept blowing, and the dawn
   came soon.
We were very tired, we were very merry—
We had gone back and forth all night on the ferry;
And you ate an apple, and I ate a pear,
From a dozen of each we had bought somewhere;
And the sky went wan, and the wind came cold,
And the sun rose dripping, a bucketful of gold.
We were very tired, we were very merry,
We had gone back and forth all night on the ferry.
We hailed, "Good morrow, mother!" to a
   shawl-covered head,
And bought a morning paper, which neither
   of us read;
And she wept, "God bless you!" for the
   apples and pears,
And we gave her all our money but our
   subway fares.

Dream Boogie
by Langston Hughes

Ain't you heard
The boogie-woogie rumble
Of a dream deferred?
Listen closely:
You'll hear their feet
Beating out and beating out a—
You think
It's a happy beat?
Listen to it closely:
Ain't you heard
something underneath
like a—
What did I say?
Sure,
I'm happy!
Take it away!
Hey, pop!
Re-bop!
Mop!
Y-e-a-h!

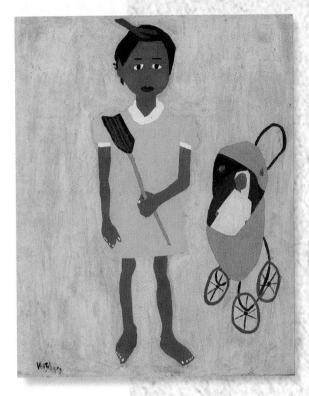

▲ *Li'l Sis* BY WILLIAM H. JOHNSON, 1944

▲ *Ferry Boat Trip* BY WILLIAM H. JOHNSON, 1934

Responding to Literature

1. What period of time is covered in "Recuerdo"?

2. How many speakers are there in "Dream Boogie"? What device is used to set them apart?

3. What differences and similarities in voice can you find between the authors of these selections?

4. What views of American life in the 1920s do Millay and Hughes embody?

ACTIVITY

5. Write a poem of at least 8 lines to describe a walk in the park.

★★

The "Roaring Twenties"

Guide to Reading

Main Idea

During the 1920s American society underwent significant changes.

Reading Strategy

Organizing Information As you read about the "Roaring Twenties," use a diagram like the one shown here to describe changes in the personal and economic status of women.

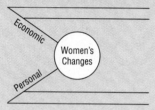

Objectives

After studying this section, you should be able to

★ describe changes in women's lives during the 1920s.

★ outline developments in the arts and education during this period.

Key Term

postwar disillusionment

▶ **COOLIDGE CAMPAIGN POSTER, 1924**

From a Long Island airfield on May 20, 1927, a small plane called the *Spirit of St. Louis* took off for France. Twenty-five-year-old Charles Lindbergh set off to make the first nonstop solo flight across the Atlantic. Thirty-three and one-half hours later, Lindbergh landed near Paris. Huge crowds greeted him. An American naval vessel brought him home, and even greater crowds welcomed him back to the United States. "Lucky Lindy," as he was called, became a hero of the age.

In an era when the ideals and heroes of history were questioned, when politics was riddled with graft, and when machines seemed to be replacing people, Lindbergh helped people restore some confidence in themselves. He proved that Americans were still capable of pioneering, even in the machine age. Quiet, courageous, and self-reliant, Lindbergh showed that not all the old values of life had disappeared, despite the changing priorities of modern society.

■ New Directions in Society

The rapid changes caused by the progress of technology in the 1920s brought with them some serious problems. Automobiles, though they offered an exciting new freedom of movement, also killed as many Americans in 1928 and 1929 as had lost their lives in battle during World War I. Cities lost some of their attractiveness as automobiles enabled people and businesses to move to the suburbs. The easily available "canned entertainment" provided by radio and motion pictures seemed to discourage Americans from creating their own amusements.

▲ **LINDBERGH'S HISTORIC FLIGHT** Because a huge fuel tank blocked his plane's windshield on his transatlantic flight, Lindbergh used a periscope to see. Lindbergh's heroics inspired other pilots like Amelia Earhart (right). *In what way was Lindbergh a symbol of the 1920s?*

Prohibition

Unfortunately, during the 1920s crime became big business. Gangsters such as Al Capone and Dutch Schultz consolidated the illegal liquor trade on many of the same principles used to consolidate the automobile and steel industries. The Prohibition Bureau, set up to enforce the law against the distilling and sale of liquor, was understaffed, underpaid, graft-ridden, and ineffective. Although liquor consumption dropped substantially during Prohibition, illegal drinking by millions created an illegitimate billion-dollar industry. The entrepreneurs in this illegal business became wealthy enough to buy beautiful homes in Florida and steel-plated limousines. Some gangsters became powerful enough to corrupt local governments.

Rural America, with its traditional values and churchgoing ways, tended to support Prohibition, but the cities generally opposed it. The customary diets of several urban ethnic groups included liquor, and many city dwellers resisted Prohibition as the work of religious crusaders.

Despite the success of the illegal liquor trade, Prohibition actually gained in popularity during the 1920s. In 1928 voters elected more supporters of Prohibition to

HISTORY Online

Student Web Activity
Visit the *American History: The Modern Era Since 1865* Web site at **me.glencoe.com** and click on *Chapter 16—Student Web Activities* for an activity about Al Capone.

▲ Movie poster, 1920s

Congress than ever before, as well as a "dry" President, Herbert Hoover. The popularity of Prohibition was a sign of continuing faith in the possibility of achieving a better life, of a longing for the ideals that had eroded in the horrors of World War I. Traditional standards of behavior were changing as Americans left the villages for the cities and the farms for the factories. Prohibition seemed a way to halt this change in values.

Women in the 1920s

The 1920s saw women express greater personal freedom. A dramatic new woman of the 1920s—the "flapper"—demanded the same freedom enjoyed by men. She sometimes smoked cigarettes and drank liquor and dressed in a way her mother and grandmother would not have believed possible. While most women in the 1920s

• •

Footnotes to History

Pastimes Recreation became the order of the day in the 1920s. Crossword puzzles, word games, and the Chinese game of Mah Johng became national obsessions. Thanks in great part to the efforts of sports journalists, athletes became larger-than-life heroes.

were not flappers, these new women demonstrated how modern behavior was changing.

American family life was also changing. Couples had fewer children because of increased knowledge about family planning, divorce rates increased, and more women than ever before sought employment outside the home.

Women in the Workplace

Having achieved the right to vote, women sought financial independence as well. Many young single women became salesclerks in department stores, secretaries, or telephone operators, for example. In 1920, 25 percent of female workers were in clerical and sales work. Eventually the employees in those particular jobs became almost exclusively female. Graduates of women's colleges began to seek jobs in business rather than in more traditional jobs such as teaching. But many women, especially married women who had to work to support families, were confined to jobs with long hours, poor conditions, and low wages. Women who worked outside the home suffered severe discrimination, often receiving only 50 to 60 percent of a man's wages for the same work. Further, women continued to meet with difficulty when trying to enter prestigious professions such as science and law.

Individual women made great contributions in many fields—often under difficult circumstances. Amelia Earhart learned to fly planes and became the first woman to complete a solo flight across the Atlantic. Singers Bessie Smith and Billie Holliday were innovative interpreters in jazz and blues. Dorothy Thompson became a famous journalist. Mary McLeod Bethune—an African American woman born into poverty—founded her own college, founded the National Council of Negro Women, and served as a government consultant.

Women in the Home

Most Americans—both men and women—continued to believe that a married woman's place was in the home. Thus, in

Commercial Radio

The 1920s ushered in a host of technologies still used today. Among the most significant breakthroughs was commercial radio.

Then

The 1920s

In one of the first commercial broadcasts, radio station KDKA in Pittsburgh broadcast news of President Harding's landslide victory in November 1920. Within the next two years, nearly 600 radio stations began operation. One million Americans tuned in daily to hear their favorite radio

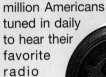

► RADIO, 1920s

programs. Dramas, adventures, and comedies, each with a cast of actors and a sound effects technician, were performed live in the radio studio as the broadcast aired. Radio, like so many technologies that emerged in the post-World War I period, served to shrink the world, bringing immediate contact and communication, and a common experience to people in all parts of the world.

Now

The Scope of Broadcasting

By 2000, nearly 11,000 radio stations operated in the United States, and Americans owned more than 500 million radios—on average, each household has about six. One survey indicates that four of every five American teenagers and adults listen to radio every day.

▲ RADIO AND CASSETTE PLAYER

Many of the radiocasts in the United States are designed for entertainment, chiefly recorded music. Most stations focus on one kind of music, such as rock, classical, or country and western. Other stations specialize in providing information such as newscasts, talk shows, and sporting events. Long a staple of radio, the talk show gained many listeners during the 1980s and 1990s. Talk shows provide a forum for discussion on a variety of topics and interviews with people from many professions.

---

spite of a spirit of independence, most women continued to be bound by the belief that their role was different from that of men, that they were to be mothers and homemakers. With new electric technology, the nature of being a homemaker changed. New household appliances, such as refrigerators and vacuum cleaners, commercial laundries, and canned food made hard, time-consuming domestic duties much easier. Many who stayed at home and became mothers, particularly in middle-class families, managed motherhood by listening to child-rearing experts who promoted regularly scheduled feedings for children and regimented routines for such children's extracurricular activities as music lessons and clubs.

■ Cultural Achievements

American culture thrived in the 1920s. Literature, architecture, music, painting, movies, radio—all flourished during this time.

American Literature

Some writers of the period, such as novelist Willa Cather and poet Robert Frost, tried to recapture the spirit and traditions of rural America; others, such as poet Carl Sandburg, examined what was happening in America's cities. In Eugene O'Neill, the United States produced its finest playwright. O'Neill found material in many aspects of American life—from the rage of a worker in

▲ WORKING FOR JUSTICE Activists like Mary McLeod Bethune fought to pass a federal law against lynching. *What attitudes might explain why lynching and other such incidents increased in the 1920s?*

the myths of many American heroes. Many American writers did the same. In his novels *Main Street* and *Babbitt,* Sinclair Lewis depicted the absurdities of life in small-town America. H. L. Mencken mocked the "vast . . . herd of good-natured animals" who made up most of the machine-age society. Mencken saw no hope for improvement. "If I am convinced of anything," he wrote, "it is that Doing Good is in bad taste."

The Arts

Achievements in American literature were matched in the arts. New city skyscrapers and suburban homes expanded the opportunities of architects like Frank Lloyd Wright, who achieved worldwide fame for his bold use of new materials and for architectural designs free of traditional influence. In jazz, which started with African American Dixieland bands in New Orleans, America produced a new form of music. At first seen as corrupting the morals of young people, jazz was soon accepted as an important art form. In the fine arts, the American scene was brilliantly portrayed by such painters as Reginald Marsh, Thomas Hart Benton, George

◄ SINGER AND ACTRESS ETHEL WATERS

the hold of a steamship in *The Hairy Ape,* to family tension in a decaying New England town in *Desire Under the Elms.* Ernest Hemingway, who had driven an ambulance on the Italian front during World War I, wrote about the meaningless violence of war in *A Farewell to Arms.* His fiction created a new literary style characterized by direct, simple, spare prose. The poet T. S. Eliot saw a world filled with "hollow men" and, in *The Wasteland,* one that would end "not with a bang but a whimper."

Postwar disillusionment, disappointment or dissatisfaction with the way things were after the war, was often manifested as criticism of American life. Henry Ford said that "history is bunk," and a school of "debunking" historians reexamined the past and reevaluated more accurately the facts behind

504   UNIT 5 Crusade and Disillusion: 1914–1932

Bellows, and Edward Hopper. In photography, Alfred Stieglitz achieved an international reputation.

Also during this period, the young motion-picture industry mushroomed. The first feature-length film appeared in 1915. By 1929 there were about 100 million paid admissions to movie theaters every week—proof that moviegoing had gained respectability. During the 1920s the motion-picture industry moved from New York to southern California. Mary Pickford, Charlie Chaplin, Douglas Fairbanks, Gloria Swanson, and Clara Bow were among the first stars of the silent screen. In 1927 Warner Brothers introduced "talking" pictures, which made the movies more popular than ever.

Visualizing History

▲ THE SCOPES TRIAL Opposing attorneys Clarence Darrow (left) and William Jennings Bryan pose during the Scopes trial. Scopes was later freed on appeal, but the trial proved too much for Bryan, who died a week after it ended. *What basic clash of values in 1920s society did the trial illustrate?*

Changes and Challenges in Education

A significant amount of the new wealth of the 1920s went into education, both through taxes for new public schools and through private donations to colleges and universities. The introduction of the school bus made possible the gradual replacement of bare, one-room country schoolhouses with large, well-equipped central schools. High school was no longer the privilege of the well-off but was also attended by the children of farmers and workers—although graduation from high school remained the exception rather than the rule. Both high school and college enrollment increased steadily.

A philosophy of education, long championed by John Dewey, emphasized learning through direct experience and experiment rather than through memorization. Greater emphasis was placed on science, which Dewey viewed as a way of using both thought and activity to investigate nature.

Some religious groups found these new educational theories threatening and were able to gain laws in some states to prevent the teaching of evolution in public schools. This set the stage for a battle between science and religion. It came in 1925, at the trial of John T. Scopes, a teacher in Dayton, Tennessee, who was willing to be arrested for teaching evolution to his high school class. The American Civil Liberties Union (ACLU) had raised money to test the new antievolution law in Tennessee and had asked Scopes if he would volunteer for the cause. The famous attorney Clarence Darrow defended Scopes, while William Jennings Bryan aided the prosecution for the antievolution forces. After a sensational trial, Scopes was convicted, but Bryan, who took the witness stand as an expert on the Bible, was made to look foolish through Darrow's penetrating questioning. The Scopes case symbolized the tensions of the 1920s, as some Americans tried to resist the tide of social change and to preserve older values and beliefs.

The Harlem Renaissance

World War I had been a liberating experience for many African Americans. This was especially true of those who went abroad.

For the first time they were freed from the second-class citizenship they suffered in the United States. But the prejudice and discrimination that awaited them at home helped to create a spirit of pride and protest, forging a new unity and a new African American:

" *. . . who had pride in heritage and self and who, through poetry, music, dance, and the theater, was able to create works of beauty out of travail and sufferings, as well as out of the more humorous facts of life.* "

A striking outcome of this new spirit among African Americans was the "Harlem Renaissance." In New York City, the intellectual capital of the United States, a number of highly talented African Americans rose to fame. Some were in the performing arts, including actors Charles Gilpin and Richard B. Harrison, singers Roland Hayes and Ethel Waters, dancer Bill Robinson, and singer-actor Paul Robeson. Others were scholars, including sociologist E. Franklin Frazier and economist Abram L. Harris. Still others were writers, such as poets Countee Cullen and Langston Hughes and novelists Jessie H. Fauset, Zora Neale Hurston, and Walter White. The use of the American experience as a theme for novels, poems, paintings, and sculpture was new in a society that until now had recognized few African American artists.

▲ WRITER COUNTEE CULLEN

More influential than the intellectuals and artists among African Americans themselves was a dynamic leader from Jamaica, Marcus Garvey. A spokesman for "Negro Nationalism," which exalted African American culture and traditions, Garvey formed the Universal Negro Improvement Association, which soon boasted a million members. Garvey told his followers they would never find justice in America and proposed to lead them to Africa. People were not interested, but Garvey stimulated the pride of African Americans in their history and heritage.

Section 3 ★ Assessment

Checking for Understanding

1. **Define** postwar disillusionment.
2. **Cite** the factors that resulted in increased crime in the 1920s.
3. **Discuss** significant contributions that the Harlem Renaissance made to the arts.

Critical Thinking

4. **Evaluating Achievements** How are the advances made by women in the 1920s significant to the lives of American women today?

5. **Summarizing** Re-create the diagram shown here, and describe the developments in arts and education during the 1920s.

Cultural Development in the 1920s	
The Arts	Education

INTERDISCIPLINARY ACTIVITY

6. **The Arts** Read a short story or poem by one of the Harlem Renaissance writers. Make a collage of photographs that express the work's main ideas.

BUILDING SKILLS
Critical Thinking Skills

Distinguishing Fact from Opinion

A fact is a statement or piece of information that can be verified by evidence. An opinion, on the other hand, presents a personal viewpoint that cannot be proved true or false.

Learning the Skill

Use these steps to help distinguish between fact and opinion.

- **Read** the statement carefully.
- **Ask:** What evidence supports this statement? What makes me confident that this statement is valid?
- **Look** for words and phrases that indicate opinion. Examples are *I think, I believe, probably, seems to me, may, might, could, ought, in my judgment,* or *in my view.*
- **Examine** the material for expressions of approval and disapproval such as *good, bad, poor,* and *unsatisfactory.* Be aware of such superlatives as *greatest, worst, finest,* and *best.*
- **Locate** and analyze such superlatives as *greatest, worst, finest,* and *best.*
- **Look** for words that have negative meanings such as *squander, contemptible,* and *disgrace.*
- **Note** the use of generalizations that include words like *none, every,* and *always.*
- **Look** for specific data that supports a statement of fact. If the statement can be proven, it is factual. For example, it is a fact that *George Washington served as the first President.*
- **Determine** whether information is fact or opinion.

If the statement refers to situations that are desirable or undesirable, important or unimportant, or likely or unlikely, then the statement is an opinion. For example, it is an opinion that *George Washington was the greatest President.* This assertion is based on someone's preferences or ideas.

▲ *THE CREATION* BY AARON DOUGLAS

Practicing the Skill

Decide whether each statement below is fact or opinion and explain what evidence would be needed to support it.

1. Aaron Douglas was the best-known visual artist, but equally accomplished work was produced by Laura Wheeler Waring.

2. The painting *The Creation* is the best work of American art of the 1900s.

 Glencoe's **Skillbuilder Interactive Workbook, Level 2** provides instruction and practice in key social studies skills.

APPLYING THE SKILL

3. Paste a photo or drawing of one of your favorite musical or visual artists on a poster. List at least three facts and three opinions about the artist.

507

Using Vocabulary

Imagine that you are the chairperson of a large industrial company in the 1920s. Write a letter to the President using the terms below.

welfare capitalism
technological unemployment

Reviewing Facts

1. Summarize foreign-policy actions of Harding and Coolidge.

2. List three ways that Harding and Coolidge helped stimulate business in America.

3. Cite evidence that the 1920s changed the arts and the lives of women and African Americans.

Understanding Concepts

Economic Change

1. Explain why urban dwellers of all economic levels would support the economic changes of the 1920s.

Social Change

2. Re-create the diagram shown here, and list examples of how women and minorities experienced both gains and setbacks with regard to civil rights and liberties during the 1920s.

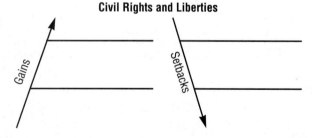

Civil Rights and Liberties

Gains

Setbacks

Critical Thinking

1. **Drawing Conclusions**   Explain how changes in business and manufacturing during the 1920s sparked a revolution in social customs, arts, and entertainment.

2. **Analyzing Fine Art**   Study the painting of singer and actor Paul Robeson on this page by artist Betsy Graves Reyneau, then answer the questions that follow.

   a. What does the painting tell you about the artist's view of Robeson?

   b. What title would you give this painting?

▲ PAUL ROBESON IN THE ROLE OF OTHELLO

History and Geography

Immigration

1. **Movement**   Why did levels of immigration fall after 1921?

2. **Human/Environment Interaction**   Why do you think homogeneous ethnic communities develop in many major cities?

Interdisciplinary Activity: Language Arts

Cooperative Learning

Work in groups of four to evaluate the changes that took place in the 1920s. One member of each group should assume one of the following roles: business owner, farmer, African American, flapper. The goal of your group is to write four paragraphs that discuss the changes from these four perspectives. Have each group member read his or her paragraph aloud.

Practicing Skills

Distinguishing Fact from Opinion

Read the following passages. Review the information on distinguishing fact from opinion on page 507. Then tell whether each sentence expresses factual information or an opinion.

Passage A

In 1917 Congress adopted and submitted to the States the Eighteenth Amendment, known as the Prohibition Amendment. It prohibited the "manufacture, sale, or transportation of intoxicating liquors."

Prohibition was more than a protest against "Demon Rum." It also was a defense of the old rural America against the threat of urbanization and social change. As such, it was a legal triumph for the conservatives in American society.

Passage B

The Republican party isn't a "poor man's party." Republican prosperity has erased that degrading phrase from our political vocabulary. Republican efficiency has filled the working-man's dinner pail—and his gas tank besides—made the telephone, radio, and sanitary plumbing standard household equipment. And placed a whole nation in the silk stocking class. Republican prosperity has reduced hours and increased earning capacity, silenced discontent, put the proverbial "chicken in every pot" and a car in every backyard to boot.

Passage C

Advertising aimed at the emotions rather than at the mind, selling a way of life centered on the happy home and the healthy family. Photographs were skillfully contrived to make people believe they were denying themselves unnecessarily if they did not share the joy others derived from owning, eating, or using a certain product. Advertising copywriters played on the desire for prestige. In the words of one author of the time: "When all is said and done, this much can be said in behalf of advertising, that it gives a certain illusion, a certain sense of escape in the machine age. It creates a dream world."

Still another factor was the motion picture, which did more than just entertain. It gave Americans who lived in small towns a glimpse of a glamorous lifestyle far different from the one they and their neighbors knew.

Technology Activity

Using a Word Processor The 1920s was a time of fads. Think of a fad today that you find interesting. Write a brief report describing the fad, why you think the fad developed, and why it might or might not last. Share your report with the class.

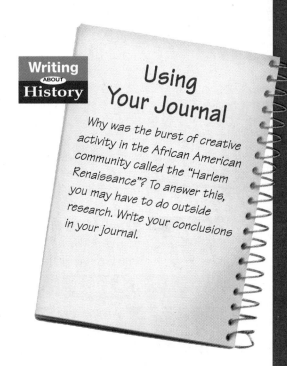

Writing ABOUT History

Using Your Journal

Why was the burst of creative activity in the African American community called the "Harlem Renaissance"? To answer this, you may have to do outside research. Write your conclusions in your journal.

CHAPTER 17

★★★

The Depression Begins
1928–1932

▶ APPLE VENDOR DURING THE DEPRESSION

Setting the Scene

Focus

Most Americans believed that the election of Herbert Hoover as President in 1928 would continue a decade of prosperity. This optimism quickly disappeared. A prolonged slump in agriculture, industrial overproduction, high tariffs, and the stock market crash all contributed to the worst economic depression in the nation's history. By 1932 millions of Americans were out of work. When Hoover's best efforts to revive the economy proved unsuccessful, the nation turned to a new President.

Journal Notes

As you read the chapter, record in your journal how the American people conflicted with the government during the Depression.

Concepts to Understand

★ Why **economic change** from prosperity to depression was triggered by the stock market crash

★ How **political policy** changed as a result of the Depression

Read to Discover . . .

★ how President Hoover tried to lift the country out of the Depression.

★ why Hoover's political leadership was not more successful.

HISTORY
Online

Chapter Overview
Visit the *American History: The Modern Era Since 1865* Web site at **me.glencoe.com** and click on ***Chapter 17—Chapter Overviews*** to preview chapter information.

CULTURAL	• First color motion pictures are demonstrated by George Eastman	• Ernest Hemingway publishes A Farewell to Arms	• Sinclair Lewis is the first American to win Nobel Prize for Literature
	1928	**1929**	**1930**
POLITICAL	• Hoover is elected	• Stock market crashes	• Hawley-Smoot Tariff is passed

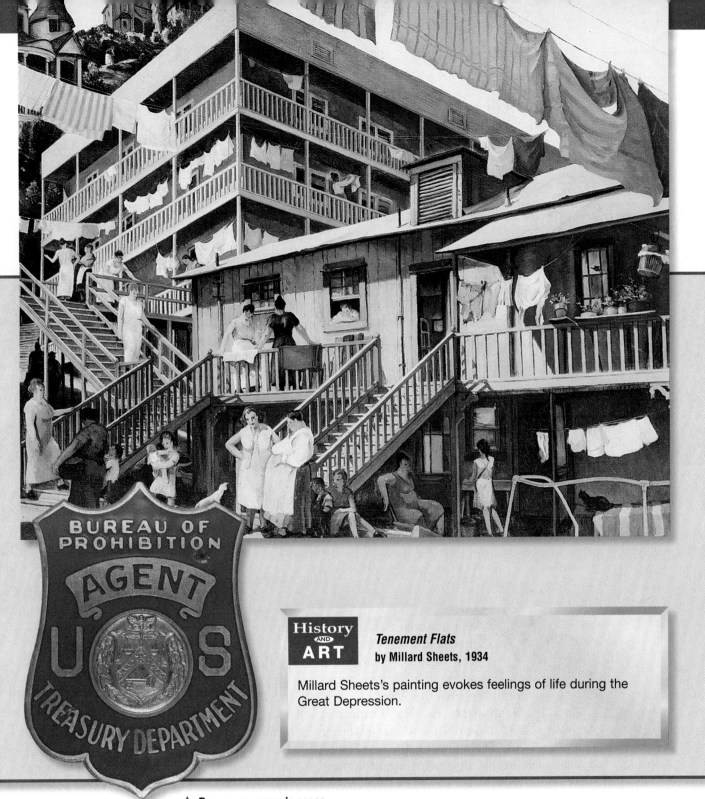

History AND ART

Tenement Flats
by Millard Sheets, 1934

Millard Sheets's painting evokes feelings of life during the Great Depression.

▲ PROHIBITION AGENT'S BADGE

- "The Star-Spangled Banner" becomes official U.S. national anthem

- Amelia Earhart is first woman to fly solo across the Atlantic

- San Francisco Ballet founded

1931	1932	1933

- Hoover vetoes Veteran Bonus

- RFC is established
- Bonus Army marches on Washington, D.C.

- Franklin D. Roosevelt becomes President

★★

The Stock Market Crashes

Guide to Reading

Main Idea
Shortly after Herbert Hoover became President, the stock market crashed, and the nation tumbled into economic chaos.

Reading Strategy

Organizing Information As you read about the beginning of the nation's economic crisis, use a diagram like the one shown here and list four causes of the Great Depression.

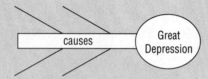

causes → Great Depression

Objectives

After studying this section, you should be able to

★ explain how Hoover's philosophy affected his economic policy.

★ explain the major causes of the Great Depression.

Key Terms

armory, securities, speculation, on margin, installment buying

▶ HOOVER CAMPAIGN BUTTON, 1928

---

*H*erbert Hoover easily won the Republican nomination in 1928. A successful geologist, he had spent eight years as secretary of commerce in the Harding and Coolidge administrations. The Democrats chose Alfred E. Smith, four-time governor of New York. Their race for the presidency was marked by the influence of a new invention—the radio.

■ The Election of 1928

The most visible issue in the election campaign was Prohibition. Both candidates vowed to continue enforcing Prohibition. The Prohibition issue, however, masked other important differences between the candidates. Hoover represented rural, agrarian

interests; Smith represented urban, industrial interests.

Religion was at the core of a smear campaign against Smith's Catholicism. Wild tales circulated alleging that Catholics had turned certain Washington church sites into **armories,** or storehouses for guns. Some believed that the White House under Smith would become a branch of the Vatican. Hoover was embarrassed by these accusations and tried to quash them.

Late in the campaign, Hoover made a speech to offer his ideas on the proper relationship of government to business. Government, Hoover claimed, should be "an umpire instead of a player in the economic game." Government had a part to play—conservation of natural resources, scientific research, and flood control were places where Hoover believed government could make useful contributions. To him, personal liberty depended on economic freedom. He reminded his listeners that:

> *Our experiment in human welfare has yielded a degree of well-being unparalleled in the world. . . . We are nearer to the ideal of abolition of poverty and fear from the lives of men and women than ever before in any land.*

Prosperity was the campaign issue that proved most damaging to the Democrats. The almost uninterrupted prosperity the country had enjoyed during the 1920s was associated in the minds of many voters with the Republican party. Republican campaign slogans such as "two cars in every garage" gave the Democrats no chance of winning the election.

Hoover won an impressive victory in the electoral college with a vote of 444 to 87, taking 58 percent of the popular vote and carrying all but 8 states. His appeal to rural Protestant voters even broke the Democrats' traditional hold on the Solid South, resulting in a Republican win in 5 Southern states. Although Smith lost the election, he won nearly twice as many votes as had the Democratic candidate in 1924. Of greater significance, Hoover became the first presidential winner to lose in the nation's 12 largest cities. A shift in the rural-urban balance of political power in America was in the wind.

■ Hoover in the White House

When he took office in March 1929, Herbert Hoover still radiated optimism. In his Inaugural Address, he predicted that the United States would soon be "in sight of the day when poverty will be banished from this nation."

▲ CRIME FIGHTER ELIOT NESS

▲ *PROHIBITION RAID* by Thomas Hart Benton, 1929 An unwanted result of Prohibition was the stimulus it gave to illegal activity. Thomas Hart Benton's *Prohibition Raid* is symbolic of the time. **What did the Wickersham Commission recommend?**

The Stock Market Crash of 1929

CAUSES

- Unrestricted availability of credit
- Greatly inflated sense of prosperity
- The government's "hands-off" policy toward business

• The Market Crashes

EFFECTS

- Massive unemployment
- Economic downturn
- Loss of confidence in financial institutions
- Questioning of government policy
- Trend toward social consciousness

Prohibition

Hoover did not believe that government should let economic events run their course but rather that it should help people to help themselves. He appointed commissions to investigate problems such as housing, retirement pensions, unemployment insurance, child welfare, and conservation. One commission, headed by former Attorney General George W. Wickersham, devoted 2 years to investigating Prohibition. The 11 members of the commission disagreed among themselves on whether Prohibition should continue. Most felt that the "noble experiment" was ineffective and promoted crime, yet the commission as a whole recommended that Prohibition be continued.

Farmers' Problems

The plight of farmers was an issue that demanded more immediate action. In April 1929, Hoover called Congress into special session to pass farming legislation. Members of Congress from farm states demanded that the federal government buy surplus farm products and sell them abroad. Hoover opposed this. Instead, the President proposed that the federal government help farmers use their own organizations to market produce more efficiently and adjust supply to demand.

Following this recommendation, Congress passed the Agricultural Marketing Act of 1929, which created a Federal Farm Board with $500 million at its disposal to help existing farm organizations and to

Visualizing History

▲ EFFECTS OF THE CRASH One day after the stock market crash, Walter Thornton advertised his car for sale. Panic hit the stock market as people frantically tried to sell. *What effect did speculation have on the stock market in 1929?*

form new ones. The Farm Board established national cooperatives—such as the National Livestock Marketing Association and the American Cotton Cooperative Association—and then loaned these organizations money to help keep prices stable. It was too little, too late. Farmers were soon worse off than ever.

$ ECONOMICS

The Crash of 1929

The market value of **securities,** or stocks and bonds, on the New York Stock Exchange more than tripled between 1925 and 1929—from $27 billion to $87 billion. In the summer of 1929, for example, a share of General Motors rose from $268 to $391 and by September 2 rose even higher—to $452 per share.

Speculation

As prices rose, more and more people began speculating. **Speculation** is engaging in a risky business venture on the chance that a quick or sizable profit can be made. People bought shares they thought would rise in price quickly, and after prices went up they would sell the stocks for a profit.

To maximize the potential profits on their investments, speculators commonly bought stock **on margin.** To buy stock in this way one made a small cash down payment and borrowed the rest from a stockbroker. For example, for $2,000 a person could buy 100 shares on margin rather than pay cash for 10 shares of stock at $200 per share. The purchaser simply put down 10 percent of the price (or $20 per share) and borrowed the other $18,000 from a broker, who would then hold the shares of stock as collateral for the loan. So long as prices continued to rise, investors could sell the stock later, repay the loan, and reap the profit.

Stock Market Begins to Decline

Some bankers, brokers, and economists were concerned, however, because they knew the stocks for many companies were greatly overpriced in comparison to the earnings and profits the companies were making. Yet most investors were swept

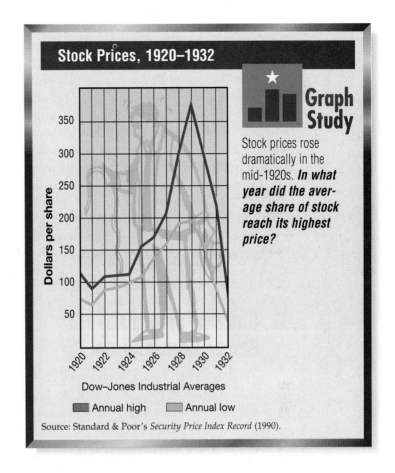

Stock Prices, 1920–1932

Graph Study

Stock prices rose dramatically in the mid-1920s. *In what year did the average share of stock reach its highest price?*

Dollars per share / Dow–Jones Industrial Averages

■ Annual high   ■ Annual low

Source: Standard & Poor's *Security Price Index Record* (1990).

along on the tide of the day's optimism. Meanwhile, the market continued its dizzying climb.

In September 1929, the market started to waver as some professional speculators sensed danger and began to pull out, and prices slipped. Late in October real disaster struck. On Thursday, October 24, almost 13 million shares of stocks were frantically traded. As stocks' values dropped below the amounts borrowed to purchase them, brokers demanded that investors repay their loans. If they could not, the brokers offered the stock for sale.

Black Tuesday

Recognizing what was going on, investment bankers tried to shore up market prices by purchasing as many shares as they could. The effort was not enough to stabilize an overvalued market. On October 29—Black Tuesday—the bottom fell out. Some 16 million shares were sold, causing such a collapse that by mid-November the average price of securities had been cut nearly in half. This cost investors about $30 billion, a sum that represented almost one-third of the value of all goods and services produced in the United States in 1929. The loss was equal to the total wages of all Americans that year.

It was the failure of banks that hit the hardest. Banks loaned money to brokerage houses, which in turn bought stock themselves or loaned money to investors for stock purchases. When loan payments were not forthcoming, many banks went bankrupt. In the aftermath, millions of people who had never bought stock but had trustingly kept their money in savings accounts lost everything as the banks closed. $

■ Causes of the Great Depression

The collapse of the stock market was only a prelude to a catastrophic economic decline from which the United States did not recover for 12 years. The causes of the Great Depression were so complex that economists have debated the issue ever since.

Overproduction and Underconsumption

One cause of the Depression was overproduction. Laborsaving machinery had increased the production capacity of the nation's industries so much that far more goods were produced than the American population could consume. For a time, consumer purchasing power was bolstered by **installment buying**—an agreement whereby a purchaser made a down payment and paid the rest of the cost in periodic regular installments to which an interest charge was added. By the late 1920s, most consumers who could afford high-cost items such as refrigerators, cars, or stoves had bought them on an installment plan. Consumer spending began to decrease. From January to September 1929, for example, the number of automobile purchases dropped by one-third.

Another cause of the Depression was underconsumption. In the 1920s the rich got richer much faster than the rest of the people. Some 30,000 families at the top of the eco-

nomic pyramid had as much income as did the 11 million families at the bottom. Though production increased, employment stood still and workers' wages went up very slowly. In 1929 more than two-thirds of the nation's families were earning less than $2,500 per year, a sum said to be the minimum income for a decent quality of life. About one-fifth of the nation lived in dire poverty. Thus there was insufficient purchasing power to support the nation's mass-production industries.

Agricultural Slump and Surpluses

A prolonged slump in agriculture, which affected the economic life of the entire country, was another factor. Farmers were heavily indebted to banks, which held mortgages on farmlands throughout the nation. The declining value of farms made it harder for farmers to get credit. Banks that had invested heavily in farm mortgages were in danger of failing.

In addition, huge farm surpluses produced a drop in farm prices so great that farmers often spent more money growing and marketing their products than they received in selling them. The resulting loss in farmers' purchasing power further reduced the consumption of manufactured goods—a condition that only added to the problem of underconsumption.

Tariffs and Taxes

The Great Depression was not solely a result of economic practices. Many of the economic policies of the Harding and Coolidge administrations during the 1920s set the stage for problems by the end of the decade. Policies such as the high Fordney-McCumber Tariff, combined with an insistence on collecting war debts, interfered with world trade and destroyed foreign markets for American products, especially in agriculture. The Mellon tax policies, which aided the upper class, contributed to the uneven distribution of wealth. Failure to curb or discourage the stock market's early boom made the ultimate crash more severe.

Once started, the Great Depression took on a momentum of its own. Individuals with mortgages on their homes, who had bought cars and other goods on credit and who had purchased stocks on margin, "lost their shirts." They stopped buying, for example, luxuries like radios, causing radio manufacturers to close down plants or run them only part-time. Thousands of workers were laid off as orders were canceled for copper, wood cabinets, and glass radio tubes. Montana copper miners, Minnesota lumberjacks, and Ohio glassworkers in turn lost their jobs.

Because these jobless workers could not meet mortgage payments or repay loans, they lost their property. Banks that had lent them money failed, wiping out the savings of their depositors. Such chain reactions closed down more and more factories, drove more and more firms into bankruptcy, and put more and more Americans out of work.

Russell Hunter, a brass worker in the Naugatuck Valley region of Connecticut, known as the "Brass Valley," describes what the early years of the Depression were like:

❝ *During Hoover's time, we went on short time. After a while, when things really were bad, in 1932, we were working sometimes five hours a week, one day a week. That was tough, trying to raise a family. Nobody lost their jobs completely. They shared [the work] to give everybody something to do. Still, you* *had to go on welfare. People got by going on the welfare. At that time, people were losing their homes, automobiles. . . .* ❞

The mood of the country was changing. Feelings of optimism were giving way to feelings of fear.

GNP, Stock Values, and Unemployment

Year	Gross National Product (in billions)	Stock Values, New York Stock Exchange (in billions)	Unemployment (Percent)
1920	$140.0	$5.5	5.2
1921	127.8	4.7	11.7
1922	148.0	5.7	6.7
1923	165.9	5.9	2.4
1924	165.5	5.9	5.0
1925	179.4	7.6	3.2
1926	190.0	8.6	1.8
1927	189.8·	10.5	3.3
1928	190.9	13.7	4.2
1929	203.6	17.9	3.2
1930	183.5	14.4	8.7
1931	169.3	7.5	15.9
1932	144.2	3.8	23.6

Chart Study Study each column heading, noting the years that show the greatest change. *What was the worst year of the Great Depression for both business and labor?*

Section 1 ★ Assessment

Checking for Understanding

1. **Define** armory, securities, speculation, on margin, installment buying.

2. **State** two reasons Hoover won the presidential election in 1928.

3. **Explain** how speculation caused the stock market to rise.

Critical Thinking

4. **Synthesizing Ideas** Who was to blame for stock market speculation? Explain.

5. **Analyzing Issues** Re-create the chart shown here, and describe Hoover's views on how the government should manage the economy. Provide an example of each.

Hoover's Economic Philosophy	Example

INTERDISCIPLINARY ACTIVITY

6. **Economics** For one week, keep track of references in the media to unemployment, consumer spending, manufacturing trends, recession, and prices. After each entry, indicate whether the information was, in your view, positive or negative.

The Stock Market

"Sooner or later," said economist Roger Babson on September 5, 1929, "a crash is coming . . . factories will be shut down . . . men will be thrown out of work . . . the result will be a serious business depression." However, most analysts assured Americans that the stock market was healthy and thriving.

A stock exchange is an organized system for buying and selling shares, or blocks of investments, in corporations. In the late 1920s, the value of stocks on the New York Stock Exchange climbed to dizzying heights. To take advantage of the boom, investors borrowed money to buy stocks, a practice known as buying on margin.

In other words, speculators were using their own money to make a relatively small down payment on the stock and borrowing the remainder of the purchase price from a stockbroker. The broker in turn borrowed the money lent to the speculator from a bank. The brokers' loans were call loans—loans that could be called in at any time by the borrower or lender.

The 1920s seemed to be a period of never-ending prosperity. The values of common stock had been increasing steadily year after year. In 1926 more than 450 million shares of stock were traded on the New York Stock Exchange. In 1927 the total rose to more than 570 million. Speculators believed they could make a quick profit in the market. Bankers knew they could make money by lending to brokers. Brokers knew they could come out ahead by lending to customers. Everyone, it seemed, was trying to get rich quickly.

The boom could last only as long as investors added money to the pool. By 1929 everyone with money to invest had bought into the market, and it ran out of new customers. Prices stopped rising. People sold shares to pay the interest on their loans. As shares were sold, prices fell. Panicked investors tried to minimize their losses.

On October 29, less than two months after Babson's prediction, the market crashed. The crash was a symptom, not a cause, of the Great Depression.

▼ WALL STREET

Making the Economics Connection

1. What series of events occur when the stock market crashes?

2. Why did people begin selling shares of stock in the fall of 1929?

ACTIVITY

3. Research information on stock market figures during the months of September and October 1929. Compare these figures with those from a two-week period today. Are any of the companies the same? How much do their shares cost today?

★★★★★★★★★★★★★★★★★★★★★★★★★★★★★★★

Hoover's Policies

Guide to Reading

Main Idea
The Hoover administration struggled to solve the nation's vast economic problems.

Reading Strategy

Organizing Information As you read about Hoover's policies for ending the Depression, use a diagram such as the one shown here to highlight Hoover's indirect approach to help the economy.

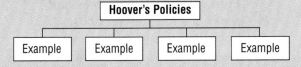

Hoover's Policies

| Example | Example | Example | Example |

Objectives

After studying this section, you should be able to

★ list the ways in which Hoover tried to end the Depression.

★ describe the change in policy toward Latin America under Hoover.

★ describe the Hoover-Stimson Doctrine and evaluate its effectiveness.

Key Term

moratorium

▶ UNION LABEL SYMBOL

---

*N*o sooner had the stock market collapsed than President Hoover asked leaders of industry, finance, and labor to come to the White House. The President asked labor leaders to abandon or postpone wage demands, industry leaders to keep employment high, and bankers to continue lending.

Hoover and other leaders tried to restore public confidence by issuing optimistic statements. Their rosy predictions were contradicted by worsening conditions, however, and the phrase "prosperity is just around the corner" became a joke. The Republican campaign slogan "Two cars in every garage" had become "Two families in every garage." The President's position was made all the more difficult because he was blamed for the Depression.

■ Domestic Economic Concerns Loom

In dealing with Congress and the public, Hoover was limited by his inflexible views. A man of great ability and possessing a sincere desire to serve the nation, he lacked the practical political experience that comes from being a legislator or state executive. Even with such skills, his position would have been difficult. Republican party leaders never gave him their whole-hearted support, and members of the Farm Bloc were in open revolt. As a result of the midterm elections of 1930, the Democrats made gains in the Senate and won control of the House of Representatives. This shift in power led to a Congress that was hostile to Hoover's policies during the last two years of his administration.

Tariffs

Like President Taft in 1909, Hoover was unable to control Congress on the tariff issue. The Hawley-Smoot Tariff started in the House as a protection for farmers, but by the time it passed the Senate, it had turned into the highest protective tariff in peacetime history. It raised the average duty on raw agricultural materials and other items above the Fordney-McCumber Act levels.

By the time the Hawley-Smoot bill reached the President's desk in 1930, more than 1,000 leading economists had signed a letter urging him to veto it. They argued that it would help inefficient producers, raise consumer prices, reduce foreign markets, and cause ill will toward the United States in other countries. This opinion was voiced by many newspapers, bankers, and even by a number of manufacturers. Now Hoover faced a dilemma. If he used his veto power, he would isolate himself politically by breaking with the Republican values he held so strongly. Furthermore, he would abandon the one feature of the bill he had fought so hard for—a revised Tariff Commission with the authority to raise and lower rates. He therefore signed the bill in spite of the warnings.

Within a year, 25 nations retaliated with laws to restrict purchases of American goods, causing foreign trade with the United States to drop rapidly. Some American corporations managed to avoid international barriers by establishing factories overseas. Ironically, an act designed to promote American economic recovery instead created employment overseas.

Farmers

American farmers, beleaguered throughout the 1920s, were hit even harder. Farmers' income was cut by more than half between 1929 and 1932; their burden of debt became unbearable. During this crisis the Farm Board tried to maintain the price of wheat and cotton by buying up the surplus of these crops. The Farm Board also attempted—without success—to persuade farmers to plant less, in order to reduce the amount of farm produce grown and thus to prevent further surplus crops. The immense quantities of wheat and cotton held by the government actually drove prices down, however, because buyers feared that the government would sell these surpluses as soon as prices rose. Finally, in 1931 the Farm Board acknowledged defeat and stopped its purchases. Immediately prices dropped even lower. By 1932 farmers were receiving only 38 cents a bushel for wheat that in 1929 had sold at $1.04. Even Hoover's relatives in Iowa suffered from the depressed farm economy. Harry Terrell, a farmer who lived in the same neighborhood as President Hoover in Iowa, described conditions in the following way:

> *I was born across the road from the farm of Herbert Hoover's uncle. I knew the Hoover family, distant cousins of the President. Even people like them, they had times just like the rest of us. . . . Corn was going for eight cents a bushel. One county insisted on burning corn to heat the courthouse, 'cause it was cheaper than coal."*

■ Hoover's Strong Resolve

Hoover was deeply affected by all the misery and poverty around him, but as a staunch believer in private enterprise, he feared direct government handouts would destroy personal initiative. Hoover therefore offered government help to banks and businesses in the hope that restored financial health at the top of the economic pyramid would eventually trickle down to relieve unemployment at the bottom. Keeping his attitude positive and his resolve strong, Hoover sought to inspire confidence in a people ravaged by hopelessness and despair: "Ninety percent of our difficulty in depression is caused by fear."

▲ *DROUGHT-STRICKEN AREA* by Alexander Hogue, 1934 The collapse of farm prices was compounded by a terrible drought in 1930. **How did President Hoover feel about providing direct relief to the unemployed?**

In 1932, after Hoover's initial resistance, Congress established the Reconstruction Finance Corporation (RFC). With $2 billion in resources, the RFC made loans to hard-pressed railroads, insurance companies, banks, and even state and local governments—but not to individuals. The RFC favored projects that were "self-liquidating"; that is, projects designed to pay their way so the government would eventually get back its money. Thus projects such as toll bridges and dams that would produce electric power were favored over those that could have been socially useful but brought in no revenue, such as playgrounds, schools, and city halls.

There was a point beyond which Hoover refused to use the power of the federal government. He feared that too much reliance on federal action would result in the "paternalism" and "state socialism" he had warned against in 1928. He opposed direct federal relief for the unemployed because he believed it would weaken the self-respect of those who received it, undercut the efforts of private charity, and that it would destroy the tradition of local responsibility for the unfortunate. Hoover, therefore, vetoed the Garner-Wagner bill in 1932, which would have given direct aid to the unemployed. He also

vetoed the Norris bill, which would have put the government in the business of producing and selling electricity in the Tennessee Valley—thus setting up direct competition with private companies.

■ Efforts for Peace

The desire for world peace was strong during these hard times, partly because preparation for war was costly, and partly because few had forgotten the horrors of World War I.

As a Quaker and a pacifist, Herbert Hoover believed that war was morally wrong; as administrator of Belgian relief between 1914 and 1917, he saw firsthand the devastation of World War I. Hoover was committed to world peace. As he stated in 1928:

❝ *I think I may say that I have witnessed as much of the horror and suffering of war as any other American. From it I have derived a deep passion for peace. Our foreign policy has one primary objective, and that is peace.* ❞

Hoover's peace efforts were aided by his many years spent overseas. The most widely traveled man ever to occupy the White House, he had visited every continent and knew many foreign leaders personally.

Latin America

As secretary of commerce, Hoover had come to understand Latin America's distrust of the United States. Before his inauguration in March 1929, he made goodwill tours of 10 Latin American countries. Hoover stressed that the United States wished to be a friend to its neighbors in Latin America. Many expressed doubts about how effective Hoover's efforts would be. Hoover's Latin American policies reflected a sincere desire to improve relations. In addition to successfully arbitrating a long-standing boundary dispute between Chile and Peru, Hoover abandoned military intervention in Latin American countries.

The Clark Memorandum, written by Undersecretary of State J. Reuben Clark, argued the position that the Roosevelt Corollary to the Monroe Doctrine had no historical basis. Clark wrote, "The Monroe Doctrine states a case of the United States v. Europe, not of the United States v. Latin America." In other words, the Monroe Doctrine could no longer be used to justify American intervention in Latin America.

In accordance with this principle, Hoover withdrew troops from Nicaragua and refused to intervene in the affairs of Latin American states that, because of political chaos, had repudiated their debts to the United States. While this nonintervention policy helped to convince many Latin Americans that the United States had no aggressive intentions, it won Hoover little goodwill. The Hawley-Smoot Tariff had hurt Latin America's economy, and the region's resentment of the power of the United States did not disappear.

Visualizing History

▲ SOUP KITCHEN People line up at a 1930s Chicago soup kitchen, operated by gangster Al Capone. Government made few efforts to help citizens fight the effects of the Depression. *What was the Garner-Wagner bill intended to provide?*

Disarmament

Hoover strongly favored disarmament, not only because of his personal beliefs but also because military spending and increased taxes depleted valuable resources. Shortly after taking office, Hoover made arrangements for a new conference in London on naval disarmament. Its goal would be to extend the limits on battleships that had been set in the Five-Power Treaty signed in 1921–1922.

After four months of talks, the London Naval Conference of 1930 produced a treaty fixing ratios for the submarines, cruisers, and destroyers of the United States, British, and Japanese navies. Italy refused to sign. France, fearing aggression by Germany and Italy, said that it favored disarmament only if other powers would agree to give France assurance of protection. In the end, France chose not to sign.

Ever since 1927 a disarmament conference hosted by the League of Nations had been meeting at Geneva. Its work was hampered by the activities of lobbyists for arms manufacturers and by mutual mistrust among the delegates. For five years it had gotten nowhere, focusing on such trivial issues as the influence of fog on war. In 1932 President Hoover proposed to the Geneva Conference that the nations of the world either entirely abandon aggressive weapons or cut existing arms by one-third. No action resulted. With Adolf Hitler's rise to power in Germany, however, and Japanese invasions into China, disarmament now seemed like an invitation to aggression. Hoover's proposal could have succeeded only if the United States had been willing to join an alliance of nations committed to "collective security," whereby members would all agree to come to the aid of any member nation who was threatened with aggression.

War Reparations

By 1931 Germany was in the throes of a serious depression. Germans could not continue paying war reparations to the Allies without defaulting on their debts to American private investors. Hoover, like Harding and Coolidge before him, believed that

Visualizing History

▲ WAR DEBTS This cartoon suggests that Germany, despite its ability to pay, was making little effort to make payments owed to the United States and its allies. ***What political movements did Germany's economic woes help bring about?***

reparations were "a European problem." But heavy war debts and rising unemployment caused great discontent among the German people and led directly to the rapid growth of two antidemocratic parties—the Communist party and the Nazi party.

Moratorium

The Allies were unlikely to cancel German reparation payments, which they used to pay off their own war debts to the United States. To address the problem, in 1931 Hoover proposed an international **moratorium,** or suspension, for one year of all war-debt payments to the United States. Hoover's aim was to protect United States investments in Germany and to save the German Republic from collapse, as well as to stimulate international trade. Secretary of State Henry L. Stimson urged that war debts and reparations be canceled completely, but Hoover refused. To do so would have been a highly unpopular measure and would have worsened Hoover's already poor relations with Congress.

The Hoover-Stimson Doctrine

The Hoover administration encountered problems in the Far East. In September 1931, Japan took advantage of the civil war in China and invaded Manchuria. This action was in direct violation of the Nine-Power Treaty of 1922, which guaranteed China's sovereignty, and the Kellogg-Briand Pact, which outlawed wars of aggression. It also breached the Charter of the League of Nations, to which both China and Japan belonged.

The Intent of the Doctrine

China appealed to the League of Nations, which turned to the United States for help. President Hoover, however, refused to consider either economic or military action. Instead, he sent an army officer to serve on a League commission to investigate Japanese actions in Manchuria. Secretary Stimson proclaimed in 1932 that the United States would refuse to recognize the legality of any territorial arrangement that violated the Kellogg-Briand Pact. The Hoover-Stimson Doctrine, designed to enlist world opinion against aggressor nations, did nothing to aid China and served only to irritate the Japanese.

Although the nonrecognition policy had been worked out by Hoover and Stimson together, it meant different things to each of them. Stimson wanted the policy to act as a warning, which later might be backed up by economic or military aid. According to

Hoover, the statement itself was enough. The United States, he said, did not exist to police the world. Economic sanctions might lead to war, he said, and Japanese aggression in Asia did not "imperil the freedom of the American people." Hoover then said that should the United States be obliged to

> " . . . arm and train Chinese, [we would] find ourselves involved in China in a fashion that would excite the suspicions of the whole world. "

Nor were the British and French governments willing to apply sanctions. The failure of Western nations to take action only encouraged Japanese expansion into China and Southeast Asia.

Public Opinion

The American public was not prepared to support any interventionist effort that could potentially involve the United States in war once again. This feeling was evident in 1931 when Congress overwhelmingly overrode Hoover's veto and voted to give independence to the Philippines within 10 years. This measure pleased Filipino leaders; it also pleased the United States business community, who wanted to keep Filipino products out of America. However, a major reason for passage of the bill was that the American people no longer wanted to defend the islands, upholding the American anti-imperialist past.

Section 2 ★ Assessment

Checking for Understanding

1. **Define** moratorium.
2. **Describe** the Hoover-Stimson Doctrine and its overall effectiveness.

Critical Thinking

3. **Predicting Consequences**   What message did the United States and its allies send by not taking action against Japan?
4. **Summarizing**   Re-create the diagram shown

here, and list the reasons why Hoover disapproved of relief programs and help for business.

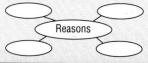

Reasons

INTERDISCIPLINARY ACTIVITY

5. **The Arts** Create newspaper headlines to announce the major events covered in this section related to Latin America.

Writing a Persuasive Argument

A persuasive argument is one in which the audience is urged to do something or believe in the same thing as does the writer.

Learning the Skill

The following guidelines will help you organize and write a persuasive argument:

a. Research the topic. What are the facts, and how do people feel about it?

b. Tailor your argument to your audience. Exactly who are you trying to persuade? Many people will share your point of view if they see some benefits for themselves.

c. Support your argument with solid facts and examples.

d. Save the most persuasive arguments for last, then end your paper by summarizing.

Imagine that the following is a paper that you wrote as Herbert Hoover defending his war-debt moratorium.

I am writing to you, the people of France, as you continue to heal the wounds inflicted by the Great War. My heart and thoughts are with you. Look around you. In what condition is Europe? There is depression, unemployment, and debt. Germany, for all its past offenses, is teetering on the brink of collapse. Europe, like America, is fighting the effects of this demoralizing depression. International trade is at dangerously low levels, and the spectre of debt hangs over all of us like a shadow. The time has come to close the gap between how we feel about that Great War, and what we know to be the just and proper way to revive our ailing economies. Let us consider our children's future, and not so much our temporary feelings of outrage for a war that is over. Abide with me in my decision to place a one-year, international moratorium on all war debts. It is time to let go of the past and resurrect the quality of life that has been obscured by this spectre of debt.

▲ PRESIDENT HERBERT HOOVER

Practicing the Skill

1. To whom did President Hoover address his views?

2. What do you think is his most persuasive argument? Explain.

3. How did Hoover summarize his argument?

 Glencoe's **Skillbuilder Interactive Workbook, Level 2** provides instruction and practice in key social studies skills.

APPLYING THE SKILL

4. Use the guidelines above to write a persuasive argument for or against the Hawley-Smoot Tariff.

★★

The Depression Worsens

Guide to Reading

Main Idea

As Franklin Roosevelt entered the White House, thousands of businesses and banks shut down and millions of families struggled to get by.

Reading Strategy

Organizing Information As you read about the worsening Depression, use a diagram such as the one shown here to describe how Americans felt as the economic crisis worsened.

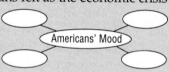

Objectives

After studying this section, you should be able to

★ compare the condition of workers and farmers in the early 1930s.

★ discuss the mood of the country as the election of 1932 approached.

Key Term

lame duck

▶ **DEPRESSION SCRIP, EMERGENCY MONEY**

The Depression was uneven in its impact. While many people lost their jobs, the majority of Americans did not. Instead, many found their hours reduced. The few who kept their jobs and did not have their hours or wages cut actually were better off because prices declined. Even so, for most Americans the mood was gloomy—and for good reason. In 1932 over 30,000 companies closed. In just 2 months in 1931 over 800 banks failed, wiping out the life savings of thousands of depositors.

All over the United States, families not able to pay their rent or mortgages were evicted from their homes. Some ended up in communities of makeshift shacks on the outskirts of cities.

■ Want in the Land of Plenty

As the Depression deepened, fear and despair replaced the buoyant optimism of the 1920s. "I'm afraid, every man is afraid," steel industrialist Charles M. Schwab admitted. "I don't know, we don't know, whether the values we have are going to be real next month or not."

Fear

Loss of confidence affected all sorts of people. Some who lost their jobs suffered such emotional effects that they became unemployable. "My father spent two years painting his father's house," one man later remembered. "He painted it twice. It gave him something to do."

Business leaders hesitated to build new factories or to bring out new products. Frightened bankers became unwilling to lend money, even to borrowers with good character and ample collateral. On the stock market, security prices dropped dramatically. Stock in Radio Corporation of America (RCA) dropped from $101 per share in 1929 to $2.50 in 1932.

Starvation

One of the great ironies of the Depression was that starvation existed in the midst of plenty. The productive capacity of farmers did not slacken. On the contrary, farmers' problems resulted, in part, from their ability to grow more food than they were able to sell. Already in a depression throughout most of the 1920s, the collapse of the farm economy after 1929 wreaked havoc on rural America. Despite Hoover's programs, grain prices dropped so low that farmers heated their homes by shoveling their crops into their furnaces. They protested low agricultural prices by declaring "farmers' holidays" and tried to prevent food shipments to cities. In Iowa farmers blockaded highways and dumped milk trucks in an attempt to make milk scarce and raise its price. In Oregon they slaughtered sheep because mutton prices were lower than what it cost to ship the animals to market. Meanwhile, in America's cities people picked through garbage looking for scraps of meat.

Virginia Durr, an Alabama activist for tenant farmers' rights, described the suffering when she said, "Have you ever seen a child with rickets shaking, as with palsy? No proteins, no milk. And the companies pouring milk into the gutters. . . . People with nothing to eat and they killed the pigs."

▶ APPLE SELLER, NEW YORK CITY, 1932

Visualizing History

▲ "HOOVERVILLES" Many families lost their homes during the Great Depression because they were unable to meet mortgage payments or pay rent. Some of the homeless found living quarters in shacks constructed of tin and old crates. Villages of these makeshift shacks, such as this one in Seattle, Washington, sprouted up throughout the nation. *How did the rate of unemployment change between 1930 and 1933?*

The Game of Monopoly

Board games are a favorite American pastime, and one of the more popular is Monopoly. The game, in which each player's goal is to make money while forcing the opponents into bankruptcy, originated and flourished, oddly enough, during the height of the Great Depression.

Then

Atlantic City Vacations

Charles Darrow was a tinkerer, continually designing puzzles,

games, and toys. The unemployed Philadelphia engineer hoped that if one of his creations proved popular, his family could once more afford their cherished excursions to Atlantic City. One thought prompted another, and one night in 1931 Darrow sat down at his kitchen table to design a game. He sketched in the name of Atlantic City streets on a board. He carved little wooden houses, hotels, and tokens. He printed direction cards and title deeds, and added dice and play money. Soon Darrow was taking orders from Philadelphia department stores. The popularity of the game spread when the Parker Brothers Game Company began distributing Monopoly nationwide. Within a short time, the company was producing nearly

20,000 sets a week—and Darrow could afford as many Atlantic City vacations as he wanted.

Now

Worldwide Popularity

Monopoly has become popular in many other parts of the world. Published in more than 25 nations in 19 languages, Monopoly is challenged only by Scrabble as the best-selling trademarked game in the world. Sets merchandised in other nations are adapted to represent native locales. The British version of the game, for example, uses the names of London streets.

★★★

Chance — TAKE A WALK ON THE BOARD WALK **ADVANCE TOKEN TO BOARD WALK**
© 1936 PARKER BROTHERS

■ The Human Cost of the Depression

Although business leaders promised Hoover that they would not cut wages of remaining workers, as the Depression deepened, their situation changed.

Wage Cuts and Unemployment

In October 1931, United States Steel Corporation cut salaries and wages by 10 percent, and employers in other industries soon followed. By 1933 salaries had decreased 40 percent and hourly wages by 60 percent. The

average family's income fell from $2,300 in 1929 to $1,600 in 1932. More layoffs followed the wage cuts. In 1930, 4 million workers were unemployed; by 1933 the number of jobless Americans more than tripled.

In cities throughout the country breadlines and soup kitchens appeared on sidewalks as local governments and private charities struggled to feed the poor. In some cases the lines stretched for blocks as people waited for their only good meal each day.

As unemployment grew, Hoover's Reconstruction Finance Corporation began to loan money to state governments for relief, but these and other relief funds proved woefully inadequate. In many cities, after private charity was exhausted, there was nothing to help the unemployed.

Hoovervilles

Throughout the nation, families who could not pay their rent or make their mortgage payments were evicted from their homes.

HISTORY Online — **Student Web Activity**

Visit the *American History: The Modern Era Since 1865* Web site at **me.glencoe.com** and click on **Chapter 17— Student Web Activities** for an activity about glimpses of Depression life.

Some moved in with relatives if they could. The less fortunate ended up in makeshift communities dubbed "Hoovervilles" on the outskirts of cities. One woman later remembered Oklahoma City's Hooverville:

> *Here were all these people living in rusted-out car bodies. I mean that was their home. There were people living in shacks made of orange crates. One family with a whole lot of kids was living in a piano box. This wasn't just a little section, this was maybe ten miles wide and ten miles long. People living in whatever they could junk together.*

People who were even less fortunate slept in doorways or on park benches. Desperate men grubbed in garbage cans to feed their families. Nearly every street corner had its apple seller. So many apples were available because of a surplus of the fruit in the Pacific Northwest. To reduce the surplus, the International Apple Shippers Association set up a system for unemployed people to sell the apples. A person could get a credit for $1.75 for a crate of 100 to 120 apples, then turn around and sell the apples for 5 cents each, making a small profit.

Other jobless Americans banded together in hunger riots, smashing into grocery stores and grabbing whatever food they could carry. Begging increased dramatically, and the song "Brother, Can You Spare a Dime?" became a bitter testimony to veterans who remembered fighting a war to protect American values and to make the world safe for democracy.

■ The Bonus Army

In May 1932, some 1,500 unemployed army veterans and their families marched on Washington, D.C., to demand early payment of the bonus Congress had promised to pay them in 1945. Within sight of the White House, some set up a Hooverville in an area across the Potomac River known as Anacostia Flats. Others occupied abandoned buildings in the area. As they demonstrated daily in front of the White House and the Capitol, their numbers increased to more than 20,000.

The government tried to keep the protesters peaceful. President Hoover supported their right to express their views and even provided them with army tents, cots, and field kitchens. When Congress

★★★★A★★★★★★★★
AMERICAN PORTRAITS

Dorothea Lange
1895–1965

By the time she finished high school, Dorothea Lange had chosen her career. She wanted to be a photographer—even though she had never used a camera.

After taking a photography course, Lange journeyed from New York to San Francisco, where she ran a portrait business for 10 years. Then the Depression struck. Lange became a documentary photographer, her compassion showing clearly in her photos. By the mid-1930s she was documenting the life of California's migrant laborers, work that earned her a position with the Farm Security Administration (FSA). Her FSA photos revealed poverty's brutal effects on rural Americans. Lange later traveled through the dust bowl states, capturing people's suffering in a book called *An American Exodus, A Record of Human Erosion.*

rejected their demands, most of the veterans left Washington. About 2,000 refused to leave, however. After a clash between the veterans and the local police, Hoover called in the army. General Douglas MacArthur, commander of the troops, carried out the President's orders to clear the veterans from federal buildings. Using tanks, machine guns, and tear gas, his troops drove the veterans out of Washington and burned their camp. Historian Frederick Lewis Allen described the sudden chaos that resulted:

> ❝ Cavalrymen were riding into the crowd, infantrymen were throwing tear-gas bombs, women and children were being trampled and choking from the gas; . . . [People] were running wildly, pell-mell across uneven ground, screaming as they stumbled and fell. The troops moved slowly on, scattering before them veterans and homegoing government clerks alike. . . . That evening, the Washington sky glowed with fire. Even after midnight the troops were still on their way with bayonets and tear-gas bombs. ❞

Many Americans blamed Hoover for the use of brutal and excessive force against the veterans. He seemed more than ever an inflexible leader.

■ Fear of Revolution

During this time of bewilderment and despair, fear of revolution started to spread. Lloyds of London, a British insurance company, began to write policies for riot insurance in the United States. Looking for scapegoats, Americans blamed the Depression on the very people they had admired and willingly followed a few years earlier—industrialists and bankers. Public outrage

▲ THE BONUS ARMY Veterans of World War I converged on Washington, D.C., in 1932. They hoped to persuade Congress to grant them immediate payments of a bonus, not due until 1945. *How did the federal government react to the bonus marchers?*

increased when a Senate investigation charged that some of the nation's wealthiest were trying to get away without paying taxes on their huge incomes. Others were accused of using unscrupulous business practices to increase their own wealth in the midst of such widespread poverty and suffering.

Radical Alternatives

The unrest in society offered hope to both Socialists and Communists, who preached that the Depression marked the end of capitalism, which would soon be replaced by a system that distributed goods more fairly. Both groups proposed that government control the means of production and distribution. Both promised that a planned economy would result in greater abundance for all. "Folks are restless," observed Mississippi Governor Theodore Bilbo, "communism is gaining a foothold. . . . In fact, I'm getting a little pink myself."

Such radical alternatives were weakened because Socialists and Communists bitterly opposed each other and destroyed each other's credibility. The Socialists proposed to gain their power by persuasion and the ballot box. The Communist party, however, held that capitalism could not be overthrown without violent revolution—what Earl Browder, the general secretary of the party, called the "omelet theory." Just as it was impossible to make an omelet without breaking eggs, Browder explained, it was impossible to make a revolution without breaking heads.

Using the Forces of Democracy

Fears of a revolution in the United States proved to be unfounded, however. Although many Americans were suffering, were angry, and wanted a change, protest movements tended to be splintered. No single leader emerged to galvanize them or act as a unify-

ing force. Most Americans clung to their democratic traditions and expressed their anger at the ballot box.

■ The Election of 1932

As the presidential election of 1932 approached, the Democrats sensed victory for the first time since 1916.

The Candidates

The Democratic national convention rejected Al Smith's bid for renomination and instead chose New York Governor Franklin D. Roosevelt as their candidate. The former assistant secretary of the navy had run as the candidate for Vice President in 1920. In 1928, while Smith was losing the presidential election to Hoover, Roosevelt had won New York's race for governor and

▲ *HOME RELIEF STATION* by Louis Ribak, 1935–1936 The painting expresses the frustration felt by the American people during the Depression years. *What did the election of 1932 reveal about American public opinion concerning the Hoover administration and its response during the most difficult years of the Depression?*

▲ **INAUGURATION DAY** During the ride to Roosevelt's inauguration, Hoover seemed glum while Roosevelt appeared confident. *What happened to the American economy between Election Day 1932 and Inauguration Day 1933?*

in the process proved himself to be a remarkable vote-getter. In 1930 he had been reelected by a huge majority.

The Campaign

The Democratic platform of 1932—the briefest in United States political history—urged the repeal of Prohibition and made general proposals for reform and recovery. The Democrats' most effective asset, however, was Roosevelt himself. Setting the tone for

• •

Footnotes to History

The Roosevelt Campaign Franklin D. Roosevelt had been stricken with polio in 1921 and could not walk without braces and canes. Very few photographs were taken of Roosevelt in a wheelchair. Determined to prove that his disability would not affect his performance as President, Roosevelt set out on a grueling cross-country campaign trip.

what became a whirlwind campaign, he flew by plane to the Democratic convention to become the first candidate to accept a presidential nomination in person.

In his acceptance address, he pledged "a new deal for the American people." In later speeches, however, he was vague and described the "New Deal" in broad terms only. It remained clear that Roosevelt intended to take action that would help "the forgotten man at the bottom of the economic pyramid." He summed up the history of the Hoover administration in four sentences:

> ❝ *First, it encouraged speculation and overproduction through its false economic policies. Second, it attempted to minimize the crash and misled the people as to its gravity. Third, it erroneously charged the cause to other nations of the world. And finally, it refused to recognize and correct the evils at home which it had brought forth; it delayed reform, it forgot reform.* ❞

The Republicans, meanwhile, gloomily renominated Hoover, who suffered the problem of having to defend his policies in the midst of a terrible depression. He maintained that hard times were the result of economic collapse abroad—for which his administration could not be held responsible. Hoover flatly rejected Roosevelt's position that government had "a positive duty to see that no citizen shall starve." "You cannot," warned Hoover, "extend the mastery of government over the daily life of a people without somewhere making it master of people's souls and thoughts."

On Election Day, the Republican victories of the 1920s were completely reversed as Roosevelt carried 42 of the 48 states. This landslide revealed not only a widespread willingness to blame the Republicans for the Depression but also a desire to use government as an agency for human welfare.

Yet even at the bottom of the worst depression in history, few Americans favored the overthrow of capitalism, either by violent or peaceful means. The election results revealed that the Socialists polled 900,000 votes and the Communists only 100,000. This meant that their combined share was a little more than 2 percent of all of the votes cast.

Banking Panic

In the time between Roosevelt's election in November and his inauguration in March, the Twentieth Amendment was added to the Constitution, changing the date of the presidential inauguration from March 4 to January 20. Had this amendment gone into effect sooner, it would have been better for the country. For four months Hoover as President was a **lame duck,** an officeholder with little influence, because his term was about to end. During this time the nation was virtually leaderless. The new President—Franklin D. Roosevelt—was without power to act.

During this short time, the entire banking system disintegrated, and the economy ground almost to a standstill. Although thousands of smaller banks had already failed, most of the larger banks seemed to be able to hold firm during this time. Despite Roosevelt's promise that upon becoming President he would take action to rescue the nation from the Depression, in early 1933 the entire country was seized by a banking panic. Having lost faith in the nation's economy, thousands of depositors withdrew their money from banks and hoarded cash and gold. Given such a situation, even the most stable banks were bound to stop payments

Visualizing **History**

▲ **DEPRESSION LIFE** These three children, ages 5, 12, and 7, were discovered living in an abandoned house. Many Americans demanded action to escape such economic woes. **What candidate won the 1932 election?**

eventually because there was not enough gold in circulation to cover all deposits.

As the situation deteriorated, state governors issued proclamations closing the banks of their states until confidence could be restored. By March 4—the day Roosevelt would take the oath of office—almost every private bank in the country was closed or placed under restriction by state regulation. From 1930 to the eve of the inauguration, more than 5,400 banks had shut down. The people of the nation waited anxiously to see what the new President would do.

Section 3 ★ Assessment

Checking for Understanding

1. **Define** lame duck.

2. **Explain** why farmers destroyed crops and livestock even though people were hungry.

Critical Thinking

3. **Identifying Problems** What part did the public's lack of confidence in government play in the banking crisis?

4. **Comparing and Contrasting** Re-create the diagram shown here, and identify similarities and

differences between the conditions of workers and farmers in the early 1930s.

Farmers　　Workers

INTERDISCIPLINARY ACTIVITY

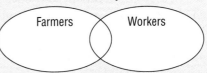

5. **The Arts** Write a day's entry in the diary of a 17-year-old looking for work during the Great Depression.

CHAPTER 17 ★ ASSESSMENT

Self-Check Quiz

Visit the *American History: The Modern Era Since 1865* Web site at **me.glencoe.com** and click on *Chapter 17—Self-Check Quizzes* to prepare for the chapter test.

Using Vocabulary

Imagine that you must write a handbook on tips for investing in the stock market. Write an entry about speculation that explains the pros and cons. Use these terms:

speculation   on margin

securities   installment buying

Reviewing Facts

1. **Explain** how overproduction or underconsumption was one cause of the Great Depression.

2. **Describe** the effects of the Hawley-Smoot Tariff.

3. **Summarize** Hoover's actions to combat the Depression and the philosophy behind the actions.

4. **List** two defeats Hoover had in foreign policy.

Understanding Concepts

Political Policy

1. Re-create the diagram shown here to cite the reasons for the rise of communism and socialism during the Depression, as well as the reasons for their quick demise.

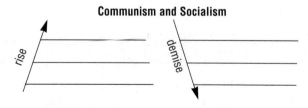

Communism and Socialism

rise   demise

Economic Change

2. Was America's appetite for money and consumer goods a cause of the Great Depression? Explain how activities such as stock market speculation and installment buying contributed to the crisis.

Critical Thinking

1. **Contrasting Ideas** Explain the difference between laissez-faire economics and Hoover's beliefs about government in the economy.

2. **Analyzing Trends** Study the graph on farm prices, then answer the questions that follow.

   a. When were wheat and corn prices the highest? The lowest?

   b. What is the overall trend in the prices of wheat, corn, and cotton?

   c. How did this trend affect farmers during the Great Depression?

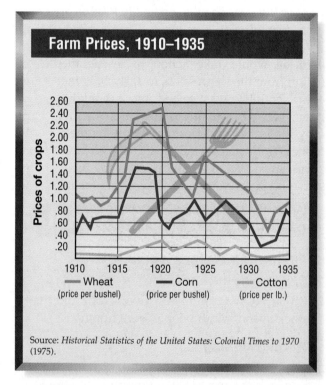

Farm Prices, 1910–1935

Prices of crops

2.60
2.40
2.20
2.00
1.80
1.60
1.40
1.20
1.00
.80
.60
.40
.20

1910   1915   1920   1925   1930   1935

— Wheat (price per bushel)   — Corn (price per bushel)   — Cotton (price per lb.)

Source: *Historical Statistics of the United States: Colonial Times to 1970* (1975).

3. **Analyzing Choices** Explain why the Hoover-Stimson Doctrine was ineffective. Make a list of

reasons why Americans might have been unwilling to go to war in the early 1930s.

4. **Identifying Assumptions** Compare the Democratic and Republican platforms in the election of 1932. What assumptions did the Republicans make about what American voters were thinking?

History and Geography

Agriculture and the Depression

1. **Human/Environment Interaction** Why did the Farm Board want farmers to plant fewer crops?

2. **Human/Environment Interaction** What conservation measures did Hoover support?

Interdisciplinary Activity: Economics

Work in groups of three to analyze the causes of the Great Depression. Assign each group member two of the causes listed on pages 515–517 of your text. Have each group member make a list of economic and social effects that might have resulted from his or her cause. When you have finished your individual lists, create a master list entitled "How the Great Depression Changed America."

Practicing Skills

Writing a Persuasive Argument

Refer to the skills lesson on Writing a Persuasive Argument on page 525 to help you practice this skill.

Imagine that you are an American citizen at the time of the Great Depression. Use information from Chapter 17 to write a persuasive argument on one of the following topics.

1. Why President Hoover was/was not justified in his refusal to give direct aid to victims of the Great Depression.

2. The United States should/should not follow a policy of isolation.

3. Documentary photography captured/did not capture the sufferings during the Great Depression.

▲ DEPRESSION FAMILY PHOTOGRAPHED BY DOROTHEA LANGE

Technology Activity

Using a Word Processor

Use the Internet and other library resources to compile a brief oral history of the Depression. Find quotes that you find compelling from people who lived through the economic crisis, and organize them in a report.

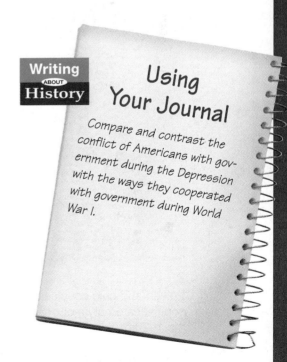

Writing ABOUT History

Using Your Journal

Compare and contrast the conflict of Americans with government during the Depression with the ways they cooperated with government during World War I.

Cultural Kaleidoscope

The 1920s

Fashions in the 1920s

During the 1920s, postwar America rebelled against many of the social values that were in place at the turn of the century. Nowhere was this revolution more evident than in the fashions of the period. The flapper, embodying independence and social rebellion, became the model for the new woman.

During the 1920s straight, unfitted dresses were in vogue. Skirts seemed to rise and fall with the stock market. When Wall Street boomed during the 1920s, skirt lengths rose above the knee.

▼

The straw hat, or boater, was the common headwear for men.

▲ Poised and chic couples set a sophisticated style of dress in the 1920s.

► Many women adopted a new kind of hat style, a drooping, bell-shaped hat called a cloche.

◄ Bow tie

▼ Artist John Held, Jr., helped create the image of youth in the 1920s. His art often appeared on the cover of popular magazines.

► Woman's earring

► The changes in society gave women a greater measure of intellectual and economic independence.

Life

Price 15 cents

April 28 1927

SHE MISSED THE BOAT

537

Standardized Test Practice

Directions: Choose the *best* answer to each of the following multiple choice questions. If you have trouble answering a question, use the process of elimination to narrow your choices. Write your answers on a separate piece of paper.

1. Based on the maps below, which of the following was an effect of World War I?

A World War I created larger empires.

B The country of Palestine was created for war refugees.

C Austria-Hungary became Latvia and Lithuania.

D The Central European nations were divided up into many smaller countries.

> **Test-Taking Tip:** Look carefully at the maps to understand what they represent. Notice that each map has its *own* key. Since the question says that you should base your answer on the maps, make sure that you double check each answer choice against the information *on the maps.* What is the most striking difference between the two maps? What does that most likely mean?

2. Which of the following was one of the primary causes of World War I?

F A complex set of alliances among European nations

G The exile of General Victoriano Huerta

H The dissatisfaction of Russian peasants

J The breakup of the Austro-Hungarian empire

> **Test-Taking Tip:** Eliminate answers you know are incorrect. For example, *the dissatisfaction of Russian peasants* (answer H) was a cause of the Russian Revolution, not World War I, so you can eliminate that answer. Similarly, the exile of Huerta (answer G) occurred in Mexico, which had little effect on European nations. You also can eliminate that answer.

3. One of the effects of World War I on the American economy was

   A a sharp rise in unemployment.

   B stronger government control over industry.

   C a sharp decrease in taxes.

   D the abolition of labor unions, which were seen as unpatriotic.

Test-Taking Tip: This question is asking for a cause-and-effect relationship. Look for an answer that can be *directly related* to the needs of a wartime economy. During the war, it was necessary to produce supplies and munitions for the armed forces (which also needed expanded manpower), so answer A must be incorrect. In fact, there were more jobs and fewer workers to fill them, so unemployment is not a logical choice.

---

4. Which of the following did NOT occur during the 1920s?

   F Secondary education became available to a large number of Americans.

   G A large number of people migrated from cities to farms.

   H Motion pictures became an extremely popular form of entertainment.

   J A new generation of African American artists arose in Harlem.

Test-Taking Tip: Be careful—overlooking the words NOT or EXCEPT in a question is a common error. Look for the answer choice that does NOT fit. Since the availability of secondary education, the rise of motion pictures, and the Harlem Renaissance all *did* occur during the 1920s, answers F, H, and J cannot be the correct choices.

---

5. The Great Depression followed soon after

   A the rise of organized crime during Prohibition.

   B an increase in the value of agricultural products.

   C a large and sudden drop in the value of stocks.

   D an increase in the number of unemployed workers.

Test-Taking Tip: This question involves a sequence of events. The Great Depression resulted in increased unemployment (answer D). The Depression did not follow after an increase in unemployment. Therefore, answer D is incorrect. Make sure you read each answer choice carefully so that you pick the *best* one.

---

6. The United States refused to take action against the Japanese invasion of China because

   F the United States supported the Japanese government.

   G most Americans did not want to get involved in another war.

   H the Kellogg-Briand Pact prevented the United States from defending China.

   J Japan did not belong to the League of Nations.

Test-Taking Tip: If you are not sure of the answer to a question, use the process of elimination. For example, the Japanese invasion of China was, itself, a violation of the Kellogg-Briand Pact, so answer H is not a likely answer.

UNIT SIX
TIMES OF CRISIS
1932–1960

| CHAPTER **18** The New Deal 1932–1939 | CHAPTER **19** World War II 1933–1945 | CHAPTER **20** The Cold War 1945–1952 | CHAPTER **21** Search for Stability 1952–1960 |

▲ WPA PLAY POSTER, 1936

▲ M-1 RIFLE, FIRST USED DURING WORLD WAR II

History AND ART

B-17 Base in England
by Peter Hurd, 1943

Less than 25 years after World War I, the United States found itself at war again. This war, however, was far different. It was a fight for survival, and before it was over, it involved almost every nation in the world.

Why It's Important

Several major crises deeply affected the United States between 1930 and 1960. A great depression endangered the nation's economic system, and foreign military powers threatened its national security. Americans committed themselves to economic recovery and to fighting—first, the Axis Powers in World War II, and later, the spread of communism. America would emerge from these trying times as the most dominant nation in the world.

 To learn more about America's years of crisis, view the *Historic America: Electronic Field Trips* Side 2, Chapter 8; Side 2, Chapter 9 video lessons:
- *The USS Arizona Memorial*
- *The Holocaust Museum*

Themes

- American Democracy
- Civil Rights and Liberties
- Conflict and Cooperation
- U.S. Role in World Affairs

Key Events

- New Deal legislation
- Japanese attack Pearl Harbor
- Surrender of Germany and Japan
- United Nations Charter
- Cold War
- Truman Doctrine
- North Atlantic Treaty Organization
- Korean War
- Suez Crisis
- Castro controls Cuba

 **PRIMARY SOURCES Library** See pages 866–867 for primary source readings to accompany Unit 6.

▼ **WORLD WAR II POSTER**

Together We WIN

Portfolio Project

Identify something you consider a symbol of the era and describe the ideas and emotions connected with it. Try to include visual materials.

▲ **FLYING GRUMMAN WILDCAT FIGHTER, 1942**

Global Perspectives

★★★★★★★★ ★★★

The World

		1930	1940
Asia and Oceania			
Europe		◄ **1934** *Hitler becomes Der Führer of Germany*	**1939** *World War II begins in Europe*
Africa			
South America			**1938** *Venezuela becomes the third-largest oil-producing nation in the world*
North and Central America			

The United States

		1930	1940
Pacific and Northwest			◄ **1941** *Japanese attack on Pearl Harbor brings United States into World War II*
Southeast			
Midwest			
Southwest			**1937** *Parts of the Southwest and the Great Plains become a dust bowl*
Atlantic Northeast		◄ **1933** *Newly inaugurated President Franklin D. Roosevelt launches New Deal*	

Linking Across TIME

The Chinese and Japanese have played a major role in American life, especially in California and Hawaii, since the mid-1800s. They may have set foot on the North American continent hundreds of years before. Some scholars believe that Hui Shen, a Chinese missionary, explored the Pacific coast of North America as early as the 400s! There is solid evidence to suggest that Chinese sailors regularly visited California in the mid-1500s. Before the closing of Japan in the 1600s, Japanese sailors, too, probably ventured as far as California.

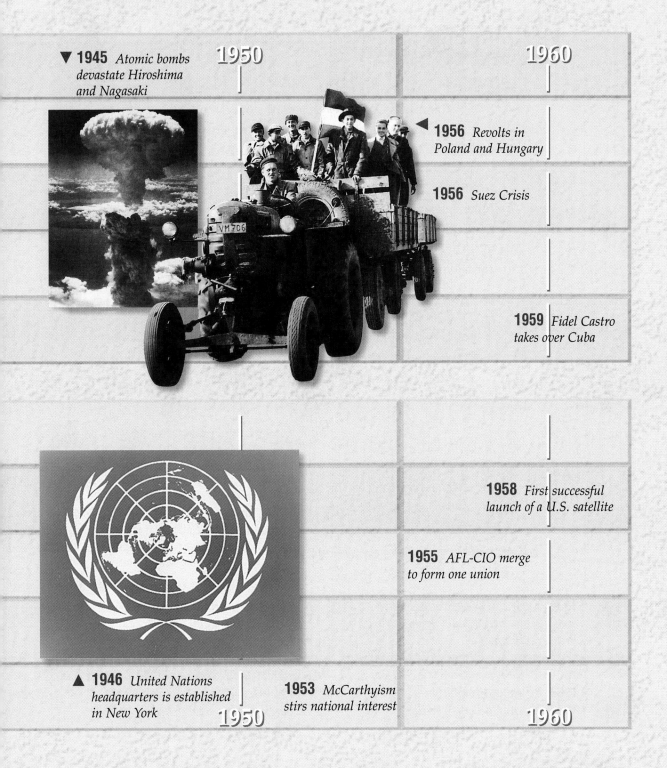

▼ **1945** *Atomic bombs devastate Hiroshima and Nagasaki*

1950

1960

◄ **1956** *Revolts in Poland and Hungary*

1956 *Suez Crisis*

1959 *Fidel Castro takes over Cuba*

1958 *First successful launch of a U.S. satellite*

1955 *AFL-CIO merge to form one union*

▲ **1946** *United Nations headquarters is established in New York*

1953 *McCarthyism stirs national interest*

1950

1960

CHAPTER 18

★★

The New Deal
1932-1939

▶ SHOVEL, CIVILIAN CONSERVATION CORPS

Setting the Scene

Focus

When Franklin D. Roosevelt took the oath of office, Congress and the American people were eager to follow the President's leadership. Within months, laws were passed to provide relief, recovery, and reform of the economic system. Two years later, however, millions of Americans were still unemployed, and the New Deal came under increasing criticism. Throughout Roosevelt's second term, many programs were reshaped to permanently change the way government relates to its citizens.

Concepts to Understand

★ How New Deal **economic reform** differed from previous policies

★ Why the **political leadership** of Roosevelt was effective at bringing about New Deal reforms

Read to Discover . . .

★ how New Deal legislation attempted to end the Depression.

★ what long-term effects the New Deal programs had on American society.

Journal Notes

What role did women play in the Roosevelt administration? Note the details in your journal.

HISTORY Online

Chapter Overview
Visit the *American History: The Modern Era Since 1865* Web site at **me.glencoe.com** and click on *Chapter 18—Chapter Overviews* to preview chapter information.

CULTURAL	• **1932** *American speed skaters and bobsledders earn medals in the Winter Olympics*	• **1934** *Severe drought in the Great Plains creates a dust bowl* • **1935** Middletown *is published*
	1932	**1934**
POLITICAL	• **1933** *Repeal of Prohibition* • **1933** *"Hundred Days" begins after Roosevelt's inauguration*	• **1934** *Securities and Exchange Commission is established* • **1935** *Social Security Act is passed*

▲ NEW DEAL POSTERS

 History AND ART

We Demand
by Joe Jones, 1934

Depression painter Joe Jones emphasized working people in his art. In *We Demand*, he concentrated on the efforts of workers to organize the protest to improve their wages and conditions of employment.

- **1936** *Tornadoes kill more than 400 Southerners in 5 states*

- **1938** *Thornton Wilder's play* Our Town *wins Pulitzer Prize*

1936

- **1936** *Roosevelt is reelected*
- **1937** *Roosevelt attempts to pack the Supreme Court*

1938

- **1938** *Fair Labor Standards Act passes*

★★★

Roosevelt Takes Charge

Guide to Reading

Main Idea

Responding to Americans' desire for greater leadership, President Roosevelt took action against the Depression.

Reading Strategy

Organizing Information As you read about the first months of Franklin Roosevelt's presidency, use a diagram such as the one shown here to list the steps Roosevelt took to end the banking crisis.

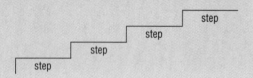

Objectives

After studying this section, you should be able to

★ identify the traits that made Franklin Roosevelt an effective leader.

★ describe how Roosevelt garnered ideas and support for his New Deal.

Key Term

fireside chat

▶ PERSONAL BANK CHECKS

W ithin his Inaugural Address Franklin D. Roosevelt made the same promises about the nation's recovery that Herbert Hoover and his advisers had been making since 1929. Roosevelt promised that the nation "will endure as it has endured, will revive and will prosper." Unlike Hoover, however, the new President reflected the popular mood of the nation by blaming bankers, "the unscrupulous moneychangers," for allowing starvation in the midst of plenty. The nation was in a kind of war, he said, and strong presidential leadership was needed. Sketching the need for various relief and reform measures, the new President called for immediate legislation. If Congress failed to act quickly, Roosevelt promised to ask for executive authority "as great as the power that would be given to me if we were in fact invaded by a foreign foe."

■ A Strong Leader

Before taking office, Roosevelt displayed little evidence of the leadership he would offer in his 12 years in the White House. One writer described him as "an amiable man . . . who without any important qualifications for the office, would very much like to be President." His outstanding attribute was his name, which his cousin Theodore Roosevelt had made well known in American politics.

Early Life

The only son of wealthy parents, FDR, as his friends called him, attended the best schools. At the time of his election, Roosevelt had been in politics for more than 20 years, yet his views on many issues were unknown. Nor did many Americans realize that he had overcome a serious physical handicap.

In 1921, at age 39, Roosevelt was stricken with polio. Fighting back against the crippling disease, he regained the use of his hands and arms, but he remained paralyzed from the waist down. His painful recovery toughened him and, at the same time, gave him genuine sympathy for the less fortunate. Playwright Robert Sherwood, a close associate, described his toughness and compassion:

“ *I tried continually to study him, to try to look beyond his charming and amusing and warmly affectionate surface into his heavily forested interior. But I never understood what was going on in there. . . . He could be a ruthless politician, but he was the champion of friends and associates who for him were political liabilities . . . and of causes which apparently competent observers assured him would be political suicide.* ”

A Master Politician

Both friends and foes agreed that, despite his complexity, Roosevelt was master of the art of politics. Few Presidents had such varied political training—at local, state, and federal levels—in elected and appointed offices. Elected to the New York legislature in 1910, at the height of the Progressive Era, Roosevelt learned about local government. As assistant secretary of the navy during World War I, he had an insider's view as the Wilson administration organized the federal government to wage war. As governor of New York when the stock market crashed, FDR dealt with many of the same problems he would face as President.

Perhaps Roosevelt's greatest strength as a politician was his warm and understanding approach to people. Where Hoover had withdrawn to the isolation of the White House as the Depression settled in, Roosevelt reached out by radio to the American people in a series of **fireside chats.** These were informal talks in which the President calmly but confidently explained in simple

Visualizing History ▲ A MANDATE FOR CHANGE Farmers in debt, workers without jobs, and bankrupt business owners wanted the government to take bolder action. Americans responded enthusiastically to Franklin D. Roosevelt's call for action to fight the Great Depression. *What personal qualities did Roosevelt bring to the presidency?*

terms the nation's problems and how the New Deal planned to defeat the Depression. Millions of radio listeners felt that the President was talking directly to them. After a fireside chat, Roosevelt sometimes received as many as 50,000 letters a day.

Roosevelt also knew how to use the press better than his predecessor. Hoover had avoided reporters and refused to answer questions unless they were written out in advance. In contrast, FDR allowed reporters to barrage him with questions during frequent press conferences. This approach made him popular with the press—important shapers of public opinion—and focused public attention on Washington, D.C., and his New Deal programs. "Gone is the fortress that was the White House," wrote one reporter after Roosevelt took office.

Getting Things Done

A product of the Progressive Era, FDR retained the progressives' approach to solving society's problems. As President he was a pragmatist and an experimenter. He sometimes asked three or four people with conflicting opinions to do the same job and compared the results. FDR compared himself to a quarterback on a football team who called a play, and if it did not work, tried another. Action, he felt, was better than inaction. Most Americans, desperate for relief from the effects of the Depression, agreed with him.

The "Brain Trust"

Roosevelt also had trust in the ability of experts to plan for society. Even before receiving the Democratic nomination for President, he gathered a group of professors from Columbia University to advise him. This group of economists, political scientists, and attorneys was nicknamed the "brain trust" by the press. After Roosevelt became President, the brain trust stayed on to help him plan New Deal recovery programs. In selecting his cabinet, FDR named people who presented a variety of viewpoints and ideas—Northerners and Southerners, liberals and conservatives. He

named Republican Harold Ickes as secretary of the interior, and for secretary of agriculture he chose Henry A. Wallace, whose father had the job under Harding. For secretary of labor Roosevelt named the first woman cabinet officer, former child labor reformer Frances Perkins. Other women held important positions in almost every New Deal agency. Like Secretary Perkins, many of these women had been social workers. Now the President was calling upon them to administer the federal government's social and relief programs.

Eleanor Roosevelt as Adviser

Outside the brain trust, the adviser that Roosevelt relied on most was his wife, Eleanor. Because of his paralysis, FDR moved with difficulty in a wheelchair or with heavy braces on his legs. As a result, he asked Eleanor to assume a significant role in his administration. The President called her his "eyes and ears" outside the White House. During the first year of the New Deal, she traveled extensively to attend political rallies, tour factories, visit coal mines, and contact many people that FDR might not otherwise have met. At cabinet meetings, the President

Visualizing History ▲ SECRETARY OF LABOR Frances Perkins was appointed secretary of labor by Roosevelt. A long-time advocate of minimum wage and maximum hour laws, child-labor restrictions, and other progressive reforms, she was one of only two cabinet members to serve throughout Roosevelt's four terms. *What was unique about her appointment?*

Eleanor Roosevelt
1884–1962

Eleanor Roosevelt did not herself hold public office until she was a 61-year-old widow. But as First Lady she fought tenaciously for social justice and added a sense of compassion to the New Deal.

Although painfully shy as a young girl, Eleanor Roosevelt emerged as a vibrant public personality during the 1920s when her husband, FDR, was recovering from polio. She did all she could to keep his name in the public mind. After Roosevelt's election, she spoke for people who otherwise would have been ignored—women, the poor and the underprivileged, and African Americans.

Sensitive to racial injustice, she spoke up so strongly for civil rights that she won African American support for the New Deal. A lecturer and columnist, Eleanor Roosevelt later worked for global human rights in the United Nations.

would report, "My missus says that people are working for wages well below the minimum . . . in the town she visited last week." Eleanor Roosevelt shared Franklin's concern for the victims of the Depression—close friends thought that her concern was even deeper than his—and the belief that decisive government action was needed to conquer society's ills.

■ The First New Deal

President Roosevelt fulfilled his promise to provide "action now." Americans waited to see what he would do.

Restoring Faith in Banks

On Sunday, March 5, 1933, the day after his inauguration, Roosevelt called a special session of Congress. On Monday he used an old law still on the books to suspend the nation's banking activity. Many Americans had lost faith in banks after the crash, withdrew their money, and kept it at home. Banks needed depositors' funds to make loans that would help recovery, but, in many areas, the loss of deposits was so great that banks had to close their doors. After a week in office, the President went on the radio with his first fireside chat. He explained that only healthy banks would be allowed to reopen. He assured Americans that it would be "safer to keep money in a reopened bank than under the mattress." The next day most banks began to do business again, and in a few days deposits exceeded withdrawals. As the President's calm assurances restored public confidence in the nation's financial system, the bank crisis ended.

The Hundred Days

That first week was just the beginning of feverish activity. In the "Hundred Days" between March 9 and June 16, 1933, Congress passed 15 major bills, more than had ever been enacted in such a short time. Most were bills that the President submitted and that Congress passed with little debate. Seldom had a President enjoyed such overwhelming support.

Meeting "Each Day's Troubles"

Roosevelt took office with no clear idea of how to solve the nation's economic crisis. "There's nothing to do," he said, "but meet each day's troubles as they come." The New Deal, therefore, was not a carefully worked

▲ BANK CLOSINGS Afraid for the safety of their savings, panicked depositors line up outside a bank. Such "runs"—when all depositors tried to withdraw their money at the same time—usually caused those banks to fail, making their depositors' fears come true. *How did Roosevelt handle the bank crisis?*

out reform plan. Instead, it was a series of measures quickly drawn up to attack the Depression in many ways at once. Some laws were in response to special demands. Some were even passed against the President's wishes, but he signed them to avoid holding up other legislation. However, New Deal programs had three general purposes: recovery from the Depression, relief for its victims, and reform of the economic system.

From 1933 to early 1935, the dominating goals of the Roosevelt administration were recovery and relief. During the "First New Deal," as this phase was called, the President and his advisers thought that a series of temporary measures could get the economy moving again. From this beginning, recovery would come on its own momentum. Therefore, little additional legislation followed the Hundred Days of the First New Deal. The administration merely implemented the laws that the Senate and the House had created and waited for recovery to occur.

Section 1 ★ Assessment

Checking for Understanding

1. **Define** fireside chat.
2. **Cite** the political experience that prepared Roosevelt to lead the nation out of the Depression.
3. **Explain** Roosevelt's approach to solving problems.

Critical Thinking

4. **Making Comparisons** Re-create the chart shown here to compare Roosevelt's style in managing the nation's economic crisis to Hoover's.

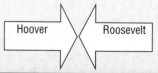

Hoover   Roosevelt

INTERDISCIPLINARY ACTIVITY

5. **The Arts** Analyze the painting that opens this chapter. Draw a political cartoon that expresses the painting's main idea.

★★★

Reform, Relief, and Recovery

Guide to Reading

Main Idea
The Roosevelt administration established programs to boost the economy and provide relief to jobless Americans.

Reading Strategy

Organizing Information As you read about the various relief and recovery acts, use a diagram like the one shown here to describe Roosevelt's efforts to help farmers.

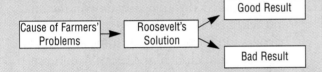

Objectives

After studying this section, you should be able to
★ give examples of how Roosevelt's policies helped and hurt the rural poor.
★ compare the effectiveness of measures aimed at farmers and city workers.

Key Terms

deficit spending, pump priming, dole, foreclosure

▶ **WPA POSTER, LATE 1930S**

Both Hoover and Roosevelt believed that prosperity would return with a little help to spark the economy. So, like Hoover, FDR sought the help of the business community. But he differed from Hoover in the amount and variety of legislation he proposed and in his willingness to call on the full powers of the federal government to solve national problems.

$ ECONOMICS

■ Financial Reform

In June 1933 Congress passed the Glass-Steagall Act. This law prohibited banks from investing in the stock market and created a Federal Deposit Insurance Corporation (FDIC) to insure depositors' savings. Although the program was opposed by the American Bankers' Association as "unscientific, unjust, and dangerous," federal insurance made people feel that their money would be safe in banks.

Congress also responded to the demand that the government prevent stock market fraud. The Federal Securities Act of 1933 required companies that issued or marketed stocks and bonds to provide complete and truthful information to purchasers. Congress followed this act in 1934 with the Securities and Exchange Commission (SEC) to regulate the stock market.

When Roosevelt took office, he faced strong pressure to inflate the currency. A number of senators and representatives wanted to stimulate recovery by putting into circulation billions of dollars in new paper money. Roosevelt, however, rejected inflation and took a conservative approach in his early efforts to achieve recovery. Still, he realized that to keep relief agencies from

◀ CHILDREN PICKETING,
ST. PAUL,
MINNESOTA, 1937

closing and millions of Americans from
starving, **deficit spending** was necessary. In
other words, the federal government's
annual spending would have to exceed its
income. $

■ Help for the Jobless

From deficit spending, the New Deal
moved to **pump priming**—pouring government money into the economy through
loans and federal spending in the hope of
stimulating recovery. Roosevelt called for
government to give money directly to people who would spend it. Increased spending
would increase demand for consumer
goods, New Dealers claimed, which would
stimulate production and create jobs.

By 1933, 12 million to 15 million Americans—1 of every 4 workers—was unemployed, and many were on the verge of
starvation. At first Roosevelt, like Hoover,
thought that local agencies should handle
relief until industry and agriculture recovered enough to provide jobs. It soon
became clear, however, that states, cities,
and local charities had exhausted their
resources.

The Federal Government Steps In

In May 1933 Congress established a Federal Emergency Relief Administration
(FERA). FERA made outright grants to
states and municipalities to distribute as
they chose. They generally provided a
dole—direct gifts of money, food, and clothing. Although the dole was the cheapest and
quickest form of relief, its critics were concerned that people who received handouts
would lose their self-respect and job skills,
making them even more unemployable. So
once the federal government had met the
need for emergency relief, New Dealers
searched for alternatives to the dole.

The Public Works Administration (PWA),
created in June 1933, offered jobs instead of
handouts. Under the direction of Secretary
of the Interior Harold Ickes, the program
provided jobs on construction projects—
improving highways and building dams,
sewer systems, waterworks, schools, and
other government buildings. The PWA generally worked through private contractors,
and Ickes broke down long-standing racial
barriers in the construction trades by insisting that contractors hire African Americans.

In the autumn of 1933, Harry Hopkins,
head of the FERA, won approval for a Civil
Works Administration (CWA) to hire jobless
persons. During the winter of 1933–1934, the
CWA employed 4 million people—300,000
of them women. The CWA built or
improved 1,000 airports, 500,000 miles of
roads, 40,000 school buildings, and 3,500
parks, playgrounds, and playing fields. But
the cost of all this was tremendous—$1 bil-
lion in just five months. In the spring of 1934,
Roosevelt gave in to fierce criticism from
conservatives and cancelled the program.

The TVA

One early New Deal program combined
emergency relief and pump priming with
long-term economic and social planning. In
May 1933, after Roosevelt's prodding, Congress established the Tennessee Valley
Authority (TVA), designed to promote the
development of a seven-state region.

Before the TVA, the natural resources of
the Tennessee Valley had long been exploited.

Forests were leveled, and heavy rainfalls caused erosion and disastrous floods. Poor farmers attempted to work worn-out land, and many people were on relief.

Employing as many as 40,000 workers at a time, the TVA built 20 dams for flood control and improved 5 others. The TVA also moved farmers from marginal lands, reforested millions of acres, built power plants and fertilizer factories, and even started new towns. But the most notable change was the immense amount of cheap electricity that the TVA produced. Its increased availability allowed farmers to install refrigerators, milking machines, and other equipment. Cheap power also attracted industry.

Despite its obvious benefits, the TVA had its critics. Some charged that funds for the TVA should be used to support programs nationwide. Above all, the TVA was attacked by the power companies. One goal of the TVA was to provide a basis to determine fair electricity rates all over the country. But private power companies argued that to use the TVA for this purpose was unfair because the government charged large parts of the cost of electricity production to the cost of flood control and navigation. For the federal government to take over the production of private power, they argued, was unfair and communistic. Although the power companies were powerful enough to prevent any more regional authorities like the TVA, the New Deal did build other power plants, the most famous of which was the Grand Coulee Dam in Washington state.

The CCC

The most generally admired New Deal relief agency was the Civilian Conservation Corps (CCC), established in March 1933. It offered outdoor work to unemployed single men, 18 to 25 years old, at $30 per month, $22 of which went back to their families. By midsummer the CCC had established 1,500 camps. During its existence, the CCC helped conserve the nation's natural resources by putting 3 million young men to work planting trees, fighting forest fires, building reservoirs, and stopping soil erosion.

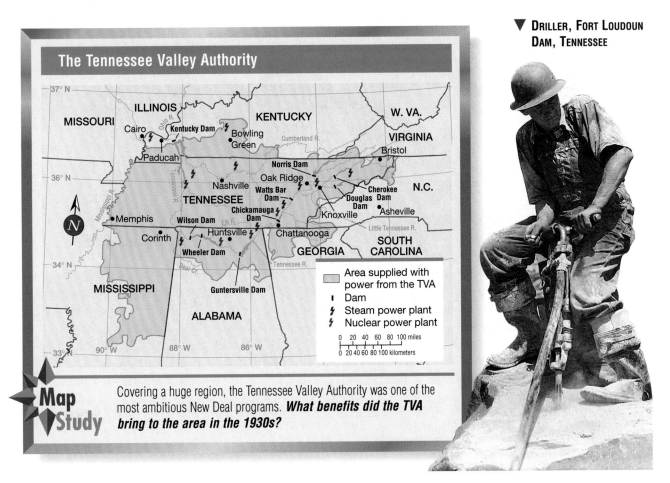

▼ DRILLER, FORT LOUDOUN DAM, TENNESSEE

The Tennessee Valley Authority

Area supplied with power from the TVA
ı Dam
⚡ Steam power plant
⚡ Nuclear power plant

Map Study Covering a huge region, the Tennessee Valley Authority was one of the most ambitious New Deal programs. *What benefits did the TVA bring to the area in the 1930s?*

■ Relief for Agriculture

The impoverished condition of farmers in the Tennessee Valley was by no means unique in 1933. Since 1929 banks had foreclosed on the property of 10 percent of the nation's farmers. In **foreclosure** actions, when a borrower cannot make loan payments, the bank seizes the property that was put up as security for the loan. Farmers threatened to stop producing food unless their debt burden and agricultural prices improved. The New Deal provided relief for heavily indebted farmers by placing a five-year moratorium, or freeze, on mortgage foreclosures. But New Dealers recognized that the root of the farmers' plight was low agricultural prices, and that this situation was related to a problem that had plagued farmers since the end of World War I —overproduction.

The Agricultural Adjustment Act

Roosevelt proposed an unusual approach: stop agricultural surpluses by paying farmers to *not* produce crops. In May 1933, Congress passed the Agricultural Adjustment Act (AAA), under which the government paid farmers who reduced production of basic crops like cotton, wheat, tobacco, hogs, and corn. Funds for these payments came from a tax levied on flour mills, slaughterhouses, and other businesses that processed food.

In 1933 cotton farmers plowed under a quarter of their acreage, and hog producers killed 6 million piglets instead of fattening them for market. In 1934 and 1935, farmers withdrew 10 million acres from production and received more than $1 billion in benefit payments. Surpluses were greatly reduced by 1936, and total farm income rose by more than 50 percent.

Large commercial farmers, who concentrated on one crop, benefited more than smaller farmers who raised several. The crop reduction program actually hurt some people. In the West and Southwest, Mexican migrant workers suffered when growers raised less produce and so hired fewer pickers. Tenant farmers and sharecroppers were forced off the land they worked as owners took it out of production. About 150,000 white tenants and almost 195,000 African American tenants left farming during the 1930s. To stop this trend, the New Deal created the Farm Security Administration to give loans to help tenants purchase land.

▲ Jobs Unemployment was a major problem during the Depression. Many New Deal programs were aimed at putting men and women back to work. *Why were jobs important to economic recovery?*

▲ **THE CCC** Many work programs for the unemployed were started during the Roosevelt administration. The CCC offered outdoor work to unemployed single men. *What work did the CCC do?*

But only 3,400 African American farmers received any of this money. Landless farmers joined other urban and rural migrants who wandered the country in search of jobs.

The Dust Bowl

In 1934 and 1935 a terrible disaster struck the Great Plains and added to the number of farmers on the move. The origins of the disaster arose during World War I, when high crop prices tempted farmers to grow wheat and cotton on what traditionally had been grazing lands. Plows broke up the deep, tough sod that had prevented erosion and conserved moisture in this semiarid region. When the years from 1933 to 1935 were unusually dry, the area began to turn to desert. Dust storms carried away so much topsoil that a haze obscured the sun, sometimes as far away as the Atlantic coast. Between 1934 and 1939, nearly 350,000 farm families left the dust bowl.

To take care of immediate distress, Congress provided the farmers in the dust bowl with funds for new seed and livestock. For long-term solutions, the Department of Agriculture helped farmers plant millions of trees in shelter belts to cut wind velocity and help retain moisture. The government also encouraged farmers to return the land to grazing. Yet there was much criticism of New Deal farm policies. Many farmers did not like being told what to raise or how much to plant. To others, decreasing food supplies when people were hungry seemed immoral. However, the New Deal provided more direct assistance to farmers than to

HISTORY Online

Student Web Activity
Visit the *American History: The Modern Era Since 1865* Web site at **me.glencoe.com** and click on *Chapter 18— Student Web Activities* for an activity on the dust bowl.

any other group, and saved thousands of farm families from poverty and despair.

Native Americans and the New Deal

The New Deal worked to change long-standing government policies affecting Native Americans, including a reversal of the gradual loss of land and tribal authority. Earlier, the federal government had opted for a number of different policies with widely divergent goals. These policies were based on the idea that the best thing for Native Americans was to make them as much like other Americans as possible.

The education system reinforced this idea: children were taken from home at an early age, crowded into boarding schools, and given some "book learning" before being sent back to the reservation. They acquired little knowledge of the culture of their ancestors. Meanwhile, older people received just enough food to sustain them.

However well-meaning, this policy was scarcely better than the old policy. By 1934 Native Americans held only 48 million of the 133 million acres they had possessed in 1887. Although Native Americans were citizens of the United States, state laws often discriminated against them, and the federal government generally ran their affairs for them.

Some improvement began during the Coolidge administration with a reorganization of health services for Native Americans. Later, President Hoover appointed two dedicated individuals as commissioner and deputy commissioner of Indian Affairs. They began to reform of the workings of the department.

The Indian Reorganization Act

More action on Native American affairs was taken during the New Deal years. The Roosevelt administration promoted a new approach that was made law in the Indian Reorganization Act in 1934. This act repealed the allotment policy and returned to tribal ownership Native American lands previously open to sale.

According to John Collier, commissioner of Indian Affairs, the act had a worthwhile purpose. It would enable Native Americans "to earn a decent livelihood and lead self-respecting, organized lives in harmony with their own aims and ideals."

Instead of promoting individual ownership, the federal government now encouraged Native Americans to revert to their own traditions. Instead of being weakened, tribal organization was strengthened. Native Americans were encouraged to become members of the federal Indian Service. Children were now taught the traditions of their own people in school. Ceremonies, art forms, and handicrafts were revived.

New Benefits

The new arrangements brought benefits that could be seen in the reversal of two disturbing trends: Native American landholdings increased after 1934, and the Native American population once again began to increase. Since then Native Americans, now a rapidly growing minority group, have continued to fight in the courts and legislatures for religious freedom, water rights, and land claims.

■ Industrial Relief

Roosevelt's advisers believed that industry, like agriculture, suffered from overproduction. In June 1933 the New Deal tried to help industry with the National Industrial Recovery Act (NIRA).

The NIRA

To control production, the NIRA provided that representatives of labor and of management from competing companies draw up "codes of fair competition" in each industry. These codes set the prices of products to eliminate discount selling. They shortened workers' hours in order to create more jobs, and they established minimum-wage levels. To spread production among as many firms as possible, factories were limited to two shifts a day. To direct this complex program, the act created the National Recovery Administration (NRA).

Power to enforce the codes was very limited, so the NRA used the power of public opinion to enlist the cooperation of business. Those that signed code agreements were given signs with blue eagles and the words "We Do Our Part." Consumers were encouraged to purchase goods only from businesses that displayed the signs. The NIRA, however, never worked out as planned. Prices rose faster than wages. Businesses complained that large companies wrote the codes to favor themselves and to put small competitors out of business.

Workers Turn to Unions

Probably no group suffered more than people who worked for hourly wages. By 1933 one-third of these workers were unemployed. The earnings of the rest had shrunk as their rates or hours were cut. The idea spread that the best way to restore workers' wages and purchasing power was to strengthen labor unions. Under Section 7a of the NIRA, every NRA code guaranteed workers the right to organize unions and to bargain collectively with their employers. As a result, between May and October 1933, American Federation of Labor (AFL) membership jumped by about a million workers.

In 1934 a wave of strikes swept the nation as workers demanded the right to organize for improved wages and job security. Many of these strikes became violent, and most resulted in defeat for the workers, as police generally sided with employers. Although sympathetic to organized labor, the only

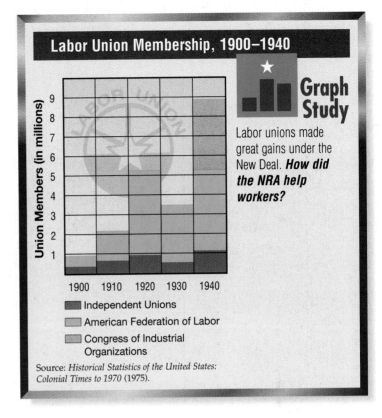

Labor Union Membership, 1900–1940

Graph Study

Labor unions made great gains under the New Deal. *How did the NRA help workers?*

Union Members (in millions)

- ■ Independent Unions
- ■ American Federation of Labor
- □ Congress of Industrial Organizations

Source: *Historical Statistics of the United States: Colonial Times to 1970* (1975).

way the NRA could punish a company was to take away its Blue Eagle symbol. Workers began to demand stronger labor laws.

New Solutions Needed

As the nation entered 1935, American spirits sagged. Despite the New Deal, farm prices and industrial wages were well below 1929 levels, and workers remained unemployed and poor. To many Americans, the New Deal was taking too long and accomplishing too little. FDR clearly saw that he must find other means to restore prosperity.

Section 2 ★ Assessment

Checking for Understanding

1. **Define** deficit spending, pump priming, dole, foreclosure.

2. **State** effects of the farm program.

Critical Thinking

3. **Making Judgments** During widespread unemployment, is government money better used as a dole or for more expensive work-relief programs? Why?

4. **Summarizing** Re-create the chart shown here to describe three programs designed to create jobs while benefiting the nation.

Program	Description

INTERDISCIPLINARY ACTIVITY

5. **Government** Create a table that describes the various New Deal programs.

▲ FARM IN THE DUST BOWL

The Dust Bowl

As the entire nation struggled to cope with the Depression, farmers in Kansas, Oklahoma, and Texas suffered from the scourges of drought and dust. From the 1890s to the 1920s, grasslands in this part of the Great Plains were put to the plow, and when rain fell, they were bountiful. But in the 1930s, the rains failed. As crops withered, leaving bare dirt exposed, the region's high winds lifted the fine topsoil to create dust storms called "dusters."

Large-scale mechanized farming on the plains after 1900 exposed huge areas of soil. Farmers eager to maximize yields overtilled the soil and burned wheat stubble to kill weeds. These poor soil-conservation practices and the long drought created a dust bowl on the plains throughout most of the 1930s, as millions of tons of airborne powdery topsoil buried crops and killed livestock.

The dust bowl took its toll on people too. People sat helpless while their farms blew away. They sometimes lost their way and died in the thick storms while only yards from their houses. Thousands of families abandoned their land to seek work in the fields and orchards of California, Oregon, and Washington. Many migrants, however, could not find work even after they reached their destination. Those who stayed on their land were encouraged to plant crops that conserved the soil.

Making the Geography Connection

1. How did humans change the natural environment of the Great Plains in the early twentieth century?

2. How was a dust bowl created in this region?

ACTIVITY

3. On a piece of posterboard, paste photographs that show modern methods of irrigation and agricultural practices. Write a paragraph in which you argue whether another dust bowl in the United States is possible.

★★★★★★★★★★★★★★★★★★★★★★★★★★★★★★★★★★★★★★

The Second New Deal

Guide to Reading

Main Idea

Some Americans openly opposed President Roosevelt's New Deal programs.

Reading Strategy

Organizing Information As you read about the Second New Deal, use a diagram like the one shown here to list those people who challenged Roosevelt and their reasons for taking such action.

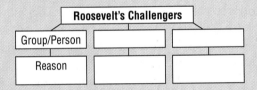

Roosevelt's Challengers		
Group/Person		
Reason		

Objectives

After studying this section, you should be able to
★ list the special-interest groups that challenged Roosevelt.
★ outline the steps the Second New Deal took to achieve reform.
★ identify the events that led to the end of the New Deal.

Key Terms

coalition,
craft union,
industrial
union,
recession

▶ UNION CARDS

---

or the 10 million unemployed Americans in 1935, Senator Huey Long's slogan, "Every Man a King," was an appealing fantasy but a far cry from their reality. They received just enough relief to keep themselves and their families alive. Their miserable dole seemed hardly worth the humiliation it caused. Millions of elderly Americans faced a similar stark reality, without savings, without adequate medical care, and without hope.

■ Attacks on the New Deal

The radical critics of the New Deal posed a strong threat to the Roosevelt administration. As time passed, the ranks of New Deal critics grew. Some wanted a more active government. Others felt that the government was interfering too much in American life.

Three Prominent Attackers

Every week Father Charles E. Coughlin, the "Radio Priest" whose broadcasts reached 40 million listeners, bitterly attacked Roosevelt. Originally a New Deal supporter, Coughlin accused the President of turning the New Deal into a "raw deal." His political organization, the National Union for Social Justice, called for such socialistic measures as heavy taxes on the wealthy and a guaranteed income for everyone. Gradually, Coughlin began expressing anti-Semitic, or anti-Jewish, views. In 1942 Catholic leaders ordered him to stop broadcasting.

An even more dangerous rival to Roosevelt was Huey Long, senator from Louisiana. With the backing of the rural poor, he became extremely powerful in his home state and used it as a base on which to build national popularity. With his folksy, humorous manner, Long knew how to win

▲ **NEW DEAL CRITICS** Father Charles Coughlin (left) reached millions of listeners before the Catholic Church made him stop his radio broadcasts. Until his assassination, Senator Huey Long (right) was equally popular. *What idea did these leaders share?*

audiences. He proposed confiscating the property of the rich and giving every family a home, $2,000 a year, and a free college education for their children. His followers organized hundreds of "Share-Our-Wealth" clubs.

Less colorful than Father Coughlin or Senator Long, but just as threatening, was Dr. Francis Townsend. A former public health official, Townsend was shocked by the plight of older Americans who were no longer able to compete for jobs. He proposed a plan that he claimed would provide relief for the elderly and at the same time stimulate economic recovery, calling for the federal government to pay all Americans over age 60 a pension of $200 per month. Recipients would be required to spend their entire pension check within 30 days. Townsend claimed that not only would this help older Americans, but the money they pumped into the economy would create jobs. The pensions could be financed by a national sales tax on consumer goods, Townsend argued. His innovative plan attracted millions of devoted advocates.

Fighting Back

Roosevelt's annual address to Congress in January 1935 answered his attackers. He admitted that "we have not weeded out the

overprivileged and we have not effectively lifted up the underprivileged." The President announced a "Second New Deal" to put recovery on a new course. This new phase showed greater concern for the less fortunate and abandoned efforts to enlist the support of business.

The political groups supporting the New Deal also changed. Roosevelt had played down partisanship to gain the support of moderate and progressive Republicans. Now he devoted his energies to achieving his goals through the Democratic party alone. To strengthen it, he attempted to form a **coalition,** or combination, of separate groups whose members could be counted on to vote for Democrats. To the traditional source of Democratic political power—the South and Northern urban political machines—Roosevelt attempted to add labor unions, farmers, and African Americans. Many of the Second New Deal's programs were intended to appeal to these groups.

■ Work Relief and Social Security

The most immediate result of the New Deal's shift in attitude was the President's demand for large-scale work relief.

Responding to Roosevelt's request, Congress appropriated funds in April 1935 for "work relief and to increase employment by providing useful projects." An immense new agency, the Works Progress Administration (WPA) was set up under the direction of Harry Hopkins to provide a chance for all people to use their skills to earn an income.

The WPA employed writers, teachers, librarians, actors, musicians, and artists. A "junior WPA," the National Youth Administration (NYA) helped high school and college students stay in school by giving them part-time work, such as typing and library cataloguing. Existing work-relief programs were expanded. The government, through the Reconstruction Finance Corporation, lent large sums to businesses and to local governments. The Civilian Conservation Corps increased the number it employed. The Public Works Administration finally rolled into high gear and provided hundreds of thousands of jobs.

Unemployable men and women needed help during the Depression as much as the unemployed. Persons with no source of support and no ability to earn an income had no place to go. To remedy this problem, Congress in 1935 passed the Social Security Act. Under this program, the federal government financed state unemployment insurance plans through payroll taxes paid by employers. Federal grants to states provided care for dependent mothers and children. The core of the program was retirement benefits, paid for by taxes on workers and employers, that people could collect when they stopped working at age 65.

The Social Security Act had flaws. For example, the act did not protect some groups who needed it most, such as farm workers and domestic help. Since 65 percent of all African American employees in the 1930s fell into these two categories, the act neglected this group the most. Yet the Social Security Act was a landmark in reforming society. It set the policy that an industrial society was responsible for those who, through no fault of their own, are unable to work.

■ Business and Labor

Several pieces of legislation demonstrated Roosevelt's efforts to appeal to the political coalition he was forming. Early in the New Deal, taxes remained at levels set in the 1920s. Now Congress passed tax increases on the incomes of wealthy Americans, inheritance taxes on the property of deceased persons, and higher taxes on corporations. Although the law was attacked as communistic, Roosevelt was more interested, some felt, in heading off the various "share-the-wealth" schemes than he was in actually redistributing the nation's wealth.

The Wagner Act

Next to the Social Security Act, the most important and lasting legislation of the Second New Deal was the National Labor Relations Act, also called the Wagner Act,

Visualizing History

▲ **ATTACK ON THE NEW DEAL** Some Americans thought the New Deal was too restrictive to free enterprise. This cartoonist shows Uncle Sam tied down by New Deal agencies and laws, much as Gulliver was bound by the Lilliputians in the book *Gulliver's Travels*. **Why might critics have thought this way?**

▲ *An Incident in Contemporary American Life, 1942*, by Mitchell Jamieson WPA artists painted murals in many government offices. Mitchell Jamieson's mural of African American opera singer Marian Anderson's famous concert before an integrated audience of 73,000 at the Lincoln Memorial is in the offices of the United States Department of the Interior in Washington, D.C. *What political favor did Roosevelt want from African Americans?*

passed in July 1935 after the Supreme Court declared the National Industrial Recovery Act unconstitutional. The Wagner Act set up a National Labor Relations Board (NLRB), which could hold secret elections in factories to find out whether workers wanted to unionize. The board could arbitrate griev-ances, reinstate workers fired for support-ing unions, and order employers to stop antiunion activities.

The Wagner Act stimulated a burst of labor union activity. But the AFL was ill-equipped in both philosophy and structure to organize workers in mass-production indus-tries such as radio, steel, automobiles, and textiles. The AFL was a federation of **craft unions**—unions where all members had the same skill. In mass-production industries, however, workers from many crafts or skills often worked in a single plant. To have sever-al unions undermined unity. So some labor leaders proposed that factory workers be organized in an **industrial union**—a union to which all workers in a single industry belong, regardless of the job they perform. When the AFL rejected this approach, these leaders abandoned it to form the Congress of Indus-trial Organizations (CIO).

The CIO

"If I went to work in a factory, the first thing I'd do would be to JOIN A UNION," read the slogan signed by President Roo-sevelt on union recruiting posters, as the CIO moved into industries that the AFL had long neglected. By 1936 the CIO had signed up enough steelworkers to threaten a nation-wide strike. Instead, in March 1937 the nation's largest steel producer, the United States Steel Corporation, recognized the union as bargaining agent for its workers, established a 40-hour workweek, and increased wages. Just beginning to recover from the Depression, the company was not willing to risk a major strike. The smaller producers did not follow this lead, however, and bloody strikes broke out around the country. But by 1941, the steelworkers' union had contracts with the entire industry.

Meanwhile, the CIO moved into the auto-mobile industry, where management dis-couraged worker unity by exploiting racial and religious tensions among African Amer-icans, Southern whites, and Catholic ethnic groups. Although hourly wages in the industry were high, seasonal layoffs reduced the average worker's annual earnings to less than $1,000. Workers also resented the "speed-ups" that occurred when management increased the rate at which cars moved along the assembly line.

The Autoworkers Strike

The CIO did not want to challenge the auto industry until the struggle with the steel companies had ended. The nation's autoworkers, however, were impatient for change and took matters into their own hands. They instituted a strike strategy called the sit-down strike. Rather than walking off their jobs, the striking autoworkers remained in the factory. The company could not hire new workers to continue production, nor could it remove the strikers by force without risking violence to the factory. One striker later remembered:

> 66 We were nervous. We didn't know we could do it. Those machines had been kept going as long as we could remember. When we finally pulled the switch and there was some quiet, I finally remembered something . . . that I was a human being, that I could stop those machines. . . . 99

The sit-down strike was not originated by the autoworkers, nor was it unique to them. The radical International Workers of the World first used the technique against General Electric in 1906. But in the late 1930s factory workers, taxi drivers, maids, secretaries, and salesclerks sat down at their jobs to protest their pay and working conditions.

Union success in the auto, steel, and other industries swelled the ranks of organized labor during the Second New Deal. The CIO grew especially rapidly because it was willing to organize women workers, whom the AFL had ignored. From less than 3 million in 1933, union membership more than tripled by 1939. Organized labor showed its appreciation for the Wagner Act and other New Deal programs by giving political support to the Democrats.

■ The 1936 Election

The Democrats renominated Roosevelt for President in 1936, and they enthusiastically endorsed the New Deal. The business community, however, contributed to his 1936 campaign only about one-fifth as much as it contributed in 1932, and many newspapers turned against FDR. The Republican nominee, Kansas governor Alfred M. Landon, denounced Roosevelt for endangering the "American system of free enterprise." He labeled Social Security as "unjust, unworkable, stupidly drafted, and wastefully financed," and attacked many other New Deal programs.

Four years of New Deal programs, however, had forged a new political coalition for the Democrats. Farmers, labor unions, retirees, and many ethnic groups supported Roosevelt and his programs. African American voters abandoned an allegiance to the Republican party that dated back to Reconstruction to support the party of Roosevelt. FDR's New Deal had not offered special programs for African Americans, but it had not tried to exclude them either. African American workers, who often were the first fired when hard times hit, owed much to New Deal relief programs, and they showed their gratitude at the polls. On Election Day, Roosevelt won in a landslide, and Democrats elected huge majorities to the House and Senate.

■ The New Deal and the Supreme Court

Before he could continue the New Deal in his second term, Roosevelt believed he had to eliminate opposition on the Supreme Court. During 1935 and 1936 the Court struck down New Deal programs, including the NIRA and AAA. Never before had the Court declared so much legislation unconstitutional. Roosevelt and his supporters believed that "9 old men" on the Court, 7 of whom had been appointed by Republican Presidents, were interfering with the New Deal's attempts at recovery. Laws that helped millions of people,

★★★★★★★★★★★★★★★

Government and the Farmer

When their problems became widespread, farmers joined cooperatives and turned to the government for help. In farm crises before the 1930s, the federal government always left competition and the free enterprise system intact among farm businesses.

Then

New Deal Policies

The Great Depression of the 1930s, however, triggered actions that altered the face of agriculture. Farmers, long thought of as free and independent, became largely dependent on government assistance. The Agricultural Adjustment Act of 1933, for example, offered farmers payments to reduce production.

Now

Supports and Controls

The period since World War II has seen almost continuous battles over how much government control should be exercised over farm production. The farmers' own efficiency sometimes works against the government's solution. When production is slowed by one method, such as limiting acreage planted, farmers turn to technology to pull ahead again. They improve their farming meth-

▲ WHEAT HARVESTING TODAY

ods to make those fewer acres yield more than before.

Nor have price supports, another New Deal remnant, been the answer. Under this program, if market prices for certain crops fall below a guaranteed price, the government buys them. An immensely expensive program, it reaches few small farmers. Government efforts to preserve the independent farmers continue. But with each farm crisis, large agribusinesses gradually replace smaller farms.

◀ FARMING IN VIRGINIA, 1930S

★★★★★★★★★★★★★★★★★★★★★★★★★★★★★★★★★★★★

passed by large majorities in Congress, were being rejected by the Court, often by margins of 5 to 4.

Roosevelt considered his landslide reelection to be a mandate to curb the Supreme Court. In February 1937 the President presented legislation allowing him to appoint an additional justice to the Supreme Court for each justice over 70 years of age. Although the Court's size would increase from 9 to 15, Roosevelt argued that it needed "an infusion of younger blood." The "court-packing" bill caused a furor even in the President's own party. Many Americans were alarmed by the threat it posed to the system of checks and balances. Enough Democrats joined the Republicans in Congress to defeat Roosevelt's proposal. Although he suffered a major setback and lost many supporters, the President claimed that he had "lost the battle but won the war." While debate on the "court-packing" bill raged in Congress, in

two 5-to-4 decisions, the Court upheld the constitutionality of the two major laws of the Second New Deal—the Social Security Act and the Wagner Act.

■ Later New Deal Measures

By 1937 the economy had recovered nearly to 1929 levels, although widespread unemployment still remained. Roosevelt's financial advisers urged a cutback in spending and a balanced federal budget. Federal Reserve banks tightened credit, and the WPA cut the number of its employees in half.

The economy quickly slumped into a **recession,** a mild downturn in the business cycle, that critics called a "Roosevelt Depression." Huge crop surpluses collapsed agricultural prices, and industrial production dropped by one-third, almost to 1932 levels.

The President blamed the slump on businesses that, he claimed, failed to reinvest profits in production and on monopolies that kept prices artificially high. To meet the economic crisis, the President again expanded the work-relief programs of the WPA and stepped up military spending. People went back to work and prices rose. But the recession proved that hard times were not yet over.

In 1938 Congress passed a number of New Deal measures that carried out earlier policies. A Fair Labor Standards Act abolished child labor and placed a ceiling on hours and a floor under wages, at least for workers in businesses classified as "interstate commerce." A new Farm Security Administration promoted the well-being of impoverished farmers. A new AAA attempted to cope with surpluses by paying farmers not only to produce less but also to improve the soil and to control erosion. In addition, a food-stamp plan helped to distribute farm surpluses among those on relief.

These were some of the last New Deal programs. In the fall of 1937, when Roosevelt called a special session of Congress, not one of his proposals was enacted. Both in 1937 and in 1938 Congress rejected the President's request to reorganize the executive branch. These defeats were largely the result of a coalition of Republicans and conservative Southern Democrats who increasingly opposed the President in Congress. Roosevelt tried to weaken this coalition by supporting liberal Democrats against incumbents in the 1938 primary.

Visualizing History

▲ **PACKING THE COURT** Although Roosevelt was overwhelmingly reelected in 1936, most people reacted negatively in 1937 to his attempt to pack the Supreme Court. *In this cartoon, what does the donkey's reaction symbolize?*

Roosevelt's attempted "purge" of his own party ended in defeat. In most cases, the conservative Democrats won. In the November election the Republicans staged a modest comeback, picking up seats in both houses of Congress. The coalition of Republicans and Southern Democrats was growing powerful and could block further extension of the New Deal.

Roosevelt accepted the judgment of the voters in the 1938 election. In January 1939 he announced that he would propose no further New Deal programs. Instead, he turned his attention to the growing threat of war in Europe.

Section 3 ★ Assessment

Checking for Understanding

1. **Define** coalition, craft union, industrial union, recession.

2. **Explain** the steps in Dr. Townsend's recovery plan.

Critical Thinking

3. **Contrasting Ideas** How did the second New Deal differ from the first in its objectives, support base, program focus, and success?

4. **Summarizing** Re-create the diagram shown here, and list what steps the Second New Deal took to achieve reform.

step

step

step

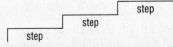
INTERDISCIPLINARY ACTIVITY

5. **Government** Draw a cartoon depicting opponents Huey Long and Franklin Roosevelt or labor unions and the New Deal.

BUILDING SKILLS
Critical Thinking Skills

Predicting Consequences

Consequences are the effects and repercussions that result from a decision or action. With a little forethought you can anticipate possible consequences.

Learning the Skill

To help predict consequences you can:

- **Restate** the action or decision under consideration.

- **Link** the action with relevant prior circumstances.

- **Map** out all possible outcomes or consequences.

- **Analyze** the possibilities. Are some consequences more likely to occur than others?

The American labor movement worked toward improving economic conditions and employment opportunities long before Roosevelt's New Deal. But the progress of the labor movement was impacted, either negatively or positively, by the actions and decisions of employers, Congress, and the courts.

Read each of the items described below. Predict what might have happened to the American labor movement if these events had *not* occurred.

- Court interpretation of the Sherman Antitrust Act of 1890 finds that union strikes are "in restraint of trade or commerce."

- Clayton Act of 1914 holds that the courts cannot stop peaceful strikes, pickets, or boycotts.

- Fair Labor Standards Act of 1938 outlaws child labor and limits workday hours.

- Taft-Hartley Act of 1947 halts strikes that might endanger national health and safety.

Practicing the Skill

1. Predict the effect of the Clayton Act on a local factory owner whose workers are on strike.

2. Predict the effect of the Fair Labor Standards Act on a family's financial situation.

3. Predict the effect of the Taft-Hartley Act on police and firefighters.

 Glencoe's **Skillbuilder Interactive Workbook, Level 2** provides instruction and practice in key social studies skills.

APPLYING THE SKILL

4. On a sheet of paper, paste a copy of a current newspaper article that discusses a public policy. Predict one or more consequences that may occur from the policy. On what basis did you make your predictions? How confident are you of your predictions?

566

The Impact of the New Deal

★★★

Guide to Reading

Main Idea
The New Deal had a great impact on American society and government.

Reading Strategy

Organizing Information As you read about the impact of the New Deal, use a chart like the one shown here to show how the New Deal changed American society.

Groups	Effect of New Deal
Artists	
Farmers	
Industrial Workers	
Elderly, Poor	

Objectives

After studying this section, you should be able to

★ identify changes that the New Deal caused in American society.

★ evaluate the effects of the New Deal on life today.

Key Term

ethnic group

► **WPA POSTER, 1940**

Sociologists Robert and Helen Lynd in 1929 published a study of values, behaviors, and everyday life in the 1920s in a typical American city that they called "Middletown." (It was actually Muncie, Indiana.) In 1935 they returned to "Middletown" for a follow-up study and found that the Depression and the New Deal had profoundly affected the families living in that community.

■ The New Deal and Society

The Depression affected every part of society. Its impact was felt at home and at work. The New Deal brought relief for some, but problems remained. In 1937 President Roosevelt said, "I see one-third of a nation ill-housed, ill-clad, ill-nourished."

Adapting to the Depression at Home

During the Depression, both births and divorces decreased as people could not afford either event. Older people moved in with working relatives. Many families rented rooms to boarders or moved to smaller and less expensive homes. Housewives took in laundry and sewing to help support their families. Sales of prepared food declined, and many people canned foods at home.

Changes at Work

Competition among adults for jobs resulted in stronger child labor laws, and the number of working children declined during the 1930s. Consequently, the number of high school and college students rose.

In Middletown, the Lynds noted that when a man lost his job and could not find

Visualizing History ▲ A. PHILIP RANDOLPH As a young man, A. Philip Randolph quickly became aware of the discrimination African Americans faced in employment. He became a leader in the labor movement. *What civil rights measures were enacted during the New Deal?*

another, traditional family roles often were reversed, "with the woman taking a job for whatever money she could earn and the man caring for the household." Still, women were accused of taking men's jobs, and businesses often refused to hire married women.

Most women who worked outside the home, with the exception of farm and domestic workers, benefited from the New Deal. Women's wages rose and working conditions improved. The greatest direct assistance to women came from the Women's Division of the WPA. It employed between 300,000 and 400,000 women, some in traditionally female white-collar jobs such as teacher, nurse, and librarian. But most worked on canning and sewing projects. Their pay was low, but it often made the difference between food and famine.

■ Minorities

African Americans did not fare well under the New Deal. In addition, the government failed to enact any major civil rights measures during this period.

African Americans Get Mainly the Same Old Deal

As the poorest of the poor, African Americans often fell through the cracks of broad legislation such as the AAA and the Social Security Act. For example, although the AAA gave money to rural landowners, in the South 80 percent of all African American farmers owned no land. In addition, Roosevelt offered no civil rights program and did little to challenge the segregation that continued to exist throughout the nation, and he tolerated job discrimination. Even some government agencies refused to hire African Americans. Those that did, such as the CCC and armed forces, segregated African Americans and whites. In addition, African Americans received lower wages than white workers and were not assigned to certain jobs.

Nevertheless, Roosevelt appointed more African Americans to government posts than any President before him. Although most African American officials filled secondary posts, they influenced the President as an unofficial "black cabinet." Heading the cabinet was Mary McLeod Bethune, director of the Negro Affairs Division of the National Youth Administration. A personal friend of Eleanor Roosevelt, she often expressed the cabinet's concerns to the First Lady, who then carried them to FDR.

One concern of African Americans during the Depression was an increase in lynching and other acts of mob violence against them. Roosevelt supported a 1934 federal antilynching bill that held local sheriffs accountable for the frequent lynchings of African Americans in the South. But he never made the bill a legislative priority, and it finally died in the Senate in 1938.

One reason New Deal programs for African Americans were so limited was the opposition of powerful congressional committee heads who were from the South. As a result Roosevelt accepted NRA codes, for example, that permitted a lower minimum wage in the South than in the rest of the nation. FDR felt that if he pushed these Southern legislators too strongly, he would lose their support.

White Ethnic Groups Do Well

In general, the federal government responded more favorably to white **ethnic groups,** groups of people who shared the same culture, religion, and customs. During the 1930s the federal Office of Education sponsored a radio series called "Americans All . . . Immigrants All." The show celebrated the cultural vitality of a democracy made up of people from many lands. It also indicated the Democrats' awareness of the political power that ethnic groups could exercise if they were organized. Immigrants and their children made up 40 percent of the white population at that time. They tended to vote in groups and could swing elections, especially in large urban areas. Americans of Irish, Italian, and Polish descent became major partners in the New Deal coalition.

■ Popular Culture

The 1930s were somber years compared to the fads and frivolity of the 1920s. Literature and the arts generally turned to more realistic themes about poverty and human suffering.

Literature

Grim times provided powerful themes for American authors such as John Dos Passos, whose trilogy of novels called *U.S.A.* focused on fictional characters who lost their ideals and became hardened by society. Perhaps the most powerful novel of the era was John Steinbeck's *Grapes of Wrath,* the story of a family who left their Oklahoma farm in the dust bowl and headed to the migrant labor camps of California.

There was also much escapism in popular culture, as people turned to entertainment when things became grim. The best-selling book of the decade was Margaret Mitchell's *Gone With the Wind.* Although set in the South during the Civil War and Reconstruction, it offered a hopeful account of Scarlett

▲ AT THE MOVIES The decade of the 1930s was a golden era for motion pictures. Popular fare included the Fred Astaire and Ginger Rogers musicals and Disney favorites such as *Snow White and the Seven Dwarfs.* **How many Americans attended the movies every week?**

▲ **MASS ENTERTAINMENT** Clark Gable and Vivien Leigh starred in the movie of the 1930s best-selling novel, *Gone With the Wind.* The film was a big hit because people got nearly 4 hours of entertainment for just 10 to 25 cents. *What other mass entertainment medium was popular in the 1930s?*

O'Hara's efforts to rebuild her life and had much meaning for readers who had gone through the 1929 crash and the Depression.

Entertainment

As "talkies"—films with sound—became common during the 1930s, about 85 million people escaped the realities of the Depression for a few hours each week at the movie theater. There they watched movies that were often about the lives of happy and successful people. Continued improvements in sound technology ushered in the era of musicals, and audiences delighted at the dance routines of Fred Astaire and Ginger Rogers. Cartoon characters, such as Mickey Mouse, made audiences laugh, and as color-film technology spread, full-length animated features like Walt Disney's *Snow White and the Seven Dwarfs* provided more fantasy and escape.

Footnotes to History

The 40-Hour Workweek During the 1930s, more leisure time was available, partly because working hours were reduced. The 40-hour week became standard. With the growth of unions, NRA codes and, finally, the Fair Labor Standards Act, the shorter work-week remained.

At home families could listen to network radio programs broadcast coast-to-coast. Daytime radio offered "soap operas," where characters suffered through daily crises. At night comedy, adventure, and musical variety programs dominated the airwaves. And the performances of Arturo Toscanini conducting the NBC Symphony of the Air brought classical music for the first time to millions of radio listeners.

The Automobile

Just as books, movies, and the radio provided Americans with an emotional outlet from the realities of the Depression, the automobile made them feel that they could physically escape their problems. Americans' love affair with cars, which began during the prosperity of the 1920s, continued throughout the poverty-stricken 1930s. The number of automobiles increased from 26 million in 1933 to 32 million by 1940. During the depths of the Depression, almost half the families in the United States owned a car, even though many could not afford to buy gasoline.

Yet despite the expense, many Americans continued to drive their cars during the 1930s. By late in the decade, thanks to government work projects, a maze of paved highways crisscrossed the nation. Large numbers of people took off down these two-lane roads, some searching for employment and others pioneering what became an American institution—the family vacation by car.

The Influence of the New Deal

In the arts, as in so many other areas of society, the New Deal played a role. The WPA helped unemployed actors, artists, writers, and musicians. The Federal Theatre Project sponsored performances of Shakespeare as well as children's plays. Some 6,500 writers put together state and regional guidebooks and recorded life stories of formerly enslaved people, immigrants, and Native Americans.

The Federal Arts Project had artists paint murals and sculptors create statues, many of which still can be viewed today. The artistic works of William Gropper, Peter Blume, and Jack Levine reflected social concerns. Photographers like Dorothea Lange and artists like Ben Shahn documented people's lives during the Depression. Arts projects were among the most controversial New Deal programs, however. Critics called them socialistic. In 1939 Congress cut off funds for the theater project, and the other arts programs were discontinued as employment rose during World War II.

To many people who lived through it, the New Deal seemed to have changed American society. Yet it was not the revolutionary assault on capitalism that some of its critics charged. The New Deal changed the lives of farmers through crop subsidies and rural electrification. It changed the lives of indus-

▲ COMIC STRIP HERO LITTLE ORPHAN ANNIE

trial workers by strengthening labor unions and expanding collective bargaining. It provided Social Security and welfare programs for the aged, the unemployed, and dependent children. In so doing, it turned a government that previously had responded more to business groups into a government open to labor, farmers, and other interests.

Yet the New Deal did not adopt national planning of the economy, as some of Roosevelt's advisers had expected. Rather than government owning industry, the New Deal emphasized federal regulation of private enterprise. Rather than overturning capitalism, New Dealers believed that they had helped to save it.

Section 4 ★ Assessment

Checking for Understanding

1. **Define** ethnic group.
2. **Discuss** popular forms of entertainment in the 1930s.

Critical Thinking

3. **Seeing Relationships** Analyze how the Depression influenced art and literature.
4. **Analyzing Issues** Re-create the diagram shown here, and list what impact the New

Deal had on African Americans.

Impact on African Americans

INTERDISCIPLINARY ACTIVITY

5. **Government** Research the effect of the New Deal in your community. Find out if the federal government supported any local projects in conservation, construction, or the arts.

▲ JOHN STEINBECK

In *The Grapes of Wrath*, John Steinbeck chronicles the hardships of the Joads, an Oklahoma farm family whose plight resembles that of the downtrodden everywhere. As you read the excerpt from Steinbeck's novel, look for statements that reveal the beliefs, concerns, and attitudes of tenant farmers during the 1930s.

Read to Discover

When the economy collapsed in 1929, millions of American lives collapsed with it. People everywhere lost their jobs. In the nation's Dust Bowl, farmers had to leave the land that their families had worked for generations.

Reader's Dictionary

auger	large tool for boring into the earth
tenant	one who holds or possesses land

The Grapes of Wrath (excerpts)

The owners of the land came onto the land, or more often a spokesman for the owners came. They came in closed cars, and they felt the dry earth with their fingers, and sometimes they drove big earth augers into the ground for soil tests. The tenants, from their sunbeaten dooryards, watched uneasily when the closed cars drove along the fields. And at last the owner men drove into the dooryards and sat in their cars to talk out of the windows. . . .

If a bank or a finance company owned the land, the owner man said, The Bank—or the Company—needs-wants-insists-must have-as though the Bank or the Company were a monster, with thought and feeling, which had ensnared them. . . . The owner men sat in the cars and explained. You know the land is poor. You've scrabbled at it long enough, God knows. . . .

The owner men went on leading to their point: You know the land's getting poorer. You know what cotton does to the land; robs it, sucks all the blood out of it.

The squatters nodded—they knew, God knew. If they could only rotate the crops they might pump blood back into the land. Well, it's too late. And the owner men explained the workings and the thinkings of the monster that was stronger than they were. . . .

The squatting men raised their eyes to understand. Can't we just hang on? Maybe the next year will be a good year. God knows how much cotton next year. And with all the wars—God knows what price cotton will bring. Don't they make explosives out of cotton? And uniforms? Get enough wars and cotton'll hit the ceiling. Next year, maybe. They looked up questioningly.

We can't depend on it. The bank—the monster has to have profits all the time. It can't wait. It'll die. . . .

The squatting men looked down again. What do you want us to do? We can't take less share of the crop—we're half starved now. The kids are hungry all the time. We got no clothes, torn an' ragged. If all the neighbors weren't the same, we'd be ashamed to go to meeting.

And at last the owner men came to the point. The tenant system won't work any more. One man on a tractor can take the place of twelve or fourteen families. Pay him a wage and take all the crop. We have to do it. We don't like to do it. But the monster's sick. Something's happened to the monster.

But you'll kill the land with cotton. We know. We've got to take cotton quick before the land dies. Then we'll sell the land. Lots of families in the East would like to own a piece of land.

The tenant men looked up alarmed. But what'll happen to us? How'll we eat?

You'll have to get off the land. The plows'll go through the dooryard. . . .

It's not us, it's the bank. A bank isn't like a man. Or an owner with fifty thousand acres, he isn't like a man either. That's the monster.

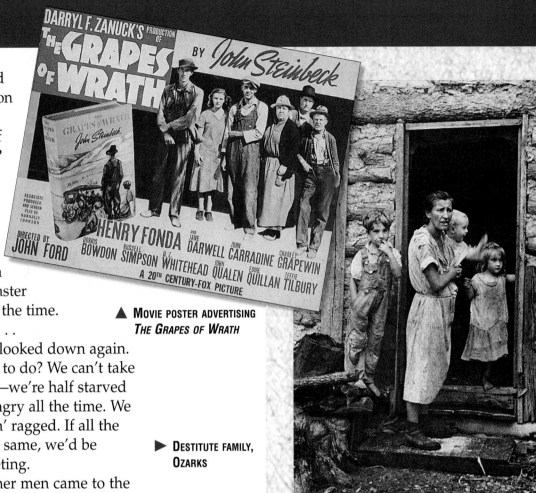

▲ MOVIE POSTER ADVERTISING *THE GRAPES OF WRATH*

▶ DESTITUTE FAMILY, OZARKS

Responding to Literature

1. Locate passages where the tenant men are beseeching or protesting.

2. What is the "monster"? Do you think this is an apt metaphor? Why or why not?

3. Steinbeck clearly sides with the tenant farmers. What arguments could be made for the banks and the owners? Which viewpoint do you favor?

ACTIVITY

4. Write a dialogue in which a parent explains to a son or daughter why they must move from their home in the Dust Bowl.

HISTORY Online

Self-Check Quiz

Visit the *American History: The Modern Era Since 1865* Web site at **me.glencoe.com** and click on *Chapter 18—Self-Check Quizzes* to prepare for the chapter test.

Using Vocabulary

Write sentences about Roosevelt's New Deal using these vocabulary words.

deficit spending   foreclosure

dole   recession

pump priming

Reviewing Facts

1. **Explain** the purpose of the bank holiday in the first Hundred Days.

2. **Compare** the purposes of New Deal legislation before and after 1935.

3. **Cite** the means Roosevelt used to advocate, promote, and gain public support for his New Deal programs.

4. **Describe** Roosevelt's attempts to help farmers.

5. **Specify** groups that did not fully share in the benefits of the New Deal.

6. **Explain** the lasting effects that came from the New Deal policy.

Understanding Concepts

Economic Reform

1. Re-create the diagram shown here, and cite specific New Deal programs that provided help to the needy groups listed here.

```
                    New Deal
        ┌───────────┬───────────┬───────────┐
     Farmers     Workers   Unemployed  Unemployable
        │           │           │           │
    Programs    Programs    Programs    Programs
```

Political Leadership

2. One mark of a good leader is the ability to choose and utilize able administrators. Explain to what extent this was true of Franklin Roosevelt.

Critical Thinking

1. **Finding Explanations** Though farmers received substantial assistance during the New Deal and have since, many farmers have continued to suffer economically. What problems inherent in farming could possibly account for this recurring difficulty?

2. **Analyzing Statistics** Use the table on this page and information from the chapter to help you answer these questions.

   a. What is the subject of the table? How many years does the information presented in the table cover?

The Federal Budget and Deficit

	Federal Receipts (in billions of dollars)	Federal Deficit (in billions of dollars)	Gross Federal Debt (in billions of dollars)	Per Capita Federal Debt (total dollar amt.)
1940	6.9	–2.7	43.0	325
1939	6.6	–2.9	40.4	309
1938	7.0	–.1	37.2	286
1937	5.6	–2.8	36.4	283
1936	4.2	–3.5	33.8	264
1935	3.8	–2.4	28.7	226
1934	3.1	–3.3	27.1	214
1933	2.1	–2.6	22.5	179
1932	2.0	–2.7	19.5	156

Source: *Historical Statistics of the United States: Colonial Times to 1970* (1975).

   b. What year was the federal deficit at its highest level? What was happening in the United States at that time?

   c. During the time period shown, did the government ever spend less than it received?

d. If the federal deficit decreased in 1940, why didn't the federal debt also decrease?

3. Understanding Cause and Effect Why do you suppose Roosevelt abandoned his efforts to enlist the support of the business community for the New Deal reforms that he launched during his second term as President?

4. Demonstrating Reasoned Judgment Assume the nation has entered a depression today. As a member of Congress devoted to economic reform, write an argument proposing and supporting deficit spending to stimulate the economy and to finance expanded government assistance programs. Think carefully about the reasons why some of your constituents would favor such policies and why others would oppose them.

History and Geography

The Effects of the Great Depression

1. Place How did the problems of urban people compare with those in agricultural areas?

2. Region What problems faced residents of the Dust Bowl?

3. Human/Environment Interaction Could the problems of the Dust Bowl have been prevented? If so, how? If not, why?

Cooperative Learning **Interdisciplinary Activity: Debate**

Working in a group of three, assume roles of government officials during Roosevelt's term. One member should assume the role of a Roosevelt supporter in Congress and present an argument to Congress for enlarging the Supreme Court. The second member should assume the role of an anti-Roosevelt senator and address Congress, refuting the need to enlarge the Court. The third member will listen to both arguments and decide which is the more effective. All group members should then be prepared to argue either position before the class.

Practicing Skills

Predicting Consequences

Review the skill on predicting consequences on page 566. Then read the following statements and predict consequences for each.

1. Engineers develop an effective, efficient electric-powered automobile.

2. The laws are changed to provide for the direct election of the Supreme Court.

3. You decide to work in a field that does not appeal to you but that will provide financial security.

Technology Activity

Using a Word Processor

Use the Internet and other library resources to find information about the current Social Security Administration and its activities. Write a brief report detailing the benefits and services that this organization provides Americans today.

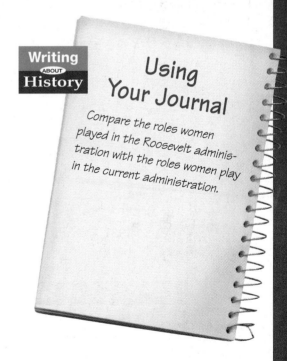

Writing ABOUT History

Using Your Journal

Compare the roles women played in the Roosevelt administration with the roles women play in the current administration.

CHAPTER 19

★★

World War II
1933–1945

► **SILVER STAR, AWARDED
FOR GALLANTRY IN ACTION**

Setting the Scene

Focus

The Depression of the 1930s was worldwide. When a new war engulfed Europe, Roosevelt sought to aid the British. After Japan attacked Pearl Harbor in 1941, America entered the war directly. Initially, Allied prospects were bleak, but by 1944 the tide had turned. Victory in the Pacific, however, came only after the use of nuclear weapons.

Concepts to Understand

★ Why **international alliances** were formed between Germany, Italy, and Japan

★ How the Allies prevented Germany and Italy from winning the **military conflict** in Europe

Read to Discover . . .

★ what events led the American people to abandon isolationism and neutrality.

★ why Roosevelt was more successful than Wilson in helping to form a world peacekeeping body.

Journal Notes

Consider the interests, fears, and concerns of the nations involved in World War II. Record examples in your journal as you read the chapter.

Chapter Overview
Visit the *American History: The Modern Era Since 1865* Web site at **me.glencoe.com** and click on **Chapter 19—Chapter Overviews** to preview chapter information.

CULTURAL

● **1931** *Pearl Buck publishes* The Good Earth

● **1936** *Babe Ruth and Ty Cobb named to baseball's Hall of Fame*

| 1930 | 1935 |

● **1933** *United States recognizes the government of the Soviet Union*

POLITICAL

● **1939** *Germany attacks Poland; war in Europe begins*

The Landing at Bougainville
by William Franklin Draper

The artist depicts the November 1943 landing at Bougainville, in the Northern Solomons. The battle was part of the U.S. South Pacific offensive that cracked the Japanese defense perimeter.

◀ TANK BOOTS, 1943

- **1940** *Color television is demonstrated by the Columbia Broadcasting System*
- **1942** *Sugar and gasoline are rationed*

- **1945** *Tennessee Williams's play* The Glass Menagerie *opens in New York*

1940	1945

- **1940** *Selective Service Act passed*
- **1941** *Japanese attack Pearl Harbor*

- **1944** *Allies invade Normandy*
- **1945** *Nuclear weapons first used*

★★★

World Affairs, 1933–1939

Guide to Reading

Main Idea

As the United States worked to pull itself out of the Great Depression, Europe again moved toward war.

Reading Strategy

Organizing Information As you read about events overseas during the 1930s, use the diagram shown here to list the characteristics of America's Depression-era foreign policy.

> New Deal Foreign Policy

Objectives

After studying this section, you should be able to

★ discuss how the Depression influenced American foreign policy.

★ explain the reasons for Japan's aggression in Asia.

Key Terms

fascism, totalitarian, appeasement

► **MILITARY ALUMINUM CANTEEN**

*L*ike his distant cousin Theodore, Franklin D. Roosevelt was acquainted with the world beyond the shores of the United States. He had made more than a dozen trips to Europe, and he had firsthand knowledge of the Caribbean area. Through family connections with the China trade, he had acquired an interest in Asia. He resembled Theodore Roosevelt, too, in realizing that as a world power the United States had a commitment to help preserve the peace of the world. As a former associate of Woodrow Wilson, he believed in world organization to promote international cooperation and to solve disputes.

For most of his first two terms, however, Franklin D. Roosevelt focused on domestic affairs. Events in Europe and Asia seemed distant when compared to the crisis of the Depression. In addition, the President rec-ognized that Americans, pressed by hard times at home, cared little about the world at large. So although Roosevelt believed that German expansion posed a threat to the United States, he was cautious in his efforts to alert the nation to this danger. Only when dealing with affairs in the Western Hemisphere did Roosevelt act with his typical bold political style.

■ New Deal Foreign Policy

At his first inaugural in 1933, President Roosevelt pledged that the United States would be a "good neighbor" in the family of nations. He pledged to respect the sovereign rights of all nations in the Western Hemisphere. A few weeks later, he applied the phrase "Good Neighbor" specifically to the administration's Latin American policy.

Peaceful Intentions in Latin America

President Roosevelt and Secretary of State Cordell Hull worked to improve relations with the United States's southern neighbors. Later that year, at the Pan-American Conference at Montevideo, Uruguay, the United States agreed to a resolution that "no state has the right to intervene in the internal affairs of another." Roosevelt demonstrated his commitment to the Good Neighbor policy by recalling American troops from Haiti and Nicaragua, where they had been protecting American property since the 1920s. When Cuba erupted in revolution in 1933, Roosevelt used diplomacy, not troops, to help restore order. When Mexico seized American-owned oil companies in 1938, Roosevelt resisted demands for military action and sought a peaceful settlement.

Domestic Recovery Determines Foreign Decisions

During Roosevelt's first years in office, the United States seemed less inclined to cooperate with Europe. The New Deal adopted a policy of economic isolation, and its recovery programs included attempts to solve agricultural and industrial production problems without considering the rest of the world. In 1933 delegates from more than 60 nations met in London to bring about cooperation in confronting world depression. Roosevelt wrecked the conference by rejecting proposals to peg the value of the dollar to any other currency. He feared that such a move would hurt his efforts to raise American farm prices.

Only when the United States had achieved some recovery from the Depression was the President willing to consider economic cooperation with other nations. Secretary of State Hull believed world prosperity and goodwill could be gained by reducing tariffs. At Hull's urging, Congress passed the Reciprocal Trade Agreements Act of 1934, allowing the State Department to make treaties with other countries to mutually lower import duties. Within six years, the United States had reached such agreements with more than a dozen nations.

Recognition of the Soviet Union

Another change in foreign policy took place when the United States recognized the government of the Soviet Union. Since the Bolshevik Revolution of 1917, the United States had refused to recognize the communist government. After their revolution, the Soviets tried to encourage communism throughout the world. By 1933, however, the USSR was beset by serious economic problems at home and seemed less of a threat. Much more threatening was the rising power of Japan, the Soviets' rival in Asia. The President hoped that a strong Soviet Union could slow Japanese expansion. In addition, Roosevelt saw the Soviets' need for food and industrial equipment as a market for American farmers and manufacturers. "The United States would probably

Visualizing History ▲ **JAPANESE EXPANSION** Japanese forces first moved into Manchuria in 1931. Japan established the puppet state of Manchukuo a year later. ***How did Roosevelt hope to slow Japan's aggression in Asia?***

▲ MUSSOLINI Italy's dictator Benito Mussolini gives the Fascist salute during an address. After Italy surrendered to Allied forces, Mussolini was captured and executed by the Italian people. *What plans did Mussolini have in common with Adolf Hitler?*

recognize the Devil," Will Rogers joked, "if it could sell him pitchforks." Recognition of the Soviet Union helped improve relations but did little to increase trade or to check Japanese militarism.

Aggression and Appeasement

American hopes to concentrate on domestic affairs, relatively isolated from foreign concerns, were quickly dashed. Events in the world began to send off alarms of trouble ahead.

Japanese Expansion in the Pacific

Between 1872 and 1925, Japan's population nearly doubled, causing severe problems for that small island nation. To sustain industrial growth, Japan needed larger markets for its products and more raw materials for its factories. To meet these needs and to ease overcrowding in the home islands, Japan pursued a policy of expansion in the Pacific.

During World War I, Japan supported the Allies but used the war to increase its influence in China. After the war Japan was bitter toward the West. The Washington Conference of 1921 cost Japan most of its gains in China and limited Japan's naval power. When the United States joined other Western nations in 1924 in banning immigrants from Japan, its leaders looked to military solutions for their nation's problems.

In September 1931, Japanese troops invaded and occupied mineral-rich Manchuria in northeastern China. When the League of Nations demanded that Manchuria be returned to China, Japan ignored the order.

Threats From Germany and Italy

On March 5, 1933, the day after Roosevelt took office, the German parliament voted Adolf Hitler, the National Socialist (Nazi) leader, the power he needed to begin a program of conquest in central and eastern Europe. In Italy, dictator Benito Mussolini made similar plans to control the Mediterranean and to expand Italy's empire in Africa.

Mussolini and Hitler followed a new political doctrine known as **fascism** (FASH•ihz•uhm), a form of government in which a dictator and supporters cooperate to seek more power for their nation, usually at the expense of rights for individuals. Each ruler established a **totalitarian** state—a nation that totally controls the life of its people. The Fascists in Italy and the Nazis in Germany set up all-powerful official parties. Both whipped up support with huge patriotic rallies, parades, music, and appeals to national pride and racial hatred, and both used force to silence all opposition.

Each dictator blamed his country's problems after World War I on undesirables in society. Mussolini accused Italy's Communists of causing strikes and social unrest.

The Nazis blamed Germany's economic chaos on its Jewish population. They restricted Jews, boycotted Jewish-owned stores, and destroyed synagogues. Both Hitler and Mussolini hinted that another war might be necessary to right the wrongs they felt had been done to their countries by the Treaty of Versailles.

The glorification of war by Italy, Germany, and Japan was not idle talk. In 1935 Mussolini attacked and took control of Ethiopia in Africa. In 1937 Japanese armies invaded the rest of China. In March 1938 Hitler marched into Austria. In 1936 General Francisco Franco rebelled against the republican government of Spain, and German and Italian tanks, bombers, and troops helped Franco win a bitter civil war that lasted until 1939.

Bargaining for Peace

The response of Great Britain and France was **appeasement**, a policy of giving aggressor nations what they wanted in order to avoid war. Like the Americans, the British and French were disillusioned by World War I and wanted peace. Much as they disliked Italian, German, or Japanese expansion, they disliked the thought of war

Visualizing History | **GERMANY UNDER HITLER** In 1935 Adolf Hitler announced that he intended to ignore the Versailles treaty and began to rearm Germany. In 1936 his army reoccupied the Rhineland on Germany's border with France. *How did Great Britain and France respond when Hitler began to act aggressively in Europe?*

even more. Pacifism reached new heights: a majority of the students in the debating union at Britain's Oxford University voted that on no account would they go to war for king or country. Appeasement reached its peak at the Munich Conference of September 1938 when British and French leaders allowed Hitler to annex part of Czechoslovakia in return for his promise to make no further territorial demands. British Prime Minister Neville Chamberlain returned from Germany to tell a jittery world that the Munich Pact meant "peace for our time." Winston Churchill, however, who soon would replace Chamberlain as prime minister, observed that "Britain and France had to choose between war and dishonor. They chose dishonor. They will have war."

Neutrality

The American people were also determined to avoid war. World War I had left the United States with a huge domestic debt and billions of dollars in foreign debts that could not be collected. Americans also wanted to avoid war for a number of other reasons. A congressional investigation of the munitions industry revealed that American manufacturers had made large profits by supplying arms and credit to the Allies during the years 1914–1917. This led to the notion that American participation in World War I had been arranged by "merchants of death," assisted by British propagandists. There was increasing feeling that William Jennings Bryan had been correct in 1914 in urging that the United States supply no arms to the belligerents,

make them no loans, and abandon defense of neutral rights on the high seas. To prevent being drawn into war again, Congress passed Neutrality Acts in 1935, 1936, and 1937. These laws barred the transportation or sale of arms to warring nations and banned loans to nations at war outside the Western Hemisphere.

The restrictions of the Neutrality Acts did not please Roosevelt who believed they would "drag us into the war instead of keeping us out." He had wanted legislation that would allow him more discretion—for example, to embargo supplies on one side but not to the other. On October 5, 1937, he warned the American people that war was contagious:

66 *Innocent people are being cruelly sacrificed to a greed for power and supremacy. . . . Let no one imagine that America will escape. . . . War is contagion, whether it be declared or not.* 99

Roosevelt signed the Neutrality Acts without protest. However, he would have preferred some freedom to distinguish between aggressors and victims. The President believed that Germany, Italy, and Japan were "bad neighbors" who were bent on war. In a speech in October 1937, Roosevelt called for the abandonment of isolation, but American public opinion forced him to drop any idea of collective action against aggressor nations. "It's a terrible thing," Roosevelt remarked, "to look over your shoulder when you're trying to lead—and find no one there."

Section 1 ★ Assessment

Checking for Understanding
1. **Define** fascism, totalitarian, appeasement.

Critical Thinking
2. **Evaluating Policy**   Should one country intervene militarily in the affairs of another to protect property owned by its citizens? Explain.

3. **Recognizing Causes**   Re-create the diagram shown here, and list Japan's objectives in its expansion in Asia.

Japan's Objectives

INTERDISCIPLINARY ACTIVITY
4. **Government** Create a time line depicting the main events that led to war.

★★★★★★★★★★★★★★★★★★★★★★★★★★★★★★★★★★★★★★★

Moving Closer to War

Guide to Reading

Main Idea

As Europe once again plunged into war, Americans debated whether the United States should become involved.

Reading Strategy

Organizing Information As you read about the start of World War II, use a diagram like the one shown here to list Germany's military conquests in the late 1930s and early 1940s.

Objectives

After studying this section, you should be able to

★ discuss Germany's military conquest of Europe during the late 1930s and early 1940s.

★ list the steps by which the Roosevelt administration increased American support to the Allies and the effects these steps had.

Key Terms

blitzkrieg, lend-lease

► **BRONZE STAR,** AWARDED FOR HEROISM

The most outspoken isolationists in Congress were progressive Republicans mainly from the Midwest and the West. Their primary support came from a number of newspapers, most notably those in the William Randolph Hearst chain. On the radio Roosevelt's New Deal critic, Father Charles Coughlin, also lined up with the isolationists. An America First Committee sponsored rallies around the country against the war. A frequent speaker was the popular pilot Charles Lindbergh who warned that "the only way our American life and ideals can be preserved is by staying out of this war." The internationalists were strongest in the Democratic party and generally represented states in the South and the Northeast. They looked to President Roosevelt for leadership.

■ Europe at War Again

As Churchill had predicted, the Munich agreement failed to appease Hitler, who in March 1939 swallowed up the rest of Czechoslovakia and demanded territory in Poland. Britain and France pledged to defend Poland from Hitler, and they asked the Soviet Union to join in an alliance to contain Germany. In August 1939, however, Soviet dictator Joseph Stalin signed a nonaggression pact with Germany. By removing the threat of war on two fronts, the pact cleared the way for Hitler to invade Poland. Hitler still doubted that Britain and France would resist him, however.

▲ **PURPLE HEART**

▲ THE FALL OF POLAND By the late 1930s, Hitler had rebuilt the German military force, and he was ready to embark upon a course of intimidation and conquest. German forces invaded Poland in September 1939. The conquest of Poland took little more than a month. *What point does the cartoon express?*

Outbreak of War

Before dawn on September 1, 1939, German forces crossed into Poland in an attack so fast and brutal that a new word was coined—**blitzkrieg,** meaning "lightning war." This time Britain and France decided to fight, and on September 3 they declared war on Germany.

President Roosevelt declared that the United States would remain neutral, but he added, "Even a neutral cannot be asked to close his mind or his conscience." Within weeks he asked Congress to lift the Neutrality Acts' arms embargo that prevented Britain and France from buying American weapons. Although Congress was flooded with telegrams urging it to "keep America out of the blood business," after weeks of debate, it agreed to sell arms to the Allies if they paid cash and carried the goods in their own ships.

Near Disaster at Dunkirk

After a lull in the fighting over the winter of 1939–1940, Hitler launched an invasion of Norway and Denmark. Next, the German armies swept into the Netherlands and Belgium, where for the first time they met resistance from British and French troops. In May 1940, German forces defeated the Allied army and drove it to the sea at the French town of Dunkirk on the Belgian border. Cut off from retreat by land, the army was saved when 300,000 British and French troops were evacuated across the English Channel in a heroic nine-day rescue effort aided by 600 private boats.

Battle of Britain

In June 1940, Italy invaded France and declared war on Great Britain. In response, President Roosevelt announced that, although the United States would not enter the war, it would extend as much aid as possible to the democracies. On June 22 France surrendered, and Britain faced the threat alone.

As the German air force bombed British airfields, factories, and cities to prepare the way for German armies to cross the English Channel, Britain found leadership in its new prime minister, Winston Churchill. Offering only "blood, toil, tears, and sweat," he pledged:

> 66 . . . we shall defend our island, whatever the cost may be. We shall fight on the beaches. We shall fight on the landing grounds. We shall fight on the fields and in the streets. We shall fight in the hills. We shall never surrender . . . until, in God's good time, the New World, with all its power and might, steps forth to the rescue and liberation of the Old. 99

■ America Abandons Neutrality

Prime Minister Churchill asked the United States for a loan of 50 destroyers to protect British shipping from German submarines. Recognizing that the isolationists in Congress would block approval of the loan, Roosevelt decided to act on his own. In September 1940, by executive order, he transferred 50 old World War I destroyers to Britain in return for the use of bases in Newfoundland and the Caribbean.

Meanwhile, for months London suffered bombing day and night by hundreds of German planes. The fighter pilots of the Royal

▶ WATCHING THE GERMAN ARMY ENTER PARIS

Visualizing History

▲ DUNKIRK As the trapped British and French armies awaited evacuation at Dunkirk, they were bombarded by German planes and artillery. The largest retreat in military history was accomplished by the British navy and private boats ranging from yachts to tugboats, all protected by the Royal Air Force. Huge amounts of equipment were left behind, but Britain's army was saved from total destruction. *What effect did the fall of France have on American foreign policy?*

Visualizing History

▲ **ARRESTING OPPONENTS** Hitler's secret police, the Gestapo, arrested Jews and other opponents of the government by the thousands. Many were sent to large prisons called concentration camps. Resistance by the imprisoned against Nazi atrocities took many forms, including trying to escape and rebelling against their captors. *How did Americans react to the fall of France and the threat to Britain?*

Air Force, however, kept the Germans from gaining control of the skies over Britain and forced Hitler to abandon his invasion plans. "Never in the field of human conflict," said Churchill, "was so much owed by so many to so few."

America Realizes Its Peril

The fall of France and the threat to Britain shook many Americans out of their belief that events outside the Western Hemisphere were none of their business. The possibility that Hitler and Mussolini might add the British and French fleets to their own made the Atlantic Ocean suddenly seem narrower, and Congress began to heed Roosevelt's warnings. It appropriated billions of dollars for defense and passed a Selective Service Act in September 1940, the first peacetime draft in American history, adding 800,000 men to the armed forces.

Roosevelt's Leadership Endorsed

In the presidential election of 1940, the debate between internationalists and isolationists was carried on in both major parties. The Republicans nominated a newcomer to politics—Wendell Willkie, a Wall Street lawyer and utility company executive, best known for his criticism of the New Deal. For Democrats the question was whether Roosevelt would seek a third term, breaking the precedent set by George Washington. With the United States facing war in Europe and Asia, Roosevelt felt his experience was needed. He kept silent until the Democratic convention, then announced that he would accept the nomination.

At first, both candidates agreed on foreign-policy issues. But when Willkie slipped in the polls, he began to warn that Roosevelt's reelection would mean war. Roosevelt's promise to keep American troops out of war, Willkie said, was no better than his promise to balance the budget. In November 1940, Roosevelt won reelection. With the world in crisis, most American voters did not want to gamble on a change in leadership.

Aid to a Desperate Britain

The British government was running out of money to pay for weapons, so the President proposed that the United States abandon its "cash and carry" policy. But not wanting to revive the old war-debts controversy, Roosevelt suggested a **lend-lease** policy, wherein the United States would merely lend goods to Britain, which the British could return or replace after the war. Lend-lease again stirred debate, but public opinion was shifting in Roosevelt's favor. A poll in January 1941 showed that 60 percent of Americans believed that it was more important to help Britain than to keep out of war. In March 1941, large majorities in both houses of Congress passed lend-lease, authorizing the President to send American supplies and weapons to other nations on any terms he thought would protect the security of the United States.

Battle for the Atlantic

It was one thing to enact lend-lease, however, and another to get supplies across the Atlantic in time to help. When Hitler attacked Yugoslavia and Greece in the spring of 1941, the Nazis overran those countries before lend-lease aid could reach them. When Hitler's bombers failed to knock out Britain, he ordered his submarine fleet to starve that nation into submission.

In trying to make sure that lend-lease supplies reached their destination, the United States was drawn step-by-step into the critical battle of the Atlantic. As German U-boats sank British and American supply ships almost daily, Roosevelt ordered the United States Navy to protect merchant shipping. By the fall of 1941, American and German warships were exchanging fire, and in October a German U-boat sank an American destroyer, killing more than 90 members of its crew. Congress responded by revising the Neutrality Acts to allow merchant ships to be armed.

Germany Turns on a Former Ally

While German-American tensions were escalating in the Atlantic, in June 1941 Hitler, wanting Russia's vast wheat and oil supplies, suddenly attacked the Soviet Union. As German armies quickly advanced into the USSR, Stalin signed an alliance with Great Britain, and the United States offered lend-lease aid. American isolationists were outraged that Roosevelt would aid the Soviets. But Churchill knew that American aid to the Soviet Union would reduce German pressure on Britain. In supporting Roosevelt's decision, he remarked:

> **❝** *I have only one purpose, the destruction of Hitler. . . . If Hitler invaded Hell I would at least make a favorable reference to the Devil in the House of Commons.* **❞**

By the end of November 1941, very few Americans were preaching isolation. Most agreed with Roosevelt that the United States must be an "arsenal of democracy" to sup-

Visualizing History ▲ **STRATEGY SESSION** Before the United States entered the war, Roosevelt and Churchill met to coordinate Allied strategy and to make peacetime plans. Out of this meeting off the North American coast in August 1941, plans emerged for the United Nations. *How did Churchill feel about helping Stalin?*

ply Great Britain and the Soviet Union against Hitler. In fact, about 15,000 Americans were already at war, most in British or Canadian uniforms.

■ Aggression in the Pacific

While the American public's attention was fixed on the Atlantic and Europe, events were taking place in the Pacific and Asia that would eventually plunge the United States into war. Already in China, Japan moved against European colonies in Southeast Asia. This vast region contained the rice, rubber, tin, zinc, and oil needed for Japan's expanding industries. With France defeated, Britain on its knees, and the Soviets retreating in front of German armies, the United States was the only remaining obstacle to Japanese ambitions in the Pacific.

Embargo

In September 1940, Japan allied with the Axis Powers, the countries of Germany and Italy. The United States quickly responded by cutting off exports of scrap metal to Japan. As Japan continued its aggression in Asia, President Roosevelt extended the embargo to include other products that had possible military uses. In July 1941, he told the Japanese that the United States would help them find raw materials if they abandoned their policy of conquest. When Japan rejected his proposal, the President halted all trade with Japan and ordered American forces in the Pacific to prepare for war.

Appeal for Peace

On October 18, 1941, the Japanese prime minister, Prince Fumimaro Konoye, resigned. Konoye had been willing to negotiate with the United States because he did not believe Japan could defeat America in a war. The new prime minister, General Hideki Tojo, did not share Konoye's views. He favored war to eliminate American and British influence in Asia.

By late November, as the United States continued to insist that Japan honor the Open Door policy, Japanese leaders decided that if the dispute did not quickly come to a favorable conclusion, they would attack. Nonetheless, on November 20, negotiations were opened in Washington, D.C. Representing the United States was Secretary of State Cordell Hull. Ambassador Admiral Kichisaburo Nomura and special envoy Saburo Kurusu represented Japan.

The Talks Stall

As negotiations deadlocked, Roosevelt realized that war was inevitable. On December 6, the President appealed for peace directly to Japan's Emperor Hirohito. American officials did not know that, on November 26, a Japanese fleet had put to sea, headed for the United States's main naval base in the Pacific—Pearl Harbor in Hawaii.

Section 2 ★ Assessment

Checking for Understanding

1. **Define** blitzkrieg, lend-lease.

2. **Describe** why hostilities developed between the United States and Japan.

3. **Explain** the importance of the presidential election of 1940.

Critical Thinking

4. **Summarizing** Re-create the diagram shown here, and list the steps the Roosevelt adminis-tration took to support the Allies during the early days of World War II.

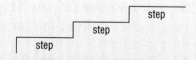

INTERDISCIPLINARY ACTIVITY

5. **The Arts** Write a radio news story on a bombing raid on London.

★★★

The United States at War

Main Idea

After the Japanese attacked Pearl Harbor, the United States entered World War II and helped the Allies win.

Reading Strategy

Organizing Information As you read about World War II, use a diagram like the one shown here to summarize the war in Europe and the Pacific after the Allied offensives in Africa and Italy.

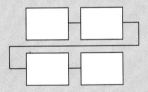

Objectives

After studying this section, you should be able to

★ discuss the course of the war in Europe and in Asia.

★ describe the Atlantic Charter and the agreements the Allies reached at the Yalta Conference.

Key Term

Holocaust

► UNITED STATES POSTER AFTER BOMBING OF PEARL HARBOR

With little warning, Japanese bombers attacked the American fleet based at Pearl Harbor. Shortly after noon on Sunday, December 7, 1941, President Roosevelt had just finished lunch when he received an urgent telephone call from Frank Knox, the secretary of the navy. The secretary had just received a wire from Hawaii: "Air Raid on Pearl Harbor. This is no Drill."

In 2 hours, Japanese planes sank many vessels, including 5 battleships and 3 destroyers, and heavily damaged many others. The attack also destroyed about 250 airplanes, and about 4,500 people were killed or wounded. Only the fleet's aircraft carriers, out of the harbor on maneuvers, escaped the devastation.

■ The World at War

However determined the American people were to defeat the Axis Powers—Germany, Italy, and Japan—the immediate outlook was bleak.

Japanese Victories in the Pacific

The destruction of the American fleet removed Japan's only obstacle in the Pacific. For six months the Japanese won victory after victory, capturing American bases at Guam and Wake Island, conquering Britain's colonies at Hong Kong and Singapore, and occupying the independent kingdom of Thailand. In April 1942, American forces on the peninsula of Bataan in the

Philippines finally surrendered. Meanwhile, the Japanese forces conquered Burma and the East Indies.

German Success in Europe

Axis forces occupied nearly all of Europe, and Britain was besieged. In North Africa, German General Erwin Rommel, "the Desert Fox," led an Italian-German force toward the Suez Canal, pushing the British back to the borders of Egypt. By summer 1942 the Germans had pushed deep into the Soviet Union, capturing the rich farmland of Ukraine and threatening the cities of Stalingrad, Leningrad, and Moscow. Success or failure of the war in Europe depended on whether the Soviet Union could hold out until the United States and Britain could launch an offensive on the western front.

Even before Japan attacked Pearl Harbor, American strategists had decided that in the event of war, United States forces would concentrate on defeating Hitler before dealing with Japan. Not only did the United States have closer ties with the countries occupied by Germany, but Germany seemed a greater threat to the Western Hemisphere, where Nazi sympathies were strong in several Latin American nations. Churchill agreed with this plan, observing that

> " ... [T]he defeat of Germany ... will leave Japan exposed to an overwhelming force, whereas the defeat of Japan would by no means bring the World War to an end. "

Turning Point of the War

Meanwhile, German troops launched a second attack on the Soviets in 1942. In the spring they moved toward the oil fields near the Caspian Sea, and by midsummer

Visualizing
History

▲ **PEARL HARBOR** Japan's surprise attack on Pearl Harbor severely damaged the United States Pacific Fleet. In addition, about 250 warplanes were destroyed and more than 2,400 Americans were killed. *How did the attack affect American public opinion about isolationism?*

World War II in Europe and Africa

Legend:
- Major Axis Powers
- Greatest extent of Axis control
- Allied or Ally-controlled
- Allied forces
- Supply lines

SUPPLY LINES FROM U.S.

D-DAY June 6, 1944

FINAL SOVIET DRIVE July-August, 1944

Nov. 8, 1942

Aug. 15, 1944

July 10, 1943

Oct. 23, 1942

SUPPLY LINE TO SOVIET UNION

Map Study

Churchill and Roosevelt delayed an attack in Europe to first fight in the Mediterranean. Some historians believe this was a plan to weaken Soviet power in postwar Europe. *What reasoning might support such a theory?*

they were more than halfway to their goal. Stalin pleaded with the Allied leaders Roosevelt and Churchill for an invasion of western Europe that would take some pressure off the Soviet Union. Churchill told him that such a second front in Europe was a year away. Soviet troops were left to face the Germans alone.

In September 1942, the Red Army made a desperate and heroic stand at Stalingrad. For four months, Soviet and German troops battled house-to-house for control of the city. Although the German invasion was halted, Stalingrad was reduced to rubble and the Soviets suffered more casualties defending it than the United States did in the entire war. Stalin never forgave Roosevelt and Churchill for allowing this to happen.

In November the Soviet army counterattacked. Taking advantage of the Russian winter, the Red Army surrounded Hitler's freezing forces. In February 1943, the tattered remains of the invading German army, only one-third of its 330,000 men still alive, surrendered.

German Weak Point Exposed

In North Africa, American and British forces, working first separately and then together, pushed Rommel and his Afrika Korps into Tunisia. Under the command first of Major General Lloyd R. Fredendall and then of Major General George S. Patton, American forces checked Rommel's drive at Kasserine Pass and took El Guettar and Bizerte. Under General Bernard L. Montgomery, the British took Tripoli and Tunis. By May, Rommel had fled, nearly 250,000 Axis troops had surrendered, and the campaign in North Africa was over.

In August 1943, British and American forces took Sicily, and in September they invaded the Italian mainland. After his defeat in Sicily, Mussolini was overthrown, and the new Italian government quickly surrendered. German troops still occupied Italy, however, and put up fierce resistance in the mountainous terrain. Not until June 1944 did the Allies enter Rome.

■ Victory in Europe

Allied air forces had already begun round-the-clock bombing of German industrial and transportation centers. But Hitler's armies had to be defeated on the ground.

Normandy Invasion

On June 6, 1944, the greatest amphibious force in history—176,000 troops carried in 5,000 vessels—crossed the English Channel to land along a 60-mile stretch of coastline in France. This invasion at Normandy was known as "D-Day."

Under the command of American General Dwight D. Eisenhower, a million Allied forces were in France within a month after D-Day. On July 25 the Americans broke through the German line. By early August, General George Patton and his forces were racing across northern France through open countryside. In August American and

▼ AMERICAN SOLDIER IN FRANCE, 1944

Visualizing History

▲ **D-DAY** American troops, under heavy fire from German defenders, stormed the coast of France from Coast Guard landing barges. British, Canadian, and free French forces also participated in the invasion. *How did the Normandy invasion take pressure off Soviet forces?*

British troops broke out of Normandy and struck rapidly eastward, entering Paris on August 25, 1944. In September they crossed the western border of Germany.

Rapid Soviet Advance From the East

At the same time, the Soviets closed in from the east. In January 1944, the Red Army freed Leningrad from an 890-day German siege, during which 800,000 residents died. By spring Soviet troops had freed Ukraine, and in July they entered Poland. In August Romania and Bulgaria surrendered, opening the Balkans to the Soviets. In December they entered Hungary. By the end of 1944, most of eastern Europe was in Soviet hands.

Germany Surrenders

In December 1944, Hitler ordered a counterattack in Belgium. Although Allied lines "bulged," the Germans could not break through. The Battle of the Bulge was the last German offensive. In March 1945, the Allies crossed the Rhine River and moved into the heart of Germany. Meanwhile, the Soviets pushed from the east, taking Berlin in April 1945. In April, Hitler committed suicide in his underground shelter in Berlin, and on May 7, 1945, German leaders agreed to an unconditional surrender. Franklin D. Roosevelt, who led the nation through the Depression and the war, however, did not witness this event. Only days before Hitler's suicide, the President died of a massive cerebral hemorrhage.

Crimes Against Humanity

As they entered Germany, Allied armies discovered evidence of one of the most terrible acts of the war—the Nazi **Holocaust,** or deliberate extermination of millions of European Jews and other civilians. As early as 1942, the United States government had received reports that Hitler had ordered the murder of all Jews in German-occupied territories. Only in 1944 did Roosevelt respond to criticism within his own administration that the United States was passively accept-

Visualizing History

▲ **CONCENTRATION CAMPS** The condition of survivors in Nazi death camps such as Belsen, Auschwitz, and Buchenwald horrified the world. *Why were the death camps created?*

ing the murder of Jews. He created a War Refugee Board, but for 6 out of 10 Jews in Europe, action came too late. Not until Allied troops reached the Nazi death camps—at Auschwitz, Dachau, Buchenwald, and elsewhere—and found the survivors and the gas chambers in which so many had died was the horrible truth fully realized. The Nazis had killed 12 million people, of whom 6 million were Jews.

HISTORY Online

Student Web Activity Visit the *American History: The Modern Era Since 1865* Web site at **me.glencoe.com** and click on *Chapter 19— Student Web Activities* for an activity about D-Day.

War in the Pacific

In May 1942, American warships defeated a Japanese fleet in the Battle of the Coral Sea. In June Japanese forces tried to take the Midway Islands, an atoll in the central Pacific about 1,200 miles (1,920 kilometers) northwest of Hawaii. The naval and air

Battle of Midway that ensued was a great victory for the Allies, resulting in the first major defeat of the Japanese navy. It slowed the Japanese advance across the central Pacific, brought an end to the threat to Hawaii, and ended Japanese naval superiority in the Pacific. Japan still held many heavily fortified Pacific islands. So the Allies

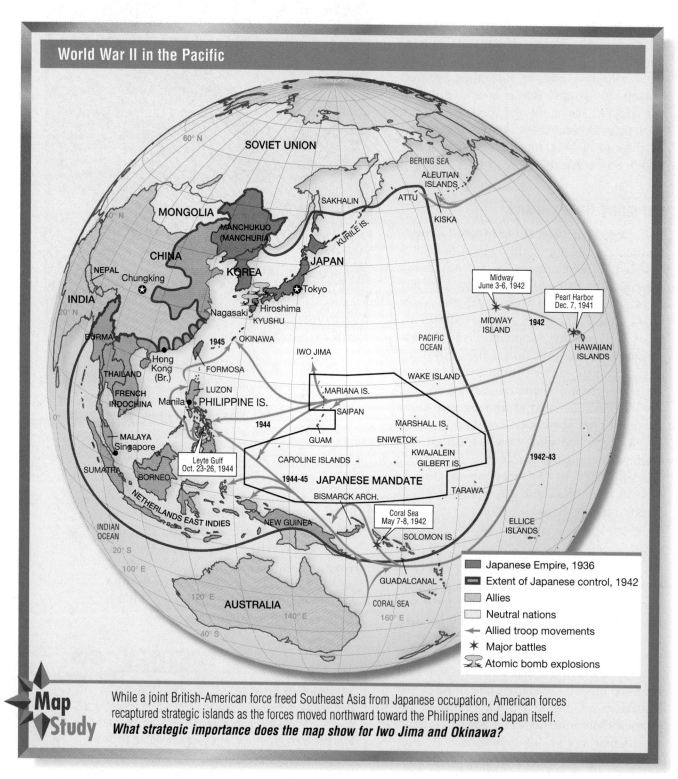

World War II in the Pacific

Japanese Empire, 1936
Extent of Japanese control, 1942
Allies
Neutral nations
Allied troop movements
Major battles
Atomic bomb explosions

Map Study

While a joint British-American force freed Southeast Asia from Japanese occupation, American forces recaptured strategic islands as the forces moved northward toward the Philippines and Japan itself.
What strategic importance does the map show for Iwo Jima and Okinawa?

adopted a military strategy called "island hopping"—to cut Japanese supply lines by capturing key islands and to use them as bases to attack other Japanese strongholds, especially the Philippines and eventually Japan itself.

Guadalcanal

In August 1942, Americans took the first step in the long and bloody road to Tokyo when marines landed on Guadalcanal in the Solomon Islands. The struggle for Guadalcanal was fought on the ground, at sea, and in the air, lasting six months. Not until 1943 did Japan's resistance there come to an end.

In attacking the United States, Japan had failed to realize the industrial power of America and its ability to mobilize that power rapidly. Of the 19 ships sunk at Pearl Harbor, 17 were returned to duty by December 1942, and new ships were constantly added. The navy worked out new ways of fueling and repairing ships at sea, allowing fleets to stay at sea for long periods of time.

During 1943 and 1944, American forces "island-hopped" toward the Philippines and Japan. In October 1944, Allied forces under the leadership of American General Douglas MacArthur landed in the Philippines. MacArthur's advance was matched by amphibious operations directed by Admiral Chester Nimitz against Japanese-held islands in the central Pacific.

Iwo Jima and Okinawa

In 1945 the last of Japan's island outposts fell with the taking of Iwo Jima (EE•woh JEE•muh) in March and Okinawa (oh•kuh•NAH•wuh) in June. Though Iwo Jima measures only a few square miles, American marines suffered more than 20,000 casualties in capturing it. Japan now began to use kamikazes (KAH•mih•KAH•zeez), suicide pilots who flew bomb-laden planes into American ships. During the invasion of Okinawa, kamikazes scored 279 hits on United States vessels.

By the summer of 1945, after Germany was defeated, all Allied power was turned against Japan. The Soviet Union agreed to declare war on Japan and confront Japan's forces in Manchuria. But the conquest of the Japanese islands was left to the United States. America's long-range B-29 bombers had been bombing Japan from bases on recaptured Pacific islands since June 1944. In one raid alone in March 1945, more than 83,000 Tokyo civilians were incinerated by American incendiary bombs. But despite such heavy casualties, Japan's military leaders rejected calls for unconditional surrender. American commanders worried that an invasion of Japan would meet heavy resistance and might cost a million lives.

Hiroshima and Nagasaki

Since early in the war, American scientists had secretly been developing an atomic bomb. First tested in New Mexico in July 1945, it gave Harry Truman, who became President after Roosevelt's death, another choice, and Soviet leader Stalin told Truman to "make good use of it."

After the Japanese government rejected Truman's final warning to surrender or risk "utter destruction," on August 6 an atomic bomb destroyed 60 percent of Hiroshima, a major Japanese industrial city. When Japan still refused to surrender, a second bomb was dropped on the city of Nagasaki on August 9, causing almost as much destruction as the first. The two attacks took about 150,000 Japanese lives. When reports of the death and devastation reached Tokyo, the stunned emperor, telling his people that "the unendurable must be endured," asked for peace. The final surrender took place on September 2, 1945, on the battleship *Missouri* anchored in Tokyo Bay.

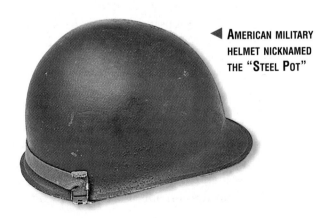

◄ AMERICAN MILITARY HELMET NICKNAMED THE "STEEL POT"

▲ **Meeting at Yalta** Looking tired and drawn, Roosevelt (center) poses with Stalin (right) and Churchill during a break in their meetings at Yalta. Two months later, Roosevelt was dead. *What agreements were reached at Yalta?*

■ Wartime Diplomacy

The first planning for peace took place in August 1941 when Roosevelt and Churchill met on a ship off the coast of Newfoundland. At that meeting they issued the Atlantic Charter, a statement of principles on which depended "hopes for a better future for the world." Much like Wilson's Fourteen Points, the Atlantic Charter looked forward to a world where people would have the right to choose their form of government.

After Pearl Harbor, Roosevelt turned his attention to forming an alliance among the nations fighting against Hitler. On January 1, 1942, representatives of the 26 countries at war with the Axis Powers agreed to support the principles of the Atlantic Charter. They promised full economic and military support in the war, and they agreed not to make a separate peace.

In holding the great alliance together, Roosevelt and Churchill kept constantly in touch. Although they often did not agree on strategy, neither wavered in admiration for the other. Working closely with the other major Allies was more difficult. Japanese troops had pushed China's government deep into the interior, and Chinese leaders were unhappy that the war in Europe was the top priority. General Charles de Gaulle (dih•GOHL), leader of the French government in exile, disapproved of the United States's recognizing a government in south France that was friendly to the Nazis.

Cooperation with the Soviet Union proved the most difficult problem. Stalin had almost never been outside of his country and was suspicious of capitalist nations. Even so, the alliance between the United States and Great Britain and the Soviet Union lasted until the end of the war. Germany could not be defeated without Soviet aid, and the Soviets depended on supplies from Britain and the United States.

Planning for War and Peace

Cooperation in plans for war and peace was worked out in a series of international conferences. At Casablanca, Morocco, in January 1943, Roosevelt and Churchill agreed to demand "unconditional surrender" from the Axis Powers, assuring the Soviet Union that its allies would not sign a separate peace treaty with Germany.

At Cairo, Egypt, in November 1943, Roosevelt and Churchill met Chinese leader

Chiang Kai-shek (jee•AHNG ky•SHEHK) and agreed that Japan should be stripped of its Pacific empire and Korea given independence. From Cairo, Roosevelt and Churchill flew to Tehran, capital of Iran, to meet with Stalin. There they promised that the D-Day invasion of France would be launched the next year. In return Stalin agreed to begin a new offensive against Germany at the same time from the east.

The Yalta Conference

In February 1945, Roosevelt, Churchill, and Stalin met for the last time at Yalta, in the Soviet Union. They agreed publicly that the United States, Britain, and the Soviet Union, along with France, should occupy Germany after the war, but they promised to encourage some form of representative government for the other peoples of Europe. They also agreed on a conference to be held at San Francisco in April 1945 to establish a world peace organization.

Secret agreements at Yalta covered the terms on which the Soviet Union could enter the war against Japan after Germany was defeated. The Soviets were promised Japanese territories, and that they could keep Outer Mongolia, in China, and obtain an ice-free naval port. In return, Stalin agreed to support the Nationalist government of Chiang Kai-shek instead of the Chinese Communists who were challenging Chiang for power.

Although the Yalta agreements later were attacked as a "sellout," at the time it seemed vital to keep the Soviet Union from making a separate peace with Germany when American and British forces were still fighting in the west. Even more important, the United States wanted Soviet support in the war against Japan.

Roosevelt's Death

When he reported to Congress on his Yalta trip, Roosevelt looked tired and pale. Two months later, on April 12, 1945, the President died suddenly at Warm Springs, Georgia. The nation he led for more than 12 years was shocked, and newspapers that printed daily lists of soldiers and sailors who had died in action added the name: "Roosevelt, Franklin D., Commander in Chief."

The United Nations

Two weeks after Roosevelt's death, representatives of 50 nations met at San Francisco to make plans for a new world organization. But the talks at San Francisco were made more difficult by rising suspicions among the Allies. The Soviet Union was keeping a firm hand on Poland and seemed to be breaking its Yalta promises. Still, the meeting at San Francisco produced a charter for the United Nations (UN). The preamble of the UN Charter pledged all the countries signing it to "faith in fundamental human rights," to "justice and respect" for the terms of peace treaties, and to the goal of living together. In July 1945, when the Senate ratified the Charter by a vote of 89 to 2, the United States became the first nation to join the UN.

Section 3 ★ Assessment

Checking for Understanding

1. **Define** Holocaust.

2. **List** the meetings held among Allied leaders between 1941 and 1945.

Critical Thinking

3. **Anticipating Consequences** In a wartime alliance, what risk is carried by each nation that agrees not to make a separate peace?

4. **Analyzing Issues** Re-create the diagram shown here, and list the agreements the Allies reached at the Yalta Conference.

Yalta Agreements

INTERDISCIPLINARY ACTIVITY

5. **Government** Research information on the United Nations. Make a chart illustrating the organization's various roles.

The Atomic Bomb

"We must not be the most hated and feared people in the world," a physicist wrote, urging President Truman not to use the atomic bombs that would kill some 150,000 mostly civilian Japanese.

Rumors that the Nazis might develop an atomic bomb spurred American and British efforts to build one. Scientist Albert Einstein wrote President Roosevelt urging that a major research program begin at once so that the nation would be the first with the bomb.

The secret project, later called the Manhattan Project, was carried out primarily at facilities in Oak Ridge, Tennessee and, later, at Los Alamos, New Mexico. American physicist J. Robert Oppenheimer was the director, and he persuaded many top physicists to join the project. On July 16, 1945, the bomb was tested atop a steel tower in a lonely desert track at Alamogordo, New Mexico, called *Jornada del Muerto*, Journey of Death.

President Truman did not know the bomb existed until a few weeks before his decision to use it. Truman, who had taken office after President Roosevelt's death on April 12, received word of the test results in Potsdam, Germany, where he was in conference with Churchill, Stalin, and their top advisers. Roosevelt had told Churchill about the bomb. Although some historians disagree about why atomic bombs were dropped on Japan and about the ethical issues involved, President Truman believed the bombing was justified: "The dropping of the bombs stopped the war, saved millions of lives."

▲ **THE DEVASTATION AT HIROSHIMA**

Making the Science Connection

1. Why did the United States start the Manhattan Project?

2. Given the present concerns about the dangers of nuclear war, do you think the United States was right to develop nuclear weapons? Why or why not?

ACTIVITY

3. Research information on nuclear testing. Present findings in a written report about how current testing regulations differ from the 1940s and 1950s.

★★★

War on the Home Front

▶ ROSIE THE RIVETER, SYMBOL OF WOMEN
WORKERS DURING WORLD WAR II

Guide to Reading

Main Idea

To defeat the Axis Powers, United States citizens from all walks of life committed to the war effort.

Reading Strategy

Organizing Information As you read about the war effort on the home front, use a diagram like the one shown here to list examples of how the nation mobilized for war.

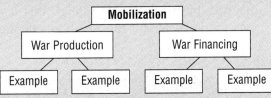

Mobilization
- War Production
  - Example
  - Example
- War Financing
  - Example
  - Example

Objectives

After studying this section, you should be able to

★ discuss efforts to mobilize the economy for war production.

★ explain the war's impact on women, African Americans, and Japanese Americans.

Key Term

wildcat strike

Americans were amazed at the speed with which industry turned to making war materials. When in May 1940 President Roosevelt talked of producing 50,000 airplanes a year, some thought he was asking the impossible. Yet, by 1944 the number of planes produced annually had risen to about 100,000. Mass production was so effective in the ship industry that the average time for building a freighter dropped from a year to less than 2 months.

🏛 GOVERNMENT

■ The Production Battle

As in World War I, federal agencies took on the direction of private companies doing war work. After a Senate investigation revealed corruption and mismanagement among companies involved in war production, in January 1942 Roosevelt gave a War Production Board strong regulatory power. Its head, Donald Nelson, could seize vital materials, order industrial plants to convert to war production, and prohibit manufacture of products he considered unessential to the war effort.

Rapid Conversion to War Production

Within weeks of Pearl Harbor, production of bicycles, beer cans, refrigerators, toothpaste tubes, and more than 300 other items was cut back or banned. Automobile manufacturers were ordered to convert production to tanks and other war supplies. Entire new industries were created. Synthetic rubber, for example, became important when Japan's conquest of Southeast Asia cut off America's supply of natural rubber. By the end of 1942, nearly 33 percent of American production went to war materials, and by 1944 nearly 50 percent. Production of all goods nearly doubled, and America's production of war materials matched the total output of Germany, Italy, and Japan combined.

In May 1941, Roosevelt set up the Office of Scientific Research and Development to mobilize science and technology for the war effort. Among the many inventions that came from this agency were DDT, which controlled insects and made jungle fighting more tolerable; the bazooka, a weapon that enabled an infantry soldier to destroy a tank; and radar, which determined the position and speed of airplanes and ships.

Financing the War

To raise funds for the war effort, the federal government increased taxes and sold war bonds in amounts ranging from $25 to $10,000. In 1942 the government extended the income tax for the first time to include middle- and lower-income people. To make collection easier, the government in 1943 began to require that employers deduct taxes from workers' paychecks before they received them.

The war increased employment, and workers' earnings rose as war production brought longer workweeks and overtime. As people had more money to spend, and as the shift to war materials made consumer goods scarce, prices rose. To combat inflation, in 1942 Congress created the Office of Price Administration, which set price ceilings on consumer products and began to ration goods that were in short supply. By war's end 20 items—including sugar, meat, butter, coffee, gasoline, fuel oil, and shoes—required government-issued rationing coupons to be presented at the time of purchase. Despite attempts to hold down prices, however, the cost of living rose 29 percent during the war, leading to demands for higher wages.

To help prevent strikes, a National War Labor Board was established to settle labor disputes by mediation. Although this task was made easier by the no-strike pledges

Linking Past and Present

★★★

The Jeep

General George C. Marshall, U.S. Army chief of staff during World War II, once described the jeep as "America's greatest contribution to modern warfare." From Normandy to North Africa, from World War II to the Gulf War, the Jeep played a vital military role.

Then_____

General Purpose

The small, durable military motor vehicle called the jeep derived its name from the initials G.P., an abbreviation for "General Purpose Vehicle," its official title. Supremely functional, the jeep had an 80-inch wheel base, 1/4

ton capacity, and three seats, with room for a .30-caliber machine gun mount. Equipped with four-wheel drive, the jeep was able to overcome such battlefield stumbling blocks as ice or mud and was sturdy enough to be dropped by parachute onto rugged terrain. Nearly 650,000 jeeps were manufactured during World War II.

Now_____

Clones and Copies

Imitations, clones, and copies of the jeep design mushroomed after the war. Research and development yielded, among other military land vehicles, an all-steel vehicle, an all-aluminum version, and the High Mobility Multi-Purpose Wheeled Vehicle (the Humvee).

▼ CIVILIAN HUMVEE

★★

▲ RATIONING Ration stamps were used during World War II in an attempt to distribute essential goods fairly. Meat, butter, sugar, and gasoline were among the items that were rationed. *How did the cost of living change during the war years?*

that both the AFL and the CIO made after Pearl Harbor, there were many small **wildcat strikes**—work stoppages without union approval—and a short national strike by 500,000 coal miners. Even though most labor unions kept their no-strike pledge, an act passed in 1947 outlawed strikes against war industries. ▲

■ The War and Social Change

The need for defense workers altered traditional patterns of American society. As millions of men joined the armed services, more women than ever before entered the labor force. "If you can drive a car, you can run a machine" became an advertising slogan for industries.

Women Assume Nontraditional Roles

The government, newspapers, radio, and newsreels encouraged women to take factory jobs as a patriotic duty, and 5 million American women entered the workforce during the war. "Rosie the Riveter," who first appeared in overalls in a Lockheed Aircraft poster, became a national symbol of the vital contribution women were making to the war effort.

More than ever before, women filled jobs that were not traditional for females. They worked on production lines, in steel mills, on the docks, and in other jobs that required heavy manual labor. Outside war industries, women also took over such traditionally male jobs as driving buses and trucks and working as train conductors, lumberjacks, and barbers. Most of these new workers were married and had children. Yet women still encountered resistance from male workers. As one female aircraft worker described it:

• •

Footnotes to History

Women Pilots Of the more than 25,000 women who applied to become members of the Women's Airforce Service Pilots (WASPs), about 2,000 were accepted, and 1,074 won their wings. Their duties included ferrying planes from the factories to the airfields, testing rebuilt aircraft, and hauling gunnery targets. After the war, women were not permitted to fly for the military again until 1977.

> *The men really resented the women very much. . . . [A]fter a while they realized that it was essential that the women worked there, 'cause there wasn't enough men, and the women were doing a good job.*

To encourage women to work, the government offered job-training courses, and Congress appropriated funds for child-care centers, but even this was not enough to meet the need. Federal and state governments suspended laws that limited the hours women could work, and women's wages rose as the concept of equal pay for equal work spread. Although at first most women considered their new employment to be temporary, by war's end 80 percent said they wanted to keep their jobs.

Opportunities for African Americans

The need for workers also speeded the shift of African Americans from farming to manufacturing. Many African Americans left the South and moved to cities in the Northeast, the Midwest, and California to work in war industries. Some companies hired few African Americans before the war, but by 1945 thousands of African Americans had jobs in defense plants.

Resentment Toward Social Change

Between 1941 and 1945, one of every five Americans relocated to another part of the country. The movement of so many Americans to fill jobs in war industries created housing shortages, crowded schools, and heightened social tensions. Old-timers resented the newcomers, regardless of their race. In California there were prejudices against "Okies," white migrants from Oklahoma and Texas who arrived in the 1930s to look for work after losing their farms in the Dust Bowl. In many cities prejudices arose against newly arrived African Americans. The police were needed to help African American families move into public housing in Detroit, when angry mobs tried to block them. It took federal troops to break a strike of streetcar operators in Philadelphia, who protested against the promotion of African American workers.

The federal government's response to racial discrimination during the war was uneven. In 1941 African American labor leader A. Philip Randolph threatened to lead 100,000 protesters on Washington, D.C., to

Visualizing History

▲ NEW OPPORTUNITIES World War II offered increased job opportunities for women and for African Americans. Although women's wages rose, they still averaged 60 percent less than men's wages. *How did the government encourage women to work?*

AMERICAN PORTRAITS

Charles Drew
1904–1950

Born and raised in the segregated city of Washington, D.C., Charles Drew refused to let racial prejudice bar him from professional success. After graduating from Amherst College in Massachusetts, he earned his M.D. degree at Canada's McGill University.

In the 1930s Drew conducted pioneering research on blood plasma, and he established a model blood plasma bank. When the United States entered

World War II, Drew was asked to head the military's blood plasma program. By collecting, storing, transporting, and transfusing donated blood plasma, this program saved the lives of countless wounded soldiers. But in 1942 Drew resigned when the military refused to accept blood donations from African Americans unless their blood was segregated from the blood of white donors and was given only to black soldiers.

demand an end to discrimination in defense jobs and the armed forces. In order to stop the march, Roosevelt established the Fair Employment Practices Commission to promote minority hiring in government offices and in companies that had war contracts. But while it opposed discrimination, the commission did not reject segregation. Even the military remained segregated, and although hundreds of thousands of African Americans served in uniform in every capacity from cooks to fighter pilots, most served in all-black units.

Detention of Japanese Americans

The most significant racial discrimination of the war involved the removal of Japanese Americans from the West Coast. About 90 percent of all Japanese Americans, outside Hawaii, lived in California and the Pacific Northwest. Because of immigration restrictions after 1924, two-thirds had been born in the United States and were citizens by birth. Yet government officials were suspicious of their loyalty. When war broke out, residents of California, Oregon, and Washington feared that with the Pacific fleet at Pearl Harbor severely damaged, they were vulnerable to invasion at any time. Californi-

ans, in particular, were concerned that their neighbors of Japanese descent might engage in sabotage. Army General John DeWitt investigated and reported that:

> The Japanese race is an enemy race and while many second and third generation Japanese born on United States soil have become 'Americanized,' the racial strains are undiluted.... It, therefore, follows that along the vital Pacific Coast over 112,000 potential enemies of Japanese extraction are at large today.

Based on such reports, beginning in February 1942, the government moved 110,000 Japanese Americans to detention centers surrounded by barbed wire and patrolled by soldiers and confined them there for the duration of the war.

The order to evacuate Japanese Americans from the West Coast came quickly. Detainees had as little as 48 hours to make arrangements for their homes, businesses, and farms. Many had to sell their property at a loss or abandon it. Bargain hunters descended on them, taking advantage of their plight.

▲ INTERNMENT OF JAPANESE AMERICANS During World War II, persons of Japanese descent were sent to internment camps. More than 70,000 were Nisei, or American-born. *How did the Supreme Court rule on the detainees' appeal to protect their rights?*

Arriving at one of 10 detention camps in isolated areas of Utah, Wyoming, Arizona, and other sparsely settled Western states, they were put to work at menial, low-paying jobs. Their military guards searched their quarters for "weapons," sometimes confiscating kitchen knives, scissors, and even knitting needles. Entire families lived out the war in a single room in army-style barracks furnished with cots and bare light bulbs. Since the authorities had no plans for running the camps, the detainees established their own camp governments, schools, and newspapers.

Almost immediately detainees appealed to the courts to protect their rights. When the issue came before the Supreme Court in December 1944, in *Korematsu* v. *United States*, the justices upheld the government's policy as necessary for national security.

Despite their unhappy experience, most Japanese Americans remained loyal to the United States. Thousands served in segregated military units. A Japanese American army unit recruited from detention camps fought in the Italian campaign and was the army's most decorated unit in American military history. However, the government's policy toward Japanese Americans at home became a blot on the nation's war record.

Section 4 ★ Assessment

Checking for Understanding

1. **Define** wildcat strike.

2. **Explain** how the productive capacity of American industries aided the war effort.

Critical Thinking

3. **Formulating Hypotheses** Why were Japanese Americans detained during the war while Americans of German or Italian descent were not?

4. **Comparing and Contrasting** Re-create the diagram shown here, and describe the similarities and differences between the lives of these minorities during the war.

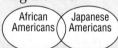

African Americans   Japanese Americans

INTERDISCIPLINARY ACTIVITY

5. **Economics** Write a diary entry describing a day as a World War II defense worker.

BUILDING SKILLS
Critical Thinking Skills

Interpreting Points of View

A person's point of view is the way in which he or she interprets topics or events. There are a number of factors that affect a person's point of view, including age, gender, ethnic background, and religion. The ability to interpret points of view will help you to determine the objectivity of an argument or the accuracy of a description.

Learning the Skill

Use these steps to help you interpret written points of view:
- **Read** the material and identify the main idea.
- **Gather** background information on the topic and the author.
- **Identify** points that the author has emphasized or excluded.
- **Identify** any words or phrases that suggest a personal opinion.
- **Identify** the author's point of view.

Read this excerpt from "The Good War, An Oral History of World War Two." The speaker, Peter Ota, was 15 when he was sent to a detention camp for Japanese Americans in 1942. Later, he served in the U.S. military.

We came back to Los Angeles at the end of the war, believing that there was no other way but to be American. We were discouraged with our Japanese culture. My feeling at the time was, I had to prove myself. I don't know why I had to prove myself. Here I am, an ex-GI, born and raised here. Why do I have to prove myself? We all had this feeling. We had to prove that we were Americans, okay?

. . . My children were denied a lot of the history of what happened. . . . I think this stems from another Japanese characteristic: when shame is put on you, you try to hide it. We were put into camp, we became victims, it was our fault. We hide it.

▲ **JAPANESE AMERICAN CHILDREN AT INTERNMENT CAMP**

Practicing the Skill

1. What is Ota's background?

2. How does Ota explain the silence of Japanese Americans on the internment camps? Do you agree or disagree with Ota's explanation?

Glencoe's **Skillbuilder Interactive Workbook, Level 2** provides instruction and practice in key social studies skills.

APPLYING THE SKILL

3. Think about a topic on which you and a friend disagree. Analyze each point of view. Then, in a brief paragraph, describe the compromises each side might make to resolve your differences.

605

Using Vocabulary

Use each of the following words in a statement about the aggressor nations in World War II, the kind of warfare they conducted, and world response.

appeasement   Holocaust
fascism   totalitarian

Reviewing Facts

1. **List** reasons for isolationist policies in the United States and appeasement in Europe.

2. **Discuss** the priorities and sequence of the Allies' military campaigns in World War II.

3. **Explain** the difficulties Roosevelt and Churchill faced in dealing with Chiang Kai-shek, de Gaulle, and Stalin.

Understanding Concepts

International Alliances

1. How did World War II underscore the importance of an international organization such as the United Nations?

Military Conflict

2. Re-create the diagram shown here, and list where Hitler went wrong after his early victories.

```
         Hitler's Mistakes
    ┌──────────┼──────────┐
 ┌─────┐   ┌─────┐    ┌─────┐
 │     │   │     │    │     │
 └─────┘   └─────┘    └─────┘
```

Critical Thinking

1. **Evaluating Policy** Economic problems at home was one reason that the United States initially avoided involvement in World War II. What subsequent developments suggest that this policy may have been self-defeating?

2. **Analyzing Fine Art** Study the painting of V-J Day on this page and explain the central focus.

3. **Analyzing Trends** How did the nation's role in the United Nations illustrate the dramatic change World War II had made in long-range United States foreign policy?

▲ *V-J Day—Crowds cheering at Times Square* by Edward Dancig, 1947

4. **Analyzing Graphs** Study the graph on page 607 and answer the questions that follow.

   a. Which decade depicted on the graph shows the smallest increase in the number of women joining the labor force? The largest increase?

   b. Summarize the apparent relationship between the world wars and the employment of women.

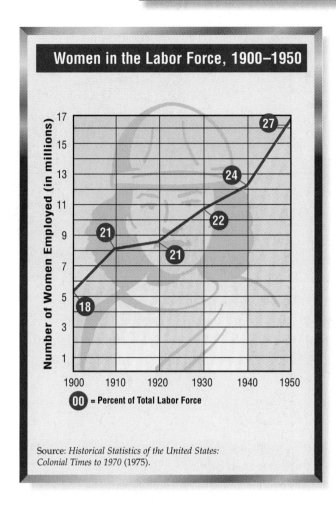

Women in the Labor Force, 1900–1950

Number of Women Employed (in millions)

18 — 1900
21 — 1910
21 — 1920
22 — 1930
24 — 1940
27 — 1950

00 = Percent of Total Labor Force

Source: *Historical Statistics of the United States: Colonial Times to 1970* (1975).

History and Geography

War in the Pacific

Study the map on page 594, then answer the questions that follow.

1. **Region** Compare the area under Japanese control in 1942 with that of 1936.

2. **Location** Between which lines of latitude is Iwo Jima located?

Cooperative Learning ### Interdisciplinary Activity: Law

As a class, create a courtroom with students role-playing a panel of judges, a three-member prosecution team, three defense attorneys, a jury, three defendants, and an audience. Put the following people on trial for crimes against humanity: Adolf Hitler—for beginning World War II and establishing the Nazi death camps; a German military officer—for carrying out orders to execute Jews in a death camp; General Hideki Tojo—for ordering kamikaze attacks against Allied forces.

Practicing Skills

Interpreting Points of View

Read the editorial page of a newspaper and choose an editorial, column, or letter to the editor with a point of view that conflicts with your own. Analyze the author's view, and write a brief paragraph comparing his or her view with your own.

Practicing Skills

Using the Internet

Search the Internet for the memoirs or recorded personal experiences provided by soldiers and/or civilians during World War II. Copy or print a part of the memoirs that you find interesting. Post these excerpts on the classroom bulletin board under the heading "Voices of World War II."

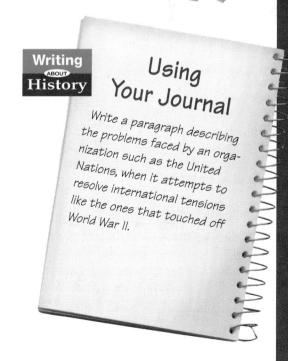

Writing ABOUT History

Using Your Journal

Write a paragraph describing the problems faced by an organization such as the United Nations, when it attempts to resolve international tensions like the ones that touched off World War II.

CHAPTER 20

★★★

The Cold War
1945–1952

▼ REBUILDING BERLIN, THE MARSHALL PLAN AT WORK

Setting the Scene

Focus

Within months after the end of World War II, the United States and the Soviet Union entered into a period of intense confrontation and rivalry. American leaders sought to maintain workable links with the Soviets while trying to check communism in Europe. Later this containment policy was applied to China, but it could not prevent the outbreak of war in Korea. At home, Americans sought to adjust to a peacetime economy.

Concepts to Understand

★ Why the **political and economic power** of the United States and the Soviet Union were set against each other

★ How effective presidential **leadership** resulted in aggressive foreign and domestic policies

Read to Discover . . .

★ ways the United States sought to contain the Soviet Union.

★ the effect the cold war had on Americans at home.

Journal Notes

How did the fear of communism become a serious threat to American democracy during the Truman administration? Record relevant points as you read the chapter.

HISTORY *Online*

Chapter Overview
Visit the *American History: The Modern Era Since 1865* Web site at **me.glencoe.com** and click on *Chapter 20—Chapter Overviews* to preview chapter information.

CULTURAL	●**1945** Harvey *by Mary Chase wins Pulitzer Prize for plays*
	●**1947** *Jackie Robinson first plays for Brooklyn Dodgers*

1944	**1946**

POLITICAL	●**1945** *Harry S Truman becomes President on death of Franklin D. Roosevelt*
	●**1946** *Winston Churchill makes "iron curtain" speech*
	●**1947** *Truman Doctrine announced*

History AND ART

The Homecoming
by Norman Rockwell, 1945

New opportunities for housing and education eased the transition from military to civilian life for returning veterans. At the same time, Americans faced new challenges at home and abroad.

▲ PRESIDENT HARRY S TRUMAN AND GENERAL DOUGLAS MACARTHUR

• **1948** *Largest telescope in the world is dedicated at Mount Palomar Observatory*

• **1950** *National Council of Churches of Christ is formed, representing 30 denominations*

1948	1950

• **1948** *Berlin airlift*
• **1949** *Communist forces take China*
• **1949** *NATO created*

• **1950** *North Korea invades South Korea*

★★★

The Start of the Cold War

▶ **UN** FLAG

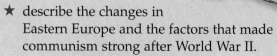

Guide to Reading

Main Idea

The Soviet Union imposed communist rule throughout Eastern Europe after the war.

Reading Strategy

Organizing Information As you read about the start of the cold war, use a diagram like the one shown here to list the events that led to the establishment of communism in Eastern Europe.

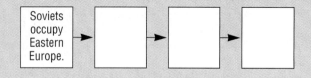

Objectives

After studying this section, you should be able to

★ describe the changes in Eastern Europe and the factors that made communism strong after World War II.

★ outline the foreign policy goals of the Truman administration.

★ explain how the United States became a world power after World War II.

Key Terms

communism, satellite nation, purge, buffer, guerrilla, containment, collective security

---

*P*resident Truman's policies from the beginning of his administration showed his determination and the high degree to which he was personally involved in handling both domestic and international affairs. On his desk he kept a sign: "The buck stops here." In times of great crisis, Truman showed an extraordinary capacity for quick, effective, yet restrained action.

■ East-West Suspicions

In 1945, during the first months of his administration, President Truman concentrated his attention on winning the war against Germany and Japan. Like Roosevelt, he supported the creation of the United

Nations as a world peacekeeping organization. But Truman was much more suspicious than Roosevelt had been of the Soviet Union and its dictator, Joseph Stalin.

Soviet Control of Eastern Europe

When the war ended, the alliance between the United States, Great Britain, and the Soviet Union unraveled. While there was a common enemy, Western democracies and Soviet leaders had overlooked their political, economic, and social differences. After the war, suspicions returned. Soviet expansion into Eastern Europe heightened American fears of **communism,** a system in which society as a whole, represented by the Communist party, owns and controls property and the means of production.

As fighting ended, Soviet troops occupied much of Eastern Europe. The Soviet leaders, who had promised free elections in these nations, did not follow through. In Hungary, where free elections were held in November 1945, communist candidates received only 17 percent of the vote. Unwilling to lose control, Stalin later suppressed elections in Hungary and in the other nations of Eastern Europe. Then, under elections supervised by Soviet troops, voters gave 90 percent of the vote to communist candidates in Poland. This pattern was repeated in all Soviet-occupied areas, helping to establish communist governments throughout Eastern Europe. Nations that were held under Soviet domination came to be called **satellite nations.**

To restore the devastated Soviet economy, the Soviets removed whole factories, transportation equipment, and machinery from the satellite nations. Stalin also ordered **purges,** or forced removals, of leaders of satellite nations who were deemed disloyal.

The Iron Curtain

The leaders of Western Europe and the United States watched with grave concern as the Soviet Union crushed all opposition in the nations of Eastern Europe after 1945. Former Prime Minister Winston Churchill identified the new threat in a speech in March 1946 at Fulton, Missouri. With President Truman on the platform, Churchill warned:

66 *. . . [F]rom Stettin on the Baltic to Trieste on the Adriatic, an iron curtain has descended across the continent. Behind that line lie all the capitals of the ancient states of central and eastern Europe.* 99

The phrase "iron curtain" would be used to describe Soviet policy in Europe from 1945 to 1989. The West, said Churchill, must meet this challenge with force, if needed, because the Communists had no respect for weakness. Truman and his advisers agreed that a "get tough" policy was their only choice.

▲ **AN IRON CURTAIN** Former Prime Minister Winston Churchill and President Truman appear together during Churchill's speech at Fulton, Missouri. *What message did Churchill give to the American people?*

The Strength of Communism

Following World War II, the United States began to withdraw troops from Europe, leaving the Soviet army as the most powerful military force in Europe. As a result of the German invasion, the Soviet Union had lost 20 million people and suffered devastation of land, property, and industry. Feeling threatened by Western powers, the Soviet Union wanted to create a **buffer,** or safety zone, on its western border. Soviet troops stationed there ensured that the nations of Eastern Europe would remain its allies.

Communism's Promises

The Communists promised to abolish poverty, privilege, and private property. They guaranteed productive work, shelter, education, health care, and a classless society in the new "people's democracies" of war-torn Eastern Europe.

The Communists saw the world as divided between forces of progress and forces of oppression. Soviet rhetoric incited revolts in other impoverished nations, as people living in poverty listened eagerly to the Communists' plans. Communists began to organize resistance to governments they considered to be reactionary and imperialist. Sometimes they organized groups of **guerrilla** forces—armed bands that were not a part of a regular military unit—to foment civil war.

Containment

President Truman responded with a policy of **containment**—preventing the further spread of communism. This policy was based on the belief that foreign policy goals of Soviet leaders included conquering other nations—not simply the securing of their own borders. Containment, however, did not win universal support.

Some who opposed the policy believed that it was too soft. Angry with the advance of communism, they called for a quick and decisive victory over the Soviet Union. Another view was expressed by Walter Lippmann, a newspaper columnist. Lippmann argued that Soviet troops remained in Eastern Europe to protect the Soviets' western border. He warned that the United States could not contain the Soviet Union everywhere. Such a policy, he said, would require the United States to defend all anticommunist governments—no matter how repressive or unpopular they might be.

Lippmann published his newspaper columns on containment in a book called *The Cold War*. The title, a term coined by Lippmann to refer to a state of war that did not involve actual bloodshed, came to be used by everyone, including the President, to describe the icy rivalry that existed between the United States and the Soviet Union.

Aid to Europe

The cold war was like no other struggle that had ever engaged the United States. It required a constant state of military preparedness; it called for military support for countries believed to be in danger of a communist takeover. It had other economic costs, as both the United States and the Soviet Union tried to "buy" allies with gifts ranging from food to steel mills.

The Truman Doctrine

The policy of containment began in Europe. Great Britain, in financial trouble, was forced to notify United States officials early in 1947 that it would withdraw its soldiers from Greece and end aid to Turkey. United States diplomats in Greece warned that this could lead to a communist takeover. Already, they said, Soviet-supported guerrillas were controlling much of the country. It was feared that if Greece fell to the Communists, Turkey would be next.

President Truman decided that the United States must act. In March 1947 he told Congress that if the United States was not willing to give aid to Greece and Turkey to contain communism, democratic governments everywhere would be threatened. Truman's warning that the nation faced a crisis was clear:

> **"** *I believe that it must be the policy of the United States to support free peoples who are resisting attempted subjugation by armed minorities or outside pressures. . . . If we falter in our leadership, we may endanger the peace of the world—and we shall surely endanger the welfare of our own nation.* **"**

Truman's policy, known as the Truman Doctrine, proposed that the United States provide military and economic aid to Greece and Turkey. Immediately approved by Congress, the Truman Doctrine superseded the Monroe Doctrine, shifting the United States away from peacetime isolationism.

The Marshall Plan

Soon after the Truman Doctrine went into effect, the administration proposed a plan for economic aid to Europe. The situation in Europe was desperate in 1947. There were shortages of food, fuel, and raw materials, and European nations needed money to rebuild industries and transportation systems.

The Truman administration realized that economic woes in France, Italy, and other Western European countries might lead to the election of communist governments. The nation's leaders were also concerned that Europe's faltering economy would affect United States markets.

In June 1947, Secretary of State George C. Marshall went beyond the Truman

Europe After World War II

British — Air corridors
French — Iron Curtain
American ◎ Jointly occupied cities
Russian

Map Study After being invaded twice in less than 30 years, the Soviets especially feared future German power. Thus, after World War II, the Allies agreed to divide and occupy Germany. *What other nation was divided after the war?*

▲ THE BERLIN AIRLIFT When the Soviets closed off the routes from the West to Berlin, American and British cargo planes carried on an around-the-clock airlift. Berlin children, standing in the rubble of their shattered city, watch an American bomber fly in with supplies. *What effect did the airlift have on the Soviet blockade?*

Doctrine to propose a massive recovery plan for European nations. Under the Marshall Plan, American aid in the form of money, supplies, and machinery would help to end Europe's "hunger, poverty, desperation, and chaos." The United States offered the Marshall Plan to all nations in Europe—including the Soviet Union. Believing that the plan would promote the interests of United States capitalism, the Soviet Union and Eastern European communist nations turned it down.

The nations of Western Europe, on the other hand, welcomed the Truman administration's offer. Drawing up detailed plans for restoring production and controlling inflation, they also agreed to change trade laws—tariffs and quotas that blocked the flow of commerce.

The Marshall Plan was an enormous success. During the Truman years, the United States gave more than $13 billion in loans and grants to the nations of Western Europe. To administer aid effectively, the 16 Western European nations formed the Organization for European Economic Cooperation, the first step toward European economic unity.

■ The Berlin Airlift

At the end of the war, the Allies had decided on a joint occupation of Germany. The United States, Great Britain, France, and the Soviet Union each controlled a zone, or section, of Germany. They also each controlled a section of the capital, Berlin, in the Soviet-controlled zone.

Failing to reach agreement with the Soviet Union, the Western powers in May 1948 announced plans to join their three sections of Germany to form an independent nation. The Soviet Union responded by closing off all traffic from West Germany to Berlin. They thought that this move would force the West to back down from its control of West Berlin. President Truman saw this action as a test of Western determination. Instead of sending troops through the land corridor to Berlin and risking war, Truman ordered a massive airlift to supply Berlin's 2 million people. Night and day for more than 10 months, British and United States cargo planes carried food, medicine, clothing, raw materials, and even coal to Berlin. In May 1949, the Soviet Union finally lifted its blockade.

North Atlantic Treaty Organization

Believing that rebuilding their economies without rebuilding their military strength might invite Soviet aggression, five Western European states formed an alliance in March 1948. They invited the United States, the world's only atomic power, to join their alliance. With Senate approval, Truman began talks to create a North Atlantic Treaty Organization (NATO), which formed in April 1949.

NATO linked into a military alliance the United States, Great Britain, Canada, Belgium, Italy, France, the Netherlands, Luxembourg, Iceland, Denmark, Norway, and Portugal. Greece, Turkey, and West Germany joined later. NATO was based on **collective security,** an agreement by which "an armed attack against one or more of them in Europe or North America shall be considered an attack against all of them." General Dwight D. Eisenhower, commander of NATO's forces, exercised sole authority over the atomic weapons that the United States committed to the defense of NATO.

Then, in September 1949, the Soviet Union exploded its first atomic bomb. Much sooner than military experts had expected, the United States had lost its nuclear monopoly. Faced with this new threat, Congress quickly passed the NATO appropriations bill. In 1955 the Soviet Union and its satellites countered NATO by establishing their own military alliance—the Warsaw Pact. The arms race was well under way.

Within a few years, both the United States and the Soviet Union developed a new and more powerful weapon—the hydrogen bomb. Later, other nations, including Great Britain, France, and China, also built nuclear weapons.

Rebuilding Europe

CAUSES

- Communist guerrillas control much of Greece
- European countries suffer economic devastation after World War II

The Marshall Plan

EFFECTS

- Congress responds by voting military and economic aid to Greece
- Western European economies prosper

Section 1 ★ Assessment

Checking for Understanding

1. **Define** communism, satellite nation, purge, buffer, guerrilla, containment, collective security.

2. **Explain** how the Soviet Union controlled its satellite nations.

Critical Thinking

3. **Analyzing Policies** How did exercising the Truman Doctrine in Greece nullify the Monroe Doctrine of 1823?

4. **Summarizing** Re-create the diagram shown here, and list the Truman administration's major foreign policy goals.

Foreign Policy Goals

INTERDISCIPLINARY ACTIVITY

5. **Government** Select a nation mentioned in Section 1 and create a time line of important events in the nation's history between World War II and the present.

BUILDING SKILLS
Critical Thinking Skills

Hypothesizing

Hypothesizing is the process of forming a tentative explanation based on available evidence. A hypothesis offers a possible answer to a problem, or an explanation for why a situation or condition exists.

The Occupation of Berlin

Tegel
EAST BERLIN
Gatow
WEST BERLIN
Brandenburg Gate
Spree R.
Tempelhof

Allied Sectors in Berlin
- British
- American
- French
- Russian
- Airports

0   5   10 miles
0   5   10 kilometers

Learning the Skill

A hypothesis cannot be judged right or wrong until it is confirmed or disproved by additional evidence. The following guidelines will help you form hypotheses.

- **Analyze** the information that is being presented and write it as a statement.

- **Form** possible hypotheses that may explain the statement you have written.

- **Gather** additional evidence about the situation and test each hypothesis.

- **Accept** or reject each hypothesis.

Study the map on this page showing the Allied occupation of Berlin. Note how the guidelines on hypothesizing have been applied.

a. Berlin was divided and occupied by the Allies. The Soviets occupied East Berlin. West Berlin was divided into French, British, and American sectors.

b. *Hypothesis:* Berlin was divided among the Allies because the Western nations did not want the Soviets to have control of it.

Hypothesis: Berlin was divided so that its citizens would have self-government.

Hypothesis: Berlin was divided because the Western Allies feared Soviet intentions.

c. Gather additional evidence to test these hypotheses. Written primary sources are often the most reliable record of what happened.

d. The information provided from reading Chapter 20 and from doing additional research might indicate that the second hypothesis best explains the statement.

Practicing the Skill

1. Form a hypothesis to explain why the United States instituted the Marshall plan.

2. Accept or reject the following hypothesis and explain your reasoning: The policy of containment was intended to hold back the spread of communism.

Glencoe's **Skillbuilder Interactive Workbook, Level 2** provides instruction and practice in key social studies skills.

APPLYING THE SKILL

3. On Saturday morning you find a note in your pocket in your own handwriting that says "study Tues./Wed. civics/multiple choice." You do not remember writing the note or what it means. Explain how you can use hypothesizing and your knowledge of your own habits to figure out the note.

★★★

The Cold War in Asia

Guide to Reading

Main Idea

The cold war escalated into a hot war in Asia.

Reading Strategy

Sequencing Information As you read about the cold war in Asia, use a diagram like the one shown here to trace the events that led to the Korean War.

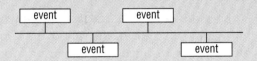

Objectives

After studying this section, you should be able to

★ cite the outcome of the United States's occupation of Japan.

★ explain the political situation in China after the war.

★ explain why the United Nations waged a limited war in Korea.

Key Term

defense perimeter

▶ CHINESE COMMUNIST LEADER MAO ZEDONG

At the close of World War II, the aims of the United States in Asia were to restore peace, help Asian peoples to resist foreign rule, and restore Asian trade with the world. The United States felt it had a special commitment to the Philippines, Japan, and China.

On July 4, 1946, the United States carried out its promise of independence for the Philippines. In return for special business rights and the lease of military bases, the United States gave the Philippine nation tariff concessions in American markets and $600 million to repair war damage. Later, when communist-led guerrilla groups revolted against the government, the United States sent money and weapons to put down the rebellion. Despite difficult economic and political problems, the Philippines became an independent, democratic nation.

■ The Occupation of Japan

In July 1945, shortly before the United States dropped atomic bombs on Hiroshima and Nagasaki, the leaders of Great Britain, the United States, and the Soviet Union met in Potsdam, near Berlin. They discussed how they would deal with Germany and Japan after the war.

The agreement regarding Japan provided that Japanese militarists be punished and Japan disarmed, Japanese rule be restricted to their home islands, and the Japanese be reeducated so that a democratic Japanese nation could be formed. American troops would occupy Japan until these aims were accomplished. To carry out this Potsdam Declaration, General Douglas MacArthur was named Supreme Commander of the Allied Powers.

Under MacArthur's leadership, Japan's military was dismantled. A few militarists were tried and convicted of war crimes and hanged. Under American direction, a new constitution provided for elected representative government and woman suffrage. Most other aspects of Japanese culture remained intact. The emperor remained as a symbol of Japan's unity, but he was no longer to be looked upon as a god.

MacArthur encouraged economic opportunity and trade unionism, and he attempted to redistribute large rural tracts to landless Japanese. A reorganized school system taught democratic values. The Allies had planned to make Japan pay reparations for war damages, but MacArthur realized that the Japanese lacked the resources to pay such compensation. Instead, Japan received nearly $2 billion in aid. The Japanese people accepted the reforms. In a treaty signed in San Francisco in 1951, the country gained back its independence. Japan achieved a remarkable recovery, eventually establishing itself as the leading economy of Asia.

■ Communist Triumph in China

Japan's surrender left China a divided nation. The Communists under Mao Zedong [MAU dzuh•DUNG] controlled the north, the Nationalists led by Chiang Kai-shek held the southwest, and Japanese armies occupied the center. The United States helped the Nationalist armies take the land the Japanese had held. In planning for peace, President Roosevelt had insisted to Churchill and Stalin that China be treated as a power. As a result, China gained a permanent seat on the UN Security Council.

Civil War

Since the early 1930s, a civil war between the Nationalist government and the Communists had ravaged China. During World War II, both sides stopped fighting one another and fought the Japanese. In the war against Japan, Mao's Communists grew to

Douglas MacArthur
1880–1964

★★★★ AMERICAN PORTRAITS

Douglas MacArthur was born into a military family. His father won the Congressional Medal of Honor during the Civil War and later became the army's top-ranking general. Following in his father's footsteps, MacArthur saw action during World War I and was twice wounded. By 1918 he had risen to the rank of general. When Japan attacked Pearl Harbor, MacArthur was stationed in the Philippines, where he led its defense.

Ordered to retreat in 1942, he pledged: "I shall return." He kept his promise in 1944 by leading the liberation of the islands. After the war, as commander of U.S. occupation forces in Japan, he wrote its constitution. From July 1950 until President Truman fired him in April 1951, MacArthur commanded UN forces in Korea. Some Republican leaders urged MacArthur to run for President, but he declined and retired.

▲ **AMERICANS IN KOREA** President Truman ordered American forces to the Korean peninsula in June 1950 after North Korean troops invaded South Korea. In the conflict with North Korea, the United States was directly fighting a communist nation for the first time. *What was the outcome of the conflict?*

be a strong guerrilla force. Through his promise of land reform, as well as military and political pressure, Mao's forces were able to extend their control over much of mainland China. The civil war of the 1930s had greatly weakened the Nationalists.

After Japan surrendered, the conflict between the Communists and the Nationalists again flared. To prevent the extension of communist power, Truman sent General George C. Marshall to China. Marshall was unsuccessful. As the Communists gained strength, Chiang asked Truman to send military aid. Marshall, now secretary of state, advised that it was more important to spend the limited foreign-aid resources of the United States on saving Western Europe from Stalin rather than on saving China from Mao. In addition, a fact finder Truman sent to China reported no attempt to save it from the Communists could succeed because:

> " *The only basis on which national Chinese resistance to Soviet aims can be revitalized is through the presently corrupt, reactionary and inefficient Chinese National government.* "

Having already given Chiang's forces $2 billion in aid, the State Department judged that further help would not save the Nationalists from their own internal weaknesses. By the end of 1949 Mao Zedong's forces had forced Chiang's army off the mainland to Taiwan and a few other small islands.

Aftermath of Communist Victory

Truman's China policy came under bitter political attack. Nationalist supporters accused Truman of "writing off" Chiang and losing China to the Communists. Truman believed, however, that most Americans would not support the massive military intervention needed to save Chiang's government.

The United States recognized the Nationalist government in Taiwan as the government of all of China and blocked attempts by Mao's government to gain a seat in the United Nations. To protest the exclusion of the Chinese communist government, the Soviet Union walked out of the United Nations Security Council and boycotted its proceedings.

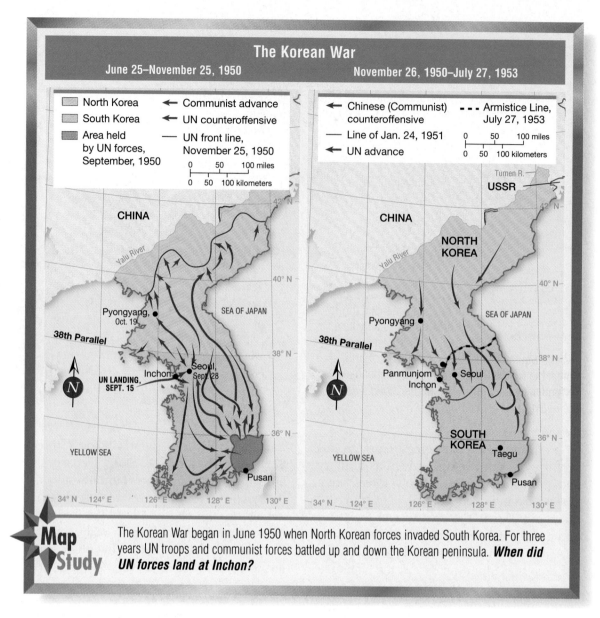

The Korean War

| June 25–November 25, 1950 | November 26, 1950–July 27, 1953 |

North Korea   ← Communist advance
South Korea   ← UN counteroffensive
Area held   — UN front line,
by UN forces,   November 25, 1950
September, 1950

0   50   100 miles
0   50   100 kilometers

← Chinese (Communist)   - - - Armistice Line,
counteroffensive   July 27, 1953
— Line of Jan. 24, 1951
← UN advance

0   50   100 miles
0   50   100 kilometers

CHINA

Yalu River

43° N
40° N
38° N
36° N
34° N

Pyongyang, Oct. 19

SEA OF JAPAN

38th Parallel

Seoul, Sept. 28
Inchon

UN LANDING, SEPT. 15

N

YELLOW SEA

Pusan

124° E   126° E   128° E   130° E

USSR
Tumen R.

CHINA

NORTH KOREA

Yalu River

Pyongyang

SEA OF JAPAN

38th Parallel

Panmunjom
Inchon
Seoul

N

SOUTH KOREA

Taegu

YELLOW SEA

Pusan

124° E   126° E   128° E   130° E

Map Study

The Korean War began in June 1950 when North Korean forces invaded South Korea. For three years UN troops and communist forces battled up and down the Korean peninsula. *When did UN forces land at Inchon?*

War in Korea

When the Japanese surrendered, Soviet Union troops occupied Korea north of the 38th parallel and set up a communist government. As with other Soviet satellite states, North Korea sealed itself off from other countries of the world. A 1948 UN fact-finding commission was not allowed to travel north of the 38th parallel.

In the south the United States supported the government of Syngman Rhee, who was chosen in UN-supervised elections. In 1948 the UN recognized the South Korean Republic as the government of all Korea.

United States military and diplomatic experts advised that Korea should be viewed as outside the **defense perimeter,** or

area that could be protected, of the United States because of the great cost of defending it. The next year the United States withdrew most of its troops from Korea.

On June 25, 1950, North Korean troops invaded South Korea. The Truman administration was not sure whether North Korea was acting by itself or as the agent of the Soviet Union or China. The invasion, however, became a vital test for the UN. Calling an emergency meeting of the Security Council, the United States won a vote to order North Korea to withdraw its troops. On June 27, 1950, as the invasion continued, the Security Council called on all UN members to aid South Korea.

President Truman appointed General MacArthur to command all UN troops in

Korea and instructed him to limit the fighting to South Korean territory below the 38th parallel. Truman also ordered United States military forces to Korea without asking Congress to declare war.

During the summer of 1950, North Korean troops pressed UN forces down the Korean peninsula until they had their backs to the water at Pusan (POO•SAHN), a major port in South Korea. In the fall, however, General MacArthur planned a surprise landing midway up the peninsula at the South Korean port of Inchon.

This landing gave the UN troops the offensive, and MacArthur was given authority by the UN Security Council to liberate North Korea and unite it with the South. By November, UN troops were as far north as the Yalu River valley, bordering communist China, when 200,000 Chinese troops crossed the border to aid the North Koreans. MacArthur's troops were once again pushed back.

Truman Fires MacArthur

A major disagreement soon developed between MacArthur and Truman over the conduct of the war. MacArthur wanted the United States to bomb China and to help Chiang Kai-shek invade China from Taiwan. Truman, however, did not want to risk war with China. In April 1951, Joseph Martin, Republican leader of the House of Representatives, released a letter he had received in which MacArthur criticized the President. MacArthur's letter was a deliberate challenge to the principle that the civilian power of the President must be superior to that of the military. Truman felt he had no choice but to remove MacArthur from command. He explained, "I could do nothing else and still be President of the United States."

The Senate Foreign Relations and Armed Services Committee opened hearings to determine the circumstances of MacArthur's dismissal. Two months of hearings dispelled much of the controversy. Truman's decision emerged as acceptable to the country.

The Conflict Ends

Years of fighting had produced a stalemate in Korea. Presidential candidate Dwight Eisenhower in 1952 pledged to "go to Korea," to settle hostilities. The war continued until 1953, when a cease-fire was declared. Korea was left a divided country, much as it had been before the war began. The Korean struggle was costly for the United States, which lost more than 54,000 troops. But as a result, many neutral nations drew closer to the United States, and noncommunist ones began to arm for their own defense.

• •

Footnotes to History

A New Korea The division of Korea left South Korea with a weakened economy. Today, however, industrial development has made South Korea's economy one of the world's fastest-growing. Among its most important industries are electronics, textiles, and automobiles.

Section 2 ★ Assessment

Checking for Understanding

1. **Define** defense perimeter.

2. **What** was the outcome of the United States's occupation of Japan?

Critical Thinking

3. **Choosing a Position**   Explain the two positions represented by Truman and MacArthur on Korea. Which position would you have chosen?

4. **Analyzing Issues**   Re-create the diagram shown here, and list the reasons why the United States's China policy failed.

Reasons for Failure

INTERDISCIPLINARY ACTIVITY

5. **Government** Create a chart that lists the advantages and disadvantages of civilian control of the military.

★★★★★★★★★★★★★★★★★★★★★★★★★★★★★★★★★

Cold War America

Guide to Reading

Main Idea

As African Americans and women sought to keep the gains they had made during the war, many others in cold war America searched for a sense of security in an increasingly turbulent world.

Reading Strategy

Organizing Information As you read about cold war America, use a diagram such as the one shown here to list the positive and negative aspects of Truman's presidency.

Truman Presidency	
Positive	Negative

Objectives

After studying this section, you should be able to

★ explain changes in the American labor force after the war.

★ describe the condition of African Americans during the 1940s.

★ evaluate the Truman presidency.

Key Terms

jurisdictional strike, featherbedding, subversive

▶ SENATOR ROBERT TAFT

World War II brought great changes to the nation's economy. War industries solved the unemployment problem of the Depression. In fact, with 16 million people in the United States armed services, there was actually a shortage of workers in industry. The number of African American workers in defense industries more than tripled. Six million women joined the labor force, a rise of nearly 60 percent.

■ Prosperity Continues

When the war ended in 1945, people were fearful of depression. In the past, when government spending for war materials stopped and soldiers returned home to look for jobs, unemployment spread. Even if the factories kept running, some newly hired African American and women workers now feared that they would be replaced by returning soldiers.

Fears of a depression proved groundless. After a slight drop in business activity, the number of Americans with jobs actually increased. Several factors contributed to the continuing prosperity. As the United States kept feeding not only its own people but millions of people overseas, farm income remained high. During the war Americans, due to rationing and scarcity of consumer goods, had saved $30 billion. Now they spent their savings for postponed purchases. In addition, Congress stimulated postwar business by cutting wartime taxes nearly $6 billion. Instead of depression, consumer demand stimulated a sharp rise in prices, or inflation. Defense spending, which had dropped to $15 billion by 1949, escalated to $50 billion by 1953, pouring even more money into the economy. In addition, the Marshall Plan restored markets in Europe for American goods.

In some ways the cold war economy of the 1950s resembled the wartime economy of the 1940s. The government's military spending continued to stimulate industrial production, while a portion of the labor force continued in military service.

Women

Immediately following World War II, soldiers returning from service took the places of many women who were employed in factories. In the automobile plants the proportion of women on assembly lines dropped from 25 percent in 1944 to 7.5 percent in 1946. The head of the Women's Bureau, a federal agency set up to protect women's interests, stated that "women ought to be delighted to give up any job and return to their proper sphere in the kitchen." Federal and state aid to child-care centers in factories was stopped.

Yet continued prosperity created new job opportunities. By 1952 more than 2 million more women were employed than in 1946. The kinds of work available to women were changing. This change was dramatically reflected in the experience of African American women. Between 1940 and 1950 the percentage of African American women employed as domestic servants dropped from 72 to 48 percent. The number of those working as farm laborers fell from 20 percent to 7 percent. At the same time, the percentage hired by factories rose from 7 percent to 18 percent. The rise in female employment did not mean that women had gained economic equality, however. Women in industries earned less than two-thirds as much as men.

■ Gains for African Americans

As a group, African Americans benefited from the postwar economic boom. Many made the transition from farming to manufacturing, from rural areas to cities, from the South to other regions of the country. The number of African American workers in white-collar, skilled, and supervisory jobs nearly tripled, increasing from about 300,000 to nearly 900,000. As opportunities for African Americans opened up fields such as law, nursing, and professional sports, average income—even adjusted for inflation—almost doubled.

▼ **1953 Packard convertible**

▲ **Purchasing Power** The United States enjoyed an economic boom in the early postwar years. Increasing consumer demand for necessities as well as luxury items fueled inflation, however. *How did job opportunities for women change during the early 1950s?*

Changing social attitudes helped these advances. The war against Germany and the cold war both played a part. The horrifying racism of the Nazis helped to make some Americans more sensitive to racism in their own country. They began to realize that not only African Americans, but also Asian Americans, Hispanic Americans, and other minorities had been treated unfairly and denied social and economic opportunities.

During this period, African Americans worked hard to gain civil rights. During the war, the membership of the National Association for the Advancement of Colored People (NAACP) rose from 100,000 to 351,000. The NAACP hired teams of able lawyers to bring a series of lawsuits to the federal courts to end violations of the constitutional rights of African American citizens. Like women, however, African Americans fell short of gaining full equality in the 1940s.

In the North, African Americans often lived in crowded inner-city areas. Wages averaged about 60 percent of those paid to white workers. African American workers were still likely to be "last hired, first fired." In the South old patterns of segregation and racism remained. African American Southerners resented that their children had to attend separate schools that were often ill-equipped and understaffed. They objected to Jim Crow laws that forced them to use segregated facilities. Even worse, most African American Southerners were denied the vote, either by custom or by law. Almost none held political office.

■ Inflation in the Postwar Years

Government spending on wartime military programs and for postwar domestic programs brought prosperity and inflation. During periods of inflation the amount of money in circulation increases and prices rise sharply as the demand for goods exceeds the supply.

Because increased taxes were not sufficient to pay the costs of war, the federal government ran a large deficit during World War II. The national debt rose from $50 million to nearly $270 billion. The government borrowed much of this money from Federal Reserve Banks. Using the federal bonds that the government gave as security, the banks issued new money. As a result, there was four times as much money in circulation in 1945 as there was in 1938.

As inflation drove prices up, the purchasing power of paychecks decreased. When consumers could not buy as much, factories slowed production, returning to a 40-hour week, and employers stopped paying overtime. Workers, losing purchasing power, demanded pay raises and often went on strike. In 1946 there were nearly 5,000 strikes, in which nearly 4.6 million workers took part—a record that is unlikely to be surpassed. Some strikes hit industries basic to the national economy such as steel, transportation, and coal. When railroad workers went on strike, President Truman asked Congress for power to draft them into the army. Fortunately, however, the strike ended before this measure was necessary.

■ The Taft-Hartley Act

Union activities were a major issue in the congressional elections of 1946. The anxiety caused by the strikes in basic industries helped conservative, antilabor candidates. The Republicans showed new vigor as they ran on the slogan, "Had enough?" For the first time in 18 years, they gained control of both the Senate and the House.

An immediate result of this swing toward conservatism was the Taft-Hartley Act, passed over President Truman's veto in 1947. Intended to keep unions from abusing their power, the act outlawed practices such as the closed shop, which forced business owners to hire only union members; **jurisdictional strikes,** which forced businesses to recognize one union instead of another; **featherbedding,** which limited workers' output in order to create more jobs; and high fees charged to workers for joining a union. In addition, unions were forbidden to use their money to support political campaigns.

Linking Past and Present

Women and Sports

Over the past 50 years, a revolution has taken place in women's sports. Still, resistance to women's sports did not disappear overnight.

Then

Play Days

Even in the 1950s American physical educators disparaged women's sports. Arguing that organized, competitive sports were "unfeminine" and a "male domain," they tried to channel female athletes' energy into "Play Days" and other forms of mild exercise. Opportunities for females in interscholastic and intercollegiate sports, in which schools compete against one another, were limited. Males outnumbered females in interscholastic competition by as much as 20 to 1. At the intercollegiate level, the ratio approached 10 to 1.

► BABE DIDRICKSON ZAHARIAS

Now

Changing Attitudes

The rise in the level of women's sports participation is undeniable evidence of strong and dramatic change. Part of the change is due to new attitudes. Campaigns on behalf of female athletics by Billie Jean King, Wilma Rudolph, and many others helped shatter the myth that women and competitive sports did not mix. By the 1990s, nearly 2 million females were taking part in interscholastic sports participation—an increase of 600 percent in a 20-year span—and nearly 100,000 on the intercollegiate level.

The Taft-Hartley Act was a very controversial measure. Its supporters claimed the law held irresponsible unions in check the way the Wagner Act of 1935 restrained antiunion activities of employers. Labor leaders called the act a "slave labor" law. They claimed it erased many of the gains that unions had made since 1933. In addition, they deeply resented that union leaders had to swear they were not members of the Communist party.

■ Election of 1948

As the presidential election of 1948 drew near, the Democratic party was divided. Southern Democrats objected to Truman's civil rights program, which included proposals to end racial, religious, and ethnic discrimination, to abolish immigration quotas, and to integrate the armed forces.

The Candidates

Many white Southerners left the Democratic party to form the "Dixiecrat" party, which nominated South Carolina Governor Strom Thurmond for President. Other Democrats thought Truman was taking too hard a line against the Soviet Union. They supported the Progressive party ticket led by former Vice President Henry Wallace. Truman appeared certain to lose the election; he had lost the support of both the right wing and the left wing of his party. The Democrats renominated Truman only after party leaders failed to persuade General Eisenhower to accept the nomination.

The Republicans united behind their candidate for President, Governor Thomas E. Dewey of New York. Dewey was so confident that he would win that he avoided discussing issues and simply called on Americans to join him in building unity.

The Campaign

Far behind in the public-opinion polls, President Truman pursued an aggressive campaign from the beginning. First, he called the Republican Congress back into special session and asked them to carry out the promises of the Republican party platform by passing civil rights and other progressive legislation. When they failed to act, Truman had his campaign theme: The "do-nothing, good for nothing" Republican 80th Congress. Setting out on a "whistle stop" tour of the country by train, Truman covered 30,000 miles, giving some 350 speeches along the way.

Right up to Election Day, the pollsters predicted a Republican victory. But Truman won 2 million more votes than Dewey and piled up a 303-to-189 margin in the electoral college. Truman had held together the New Deal coalition. He won labor support for his veto of the Taft-Hartley Act. He won support from African American voters for his civil rights proposals. He won the farmers' vote for his support of high farm price supports. Not only did Truman defeat Dewey, but the Democrats regained their majority in Congress.

The Fair Deal

In his Inaugural Address in January 1949, Truman called for a Fair Deal, a return to and expansion of Roosevelt's New Deal policies. President Truman asked for slum clearance, federal subsidies for public schools, government-backed medical insurance, aid to farmers, and higher minimum wages. Although the Democrats held a majority, the new Congress was still influenced by an alliance of Republicans and conservative Southern Democrats. Together they blocked most of Truman's proposals to Congress.

In 1949 postwar prosperity slipped into a recession. Unemployment reached 7 percent of the labor force. The recession lasted only a few months, however. A tax cut passed in 1948 took effect, making more money available. The New Deal's built-in stabilizers such as price supports for agriculture and Social Security benefits helped to lessen the effect of the economic downturn. Beginning in 1950, the Korean War changed the economic picture sharply. Rearmament now competed with the demand for consumer goods. The war also fueled anticommunist sentiment at home.

▲ TRUMAN DISPLAYS HEADLINE THAT WRONGLY PROJECTED DEWEY AS THE WINNER

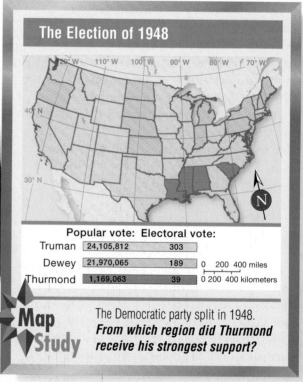

The Election of 1948

Popular vote: Electoral vote:

	Popular vote	Electoral vote
Truman	24,105,812	303
Dewey	21,970,065	189
Thurmond	1,169,063	39

Map Study

The Democratic party split in 1948.
From which region did Thurmond receive his strongest support?

■ Fear of Communists

The cold war and the Korean War heightened fear of communism in the United States. A communist spy ring, which had been sending atomic secrets to the Soviet Union, was uncovered in Canada. To Americans, this explained the Soviets' success in developing an atomic bomb so early. Americans began to suspect that there might be other communist sympathizers and spies in the government, universities, press, and the arts—all working to undermine American democracy. In a period of international tensions, national insecurity led to a search for scapegoats.

Constitutional Rights

The question arose: Should the rights of Communists be protected by the Constitution? In 1949, 11 members of the Communist party in the United States were convicted of conspiracy. The courts held that since the Communist party was organized to overthrow the United States government by force, its members were not entitled to protection by the free speech rights of the First Amendment. Although there were relatively very few Communist party members in the United States, the suspected communist conspiracy led to extensive precautions. Many people were forced to take loyalty oaths before being hired for jobs. Government officials were subjected to security checks.

Loyalty Oaths

During the postwar period, a tendency grew among many Americans to mistake criticism of American institutions for disloyalty. As Judge Harold Medina told the jury that convicted the 11 Communists of conspiracy, taking away the right to criticize does not make a country stronger. Instead, allowing abuses of rights to go unchecked makes it weaker. In several rulings during this period, however, the Supreme Court found state loyalty oaths to be constitutional. The Court noted that the states had a constitutional right to assurance that an employee was not engaged in subversive activity.

Visualizing History

▲ CHARGES OF SUBVERSION In the early 1950s, Senator Joseph R. McCarthy (left) claimed that Communists had infiltrated educational institutions and high levels of government. *What cold war events stirred McCarthy and others?*

Subversives

The "loss" of China to the Communists and the stalemated Korean War helped to create this mood in the United States that was much like the Red Scare in the years following World War I. Critics of Truman accused the President of having lost China, alleging that his close advisers were Communists or communist tools. Senator Robert A. Taft, Republican leader in the Senate, claimed that the State Department was "riddled" with **subversives,** or individuals attempting to overthrow the government.

In 1948 the House Committee on Un-American Activities heard testimony from Whittaker Chambers. Chambers admitted that he had been a communist spy in the 1930s and that he had received secret documents from Alger Hiss, a State Department official. At first, few people believed Chambers's story. However, Richard M. Nixon, a

HISTORY Online

Student Web Activity
Visit the *American History: The Modern Era Since 1865* Web site at **me.glencoe.com** and click on **Chapter 20— Student Web Activities** for an activity about McCarthyism.

young representative from California, pressed the case forward. Finally, Chambers produced several rolls of microfilm of secret documents he claimed to have received from Hiss. Hiss denied these charges. Though not convicted of spying, Hiss was found guilty of lying under oath.

McCarthyism

Increased fears of communist subversion were fertile ground for more reckless voices. At a Lincoln's Day speech in February 1950, Senator Joseph R. McCarthy of Wisconsin accused the Democratic party of "twenty years of treason." McCarthy charged that Roosevelt had deliberately sacrificed the navy at Pearl Harbor and had "sold out" to the Soviet Union at Yalta. In addition, McCarthy claimed to have a list of "card-carrying Communists" in the State Department.

While McCarthy never produced the list, nor a shred of evidence to support his charges, he ruined the careers of many government officials. A growing atmosphere of hysteria inspired other "witch-hunts." Private groups used the communist label to drive liberal professors out of colleges. They made sure books they believed to be subversive were removed from schools. They had many broadcasters, writers, and entertainers barred from television and kept many actors from working on the stage and in films.

Years later a Senate committee determined that McCarthy's accusations and investigations had been groundless. The use of indiscriminate, unfounded political accusations to destroy or assassinate the character of one's opponent came, in time, to be known as McCarthyism.

■ Truman's Legacy

In 1952 President Truman announced that he would not run for reelection. By the time Truman left office, he had become unpopular. The successful Soviet atomic bomb explosion, the defeat of the Nationalists in China, and the problems with carrying out the war in Korea, all contributed to charges that Truman was "soft on communism." Other Americans thought his loyalty program had hurt innocent people.

Instances of corruption in high places were also discovered—some of the President's closest aides had received valuable gifts in return for political favors. Although Truman was not personally involved, the "Truman scandals" gave the Republicans a ready-made issue for the 1952 elections.

The problems Truman faced were new and complex. Congress was often suspicious or hostile, yet Truman got many of his programs enacted. Americans were tired of foreign involvements, yet he managed to keep the nation from retreating into isolationism. Truman's reputation as leader rose after he left the White House. Most of the Fair Deal measures he called for eventually became law. His policy of "containment" was continued by other Presidents. He set the United States on a course that included an unwavering defense of democracy everywhere.

Section 3 ★ Assessment

Checking for Understanding

1. **Define** jurisdictional strike, featherbedding, subversive.

2. **List** reasons why economic growth continued after World War II.

Critical Thinking

3. **Analyzing Issues** Re-create the diagram shown here, and list both the gains made and the limitations faced by African Americans in their struggle for equality.

INTERDISCIPLINARY ACTIVITY

4. **The Arts** Draw a political cartoon that focuses on the effect Senator Joseph McCarthy had on the American people.

▲ FLORIDA FAMILY MOVING NORTH

African American Migration

African American migration from the rural South to Northern and Western cities between 1910 and 1950 was one of the largest migrations in American history. African Americans migrated in search of greater economic opportunity and a better life than the drought, boll weevils, racism, and poverty they were accustomed to in the South. Much of the African American migration took place during the two world wars.

During World War I, industrial agents traveled the South promising jobs with high wages and free transportation to the North. Soon the African American population of cities such as Chicago, Cleveland, and Detroit swelled. Detroit alone saw an increase of over 600 percent.

In the 1940s rural Southern African Americans streamed into Northern and Western cities for two main reasons. First, around 1940 cotton farming became mechanized. Far fewer workers were needed, and many African Americans became jobless. Second, many saw great opportunity in wartime industries.

Although social and economic gains in the cities were limited by racial prejudice, African Americans acquired a political voice. Their migration forever changed the face of American politics and society.

Making the Geography Connection

1. Where did African Americans migrate to during the period from 1910 to 1950?

2. Why did they migrate from the rural South?

ACTIVITY

3. Prepare a chart of population in 1970, 1980, and 1990 for several cities in your state. Write a paragraph that accounts for the population trends.

Using Vocabulary

Use the following vocabulary terms to write a paragraph describing the Soviet establishment of an iron curtain and the development of the cold war.

communism   satellite nation
containment   subversive

Reviewing Facts

1. Discuss how and why the Soviets created a buffer of satellite states.

2. Explain why communism appealed to people in certain parts of the world.

3. Summarize arguments for and against containment and the Truman Doctrine.

4. Explain how the Truman agenda for prosperity at home and abroad enabled him to win in 1948.

Understanding Concepts

Political and Economic Power

1. How did the United States use its power to shape economic recovery in Europe?

Leadership

2. Re-create the diagram shown here, and explain how the goals and leadership styles of Stalin and Mao Zedong were similar.

Stalin and Mao Zedong

Goals

Styles

Critical Thinking

1. **Applying Ideas**   What does the term "cold war" mean and how does it apply to this era?

2. **Testing Conclusions**   According to some experts, the United States failed to save China because of its loyalty to the Nationalists and its ignorance of China's true situation. Test this theory using information from the text.

3. **Making Comparisons** Write a report comparing the purposes and provisions of the Monroe Doctrine and the Truman Doctrine. Address such questions as: What were the foreign policy objectives that the United States tried to accomplish in each case? What commitment of resources was required to support each doctrine? Explain what the differences indicate about fundamental change in foreign policy between the 1820s and the 1940s. Share your findings with the class.

4. **Analyzing Political Cartoons** Study the political cartoon on this page and answer the questions that follow.

   a. Whom do the individuals in the cartoon represent?

   b. What is the cartoonist saying about Truman's power?

History and Geography

Postwar Europe

Study the map on page 613 and answer the questions that follow.

1. **Location** What countries occupied Germany?
2. **Movement** Into what city did air corridors flow? What was the purpose of the corridors?

Cooperative Learning Interdisciplinary Activity: Debate

Working in groups of three, conduct a debate about the possible alternatives of United States foreign policy in Europe after World War II. One member should propose and support pulling troops out of Europe to lessen the Soviets' perceived need for a buffer of satellites. Another should support the contention that a heavy military presence is needed in Europe to contain them. The third member should decide which position was best supported and explain why.

Practicing Skills

Hypothesizing

Study the graphs on the Marshall Plan and European recovery on this page. Indicate whether each hypothesis below is correct, incorrect, or not answerable.

1. A large majority of the Plan's funds went to Eastern European nations.
2. Agricultural production grew at a faster rate than industrial production.
3. Industrial production grew at its fastest rate in Western Europe.

Technology Activity

Using the Internet Search the Internet for the nation's yearly inflation figures from 1946 to the present. Draw a bar or line graph showing your data. Beneath the graph, list the years with the highest and lowest inflation as well as any trends you determined from the graph.

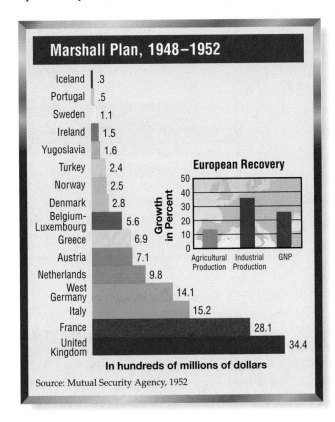

Marshall Plan, 1948–1952

Iceland	.3
Portugal	.5
Sweden	1.1
Ireland	1.5
Yugoslavia	1.6
Turkey	2.4
Norway	2.5
Denmark	2.8
Belgium-Luxembourg	5.6
Greece	6.9
Austria	7.1
Netherlands	9.8
West Germany	14.1
Italy	15.2
France	28.1
United Kingdom	34.4

In hundreds of millions of dollars

Source: Mutual Security Agency, 1952

European Recovery

Growth in Percent (0–50)

Agricultural Production, Industrial Production, GNP

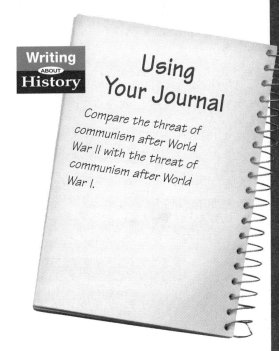

Writing ABOUT History

Using Your Journal

Compare the threat of communism after World War II with the threat of communism after World War I.

CHAPTER 21

★★★

Search for Stability
1952–1960

▼ 1957 CHEVROLET

Setting the Scene

Focus

A war hero, Dwight D. Eisenhower became one of the most popular Presidents of modern times. His domestic and foreign policies were stable and consistent. At home, the nation was generally prosperous. In foreign policy he continued Truman's efforts at containment. The cold war expanded into the Middle East, Africa, and Latin America. Covert operations increased, and American troops were sent into Lebanon.

Concepts to Understand

★ Why the United States's **international leadership** led to the use of covert operations in other countries

★ How **economic growth** stimulated the economy during the 1950s

Read to Discover . . .

★ how President Eisenhower viewed his role as President.

★ how the lives of most Americans improved following World War II.

Chapter Overview
Visit the *American History: The Modern Era Since 1865* Web site at **me.glencoe.com** and click on ***Chapter 21—Chapter Overviews*** to preview chapter information.

Journal Notes

As you read the chapter, record in your journal the efforts of the United States to contain the spread of communism.

CULTURAL

• **1952** *Ralph Ellison publishes* Invisible Man

• **1955** *Jonas Salk develops vaccine to prevent polio*

| 1950 | 1953 |

• **1950** *McCarthy charges communist influence in government*
• **1952** *Eisenhower elected President*

POLITICAL

• **1953** *Truce in the Korean War reached*
• **1954** *Geneva Conference divides Vietnam*

Snack Bar
by Isabel Bishop, 1954

The 1950s was an era of social change for many Americans. Artist Isabel Bishop captures the lonely aspects of urban life and the nature of the fast-food culture.

◀ BASEBALL PLAYER JACKIE ROBINSON

• **1957** *The musical West Side Story premieres in New York*

1956

• **1955** *Formation of the AFL-CIO*
• **1956** *Suez crisis erupts*

• **1960** *There are more than 45 million television sets in American homes*

1959

• **1959** *Castro comes to power in Cuba*
• **1960** *Soviets shoot down a United States U-2 surveillance plane*

★★

The Eisenhower Years

Guide to Reading

Main Idea

The United States looked to a hero of World War II to guide them through the unstable cold war years.

Reading Strategy

Organizing Information As you read about the Eisenhower years, use a diagram like the one shown here, and list reasons for Eisenhower's appeal to moderate Democrats.

Eisenhower's Appeal

Objectives

After studying this section, you should be able to

★ describe President Eisenhower's style of leadership.

★ explain how Senator Joseph McCarthy's influence came to an end.

Key Term

presidential succession

▶ **EISENHOWER CAMPAIGN BUTTON**

After 7 years of the Truman administration and 20 years of Democratic leadership, the Republicans hoped that 1952 would be their year. They knew Americans were worried about the continuing war in Korea and the tense cold war. Americans were also concerned with the charges of communist infiltration in the government. President Truman's reputation was damaged by news reports that some of his officials had accepted bribes. These issues gave the Republicans their rallying cry for the election. They ran against "Korea, communism, and corruption."

■ The Election of 1952

As their candidate, the Republicans picked one of the most popular war heroes, Dwight D. Eisenhower.

When asked to run for President in 1948, Eisenhower refused. By 1952, however, he became concerned that isolationists might regain the White House and agreed to run. He won the Republican nomination after a hotly contested race with Senator Robert A. Taft of Ohio. As his running mate, Eisenhower chose Richard M. Nixon, a 39-year-old senator from California who had made his reputation pursuing alleged Communists in government.

"I Like Ike"

The Republicans adopted the slogan "It's time for a change!" Eisenhower, known as "Ike," promised to end the war in Korea and took a hard line against corruption. "I like Ike" became the Republican rallying cry.

Eisenhower's promise to keep his administration clean was soon regarded with skepticism. Charges were disclosed that Richard

Nixon had received gifts from California businesspeople totaling $18,000 while he was a senator. For a while, it looked as though Nixon might be dropped from the ticket. But in a nationwide speech broadcast on radio and television, he insisted the funds had been used for legitimate political purposes. He did admit that his family had kept one gift, a cocker spaniel puppy named "Checkers." The "Checkers speech" saved Nixon, who remained on the Republican ticket.

Eisenhower Defeats Stevenson

The Democrats nominated Adlai Stevenson, governor of Illinois. Stevenson was a thoughtful and eloquent liberal, but his campaign was burdened by the need to defend the actions of the Truman administration.

It is doubtful that Stevenson ever had a chance to win against the popular Eisenhower. If he did, he lost it two weeks before Election Day, when Eisenhower promised to make a trip to Korea if elected. The election was a landslide for Eisenhower. He received in excess of 6 million popular votes more than Stevenson and carried the electoral

college by 442 to 89 votes. The Republicans also gained an eight-seat majority in the House. The Senate was evenly divided between Democrats and Republicans.

■ A New Style of Leadership

Although Eisenhower was a career soldier, he did not run the White House like an officer commanding an army. Instead, he acted as the chief administrator or leader of the White House team.

Hidden-Hand Presidency

Under Eisenhower the cabinet assumed new importance and acted as a genuine advisory board. For the first time in history, the cabinet had a full-time secretary, an agenda, and regularly kept minutes. Eisenhower made Sherman Adams, former governor of

Visualizing History ▲ EISENHOWER BECOMES PRESIDENT Dwight D. Eisenhower proved to be a popular campaigner and was the first Republican to be elected President since 1928. *How great was his margin of victory over Stevenson in 1952?*

New Hampshire, his chief of staff. Adams wielded great power by controlling access to the President.

The advantages of Eisenhower's kind of administration were clear. If, for some reason, the President was unable to lead, the government would not come to a standstill. Cabinet members could easily take over day-to-day operations. Indeed, Eisenhower suffered serious illnesses three times during his presidency, and each time the White House staff carried on with little difficulty. Critics claimed that the President was abdicating his responsibilities. At crucial times he seemed unaware of decisions made by his aides. Historians later described Eisenhower's management style as a "hidden-hand presidency."

The Bricker Amendment

Eisenhower hoped to establish good working relations with Congress, but members of his own party sometimes made this difficult. Still angry over the secret agreements that President Roosevelt had made with Stalin and Churchill at Yalta, Republican senator John Bricker of Ohio introduced a bill to limit presidential power. The Bricker Amendment required Senate ratification of all agreements made by the President with other nations. It also prohibited the President from making a treaty that conflicted with the laws of any state.

A Narrow Victory

Eisenhower believed that the Bricker Amendment would limit the President's

- -
Footnotes to History

A New Cabinet Post During his first term, President Eisenhower worked to reorganize the government. The Department of Health, Education, and Welfare was created in 1953. Oveta Culp Hobby, commander of the Women's Air Corps during World War II, became the head of the department. She was the second woman in American history to hold a cabinet post. Frances Perkins, secretary of labor during Franklin Roosevelt's presidency, was the first.

power to deal effectively with other nations. It would also allow any state to disrupt United States foreign policy. Although most Republicans in Congress supported the Bricker Amendment, the Eisenhower administration fought hard against it. In February 1954, the bill was defeated by a single vote. Wearily, the President commented:

> **If it is true that when you die the things that bothered you most are engraved on your skull, I am sure I'll have there the mud and dirt of France during the invasion and the name of Senator Bricker.**

■ McCarthy's Influence Ends

Some Americans believed that a Republican President would put an end to Senator Joseph McCarthy's charges that the government was filled with Communists. But McCarthy continued his crusade and subjected many government officials to humiliating investigations.

For a time McCarthy succeeded in giving the impression that he was saving the country from communism. A public opinion poll taken in 1954 reported that 50 percent of the people favored him and 29 percent opposed him. Senators wary of McCarthy's influence with the voters were reluctant to oppose him.

Although the President privately disapproved of McCarthy and his methods, Eisenhower refused to attack him publicly. The President believed that if he fought McCarthy, he would only give him more publicity. This tactic, however, deprived McCarthy's opponents in Congress of Eisenhower's leadership.

McCarthy's underhanded tactics were finally exposed to the public in 1954. In televised hearings regarding possible communist subversion in the army, Americans observed McCarthy's callous disregard of law and fairness. After the hearings ended, the Senate passed a resolution condemning McCarthy for his conduct.

◼ The Election of 1956

In September 1955, President Eisenhower suffered a heart attack. Although the President recovered rapidly, the nation's confidence was shaken. The stock market dropped more sharply than it had since 1929. Then, within the next two years, Eisenhower suffered two major illnesses.

Presidential Disability

The President's health focused attention on the question of **presidential succession,** the order in which others fill the office of President. Although Eisenhower had kept the government running smoothly during his illnesses, Americans wondered what would happen if the President remained ill. The Constitution provides that the Vice President becomes President if the President is unable to handle the duties of office. However, it does not say who is to decide whether the President is, or is not, able to serve.

The matter was addressed in 1967 after ratification of the Twenty-fifth Amendment, which outlines procedures when the President is disabled. Moreover, it deals with the situation when a President feels capable of continuing in office but is thought by others to be incapable.

In 1956 the Republicans renominated Eisenhower. The Republicans claimed that the Eisenhower administration had brought peace and prosperity to the nation. Eisenhower had ended the war in Korea and avoided other world conflicts. The Democrats, nominating Adlai Stevenson for a second time, capitalized on fear about the President's health. They played upon the public's concern that Vice President Nixon might become President.

Eisenhower Is Reelected

Eisenhower won by a greater margin than in 1952. Eisenhower's personal popularity led him to a decisive victory. He won 35.6 million popular votes to Stevenson's 26 million. Eisenhower had 457 electoral votes while Stevenson had 74. The President's popularity did not rub off on his party, however. Democrats won control of both the House of Representatives and the Senate. The Democrats had a slight majority in the Senate, 49 to 47 seats, and a sizable majority in the House. Consequently, Eisenhower became the first President in more than 100 years to take office without his party controlling either house of Congress.

In his second term, Eisenhower was more independent of his party than any other President in the twentieth century. Many conservative Republicans regarded Eisenhower as too liberal in domestic affairs and too interventionist in foreign affairs. However, "modern Republicans" and some Democrats supported the President. His policies won support from the two Democratic leaders in Congress, House Speaker Sam Rayburn and Senate Majority Leader Lyndon Johnson. On domestic issues, an alliance developed between "modern Republicans" and moderate-to-liberal Democrats.

Section 1 ★ Assessment

Checking for Understanding

1. **Define** presidential succession.

2. **How** did Senator Joseph McCarthy's influence come to an end?

Critical Thinking

3. **Examining Issues** Re-create the diagram shown here to describe Eisenhower's leadership style and to discuss the advantages and disadvantages of the President's leadership.

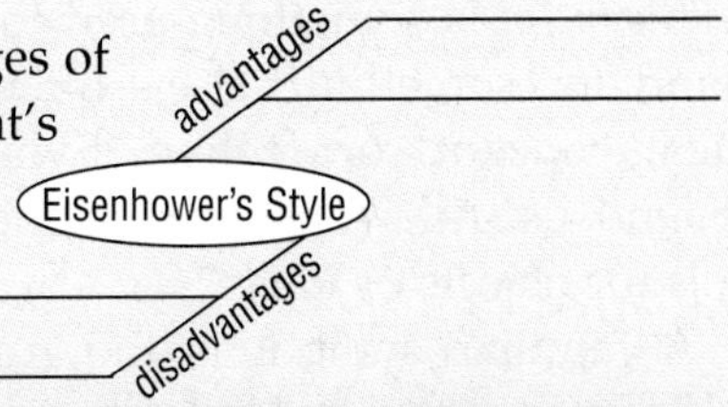

advantages

Eisenhower's Style

disadvantages

INTERDISCIPLINARY ACTIVITY

4. **Government** Write an editorial in which you argue whether or not a military official should be President.

Analyzing Symbols

▲ COLD WAR CARTOON

Neil Armstrong was the first person to walk on the moon. This accomplishment had a powerful impact on people all over the world. One reason was that people saw his walking on the moon as a symbol, and they attached extra meaning to it.

Learning the Skill

A *symbol* is something used to represent or stand for something else—often an abstract idea, concept, or feeling. Symbols are all around us. All words, for example, are symbols for objects or ideas.

A familiar symbol is the American flag, which stands for the United States and patriotic pride. Other familiar symbols include the color purple, which stands for royalty; and lions, which stand for courage.

Armstrong's moon walk symbolizes human progress, the power of modern technology, and our never-ending curiosity about the universe. The following guidelines will help you discover symbolism in history:

- Think about the event or condition being studied. What is the main activity in it?
- What overall condition led to this main activity?
- Who or what situation could be affected by this activity?
- What consequences could there be for those who are affected?
- What statement could be made that would demonstrate the symbolism, or meaning, of this event?

For example, possible statements of the symbolism in McCarthyism include:

   a. McCarthyism symbolized a callous disregard for law and fairness.

   b. McCarthyism symbolized cold war mistrust between two superpowers.

Practicing the Skill

1. Analyze the political cartoon on this page. What do the two figures symbolize?

2. Why do you think the cartoonist used those two figures? What other figures might he have chosen?

 Glencoe's **Skillbuilder Interactive Workbook, Level 2** provides instruction and practice in key social studies skills.

APPLYING THE SKILL

3. Create a table with two columns. In the first column, write down the symbols used to represent your school. In the second column, answer these questions: What does each symbol stand for? How does the symbol represent that idea?

★★★

"The Straight Road"

Main Idea
During Eisenhower's presidency, the nation enjoyed prosperity and rapid economic growth.

Reading Strategy
Organizing Information As you read about business affairs under Eisenhower, use the diagram shown here to trace the development of America's economic growth.

Objectives
After studying this section, you should be able to
★ explain the Eisenhower administration's economic policies.
★ discuss the plight of the small farmer in the 1950s.

Key Term
agribusiness

▶ LABOR UNION SYMBOL

Throughout both of his administrations, Eisenhower steered a course between conservatism and liberalism. Ike's middle course pleased most Americans. At the beginning of his administration it looked as though he might try to undo the New Deal. Like Hoover, Eisenhower believed that the role of government should be limited. Eisenhower advocated cutting the budget, reducing taxes, and ending government regulation of business. He condemned the Tennessee Valley Authority as "creeping socialism" and tried unsuccessfully to arrange for private industry to build new power plants in Tennessee, Alabama, and Kentucky.

Eisenhower and the New Deal

Despite this conservative agenda, Eisenhower recognized that New Deal programs were strongly supported by most Americans. He wrote in a private letter:

❝ *Should any political party attempt to abolish Social Security, unemployment insurance, and eliminate labor laws and farm programs, you would not hear of that party again in our political history.* ❞

The debate during Eisenhower's presidency was not over ending such New Deal programs as Social Security or the minimum wage, but over how much larger to allow them to become. With President Eisenhower's encouragement, Congress extended Social Security to 7 million more people and increased benefits. Congress also extended unemployment compensation to 4 million more people. Eisenhower tried to persuade Congress to enact a health insurance program partly funded by the federal government, but Congress rejected the legislation.

■ Business and Labor

Big business also had an ally in the White House. During the 1950s, 3,000 companies merged with the 500 largest corporations without any antitrust challenges by the government. The nation's 100 largest companies controlled more than 30 percent of all industrial production. Some corporations, such as General Motors and American Telephone and Telegraph, had annual budgets that were larger than those of many countries.

The American labor movement grew more slowly than big business, but it continued to gain strength. In 1955 the American Federation of Labor (AFL) and the Congress of Industrial Organizations (CIO) merged, forming the AFL-CIO. The merger increased the strength of organized labor and made it easier for workers to form local unions.

Organized labor tried hard to win pay increases. During the 1950s, take-home pay and buying power rose sharply. Workers also enjoyed longer paid vacations. Walter Reuther, United Auto Workers president, observed that the movement was developing a "whole new middle class."

Organized labor was not very successful in its efforts to organize the lowest-paid factory workers and office workers. Often, these workers were women or minorities. The growth in AFL-CIO membership actually slowed by 1957.

Union growth was also adversely affected by congressional investigations into corrupt union practices. The investigations revealed that strong-arm tactics were used by some unions to force employers into accepting the unions. The Teamsters' Union, accused of misappropriating funds, was expelled from the AFL-CIO. These revelations began to turn public opinion against unions.

■ Farm Problems

Despite the prosperity of the 1950s, it was a difficult time for many of the nation's farmers. Between 1948 and 1956, the farmers' share of the national income dropped from 9 to 4 percent. While the average American enjoyed a per capita income of $1,629, the farm population averaged $632 a year.

Visualizing History

▲ **LABOR UNIONS MERGE** George Meany (left), president of the AFL, and Walter Reuther, president of the CIO, shake hands on the merger of the two unions. *How did the joining of these unions help organized labor?*

Betty Friedan (free•DAN) was one of the first to analyze the lives of women. When she began her analysis, most women were homemakers or worked in low-paying jobs.

In 1957 she began a year-long study of her Smith College classmates. She discovered that many of these well-educated women were leading unhappy lives. With additional research it became clear to Friedan that American women were failing to find fulfillment in life. Instead, they were succumbing to "the feminine mystique"—a belief that they were supposed to ignore their talents and interests and live only for the achievements of their family.

In 1963 Friedan published *The Feminine Mystique*, a book that sparked the modern women's liberation movement. In 1966 she helped found the National Organization for Women (NOW) to lead the fight for equal rights.

Question of Price Supports

Eisenhower was reluctant to have the government continue to guarantee farmers set prices for their products. The heart of the issue, according to the administration, was

> " *... whether our farms are to continue to be operated by freemen. Or ... to offset some very real and obvious problems that farmers now face, will government go in the opposite direction and subsidize agriculture in such a manner that it also takes control?* "

But without strong price supports from the government, the small family farmer faced economic ruin. Overproduction from better seeds, fertilizers, and mechanization kept farm prices low. Legislation reduced but did not end price supports or the farm surplus.

Many small farm families gave up and sold out to large farm owners who raised only a single crop and used the latest machinery and agricultural methods. Because of their efficiency, the large farm owners could cut their costs and still make a profit. More small farmers were unable to compete with the **agribusinesses,** or modern large-scale farms that covered 1,000 acres or more. By 1959 half of the nation's farmland belonged to 4 percent of the farmers.

Seasonal Workers

There were other problems associated with America's changing agricultural patterns. Large farm owners hired seasonal workers to cultivate and harvest their crops. Many of the workers were Mexican Americans from California and the Southwest, but as many as 400,000 workers were Mexicans allowed into the United States on short-term visas. Unprotected by the National Labor Relations Act or federal minimum wage laws, these migrant workers labored long hours for little pay and endured terrible living conditions. Their children grew up with little, if any, education.

■ Prosperity and Recession

Much of the economic growth of the 1950s was due to a tremendous increase in consumer credit. Effective advertising enticed Americans to borrow more money to buy houses, cars, and consumer goods.

This growing demand, in turn, encouraged industries to produce more goods and hire more people.

President Eisenhower worried that this rapid growth of the economy would lead to inflation, or rapidly rising prices. Because of this he tried to hold down domestic and military spending. But in 1957 and 1958, his attempts to balance the budget set off a recession. Sales dropped and manufacturers laid off workers. Unemployment rose to 7.6 percent of the workforce. Eisenhower resisted congressional pressure for a tax cut to stimulate the economy. Finally, late in 1958, boom times returned again.

Although President Eisenhower remained a popular leader during the late 1950s, he was sharply blamed by some critics for not moving quickly enough. Some detractors charged that the President ignored important national issues such as civil rights and the protection of natural resources.

At the same time, the administration also had to deal with a number of scandals. The most publicized scandal revolved around Sherman Adams, the President's closest adviser. In the spring of 1958, congressional hearings disclosed that Adams had received gifts from a wealthy Boston industrialist who was under investigation by the government. Adams was forced to resign. The recession and the scandals hurt the Republican cause during the 1958 elections, and the Democrats strengthened their control of both houses, winning 15 additional seats in the Senate and 48 seats in the House. Despite these difficulties, Eisenhower received praise for some of his efforts. In foreign policy, he sought to ease world tensions. During his last year in office, the President visited an unprecedented number of nations on a goodwill tour. He affirmed that

> 66 *Our basic aspiration is to search out methods by which peace in the world can be assured with justice for everybody.* 99

At home, he backed government grants to help in the building of more schools for the nation's expanding school-age population. Eisenhower also supported the National Defense Education Act of 1958. This law provided a $295 million fund to provide loans to college students for their education.

In 1959 two new states were added to the union. On January 3 Eisenhower issued a proclamation making Alaska the 49th state—the first new state since Arizona and New Mexico joined the Union in 1912. On August 21, Hawaii became the 50th state.

★★★ **AMERICA'S FLAGS** ★★★

The Stars and Stripes Today The 50-star flag of the United States was raised for the first time on July 4, 1960. New stars were added in 1959 for Alaska and in 1960 for Hawaii. The Stars and Stripes has been through 27 versions in all.

★★★★★★★★★★★★★★★★★★★★★★★

Section 2 ★ Assessment

Checking for Understanding

1. **Define** agribusiness.

2. **Characterize** the economic philosophy and practice of Eisenhower.

Critical Thinking

3. **Comparing Trends** Compare developments in business and agriculture during the 1950s, including the impact on workers.

4. **Summarizing** Re-create the diagram shown here, and list the problems farmers faced during the 1950s.

Farmers' Problems

INTERDISCIPLINARY ACTIVITY

5. **Economics** Imagine you are President Eisenhower's speech writer. Write a short speech incorporating the President's economic goals.

★★★★★★★★★★★★★★★★★★★★★★★★★★★★★★★★★★★

An Affluent Society

► THE TELEVISION GENERATION

Guide to Reading

Main Idea

The prosperity of the 1950s brought great changes, as many Americans for the first time enjoyed a life of comfort and abundance.

Reading Strategy

Taking Notes As you read about the affluent society in the 1950s, describe the technological and medical breakthroughs made during this time. Use an outline form like the one shown here.

Breakthroughs

I. Technological
  A.
  B.

II. Medical
  A.
  B.

Objectives

After studying this section, you should be able to

★ describe the effect of affluence on American life.

★ give examples of advances in medical technology.

★ explain the pressures of conformity in the 1950s.

Key Term

automation

After World War II, Americans were ready to settle down and enjoy a period of peace and prosperity. Industry responded to the demands of Americans by turning out huge quantities of new goods. New communities and housing developments were built as people moved from the cities to the suburbs. Americans were on the move, and they relied heavily on the automobile for this new mobility. People anxiously awaited each year's new car models with their added gadgets and longer "tail fins." Highways stretched across the country carrying more and more traffic. A new suburban lifestyle evolved among middle-class Americans.

New technology and continuing prosperity allowed many Americans to enjoy more leisure time. At the same time, the number of available leisure activities increased.

■ An Economy of Abundance

In 1958 economist John Kenneth Galbraith published *The Affluent Society*, in which he claimed that America's postwar prosperity was a new phenomenon. In the past, Galbraith said, all societies were based on an "economy of scarcity," in which the productivity of the economy was limited by a lack of resources and overpopulation.

In the 1950s, however, the United States and a few other highly industrialized nations were experiencing what Galbraith called an "economy of abundance." Up-to-date technology enabled these nations to produce an endless variety and amount of goods and services for their people. Many citizens of these countries were enjoying a standard of living never before thought possible.

▲ COMPUTERS COME OF AGE Early computers, such as the UNIVAC, occupied entire rooms and used vacuum tubes rather than microchips to process information. *How did most businesses first use computers?*

Some critics accused Galbraith of overstating the situation, but the facts and figures seemed to support it. Americans produced more than they could use, and this new wealth was being distributed throughout the population. During the 1920s the wealthiest 5 percent of the population received 35 percent of the country's income, but by 1960 this group received only 18 percent.

Life for most Americans was easier than ever before. They earned more money than they needed for such necessities as food and housing. With their surplus income, they purchased automobiles, household appliances, and other luxury items. The number of Americans owning their own homes went up from 40 percent to 60 percent between 1940 and 1960.

Student Web Activity
Visit the *American History: The Modern Era Since 1865* Web site at **me.glencoe.com** and click on *Chapter 21— Student Web Activities* for an activity about economics.

■ Technological and Scientific Progress

The United States made spectacular leaps in the field of science. With more money to spend, an increase in the number of university-trained scientists, and a growing commitment to the future, the United States led the world in new technological developments. America's factories and industries began to use **automation,** the technique of operating a production system using mechanical or electronic devices. With automated production methods, goods could be produced more efficiently and quickly than with human workers.

During the 1950s the use of computers began to revolutionize American industry. Businesses used computers for many purposes. Computers took over bookkeeping functions such as billing and inventory control. They were also used for such things as making hotel reservations, sorting bank checks, guiding satellites, predicting election results, forecasting weather conditions, identifying fingerprints, and setting type for printing.

Automation and computers in the workplace caused many workers to lose their jobs. In the long run, however, computers and automation created more jobs than they eliminated. And the new jobs usually demanded a higher level of education.

Breakthroughs in medicine during the 1950s were also impressive. In April 1955, Americans learned of one of the most important discoveries in the history of medicine. After many years of research, United States scientist Dr. Jonas Salk had developed a vaccine for preventing the dreaded childhood disease known as polio. Within a few years, cases of polio nearly disappeared.

By 1960 other major illnesses, including pneumonia, tuberculosis, and diphtheria, were nearly wiped out. Life expectancy in the United States increased. While cancer and heart disease continued to be serious threats to the lives of Americans, researchers made important advances in diagnosing and treating these diseases.

less-crowded places. This migration of city residents caused rapid growth of suburbs. In the years after World War II, cities became ringed by seemingly endless housing developments carved out of the less densely settled country land. Shopping centers with vast parking lots were built to serve the new suburban population. Businesses and factories also began relocating from the cities to the suburbs, where their workers now lived. The Highway Act of 1956 contributed to the growth of the suburbs by adding 41,000 miles to the interstate highway system.

Meanwhile, cities began to experience serious problems. To handle the flood of automobile traffic, new highways had to be built, often destroying whole urban neighborhoods. Those who were left behind to live in the cities often included poor people and the members of minority groups. With a declining population, cities faced growing financial problems. Taxes could no longer keep up with the demands for such services as public transportation, police protection, housing, and education. ⊕

GEOGRAPHY

■ From Cities to Suburbs

In the 1950s the automobile changed the face of America. No longer did people have to live near their places of work. Those who lived and worked in the city could move to

■ Pressures to Conform

In the affluent 1950s, a new house in the suburbs, a larger television in the living room, and the newest model automobile in the garage represented the fulfillment of the

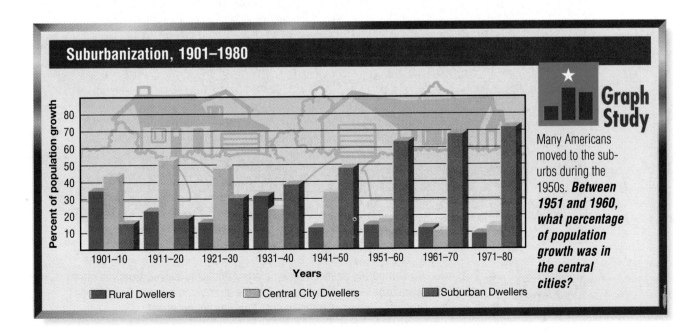

Suburbanization, 1901–1980

Percent of population growth — Years: 1901–10, 1911–20, 1921–30, 1931–40, 1941–50, 1951–60, 1961–70, 1971–80

■ Rural Dwellers ■ Central City Dwellers ■ Suburban Dwellers

Graph Study

Many Americans moved to the suburbs during the 1950s. *Between 1951 and 1960, what percentage of population growth was in the central cities?*

"American Dream." For many young couples, the suburbs offered comfort, security, and a pleasant place to raise their children. Yet it soon became clear that this new lifestyle had problems of its own.

Critics noted that a strong pressure to conform characterized American suburban life. Suburban neighborhoods were usually filled with people who were very much alike. They were generally typified as being young, with comfortable incomes, and having jobs in the service industries. Often this conformity led to discrimination or ostracism of those who seemed "different." For example, in many suburbs racial and religious minorities were unable to buy homes. To some extent, the high cost of homes in the suburbs was the reason, but prejudice was an even more important factor. Often suburban residents refused to sell homes to minority families. If minority families did move to the suburbs, others in the community made them feel unwelcome.

Many writers criticized the trend toward conformity in American life in the 1950s. Nonfiction works, such as David Reisman's *The Lonely Crowd* (1950) and William H. Whyte's *The Organization Man* (1956), and novels such as Sloan Wilson's *The Man in the Gray Flannel Suit* (1956), tried to explain the pressure to conform. Sometimes, as represented in *The Man in the Gray Flannel Suit*, these pressures were so subtly pervasive as to make people feel they had little control over their own lives:

> **❝** *[I]t seemed as though all I could see was a lot of bright young men in gray flannel suits rushing around New York in a frantic parade to go nowhere. They seemed to be pursuing neither ideals nor happiness— they were pursuing a routine. . . . I thought I was on the sidelines watching that parade. . . . It was quite a shock to glance down and see that I too was wearing a gray flannel suit.* **❞**

The pressures to conform in business were especially great. Employees who wanted to advance to better positions took care to adhere to the company's rules. This often meant being loyal to the corporation and being "one of the team." Outside work

Visualizing
History

▲ **SUBURBAN LIFE** During the postwar years, many Americans moved from the farms and cities to the suburbs—and many young people discovered a new cast of heroes such as Davy Crockett. ***What advantages did suburban living offer?***

Linking Past and Present

The Drive-in Theater

The drive-in movie theater is a uniquely American institution. By the very early 1950s, the drive-in had fully arrived.

Then

Movies Under the Stars

Part of the drive-in's appeal was that it met a wish on the part

▼ DRIVE-IN, EARLY 1950s

of families to spend more time together—an important aim, particularly after the disruptions of World War II. Drive-ins provided an inexpensive night out and erased the problem of hiring a baby-sitter. Theater operators provided play areas for children; by the mid-1950s, an estimated 90 percent of drive-ins either contained a children's playground or planned to build one.

Operators provided patrons with such items as car heaters in the winter and window nets in the summer to keep out insects. Other enticements included baby bottle warmers, barbecue pits, and laundromats. Some of the measures to attract customers were clever, but decidedly offbeat. One theater in Asbury Park, New Jersey, provided space for 500 cars and 25 airplanes.

Now

Industry in Decline

Spiraling real estate costs and competition from indoor theaters, television, and the video stifled the drive-in's appeal. From a peak of more than 4,000 in 1958, the number of drive-in theaters has plunged to less than 1,000 today. Yet so deep-rooted is the drive-in experience that for many Americans it is still the perfect night out.

---

it meant having the "right" type of family life and belonging to the "right" clubs and religious groups. Social critics complained that Americans were in danger of losing their individuality.

■ Changes in Family Life

During the 1950s there were renewed social pressures on women to remain at home. Women's magazines ran articles such as "Should I Stop Work When We Marry?" and "The Business of Running a Home." The immensely popular *Pocket Book of Baby and Child Care* by Dr. Benjamin Spock said that raising children was more important and rewarding than the extra money or satisfaction that a woman might get from a job. Many women who had gone to college or had careers traded their aspirations and jobs for marriage and motherhood. The number of women who worked continued to rise,

but women lost ground in the workplace. They were still paid less than men for doing the same work. They were also shut out of better jobs with higher salaries.

After World War II, more women dropped out of school and married at an early age. The nation's birthrate increased so rapidly that people refer to the period between 1945 and 1961 as the "baby boom." During the baby boom, more than 65 million children were born in the United States.

Parents in the prosperous 1950s wanted their children to have all the things that they had not been able to have during the Depression and war years. They gave their children an increasing amount of material goods and emphasized the benefits of living the "good life." Parents also allowed their children greater freedom than they themselves had known as youngsters. Critics pointed to this new "permissiveness" as the major cause of the rise in juvenile delinquency.

▲ **WATCHING TELEVISION** The most popular of the 1950s television shows were comedies, variety shows, and "Westerns" starring Roy Rogers (above), Hopalong Cassidy, and other stars. *Why were some people worried about the effects of watching television?*

■ The Impact of Television

One of the symbols of the prosperity of the 1950s was the television set. In 1945 fewer than 1 in every 20,000 people had a television. But within a few years, televisions were everywhere, and they were almost as common as telephones.

Beginning with the election of 1952, television brought national politics into American living rooms. During the campaign, both the Republican party and the Democratic party spent millions on television advertising and broadcasts. Although television stirred greater interest in voting, it also posed disturbing questions. Would television give an unfair advantage to the candidate who used television most effectively and who could afford to buy the most airtime?

Some critics also worried that television would have a negative effect on American culture. In the early 1950s, pollster George Gallup voiced concern that:

❝ *[O]ne of the real threats to America's future place in the world is a citizenry which daily elects to be entertained and not informed.* ❞

Supported by advertisers trying to reach the widest audience, television programs often appealed to the lowest common denominator of public taste. In order to avoid offending potential customers, advertisers would not buy time on programs that dealt with controversial issues. As a result, television furnished entertainment that was intended "to fix the attention but not engage the mind."

Yet the 1950s has often been called the "Golden Age of Television." Many of the country's most talented writers, comedians, musicians, and actors flocked to the new medium. There they could reach an audience of millions.

Section 3 ★ Assessment

Checking for Understanding

1. **Define** automation.

2. **Discuss** changes that occurred in American life as a result of affluence and medical technology.

3. **Report** how minority groups were adversely affected by pressures to conform.

Critical Thinking

4. **Determining Effects** Re-create the diagram shown here, and explain the ways television and the automobile changed the American lifestyle during the 1950s.

Television → Effect on American Life ← Automobile

INTERDISCIPLINARY ACTIVITY

5. **Math** Research the distribution of population by age for each decade from 1940 to 1990. Present your findings in graph form. Write three generalizations.

◀ ELVIS PRESLEY, ROCK-AND-ROLL STAR OF THE 1950S

▲ CHUCK BERRY

Origins of Rock and Roll

During the Eisenhower years, many teenagers rebelled against the pressure to conform by rejecting the mellow pop music favored by their parents. Teens of the 1950s preferred the heavily accented beats and repetitious lyrics of rock and roll.

Rock and roll developed in the mid-1950s. It was a derivation of the rhythm and blues that African American musicians had created for black audiences years before. It also often had some elements of country music. In rock and roll, the tempo was quicker, the accented beats were moved, and electrically amplified instruments—mostly guitars—were used.

Because rock and roll was such a departure from the sentimental love songs of the past, it shocked and dismayed many parents. Teenagers, however, were sold. One of the first rock hits, recorded in 1955, was Bill Haley and the Comets' *Rock Around the Clock,* which sold 17 million copies. In 1956 Elvis Presley came on the rock scene. In his performances he moved to the beat of the music. With songs like *Don't Be Cruel* and *Jailhouse Rock,* Presley set the musical style for a decade. The lyrics of most rock-and-roll music remained about love, although some writers and performers, most notably Chuck Berry, treated the subject with wit and humor.

Making the Art Connection

1. How did rock-and-roll music evolve?

2. Why did rock and roll shock and dismay parents?

ACTIVITY

3. Paste photographs or drawings on a posterboard of the musician or musical group that you think represents the best of modern rock and roll. Write a caption that includes your definition of rock and roll.

649

★★★★★★★★★★★★★★★★★★★★★★★★★★★★

Foreign Policy

▶ ASTRONAUT JOHN GLENN

Guide to Reading

Main Idea

President Eisenhower used a combination of diplomacy, military power, and secret activities to contain communism and promote world peace.

Reading Strategy

Organizing Information As you read about foreign policy under Eisenhower, use a diagram like the one shown here to list the reasons why American relations with Latin America were poor in the 1950s.

Latin American Hostility

Reason | Reason

Objectives

After studying this section, you should be able to

★ discuss Eisenhower's approach to foreign policy and the Eisenhower Doctrine.

★ describe how the fear of nuclear war affected the cold war.

★ discuss why American relations with Latin America were poor in the 1950s.

Key Term

covert

---

*D*uring the 1950s the Eisenhower administration labored to contain communism, particularly in newly independent nations in Asia and Africa. Eisenhower used diplomacy, military power, and secret activities to achieve these goals.

President Eisenhower and Secretary of State John Foster Dulles (DUH•luhs) expanded the nation's network of alliances in order to contain communism. In Western Europe, the United States took a leading role in NATO. In Southeast Asia, the United States helped to create the Southeast Asian Treaty Organization (SEATO). In the Middle East, the United States counted on the cooperation of the Central Treaty Organization (CENTO), and in Latin America, the United States promoted the Organization of American States (OAS). These alliances created a formidable counterbalance to the influence of the Soviet Union.

■ The Influence of Dulles

President Eisenhower's foreign policy was greatly influenced by Dulles. After serving in the United States Senate in the late 1940s, Dulles had years of experience in high-level diplomacy, particularly with Asian nations. Secretary Dulles favored a vigorous foreign policy, denouncing Truman's "containment" policy as inadequate. Instead, he advocated "liberation" of Eastern European nations that were under Soviet domination:

❝ *If our policy is to stay where we are, we will be driven back. It is only by keeping alive the hope of liberation, by taking advantage of that wherever opportunity arises, that we will end this terrible peril which dominates the world. . . .* ❞

Dulles threatened "massive retaliation" against communist aggression. "If you are scared to go to the brink [of nuclear war], you are lost," he said. Accordingly, the Department of Defense reduced the size of the regular army and increased its nuclear arsenal.

Eisenhower tempered Dulles's tough stance and took a more cautious approach. He insisted that "there is no alternative to peace." A nuclear war might well mean the end of civilization. Therefore, the Eisenhower administration continued Truman's policy of containment.

■ War and Peace in Asia

Containing communism became a global challenge for Eisenhower. In Asia the end of one conflict was followed by the start of another one.

End of the Korean War

Carrying out his campaign promise, Eisenhower went to Korea in December 1952. Peace negotiations to end the Korean War, however, seemed to go nowhere. Exasperated, Eisenhower threatened the Communists with possible use of nuclear weapons. Finally in July 1953, after long and bloody fighting, the United Nations Command and the North Koreans reached a settlement. Korea was divided along a line close to the 38th parallel.

Southeast Asia

The United States then was faced with a new problem in Southeast Asia. After Japan surrendered Indochina in 1945, France tried to regain control of its colonies. The people, however, wanted to rule themselves. Ho Chi Minh, a Communist, headed an independence movement called the Vietminh to drive the French from Vietnam, one of the countries of Indochina. The United States stayed out of the fighting but supplied weapons and supplies to the French.

In 1954 the Vietminh surrounded French troops at Dien Bien Phu. The French asked the United States to bomb communist positions. Eisenhower believed that a French defeat might lead to communist domination of all of Southeast Asia.

Secretary Dulles favored giving military support to France. But when Eisenhower could get no support from the leaders of Congress or from other Western nations, he decided to stay out of the war. Dien Bien Phu fell in May 1954, and the French soon withdrew from Indochina.

▲ EISENHOWER AND DULLES President Eisenhower delegated much of the conduct of foreign affairs to his secretary of state, John Foster Dulles (left). *What policy did Dulles favor to fight communist aggression?*

▲ THE UNITED STATES AND IRAN Shah Mohammad Reza Pahlavi came to power in Iran in 1953 with the help of secret American funds. He was later overthrown during the Iranian revolution of 1979. *Why did Eisenhower involve the CIA in Iran?*

At a conference in Geneva, Switzerland, in 1954, Vietnam was divided along the 17th parallel. North of that line, Ho Chi Minh's communist forces took control. To the south, a United States-supported government under Ngo Dinh Diem was set up. Diem's regime was dictatorial, inefficient, and unpopular. Communist-supported guerrillas began to fight against Diem's government. The United States provided most of the money for South Vietnam's defense. President Eisenhower had avoided war in Vietnam, but he had tied American prestige to the survival of Diem's unpopular and dictatorial government.

The Eisenhower Approach

When it came to solving foreign problems, Eisenhower preferred using diplomacy and **covert**, or secret, activities carried out by the Central Intelligence Agency (CIA).

In Iran and Guatemala

In 1953 President Eisenhower became concerned when the Iranian prime minister seized control of the Anglo-American Oil Company. The President feared that Iran was aligning itself with the Soviet Union, which would endanger oil supplies to Western nations. Under Eisenhower's orders, the CIA secretly funded a successful revolt by the young shah of Iran. Later Iran signed an agreement allowing United States, British, and French companies to share in Iranian oil production.

In 1954 the CIA helped to remove another unfriendly government. The Guatemalan government of Colonel Jacobo Arbenz Guzman had seized property of the American-owned United Fruit Company. The United States learned that Guzman was getting weapons from communist nations. Concerned that Guatemala would become a communist foothold in Latin America, the Eisenhower administration funded a coup that overthrew the government.

In both Iran and Guatemala, the revolutions appeared to have been inspired from within the nation. Only later did people learn of the CIA's role.

Secretary Dulles believed the events in Vietnam, Iran, and Guatemala were evidence of the Soviet Union's intention to spread communism. He argued that newly emerging nations should choose sides in the worldwide struggle between communism and democracy.

"Third World" Neutrality

In 1955 representatives from 29 Asian and African states met and signed an agreement calling for racial equality and self-determination. Two thousand delegates, from countries containing more than half the world's population, saw themselves as the "Third World." They declared their intention to remain independent of both the "First World"—the West—and the "Second World"—the Soviet Union.

The policy of neutralism was hotly debated. Some observers compared neutralism to isolationism and defended it as necessary for new and comparatively weak nations. Others attacked neutralism. Secretary Dulles took the position that no nation had the right to remain neutral in a conflict between "tyranny and freedom."

■ Middle East Powder Keg

During the 1950s the United States was drawn into the affairs of the Middle East. Before World War II, American businesses had begun to exploit the area's rich oil supplies. After the war the United States became increasingly dependent on Mideast oil. Americans were anxious to protect this oil supply. Many Americans also were interested in the survival of Israel, established in 1948 as a Jewish homeland.

The Middle East was like a "powder keg ready to explode." Arab nations believed that Israel was on land belonging to the Palestinians. They threatened to destroy Israel. Also, deep divisions existed among the Arab nations. Poverty and discontent were widespread. Finally, Soviet expansion posed a threat to Western oil supplies.

The first explosion came in 1956 in Egypt. Egypt's President Gamal Abdel Nasser was anxious to gain military superiority over the Jewish state. To get weapons, Egypt signed a commercial treaty with the Soviet Union, exchanging cotton—Egypt's major cash crop—for tanks and guns. The United States had tried to forge friendly relations with Egypt by offering to loan the nation money to build a giant dam across the Nile River. But Nasser's overtures toward the People's

Republic of China and the Soviet bloc forced Dulles to cancel the loan. Nasser responded by seizing the Suez Canal in July 1956.

The British, French, and Israelis decided to attack Egypt and reclaim the Suez Canal, which provided a vital trade link between Europe, the Middle East, and Asia. Acting independently of the United States, they invaded Egypt in October.

The world seemed on the verge of another major war. During a heated debate in the United Nations, the United States voted with the Soviet Union to condemn the actions of Israel, Great Britain, and France. This pressure forced the three nations to agree to withdraw from Egypt.

The Suez crisis greatly embarrassed the United States. Three of its strongest allies had acted alone. The affair might have shattered the Western alliance if Soviet action to crush the Hungarian revolution had not persuaded them to close ranks again.

Visualizing History

▲ NASSER AND THE SUEZ CRISIS Warfare in the Middle East was close at hand after Egyptian leader Nasser seized the Suez Canal. Then Egypt was invaded by Britain, France, and Israel. *What caused Britain, France, and Israel to withdraw?*

▲ **CONFLICT IN HUNGARY** The Hungarian revolt began when workers and students demonstrated for reform in 1956. Here, Hungarian citizens capture a Soviet tank in strife-torn Budapest. *How did the revolt end?*

■ The Eisenhower Doctrine

After the Suez crisis, the Soviets supported Egypt and offered to help build a new dam, the Aswan, across the Nile. President Eisenhower worried that the Soviets would gain new strength in the region. In January 1957, Eisenhower asked Congress to give him authority to use United States military forces to defend any Middle Eastern country that requested help against the forces of "international communism." Congress overwhelmingly approved the so-called Eisenhower Doctrine.

A year later the president of Lebanon asked Eisenhower to send troops to protect his government. He feared that Nasser and the Soviet Union might encourage a revolt in Lebanon.

In July 1958, American soldiers entered Lebanon. American troops remained in Lebanon until new elections established a stronger government. By taking this action, the United States showed that it intended to play a leading role in the Middle East. Yet the basic problems of the Middle East—poverty, rivalry and strife, and the threat of communist aggression—still defied solution.

■ The NATO Alliance

After President Eisenhower took office in 1953, he attempted to strengthen NATO under a unified command. But France was fearful of German resurgence and strongly opposed the plan. Western defenses were strengthened, however, when West Germany was allowed to rearm and join NATO.

The NATO alliance faced other difficulties. Europeans had mixed feelings about the United States. European Socialists and Communists regarded the United States as a materialistic nation where workers were exploited in order to increase the profits of a few great trusts. Conservatives believed Europe would be Americanized. In Britain and France, many people blamed the United States for their nation's loss of power in the world. But Soviet aggression persuaded Western Europe and the United States to maintain a common front.

Political uprisings in two of its satellites prompted the Soviet Union to reassert its control over Eastern Europe. In October 1956, anti-Soviet riots broke out in some Polish cities. The Soviet Union ultimately agreed to Polish demands for more freedoms. In Hungary, however, what began as peaceful protests ended with open fighting. When communist leaders tried to put down the unrest, the Hungarians turned against them. On October 30, 1956, after less than a week of fighting, Budapest radio told the Hungarians: "You have won!" For five days jubilant Hungarians tasted freedom. Then on November 4, Soviet tanks and troops rolled through Budapest and overwhelmed its defenders. In the United States there was sympathy for the Hungarians, but little could be done without risking war.

■ Trouble in Latin America

While the United States worried about communist gains in Europe, Asia, and Africa, it ignored Latin America. There, the great poverty of the majority of the people and the concentration of land and power in the hands of a few created a breeding ground for political instability.

Latin Americans had good cause to believe they were "forgotten neighbors." They saw the United States pouring billions of dollars into remaking Europe's economy and strengthening weak governments in Asia. Yet Latin America received little United States foreign aid.

In 1958 Vice President Nixon made a goodwill visit to Latin America. In some of the countries he visited, Nixon faced hostile demonstrations. In Peru and Venezuela, mobs threw stones and beat sticks against Nixon's car. This shocking attack on the Vice President brought home to people of the United States their neglect of Latin America's problems.

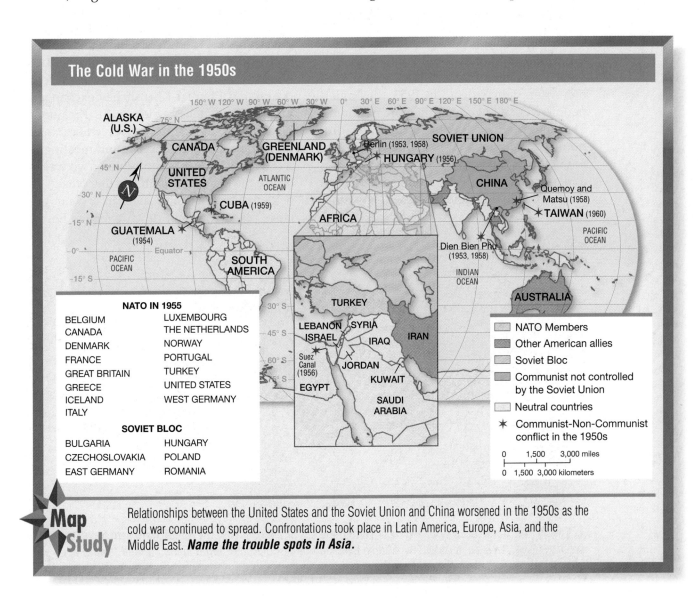

The Cold War in the 1950s

NATO IN 1955

BELGIUM	LUXEMBOURG
CANADA	THE NETHERLANDS
DENMARK	NORWAY
FRANCE	PORTUGAL
GREAT BRITAIN	TURKEY
GREECE	UNITED STATES
ICELAND	WEST GERMANY
ITALY	

SOVIET BLOC

BULGARIA	HUNGARY
CZECHOSLOVAKIA	POLAND
EAST GERMANY	ROMANIA

■ NATO Members
■ Other American allies
■ Soviet Bloc
■ Communist not controlled by the Soviet Union
☐ Neutral countries
✳ Communist-Non-Communist conflict in the 1950s

0   1,500   3,000 miles
0   1,500 3,000 kilometers

Map Study

Relationships between the United States and the Soviet Union and China worsened in the 1950s as the cold war continued to spread. Confrontations took place in Latin America, Europe, Asia, and the Middle East. *Name the trouble spots in Asia.*

Events in Cuba further soured United States-Latin American relations. In 1959 a resistance movement headed by Fidel Castro forced the resignation of Cuba's corrupt dictator, Fulgencio Batista. Castro became a popular figure in the United States, and there was hope that the two nations would establish friendly relations. But American enthusiasm for Castro waned when he made friendly moves toward the Communists, denounced the United States, and seized private property. Castro also sought the military support of the Soviet Union. In response, President Eisenhower cut the quota of sugar the United States imported from Cuba and broke off relations with the Castro government.

■ Thaws in the Cold War

During the Eisenhower administration, the cold war spread to all continents. Yet there were signs that a "thaw" was possible. After Stalin's death in 1953, the Soviet people were allowed a little more freedom. The new premier, Nikita Khrushchev, denounced Stalin as a brutal tyrant. The Soviets now talked of peaceful coexistence and said that war in the atomic age would be so horrible that "the living will envy the dead."

In July 1955, Eisenhower met with the leaders of the Soviet Union, France, and Great Britain in Geneva, Switzerland. He made a strong plea for nuclear disarmament, saying that it would:

❝ . . . ease the fears of war in the anxious hearts of people everywhere. . . . It would make [it] possible for every nation, great and small, developed and less developed, to advance the standards of living of its people. . . . ❞

The summit, however, settled nothing. In 1958 tensions between the superpowers escalated once more, this time over the divided city of Berlin. The Soviets threatened to cut off Western access to Berlin unless the West recognized the East German government. When the crisis cooled down, both sides made new efforts to reduce world tensions. In 1959 Vice President Nixon and Premier Khrushchev exchanged visits. Khrushchev met with President Eisenhower at Camp David, where they made plans for a second summit meeting.

The new thaw was short-lived. Two weeks before the second summit meeting was to be held, in May 1960, an American U-2 surveillance plane was shot down over the Soviet

Visualizing History

▲ **COLD WAR RELATIONS** During the era of the cold war, UN forces were sent to keep peace in Africa, the Middle East, and other hot spots. *What signs pointed toward a thaw in the cold war?*

Eisenhower's Farewell

The U-2 incident and the failure of East-West negotiations brought Eisenhower's years in office to a frustrating close. After the death of Secretary Dulles in 1959, Eisenhower took over more of the direction of foreign policy himself. He traveled widely in Europe, Asia, the Middle East, and Latin America to promote "peace and goodwill" and a "better understanding of America." But he was unable to lessen the tensions of the cold war and the threat of nuclear confrontation.

Still, Eisenhower remained a popular President, as near to a "father figure" as any President since George Washington. Like Washington, Eisenhower gave a farewell address. In it he warned against the influence of the military-industrial complex:

> *We must never let the weight of this combination (of the military and industry) endanger our liberties or democratic processes. We should take nothing for granted. Only an alert and knowledgeable citizenry can compel the proper meshing of the huge industrial and military machinery of defense with our peaceful methods and goals, so that security and liberty may prosper together.*

▲ U-2 PILOT GARY POWERS

Union. The CIA had sent it to spy on and photograph Soviet nuclear sites and missile bases. Khrushchev denounced Eisenhower as a prisoner of the "war mongers" and refused to take part in the meeting. Relations between East and West once again turned colder.

The President's message was impressive because it came from a man who had spent most of his life as a soldier.

Section 4 ★ Assessment

Checking for Understanding

1. **Define** covert.

2. **State** reasons why European attitudes toward the United States changed in the 1950s.

Critical Thinking

3. **Making Predictions** How might economically developing nations view the cold war?

4. **Summarizing** Re-create the diagram shown here, and list the characteristics of the

Eisenhower administration's foreign policy.

INTERDISCIPLINARY ACTIVITY

5. **The Arts** Imagine you were a journalist when Eisenhower left office. Write a profile of him for a magazine.

Using Vocabulary

Use these vocabulary words in a statement about the influence of technology on business and agriculture.

agribusiness   **automation**

Reviewing Facts

1. **State** reasons why Americans elected Ike by overwhelming majorities in 1952 and 1956.

2. **Explain** the Eisenhower administration's dilemma regarding the farm problem.

3. **Cite** the differences between Dulles's and Eisenhower's approaches to foreign policy.

4. **Discuss** how the following groups were affected by the pressure to conform: (1) middle-class families, (2) African Americans, (3) women.

5. **Speculate** about the effects of the nuclear threat on the conduct of the cold war.

Understanding Concepts

International Leadership

1. What is your opinion of Eisenhower's use of covert operations to remove unfriendly foreign governments? Explain.

Economic Growth

2. Re-create the diagram shown here, and list the factors that stimulated economic growth in the 1950s.

Economic Growth

Critical Thinking

1. **Demonstrating Judgment** Find an example of Eisenhower's actions that supports both national security and global security. Did he take any steps in the interest of national security at the risk of global security? Support your answer.

2. **Locating Examples** What lifestyle changes reflected the "economy of abundance" during the 1950s?

3. **Analyzing Photographs** Study the photograph of the bomb shelter on this page, then answer the questions that follow.

   a. What do you think the photographer was trying to show with this picture?

   b. Do you think this photograph was part of an advertisement or a news story? Explain.

CHAPTER 21 ★ ASSESSMENT

4. **Supporting an Opinion** Respond to President Eisenhower's domino theory. Do you believe it justifies the containment policy? Explain.

5. **Assessing Outcomes** Do you agree with President Eisenhower's statement that control of the military-industrial complex is necessary "so that security and liberty may prosper together"? Why or why not?

6. **Making Comparisons** When NATO was established in 1949, each country promised to come to the aid of the others in case of attack. In 1991 NATO dispatched three squadrons of German, Italian, and Belgian jet fighters to Turkey, a member of NATO, to strengthen its border with Iraq in case of war. How does this 1991 NATO action carry out the intent of the charter?

History and Geography

The Western and Eastern Blocs

Use the map on page 655 and information from Chapter 21 to help you answer these questions.

1. **Location** What conflicts took place in Europe?

2. **Place** What features of the Suez Canal made it the center of conflict in the mid-1950s?

Cooperative Learning Interdisciplinary Activity: Sociology

Working in a group of four, research life in the United States during the Eisenhower administration. Divide the research assignments so that different members are responsible for finding information about news events, movies, television shows, popular music, theater, art achievements, literary publications, advances in science and technology, sports events, and fashion trends for those years. Combine the reports to form a history of American life back then.

Practicing Skills

Analyzing Symbols

Refer to the skills lesson on page 638 to help you practice this skill. For each of the following names, phrases, or terms, select an appropriate symbol, draw the symbol, and write a caption that explains the association.

- *The Affluent Society*
- suburbanization
- automation
- baby boom
- Fidel Castro
- Middle East powder keg
- cold war thaw
- U-2

What does each item below symbolize to you?

- The American Flag
- The Constitution
- The White House
- The Statue of Liberty

Technology Activity

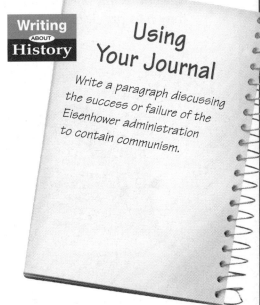

Using a Word Processor The 1950s was a time when inventions such as television became available to many Americans. Make a list of the devices you use on a regular basis (e.g., television, compact disc player). Under the list, name which devices you could or could not give up, with reasons why or why not. Then compare your list with classmates.

Writing ABOUT History

Using Your Journal

Write a paragraph discussing the success or failure of the Eisenhower administration to contain communism.

Cultural Kaleidoscope

A Changing Society

Innovations

From important discoveries and innovations like computers, penicillin, open heart surgery, and the polio vaccine to more mundane accomplishments like TV dinners, the period from the 1930s to the 1960s was a time of discovery and unbounded imagination. New technology transformed the nature of work and helped Americans enjoy more leisure time. At the same time, the number of available leisure activities increased. By the 1950s Americans were enjoying a standard of living far beyond any they had previously known.

◄ Progress in electronics began to revolutionize home entertainment. Probably no form of entertainment has matched the effects of television. Developed in the 1930s, television went on the market in the late 1940s. Fewer than 1 million households had a set in 1949. Within four years, the number had soared to 20 million.

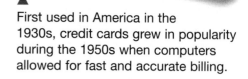

▲ First used in America in the 1930s, credit cards grew in popularity during the 1950s when computers allowed for fast and accurate billing.

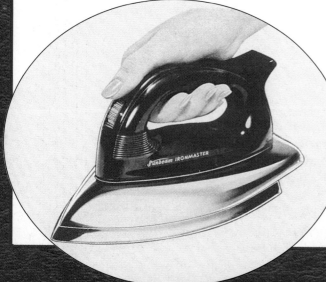

◄ The electric iron, like this model, became a necessary domestic appliance.

With new means of refrigeration widely available after World War II, Americans could store quantities of food for months on end. By 1956, 9 of 10 American families owned a refrigerator. Other symbols of the affluent society: by 1956, 3 of 4 families owned at least one auto, 3 out of 5 owned their own home. In 1945 only 9,000 private swimming pools were in use. In 1957 alone more than 50,000 pools were installed.

The General Electric Two-Door Refrigerator—Home Freezer Combination

Now . . . a new 10-cubic-foot model of today's outstanding refrigerator!

Home Freezer Compartment. Full 2 cubic feet. Separately refrigerated, separately insulated, with its own separate outside door.

Freezes foods and ice cubes quickly. AND LOOK at all the frozen food it will keep under long-time storage at zero temperature.

Refrigerator Compartment. Separately refrigerated, separately insulated, with its own separate outside door.

AND LOOK at all the fresh food it holds under refrigeration—as much as the ordinary 9-cubic-foot refrigerator! Moisture-conditioned cold keeps humidity just right. No need to cover dishes. Never needs defrosting.

Famed General Electric dependability—in a refrigerator designed for years of better living.

WHEN YOU BUY a refrigerator like this great, new Two-door Refrigerator-Home Freezer Combination, you're making a major investment in better living for yourself and your family.

You have every right to expect years and years of dependable, efficient, and economical refrigeration . . . 24 hours a day, day in, day out. And you'll get it—in this refrigerator. For it's equipped with the famous General Electric sealed-in refrigerating system that has set an unexcelled record for years and years of reliable performance.

See this most advanced of all refrigerators at your retailer's. General Electric Company, Bridgeport 2, . . .

More than 1,700,000 in service 10 years . . .

GENERAL ELECTRIC

Between the 1920s and the advent of the television age, millions of Americans learned about the important events of the day from radio. By the mid-1930s, two-thirds of American homes had at least one radio—less than half that many had telephones.

More and more Americans, it seems, were eating canned foods. Hormel's Spiced Ham, better known as Spam, quickly established a strong position. Part of the impetus came during World War II when Spam's price and shelf life made it a staple of the soldier's diet. In Korea, Spam is considered an imported luxury item.

SPAM A NEW HORMEL MEAT NET WEIGHT INCLUDING JUICES 12 OZ.

Standardized Test Practice

Directions: Choose the *best* answer to each of the following multiple choice questions. If you have trouble answering a question, use the process of elimination to narrow your choices. Write your answers on a separate piece of paper.

1. **When Franklin D. Roosevelt began his term as President a reporter remarked, "Gone is the fortress that was the White House." What was this comment intended to mean?**

   A The White House was no longer as heavily defended as it was before.

   B Roosevelt was more accessible to the American people than earlier Presidents.

   C The White House was destroyed and rebuilt to meet new building codes.

   D Roosevelt redesigned the interior of the White House to look less like a fortress.

   Test-Taking Tip: Think about the meaning of the word *fortress*. It's a military term, referring to a place that is heavily defended (a *fort*). Since the U.S. does not have a military government, nor was it at war at the beginning of FDR's presidency, a literal answer (such as answer A) is unlikely.

2. **Each of the following is true of the bills passed during the first Hundred Days of Roosevelt's Presidency EXCEPT that**

   F they were intended to provide immediate relief to American citizens.

   G they were known as the New Deal.

   H they were designed as temporary measures to restart the economy.

   J they were the subject of divisive and protracted debate in Congress.

   Test-Taking Tip: Remember, this question asks for the *exception*. Read through each answer carefully to see if it is true of FDR's first Hundred Days. You are looking for the answer that is false. For example, you probably remember that these bills were intended to combat the effects of the Great Depression, so answer F is true, and therefore, definitely not the correct answer.

3. **The Public Works Administration, the Tennessee Valley Authority, and the Civilian Conservation Corps were all examples of**

   A programs that spent large amounts of money to create new jobs.

   B laws intended to help insure the stability of banks.

   C reforms to insure the stability of the stock market.

   D programs intended to increase the size and readiness of the military.

   Test-Taking Tip: The important word in this question is *all*. Think about what *all three* of these programs had in common. There are also clues in the names of the programs. For instance, what does *public works* most likely mean? Does it sound like something that would have to do with the stock market or the stability of banks? Probably not. Therefore, you can eliminate answers B and C.

4. **The United States' policy during the Cold War can best be described as**

   F maintaining isolation and neutrality.

   G destroying communism through expansionism.

   H preventing the spread of communism through containment.

   J sending aid to communist countries to rebuild their economies.

   Test-Taking Tip: The *Cold War* was a time of tension between the Soviet Union and the United States caused, in part, by Soviet expansion into Eastern Europe. Therefore, there is no reason that the United States would send aid to communist-block countries. Answer J can be eliminated.

5. This political cartoon, published in 1938, makes a statement about the dictatorships that developed in Europe after World War I and the reaction of the Western democracies toward the newly formed dictatorships. What is the main idea of this cartoon?

A Dictatorships should be more respectful toward democracies.

B Dictatorships are necessary to support democracies.

C Democracies are helping the dictatorships be destructive.

D Democracies should help dictatorships with military aid.

WOULD YOU OBLIGE ME WITH A MATCH PLEASE ?

Test-Taking Tip: Look carefully at the cartoon before answering this question. Cartoonists often use *caricature* (exaggerated details) and *symbols* (familiar pictures that stand for ideas) to communicate a message. Why do you think the standing figure is so large? What is he holding? If you look closely, you'll notice that the cartoonist has labeled the jackets of the two figures to help you understand what the figures represent.

6. Why did Britain and France finally declare war in 1939?

F Because Germany annexed part of Czechoslovakia

G Because Germany invaded Poland

H Because Italy invaded France

J Because of the non-aggression pact between Russia and Germany

Test-Taking Tip: This question requires you to remember one of the primary events that led to World War II. If you are not certain, use the process of elimination to rule out answers you know are wrong. For example, it is unlikely that a non-aggression pact between *Russia and Germany* would cause *Britain and France* to declare war, so this answer can be eliminated.

7. After World War II, the division of Germany into East and West Germany and the division of Korea into North and South Korea were both the result of

A the occupation by different Allied armies.

B invasions by the Soviet Union.

C the withdrawal of Japanese troops.

D civil wars in those countries.

Test-Taking Tip: Make sure that you read the question and all the answer choices carefully. Although civil war is often a reason why a country has divided, it was not the reason for the division of Germany or Korea after WWII. Therefore, you can eliminate answer D.

UNIT SEVEN
REDEFINING AMERICA
1954–PRESENT

★★

CHAPTER **22**	CHAPTER **23**	CHAPTER **24**	CHAPTER **25**	CHAPTER **26**
The Civil Rights Era 1954–1975	The Vietnam Era 1954–1975	Camelot to Watergate 1960–1976	Search for Solutions 1976–1992	Toward a New Century 1992–

▲ VIETNAM VETERAN'S HAT

History AND ART

Mural on Building
Davenport, Iowa

Vivid images abound in this colorful mural commemorating American leaders and important events.

Why It's Important

American society from the mid-1950s to the present has been described as a roller coaster. Americans have ridden not only to new heights of optimism and confidence but to lows of frustration as well. In addition, new technology has redefined the way Americans live and work. The events of the last part of this century have presented the nation with a new set of challenges and opportunities as it starts the next century.

To learn more about modern America, view the *Historic America: Electronic Field Trips* Side 2, Chapter 10 video lesson:

- *The Vietnam Veterans Memorial*

Themes

- Civil Rights and Liberties
- Conflict and Cooperation
- Cultural Diversity
- U.S. Role in World Affairs

Key Events

- Desegregation in public schools
- War in Vietnam
- Watergate scandal
- Camp David Peace Accords
- Persian Gulf War
- Congress approves NAFTA

PRIMARY SOURCES Library See pages 868–869 for the primary source readings to accompany Unit 7.

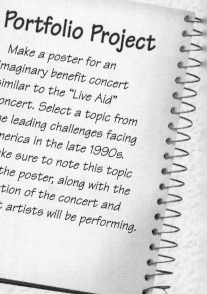

▲ TALL SHIPS, PART OF BICENTENNIAL CELEBRATION

◀ POLITICAL CAMPAIGN BUTTONS

Portfolio Project

Make a poster for an imaginary benefit concert similar to the "Live Aid" concert. Select a topic from the leading challenges facing America in the late 1990s. Make sure to note this topic on the poster, along with the location of the concert and what artists will be performing.

Global Perspectives

The World

	1950		1965	
Asia and Oceania		**1954** *French are defeated in Vietnam*		**1966** *China's Cultural Revolution begins*
Europe			**1961** *Berlin Wall built*	
Africa			◄ **1960** *"Year of Africa" —many countries become independent*	
South America				
North and Central America			**1959** *St. Lawrence Seaway opens*	

The United States

Pacific and Northwest			◄ **1959** *Alaska and Hawaii become states*	
Southeast		**1955** *Rosa Parks inspires Montgomery bus boycott*		**1965** *Freedom March from Selma to Montgomery*
Midwest		**1954** *Brown v. Board of Education decision*		
Southwest				◄ **1966** *First artificial heart implanted*
Atlantic Northeast	1950		1965	

The United States has long been known as a nation of immigrants. Throughout its history, people from other countries came to its shores seeking a better way of life. In the late 1980s, the major sources of immigration to the United States were Asia, the Caribbean, and Latin America. Among the countries that sent the most immigrants were China, Colombia, the Dominican Republic, Ecuador, Guyana, Haiti, India, Jamaica, the Philippines, and South Korea. At the same time, however, immigrants came from another 150 countries. It is not surprising then that some people have called the United States the world in microcosm, or miniature.

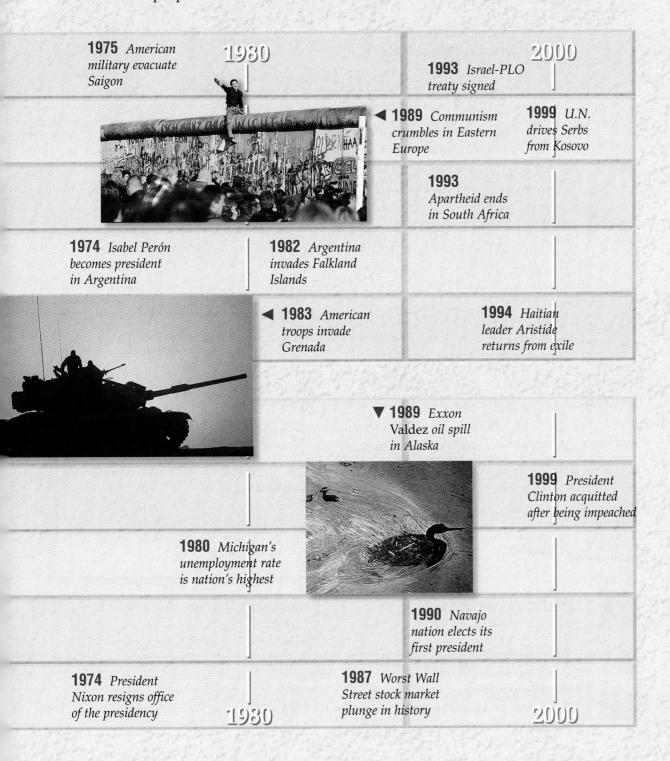

1975 *American military evacuate Saigon*

1980

1993 *Israel-PLO treaty signed*

2000

◄ **1989** *Communism crumbles in Eastern Europe*

1999 *U.N. drives Serbs from Kosovo*

1993 *Apartheid ends in South Africa*

1974 *Isabel Perón becomes president in Argentina*

1982 *Argentina invades Falkland Islands*

◄ **1983** *American troops invade Grenada*

1994 *Haitian leader Aristide returns from exile*

▼ **1989** *Exxon Valdez oil spill in Alaska*

1999 *President Clinton acquitted after being impeached*

1980 *Michigan's unemployment rate is nation's highest*

1990 *Navajo nation elects its first president*

1974 *President Nixon resigns office of the presidency*

1980

1987 *Worst Wall Street stock market plunge in history*

2000

CHAPTER 22

★★

The Civil Rights Era
1954–1975

► CELEBRATING KWANZAA, HOLIDAY BASED ON TRADITIONAL AFRICAN FESTIVAL

Setting the Scene

Focus

During the 1950s, African Americans rebelled against their second-class status. The ranks of civil rights advocates swelled, and African Americans, joined by some white liberals, began following the nonviolent ideas of Dr. Martin Luther King, Jr. They fought for equality first in the South and eventually in the North. Met with violence at every turn, many African Americans abandoned King's ideas and developed new philosophies. Whatever their ideas, these civil rights activists inspired hope to other minorities.

Concepts to Understand

★ Why efforts to gain **civil rights** created an effective movement for change

★ How the **civil rights** movement led to social upheaval

Read to Discover . . .

★ legislation that addressed civil rights issues.

★ the kind of impact the civil rights movement had on other minorities.

Journal Notes

What was life like for civil rights activists during the 1950s and 1960s? Note details about it in your journal as you read the chapter.

HISTORY Online

Chapter Overview
Visit the *American History: The Modern Era Since 1865* Web site at **me.glencoe.com** and click on *Chapter 22— Chapter Overviews* to preview the chapter.

CULTURAL
- **1959** *Jazz pioneer Ornette Coleman releases* The Shape of Jazz
- **1962** *Richard Wright pens* Another Country
- **1964** *Dr. King wins Nobel Peace Prize*

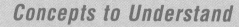

1954	1960

POLITICAL
- **1955** *Montgomery bus boycott begins*
- **1957** *Congress passes the first civil rights legislation since Reconstruction*
- **1964** *Civil Rights Act is passed*
- **1965** *"March for Freedom" begins*
- **1965** *Voting Rights Act is passed*

Visualizing
History

The March on Washington, 1963

The August 1963 March on Washington for equal rights was the largest and most peaceful protest in the nation's history. Dr. Martin Luther King, Jr., electrified the listeners with his "I Have a Dream" address.

◀ STATUE OF LIBERTY

● **1966** Soul on Ice *states Black Panther aims*

● **1967** *Carl Stokes is elected mayor of Cleveland, Ohio*
● **1968** *Martin Luther King, Jr., is assassinated*

● **1972** *Joseph Walker publishes* The River Niger
● **1973** *Toni Morrison publishes* Sula

1966

1972

● **1972** *Congress approves Equal Rights Amendment*

★★★★★★★★★★★★★★★★★★★★★★★★★★★★★★★★

A New Beginning

Main Idea

Beginning in the 1950s, African Americans escalated the effort to achieve equality in society.

Reading Strategy

Sequencing Information As you read about the beginning of the modern civil rights movement, create a time line of major events. Use the dates provided as a guide.

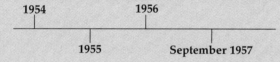

1954	1956
1955	September 1957

Objectives

After studying this chapter, you should be able to

★ discuss the effects of the *Brown* v. *Board of Education* decision.

★ describe major events in the early civil rights movement.

Key Terms

nonviolent resistance, federalized

▶ **DR. MARTIN LUTHER KING, JR.**

The end of Reconstruction left African Americans economically and politically second-class citizens. The sharecropping system and "Jim Crow" segregation laws worked to deny them their rights as citizens. African American leaders began to work toward restoring their full civil rights in the early decades of the twentieth century, but the movement did not come into full flower until almost 50 years later.

During the 1950s and the early 1960s, African Americans boldly rejected their second-class status and the humiliating practice of forced separation. They fought for equal opportunities in jobs, housing, and education. They fought against segregated schools, buses, and trains; they fought against separate facilities in restaurants, hotels, libraries, and hospitals. They won an important ally when the Supreme Court issued several decisions against racial discrimination. But the main force behind the civil rights movement came from citizens—African American and white—who banded together in an effective protest movement.

■ Brown v. Board of Education

One of the Supreme Court's most significant rulings of the 1950s came in May 1954. Three years earlier, Linda Brown's parents had sued the school board of Topeka, Kansas, for not allowing their daughter to attend an all-white school, miles closer to their home than the segregated elementary school she was assigned to attend.

The Supreme Court ruled in *Brown* v. *Board of Education of Topeka, Kansas* that it was unconstitutional to separate schoolchildren by race. The *Brown* decision reversed the

Court's decision in *Plessy* v. *Ferguson,* an 1896 ruling that had upheld the constitutionality of "separate but equal" public accommodations. *Plessy* had become the basis for Jim Crow laws and legal segregation in many states.

The Southern Manifesto

The Supreme Court's ruling in *Brown* v. *Board of Education* called for major changes in many states, especially those in the South. Some border states integrated their schools, but the South remained segregated. The governor of Virginia threatened to close the state's public schools and send white children to private schools. A group of 101 southern members of Congress signed a "Southern Manifesto," which called the Court's ruling "a clear abuse of judicial power" and pledged use of "all lawful means to bring about a reversal of this decision."

■ Boycotts and Demonstrations

The decisions of the Warren Court gave legal support to African Americans' struggle for civil rights. But most civil rights battles, particularly in the South, were fought by brave men and women who broke down barriers of segregation one by one.

Rosa Parks Takes a Stand

In December 1955, an African American seamstress from Montgomery, Alabama, became one of the first to take a stand. At the end of the workday, Parks boarded a segregated bus in which all the seats allotted for African Americans were filled; she took a seat in the front, which was reserved for white riders. Because Parks refused to give up her seat, she was arrested.

The arrest of Rosa Parks aroused anger in Montgomery's African American community. Many of its leaders believed that now was the time to challenge Alabama's segregation laws. At a meeting held at the Dexter Avenue Baptist Church, a boycott of the city's buses was called. The 26-year-old minister of the church, Dr. Martin Luther King, Jr., was asked to lead the boycott.

On the day of Rosa Parks's trial, almost all the African American riders who usually took the buses began a nearly year-long boycott. Because a majority of the regular bus riders were African American, the bus company lost much of its business.

Visualizing History

▲ **ROSA PARKS** Rosa Parks refused to give up her seat to a white bus rider. She meets with her lawyer after she was charged with breaking the law. ***What actions did civil rights leaders take to protest Parks's arrest?***

Linking Past and Present

violence and confrontation without conflict.

Then_____

Organizing for Freedom

Many leaders of the Southern Christian Leadership Conference (SCLC) and other organizations were ministers. In 1957 Martin Luther King, Bayard Rustin, and others had founded the SCLC in the wake of the Montgomery bus boycott.

The SCLC took a leading role in the Freedom Rides challenging segregation on public transportation and other public accommodations. Dr. King's first SCLC drive in the North was launched in Chicago in July 1966 for open housing.

Now_____

New Directions

Led by Dr. King's family and friends, the SCLC continues the fight against segregation and discrimination through nonviolent civil protest. In expanding its scope, the SCLC today also concentrates on such problems as crime and drug abuse. Membership in the organization is open to all, but most of the leaders are African American Protestant ministers.

Churches and Civil Rights

From the beginning of the civil rights movement, African American churches played a central role in devising strategies and mobilizing volunteers. The message of the gospel became the message of the movement. The churches called for protest without retaliatory

---

Rosa Parks was convicted and fined $10. Dr. King and other African American leaders were arrested for sponsoring an "illegal boycott." Then, in November 1956, the Supreme Court ruled that segregation in public transportation was illegal. The bus company ended its policy of segregation. The African American citizens of Montgomery, assured of equal treatment, resumed riding the buses. The Montgomery bus boycott galvanized the civil rights movement, and in Martin Luther King, Jr., that movement found an inspiring leader.

King Preaches Nonviolence

African American churches and their ministers took the lead in organizing the civil rights movement. Dr. King, a Baptist minister, drew from his own faith and also from techniques of the Indian leader Mohandas Gandhi. Like Gandhi, King encouraged the use of **nonviolent resistance,** or peaceful

means to effect change. He told people to disobey unjust laws but asked them to love their oppressors and never fight with them even if provoked. He explained that public opinion, not violence, would force authorities to change unjust laws:

> " *Injustice must be exposed, with all the tension its exposure creates, to the light of human conscience and the air of national opinion before it can be cured.* "

In 1957, to carry on this nonviolent struggle against discrimination in public places all over the South, King and other African American leaders founded the Southern Christian Leadership Conference (SCLC). In addition to the SCLC and its student branch—the Student Nonviolent Coordinating Committee—there were many other groups organized to promote civil rights.

Among them were such long-established African American organizations as the National Association for the Advancement of Colored People (NAACP), which fought discrimination in many legal cases, including *Brown* v. *Board of Education;* the National Urban League, which established community programs for minorities in cities; and the Congress of Racial Equality (CORE), which worked for economic and political opportunities for African Americans. Dr. King remained at the forefront of the movement as it continued to grow in the 1960s. In 1964 he received the Nobel Peace Prize for his nonviolent leadership.

■ Crisis in Little Rock

Not wanting to create controversy, the Eisenhower administration and Congress refused to pass civil rights legislation. As a result, civil rights groups turned to the courts for settlement of their grievances.

In 1953 Eisenhower appointed Earl Warren as chief justice of the United States Supreme Court. Warren began to move the Court toward a more liberal interpretation of the Constitution in decisions on individual rights. Also in 1953 the NAACP brought a number of civil rights cases before the Court. Thurgood Marshall, the NAACP's leading lawyer, wanted the Court to strike down state laws that required racial segregation in public schools. He argued that African American children were not getting the same quality of education as white children.

On May 17, 1954, the Court handed down a historic decision in *Brown* v. *Board of Education of Topeka.* It overturned the 1896 *Plessy* v. *Ferguson* decision that segregation was constitutional so long as equal facilities were provided for both races. The Court declared

66 *We conclude that in the field of public education, the doctrine of "separate but equal" has no place. Separate educational facilities are inherently unequal.* 99

In *Brown* v. *Board of Education of Topeka,* the Supreme Court did not set a deadline for ending segregation. However, in May 1955, the Court called for the implementation of integration "with all deliberate speed."

Civil Rights Legislation

The ruling needed the active support of President Eisenhower, but the President believed that the federal government should remain neutral concerning controversial issues that affected state and local governments. He remarked, "I don't believe you can change the hearts of men with laws and decisions."

In 1957 Congress passed the first civil rights law since Reconstruction. The act created a civil rights division within the Department of Justice and gave the government the power to seek court injunctions against those who denied any citizen's constitutional rights.

Confrontation

In September 1957, the state of Arkansas tested the federal government's policies on civil rights. A federal court had ordered that nine African American students be admitted

Visualizing History

▲ Crisis in Little Rock Central High School in Little Rock, Arkansas, became the focus of court-ordered desegregation in 1957. After Governor Orval Faubus used the Arkansas National Guard to prevent nine African American students from attending, Eisenhower sent federal troops to Little Rock. *How was the crisis resolved?*

▲ PROTESTING FOR RIGHTS

to the all-white Central High School in Little Rock, Arkansas. The state's governor, Orval Faubus, defied federal authority and sent National Guard troops to prevent the students from attending.

President Eisenhower tried to persuade Governor Faubus to obey the court order. The governor withdrew the troops, but without their presence the African American students were exposed to an angry mob that threatened them with physical harm. Forced to act to maintain order, Eisenhower sent in 1,000 paratroopers and **federalized,** or put

under the jurisdiction of the federal government, 10,000 members of the Arkansas National Guard to surround the school so that the students could enter safely.

As Daisy Bates, then the president of the Arkansas NAACP, later remembered:

❝ . . . the nine [African American] pupils marched solemnly through the doors of Central High School, surrounded by twenty-two soldiers. An Army helicopter circled overhead. Around the massive brick schoolhouse 350 paratroopers stood grimly at attention. . . . Within minutes a world that had been holding its breath learned that the nine pupils . . . had finally entered the 'never-never-land.' ❞

Troops remained in Little Rock for the rest of the year, however, and Central High School was closed for the 1958–1959 academic year.

As the Eisenhower administration drew to a close, the nation remained racially divided. Custom and years of intimidation kept many African Americans from voting. Between 1957 and 1960, the Justice Department brought only 10 suits to secure voting rights for African Americans. Only 25 percent of African American adults voted in states of the Deep South, and only 5 percent in Mississippi. The movement for civil rights was just beginning.

Section 1 ★ Assessment

Checking for Understanding

1. **Define** nonviolent resistance, federalized.

2. **Explain** Martin Luther King's philosophy of nonviolence.

Critical Thinking

3. **Analyzing a Viewpoint** How would you evaluate Eisenhower's stand on civil rights? Explain why many African Americans in the South would not be content with this approach.

4. **Determining Effects** Re-create the diagram shown here to list the effects of the *Brown* v. *Board of Education* decision.

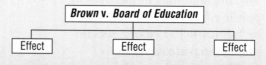

| Brown v. Board of Education |
| Effect | Effect | Effect |

INTERDISCIPLINARY ACTIVITY

5. **Journalism** Write headlines for three events of the civil rights movement.

African American Women Pioneers in Film

In a 1946 issue, the NAACP magazine, the *Crisis*, noted "There are very few [African American men] working on the technical and production side of film-making. There have been one or two . . . writers, a few musicians, and a handful of dance directors." The situation was even more limiting for African American women. Some had made their mark on the other side of the camera. Performers such as Hattie McDaniel, Dorothy Dandridge, and Louise Beavers showcased their talents in many films—almost always, however, playing servant roles.

In the 1980s and 1990s, African American women began to make their mark in film directing, writing, and in other areas of movie production. One of the most influential remains Kathleen Collins. Her work as a teacher, director, playwright, and screenwriter inspired a generation of African American women filmmakers. In such films as *The Cruz Brothers and Mrs. Malloy* (1980) and *Losing Ground* (1982), Collins worked on the belief that "if I can be very faithful to [my own view] and manage to find a way to say it, it will mean something to other people."

Documentary filmmaker Michelle Parkerson has won acclaim for a number of compelling profiles of artists and performers.

Her first film, *But Then, She's Betty Carter* (1980), offers the story of the noted jazz stylist. *Gotta Make This Journey* (1983) tells the story of a female a cappella singing group. *A Litany of Survival* (1993) chronicles the story of one of Parkerson's heroes, poet and essayist Audre Lord.

Writer, producer, and director Julie Dash garnered acclaim and honors for *Daughters of the Dust* (1992). This poignant film, set in the Georgia Sea Islands, tells the story of the women of a family at the turn of the century. For Dash, the film's essence is "the fear of going away from home and not being able to come back, the fear of abandoning one's culture."

▲ FILMMAKER JULIE DASH

Ruth Carter has made a significant contribution in costume design. Her responsibilities include both designing and making costumes. In works such as *School Daze* and *What's Love Got to Do With It* she has taken on the challenging assignments of re-creating the clothes and styles of the 1950s and 1960s. She was nominated for a 1992 Academy Award for Best Costume Design for her work on *Malcolm X*.

Making the Art Connection

1. What positions in film were open to African American women before the 1940s?

2. Who are the subjects of Michelle Parkerson's documentaries? What do they have in common?

3. In what area of filmwork has Ruth Carter contributed?

ACTIVITY

4. View a film written, directed, or produced by an African American woman. Write a review of the film describing the plot, technique, and main point of the story.

★★

Successes and Setbacks

Guide to Reading

Main Idea

During the Kennedy-Johnson years, the civil rights movement experienced both successes and setbacks.

Reading Strategy

Organizing Information As you read about the successes and setbacks or the civil rights movement, use a diagram like the one shown here to list the provisions of the Civil Rights Act of 1964.

Civil Rights Act of 1964

Objectives

After studying this section, you should be able to

★ describe advances made in civil rights during the Kennedy-Johnson administrations.

★ describe the setbacks and difficulties the civil rights activists faced during the 1960s.

Key Term

sit-in

▶ "IN A FREE GOVERNMENT . . . " BY JACOB LAWRENCE

As the 1960s began, leaders for the civil rights movement—both African Americans and liberal whites—stepped up the tactics of nonviolent resistance throughout the South. Although eventually many of these tactics resulted in great gains for the movement, they generally were met with violence. People were attacked and killed, and only the federal government was strong enough to do something about it.

■ Students Stage Sit-ins

During the winter of 1959 and 1960, civil rights groups held marches, demonstrations, and boycotts to end segregation in public places. They especially challenged the practice of not serving African Americans at many southern lunch counters. In February 1960, four African American students sat down at a segregated lunch counter in a local store in Greensboro, North Carolina. They refused to leave until they were served. Their action was known as a **sit-in**, and before long students were staging sit-ins all over the South. By September 1961, 70,000 students were using this tactic to produce social change.

By 1960 the crusade for civil rights had become a national movement. As a result, many Americans were now beginning to recognize the moral evil of racial discrimination. King wrote:

> ❝ *The law cannot change the heart—but it can restrain the heartless. It will take education and religion to change bad internal attitudes—but legislation and court orders can control their external aspects.* ❞

■ Kennedy and Civil Rights

In contrast to Eisenhower's cautious stand on civil rights, President Kennedy had promised vigorous support of the movement. Kennedy was aware of the support he needed from African American voters to win the 1960 election. Yet his slim victory over Nixon, coupled with the fear of losing southern Democratic support in Congress, made him act less forcefully than the words of his campaign had seemed to promise.

Kennedy's cautious attitude disappointed white liberals and African American leaders. He waited until 1962 to sign an executive order ending segregation in government-owned housing. And although Kennedy appointed African Americans to his administration as well as to federal judicial positions, he also appointed some judges who supported segregation. Events in the South, however, soon forced Kennedy to take a more active role in civil rights.

The Freedom Riders

In the spring of 1961, civil rights activists volunteered as "Freedom Riders" to ride buses into segregated terminals throughout the South. In May busloads of Freedom Riders were attacked by mobs in the Alabama cities of Anniston and Birmingham. A bus was fire-bombed and riders were beaten and clubbed. As more and more Freedom Riders poured into southern cities, local police were unable or unwilling to protect them. The President was forced to use federal marshals to restore order. The Justice Department also pressured the Interstate Commerce Commission to bring lawsuits against those terminals that refused to comply with regulations on desegregation.

While Kennedy was in office, from 1961 to 1963, the Department of Justice brought six times as many lawsuits to protect African American voting rights as it did under Eisenhower, from 1958 to 1960. As a result, by 1964, the percentage of African American citizens registered to vote in the Deep South had risen from 25 to 40 percent, largely because of the work of the Freedom Riders.

Violence in Birmingham

Violence that broke out in Birmingham was the last straw for Kennedy. From that point on, Kennedy wholeheartedly sided with Martin Luther King and the civil rights

Visualizing History

▲ **CHALLENGING SEGREGATION** Civil rights groups challenged the practice of not serving African Americans at many southern diners. Here, two African Americans refuse to leave a segregated Raleigh, North Carolina, lunch counter until they are served. *What was their tactic called?*

Visualizing History

▲ THE ROAD TO MONTGOMERY Dr. Martin Luther King, Jr., led a five-day march from Selma to Montgomery, Alabama, in March 1965. Marches were an effective way for African Americans to protest discrimination. *What demonstration did King lead in April 1963?*

activists. In April 1963, King led a demonstration in Birmingham, Alabama. On the orders of Police Commissioner Eugene "Bull" Connor, police used fire hoses, clubs, and snarling dogs on demonstrators. National television carried the sight of this violence into millions of homes. Viewers were outraged. Kennedy sent 3,000 troops to restore peace in the city. In June he proposed a new civil rights bill that would outlaw segregation throughout the nation.

■ Trouble in Southern Universities

During Kennedy's administration the Department of Justice brought numerous suits for desegregation of schools. In Sep-

HISTORY Online — **Student Web Activity**

Visit the *American History: The Modern Era Since 1865* Web site at **me.glencoe.com** and click on *Chapter 22— Student Web Activities* for an activity about the march on Birmingham.

tember 1962, James Meredith, a 29-year-old African American air force veteran, sought entrance to the University of Mississippi. The state's governor refused. Kennedy sent in federal marshals and eventually the Mississippi National Guard to enable Meredith to enter the university.

Another confrontation between state and federal powers took place in June 1963—this time in Alabama. Governor George Wallace symbolically stood in a doorway to prevent desegregation of the University of Alabama at Tuscaloosa. Kennedy immediately federalized the Alabama National Guard and ordered the troops to make sure African Americans were allowed to enter. As a result, Wallace backed down.

The violence of such confrontations convinced Kennedy that federal legislation against segregation and discrimination was needed. Kennedy quickly proposed laws that would forbid segregation in stores, restaurants, hotels, and theaters and that would prohibit discrimination in employment. But progress on school desegregation was slow. Most African American school children in the South continued to attend all-black schools.

■ The March on Washington

In August 1963, for the 100th anniversary of the Emancipation Proclamation, African American leaders planned to hold the largest civil rights demonstration in the nation's history. This "March on Washington for Jobs and Freedom" would press for the passage of Kennedy's proposed civil rights bill, which was being debated in Congress.

King's Dream of Freedom

More than 200,000 demonstrators, both African American and white, converged on the nation's capital. They sang hymns and spirituals as they gathered near the Lincoln Memorial.

At the Lincoln Memorial the marchers heard eloquent speeches, especially from Dr. Martin Luther King, Jr., who, in a famous address, described his dream of freedom and equality for all people:

❝ *I have a dream that one day this nation will rise up and live out the true meaning of its creed: 'We hold these truths to be self-evident; that all men are created equal' . . . And when this happens, and when we allow freedom to ring, when we let it ring from every village and hamlet, from every state and every city, we will be able to speed up that day when all God's children . . . [will] join hands and sing in the words of the old . . . spiritual: 'Free at last, Free at last, Thank God Almighty, we're free at last.'* ❞

The leaders of the march then left for a meeting with President John F. Kennedy at the White House.

🏛 GOVERNMENT
A New Civil Rights Act

The March on Washington was a historic event for the civil rights movement. It not only awakened millions to the plight of African Americans living in the South but also confirmed for Congress the widespread support for a civil rights bill.

Progress was slow. In 1963, 9 years after the *Brown* decision, only one-half of one percent of African American public school children in the 11 former Confederate states were attending desegregated schools. Some southern communities desegregated public facilities only after boycotts and sit-ins. Others, however, refused.

After President Kennedy's assassination on November 22, 1963, President Johnson was determined to continue Kennedy's civil rights policies. So he accepted the challenge

---

The Move Toward Equality

CAUSES

- 1955 Rosa Parks is arrested
- 1955 Montgomery bus boycott
- 1957 Conflict at Little Rock
- 1957 SCLC is organized
- 1960 Students stage sit-ins
- 1963 March on Washington

• Toward Equality

EFFECTS

- 1962 James Meredith enters University of Mississippi
- 1967 Thurgood Marshall appointed to Supreme Court
- 1968 Shirley Chisholm elected to House
- 1972 Barbara Jordan and Andrew Young are first Southern African Americans elected to House since 1901

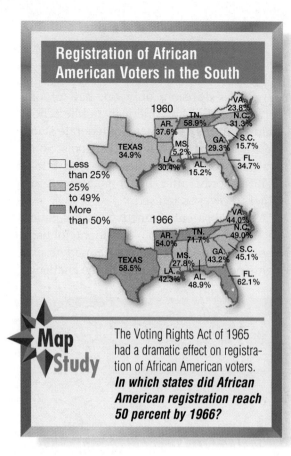

Registration of African American Voters in the South

1960

VA. 23.8%
TN. 58.9%
N.C. 31.3%
AR. 37.6%
TEXAS 34.9%
MS. 5.2%
GA. 29.3%
S.C. 15.7%
LA. 30.4%
AL. 15.2%
FL. 34.7%

☐ Less than 25%
☐ 25% to 49%
☐ More than 50%

1966

VA. 44.0%
TN. 71.7%
N.C. 49.0%
AR. 54.0%
TEXAS 58.5%
MS. 27.8%
GA. 43.2%
S.C. 45.1%
LA. 42.3%
AL. 48.9%
FL. 62.1%

Map Study

The Voting Rights Act of 1965 had a dramatic effect on registration of African American voters. *In which states did African American registration reach 50 percent by 1966?*

66 *No memorial . . . could more eloquently honor President Kennedy's memory than the earliest possible passage of the civil rights bill. . . .* 99

On July 2, the President signed into law the Civil Rights Act of 1964. The strongest civil rights act since Reconstruction stated that all citizens should have equal access to such public facilities as parks and libraries and to such private businesses serving the public as restaurants and theaters. It forbade discrimination in education and strengthened the right to vote. It also outlawed job discrimination because of race, sex, religion, or national origin. Passage of the Voting Rights Act of 1965 helped pave the way for more African Americans to vote. Activist John Lewis said:

66 *These elections signal a new level of maturation in American politics. They demonstrate the willingness of white voters to set aside racial differences, and they reflect the fact that many minorities have gained the broad political experience and skills to make them solid candidates for major office.* 99

The Voting Rights Act of 1965 also helped other minorities. It set aside a New York state law requiring voters to be able to read English, enabling such groups as Mexican Americans to vote. 🏛

of getting Kennedy's proposed bill passed. It had passed the House of Representatives in February 1964 but was stalled in the Senate where southern segregationists intended to kill it. Even though Johnson himself was from the South, he had broken with the segregationists early in his career. Johnson was aided in his goal by national remorse over Kennedy's assassination. To take advantage of this, the President called for speedy action:

Section 2 ★ Assessment

Checking for Understanding

1. Define sit-in.

Critical Thinking

2. **Evaluating Events** The March on Washington is seen as one of the major events of the civil rights movement. Why is this so?

3. **Summarizing** Re-create the diagram shown here to list the advances and setbacks of the

civil rights movement during Kennedy's presidency.

Civil Rights Movement

Advances ↗   Setbacks ↘

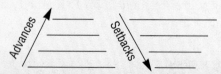

INTERDISCIPLINARY ACTIVITY

4. **Government** Create a poster encouraging people to vote. Include a slogan.

BUILDING SKILLS
Critical Thinking Skills

Identifying Cause and Effect

▲ REGISTERING TO VOTE, BATESVILLE, MISSISSIPPI

Understanding cause and effect involves considering why an event occurred. A cause is the action or situation that produces an event. An effect is the result or consequence of an action or situation.

Learning the Skill

To understand cause and effect, follow these steps:

- Identify two or more events or developments.

- Decide whether one event caused the other. One useful way to determine this is to look for language clues. Such words as *because, as a result of, for this reason,* and *thus* often indicate a cause-and-effect relationship.

Read the following passage, then answer the questions that follow.

Despite federal laws that granted them the right to vote, many African Americans in the South were deprived of their rights by threats and violence or by unfair eligibility tests. Dr. Martin Luther King,

Jr., decided it was time to push for voting rights, and selected Selma, Alabama, as the starting point for the campaign. This was because in Selma most of the African Americans who applied to vote were turned down. Dr. King wanted to dramatize this injustice.

In January 1965, King organized a voter registration drive in Selma. The county sheriff, however, deputized whites and attacked groups of African Americans with dogs and cattle prods as they tried to register. In March, King organized a "march for freedom" from Selma to the state capitol in Montgomery, 50 miles away. Police armed with billy clubs attacked the marchers.

National outrage over the events in Selma helped speed the passage of the Voting Rights Act of 1965. It did away with literacy tests in many southern states and provided for federal assistance in registering African Americans. Steps were also taken to eliminate the poll tax, forbidden by the Twenty-fourth Amendment yet still used to keep the poor from voting. As a result, more than 400,000 people, mostly African Americans who had not previously voted, were registered within a single year.

Practicing the Skill

1. Why did Dr. King select Selma to start the voting campaign?

2. What effect did the events at Selma have on subsequent legislation?

 Glencoe's **Skillbuilder Interactive Workbook, Level 2** provides instruction and practice in key social studies skills.

APPLYING THE SKILL

3. Write three sentences that show a cause-and-effect relationship. For each sentence, construct a cause-and-effect diagram by writing the cause on the left and the effect on the right. Connect the two parts of the sentence with an arrow. Show any words that indicate cause and effect.

★★★★★★★★★★★★★★★★★★★★★★★★★★★★★★★★★

New Directions

Guide to Reading

Main Idea
Frustrated by the slow pace of change, some African Americans adopted new strategies to gain equality.

Reading Strategy

Organizing Information As you read about new directions in the civil rights movement, use a diagram like the one shown here to list the factors responsible for discontent among some African Americans.

Reasons for Discontent

Objectives

After studying this section, you should be able to

★ list some of the factors responsible for discontent among some African Americans.

★ explain what new philosophies were developed by African Americans to deal with the discontent.

Key Terms

racism, black nationalism, black power, assimilation, busing

▶ MALCOLM X HAT

espite gains made at the national, state, and local levels through peaceful change in cooperation with whites, progress in civil rights was slow. It was especially slow in social and economic areas. Unemployment for African Americans, for example, was much higher than the national average. As a result, by the mid-1960s a growing number of African Americans adopted a new, more radical approach to the problem of **racism,** that is, racial prejudice or discrimination. They believed in taking immediate action not only to gain political and legal rights, but to end discrimination in housing, education, and employment. Instead of following King's philosophy of integration and nonviolence, radical groups began to put forward a new theory and expressed their willingness to use violence to protect themselves and to achieve just treatment.

■ New Leadership

Many whites reacted with alarm to the new direction in the civil rights movement. They were especially worried about groups that openly preached black revolution. These whites felt the new philosophies African Americans were developing threatened their way of life.

The Black Muslims

The Nation of Islam, known as the Black Muslims, was originally founded in the early 1930s, and was led by Elijah Muhammad. This group appealed to African Americans to embrace the Islamic faith and preached **black nationalism.** This philosophy stated that African Americans should completely separate themselves from whites and form their own self-governing communities—their own nation. They also advocated a program of self-defense. Their ideas—popularized by a talented speaker and minister known as Malcolm X—received national attention in the early 1960s. In his autobiography, Malcolm X talked about his views:

> 66 ... I'm not for wanton violence, I'm for justice. ... I feel that when the law fails to protect [African Americans] from whites' attacks, then those [African Americans] should use arms, if necessary, to defend themselves. ... 99

By 1964, however, Malcolm X came to favor an integrated society instead of separatism. Therefore, he broke with the Black Muslims. Apparently as a result of his public disagreements with them, he was shot and killed in February 1965. Although in the end Malcolm X came to favor integration, his earlier ideas continued to influence many young African Americans after his death. By the late 1960s, the Student Nonviolent Coordinating Committee (SNCC) and the Congress of Racial Equality (CORE), which had originally supported King's tactics, had become more radical.

Black Power

In May 1966, the head of SNCC, Stokely Carmichael, developed the idea of **black power** to further racial equality. This philosophy stated that blacks should "take back control of all aspects of their lives—social, political, and economic. As expounded by the black nationalists, it meant separation from white society, by violent means if necessary."

The philosophy of black power moved away from the idea of **assimilation**—the policy of incorporating different racial or cultural groups into the dominant society—and preached racial distinctiveness, pride, and leadership.

Many members and leaders of the civil rights movement had been white liberals. Now groups like SNCC and CORE moved whites out of leadership positions. African Americans began to reexamine their African heritage. Some took African names or wore "Afro" hairstyles and African-style clothing. They demanded that schools adopt programs in African-American studies.

Black power created a deep division among civil rights activists. This new idea was firmly rejected by such groups as the NAACP, which saw it as a threat to law and order. However, it would be black power that, from this point on, would more strongly influence the future development of the civil rights movement.

The Black Panthers

One of the most militant black-power groups was the Black Panthers. Founded in 1966 by Huey Newton, Bobby Seale, and Eldridge Cleaver, the Black Panthers urged African Americans to arm themselves and confront white society in order to force whites to grant them equal rights. Cleaver's *Soul on Ice* (1967) served as a statement of Black Panthers' aims:

 ▲ NATION OF ISLAM The Nation of Islam, founded in Detroit, Michigan, by Wali Farad, gained many converts during the 1950s and 1960s. *What were the goals and objectives of black nationalism?*

> **What the white man must be brought to understand is that the black man . . . does not intend to be tricked again into another hundred-year forfeit of freedom. Not for a single moment or for any price will the black men now rising up in America settle for anything less than their full . . . share . . . in the sovereignty of America.**

■ The Battle in the North

Although the major battles for civil rights were fought in the South, the movement's leaders recognized that segregation and prejudice also existed in the North. King shifted his demonstrations from the South to such northern cities as Chicago, where he protested housing discrimination, unemployment, and urban poverty. Northern African American populations tended to be concentrated in the inner cities, where poverty was widespread and discontent was high.

Discontent Leads to Riots

Frustration over urban conditions led to a series of riots in many cities. Often occurring in the heat of summer, these riots were sometimes triggered by an incident between police and African American citizens. When riots erupted, looting and burning also broke out.

The first major riot took place in the Harlem section of New York City in July 1964. Other riots broke out that year in Philadelphia and Chicago. In August 1965, a riot in the African American neighborhood of Watts in Los Angeles left 34 people dead, more than 3,000 arrested, and $20 million in property damage. The summer of 1966 brought new disruptions in New York, Atlanta, Cleveland, Detroit, Chicago, San Francisco, and Los Angeles. Federal troops and National Guardsmen entered Detroit in July 1967, after much of the city was in flames. When the riot was over, 40 people had been killed and hundreds more were injured. Thousands were left homeless, and many businesses were in ashes.

Most of the riots took place outside the South, in parts of the United States where African Americans supposedly enjoyed

Malcolm X
1925–1965

★★★★★★★★★★ AMERICAN PORTRAITS

Born Malcolm Little in Omaha, Nebraska, this future religious leader and activist became a member of the Nation of Islam while serving a prison sentence for burglary. As was the custom in this religious sect, Malcolm dropped his "slave" name in favor of the letter X.

Malcolm X became a powerful and eloquent minister in the Nation of Islam. He taught the religious faith while advocating a position of independent African American political action, black power, pride, and self-defense. The Nation of Islam, sometimes referred to as the Black Muslim movement, stressed the need for African American unity, and advocated a position of separation in a time when most civil rights workers dedicated themselves to achieving racial and economic integration.

Malcolm X eventually broke with the Nation of Islam, moderated his separatist stance, and agreed to work with other civil rights activists to fight racism, discrimination, and injustice. However, Malcolm was assassinated shortly thereafter by rival members of the Nation of Islam.

Visualizing History

▲ SUMMER OF 1965 Members of the National Guard patrol the streets of the Watts section of Los Angeles in August 1965. Watts was the site of one of many urban racial confrontations to erupt in the United States during the middle and late 1960s. *What event set off a wave of riots in April 1968?*

equal rights. Adam Clayton Powell, Jr., an African American member of Congress from New York City, offered an explanation. In the South, he said, what African Americans wanted was relatively easy for whites to give: the right to sit at a drugstore counter or in the front of a bus. In the North, African Americans had long been able to sit where they pleased. Now they wanted "a bigger piece of the pie"—better jobs, more money, better places to live. Some white jobholders and property owners felt threatened.

The Kerner Commission

In response to the violence spreading across America, President Johnson appointed a National Advisory Commission on Civil Disorders, known as the Kerner Commission, to look into the problem. The Kerner Commission laid responsibility for the ghettos at the feet of white society.

Although African Americans suffered greater loss of life and property, the riots tended to harden white prejudices. The urgently requested commission report was quietly received and produced little change.

The Death of Martin Luther King, Jr.

Despite the Kerner Commission report, violence continued to grow. Then in 1968 the violence reached a climax with the assassination of Dr. Martin Luther King, Jr. In April of that year, King was in Memphis, Tennessee, to support a strike of African American sanitation workers. He was planning a national poor people's campaign to promote economic gains for African Americans and all poor people.

There had been many threats against King's life over the years. Dr. King, however, had always dismissed them. Yet prophetically, King told a church meeting the night of April 3:

❝ . . . I've been to the mountain top, and I don't mind. . . . I've looked over and I've seen the Promised Land. I may not get there with you, but I want you to know tonight that we as a people will get to the Promised Land. ❞

The next day, he was killed by a sniper. Ironically, the murder of the great teacher of

◄ **STOKELY
CARMICHAEL**

nonviolence set off a week of rioting, arson, and looting in 125 American cities. It was as if King's death swept away the last bit of faith in a peaceful solution. "America," announced Stokely Carmichael, "must be burned down in order for us to survive." Rioting took place in Washington, D.C., just blocks from the White House. President Johnson ordered troops to enforce a curfew and protect government buildings.

■ The Civil Rights Movement After 1968

Between the *Brown* decision and King's death, the civil rights movement made great gains. After King died, however, the movement's leaders feared that they would begin to lose some of their hard-won victories.

Richard Nixon, who won the presidency in 1968, had his own agenda. He wanted the Republicans to win control of both the White House and Congress in 1972. To do that, he needed to lure southern Democrats into the Republican ranks.

To this end, Nixon developed a "southern strategy." He appointed a southern justice to the Supreme Court. The President also reversed a Johnson administration policy that cut off federal funds to racially segregated school systems. Although federal policy had been affirmed in 1968 by the Supreme Court in *Green* v. *County School Board,* Nixon ignored the Court's ruling and instructed the Justice Department to support school boards that were seeking to delay desegregation.

Contrary to Nixon's hopes, his appointments to the Supreme Court did not guarantee a reversal of the *Green* decision. Instead, the Court affirmed integration by means of **busing**—transporting children to a school outside their residential area to achieve racial balance in that school. White Americans in the South and most other regions of the nation resisted busing, and Nixon denounced it. The Nixon administration's open opposition to busing for desegregation intensified public controversy over the issue.

Nixon's agenda moved many people and much of government policy to the right, away from the liberal policies of the Kennedy-Johnson years. Many civil rights gains were lost or delayed. However, despite the setback, the movement continued. It would make gains in the future and strongly influence other minorities.

Section 3 ★ Assessment

Checking for Understanding

1. **Define** racism, black nationalism, black power, assimilation, busing.
2. **Summarize** the goals of the black-power movement.

Critical Thinking

3. **Making Comparisons**   Re-create the diagram shown here to describe how Malcolm X and

Martin Luther King, Jr., differed in their views on how to combat racism.

INTERDISCIPLINARY ACTIVITY

4. **The Arts** Use photographs and drawings to illustrate a poster on the life and accomplishments of Dr. Martin Luther King, Jr.

★★★

The Impact of Civil Rights

Guide to Reading

Main Idea
Women, Hispanics, and Native Americans fought for greater equality during the 1960s and 1970s.

Reading Strategy

Classifying Information As you read about the civil rights efforts of other groups, use a chart like the one shown here to list their gains.

Civil Rights Gains		
Women	Hispanics	Native Americans

Objectives
After studying this section, you should be able to

★ describe the gains made by women and minorities.

★ explain why the Equal Rights Amendment was not ratified.

Key Terms

feminist, sexism, bilingualism

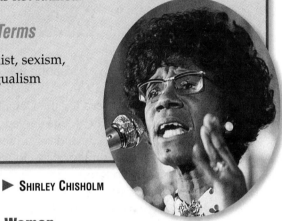

▶ SHIRLEY CHISHOLM

During the 1960s and 1970s, young Americans became leaders in promoting social justice. They were determined to close the gap between the realities of American life—discrimination, poverty, and social inequalities—and the nation's ideal of "liberty and justice for all."

■ The Women's Rights Movement

Women constituted more than 50 percent of the population in the United States in the 1970s. However, their political, economic, legal, and social status resembled that of a disadvantaged minority. Minority women faced a special problem in that they encountered sexual and racial discrimination at the same time.

Status of Women

In 1977 women held less than 5 percent of the elective offices in the United States. There had been few female senators or governors, no Supreme Court justices, and no mayors of major cities in the history of the republic. Of the 435 members of the House of Representatives, only 18 were women. In her autobiography *Unbought and Unbossed*, Shirley Chisholm, the first African American woman to serve in the House of Representatives, wrote:

❝ *When I decided to run for Congress, I knew I would encounter both anti-black and anti-feminist sentiments. What surprised me was the much greater virulence of the sex discrimination.* ❞

▼ GLORIA STEINEM

► PHYLLIS SCHLAFLY

Visualizing History

▲ **ERA MARCHERS** The Equal Rights Amendment, submitted to the states in 1972 for ratification, aroused strong feelings among supporters and opponents. ***What happened to the Equal Rights Amendment?***

Representative Chisholm was elected for a second term in 1970. In 1972 she ran against George McGovern for the Democratic nomination for President. She served in Congress for the next decade and continued to support equal rights for minorities and women. After serving in Congress, she then turned her talent to teaching on the college level. About her accomplishments, she noted:

> *I hope that my having made it, the hard way, can be some kind of inspiration, particularly to women.*

In 1960 women made up one-third of the nation's workforce. Yet, most of their jobs offered less pay and prestige than those positions that men held. For every dollar on average that a man earned on a job in the 1960s, a woman with the same job earned only 59 cents. During the rest of the 1960s and into the next decade the economic situation of women improved slightly.

In 1976 the United States Department of Labor reported that full-time working men averaged 75 percent more pay than full-time working women. Dissatisfied with the slow progress, many women began calling for stronger action.

The publication in 1963 of *The Feminine Mystique* by Betty Friedan had inspired demands for change. Friedan rejected the notion that the destiny of women was only to be wives and mothers. She described how the media had created an image of women that was designed to imprison them in their households and bar serious consideration of them as competitors in the labor market.

National Organization for Women

In 1966 Betty Friedan joined with other **feminists,** or women activists, to establish the National Organization for Women (NOW). The organization's Statement of Purpose read:

> *. . . [To] take action to bring women into full participation in the mainstream of American society now, assuming all the privileges and responsibilities thereof in truly equal partnership with men.*

Among its early successes, NOW helped end separate classified employment ads for men and women, and airline rules that required female flight attendants to retire at age 32. In the 1960s and 1970s, NOW and similar groups helped increasing numbers of women to enter professions. Banks, realtors, and department stores were forced to grant loans, mortgages, leases, and credit that they long had denied to female applicants.

The Equal Rights Amendment

Following intense lobbying by women's groups, in 1972 Congress voted to submit the Equal Rights Amendment (ERA) to the states for ratification. This amendment stated that "equality of rights under the law shall not be denied or abridged by the United States or by any state on account of sex."

Not all women supported ERA, however. Phyllis Schlafly, founder of STOP ERA, dismissed the women's rights movement as "a series of sharp-tongued, high-pitched, whining complaints by unmarried women." STOP ERA supporters contended that the ERA would force women to give up their traditional roles as wives and mothers, and that they would lose certain legal protections in the family and in the workplace. As a result of a vigorous campaign by STOP ERA and other groups, the Equal Rights Amendment failed to obtain the votes needed for ratification.

Women Make Progress

Despite the failure of the ERA, women continued to make progress. **Sexism**—treating people differently because of their gender—was recognized and outlawed in the workplace by 1971. Princeton, Yale, and other traditionally all-male colleges began to open their doors to females.

Women were also becoming increasingly important in the business world. By the mid-1970s, nearly half of all married women worked outside the home; almost all who had graduated from college worked.

Women also were becoming an important force in politics in the 1970s. By the 1980s, there were more women than ever in both the Senate and the House of Representatives, as well as on the Supreme Court, in the cabinet, and in state government offices. In 1984, Representative Geraldine Ferraro became the first female major-party candidate to run for Vice President.

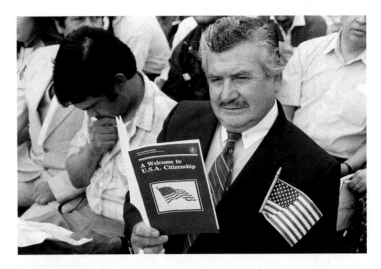

Visualizing History

▲ HISPANIC AMERICANS By the 1970s Hispanic Americans were the second-largest minority in the United States. *What group made up the largest number of Hispanics?*

■ Hispanic Activism

At this time, Hispanics also became active in campaigning for equal rights. By the 1970s Hispanic Americans had become the second-largest minority in the United States, next to African Americans. Spanish-speaking people made up almost 8 percent of the population and were the largest minority group in several states. New York City alone had about 2 million Spanish-speaking people. Part of Miami, Florida, became known as "Little Havana" because it was home to hundreds of thousands of Cuban immigrants.

Mexican Americans made up the largest group of Hispanic peoples. For years, thousands of Mexican Americans labored as

●●●●●●●●●●●●●●●●●●●●●●●●●

Footnotes to History

Muñoz Marín and Puerto Rico Puerto

Rican newspaper editor Luis Muñoz Marín formed his own political party after Liberal party leaders expelled him, partly because he called for independence from the United States. Muñoz Marín founded his own party and, in 1942, organized Operation Bootstrap to attract mainland industry to the island. In 1948 Muñoz Marín was overwhelmingly elected Puerto Rico's first governor. He persuaded the United States to approve a commonwealth status for the island in 1952. When he died in 1980, he was mourned as a national hero.

migrant farm workers, moving from place to place to harvest seasonal crops. They were not protected by federal minimum-wage laws, unemployment insurance, or Social Security.

In 1965 Cesar Chavez organized a nation-wide coalition and asked Americans to boycott California grapes picked by nonunion labor. After enduring five years of such persistent protest, most California grape growers relented and agreed to sign a contract with Chavez's union, the United Farm Workers.

During the 1970s, Hispanic Americans began to organize. The League of United Latin American Citizens (LULAC) won suits in federal courts to guarantee Hispanic Americans the right to serve on juries, to send their children to unsegregated schools, and to be taught in Spanish as well as in English. The use of two languages is called **bilingualism.** As their political strength grew, more Hispanic Americans were elected to local and state offices as well as to Congress.

◀ RUSSELL MEANS, AIM LEADER

▲ AMERICAN INDIAN MOVEMENT FLAG

■ Native Americans Organize

Like the Hispanics, Native Americans organized during the 1960s and 1970s. Their plight captured national attention when a 1966 study revealed that Native Americans suffered from malnutrition and disease to such an extent that their life expectancy was only 46 years. They had less formal education than any other minority group, and their family income was less than one-half the national average.

Termination Policy

After World War II, the federal government tried to incorporate Native Americans into white society. A new policy called "termination" was established in 1953. This meant that the federal government stopped recognizing Native American nations as legal entities that were separate from state government. Now, the nations would be subject to the same local governments as whites. The government in Washington worked to make Native Americans give up their cultures and adapt to white society.

Native Americans were so angry that they began speaking out more forcibly. A group of younger Native Americans had breathed life into the National Congress of American Indians (NCAI), set up in 1944. As a result of their activity, President Eisenhower put a stop to termination without consent. Later Presidents did not revive it during the 1960s. They made some efforts to provide tribes with government money.

Declaration of Indian Purpose

In 1961, more than 400 representatives of 67 Native American nations met in Chicago to draw up a bill of rights for Native Americans. They called it the Declaration of Indian Purpose, and in it they committed themselves to Indian nationalism and intertribal unity. The delegates also stated their belief in "red power," and demanded an end to federal control of Native American affairs. "We simply want to run our lives our own way," said one young leader.

As a result, in 1968, the Congress passed the Indian Civil Rights Act, which guaranteed Native American reservation dwellers some of the rights provided to other citizens under the Bill of Rights.

However, some Native Americans wanted to take more direct action. In the state of Washington, men from more than 50 Native American groups led a "fish-in." They deliberately broke game laws and risked imprisonment to protest the loss of their former fishing and hunting grounds.

In 1973 a more militant group, the American Indian Movement (AIM), seized the reservation at Wounded Knee, South Dakota. They demanded that lands taken from Native Americans in violation of federal treaties be returned. They also demanded that development programs on reservations be managed by their own governments, and not the federal Bureau of Indian Affairs. The takeover ended after a standoff between federal agents and Native Americans, and federal policies toward Native Americans began to change.

The Pueblo of Taos, New Mexico, regained Blue Lake, a place sacred to their religious life. In 1975 a federal court declared that the Passamaquoddy and the Penobscot nations had a valid claim to more than half the state of Maine and to $25 billion in damages and unpaid rents.

Visualizing History

▲ **NATIVE AMERICANS** Native Americans fought in the nation's wars and honored those who gave their lives for freedom. Many pressed for economic and political equality and compensation for the loss of their land. *What action did Native Americans take at Wounded Knee in 1973?*

Section 4 ★ Assessment

Checking for Understanding

1. **Define** feminist, sexism, bilingualism.

2. **State** two demands that were made by Hispanics and Native Americans.

Critical Thinking

3. **Analyzing Point of View** Analyze the women's rights movement in the 1970s. What stereotypes of women persist today?

4. **Summarizing** Re-create the diagram shown here to list three inequalities that existed between men and women in the 1970s.

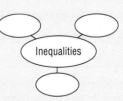

Inequalities

INTERDISCIPLINARY ACTIVITY

5. **The Arts** Write a one-page report about the history of one of the immigrant groups in your community.

Using Vocabulary

Using the following vocabulary terms, write a paragraph describing the development of the civil rights movement.

nonviolent resistance   sit-in
federalized   racism
black nationalism   black power

Reviewing Facts

1. **List** two results of the Supreme Court's *Brown* v. *Board of Education* ruling.

2. **List** two results of the black-power movement.

3. **Describe** the aims and objectives of the women's rights movement.

4. **Summarize** advances made by Native Americans.

Understanding Concepts

Civil Rights

1. Re-create the chart shown here to describe the significance of each listed person to the civil rights movement.

Person	Significance
Rosa Parks	
Martin Luther King, Jr.	
Malcolm X	

2. Explain the factors in American society that helped the civil rights movement grow.

3. Why did the civil rights movement cause so much turmoil? Explain how the demands of African Americans affected other minorities and what the results were.

Critical Thinking

1. **Evaluating Tactics** Though Martin Luther King, Jr.'s, methods for change were nonviolent, they were not passive. What were some challenges faced by nonviolent demonstrators? Why was their nonviolence an effective tactic?

2. **Analyzing Fine Art** Study the mural that appears on this page. Then answer the questions that follow.

   a. Describe what the mural is showing.

   b. Based on the mural, what are the artist's feelings toward African American culture?

3. **Interpreting Demographic Data** *Demographics* is the data used to show the characteristics of a human population in terms of size, growth, density distribution, and vital statistics. Study the graph on page 693 and answer the questions.

   a. What demographic information does the graph show?

   b. What do the numbers in parentheses represent? What change does this data show?

   c. What does the information indicate about the problems a small group might have effecting change through the political process?

CHAPTER 22 ★ ASSESSMENT

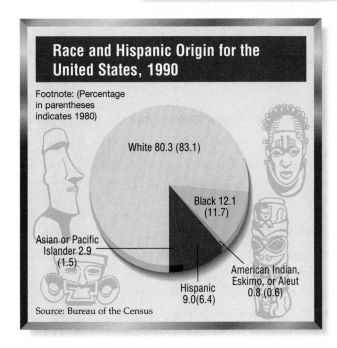

Race and Hispanic Origin for the United States, 1990

Footnote: (Percentage in parentheses indicates 1980)

White 80.3 (83.1)

Black 12.1 (11.7)

Asian or Pacific Islander 2.9 (1.5)

Hispanic 9.0(6.4)

American Indian, Eskimo, or Aleut 0.8 (0.6)

Source: Bureau of the Census

History and Geography

Native Americans and the Land

1. **Human/Environment Interaction** What effect did the Indian Civil Rights Act have on Native American reservations?

2. **Human/Environment Interaction** What action did Native Americans take to protest the loss of their fishing and hunting grounds?

 Interdisciplinary Activity: Sociology

You will work in a group with two others to analyze three activist movements of the 1970s: the women's rights movement, the Hispanic movement, and the Native American movement. The goal of your group is to find as many similarities between these movements as you can. Each group member should choose one of these movements. First, work individually to make a list of the goals of each movement and the methods used to attain them. Next, work with your partners to compile a master list of similarities between the three movements. Present your list to the class and discuss the findings.

Practicing Skills

Identifying Cause and Effect

Consider the following statements. Each statement includes a cause and an effect. For each statement make a cause-and-effect diagram by writing the cause on the left and the effect on the right. Then connect the two parts with an arrow.

1. As a result of serving in the military during wartime, African Americans were in a better position to demand their full rights as Americans.

2. President Truman could not get Congress's support for his civil rights program, largely because of a split in the Democratic party.

Technology Activity

Using the Internet The United Farm Workers are still active today. Working with another classmate, search the Internet for information about this organization and create a brochure that explains its goals. Share your brochure with the class.

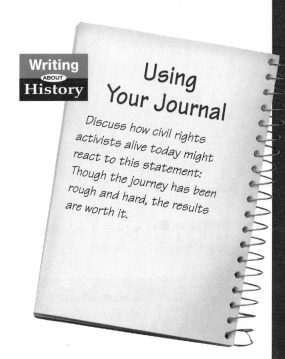

Writing ABOUT History

Using Your Journal

Discuss how civil rights activists alive today might react to this statement: Though the journey has been rough and hard, the results are worth it.

CHAPTER 23

★★★

The Vietnam Era
1954–1975

▶ SOLDIER STANDING GUARD

Setting the Scene

Focus

President Kennedy's handling of foreign policy was tested strenuously as cold war challenges arose during the Vietnam Era. Kennedy faced a failed Cuban invasion, a missile crisis, quarrels over nuclear testing, and the beginnings of the war in Vietnam. During the Johnson years, this conflict became the focus of attention for the nation. More and more, the American people became divided over this issue.

Concepts to Understand

★ How social upheaval divided the nation and affected **foreign policy** during the Vietnam Era

★ Why public opinion was divided over the conduct of the **war** in Vietnam

Read to Discover . . .

★ lessons Kennedy learned from his handling of foreign policy.

★ what events set off political turmoil during this period.

Journal Notes

What do you think it would have been like to be President of the United States during the Vietnam War? Note details about it in your journal as you read the chapter.

HISTORY Online

Chapter Overview
Visit the *American History: The Modern Era Since 1865* Web site at **me.glencoe.com** and click on *Chapter 23—Chapter Overviews* to preview chapter information.

CULTURAL	• **1955** *Ford offers seatbelts as optional equipment*	• **1964** *The Beatles appear on* The Ed Sullivan Show
	1955	**1960**
POLITICAL	• **1959** *Castro takes power in Cuba*	• **1961** *Peace Corps is established* • **1962** *Cuban missile crisis*

Con Thien
by John Gordon, 1967

An American soldier in a Vietnam bunker waits out heavy shelling during an attack near the demilitarized zone.

◄ VIETNAM VETERANS STATUE, WASHINGTON, D.C.

- **1967** *Green Bay Packers win first Super Bowl, 35–10, over Kansas City Chiefs*

- **1970** *First Earth Day observed as millions protest pollution*

1965	1970

- **1968** *Peace talks to end Vietnam War begin in Paris*
- **1968** *Robert Kennedy is assassinated; Nixon becomes President*

- **1970** *Kent State University students riot*
- **1971** Pentagon Papers *are published*
- **1972** *President Nixon visits China*

★★★

Cold War Challenges

Guide to Reading

Main Idea
President Kennedy tasted both success and failure when he addressed a series of foreign affairs challenges.

Reading Strategy

Classifying Information As you read about the Cold War challenges faced by President Kennedy, use a chart like the one shown her to describe the purpose of each organization.

Group	Purpose
Alliance for Progress	
Peace Corps	

Objectives
After studying this section, you should be able to
★ discuss Kennedy's responses to Soviet and international communism.
★ explain the purposes of the Alliance for Progress and the Peace Corps.

Key Terms
reactionary government, credibility gap

► CUBAN LEADER FIDEL CASTRO

*P*resident Kennedy's basic aims in foreign policy were similar to those of Truman and Eisenhower. His major concern was the threat of communism, and he declared that he would not relax efforts to contain it.

■ Crises in Cuba

In 1959 Fidel Castro had led a movement to overthrow Fulgencio Batista—the corrupt dictator then ruling Cuba—and had set up a new government. Castro soon established ties with the Soviet Union and began to adopt Marxist-influenced policies. As a result, the Eisenhower administration began to view Cuba as a threat to democracy in the Western Hemisphere. Eisenhower authorized the Central Intelligence Agency to train and arm Cuban exiles secretly for the overthrow of Castro.

The Bay of Pigs Invasion

The CIA believed that an invasion of Cuba by these exiles would touch off a popular uprising against Castro. Kennedy's military advisers approved the project. In office less than three months, Kennedy agreed that the invasion should proceed.

On April 17, 1961, a force of 1,400 Cuban exiles came ashore at the Bay of Pigs on the south coast of Cuba. From the start the invasion went poorly. There was no popular uprising by the Cuban people. Within hours Castro's forces had the invaders surrounded.

The failed invasion hurt the prestige of the new Kennedy administration and strengthened Castro's position in the world. It also allowed Soviet leader Nikita Khrushchev to pose as the defender of Latin America against United States imperialism.

The Alliance for Progress

The Castro movement, known as "Fidelismo," threatened to spread to other countries in Latin America. Promoted by Cuban agents, it often found support among the poverty-stricken and those seeking more political power. Kennedy announced a new economic program for Latin America—called the Alliance for Progress—that emphasized social reform and political freedom. Its purpose was to develop long-term economic growth among 19 Latin American nations, thus making it less likely that poverty would drive people in these countries to support communist-inspired revolutions. Over a 10-year period, the United States pledged $20 billion to help Latin American countries provide better schools, housing, and health care.

Even though United States aid to Latin America quadrupled, the results were uneven. In some countries—notably Chile, Colombia, Venezuela, and the Central American republics—the Alliance succeeded in promoting reform. In others, however, much of the money was diverted for the benefit of the military and the wealthy.

The Cuban Missile Crisis

On October 22, 1962, President Kennedy appeared on television and made a chilling announcement. U-2 spy planes from the United States had taken photographs proving that the Soviet Union had placed missiles in Cuba. The medium-range missiles were capable of reaching Atlanta and New Orleans; intermediate-range missiles were capable of reaching as far north as Pittsburgh and Detroit and as far west as Denver. Kennedy ordered a naval blockade to keep the Soviets from delivering any more missiles, and he demanded that the Soviets

• •

Footnotes to History

The Brink of War The Cuban missile crisis grew volatile because installation of Cuban missile bases would cut the warning time for an attack on the United States from 15 minutes to under 3 minutes. Kennedy's firmness and cool judgment erased the shame of the Bay of Pigs and boosted the United States's prestige.

dismantle all their missile sites in Cuba. War seemed imminent.

Secretly, the Soviet Union offered to remove the missiles if the United States promised never to invade Cuba. As negotiations continued, Khrushchev added another demand: that the United States remove its own missiles from the Soviet border of Turkey. President Kennedy rejected this demand because it would weaken the NATO alliance. The President's brother, Attorney General Robert Kennedy, suggested they ignore the new proposal and accept the Soviet Union's first offer.

After five agonizing days, when the world appeared on the brink of nuclear disaster, the Soviet ships turned back from the blockade. Soviet leaders also decided to withdraw their missiles from Cuba. President Kennedy won strong public support for his firm stand.

■ The Peace Corps

To help developing nations fight poverty and disease, Kennedy set up the Peace Corps in 1961. Like the Alliance for Progress, the Peace Corps was organized to help prevent the spread of communism.

Peace Corps Volunteers

After a period of rigorous training, Peace Corps volunteers went to countries that had asked for their assistance. There they lived among the people and helped them solve local problems. They laid out sewage systems in Bolivia, trained medical technicians in Chad, and built a model town in Pakistan. A high proportion of volunteers taught English and practical skills. In return they received only a living wage and a small vacation allowance. By late 1963 there were 11,000 Peace Corps volunteers serving in 40 countries.

Peace Corps volunteers in economically developing nations of Africa, Asia, and Latin America witnessed firsthand the problems and potential of newly independent nations. Many countries often lacked the necessary institutions to make the transition from colonial status to political and economic independence.

▲ SUMMIT MEETING When Khrushchev and Kennedy met at Vienna in June 1961, the two leaders treated one another with wary politeness. *What agreement did they reach on nuclear testing?*

Nationalism in Africa

By 1961, 27 newly independent nations had been formed from European colonies in Africa. When Europeans established boundary lines of the colonies in the 1800s and early 1900s, they failed to take into account the existing ethnic and cultural divisions. Even decades later, it was difficult to obtain loyalty to the new nation-states.

Since the beginning of colonial rule, nationalist groups in Africa had resisted European control, often violently. Following World War II, these relatively small efforts for freedom swelled into powerful mass movements.

In 1961 ethnic rivalries in the Congo, later renamed Zaire, broke out into civil war. When the mineral-rich province of Katanga attempted to secede because of tribal and regional differences, two Congolese leaders called for Soviet military aid. The United States, however, backed the efforts of the United Nations to arrange a cease-fire. In 1963, after intervention by UN troops, the Congo was reunited. Other attempts at superpower intervention were generally rebutted as most African nations developed a policy of nonalignment.

■ Challenges From the Soviet Union

Although holding to the containment policy, Kennedy sought means of relieving the tensions of the cold war. In his Inaugural Address he had said, "Let us never negotiate out of fear, but let us never fear to negotiate." In June 1961, he met with Khrushchev in the Austrian capital, Vienna. The two men treated each other with wary politeness, but they could find no area of agreement. Khrushchev may have thought that he could intimidate Kennedy, who had recently been embarrassed by the Bay of Pigs disaster. The Soviet leader handed Kennedy a near-ultimatum on East Germany and Berlin. He insisted that the Western powers recognize the German puppet state and that the four-power postwar occupation of Berlin, which was completely surrounded by East Germany, come to an end. The President refused.

The Berlin Wall

The communist answer was to build a wall through Berlin, blocking free movement between their section of Berlin and the rest of the city. This weakened the economy of West Berlin, which had drawn much of its labor from the Soviet sector. The wall also prevented the flight of refugees seeking to escape the oppression of East Germany. Those attempting to escape were shot down by East German police.

In June 1963, Kennedy visited West Berlin. A vast, cheering crowd gathered to hear him at the city hall. The President told them:

> ❝ *Freedom has many difficulties and democracy is not perfect, but we have never had to put up a wall to keep our people in. . . . All free men, wherever they may live, are citizens of Berlin, and therefore, as a free man I take pride in the words, 'Ich bin ein [I am a] Berliner.'* ❞

The Berlin Wall stood for nearly 30 years as a menacing symbol of the cold war division between East and West.

Quarrels Over Nuclear Testing

In 1961 the Soviet Union broke a three-year moratorium on testing nuclear weapons in the atmosphere. The Soviets exploded more than 40 bombs, one with 3,000 times the power of the bomb that destroyed Hiroshima. Kennedy attempted to persuade the Soviets to ban above-ground testing because nuclear fallout pollutes the atmosphere of the whole world. The Soviets would not agree to a method of inspection satisfactory to Americans. Not wanting the Soviet Union to gain nuclear superiority, the United States also resumed testing.

In August 1963, the United States, the Soviet Union, and Great Britain signed a test-ban treaty that prohibited atomic tests in the atmosphere, in outer space, and underwater. It did not, however, ban underground testing or reduce the total number of nuclear weapons. In September 1963, the Senate ratified the treaty by a vote of 80 to 19.

Dominican Intervention

Cold war tensions were again heightened when the United States intervened in the Dominican Republic. In April 1965, Lyndon Johnson, who was then in the White House, received word that rebels were trying to overthrow the rightist military government that controlled the island country. Fearing that the rebels

Visualizing History

▲ **Barrier to Freedom** The Berlin Wall dividing the East German and West German parts of the city was hastily constructed in August 1961. West Berliners decorated their side and questioned the wall's existence. ***Why was the wall built?***

were controlled by communists, Johnson ordered 20,000 marines to the Dominican Republic. This was the first time the United States had openly sent troops to the Caribbean since 1926.

Many Latin Americans criticized this military action. They charged that fear of a communist takeover, similar to that of Cuba by Fidel Castro, was leading the United States to support **reactionary governments,** or extremely conservative governments with oppressive policies. Nonetheless, most members of Congress continued to support the President. By a margin of 312 to 52, the House of Representatives voted in support of sending American troops to prevent a communist takeover anywhere in Latin America. But the Dominican incident raised suspicions of a **credibility gap,** a lack of believability growing out of the difference between official statements and practices.

■ Israel and Korea

Two other incidents caused friction with the Soviet Union during the 1960s. One had to do with Israel. The other was the *Pueblo* incident in Korea.

Arab-Israeli War

Hostilities between Israel and the Arab nations in the Middle East were common and continuing. The United States, which had traditionally supported Israel since its founding in 1948, continued that support during the Arab-Israeli War of 1967. The Soviet Union, on the other hand, backed and armed Egypt, Syria, and Jordan, the three Arab nations involved. Being on opposite sides in this conflict heightened cold war tensions between the two superpowers. However, the speed of Israel's victory prevented an out-and-out clash between the two countries.

Later in 1967, President Johnson met with Soviet Premier Aleksey Kosygin at Glassboro, New Jersey, to try to smooth relations between the United States and the Soviet Union. Although they discussed their nations' views and goals, they came to no agreement.

The *Pueblo* Incident

In January 1968, the North Koreans seized a United States ship, the *Pueblo,* and its 83 crew members. The *Pueblo* was a spy vessel, which used electronic equipment to obtain information about communist North Korea. As long as the ship stayed in international waters at least 12 miles from shore, its activities were considered legal. North Korea, however, claimed that the *Pueblo* had illegally entered its waters.

American officials were stunned. Some people wanted to retaliate, but President Johnson could not afford a conflict with North Korea while the United States was involved in the Vietnam War. As a result, the crew members remained prisoners for nearly a year.

Section 1 ★ Assessment

Checking for Understanding

1. **Define** reactionary government, credibility gap.

2. **Explain** why the Bay of Pigs invasion failed.

Critical Thinking

3. **Making Inferences** Besides being an economic policy, the Alliance for Progress was an attempt to stop communism. Explain this aspect of the program.

4. **Summarizing** Re-create the diagram shown here to list the regions where the United States and the Soviet Union fought the cold war.

Cold War Conflicts

INTERDISCIPLINARY ACTIVITY

5. **Government** Write a speech in which you defend or criticize President Kennedy's actions during the Cuban missile crisis.

Changing Nature of Warfare

Technology always affects the conduct of war. In fact, changes in the way wars are fought are often the result of changes in technology.

During the Revolutionary War, armies were outfitted with flintlock muskets—notoriously inaccurate. The soldier fired at the enemy when he saw "the whites of his eyes," a distance of less than 50 yards. With the Civil War and the introduction of a more accurate bullet, rifles were deadly up to 300 yards.

In some ways the Civil War was the first modern war. It was the first war in which railroad lines were vital, and the first in which telegraph lines, ironclad ships, and observation balloons were used as a matter of course. It foreshadowed World War I, since the armies often dug in, and sometimes fought from elaborate trenches. It also represented a step toward the concept of "total war," with less and less distinction between civilians and soldiers.

Over time, battles became increasingly impersonal, as soldiers killed and were killed by unseen enemies. Field telephones, first used in World War I, enabled soldiers to direct their fire thousands of feet behind enemy lines.

Airplanes were introduced, and pilots dropped bombs by hand from open cockpits. Bombing quickly became more sophisticated, and by World War II, bombers flying over enemy territory in Europe dropped hundreds of bombs in a single mission.

Modern-day warfare has become even more detached. Weapons systems are computer-controlled. Pilots use radar to direct heat-seeking missiles at enemies miles away.

During the Vietnam War, United States pilots flew huge B-52s on bombing raids over North Vietnam. Helicopters supplied food and ammunition to United States field forces, transported troops, and promptly evacuated the wounded.

▶ MARINE DURING GULF WAR

▲ WORLD WAR I SOLDIERS

Making the Science Connection

1. How did technological advances affect battlefield tactics? Which advance do you think has had the greatest effect on modern warfare?

2. How do today's radio and television influence the perception of war on the home front?

ACTIVITY

3. Select an implement of modern warfare and research its development. Place your findings on a time line.

War in Vietnam

Main Idea

Seeking to stop the spread of communism in Southeast Asia, the United States sent troops to fight in the Vietnamese civil war.

Reading Strategy

Sequencing Information As you read about the war in Vietnam, create a time line of key events regarding U.S. involvement in the conflict. Use the dates provided as a guide.

1963	April 1965
August 1964	1968

Objectives

After studying this section, you should be able to

★ explain how the Gulf of Tonkin incident led to the escalation of the war in Vietnam.

★ explain why the Tet offensive was the turning point of the Vietnam War.

Key Terms

war of national liberation, escalation, search-and-destroy strategy

▶ SOLDIER'S BOOTS, VIETNAM WAR

*I*n setting United States policy in Vietnam, both Kennedy and Johnson were torn between a wish to limit American involvement in a country halfway around the world and fear of a communist victory that would swallow up all of Southeast Asia. Ultimately, however, involvement increased and, before long, American troops were engaged in combat.

■ Trouble in Southeast Asia

During the Kennedy years, the Soviet Union lent its support to **wars of national liberation.** These were wars to free a nation from the control of another country, and they took place in many economically developing nations.

War in Laos

When Kennedy took office in 1961, the Southeast Asian nation of Laos was in danger of falling to communist guerrilla forces. The CIA and the Joint Chiefs of Staff pressed for a strong defense of Laos. Kennedy, on the other hand, believed a diplomatic solution could be found. In the end Kennedy avoided war by striking a compromise with Khrushchev—first by agreeing to a cease-fire and then by establishing a neutral government. Fighting between the Laos government and the guerrilla forces soon resumed, however.

Kennedy and Vietnam

Another hot spot was Vietnam, a former French colony in Southeast Asia. It had been divided into North and South Vietnam in 1954. North Vietnam was controlled by the communist government of Ho Chi Minh.

South Vietnam was controlled by a noncommunist government supported first by France and then by the United States. In the late 1950s the Vietcong—South Vietnamese communist guerrillas—began fighting to overthrow the United States-backed government of Ngo Dinh Diem and to reunite South Vietnam with the North. Both Eisenhower and Kennedy responded by sending military aid and advisers to South Vietnam. By late 1963 Kennedy had increased the number of advisers to 16,000.

Kennedy's Vietnam policy was complicated because Diem was a corrupt and unpopular dictator, a French-educated, upper-middle-class Catholic who ruled a largely Buddhist country. Middle- and lower-class Buddhists distrusted both Diem and the West. In his efforts to remain in power, Diem took increasingly harsh and undemocratic measures.

■ Johnson's Choices

During the 1964 campaign Johnson ran as the candidate of peace and restraint. At the same time, the President did not want to leave the door open for a communist victory in Vietnam.

As the military situation in Vietnam continued to deteriorate, the war dominated the foreign policy of the administration. When President Johnson entered the White House, South Vietnamese President Ngo Dinh Diem had just been assassinated. Within three months, another revolution took place in South Vietnam. This was followed by a series of governments, as one military faction after another gained power in South Vietnam.

The President faced disagreeable choices. He could admit defeat and pull out. If the "domino theory" was correct, the rest of Southeast Asia would soon fall to the communists. Another option was continuing limited support of South Vietnam's government, but the instability of that government would probably mean eventual defeat. Finally, he could actively enter the war and attack North Vietnam. This would mean the loss of lives and vast expense, and also the possibility of war with the People's Republic of China.

By the summer of 1964 Johnson began to move cautiously toward the third alternative. In secrecy the United States began limited bombing of positions held by the Vietcong and supported limited commando raids on North Vietnam's coast.

Visualizing History

▲ ESCALATION By the end of 1965, there were nearly 200,000 American troops in Vietnam. By the end of 1968, the total had increased to more than 500,000. *What was the Gulf of Tonkin Resolution?*

▲ THE AIR WAR As American involvement in Vietnam grew, helicopters were used extensively because they were effective at pinpointing enemy positions. *What were the goals of search-and-destroy missions?*

■ Escalation

Johnson reported that North Vietnamese torpedo boats fired on two American destroyers in the Gulf of Tonkin on August 2 and 4, 1964. Calling these attacks unprovoked, he asked Congress for authorization to bomb North Vietnam.

Gulf of Tonkin Resolution

On August 7 the Senate and House quickly passed the Gulf of Tonkin Resolution, authorizing the President to "take all necessary steps, including the use of armed force" to prevent further aggression. In effect, Congress, with only two dissenting votes, handed its war powers over to the President.

Johnson, however, had kept important information from Congress. The American ships had been assisting the South Vietnamese

Student Web Activity

Visit the *American History: The Modern Era Since 1865* Web site at **me.glencoe.com** and click on *Chapter 23— Student Web Activities* for an activity about America's wars.

military in spying on North Vietnam. It was unclear whether the ships had been attacked. Furthermore, Johnson did not reveal that a draft of the resolution had been prepared before the attack, in case such an event occurred.

President Johnson regarded the Gulf of Tonkin Resolution as a blanket approval of the war effort from Congress. At the suggestion of his military advisers, he ordered the bombing of bases in North Vietnam.

Until August 1964, the fighting in South Vietnam had been between South Vietnamese government troops and the Vietcong. After the Gulf of Tonkin incident, however, North Vietnam began sending its own troops to fight in the South. As the United States expanded its role, the civil war grew into a major conflict between American and communist forces.

In February 1965, after the Vietcong attacked an American base in South Vietnam, Johnson ordered an **escalation,** or military expansion, of the war. In April 1965, he made the fateful decision that American ground forces should engage in combat.

In the Vietnam War the United States faced a far more difficult situation than it had in Korea. In Korea the United States fought as an agent of the United Nations, with widespread support from noncommunist countries. Now the United States stood almost alone in its military support of South Vietnam's government, and much of world opinion was hostile to American policy in Vietnam. The South Vietnamese communists had strong support in rural areas and military aid from North Vietnam. Most noncommunist South Vietnamese were indifferent or opposed to their government, no matter what group happened to be in power.

🌐 **GEOGRAPHY**

A Different Kind of War

Military operations turned into a war without a battlefront. The Vietcong guerrillas used hit-and-run tactics. Not as well equipped as the Americans, the Vietcong and North Vietnamese used ambushes, boobytraps, and small-scale attacks. They moved swiftly by night and by day hid in the jungles or in friendly villages. Using terrorism against civilians, the Vietcong controlled much of the countryside.

Search and Destroy

To counter such tactics, American troops adopted a **search-and-destroy strategy.** American forces tried to search out enemy troops, bomb their positions, destroy their supply lines, and force them out into the open for combat. By 1966 American planes had dropped nearly the same tonnage of bombs in Vietnam as had been dropped in the Pacific in World War II.

Napalm, a jellied gasoline that explodes, splatters, and clings to whatever it touches, was dropped from airplanes. In order to improve visibility, American planes sprayed chemical defoliants—Agent Orange, for example—that stripped leaves from trees and shrubs. American troops burned villages believed to be hiding communist supporters. 🌐

■ Resistance to Peace

The United States poured increasing numbers of troops into Vietnam. During the height of the conflict, more than 500,000 American soldiers were serving in Vietnam. The number of American dead continued to rise: from 5,008 in 1966 to 9,377 in 1967 and 14,489 in 1968.

Once the United States had escalated the fighting, there seemed to be no way of leaving without damaging its international prestige. North Vietnam's leader, Ho Chi Minh, kept his forces in battle despite the massive bombing of his country, believing that North Vietnam could simply outlast the United States in the war.

Between 1965 and 1967, American officials estimated that some 2,000 attempts were made to open direct negotiations, all unsuccessful. Other nations, including Great

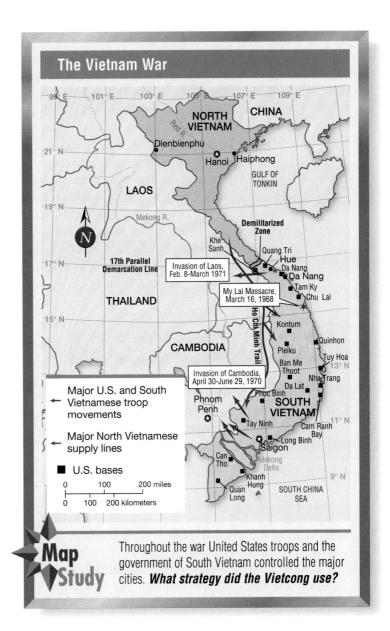

The Vietnam War

Map Study

Throughout the war United States troops and the government of South Vietnam controlled the major cities. *What strategy did the Vietcong use?*

Britain, Poland, and the Soviet Union, offered plans to negotiate between the two sides. None succeeded.

■ Tet and Retreat

At the end of 1967, General William Westmoreland, American commander in Vietnam, had assured the country that the end of the war was in sight. Vastly enlarged American forces expanded the "search-and-destroy" missions. American bombers destroyed North Vietnamese factories, roads, bridges, and cities. Secretary of State Dean Rusk said the enemy "was hurting very badly."

Vietcong Attack Turns the Tide

January 30, 1968, marked a turning point in the war. The supposedly exhausted communist guerrillas abruptly launched major offensive strikes. Early that morning a handful of Vietcong soldiers attacked the United States Embassy compound in Saigon—the very center of the American presence in South Vietnam. Together, the Vietcong and the North Vietnamese then launched massive attacks on all American bases in South Vietnam and on most of South Vietnam's major cities and provincial capitals. Taken by surprise by the assault during the celebration of Tet, the Vietnamese lunar New Year, Americans and South Vietnamese sustained heavy losses. After fierce fighting, they finally drove back the communist offensive.

Militarily, the communists were defeated. Politically, however, they scored a victory. The American people were shocked that the enemy that was supposedly on the verge of defeat could launch such a large-scale attack. Television coverage of the attack and the destruction that followed shook the nation's confidence. When General Westmoreland requested an additional 209,000 troops for Vietnam—in addition to the 500,000 already there—it seemed like another admission that the United States could not win the war.

Peace Talks Begin

Finally, on March 31, 1968, Johnson announced that he would halt nearly all bombing of North Vietnam. He offered to send special negotiators to hold peace talks with the North Vietnamese and the Vietcong. A few days later, on April 3, North Vietnam accepted Johnson's offer to begin peace negotiations. Diplomats from the United States and North Vietnam met in Paris in May 1968, but they could not agree on terms. Prospects for peace in Vietnam grew dim. After a lull, the war continued, and the number of American troops in Vietnam reached a new high. It would be five long years of continued bitter struggle, however, before the United States left the war in Vietnam behind.

Section 2 ★ Assessment

Checking for Understanding

1. **Define** war of national liberation, escalation, search-and-destroy strategy.

2. **Explain** why the Tet offensive was the turning point of the Vietnam War.

Critical Thinking

3. **Expressing Problems Clearly** Some political analysts called Vietnam a "quagmire." Write two statements that explain the difficult choices the United States faced in Vietnam.

4. **Analyzing Issues** Re-create the diagram shown here to describe the Gulf of Tonkin Resolution and how it led to war escalation in Vietnam.

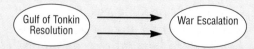

INTERDISCIPLINARY ACTIVITY

5. **Journalism** Interview friends and relatives who lived during the Vietnam War era. Present a written summary of your findings.

BUILDING SKILLS

Social Studies Skills

Interpreting Military Maps

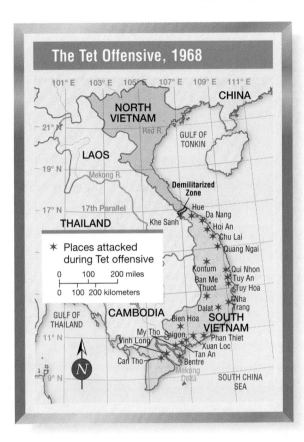

The Tet Offensive, 1968

CHINA

NORTH VIETNAM

Red R.

GULF OF TONKIN

LAOS

Mekong R.

Demilitarized Zone

17th Parallel

THAILAND

Hue
Khe Sanh
Da Nang
Hoi An
Chu Lai
Quang Ngai

Kontum   Qui Nhon
Ban Me   Tuy An
Thuot   Tuy Hoa
          Nha
Dalat   Trang
Bien Hoa SOUTH VIETNAM

GULF OF THAILAND
CAMBODIA

My Tho Saigon Phan Thiet
Vinh Long   Xuan Loc
        Tan An
Can Tho   Bentre
          Mekong Delta

SOUTH CHINA SEA

* Places attacked during Tet offensive

0   100   200 miles

0   100 200 kilometers

In your study of American history, you often use maps. Maps are especially helpful for studying the progression of war. A military map shows the area where battles occur, where victories have been won, and who controls various sites.

Military maps vary in the level of detail provided. Some military maps show only the major battles fought over the course of a war. Others may show detailed troop movements and defensive positions during a particular battle or over a specific period of time.

Learning the Skill

On January 30, 1968, Vietcong and North Vietnamese forces launched a major attack throughout South Vietnam. This was unexpected, as a truce had been declared for Tet, or the lunar New Year. Study the map of the Tet offensive. Nearly 8,400 communist troops infiltrated South Vietnam's major cities and government installations during the offensive. Although the invading troops failed to capture any major cities, more than 30 cities were attacked, with the heaviest fighting in Saigon and Hue. After you read the guidelines that follow, answer the questions.

a. **Read** the map title. This will indicate the location and time period covered on the map.

b. **Read** the items listed in the map key. This tells what the symbols on the map represent. For example, areas under the control of a particular nation or region may be represented by a color. Battle sites may be symbolized by crossed swords, a shell burst, or a star. Military movements may be illustrated with solid or broken lines and arrows.

c. **Study** the map itself. This will reveal the actual events or sequence of events that took place. Notice the geography of the area and try to determine how it would affect military strategy.

Practicing the Skill

1. What time period is represented on the map?

2. From the map, can you tell the outcome of the attacks?

3. Where are the attack sites with respect to North Vietnam?

Glencoe's **Skillbuilder Interactive Workbook, Level 2** provides instruction and practice in key social studies skills.

APPLYING THE SKILL

4. Locate a map of the Vietnam War. List the information presented in the map. Answer the question: How do such maps help summarize the events in a war?

★★★

Protest and Reaction

Main Idea

As U.S. casualties mounted in Vietnam, a growing number of Americans voiced their opposition to the war.

Reading Strategy

Organizing Information As you read about protest at home against the Vietnam War, use a diagram like the one shown here to list the reasons why some Americans opposed the war.

Reasons for Opposition

Objectives

After studying this section, you should be able to

★ list reasons for opposition to the war.

★ describe the values and beliefs of the youth counterculture.

Key Terms

student deferment, conscientious objector, teach-in, commune, counterculture

▶ **ANTIWAR BUTTON**

fter Tet, criticism of American involvement in Vietnam increased. One of the nation's most trusted news broadcasters, Walter Cronkite, reported:

> We have too often been disappointed by the optimism of the American leaders to have faith any longer in the silver linings. . . . To say that we are closer to victory today is to believe, in the face of evidence, the optimists who have been wrong in the past. To suggest we are on the edge of defeat is to yield to unreasonable pessimism. To say that we are mired in stalemate seems the only realistic, yet unsatisfactory conclusion. "

Hearing Cronkite's broadcast, President Johnson turned to his aides and said, "It's all over." He recognized that he had lost the battle for public opinion.

■ Growing Opposition to War

Gradually, as America moved deeper into the Vietnam War, opposition grew. The United States's reasons for fighting in Southeast Asia began to be questioned.

Senate Hearings on the War

Beginning in January 1966, the Senate Foreign Relations Committee held "educational" hearings on Vietnam. The televised hearings carried the senators' doubts about the war to millions of American homes.

Hawks and Doves

Before long, Americans became divided into two groups. Those who supported the war were called "hawks" and those who opposed, "doves." For a long time, polls showed that most Americans sided with the "hawks." But doubts began to grow. By May 1967, even Secretary of Defense Robert McNamara had begun to question America's role in the war.

■ Student Protests

Many of those opposed to the war were students who openly protested America's involvement in Vietnam. The antiwar movement was centered on college campuses, which had also been the source for activists in the civil rights movement.

Protests Against the Draft

A number of the antiwar protests focused on the draft. Many of those facing the draft did not understand why the war was being fought or why they should go. Students also protested against the government's unfair practices. A person with a limited education from a low-income family was far more likely to be sent to fight in Vietnam than someone with a good education from an upper-income family, and African American soldiers made up a disproportionately large number of American soldiers fighting overseas.

One policy that contributed to this inequity was the practice of giving **student deferments.** Young men were safe from the draft as long as they were enrolled in college. In 1966 alone, there were 1.8 million deferments. Some men who did not serve were **conscientious objectors.** They received this status by belonging to an organized religious body with pacifist views. About 500,000 young men simply refused to report when they were drafted. Some fled to other countries, such as Canada or Sweden. Around 3,000 young men went to prison rather than fight in a war they opposed. Some antiwar protesters used the tactics of civil disobedience and demonstrations that they had learned from the civil rights movement.

▲ **DEMONSTRATIONS AND CONFRONTATION** Reacting against the antiwar demonstrations, many Americans began to counter with demonstrations in support of American troops. Many antiwar demonstrations were accompanied by violence. In May 1970, six students were killed during separate confrontations at Jackson State and Kent State (above right). ***Why did many students protest the war?***

Surviving the War

The military kept accurate records of Americans who died fighting in Vietnam. No one, however, was keeping track of what happened to those who survived.

Then_____

Coming Home

Many Vietnam veterans adjusted smoothly to civilian life. Others, however, were left with deep

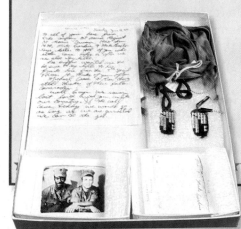

◀ **COLLECTION OF VETERAN'S ITEMS**

psychological problems. These veterans were often described as suffering from "shell shock" or "combat fatigue." Yet a significant number continued to suffer trauma years later.

Now_____

PTSD

Research indicated that these veterans were experiencing post-traumatic stress disorder (PTSD), a condition in which a person who has experienced a traumatic event feels severe and long-lasting aftereffects. The event that triggers the disorder overwhelms a person's normal sense of reality and ability to cope. Typical symptoms include involuntary "flashbacks" or recurring nightmares during which the victim reexperiences the ordeal.

The National Vietnam Veterans Readjustment Study indicated that one-third of male Vietnam veterans and more than one-fourth of females serving in the Vietnam theater had full post-traumatic stress disorder at some time during their lives.

PTSD is also common among survivors of natural disasters, such as floods or tornadoes, and victims of human aggression, such as assault. PTSD can be extremely long-lasting. Studies show that survivors of Nazi concentration camps and soldiers returning from war may display symptoms decades after the traumatic event.

The Veterans Administration provides counseling to veterans who have postwar readjustment problems in the areas of family relationships, education, and in their personal lives.

Some university students and teachers held **teach-ins** to study the history of the war and to protest against its expansion.

Violence on Campus

While most protests were peaceful, some turned violent. One occurred in April 1968 at Columbia University in New York City. It began when students seized college buildings and ended in a riot marked by both police brutality and student retaliation.

Two of the most tragic episodes of the anti-war movement took place in May 1970. After President Nixon announced the invasion of Cambodia, protests erupted on scores of campuses. At Kent State University in Ohio, rioting reached such an intensity that the National Guard was sent in. On May 4, a contingent of guardsmen, harassed by students,

fired into the crowd, killing 4 students and wounding 9. On May 14, at Jackson State University in Mississippi, student protest was suppressed by the state police, who fired randomly into a dormitory. Two students were killed, 12 were wounded. These events precipitated a nationwide student strike. Hundreds of colleges and universities suspended classes or closed down completely.

The campus violence that erupted was not limited to the United States. During this time and before, there were student riots in Rio de Janeiro, London, Paris, Rome, Madrid, Warsaw, and Prague. In Prague, student protests triggered a rebellion that led to the overthrow of the communist regime that had ruled Czechoslovakia since 1948. However, after a few months 200,000 Soviet troops crushed the revolt and reestablished control.

New Beliefs and Values

Some young people rebelled against established values and searched for a new set of beliefs. They studied different religions and philosophies. In an attempt to achieve expanded awareness, some experimented with drugs that cause hallucinations. They proclaimed their freedom of expression and individuality by wearing long hair and unconventional clothing. Some even left family and comfortable homes to live in **communes**—communities in which living quarters, food, and work were shared.

In their rejection of their parents' values, the "hippies," or "flower children" as they were frequently called, were said to have established a **counterculture**—with values and practices that conflicted with those of established society. The counterculture was symbolized in an outdoor rock concert, the Woodstock festival held in New York in August 1969. More than 400,000 people attended what *TIME* called "history's biggest happening."

A Conservative Backlash

The actions and protests of the Woodstock generation caused a reaction among a growing number of conservative Americans who had become angry over the demonstrations, the riots, and a war that seemed to be going nowhere. The sight of long-haired draft protesters outraged many who did not hesitate to support their government in time of war. Many working-class Americans were offended by the actions of students they considered privileged. The deep anger these Americans felt soon developed into a backlash against the antiwar movement.

■ 1968: The Turning Point

By 1968, a kind of turning point had been reached in American society. With the Tet offensive and the protests, polls showed that the majority of Americans had turned against the President's handling of the war.

Johnson had become so unpopular that he seldom appeared in public for fear of hostile crowds. Even the President's own party was divided over the war.

The Race for President

By this time, Eugene McCarthy, a Democratic senator from Minnesota—and a dove—had announced that he was going to challenge Johnson for the Democratic party's presidential nomination. Although Johnson won the first primary election in New Hampshire, his margin of victory was narrow. McCarthy received more than 40 percent of the votes. Then, four days after this primary, Democratic Senator Robert Kennedy, who also opposed the war, announced that he too would run for the nomination.

Johnson had always intended to run for reelection in 1968. When he realized just how little support he had, however, he made a decision that was surprising to many. The President decided to drop out of the race. On March 31, 1968, he stunned the nation by announcing, "I shall not seek, and I will not accept, the nomination of my party for another term as your President." With Johnson withdrawn, Vice President

Visualizing History

▲ **ASSASSINATION** During the 1968 Democratic primaries, Robert F. Kennedy won a number of victories. On June 5, 1968, the night of his victory in the California primary, Kennedy was assassinated. ***What two Democratic candidates remained in the race?***

Hubert Humphrey became the administration candidate and the preferred choice for many longtime Democrats.

Soon it appeared that Kennedy was pulling in front of McCarthy and Humphrey. Kennedy's program and popularity seemed broad enough to rebuild the Democratic coalition shattered by Vietnam. Then on June 5, 1968, just after winning the Democratic primary in California, Kennedy was assassinated by an Arab nationalist, angry at Kennedy for his support of Israel.

In August the Democrats held their national convention in Chicago. Now that Kennedy was dead, Humphrey was expected to win the nomination. However, furious at the Vice President's support of the war, about 10,000 protesters gathered in Chicago. Chicago Mayor Richard Daley, himself a Democrat, advised his police to get tough with the protesters. While violence reigned outside, the convention nominated Hubert Humphrey for President and Senator Edmund Muskie of Maine for Vice President.

The Candidates

The splintering of the Democratic party made the Republican candidate, Richard M. Nixon, the front-runner in the election of 1968. Although defeated in his campaign for President in 1960 and for governor of California in 1962, Nixon had remained active in national politics. For his vice-presidential running mate, Nixon chose Spiro T. Agnew, governor of Maryland.

In his campaign, Nixon promised to unify the nation, return dignity to the presidency, stabilize American foreign policy, and lead a war against crime in the streets. He said he had a plan for ending the war in Vietnam, but he did not provide details.

A third candidate, George Wallace, governor of Alabama, ran as an Independent in all 50 states. Wallace was against federally enforced civil rights, including desegregation and busing; black power; "pointy-headed intellectuals"; and social unrest. As a result of his civil rights stand, he attracted support in the South. Wallace also appealed to blue-collar workers in the North as well as the South. Leaders of organized labor, however, campaigned hard for Humphrey and moved much of the blue-collar vote back to the Democrats.

The Election of 1968

On Election Day, Nixon won, though the vote was very close. He received 31.8 million votes, while Humphrey had 31.3 million and Wallace, 9.9 million. In the electoral college, Nixon won 301 votes to 191 for Humphrey and 46 for Wallace. However, although the people had elected a Republican President, the Democrats kept their majorities in both houses of Congress.

Speaking to reporters after his election, Nixon recalled seeing a young girl carrying a sign at one of his rallies that said: "Bring Us Together." This, he promised, would be his chief effort as President.

Section 3 ★ Assessment

Checking for Understanding

1. **Define** student deferment, conscientious objector, teach-in, commune, counterculture.

2. **Explain** how the conservative backlash developed.

Critical Thinking

3. **Synthesizing Ideas** How did the war in Vietnam and increasing violence at home affect Americans' confidence in President Johnson?

4. **Summarizing** Re-create the diagram shown here to list the practices of the youth counterculture during the 1960s.

INTERDISCIPLINARY ACTIVITY

5. **The Arts** Create a cartoon illustrating the growing division between the "hawks" and "doves." Give your cartoon a title.

★★

Secrecy and Summitry

Guide to Reading

Main Idea
After years of bloody fighting that resulted in a stalemate, American forces finally withdrew from Vietnam.

Reading Strategy

Organizing Information As you read how President Nixon handled foreign affairs, use a diagram such as the one shown here to list the steps Nixon took to end U.S. involvement in Vietnam.

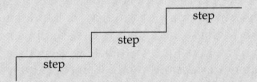

Objectives

After studying this section, you should be able to

★ explain why Nixon pursued détente in foreign policy.

★ list and describe the steps that President Nixon took to end American involvement in Vietnam.

Key Terms

détente,
summit,
shuttle
diplomacy

▶ VIEW AT THE VIETNAM MEMORIAL

---

*S*urprising both his supporters and his critics, Richard Nixon as President shed his long-held image as a "cold warrior." He opened a dialogue with the communist leaders of China and entered into a series of agreements with the Soviet Union. Nixon recognized the legitimacy of the communist regimes of Eastern Europe.

■ A New Policy

Like Woodrow Wilson, President Nixon took almost sole charge of foreign policy. To help him handle foreign policy matters, Nixon appointed Henry A. Kissinger, a brilliant political scientist, as his national security adviser. Kissinger's job was to present the President with policy options in which the probable consequences of each policy were outlined. Kissinger also undertook secret missions abroad. In 1973 Nixon appointed Kissinger secretary of state.

Nixon, like Wilson, wanted to be remembered as a peacemaker. In his Inaugural Address he proclaimed:

❝ *After a period of confrontation, we are entering an era of negotiation. Let all nations know that during this administration our lines of communication will be open. We seek an open world—open to ideas, open to the exchange of goods and people....* ❞

▲ OPENING THE LINES OF COMMUNICATION President Richard Nixon worked to improve relations with the communist superpowers. The thaw in relations was reflected in the President's visits to the Soviet Union (left) and China (right). *What is détente?*

Nixon Proclaims Détente

Nixon proclaimed a policy of **détente,** or relaxation of tensions between the United States and the communist bloc. He maintained that it would be a "safer world and a better world if we have a strong, healthy United States, Europe, China, Russia, and Japan, each balancing the other."

To achieve this balance Nixon proposed a meeting between the United States and the Soviet Union to discuss strategic arms limitations. The SALT negotiations, as they were called, began in Helsinki, Finland, in 1969. Before the conclusion of SALT I in 1972, the two sides had agreed to ban biological warfare and limit the growth of nuclear weapons.

SALT culminated in the May 1972 Moscow **summit,** or diplomatic meeting, between the superpowers. In addition to signing the SALT agreement, Nixon and the Soviet leader, Leonid Brezhnev, also agreed to increase trade, exchange scientific information, and cooperate in preventing pollution.

Nixon and China

President Nixon also sought improved relations with China. He began by lifting trade and travel restrictions. The President also withdrew the Seventh Fleet from defending Taiwan, an island which China claimed as its own.

The Chinese responded to Nixon's initiatives in a variety of ways. More important, the Chinese accepted Henry Kissinger's proposal that he visit Beijing secretly to open discussions with Chinese leaders. During Kissinger's meeting with Chinese Premier Zhou En-lai (JOH EHN•lye), he arranged for President Nixon to visit China in February 1972. President Nixon's sensational announcement that he would visit Beijing foreshadowed the 1971 admission of the government of the People's Republic of China to the United Nations.

■ War in Vietnam

During the 1968 presidential campaign, Nixon declared that he had a plan for ending the Vietnam War. After his inauguration he resumed negotiations with the North Vietnamese, but they produced little.

The President faced a dilemma: if he continued United States involvement in the war, public opposition would increase. If he withdrew United States troops without a peace agreement, he would be the first President of the United States ever to lose a war.

The Pentagon Papers

To make matters worse, in June 1971, the *New York Times* published a secret Department of Defense study. *The Pentagon Papers,* as they were called, documented that for two decades, four Presidents had escalated the nation's involvement in Indochina.

The Pentagon Papers were evidence of the growing power of the executive branch. They contained details of decisions made by Presidents and their advisers without the consent of Congress. *The Pentagon Papers* also showed how the administrations acted to deceive Congress and the public about Vietnam.

President Nixon was outraged over the "leaking" of the secret documents. He ordered the Justice Department to go to court to stop further publication of the papers. Nixon hoped the Supreme Court would affirm the government's right to restrain publication in matters of national security, but the Court decided that *The Pentagon Papers* were not vital to national security.

The federal government then brought charges against Daniel Ellsberg, one of the authors of *The Pentagon Papers,* for leaking the documents to the press. President Nixon also authorized a group of people who were called "the Plumbers" to break into the office of Ellsberg's psychiatrist to collect information about him. When their activities came to light, the charges against Daniel Ellsberg were dropped.

The United States in Vietnam, 1950–1975

1950	**May 8** President Truman sends U.S. aid and advisers to French forces in Indochina
1954	**May 7** French defeated by Communists at Dien Bien Phu
	July 20–21 Geneva Conference provides cease-fire and divides Vietnam
1957	Vietcong begin attacks in South Vietnam
1960	**Dec. 20** Vietcong form National Front for the Liberation of South Vietnam
1961	**Nov. 16** President Kennedy increases number of U.S. advisers in Vietnam
1963	**Nov. 1** Ngo Dinh Diem assassinated
1964	**July 24** U.S. rejects French President de Gaulle's plan to neutralize all of Indochina
	Aug. 2–4 Gulf of Tonkin—N. Vietnam attacks a U.S. destroyer and U.S. retaliates
	Aug. 7 Gulf of Tonkin Resolution—Congress grants President Johnson authority to use force against aggression
1965	**Feb. 7–8** First U.S. bombing of North Vietnam
	March 2 Rolling Thunder bombing campaign begins against North Vietnam
	March 8–9 President Johnson sends 3,500 Marines (first combat troops) to join 23,500 U.S. advisers
1966	**March 2** U.S. forces number 215,000
	Dec. 31 U.S. forces number 389,000
1967	**May 19** First U.S. air strike against central Hanoi
1968	**Jan. 30–Feb. 24** Tet offensive by Vietcong
	March 31 President Johnson announces cessation of bombing of N. Vietnam north of 20th parallel and that he will not seek reelection
	May 10 Paris Peace Talks begin between U.S. and N. Vietnam
1969	**January 25** First full session of Paris Peace Talks with Vietcong and S. Vietnam also represented
	March 16 My Lai massacre (revealed in November 1969)
	June 8 President Nixon announces the withdrawal of 25,000 U.S. troops from Vietnam
	Sept. 3 Death of Ho Chi Minh
	Oct. 15 Vietnam Moratorium Day—nationwide antiwar demonstrations across the U.S.
1970	**Feb. 20** Presidential adviser Henry A. Kissinger opens secret peace negotiations in Paris
	April 29 U.S. troops invade Cambodia
	May 4 Four antiwar students killed during demonstrations at Kent State University, Ohio
	July 24 Senate votes to repeal Gulf of Tonkin Resolution
1971	**Nov. 12** President Nixon limits U.S. ground forces in Vietnam to a defensive role
1972	**April 15–20** Widespread antiwar demonstrations in U.S.
	June 17–22 Watergate break-in and arrests
	Aug. 12 Last U.S. ground combat troops leave Vietnam
	Dec. 18–30 Bombing of Hanoi and Haiphong resumed to break stalled peace negotiations
1973	**Jan. 27** Cease-fire in Vietnam agreed upon
	Feb. 12 N. Vietnam releases first U.S. prisoners of war
1974	**Aug. 9** President Nixon resigns
1975	**April 29–30** North Vietnamese capture Saigon; American personnel evacuated; Vietnam War ends

Source: *The New York Times,* April 30, 1985; *An Encyclopedia of World History,* 5th ed. (1972); Gorton Carruth, *What Happened When* (1989); James S. Olson, *Dictionary of the Vietnam War* (1988)

Chart Study

American involvement in Vietnam grew rapidly after the first combat troops arrived in 1965. In 1975 troops from North Vietnam moved into South Vietnam, and it came under communist control. **When did the Tet offensive take place?**

Maya Lin
1959–

Maya Lin was a 21-year-old architecture student at Yale University when her design for the Vietnam Veterans Memorial was selected in a national competition. Lin's simple but powerful and unique design joined two gleaming black granite walls inscribed with the names of the war's 58,000 dead and missing. While Maya's work was initially controversial, today the memorial is a symbol of national healing.

Maya was born and raised in Athens, Ohio. Her parents, both of whom had emigrated from China in the 1940s, were college professors. Maya was a good high school student, with a particular aptitude for mathematics.

In 1988, Maya Lin designed the Civil Rights Memorial in Montgomery, Alabama. Recently she completed a memorial at Yale University and designed the interior of the Museum of African Art in New York City.

President Nixon's response to the publication was a further sign that the credibility of his administration was eroding. Nixon himself, it was revealed, had ordered the secret bombing of North Vietnamese sanctuaries in Cambodia in 1969. In April 1970, Nixon, without consulting Congress, ordered an invasion of Cambodia to drive the North Vietnamese out of the country. Protests against the war now intensified.

Nixon Announces Vietnamization

To quiet opposition to the war, Nixon announced a policy of "Vietnamization." Vietnamization consisted of two steps: the phased withdrawal of United States troops, and their replacement by conscripts from Vietnam. Nixon hoped that Vietnamization, combined with saturation bombing of North Vietnam, would allow the United States to withdraw from the war "with honor."

By the end of the war, the total tonnage of bombs dropped by the United States on Vietnam was more than twice that dropped by the United States on all targets in both World War II and the Korean War.

Finally, on January 23, 1973, the United States, South Vietnam, North Vietnam, and the Vietcong signed a cease-fire agreement, ending the military presence of the United States in Vietnam. The war, however, did not end for the people of Vietnam. Although United States troops withdrew from South Vietnam, North Vietnamese troops did not.

The End of the War

In 1974 the weakened forces of South Vietnam abandoned distant outposts they could no longer defend, and North Vietnamese forces captured several provincial capitals. In January 1975, North Vietnam launched a major offensive. By late March they drove South Vietnamese troops from a region known as the Central Highlands, approximately 160 miles north of Saigon. While thousands of civilians retreated with the soldiers, many died in the gunfire or from starvation. The South Vietnamese army soon collapsed, and by early April, the North Vietnamese army had reached the outskirts of Saigon.

Hoping to stall the communist drive, President Gerald Ford, Nixon's successor, requested more than $700 million in military aid for South Vietnam. Congress, however, approved only $300 million, to be used chiefly to evacuate Americans from Saigon. On April 29, as North Vietnamese troops overtook Saigon, the United States carried out an emergency evacuation of all remaining Americans and many South Vietnamese refugees.

The war ended when the Saigon government surrendered on April 30, 1975. North and South Vietnam were formally united as the Socialist Republic of Vietnam on July 2, 1976.

■ War in the Middle East

On October 6, 1973, the Jewish holiday of Yom Kippur, Egyptian and Syrian troops launched surprise attacks against Israeli forces. Their objective was to recapture the territory Egypt and Syria had lost to Israel during the Six-Day War of 1967. Caught by surprise, the Israeli troops were pushed back, but they quickly regrouped and launched their own attack, pushing into Syria and across the Suez Canal into Egypt.

Israel appealed to the United States for help, and President Nixon responded with a massive airlift of $2 billion in military supplies. At the same time, the Soviet Union continued to supply Egypt and Syria.

Even as the United States and the Soviet Union gave aid to the opposing sides, they worked through the United Nations Security Council to arrange a cease-fire. In late October, the nations of Israel, Egypt, and Syria agreed to terms. By the end of 1973, a UN peacekeeping force had been sent to the Middle East to police the region.

After the conflict, Secretary of State Henry Kissinger worked with Israel and Egypt to reduce tensions in the Middle East. For the next two years, he engaged in **shuttle diplo-**

Visualizing (H)istory

▲ THE FALL OF SAIGON On April 28, 1975, President Ford ordered the emergency helicopter evacuation of all Americans remaining in Vietnam. *When did the United States end its military involvement in Vietnam?*

macy, flying back and forth between the capitals of the two nations in an effort to produce a lasting peace. Kissinger's efforts yielded two important results. Early in 1974 Golda Meir, the prime minister of Israel, and Anwar el-Sadat, the president of Egypt, agreed to establish diplomatic relations again between their countries. Then in September 1975, Israel and Egypt agreed to withdraw their forces from the cease-fire line. Although significant problems remained, a measure of peace had been achieved in the Middle East.

Section 4 ★ Assessment

Checking for Understanding

1. **Define** détente, summit, shuttle diplomacy.
2. **Describe** how Henry Kissinger's shuttle diplomacy helped to end war in the Middle East.

Critical Thinking

3. **Evaluating Foreign Policy** Evaluate the pros and cons of Nixon's use of secrecy in China and Vietnam.
4. **Analyzing Issues** Re-create the diagram shown here to list two examples of President

Nixon's policy of détente that was designed to lessen world tensions.

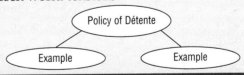

Policy of Détente

Example   Example

INTERDISCIPLINARY ACTIVITY

5. **Government** Study the chart on page 715 and answer the following in a paragraph: Why is the Vietnam War called the nation's most tragic war?

Using Vocabulary

Use the following vocabulary words to write an article describing the history of the United States's cold war struggle against communism.

credibility gap   escalation
search-and-destroy strategy   détente

Reviewing Facts

1. **Summarize** Kennedy's relations with Khrushchev.

2. **Explain** the many foreign policy challenges that Kennedy faced in Southeast Asia.

Understanding Concepts

Foreign Policy

1. Explain how Americans' perceptions of communism influenced United States policy to support South Vietnam.

War

2. Re-create the diagram shown here to list the reasons why the United States was unable to win the war in Vietnam.

Reasons for Difficulty
in Vietnam

Critical Thinking

1. **Analyzing Art**   Study the photograph on this page of the Vietnam Veterans Memorial. This

Memorial is one of the most visited of our nation's monuments. Why do you think this is so?

History and Geography

The Vietnam War

Study the map on page 705 and answer the questions that follow.

1. **Region**   What nations besides North and South Vietnam were the sites of battles or invasions?

2. **Location**   What is the relative location of China to North Vietnam?

Interdisciplinary Activity: Political Science

Work with two other group members to explore the options facing President Kennedy during the Cuban missile crisis. List two potential consequences of each option.

Practicing Skills

Interpreting Military Maps

Two kinds of terrain maps are shown on page 719—a terrain model and a topographic map. The two maps show roughly the same area of Vietnam. The terrain model is a representation of the shape of the land, with hills and valleys shown.

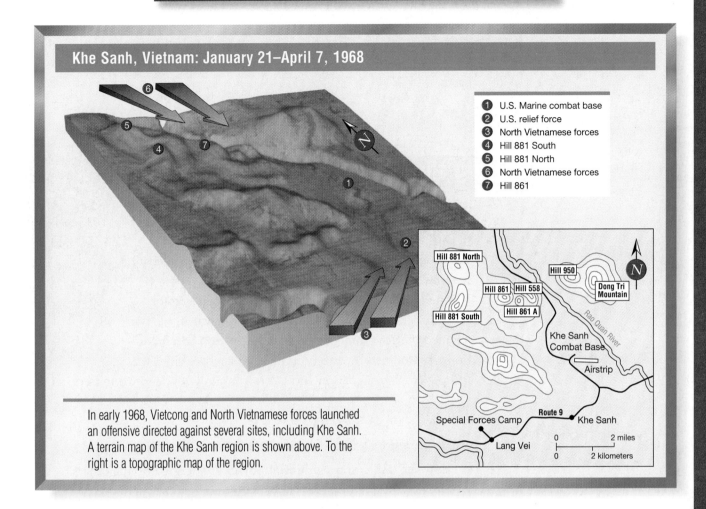

Khe Sanh, Vietnam: January 21–April 7, 1968

1 U.S. Marine combat base
2 U.S. relief force
3 North Vietnamese forces
4 Hill 881 South
5 Hill 881 North
6 North Vietnamese forces
7 Hill 861

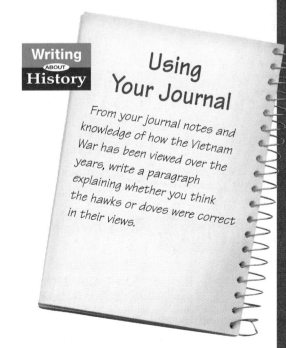

Hill 881 North
Hill 861   Hill 558
Hill 881 South
Hill 861 A
Hill 950
Dong Tri Mountain
Rao Quan River
Khe Sanh Combat Base
Airstrip
Special Forces Camp
Route 9
Khe Sanh
Lang Vei

0   2 miles
0   2 kilometers

N

In early 1968, Vietcong and North Vietnamese forces launched an offensive directed against several sites, including Khe Sanh. A terrain map of the Khe Sanh region is shown above. To the right is a topographic map of the region.

The topographic map is a two-dimensional map showing elevations using contour lines. A contour line represents points that are all at the same elevation. Each contour line represents a successively higher or lower elevation.

1. Why do you suppose there are no distance or elevation scales on the three-dimensional model?

Technology Activity

Building a Database

Prepare a database of the major battles of the Vietnam War involving United States troops. Use the Internet and other library sources to find information about each battle. Share your database with the rest of the class.

Writing ABOUT History

Using Your Journal

From your journal notes and knowledge of how the Vietnam War has been viewed over the years, write a paragraph explaining whether you think the hawks or doves were correct in their views.

CHAPTER 24

★★★

Camelot to Watergate
1960–1976

▶ **HYDRANT DECORATED FOR NATION'S BICENTENNIAL**

Setting the Scene

Focus

During the brief administration of John F. Kennedy, his leadership and the American people were repeatedly tested by staggering challenges at home and abroad. During Johnson's administration federal spending for social programs, along with the cost of the war in Vietnam, strained the government's budget. The Nixon administration was troubled by questions about illegal activities that led to Nixon's resignation and left the nation with deep wounds.

Concepts to Understand

★ How presidential leadership shaped **domestic policy**

★ How the limits of **presidential power** are defined by the other branches of government

Read to Discover . . .

★ how Kennedy's and Johnson's approaches to economic problems

Journal Notes

In what ways has corruption affected politics in America? Note details in your journal as you read the chapter.

HISTORY Online

Chapter Overview
Visit the *American History: The Modern Era Since 1865* Web site at **me.glencoe.com** and click on *Chapter 24—Chapter Overviews* to preview the chapter.

CULTURAL

• **1964** *The Beatles come to America*

• **1968** *Cost of mailing a letter increases to 6 cents*
• **1969** *Neil Armstrong walks on the moon*

1960

1965

• **1963** *Kennedy assassinated; Lyndon Johnson becomes President*

POLITICAL

• **1968** *Nixon appoints Warren Burger head of Supreme Court*
• **1969** *Nixon announces new federalism*

History
AND
ART

The Peace Corps in Ethiopia, 1966
by Norman Rockwell

Rockwell's painting depicts a young American volunteer giving instructions on the use of a plow. Peace Corps volunteers worked in many developing countries around the world.

◄ PRESIDENT JOHN F. KENNEDY

● **1971** *Amtrak passenger service begins*

● **1976** *Bicentennial celebration of the United States*

1970	1975

● **1973** *Vice President Agnew resigns*
● **1974** *Watergate scandal unfolds; Nixon resigns*

● **1975** *Several of Nixon's aides are convicted*

★★

Kennedy's New Frontier

Guide to Reading

Main Idea
President Kennedy captured the nation's imagination with his energy and charisma, but an assassin's bullet cut his presidency short.

Reading Strategy
Organizing Information As you read about the Kennedy presidency, use a diagram like the one shown here to list three economic programs initiated by Kennedy.

Economic Programs

Objectives
After studying this section, you should be able to
★ describe important legislation Kennedy proposed during his term of office.
★ describe the impact of Kennedy's death on the nation.

Key Terms
mandate,
pragmatist,
urban
renewal

▶ DECORATIVE FLAG, COMPUTER ART

Washington, D.C., glittered during the Kennedy years. As never before, millions became familiar with the occupants of the White House. The public's enchantment with Kennedy was not shared by Congress, however. Many of Kennedy's most important legislative efforts would have to wait until after his death to become law.

The Election of 1960

In the 1960 presidential campaign, the Republicans chose Vice President Richard M. Nixon and the Democrats chose Senator John F. Kennedy of Massachusetts. As his vice-presidential running mate Nixon chose UN Ambassador Henry Cabot Lodge. To win Southern support, Kennedy chose Texas Senator Lyndon B. Johnson.

The backgrounds of the two presidential candidates presented striking contrasts. Kennedy was a Catholic and the second-oldest son of a wealthy family. Nixon, born in California, was from far more humble origins, and his Quaker mother had struggled to keep the family together.

There were also similarities between the two men. Both were young: Nixon was 47 years old, and Kennedy was 43. Nixon and Kennedy were experienced legislators, both having served in the House of Representatives or in the Senate. Nixon had also served eight years as Eisenhower's Vice President.

The Impact of Television

The political differences between the candidates were small. Both were considered "cold warriors" who believed that communism was the chief threat to the way of life in the United States. Senator Kennedy hoped to take advantage of Republican weaknesses and challenged Nixon to a series of televised debates. Nixon was the more skilled debater, and most who heard the debates on radio declared Nixon the winner. Yet, the millions more who watched on television thought a well-prepared, poised, and youthful Senator Kennedy won the debates. The debates were one of the earliest examples of the strong impact television would have on politics in the United States.

The Issue of Religion

Political observers wondered whether Kennedy's religion would be an obstacle to his election. No Catholic had ever been elected President, and some believed that a Catholic could not make official decisions independent from the Roman Catholic Church. Kennedy answered by stressing his belief in the separation of church and state. He declared he would resign, rather than violate either his conscience or the interests of the nation.

Kennedy won the election, finally laying to rest the idea that a Roman Catholic could not be elected President. Analyzing his victory, Kennedy concluded, "It was TV more than anything else that turned the tide." However, he carried the election by one of the narrowest margins in American history. He won the popular vote by 120,000 out of 68 million votes cast and the electoral college by 303 to 219. In several states a difference of only a few thousand votes would have swung the electoral votes the other way. As a result, Kennedy did not enter office with a clear **mandate,** or endorsement of his ideas, from the American people. Nevertheless, though he was cautious at first, the new President moved ahead with his domestic program.

▶ **KENNEDY-NIXON** DEBATE

Visualizing History

▲ **THE 1960 ELECTION** At the start of the 1960 election campaign, polls showed Richard Nixon in the lead. Kennedy, who had been less in the public eye than Nixon, began to draw enthusiastic responses on the campaign trail and revealed that he was highly informed and poised under fire. ***What impact did the televised debates have on voters?***

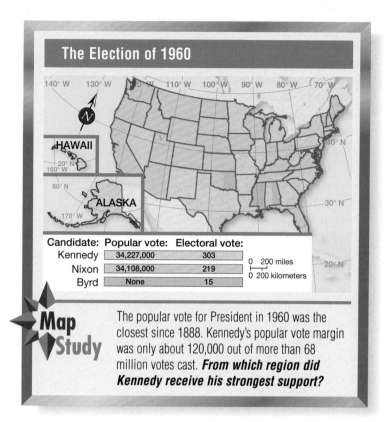

The Election of 1960

Candidate:	Popular vote:	Electoral vote:
Kennedy	34,227,000	303
Nixon	34,108,000	219
Byrd	None	15

Map Study

The popular vote for President in 1960 was the closest since 1888. Kennedy's popular vote margin was only about 120,000 out of more than 68 million votes cast. *From which region did Kennedy receive his strongest support?*

■ The New Frontier

Kennedy devoted his Inaugural Address to defining the role of the United States in a divided world. The torch, he said, had been "passed to a new generation," committed to the rights for which the United States had stood since the Revolution. He warned the communist world that the United States would remain strong, but he also urged both sides to renew the search for peace. He wanted both to join forces against the common enemies of "tyranny, poverty, disease, and war itself." In ringing tones, he declared:

❝ *My fellow Americans, ask not what your country can do for you. Ask what you can do for your country. My fellow citizens of the world: Ask not what America can do for you, but what together we can do for the freedom of man.* ❞

The Kennedy administration became known as the "New Frontier." For the first time, the future of the United States lay in the hands of those born in the twentieth century. The President and his closest advisers were intelligent and tough-minded. They were sure of their ability to make the country and the world better places to live in.

In public the new President mixed idealism with realism and informality with dignity. Although he showed a great deal of idealism, Kennedy was also a **pragmatist**—one who searches for practical solutions to problems. Above all, Kennedy seemed to have the gift of leadership that inspired trust and devotion. Kennedy's qualities seemed to appeal not only to those in the United States but to people all over the world.

■ Kennedy's Economic Program

Essentially, Kennedy's New Frontier was a continuation of Roosevelt's New Deal and Truman's Fair Deal. Kennedy promised to stimulate the economy with tax cuts and increased federal spending.

Promoting Economic Growth

In 1960, though the country was still prosperous, the economy was slowing down. When Kennedy became President, the nation's rate of economic growth was only 3 percent a year. Kennedy looked for ways to increase growth and create more jobs. In stimulating the economy, he chose not to rely on federal spending, which tends to cause inflation. Instead, he sought to increase business production and efficiency. His administration also asked businesses to hold down prices and labor leaders to hold down requests for pay increases.

Conflicts With Steel Companies

Prodded by Secretary of Labor Arthur Goldberg, labor unions in the steel industry agreed to reduce their demands for higher wages. Despite this agreement, several steel companies raised prices sharply in 1962. Kennedy denounced the steel company executives and threatened to have the Department of Defense buy cheaper steel from foreign companies. He also instructed the Justice Department to investigate whether the steel industry was guilty of price-fixing. The steel companies backed down and cut their prices. To achieve this victory, however, Kennedy had strained his relations with the nation's business leaders. As a result of his actions to stimulate the economy, Kennedy achieved his aim of raising the growth rate, which doubled during his administration.

Legislative Victories

Kennedy was able to win some legislative victories in his domestic program. After getting a bill for federal aid to public schools passed, he tried to wipe out areas of poverty, notably in the Appalachian Mountain region, in much of the South, and in the nation's inner cities. Kennedy supported the Area Redevelopment Act, designed to encourage industries to move into economically depressed areas. His Housing Act of 1961 called for $5 billion for **urban renewal,** or programs to improve homes and neighborhoods in the inner cities.

Perhaps his most significant victory was increased funding for the National Aeronautics and Space Administration (NASA). Kennedy challenged the nation and NASA with the goal of putting an astronaut on the moon by 1970. There were those who objected to spending an estimated $20 billion for the space program, but Kennedy saw space exploration as a challenge to the nation's prestige and a symbol of cold war rivalry with the Soviet Union.

Conflict With Congress

Although Kennedy achieved some legislative victories, conflict with Congress prevented him from getting much of his domestic program passed. Despite the fact that the Democratic party enjoyed large majorities in both houses, a coalition of conservative Southern Democrats dominated Congress, rejecting many New Frontier measures.

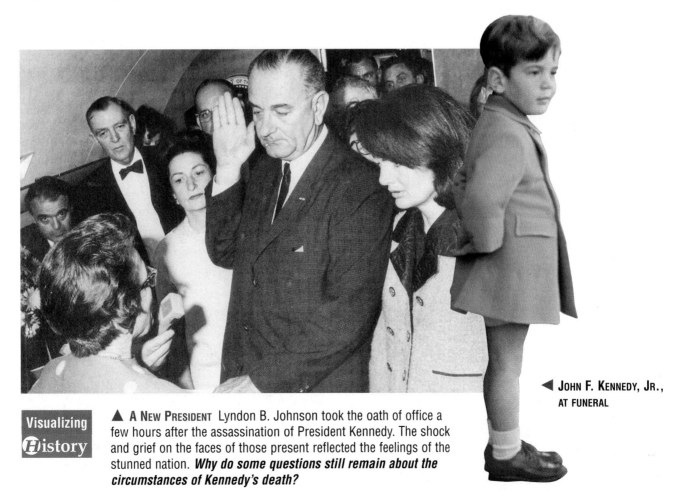

◄ JOHN F. KENNEDY, JR., AT FUNERAL

Visualizing History ▲ A NEW PRESIDENT Lyndon B. Johnson took the oath of office a few hours after the assassination of President Kennedy. The shock and grief on the faces of those present reflected the feelings of the stunned nation. *Why do some questions still remain about the circumstances of Kennedy's death?*

When Kennedy proposed that the government recognize the problems of cities by creating a new cabinet department for urban affairs, Congress voted down the proposal. Kennedy also asked for a national health insurance program, Medicare, to help older citizens pay their medical bills. The Senate defeated this bill, which was opposed by many doctors. The President called the Senate's action a "serious defeat for every American family."

■ Tragedy in Dallas

Kennedy hoped to achieve a greater mandate for his domestic program in the election of 1964. To that end, he traveled to Dallas, Texas, to smooth party differences and gather support. In Dallas, on November 22, 1963, the President was assassinated.

The sense of tragedy and grief that many felt was caught by a conversation between the newspaper columnist Mary McGrory and Daniel Moynihan, a member of Kennedy's staff. In response to McGrory's remark that "we'll never laugh again," Moynihan replied, "Heavens, Mary, we'll laugh again. It's just that we'll never be young again." It was this feeling of youth snuffed out, of promise unfulfilled, that made Kennedy's death seem peculiarly tragic to many.

The country and the world were deeply shocked and saddened at this loss. Americans everywhere grieved over the President's death. In Italy, people brought flowers to the gates of the American embassy in Rome. In India, crowds wept in the streets of New Delhi. In Africa, President Sékou Touré of Guinea said, "I have lost my only true friend in the outside world."

The Warren Commission

Kennedy's alleged assassin, Lee Harvey Oswald, was himself shot to death only two days after the assassination. This event led to speculation that Oswald was killed to protect others who may have helped plan the crime. In 1964, a national commission headed by Chief Justice Warren concluded that Oswald was indeed the assassin and that he acted alone. The commission's report did leave important questions unanswered, though, and theories still persist that Oswald acted as part of a conspiracy. None of those theories have gained wide acceptance, however.

Johnson Takes Over

Kennedy was succeeded in office by Vice President Lyndon B. Johnson. Johnson took the oath of office on the plane that carried Kennedy's body from Dallas back to Washington, D.C. From Kennedy, Johnson inherited both unsolved problems and unfulfilled promises.

In domestic policy, Kennedy's New Frontier program was stalled in Congress. Yet, only two years after his death, most of these programs became law. The public reaction to the young President's tragic death, combined with the political skills of Lyndon Johnson, made possible sweeping social reform.

Section 1 ★ Assessment

Checking for Understanding

1. Define mandate, pragmatist, urban renewal.

2. Explain why many of Kennedy's domestic programs were not passed.

Critical Thinking

3. Analyzing Results   How did the lack of a mandate affect Kennedy's ability to govern?

4. Analyzing Issues   Re-create the diagram shown here to list the victories and defeats that President Kennedy's programs faced in both houses of Congress.

Kennedy's Legislative Efforts

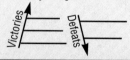

INTERDISCIPLINARY ACTIVITY

5. Government Make a collage using photographs of important events during the Kennedy administration.

▼ PHOTOGRAPH OF EARTH FROM THE MOON

▲ ASTRONAUT IN SPACE

Space Race

Americans were stunned by the news that the Soviets had put a satellite—*Sputnik I*—into orbit around the earth in October 1957. Physicist Edward Teller called the launch a Soviet victory in "a battle more important and greater than Pearl Harbor." President Eisenhower told the panicked nation that only its pride, not its security, was damaged.

Americans, however, were threatened by what they considered Soviet technical superiority. In response, Congress passed the National Defense Education Act, which financed science and foreign-language programs in schools. In addition, the National Science Foundation's curriculum-development budget was dramatically increased. Congress also created the National Aeronautics and Space Administration (NASA) in 1958. Huge sums of money were allocated to develop space technology and to compete with the Soviets in space.

In the spring of 1961, Alan Shepard, Jr., became the first American to make a space flight. On February 20, 1962, Lieutenant Colonel John Glenn became the first American to orbit the earth. Shortly after Shepard's flight,

Kennedy challenged the nation to a great undertaking. He pledged that America would land an individual on the moon by 1970. In July 1969 Commander Neil A. Armstrong, Colonel Edwin E. Aldrin, Jr., and Lieutenant Colonel Michael Collins took off in Apollo.

When they reached the moon, Collins remained aboard the command spacecraft while Aldrin and Armstrong descended to the surface in a lunar module. Millions watched on television as Armstrong became the first human being to set foot on the surface of the moon.

Making the Science Connection

1. How did Americans feel about the success of *Sputnik*?

2. What actions were taken in response to *Sputnik*?

ACTIVITY

3. Investigate major events in the American space program from 1960 to the present. Use your findings to create a space time line.

★★★★★★★★★★★★★★★★★★★★★★★★★★★★★★★

The Great Society

Guide to Reading

Main Idea
President Lyndon Johnson worked with Congress to pass the most significant program of domestic legislation since the New Deal.

Reading Strategy

Classifying Information As you read about President Johnson's domestic agenda, use a chart like the one shown here to list and explain four programs that were part of the War on Poverty.

Program	Description

Objectives
After studying this section, you should be able to

★ explain how Johnson's belief in consensus helped him win the 1964 election.

★ discuss Johnson's efforts to fight poverty in the United States.

Key Term
consensus

► *SILENT SPRING* BY RACHEL CARSON

ided by the Kennedy cabinet and relying on his long experience in government, Lyndon Johnson quickly made the transition from Vice President to President. On November 27, 1963, five days after John F. Kennedy's assassination, Johnson appeared before a joint session of Congress. His words assured the nation's representatives that he intended to carry out Kennedy's programs:

❝ *. . . the ideas and ideals which [Kennedy] so nobly represented must and will be translated into effective action. John Kennedy's death commands what his life conveyed—that America must move forward.* ❞

Elected to the House of Representatives in 1937 and the Senate in 1948, Johnson was at home in Congress. During the 1950s he was the powerful Democratic majority leader of the Senate. Although a Southerner, Johnson had taken a moderate position on most issues and had been a leader in passing the Civil Rights Act of 1957.

■ The Election of 1964

As President, Johnson continued an effective policy of working through **consensus,** or general agreement, that he had developed in Congress. With skilled bargaining, compromising, and even verbal arm-twisting, Johnson reinforced his favorite biblical quotation, "Come let us reason together." He took over the responsibilities of the Chief Executive with firmness and strength, determined to pursue the Democratic party's goals of social justice.

In the election of 1964, Johnson used these goals to campaign for President. His campaign plan offered something for everyone: business and labor, rich and poor, young and old, African American and white. Known as "the Great Society," Johnson's domestic program was an effort to expand upon Kennedy's ideas as well as to make a contribution of his own. It was designed to fight poverty, discrimination, unemployment, pollution, and other social ills of America. At the same time, he pledged to provide major tax cuts for individuals and corporations.

To offer voters "a choice, not an echo," Republicans selected an outspoken conservative, Barry Goldwater, to run against Johnson and his liberal running mate, Hubert Humphrey. The Arizona senator ran a determined, uncompromising campaign. His opposition to the Civil Rights Act of 1964 turned away African American voters. His coolness to Social Security made older people fearful. His support of the open shop hurt him with organized labor. Above all, Goldwater's suggestion that military commanders should be allowed to decide for themselves whether to use nuclear weapons made many people nervous.

As predicted, Johnson's wide appeal won him more than 60 percent of the popular vote. Goldwater carried only his home state of Arizona and five Southern states, where former "Dixiecrats" switched to the Republican party. In addition, the Democrats increased their majorities in both houses of Congress. The Great Society had won an overwhelming mandate.

■ War on Poverty

In the mid-1960s the United States had the highest standard of living in the world. But behind the Great Society program was a new awareness that many Americans did not share in the general prosperity.

The Other America

Contributing to this awareness was a book by Michael Harrington entitled *The Other America*, published in 1962. In response to economist John Kenneth Galbraith, who wrote in *The Affluent Society* that only "pockets" of poverty remained, Harrington claimed that as many as 40 million Americans—one-fourth of the population —were poor. He charged:

▲ HELP FOR NEGLECTED AMERICANS The War on Poverty reached into Appalachia where poor soil and lack of education affected many lives. *Why did some writers and leaders call for the government to help the poor?*

Cesar Chavez
1927–1993

Born to Mexican American migrant workers, Cesar Chavez picked crops in the Southwest as a child and young man. At age 25, he began organizing farm workers to win better pay and working conditions.

Early in the 1960s, Chavez founded a union for migrant farm workers and later merged it with another to form the first large-scale organization of farm workers. He then organized a strike against grape growers.

The strike drew national attention as Chavez borrowed tactics from the civil rights movement— marches and a 25-day fast.

Yet the grape growers would not settle. The tide began to turn in 1968 when Chavez asked the American people to boycott grapes. Growers' profits tumbled as consumers began to side with the workers. The strike lasted until 1970, when the growers finally agreed to settle.

> *The United States contains an underdeveloped nation, a culture of poverty. Its inhabitants do not suffer the extreme poverty of the peasants of Asia . . . yet the mechanism of the misery is similar.*

Most of the American people knew little of the great mass of human misery, said Harrington. The poor were hidden away in the slums of central cities, in rural areas, and on Native American reservations.

Automation had done away with the jobs of many workers, and small farmers could no longer compete with agribusiness. Then, too, displaced factory workers and farmers did not have the opportunity for the training and work experience needed for new jobs. Further, pensions and Social Security did not adequately cover medical expenses for older citizens.

HISTORY Online

Student Web Activity

Visit the *American History: The Modern Era Since 1865* Web site at **me.glencoe.com** and click on **Chapter 24— Student Web Activities** for an activity about poverty.

Johnson Declares War

Johnson announced his strategy in his first State of the Union Address on January 8, 1964: "This administration . . . declares unconditional war on poverty in America." A new Office of Economic Opportunity (OEO) aimed its billion-dollar budget at illiteracy, unemployment, and disease. The OEO-sponsored VISTA (Volunteers in Service to America) sent workers to improve conditions in poor neighborhoods. Job Corps provided training for the unskilled, while Project Head Start helped poor children prepare for school. The Elementary and Secondary Education Act of 1965 gave direct massive federal aid to public and parochial schools. A similar act provided college scholarships for needy students.

The Great Society's War on Poverty extended federal influence into areas that had traditionally been handled by local governments, private enterprise, or religious groups. In some cases OEO was granted power to overrule local governments.

The emphasis was not simply on relief but on helping poor people help themselves. For example, community action programs taught people to organize protests and put pressure on landlords, employers, and even government agencies to effect change.

Medicare

After nearly 20 years of opposition by those who believed that the government should stay out of health care, Congress passed the Medicare Act. Medicare provided people over age 65 with hospital care. Medical centers were to be set up in areas where such facilities were lacking. The act provided funds for medical schools to increase enrollments and reduce the shortage of doctors.

■ Immigration Reform

To many thousands of immigrants, the United States already represented a "great society"—a land of newfound opportunity and freedom. The doors of this great society had opened wide to immigrants from northwestern Europe and nearly closed to others, because of a quota system that the United States established in 1924.

Out of 157,000 immigrants admitted each year, Great Britain and Ireland were allotted 83,000; India, with a population of 450 million, and Andorra, with a population of 6,400, each were allotted 100. Presidents Truman, Eisenhower, and Kennedy had been unable to persuade Congress to change this system.

Standing beneath the Statue of Liberty, which welcomed immigrants to the country, Johnson signed the Immigration Act of 1965. The law replaced national quotas with global quotas and favored those with special skills. As a result, immigration to the United States from Asia and Latin America increased sharply.

Under Johnson's leadership Congress passed a great number of other important laws in a few months. "We did reach consensus," he concluded. "I think we did convince the vast majority of Americans that the time for procrastinating had passed."

His programs were well-received in part because people saw benefits for themselves. Some businesspeople, for example, benefited from the War on Poverty because of the increased purchasing power of poor people. Johnson's program also included subsidies to farmers.

■ Rising Costs End Great Society

Great Society programs required large sums of money. Federal spending for social purposes rose from $54 billion in 1964 to $98 billion in 1968. Federal budget problems and national inflation made Great Society spending an issue for debate. The $20-billion-a-year cost of the Vietnam War made things worse.

Guns and Butter

At first, Johnson tried to finance the war with taxes, explaining that the nation could afford both guns and butter. New social programs and rising war costs made the federal deficit climb to $28 billion by 1968. The President realized that without additional taxes, either social or military programs would have to be cut. He asked Congress for a tax increase. Congress refused unless the President would cut the budget. Johnson chopped $6 billion out of proposed domestic spending, marking the end of the Great Society.

End of an Era

Lyndon Johnson left office in January 1969 a discouraged man. Unable to build a Great Society at home and wage a war at the same time, he had to waive his chance for another term. The American people had rejected Johnson's policies in Vietnam. Supporters of Nixon, he knew, were not sympathetic to the Great Society programs. The nation had become deeply divided.

The 1960s had begun as a time of youth, optimism, and confidence in the future and ended in war, riots, and extreme violence. Three national heroes—President John F. Kennedy, Dr. Martin Luther King, Jr., and Senator Robert Kennedy—had been assassinated. Tens of thousands of young Americans had been killed or wounded in the most unpopular war the United States had ever fought. The New Frontier and the Great Society programs, designed to make life better for the poor and the needy, had also become casualties of the war.

▲ END OF THE GREAT SOCIETY
President Johnson felt increasing criticism because of the growing dissent over the war and increasing opposition within his own party. *What decision did the President make in 1968 regarding his political future?*

After the unhappy events of 1968, the year itself ended on an ironic note of hope and progress. Late in December 1968 the United States succeeded in sending the first astronauts into orbit around the moon. During one of the most difficult years in American history, the nation had scored a great technological achievement. The photographs sent back from space made planet Earth seem small, peaceful, and beautiful. It brought a new feeling to Americans that no matter how difficult, the problems they faced could be solved.

Growing Concern for the Environment

During the 1960s, greater emphasis was placed on the environment. Many conservation projects had been started during the Great Depression, mostly as a means of providing work for the unemployed. During the same period, the dust bowl demonstrated the need for soil conservation. As time went on, scientists discovered more about the effects of pollutants on the environment, and people became more concerned with environmental health.

The individual most responsible for launching the environmental movement and prompting new regulations was Rachel Carson. An aquatic biologist by training, Carson wrote about the sea with great insight. Her most important book, *Silent Spring* (1962), dealt with the environment. Long aware of the threat posed by careless use of toxic chemicals, she researched carefully and wrote movingly about how modern industry and agriculture were poisoning the planet. *Silent Spring* sparked a federal investigation that backed her conclusions and led to tougher laws regarding harmful chemicals. Rachel Carson died soon after publication of *Silent Spring*, unaware of the ecology movement that her work would inspire.

Section 2 ★ Assessment

Checking for Understanding

1. Define consensus.
2. Identifying Central Issues   How did the war in Vietnam and violence in the United States affect confidence in President Johnson?

Critical Thinking

3. Classifying Information   Make a list of guidelines that you would use to classify Americans who live in poverty. Would your classification meet government standards?

4. Determining Effects   Re-create the diagram shown here to explain how the Vietnam War helped to end Johnson's Great Society.

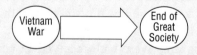

INTERDISCIPLINARY ACTIVITY

5. The Arts   Make a pictorial history of the 1960s using photographs from magazines. Include an introduction and captions.

BUILDING SKILLS
Critical Thinking Skills

Drawing Conclusions

Drawing conclusions allows you to understand ideas that are not stated directly. To draw conclusions, use the available facts and your own knowledge and experience to form a judgment or opinion about the material.

Learning the Skill

Here are some steps to follow in learning to draw conclusions.

- **Review** the facts that are stated directly.
- **Use** your knowledge and insight to develop some conclusions about these facts.
- **Look** for information to check the accuracy of your conclusions.

Read the selection about artist Robert Rauschenberg, then answer the questions that follow.

The decade of the 1960s was a fresh period in American art when artists experimented with a variety of media, materials, techniques, and styles. Robert Rauschenberg mastered the technique of *collage,* a two-dimensional art form using a variety of images.

Rauschenberg incorporated pieces of discarded cloth, wood, crumpled printed materials, and other manufactured objects, such as tin cans or bottles, onto his canvases. He referred to these works as "combine paintings."

The bold drips and splatters of Rauschenberg's brushwork, as well as his use of geometric shapes and colors, reflect his debt to abstract expressionism, an artistic movement that came into vogue after World War II. Yet his works also point to the emergence of pop art in the 1960s, an artistic style that used commonplace subject matter from popular culture.

▼ *KITE* BY ROBERT RAUSCHENBERG, 1963

Practicing the Skill

1. Interpret the meaning of Rauschenberg's title *Kite.*

2. How does *Kite* capture the dynamic change of a nation?

3. What conclusions can you draw about the artist's intent in using images of the bald eagle and the military flag? Troops and an army helicopter?

Glencoe's **Skillbuilder Interactive Workbook, Level 2** provides instruction and practice in key social studies skills.

APPLYING THE SKILL

4. Study a physical-political map of your state, then draw conclusions about the economic future. Consider such questions as: How might the state's bodies of water be used in the future? Does the land have agricultural potential? Present your findings in a one-page report.

★★

An Imperial Presidency

Guide to Reading

Main Idea

Richard Nixon greatly increased the power of the presidency as he grappled with a host of domestic problems.

Reading Strategy

Classifying Information As you read about Nixon's presidency, use a chart like the one shown here to list Nixon's economic policies and their results.

Problem	Nixon's Policy	Result
Inflation		
Recession		

Objectives

After studying this section, you should be able to

★ describe how Nixon tried to deal with the economic problems of the early 1970s.

★ explain how Nixon handled the war on crime and the energy crisis.

Key Terms

stagflation, balance of payments, new federalism, revenue sharing

◀ **SEAL OF THE REPUBLICAN NATIONAL COMMITTEE**

To Americans and foreigners alike, the United States in the late 1960s had lost its direction. Not only was it losing the war in Vietnam, but its industries were losing their competitive edge. A sense of defeat and decay became apparent. Deep social, political, and racial divisions were threatening to tear society apart. Richard Nixon claimed that he had a "plan to end the war in Vietnam" and "bring Americans together." His promise of peace in Vietnam and tranquility at home appealed to many.

■ Nixon's Political Career

Richard M. Nixon was the first President in modern times to be elected after having lost a previous bid for the presidency. After losing the 1962 California gubernatorial race, his political career seemed over. In the 1968 campaign, however, he changed his public image. The old Nixon had been intensely partisan and ruthless. When he had run for Congress from California in 1946 as a newly discharged naval officer, he charged that his opponent had strong ties to communist organizations. Political opponents called him opportunistic and self-serving.

The new Nixon, however, impressed observers as calm, broad-minded, and statesmanlike. He promised that his administration would be "open to new ideas, open to men and women of both parties, open to the critics as well as those who support us." Bringing the nation together proved difficult, however. With the Democrats in control of Congress, Nixon saw many of his domestic proposals rejected.

◼ The War Against Crime

One of Nixon's domestic successes was his war against crime. During the 1968 campaign, Nixon spoke out against permissive attitudes toward the rights of those accused of crimes. Nixon criticized the record of the Supreme Court under Chief Justice Earl Warren. He denounced Supreme Court decisions that curtailed the powers of the police in the interrogation of suspects and that forbade the use of electronic "bugging" equipment for gathering evidence. Such decisions, Nixon maintained, violated "the first civil right of every American to be free of domestic violence." He promised to fill vacancies on the Supreme Court with judges who would not "weaken the peace forces as against the criminal forces."

Nixon eventually succeeded in his campaign to change the liberal thrust of the Court. When Chief Justice Warren resigned shortly after Nixon took office, the President nominated Warren Burger, a respected conservative judge, to take his place. He also placed three other conservative justices on the Court. The Burger Court, known to critics as the Nixon Court, did not abolish the pro-

tections of criminal suspects set up by the Warren Court. It did, however, whittle them down. Its harder line against criminals was dramatically revealed when it reversed the opinion of the Warren Court that capital punishment was a violation of the Bill of Rights.

◼ Nixon's Economic Policies

Nixon inherited difficult economic problems. The combined costs of President Johnson's War on Poverty and the Vietnam War had produced a large federal budget deficit and mounting inflation. Between 1964 and 1969, the dollar lost one-fifth of its purchasing power.

Stagflation

The President tackled inflation by curtailing the supply of money. By the end of 1970, however, it was apparent that the plan was not working. Restricting the supply of money drove interest rates up, and higher interest rates discouraged investment. Unemployment increased, and the stock market

Visualizing History

▲ THE BURGER COURT The Supreme Court is generally referred to by the name of its chief justice. Thus, in 1969, when Warren E. Burger became chief justice, the Supreme Court became known as the Burger Court. *Why had President Nixon criticized the Warren Court?*

Shopping Malls

A 1973 report on New Jersey's Cherry Hill Mall observed that the shopping mall had become to the suburb what Main Street once was to the small town—the focus of community life.

Then_____

Something for Everyone

Mall construction was at a peak during the early 1970s.

Cities and suburbs across the United States became home to enclosed malls featuring, under one roof, a fairly predictable array of small specialty stores for books, gifts, and shoes.

Large malls typically included major department stores as dependable "anchors" for sales and customers, as well as several popular restaurants. Malls were enormously successful in not only attracting shoppers, but also walkers and joggers.

Now_____

A City Under One Roof

Compared to its early counterpart, the mall in the 1990s grew in size and in scope—serving as an entertainment complex as well as a retail center. The nation's largest is Bloomington, Minnesota's Mall

▲ MALL OF AMERICA, BLOOMINGTON, MINNESOTA

of America. Opened in the summer of 1992, the mall contains 350 stores, 8 night clubs, a 14-screen movie theater, an 18-hole miniature golf course, and a 7-acre amusement park over its 4.2 million square feet. On average, the mall attracts more than 700,000 shoppers per week—200,000 on Saturday nights alone. A special Christmas season promotion offers bargain airfares to passengers who fly in for a day of shopping.

---

declined. The slowdown in business activity reduced federal revenues, and inflation accelerated. This economic slowdown, coupled with inflation, was called **stagflation.**

To meet the problem of stagflation, Nixon turned to other, less conservative measures. In August 1971 he announced his New Economic Policy, which called for a 90-day freeze on wages, prices, and rents. This was followed by a system of wage and price controls in November. In January 1973 the President relaxed controls, and prices rose sharply. In response, a new freeze was imposed in June.

President Nixon also took steps to end the recession by stimulating the economy. He proposed tax cuts for both businesses and individuals, hoping that when the demand went up, production would rise and unemployment would fall. After making some revisions in the President's proposals, Congress enacted tax cuts in December 1971.

The President also used deficit spending to fight recession.

These measures, however, failed to solve the problem of stagflation. Although the tax cuts and deficit spending helped to ease the recession, they added to inflation. On the other hand, while the controls slowed inflation for a time, they did little to help the economy grow or to lower unemployment.

A Balance of Payments Deficit

Inflation caused prices to rise not only on domestic goods, but on exports. So, fewer exports were purchased. This resulted in a balance of payments deficit. The **balance of payments** is the difference between the money paid to and received from other nations. In this case, the nation was spending more than it received. Between 1970 and 1971, the nation's balance of payments deficit jumped from $4 billion to $22 billion.

The deficit was evidence that the United States had lost its dominance in world markets. Between 1950 and 1970, for example, the United States's share of world automobile production dropped from 76 to 31 percent, and the same phenomenon was occurring in the textile, shoe, and electrical equipment industries.

A serious effect of the balance of payments deficit was that it weakened other nations' confidence in the value of the dollar. Because world trade depends on stable money and because the dollar was the major currency in the world, the dollar crisis threatened to disrupt trade.

Trying to improve the economic situation, Nixon acted decisively. To combat inflation, in August 1971 he announced, as noted earlier, a 90-day freeze on prices and wages. To discourage imports, he placed an additional duty of 10 percent on all goods purchased from abroad. He also allowed the dollar to decline in value in relation to foreign currencies, making it more expensive for Americans to buy goods from other countries. Therefore, goods made in the United States became cheaper than foreign-made goods, and that promoted exports.

Although Nixon's policies brought some relief, inflation, chronic unemployment, and the loss of foreign markets remained a problem throughout his presidency. The measures also caused ill will in nations that depended on American markets for their products.

The New Federalism

Nixon also announced his **new federalism,** which was intended to reduce the federal government's role in the economy and turn many of its tasks over to state and local governments. Following the President's lead, Congress passed a series of **revenue-sharing** bills that granted federal funds to local agencies to use as they saw fit.

■ The Energy Crisis

Another problem concerned energy. In the fall of 1973, Arab nations placed an embargo on crude oil shipments from the Middle East.

The purpose of the embargo was to force the United States to stop supporting Israel in its struggle with the Arab states. Support for Israel did not change, but the embargo produced an energy crisis in America—and near panic. In some areas the price of petroleum shot up nearly 400 percent, and there were shortages of gasoline for cars and heating oil for homes, schools, and businesses.

Although the United States had about one-sixteenth of the world's population, Americans consumed about one-third of the world's energy. Most of this energy came from such nonrenewable resources as oil, gas, and coal. Coal reserves were abundant in America but supplied less than 20 percent of the nation's energy needs. By 1973, the United States was importing about 6 million barrels of oil each day, or about 36 percent of the oil needed to heat homes and to keep factories and automobiles running.

President Nixon announced a plan to make the country self-sufficient in energy by 1980. He called for higher taxes on imported oil and encouraged Americans to take conservation measures, such as lowering their thermostats at home and at work. Congress passed a law requiring states to lower the speed limit on highways to 55 miles per hour to save gasoline and approved the construction of a pipeline in Alaska for the shipment of newly discovered oil to refineries. Congress provided some tax incentives to

▼ SIGN OF THE TIMES

Temporarily... 10 GALLONS PER CUSTOMER We appreciate your business & cooperation.

▲ **ENERGY CRISIS** One of the nation's most important concerns during the Nixon administration was the energy crisis. Long lines of cars at gas stations were a sign of the times. *What actions did the administration take to conserve energy?*

encourage energy research and put the nation on year-round daylight saving time for two years.

After the Arab nations lifted the oil embargo in March 1974, most Americans forgot about the energy crisis mentality. They began once again to use fuel in increasing quantities. However, fuel prices began a steep rise as the oil shortage continued. In the 1960s the major

oil-exporting nations had formed the Organization of Petroleum Exporting Countries (OPEC). By 1970 OPEC had begun to raise prices, and over the next decade the cost of oil increased from less than $2 a barrel to more than $30 a barrel. The increases in the price of oil by the OPEC members contributed to the problems that plagued the American economy throughout the 1970s.

Section 3 ★ Assessment

Checking for Understanding

1. **Define** stagflation, balance of payments, new federalism, revenue sharing.

2. **Point out** how Nixon affected the criminal justice system.

Critical Thinking

3. **Evaluating Policy** Write an evaluation of Nixon's policy for handling inflation.

4. **Summarizing** Re-create the diagram shown here to explain what steps the President and Congress took to combat the energy crisis.

Step

Step

Step

Step

INTERDISCIPLINARY ACTIVITY

5. **Government** Write a press release in which you detail President Nixon's plans to fight inflation and unemployment.

★★

The Watergate Scandal

Guide to Reading

Main Idea

President Nixon became involved in a political scandal that ultimately forced him to resign.

Reading Strategy

Sequencing Information As you read about the Watergate scandal, use a diagram such as the one shown here to list the key events that led to President Nixon's resignation.

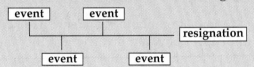

Objectives

After studying this section, you should be able to

★ explain how the constitutional process solved the Watergate crisis.

★ list the ways in which Congress sought to reassert its constitutional powers.

Key Terms

executive privilege, impound, deregulation

▶ STREET SIGN, WASHINGTON, D.C.

Not surprisingly, the Republican party nominated President Nixon as its candidate in the election of 1972. Nixon ran against Senator George McGovern of South Dakota, who won the Democratic nomination with the support of a coalition of activists—young people, African Americans, and women.

■ A Crisis in the Presidency

Almost from the beginning, however, the McGovern campaign derailed itself. McGovern's running mate, Senator Thomas Eagleton, was forced to withdraw when it was disclosed that he had been hospitalized for depression. In addition, Democratic party regulars and labor union leaders were cool, if not hostile, toward the liberal McGovern's candidacy.

In contrast, President Nixon conducted a perfect campaign. The almost-complete withdrawal of United States troops from Vietnam defused the war issue, and the summits in Beijing and Moscow signaled an easing of cold war tensions. Moreover, the President solidified his support among "middle Americans" by calling for law and order, by opposing busing, and by making continuous appeals to patriotism.

On Election Day the President received 61 percent of the popular vote and won every electoral vote except those of Massachusetts and the District of Columbia.

CREEP

It was later learned, however, that this tremendous victory was not won entirely fairly. During the campaign the President and his political advisers organized the Committee to Reelect the President (CREEP) and collected more than $50 million for Nixon's reelection campaign, some of which was illegally received. Some campaign contributions were used to finance "dirty tricks" against the Democrats.

The Watergate Break-in

A group of CREEP employees were caught "bugging" the offices of the Democratic National Committee in the Watergate building in Washington, D.C. Although the President's press secretary dismissed the break-in as a "third-rate burglary," this seemingly insignificant incident had serious consequences for the President.

Rumors began to circulate that the President himself had ordered the Watergate break-in. Stories were published in the *Washington Post* and other newspapers that linked key members of the White House staff and CREEP to the break-in. It was reported that key Nixon advisers had paid the Watergate burglars almost $1 million in "hush money" to plead guilty and say nothing else at their trials. To quiet the rumors, the President ordered his attorney general to appoint a special prosecutor, Harvard law professor Archibald Cox, to investigate the case.

The Investigation

At the same time, a special Senate committee began to hold televised hearings on the break-in and other abuses alleged to have been committed during the campaign of 1972. Starting in May 1973, millions of Americans watched in fascination as a parade of witnesses testified about illegal activities carried out by the White House staff and by CREEP. Perhaps the most startling discovery was that the President tape-recorded most of the conversations he had in the Oval Office.

Following these revelations, federal grand juries indicted members of the Nixon administration for their illegal activities, including the unauthorized wiretapping, burglaries, illegal campaign contributions, and the bribing of witnesses. Eventually 25 people connected with the administration—including former Attorney General John Mitchell and two of Nixon's closest White House aides, H. R. Haldeman and John D. Erlichman—were convicted and served prison terms for Watergate-related crimes.

■ The President Answers

Month after month President Nixon continued to deny any involvement in Watergate. Claiming **executive privilege,** or the principle that the President does not have to give information to other branches of the government, Nixon refused to turn over the White House tapes to the special prosecutor. In October 1973, he offered to provide written summaries of the tapes.

Visualizing History

▲ **WATERGATE** The Watergate hearings led to criminal charges against several top White House aides, including H. R. Haldeman (left) and Jeb Stuart Magruder (speaking at hearing). President Nixon disavowed knowledge of the break-in. *What is executive privilege?*

The Saturday Night Massacre

When the special prosecutor insisted on having the tapes, Nixon ordered the attorney general to remove Cox. Both the attorney general and his top assistant resigned rather than carry out the President's order. Finally Nixon found a Justice Department official who was willing to fire Cox. The dismissal of the special prosecutor became known as the "Saturday Night Massacre," and it provoked a wave of public protest as well as the first serious calls for Nixon's impeachment.

Agnew Resigns

October 1973 proved to be a disastrous time for Richard Nixon for other reasons as well. His Vice President, Spiro Agnew, was forced to resign in disgrace. A grand jury found that Agnew, while governor of Maryland, had taken bribes from contractors who did business with the state. It was further revealed that Agnew continued to receive such payments while he was Vice President. Nixon nominated Gerald Ford, the Republican leader of the House of Representatives, as the new Vice President.

Nixon Proclaims Innocence

In an effort to quiet public outrage over the Saturday Night Massacre, Nixon appointed another special prosecutor in November 1973. In April 1974, the President released written transcripts of 47 tape-recorded conversations. Even though the transcripts had been heavily edited, many believed the tapes indicated the President

▲ PRESIDENT NIXON LEAVES THE WHITE HOUSE

had indeed been involved in covering up the Watergate scandal. Nevertheless, the President still continued to proclaim his innocence:

> 66 *If read with an open and fair mind and read together with the record of actions I took, these transcripts will show that what I have stated since the beginning to be the truth . . . my actions were directed toward finding the facts and seeing that justice was done, fairly and according to the law.* 99

In July the Supreme Court ruled that the President had to turn over the tapes themselves, not just their transcripts. A month later Nixon complied and handed over the tapes. One tape provided direct evidence that on June 23, 1972, only six days after the Watergate break-in, the President had arranged a cover-up. With this news, even the President's strongest supporters conceded that there was sufficient evidence to

• •

Footnotes to History

Impeachment in American History

The House of Representatives has voted articles of impeachment against 15 officials. Twelve of those impeached were federal judges. The others are Senator William Blount of Tennessee in 1797, President Andrew Johnson in 1868, and Secretary of War William Belknap in 1876. The Senate has convicted 7 of the impeached judges.

support impeachment. They advised Nixon that it seemed certain the House would impeach him and that the Senate would find him guilty. On August 8, 1974, Nixon announced on national television that he would resign. He also expressed hope that his departure would begin the process of healing the country.

■ Ford Becomes President

The next day Gerald Ford was sworn in as the thirty-eighth President. President Ford appointed Nelson Rockefeller, former governor of New York, as his Vice President, making them the first unelected presidential team in the nation's history.

At first, President Ford inspired public confidence. He assured a joint session of Congress that his administration would be free of "illegal tappings, eavesdropping, buggings, or break-ins." The new President seemed to be a decent, candid, and trustworthy man.

A month after entering office, however, Ford damaged his public image by granting Richard Nixon an unconditional pardon for all crimes he committed or may have committed while in office. Ford insisted that he was acting not out of sympathy for Nixon, but in the public interest. He wanted to avoid the publicity and national division that a trial would create. Nevertheless, the pardon aroused fierce and widespread criticism of the new President.

Congress Reasserts Its Authority

When he took office, Gerald Ford promised to adopt a policy of "communication, conciliation, compromise, and cooperation" with Congress. He expected good relations with Congress, since he had served for 25 years as a representative and almost a decade as House Republican leader. However, the President and Congress were often at odds because Ford was a conservative, and liberal Democrats controlled both houses of Congress. In addition, the new President confronted a Congress that was determined to reassert its authority over what some critics called the "imperial presidency."

Congress Attacks Executive Privilege

To counter the trend toward greater presidential power and curb future abuses, Congress passed a series of laws. In the last year of the Nixon administration, as Watergate weakened the President, Congress attempted to regain some of its power. In November 1973, it passed the War Powers Act in spite of President Nixon's veto. This law required that the President report to Congress within 48 hours after sending combat troops abroad or after engaging in any military action. Unless Congress approved his action, the President had to withdraw all troops within 60 days. After the Watergate crisis, Congress passed the Congressional Budget and Impoundment Control Act of 1974, which allowed Congress to force the President to spend any appropriations that he attempted to **impound,** or withhold, unless he could justify his action to both houses.

Quarrels Over the Economy

One of the biggest problems facing President Ford and Congress was the economic recession. To Ford, inflation and the nation's dependence on foreign oil were the greatest threats to recovery. The Democratic Congress was more alarmed by the highest rates of unemployment and the lowest levels of productivity since the Great Depression of the 1930s.

Like Nixon, President Ford wanted to cut spending on social welfare programs and adopt an energy program. He favored **deregulation,** or removing price controls, of gas and oil. This would cause a rise in prices so people would use less. Increased profits would go toward helping companies find alternate forms of energy. Congress, however, did not cooperate. Ford, in turn, prevented the enactment of liberal Democratic legislation by the use of the veto power.

Ford's Foreign Policy

At first, Congress allowed the President greater leeway in foreign policy than it had to past officeholders. Ford met with leaders of NATO and the Warsaw Pact to sign the

Helsinki Accords in August 1975. Under the terms of the accords, the parties recognized the borders of the countries of Eastern Europe and committed themselves to respect and protect the human rights of their citizens.

Soon, however, in foreign policy, as in domestic affairs, Ford came into conflict with the Democratic-controlled Congress. In 1975 Congress refused President Ford's request for additional funds to aid South Vietnam and Cambodia in their continuing civil wars. As a result, the Cambodian government surrendered to the repressive Khmer Rouge forces on April 17. Twelve days later the North Vietnamese and the Vietcong overran Saigon and forced the government of South Vietnam to surrender. Communist regimes were now in control everywhere in Indochina except Thailand, which remained an ally.

The Bicentennial

Despite difficulties with Congress, President Ford headed for Boston to participate in the opening ceremonies of the Bicentennial, celebrating the nation's 200th birthday. As July 4, 1976, approached, most people in the United States caught the bicentennial spirit. Cities, towns, and villages held parades and concerts and displayed fireworks. A procession of Conestoga wagons traveled to Valley Forge, Pennsylvania, and eighteenth-century sailing ships from many countries majestically sailed into New York Harbor on the Fourth of July.

Visualizing History

▲ **THE NATION'S BICENTENNIAL** In 1976 Americans were anxious to put the tragedy of the Vietnam War and the Watergate affair behind them. A bicentennial spirit swept the nation as millions participated in parades, fireworks displays, and other activities. *Who was the nation's President during this time?*

As the Bicentennial ended, the nation felt a new sense of hopefulness. It knew that the constitutional system had curbed the abuses of the imperial presidency. The people of the United States were proud of achievements such as the space program, and they began to regain their sense of confidence.

Section 4 ★ Assessment

Checking for Understanding

1. **Define** executive privilege, impound, deregulation.

2. **Explain** why President Nixon resigned.

Critical Thinking

3. **Interpreting Viewpoints** Explain why many Americans, although dismayed by the Watergate scandal, felt proud of the way their government functioned during the crisis.

4. **Summarizing** Recreate the diagram shown here to list the actions Congress took to reassert its authority during Ford's presidency.

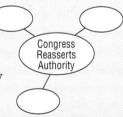

Congress Reasserts Authority

INTERDISCIPLINARY ACTIVITY

5. **The Arts** Write a poem of two stanzas. In the first stanza, describe Bicentennial America. In the second, describe America today.

Self-Check Quiz

Visit the *American History: The Modern Era Since 1865* Web site at **me.glencoe.com** and click on **Chapter 24—Self-Check Quizzes** to prepare for the chapter test.

Using Vocabulary

Each of the terms below has significance for the concept of presidential power. Use each term in a sentence, describing its relation to this concept.

mandate   executive privilege

pragmatist   impound

Reviewing Facts

1. Describe Kennedy's presidential style.
2. Describe why there was a decrease in United States dominance of world markets.
3. Explain the significance of Nixon's new federalism.

Understanding Concepts

Domestic Policy

1. Examine the Kennedy and Johnson presidencies and describe how an election mandate affected each man's ability to govern.
2. Re-create the diagram shown here to list four achievements of the Johnson administration.

Which do you consider the most important? Why?

Presidential Power

3. Some nations expressed astonishment that Americans would force their highest leader to step down over a "relatively small offense." Is it important for our nation to hold politicians accountable for their actions? Explain.

Critical Thinking

1. **Comparing and Contrasting** Explain how Kennedy and Johnson differed in their relationships with Congress.
2. **Drawing Conclusions** What are the lessons of the Watergate scandal? Would you agree that our system of government was vindicated by this affair? What long-term repercussions do you think Watergate had on Americans' views of government and politicians?
3. **Analyzing Fine Art** Study the painting that appears on this page, then answer the question that follows.

   a. What do you think the artist is expressing in this painting?

History and Geography

Reforms in the 1960s and 1970s

1. **Human/Environment Interaction** What was the purpose of urban renewal?
2. **Region** What geographic areas' problems was the War on Poverty formed to combat?
3. **Movement** How did quota reform affect levels of immigration to the United States?

Cooperative Learning ### Interdisciplinary Activity: Government

You will work in small groups to investigate testimony before the Senate subcommittee on Watergate. Each group member should select a different witness to research. Use the actual transcripts of the hearings to discover the process the committee really went through. Then meet together and discuss your findings with the class.

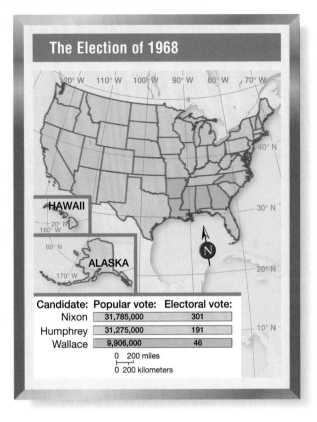

The Election of 1968

Candidate:	Popular vote:	Electoral vote:
Nixon	31,785,000	301
Humphrey	31,275,000	191
Wallace	9,906,000	46

0   200 miles
0 200 kilometers

Practicing Skills

Drawing Conclusions

Study the map on this page, then answer the questions that follow.

1. Who were the candidates in the 1968 election?
2. What conclusions can you draw about the strength of the Republican party at the national level?

Technology Activity

Using a Word Processor

Use the Internet and other library sources to find out more about a program that you read about in this chapter (e.g., the Peace Corps, Medicare). Write a brief report examining the program today. Share your report with the class.

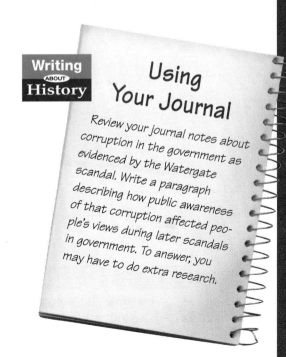

Writing ABOUT History

Using Your Journal

Review your journal notes about corruption in the government as evidenced by the Watergate scandal. Write a paragraph describing how public awareness of that corruption affected people's views during later scandals in government. To answer, you may have to do extra research.

CHAPTER 25

★★

Search for Solutions
1976–1992

► **YELLOW RIBBON TREE TIE**

Setting the Scene

Focus

Despite success in foreign affairs, Jimmy Carter rapidly lost the people's confidence. In the next election, they turned to the conservative Ronald Reagan to restore their confidence. During his administration, the economy recovered and relations with the Soviet Union improved. But Reagan left a mixed legacy, and problems with the economy were passed on to his successor, George Bush, who also had to redefine America's role in world affairs.

Concepts to Understand

★ How **political ideology** shaped events and policies

★ How **leadership** altered the world's political landscape

Read to Discover...

★ what important changes took place in the Soviet Union and Eastern Europe in the late 1980s and early 1990s.

Journal Notes

Why do you think so many Americans were ready for the conservative shift initiated by Ronald Reagan in the 1980s? Note details about it in your journal as you read the chapter.

HISTORY Online

Chapter Overview
Visit the *American History: The Modern Era Since 1865* Web site at **me.glencoe.com** and click on *Chapter 25—Chapter Overviews* to preview chapter information.

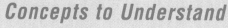

CULTURAL

• **1979** *Inflation reaches unprecedented rates*

• **1980** *United States boycotts Moscow Olympics*
• **1983** *Sally Ride is first American woman in space*

1975　　　　　　　　　　**1980**

POLITICAL

• **1978** *Camp David Accords are signed*
• **1979** *Iran seizes 52 American hostages*

• **1981** *Sandra Day O'Connor is first woman named to Supreme Court*
• **1983** *Reagan announces Strategic Defense Initiative*

Three Flags
by Jasper Johns, 1958

The paintings of American artist Jasper Johns typically featured two-dimensional objects of everyday life as subjects. Johns, for example, painted pictures that consisted entirely of flags, maps, numbers, and letters of the alphabet.

◄ UNITED STATES SOLDIERS, ACTION DURING THE GULF WAR

- **1986** *Space shuttle* Challenger *explodes*
- **1989** *Bicentennial of the Constitution*

- **1990** *Detroit Pistons win National Basketball Association championship*

1985

1990

- **1986** *Iran-contra scandal*
- **1987** *Reagan and Gorbachev sign nuclear arms reduction treaty*

- **1991** *Persian Gulf War begins*
- **1991** *The Soviet Union collapses*

★★

Crisis of Confidence

Guide to Reading

Main Idea
Americans encountered new foreign and domestic challenges during the Carter presidency.

Reading Strategy

Organizing Information As you read about the United States's crisis of confidence during the 1970s, use a diagram like the one shown here to list examples of President Carter's moral foreign policy.

Examples

Carter's Moral
Foreign Policy

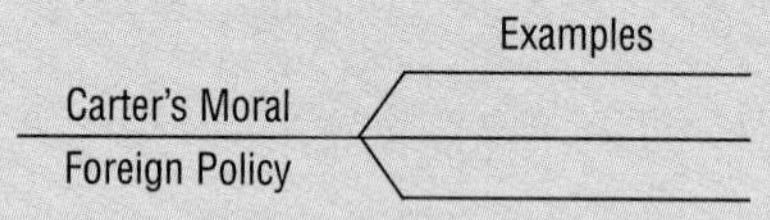

Objectives
After studying this section, you should be able to
★ state reasons for the American public's crisis of confidence.
★ explain how moral principles directed President Carter's domestic and foreign policy.

Key Terms
cartel, double-digit inflation, pork-barrel legislation

► HOSTAGE TERRY ANDERSON AFTER HIS RELEASE

*A*t the time of its Bicentennial in 1976, the United States was faced with the grim prospect of diminishing vital natural resources. One result was that the nation was no longer self-sufficient in its production of energy. By then, the United States was importing more than half of its oil. Competition from Japan, Germany, and other countries threatened America's giant automobile and steel industries. With rising inflation and unemployment, the lifestyles of many Americans were critically affected.

There were equally serious problems in foreign affairs. Political turmoil in economically developing nations upset global stability. The Soviet Union pursued an increasingly aggressive foreign policy as the nuclear arms race continued. As the United States began its third century, the American people wondered if the government was capable of meeting these challenges.

Election of 1976

Soon after Gerald Ford became President in 1974, he began to campaign for his election in 1976. The public regarded Ford as a warm, easygoing man of high integrity, but had doubts about his intellectual capabilities and competence as a leader. As a result, conservatives in the Republican party rallied behind Ronald Reagan, the former governor of California. Ford survived the challenge and won the Republican nomination, but only by a few votes.

The Democratic presidential primaries were crowded with candidates including several who were nationally known. One, however, was a political outsider. James Earl "Jimmy" Carter, Jr., a former governor of Georgia, had no previous experience in the federal government. He toured the nation meeting voters face to face. Carter made a virtue of this inexperience:

> *The people of this country want a fresh face, not one associated with a long series of mistakes at the White House and Capitol Hill.* "

To almost everyone's surprise, Carter won many of the primaries and secured the Democratic nomination for President. This was partly because his informal, down-home style appealed to Americans tired of the "imperial presidency."

During the presidential campaign, Jimmy Carter vowed to restore people's faith in the federal government by making it more open and efficient. He promised major new programs for energy development, tax reform, welfare reform, and national medical care. Conservatives liked him because he promised to balance the budget. Liberals supported him because he insisted he would not let unemployment rise as a means of lowering inflation.

Although the vote was close, Carter won the election. He took 51 percent of the popular vote and 297 electoral votes to Ford's 48 percent and 241 electoral votes. Carter achieved his victory by combining the support of the old Democratic coalition of the industrial Northeast and the Solid South

(except for Virginia). For the first time since 1848, a candidate from the Deep South had been elected President. To a great extent, Carter owed his margin of victory to African American Southern voters.

$ **ECONOMICS**

■ Domestic Trouble

President Carter believed that America's most serious domestic problem was its increasing dependence on oil as an energy source. Experts warned that world supplies of oil, a nonrenewable resource, would soon be exhausted. The oil-producing countries belonged to a **cartel,** an association of nations promoting its economic interests, the Organization of Petroleum Exporting Countries (OPEC). They set prices at ever-higher levels. Rising oil prices added substantially to the price of consumer goods.

Carter's Energy Program

To address the problem, Carter proposed a national energy program. He persuaded Congress to create a Department of Energy. In order to conserve oil, he promoted the

▲ **AN INFORMAL PRESIDENCY** Both Jimmy Carter and his wife Rosalyn lived a relatively simple life. Both came from close-knit families that stressed hard work, dedication, and religion. *What electoral group helped Carter win the 1976 election?*

Gasoline Consumption and Prices

Year	Consumption (billions of gallons)	Cents per Gallon		
		Reg.	Prem.	No lead
1973	110.5	40	45	NA
1974	106.3	53	57	55
1975	109.0	57	61	60
1976	115.7	59	64	61
1977	119.6	62	67	66
1978	125.1	63	69	67
1979	122.1	86	92	90
1980	115.0	119	128	125

Source: *Statistical Abstract of the United States, 1981*

Chart Study Gasoline prices increased steadily beginning in 1973. *In what years did prices affect consumption?*

use of coal and such renewable energy sources as solar energy. The President wanted Americans to join together in a moral crusade against rising consumption:

66 *[The nation's] decision about energy will test the character of the American people and the ability of the President and Congress to govern this nation. This difficult decision will be the 'moral equivalent of war'— except that we will be uniting our efforts to build and not to destroy.* 99

The President asked all Americans to make personal sacrifices to reduce their energy consumption. Because the sacrifices he asked people to make were voluntary, however, the public was confused about the seriousness of the crisis. When Carter later proposed stronger methods of restricting consumption, such as a 10 percent tax on all imported oil and emergency authority to impose gasoline rationing, Congress rejected them. Carter did, however, convince Congress to lift controls on domestic oil production and to impose a "windfall profits" tax on the oil companies' huge earnings.

Double-digit Inflation

Sharp rises in the price of oil and gasoline contributed to **double-digit inflation,** or a rise in the general level of prices of 10 percent or more. By 1980 it cost more than $200 to purchase the same goods that $100 would have bought only 10 years earlier. At the same time, the Federal Reserve Board raised interest rates to all-time highs in an effort to discourage borrowing and bring the economy under control. These policies helped reduce inflation but caused a severe business recession. $

■ Governmental Disunity

Even though the Democrats held the presidency and had a majority in both houses of Congress, there was a lack of unity between the two branches of government. This was largely because Carter was unwilling to play politics. For example, in 1977 he announced that he would veto appropriation bills for a series of costly dams, canals, and other water projects. Passing such **pork-barrel legislation,** or bills that benefit only a small part of the country, was a common practice. Carter's move saved the nation millions of dollars, but it cost him valuable support.

Carter's inability to sell his political position on important issues puzzled many people. He followed a cautious middle course, promising to reduce government spending while endorsing expensive social programs. The President would not "choose up sides," as newspaper columnist James Reston observed. "Confronted with a series of ambiguous questions, he simply refused to give simple answers." As a result, the public became confused about Carter's goals. By 1979 his popular support had fallen dramatically.

■ Morality in Foreign Policy

In contrast to his leadership in domestic policy, President Carter's foreign policy was clearly defined. Carter denounced past

American foreign policy as "lacking moral principle." A man of strong religious beliefs, Carter argued that instead of relying on military and economic might, the United States must try to be "right and honest and truthful and decent" in its dealings with other nations.

The Panama Canal

Carter demonstrated his new policy over the Panama Canal, which the United States had controlled since 1903. In 1978 he won Senate ratification of the Panama Canal treaties, which transferred control of the canal from the United States to Panama by the end of the century. This action removed a major symbol of United States interventionist policy and signaled a new approach to Latin American relations.

Respect for Human Rights

In his dealings with other nations, Carter expressed a "clear-cut preference for those societies which share with us an abiding respect for human rights." His administration cut off military and economic support to several Latin American governments considered dictatorial and repressive. Carter also strongly condemned the Soviet Union for imprisoning people who protested government policies and for not allowing more of its Jewish citizens to emigrate.

Tension Over Afghanistan

Tension between the United States and the Soviet Union heightened when Soviet troops invaded Afghanistan late in 1979. In keeping with Carter's noninterventionist policy, the United States refrained from sending troops to the area. Instead, the President imposed an embargo on the sale of grain to the Soviet Union and called for a boycott of the 1980 Summer Olympic Games to be held in Moscow.

■ The Troubled Middle East

Carter's greatest foreign policy triumph and his greatest failure involved the Middle East. Since its early history, the region had been troubled by deep political and religious conflicts. Carter acknowledged that:

Visualizing History

▲ **AGREEMENT AT CAMP DAVID** President Carter meets with Egyptian President Anwar el-Sadat (left) and Israeli Prime Minister Menachem Begin (right) to sign the Camp David Peace Accords. *What was the goal of the agreement?*

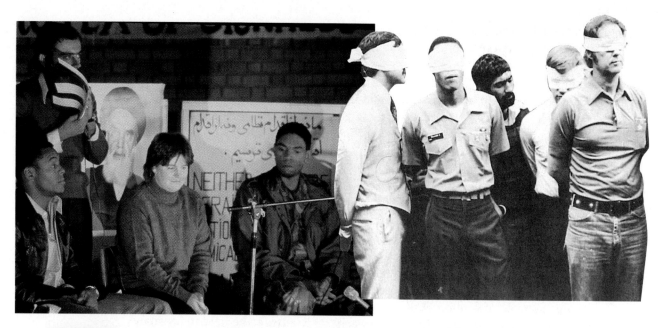

Visualizing History

▲ HOSTAGE CRISIS In November 1979 Iranian radicals seized more than 50 Americans as hostages. President Carter condemned the action as "an act of terrorism outside the boundaries of international law." *What actions did Carter take to resolve the crisis?*

" *[The Middle East] has long been a textbook for pessimism, a demonstration that diplomatic ingenuity was no match for intractable human conflicts.* "

The Camp David Accords

Despite this view, President Carter made a bold move to negotiate a peace treaty between Egypt and Israel, nations that had been bitter enemies for 30 years. In 1978 Carter brought Egypt's President Anwar el-Sadat and Israel's Prime Minister Menachem Begin together at Camp David, the presidential retreat in Maryland. The leaders talked for 14 days. More than once the discussions broke down, but Carter persisted until the leaders reached an agreement on September 17, 1978. In front of a joint session of Congress, with Sadat and Begin in the gallery, Carter announced:

" *This is the first time that an Arab and an Israeli leader have signed a comprehensive framework for peace. It contains the seeds of a time when the Middle East, with all its vast potential,*

may be a land of human richness and fulfillment, rather than a land of bitterness and continued conflict. "

The Camp David Accords, which were formally signed in 1979, established peace between Egypt and Israel. Most of the other Arab nations expressed strong opposition to the treaty because they felt Egypt should not have acted alone. Also, the issue of the Israeli-occupied territories inhabited by Palestinians was yet to be solved. Still, an important first step toward peace in the Middle East had been taken.

Crisis With Iran

This success, however, could not make up for Carter's inability to resolve the crisis with Iran in 1979. The United States had long supported the Shah of Iran. Iran served as a major supplier of oil and as a reliable buffer against Soviet expansion in the Middle East. Yet many Iranians had grown unhappy with the Shah's rule. The Shah had brought Western technology and reform to his people with immense revenues from oil, but these changes had only widened the gap between the wealthy and the extremely poor.

Some Islamic leaders objected to the Western social reforms and customs that had been introduced into Iran, claiming that they ran contrary to their religious traditions. Huge protests forced the Shah to flee in 1979, and an Islamic republic replaced the monarchy.

The new regime, headed by the religious leader Ayatollah Ruholla Khomeini (koh•MAY•nee), viewed the United States with deep distrust because of its ties with the Shah. Anti-American feelings were so strong that on November 4, 1979, militants stormed the American embassy in Tehran, the Iranian capital, and took hostage more than 50 Americans. The militants threatened to kill the hostages or try them as spies.

Negotiations for the freedom of the hostages were unsuccessful. As pressure mounted to secure their release, Carter felt he had no choice but to launch a military rescue. One morning in April 1980, Americans awoke to the shocking news that a mission to rescue the hostages had failed. Eight members of the rescue team had died in a helicopter crash in Iran. Despite this setback, Carter persisted in his diplomatic efforts to free the hostages.

■ Election of 1980

The hostage crisis became a key issue in Carter's bid for reelection. Carter fought off a strong challenge from Senator Edward Kennedy of Massachusetts for the Democratic nomination. As Election Day grew near, however, the American people became increasingly impatient with the situation in Iran.

The Republicans chose former California governor Ronald Reagan as their candidate. Reagan's chief opponents in the primaries were two moderate Republicans, former United Nations Ambassador George Bush and Illinois Representative John Anderson. After his nomination, Reagan picked Bush as his running mate.

The Republicans adopted a conservative platform calling for reductions in taxes and government spending in order to restore prosperity. The party did endorse higher defense spending to strengthen the role of the United States in world affairs.

Throughout the campaign, Reagan hammered at Carter's lack of leadership and the nation's weak economy. He promised voters economic growth and development. On Election Day, Reagan claimed victory with 51 percent of the popular vote and 489 electoral votes. Carter won 41 percent, with 49 electoral votes. John Anderson and other candidates of minor parties split the rest of the vote. The conservative tide that elected Reagan resulted in a Republican Senate and reduced the Democratic House of Representatives.

President Carter's failure to obtain release of the hostages sealed his defeat. Only after Ronald Reagan was sworn in on January 20, 1981, did Iran release the Americans, ending their 444 days in captivity.

Section 1 ★ Assessment

Checking for Understanding

1. **Define** cartel, double-digit inflation, pork-barrel legislation.

2. **List** three features of Carter's energy program.

Critical Thinking

3. **Evaluating Leaders** Explain why Carter's unwillingness to play politics eroded his support in Congress.

4. **Summarizing** Re-create the diagram shown here to list President Carter's successes and failures in dealings with the nations of the Middle East.

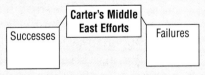

INTERDISCIPLINARY ACTIVITY

5. Government Write an appropriate speech for Jimmy Carter during his reelection campaign.

★★★

A Conservative Shift

Main Idea

Frustrated by the nation's foreign and domestic problems, Americans elected a new President, Ronald Reagan, to restore their confidence in the future.

Reading Strategy

Classifying Information As you read about Ronald Reagan's presidency, use a chart like the one shown here to list Reagan's economic measures, called "Reaganomics," and their ultimate results.

Reaganomics	
Measures	Results

Objectives

After studying this section, you should be able to

★ explain the conservative shift in Americans' political convictions in the late 1970s and early 1980s.

★ describe President Reagan's economic recovery plan, which included cutting taxes and reducing spending.

★ describe Reagan's foreign policy regarding the Soviet Union.

Key Terms

supply-side economics, federal deficit, glasnost, perestroika, privatized

▶ REPUBLICAN PARTY SYMBOL

Reagan's election indicated a significant conservative shift in Americans' political convictions. In addition to support from traditionally conservative groups such as fundamentalist Christians and antifeminists, many groups that had historically voted Democratic broke with their party and supported Reagan. These included former liberals, blue-collar workers, ethnic voters, and Southerners, who became known as "Reagan Democrats." The 69-year-old Reagan also attracted many older voters.

As a whole, the Reagan conservatives believed that the federal government should withdraw from most areas of domestic life.

They were against liberal social programs and government restrictions on business. In foreign policy, they favored a strong military to stand against communism.

■ Reagan's Economic Program

President Reagan acted quickly to limit the size of the federal government. His first act as President was to place a freeze on the hiring of federal employees. At the same time, he began to ease government controls on many business activities. He set up a task force headed by Vice President Bush to review federal regulations. As President, Reagan moved to fulfill his campaign promise to get the economy going again. In February 1981, he told Americans:

❝ *Since 1960 our government has spent $5.1 trillion. Our debt has grown to $648 billion. Prices have exploded by 178 percent. . . . [We] know we must act and act now. We must not be timid. . . .* ❞

To take care of the problem, Reagan proposed a new economic program, which came to be called "Reaganomics."

Cutting Taxes

The first part of the President's program was to make deep cuts in federal taxes. He predicted that income tax reductions would increase consumer spending and would also encourage investments, especially by the wealthy. Similarly, cuts in corporate taxes would allow companies to expand production and hire more workers. Reagan's beliefs were based on an economic theory called **supply-side economics,** which claimed that the economy could best be stimulated by increasing the supply of goods rather than the demand.

Reducing Government Spending

The second part of Reagan's program was to reduce government spending by ending federal job-training programs and cutting back the amount of federal money going into Medicare, food stamps, and education. Critics predicted that Reagan's proposal would cause great suffering for the economically disadvantaged. Reagan denied this, claiming that there would always be a "safety net" of government aid for truly needy Americans.

■ Results of Reaganomics

Although the President faced opposition to his proposals, he had personal qualities that helped to promote his position: a great ability to communicate with his audience and a sense of humor. In March 1981, when he was shot and seriously wounded, the

Visualizing History

▲ **ASSASSINATION ATTEMPT** In March 1981 President Reagan survived an attempt on his life outside a Washington hotel. His press secretary, a police officer, and a Secret Service agent were also wounded. *What was Reagan's chief concern when he took office?*

▲ A POPULAR PRESIDENT Some observers noted that President Reagan's strong victories in the 1980 and 1984 elections were due to his personal appeal as well as to growing public support for his conservative policies. *Who were the Democratic candidates in 1984?*

President's aides visited him in the hospital. They assured him that the business of government was continuing as usual. "What makes you think I'd be happy about that?" Reagan quipped.

With his great popularity and shrewd handling of Congress, Reagan soon got much of his economic program passed. The final bill included $39 billion in tax cuts and a 25 percent cut in income taxes. The results of Reaganomics, however, were not quite what the President had hoped. Spending cuts, together with high interest rates, brought inflation down, but at first the cure was painful.

Recession

In 1982 a severe economic recession occurred. Business bankruptcies, factory closings, and farm foreclosures increased at alarming rates. By the end of the year, more than 11 million Americans—10 percent of the workforce—were jobless. Blaming President Reagan's economic programs for the recession, the Democrats won back many seats in the congressional elections.

Recovery

By 1983, however, the economy began to turn around. The Federal Reserve Board lowered interest rates, making it easier for businesses and individuals to borrow money. The inflation rate dropped just as the 25-percent cut in income taxes was putting more money into the hands of consumers. Feeling new confidence in the economy, Americans made purchases they had put off during the recession. Sales of every type of goods and service shot upward, and industries hired back workers who had been laid off during the recession. By the end of Reagan's second term in 1988, unemployment had dropped to 5.5 percent—the lowest in 14 years.

To hail the recovery, President Reagan declared to Congress in 1984, "America is back—standing tall, looking to the '80s with courage, confidence, and hope. . . . Send away the hand-wringers and doubting Thomases."

The Federal Debt Increases

Although Reagan promised to balance the budget, the federal debt greatly increased during his first term. He cut taxes, which meant the government received less revenue. In addition, Congress, now controlled by the Democrats, refused to make the deeper cuts in social programs that Reagan requested. On top of that, Reagan himself increased government spending in certain areas, especially defense. The result was the most unbalanced budget in American history.

By 1984 the **federal deficit,** or the difference between the amount of money the government took in and what it spent, was nearly $200 billion a year. When the government spends more money than it collects, it has to borrow to make up the difference. The more the government borrows, the more interest it owes on its debts. In 1984 the interest alone on the federal debt amounted to $153.8 billion, an increase of more than $55 billion from Reagan's first year in office.

■ Election of 1984

Despite the federal deficit, Reagan was still popular, and the economy had made a healthy recovery. These factors made Reagan a formidable candidate for President in the 1984 election. To run against him, the Democrats nominated a traditional liberal, former Vice President Walter Mondale. Mondale created a precedent by choosing Representative Geraldine Ferraro of New York to run as his Vice President. She was the first woman candidate from a major party to run for this office.

Mondale claimed that Reagan's tax and budget cuts benefited only the wealthy. Reagan countered that his economic program had aided all Americans by sharply reducing inflation. To cut the deficit, Mondale proposed raising taxes, always an unpopular step. Reagan, however, continued to oppose any increases and insisted that economic expansion and deeper cuts in government spending would reduce the deficit.

In November Americans gave the President an overwhelming vote of confidence. On Election Day, Reagan won the biggest electoral margin in history.

■ A Conservative Court

With this tremendous mandate, Reagan began his second term confident in his policies. One of his priorities was to appoint conservative justices to the Supreme Court and the lower federal courts. In 1981, the President had appointed Sandra Day O'Connor, the first woman to serve on the Court. In 1986 Reagan selected Antonin Scalia, and a year later he chose Anthony M. Kennedy.

With Reagan's appointees in place, the Supreme Court began to hand down the kind of conservative rulings for which Reagan had hoped. For example, one decision cut back affirmative action programs that had benefited minorities.

■ Strengthening America's Defenses

President Reagan supported America's space program, both as a means of restoring the nation's self-confidence and strengthening its defenses. Americans took pride in their successes in space exploration, and the launch of reusable space shuttles marked a new era in the space program.

Support for SDI

Reagan had a special interest in the military aspects of the space program. In 1983 he announced a new research project to create a shield that would intercept and destroy nuclear ballistic missiles. It was called the Strategic Defense Initiative (SDI), nicknamed "Star Wars." Opponents feared that SDI would stimulate an intensified nuclear competition between the United States and the Soviet Union. Reagan and the project's supporters, however, believed SDI would improve chances of nuclear disarmament.

HISTORY Online

Student Web Activity
Visit the *American History: The Modern Era Since 1865* Web site at **me.glencoe.com** and click on *Chapter 25— Student Web Activities* for an activity about NASA.

Military Buildup

In addition to Star Wars, Reagan also promoted a military buildup, including new bombers, submarines, and missiles and better training for ground troops. Other aspects of his defense program included placing new nuclear missiles in Europe, basing intercontinental missiles in Western states, and developing expensive new B-2 "stealth" bombers. Stealth bombers are military aircraft designed so that radar cannot easily detect them.

The Cost of Defense

Aside from Star Wars, Reagan's military buildup cost $1 trillion. This caused a sharp rise in the federal deficit. As the deficit increased, a greater share of tax revenues went to pay the interest on the national debt. This left less money available for new programs in education, the environment, and public housing.

Congress responded in 1985 by passing the Gramm-Rudman Act, which put greater pressure on Congress and the President to reach agreement on reducing the budget. If they were unable to reduce the annual deficit to certain limits, this legislation set up automatic, across-the-board federal spending cuts.

Reagan, however, still refused to increase income taxes. He was able to maintain this position only because in 1986 a great drop in oil prices occurred. Fear of inflation lessened as interest rates dropped. Nevertheless, by 1988 the national debt had reached $2.3 trillion.

■ Improved Relations with the Soviet Union

Reagan's desire for a strong defense was based on his belief that the Soviet Union, which he called an "evil empire," was a serious threat to the United States. He aimed to contain and counter communism throughout the world, and he followed this policy until relations with the Soviet Union suddenly began to improve.

When Mikhail Gorbachev (GAWR•buh•CHAWF) became Soviet premier, his country's economy, which was highly centralized under the control of the Communist party, was on the verge of collapse. For decades,

 Visualizing History

▲ THE CHALLENGER DISASTER On January 28, 1986, the space shuttle *Challenger* exploded in space, killing all seven astronauts on board. The tragedy temporarily halted the space program. ***What innovation had the shuttle introduced?***

Physical Fitness

Ronald Reagan was one of the oldest Presidents and one of the fittest. He kept trim by riding horses and chopping wood. Thanks in part to Reagan's example, interest in physical fitness bloomed.

Then

The Benefits of Exercise

Tracking individuals over many years, scientists studied the effect of exercise on the body. They concluded that physical inactivity is a significant factor in the development of several major illnesses including heart disease. They also found that regular exercise increased fitness and health. Health professionals of the 1970s and 1980s stressed the benefits of aerobic exercise. Jogging, aerobic dance, exercise bikes, rowing machines, and mini-trampolines were familiar fitness activities of the time.

Now

A Healthy Trend

The fitness boom of the 1980s continued in the mid-1990s. Walking and jogging trails and bicycle paths were developed in neighborhoods all over the country. About 70 million Americans made exercise a part of their regular schedule.

In one year, about 300,000 Americans took part in middle-distance triathlons, three-part races in which they biked for 25 miles, ran 6.2 miles, and swam 1 mile. In that same year, about 250,000 Americans ran in marathons, which are 26.2 miles long.

---

the party had focused on building up the Soviet Union's position as a superpower and neglected the needs of the people. As a result, farms and factories underproduced and the standard of living was low. The centralized communist system of government was also showing serious strain. The people had no voice and had grown very apathetic in the face of total party control.

Gorbachev Sets New Policy

To save his country and party, Gorbachev set some new policies. First, he introduced **glasnost,** meaning "openness." This policy gave people the right to speak freely—and, Gorbachev hoped, in support of his reforms. Then Gorbachev began **perestroika,** a restructuring of the economy and the government. Instead of party officials deciding everything from Moscow, local farm and factory managers now had the power to make some decisions. The nation's businesses were **privatized,** or transferred from government to private ownership. To lessen the party's control of government, Gorbachev scheduled the first elections in 70 years in which the people had a real choice.

Gorbachev Makes an Astounding Offer

Gorbachev knew that if the arms race could be halted, it would free people and money to produce consumer goods in the Soviet Union. Peace would also allow him to concentrate all his energies on domestic reforms, and could lead to trade agreements and economic aid from the West. So, Gorbachev made the United States an astounding offer, announcing that the Soviet Union would reduce its nuclear weapons.

Reagan and Gorbachev Hold Summit Meeting

When Reagan and Gorbachev met at Reykjavík, Iceland, in 1986, the two leaders tried but could not come to an agreement on the issue of the Strategic Defense Initiative.

Reagan insisted on pursuing it, and Gorbachev opposed it. When they met again a year later at Washington, D.C., however, they signed a treaty calling for the removal of all intermediate-range nuclear weapons from Europe. This was the first agreement that eliminated an entire class of nuclear weapons. Unbelievably, the cold war was slowly coming to an end.

Along with agreeing to limit nuclear weapons, Gorbachev took other surprising steps that affected international relations. Admitting that the Soviet Union's intervention in Afghanistan had been "morally wrong," he withdrew Soviet troops. He also released political prisoners and allowed freer emigration of Soviet Jews.

■ A Hands-Off Presidency

Although Reagan was a strong leader when it came to establishing public policy, he adopted a "hands-off" attitude toward the day-to-day operations of the presidency. This attitude led to scandals that would tarnish Reagan's final years in office, though he remained popular.

A Master of Delegation

Reagan gave far greater responsibilities to his staff than any other recent President had. The President's detachment allowed his subordinates to function independently. Some acted for financial gain. Others made policy on their own.

The Iran-Contra Scandal

The worst fiasco to hit the Reagan administration was the Iran-contra scandal of 1986. Several of the President's national security aides, including John Poindexter, Robert McFarland, and Lieutenant Colonel Oliver North, had schemed to sell weapons to the Iranians to win the release of American hostages in the Middle East. Then they had diverted the profits from these arms sales to the *contras*, Nicaraguan guerrillas who were fighting to topple the Sandanista government ruling the nation. This was a violation of a congressional ban on such financing.

Critics charged that an undercover foreign policy was being carried out against the express will of Congress. Defenders maintained that the executive branch was forced to take these measures because of congressional interference with the President's authority to conduct foreign policy. A special commission was set up to study the Iran-contra case. Although the commission cleared the President of direct blame, it found fault with Reagan for allowing aides to make policy decisions without his knowledge.

The Iran-contra scandal helped the Democrats win back a Senate majority in 1986. The election produced a divided government—with the presidency held by the Republican party and control of Congress held by the Democrats. Democratic majorities in Congress acted as a brake on the Reagan administration.

Section 2 ★ Assessment

Checking for Understanding

1. **Define** supply-side economics, federal deficit, glasnost, perestroika, privatized.
2. **Describe** the political philosophy of Reagan conservatives.

Critical Thinking

3. **Evaluating Policies** Evaluate whether technology such as the SDI will help prevent nuclear war.

4. **Analyzing Issues** Re-create the diagram shown here to list the key events in President Reagan's dealings with the Soviet Union.

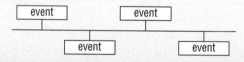

INTERDISCIPLINARY ACTIVITY

5. **Government** List in order the three qualities you think are most important for a President and explain why.

BUILDING SKILLS
Social Studies Skills

Reading a Bar Graph

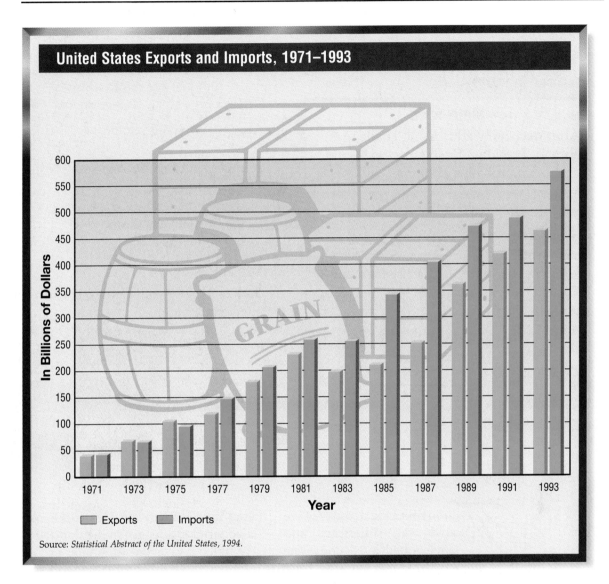

United States Exports and Imports, 1971–1993

In Billions of Dollars

Year

☐ Exports   ☐ Imports

Source: *Statistical Abstract of the United States, 1994.*

Learning the Skill

Like line graphs, bar graphs are used to compare facts involving numbers. Bars, or columns, of different lengths are used to represent quantities or totals. Some bar graphs show changes over time much like line graphs. Bar graphs can also be used to compare quantities during the same time period. Like line graphs, bar graphs have horizontal and vertical axes that describe the information presented in the graph. Study the graph and answer the question that follows.

Practicing the Skill

1. Analyze the trends for both exports and imports from 1971 to 1993.

Glencoe's **Skillbuilder Interactive Workbook, Level 2** provides instruction and practice in key social studies skills.

APPLYING THE SKILL

2. Review the subsection on page 757 entitled "Election of 1984." Create a bar graph that depicts the electoral vote totals.

761

★★★★★★★★★★★★★★★★★★★★★★★★★★★★★★★

A New Presidency

Guide to Reading

Main Idea

After decisively addressing challenges abroad, President Bush struggled with economic problems at home.

Reading Strategy

Organizing Information As you read about George Bush's presidency, use a diagram like the one shown here to describe the changes in Eastern Europe that resulted from the collapse of the Soviet Union.

```
Changes in
Eastern Europe
```

Objectives

After studying this section, you should be able to

★ describe America's role in the post-cold war world.

★ discuss the reasons for discord between the legislative and executive branches of government under Bush.

Key Terms

coup d'état, drawdown, user tax, junk bond, underemployed

ROAD SIGN IN KUWAIT ▶

Throughout the decades of the cold war, Americans and Soviets had lived under the threat of nuclear war as each side built mighty arsenals and viewed almost all disputes around the world in terms of the East-West struggle. Then, with almost surprising suddenness, democratic movements erupted throughout the Soviet Union's Eastern European satellites. Popular demands for political, social, and economic reform toppled one communist government after another. Eventually, even the Soviet Union itself split into independent republics.

Without a Soviet adversary, the United States was the only superpower left. It faced the critical challenge of establishing a new role in world affairs, which was tested when

Iraq invaded Kuwait. Meanwhile, America also faced challenges in the domestic arena. Troubled by severe economic problems, a divided government tried to work toward a solution.

■ Election of 1988

In the election of 1988, there was tough competition for both the Republican and Democratic presidential nominations. In the end, the Republicans selected Vice President George Bush. The final Democratic contenders were the Reverend Jesse Jackson and Massachusetts Governor Michael Dukakis. Jackson, who appealed to a "rainbow coalition" of minorities and reformers, picked up support along the way and ran a much stronger race than expected. Dukakis, however, won the nomination.

Early in the race, Dukakis led Bush in the public polls. Then Bush's campaign team unleashed a string of negative television advertisements that portrayed the liberal Dukakis as unpatriotic and soft on criminals. Dukakis, however, failed to respond strongly to these charges. As a result, Dukakis lost his lead to Bush. Slick television commercials seemed to replace debating real issues.

Saying, "Read my lips," the Vice President pledged not to raise taxes. Bush also promised the nation that if elected he would follow Reagan's economic policies. On Election Day he won a resounding victory, taking 40 of the 50 states, with 49 million popular votes and 426 electoral votes. Dukakis had 42 million popular votes and 112 electoral votes.

■ A Tidal Wave of Change

George Bush came to the presidency with a great deal of experience in foreign policy.

In addition to being Vice President, he had been ambassador to the United Nations, ambassador to China, and director of the CIA. This training served Bush well, for he was immediately confronted with a tidal wave of change around the world.

Change in Eastern Europe

Gorbachev's new policies in the Soviet Union triggered demands for change in Eastern Europe. In 1989 the people of the satellite nations of Poland, Hungary, Czechoslovakia, Bulgaria, Romania, and East Germany overthrew their communist rulers and forced democratic elections. When the East German government fell, crowds tore down the Berlin Wall that had divided Germany and symbolized the "iron curtain" that separated Eastern Europe and Western Europe.

The end of the cold war allowed some countries to renew and rethink relationships. In October 1990, East Germany and West Germany reunited. As Western European nations took steps toward political and economic union, Eastern Europe sought to

Visualizing History

▲ THE BARRIER FALLS In November 1989 the Berlin Wall, which had separated the two Germanys since 1961, was opened. On the first weekend after the wall was opened, 3 million visitors crossed from East Berlin to visit West Berlin. *What had the Berlin Wall symbolized?*

forge new ties with them—especially economic ones. In July 1991, the Warsaw Pact between Eastern Europe and the Soviet Union was terminated. This left the future of NATO, which was also a military alliance, in doubt.

The Collapse of the Soviet Union

The loss of Eastern Europe was only the beginning. Despite Gorbachev's efforts to save his country, the Soviet Union itself collapsed. Glasnost and perestroika had unleashed two forces that would bring it down. One was the people's demand for democracy. The other was the desire of different ethnic groups for self-rule; the Soviet Union had been organized without regard for ethnic boundaries. As rumblings for independence began, Gorbachev even dispatched troops to preserve the Soviet Union.

The catalyst came in August 1991 when a group of hard-line Communists attempted a **coup d'état,** or a sudden revolt, and proclaimed an old-style communist government. The plotters arrested Gorbachev and ordered troops to Moscow. They failed, however, to take into account Boris Yeltsin, the recently elected president of the Russian Republic. Appearing before crowds gathered in front of the Russian parliament building, Yeltsin condemned the coup and called for the people's help. To protect him, tens of thousands of Moscow's citizens stood guard unarmed, ready to face down an expected attack. The soldiers refused to carry out orders, and the coup collapsed. Gorbachev was back in office, but Yeltsin now held the real power.

Both men knew that the Communist party had been behind the coup. Soon, Gorbachev stepped down as general secretary and abolished the party. Without communism holding the Soviet state together, the country itself shattered. Republic after republic declared its independence.

On December 25, 1991, Gorbachev formally resigned as Soviet president, saying, "We are living in a new world." His resignation marked the end of what was left of the Soviet Union. By this time, 11 of the 15 former republics had organized a loose union called the Commonwealth of Independent States (CIS).

Colin Powell
1937–

★★★★★★★★★★★ AMERICAN PORTRAITS

Born in New York of Jamaican immigrants, Colin Powell grew up in Harlem and the South Bronx. He recounts in his 1995 autobiography *My American Journey* that his "inability to stick to anything became a source of concern to my parents." Only after he enrolled in his college's Reserve Officers Training Corps (ROTC), did he find a focus: "I put the uniform on and looked in the mirror. I liked what I saw. . . . I felt distinctive."

An infantry officer in the Vietnam War, he was decorated for bravery. In the 1970s, Powell began to rise up the chain of command, receiving ever more important military and political appointments. Then, in 1988, he was named Chairman of the Joint Chiefs of Staff, the first African American to hold the office.

Military experts consider Powell a talented officer with tremendous organizational and leadership qualities. Some even called his management of Operations Desert Shield and Desert Storm "masterful." Powell retired in 1993 as Chairman of the Joint Chiefs of Staff, leaving open the possibility of a political career.

Troubles in the New States

All the former Soviet and communist bloc states faced serious economic troubles. In trying to set up capitalist economies, the new governments began lifting state controls on economies already in decline. So production fell, prices rose, and unemployment spread. People suffered from shortages of fuel, food, medicine, and housing.

Another problem was ethnic rivalry. Without tight communist control there was a rise of nationalism, and old hatreds surfaced. These hatreds led to the outbreak of bloody civil wars in many states. The worst was in what was formerly Yugoslavia.

Although Western nations, including the United States, quickly recognized the new countries, they were uncertain what kind of aid to send. Some people wanted to send cash to help support the new democracies. Others feared even a non-communist Russia might someday threaten world security and favored increasing trade and sending advisers, along with food and medicine. For the most part the United States government followed the latter course.

Part of the reason the United States was concerned about Russia was that it had most of the former Soviet Union's nuclear weapons. In 1992, Bush and Yeltsin met at Camp David and agreed to drastic reductions. Afterward, the President declared that the meeting marked "a new relationship based on trust, based on a commitment to economic and political freedom."

■ The Persian Gulf War

Meanwhile, the Persian Gulf War gave President Bush an opportunity to further define America's role in the post-cold war world. On August 2, 1990, Iraq's president, Saddam Hussein, sent invasion forces into Kuwait, its oil-rich neighbor. To punish this aggression, Bush froze $20 billion of Iraqi money in American banks and banned imports of Iraqi oil. The United Nations demanded that Saddam Hussein withdraw his forces and called for countries throughout the world to halt all trade with Iraq. But Iraqi troops remained in Kuwait.

Operation Desert Shield

Bush, with assistance from 25 nations around the world, assembled a huge military coalition he called "Operation Desert Shield." The United Nations then authorized military action to restore Kuwait's independence. The coalition waited for 6 months, however, hoping that diplomacy and the threat of force would prevent a war.

Operation Desert Storm

Finally, Bush initiated Operation Desert Storm. He ordered massive air strikes against Iraq on January 16, 1991, rejecting calls for further delay:

Visualizing History ▲ THE PERSIAN GULF WAR In January 1991 the United States launched a massive air and missile assault on Iraq after Iraq refused to withdraw from Kuwait. *Why had Iraq invaded Kuwait?*

▲ COMING HOME American military personnel return after taking part in Operation Desert Storm. Coalition forces took part in the military action after diplomatic efforts failed. *Who was the military leader of the operation?*

66 *The world could wait no longer. ... While the world waited, Saddam Hussein met every overture of peace with open contempt. While the world prayed for peace, Saddam Hussein prepared for war.* 99

After a month of bombing, General Norman Schwarzkopf led a lightning-swift ground assault. Just 100 hours later, Allied forces had crushed the Iraqi army and freed the Kuwaiti people. "Kuwait is liberated," Bush announced. "America and the world have kept their word."

■ Rethinking America's Military Role

The Persian Gulf War caused people in the United States to begin rethinking America's military role in the world. Some leaders felt the United States should scale down its military. They pointed out that the source of a country's power in the new world order promised to be its economy rather than its military. Examples of just such a change were evident by the emergence of Germany and Japan. So, as the federal deficits skyrocketed, Bush called for cuts in defense spending, and Congress made even greater reductions. The Pentagon planned a **drawdown** that would bring troops home from overseas bases in Europe and Asia.

Other experts, however, warned that the United States should maintain a strong military—and that the cost would be worth it. They pointed out that Cuba, North Korea, Vietnam, and the People's Republic of China remained communist nations. Although China had shown some signs of change by instituting various free-market programs, its Communist party leaders had massacred pro-democracy demonstrators at Beijing's Tiananmen Square in 1989.

■ Divided Government

Whereas President Bush acted decisively in foreign affairs, he was accused of wavering leadership at home. Part of the problem was that the government was divided again, with the presidency held by one party and Congress controlled by the other. During the Bush administration, this hindered the process of government.

Bush and Congress in Gridlock

Congress ignored or drastically changed many of the President's proposals. The President, in turn, vetoed many bills, knowing that the Democrats generally lacked the two-thirds vote needed to override his vetoes. The executive and legislative branches of the government quickly became gridlocked over such issues as reforming campaign financing, improving public education, recharging the economy, reducing the federal deficit, and balancing the budget.

Taxation Issues

When the federal deficit rose to a record level of $300 billion, Bush realized he would have to increase revenues. To do so, however, he was forced to break his campaign pledge of "no new taxes." In 1992, after weeks of negotiations with Democratic congressional leaders, Bush agreed to raise some taxes. Among these were gasoline, tobacco, and other **user taxes,** or taxes on products used by consumers. The President also agreed to make deep cuts in Medicare and military spending. Although this plan was defeated by conservative Republicans, the President and congressional leaders finally hammered out a compromise bill.

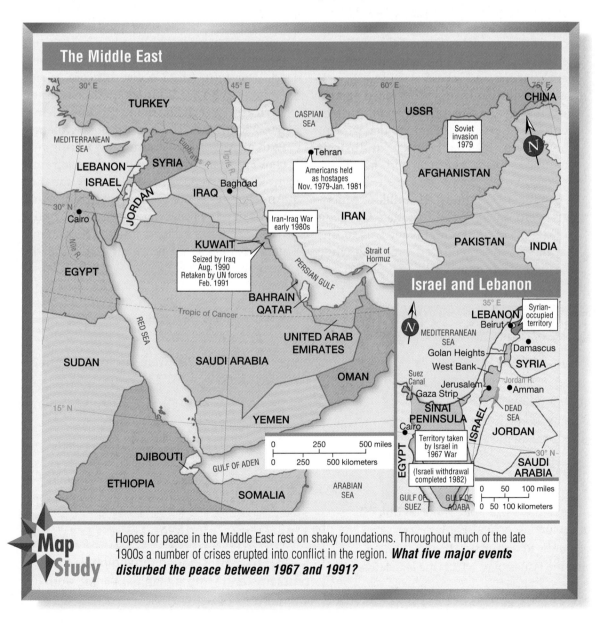

The Middle East

Israel and Lebanon

Map Study

Hopes for peace in the Middle East rest on shaky foundations. Throughout much of the late 1900s a number of crises erupted into conflict in the region. *What five major events disturbed the peace between 1967 and 1991?*

■ Economic Woes in the Early 1990s

During the Bush administration, the economy grew more slowly than at any time since the end of World War II. Among other factors, sharply rising oil prices following Iraq's invasion of Kuwait threw America into a recession that persisted longer than expected.

The long recession was partly caused by consumer and corporate debts incurred during the Reagan era. Deregulation had allowed banks and savings and loans (S&Ls) to lend money more freely. Corporations funded mergers with **junk bonds,** or high-risk bonds that offer high yields.

Consumers ran up large debts on credit cards and home mortgages. The federal government, too, spent far more than it received. These debts limited the ability of consumers, corporations, and the government to spend and invest.

As a result, banks and S&Ls failed at rates unseen since the Great Depression. Airlines went out of business. Famous department stores filed for bankruptcy. Industries announced plant closings and layoffs of workers.

By mid-1992, almost 10 million Americans were unemployed. Another 6 million workers were **underemployed.** This means that these people held part-time jobs while looking for full-time work.

The Problem of Homelessness in America

As unemployment rose, people migrated from one state to another in search of jobs, and some found themselves homeless. Homeless people included battered women, runaway children, alcoholics, drug abusers, deinstitutionalized mental patients, and people lacking family support. Homelessness reflected rising rents, lower wages for unskilled workers, and the urgent need for low-cost housing. Estimates of the number of homeless people in America ranged as high as 3 million.

The Los Angeles Riots

The recession, poverty, and homelessness hit particularly hard at African Americans, Hispanics, and other minorities living in inner cities. Racial tensions ignited after four white police officers in Los Angeles who were videotaped beating an African American man, Rodney King, were acquitted. The city erupted violently with acts of arson, looting, and rioting that claimed more lives than had the 1965 riots in Watts. Conservatives blamed the Los Angeles riots on welfare programs that weakened the family and individual initiative. Liberals blamed the government's general neglect of inner cities during the Reagan-Bush years.

Section 3 ★ Assessment

Checking for Understanding

1. **Define** coup d'état, drawdown, user tax, junk bond, underemployed.

2. **Discuss** the reason why the United States resorted to force against Iraq.

Critical Thinking

3. **Identifying Alternatives** In your opinion, should Presidents concentrate more on domestic issues or on foreign policy? Explain your answer.

4. **Summarizing** Re-create the diagram shown here to list the issues over which the legislative and executive branches were gridlocked during the Bush presidency.

Issues Affected by Gridlock

INTERDISCIPLINARY ACTIVITY

5. **Government** Choose three global problems and write a plan explaining your solutions.

As the Brain Grows Older

Life expectancy in the United States increased dramatically in the twentieth century. In the early 1900s, most people died before the age of 50. By the year 2000, the average life expectancy will be 80 years for women and 76 for men. Even more significant is the fact that by 2000, 13 percent of all Americans will be 65 years of age or older. By 2025, one-fourth the population will be over age 65.

The aging population has prompted scientists to study the changes that occur in the brain with age. What these studies show is that the brain loses little functioning during most of the adult years. After age 65, deterioration in memory, spatial skills, and reasoning begins. What is most noticeable in the over-65 population, however, is the greater variation in brain function between individuals. That is, some people show only slight mental decline, while others show very noticeable losses. Alzheimer's disease, a

▲ SENIOR CITIZENS HIKING

condition that limits brain functioning, especially in memory, language, reasoning, and spatial abilities, afflicts millions of older adults in this country.

Research in the 1990s has centered on ways that older individuals can maintain or regain their intellectual strength. Just as diet and exercise have been shown to have a direct impact on physical fitness, researchers hope to identify educational, nutritional, and medical breakthroughs that can build mental fitness.

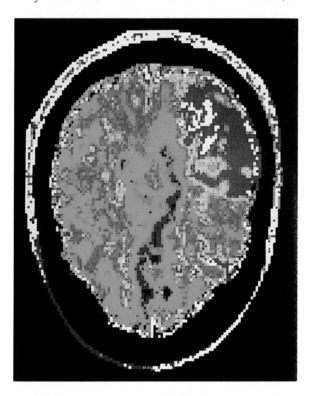

▲ BRAIN SCAN

Making the Science Connection

1. How does brain functioning change with age?

2. Describe two educational or nutritional factors that could be studied in relation to brain function.

Linking Past and Present

3. Why are declines in brain function and diseases such as Alzheimer's of particular significance at this time?

ACTIVITY

4. Research and write a report showing medical progress during the past 25 years on Alzheimer's disease.

Using Vocabulary

On a separate sheet of paper, write three headings: *Carter, Reagan, Bush.* Classify each of the following terms under the Presidents to which they are related. Some terms belong in more than one category.

double-digit inflation	pork-barrel legislation
supply-side economics	federal deficit
coup d'état	perestroika
user taxes	drawdown
	underemployed

Reviewing Facts

1. Explain how Carter's election was partly a result of Watergate.

2. Describe why Ronald Reagan appealed to the American people.

3. Explain how the problems between Kuwait and Iraq helped define America's new role in world affairs.

Understanding Concepts

Political Ideology

1. Re-create the diagram shown here, and describe the images of Carter and Reagan and how the images affected their public support.

Carter's Image	→	Public Support
Reagan's Image	→	Public Support

Leadership

2. How does the role of the United States government in the economy during the 1980s and 1990s compare to its role during the early 1900s?

Critical Thinking

1. **Assessing Programs** The United States has had difficulty implementing an energy policy. Evaluate Carter's energy program. Explain why it was only partially successful.

2. **Analyzing Media** Television in the 1990s has exposed Americans to an unprecedented amount of news and information.

   a. In what ways does television benefit society?

   b. Do you think the overall effect of television is a positive one or a negative one? Explain.

History and Geography

The Middle East

Use the map on page 767 and information from Chapter 25 to help you answer these questions.

1. **Region** What body of water separates Saudi Arabia from Sudan?

2. **Place** Why did Iraq invade Kuwait?

Federal Budget, 1945–1994

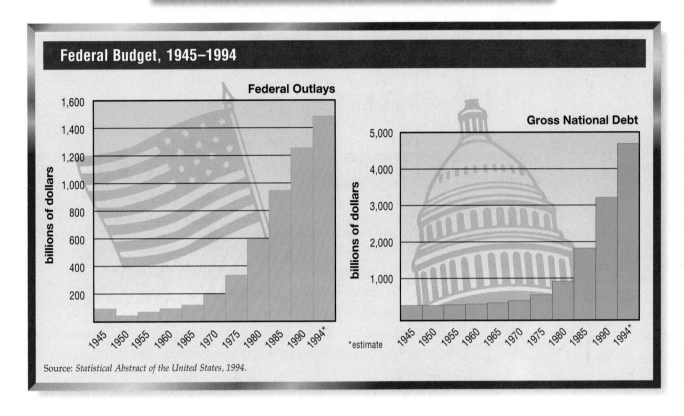

Federal Outlays

Gross National Debt

Source: *Statistical Abstract of the United States, 1994.*

Interdisciplinary Activity: Economics

Cooperative Learning

Organize into four groups to research and analyze the two ways to reduce the federal deficit. Two groups will research and present arguments for and against raising taxes. The other two groups will research and present arguments for and against reduced government spending.

Practicing Skills

Reading a Bar Graph

Study the bar graphs on this page, then answer the questions that follow.

1. When did federal outlays surpass $400 billion?

2. Describe the trends shown in each graph.

Technology Activity

Using the Internet

Search the Internet for information about one of the foreign countries mentioned in this chapter. Write a short description of what a traveler visiting this nation might expect to find.

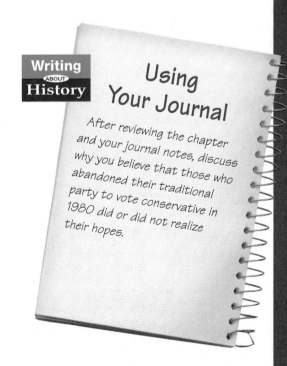

Writing ABOUT History

Using Your Journal

After reviewing the chapter and your journal notes, discuss why you believe that those who abandoned their traditional party to vote conservative in 1980 did or did not realize their hopes.

CHAPTER 26

Toward a New Century
1992–Present

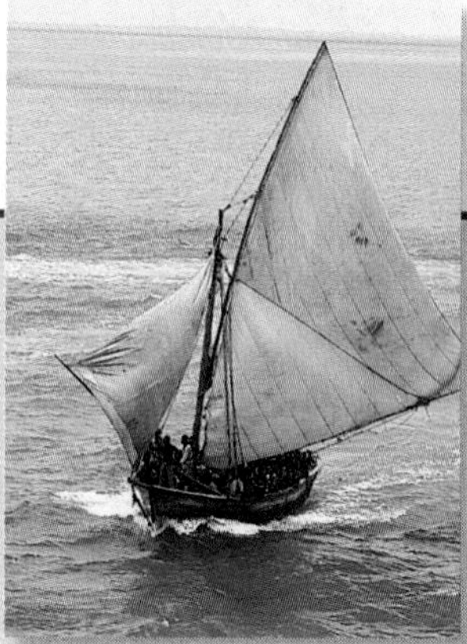

▶ HAITIAN REFUGEE BOAT

Setting the Scene

Focus

As 1992 dawned, the cold war had ended and a new world order was emerging. Instead of being sharply divided by the East-West conflict, nations were becoming more integrated, and their leaders were acquiring a more global outlook. As the United States struggled to define its role in this new world, urgent concerns at home threatened changes in government. Despite attempts by political leaders to be more responsive to the needs of the American people, voter dissatisfaction continued to grow.

Concepts to Understand

★ What **changes** occurred in government as a result of Clinton's election

★ How Americans were dealing with the **challenges** they faced

Read to Discover . . .

★ how Clinton's policies—both domestic and foreign—affected Americans.

★ what challenges face the American government and people in the future.

Journal Notes

What do you think it would be like to be an immigrant from another country coming to the United States during the 1990s? Note details about it in your journal as you read the chapter.

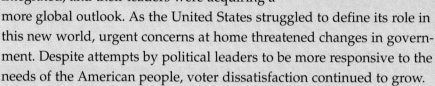

HISTORY Online

Chapter Overview

Visit the *American History: The Modern Era Since 1865* Web site at **me.glencoe.com** and click on ***Chapter 26—Chapter Overviews*** to preview chapter information.

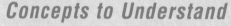

	1992	1993	1994
CULTURAL	• *Eric Clapton's "Unplugged" wins Grammy award*	• *Americorps helps student education* • *Projections show Hispanics as largest minority by 2010*	• *Scientists estimate 1 million Americans have HIV*
POLITICAL	• *Bill Clinton is elected President* • *Yugoslav Federation breaks up*	• *Israel and PLO negotiate peace with American help* • *Congress approves NAFTA*	• *Israel and Jordan, assisted by United States, sign peace treaty* • *Republicans sweep midterm elections*

History AND ART

Earth
by David Lawrence, 1994

New technology has opened new avenues for artists. Computer-manipulated art combines actual photography and computer art to create a new image.

◀ **DNA,** COMPUTER MODEL

- *Internet revolutionizes communications*
- *Myrlie Evers-Williams leads NAACP*

- *Number of reported AIDS cases drops for first time*

- *Denver Broncos win second straight Super Bowl*

1995	1996	1999

- *President Clinton authorizes $20 billion in loans and loan guarantees to Mexico*

- *Welfare Reform Act ends "welfare as we know it"*
- *President Clinton is elected to second term*

- *President Clinton is acquitted by the Senate after being impeached*

★★★

Reinventing Government

Guide to Reading

Main Idea

Elected amid cries for change, President Clinton had a stormy relationship with Congress and weathered the first presidential impeachment since 1868.

Reading Strategy

Organizing Information As you read about the Clinton presidency, use a diagram like the one shown here to list the reasons for Americans' anti-incumbent mood in the early 1990s.

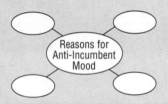

Reasons for Anti-Incumbent Mood

Objectives

After studying this section, you should be able to

★ explain why many Americans demanded a change in government in 1992.

★ explain how gridlock between Congress and the President affected the process of government.

★ explain why Clinton won a second term.

Key Terms

incumbent, line-item veto, appropriations bill, filibuster, downsizing

► MEMORIAL BUTTON, INAUGURATION DAY 1993

At the beginning of the twentieth century, progressives had worked to strengthen and enlarge the small federal government. Their purpose in moving toward this objective was to equip government to handle the social and economic problems caused by industrialization. Toward the end of the century, government had grown so large that more Americans worked in local, state, and national government than in the manufacturing industries.

Many Americans believed government had grown too large, that it taxed too heavily and spent too much. Leaders from both major political parties promised to renovate government and make it more responsive to the needs of the people.

■ Demands for Change

As the election of 1992 approached, many people in the United States expressed demands for change in government. Public opinion had turned against Washington, D.C., "insiders" and **incumbents,** or people currently holding office. Voters blamed incumbents for the recession, the federal deficit, and government gridlock.

Government Scandals

Scandals deepened Americans' anger at incumbents. Revelations that some members of the House of Representatives had bounced checks repeatedly at the House bank outraged the public. They asked

▲ **A Presidential Debate** During the 1992 presidential election, the candidates faced each other in several debates. *Who won the 1992 presidential election?*

how these officials could manage the nation's economy when they bungled their personal finances. Further angered when members of Congress voted to raise their own salaries, many political leaders and citizens took action. Ultimately, the movement led to the ratification in 1992 of the Twenty-seventh Amendment to the Constitution. This amendment prohibited any congressional pay raise from taking effect until after the following election, thus giving the voters a chance to act.

Another uproar followed President Bush's nomination of Clarence Thomas to the Supreme Court in 1991. One of Thomas's former coworkers, law professor Anita Hill, testified before the Senate Judiciary Committee that Thomas had sexually harassed her. Thomas denied the charge.

The Senate narrowly confirmed Thomas to the Supreme Court, but many Americans were angry. Noting the absence of any women on the Senate Judiciary Committee and seeing that only 2 of the 100 senators were women, they argued that "2 percent is not enough." Building on the rising discon-

tent, more women ran for political office. As "outsiders" in politics, women candidates drew support from both women and men.

The Race for President

After victory in the Persian Gulf War, President Bush's reelection seemed assured. Several Democrats declined to run against him. The lengthening recession, however, raised new doubts about his leadership and encouraged challengers to enter the race.

Among the leading Democratic candidates for President was Governor Bill Clinton of Arkansas. Early in the campaign, the press raised questions about Clinton's character and his failure to serve in the armed forces during the Vietnam War. Yet, after victories in the primaries, Clinton won the nomination.

Texas billionaire H. Ross Perot fashioned a strong third-party challenge. Perot had promised to run if volunteers could collect enough petitions to place his name on all 50 state ballots. The outpouring of volunteers expressed demand for change as well as unhappiness with the two major parties.

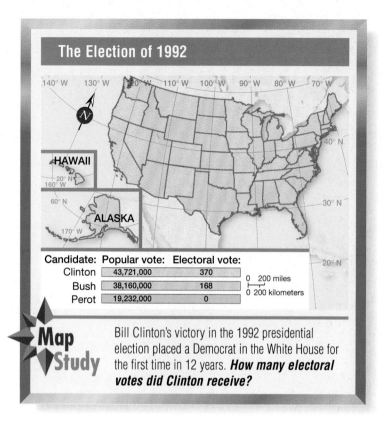

The Election of 1992

Candidate:	Popular vote:	Electoral vote:
Clinton	43,721,000	370
Bush	38,160,000	168
Perot	19,232,000	0

0   200 miles
0 200 kilometers

Map Study

Bill Clinton's victory in the 1992 presidential election placed a Democrat in the White House for the first time in 12 years. *How many electoral votes did Clinton receive?*

Election of 1992

During the campaign, Clinton painted the recession as President Bush's most glaring failure. The challenger made the economy his number-one issue.

About 104 million Americans—the largest number of people ever to go to the polls—voted in the presidential election of 1992. Clinton received 43 percent of the popular vote, while Bush captured 38 percent and Perot 19 percent. Clinton received less than a majority because of Perot's strong showing, the highest for any third-party candidate since 1912.

Democrats retained control of both houses of Congress. Moreover, voters defeated a large number of incumbents and elected a record number of women and minority candidates.

Twenty-four new women members were elected to the House, and four won Senate seats. Nydia Velazquez became the first Puerto Rican woman in the House of Representatives. Carol Moseley Braun of Illinois was the first African American woman senator.

A New Democrat

President Clinton identified himself as a "New Democrat" who put less faith in big government to solve problems than did earlier Democrats. Only 46 years old, Clinton was a complex person who, at times, presented different images to different people. He embraced middle-class values, playing music, jogging, and exhibiting a taste for fast foods.

Yet Clinton had graduated from such elite institutions as Georgetown University and the Yale Law School and had attended Oxford University as a Rhodes scholar. Reflecting a tension between these two facets of his personality, Clinton changed positions on a number of issues as he sought a middle ground. Critics complained that these shifts showed that Clinton was a compromiser rather than a committed leader.

Taxes

As a candidate, Clinton had called for a tax cut along with new spending to stimulate the economy. Soon after he took office, Clinton learned that the federal deficit would be even bigger than estimated. As a result, Clinton concluded that reducing the deficit would put the government in a stronger position to respond to future economic problems. He abandoned plans for the tax cut and instead supported tax increases to raise more revenue.

Congress narrowly passed the deficit reduction plan but then defeated the Clinton administration's $16 billion spending plan that had been intended to stimulate the economy. Opponents of the spending plan had successfully argued that increasing spending while trying to cut the deficit sent a mixed message to Americans.

Shrinking the Bureaucracy

The President and Vice President Al Gore planned ways to "reinvent" or redesign the national government. They called for greater and more efficient use of computer technology to sustain services with fewer workers, and they launched a National Performance Review to examine each government agency. The purpose of the review was to eliminate outdated and unnecessary functions and to shrink the bureaucracy to create a government that "works better and costs less." During Clinton's presidency, the size of the federal government shrank by 15 percent.

The Clinton Health Plan

A central goal for the administration was to set up a system of health care to provide for the 15 percent of Americans with no insurance. The President named his wife, Hillary Rodham Clinton, an experienced attorney, to lead a task force that would recommend changes in the health-care system. The Clinton plan would have guaranteed basic health benefits to all Americans. The plan, however, required employers to shoulder much of the burden for health insurance for their employees. Many small-business owners opposed the plan out of fear that they could not afford it.

The insurance industry, which stood to lose revenue, also opposed the plan. This industry sponsored a series of television commercials featuring a fictitious couple

who worried what impact the Clinton health plan would have on their lives. The majority of Americans already had medical insurance. As a result, the commercials encouraged people to worry that universal health care might increase their costs and reduce the quality of care they were currently receiving in order to pay for the uninsured.

The Republicans also challenged the Clinton health-care plan, deriding it as too big, complicated, and costly. Soon, many Democrats deserted the President's plan and proposed a variety of alternatives. None of their plans, however, attracted enough support to be passed into law. Conservative radio talk-show hosts attacked the Clinton health-care plan and criticized the President and his wife, causing Clinton's popularity to dwindle.

A Contract With America

In 1994 mounting criticism of the Clinton adminstration led voters to turn control of Congress over to the Republicans for the first time in 40 years.

A key to the Republican victories was their "Contract with America," which proposed lower taxes, stronger restrictions on immigration, tougher anti-crime laws, limits

★★★★ **A**★★★★★★★
AMERICAN PORTRAITS

Ruth Bader Ginsburg

1933–

On August 10, 1993, Ruth Bader Ginsburg was sworn in as the 107th justice of the United States Supreme Court. The second woman ever to serve on the Court, Justice Ginsburg attended law school at a time when women often suffered discrimination. Ginsburg experienced discrimination firsthand when, in 1960, Supreme Court Justice Frankfurter refused to hire her as his law clerk because she was a woman. Having a keen sense of fairness, Ginsburg successfully argued against a number of laws that treated men and women differently, even when the laws gave women favorable treatment.

When Ginsburg became a judge on the United States Court of Appeals, she carefully thought out her decisions just as she had carefully prepared her cases when she was a lawyer. Largely because of those decisions, the Senate approved her appointment to the Supreme Court.

▲ CLINTON AND GORE From the beginning, the Clinton administration worked to streamline government. *What plans did the administration put in place for redesigning the government?*

on congressional terms, a balanced budget, and the **line-item veto.** This kind of veto would allow the President to veto particular items in an **appropriations bill** without having to veto the entire bill. An appropriations bill sets aside money for specific purposes.

Republicans saw their victory as a mandate to dismantle the welfare system and to transfer power from the federal government back to the states. The new Republican Speaker of the House, Newt Gingrich of Georgia, blamed the New Deal and Great Society programs for creating a culture of poverty and violence. Condemning the growth of large government, Gingrich vowed to "erase the slate and start over."

■ Republican Agenda in Congress

As they promised, House Republicans enacted most of the "Contract with America" during their first hundred days in the majority. Congress also restricted "unfunded mandates," laws that required states to take action without providing federal funds to pay for it. In addition, Congress passed the line-item veto, giving the President the power to cancel particular spending items.

The Supreme Court later struck down the line-item veto as unconstitutional.

While congressional Republicans attempted to set the government's agenda, the President responded with vetoes and threats of vetoes. Clinton forced Congress to restore funds for education, job training, child care, and the environment. He also made protection of Social Security, Medicare, and Medicaid administration priorities.

■ Government Shutdown

Throughout Clinton's presidency, Republicans remained united in their opposition to most administration programs. In the Senate, Republicans used delaying tactics to block passage of certain bills. The main weapon they used was the **filibuster.** To filibuster means to keep talking for hours until a majority of the Senate either abandons the bill or agrees to modify its most controversial provisions.

Late in 1995 tensions between Congress and the White House heightened, as the two sides reached a showdown over the federal budget. To reduce deficits, Republicans wanted to turn Medicaid—health care for the poor—over to the states. President Clinton objected, arguing that this plan would hurt poor children. He refused to sign the bill.

Neither side would back down, and the resulting stalemate forced the federal government to close for lack of operating funds. Many citizens blamed Congress for the government shutdown, and as a result, President Clinton's approval ratings rose.

Congress and the President finally agreed to balance the budget. Congress increased the minimum wage as the President had requested. Congress also passed a health-care bill. Although smaller than Clinton's original proposal, the new law made it easier for workers to keep their health insurance when they changed jobs.

In addition, the President signed a welfare reform bill—after twice vetoing Republican-backed welfare legislation. The new law significantly revised the 60-year-old welfare system and fulfilled Clinton's promise to "end welfare as we know it."

Clinton Is Reelected

During the 1996 elections, Republicans chose the Senate majority leader, Kansas senator Bob Dole, as their candidate. Dole, a 73-year-old veteran of World War II, described himself as a bridge to better times in the American past. By contrast, President Clinton offered himself as a bridge to the future.

By 1996, the U.S. economy had grown strong. Some Americans did worry about layoffs and **downsizing,** the process by which companies seek to increase profits by reducing the number of midlevel employees. In the end, however, many voters felt comfortable with the economy and optimistic about the future. As a result, Clinton easily won reelection.

Impeachment and Acquittal

Scandal beleaguered President Clinton's second term. An independent prosecutor, Kenneth Starr, had begun looking into a questionable financial deal in the President's past. During his investigation, Starr learned that Clinton had had an affair with a young White House intern. Clinton angrily denied the charge, but he later admitted to having the affair. Starr then accused the President of lying under oath about the relationship.

Starr submitted a report to Congress, outlining charges of perjury and obstruction of

Visualizing History

▲ THE IMPEACHMENT TRIAL OF PRESIDENT CLINTON History is made in the U.S. Senate as President Clinton is acquitted in both votes on articles of impeachment. Supreme Court Chief Justice William Rehnquist presided over the trial. *On what two charges did the House of Representatives impeach President Clinton?*

justice against Clinton. Voting along party lines, the House impeached the President in December 1998. In the Senate trial, many senators did not believe that the President's offenses were serious enough to merit removal from office. Clinton was acquitted, and he remained in office.

Section 1 ★ Assessment

Checking for Understanding

1. **Define** incumbent, line-item veto, appropriations bill, filibuster, downsizing.

2. **Explain** how gridlock between Clinton and Congress affected the nation.

Critical Thinking

3. **Identifying Alternatives** In your opinion, should President Clinton have shifted his political position on key issues, such as the deficit, once he took office? Explain your answer.

4. **Summarizing** Re-create the chart shown here to highlight Clinton's major actions during his tenure as President.

Clinton's Major Actions

INTERDISCIPLINARY ACTIVITY

5. **Government** Imagine you are a member of Congress. Write a one-page paper identifying two bills you would introduce. Discuss your choices.

★★

America in a Changing World

Guide to Reading

Main Idea

The collapse of the Soviet Union ended the cold war, but the United States still had to deal with complex and often volatile issues around the world.

Reading Strategy

Sequencing Information As you read about the United States's role in a changing world, create a time line of key events in the Middle East peace process. Use the dates provided as a guide.

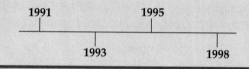

Objectives

After studying this section, you should be able to

★ describe the development of Clinton's foreign policy in the new world order.

★ explain what key role the United States played in bringing about major breakthroughs between old enemies.

Key Terms

multinational state, genocide, ethnic cleansing, global economy, trade deficit, creditor nation, debtor nation

▶ TRAVEL PASSPORT

The struggle between communism and democracy was virtually over. Yet throughout the world, wars erupted over ethnic hatreds, political boundaries, and religion.

■ Clinton's Foreign Policy

Two traumatic episodes in the twentieth century helped influence the United States's efforts to shape foreign policy after the cold war. The first was the Holocaust, which claimed millions of lives in Europe during World War II. From that tragedy, many policy makers drew the lesson that appeasement of dictators would not work and that strong nations had a moral obligation to aid the victims of genocide, even if it meant war. The second episode was the U.S.

involvement in the Vietnam War, from which other foreign affairs analysts argued that military power could not always accomplish diplomatic goals. They believed that the United States needed to set clear foreign policy goals and rely as much as possible on diplomacy but be willing to employ overwhelming force to prevent a limited war from turning into another Vietnam-like quagmire.

As President, Clinton tried to balance that anti-war impulse with the need to defend victims of tyranny and aggression. He generally sought to achieve his foreign policy goals through diplomacy or by applying economic pressures. Whenever the prospect of using military force arose, the President tried to work cooperatively through the United Nations or NATO.

Civil War in Somalia

The first crisis to confront the Clinton administration was civil war in the East African nation of Somalia. Beginning in the 1980s, warring factions battled for control of the government while thousands of civilians died of hunger. When Clinton took office, 28,000 American troops were already in Somalia protecting deliveries of food to the starving Somalis as part of a United Nations mission.

The longer American troops remained in Somalia, the more they were drawn into the conflict. President Clinton eventually decided to withdraw all United States personnel from Somalia. In 1995 United States forces left and rival factions signed a peace agreement. Continued fighting, however, has delayed the formation of a stable government.

Bloodshed in the Balkans

The United States and the world confronted mounting tension in the Balkans, a peninsula in southeastern Europe. During the cold war, Yugoslavia was a **multinational state,** a state with many different ethnic groups. Although its six republics each had a dominant ethnic group, their populations were mixed. Dividing the people were centuries-old differences of ethnicity, religion, and territorial claims. Communist rule had suppressed ethnic divisions, but when the communist government collapsed, old rivalries resurfaced.

In 1991 the republics of Slovenia, Croatia, Bosnia-Herzegovina, and Macedonia declared their independence. They did so after Serbia, the largest of the former republics, refused to allow the other republics greater autonomy. Under its leader, Slobodan Milosevic, Serbia began waging war against the breakaway states.

The creation of an independent Bosnia led to war among the Serbs, Croats, and Muslims. Bosnian Serb forces followed a policy of **genocide**—the systematic destruction of an ethnic, political, or cultural group—of the Muslims and Croats. They also engaged in a policy of **ethnic cleansing,** the expulsion of Bosnian Mus-

▲ **KEEPING PEACE IN BOSNIA** In 1995 the warring groups in the Balkans agreed to lay down their arms. NATO then sent troops to the region to help maintain the fragile peace. *What was the name of the peace agreement?*

lims and other non-Serbs from areas under Bosnian Serb control. As a result of the fighting, some 200,000 people died and nearly 3 million lost their homes.

A New Role for NATO

The United Nations instituted an arms embargo against all the former Yugoslav states, placed trade sanctions on Serbia, and sent a peacekeeping force into Bosnia. In addition, the United States and its NATO allies staged air strikes against Bosnian Serb military sites—the first time NATO ever launched a military offensive.

Combined with a successful Croatian ground offensive against the Serbs, the NATO air strikes helped turn the tide of the war. Bosnian Serbs, Muslims, and Croats agreed to attend a peace conference in Dayton, Ohio. The Dayton peace accords, reached in November 1995, established a Bosnian state divided into two separate regions, one Croat-Muslim and the other Serbian. It also provided for arms control, free elections, and protection of human rights in Bosnia. To enforce the Dayton agreement, NATO furnished

◄ **WAR REFUGEES** The war in Kosovo forced thousands of ethnic Albanians to flee their homes. *How did NATO respond to the crisis in Kosovo?*

60,000 troops—including 20,000 Americans—to maintain peace in Bosnia.

The Kosovo Crisis

In 1999 the Clinton administration grew concerned about the crisis in Kosovo, a province of Yugoslavia. Although Serbia claimed Kosovo, Serbs represented less than ten percent of its population, while the rest were ethnic Albanians and Muslims. When the Kosovo Liberation Army fought to achieve independence for the region, Yugoslav president Milosevic sent Serb police and military forces to push ethnic Albanians out of their villages. Serb forces resorted to torture and mass killings. After diplomatic negotiations failed, NATO launched air strikes against Yugoslavia.

Milosevic had anticipated an air war. As soon as the bombing began, Serb forces launched a campaign to drive all ethnic Albanians out of Kosovo. Some 800,000 refugees crossed the borders into neighboring countries, while another half million people remained in Kosovo but were displaced from their homes. After months of NATO bombing, Serbia agreed to remove its forces and permit NATO troops to restore order in Kosovo.

Unrest in Haiti

Closer to home, unrest in the Caribbean nation of Haiti posed difficult challenges for the United States. In 1991, the Haitian military had overthrown a democratically elected government. The new rulers of Haiti used violence—even murder—to put down opposition, causing thousands of Haitians to flee to the United States.

Seeking to topple the Haitian military government and restore democracy, the United Nations used economic pressure. The UN imposed an embargo on arms and other trade, and President Clinton banned all financial transactions between the United States and Haiti. Despite these pressures, Haiti's rulers retained their tight grip.

When economic pressures failed, the United Nations authorized the United States to lead an invasion to drive the military rulers out of Haiti and reinstate a civilian government. In September 1994, on the eve of the planned invasion, President Clinton sent former President Jimmy Carter to negotiate with Haiti's military rulers. The threat of an invasion persuaded the generals to step down peacefully. The next day, 2,000 American troops met no resistance when they landed in Haiti. By December 1995, a peaceful election restored democratic government there.

■ Peace Efforts in Ireland and the Middle East

Although bloody wars seemed to be raging all over the post-cold war world, there were significant breakthroughs toward peace. The United States acted as a peacemaker in Northern Ireland and the Middle East.

Peace in Northern Ireland

For many years, sectarian violence between the Protestant majority and Roman Catholic minority had torn Northern Ireland apart. Roman Catholics protested the economic and social discrimination they suffered in Northern Ireland, and they sought to reunite with the predominantly Roman Catholic Irish Republic. Protestants insisted that Northern Ireland remain part of Great Britain. Indiscriminate bombings and shootings killed or wounded thousands of people in Ireland and Great Britain.

Hoping to break the impasse, President Clinton sent former Senate Majority Leader George Mitchell to help negotiate a peace settlement. In 1997, after three years of negotiations, Mitchell announced that leaders on both sides had agreed to disarm and accept a cease-fire. The plan established new ties between Northern Ireland and the Irish Republic, promised protection of all citizens' human rights, and agreed that no change in the political status of Northern Ireland would take place unless a majority of its voters approved. In referendums in both the North and South, the Irish public overwhelmingly approved the peace plan.

Israeli-PLO Agreement

Another enduring and difficult struggle was the Arab-Israeli conflict in the Middle East. When Israel was created from British-occupied Palestine in 1948, Palestinian Arabs were forced to move to the West Bank of the Jordan River. This area soon came under the control of Jordan. In 1964, with the support of Arab leaders, some of these displaced people formed the Palestine Liberation Organization (PLO) to work toward the elimination of Israel and the creation of an independent Arab Palestine.

Fearing attack by its Arab neighbors, in 1967 Israel seized the Gaza Strip from Egypt as well as Jordanian territory west of the River Jordan, including Jordan's part of Jerusalem. For 20 years after the 1967 war, Arabs and Israelis could not agree on the future of the Israeli-occupied territories. Then in 1987 the Palestinians in both areas began an uprising. Finally, in 1991 the United States helped start peace talks between the Israelis and the Arabs. Peace negotiations continued after President Clinton took office.

The peace talks proceeded erratically until September 1993, when Israeli Prime Minister Yitzhak Rabin and Palestine Liberation Organization leader Yasir Arafat reached an agreement. The PLO recognized Israel's right to exist as an independent nation, and Israel recognized the PLO as the representative of the Palestinians. In addition, both parties agreed on a framework for limited Palestinian self-rule in the Gaza Strip and the West Bank. In 1995 Israel and the PLO agreed on significant Palestinian self-rule and the removal of Israeli forces from other Palestinian areas.

Preserving the Peace

There remained, however, strong opposition to the peace plan. Palestinian leaders contended that expanding Israeli settlements on the West Bank violated the spirit of the agreement. Israelis feared that a fully independent Palestinian state would be a threat to their nation. Israeli leaders drew away from implementing the agreement when Palestinian military groups attacked Israeli settlements.

In November 1995 an Israeli student who opposed his government's policies with the Palestinians assassinated Prime Minister Rabin. A series of terrorist attacks further rocked Israel, and the 1996 election of a more hard-line prime minister, Benjamin Netanyahu, dealt a major setback to the peace plan.

After a lengthy stalemate, President Clinton invited Netanyahu and Arafat to meet together near the Wye River in Maryland, in 1998. After intense negotiations, they signed the Wye River Memorandum, which detailed the steps needed to implement the peace agreement. Both sides credited Clinton with facilitating the Wye River agreement. Middle East peace advanced further

▲ **ISRAEL'S PRIME MINISTER** Israeli Prime Minister Ehud Barak (far left) and his wife, Nara (far right), pose with President Clinton and his wife, Hillary. **Why did Barak's election advance the peace process?**

when Israel elected a new prime minister, Ehud Barak, who vowed to revive the peace settlement with the Palestinians.

■ A Global Economy

By the end of the twentieth century, innovations in technology and economics had transformed national and regional

• •

Footnotes to History

The West Bank *The West Bank* refers to lands west of the Jordan River between Israel and Jordan. The area, which encompasses 2,200 square miles, includes many places of religious and cultural importance for Jews, Christians, and Muslims. Under British rule in the early 1900s, the West Bank was seized by Jordan in 1948. Israel secured the area during the 1967 Mideast War and placed it under military occupation. In December 1987 Palestinians launched work stoppages and demonstrations called the *intifada* to focus world attention on the plight of the Palestinians and to bring international pressure to deal with their conditions.

economies into a **global economy**—an economic world with interdependence among countries. Developments in transportation and communication made international trade an economic driving force in the world. Part of this pattern was the growth of multinational corporations, companies that produce and market goods in different countries.

The United States had long based its economic prosperity on selling its goods abroad. By the 1970s, however, the United States was losing its economic dominance. America experienced **trade deficits**, purchasing more from foreign nations than it sold in foreign markets. By the early 1970s, the United States had changed from a **creditor nation**, or a lending nation, to a **debtor nation**, or a borrowing one.

The United States reacted to its declining economic position by competing harder in the global marketplace, streamlining industries, using new technology, and opening new markets. Leading American companies became globalized corporations, ones that operated throughout the world.

Free Trade Agreements

The government also pursued ways to strengthen America's economic position in an increasingly interdependent and global marketplace. In 1992 the United States, Canada, and Mexico signed the North American Free Trade Agreement (NAFTA), which lifted all tariffs among the three nations, making North America the world's largest free trade area.

The North American Free Trade Agreement offered American companies a chance to open factories in Mexico, where labor costs were lower than in the United States. Mexican and Canadian markets became more open to American products and services. Critics argued that American workers would be displaced when industrial jobs moved to Mexico. However, the Senate approved the treaty after an almost year-long battle.

The American economic picture improved during the 1990s as exports rose steadily. The United States achieved a trading surplus with nearly every nation, although it continued to carry an overall trade deficit. Some economists now saw these trade deficits as a sign of strength, since Americans could afford to import more they exported. American trade deficits especially helped to stabilize national economies in Asia and Latin America, whose economies depended heavily on their exports to the United States.

Trade and Tensions With China

The United States suffered one of its largest trade deficits with China, one of its most rapidly growing trading partners. By 1998, after a long period of political isolation, China exported some $85 billion in goods to the United States, mostly consumer items such as toys, clothing, shoes, radios, televisions, and other electronic appliances. Although China exported five times the amount it imported from the United States, it resisted opening its markets to American products. American officials sought to prevail on China to reduce tariff barriers and allow greater foreign investment. President Clinton also called on China to improve its record on human rights. The President urged the Chinese government to allow its people more freedoms.

Complaints from American computer manufacturers persuaded the Clinton administration to relax restrictions on the types of technology they could export to China and other nations. This policy bolstered the U.S. economy, but Republicans in Congress objected, saying that it gave China computer technology that it could use militarily. Evidence also surfaced that China had conducted espionage in American nuclear technology. Such charges strained the uneasy relationship between the United States and China, the world's largest remaining communist power.

Section 2 ★ Assessment

Checking for Understanding

1. **Define** multinational state, genocide, ethnic cleansing, global economy, trade deficit, creditor nation, debtor nation.

2. **Explain** why President Clinton found it difficult to decide when and how to intervene in another nation's affairs.

Critical Thinking

3. **Examining Issues** Re-create this diagram to list the pros and cons of American companies' moving factories to foreign countries to take advantage of lower real estate costs and lower wages in those countries.

INTERDISCIPLINARY ACTIVITY

4. **Geography** Create a chart titled "World Trouble Spots in the 1990s, and describe the various conflicts discussed."

BUILDING SKILLS
Social Studies Skills

Interpreting Statistics

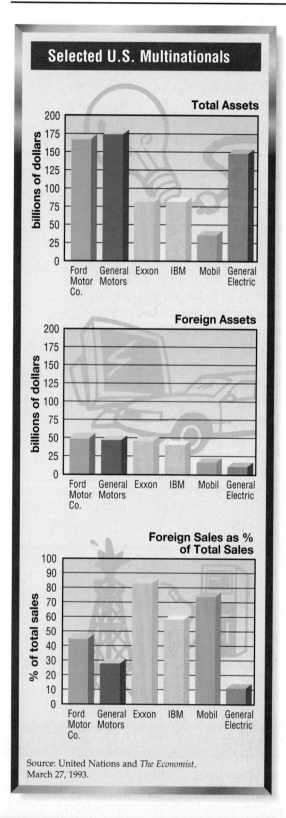

Selected U.S. Multinationals

Total Assets

billions of dollars

200
175
150
125
100
75
50
25
0

Ford Motor Co. | General Motors | Exxon | IBM | Mobil | General Electric

Foreign Assets

billions of dollars

200
175
150
125
100
75
50
25
0

Ford Motor Co. | General Motors | Exxon | IBM | Mobil | General Electric

**Foreign Sales as %
of Total Sales**

% of total sales

100
90
80
70
60
50
40
30
20
10
0

Ford Motor Co. | General Motors | Exxon | IBM | Mobil | General Electric

Source: United Nations and *The Economist*, March 27, 1993.

Often presented in graphs and tables, statistics, or numerical data, need to be carefully examined to determine their real significance. The ability to interpret statistics allows us to understand probable effects and make predictions.

Learning the Skill

Use the following steps to help you interpret statistical information.

- Scan the graphs, reading the title and labels to get an idea of what is being shown.
- Check the graphs for unfamiliar terms. When you find one, look up the term in your book's glossary or in a dictionary.
- Examine the statistics, looking for increases and decreases, similarities and differences.
- Determine the conclusions you can draw from the statistics.

Practicing the Skill

1. What subject do all these graphs deal with?
2. What do the graphs' keys tell you?
3. What do the labels on the horizontal axes tell you?
4. Which company has the greatest total assets?
5. How are assets and sales related?
6. Which companies sell more of their products nationally than internationally?

 Glencoe's **Skillbuilder Interactive Workbook, Level 2** provides instruction and practice in key social studies skills.

APPLYING THE SKILL

7. List five household items you use. Visit three stores that have these items. Price the items by store and brand and organize your data into five separate graphs. Summarize your findings.

★★

Challenges and Opportunities

Guide to Reading

Main Idea

As America approached the twenty-first century, the nation faced a host of exciting opportunities as well as difficult challenges.

Reading Strategy

Organizing Information As you read about American challenges and opportunities, use a diagram like the one shown here to list the nation's environmental concerns at the beginning of the twenty-first century.

Environmental Concerns

Objectives

After studying this section, you should be able to

★ identify the challenges facing the United States in the 1990s.

★ describe some of the proposed solutions to these challenges.

Key Term

ratification

▶ **AIDS** RIBBON

---

*V*oters' demands for change in government during the 1990s reflected great concern among the American people. While the United States was on the verge of new opportunities, difficult challenges threatened to diminish the quality of life on the United States.

■ Welfare Reform

Even in times of prosperity, poverty remained a problem. Since the 1930s, the federal government had helped many low-income families who had no other alternative. Yet these efforts did little to reduce the growing number of Americans in poverty. By 1996 one out of every eight children received Aid to Families with Dependent Children (AFDC). One of the most troubling aspects of poverty was how it contributed to crime and violence and how crime and vio-

lence affected the young. In many cities, gang activities rose.

Both Democrats and Republicans called for reform of the welfare system, but for different reasons. Some sought reform because of welfare's great cost to America and the need to decrease the deficit. Others argued that the system had to change because it created a "culture of poverty" in which the poor were trapped by their dependence on welfare.

President Clinton proposed a welfare reform plan that increased education and training for welfare recipients so that they might find work. House Speaker Newt Gingrich argued instead for cutting public assistance and emphasized that it was up to the poor to find work. Gingrich preferred relying on private charities, not the government, to rescue the most impoverished.

In 1996 the Republican Congress passed and President Clinton signed a welfare reform bill that ended Aid to Families with Dependent Children. The federal government would now offer states block grants of aid, rather than pay poor people directly. States would be able to take money formerly used for welfare and use it as incentives for businesses to hire people currently on welfare.

Changes in the American Economy

The booming economy eased the impact of welfare reform. In the past, the wide range of good jobs in industry had helped people with high school educations enter the middle class. In the latter part of the twentieth century, however, low-skill manufacturing declined while high-technology and service companies flourished. Workers who had the skills to take advantage of the technological revolution did better.

Low unemployment and tight labor markets in the 1990s helped boost many people out of poverty. Many of the new jobs were in service industries, while the number of jobs in manufacturing continued to shrink. As the employment rate among young people in particular improved, the crime rate fell dramatically.

Students as a Resource

Seeking to help students who had left school early, some cities started volunteer programs to provide them with job skills and scholarship opportunities. In addition, President Clinton helped establish Ameri-

Corps in 1993. This program employed students to deal with issues such as improving low-income housing and cleaning up the environment. Students earned a salary and, after completing their services, a scholarship to continue their education.

■ Social Issues

In addition to grappling with the issues of poverty and unemployment, the government addressed other pressing social problems.

School Violence

Although crime rates dropped significantly in the 1990s, Americans were shocked by an outburst of school violence. Tragic shootings at schools in Jonesboro, Arkansas; Paducah, Kentucky; and Littleton, Colorado, showed that adolescent alienation and violence was not limited to impoverished inner cities but had spread to small towns and affluent suburbs. These incidents raised questions about the easy accessibility of firearms and about the negative effects on juveniles of violent television programs, movies, and video games. School violence stimulated a national debate, and Congress responded to public opinion by enacting stricter gun control legislation.

The Cost of Terrorism

Escalating terrorism also posed new dangers to Americans of all ages. In 1993 Islamic radicals bombed New York City's World Trade Center in an effort to force the United States to abandon its support for Israel and Egypt. In 1995 the bombing of a federal office building in Oklahoma City claimed the lives of 168 people, among them 15 children in the building's day care center. The men convicted of the bombing had ties to a private American militia group. Militia members often believed that the federal government and other powerful interests were conspiring to rob them of their freedom.

To combat terrorism, the government sought new powers, such as increased wiretapping authority. This raised the question

• •

Footnotes to History

Medicare and the Elderly Reports indicate that by the year 2002 Medicare's hospital trust fund will run out of money. What caused the depletion? One reason is that elderly Americans are living longer because of improved medical science and the access to health care that Medicare provides. In addition, the number of retirees continues to grow in comparison to the number of workers. There were 5.6 workers for every retiree in 1965. By 1995 the ratio of workers to retirees was 3.3 to 1. Estimates indicate that by 2035 the ratio will be 2 to 1.

Linking Past and Present

★ ★

Third Parties

The Republican and Democratic parties dominate the two-party system, yet the United States has a long history of other political parties that have risen to challenge the major parties.

Then

Voices for Change

The Republican party was itself a third party in 1856; just four years later, it captured the White House.

At the turn of the century, the Populists seriously threatened

◀ PROGRESSIVE PARTY CARTOON

the two-party monopoly. The Populist party had an impact on politics and government far beyond its showing in national elections. Most importantly, minor parties have served as vehicles for reform by taking clear-cut stands on controversial issues and proposing bold and original solutions. Other significant third parties include the Free Soil party (1848-1852), the Know Nothings (1856), the Progressive party (1912-1948), and the American Independent party (1968-1972).

Now

The Reform Party

In 1995 business leader and 1992 presidential candidate H.

UNITED WE STAND, AMERICA

Ross Perot formed a third political party—the Independence party.

The Independence party, now known as the Reform party, focuses on several key issues, including reforming congressional campaign practices and passing a balanced budget amendment. Perot contended that his party was for Americans "who don't feel represented by either the Republicans or the Democrats."

---

of whether Americans would accept infringements of their civil liberties in order to suppress terrorist violence. After the Oklahoma City bombing, concrete barriers closed off Pennsylvania Avenue in front of the White House. These barriers served as a reminder of terrorism's cost.

■ The Environment

Threats to the environment mounted as the twentieth century ended. The battle continued between those who wanted to preserve natural wilderness and those who favored greater development of natural resources.

Clinton and the Environment

President Clinton wanted to protect the environment, but he also promised to "grow the economy." The President tried to placate

both developers and environmentalists through a series of compromises. One compromise between the logging industry and environmentalists balanced the needs of loggers in the Pacific Northwest with protection of the spotted owl. President Clinton also took steps to stop further loss of America's wetlands, areas such as tidal flats and swamps. Moreover, in 1996 the President protected Utah's southern red-rock cliffs and canyons from mining by declaring them a national monument.

Acid Rain

One of the more controversial environmental issues concerned acid rain, precipitation contaminated by acidic gases given off when environmental pollutants such as oil, gas, or coal burn. Environmentalists, calling for stricter regulations, contended that acid rain kills

▶ **LANDFILLS**
This landfill in Massachusetts is a repository for trash from all over the state. The largest landfill in the world is Fresh Kills in New York. It receives 17,000 tons of garbage each day. The landfill covers 3,000 acres and takes up 2.4 billion cubic feet of space. Contents of the landfill include paper (50%), miscellaneous (20%), organic (13%), metal (6%), glass (1%), and plastic (less than 1%). *How is Fresh Kills affected by the Clinton administration's environmental policy?*

fish, damages crops, and strips forests. Developers warned that more regulations meant higher costs for companies that burn fossil fuels, forcing them either to find other energy sources or to install pollution-control devices. Accepting either option, they argued, would increase production costs, sending fuel prices spiraling upward and leading to the loss of jobs.

Global Warming

In 1995 the earth's surface reached a record high. Scientists think this was caused by global warming—warming created as gases released by burning fuels, such as coal and natural gas, trap the sun's heat. Some predicted that this "greenhouse effect" of heating up the earth's atmosphere could lead to problems such as erratic weather patterns and the spread of tropical diseases.

A United Nations-sponsored meeting on global warming in Kyoto, Japan, produced the Global Climate Change Treaty, which called on nations to take steps to reduce the emission of "greenhouse" gases. The Clinton administration signed the treaty, but opponents in the Senate blocked its **ratification**, or official approval. They argued that the treaty would require the United States to reduce its use of fuel drastically and would limit the growth of the U.S. economy.

■ Increasing Risks to Health

The 1990s saw mounting risks to people's health. Diseases such as AIDS (acquired immune deficiency syndrome) killed thousands in the United States and worldwide. Continued concern about drug addiction caused many people to demand more government efforts to halt the problem.

The Spread of AIDS

During the 1980s and 1990s, AIDS spread rapidly throughout the world. By the mid-1990s, AIDS became the third-leading cause of death among Americans aged 25 to 44. Since 1981, over 600,000 AIDS cases were diagnosed in the United States, and estimates placed the number of Americans infected with HIV (human immunodeficiency virus, which often leads to AIDS) at over 1 million.

Responding to these alarming statistics, the federal government launched programs to educate Americans about the dangers of AIDS. President Clinton appointed a federal AIDS policy coordinator, and Congress significantly increased funding for AIDS research. In 1996 new drugs caused the first drop in the number of Americans diagnosed with AIDS. Many Americans remain infected with the disease, however.

Drug Abuse

Drug abuse also spread toward the end of the twentieth century. During the 1990s a significant increase in marijuana use occurred among high school students. The head of Columbia University's Center on Addiction and Substance Abuse, said:

> *. . . [T]he most frightening thing is that smoking marijuana is clearly a stepping stone to more serious problems. Children who smoke pot are 85 times more likely to use cocaine.*

Indeed, the use of cocaine and crack cocaine, a more potent form of the drug that is smokable, rose among men, women, and young people. Moreover, some of the women who used cocaine during pregnancy had babies who were born addicted. These children, sometimes called cocaine babies, often suffered serious and lasting health problems.

■ Diversity and Equal Rights

Economic and political problems in places such as Mexico, the former Soviet Union, and Haiti brought a new tide of immigration to the United States. Between 1970 and 1998 the number of immigrants living in the United States nearly tripled from 9.6 million to 26.3 million. Some newcomers were illegal aliens, people who enter a country without legal permission. Total legal immigration reached nearly 1 million a year during the late 1980s, yet declined by nearly 200,000 in the 1990s.

Illegal Aliens

Many Americans blamed increased immigration for lost jobs and higher taxes. Immigration took on especially emotional tones in states with large concentrations of illegal immigrants, such as Florida, Texas, and California. For example, California's governor Pete Wilson blamed much of his state's economic problems on the costs of providing state services for illegal immigrants. Wilson argued, "We can no longer allow compassion to overrule reason."

In California, where illegal immigrants crossed the border from Mexico, voters in 1994 approved Proposition 187, which banned illegal aliens from enrolling in public schools and using nonemergency medical care and other social services. In 1996 California Proposition 227 abolished bilingual education in the public schools. These propositions stirred protests among legal immigrants, who reacted strongly to what they considered ethnic prejudice.

The Treatment of Legal Immigrants

Congress also limited the rights of legal immigrants by limiting their access to welfare benefits. Although immigrants applied for welfare benefits less often than American citizens, the number of legal immigrants in the welfare system kept rising. This growth in population increased costs for the government.

As part of its welfare reform bill in 1996, Congress barred legal immigrants who were not yet citizens from receiving many benefits, including food stamps and Social Security. Family members who sponsored immigrants were expected to bear more of the financial burden. President Clinton called these benefit cuts unjustified and pledged to restore them.

The Question of Diversity

Tied directly to the debate on immigration was the question of diversity. Some Americans believed that the different people who make up the United States should retain their individual cultural heritages. They saw the United States as a multicultural society in which everyone should respect each other's uniqueness. As Mayor Sharpe James of Newark, New Jersey, said, "Our diversity is our strength." Others believed, as many had in years past, that the United States should be a melting-pot society in which immigrants from around the world blend into one unique people.

Americans With Disabilities

Among the groups that sought equal rights during the 1990s were Americans with disabilities. In 1990 Congress passed the Americans with Disabilities Act. This law prohibited discrimination against the more than 40 million Americans who had physical, hearing, or visual impairments. Television news correspondent John Hockenberry, who himself used a wheelchair, commented: "Our struggle for inclusion in this society is a test of whether American society truly wants diversity and freedom for all."

■ The Information Superhighway

As the United States entered the twenty-first century, a creative new form of communication became available via computer networks, forming an "information superhighway." This superhighway carried vast amounts of digitized information across fiber-optic telecommunications circuits at rapid speed.

The cold war gave rise to the original network, the Advanced Research Projects Agency Network (ARPANET), in 1969. ARPANET allowed the Department of Defense to communicate with contractors and universities working on defense projects.

By the 1990s millions of people gained access to an international computer network, the Internet. The Internet offered easy access to information on a global scale, and it grew rapidly toward the end of the century. Users could browse library catalogs, read magazines, listen to music, invest in stocks, buy consumer goods, and chat electronically with others who shared similar interests. The World Wide Web provided a powerful search tool that enabled users to retrieve a limitless variety of information—whether text, graphic, audio, or visual material—from the Internet.

The Internet offered unprecedented freedom of expression. Anyone with a modem could post information. This raised questions about the Internet's tendency to spread rumors and misinformation along with its more reliable services. Handled with responsibility, however, the Internet seemed poised to shape the future as the most universal and democratic means of global communication yet devised.

Section 3 ★ Assessment

Checking for Understanding

1. **Define** ratification.

2. **Describe** how the United States tried in the early 1990s to stop illegal immigration.

Critical Thinking

3. **Evaluating Tactics** Do you think the government's efforts in the war on drugs should be focused on stopping the supply of drugs from other countries or on reducing demand?

4. **Summarizing** Re-create the diagram shown here to describe the components of the welfare reform bill.

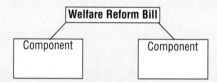

INTERDISCIPLINARY ACTIVITY

5. **Government** Design a poster that illustrates one of the issues mentioned in this section. Make the focus of the poster why young Americans should be concerned.

Environmental Issues of the Twenty-First Century

The industrialized world has purchased prosperity at the expense of the environment. The conflict between economic growth and environmental protection may well become the central issue of the twenty-first century.

The disappearing ozone layer—part of the upper atmosphere—is linked to the widespread use of chlorofluorocarbons (CFCs), commonly found in such products as aerosols and foam packaging. Ozone depletion may cause an increase in skin cancer. Another concern is global warming caused by high levels of carbon dioxide and other gases that trap heat from the sun in the atmosphere and cause a greenhouse effect. The destruction of rain forests, which absorb carbon dioxide and release oxygen, compounds the problem. Many scientists believe that global warming could cause polar ice caps to melt, raising ocean levels and flooding coastal cities.

Disposal of wastes, especially toxic and nuclear materials, will also be a continuing issue. The United States alone produces 40 million tons of toxic wastes annually.

▲ SCIENTISTS TAKING WATER SAMPLES, ARCTIC RESEARCH PROJECT

Making the Geography Connection

1. What is the cause of global warming?

2. How do you think future technology will affect environmental problems?

ACTIVITY

3. Prepare a set of 10 questions to use as a survey. Ask 10 adults and 10 students to answer questions about environmental concerns such as "What do you consider the most pressing environmental issue?" Write a one-page report summarizing the results of the survey.

▲ EFFECTS OF ACID RAIN

▲ RICHARD RODRIGUEZ

Hispanic Americans cherish their heritage, and many speak only Spanish among their friends and family. However, most of their children's teachers speak only English. As a result, Hispanic students often find school confusing and humiliating. Richard Rodriguez describes his struggle to become "educated" in his autobiography, *Hunger of Memory.*

Read to Discover

Analyze how the author's attitude toward books changes. What difficulties did the author face? How was a yearning to read more complicated, more adult materials expressed by Rodriguez?

Reader's Dictionary

fellowship	companionship
bookish	fond of books or reading

*H*unger of Memory (excerpts)

From an early age I knew that my mother and father could read and write both Spanish and English. . . . For both my parents, however, reading was something done out of necessity and as quickly as possible. . . . Their reading consisted of work manuals, prayer books, newspapers, recipes. . . .

. . . I privately wondered: What was the connection between reading and learning? Did one learn something only by reading it? . . . [A sign said:] CONSIDER BOOKS YOUR BEST FRIENDS. Friends? Reading was, at best, only a chore. I needed to look up whole paragraphs of words in a dictionary. Lines of type were dizzying, the eye having to move slowly across the page, then down, and across. . . . What bothered me most, however, was the isolation reading required. To console myself for the loneliness I'd feel when I read, I tried reading in a very soft voice. Until: "Who is doing all that talking to his neighbor?" Shortly after, remedial reading classes were arranged for me with a very old nun.

At the end of each school day, for nearly six months, I would meet with her in the tiny room that served as the school's library. . . . Most of the time we took turns. I began with my elementary text. Sentences of astonishing simplicity seemed to me lifeless and drab: "The boys ran from the rain. . . . She wanted to sing. . . . The kite rose in the blue." Then the old nun would read from her favorite books, usually biographies of early American presidents. Playfully she ran through complex sentences, calling the words alive with her voice, making it seem that the author somehow was speaking directly to me. I smiled just to listen to her. I sat there and sensed for the very first time some possibility of fellowship between a reader and a writer, a communication. . . .

I entered high school having read hundreds of books. My habit of reading made me a confident speaker and writer of English. Reading also enabled me to sense something of the shape, the major concerns, of Western thought. . . . In these various ways books brought me academic success as I hoped that they would. But I was not a good reader. Merely bookish, I lacked a point of view when I read. Rather, I read in order to acquire a point of view. I vacuumed books for epigrams, scraps of information, ideas, themes—anything to fill the hollow within me and make me feel educated. . . .

. . . One day I came across a newspaper article about the retirement of an English professor at a nearby state college. The article was accompanied by a list of the "hundred most important books of Western Civilization." "More than anything else in my life," the professor told the reporter with finality, "these books have made me all that I am." . . . I clipped out the list and kept it for the several months it took me to read all of the titles. Most books, of course, I barely understood. While reading Plato's *Republic*, for instance, I needed to keep looking at the book's jacket comments to remind myself what the text was about. Nevertheless . . . I looked at every word of the text. And by the time I reached the last word, relieved, I convinced myself that I had read *The Republic*. In a ceremony of pride, I solemnly crossed Plato off my list.

▲ *THE LIBRARY* BY JACOB LAWRENCE, 1960

Responding to Literature

1. How did the writer's attitude toward reading change over time?

2. What benefits from reading do you think the writer especially appreciated because he was Hispanic American?

3. Why do you think Rodriguez's parents viewed books differently from his teachers?

ACTIVITY

4. Think about a book that has had a strong influence on you. Write a one-page report explaining the power and fascination the book holds.

CHAPTER 26 ★ ASSESSMENT

Using Vocabulary

Assume that you are a magazine reporter covering the state of the economy during the Clinton administration. Write an article detailing your findings using the following vocabulary words.

> **global economy**
> **trade deficit**
> **multicultural society**

Reviewing Facts

1. **Explain** why Bill Clinton focused on the economy during his campaign against President Bush.

2. **Explain** why gridlock in Congress reappeared after the 1992 elections, despite the fact that the Democrats controlled the presidency and held majorities in both the House and the Senate.

3. **Summarize** the purpose of the Contract with America.

4. **Describe** the positive breakthroughs in world affairs in which the United States played a part.

Understanding Concepts

Challenges

1. Re-create the diagram shown here to list the challenges that Americans faced as they entered the twenty-first century.

Twenty-First Century Challenges

Changes

2. Why did Americans demand that politicians "reinvent government," and how did Clinton proceed to carry out this charge?

Critical Thinking

Analyzing Art   The personal computer has revolutionized graphic, illustrated, and animated art. Study the art on this page and answer the questions that follow.

a. Does the computer extend the creative capacity of artists? Explain.

b. What do you think the artist is trying to say in this work?

c. What title would you give it?

History and Geography
Global Issues

1. **Location**   Why was Chechnya the site of much conflict?

2. **Location**   Where is the West Bank?

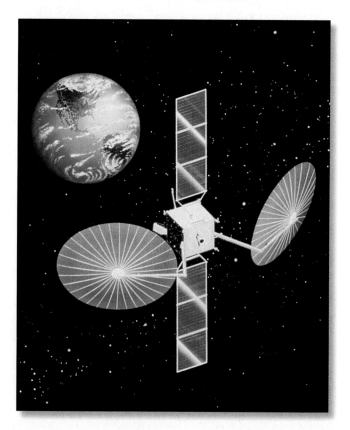

3. **Human/Environment Interaction** Why do some developers call for more lenient environmental regulations?

Cooperative Learning ## Interdisciplinary Activity: Environmental Studies

Many recycling centers depend on volunteers to unload cars, sort materials, or bundle newspapers. Work in groups of three to find out how you can participate in your community's recycling program. Share your information about the programs with the class in the form of a poster or leaflet.

Practicing Skills

Interpreting Statistics

Use the table on this page to answer the following questions.

1. What are the three parts of the table?

2. Summarize the changes in the total workforce.

3. Did earnings for female workers compared to earnings for male workers rise or drop between 1985 and 1997? Explain.

4. Are minorities and women achieving equality of earnings in the workplace?

5. How do the percentages of minorities in the workforce compare with the percentages of those minorities in the population? Analyze the graph on page 693 to help you answer this question.

Technology Activity

Using E-Mail

Determine what you consider to be the most pressing challenges facing your community or the nation at the start of the new century. Then send an electronic message to your representative in Congress describing the challenge you selected and the possible solution you worked out.

The Labor Force, 1983–1997

	1985	1990	1995	1997
Total workforce (in thousands)	115,461	125,840	132,304	136,300
Percentage of total workforce				
Male	59.2	57.6	53.9	53.7
Female	40.8	42.4	46.1	46.2
White	86.3	85.4	84.7	84.2
Black	10.9	11.3	10.6	11.4
of Hispanic origin	NA	8.2	8.9	10.1
Ratio of weekly median earnings for full-time workers				
Females to Males	68.2	71.9	75.5	74.4
Blacks to Whites	78.0	77.6	77.5	77.1
Hispanics to Whites	NA	71.7	66.6	67.7

Source: *Statistical Abstract of the United States*, 1998.

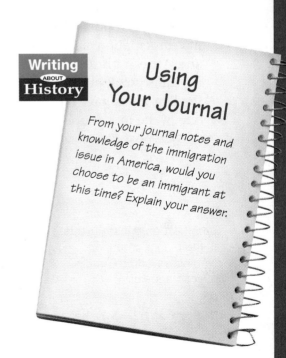

Writing ABOUT History

Using Your Journal

From your journal notes and knowledge of the immigration issue in America, would you choose to be an immigrant at this time? Explain your answer.

Cultural Kaleidoscope

The World of Music

ROCKING INTO THE FUTURE

Rock and roll music has been one of the most popular forms of musical expression in the twentieth century. It began as a mixture of styles, borrowing elements from rhythm and blues and country music as well as the popular ballads of the 1950s. Today's rock musicians show the willingness to explore new boundaries. In pushing for new sounds, they have made use of synthesizers and electronic sounds, classical instrumentation, and Latin and African phrasings and rhythms. Rock performers in the late 1900s have created one of the most popular and unique postwar arts.

▲

In the late 1970s and early 1980s, Janet Jackson was best known as the sister of Michael Jackson and for her appearances in televised situation comedies. Her musical albums *Rhythm Nation* and *Janet* pushed her to the top echelon of rock performers.

►

Such keyboard instruments as the piano, organ, and synthesizer add to rock's eclectic appeal.

► Innovations ranging from the jukebox to the compact disc have helped the popular appeal of rock and roll.

▼ Whitney Houston's billowy soprano voice made "I Will Always Love You" one of the top-selling singles of the 1990s.

▼ The appeal of Seattle's Pearl Jam is based on the group's hard-rocking sound and the expressive vocals of lead singer Eddie Vedder.

Standardized Test Practice

Directions: Choose the *best* answer to each of the following multiple choice questions. If you have trouble answering a question, use the process of elimination to narrow your choices. Write your answers on a separate piece of paper.

1. One difference between the strategies of Martin Luther King, Jr., and some later civil rights groups, such as the Black Panthers, was that King was committed to

A ending discrimination in housing and employment.

B using nonviolent forms of protest.

C demanding equal rights for African Americans.

D gaining improvements in living conditions for African Americans.

> **Test-Taking Tip:** If you read this question carefully, you will notice that it asks for one *difference* in the way that Martin Luther King, Jr., and other groups tried to accomplish their goals. In other words, three of the answer choices will represent *common goals*. Since *ending discrimination in housing and employment*, answer A, was a common goal of civil rights groups, this answer cannot be the correct choice. Read through all the answer choices to find the one that represents a *different* type of strategy.

2. Women faced all of the following kinds of discrimination in the 1960s EXCEPT

F unequal pay for performing the same tasks as men.

G being prohibited from attending certain universities.

H being denied the right to vote.

J the inability to obtain loans and credit.

> **Test-Taking Tip:** This question is also looking for the *exception*. Three of the answer choices describe types of discrimination that women faced *in the 1960s*. Women gained the right to vote in 1920, when the Nineteenth Amendment was signed into law.

3. During the Cold War, the Alliance for Progress gave money to Latin American countries in order to

A help insure that these countries did not ally with the Soviet Union.

B gain the right to install missiles in those countries.

C fund Cuban exiles who wished to overthrow Fidel Castro.

D create popular support for the naval blockade of Cuba.

> **Test-Taking Tip:** The phrase *Cold War* is an important clue to understanding this question. What was the most important goal of the United States in the Cold War? Remember, the United States pursued a policy of *containment* in order to halt the spread of communism. Which answer choice best fits with this information?

4 One of Nixon's first successful attempts to relax Cold War tensions was a result of the SALT negotiations. These talks culminated in

F increased trade with communist China.

G a series of arms-control agreements.

H a peaceful end to the war in Vietnam.

J a cease-fire agreement between Israel and Egypt.

> **Test-Taking Tip:** Eliminate answers that do not make sense. The Middle East conflict (answer J) was not directly related to the Cold War.

5. In his "War on Poverty," Lyndon Johnson helped to enact laws that led to all of the following EXCEPT

    A significantly changing the quota system for immigrants.

    B providing medical care of people who could not afford it.

    C helping the fight against illiteracy.

    D reducing the consumption of crude oil.

> **Test-Taking Tip:** Johnson's program, also known as "the Great Society," was designed primarily to combat poverty and discrimination. Which answer choice seems *least* likely to alleviate *poverty* or *discrimination*?

6. The purpose of the War Powers Act, passed in 1973, was to insure that

    F the President would have greater authority over the military in the future.

    G the President would consult Congress before sending American troops into an extended conflict.

    H the President would have the authority to sign treaties without the approval of the Senate.

    J the President would be able fight the spread of communism as effectively as possible.

> **Test-Taking Tip:** The War Powers Act was partly a reaction to the Vietnam War and to Watergate. Congress wanted to make sure that the President was not becoming too powerful in relation to the other branches of government. Three of the answer choices actually do the *opposite*—they give *more* power to the President. Which choice puts a strong limit on presidential powers?

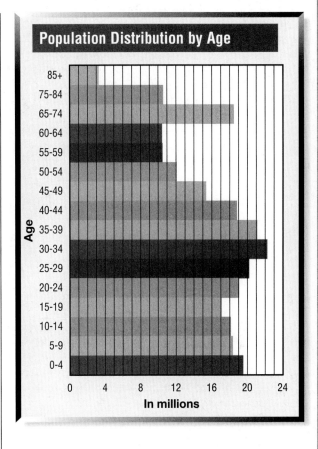

Population Distribution by Age

(Age groups, from top: 85+, 75-84, 65-74, 60-64, 55-59, 50-54, 45-49, 40-44, 35-39, 30-34, 25-29, 20-24, 15-19, 10-14, 5-9, 0-4; In millions: 0, 4, 8, 12, 16, 20, 24)

7. Based on the graph above, which of the following will be the most important future concern for the United States?

    A National education standards

    B Literacy

    C Adequate health care for the elderly

    D A shortage of trained medical doctors

> **Test-Taking Tip:** Make sure that your answer choice is supported by information on the graph. Since the question asks for a future concern, what do you think this graph will look like in 40 years? What age range will comprise the largest percentage of the population? Be careful—other choices, such as answer B, will certainly be important future concerns, but they are not supported by the information on the graph.

REFERENCE ATLAS

NATIONAL
GEOGRAPHIC
SOCIETY

ATLAS KEY

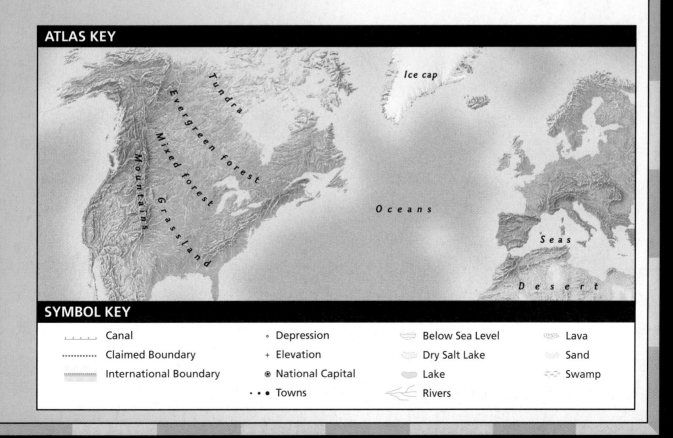

Ice cap

Tundra

Evergreen forest

Mixed forest

Mountains

Grassland

Oceans

Seas

Desert

SYMBOL KEY

⌐⌐⌐ Canal	○ Depression	⊂⊃ Below Sea Level	≈≈ Lava
·········· Claimed Boundary	+ Elevation	⊂⊃ Dry Salt Lake	≈≈ Sand
▓▓▓▓ International Boundary	⊛ National Capital	⊂⊃ Lake	⊂⊃ Swamp
	• • Towns	≪ Rivers	

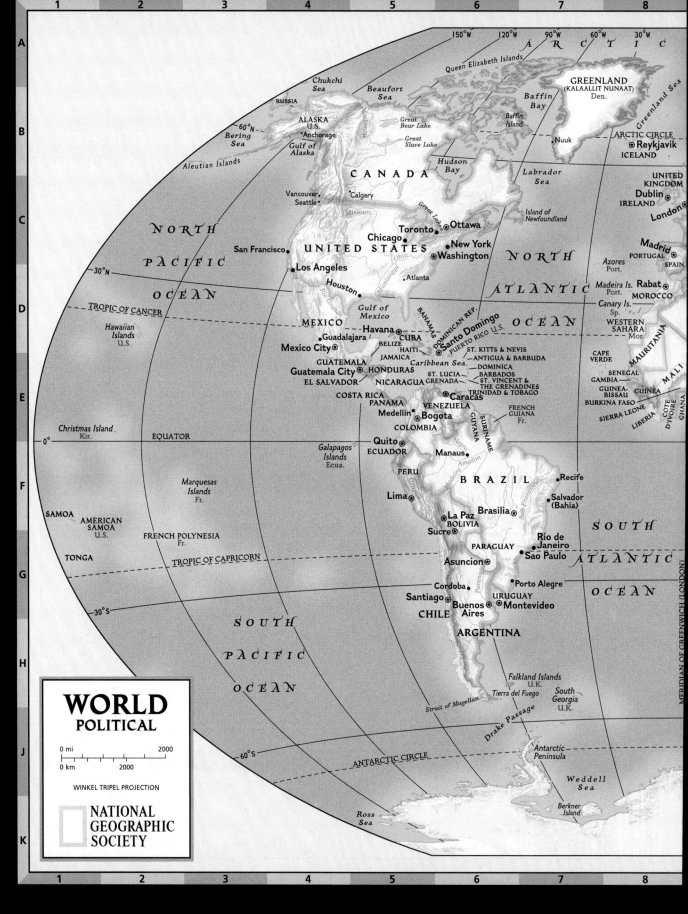

WORLD
POLITICAL

0 mi   2000
0 km   2000

WINKEL TRIPEL PROJECTION

NATIONAL
GEOGRAPHIC
SOCIETY

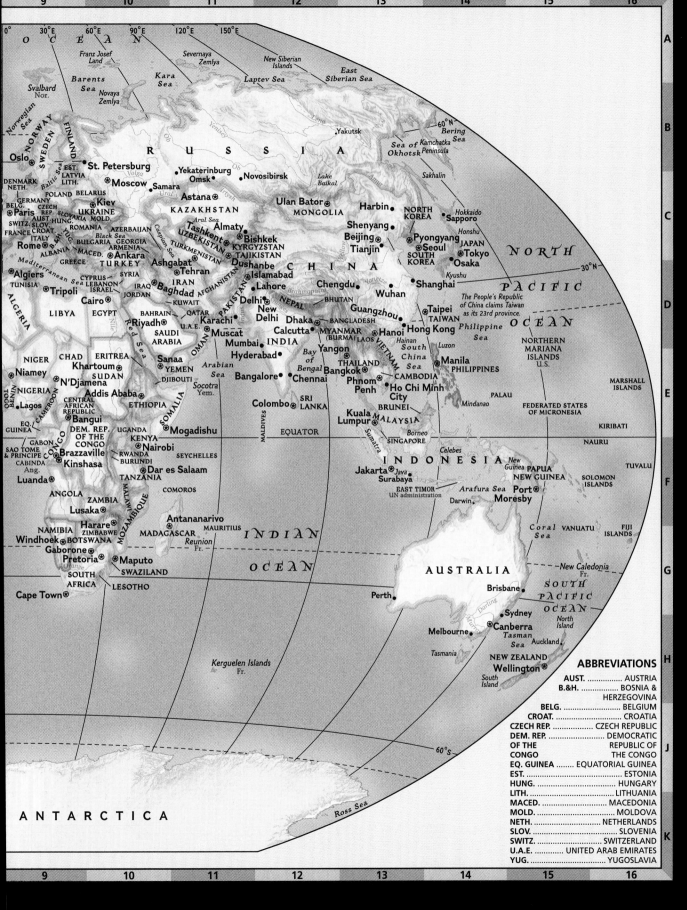

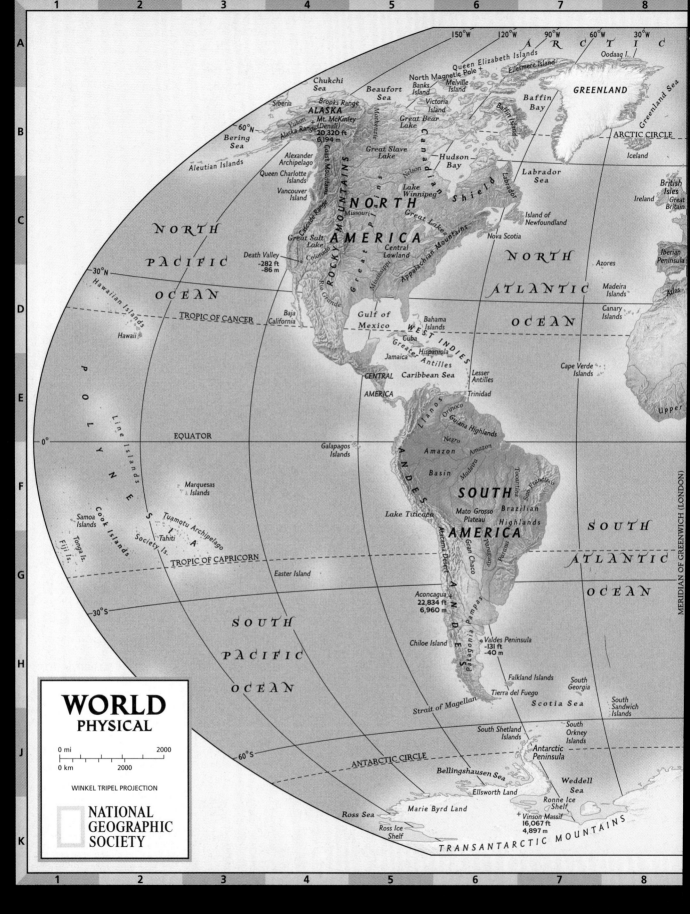

WORLD
PHYSICAL

0 mi   2000
0 km   2000

WINKEL TRIPEL PROJECTION

NATIONAL
GEOGRAPHIC
SOCIETY

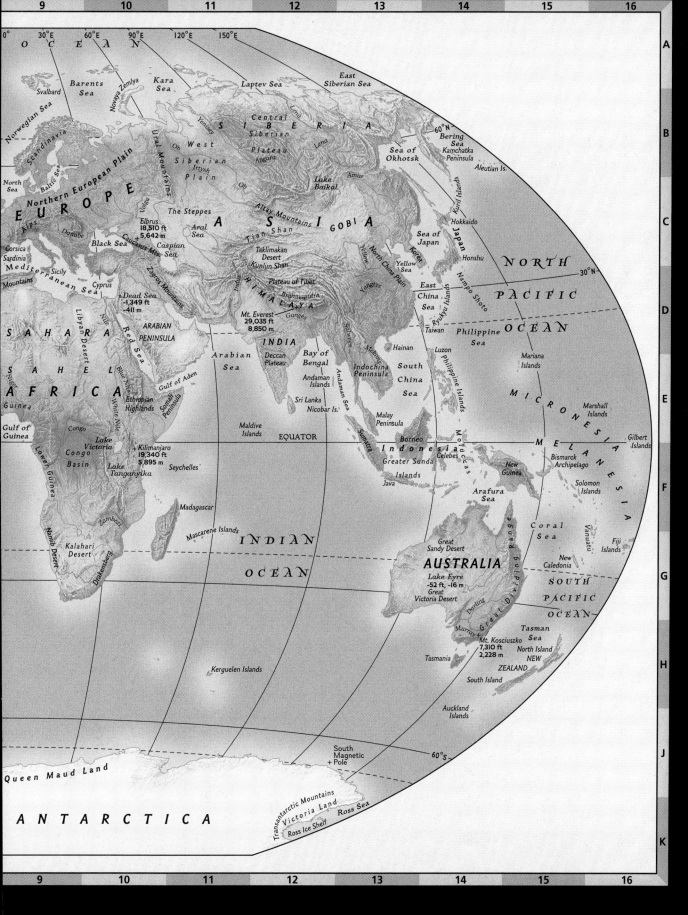

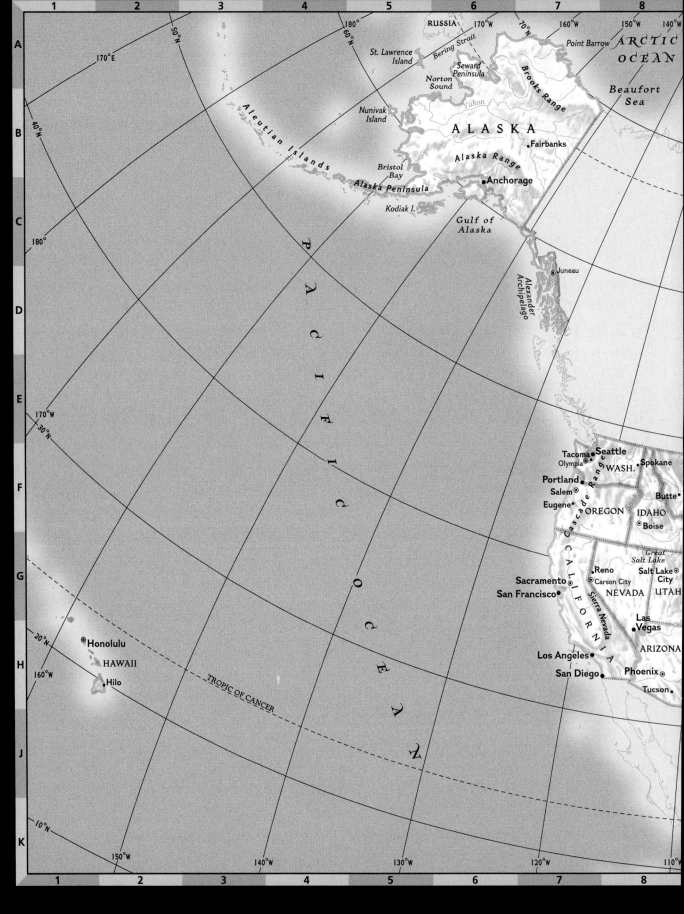

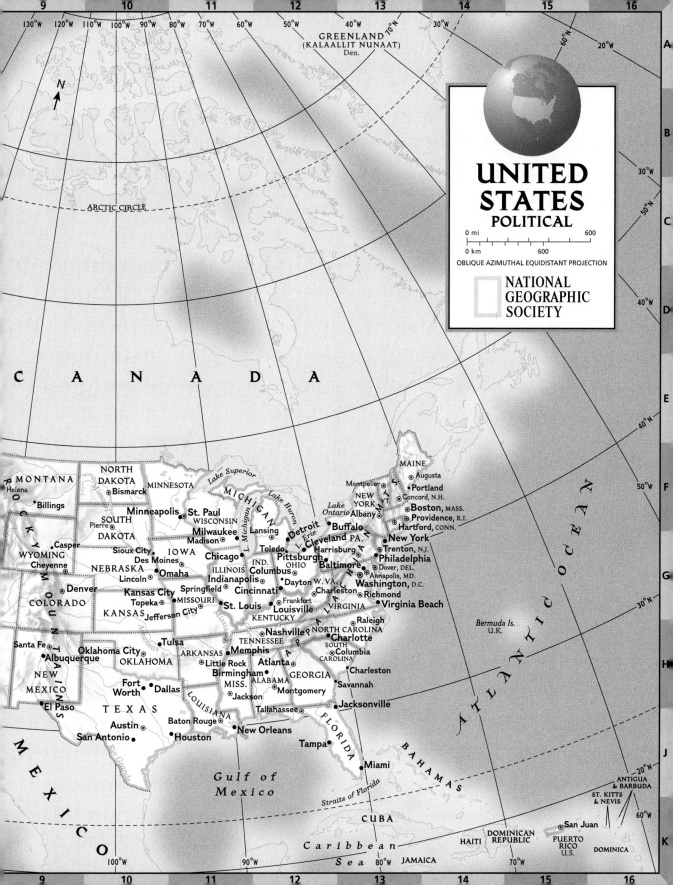

UNITED STATES POLITICAL

0 mi   600
0 km   600

OBLIQUE AZIMUTHAL EQUIDISTANT PROJECTION

NATIONAL GEOGRAPHIC SOCIETY

GREENLAND
(KALAALLIT NUNAAT)
Den.

ARCTIC CIRCLE

C A N A D A

MONTANA
• Helena
• Billings

NORTH DAKOTA
• Bismarck

MINNESOTA
Minneapolis • St. Paul

Lake Superior

MICHIGAN

Lake Huron

MAINE
• Augusta
Montpelier • Portland
NEW YORK • Concord, N.H.
Albany • Boston, MASS.
• Providence, R.I.
Hartford, CONN.

WYOMING
Cheyenne •

SOUTH DAKOTA
Pierre •

WISCONSIN
Milwaukee
Madison •

Lansing •

Detroit • Buffalo

L. Erie Cleveland
PA.

New York
Trenton, N.J.
Philadelphia

Casper •

Sioux City •

IOWA
Des Moines •

Chicago •

L. Michigan

Toledo •

Pittsburgh

Harrisburg
Baltimore
Dover, DEL.
Annapolis, MD.

NEBRASKA
Lincoln •

Omaha •

ILLINOIS

IND.
Columbus
OHIO
Dayton •

Indianapolis •

W. VA.
Washington, D.C.

Denver •

Kansas City

Springfield •

Cincinnati •

Charleston •

Richmond •

COLORADO

Topeka •
KANSAS
Jefferson City •

MISSOURI
St. Louis •

Frankfort •
Louisville •
KENTUCKY

VIRGINIA

Virginia Beach

Santa Fe •
Albuquerque •

Oklahoma City •

Tulsa •

Nashville •
TENNESSEE
Memphis •

Raleigh •
NORTH CAROLINA
Charlotte •
SOUTH
Columbia •
CAROLINA
Charleston •

NEW MEXICO

El Paso •

OKLAHOMA

ARKANSAS
• Little Rock

Birmingham •
MISS.
ALABAMA
Jackson •

Atlanta •
GEORGIA
Montgomery •

Savannah •

Jacksonville •

TEXAS
Austin •
San Antonio •

Fort Worth • Dallas •

LOUISIANA
Baton Rouge •
New Orleans •

Tallahassee •

FLORIDA

Houston •

Tampa •

Miami •

Gulf of Mexico

Straits of Florida

BAHAMAS

Bermuda Is.
U.K.

A T L A N T I C   O C E A N

CUBA

Caribbean Sea

HAITI
DOMINICAN
REPUBLIC

JAMAICA

San Juan •
PUERTO RICO
U.S.

ANTIGUA
& BARBUDA
ST. KITTS
& NEVIS

DOMINICA

M E X I C O

Rio Grande

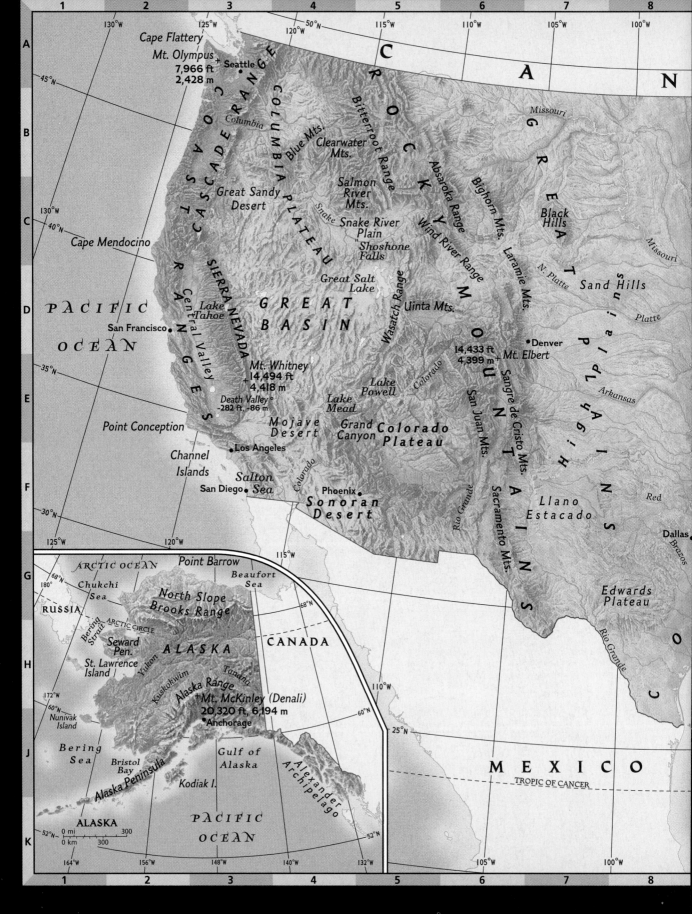

| | 1 | 2 | 3 | 4 | 5 | 6 | 7 | 8 |

A

130°W · 125°W · 50°N · 120°W · 115°W · 110°W · 105°W · 100°W

Cape Flattery
Mt. Olympus
7,966 ft
2,428 m
• Seattle

C A N A D A

B
45°N

COLUMBIA RANGE
Columbia
Blue Mts.
Clearwater Mts.
Bitterroot Range

ROCKY
Missouri
GREAT

C
130°W
40°N

Cape Mendocino

Great Sandy Desert
COLUMBIA PLATEAU
Salmon River Mts.
Snake
Snake River Plain
Shoshone Falls
Absaroka Range
Bighorn Mts.
Laramie Mts.
Black Hills
Missouri

D
130°W
40°N

PACIFIC
OCEAN

CASCADE RANGE
SIERRA NEVADA
Central Valley
Lake Tahoe
Great Salt Lake
GREAT BASIN
Wasatch Range
Uinta Mts.
Wind River Range
M O U N T A I N S
N. Platte
Platte
Sand Hills
G R E A T

San Francisco•

14,433 ft
4,399 m + Mt. Elbert
• Denver

E
35°N

Point Conception

Mt. Whitney
14,494 ft
4,418 m
Death Valley °
-282 ft, -86 m
Lake Mead
Lake Powell
Colorado
San Juan Mts.
Sangre de Cristo Mts.
Arkansas
H I G H   P L A I N S

COAST RANGES

F
125°W
30°N

Channel Islands
San Diego
Los Angeles•
Salton Sea
Mojave Desert
Grand Canyon
Colorado Plateau
Colorado
Phoenix•
Rio Grande
Sacramento Mts.
Llano Estacado
Red
Dallas•
Brazos

Sonoran Desert

G
120°W

ARCTIC OCEAN
Point Barrow
Beaufort Sea
115°W

Edwards Plateau
C O

H
180°
68°N
Chukchi Sea
RUSSIA
Bering Strait
Seward Pen.
St. Lawrence Island

North Slope
Brooks Range
ARCTIC CIRCLE
ALASKA
Yukon
Kuskokwim
CANADA
68°W
110°W

J
172°W
60°N
Nunivak Island

Alaska Range
Tanana
+ Mt. McKinley (Denali)
20,320 ft, 6,194 m
•Anchorage
60°W
25°N

Bering Sea
Bristol Bay
Alaska Peninsula
Kodiak I.
Gulf of Alaska
Alexander Archipelago

M E X I C O
TROPIC OF CANCER

K
52°N
0 mi   300
0 km   300
ALASKA
164°W
PACIFIC
OCEAN
156°W
148°W
140°W
52°N
132°W
105°W
100°W

| | 1 | 2 | 3 | 4 | 5 | 6 | 7 | 8 |

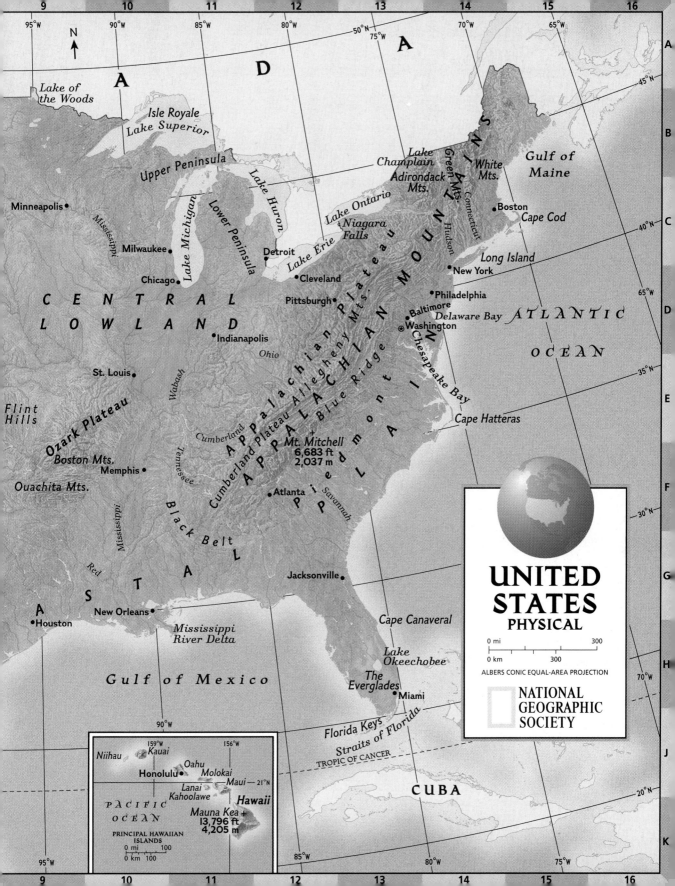

UNITED STATES
PHYSICAL

0 mi ———— 300
0 km ———— 300
ALBERS CONIC EQUAL-AREA PROJECTION

NATIONAL GEOGRAPHIC SOCIETY

Map labels:

N

Lake of the Woods

Isle Royale
Lake Superior

Upper Peninsula

Minneapolis

Milwaukee

Mississippi

Lower Peninsula

Lake Michigan

Lake Huron

Chicago

Detroit

Lake Erie

Cleveland

CENTRAL LOWLAND

Pittsburgh

Indianapolis

Ohio

St. Louis

Flint Hills

Ozark Plateau

Wabash

Boston Mts.

Memphis

Ouachita Mts.

Mississippi

Red

Black Belt

Tennessee

Cumberland

Appalachian Plateau

Allegheny Mts.

Cumberland Plateau

APPALACHIAN

Blue Ridge

Mt. Mitchell
6,683 ft
2,037 m

Atlanta

Savannah

Piedmont

COASTAL PLAIN

Lake Champlain

Adirondack Mts.

Green Mts.

White Mts.

Gulf of Maine

Boston

Cape Cod

Lake Ontario

Niagara Falls

Connecticut

Hudson

MOUNTAINS

New York

Long Island

Philadelphia

Baltimore

Washington

Delaware Bay

Chesapeake Bay

ATLANTIC OCEAN

Cape Hatteras

Jacksonville

Houston

New Orleans

Mississippi River Delta

Gulf of Mexico

Cape Canaveral

Lake Okeechobee

The Everglades

Miami

Florida Keys

Straits of Florida

TROPIC OF CANCER

CUBA

Hawaii inset:

Niihau

Kauai

Oahu

Honolulu

Molokai

Lanai

Maui — 21°N

Kahoolawe

Hawaii

Mauna Kea
13,796 ft
4,205 m

PACIFIC OCEAN

PRINCIPAL HAWAIIAN ISLANDS

0 mi ———— 100
0 km ———— 100

CANADA

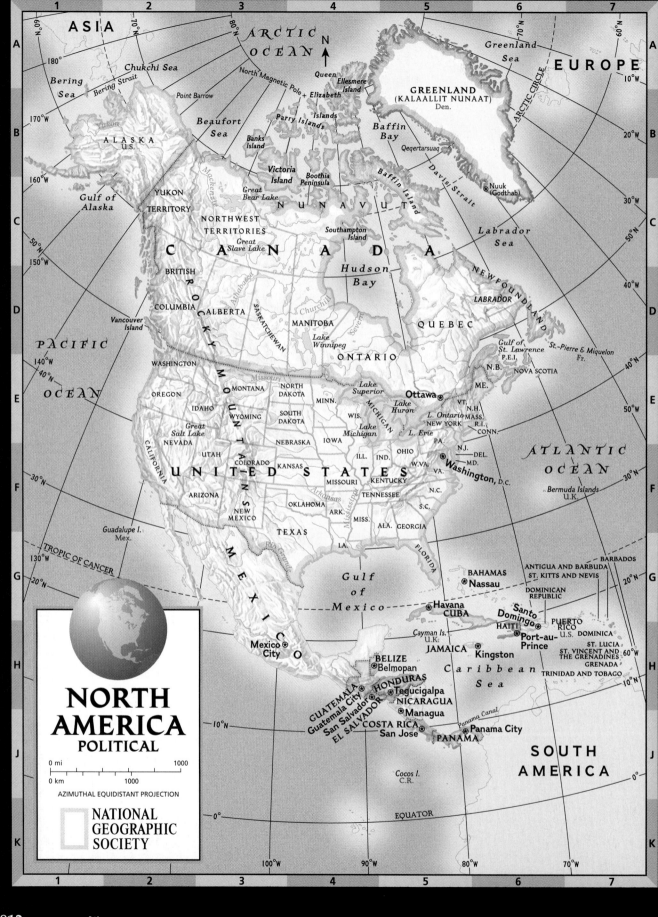

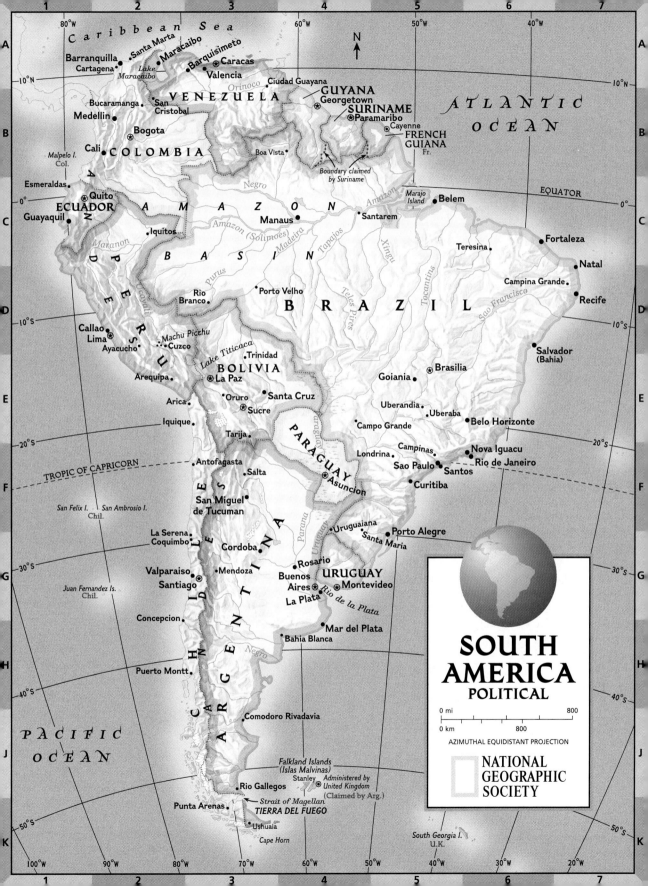

SOUTH AMERICA
POLITICAL

0 mi   800

0 km   800

AZIMUTHAL EQUIDISTANT PROJECTION

NATIONAL GEOGRAPHIC SOCIETY

CANADA
PHYSICAL/POLITICAL

0 mi — 400
0 km — 400

AZIMUTHAL EQUIDISTANT PROJECTION

NATIONAL GEOGRAPHIC SOCIETY

Ellesmere Island

Devon Island

GREENLAND
(KALAALIT NUNAAT)
Den.

ICELAND

Baffin Bay

Melville Peninsula

Baffin Island

Foxe Basin

Davis Strait

N U N A V U T

Southampton Island

Iqaluit

Hudson Strait

Labrador Sea

Ungava Bay

Hudson Bay

Belcher Islands

NEWFOUNDLAND

LABRADOR

Cartwright

Schefferville

Happy Valley-Goose Bay

Smallwood Reservoir

"Churchill Falls

Island of Newfoundland

James Bay

QUEBEC

Manicouagan Reservoir

Sept-Iles

Anticosti I.

St. John's
Avalon Peninsula

SHIELD

Gulf of St. Lawrence

St.-Pierre & Miquelon
Fr.

ONTARIO

Lake Nipigon

Chicoutimi

Gaspe Pen.

PRINCE EDWARD ISLAND

Cape Breton I.

ATLANTIC

Thunder Bay

Lake Superior

Rouyn-Noranda

Quebec

Fredericton

Charlottetown

NOVA SCOTIA

NEW BRUNSWICK

Saint John

Sudbury

St. Lawrence

Montreal

Halifax

OCEAN

Ottawa

Bay of Fundy

Lake Huron

Toronto

L. Ontario

Lake Michigan

Niagara Falls

London

L. Erie

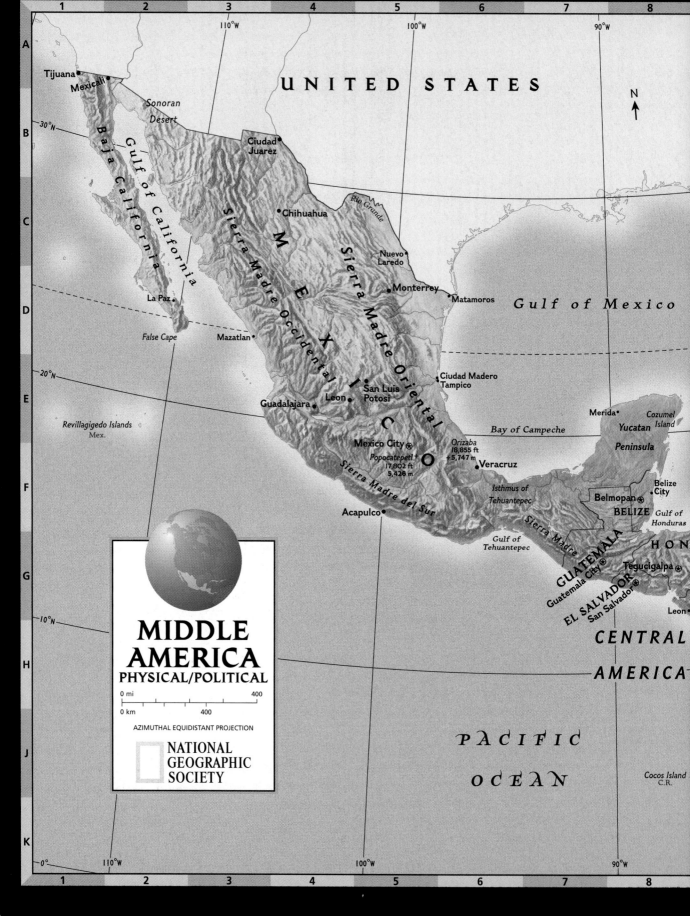

AZIMUTHAL EQUIDISTANT PROJECTION

MIDDLE
AMERICA
PHYSICAL/POLITICAL

NATIONAL
GEOGRAPHIC
SOCIETY

UNITED STATES

Tijuana
Mexicali

Sonoran
Desert

Baja California

Gulf of California

Ciudad
Juarez

Chihuahua

Rio Grande

Nuevo
Laredo

Monterrey

Matamoros

Gulf of Mexico

La Paz

False Cape

Mazatlan

Sierra Madre Occidental

M
E
X
I
C
O

Sierra Madre Oriental

Ciudad Madero
Tampico

Guadalajara

Leon

San Luis
Potosi

Merida

Cozumel
Island

Yucatan

Bay of Campeche

Peninsula

Mexico City
Popocatepetl
17,802 ft
5,426 m

Orizaba
18,855 ft
5,747 m

Veracruz

Sierra Madre del Sur

Acapulco

Isthmus of
Tehuantepec

Belize
City

Belmopan

BELIZE

Gulf of
Honduras

Gulf of
Tehuantepec

Sierra Madre

HON

GUATEMALA

Tegucigalpa

Guatemala City

EL SALVADOR

San Salvador

Leon

CENTRAL

AMERICA

PACIFIC

OCEAN

Cocos Island
C.R.

Revillagigedo Islands
Mex.

N

0 mi   400

0 km   400

30°N

20°N

10°N

0°

110°W

100°W

90°W

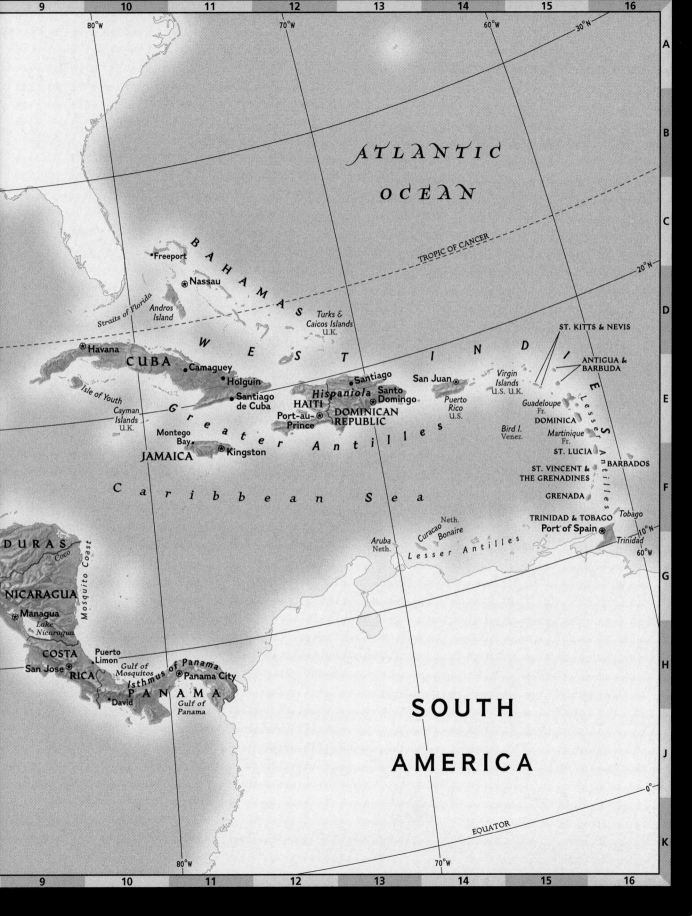

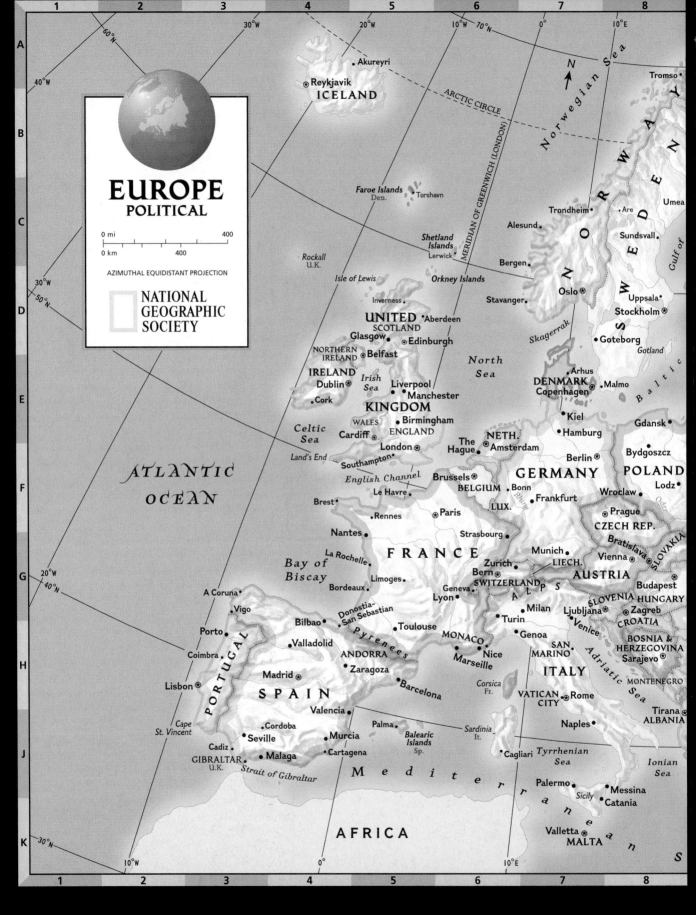

EUROPE
POLITICAL

0 mi   400
0 km   400

AZIMUTHAL EQUIDISTANT PROJECTION

NATIONAL
GEOGRAPHIC
SOCIETY

A | **B** | **C** | **D** | **E** | **F** | **G** | **H** | **J** | **K**

60°N   40°W   30°W   20°W   10°W   70°N   0°   10°E

Akureyri
⊛ Reykjavik
ICELAND

ARCTIC CIRCLE

N

Norwegian Sea

Tromso •

Faroe Islands
Den. • Torshavn

Trondheim •   • Are   Umea

Alesund •   Sundsvall •

Shetland
Islands
Lerwick

Bergen •

Gulf of

Rockall
U.K.

Orkney Islands

Isle of Lewis

Stavanger •   Oslo ⊛   Uppsala •

Inverness •

UNITED   • Aberdeen
SCOTLAND
Glasgow •   ⊛ Edinburgh

*North
Sea*

Arhus •
DENMARK
Copenhagen ⊛   • Malmo

Stockholm ⊛

• Goteborg   *Gotland*

Baltic

NORTHERN
IRELAND • Belfast

IRELAND   *Irish
Sea*
Dublin ⊛   Liverpool •
   • Manchester

• Kiel

• Hamburg   Gdansk •

• Cork

KINGDOM
WALES   • Birmingham
Cardiff •   **ENGLAND**

NETH.
The ⊛ Amsterdam
Hague

Berlin ⊛   Bydgoszcz •

*Celtic
Sea*

London ⊛

Brussels ⊛
BELGIUM   • Bonn
LUX.

GERMANY   **POLAND**
Lodz •

Land's End   Southampton •

• Frankfurt

Wroclaw •   ⊛ Prague

**ATLANTIC
OCEAN**

English Channel
Le Havre •

Brest •   Rennes •   ⊛ Paris

Rhine

CZECH REP.
Bratislava ⊛   **SLOVAKIA**
⊛ Prague

Strasbourg •

Munich •   Vienna •   **AUSTRIA**
LIECH.

Nantes •

FRANCE

Zurich •   **Budapest**

La Rochelle •   *Bay of
Biscay*
Bordeaux •

Limoges •

Bern ⊛
SWITZERLAND
Geneva •   **A L P S**
Lyon •

SLOVENIA   **HUNGARY**
Ljubljana ⊛   ⊛ Zagreb
CROATIA

20°W   A Coruna •
40°N

Vigo •

Donostia-
San Sebastian •

Milan •   • Venice

• Turin

Porto •

Bilbao •   *Pyrenees*
Valladolid •

Toulouse •   Genoa •

**BOSNIA &
HERZEGOVINA**
Sarajevo ⊛

MONACO
• Nice

**SAN
MARINO**

Coimbra •   **ANDORRA**
• Zaragoza

Marseille •

ITALY   MONTENEGRO

*Adriatic
Sea*

Lisbon ⊛   Madrid ⊛

• Barcelona

*Corsica
Fr.*

**VATICAN
CITY** ⊛ Rome
Tirana ⊛
ALBANIA

*Cape
St. Vincent*

SPAIN

Valencia •

Palma •

*Sardinia
It.*

Naples •

• Cordoba

Cadiz •   • Seville

*Balearic
Islands
Sp.*

PORTUGAL

• Murcia
• Malaga   • Cartagena

• Cagliari   *Tyrrhenian
Sea*

*Ionian
Sea*

GIBRALTAR
U.K.   *Strait of Gibraltar*

Palermo •

M e d i t e r r a n e a n

Sicily   • Messina
• Catania

30°N   10°W   0°   10°E

AFRICA

Valletta ⊛
MALTA

MERIDIAN OF GREENWICH (LONDON)

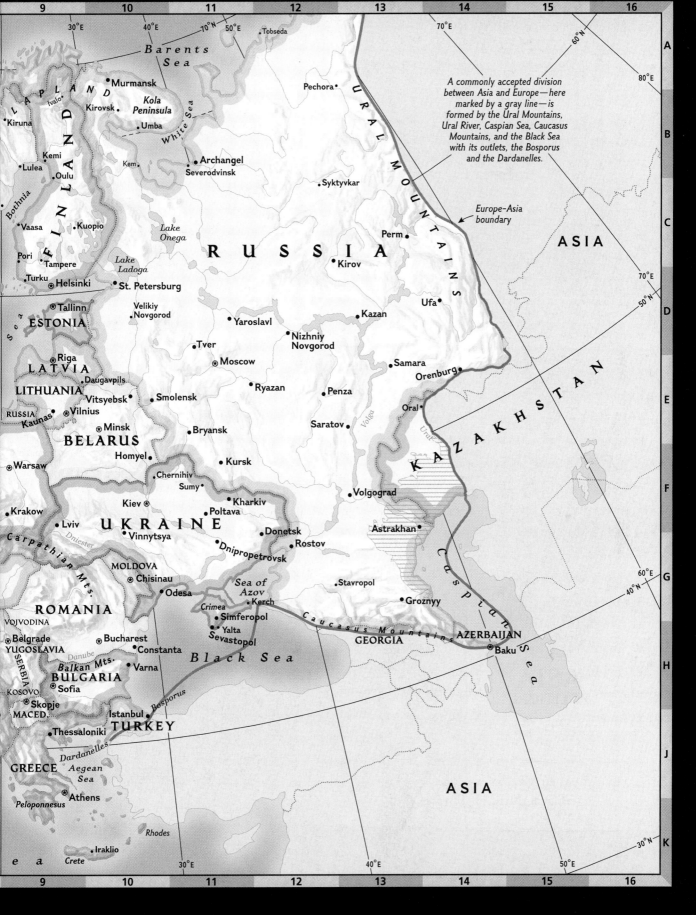

A commonly accepted division between Asia and Europe—here marked by a gray line—is formed by the Ural Mountains, Ural River, Caspian Sea, Caucasus Mountains, and the Black Sea with its outlets, the Bosporus and the Dardanelles.

Europe–Asia boundary

Barents Sea

Tobseda

Pechora

Kola Peninsula

Murmansk

Kirovsk

Umba

White Sea

Kem

Archangel

Severodvinsk

Syktyvkar

LAPLAND

Ivalo

Kiruna

Kemi

Oulu

Lake Onega

FINLAND

Bothnia

Vaasa

Kuopio

Pori

Tampere

Lake Ladoga

Turku

Helsinki

St. Petersburg

RUSSIA

Perm

Kirov

Sea

Tallinn

ESTONIA

Velikiy Novgorod

Yaroslavl

Kazan

Ufa

Riga

LATVIA

Daugavpils

Tver

Nizhniy Novgorod

Moscow

Samara

Orenburg

LITHUANIA

Vitsyebsk

Smolensk

Ryazan

Penza

Oral

Volga

Kaunas

Vilnius

Ural

RUSSIA

Minsk

Bryansk

Saratov

KAZAKHSTAN

BELARUS

Homyel

Kursk

ASIA

Warsaw

Chernihiv

Sumy

Kharkiv

Volgograd

Krakow

Kiev

Poltava

Astrakhan

Lviv

UKRAINE

Donetsk

Rostov

Vinnytsya

Dnipropetrovsk

Dniester

Carpathian Mts.

MOLDOVA

Chisinau

Sea of Azov

Stavropol

ROMANIA

Odesa

Crimea

Kerch

Simferopol

Caucasus Mountains

Groznyy

AZERBAIJAN

VOJVODINA

Yalta

Sevastopol

GEORGIA

Baku

YUGOSLAVIA

Belgrade

Bucharest

Constanta

Black Sea

Caspian Sea

SERBIA

Danube

Balkan Mts.

Varna

KOSOVO

BULGARIA

Sofia

MACED.

Skopje

Bosporus

Istanbul

Thessaloniki

TURKEY

GREECE

Dardanelles

Aegean Sea

ASIA

Athens

Peloponnesus

Rhodes

Iraklio

Crete

e   a

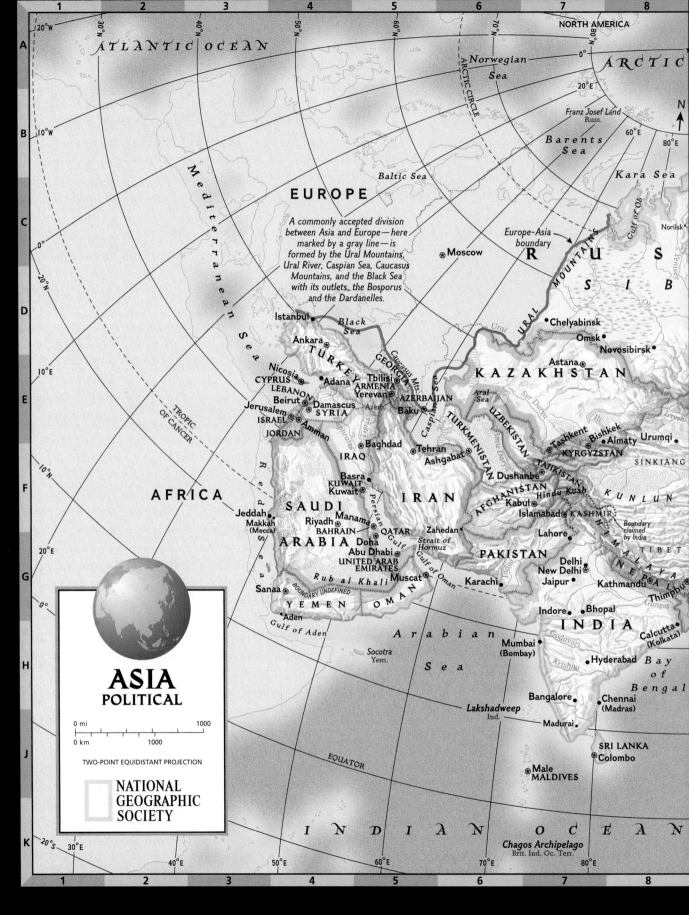

ASIA
POLITICAL

0 mi   1000
0 km   1000

TWO-POINT EQUIDISTANT PROJECTION

NATIONAL
GEOGRAPHIC
SOCIETY

9   **10**   **11**   **12**   **13**   **14**   **15**   **16**

80°N

North Pole

A R C T I C   O C E A N

North Pole

NORTH AMERICA

Bering Strait

180°

Wrangel I.

Chukchi Sea

Gulf of Anadyr

Anadyr

60°N

Bering Sea

160°W

A

170°W

B

East Siberian Sea

160°E

New Siberian Islands

North Land

120°E

100°E

Laptev Sea

Lena

Commander Is.

Kamchatka Peninsula

50°N

Cherskiy Range

Kolyma Range

Verkhoyansk Range

180°

C

20°N

Magadan

Sea of Okhotsk

A S I A

Yakutsk

Lena

S I B E R I A

Irkutsk

Lake Baikal

Yenisey

MANCHURIA

Changchun

Shenyang

Sakhalin

Kuril Islands

Hokkaido

Sapporo

170°E

D

Sea of Japan

Vladivostok

Japan

JAPAN

Tokyo

Honshu

Kyoto

Osaka

Hiroshima

Kyushu

Marcus I.
Jap.

TROPIC OF CANCER

Bonin Is.
Jap.

Volcano Is.
Jap.

10°N

160°E

E

F

Ulan Bator

M O N G O L I A

ALTAY MTS.

GOBI

Herlen

Beijing

NORTH KOREA

Pyongyang

Seoul

SOUTH KOREA

Qingdao

Yellow

Xuzhou

East China

Shanghai

Nanjing

Yellow Sea

Shijiazhuang

Lanzhou

Xian

S H A N

C H I N A

Yangtze

Yellow

Chengdu

Changsha

Nanchang

Fuzhou

East China Sea

Ryukyu Islands

Okinawa

Parece Vela
Jap.

P A C I F I C   O C E A N

160°E

G

Guiyang

Boundary claimed by China

Kunming

Guangzhou

Hong Kong

Macau

Taipei

TAIWAN

The People's Republic of China claims Taiwan as its 23rd province.

BHUTAN

BANGLADESH

Dhaka

MYANMAR (BURMA)

Yangon (Rangoon)

Hanoi

Haiphong

Vientiane

L A O S

Da Nang

South China Sea

Hainan

Luzon

Quezon City

Manila

Samar

PHILIPPINES

Mindoro

Panay

Leyte

Philippine Sea

0°

H

THAILAND

Bangkok

Andaman Islands
Ind.

Andaman Sea

CAMBODIA

Phnom Penh

Ho Chi Minh City

VIETNAM

Gulf of Thailand

Palawan

Negros

Mindanao

EQUATOR

10°S

Nicobar Islands
Ind.

Kuala Lumpur

Medan

MALAYSIA

Bandar Seri Begawan

BRUNEI

SABAH

SARAWAK

MALAYSIA

Morotai

Halmahera

Biak

Jayapura

New Guinea

Kepi

Aru
Is.

Dolak

Merauke

J

SINGAPORE

Sumatra

Jambi

I N D O N E S I A

G R E A T E R

Borneo

Celebes

Buru

Ceram

Tanimbar
Is.

Moluccas

Following East Timor's vote for independence from Indonesia, the United Nations, in October 1999, established a UN transitional administration to help East Timor's 870,000 people toward independence.

Mentawai Islands

S U N D A   I S L A N D S

Java Sea

Dili

EAST TIMOR
UN admin.

Timor

AUSTRALIA

20°S

150°E

K

Jakarta

Java

Kupang

Timor Sea

100°E   110°E   120°E   130°E   140°E

9   **10**   **11**   **12**   **13**   **14**   **15**   **16**

	1	2	3	4	5	6	7	8

120°E   130°E   140°E   150°E   160°E   170°E

A TROPIC OF CANCER

20°N

N O R T H   P A C I F I C   O C E A N

B

A S I A

M I C R O N E S I A

NORTHERN
MARIANA
ISLANDS
U.S.
⊙ Saipan

GUAM ⊙ Hagatna
U.S.

Wake Island
U.S.

Bikini Atoll MARSHALL
ISLANDS

Ralik Chain   *Ratak Chain*

10°N

C

PALAU
Koror ⊛

Yap
Islands

Truk Islands

Caroline   Islands

⊛ Palikir
Pohnpei (Ponape)

⊛ Majuro

Gilbert Islands

⊛ Tarawa

FEDERATED STATES
OF MICRONESIA

0° EQUATOR

D

M E L A N E S I A

Yaren ⊛
NAURU

TUVALU
Funafuti ⊛

New Guinea

Mt. Wilhelm
14,793 ft
+ 4,509 m

New Britain

SOLOMON
ISLANDS

PAPUA
NEW GUINEA
Port Moresby ⊛

Solomon Is.

⊛ Honiara

Santa
Cruz Is.

Torres Strait

10°S

E

Darwin •

Gulf of
Carpentaria

C
o
r
a
l

CORAL SEA
ISLANDS
TERRITORY
Austral.

VANUATU
⊛ Port-Vila

Suva ⊛

FIJI
ISLANDS

NEW
CALEDONIA
Fr.

F

20°S

*Kimberley
Plateau*

S
e
a

• Noumea

TROPIC OF CAPRICORN

GREAT DIVIDING RANGE

*Macdonnell
Ranges*

AUSTRALIA

• Brisbane

Norfolk Island
Austral.

G

30°S

GREAT VICTORIA
DESERT

Lake Eyre ○
-52 ft
-16 m

Lord Howe Island
Austral.

• Perth

*Great Australian
Bight*

Darling

• Sydney

T a s m a n

North
Island

H

Adelaide •

Murray

⊛ Canberra
+ Mt. Kosciuszko
7,310 ft
2,228 m

S e a

Auckland •

NEW
ZEALAND

Melbourne •

Wellington ⊛

40°S

J

I N D I A N   O C E A N

Tasmania

• Hobart

Mt. Cook +
12,349 ft
3,764 m

South
Island

• Christchurch

Stewart Island

50°S

K

120°E   130°E   140°E   150°E   160°E   170°E

	1	2	3	4	5	6	7	8

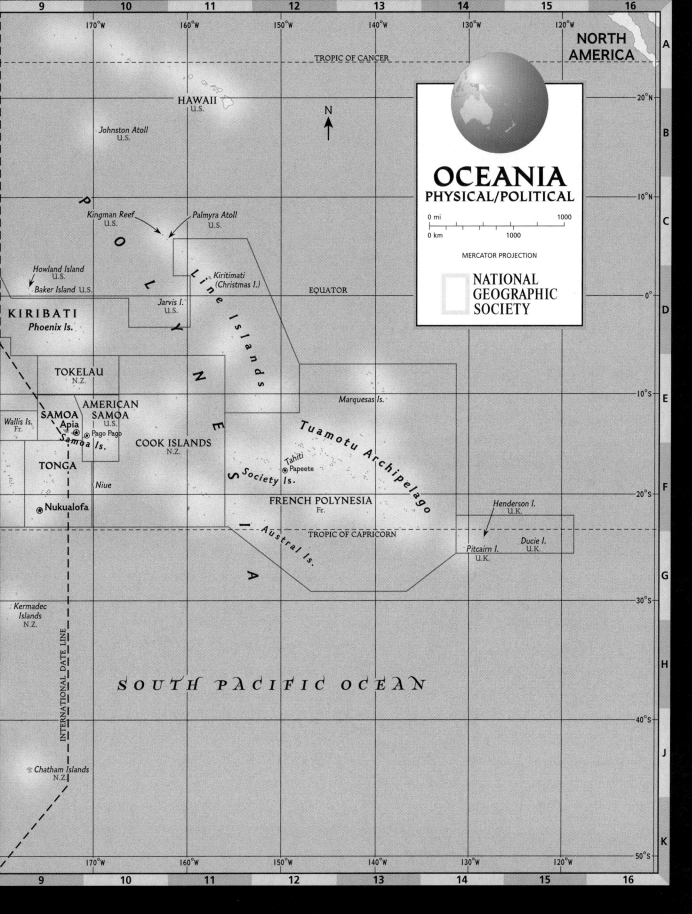

170°W   160°W   150°W   140°W   130°W   120°W

TROPIC OF CANCER

NORTH AMERICA

A

20°N

B

HAWAII
U.S.

N

Johnston Atoll
U.S.

10°N

C

OCEANIA
PHYSICAL/POLITICAL

0 mi   1000
0 km   1000

MERCATOR PROJECTION

**NATIONAL
GEOGRAPHIC
SOCIETY**

Kingman Reef
U.S.

Palmyra Atoll
U.S.

P
O
L
Y
N
E
S
I
A

Kiritimati
(Christmas I.)

Line Islands

Howland Island
U.S.

Baker Island U.S.

Jarvis I.
U.S.

EQUATOR

0°

D

KIRIBATI
Phoenix Is.

TOKELAU
N.Z.

10°S

E

Marquesas Is.

*Wallis Is.
Fr.*

SAMOA
Apia

**AMERICAN
SAMOA**
U.S.

Pago Pago

Samoa Is.

COOK ISLANDS
N.Z.

Tuamotu Archipelago

TONGA

Niue

Tahiti
Papeete

Society Is.

Nukualofa

FRENCH POLYNESIA
Fr.

Henderson I.
U.K.

20°S

F

Austral Is.

TROPIC OF CAPRICORN

Pitcairn I.
U.K.

Ducie I.
U.K.

*Kermadec
Islands
N.Z.*

30°S

G

INTERNATIONAL DATE LINE

SOUTH PACIFIC OCEAN

40°S

H

J

*Chatham Islands
N.Z.*

K

50°S

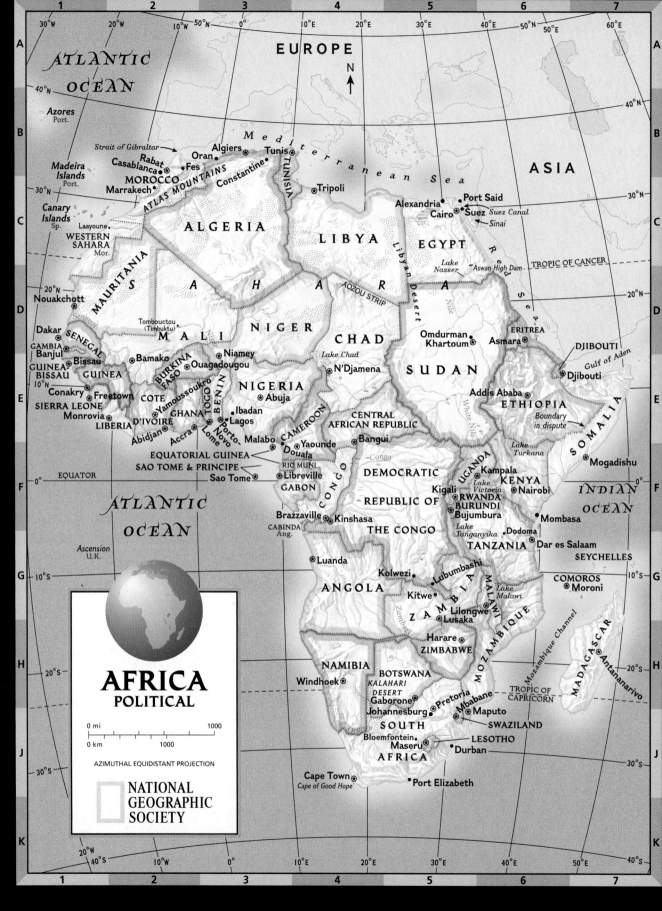

AFRICA
POLITICAL

0 mi 1000
0 km 1000

AZIMUTHAL EQUIDISTANT PROJECTION

NATIONAL GEOGRAPHIC SOCIETY

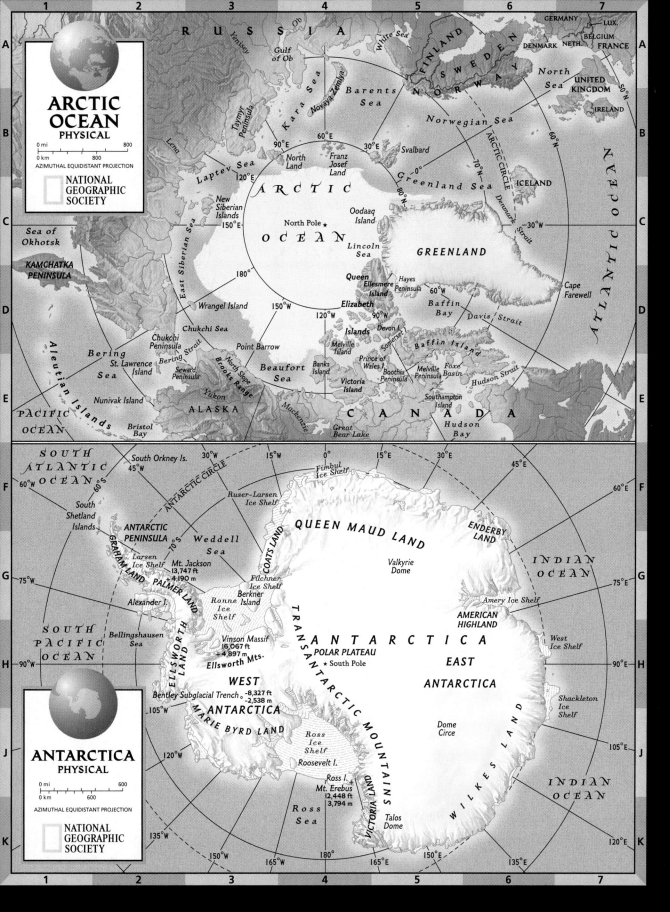

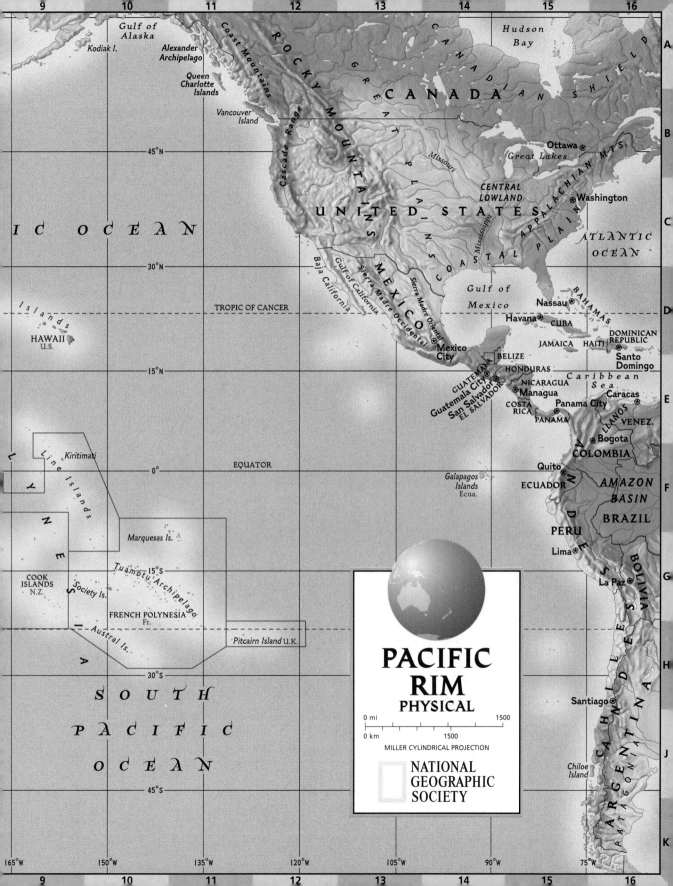

PACIFIC
RIM
PHYSICAL

0 mi ————————————— 1500
0 km ————————————— 1500

MILLER CYLINDRICAL PROJECTION

NATIONAL
GEOGRAPHIC
SOCIETY

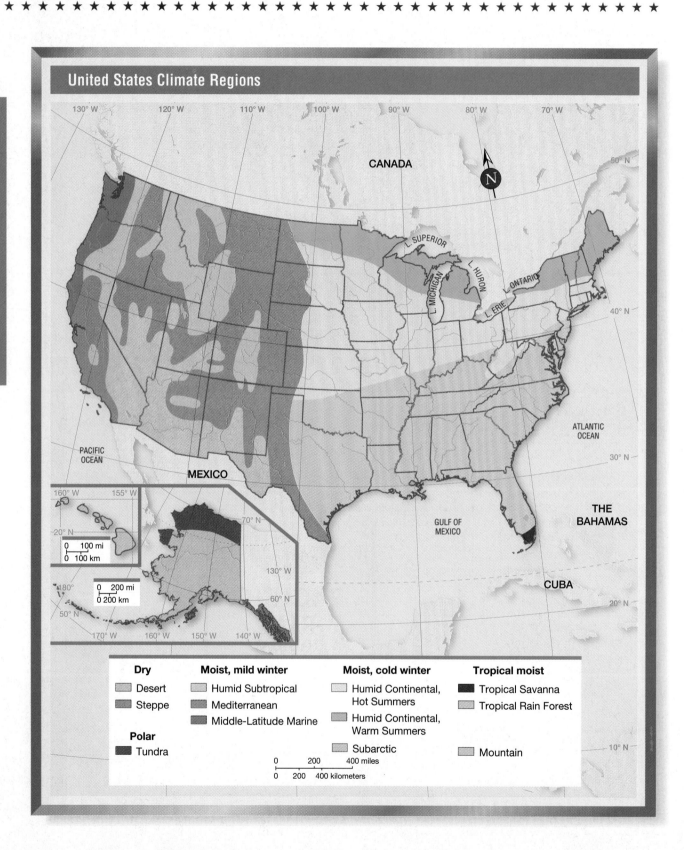

United States Climate Regions

Dry	Moist, mild winter	Moist, cold winter	Tropical moist
Desert	Humid Subtropical	Humid Continental, Hot Summers	Tropical Savanna
Steppe	Mediterranean	Humid Continental, Warm Summers	Tropical Rain Forest
Polar	Middle-Latitude Marine	Subarctic	Mountain
Tundra			

Population of the United States

Year	Population			Year	Population		
1790	3,929,214	4.5	–	1910	91,972,266	31.0	21.0
1800	5,308,483	6.1	35.1	1920	105,710,620	35.6	14.9
1810	7,239,881	4.3	36.4	1930	122,775,046	41.2	16.1
1820	9,638,453	5.5	33.1	1940	131,669,275	44.2	7.2
1830	12,866,020	7.4	33.5	1950	151,325,798	50.7	14.5
1840	17,069,453	9.8	32.7	1960	179,323,175	50.6	18.5
1850	23,191,876	7.9	35.9	1970	203,302,031	57.4	13.4
1860	31,443,321	10.6	35.6	1980	226,542,199	64.0	11.4
1870	39,818,449	13.4	26.6	1990	248,718,301	70.3	9.8
1880	50,155,783	16.9	26.0	1995	263,039,000	74.3	5.6
1890	62,947,714	21.2	25.5	2000*	271,237,000	76.7	3.2
1900	75,994,575	25.6	20.7	2020*	288,807,000	81.7	6.5

Key:

▮ Population per square mile of land

▯ Percentage increase over preceding census

*projected

Source: *Statistical Abstract of the United States*, 1996.

Population Distribution by Age

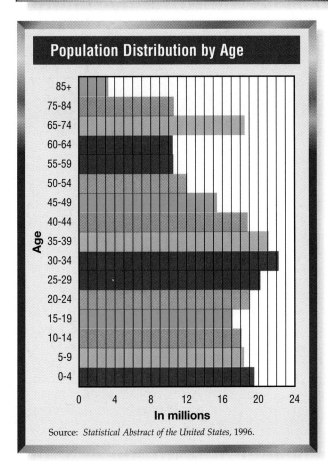

Source: *Statistical Abstract of the United States*, 1996.

Major Religions in the United States

Roman Catholic Church	61,207,914
Southern Baptist Convention	15,691,964
United Methodist Church	8,495,378
National Baptist Convention, U.S.A.	8,200,000
Jews	3,500,000
Church of God in Christ (Pentecostal)	5,499,875
Evangelical Lutheran Church in America	5,180,910
Muslims	3,332,000
Church of Jesus Christ of Latter-Day Saints (Mormon)	4,800,000
Presbyterian Church (U.S.A.)	3,637,735
African Methodist Episcopal Church	3,500,000
National Baptist Convention of America	2,500,000
Lutheran Church (Missouri Synod)	2,594,555
Episcopal Church	2,536,550
Assemblies of God	2,467,588
Orthodox Church in America	2,000,000
Churches of Christ	2,250,000
American Baptist Churches in the U.S.A.	1,503,267
United Church of Christ	1,452,565
Greek Orthodox Archdiocese of North and South America	1,950,000
African Methodist Episcopal Zion Church	1,252,369
Christian Churches and Churches of Christ	2,250,000

Source: *World Year Book 1999*.

Political Parties in Power

George Washington, 1789–1797
John Adams, 1797–1801
Thomas Jefferson, 1801–1809
James Madison, 1809–1817
James Monroe, 1817–1825
John Quincy Adams, 1825–1829
Andrew Jackson, 1829–1837
Martin Van Buren, 1837–1841
William H. Harrison/John Tyler, 1841–1845
James K. Polk, 1845–1849
Zachary Taylor/Millard Fillmore, 1849–1853
Franklin Pierce, 1853–1857
James Buchanan, 1857–1861
Abraham Lincoln, 1861–1865
Andrew Johnson, 1865–1869
Ulysses S. Grant, 1869–1877
Rutherford B. Hayes, 1877–1881
James A. Garfield/Chester A. Arthur, 1881–1885
Grover Cleveland, 1885–1889
Benjamin Harrison, 1889–1893
Grover Cleveland, 1893–1897
William McKinley, 1897–1901
Theodore Roosevelt, 1901–1909
William H. Taft, 1909–1913
Woodrow Wilson, 1913–1921
Warren G. Harding, 1921–1923
Calvin Coolidge, 1923–1929
Herbert C. Hoover, 1929–1933
Franklin D. Roosevelt, 1933–1945
Harry S Truman, 1945–1953
Dwight D. Eisenhower, 1953–1961
John F. Kennedy, 1961–1963
Lyndon B. Johnson, 1963–1969
Richard M. Nixon, 1969–1974
Gerald R. Ford, 1974–1977
James E. Carter, Jr., 1977–1981
Ronald W. Reagan, 1981–1989
George H. W. Bush, 1989–1993
William J. Clinton, 1993–2001

☐ Federalist   ☐ Democratic
☐ Democratic   ☐ Whig
   Republican
                 ☐ Republican

Graduation Rates

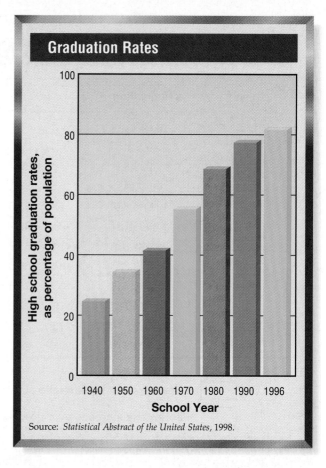

Source: *Statistical Abstract of the United States,* 1998.

Life Expectancy

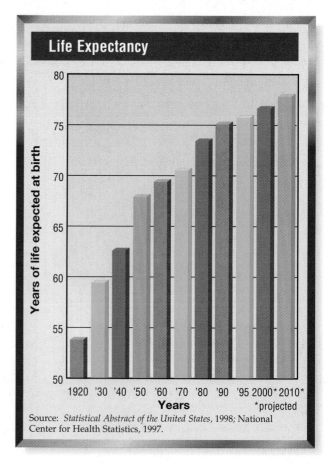

Source: *Statistical Abstract of the United States,* 1998; National Center for Health Statistics, 1997.

The United States

STATE*	YEAR ADMITTED	POPULATION (2000)	LAND AREA (sq mi)	CAPITAL	LARGEST CITY	HOUSE REP. (2000)**
1. Delaware	1787	768,000	1,954	Dover	Wilmington	1
2. Pennsylvania	1787	12,202,000	44,819	Harrisburg	Philadelphia	21
3. New Jersey	1787	8,178,000	7,418	Trenton	Newark	13
4. Georgia	1788	7,875,000	57,918	Atlanta	Atlanta	11
5. Connecticut	1788	3,284,000	4,845	Hartford	Bridgeport	6
6. Massachusetts	1788	6,199,000	7,838	Boston	Boston	10
7. Maryland	1788	5,275,000	9,774	Annapolis	Baltimore	8
8. South Carolina	1788	3,858,000	30,111	Columbia	Columbia	6
9. New Hampshire	1788	1,224,000	8,969	Concord	Manchester	2
10. Virginia	1788	6,997,000	39,597	Richmond	Virginia Beach	11
11. New York	1788	18,146,000	47,223	Albany	New York	31
12. North Carolina	1789	7,777,000	48,718	Raleigh	Charlotte	12
13. Rhode Island	1790	998,000	1,045	Providence	Providence	2
14. Vermont	1791	617,000	9,249	Montpelier	Burlington	1
15. Kentucky	1792	3,995,000	39,732	Frankfort	Louisville	6
16. Tennessee	1796	5,657,000	41,219	Nashville	Memphis	9
17. Ohio	1803	11,319,000	40,952	Columbus	Columbus	19
18. Louisiana	1812	4,425,000	43,566	Baton Rouge	New Orleans	7
19. Indiana	1816	6,045,000	35,870	Indianapolis	Indianapolis	10
20. Mississippi	1817	2,816,000	46,913	Jackson	Jackson	5
21. Illinois	1818	12,051,000	55,593	Springfield	Chicago	20
22. Alabama	1819	4,451,000	50,750	Montgomery	Birmingham	7
23. Maine	1820	1,259,000	30,864	Augusta	Portland	2
24. Missouri	1821	5,540,000	68,898	Jefferson City	Kansas City	9
25. Arkansas	1836	2,631,000	52,075	Little Rock	Little Rock	4
26. Michigan	1837	9,679,000	56,809	Lansing	Detroit	16
27. Florida	1845	15,233,000	53,997	Tallahassee	Jacksonville	23
28. Texas	1845	20,119,000	261,194	Austin	Houston	30
29. Iowa	1846	2,900,000	55,874	Des Moines	Des Moines	5
30. Wisconsin	1848	5,326,000	54,313	Madison	Milwaukee	9
31. California	1850	32,521,000	155,973	Sacramento	Los Angeles	52
32. Minnesota	1858	4,830,000	79,616	St. Paul	Minneapolis	8
33. Oregon	1859	3,397,000	96,002	Salem	Portland	5
34. Kansas	1861	2,668,000	81,823	Topeka	Wichita	4
35. West Virginia	1863	1,841,000	24,086	Charleston	Charleston	3
36. Nevada	1864	1,871,000	109,805	Carson City	Las Vegas	2
37. Nebraska	1867	1,705,000	76,877	Lincoln	Omaha	3
38. Colorado	1876	4,168,000	103,729	Denver	Denver	6
39. North Dakota	1889	662,000	68,994	Bismarck	Fargo	1
40. South Dakota	1889	777,000	75,897	Pierre	Sioux Falls	1
41. Montana	1889	950,000	145,556	Helena	Billings	1
42. Washington	1889	5,858,000	66,581	Olympia	Seattle	9
43. Idaho	1890	1,347,000	82,750	Boise	Boise	2
44. Wyoming	1890	525,000	97,104	Cheyenne	Cheyenne	1
45. Utah	1896	2,207,000	82,168	Salt Lake City	Salt Lake City	3
46. Oklahoma	1907	3,373,000	68,678	Oklahoma City	Oklahoma City	6
47. New Mexico	1912	1,860,000	121,364	Sante Fe	Albuquerque	3
48. Arizona	1912	4,798,000	113,642	Phoenix	Phoenix	6
49. Alaska	1959	653,000	570,373	Juneau	Anchorage	1
50. Hawaii	1959	1,257,000	6,423	Honolulu	Honolulu	2
District of Columbia (Washington, D.C.)	–	523,000	61	–	–	–
United States of America	–	274,634,000	3,536,341	Washington, D.C.	New York	435

* Numbers denote the order in which states were admitted.
** Number of members in House of Representatives

Source: *Bureau of the Census*

United States Databank

Presidents of the United States

★ ★ ★ ★ ★ ★ ★ ★ ★ ★ ★ ★ ★ ★ ★ ★ ★

** The Republican party during this period developed into today's Democratic party. Today's Republican party originated in 1854.

George Washington

1

1789–1797

Born: 1732
Died: 1799
Born in: Virginia
Elected from: Virginia
Age when elected: 56
Occupations: Planter, Soldier
Party: None
Vice President: John Adams

John Adams

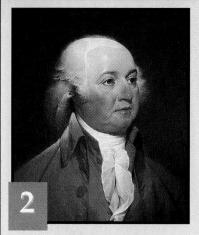

2

1797–1801

Born: 1735
Died: 1826
Born in: Massachusetts
Elected from: Massachusetts
Age when elected: 61
Occupations: Teacher, Lawyer
Party: Federalist
Vice President: Thomas Jefferson

Thomas Jefferson

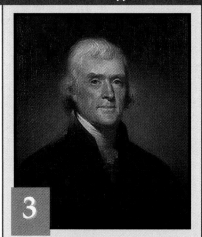

3

1801–1809

Born: 1743
Died: 1826
Born in: Virginia
Elected from: Virginia
Age when elected: 57
Occupations: Planter, Lawyer
Party: Republican**
Vice Presidents: Aaron Burr, George Clinton

James Madison

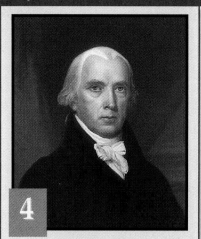

4

1809–1817

Born: 1751
Died: 1836
Born in: Virginia
Elected from: Virginia
Age when elected: 57
Occupation: Planter
Party: Republican**
Vice Presidents: George Clinton, Elbridge Gerry

James Monroe

5

1817–1825

Born: 1758
Died: 1831
Born in: Virginia
Elected from: Virginia
Age when elected: 58
Occupation: Lawyer
Party: Republican**
Vice President: Daniel D. Tompkins

Presidents

John Quincy Adams

6

1825–1829

Born: 1767
Died: 1848
Born in: Massachusetts
Elected from: Massachusetts
Age when elected: 57
Occupation: Lawyer
Party: Republican**
Vice President: John C. Calhoun

Andrew Jackson

7

1829–1837

Born: 1767
Died: 1845
Born in: South Carolina
Elected from: Tennessee
Age when elected: 61
Occupations: Lawyer, Soldier
Party: Democratic
Vice Presidents: John C.
  Calhoun, Martin Van Buren

Martin Van Buren

8

1837–1841

Born: 1782
Died: 1862
Born in: New York
Elected from: New York
Age when elected: 54
Occupation: Lawyer
Party: Democratic
Vice President: Richard M.
  Johnson

William H. Harrison

9

1841

Born: 1773
Died: 1841
Born in: Virginia
Elected from: Ohio
Age when elected: 67
Occupations: Soldier, Planter
Party: Whig
Vice President: John Tyler

John Tyler

10

1841–1845

Born: 1790
Died: 1862
Born in: Virginia
Elected as V.P. from: Virginia
Succeeded Harrison
Age when became President: 51
Occupation: Lawyer
Party: Whig
Vice President: None

James K. Polk

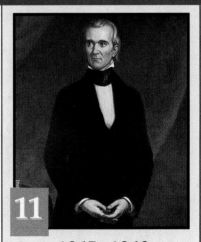

11

1845–1849

Born: 1795
Died: 1849
Born in: North Carolina
Elected from: Tennessee
Age when elected: 49
Occupation: Lawyer
Party: Democratic
Vice President: George M. Dallas

Presidents

Zachary Taylor

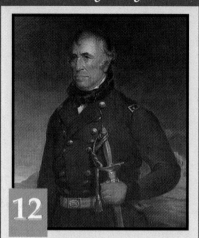

12

1849–1850

Born: 1784
Died: 1850
Born in: Virginia
Elected from: Louisiana
Age when elected: 63
Occupation: Soldier
Party: Whig
Vice President: Millard Fillmore

Millard Fillmore

13

1850–1853

Born: 1800
Died: 1874
Born in: New York
Elected as V.P. from: New York
Succeeded Taylor
Age when became President: 50
Occupation: Lawyer
Party: Whig
Vice President: None

Franklin Pierce

14

1853–1857

Born: 1804
Died: 1869
Born in: New Hampshire
Elected from: New Hampshire
Age when elected: 47
Occupation: Lawyer
Party: Democratic
Vice President: William R. King

James Buchanan

15

1857–1861

Born: 1791
Died: 1868
Born in: Pennsylvania
Elected from: Pennsylvania
Age when elected: 65
Occupation: Lawyer
Party: Democratic
Vice President: John C.
   Breckinridge

Abraham Lincoln

16

1861–1865

Born: 1809
Died: 1865
Born in: Kentucky
Elected from: Illinois
Age when elected: 51
Occupation: Lawyer
Party: Republican
Vice Presidents: Hannibal
   Hamlin, Andrew Johnson

Andrew Johnson

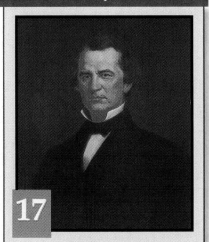

17

1865–1869

Born: 1808
Died: 1875
Born in: North Carolina
Elected as V.P. from: Tennessee
Age when became President: 56
Succeeded Lincoln
Occupation: Tailor
Party: Republican
Vice President: None

Ulysses S. Grant

18

1869–1877

Born: 1822
Died: 1885
Born in: Ohio
Elected from: Illinois
Age when elected: 46
Occupations: Farmer, Soldier
Party: Republican
Vice Presidents: Schuyler Colfax,
Henry Wilson

Rutherford B. Hayes

19

1877–1881

Born: 1822
Died: 1893
Born in: Ohio
Elected from: Ohio
Age when elected: 54
Occupation: Lawyer
Party: Republican
Vice President: William A.
Wheeler

James A. Garfield

20

1881

Born: 1831
Died: 1881
Born in: Ohio
Elected from: Ohio
Age when elected: 49
Occupations: Laborer, Professor
Party: Republican
Vice President: Chester A. Arthur

Chester A. Arthur

21

1881–1885

Born: 1830
Died: 1886
Born in: Vermont
Elected as V.P. from: New York
Succeeded Garfield
Age when became President: 50
Occupations: Teacher, Lawyer
Party: Republican
Vice President: None

Grover Cleveland

22   **24**

1885–89, 1893–97

Born: 1837
Died: 1908
Born in: New Jersey
Elected from: New York
Age when elected: 47; 55
Occupation: Lawyer
Party: Democratic
Vice Presidents: Thomas A. Hendricks, Adlai E. Stevenson

Benjamin Harrison

23

1889–1893

Born: 1833
Died: 1901
Born in: Ohio
Elected from: Indiana
Age when elected: 55
Occupation: Lawyer
Party: Republican
Vice President: Levi P. Morton

William McKinley

25

1897–1901

Born: 1843
Died: 1901
Born in: Ohio
Elected from: Ohio
Age when elected: 53
Occupations: Teacher, Lawyer
Party: Republican
Vice Presidents: Garret Hobart, Theodore Roosevelt

Theodore Roosevelt

26

1901–1909

Born: 1858
Died: 1919
Born in: New York
Elected as V.P. from: New York
Succeeded McKinley
Age when became President: 42
Occupations: Historian, Rancher
Party: Republican
Vice President: Charles W. Fairbanks

William H. Taft

27

1909–1913

Born: 1857
Died: 1930
Born in: Ohio
Elected from: Ohio
Age when elected: 51
Occupation: Lawyer
Party: Republican
Vice President: James S. Sherman

Presidents

Woodrow Wilson

28

1913–1921

Born: 1856
Died: 1924
Born in: Virginia
Elected from: New Jersey
Age when elected: 55
Occupation: College Professor
Party: Democratic
Vice President: Thomas R.
   Marshall

Warren G. Harding

29

1921–1923

Born: 1865
Died: 1923
Born in: Ohio
Elected from: Ohio
Age when elected: 55
Occupations: Newspaper Editor,
   Publisher
Party: Republican
Vice President: Calvin Coolidge

Calvin Coolidge

30

1923–1929

Born: 1872
Died: 1933
Born in: Vermont
Elected as V.P. from: Massachusetts
Succeeded Harding
Age when became President: 51
Occupation: Lawyer
Party: Republican
Vice President: Charles G. Dawes

Herbert C. Hoover

31

1929–1933

Born: 1874
Died: 1964
Born in: Iowa
Elected from: California
Age when elected: 54
Occupation: Engineer
Party: Republican
Vice President: Charles Curtis

Franklin D. Roosevelt

32

1933–1945

Born: 1882
Died: 1945
Born in: New York
Elected from: New York
Age when elected: 50
Occupation: Lawyer
Party: Democratic
Vice Presidents: John N. Garner,
   Henry A. Wallace, Harry S Truman

Harry S Truman

33

1945–1953

Born: 1884
Died: 1972
Born in: Missouri
Elected as V.P. from: Missouri
Succeeded Roosevelt
Age when became President: 60
Occupations: Clerk, Farmer
Party: Democratic
Vice President: Alben W. Barkley

Dwight D. Eisenhower

34

1953–1961

Born: 1890
Died: 1969
Born in: Texas
Elected from: New York
Age when elected: 62
Occupation: Soldier
Party: Republican
Vice President: Richard M. Nixon

John F. Kennedy

35

1961–1963

Born: 1917
Died: 1963
Born in: Massachusetts
Elected from: Massachusetts
Age when elected: 43
Occupations: Author, Reporter
Party: Democratic
Vice President: Lyndon B. Johnson

Lyndon B. Johnson

36

1963–1969

Born: 1908
Died: 1973
Born in: Texas
Elected as V.P. from: Texas
Succeeded Kennedy
Age when became President: 55
Occupation: Teacher
Party: Democratic
Vice President: Hubert H. Humphrey

Richard M. Nixon

37

1969–1974

Born: 1913
Died: 1994
Born in: California
Elected from: New York
Age when elected: 55
Occupation: Lawyer
Party: Republican
Vice Presidents: Spiro T. Agnew,
 Gerald R. Ford

Presidents

Gerald R. Ford

38

1974–1977

Born: 1913
Born in: Nebraska
Appointed by Nixon as V.P. upon
Agnew's resignation; assumed
presidency upon Nixon's resignation
Age when became President: 61
Occupation: Lawyer
Party: Republican
Vice President: Nelson A. Rockefeller

James E. Carter, Jr.

39

1977–1981

Born: 1924
Born in: Georgia
Elected from: Georgia
Age when elected: 52
Occupations: Business, Farmer
Party: Democratic
Vice President: Walter F. Mondale

Ronald W. Reagan

40

1981–1989

Born: 1911
Born in: Illinois
Elected from: California
Age when elected: 69
Occupations: Actor, Lecturer
Party: Republican
Vice President: George H.W. Bush

George H.W. Bush

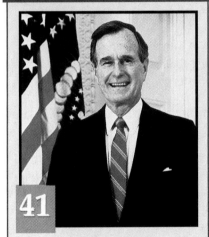

41

1989–1993

Born: 1924
Born in: Massachusetts
Elected from: Texas
Age when elected: 64
Occupation: Business
Party: Republican
Vice President: J. Danforth Quayle

William J. Clinton

42

1993–2001

Born: 1946
Born in: Arkansas
Elected from: Arkansas
Age when elected: 46
Occupation: Lawyer
Party: Democratic
Vice President: Albert Gore, Jr.

When Am I Ever Going to Use This?

*A*lthough your future career may seem far off, now is a good time to start thinking about what you will do when you finish your formal education. What you learn in this textbook will help you build a foundation of knowledge that will be extremely valuable to you when you start to work.

This Handbook helps you start thinking about one of the most important decisions you will ever make—choosing a career. Over the past 20 years the job market in the United States has changed dramatically. Many jobs that required little or no skills have disappeared, replaced with new jobs that require a high level of many different skills. Increasingly, these new jobs require workers with good educational backgrounds, particularly in fields such as Social Studies. Studying Social Studies helps establish a foundation of knowledge that will be invaluable to you when you enter the world of work.

Tomorrow's worker will need a broader educational background and better job skills. According to one senior executive, "The movement to a global economy means a very harsh, competitive environment. A degree of worry is legitimate, but not if you have world-class skills. You will be competing against Chinese, Russians, Poles, English, Brazilians, and Kenyans. You will have to do a better job and raise your skills."

PLANNING YOUR CAREER

*W*hether you plan to attend college after high school or begin working immediately, now is a good time to start thinking about what you want to do when you finish your high school education. As you will learn in this section, your generation will require a higher level of skills than previous generations, and a good background in Social Studies will be more important than ever.

Thinking About What You Want from a Career

Choosing a career depends on many factors, including your interests and skills, your level of education and training, and the opportunities available. To help you think about what kind of career you would like to pursue, use the self-assessment checklist to identify skills, weaknesses, and interests.

SELF-ASSESSMENT CHECKLIST

✔ What are my interests?
✔ What are my strengths?
✔ What are my goals?
✔ Do I like working with people, or do I prefer working alone?
✔ Do I like working in an office, or do I prefer working outdoors?

Researching Job Opportunities

Once you identify your strengths, weaknesses, and interests, you will want to try to identify what kinds of jobs could make use of those interests and skills. Several sources can help you learn about different types of jobs. Three government publications are particularly helpful.

JOB RESOURCES

✔ *The Occupational Outlook Handbook* provides detailed information on 250 occupations. Included are job duties, working conditions, levels and places of employment, education and training requirements, advancement possibilities, job trends, and average earnings.

✔ *The Dictionary of Occupational Titles* lists 20,000 different jobs and is a good source for finding out about jobs you never knew about. The *Dictionary* provides detailed explanations of job responsibilities, but it does not provide information on education or training requirements.

✔ *The Guide for Occupational Exploration* focuses on career interests and indicates the kinds of jobs that match different interests. It also indicates how to prepare for a career and find a job in a particular field.

Other good sources of information are schools and libraries, which often have career resource centers, and the Internet, which has many useful Web sites. Many schools also have computerized guidance programs that you can use to find out about different careers.

School to Work Activity: Researching the Job Market

Identify three different fields that interest you that are not listed in this handbook. Use the job resources list and any other resources, including the Internet, to learn as much as you can about jobs in these fields. In particular, find out what educational requirements are demanded, what projected future demand for these jobs will be, and what kind of salaries these jobs offer. Using a word processor, prepare a one-page report of your findings.

Finding a Job

Once you have identified the kind of job you would like, you need to find out what opportunities are available in your community. You can find out about jobs by:

- talking to people you know, including your guidance counselor
- checking the classified ads in your local news-paper
- contacting an employment agency
- using the Internet

Career Connections

Applying for a Job

You can apply for a job by writing a cover letter with a résumé. Send a clean, neatly typed letter, indicating the job you are interested in and how you found out about it, why you would be good for the job, and what your educational and work experience is.

In the last paragraph of your letter, request an appointment at the employer's convenience and indicate how the employer can reach you.

Be sure to include a copy of your résumé. A well-written résumé is critical to obtaining a good job. Before you can prepare a résumé, you will need to complete the worksheets described in the checklist.

RÉSUMÉ WORKSHEET CHECKLIST

✔ **Employment Worksheet**
List all of your previous jobs, as well as any volunteer work. Identify the name and address of the company, your duties and accomplishments, and the length of time you worked for the company.

✔ **School Worksheet**
Write the name, address, and phone number of your school, the years you have attended, the kind of program you are in (academic, vocational), your grade point average and class rank, any honors you may have received, and any important courses you have taken.

✔ **Activities Worksheet**
List all clubs, sports, and other activities in which you have participated, describe each, and identify any positions you held.

Going to a Job Interview

The job interview is probably the most important part of the hiring process; it can determine whether you are hired for a job or not. There are several things you will want to keep in mind in going through a job interview.

JOB INTERVIEW CHECKLIST

✔ Go to the interview well dressed and groomed. Dress neatly and conservatively, and avoid flashy jewelry and strong perfume/cologne.

✔ Arrive 5–10 minutes early for the interview, so that you do not appear rushed or nervous when the interviewer arrives.

✔ Shake hands firmly with the person you meet and establish good eye contact, even if you feel nervous.

✔ Be very polite. Sit down only when the interviewer asks you to have a seat. Never interrupt.

✔ Speak clearly, and avoid using slang.

After you have interviewed for a job, it is important to write a letter to the person who interviewed you, thanking him or her for meeting with you.

School to Work Activity: Writing a Cover Letter

You have often thought that you might like to become a lawyer. The following help wanted ad catches your eye.

HELP WANTED

Immediate opening for office assistant in large law firm. Duties will include creating computerized index of files.

Write a cover letter that is interesting and expresses your interest in interviewing for the job. Convince the reader that you should be considered for the job.

Career Connections

FUTURE CAREER TRENDS

The Changing Job Market

The job market has changed radically since the 1970s.

- Companies that once used American materials to produce goods exclusively for the American market now purchase materials abroad and sell their products all over the world—a trend known as globalization.
- Computerization and other technological innovations have changed the nature of the production process and the very way in which companies do business. Routine tasks, such as coding information or tightening screws, are now performed by computers or robots.
- Improvements in communications have made doing business internationally easier than ever before. Fax and Internet technologies allow firms separated by thousands of miles to communicate with each other as if they were in the same building. Overnight delivery services mean that goods can be shipped almost anywhere in the world within 24 hours.

These changes have several important implications for the United States job market:

- Many unskilled or semi-skilled manufacturing jobs are now performed abroad, where labor costs are much lower than they are in the United States. This decline in the manufacturing sector has meant that most new jobs are in the service sector. The service sector includes jobs in banking, insurance, communications, wholesaling and retailing, education, health care, engineering, architecture, construction, advertising, accounting, legal services, entertainment, tourism, and other industries in which services are provided.
- The best paying jobs in the United States now demand more education than they once did. Half of all new jobs created in the 1990s will require some education beyond high school, and almost a third of these jobs will require a college education.
- As many as 70 percent of the jobs created in 2010 will be jobs that do not exist today. To be ready to assume these new positions, workers will need to have broad-based educations and be flexible, innovative, and adaptable.

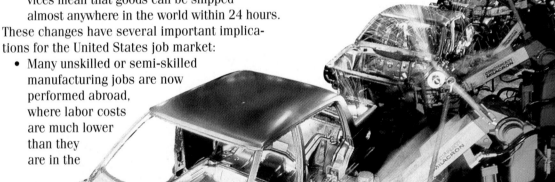

School to Work Activity: Expanding Your Horizons

Use "The Dictionary of Occupational Titles" and "The Occupational Outlook Handbook" to identify two jobs related to Social Studies in each of the following categories:

- Executive, administrative, and managerial occupations
- Professional specialty occupations
- Marketing and sales occupations
- Administrative support occupations
- Service occupations

For each job write a short report on the working conditions, levels and places of employment, education and training requirements, advancement possibilities, job trends, and average earnings.

ANTHROPOLOGIST

Job Description
Anthropologists analyze the physical, social, and cultural development of different groups of people. Some anthropologists travel to remote areas of the world to live with and learn about different cultural groups, while others study cultural groups in cities. Most anthropologists work in academic settings, teaching and doing research at colleges or universities.

Education/Training
Anthropologists almost always have doctoral degrees (Ph.D.s). Most anthropologists choose one area in which to specialize, such as sociocultural anthropology (the study of different customs and cultures), biological-physical anthropology (the study of human evolution), or linguistics (the study of the role of human speech).

Salary
Average salary: $17,800–$40,300 a year

Volunteer/Related Opportunities
Offer to help your history teacher by researching and preparing a short report for the class on the next cultural group you will study in your text.

Outlook
Growth of jobs in anthropology is projected to be slow to average, and competition for the 7,000 jobs in the field is expected to be fierce.

School to Work Activity
Choose one of these famous anthropologists to study: Louis Leakey, Davidson Black, Margaret Mead, Franz Boas, or Ralph Linton. Use your library's resources or the Internet to identify one significant contribution of the anthropologist you chose. Using a word processor, write a one-page report describing the person's main contribution.

BOOK EDITOR

Job Description
Book editors select, acquire, and edit manuscripts for publication. They work closely with authors, beginning with negotiations for the work itself and continuing as the editor directs author rewrites. They also edit manuscripts for grammar, style, and consistency.

Education/Training
Book editors usually have bachelor's degrees, most often in journalism, English, or communications.

Salary
Average salary: $26,700–$45,400

Volunteer/Related Opportunities
At the library find a list of proofreader's marks. Edit your next English paper using the correct proofreader's symbols.

Outlook
Jobs in this field are expected to grow at an average rate through 2005. Turnover in the field is high.

School to Work Activity
Editors must ensure that the reading level of a manuscript is appropriate for the intended audience. Choose two paragraphs from your history book. Rewrite them so that they are suitable for third graders.

COLLEGE PROFESSOR

Job Description
College professors teach students at colleges and Universities. Professors at universities and some research-oriented colleges also perform research. Professors spend 3-16 hours a week teaching and 3-6 hours a week meeting individually with students. The rest of the work week is spent on research, writing, and class preparation.

Education/Training
Most college professors at four-year colleges have doctoral degrees (Ph.D.s). Some two-year colleges hire faculty with master's degrees.

Salary
Average salary: $27,000–$60,000

Volunteer/Related Opportunities
Contact a local college and university and arrange for a professor to speak to your class about his or her job.

Outlook
Jobs in this field are expected to grow at an average rate through 2005. Although more jobs will open up, colleges and universities are expected to fill many positions with part-time or non-tenure-track professors as a cost-saving measure. Competition for the available positions will remain stiff.

School to Work Activity
Borrow a college course catalog from your school counselor. Imagine you are a professor of history. Look through the catalog and choose the five history courses you think would be most interesting to teach. Then write a one-page paper describing a day in your life as a history professor.

CORPORATE TRAINING SPECIALIST

Job Description
Corporate training specialists develop and conduct programs to train employees in a variety of fields related to a corporation's business.

Education/Training
Although many corporate trainers have bachelor's degrees, no specific educational training is required. Because the nature of the job is constantly changing, continuing education is usually necessary.

Salary Range
Average salary: $31,900–$49,000

Volunteer/Related Opportunities
Offer to teach another student something you know about computers, such as how to access the Internet or print a document.

Outlook
The explosion in computer use in the workplace means that the field of corporate training specialist is expected to be one of the nation's fastest-growing fields through the year 2005.

School to Work Activity
Imagine that you are a corporate training specialist preparing a manual for an upcoming course. Write the manual's first paragraph, emphasizing the importance of continuing education in the workplace.

CURATOR

Job Description
Curators collect and preserve objects—including works of art, textiles, and preserved animals and plants—for museums and private collections. Curators also arrange exhibits of the works, solicit money, and sometimes supervise research on various pieces or collections.

Education/ Training
Curators have master's or doctoral (Ph.D.) degrees.

Salary
Average salary: $47,000

Volunteer/Related Opportunities
Offer to create a class display of art, artifacts, or other items based on the next chapter of your history text.

Outlook
The number of curator jobs is expected to increase, but competition for those jobs will be stiff.

School to Work Activity
Go to your local history museum and choose one exhibit for study. List five items that appear in the exhibit. Then write a paragraph telling why the curator would have included each item.

ECONOMIST

Job Description
Economists study the economic decisions individuals and companies make both nationally and internationally. They identify possible trends in economic variables, such as interest rates, inflation, and unemployment levels. Some economists create mathematical models to help them forecast economic trends. They work for government and international agencies, private companies, banks, and trade associations.

Education/Training
Economists must have a master's or doctoral (Ph.D.) degree in economics.

Salary
Average salary: $26,700–$80,000

Volunteer/Related Opportunities
Volunteer to monitor the sale of T-shirts or other items from the school's store for a month. Then forecast how large the next T-shirt printing order should be.

Outlook
The job market for economists is expected to grow faster than average through 2005, with most new jobs opening up in the private sector.

School to Work Activity
Read the material in your textbook on the North American Free Trade Agreement (NAFTA). Now imagine you are a government economist assigned to study the potential impact of NAFTA on the United States economy. List five pieces of information that would help you determine the impact of NAFTA on the economy. Then write down where you might look for each piece of information.

FOREIGN SERVICE OFFICER

Job Description
Foreign service officers work for the United States Department of State. They represent the United States abroad, help United States citizens abroad, collect information about foreign countries, and help formulate foreign policy in particular regions of the world. They use their diplomatic skills to serve as official spokespeople for the United States.

Education/Training
Foreign services must have bachelor's degrees, and they must be United States citizens. Candidates for the foreign service must pass the foreign service exam. Proficiency in one or more foreign languages is recommended.

Salary
Average salary: $26,708–$116,000

Volunteer/Related Opportunities
Volunteer to serve as a study partner with your school's foreign exchange student.

Outlook
The number of jobs will remain small, and competition for those jobs will remain strong.

School to Work Activity
Imagine that war breaks out between two South American countries. Make a list of the things that would concern you if you were a foreign service officer working in one of the countries.

HISTORIAN

Job Description
Historians research and analyze past events and their impact on the present and future. They usually specialize in a particular part of the world, era, or field. Many historians become teachers. Others become writers or researchers, working independently or for museums or foundations. Historians also work for the military and for corporations.

Education/Training
Historians must have at least a bachelor's degree in history. Advanced degrees are recommended.

Salary Range
Average salary: $23,200–$52,600

Volunteer/Related Opportunities
Use interviews and documents to research and write a family history, going back to 1960.

Outlook
Jobs in this field are expected to grow at an average rate through 2005.

School to Work Activity
Research and write an article that recounts the history of your school.

Career Connections

•Career Connections

JOURNALIST

Job Description
Journalists research, collect, and report the news. Some work in radio and television. Others work for newspapers and magazines, including specialized magazines, such as those published by industry groups. Many journalism jobs require travel and the ability to work under tight deadlines.

Education/Training
Journalists must have bachelor's degrees. Many job candidates have experience working at their local or school newspapers.

Salary
Average salary: $16,000–$55,000

Volunteer/Related Opportunities
Offer to work on your school's newspaper or yearbook.

Outlook
The number of journalists is expected to decline in the coming years, giving those with training in a specific field or knowledge of languages an edge in the job market.

School to Work Activity
Read and take notes on the coverage of the top story in your local newspaper. Using your notes, write your own version of the same story. Videotape your story for the class as if you were presenting it on the evening news.

- -

MAPPING SCIENTIST (CARTOGRAPHER)

Job Description
Cartographers measure and map areas of the earth. They rely on information from sources such as surveys, aerial photographs, satellites, and computer databanks to do their work.

Education/Training
Cartographers must have college degrees, often in engineering or a physical science. Computer proficiency is necessary in most positions. Many cartographers have advanced degrees.

Salary
Average salary: $47,700

Volunteer/Related Opportunities
Offer to create a map of your school that can be duplicated and given to new students on their first day.

Outlook
The number of jobs for cartographers is expected to decrease because of budget cuts and improved technology.

School to Work Activity
Use your textbook to find a historical map of a particular region. Then use the resources in your library to locate a current map of the same region. Write a paragraph explaining what kinds of details have been added to the current map since the original map was created.

MARKET RESEARCHER

Job Description
Market researchers collect information that will help companies determine the potential sales, distribution, and pricing of various products. This information can be gained from telephone, mail, and personal interviews and surveys, which have been designed by the market researcher. After they have collected the information, market researchers evaluate the data and make recommendations based on their evaluations.

Education/Training
Market researchers usually have a minimum of a bachelor's degree in marketing, psychology, or another related field.

Salary
Average starting salary: $25,000

Volunteer/Related Opportunities
Conduct market research to determine what fruits not offered by your school cafeteria might sell well.

Outlook
The need for market researchers will be strong for the next decade.

School to Work Activity
Observe buyer behavior in your school cafeteria for five lunch periods. Then write down a list of the three food items that sell the best, based on your market research.

MILITARY SERVICE

Job Description
Members of the armed services protect the nation and the nation's interests. There are five branches of military service: the Army, which is responsible for military operations on land; the Air Force, which is responsible for military operations in the air; the Navy, which is responsible for military operations at sea; the Marines, which provides the Navy with a land force; and the Coast Guard, which guards the coast during peacetime and works with the Navy during war.

Education/Training
No formal education is required to join the military, although about 95 percent of all recruits are high school graduates, and a high school diploma is a requirement for some military jobs. All military personnel must sign an enlistment contract that commits them to serving in the military for up to 8 years.

Salary
Average salary: $29,300, including housing and subsistence allowances.

Volunteer/Related Opportunities
Volunteer to participate in your high school's unit of the Reserve Officer Training Corps (ROTC).

Outlook
Although political changes in Eastern Europe and in the former Soviet Union have led to recent downsizing, opportunities in the military are expected to remain constant through 2005.

School to Work Activity
Choose one branch of the military. Use your library's resources or the Internet to research your chosen branch. Then write a paragraph or two describing various skills that can be acquired while serving in the military.

Career Connections

MULTIMEDIA PRODUCER

Job Description
Multimedia producers use video and audio elements in an interactive environment to create various multimedia products, such as CD-ROM disks. Responsibilities range from choosing and acquiring titles to writing, directing, and editing the work itself.

Education/Training
No specific educational background or degree is required. Producers must be proficient in computers. Most start in lower-level multimedia jobs and work their way up to producer.

Salary
Average salary: $30,000–$90,000

Volunteer/Related Opportunities
Offer to videotape your high school's next graduation ceremony.

Outlook
The number of multimedia jobs, especially in educational products, is expected to grow through 2005.

School to Work Activity
Imagine you are an independent multimedia producer who has received funding to create a CD-ROM on American history. Write a paragraph explaining which time period you would choose to illustrate with your product. Then identify the first steps you would take as the project begins.

PARALEGAL

Job Description
Paralegals assist lawyers in many ways. They use documents, law books, and other resource materials to research cases and laws that may have a bearing on a case the lawyer is trying. They also may help check the facts of the case itself. Most paralegals are employed by medium- to large-sized law firms.

Education/Training
Paralegal positions usually require a degree from a two- or four-year paralegal program.

Salary
Average salary: $28,300

Volunteer/Related Opportunities
Help a family member prepare to write a will by finding examples of wills in the library.

Outlook
The number of paralegals is expected to increase by as much as 100 percent by 2005.

School to Work Activity
Suppose that you have just been hired as a paralegal by a law practice. One of your first research assignments is to prepare a promotional brochure providing a step-by-step guide on how someone in your community can file a claim in small claims court. Based on your findings, use a word processor to write the copy for this pamphlet.

TRAVEL AGENT

Job Description
Travel agents make travel arrangements for their clients. Duties can include finding the most cost-effective travel arrangements, booking hotel rooms, advising clients on things to do at their destinations, and arranging for car rentals. Travel agents rely heavily on their computers for up-to-date travel information. Many travel agents periodically travel to evaluate accommodations and other arrangements firsthand.

Education/Training
Many travel agents have bachelor's degrees, although a degree is not required. Travel agents also take a 6- to 12-week travel course.

Salary
Average salary: $21,300

Volunteer/Related Opportunities
Offer to make travel arrangements for your next class trip.

Outlook
The number of travel agent jobs is expected to increase at a faster than average rate through 2005.

School to Work Activity
Choose a vacation destination that interests you, and compile a list of all the arrangements you would need to make if you were arranging for a one-week stay.

URBAN AND REGIONAL PLANNER

Job Description
Urban and regional planners try to identify the best way to use an area's resources based on human needs and wants. They consider issues such as traffic, pollution, the availability of water and sewer lines, and the number of schools, hospitals, and recreational areas, as they plan for future growth in an area. About two-thirds of all urban planners are employed by local governments.

Education/Training
Urban and regional planners usually hold master's degrees in urban planning or urban design.

Salary
Average salary: $30,000–$63,000

Volunteer/Related Opportunities
Contact your local highway department and offer to participate in a traffic study of your area.

Outlook
The demand for urban and regional planning work has grown in the past few years as a result of the continuing expansion of the United States econ-omy. The number of urban planning jobs is expected to increase at a faster than average rate through 2005.

School to Work Activity
Washington, D.C., is an example of a planned community. Obtain a map of the city. Study the map and make a list of three things that indicate that Washington was planned before it was built.

The American Flag

For Americans, the flag has always had a special meaning. It is a symbol of our nation's freedom and democracy.

The Flag of 1795

The flag of the United States symbolizes the nation's unity and independence. In addition, the flag stands for the hopes and ideas of the American people. Throughout its history, the American flag has undergone numerous changes. The flag of 1795 had 15 stripes, as well as 15 stars, to represent the 15 states.

Rules and Customs

Over the years, Americans have developed rules and customs concerning the use and display of the flag. One of the most important things every American should remember is to treat the flag with respect:

★ The flag should be raised and lowered by hand and displayed only from sunrise to sunset. On special occasions, it may be displayed at night.

★ The flag may be displayed on all days, weather permitting, particularly on national and state holidays and on historic and special occasions.

★ No flag should be flown above the American flag or to the right of it at the same height.

★ The flag may be flown at half-mast to mourn the death of public officials.

★ The flag should never touch the ground or floor beneath it.

★ The flag may be flown upside down only to signal distress.

★ When the flag becomes old and tattered, it should be destroyed by burning. According to an approved custom, the Union is first cut from the flag; and then the two pieces, which no longer form a flag, are burned.

Did You Know?

★ The first official American flag, the Continental or Grand Union flag, was displayed on January 1, 1776.

★ The American flag is said to have been nicknamed "Old Glory" by William Driver, a Massachusetts sea captain.

★ The Stars and Stripes first flew around the world on the ship *Columbia of Boston* on its voyage from September 1787 to August 1790.

★ The flag was unfurled at the North Pole for the first time on April 6, 1909, by naval officer and Arctic explorer Robert Peary.

★ The flag was planted on the moon on July 20, 1969, after astronauts Neil Armstrong and Edwin Aldrin, Jr., piloted the lunar module *Eagle* to a landing on the moon's surface.

WORKING WITH PRIMARY SOURCES

Suppose that you have been asked to write a report on changes in your community over the past 25 years. Where you would get the information you need to begin writing? You would draw upon two types of information—primary sources and secondary sources.

Definitions

Primary sources are often first-person accounts by someone who actually saw or lived through the event being described. In other words, if you see a fire or live through a great storm and then write about your experiences, you have created a primary source. Diaries, journals, letters, photographs, and eyewitness reports are examples of primary sources. **Secondary sources** are secondhand accounts. For instance, if your friend experiences a fire or storm and tells you about it or if you read about the fire

or storm in the newspaper and then you write about it, you have created a secondary source. Textbooks, biographies, and histories are secondary sources.

Checking Your Sources

When you read primary and secondary sources, you should analyze them to determine if they are dependable or reliable. Historians usually prefer primary sources to secondary sources. Both can be reliable or unreliable, however, depending upon the following factors.

Time Span

With primary sources, it is important to consider how long after the event occurred that the primary source was written. The longer the time span between an event and the account, the less reliable the account is likely to be. As time passes, people often forget details or fill in gaps with events that never took place. Although we like to think we remember things exactly as they happened, we often remember them inaccurately.

Reliability

Another factor to consider when evaluating a primary source is the writer's background and reliability. First, try to determine how this person knows about what he or she is writing. How much does he or she know? Is the writer being truthful? Is the account convincing? Is the writer likely to be biased?

Opinions

When evaluating a primary source, you should also decide whether the account has been

William Clark's log book

*Opera glasses
(late 1800s)*

influenced by emotion, opinion, or exaggeration. Writers sometimes have reasons to distort the truth to suit their purposes. Ask yourself: Why did the person write the account? Do any key words or expressions reveal the author's emotions or opinions? Who is the author's intended audience? You may wish to compare the account with one written by another witness to the event. If the two accounts differ, ask yourself why they differ and which is more accurate.

Interpreting Primary Sources

To help you analyze a primary source, use the following steps:

- **Examine the origins of the document.**
  You need to determine if it is a primary or secondary source.

- **Find the main ideas.**
  Read the document and summarize the main ideas in your own words. These ideas may be fairly easy to identify in newspapers and journals, for example, but are much more difficult to determine in poetry.

- **Reread the document.**
  Difficult ideas are not always easily understood on the first reading.

- **Use a variety of resources.**
  Form the habit of using a dictionary, encyclopedia, and maps. These resources are tools to help you discover new ideas and knowledge and check the validity of sources.

Classifying Primary Sources

Primary sources fall into different categories:

 **Printed Publications**

Printed publications include books such as memoirs and autobiographies. Printed publications also include newspapers and magazines.

 **Personal Records**

Personal records are accounts of events kept by an individual who is a participant in or witness to these events. Personal records include diaries, journals, and letters.

 **Visual Materials**

Visual materials include a wide range of forms: original paintings, drawings, and sculpture; photographs; film; and maps.

 **Oral Histories**

Oral histories are chronicles, memoirs, myths, and legends that are passed along from one generation to another by word of mouth. Interviews are another form of oral history.

 **Songs and Poems**

Songs and poems include works that express the personal thoughts and feelings or political or religious beliefs of the writer, usually using rhyming and rhythmic language.

 **Artifacts**

Artifacts are objects such as tools, clothing, or ornaments. Artifacts present information about a particular culture or a stage of technological development.

A NEW NATION

The English colonists who settled in North America gradually established a culture of their own. As they grew apart from Great Britain, they yearned to be free and independent, and they risked their lives for that freedom in a war with the British rulers. The colonies emerged victorious and formed a new nation. The following readings chronicle life in colonial America during this period.

■ READER'S DICTIONARY

destitute: lacking

procure: gain or obtain

gall: to become sore by rubbing

discord: disagreement, conflict

For more primary sources to accompany this unit, use the *American History Primary Source Document Library CD-ROM.*

Poor Richard's Almanack

Printed Publications

Ben Franklin published **Poor Richard's Almanack** *every year for 25 years. An almanac is an annual collection of statistics and other useful or entertaining information. Franklin also included proverbs, or short witty sayings, like those that follow. See if you recognize any of them.*

God helps them that help themselves.

No gains without pain.

He that falls in love with himself, will have no rivals.

Love your Neighbor; yet don't pull down your Hedge.

Keep thy shop, and thy shop will keep thee.

The Cat in Gloves catches no Mice.

Military drum of the American Revolution

Surviving at Valley Forge

Personal Records

Below are excerpts from the personal records of two people who served at Valley Forge. The first selection is by Albigence Waldo, a surgeon who tended the sick and injured.

I am sick—discontented . . . Poor food—hard lodging—cold weather—fatigue—nasty cloathes—nasty cookery. . . . I can't endure it—Why are we sent here to starve and freeze? . . .

In this selection, soldier Joseph Plumb Martin remembers the hardships on the way to Valley Forge.

The army was not only starved but naked. The greatest part were not only shirtless and barefoot, but destitute of all other clothing, especially blankets. I procured a small piece of rawhide and made myself a pair of moccasins, which kept my feet (while they lasted) from the frozen ground, although, as I well remember, the hard edges so galled my ankles, while on a march, that it was with much difficulty and pain that I could wear them afterwards; but the only alternative I had was to endure this inconvenience or to go barefoot, as hundreds of my companions had to, till they might be tracked by their bloods upon the rough frozen ground.

Songs of Liberty

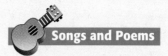

Songs and Poems

The following song is one of the many patriotic songs distributed in song books during the early 1800s.

The fruits of our country, our flocks and our
    fleeces,
What treasures immense, in our mountains
    that lie,
While discord is tearing Old Europe to pieces,
Shall amply the wants of the people supply;
New roads and canals, on the bosoms
    conveying,
Refinement and wealth through our forests
    shall roam,
And millions of freemen, with rapture
    surveying,
Shall shout out "O Liberty! this is thy home!"

INTERPRETING PRIMARY SOURCES

1. Which of Franklin's proverbs stress the importance of hard work?
2. How do the Valley Forge passages differ in the way the writers express themselves?
3. In the song, what does the phrase "treasures immense" mean?

ACTIVITY

Writing Proverbs Write a proverb about studying for school. Ask a friend to read it to see if he or she easily understands the point you are making.

For use with Unit 2
"Forging a Nation, 1815–1877"

RIFT AND REUNION

Throughout the 1800s, the new nation continued to grow—and grow apart. By the middle of the century, two distinct regions— North and South—had developed. Their differences, particularly over the issue of slavery, led to a bloody civil war. The Union eventually became one again but not before much death and destruction as some of the following readings indicate.

■ READER'S DICTIONARY

melancholy: sad

regiment: a military unit

For more primary sources to accompany this unit, use the *American History Primary Source Document Library CD-ROM.*

Settling in Texas

Personal Records

Mary Crownover Rabb moved to Texas with her family in 1823. She recalls what her first home in Texas was like:

The house was made of logs. They made a chimney to it. The door shutter was made of thick slabs split out of thick pieces of timber, and [to fasten the door] we had a large pin or peg that was drove in hard and fast [at night], and then the Indians could not get in. We had an earthen floor. . . .

I was in my first Texas house and . . . I was very much pleased, and I soon got to work to make clothing for my family.

Swing Low, Sweet Chariot

Songs and Poems

Spirituals—songs of salvation—provided the enslaved African Americans who wrote and sang them with not only a measure of comfort in bleak times but with a means for communicating secretly among themselves.

Swing low, sweet chariot,
Coming for to carry me home,
Swing low, sweet chariot,
Coming to carry me home.

I looked over Jordan and what did I see
Coming for to carry me home,
A band of angels coming after me.
Coming to carry me home.

If you get there before I do,
Coming for to carry me home,
Tell all my friends I'm coming too,
Coming to carry me home.

Swing low, sweet chariot,
Coming for to carry me home,
Swing low, sweet chariot,
Coming to carry me home.

Retreat

Personal Records

After the Confederate victory at the Battle of Chickamauga in September 1863, a Union officer described his army's retreat:

The march was a melancholy one. All along the road for miles, wounded men were lying. They had crawled or hobbled slowly away from the fury of the battle, become exhausted, and lain down by the roadside to die. Some were calling the names and numbers of their regiments, but many had become too weak to do this . . . the army is simply a mob.

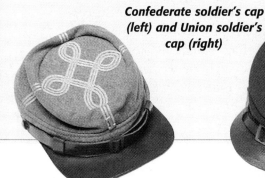
Confederate soldier's cap (left) and Union soldier's cap (right)

Looking for Relatives

Printed Publications

Families that had been separated during slavery tried to reunite after the Civil War. Newspapers carried advertisements like the one shown here from African Americans seeking information about missing relatives:

$200 reward. During the year 1849, Thomas Sample carried away from this city, as his slaves, our daughter Polly, and son, Geo. Washington, to the state of Mississippi, and [later] to Texas. . . . We will give $100 each for them, to any person who assists them, or either of them, to get to Nashville, or get word to us [about where to find them], if they are alive.

INTERPRETING PRIMARY SOURCES

1. What does "Swing Low, Sweet Chariot" show about the condition and faith of the people who sang it?
2. How does the writer describe the Union forces after the Battle of Chickamauga?
3. What is the aim of the newspaper advertisement?

ACTIVITY

Creating a Scrapbook Put together a scrapbook on the Civil War. Use your own original drawings and photocopies of maps, pictures, and other illustrations. Arrange your collection around different subjects and write a short explanation of each subject.

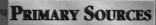

For use with Unit 3
"New Horizons, 1860–1900"

THE NATION MOVES AHEAD

After the Civil War, many Americans picked themselves up and moved on optimistically. Thousands of settlers headed west to take control of the nation's frontier. In the East, industry boomed and cities grew. Industrialization improved some citizens' standard of living—but also created an impoverished and difficult life for many workers. The following excerpts examine this eventful time in the nation's history.

■ READER'S DICTIONARY

stampede: run away in panic

inclined: slanted or leaning

kosher: approved by Jewish law

babel: a scene of noise and confusion

For more primary sources to accompany this unit, use the *American History Primary Source Document Library CD-ROM.*

On the Cattle Trail

Personal Records

Cowhand George Duffield describes the troubles along a four-month trek from mid-Texas to Iowa in 1866.

April 29
 . . . Started in evening from Salt Creek & traveled 5 miles to Alexanders Gap between Colorado & Brazos.

May 1
 . . . Big Stampede lost 200 head of cattle.

May 4
 Continued to hunt   found 40 head day pleasant   Sun shone once more. Heard that the other herd had stampeded & lost over 200.

May 13
 Big Thunder Storm last night   Stampede lost 100 Beeves [head of cattle] hunted all day found 50 all tired. Everything discouraging.

June 12
 Hard Rain & Wind   Big stampede & here we are among the Indians with 150 head of Cattle gone   hunted all day & the Rain pouring down with but poor success   Dark days are these to me   Nothing but Bread & Coffee   Hands all Growling & Swearing—everything wet and cold Beeves gone   rode all day & gathered all but 35. . . .

Child Labor

Children as well as adults suffered in unhealthy working conditions, as the following description shows:

In a little room in this big, block shed—a room not twenty feet square—forty boys are picking their lives away. The floor of this room is an inclined plane, and a stream of coal pours constantly in. They work here, in this little black hole, all day and every day . . . picking away among the black coals, bending over till their little spines are curved. . . . Not three boys in this roomful could read or write. Shut in from everything that is pleasant, with no chance to learn, with no knowledge of what is going on about them. . . . They know nothing but the difference between slate and coal.

Young coal miners in Kingston, Pennsylvania

An Emigrant's Story

In her book The Promised Land, *Mary Antin tells of leaving her native country Poland to come to America when she was 13 years old.*

What did they not ask, the eager, foolish, friendly people? They wanted to handle the ticket, and mother must read them what is written on it. How much did it cost? Was it all paid for? Were we going to have a foreign passport or did we intend to steal across the border? Were we not going to have new dresses to travel in? Was it sure that we could get kosher food on the ship?

[After we boarded the train] when the warning bell rang out, it was drowned in a confounding babel of voices—fragments of oft-repeated messages . . . [of] blessings, farewells—"Don't forget!"—"Take care of—" "Keep your tickets—" "Moshele—newspapers!—" "Garlick is best!" "Happy journey!" "God help you!" "Good-bye!" Remember—"

INTERPRETING PRIMARY SOURCES

1. What crises did George Duffield face?
2. Why could so few child workers read or write?
3. What words does Mary Antin use to describe the townspeople?

ACTIVITY

Researching Research an ethnic group in your community. Describe this group's effect on everyday life in your community.

CHANGES AT HOME AND ABROAD

During the late 1800s and early 1900s, the nation looked abroad as it sought to increase its influence on the world stage. America also looked inward as citizens worked to meet the many challenges facing society. The following readings touch on these foreign and domestic efforts.

■ READER'S DICTIONARY

score: twenty

outrage: insult

ballot: right to vote

harassing: disturbing

For more primary sources to accompany this unit, use the *American History Primary Source Document Library CD-ROM.*

The United States and Cuba

Printed Publications

Sympathy for Cubans under Spanish rule grew as newspapers competed with each other in reporting stories of Spanish atrocities. An editorial in Joseph Pulitzer's New York World is a case in point:

How long are the Spaniards to drench Cuba with the blood and tears of her people?
. . . How long shall old men and women and children be murdered by the score, the innocent victims of Spanish rage against the patriot armies they cannot conquer?
. . . How long shall the United States sit idle and indifferent . . . ?

I Cultivate the White Rose

Songs and Poems

José Martí was a Cuban political activist, journalist, and writer. Forced to flee Cuba because of his opposition to Spanish rule, Martí lived in exile in many countries, including the United States. Martí was killed fighting for Cuban independence.

I cultivate the white rose
In June as in January
For the sincere friend
Who gives me his hand frankly.

And for the cruel person who tears out
    the heart with which I live,
I cultivate neither snails nor thorns:
I cultivate the white rose.

Woman Suffrage

Oral Histories

Ernestine Hara Kettler picketed the White House in 1912 for the right to vote. She was 21 years old.

. . . It was very just for women to vote and it was highly undemocratic and an outrage that so much opposition had been placed against their getting the ballot. There were, after all, as many women in the country as men. What is this business? Is a woman so far below a man intellectually that she's not fit to vote? When I think of it, it's just incredible! I can't believe it! I condemned it. I was actually outraged that women didn't have the vote! That's why I went down to Washington.

Suffrage marcher

. . . A pretty big crowd would gather every day—at least it seemed pretty big to me. There were always men and women standing there harassing us and throwing some pretty bad insults—and pretty obscene ones. The women weren't obscene, but the men were. Our instructions were to pay absolutely no attention to them. I ignored them. I was brave. My goodness, I was fighting for a cause.

We had some support, but they took their lives in their hands. If any of the bystanders supported us, they could be beaten by the rest of the crowd. Towards the end, they started throwing stuff at the women. In fact, during this period somebody fired a shot through the windows of the Little White House, the headquarters. Any woman that happened to be in the right position for it could have been killed. And we couldn't get police protection. We just couldn't get it. The only protection we had was when we were arrested. Then we were protected!

INTERPRETING PRIMARY SOURCES

1. What action do you think the newspaper editorial wants the United States to take? Explain.
2. Why did Ernestine Kettler go to Washington, D.C.?
3. Describe the dangers Kettler and other marchers faced.

ACTIVITY

Making a Time Line Make a time line of the woman suffrage movement. Include marches, demonstrations, and people. Write a paragraph on the importance of women's clubs in the suffrage movement.

For use with Unit 5
"Crusade and Disillusion, 1914–1932"

TRYING TIMES

From a world war to a worldwide depression, Americans endured much turmoil during the first part of the twentieth century. Between these events, the nation experienced both an economic and cultural boom. The following excerpts provide a glimpse of these exciting and tumultuous years.

▰ READER'S DICTIONARY

ruefully: regretfully

starboard: the right side of the ship

stern: the rear of a ship

Harlem: New York neighborhood where many African Americans lived

treble: high-pitched musical notes

bass: low-pitched musical notes

For more primary sources to accompany this unit, use the *American History Primary Source Document Library CD-ROM.*

Aboard the *Lusitania*

Personal Records

Despite the threat of German U-boat, or submarine, attacks, American architect Theodate Pope boarded the Lusitania *to sail home from Europe. On May 7, 1915, a German torpedo sank the British luxury liner. After being rescued, Pope wrote this letter home.*

Friday morning we came slowly through fog, blowing our fog horn. It cleared off about an hour before we went below for lunch. A young Englishman at our table had been served with his ice cream, and was waiting for the steward to bring him a spoon to eat it with. He looked ruefully at it and said he would hate to have a torpedo get him before he ate it. We all laughed, and then commented on how slowly we were running. . . .

Mr. Friend [another passenger] and I went up on deck B on the starboard side and leaned over the railing, looking at the sea, which was a marvellous blue and very dazzling in the sunlight. . . . The torpedo was on its way to us at that moment, for we went a short distance farther toward the stern, turning the corner by the smoking room, when the ship was struck on the starboard side. The sound was like that of an arrow entering the canvas and straw of a target, magnified a thousand times, and I imagined I heard a dull explosion follow. The water and timbers flew past the deck. . . . The ship steadied herself a few seconds and then listed [tilted] heavily to starboard, throwing us against the wall of a small corridor. . . .

. . . [The] deck suddenly looked very strange, crowded with people. . . . An officer was shouting orders to stop lowering the boats, and we were told to go down to deck B. We first looked over the rail and watched a boat filled with men and women being lowered. The stern was lowered too quickly and half the boatload were spilled backwards into the water. We looked at each other, sickened by the sight. . . .

Dream Boogie: Variation

Songs and Poems

Langston Hughes, a leading writer of the Harlem Renaissance, often drew inspiration for his poetry from jazz music and from his Harlem neighborhood.

Tinkling treble,
Rolling bass,
High noon teeth
In a midnight face,
Great long fingers
On great big hands,
Screaming pedals
Where his twelve-shoe lands,
Looks like his eyes
Are teasing pain,
A few minutes late
For the Freedom Train.

The Long Wait

Visual Materials

Dorothea Lange was an American photographer who captured many powerful images of the Great Depression. The photograph shown here, "White Angel Bread Line," shows people waiting for food in San Francisco in 1933.

"White Angel Bread Line"

INTERPRETING PRIMARY SOURCES

1. How seriously do you think the *Lusitania* passengers took the threat of a German attack?
2. What musical instrument is being played in Hughes' poem?
3. How would you describe the mood of people in Lange's photograph?

ACTIVITY

Researching Music Research to find songs of the 1930s that reflect the mood of the Depression. Present the lyrics and/or melodies to the class.

WAR AND PROSPERITY

As the following readings indicate, the twentieth century continued to be a time of crisis. America joined in and helped win yet another, even more destructive, world war. The nation emerged from the war with a robust economy and a heightened status in the world. And yet while the United States enjoyed prosperity at home, the country's continuing involvement in world affairs led to new conflicts.

■ READER'S DICTIONARY

fallout: particles of radioactive material that drift through the atmosphere after a nuclear explosion

Conelrad: (from "Control of Electromagnetic Radiation") and emergency radio broadcasting system that would replace normal broadcasts

frugal: thrifty, careful in spending money

For more primary sources to accompany this unit, use the ***American History Primary Source Document Library CD-ROM.***

On the Home Front

The U.S. government appealed to civilians to support the war effort in many ways. This bulletin was posted in meat markets.

1) THE NEED IS URGENT—War in the Pacific has greatly reduced our supply of vegetable fats from the Far East. It is necessary to find substitutes for them. Fat makes glycerine. And glycerine makes explosives for us and our Allies—explosives to down Axis planes, stop their tanks, and sink their ships. We need millions of pounds of glycerine and you housewives can help supply it.

2) DON'T throw away a single drop of used cooking fat, bacon fat, meat drippings, fry fats—every kind you use. After you've got all the cooking good from them, pour them through a kitchen strainer into a clean, wide-mouthed can. Keep it in a cool dark place. . . .

3) TAKE THEM to your meat dealer when you've saved a pound or more. He is cooperating patriotically. He will pay you for your waste fats and get them started on their way to war industries. . . .

Family in fallout shelter

Fallout Fears

Printed Publications

By 1961 fears of nuclear war were so great that the government urged people to be prepared for a nuclear attack. LIFE magazine reminded Americans what to do during such an attack.

The standard Civil Defense signal for an alert is a steady 3- to 5-minute blast of a siren or whistle. The warning to take cover is a 3-minute period of short blasts or a wailing siren. If an attack should come, however, the first warning you may get could be the flash itself. Your first move should be to close your eyes and bury your head in your arms or clothing to block out the light. The flash may last for several seconds, so keep covered until it begins to dim.

The shockwave will come next. Take cover so you will not be knocked down. If you are in a car, roll down windows to avoid flying glass and lie on the floor. Try to count the seconds between the flash and shockwave. This will help you estimate how far away the bomb has hit and how long you have to find better cover before the fallout can reach you. . . .

Wherever you are, try to reach a radio—preferably a battery radio since the electricity may be out—and tune it to 640 or 1240 on your dial, which are the Conelrad frequencies for emergency instructions. If you have a shelter, go to it immediately. . . .

Teenage Styles

Oral Histories

Conformity was important in the 1950s. In these selections, two female teenagers remember how important it was to "fit in."

You had to have lots and lots of clothes. What mattered was variety; the more you had the better. The things that were very 'in' were just what poorer parents couldn't come up with, like cashmere sweaters. My family still didn't have much money; they were also very frugal. I was put on a clothing allowance when I started high school. I had to pay for everything except a winter coat and formal [evening dress]. So I did a lot of babysitting and sewing because I wanted a big wardrobe more than anything.

INTERPRETING PRIMARY SOURCES

1. For what purpose did the government ask people to save fats?
2. According to *LIFE* magazine, in what order would someone probably experience the effects of a nuclear attack some distance away?
3. What characteristics of the 1950s can you identify from the teenagers' comments?

ACTIVITY

Making Comparisons Create a picture comparing teenagers of the 1950s and today. You may use original art or magazine photos.

MODERN AMERICA

The following readings highlight events in the emergence of modern America. In the last half of the twentieth century, America engaged in a civil rights struggle at home and battled communism abroad. Through it all, the nation flourished and developed into a world leader. Today, many Americans look upon their country with great pride— and look ahead with great confidence.

▓ READER'S DICTIONARY

Jim Crow laws: laws passed in the South in the late 1800s that enforced segregation and barred African Americans from many public places

oppression: unjust or cruel exercise of authority or power

For more primary sources to accompany this unit, use the ***American History Primary Source Document Library CD-ROM.***

A Tired Woman's Fight

Personal Records

Rosa Parks's refusal to give up her seat on a bus helped spark the civil rights movement. In this selection, she answered a letter that asked, "How did you feel when you were on the bus?"

The custom of getting on the bus for black people in Montgomery in the 1950s was to pay at the front door, get off the bus, and then reenter through the back door to find a seat. Black people could not sit in the same rows with white people. This custom was humiliating.

When I sat down on the bus on the day I was arrested, I decided I must do what was right to do. People have said over the years that the reason I did not give up my seat was because I was tired. I did not think of being physically tired. My feet were not hurting. I was tired in a different way. I was tired of seeing so many men treated as boys and not called by their proper names or titles. I was tired of seeing children and women mistreated and disrespected because of the color of their skin. I was tired of Jim Crow laws, of legally enforced racial segregation.

I thought of the pain and the years of oppression and mistreatment that my people had suffered. I felt that way every day. December 1, 1955, was no different. Fear was the last thing I thought of that day. I put my trust in the Lord for guidance and help to endure whatever I had to face. I knew I was sitting in the right seat.

Pop Art

Visual Materials

Rebellion in the 1960s took many forms. Young people marched in the streets for social reform, protested on college campuses against the Vietnam War, and rejected the social rules of their parents' generation. Artists of the 1960s challenged traditional ideas about fine art. Andy Warhol's painting *One Hundred Cans* uses the repeated image of an ordinary object—a soup can—to comment on art, society, and values.

One Hundred Cans

Proud to Be an American

Songs and Poems

"God Bless the USA," by singer Lee Greenwood, topped the country music charts in the 1980s. It was adopted as a theme song for President Ronald Reagan's 1984 reelection campaign.

I'm proud to be an American
Where at least I know I'm free,
And I won't forget the men who died
Who gave that right to me,
And I gladly stand up next to you and defend
    her still today,
'Cause there ain't no doubt I love this land
God bless the U.S.A.

INTERPRETING PRIMARY SOURCES

1. In what way was Rosa Parks "tired" when she boarded the Montgomery bus?
2. What effect do you think Warhol was trying to create by using repeated, commercial images, like the soup cans?
3. What themes does Lee Greenwood express in his song?

ACTIVITY

Planning a Time Capsule Imagine that you are in charge of making a time capsule to be opened 100 years from now. List 10–12 items you would include and explain your choices.

Documents of America's Heritage

★ ★

The Magna Carta

The Magna Carta, signed by King John in 1215, marked a decisive step forward in the development of constitutional government in England. Later, it became a model for colonists who carried the Magna Carta's guarantees of legal and political rights to America.

1. That the English church shall be free, and shall have her rights entire, and her liberties inviolate; . . .

2. We also have granted to all the freemen of our kingdom, for us and for our heirs forever, all the underwritten liberties, to be had and holden by them and their heirs, of us and our heirs forever. . . .

39. No freeman shall be taken or imprisoned, or diseased, or outlawed, or banished, or in any way destroyed, nor will we pass upon him, nor will we send upon him, unless by the lawful judgment of his peers, or by the law of the land.

40. We will sell to no man, we will not deny to any man, either justice or right.

41. All merchants shall have safe and secure conduct to go out of, and to come into, England, and to stay there and to pass as well by land as by water, for buying and selling by the ancient and allowed customs, without any unjust tolls, except in time of war, or when they are of any nation at war with us. . . .

42. It shall be lawful, for the time to come, for any one to go out of our kingdom and return safely and securely by land or by water, saving his allegiance to us (unless in time of war, by some short space, for the common benefit of the realm).

60. All the aforesaid customs and liberties, which we have granted to be holden in our kingdom, as much as it belongs to us, all people of our kingdom, as well clergy as laity, shall observe, as far as they are concerned, towards their dependents.

63. . . . It is also sworn, as well on our part as on the part of the barons, that all the things aforesaid shall be observed in good faith, and without evil duplicity. Given under our hand, in the presence of the witnesses above named, and many others, in the meadow called Runnymede, between Windsor and Staines, the 15th day of June, in the 17th year of our reign.

Documents

The Mayflower Compact

On November 21, 1620, 41 colonists aboard the Mayflower *drafted this agreement. The Mayflower Compact was the first plan of self-government ever put in force in the English colonies.*

In ye name of God Amen. We whose names are underwritten, the loyall subjects of our dread soveraigne Lord King James, by ye grace of God, of Great Britaine, Franc, & Ireland king, defender of ye faith, &c. Haveing undertaken, for ye glorie of God, and advancemente of ye Christian faith and honour of our king & countrie, a voyage to plant ye first colonie in ye Northerne parts of Virginia, doe by these presents solemnly & mutualy in ye presence of God, and one of another, covenant, & combine ourselves togeather into a Civill body politick; for our better ordering, & preservation & furtherance of ye ends aforesaid; and by vertue hereof to enacte, constitute, and frame such just & equall Lawes, ordinances, Acts, constitutions, & offices, from time to time, as shall be thought most meete & convenient for ye generall good of ye colonie: unto which we promise all due submission and obedience. In witnes whereof we have hereunder subscribed our names at Cap-Codd ye -11- of November, in ye year of ye raigne of our soveraigne Lord King James of England, France, & Ireland ye eighteenth, and of Scotland ye fiftie fourth. Ano Dom. 1620.

The Star-Spangled Banner

During the British bombardment of Fort McHenry during the War of 1812, a young Baltimore lawyer named Francis Scott Key was inspired to write the words to "The Star-Spangled Banner." Although it became popular immediately, it was not until 1931 that Congress officially declared "The Star-Spangled Banner" as our national anthem.

O! say can you see, by the dawn's early light,
What so proudly we hail'd at the twilight's last gleaming,
Whose broad stripes and bright stars through the perilous fight,
O'er the ramparts we watched, were so gallantly streaming?
And the Rockets' red glare, the Bombs bursting in air,
Gave proof through the night that our Flag was still there;
O! say, does that star-spangled banner yet wave
O'er the Land of the free and the home of the brave!

On the shore, dimly seen through the mists of the deep,
Where the foe's haughty host in dread silence reposes,
What is that, which the breeze o'er the towering steep,
As it fitfully blows, half conceals, half discloses?
Now it catches the gleam of the morning's first beam,
In full glory reflected, now shines on the stream.
'Tis the star-spangled banner; O! long may it wave
O'er the land of the free and the home of the brave.

The Monroe Doctrine

In an 1823 address to Congress, President James Monroe proclaimed what has become known as the Monroe Doctrine. The doctrine was designed to end European influence in the Western Hemisphere. In addition, it showed the world the American spirit of strength and unity, and became a cornerstone of United States foreign policy.

. . . With the existing colonies or dependencies of any European power we have not interfered and shall not interfere. But with the governments who have declared their independence and maintained it, and whose independence we have, on great consideration and on just principles, acknowledged, we could not view any interposition for the purpose of oppressing them, or controlling in any other manner their destiny, by any European power in any other light than as the manifestation of any unfriendly disposition toward the United States. . . .

Our policy in regard to Europe, which was adopted at an early stage of the wars which have so long agitated that quarter of the globe, nevertheless remains the same, which is not to interfere in the internal concerns of any of its powers; to consider the government de facto as the legitimate government for us; to cultivate friendly relations with it, and to preserve those relations by a frank, firm, and manly policy, meeting in all instances the just claims of every power, submitting to injuries from none. . . .

Memorial and Protest of the Cherokee Nation

While Native Americans were being forced from their homeland, Cherokee leaders put their protest before the United States Senate. Their call for justice went unheard.

It cannot be concealed that the situation of the Cherokees is peculiarly distressing. In adverting to that situation it is not done to arouse, at this late day, a useless sympathy, but only as matter of history, and from necessity in giving a fair and impartial illustration of their difficulties. It is well known to those who have paid any attention to their history for the last five years, that they have been contending for the faithful execution of treaties between their nation and the United States, and that their distresses have not been mitigated; their efforts seem to have increased their difficulties. It remains for them to seek an adjustment by treaty, and an equitable acknowledgement of their rights and claims, so far as circumstances will permit.

For this purpose, this delegation has been deputed, as the proper organ of the Cherokee people, to settle, by treaty, their difficulties; and they wish, in sincerity, to have them settled, for the good, peace, and harmony of the whole nation.

The Seneca Falls Declaration

One of the first documents to express the desire for equal rights for women is the Declaration of Sentiments and Resolutions, issued in 1848 at the Seneca Falls Convention in New York. Led by Lucretia Mott and Elizabeth Cady Stanton, the delegates adopted a set of resolutions that called for woman suffrage and opportunities in employment and education. Excerpts from the Declaration follow.

When, in the course of human events, it becomes necessary for one portion of the family of man to assume among the people of the earth a position different from that which they have hitherto occupied, but one to which the laws of nature and of nature's God entitle them, a decent respect to the opinions of mankind requires that they should declare the causes that impel them to such a course.

We hold these truths to be self-evident: that all men and women are created equal; that they are endowed by their Creator with certain inalienable rights; that among these are life, liberty, and the pursuit of happiness; that to secure these rights governments are instituted, deriving their just powers from the consent of the governed. Whenever any form of government becomes destructive of these ends, it is the right of those who suffer from it to refuse allegiance to it, and to insist upon the institution of a new government, laying its foundation on such principles, and organizing its powers in such form, as to them shall seem most likely to effect their safety and happiness. Prudence, indeed, will dictate that governments long established should not be changed for light and transient causes; . . . But when a long train of abuses and usurpations, pursuing invariably the same object, evinces a design to reduce them under absolute despotism, it is their duty to throw off such government and to provide new guards for their future security. . . .

The history of mankind is a history of repeated injuries and usurpations on the part of man toward woman, having in direct object the establishment of an absolute tyranny over her. To prove this, let facts be submitted to a candid world. . . .

Now, in view of the entire disfranchisement of one-half the people of this country, their social and religious degradation, in view of the unjust laws above mentioned, and because women do feel themselves aggrieved, oppressed, and fraudulently deprived of their most sacred rights, we insist that they have immediate admission to all the rights and privileges which belong to them as citizens of the United States. . . .

The Emancipation Proclamation

On January 1, 1863, President Abraham Lincoln issued the Emancipation Proclamation, which freed all slaves in states under Confederate control. The Proclamation was a significant step toward the Thirteenth Amendment (1865) that ended slavery in all of the United States.

Whereas on the 22d day of September, A.D. 1862, a proclamation was issued by the President of the United States, containing among other things, the following, to wit: That on the 1st day of January, in the year of our Lord 1863, all persons held as slaves within any state or designated part of a state, the people whereof shall then be in rebellion against the United States, shall be then, thenceforward, and forever free; and the executive government of the United States, including the military and naval authority thereof, will recognize and maintain the freedom of such persons and will do no act or acts to repress such persons, or any of them, in any efforts they may make for their actual freedom.

That the executive will, on the 1st day of January aforesaid, by proclamation, designate the states and parts of states, if any, in which the people thereof, respectively, shall then be in rebellion against the United States; and the fact that any state or the people thereof shall on that day be in good faith represented in the Congress of the United States by members chosen thereto at elections wherein a majority of the qualified voters of such states shall have participated shall, in the absence of strong countervailing testimony, be deemed conclusive evidence that such state and the people thereof are not then in rebellion against the United States. . . .

And, by virtue of the power and for the purpose aforesaid, I do order and declare that all persons held as slaves within said designated states and parts of states are, and henceforward shall be, free; and that the executive government of the United States, including the military and naval authorities thereof, will recognize and maintain the freedom of said persons.

And I hereby enjoin upon the people so declared to be free to abstain from all violence, unless in necessary self-defense; and I recommend to them that, in all cases when allowed, they labor faithfully for reasonable wages.

And I further declare and make known that such persons of suitable condition will be received into the armed service of the United States to garrison forts, positions, stations, and other places, and to man vessels of all sorts in said service. . . .

The Gettysburg Address

On November 19, 1863, President Abraham Lincoln gave a short speech at the dedication of a national cemetery on the battlefield of Gettysburg. His simple yet eloquent words expressed his hopes for a nation divided by civil war.

Four score and seven years ago our fathers brought forth on this continent a new nation, conceived in liberty, and dedicated to the proposition that all men are created equal.

Now we are engaged in a great civil war, testing whether that nation or any nation so conceived and so dedicated can long endure. We are met on a great battlefield of that war. We have come to dedicate a portion of that field as a final resting place for those who here gave their lives that that nation might live. It is altogether fitting and proper that we should do this.

But, in a larger sense, we can not dedicate—we can not consecrate—we can not hallow—this ground. The brave men, living and dead, who struggled here have consecrated it far beyond our poor power to add or detract. The world will little note nor long remember what we say here, but it can never forget what they did here. It is for us, the living, rather, to be dedicated here to the unfinished work which they who fought here have thus far so nobly advanced.

It is rather for us to be here dedicated to the great task remaining before us—that from these honored dead we take increased devotion to that cause for which they gave the last full measure of devotion; that we here highly resolve that these dead shall not have died in vain; that this nation, under God, shall have a new birth of freedom; and that government of the people, by the people, and for the people, shall not perish from the earth.

I Will Fight No More

In 1877 the Nez Perce Indians fought the government's attempt to move them to a smaller reservation. After a remarkable attempt to escape to Canada, Chief Joseph realized that resistance was hopeless and advised his people to surrender.

Tell General Howard I know his heart. What he told me before I have in my heart. I am tired of fighting. Our chiefs are killed. Looking Glass is dead. It is the young men who say yes or no. He who led the young men is dead. It is cold and we have no blankets. The little children are freezing to death. My people, some of them have run away to the hills and have no blankets, no food; no one knows where they are—perhaps freezing to death. I want to have time to look for my children and see how many I can find. Maybe I shall find them among the dead. Hear me my chiefs. I am tired; my heart is sick and sad. From where the sun now stands, I will fight no more forever.

The Pledge of Allegiance

In 1892 the nation celebrated the 400th anniversary of Columbus's landing in America. In connection with this celebration, Francis Bellamy, a magazine editor, wrote and published the Pledge of Allegiance. The words "under God" were added by Congress in 1954 at the urging of President Dwight D. Eisenhower.

I pledge allegiance to the Flag of the United States of America and to the Republic for which it stands, one Nation under God, indivisible, with liberty and justice for all.

The Fourteen Points

On January 8, 1918, President Woodrow Wilson went before Congress to offer a statement of aims called the Fourteen Points. Wilson's plan called for freedom of the seas in peace and war, an end to secret alliances, and equal trading rights for all countries. The excerpt that follows is taken from the President's message.

. . . We entered this war because violations of right had occurred which touched us to the quick and made the life of our own people impossible unless they were corrected and the world secured once for all against their recurrence. What we demand in this war, therefore, is nothing peculiar to ourselves. It is that the world be made fit and safe to live in; and particularly that it be made safe for every peace-loving nation which, like our own, wishes to live its own life, determine its own institutions, be assured of justice and fair dealings by the other peoples of the world, as against force and selfish aggression. All the peoples of the world are in effect partners in this interest, and for our own part we see very clearly that unless justice be done to others it will not be done to us.

The program of the world's peace, therefore, is our program, and that program, the only possible program, as we see it, is this:

I. Open covenants of peace, openly arrived at, after which there shall be no private international understandings of any kind, but diplomacy shall proceed always frankly and in the public view.

II. Absolute freedom of navigation upon the seas, outside territorial waters, alike in peace and in war, except as the seas may be closed in whole or in part by international action for the enforcement of international covenants.

III. The removal, so far as possible, of all economic barriers and the establishment of an equality of trade conditions among all the nations consenting to the peace and associating themselves for its maintenance.

IV. Adequate guarantees given and taken that national armaments will be reduced to the lowest point consistent with domestic safety.

V. Free, open-minded, and absolutely impartial adjustment of all colonial claims, based upon a strict observance of the principle that in determining all such questions of sovereignty the interests of the population concerned must have equal weight with the equitable claims of the Government whose title is to be determined. . . .

XIV. A general association of nations must be formed under specific covenants for the purpose of affording mutual guarantees of political independence and territorial integrity to great and small states alike. . . .

Brown v. Board of Education

On May 17, 1954, the Supreme Court ruled in Brown v. *Board of Education that racial segregation in public schools was unconstitutional. This decision provided the legal basis for court challenges to segregation in every aspect of American life.*

The plaintiffs contend that segregated public schools are not "equal" and cannot be made "equal," and that hence they are deprived of the equal protection of the laws. Because of the obvious importance of the question presented, the Court took jurisdiction. . . .

Our decision . . . cannot turn on merely a comparison of these tangible factors in the Negro and white schools involved in each of the cases. We must look instead to the effect of segregation itself on public education.

In approaching this problem, we cannot turn the clock back to 1868 when the Amendment was adopted, or even to 1896 when *Plessy v. Ferguson* was written. We must consider public education in the light of its full development and its present place in American life throughout the nation. Only in this way can it be determined if segregation in public schools deprives these plaintiffs of the equal protection of the laws.

Today, education is perhaps the most important function of state and local governments. Compulsory school attendance laws and the great expenditures for education both demonstrate our recognition of the importance of education to our democratic society. . . . In these days, it is doubtful that any child may reasonably be expected to succeed in life if he is denied the opportunity of an education. Such an opportunity, where the state has undertaken to provide it, is a right which must be made available to all on equal terms.

We come then to the question presented: Does segregation of children in public schools solely on the basis of race, even though the physical facilities and other "tangible" factors may be equal, deprive the children of the minority group of equal educational opportunities? We believe that it does.

. . . .We conclude that in the field of public education the doctrine of "separate but equal" has no place. Separate educational facilities are inherently unequal. Therefore, we hold that the plaintiffs and others similarly situated for whom the actions have been brought are, by reason of the segregation complained of, deprived of the equal protection of the laws guaranteed by the Fourteenth Amendment. . . .

I Have a Dream

On August 28, 1963, while Congress debated wide-ranging civil rights legislation, Martin Luther King, Jr., led more than 200,000 people on a march on Washington, D.C. On the steps of the Lincoln Memorial he gave a stirring speech in which he eloquently spoke of his dreams for African Americans and for the United States. Excerpts of the speech follow.

. . . There are those who are asking the devotees of civil rights, "When will you be satisfied?"

We can never be satisfied as long as the Negro is the victim of the unspeakable horrors of police brutality. . . .We cannot be satisfied as long as the Negro's basic mobility is from a smaller ghetto to a larger one. We can never be satisfied as long as a Negro in Mississippi cannot vote and a Negro in New York believes he has nothing for which to vote. . . .

I say to you today, my friends, that in spite of the difficulties and frustrations of the moment I still have a dream. It is a dream deeply rooted in the American dream.

I have a dream that one day this nation will rise up and live out the true meaning of its creed, "We hold these truths to be self-evident, that all men are created equal."

I have a dream that one day on the red hills of Georgia the sons of former slaves and the sons of former slaveowners will be able to sit down together at the table of brotherhood.

I have a dream that one day even the state of Mississippi, a desert state sweltering with the heat of injustice and oppression, will be transformed into an oasis of freedom and justice.

I have a dream that my four little children will one day live in a nation where they will not be judged by the color of their skin, but by the content of their character. . . .

. . . When we let freedom ring, when we let it ring from every village and every hamlet, from every state and every city, we will be able to speed up that day when all of God's children, black men and white men, Jews and Gentiles, Protestants and Catholics, will be able to join hands and sing in the words of the old Negro spiritual: "Free at last! Free at last! Thank God Almighty, we are free at last!"

Gazetteer

★ ★

The gazetteer is a geographical dictionary that lists political divisions, natural features, and other places and locations. Following each entry is a description, its latitude and longitude, and a page reference that indicates where each entry may be found in this text.

A

Afghanistan country in south central Asia (33°N/63°E) 767

Africa continent of the Eastern Hemisphere south of the Mediterranean Sea and adjoining Asia on its northeastern border (10°N/22°E) 16

Alabama state in the southeastern United States; 22nd state to enter the Union (32°45'N/87°30'W) 144

Alaska state located in northwestern North America; territory purchased from Russia in 1867 (64°N/150°W) 382

Albany capital of New York; site where Albany Congress proposed first formal plan to unite the 13 colonies (40°45'N/73°45'W) 183

Allegheny River river in western Pennsylvania uniting with the Monongahela River at Pittsburgh to form the Ohio River (40°N/82°W) 44

Andes Mountains mountain system extending along western coast of South America (13°S/75°W) 10

Antarctica continent located around the South Pole (80°15'S/127°E) 16

Antietam Civil War battle site in western Maryland (39°45'N/77°30'W) 193

Appalachian Mountains chief mountain system in eastern North America extending from Quebec and New Brunswick to central Alabama (37°N/82°W) 24

Appomattox Court House site in central Virginia where Confederate forces surrendered ending the Civil War (37°N/77°W) 209

Arctic Ocean ocean in the northernmost part of the world (85°N/170°E) 10

Arizona state in the southwestern United States; 48th state to enter the Union (34°N/113°W) 177

Arkansas state in the south central United States; acquired as part of Louisiana Purchase (34°45'N/93°45'W) 144

Asia continent of the Eastern Hemisphere forming a single landmass with Europe (50°N/100°E) 16

Atlanta capital of Georgia located in the northwest central part of the state (33°45'N/84°30'W) 183

Atlantic Ocean ocean separating North and South America from Europe and Africa (5°S/25°W) 10

B

Baltimore city on the Chesapeake Bay in central Maryland (39°15'N/76°45'W) 24

Barbary Coast north coast of Africa between Morocco and Tunisia (36°45'N/3°E) 129

Baton Rouge capital of Louisiana located on the Mississippi River in the southeastern part of the state (30°30'N/91°15'W) 55

Bay of Pigs site of 1961 invasion of Cuba by U.S.-trained Cuban exiles (22°N/79°W) 696

Beijing capital of China located in the northeastern part of the country (40°N/116°30'E) 391

Berlin city in east central Germany; former national capital divided into sectors after World War II; city reunited in 1989 (52°31'N/13°30'E) 591

Black Hills mountains in southwestern South Dakota; site of conflict between the Sioux and white settlers during 1870s (44°15'N/103°45'W) 250

Boston capital of Massachusetts located in the eastern part of the state; founded by English Puritans in 1630 (42°15'N/71°W) 24

C

California state in the western United States; attracted thousands of miners during gold rush of 1849 (38°15'N/121°15'W) 10

Cambodia country in Southeast Asia bordering Gulf of Siam; official name Democratic Kampuchea (12°N/105°E) 705

Canada country in northern North America (50°N/100°W) 156

Charleston city in South Carolina on the Atlantic coast; original name Charles Town (32°45'N/80°W) 54

Château-Thierry World War I battle site in France (49°N/3°15'E) 465

Chautauqua Lake lake in western New York State (42°15'N/79°45'W) 331

Chesapeake Bay inlet of the Atlantic Ocean in Virginia and Maryland (37°N/76°W) 51

Chicago largest city in Illinois; located in northeastern part of the state along Lake Michigan (41°45'N/87°30'W) 183

China country in eastern Asia; mainland (People's Republic of China) under communist control since 1949 (36°45'N/93°E) 12

Chisholm Trail pioneer cattle trail from Texas to Kansas (34°N/98°W) 250

Cincinnati city in southern Ohio on the Ohio River; grew as result of increasing steamship traffic during the mid-1800s (39°15'N/84°30'W) 65

Colorado state in the western United States (39°30'N/107°W) 177

Columbia River river flowing through southwest Canada and northwestern United States into the Pacific Ocean (46°15'N/124°W) 120

Concord village northwest of Boston, Massachusetts; site of early battle of the American Revolution on April 19, 1775 (42°N/71°W) 73

Connecticut state in the northeastern United States; one of the original 13 states (41°45'N/73°15'W) 24

Cuba country in the West Indies, North America (22°N/79°W) 377

Czechoslovakia former country in central Europe; now two countries, the Czech Republic and Slovakia (49°30'N/16°E) 474

D

Delaware state in the northeastern United States; one of the original 13 states (38°45'N/75°30'W) 24

Detroit city in southeastern Michigan; site of significant battles during the French and Indian War and the War of 1812; center of automobile industry (42°15'N/82°15'W) 65

dust bowl area of the Great Plains where the drought of the 1930s turned the soil to wind-borne dust (37°N/98°W) 555

E

England division of the United Kingdom of Great Britain and Northern Ireland (56°30'N/1°45'W) 16

Erie Canal waterway connecting the Hudson River with Lake Erie through New York State (43°N/76°W) 144

Erie, Lake one of the Great Lakes between Canada and the United States (42°15'N/81°30'W) 19

Europe continent of the northern part of the Eastern Hemisphere between Asia and the Atlantic Ocean (50°N/15°E) 16

F

Florida state in the southeastern United States (30°30'N/84°45'W) 19

Fort Duquesne French fort on the site of Pittsburgh, Pennsylvania (40°30'N/80°W) 44

Fort Sumter Union fort during the Civil War located on island near Charleston, South Carolina; site of first military engagement of Civil War (32°45'N/80°W) 190

France country in western Europe (49°45'N/0°45'E) 16

Fredericksburg city and Civil War battle site in northeast Virginia (38°15'N/77°30'W) 194

Freeport city in northern Illinois; site of 1858 Lincoln-Douglas debate (42°15'N/89°30'W) 186

G

Galveston city on the Gulf of Mexico coast in Texas; created nation's first commission form of city government (29°15'N/95°W) 404

Georgia state in the southeastern United States (32°45'N/83°45'W) 24

Germany country in central Europe; divided after World War II into East Germany and West Germany; unified in 1989 (50°N/10°E) 461

Gettysburg city and Civil War battle site in south central Pennsylvania; site where Lincoln delivered the Gettysburg Address (39°45'N/77°15'W) 194

Great Basin interior drainage area in Nevada (40°15'N/117°15'W) 174

Great Britain commonwealth comprising England, Scotland, and Wales (56°30'N/1°45'W) 42

Great Lakes chain of five lakes, Superior, Erie, Michigan, Ontario, and Huron, in central North America (45°N/87°W) 19

Great Plains flat grassland in the central United States (45°N/104°W) 174

Great Salt Lake lake in northern Utah with no outlet and strongly saline waters (41°15'N/112°45'W) 120

Greece country in southeastern Europe (39°N/21°30'E) 474

Guadalcanal island in the Solomons east of Australia (9°45'S/158°45'E) 654

Guam United States possession in the western Pacific Ocean (14°N/143°15'E) 382

H

Harlem northern section of Manhattan in New York City; cultural center of African Americans in the early and mid-1900s (40°45'N/74°W) 506

Harpers Ferry town in northern West Virginia on the Potomac River (39°15'N/77°45'W) 186

Hartford capital of Connecticut located on the Connecticut River in the central part of the state (41°45'N/72°45'W) 127

Hawaii state in the United States located in the Pacific Ocean (20°N/157°W) 382

Hiroshima city in southern Japan; site of first military use of atomic bomb, August 6, 1945 (34°15'N/132°30'E) 594

Hispaniola island in the West Indies in North America, where Haiti and the Dominican Republic are located (17°30'N/73°15'W) 19

Hong Kong British colony along the southern coast of China in Asia (21°45'N/115°E) 382

Hudson Bay large bay in northern Canada (60°N/86°W) 43

Hudson River river flowing through New York State into the Atlantic Ocean at New York City (52°45'N/74°W) 44

Huron, Lake one of the Great Lakes between the United States and Canada in North America (45°15'N/82°45'W) 19

I

Idaho state in the northwestern United States; ranks among top states in silver production (44°N/115°15'W) 250

Illinois state in the north central United States; one of the states formed in the Northwest Territory (40°30'N/90°45'W) 144

Indian Territory land reserved by the United States government for Native Americans, now the state of Oklahoma (36°N/98°15'W) 156

Indiana state in the north central United States; one of the states formed in the Northwest Territory (39°45'N/86°45'W) 144

Indochina region in Southeast Asia (17°15'N/105°15'E) 651

Iowa state in the north central United States acquired as part of the Louisiana Purchase (42°N/94°15'W) 177

Iran country of the Middle East in southwestern Asia (31°15'N/53°30'E) 474

Iraq country of the Middle East in southwestern Asia (32°N/42°30'E) 655

Israel country of the Middle East in southwestern Asia along the Mediterranean Sea (32°45'N/34°E) 655

Italy country in southern Europe along the Mediterranean Sea (44°N/11°15'E) 461

J

Jamestown first permanent English settlement in North America; located in southeastern Virginia (37°15'N/76°45'W) 23

Japan island country in eastern Asia (36°30'N/133°30'E) 382

K

Kansas state in the central United States; fighting over slavery issue in 1850s gave territory the name "Bleeding Kansas" (38°30'N/98°45'W) 177

Kentucky state in the south central United States; border state that sided with the Union during the Civil War (37°30'N/87°30'W) 126

Kings Mountain Revolutionary War battle site in northern South Carolina (35°15'N/81°15'W) 54

Korea peninsula in eastern Asia between China, Russia, and the Sea of Japan, on which are located the countries of North Korea and South Korea (38°15'N/127°30'E) 594

Kuwait country of the Middle East in southwestern Asia between Iraq and Saudi Arabia (29°N/47°45'E) 474

L

Lexington Revolutionary War battle site in eastern Massachusetts; site of first clash between colonists and British, April 19, 1775 (42°26'N/71°13'W) 73

Little Rock capital of Arkansas located in the center of the state; site of 1957 conflict over public school integration (34°45'N/92°15'W) 183

London capital of United Kingdom located in the southeastern part of England (51°30'N/0°15'W) 585

Los Angeles city along the Pacific coast in southern California; industrial, financial, and trade center of western United States (34°N/118°15'W) 250

Louisiana state in the south central United States (30°45'N/92°45'W) 126

Louisiana Territory region of west central United States between the Mississippi River and the Rocky Mountains purchased from France in 1803 (40°N/95°W) 120

M

Maine state in the northeastern United States; 23rd state to enter the Union (45°30'N/69°45'W) 24

Maryland state in the eastern United States; one of the original 13 states (39°15'N/76°30'W) 24

Massachusetts state in the northeastern United States; one of the original 13 states (42°15'N/72°30'W) 24

Mediterranean Sea sea between Europe and Africa (36°15'N/13°30'E) 39

Mexico country in North America south of the United States (23°45'N/104°W) 174

Mexico, Gulf of gulf south of the United States and east of Mexico in North America (25°15'N/93°45'W) 16

Michigan state in the north central United States; one of the states formed in the Northwest Territory (45°N/85°W) 177

Michigan, Lake one of the five Great Lakes located in the north central United States (43°15'N/87°15'W) 19

Midway Islands United States possession in the central Pacific Ocean; site of Battle of Midway, June 1942 (28°N/177°W) 382

Milwaukee city in eastern Wisconsin along Lake Michigan (43°N/88°W) 300

Minnesota state in the north central United States; fur trade, good soil, and lumber attracted early settlers (46°15'N/96°15'W) 177

Mississippi state in the southeastern United States; became English territory after French and Indian War (32°30'N/89°45'W) 144

Mississippi River river flowing through the United States from Minnesota to the Gulf of Mexico; explored by French in 1600s (29°N/89°W) 19

Missouri state in the south central United States; petition for statehood resulted in sectional conflict and the Missouri Compromise (40°45'N/93°W) 144

Missouri River river flowing through the United States from the Rocky Mountains to the Mississippi River near St. Louis (38°45'N/90°15'W) 19

Montana state in the northwestern United States; cattle industry grew during 1850s (47°15'N/111°45'W) 177

Montgomery capital of Alabama located in the central part of the state; site of 1955 bus boycott to protest segregation (32°30'N/86°15'W) 183

Montreal city on the St. Lawrence River in southern Quebec, Canada (45°30'N/73°30'W) 19

Moscow capital of former Soviet Union and capital of Russia (55°45'N/37°30'E) 590

N

Nashville capital of Tennessee located in the north central part of the state (36°15'N/86°45'W) 183

Natchez city in western Mississippi along the Mississippi River (31°30'N/91°15'W) 144

National Road road from Baltimore, Maryland, to Vandalia, Illinois (40°N/81°30'W) 142

Nebraska state in the central United States (41°45'N/101°30'W) 177

Netherlands country in northwestern Europe (53°N/4°E) 16

Nevada state in the western United States (39°30'N/117°W) 177

New Amsterdam town founded on Manhattan Island by Dutch settlers in 1625; renamed New York by British settlers (40°45'N/74°W) 21

New Hampshire state in the northeastern United States; one of the original 13 states (44°N/71°45'W) 24

New Jersey state in the northeastern United States; one of the original 13 states (40°30'N/74°45'W) 24

New Mexico state in the southwestern United States; ceded to the United States by Mexico in 1848 (34°30'N/107°15'W) 177

New Orleans city in southern Louisiana in the Mississippi Delta (30°N/90°W) 120

New York state in the northeastern United States; one of the original 13 states (42°45'N/78°W) 24

New York City city in southeastern New York State at the mouth of the Hudson River; largest city in the United States (40°45'N/74°W) 24

Nicaragua country in Central America (12°45'N/86°15'W) 388

Normandy region along French coast and site of D-Day invasion, June 6, 1944 (48°N/2°W) 592

North America continent in the northern part of the Western Hemisphere between the Atlantic and Pacific oceans (45°N/100°W) 16

North Carolina state in the southeastern United States; one of the original 13 states (35°45'N/81°30'W) 24

North Dakota state in the north central United States; Congress created Dakota Territory in 1861 (47°15'N/102°W) 177

Northwest Territory territorial division north of the Ohio River and east of the Mississippi River (47°30'N/87°30'W) 65

O

Oberlin college and town in northern Ohio (41°15'N/82°15'W) 330

Ohio state in the north central United States; first state in the Northwest Territory (40°30'N/83°15'W) 126

Ohio River river flowing from Allegheny and Monongahela rivers in western Pennsylvania into the Mississippi River (39°N/85°W) 19

Ohio Valley valley of the Ohio River, which flows from Pennsylvania to the Mississippi River at Cairo, Illinois (37°30'N/88°W) 65

Oklahoma state in the south central United States; Five Civilized Tribes moved to territory 1830–1842 (36°N/98°15'W) 177

Ontario, Lake one of the five Great Lakes between Canada and the United States (43°30'N/79°W) 19

Oregon state in the northwestern United States; adopted woman suffrage in 1912 (43°45'N/123°45'W) 177

Oregon Trail pioneer trail from Independence, Missouri, to the Oregon Territory (42°30'N/110°W) 170

P

Pacific Ocean world's largest ocean located between Asia and the Americas (0°/175°W) 10

Panama country in the southern part of Central America, occupying the Isthmus of Panama (8°N/81°W) 393

Panama Canal canal built across the Isthmus of Panama through Panama to connect the Caribbean Sea and the Pacific Ocean (9°15'N/79°45'W) 393

Pearl Harbor naval base at Honolulu, Hawaii; site of 1941 Japanese attack, leading to United States entry into World War II (21°21'N/157°57'W) 594

Pennsylvania state in the northeastern United States (41°N/78°15'W) 24

Persian Gulf gulf in southwestern Asia between Iran and the Arabian Peninsula (27°45'N/50°30'E) 767

Philadelphia city in eastern Pennsylvania on the Delaware River; Declaration of Independence and the Constitution both adopted in city's Independence Hall (40°N/75°W) 24

Philippines island country in southeast Asia (14°30'N/125°E) 377

Pittsburgh city in western Pennsylvania; one of the great steelmaking centers of the world (40°30'N/80°W) 144

Plymouth town in eastern Massachusetts; first successful English colony in New England (42°N/70°45'W) 25

Promontory Point site in Utah where the first transcontinental railroad was completed (41°45'N/112°15'W) 270

Providence capital of Rhode Island; site of first English settlement in Rhode Island (41°45'N/71°30'W) 183

Puerto Rico United States possession in the West Indies (18°15'N/66°45'W) 19

Pullman company town south of Chicago; site of 1894 railroad strike (41°45'N/87°30'W) 291

Q

Quebec city in Canada, capital of Quebec Province, on the St. Lawrence River; first settlement in New France (46°45'N/71°15'W) 19

R

Raleigh capital of North Carolina located in the north central part of the state (35°45'N/78°45'W) 209

Rhode Island state in the northeastern United States; one of the original 13 states (41°30'N/71°45'W) 24

Richmond capital of Virginia located in the central part of the state; capital of the Confederacy during the Civil War (37°30'N/77°30'W) 209

Rio Grande river between the United States and Mexico in North America; forms the boundary between Texas and Mexico (26°N/97°30'W) 19

Roanoke island off the coast of present-day North Carolina that was site of early British colonizing efforts (35°N/75°39'W) 23

Rocky Mountains mountain range in western United States and Canada in North America (50°N/114°W) 120

Russia name of republic; former empire of eastern Europe and northern Asia coinciding with Soviet Union (60°30'N/64°E) 146

S

Sacramento capital of California located in the north central part of the state (38°30'N/121°30'W) 250

St. Augustine city in northeastern Florida on the Atlantic coast; oldest permanent existing European settlement in North America, founded in 1565 (30°N/81°15'W) 19

St. Lawrence River river flowing from Lake Ontario, between Canada and the United States, through Canada to the Atlantic Ocean (48°N/65°15'W) 19

St. Louis city in eastern Missouri on the Mississippi River (38°45'N/90°15'W) 65

St. Mihiel World War I battle site in France (49°N/5°30'E) 465

Salt Lake City capital of Utah; founded by Mormons in 1847 (40°45'N/111°45'W) 250

San Antonio city in south central Texas (29°30'N/98°30'W) 172

San Francisco city in northern California on the Pacific coast (37°45'N/122°30'W) 250

Santa Fe capital of New Mexico located in the north central part of the state (35°45'N/106°W) 250

Saratoga Revolutionary War battle site in the Hudson Valley of eastern New York State (43°N/73°51'W) 51

Savannah city in eastern Georgia (32°N/81°W) 24

Sea Islands group of islands off the coast of Georgia and South Carolina (31°15'N/81°W) 216

Seneca Falls town in New York State; site of woman's rights convention in 1848 (43°N/77°W) 161

Sierra Nevada mountain range in eastern California (39°N/120°W) 250

South Africa country in southern Africa (28°S/24°45'E) 465

South America continent in the southern part of the Western Hemisphere lying between the Atlantic and Pacific oceans (15°S/60°W) 16

South Carolina state in the southeastern United States; one of the original 13 states (34°15'N/81°15'W) 24

South Dakota state in the north central United States; acquired through the Louisiana Purchase (44°15'N/102°W) 177

Soviet Union former country in northern Europe and Asia (60°30'N/64°E) 579

Spain country in southwestern Europe (40°15'N/4°30'W) 16

Stalingrad city in the former Soviet Union on the Volga River; present name Volgograd (48°45'N/42°15'E) 591

Suez Canal canal built between the Mediterranean Sea and the Red Sea through northeastern Egypt (31°N/32°15'E) 665

Superior, Lake one of the five Great Lakes between Canada and the United States in North America (47°45'N/89°15'W) 19

T

Tampa city in west central Florida (28°N/82°30'W) 270

Tennessee state in the south central United States; first state readmitted to the Union after the Civil War (35°45'N/88°W) 126

Tennessee Valley valley of the Tennessee River, which flows from the Appalachian Mountains to the Ohio River (35°30'N/88°15'W) 553

Tenochtitlán Aztec capital on the site of present-day Mexico City (19°30'N/99°15'W) 10

Texas state in the south central United States; Mexican colony that became an independent republic before joining the United States (31°N/101°W) 177

Tokyo capital of Japan located on the eastern coast of Honshu Island (35°45'N/139°45'E) 594

Toronto city in Canada on Lake Ontario; capital of the province of Ontario (43°45'N/79°30'W) 183

Trenton capital of New Jersey located on the Delaware River; site of Revolutionary War battle in December 1776 (40°15'N/74°45'W) 51

U

Union of Soviet Socialist Republics *See* Soviet Union.

United Kingdom country in northwestern Europe made up of England, Scotland, Wales, and Northern Ireland (56°30'N/1°45'W) 470

United States country in central North America; fourth largest country in the world in both area and population (38°N/110°W) 177

Utah state in the western United States; settled by Mormons in 1840s (39°30'N/112°45'W) 177

V

Valley Forge Revolutionary War winter camp northwest of Philadelphia (40°N/75°30'W) 51

Veracruz city in eastern Mexico on the Gulf of Mexico coast (19°15'N/96°W) 174

Vermont state in the northeastern United States; 14th state to enter the Union (43°45'N/72°45'W) 177

Vicksburg city and Civil War battle site in western Mississippi on the Mississippi River (32°21'N/90°52'W) 195

Vietnam country in southeastern Asia (16°N/108°E) 707

Virginia state in the eastern United States; colony in which first permanent English settlement in the Americas was established (37°N/78°W) 24

W

Wall Street street in New York City at the center of the financial district (40°45'N/74°W) 307

Washington state in the northwestern United States; territory reached by Lewis and Clark in 1805 (47°30'N/121°15'W) 177

Washington, D.C. capital of the United States located on the Potomac River; coinciding with the District of Columbia (38°53'N/77°02'W) 126

West Virginia state in the east central United States (39°N/80°45'W) 177

Wisconsin state in the north central United States; passed first state unemployment compensation act, 1932 (44°30'N/91°W) 144

Wounded Knee site of battle between settlers and Native Americans in southern South Dakota in 1890 and of Native American movement protest in 1973 (43°26'N/102°30'W) 250

Wyoming state in the western United States; territory provided women the right to vote, 1869 (42°45'N/108°30'W) 250

Y

Yorktown town in southeastern Virginia and site of final battle of Revolutionary War (37°15'N/76°30'W) 54

Z

Zaire country in central Africa (1°S/22°15'E) 698

Glossary

★ ★

A

abolitionist 1800s reformer who worked to end slavery (p. 161)

agribusiness large farming operation that includes the cultivation, processing, storage, and distribution of farm products (p. 641)

amendment alteration to the Constitution (p. 71)

amnesty act of a government by which pardon is granted to an individual or groups of persons (p. 217)

anarchism a belief in no direct government authority over society (p. 303)

anarchist one who opposes all forms of government (p. 388)

antebellum customs, manners, and institutions that existed before the Civil War (p. 331)

appeasement policy of compromising or giving in to demands in an attempt to avoid trouble and maintain peace (p. 581)

appropriations bill draft of a law setting aside funds for a specific use (p. 778)

arbitration hearing and resolution of a disagreement between two parties through an impartial third party (pp. 296, 372)

armistice temporary suspension of hostilities between opponents (p. 467)

armory place or building where arms and military equipment are stored (p. 512)

assimilation process of one group or culture absorbing another (p. 683)

automation technique of operating a machine, manufacturing process, or system that will do a job formerly performed by humans (p. 644)

B

balance of payments difference between the value of a nation's imports and its exports; also known as balance of trade (p. 736)

bicameral political system based on two legislative chambers (p. 62)

bilingualism ability to speak two languages (p. 690)

blacklist record kept by companies of employees or former employees who are disapproved of or are to be punished or boycotted (p. 292)

black nationalism belief of militant blacks who advocate separatism from whites and forming self-governing black communities (p. 682)

black power mobilizing economic and political power of African Americans to improve their condition (p. 683)

blitzkrieg war conducted with great speed or force (p. 584)

blockade to close off something (p. 191)

bounty money paid to recruit soldiers for military service; payment to encourage an action (p. 198)

boycott refusal to buy goods or have dealings with a country or other entity, usually to express disapproval or force acceptance of certain conditions (p. 45)

buffer area designed to separate and serve as a protective barrier; neutral area separating conflicting forces (p. 612)

business cycle sequence of economic activity, usually consisting of recession, recovery, growth, and decline (p. 292)

busing transportation of children to a school outside their residential area to establish racial integration in that school (p. 686)

C

cabinet a group of advisers to the President (p. 107)

cartel an association of nations promoting its economic interests (p. 749)

closed shop system where all workers in a particular industry are required to be union members or employer agrees to hire only union members (p. 148)

coalition alliance, combination, or union of parties, people, or states formed for a specific action or purpose (p. 560)

collective bargaining negotiation between organized workers and management to reach an agreement on wages, hours, and working conditions (p. 293)

collective security an agreement to provide for common defense (p. 615)

commodity economic good; product of agriculture; article of commerce (p. 260)

commonwealth self-governing political unit of independent states associated in a common allegiance (p. 26)

commune group of people living together with collective ownership and use of property, often having shared goals, philosophies, and ways of life; large cooperative farms (p. 711)

communism system of government in which the Communist party controls the political, economic, cultural, and social life of the people; economic system in which society as a whole, represented by the Communist party, owns all means of production, distribution, and exchange of goods (p. 610)

company town village built and run by a company where workers are required to live (p. 291)

confederation nonbinding political alliance of independent countries, states, or groups (pp. 9, 63)

congregation body of church members; people meeting for worship and religious instruction (p. 26)

conquistador Spanish adventurer in sixteenth-century Americas (p. 17)

conscientious objector person who refuses to perform military service or to bear arms on the grounds of moral or religious principles or beliefs (p. 709)

conscription compulsory enrollment of people for military service (p. 190)

consensus general agreement; judgment arrived at by most of those concerned; group solidarity in sentiment and belief (p. 728)

conservation the planned management of natural resources to prevent destruction or neglect (p. 424)

conspicuous consumption lavish spending for show (p. 356)

constitution plan of government in America; basic principles and laws of a nation, state, or social group that determine the powers and duties of the government and guarantee certain rights to its people (p. 26)

containment policy of preventing the expansion of a hostile power; post-World War II foreign policy stating the United States would hold Soviet influence within its existing limits (p. 612)

contraband goods or merchandise whose importation, exportation, or possession is forbidden (p. 459)

cooperative enterprise or organization owned by and operated for the benefit of those using its services (p. 342)

corollary proposition added to another as a natural consequence or effect (p. 389)

corporation form of business consisting of a group of people authorized by law to act as a single person and having an identity that survives its incorporators (p. 274)

cotton gin a machine that cleans the seeds from cotton fibers (p. 149)

counterculture a culture with values and mores that run contrary to those of established society (p. 711)

coup d'état a sudden revolt against an existing government (p. 764)

covenant formal and binding agreement between two or more parties (p. 474)

covert secret or undercover; not openly shown or engaged in (p. 652)

craft union labor union in which all members practice the same occupation or skill (p. 562)

credibility gap lack of trust stemming from difference between official government statements and practices (p. 700)

creditor nation a nation that lends money (p. 784)

D

dark horse political candidate unexpectedly nominated, usually as a compromise between groups (p. 173)

debtor nation a country that owes money (p. 784)

defense perimeter boundary of military protection (p. 620)

deficit spending government practice of borrowing money in order to spend more money than is received from taxes (p. 552)

deflation economic condition in which the volume of available money or credit decreases, resulting in the decline of the price of goods and services (p. 345)

deport remove from a country an alien presence (p. 477)

depression economic condition marked by an extended and severe decline in production and sales, and a severe increase in unemployment (p. 66)

deregulation act of removing restrictions and regulations (p. 742)

détente relaxation of cold war tensions between the United States and the Soviet Union that began in the early 1970s (p. 714)

direct primary election in which nominations of candidates for office are made by voters (p. 406)

direct tax one paid directly to the government rather than being included in the price of goods; a tax collected directly from the person on whom the tax burden is expected to fall (p. 45)

disenfranchise having had the legal right to vote taken away (p. 221)

dole money or goods given as charity; grant of government funds to the unemployed (p. 552)

domestic market market composed of buyers and sellers within a nation (p. 495)

double-digit inflation a rise in the general level of prices of 10 percent or more (p. 750)

downsizing to reduce operations or number of employees (p. 779)

drawdown the use of soldiers stationed in Europe and Asia during the Persian Gulf War (p. 766)

E

economies of scale ability of large businesses to operate more cheaply and efficiently than smaller ones, resulting in lower per-unit costs for the products of large companies (p. 269)

emancipation freeing of enslaved persons; act or process of freeing from restraint, control, or the power of another; freedom from bondage (p. 62)

encomienda system of rewarding conquistadors with tracts of land, including the right to tax and demand labor from Native Americans who lived on the land (p. 19)

entrepreneur person who organizes, manages, and assumes the risks of a business or enterprise (p. 267)

enumerated powers those mentioned specifically one after another in the Constitution (p. 111)

escalation increase in extent, volume, number, amount, intensity, or scope (p. 704)

ethnic cleansing expulsion or extermination of a group from a country (p. 781)

ethnic group groups of people who share the same culture, religion, and customs (p. 569)

excise tax one paid by a manufacturer and passed on to those who buy the product; a tax on the manufacture, sale, or consumption of a product within a country (p. 109)

executive privilege principle that the executive branch of government is exempt from disclosing information when such disclosure would adversely affect the functions and decision-making processes of the presidency or national security (p. 740)

expatriate person who leaves his or her native country to live elsewhere (p. 332)

expedition a journey with a specific purpose (p. 119)

F

fascism system of government that is strongly nationalistic and allows private ownership of property while controlling general economic policies; government characterized by racism and militarism; a repressive one-party dictatorship (p. 581)

favorite son presidential candidate supported by the delegates of the candidate's native state at a national political convention (p. 152)

featherbedding requiring of an employer under a union rule or safety statute to hire more employees than are needed (p. 624)

federal deficit difference between the amount of money a government took in and what it spent (p. 757)

federalism system of government in which power is distributed between national and state governments (p. 70)

federalized brought under federal government jurisdiction (p. 674)

feminist person who acts on behalf of women's rights (p. 688)

feudalism a system in which powerful leaders gave land to nobles in return for pledges of loyalty and service (p. 11)

filibuster the use of delaying tactics to prevent action in a legislative assembly (p. 778)

fireside chat the name used to describe how former President Franklin D. Roosevelt talked to people by radio (p. 547)

forage to live off the land (p. 204)

foreclosure legal procedure for reclaiming a piece of property when the owner is unable to keep up the mortgage payments (p. 554)

free-trader one that practices or advocates trade without taxes or tariffs (p. 327)

frigate medium-sized warship smaller than a destroyer; used for escort and patrol duties (p. 127)

G

genocide deliberate and systematic destruction of a group (p. 781)

gentry the upper class of England (p. 29)

glasnost a Russian word for the policy of openness begun by former Soviet President Gorbachev encouraging free expression and an end to party censorship (p. 759)

global economy economic interdependence among countries of the world (p. 784)

gold standard monetary system in which a nation's currency is based on the value of gold (p. 346)

graft acquisition of money or power in dishonest or questionable ways while in public office (p. 316)

greenback paper money that was not backed by gold or silver; legal-tender notes issued by the United States government (p. 199)

guerrilla soldier who barrages the enemy with surprise attacks, harassment, sabotage, and other nontraditional warfare (p. 612)

H

habeas corpus legal principle that requires that people who are arrested be brought to court to show why they should be held; writ inquiring into the lawfulness of retaining a person who is imprisoned or detained in custody (p. 199)

holding company one that gains control of other companies by buying their stock (p. 277)

Holocaust systematic mass murder of 12 million European civilians, especially Jews, by Nazis during World War II (p. 593)

horizontal integration joining together of businesses that are engaged in similar business activities or processes (p. 277)

I

impeach to bring charges of a crime against a federal or state public official with the intent of removing the official from office (pp. 75, 223)

imperialism act of creating an empire by dominating other nations (p. 370)

implied powers those suggested but not directly stated in the Constitution (p. 112)

impound to refuse to spend congressionally allocated funds; to seize and hold in the custody of the law (p. 742)

impressment form of military and naval conscription, usually by force, practiced by Britain and other European countries (p. 121)

income tax tax on the net income of an individual or business (p. 431)

incumbent current officeholder (p. 774)

indemnity security or protection against hurt, loss, or damage; exemption from incurred penalties or liabilities (p. 391)

indentured servant person who agreed to work for an employer in colonial America for a specified time in exchange for passage to America (p. 24)

industrial union union that represents every worker in a single industry regardless of his or her job (pp. 298, 562)

inflation decline in money's value when more money is printed, resulting in increased prices of goods and services (p. 345)

inheritance tax tax on an inheritance that an heir must pay to receive the inheritance (p. 433)

initiative procedure enabling citizens to propose a bill by petitioning with a specific number of signatures from registered voters (p. 406)

injunction court order requiring an individual or company to do something or to prohibit a given action; used frequently to stop strikes (p. 299)

installment buying system of paying for goods at regular intervals, usually with interest added to the balance (p. 516)

interlocking directorate system under which the same people serve on the boards of directors of several firms within the same industry (p. 442)

internal improvements roads, canals, and other transportation needs inside a nation's boundaries (p. 140)

isolationism policy or belief that a nation should limit its alliances and involvement in international political and economic affairs (p. 370)

J

joint resolution a resolution passed by both houses of Congress requiring only a simple majority vote (p. 173)

joint-stock company form of business organization; pooled funds of many investors or stockholders who can independently sell their shares of the company (p. 14)

judicial review Supreme Court's power to review all congressional acts and executive actions and reject those it considers unconstitutional (pp. 77, 118)

junk bond high-risk bond that offers a high return to compensate for the high risk of default (p. 768)

jurisdictional strike one resulting from a dispute between unions over which union should represent the workers in a company or industry (p. 624)

K

kickback payback of a sum received from increased fees because of a confidential agreement or act of coercion (p. 317)

L

laissez-faire government doctrine of noninterference in business practices and in the economic affairs of individuals; literally, "let do" (p. 118)

lame duck elected official who continues to hold office during the period between the election and the inauguration of a successor (p. 533)

lend-lease transfer of goods and services to an ally (p. 587)

line-item veto power to veto a single part of a bill (p. 778)

line of demarcation north-south line of longitude through the Atlantic Ocean dividing lands in the Americas claimed by Spain and Portugal (p. 17)

literacy test tests to show if immigrants could read (p. 413)

lobbyist person who promotes or secures the passage of legislation by influencing public officials (p. 319)

lockout closed factory or place of employment caused by a strike; withholding of employment by an employer (p. 293)

long drive cattle run in which a large herd is moved across great distances to a railhead where they are shipped to market (p. 250)

Loyalist American colonist who supported the British government; one who is or remains loyal to a political cause, party, or government (p. 49)

M

mandate clear expression of the wishes of voters, as shown in election results (pp. 220, 723)

martial law form of military rule that suspends Bill of Rights guarantees; law administered by the military in an emergency situation when civilian law-enforcement agencies are not able to maintain order (p. 199)

maverick unbranded range animal or cattle; a motherless calf (p. 249)

mercantilism the theory that a state's power depended on its wealth (p. 20)

mercenary paid soldier hired for service in the army of a foreign country; one that serves merely for wages (p. 52)

merchandising buying and selling of goods in a business for a profit (p. 309)

meridian line of longitude; a great circle on the surface of the earth passing through the poles (p. 258)

mestizo person in the Spanish colonies born of Spanish and Native American parents (p. 19)

militia group of civilians declared by law to be called to military service and trained as soldiers to fight in emergencies (p. 43)

minutemen a group of armed men who were ready to fight the English at a moment's notice (p. 47)

moratorium official authorization to suspend payments, as with a debt; officially authorized period of waiting (p. 523)

multinational state nation with many different ethnic groups (p. 781)

N

nationalism feeling of loyalty and devotion to one's country; honoring that nation above all others and promoting its culture and interests rather than those of other nations (p. 140)

neutrality refusal to take sides (p. 375)

new federalism Richard Nixon's policy of economic partnership between the federal and state governments whereby states and municipalities received less federal funding (p. 737)

nomadic frequent roaming from place to place without a fixed pattern of movement, usually following a food source (p. 242)

nonviolent resistance objection or demonstration to gain political ends without use of violence (p. 672)

northwest passage water route to Asia through North America sought by European explorers (p. 20)

nullification state declaration of a federal law to be invalid (p. 116)

O

on margin method of buying stock with a small cash down payment and the rest borrowed from a stockbroker. Stockbroker holds shares of stock as collateral for the loan; borrower repays broker from stock resale profits (p. 515)

open shop employment practice in which eligibility is not determined by union membership (p. 487)

P

partitioned divided into two or more territorial units having separate political status (p. 390)

Patriot American colonist who favored separation before and during the Revolutionary War (p. 49)

patronage practice of elected officials to make appointments to unelected government positions for political advantage or repayment of favors (p. 323)

perestroika a Russian word for "restructuring"; former Soviet President Gorbachev's name for his economic policy, which favors less government intervention and more private initiative (p. 759)

philanthropy actions to promote human welfare and benefit society (p. 283)

platform declaration of the principles and policies adopted by a political party or candidate (p. 184)

pocket veto indirect rejection of a legislative bill by the President by retaining the bill unsigned until after Congress adjourns (p. 155)

pogrom organized massacres of unarmed people, especially Jews (p. 302)

political machine party organization in big cities that holds power by controlling votes, courts, and police (p. 317)

pooling illegal agreements among individual railroads to divide the total volume of freight among their lines and to keep rates high (p. 342)

popular sovereignty principle that the settlers within a federal territory have the power to decide the legality of slavery within that territory (p. 176)

Glossary

pork-barrel legislation the money that Congress appropriates for local federal projects (p. 750)

post-war disillusionment period after a war in which the populace is disenchanted (p. 504)

pragmatism belief that government actions should meet the needs of society; practical approach to problems and affairs (p. 400)

pragmatist one who searches for practical solutions to problems (p. 724)

presidential succession the order in which others fill the office of President (p. 637)

price-cutting reduction of prices to a level designed to cripple competition (p. 442)

privateer armed private ship commissioned by the government to attack ships of an enemy (p. 127)

privatize transfer state-owned factories and other property to private ownership (p. 759)

propaganda information, not always true, designed to help or harm a cause (p. 49)

proprietor individual who received legal and exclusive right to American colonial land from the king of England and who was expected to administer the land according to English laws (p. 24)

protectionist one who advocates government protection for domestic producers and manufacturers through restrictions on imports (p. 327)

protective tariff high tax on imports intended to protect domestic products from foreign competition rather than to yield revenue (p. 108)

protectorate country that is technically independent, but whose government and economy are controlled by a stronger power; the nation or region controlled by a stronger nation (p. 385)

public land land belonging to the national government and therefore to the people (p. 64)

pump priming government money invested in the economy to stimulate a self-sustaining economic recovery (p. 552)

purge large-scale forced removal of officials who show signs of disloyalty to their superiors (p. 611)

R

racism belief that a particular race is superior to others (p. 682)

ratification to officially approve a proposal (pp. 70, 790)

reactionary government government characterized by ultraconservative policies (p. 700)

real wages income adjusted to compensate for reduced earning power due to inflation (p. 290)

realism European-influenced literary movement that strove for accurate representation of nature or real life without idealization (p. 331)

rebate discount in the form of a refund or part of a payment for a product or service (p. 279)

recall removal of an elected official by voters in a special election (p. 406)

recession downturn in the nation's economy marked by reduced economic activity (p. 564)

reciprocity mutual lowering by nations of tariff barriers; recognition by one of two countries of the validity of privileges granted by the other (p. 372)

rediscount small fee charged to a member bank by the Federal Reserve Bank upon acceptance of a business's promissory note (p. 440)

referendum process by which people can vote directly on a proposed law (p. 406)

reparation payments made by nations defeated in war as a penalty for damages caused to other countries (p. 485)

republic a government in which the power is held by the people, who then elect representatives to act for them (p. 49)

revenue sharing plan to share or divide income (p. 737)

revenue tariff low tax on imports intended to provide income for the government rather than protection of domestic products from foreign competition (p. 108)

rider unrelated amendment attached to a bill under legislative consideration (p. 323)

S

salutary neglect policy of noninterference by a governing nation in order to produce a beneficial effect (p. 42)

satellite nations East European nations politically and economically under Soviet domination; country dominated or controlled by another more powerful country (p. 611)

scab nonunion replacement workers during a strike or union members who refuse to strike and continue working (p. 293)

scrip money that can be redeemed only at a company store (p. 291)

search-and-destroy strategy military tactic used to force an enemy into open combat (p. 705)

secession formal withdrawal from an organization (p. 187)

securities stocks, bonds, and other financial instruments traded on a stock exchange (p. 514)

segregation enforced separation of racial groups in schooling, housing, and other public areas (p. 227)

separation of powers the division of power among the legislative, executive, and judicial branches of government (p. 76)

Glossary

sexism prejudice or discrimination based on gender (p. 689)

sharecropper agricultural worker who cultivates part of another person's land, receives supplies and equipment from the landowner and, in return, gives the landowner part of the harvest (p. 213)

shogun one of a line of military governors ruling Japan until the revolution of 1867–1868; Japanese commander in chief (p. 13)

shuttle diplomacy negotiations carried out by an intermediary who shuttles back and forth between the disputants (p. 717)

sit-in occupying seats or sitting on the floor of an establishment as a nonviolent means of protest (p. 676)

social contract agreement among individuals forming an organized society that defines and limits the rights and duties of each (p. 50)

social Darwinism sociological theory that states only the fittest survive social competition and experience social advancement (p. 282)

social gospel application by religious organizations of Christian principles to social problems (p. 399)

socialism economic system in which government partly owns and controls production and distribution of goods produced (p. 164)

speculator a person who buys bonds, stocks, or land to sell at a profit when the price later goes up (p. 64)

speculation risky business venture involving buying or selling in the hope of making a large, quick profit (p. 514)

sphere of influence area in China during the late 1800s where trade was controlled by a foreign power (p. 390)

spoils system practice of dismissing government job holders affiliated with a defeated party and replacing them with supporters of the winning party (p. 155)

stagflation persistent inflation combined with static consumer demand and relatively high rate of unemployment (p. 736)

student deferment official postponement of military service (p. 709)

subversive person working secretly, attempting to overthrow or undermine a government or political system (p. 627)

summit diplomatic meeting of the superpowers; conference of highest level government officials (p. 714)

supply-side economics an economic theory that claims that the economy can best be stimulated by increasing the supply of goods rather than the demand (p. 755)

T

teach-in lecture, debate, and discussion on controversial topic (p. 710)

technological unemployment jobs lost as the result of machines doing the jobs formerly accomplished by humans (p. 487)

tenant farmer agricultural worker who rents and farms land from another person and pays the rent either in cash or with a portion of the crop (p. 213)

textile fabric, especially woven or knitted; cloth (p. 147)

third party political party operating in addition to two other major parties in a nation or state normally characterized by a two-party system (p. 347)

toll fee charged for a privilege such as the use of a means of transportation (p. 142)

totalitarian type of government controlled by a single person or party; suppressing freedom and controlling every aspect of life (p. 581)

township local unit of government within a county (p. 320)

trade deficit economic condition in which the value of a nation's imports is more than the value of its exports (p. 785)

treason attempt to overthrow the government of the state to which the offender owes allegiance (p. 49)

trust combination of companies to gain control of an industry and reduce competition (p. 277)

turnpike road barricaded by spiked poles where travelers stop to pay a fee to use the road (p. 142)

U

ultimatum a demand that would have serious consequences if ignored (p. 145)

underemployed having less than full-time, regular, or adequate employment (p. 768)

unicameral legislature consisting of a single chamber (p. 63)

urban renewal construction program to replace or restore a city or urban area (p. 725)

user tax a tax on goods or services used by consumers (p. 767)

V

vaudeville stage entertainment consisting of various acts (p. 252)

vertical integration joining together of businesses that are involved in different but related activities or processes (p. 277)

Glossary

veto action by which an executive rejects a bill submitted by a legislature; to refuse to approve (p. 62)

victory gardens gardens for raising one's own vegetables, especially during wartime (p. 470)

vigilance committee organization of citizens who take the law into their own hands for their protection (p. 252)

W

ward division of a city for representative, electoral, or administrative purposes (p. 318)

war of national liberation conflict with goal of freeing one nation from the control of another (p. 702)

welfare capitalism system of benefit programs offered to workers by employers intended to reduce the appeal of unions (p. 488)

"Western" novel, story, or Hollywood motion picture depicting life in the western United States during the latter half of the nineteenth century (p. 253)

wildcat strike work stoppage initiated by a group of workers without formal union approval or in violation of a contract (p. 601)

Y

yellow journalism type of newspaper reporting in the late 1890s that featured sensational headlines and stories (p. 333)

Glossary

Spanish Glossary

★ ★

A

abolitionist/abolicionista reformista del siglo XIX que luchó por la supresión de la esclavitud (p. 161)

agribusiness/negocio agrario operación agrícola grande que incluye cultivo, procesamiento, almacenamiento y distribución de productos agrícolas (p. 641)

amendment/enmienda alteración de la Constitución (p. 71)

amnesty/amnistía acto de un gobierno que otorga el perdón a un individuo o grupo de personas (p. 217)

anarchism/anarquismo la creencia en la ausencia de autoridad directa del gobierno sobre la sociedad (p. 303)

anarchist/anarquista persona que se opone a cualquier forma de gobierno (p. 388)

antebellum/antebellum costumbres, hábitos e instituciones que existieron antes de la Guerra de Secesión (p. 331)

appeasement/apaciguamiento política de compromiso o aceptación de exigencias con el propósito de evitar problemas y mantener la paz (p. 581)

appropriations bill/proyecto de ley de asignaciones proyecto de ley que destina fondos a un uso específico (p. 778)

arbitration/arbitraje audiencia y resolución de un desacuerdo entre dos partes a través de una tercera parte imparcial (pp. 296, 372)

armistice/armisticio suspensión temporal de hostilidades entre adversarios (p. 467)

armory/armería lugar o edificio donde se almacenan armas y equipos militares (p. 512)

assimilation/asimilación proceso en el que un grupo o cultura absorbe a otro (p. 683)

automation/automatización técnica de operación de máquinas, procesamiento industrial o sistema que realiza un trabajo previamente efectuado por seres humanos (p. 644)

B

balance of payments/balanza de pagos diferencia entre el valor de las importaciones y las exportaciones de una nación; también conocida como balanza comercial (p. 736)

bicameral/bicameral sistema político basado en dos cámaras legislativas (p. 62)

bilingualism/bilingualismo capacidad de expresarse en dos idiomas (p. 690)

black list/lista negra registro mantenido por las compañías de los empleados o antiguos empleados con los que se está en desacuerdo o se propone castigar o boicotear (p. 292)

black nationalism/nacionalismo negro creencia de los militantes negros que favorece la separación de los blancos y la formación de comunidades negras con gobierno propio (p. 682)

black power/poder negro la movilización del poder económico y político de los afroamericanos para mejorar sus condiciones de vida (p. 683)

blitzkrieg/blitzkrieg guerra relámpago que se caracteriza por su gran rapidez o fuerza (p. 584)

blockade/bloqueo aislar algo (p. 191)

bounty/recompensa dinero pagado por reclutar soldados para servicios militares; pago para alentar una acción (p. 198)

boycott/boicot rechazo a comprar productos o efectuar negociaciones con un país u otra entidad, usualmente para expresar desacuerdo o forzar la aceptación de ciertas condiciones (p. 45)

buffer/zona de amortiguación área destinada a separar y servir como una barrera protectora; área neutral que separa fuerzas en conflicto (p. 612)

business cycle/ciclo económico secuencia de actividad económica compuesta usualmente de recesión, recuperación, crecimiento y declinación (p. 292)

busing/traslado escolar obligatorio transportación de niños a una escuela fuera de su área residencial para establecer la integración racial en dicha escuela (p. 686)

C

cabinet/gabinete un grupo de asesores del presidente (p. 107)

cartel/cartel grupo de vendedores o productores que obran conjuntamente para subir los precios al restringir la disponibilidad de un producto (p. 749)

closed shop/taller sindicalizado sistema en el que a todos los trabajadores de una industria en particular se les exige ser miembros de un sindicato o cuando el patrón acuerda contratar sólo a miembros sindicales. (p. 148)

coalition/coalición alianza, combinación o unión de partidos, pueblos o estados que se forma para una acción o propósito específico (p. 560)

collective bargaining/convenio colectivo negociación entre trabajadores organizados y la administración para lograr un acuerdo sobre salarios, condiciones y horas de trabajo (p. 293)

collective security/seguridad colectiva un acuerdo para garantizar la defensa común (p. 615)

commodity/mercancía bien económico; producto agrícola; artículo comercial (p. 260)

commonwealth/mancomunidad unidad política con gobierno propio de estados independientes asociados en una lealtad común (p. 26)

commune/comuna grupo de personas que viven juntas con propiedad y uso colectivos de los bienes, compartiendo a menudo metas, filosofías y formas de vida; granjas cooperativas extensas (p. 711)

communism/comunismo sistema de gobierno en el cual el partido Comunista controla la vida política, económica, cultural y social de la población; sistema económico en el cual la sociedad como un todo y representada por el partido Comunista, controla todos los medios de producción, distribución e intercambio de bienes (p. 610)

company town/pueblo de la compañía poblado construido y administrado por una compañía en el que los trabajadores están obligados a vivir (p. 291)

confederation/confederación alianza política voluntaria de países, estados o grupos independientes (pp. 9, 63)

congregation/congregación el cuerpo de miembros de una iglesia; reunión de personas para instrucción religiosa y rendir culto (p. 26)

conquistador/conquistador aventurero español del siglo XVI en el continente americano (p. 17)

conscientious objector/objector de conciencia persona que se niega a cumplir servicio militar o a portar armas debido a principios o creencias morales o religiosos (p. 709)

conscription/reclutamiento enrolamiento obligatorio de personas en las fuerzas militares (p. 190)

consensus/consenso acuerdo general; juicio al que han llegado la mayoría de los interesados; solidaridad de grupo en sentimientos y creencias (p. 728)

conservation/conservación administración planeada de los recursos naturales para prevenir su destrucción o abandono (p. 424)

conspicuous comsumption/consumo conspicuo gastos exagerados para llamar la atención (p. 356)

constitution/constitución plan de gobierno de Norteamérica; principios y leyes fundamentales de una nación, estado o grupo social que determina los poderes y deberes del gobierno y garantiza determinados derechos a su pueblo (p. 26)

containment/contención política de prevención de la expansión de una potencia hostil; política exterior después de la Segunda Guerra Mundial que establecía que los Estados Unidos contendrían la influencia soviética dentro de sus límites existentes (p. 612)

contraband/contrabando bienes o mercancías cuya importación, exportación o posesión está prohibida (p. 459)

cooperative/cooperativa organización o empresa que pertenece y es operada para el el beneficio de áquellos que usan sus servicios (p. 342)

corollary/corolario proposición que se añade a otra como una consecuencia o efecto natural (p. 389)

corporation/corporación forma de negocio consistente en un grupo de personas autorizadas por las leyes para actuar como una entidad única que sobrevive a los que la crearon (p. 274)

cotton gin/desmotadora de algodón máquina que elimina las semillas de las fibras del algodón (p. 149)

counterculture/contracultura conjunto de valores y costumbres opuesto al establecido por la sociedad (p. 711)

coup d'état/golpe de estado el derrocamiento repentino de un gobeirno por parte de gente con autoridad, en violación deliberada de las leyes (p. 764)

covenant/convenio acuerdo formal y obligatorio entre dos o más partes (p. 474)

covert/encubierto secreto o disfrazado; que no se muestra o compromete abiertamente (p. 652)

craft union/sindicato de oficio sindicato laboral en el cual todos sus miembros practican la misma ocupación o especialidad (p. 562)

credibility gap/falta de credibilidad ausencia de confianza debida a la diferencia entre las declaraciones oficiales del gobierno y los procedimientos en la realidad (p. 700)

creditor nation/nación acreedora una nación que presta dinero (p. 784)

D

dark horse/candidato sorpresivo candidato político inesperadamente nominado usualmente debido a un compromiso entre grupos (p. 173)

debtor nation/nación deudora un país que debe dinero (p. 784)

defense perimeter/perímetro defensivo línea fronteriza que delimita un área protegida militarmente (p. 620)

deficit spending/gastos deficitarios procedimiento gubernamental de pedir prestado dinero con el propósito de gastar más dinero del que recauda en impuestos (p. 552)

deflation/deflación situación económica en la cual disminuye el volumen de dinero o crédito disponibles lo que produce una caída en los precios de los productos y servicios (p. 345)

deported/deportado sacar de un país una presencia extranjera es ilegal (p. 477)

depression/depresión situación económica caracterizada por una declinación amplia y profunda de la producción y las ventas mientras aumenta drásticamente el desempleo (p. 66)

deregulation/derogación de regulaciones ley aboliendo restricciones y regulaciones (p. 742)

détente/coexistencia pacífica relajamiento de las tensiones de la Guerra Fría entre los Estados Unidos y la Unión Soviética que se inició a principios de la década de 1970 (p. 714)

direct primary/primarias directas elecciones en las que las nominaciones de los candidatos a cargos oficiales se efectúan por los votantes (p. 406)

direct tax/impuesto directo tributo que se paga directamente al gobierno en vez de ser incluido en el precio de los bienes; un impuesto recaudado directamente de la persona sobre la que recae la carga impositiva (p. 45)

disenfranchised/privación del derecho de sufragio pérdida del derecho legal al voto (p. 221)

dole/subsidio dinero o artículos ofrecidos como donación caritativa; subvención de fondos del gobierno para el desempleo (p. 552)

domestic market/mercado interno mercado compuesto de compradores y vendedores del país (p. 495)

downsizing/reducción disminución de las operaciones o del número de trabajadores (p. 779)

E

economics of scale/economía de escala capacidad de los grandes negocios de funcionar de forma más económica y eficiente que los pequeños, lo que resulta en menor costo por unidad de los productos de las grandes compañías (p. 269)

emancipation/emancipación liberación de una persona esclavizada; acto o proceso de liberar de las restricciones, control o dominio de otro; libre de servidumbre (p. 62)

encomienda/encomienda sistema de recompensar a los conquistadores con tierras, incluyendo el derecho a imponer impuestos y exigir trabajo de los indígenas americanos que las habitaban (p. 19)

entrepreneur/empresario persona que organiza, administra y asume los riesgos de un negocio o empresa (p. 267)

enumerated powers/poderes específicos áquellos mencionados explícitamente, uno detrás del otro, en la Constitución (p. 111)

escalation/escalada aumento en amplitud, volumen, número, cantidad, intensidad o alcance (p. 704)

ethnic cleansing/limpieza étnica expulsión o exterminio de un grupo de un país (p. 781)

ethnic group/grupo étnico población que comparte la misma cultura, religión y costumbres (p. 569)

excise tax/impuesto sobre consumos tributo pagado por el fabricante y que es añadido a áquellos que compran el producto; un impuesto sobre la fabricación, venta o consumo de un producto dentro de un país (p. 109)

executive privilege/privilegio ejecutivo principio de que la rama ejecutiva del gobierno está exenta de suministrar información cuando dicha revelación afectaría adversamente las funciones y el proceso de toma de decisiones del presidente o la seguridad nacional (p. 740)

expatriate/expatriado persona que abandona su país nativo para vivir en otro lugar (p. 332)

expedition/expedición viaje con un propósito específico (p. 119)

F

fascism/fascismo sistema de gobierno que es profundamente nacionalista y permite la posesión privada de propiedades mientras controla la política económica en general; gobierno caracterizado por el racismo y militarismo; una dictadura represiva de un partido (p. 581)

favorite son/hijo favorito candidato presidencial apoyado por los delegados de su estado de origen en una convención política nacional (p. 152)

featherbedding/featherbedding solicitar de un patrón bajo una regulación sindical o estatuto de seguridad que contrate más empleados que los necesarios (p. 624)

federal deficit/déficit del presupuesto federal exceso de gastos federales sobre la recaudación de impuestos e ingresos (p. 757)

federalism/federalismo sistema de gobierno en el cual el poder está distribuido entre el gobierno nacional y los gobiernos estatales (p. 70)

federalized/federalizado llevado bajo la jurisdicción del gobierno federal (p. 674)

feminist/feminista persona que actúa en beneficio de los derechos de la mujer (p. 688)

feudalism/feudalismo sistema en el cual poderosos líderes otorgan tierras a los nobles a cambio de un juramento de lealtad y servicios (p. 11)

filibuster/obstruccionismo el uso de tácticas dilatorias para mantener inactiva una asamblea legislativa (p. 778)

fireside chat/charla al calor del hogar nombre usado para describir cómo el antiguo presidente Franklin

D. Roosevelt se dirigía a la población por la radio (p. 547)

forage/forrajear vivir de la tierra (p. 204)

foreclosure/juicio hipotecario procedimiento legal para reclamar parte de una propiedad cuando el dueño no puede estar al día en los pagos de la hipoteca (p. 554)

free-trader/librecambista alguien que practica o defiende el comercio sin impuestos ni aranceles (p. 327)

frigate/fragata navío de guerra de tamaño medio que es menor que un destructor; se utiliza como escolta y en labores de patrullaje (p. 127)

G

genocide/genocidio exterminio deliberado y sistemático de un grupo (p. 781)

gentry/nobleza la clase superior de Inglaterra (p. 29)

glasnost/glasnost término que se refiere a la política soviética de franqueza y libertad de espresión bajo Mikhail Gorbachev (p. 759)

global economy/economía global interdependencia económica entre los países del mundo (p. 784)

gold standard/patrón oro sistema monetario en el cual la moneda circulante de una nación está respaldada por el valor del oro (p. 346)

graft/soborno adquisición de dinero o poder en forma deshonesta o cuestionable mientras se ocupa un cargo público (p. 316)

greenback/nota de banco papel moneda que no estaba respaldado por oro o plata; notas de curso legal emitidas por el gobierno de los Estados Unidos (p. 199)

guerrilla/guerrilla soldado que combate al enemigo con ataques de sorpresa, acosos, sabotajes y otras formas no tradiciones de guerra (p. 612)

H

habeas corpus/hábeas corpus principio legal que exige que una persona que sea arrestada debe ser llevada ante una corte para saber la causa de su arresto; orden judicial que solicita una investigación sobre la legalidad de retener una persona que ha sido encarcelada o se halla bajo custodia (p. 199)

holding company/compañía de holding firma que obtiene el control de otras compañías mediante la compra de sus acciones (p. 277)

Holocaust/Holocausto asesinato masivo y sistemático de 12 millones de civiles europeos, especialmente judíos, llevado a cabo por los nazis durante la Segunda Guerra Mundial (p. 593)

horizontal integration/integración horizontal la unión de negocios dedicados a las mismas actividades o procesos comerciales (p. 277)

I

impeach/impugnar presentar acusaciones de un delito contra un funcionario público federal o estatal con el propósito de destituir al funcionario de su cargo (pp. 75, 223)

imperialism/imperialismo acción de crear un imperio mediante el dominio sobre otras naciones (p. 370)

implied powers/poderes implícitos áquellos sugeridos pero no expresamente enunciados en la Constitución (p. 112)

impound/embargar negarse a gastar fondos congresionales asignados; confiscar y retener bajo la custodia de la ley (p. 742)

impressment/reclutamiento forzoso forma de enrolamiento militar y naval, usualmente por la fuerza, empleado por Inglaterra y otras naciones europeas (p. 121)

income tax/impuesto sobre la renta impuesto sobre el ingreso neto de un individuo o negocio (p. 431)

imcumbent/titular funcionario ejerciendo el cargo (p. 744)

indemnity/indemnidad seguridad o protección contra lesiones, pérdida o daños; exención de penalidades u obligaciones (p. 391)

indentured servant/sirviente bajo contrato persona que acuerda trabajar para un patrón en Norteamérica colonial por un tiempo específico a cambio de la travesía a Norteamérica (p. 24)

industrial union/sindicato industrial sindicato que representa cada trabajador en una industria en particular sin importar su oficio (pp. 298, 562)

inflation/inflación descenso del valor del dinero cuando se emite más moneda circulante, lo que resulta en un aumento de los precios y servicios (p. 345)

inheritance tax/impuesto sobre la herencia gravamen sobre la herencia que el heredero debe pagar para recibirla (p. 433)

initiative/iniciativa procedimiento que permite a los ciudadanos proponer un proyecto de ley mediante una petición con un número específico de firmas de votantes inscritos (p. 406)

injunction/interdicción orden de la corte que exige que un individuo o compañía realice una acción o le prohibe que la realice; aplicada frecuentemente para detener huelgas (p. 299)

installment buying/comprar a plazos sistema de pagar por bienes a intervalos regulares, usualmente con un interés añadido al balance (p. 516)

interlocking directorate/directivas interrelacionadas sistema bajo el cual las mismas personas forman las juntas de directores de varias firmas de la misma industria (p. 442)

internal improvements/adelantos internos caminos, canales y otras necesidades de transportación dentro de las fronteras de una nación (p. 140)

isolationism/aislacionismo política o creencia de que una nación debe limitar sus alianzas y compromisos en los asuntos políticos y económicos internacionales (p. 370)

J

joint resolution/resolución conjunta una resolución aprobada por ambas cámaras del Congreso que requiere solamente una mayoría simple de votos (p. 173)

joint-stock company/sociedad en comandita por acciones forma de organización comercial; reúne fondos de muchos inversionistas o dueños de acciones que pueden independientemente vender sus participaciones en la compañía (p. 14)

judicial review/revisión judicial potestad de la Corte Suprema para revisar todas las actas congresionales y acciones ejecutivas y rechazar áquellas que considere inconstitucionales (pp. 77, 118)

junk bond/bono especulativo bono de corporación generalmente considerado por debajo del grado mediano o especulativo, que paga grandes ganancias para compensar los grandes riesgos de incumplimiento (p. 768)

jurisdictional strike/huelga jurisdiccional la que resulta de una disputa entre sindicatos sobre qué sindicato debe representar a los trabajadores en una compañía o industria (p. 624)

K

kickback/gratificación devolución de una suma recibida de honorarios aumentados debido a un acuerdo confidencial o un acto de coacción (p. 317)

L

laissez-faire/laissez faire doctrina de gobierno de no interferir en los procedimientos comerciales y en los asuntos económicos de los individuos; literalmente significa del francés "dejar hacer" (p. 118)

lame duck/titular no reelegido funcionario electo que continúa en el cargo durante el período comprendido entre las elecciones y la toma de posesión de un sucesor (p. 533)

lend-lease/préstamo-arrendamiento transferencia de bienes y servicios a un aliado (p. 587)

line-item veto/veto selectivo poder para vetar una parte de un proyecto de ley (p. 778)

line of demarcation/línea de demarcación línea de longitud Norte-Sur a través del océano Atlántico que dividió las tierras en las Américas reclamadas por España y Portugal (p. 17)

literacy test/prueba de alfabetización exámenes para comprobar si los inmigrantes sabían leer (p. 413)

lobbyist/cabildero persona que promueve o asegura la aprobación de legislación mediante su influencia sobre los funcionarios públicos (p. 319)

lockout/cierre patronal clausura de una fábrica o centro laboral debida a una huelga; negativa de empleo de un patrón (p. 293)

long drive/arriería traslado de ganado a grandes distancias hasta el ferrocarril, donde es transportado al mercado (p. 250)

Loyalist/lealista colonos norteamericanos que apoyaban el gobierno inglés; alguien que es leal o permanece fiel a una causa política, partido o gobierno (p. 49)

M

mandate/mandato clara expresión del deseo de los votantes tal como se muestra en los resultados de las elecciones (pp. 220, 723)

martial law/ley marcial forma de gobierno militar que suspende las garantías de la Declaración de Derechos; ley administrada por las autoridades civiles en una situación de emergencia cuando las instituciones civiles de aplicación de las leyes no son capaces de mantener el orden (p. 199)

maverick/maverick animal de bosque o ganado sin marcar; un ternero huérfano (p. 249)

mercantilism/mercantilismo teoría de que el poder de un estado depende de su riqueza (p. 20)

mercenary/mercenario soldado a sueldo cuyos servicios se contrataron por el ejército de una nación extranjera; alguien que realiza sus labores solamente por el pago (p. 52)

merchandising/comerciar compra y venta de bienes en un negocio con el propósito de obtener ganancias (p. 309)

meridian/meridiano medida de longitud; un gran círculo alrededor de la superficie de la Tierra que pasa a través de los polos (p. 258)

mestizo/mestizo persona en las colonias españolas nacida de padres español e indígena americano (p. 19)

militia/milicia grupo de civiles autorizados por la ley a ser llamados al servicio militar y entrenados como soldados para combatir en una emergencia (p. 43)

moratorium/moratoria autorización oficial para suspender pagos, como en el caso de deudas; período de espera autorizado oficialmente (p. 523)

multinational state/estado multinacional nación con diferentes y numerosos grupos étnicos (p. 781)

N

nationalism/nacionalismo sentimiento de lealtad y devoción a la patria, honrando esa nación por encima de las demás y promoviendo su cultura e intereses en vez de los de otros países (p. 140)

neutrality/neutralidad negativa a unirse a un bando (p. 375)

new federalism/nuevo federalismo política de Richard Nixon de asociación económica entre el gobierno federal y los gobiernos estatales en la que los estados y municipalidades recibían menos fondos federales (p. 737)

nomadic/nómada traslado frecuente de lugar a lugar sin un patrón fijo de destino, usualmente siguiendo una fuente de alimentos (p. 242)

nonviolent resistance/resistencia pacífica protesta o demostración para lograr fines políticos sin uso de la violencia (p. 672)

northwest passage/paso al noroeste ruta marina a Asia a través de América del Norte que fue buscada por los exploradores europeos (p. 20)

nullification/anulación declaración estatal que considera inválida una ley federal (p. 116)

O

on margin/al margen método de comprar acciones con un pago inicial en efectivo pequeño y un préstamo a un corredor de bolsa para cubrir el balance. El corredor retiene una parte de las acciones como colateral del préstamo; el prestatario reembolsa al corredor con las ganancias producto de la reventa de las acciones (p. 515)

open shop/taller no sindicalizado procedimiento de empleo en el cual la elegibilidad no es determinada por la membresía en un sindicato (p. 487)

P

partitioned/subdividido dividido en dos o más unidades territoriales con identidades políticas separadas (p. 390)

Patriot/Patriota colono norteamericano que favorecía la separación durante la Guerra de Independencia (p. 49)

patronage/patronazgo procedimiento de los funcionarios oficiales electos de ofrecer nombramientos en cargos gubernamentales para ventaja política o como recompensa por favores recibidos (p. 323)

perestroika/perestroika reestructuramiento fundamental de la economía soviética; política introducida por Mikhail Gorbachev (p. 759)

philanthropy/filantropía actividades para promover el bienestar de los seres humanos para beneficio de la sociedad (p. 283)

platform/plataforma declaración de la política y principios adoptados por un partido o candidato político (p. 184)

pocket veto/veto de bolsillo rechazo indirecto de un proyecto de ley legislativo por el presidente mediante la retención del proyecto sin firmar hasta el receso del Congreso (p. 155)

pogrom/pogrom masacres organizadas de población desarmada, especialmente judíos (p. 302)

political machine/maquinaria política organización de partido en las grandes ciudades que sustenta su poder mediante el control de votaciones, tribunales y policía (p. 317)

pooling/pooling acuerdos ilegales entre compañías ferrocarrileras individuales para dividir el volumen total de flete entre sus ferrovías y mantener precios elevados (p. 342)

popular sovereignty/soberanía popular principio de que los colonizadores de un territorio federal tienen el poder para determinar la legalidad de la esclavitud dentro de ese territorio (p. 176)

post-war disillusionment/desencanto de posguerra período posterior a una guerra en el que la población está desengañada (p. 504)

pragmatism/pragmatismo creencia de que las acciones gubernamentales deben resolver las necesidades sociales; enfrentamiento práctico de problemas y asuntos (p. 400)

presidential succession/sucesión presidencial el orden en que es ocupado el cargo de presidente (p. 634)

price-cutting/reducción de precios rebaja de precios hasta un nivel establecido para anular la competencia (p. 442)

privateer/corsario embarcación privada armada que era comisionada por el gobierno para atacar los barcos enemigos (p. 127)

privatize/privatizar conversión de factorías y otras propiedades del gobierno a propiedad privada (p. 759)

propaganda/propaganda comunicaciones, verdaderas o falsas, basadas en una selección cuidadosa y la manipulación de datos, con la intención de influir en los pensamientos o emociones de un grupo, y cambiar su comportamiento (p. 49)

proprietor/propietario persona que recibía del rey de Inglaterra el derecho legal y exclusivo sobre tierras coloniales en América y de quien se esperaba que administrara las tierras de acuerdo a las leyes inglesas (p. 24)

protectionist/proteccionista alguien que aboga por la protección gubernamental de productores y fabricantes domésticos mediante restricciones sobre las importaciones (p. 327)

protective tariff/arancel proteccionista impuesto elevado sobre importaciones con el objetivo más bien de proteger los productos domésticos de la competencia extranjera y no para recaudar fondos (p. 108)

protectorate/protectorado país que es técnicamente independiente pero cuyos gobierno y economía son controlados por una potencia mayor; la nación o región dominada por una potencia mayor (p. 385)

public land/tierra pública terrenos pertenecientes a un gobierno nacional y, por tanto, al pueblo (p. 64)

pump priming/inyección monetaria dinero gubernamental invertido en la economía para estimular una autorecuperación económica (p. 552)

purge/purga destitución obligatoria en gran escala de funcionarios que muestran señales de deslealtad hacia sus superiores (p. 611)

R

racism/racismo creencia de que una raza en particular es superior a las demás (p. 682)

ratification/ratificación voto de aprobación (pp. 70, 790)

reactionary government/gobierno reaccionario gobierno que se caracteriza por su política ultraconservadora (p. 700)

real wages/salario real ingreso ajustado para compensar el poder adquisitivo reducido debido a la inflación (p. 290)

realism/realismo movimiento literario de influencia europea que pretende una representación fiel de la naturaleza o de la vida real sin idealización (p. 331)

rebate/devolución descuento en forma de un reembolso de dinero o rebaja en los pagos de un producto o servicio (p. 279)

recall/elección revocatoria destitución de un funcionario electo por los votantes en elecciones especiales (p. 406)

recession/recesión retroceso en la economía de un país caracterizado por la reducción de sus actividades económicas (p. 564)

reciprocity/reciprocidad descenso mutuo de las barreras arancelarias entre las naciones; reconocimiento

de uno de dos países de la validez de privilegios otorgados por el otro (p. 372)

rediscount/redescuento honorario pequeño que el Banco de la Reserva Federal cobra a un banco miembro al aceptar el pagaré de un negocio (p. 440)

referendum/referéndum proceso mediante el cual el pueblo puede votar directamente sobre una ley propuesta (p. 406)

reparation/indemnización pagos hechos por las naciones derrotadas en una guerra como castigo por los daños causados a otros países (p. 485)

republic/república gobierno en el cual el poder descansa en los ciudadanos que votan para que otras personas los representen (p. 49)

revenue sharing/repartición de ingresos plan para compartir o dividir ingresos (p. 737)

revenue tariff/arancel sobre ingresos impuesto aduanal pequeño sobre importaciones con el propósito más bien de recaudar fondos para el gobierno y no para proteger productos domésticos de la competencia extranjera (p. 108)

rider/adición marginal enmienda no relacionada a un proyecto de ley bajo consideración legislativa (p. 323)

S

salutary neglect/negligencia saludable política de no interferencia de una nación gobernante con el objetivo de producir un efecto beneficioso (p. 42)

satellite nation/nación satélite naciones de Europa oriental bajo la dominación política y económica de la Unión Soviética; país controlado o dominado por otro más poderoso (p. 611)

scab/rompehuelga trabajadores sustitutos no sindicalizados durante una huelga o miembros del sindicato que se niegan a declararse en huelga y continúan trabajando (p. 293)

scrip/vale dinero que sólo puede ser usado en una tienda de la compañía (p. 291)

search-and-destroy strategy/estrategia de búsqueda y destrucción táctica militar empleada para forzar al enemigo a un combate abierto (p. 705)

secession/secesión retiro formal de una organización (p. 187)

securities/valores acciones, bonos y otros instrumentos financieros objetos de transacciones en un mercado financiero (p. 514)

segregation/segregación establecimiento de la separación de grupos raciales en escuelas, edificios de vivienda y otras áreas públicas (p. 227)

separation of powers/separación de poderes principio del gobierno estadounidense por el cual el poder se divide en tres ramas: ejecutiva, legislativa

Spanish Glossary

y judicial, y cada una verifique lo que efectúen las otras dos (p. 76)

sexism/sexismo prejuicio o discriminación basada en la identidad sexual (p. 689)

sharecropper/aparceros trabajadores agrícolas que cultivaban parte de la tierra de otra persona, recibían abastecimientos y equipos del dueño y en cambio le entregaban a éste parte de la cosecha (p. 213)

shogun/shogun perteneciente a la dinastía de gobernantes militares que controló Japón hasta la revolución de 1867-1868; comandante en jefe japonés (p. 13)

shuttle diplomacy/diplomacia viajera negociaciones efectuadas por un intermediario que viaja frecuentemente entre los contendientes (p. 717)

sit-in/huelga de brazos caídos ocupar asientos o permanecer sentados en el piso de un establecimiento como forma de protesta (p. 676)

social contract/contrato social acuerdo entre individuos para formar una sociedad organizada que define y limita los derechos y deberes de cada cual (p. 50)

social Darwinism/darwinismo social teoría sociológica que afirma que sólo los mejores adaptados sobreviven la competencia social y experimentan adelantos sociales (p. 282)

social gospel/evangelio social aplicación por organizaciones religiosas de los principios cristianos a los problemas sociales (p. 399)

socialism/socialismo sistema económico en el cual el gobierno es dueño en parte y controla la producción y distribución de los bienes que se producen (p. 164)

speculation/especulación empresa comercial riesgosa basada en compra o venta con la intención de obtener grandes ganancias de forma rápida (p. 64)

sphere of influence/esfera de influencia área en China a finales del siglo XIX donde el comercio era controlado por una potencia extranjera (p. 390)

spoils system/sistema de acaparamiento procedimiento de destituir a los trabajadores en cargos gubernamentales afiliados al partido derrotado por los partidarios del partido vencedor (p. 155)

stagflation/recesión con inflación inflación persistente combinada con una demanda de consumo estancada y una tasa relativamente alta de desempleo (p. 736)

student deferment/aplazamiento estudiantil posposición del servicio militar (p. 709)

subversives/subversivos personas que trabajan en secreto con la intención de derrocar o debilitar un gobierno o sistema político (p. 627)

summit/conferencia cumbre encuentro diplomático de las superpotencias; conferencia de funcionarios gubernamentales de alto nivel (p. 714)

supply-side economics/economía de oferta política económica diseñada para aumentar la oferta global o para desplazar la curva de oferta global hacia la derecha (p. 755)

T

teach-in/teach-in conferencia, debate y discusión de temas polémicos (p. 710)

technological unemployment/desempleo tecnológico empleos perdidos como resultado de maquinarias efectuando labores anteriormente realizadas por seres humanos (p. 487)

tenant farmer/agricultor arrendatario trabajador agrícola que arrendaba y cultivaba la tierra de otra persona y pagaba el arrendamiento con dinero o con una parte de la cosecha (p. 213)

textile/textil tela, especialmente tejida o de punto; paños (p. 147)

third party/tercer partido partido político menor funcionando aparte de otros dos grandes partidos en una nación o estado que se caracteriza normalmente por us sistema bipartidista (p. 347)

toll/peaje precio que se cobra por el uso de un medio de transportación (p. 142)

totalitarian/totalitario tipo de gobierno controlado por una persona o partido; supresión de la libertad y control de cada aspecto de la vida (p. 581)

township/municipalidad unidad local de gobierno dentro de un condado (p. 320)

trade deficit/déficit comercial situación económica en la cual el valor de las importaciones de una nación es mayor que el valor de sus exportaciones (p. 785)

treason/traición intento de derrocar el gobierno del estado al que la persona le debe lealtad (p. 49)

trust/trust combinación de compañías para obtener el control de una industria y reducir la competencia (p. 277)

turnpike/carretera de peaje vía cerrada con una barrera donde los viajeros se detienen a pagar un precio para poder usarla (p. 142)

U

ultimatum/ultimátum una exigencia que traerá graves consecuencias si es ignorada (p. 145)

unicameral/unicameral legislatura compuesta de una sola cámara (p. 63)

urban renewal/renovación urbana programa de construcción para reemplazar o restaurar una ciudad o un área urbana (p. 725)

V

vaudeville/vodevil entretenimiento que consiste en varios actos representados en un escenario (p. 252)

vertical integration/integración vertical unión de negocios que desarrollan diferentes, aunque relacionadas, actividades o procesos (p. 277)

veto/veto acción por la cual un ejecutivo rechaza un proyecto de ley sometido por una legislatura; negativa a aprobar (p. 62)

victory gardens/jardines de la victoria jardines donde se cosechan los vegetales propios, especialmente durante tiempos de guerra (p. 470)

vigilance committee/comité de vigilancia organización de ciudadanos que toma la ley en sus propias manos para su protección (p. 252)

W

ward/barriada electoral división de una ciudad con propósitos representativos, electorales o administrativos (p. 318)

war of national liberation/guerra de liberación nacional conflicto con el propósito de liberar una nación del control de otra (p. 702)

welfare capitalism/capitalismo de bienestar sistema de programas benéficos ofrecido a los trabajadores por los empresarios con el objetivo de reducir el atractivo de los sindicatos (p. 488)

"Western"/"Oeste" novela, narración o película de Hollywood que representa la vida en el Oeste de los Estados Unidos durante la segunda mitad del siglo XIX (p. 253)

wetland/tierras pantanosas terrenos o áreas que contienen mucha humedad (p. 789)

wildcat strike/huelga ilegal suspensión del trabajo iniciada por un grupo de trabajadores sin la aprobación formal del sindicato o en violación de un contrato (p. 601)

Y

yellow journalism/prensa amarilla tipo de reportaje periodístico a finales de la década de 1890 que presentaba titulares e historias sensacionalistas (p. 333)

Spanish Glossary

Index

★ ★

Italicized page numbers refer to illustrations. Preceding the page number, abbreviations refer to a map (m), chart (c), photograph or other picture (p), graph (g), cartoon (crt), or painting (ptg). Quoted material is referenced with the abbreviation (q) before the appropriate page number.

A

AAA, 554, 563, 565, 568
Aaron, Henry, 409
ABC powers, 457
abolition; before Civil War, 183; end of, 228; legislation, 41, 162; Southern reaction, 162. *See also* slavery, public opinion
abolitionists, 161
Accused of Witchcraft, ptg28
accused persons, rights of, 94, 735
acid rain, 789
ACLU, 505
acquired immune deficiency syndrome (AIDS). *See* AIDS
Across the Continent, ptg271
Act of Union, 136
Adams, Abigail, p55
Adams, Charles Francis, Jr., q272
Adams, Henry, 400
Adams, John, p115, 117, 118; inauguration, 104
Adams, John, administration, 114–16, 133
Adams, John Quincy, p152, 143, 145; election, 152
Adams, John Quincy, administration, 154
Adams, Samuel, ptg48, q48, 46, 68, 70
Adams, Sherman, 635–36, 642
Adamson Act, 443
Adams-Onís Treaty of 1819, 145
Addams, Jane, p306, q308, 400
adire cloth, 13
adult education, 330–31
Adventures of Huckleberry Finn, The, 331
Adventures of Tom Sawyer, The, 331
advertising, 430
affirmative action, 757
Affluent Society, The, 643, 729
Afghanistan, Soviet invasion of, 751, 760
AFL; membership before Great Depression, 487; membership during Great Depression, 557; merger with CIO, 640; organization, 297–98; role of women, 563; during World War II, 601
AFL-CIO, 543, 633, 640
AFL-CIO symbol, p639
Africa; African American colonization of, 217; commerce, m39, 12–13; independence movement, 698; prehistory, 4; U.S.-Soviet relations, 698
Africa, North, 12, 590
African Americans; African heritage, 506, 683; after American Revolution, 62; after emancipation, 213–16; in the arts, 504–06; attitudes of progressives, 415; authors, 115; in cities, 768; citizenship, 184–85, 220, 228; civil rights movement, 624, 668–86; in Civil War, 197, 200; compared to immigrants, 180; cowboys, 250; economic conditions, 682; education, p215, p228, 161, 215, 219, 222; education during progressivism, 415; effect of New Deal, 555, 563, 568; in English colonies, 30; families, 214; Harlem Renaissance, 505–06; hiring by Public Works Administration, 552; Jackson administration, 155, 156, 161; Ku Klux Klan, 492; in labor unions, 298; land ownership, 216; leaders, p664, 415–16, 502, 764; migration to North, p629, 469–70, 477, 629; Million Man March, 790; music, 137, 153, 188–89, 504, 649; names, 214; political involvement, 222, 238, 568, 739, 776; population in 1970s, 689; publishing, 138; religion, 672; in Revolutionary War, 53; rights after Reconstruction, 226–28, 401, 416; rights during Reconstruction, 219–20, 235; slavery. *See* slavery; Social Security Act, 561; in Spanish-American War, 378; support by Eleanor Roosevelt, 549; support for Carter, 749; support for Truman, 626; in Vietnam War, 709; voting rights, 224, 226, 416; voting rights, 15th amendment, 221; during Wilson administration, 443; in workforce, 623–24; in World War I, 466–67; in World War II mobilization, 602; in World War I mobilization, 469–70. *See also* discrimination, racial. *See also* racism
African Methodist Episcopal Church, 138
Afrika Korps, 592
Afro Americans. *See* African Americans
Agent Orange, 705
Age of Exploration, 4, 13, 132
aging, 769
Agnew, Spiro T., 712, 721, 741
agribusiness, 564, 641
Agricultural Adjustment Act (AAA), 554, 563, 565, 568
Agricultural Marketing Act, 514
agriculture; 1840–1860, 179–80, 363; after World War I, 475; economics, c362, 259–60, 340–41, 346; Eisenhower administration, 640–41; electrification, 553; foreign trade, 495; in Great Depression, 520, 527, 564; Great Plains, 256–60; labor, 554–55; land use, 555; legislation, 347, 496, 514; machinery, 256–57; migrant workers, 641; New Deal, 554–56; post-Civil War South, g227, 212–13; prices, g341, g534, 340–41, 346, 564, 641; public opinion, 260; in 1920s, 495–97, 516; specialization, 259; surpluses, 341, 496, 514, 516, 554
Agriculture, Department of, 407, 555
Aguinaldo, Emilio, 377, 382
AIDS, 789
AIM, 691; flag, p690
airplanes, p365; first flight, 420; Grumman fighter, p541; use in war, 466

Alabama, 187
Alabama, University of, 678
Alamo, p136, 172
Alamo, Battle of, 136
Alamogordo, New Mexico, 598
Alaska, p372; gold rush, p371, 367; Harding travel to, 490; land, 429; oil pipeline, 737; purchase, 137, 371; Russian ownership, 146; statehood, 642, 666
Albany, New York, 21
Albany Plan, 43
alcoholic beverages, prohibition. *See* prohibition
Aldrich, Nelson W., 428, 429, 437, 440
Aldrin, Edwin E., Jr., 727
Aleuts, 245
Alexander, Lamar, 788
Alexander VI, Pope, 17
algebra, 12
Alger, Horatio, p236, 274, 276
Algiers, Morocco, 129
Allen, Frederick Lewis, q530
Alliance for Progress, 697
Allies, World War I, 464; attitude during peace negotiations, 474, 479; members, 459; supplies for, 468; war debt, 485, 495, 523
Allies, World War II, 595
Allies Day, ptg455
almanacs, 115
Alsace, France, 479
Alzheimer's disease, 769
amendment, defined, 71
amendments. *See* Constitution of the United States
America, origin of name, 17
America First Committee, 583
American Bankers' Association, 551
American Civil Liberties Union (ACLU), 505
American Cotton Cooperative Association, 514
American Dream, 356, 646
American Exodus, a Record of Human Erosion, An, 529
American Federation of Labor (AFL). *See* AFL
American Independent party, 789
American Indian Movement (AIM), 691; flag, p690
American Indians. *See* Native Americans; *See also* individual Native American nations
American Library Association, 309
American Missionary Association, 215
American Protective Association, 303–04

B

Index

F

Index

K

N

Index

Index

S

Index

T

U

V

W

X

Y

Z

Index

Acknowledgments

★ ★

36 "Constitution of the Five Nations," from William N. Fenton, ed., *Parker on the Iroquois*, Copyright © 1868 by Syracuse University Press; used by permission. **37** "Navajo Song of the Rain Chant," from Nataline Curtis, ed., *The Indians' Book*, Harper and Brothers, 1907; used by permission. **123** Southgate letter from James A. Henretta, et al, *America's History*, Chicago: Dorsey Press, 1987. **254** From Mark Twain, *Roughing It.* Berkeley: University of California Press, 1972. **386** From *Official Proceedings of the Democratic National Convention. . . . 1890*, reprinted in *The Annals of America*,

vol. 12. Chicago: Encyclopaedia Britannica, 1968. **402** From Theodore Dreiser, *Sister Carrie.* New York: W.W. Norton, Critical Ed., 1970. **498** "Recuerdo" by Edna St. Vincent Millay, From *Collected Poems*, Harper & Row, Copyright © 1922, 1950 by Edna St. Vincent Millay. Reprinted by permission of Elizabeth Barnett, Literary Executor. **499** "Dream Boogie," reprinted by permission of Harold Ober Associates, Inc. Copyright © 1932, 1951 by Langston Hughes, Copyright renewed 1979 by George Houston Bass. **572** From John Steinbeck, *The Grapes of Wrath*, Copyright

© 1939, renewed © 1967 by John Steinbeck. Used by permission of Viking Penguin, a division of Penguin Books USA, Inc. **605** Ota excerpt from *"The Good War": An Oral History of World War Two* by Studs Terkel. Copyright © 1984. Reprint by permission of Pantheon Books, a division of Random House. **794** From *Hunger of Memory* by Richard Rodriguez. Copyright © 1981 by Richard Rodriguez. Reprinted by permission of David R. Godine, Publisher. **852** "I Have a Dream" copyright © 1963 by Martin Luther King, Jr. Used by permission, Joan Daves Agency.

Photo Credits

★ ★

Cover ©1995 Steve Barrett/The Stock Market; **x** (tl) North Wind Picture Archives, (tr) Bettmann Archive, (bl) Library of Congress, (bc) Henry Form Museum, (br) H. Armstrong Roberts; **xi** (tl) F. Sieb/H. Armstrong Roberts, (tr) The Auschutz Collection, Denver, CO, (cl) file photo, (cm) Courtesy Hormel Foods/Aaron Haupt Photography, (cr) file photo, (bl) C.P. George/H. Armstrong Roberts, (bc) Reuters/Bettmann, (br) Courtesy American Express; **xii** (tl,bl) Warren Motts Photographic Center, (tr) Library of Congress, (bc) Doug Martin, (br) Culver Pictures; **xiii** (tl) file photo, (tc) Culver Pictures, (tr) Focus on Sports, (cl) Bob Mullenix, (cm) Bob Daemmrich/Stock Boston, (bl) Crown Studies, (br) Ken Frick; **xiv** (tr) Lloyd Lemmerman, (l) Frank & Maria-Therese Wood/The Picture Bank, (br) Library of Congress; **xv** (tl) UPI/Bettmann, (tc) James Fee/Shooting Star, (tr) NASA, (bl) file photo, (br) Bettmann Archive; **xvi** (l) Library of Congress, (r) Courtesy, The Henry Francis du Pont Wintherthur Museum; **xvii** (t) Superstock, (bl) The Sonnabend Collection, NY, (br) Mark Burnett; **xviii** National Museum of American Art, Washington, DC/Art Resource; **xix** (tl,cr) Bettmann Archive, (tr,cl) Brown Brothers, (bl) UPI/Bettmann, (br) Courtesy David Godine Publishers; **xx** (l,cr) National Portrait Gallery, Smithsonian Institution/Art Resource, NY, (cl) file photo, (r) Bettmann Archive; **xxi** (tl) John Launois/Black Star, (tr) Richard Howard/Black Star, (tc,cbc) Bettmann Archive, (ctr)

U.S. Army Photograph, (cbl) The Oakland Museum, (cbr) Archive Photos, (bl,br) Reuters/Bettmann; **xxii** (l) Bettmann Archive, (r) AP Photo/Denis Paquin; **xxviii** William J. Weber; **xxix** (t) The Art Collection of the Boatman's National Bank of St. Louis, (b) Missouri Historical Society; **xxx** (t) Estate of Mrs. Edsel B. Ford, (b) Metropolitan Museum of Art; **xxxi** (t) Bettmann Archive, (b) H. Armstrong Roberts; **xxxii** file photo; **xxxiii** (t) Bettmann Archive, (b) Reuters/Bettmann; **xxxiv** General Electric Company; **xxxv** (t) Andy Levin/Photo Researchers, (b) Joseph Dichello; **xxxvi** (t) Architect of the Capitol, (b) Alex Maclean/Landslides; **xxxvii** (t) Superstock, (b) Lynn Stone; **xxxviii** (t) Margot Granitsas/Photo Researchers, (b) Bettmann Archive; **1** (t) North Wind Picture Archives, (b) Joe Sohm/Photo Researchers; **2** (c) Chuck O'Rear/H. Armstrong Roberts, (br) Scala/Art Resource, NY; **3** (t) Courtesy of the School of American Research, Santa Fe, (c) Boltin Picture Library, (b) Bettmann Archive; **4** (t,b) Boltin Picture Library, (c) Larry Hamill; **5** (tl) Boltin Picture Library, (tr) Bridgeman/Art Resource, NY, (bl) Courtesy American Antiquarian Society, (br) Bettmann Archive; **6** file photo; **7** (t) Bridgeman Art Library, London, (b) Scala/Art Resource, NY; **8** Bettmann Archive; **9** Schalwijk/Art Resource, NY; **10** George Hunter/H. Armstrong Roberts; **11** Giraudon/Art Resource, NY; **12** North Wind Picture Archives; **13** (l) British Museum, (r) Aldo Tutino/Art Resource, NY; **15** Erich Lessing/Art Resource, NY; **16** Werner Forman/Art Resource, NY; **17**

Bridgeman/Art Resource, NY; **18** Historical Pictures Collection/Stock Montage, Inc.; **20** The Huntington Library; **21** National Archives of Canada; **22** Frank & Marie-Therese Wood/The Picture Bank; **23** Chase Manhattan Bank; **25** (l) Courtesy of the Pilgrim Society, Plymouth, MA, (r) Bettmann Archive; **26** Historical Picture Collection/Stock Montage, Inc.; **28** Superstock; **29** Boltin Picture Library; **30 31** Bettmann Archive; **32** The Metropolitan Museum of Art, Gift of Mrs. A. Wordsworth Thompson, 1899; **33** Archive Photos; **35** North Wind Picture Archives; **37** (l) Cranbrook Institute of Science, (r) G. L. French/H. Armstrong Roberts; **38** (l) file photo, (r) Bettmann Archive; **40** The National Gallery of Art, Washington, **41** (r) Art Resource, NY, (bl) file photo; **42** file photo; **43** Historical Pictures Collection/Stock Montage, Inc.; **45** (l) Historical Pictures Collection/Stock Montage, Inc., (r) KS Studios; **46** Historical Pictures Collection/Stock Montage, Inc.; **48** Deposited by the City of Boston Courtesy, Museum of Fine Arts, Boston. **49** file photo; **50** Independence National Historical Park; **51** (t) National Portrait Gallery, Smithsonian Institution/Art Resource, NY, (b) Smithsonian Institution; **52** Courtesy American Jewish Historical Society, Waltham MA; **53** Fraunces Tavern Museum, Gift of Herbert P. Whitlock, 1913; **55** Bettmann Archive; **56** Architect of the Capitol, Washington, DC; **57** (l) Bettmann Archive, (r) Archive Photos; **59** Architect of the Capitol, Washington, DC; **62** Historical Pictures Collection/Stock Montage, Inc.;

Library of Congress; **559** Ohio Historical Society/Center of Labor and Industry; **560** (l) UPI/Bettmann, (r) Wide World Photos; **561** ©1935 (renewed 1963) by the Conde Nast Publications, Inc; **562** The U. S. Department of the Interior, Washington, DC, photographer David Allison; **564** (l) UPI Bettmann, (r) David Fraizer; **565** Franklin D. Roosevelt Library; **566** (t) Mark Reinstein/FPG International, (b) Mark Burnett; **567** Library of Congress; **568** file photo; **569** (l) Movie Still Archives, (r) Everett Collection; **570** Movie Still Archives; **571** Collection of Picture Research Consultants; **572** UPI/Bettmann; **573** (t) Everett Collection, (b) Library of Congress; **576** Warren Motts Photographic Center; **577** (t) Naval Photographic Center, (b) Warren Motts Photographic Center; **578** Warren Motts Photographic Center; **579 580** FPG International; **581** (l) Library of Congress, (r) Hugo Joeger/LIFE Magazine, Time, Inc; **583** Warren Motts Photographic Center; **584** (l) FPG International, (r) Frank & Maria-Therese Wood/The Picture Bank; **585** (t) UPI/Bettmann, (b) Imperial War Museum; **586** Yivo Institute of Jewish Research; **587** Franklin D. Roosevelt Library; **589** National Archives; **590** (l) Library of Congress, (r) Bettmann Archive; **592** (l) Wide World Photo, (r) UPI/Bettmann; **593** Bettmann Archive; **595** Warren Motts Photographic Center; **596** Franklin D. Roosevelt Library; **598** (t) USAF, (b) Wide World Photo; **599** National Archives; **600** (l) Archive Photos, (r) Dean Siracusa/FPG International; **601** (l) UPI/Bettmann, (r) Cobalt Production; **602** (l) Bettmann Archive, (r) National Archives; **603 604** Wide World Photos; **605** FPG International; **606** Courtesy D. Wigmore Fine Art, Inc, New York; **608** UPI/Bettmann; **609** (tl) White House Historical Association, (r) Printed by permission of the Norman Rockwell Family Trust, ©1945 The Norman Rockwell Family Trust, (bl) LIFE Magazine ©Time, Inc; **610** UN/J. Isaac; **611** (l) Wide World Photos, (r) UPI/Bettmann; **614** (l) FPG International, (r) UPI/Bettmann; **615** Department of the Army; **617** Wide World Photos; **618** U. S. Army Photograph; **619** (l) FPG International, (r) Wide World Photos; **622** file photo; **623** (l) Robert Reiff/FPG International, (r) FPG International; **625** (l) FPG International, (r) Duomo Photography; **626** Harry S. Truman Library; **627** Wide World Photos; **629** Library of Congress; **630** Chicago Tribune Cartoon by Carey Orr; **632** Robert Reiff/FPG International; **633** (t) Isabel Bishop/Howald Fund/The Columbus Museum of Art, #54.47, (b) UPI/Bettmann; **634** Cobalt Productions; **635** Bettmann Archive; **636 638** file photo; **639** Courtesy of Ohio AFL-CIO; **640** UPI/Bettmann; **641** Magnum Photos; **643** FPG International; **644** Erich Hartmann/Magnum Photos; **646** (l) FPG International, (r) UPI/Bettmann; **647** (l) Ken Frick, (r) Archive Photo; **648** UPI/Bettmann; **649** (l) UPI/Bettmann, (r) Bettmann Archive; **650** Ralph Morse/LIFE Magazine ©Time, Inc; **651** UPI/Bettmann; **652** Bettmann Archive; **653** UPI/Bettmann;

654 Wide World Photos; **656** UPI/Bettmann; **657** AP/Wide World Photos; **658** UPI/Bettmann; **660** (t) file photo, (c) Courtesy American Express, (b) file photo; **661** (t) file photo, (bl) Mark Steinmetz, (br) Courtesy Hormel Foods/Aaron Haupt Photography; **662** (tr) Warren Motts Photographic Center, (bl) Minnesota Historical Society/St. Paul Daily News, (br) AP/Wide World Photos; **663** (t) UPI/Bettmann, (b) AP/Wide World Photos; **664** (t) John Eastcott/Yxa Momatiuk/Stock Boston, (b) David J. Sams/Stock Boston; **665** (t) Burt Glinn/Magnum, (b) Bob Mullenix; **666** (t) United Nations, (c) Steve McCutcheon, (b) Hank Morgan/Photo Researchers; **667** (t,c) Peter Turnley/Black Star, (b) file photo; **668** Lawrence Migdale/Stock Boston; **669** (t) Flip Schulke/Black Star, (b) Tim Courlas; **670** Bob Daemmrich/Stock Boston; **671** (l) UPI/Bettmann, (r) Topham Picture Source; **672** (l) Flip Schulke/Black Star, (r) Declan Haun/Black Star; **673** UPI/Bettmann; **674** Steve Schapiro/Black Star; **675** James Fee/Shooting Star; **676** National Museum of American Art, Washington, DC/Art Resource, NY; **677** UPI/Bettmann; **678** (l) DeClan Haun/Black Star, (r) Charles Moore/Black Star; **679** Dan McCoy/Black Star; **681** UPI/Bettmann; **682** Mark Burnett; **683** UPI/Bettmann; **684** John Launois/Black Star; **685** AP/Wide World Photos; **686** Flip Schulke/Black Star; **687** Peter Southwick/Stock Boston; **688** (l,c) Allen Zak, (r) Lynda Gordon/Gamma Liaison; **689** Joe Sohm/Image Works; **690** (l) Lionel Delavingne/Stock Boston, (r) Bob Daemmrich/Stock Boston; **691** J. Jacobson/Image Works; **692** Richard Pasley/Stock Boston; **694** David Frazier; **695** (t) John Gordon/Black Star, (b) Joe Lynch/Gamma Liaison; **696** file photo; **698** UPI/Bettmann; **699** (l) UPI/Bettmann, (r) Patrick Piel/Gamma Liaison; **701** (r) UPI/Bettmann, (b) Culver Pictures; **702** Dennis Brack/Black Star; **703** (l) Bettmann Archive, (r) Robert Ellison/Black Star; **704** (l) UPI/Bettmann, (r) James Pickerell/Black Star; **708** file photo; **709** (l) L. Kalvoord/Image Works, (r) John Filo; **710** Dennis Brack/Black Star; **711** Allen Zak; **713** Tim Crosby/Gamma Liaison; **714** (l) Charlon/Gamma Liaison, (r) Gamma Liaison; **716** Richard Howard/Black Star; **717 718** UPI/Bettmann; **720** L.H. Jawitz/Image Bank; **721** (t) Photo courtesy the Archives of the American Illustrator's Gallery, New York, (b) Smithsonian Institute; **722** Joe Sohm/Chromosohm/Stock Boston; **723** (l) Photo Tiffany/Gamma Liaison, (r) UPI/Bettmann; **725** (l) UPI/Bettmann, (r) Fred Ward/Black Star; **727** NASA; **728** Life Images; **729** Owen Franken/Stock Boston; **730 732** UPI/Bettmann; **733** The Sonnabend Collection, NY; **734** Fred Ward/Black Star; **735** Photo by Robert S. Oakes, National Geographic Society, Collection of the Supreme Court of the United States; **736** Bill Pugliano/Black Star; **737** Stock Boston; **738** Randy Trine; **739** Dennis Brack/Black Star; **741** UPI/Bettmann; **742** Roland Freeman/Magnum; **743** Bill Foley/Black Star; **744** R. Hess/Image Bank; **746** ©Bill Hick-

ey/Image Bank; **747** (t) Collection of the Whitney Museum of American Art, 50th Anniversary Gift of the Gilman Foundation, Inc., The Lauder Foundation, A. Alfred Taubman, an anonymous donor, and purchase., (b) AP/Wide World Photos; **748** Theo Westenberger/Gamma Liaison; **749** KEZA/Gamma Liaison; **751** Gamma Liaison; **752** UPI/Bettmann; **754** Stock Boston; **755** Bresse/Pozarik/Gamma Liaison; **756** Bill Fitz-Patrick, The White House; **758** NASA; **759** (l) Aaron Haupt, (r) Nubar Alexanian/Stock Boston; **762** Gamma Liaison; **763** S. Ferry/Gamma Liaison; **764** Reuters/Bettmann; **765** C. Hires, G. Merillon/Gamma Liaison; **766** Todd Adank, Photo Op Inc.; **769** (t) George H. Matchneer, (b) courtesy PHYSICS TODAY Magazine; **770** William Johnson/Stock Boston; **772** Nathan Benn/Stock Boston; **773** (t) David Lawrence/Stock Market, (b) Peter Menzel/Stock Boston; **774** Mark Burnett; **775** Markel/Gamma Liaison; **777 778** Reuters/Bettmann; **779** Dennis Brack/Black Star; **780** file photo; **781** AP/Wide World Photos; **782** (l) Miami Herald/Liaison, (r) Todd Sumlin/Gamma Liaison; **783** AP Photo/Denis Paquin; **784** (l) Bettmann Archive, (r) Reuters/Bettmann; **787** Aaron Haupt; **789** (l) Ron Levy/Gamma Liaison, (r) Paul Fusco/Magnum; **790** (l) Les Stone/Sygma, (r) Larry Downing/Sygma; **793** (l) Ted Wood/Black Star, (r) Joyce Photographics/Photo Researchers; **794** Courtesy David Godine Publishers; **795** National Museum of American Art, Washington, DC/Art Resource, NY; **796** Frank Rossotto/Stock Market; **798** (tl) Reuters/Bettmann, (tr) Skip Comer, (b) Ellen Giamportone/H. Armstrong Roberts; **799** (tl) C. P. George/H. Armstrong Roberts, (bl) Reuters/Bettmann, (br) Steve Jennings/LGI Photo Agency; **801** (tl) Declan Haun/Black Star, (tr,b) Dennis Brack/Black Star; **802** (t) Peter Menze/Stock Boston, (b) AP/Wide World Photos; **832 833 834 835 836 837 838 839** White House Historical Association; **840** Tom & Deeann McCarthy/The Stock Market; **841** Betty Crews/The Image Works; **843** Charles Thatcher/Tony Stone Images; **844** Lester Sloan/Woodfin Camp & Associates; **845** Ken Kerbs/Monkmeyer Press; **846** David Austen/Tony Stone Images; **847** Leif Skoogfors/Woodfin Camp & Associates; **848** Bob Daemmrich Photo, Inc.; **849** Michael Okoniewski/The Image Works; **850** Bob Daemmrich Photo, Inc.; **851** Bob Thomas/Tony Stone Images; **852** file photo; **853** Aaron Haupt; **854** North Wind Pictures Archives; **855** Bettmann Archive; **856** Smithsonian Institution; **857** Superstock; **858** National Portrait Gallery, Smithsonian Institution, Art Resource, NY; **859** (l) Mark Burnett, (r) Smithsonian Institution; **860** (l) Photo Network, (r) Mark Burnett; **861** (t) Denver Art Museum, (b) Bettmann Archive; **862 863** UPI/Bettmann; **864** Flip Schulke/Black Star.